D1457741

THE
ALL ENGLAND
LAW REPORTS
2002

Volume 1

Editor

CRAIG ROSE   Barrister

THE LIBRARY
DLA
PRINCESS EXCHANGE
LEEDS
LS1 4BY

Butterworths
LexisNexis™

Members of the LexisNexis Group worldwide

United Kingdom	Butterworths Tolley, a Division of Reed Elsevier (UK) Ltd, Halsbury House, 35 Chancery Lane, LONDON, WC2A 1EL, and 4 Hill Street, EDINBURGH EH2 3JZ
Argentina	Abeledo Perrot, Jurisprudencia Argentina and Depalma, BUENOS AIRES
Australia	Butterworths, a Division of Reed International Books Australia Pty Ltd, CHATSWOOD, New South Wales
Austria	ARD Betriebsdienst and Verlag Orac, VIENNA
Canada	Butterworths Canada Ltd, MARKHAM, Ontario
Chile	Publitecsa and Conosur Ltda, SANTIAGO DE CHILE
Czech Republic	Orac sro, PRAGUE
France	Editions du Juris-Classeur SA, PARIS
Hong Kong	Butterworths Asia (Hong Kong), HONG KONG
Hungary	Hvg Orac, BUDAPEST
India	Butterworths India, NEW DELHI
Ireland	Butterworths (Ireland) Ltd, DUBLIN
Italy	Giuffré, MILAN
Malaysia	Malayan Law Journal Sdn Bhd, KUALA LUMPUR
New Zealand	Butterworths of New Zealand, WELLINGTON
Poland	Wydawnictwa Prawnicze PWN, WARSAW
Singapore	Butterworths Asia, SINGAPORE
South Africa	Butterworths Publishers (Pty) Ltd, DURBAN
Switzerland	Stämpfli Verlag AG, BERNE
USA	LexisNexis, DAYTON, Ohio

© Reed Elsevier (UK) Ltd 2002

All rights reserved. No part of this publication may be reproduced in any material form (including photocopying or storing it in any medium by electronic means and whether or not transiently or incidentally to some other use of this publication) without the written permission of the copyright owner except in accordance with the provisions of the Copyright, Designs and Patents Act 1988 or under the terms of a licence issued by the Copyright Licensing Agency Ltd, 90 Tottenham Court Road, London, England W1P 0LP. Applications for the copyright owner's written permission to reproduce any part of this publication should be addressed to the publisher.

Warning: The doing of an unauthorised act in relation to a copyright work may result in both a civil claim for damages and criminal prosecution.

Any Crown copyright material is reproduced with the permission of the Controller of Her Majesty's Stationery Office. Any European material in this work which has been reproduced from EUR-lex, the official European Union legislation website, is European Union copyright.

A CIP Catalogue record for this book is available from the British Library.

Printed and bound in Great Britain by William Clowes Ltd, Beccles and London

ISBN for the complete set of volumes: 0 406 85159 X
for this volume:

ISBN 0-406-95247-7

9 780406 952479

Visit Butterworths LexisNexis *direct* at www.butterworths.com

REPORTERS

James Brooks Barrister

Gillian Crew Barrister

Celia Fox Barrister

Manjit Gheera Barrister

Martyn Gurr Barrister

Alexander Horne Barrister

Melanie Martyn Barrister

Neneh Munu Barrister

Kate O'Hanlon Barrister

Victoria Parkin Barrister

Sanchia Pereira Barrister

Dilys Tausz Barrister

Lynne Townley Barrister

Gareth Williams Barrister

James Wilson Barrister (NZ)

DEPUTY EDITORS

Paul Hardy LLM

Helen O'Shea Dip Law, Dip LP

SENIOR SUB-EDITORS

Tanja Clarke LLM

Rukhsana Hasnain LLB

SUB-EDITORS

Catherine Bayliss LLB

Catherine Braund LLB

Deana Smith Barrister

PRODUCTION EDITOR

Catherine Lauder BSc

PRODUCTION ASSISTANT / INDEX MANAGER

Isabella Winter BA

House of Lords

The Lord High Chancellor of Great Britain: Lord Irvine of Lairg

Lords of Appeal in Ordinary

Lord Bingham of Cornhill
Lord Slynn of Hadley
Lord Nicholls of Birkenhead
Lord Steyn
Lord Hoffmann
Lord Hope of Craighead

Lord Hutton
Lord Saville of Newgate
Lord Hobhouse of Woodborough
Lord Millett
Lord Scott of Foscote
Lord Rodger of Earlsferry

Court of Appeal

The Lord High Chancellor of Great Britain

The Lord Chief Justice of England: Lord Woolf
(President of the Criminal Division)

The Master of the Rolls: Lord Phillips of Worth Matravers
(President of the Civil Division)

The President of the Family Division: Dame Elizabeth Butler-Sloss

The Vice-Chancellor: Sir Robert Andrew Morritt

Lords Justices of Appeal

Sir Paul Joseph Morrow Kennedy
Sir Simon Denis Brown (Vice-President of the
    Civil Division)
Sir Christopher Dudley Roger Rose
    (Vice-President of the Criminal Division)
Sir Peter Leslie Gibson
Sir Denis Robert Maurice Henry (retired 11
    January 2002
Sir Robin Ernest Auld
Sir Malcolm Thomas Pill
Sir William Aldous
Sir Alan Hylton Ward
Sir Konrad Hermann Theodor Schiemann
Sir Mathew Alexander Thorpe
Sir Mark Howard Potter
Sir Henry Brooke
Sir Igor Judge (Senior Presiding Judge for England
    and Wales)
Sir George Mark Waller
Sir John Frank Mummery
Sir Charles Barrie Knight Mantell
Sir John Murray Chadwick

Sir Robert Walker
Sir Richard Joseph Buxton
Sir Anthony Tristram Kenneth May
    (Vice-President of the Queen's
    Bench Division)
Sir Simon Lane Tuckey
Sir Anthony Peter Clarke
Sir John Grant McKenzie Laws
Sir Stephen John Sedley
Sir Jonathan Hugh Mance
Dame Brenda Marjorie Hale
Sir David Nicholas Ramsey Latham
Sir John William Kay
Sir Bernard Anthony Rix
Sir Jonathan Frederic Parker
Dame Mary Howarth Arden
Sir David Wolfe Keene
Sir John Anthony Dyson
Sir Andrew Centlivres Longmore
Sir Robert John Anderson Carnwath (appointed
    15 January 2002)

High Court of Justice

The Lord High Chancellor of Great Britain

The Lord Chief Justice of England

The President of the Family Division

The Vice-Chancellor

The Senior Presiding Judge for England and Wales

The puisne judges of the High Court

Chancery Division

The Lord High Chancellor of Great Britain

The Vice-Chancellor

Sir Francis Mursell Ferris
Sir John Edmund Frederic Lindsay
Sir Edward Christopher Evans-Lombe
Sir Robin Raphael Hayim Jacob
Sir William Anthony Blackburne
Sir Gavin Anthony Lightman
Sir Colin Percy Farquharson Rimer
Sir Hugh Ian Lang Laddie

Sir Timothy Andrew Wigram Lloyd
Sir David Edmund Neuberger
Sir Andrew Edward Wilson Park
Sir Nicholas Richard Pumfrey
Sir Michael Christopher Campbell Hart
Sir Lawrence Anthony Collins
Sir Nicholas John Patten
Sir Terrence Michael Elkan Barnet Etherton

Queen's Bench Division

The Lord Chief Justice of England

Sir Patrick Neville Garland
Sir Michael John Turner
Sir Richard George Rougier
Sir Stuart Neil McKinnon
Sir Thomas Scott Gillespie Baker
Sir Douglas Dunlop Brown
Sir Michael Morland
Sir Roger John Buckley
Sir Anthony Brian Hidden
Sir John Michael Wright
Sir Peter John Cresswell
Sir Christopher John Holland
Sir Richard Herbert Curtis
Dame Janet Hilary Smith
Sir Anthony David Colman
Sir John Thayne Forbes
Sir Michael Alexander Geddes Sachs
Sir Stephen George Mitchell
Sir Rodger Bell
Sir Michael Guy Vicat Harrison

Sir William Marcus Gage
Sir Thomas Richard Atkin Morison
Sir Andrew David Collins
Sir Maurice Ralph Kay
Sir Anthony Hooper
Sir Alexander Neil Logie Butterfield
Sir George Michael Newman
Sir David Anthony Poole
Sir Martin James Moore-Bick
Sir Gordon Julian Hugh Langley
Sir Roger John Laugharne Thomas
Sir Robert Franklyn Nelson
Sir Roger Grenfell Toulson
Sir Michael John Astill
Sir Alan George Moses
Sir Timothy Edward Walker
Sir David Eady
Sir Jeremy Mirth Sullivan
Sir David Herbert Penry-Davey
Sir Stephen Price Richards

[*continued on next page*]

Queen's Bench Division (*continued*)

Sir David William Steel
Sir Rodney Conrad Klevan (died 26 December
  2001)
Sir Charles Antony St John Gray
Sir Nicolas Dusan Bratza
Sir Michael John Burton
Sir Rupert Matthew Jackson
Dame Heather Carol Hallett
Sir Patrick Elias
Sir Richard John Pearson Aikens
Sir Stephen Robert Silber
Sir John Bernard Goldring
Sir Peter Francis Crane
Dame Anne Judith Rafferty
Sir Geoffery Douglas Grigson
Sir Richard John Hedley Gibbs
Sir Richard Henry Quixano Henriques
Sir Stephen Miles Tomlinson
Sir Andrew Charles Smith

Sir Stanley Jeffrey Burnton
Sir Patrick James Hunt
Sir Christopher John Pitchford
Sir Brian Henry Leveson
Sir Duncan Brian Walter Ouseley
Sir Richard George Bramwell McCombe
Sir Raymond Evan Jack
Sir Robert Michael Owen
Sir Colin Crichton Mackay
Sir John Edward Mitting
Sir David Roderick Evans
Sir Nigel Anthony Lamert Davis
Sir Peter Henry Gross
Sir Brian Richard Keith
Sir Jeremy Lionel Cooke
Sir Richard Alan Field (appointed 15 January 2002)
Sir Christopher John Pitchers (appointed
  16 January 2002)

Family Division

The President of the Family Division

Sir Robert Lionel Johnson
Dame Joyanne Winifred Bracewell
Sir Michael Bryan Connell (retired 11 January
  2002)
Sir Jan Peter Singer
Sir Nicholas Allan Roy Wilson
Sir Nicholas Peter Rathbone Wall
Sir Andrew Tristram Hammett Kirkwood
Sir Hugh Peter Derwyn Bennett
Sir Edward James Holman

Dame Mary Claire Hogg
Sir Christopher John Sumner
Sir Anthony Philip Gilson Hughes
Sir Arthur William Hessin Charles
Sir David Roderick Lessiter Bodey
Dame Jill Margaret Black
Sir James Lawrence Munby
Sir Paul James Duke Coleridge
Sir Mark Hedley (appointed 15 January 2002)

Official Judgment Numbers
and
Paragraph References

Since 11 January 2001, official judgment numbers have been given to all judgments delivered in the House of Lords, Privy Council, both divisions of the Court of Appeal and the Administrative Court. All such judgments have fixed paragraph numbering, as do judgments delivered on or after 11 January 2001 in those parts of the High Court which did not then adopt the system of official judgment numbers (see Practice Note (judgments: neutral citation) [2001] 1 All ER 193 for the Court of Appeal and the High Court). On 14 January 2002 the system of judgment numbers was extended to all parts of the High Court (see Practice Direction (High Court judgments: neutral citation) [2002] 1 All ER 351). We have adopted the following practice in respect of judgments with official judgment numbers and official paragraph numbering:

- The official judgment number is inserted immediately beneath the case name;
- Official paragraph numbers are in bold in square brackets;
- Holding references in the headnotes, and any other cross-references, are to an official paragraph number, not to a page of the report;
- When such a judgment is subsequently cited in another report,

    (i) the official judgment number is inserted before the usual report citations in the case lists and on the first occasion when the case is cited in the text. Thereafter, only the report citations are given;

    (ii) All 'at' references are to the official paragraph number rather than to a page of a report, with the paragraph number in square brackets but not in bold;

    (iii) The 'at' reference is only given in conjunction with the first report cited; eg [2001] 4 All ER 159 at [16], [2001] AC 61. If an 'at' reference is included on the first occasion when the case is cited, it also appears alongside the official judgment number.

For the avoidance of doubt, these changes do not apply to reports of judgments delivered before 11 January 2001 or to the citation of such cases in other reports.

CITATION

These reports are cited thus:

[2002] 1 All ER

REFERENCES

These reports contain references to the following major works of legal reference described in the manner indicated below.

Halsbury's Laws of England

The reference 14 *Halsbury's Laws* (4th edn) para 185 refers to paragraph 185 on page 90 of volume 14 of the fourth edition of *Halsbury's Laws of England*.

The reference 15 *Halsbury's Laws* (4th edn reissue) para 355 refers to paragraph 355 on page 283 of reissue volume 15 of the fourth edition of *Halsbury's Laws of England*.

The reference 7(1) *Halsbury's Laws* (4th edn) (1996 reissue) para 9 refers to paragraph 9 on page 24 of the 1996 reissue of volume 7(1) of the fourth edition of *Halsbury's Laws of England*.

Halsbury's Statutes of England and Wales

The reference 26 *Halsbury's Statutes* (4th edn) 734 refers to page 734 of volume 26 of the fourth edition of *Halsbury's Statutes of England and Wales*.

The reference 40 *Halsbury's Statutes* (4th edn) (2001 reissue) 269 refers to page 269 of the 2001 reissue of volume 40 of the fourth edition of *Halsbury's Statutes of England and Wales*.

Halsbury's Statutory Instruments

The reference 14 *Halsbury's Statutory Instruments* (1999 issue) 201 refers to page 201 of the 1999 issue of volume 14 of the grey volumes series of *Halsbury's Statutory Instruments*.

Cases reported in volume 1

Digest of cases reported in volume 1

xvii

R (on the application of Pretty) v Director of Public Prosecutions

[2001] UKHL 61

HOUSE OF LORDS

LORD BINGHAM OF CORNHILL, LORD STEYN, LORD HOPE OF CRAIGHEAD, LORD HOBHOUSE
OF WOODBOROUGH AND LORD SCOTT OF FOSCOTE

14, 15, 29 NOVEMBER 2001

d

*Criminal law – Suicide – Liability for complicity in another's suicide – Claimant
suffering from terminal disease and wishing to commit suicide – Claimant's condition
preventing her from committing suicide – Claimant seeking undertaking from DPP that
husband would not be prosecuted if he assisted her to commit suicide – DPP refusing to
give undertaking – Whether human rights convention requiring state to legalise
assisted suicide – Suicide Act 1961, s 2 – Human Rights Act 1998, Sch 1, Pt I, arts 2, 3,
8, 9, 14.*

e

*Criminal law – Proceedings – Director of Public Prosecutions – Whether DPP having
power to give prior undertaking not to prosecute.*

f

The claimant, P, suffered from motor neurone disease, a progressive degenerative
illness from which she had no hope of recovery. The disease was at an advanced
stage and she was paralysed from the neck downwards, but her intellect and
capacity to make decisions were unimpaired. She wished to be spared the
suffering and loss of dignity which was all that was left to her of life and therefore
wanted to control when and how she died. As the disease had deprived her of the
ability to commit suicide, she wished her husband to assist her. He agreed,
provided that the Director of Public Prosecutions (DPP) would undertake not to
prosecute him for the offence of assisting suicide contrary to s 2(1)[a] of the Suicide
Act 1961. Under s 2(4), no such prosecution could be instituted without the
DPP's consent. After the DPP refused to provide the undertaking sought, P
applied for judicial review, seeking a declaration that the refusal was unlawful
since it infringed certain of her rights under the European Convention for the
Protection of Human Rights and Fundamental Freedoms 1950 (as set out in Sch 1
to the Human Rights Act 1998). Alternatively, she sought a declaration that s 2(1)
of the 1961 Act was incompatible with those rights in so far as it imposed a blanket
prohibition on assisted suicide. She relied on the right to life under art 2[b] of the
convention (on the basis that it protected a person's right to self-determination in
relation to issues of life and death); the prohibition against inhuman or degrading

g

h

j

---

a Section 2, so far as material, is set out at [45], below
b Article 2 is set out at [3], below

treatment in art 3^c (on the basis that the DPP's refusal subjected her to such
treatment); the right to respect for private and family life in art 8^d (on the basis
that it recognised the personal autonomy of every individual and therefore
necessarily involved a guarantee as against the state of a right to choose when and
how to die); the right to freedom of thought under art 9^e (on the basis that it
entitled P to manifest her belief in assisted suicide by committing it); and the
prohibition by art 14^f of discrimination in the enjoyment of convention rights
(on the basis that P was treated less favourably than those who were physically
capable of ending their lives). The Divisional Court dismissed the application on
the merits, but held that in any event the DPP's decision was not amenable to
judicial review. P appealed to the House of Lords.

Held – (1) A refusal by the DPP to give an undertaking not to prosecute was not
amenable to judicial review in the absence of dishonesty, mala fides or exceptional
circumstances. In the instant case, however, there were such circumstances. It
did not concern a straightforward situation in which a person sought an assurance
after the event that he would not be prosecuted. It was therefore no answer for
P to be told that the matter should be dealt with at a criminal trial or on appeal.
There would be no criminal trial in which the issue as to whether the DPP was
acting compatibly with P's convention rights could be tested. Accordingly, it was
open to her to raise the issue by judicial review (see [67], [77], [78], [124], below).

(2) Nevertheless, the appeal would be dismissed for the following reasons—

(i) The convention did not oblige a state to legalise assisted suicide.
Article 2 did not acknowledge that it was for the individual to choose
whether to live or die and it did not protect a right of self-determination in
relation to issues of life and death. Rather, it enunciated the principle of the
sanctity of life and provided a guarantee that no individual should be
deprived of life by means of intentional human intervention. That was the
exact opposite of a right to end life by means of intentional human intervention.
Nor was art 3 engaged. The concept that no person should be subjected to
inhuman or degrading treatment was singularly inapt to convey the idea that
the state had to guarantee to individuals a right to die with the deliberate
assistance of third parties. Further, it was doubtful whether the consequences
of refusing to give the undertaking would attain the required minimum level
of severity of ill treatment in view of the palliative care available to P.
Moreover, 'treatment' should not be given an unrestricted or extravagant
meaning, and it could not plausibly be suggested that the DPP was inflicting
inhuman or degrading treatment on P, whose suffering derived from her
disease. As regards art 8, it prohibited interference with the way in which an
individual led his life and did not relate to the manner in which he wished to
die. Nor was art 9 intended to give individuals a right to perform any acts in
pursuance of whatever beliefs they might hold. Similarly, art 14 did not
assist P. Although that provision was capable of extending to discrimination
in the enjoyment of convention rights on the grounds of physical or mental
capacity, s 2(1) of the 1961 Act did not treat individuals in a discriminatory
manner. The 1961 Act conferred no right to commit suicide, and there was

c   Article 3 is set out at [10], below
d   Article 8 is set out at [16], below
e   Article 9 is set out at [63], below
f   Article 14 is set out at [32], below

a no unequal treatment before the law in respect of the offence under s 2(1). The majority of terminally ill individuals would be vulnerable, and it was the vulnerability of that class of persons which provided the rationale for making the aiding and abetting of suicide an offence under s 2(1). In any event, P's case did not engage any convention right or freedom to which art 14 could be attached. Even if convention rights were engaged, s 2(1) struck the right

b balance between the rights of individuals and the public interest which sought to protect the weak and vulnerable. It was a proportionate response for Parliament to conclude that the state's interest in protecting the lives of its citizens could only be met by a complete prohibition on assisted suicide (see [5], [9], [13], [15], [23], [26], [29], [30], [31], [34]–[37], [59]–[66], [68], [70], [87], [88], [91], [92], [97], [100]–[102], [105]– [108], [112], [124], below).

c   (ii) Section 2(4) of the 1961 Act did not empower the DPP to give the undertaking sought. A conclusion to the contrary could not be justified by the statutory language and would be inconsistent with the manifest limited purpose of s 2(4). The discretion conferred by that provision was contained in a criminal statute and was concerned with the deep-rooted sanctity of life

d principle. In that context, it was plainly beyond the power conferred by s 2(4) for the DPP to choose not to enforce s 2(1) or to disapply it. He might only exercise his discretion, for or against a prosecution, in relation to the circumstances of a specific prosecution. His discretion could therefore only be exercised in respect of past events giving rise to a suspicion that a crime under s 2(1) had been committed (see [39], [40], [70], [124], below).

e
    Per curiam. Although the DPP has no power to indicate, before the commission of a particular crime, that he will or will not prosecute if it is committed, there may be rare occasions in which it will be appropriate, and in the public interest, for the DPP to issue statements giving guidance as to how he will exercise his discretion in regard to particular offences. He is therefore entitled to form a

f policy as to the criteria that he will apply when he is exercising his discretion under s 2(4). However, the DPP cannot be compelled to issue such a statement of policy (see [66], [80], [82], [124], below).

Notes

g For the right to life, the prohibition on inhuman and degrading treatment, the right to respect for private and family life, the right to freedom of thought and the prohibition of discrimination, see 8(2) *Halsbury's Laws* (4th edn reissue) paras 123–124, 149–151, 156–157, 164, and for complicity in suicide, see 11(1) *Halsbury's Laws* (4th edn reissue) para 443.

h   For the Suicide Act 1961, s 2, see 12 *Halsbury's Statutes* (4th edn) (1997 reissue) 297.

    For the Human Rights Act 1998, Sch 1, Pt I, arts 2, 3, 8, 9, 14, see 7 *Halsbury's Statutes* (4th edn) (1999 reissue) 522, 524, 525.

Cases referred to in opinions

j *A (children) (conjoined twins: surgical separation), Re* [2000] 4 All ER 961, [2001] Fam 147, [2001] 2 WLR 480, CA.
A-G of Trinidad and Tobago v Phillip [1995] 1 All ER 93, [1995] 1 AC 396, [1994] 3 WLR 1134, PC.
A v UK (1998) 5 BHRC 137, ECt HR.
Abdulaziz v UK (1985) 7 EHRR 471, [1985] ECHR 9214/80, ECt HR.

Airedale NHS Trust v Bland [1993] 1 All ER 821, [1993] AC 789, [1993] 2 WLR 316, Fam D, CA and HL.

Alkmaar NJ (1984) No 106, 451, Neth SC.

Botta v Italy (1998) 4 BHRC 81, ECt HR.

Brown v Stott (Procurator Fiscal, Dunfermline) [2001] 2 All ER 97, [2001] 2 WLR 817, PC.

Chahal v UK (1996) 1 BHRC 405, ECt HR.

D v UK (1997) 2 BHRC 273, ECt HR.

De Freitas v Permanent Secretary of Ministry of Agriculture, Fisheries, Lands and Housing [1999] 1 AC 69, [1998] 3 WLR 675, PC.

J (a minor) (wardship: medical treatment), Re [1990] 3 All ER 930, [1991] Fam 33, [1991] 2 WLR 140, CA.

Johansen v Norway (1996) 23 EHRR 33, [1996] ECHR 17383/90, ECt HR.

Keenan v UK (2001) 10 BHRC 319, ECt HR.

Laskey v UK (1997) 24 EHRR 39, [1997] ECHR 21627/93, ECt HR.

Law Hospital NHS Trust v Lord Advocate 1996 SLT 848, Ct of Sess (IH).

Lockhart v Deighan 1985 SLT 549, HC of Just.

NHS Trust A v H [2001] 2 FLR 501.

Nyambirai v National Social Security Authority [1996] 1 LRC 64, Zim SC.

Osman v UK (1998) 5 BHRC 293, ECt HR.

R (P) v Secretary of State for the Home Dept, R (Q) v Secretary of State for the Home Dept [2001] EWCA Civ 1151, [2001] 1 WLR 2002.

R v A (No 2) [2001] UKHL 25, [2001] 3 All ER 1, [2001] 2 WLR 1546, HL.

R v Brown [1993] 2 All ER 75, [1994] 1 AC 212, [1993] 2 WLR 556, HL.

R v Croft [1944] 2 All ER 483, [1944] KB 295, CCA.

R v DPP, ex p Kebeline, R v DPP, ex p Rechachi [1999] 4 All ER 801, [2000] 2 AC 326, [1999] 3 WLR 972, DC and HL.

R v Giannetto [1997] 1 Cr App R 1, CA.

R v Howe [1987] 1 All ER 771, [1987] AC 417, [1987] 2 WLR 568, HL.

R v Richards (Isabelle) [1973] 3 All ER 1088, [1974] QB 776, [1973] 3 WLR 888, CA.

R v UK (1983) 33 DR 270, E Com HR.

Rees v UK (1986) 9 EHRR 56, [1986] ECHR 9532/81, ECt HR.

Rodriguez v A-G of Canada [1994] 2 LRC 136, Can SC; *affg* (1993) 76 BCLR (2d) 145, BC CA.

St George's Healthcare NHS Trust v S, R v Collins, ex p S [1998] 3 All ER 673, [1999] Fam 26, [1998] 3 WLR 936, CA.

Sanles v Spain [2001] EHRLR 348, ECt HR.

Smith v UK (2000) 29 EHRR 493, [1999] ECHR 33985/96, ECt HR.

Thlimmenos v Greece (2000) 9 BHRC 12, ECt HR.

Vacco v Quill (1997) 521 US 793, US SC.

Van Raalte v Netherlands (1997) 24 EHRR 503, [1997] ECHR 20060/92, ECt HR.

Washington v Glucksberg (1997) 521 US 702, US SC.

X v Germany (1983) 7 EHRR 152, E Com HR.

X v Netherlands (1985) 8 EHRR 235, [1985] ECHR 8978/80, ECt HR.

Young v UK (1981) 4 EHRR 38, [1981] ECHR 7601/76, ECt HR.

Z v UK [2001] 2 FCR 246, ECt HR.

Appeal

The claimant, Dianne Pretty, appealed with permission of the Appeal Committee of the House of Lords given on 1 November 2001 from the decision of the Divisional Court (Tuckey, Hale LJJ and Silber J) on 17 October 2001 ([2001] EWHC *a* Admin 788, [2001] All ER (D) 251 (Oct)) dismissing her application for judicial review of the refusal of the defendant, the Director of Public Prosecutions, on 8 August 2001 to give an undertaking not to prosecute Mrs Pretty's husband if he assisted her to commit suicide on the grounds set out in a letter dated 27 July 2001 to the Director from Mrs Pretty's solicitors. The Divisional Court certified that three points of law of general public importance, set out at [49], below, were

b involved in its decision. The Secretary of State for the Home Department participated in the proceedings as an interested party. The facts are set out in the opinion of Lord Bingham of Cornhill.

Philip Havers QC and *Fenella Morris* (instructed by *Liberty*) for Mrs Pretty.
David Perry and *Robin McCoubrey* (instructed by the *Treasury Solicitor*) for the
c   Director.
Jonathan Crow (instructed by the *Treasury Solicitor*) for the Secretary of State.

Their Lordships took time for consideration.

d 29 November 2001. The following opinions were delivered.

LORD BINGHAM OF CORNHILL.

[1] My Lords, no one of ordinary sensitivity could be unmoved by the frightening ordeal which faces Mrs Dianne Pretty, the appellant. She suffers from
e motor neurone disease, a progressive degenerative illness from which she has no hope of recovery. She has only a short time to live and faces the prospect of a humiliating and distressing death. She is mentally alert and would like to be able to take steps to bring her life to a peaceful end at a time of her choosing. But her physical incapacity is now such that she can no longer, without help, take her own life. With the support of her family, she wishes to enlist the help of her husband
f to that end. He himself is willing to give such help, but only if he can be sure that he will not be prosecuted under s 2(1) of the Suicide Act 1961 for aiding and abetting her suicide. Asked to undertake that he would not under s 2(4) of that Act consent to the prosecution of Mr Pretty under s 2(1) if Mr Pretty were to assist his wife to commit suicide, the Director of Public Prosecutions (the Director) has refused to give such an undertaking. On Mrs Pretty's application for judicial
g review of that refusal, the Queen's Bench Divisional Court ([2001] EWHC Admin 788, [2001] All ER (D) 251 (Oct)) upheld the Director's decision and refused relief. Mrs Pretty claims that she has a right to her husband's assistance in committing suicide and that s 2 of the 1961 Act, if it prohibits his helping and prevents the Director undertaking not to prosecute if he does, is incompatible with the
h European Convention for the Protection of Human Rights and Fundamental Freedoms (Rome, 4 November 1950; TS 71 (1953); Cmd 8969) (as set out in Sch 1 to the Human Rights Act 1998). It is on the convention, brought into force in this country by the 1998 Act, that Mrs Pretty's claim to relief depends. It is accepted by her counsel on her behalf that under the common law of England she could
j not have hoped to succeed.

[2] In discharging the judicial functions of the House, the Appellate Committee has the duty of resolving issues of law properly brought before it, as the issues in this case have been. The committee is not a legislative body. Nor is it entitled or fitted to act as a moral or ethical arbiter. It is important to emphasise the nature and limits of the committee's role, since the wider issues raised by this appeal are the subject of profound and fully justified concern to very many people. The

questions whether the terminally ill, or others, should be free to seek assistance
in taking their own lives, and if so in what circumstances and subject to what
safeguards, are of great social, ethical and religious significance and are questions
on which widely differing beliefs and views are held, often strongly. Materials
laid before the committee (with its leave) express some of those views; many
others have been expressed in the news media, professional journals and
elsewhere. The task of the committee in this appeal is not to weigh or evaluate
or reflect those beliefs and views or give effect to its own but to ascertain and
apply the law of the land as it is now understood to be.

Article 2 of the convention
   [3] Article 2 of the convention provides:

> 'Right to life
> 1. Everyone's right to life shall be protected by law. No one shall be
> deprived of his life intentionally save in the execution of a sentence of a court
> following his conviction of a crime for which this penalty is provided by law.
> 2. Deprivation of life shall not be regarded as inflicted in contravention of
> this Article when it results from the use of force which is no more than
> absolutely necessary: (a) in defence of any person from unlawful violence;
> (b) in order to effect a lawful arrest or to prevent the escape of a person
> lawfully detained; (c) in action lawfully taken for the purpose of quelling a
> riot or insurrection.'

The article is to be read in conjunction with arts 1 and 2 of the Sixth Protocol,
which are among the convention rights protected by the 1998 Act (see s 1(1)(c))
and which abolished the death penalty in time of peace.
   [4] On behalf of Mrs Pretty it is submitted that art 2 of the convention protects
not life itself but the right to life. The purpose of the article is to protect
individuals from third parties (the state and public authorities). But the article
recognises that it is for the individual to choose whether or not to live and so
protects the individual's right to self-determination in relation to issues of life and
death. Thus a person may refuse life-saving or life-prolonging medical treatment,
and may lawfully choose to commit suicide. The article acknowledges that right
of the individual. While most people want to live, some want to die, and the
article protects both rights. The right to die is not the antithesis of the right to life
but the corollary of it, and the state has a positive obligation to protect both.
   [5] The Secretary of State has advanced a number of unanswerable objections
to this argument which were rightly upheld by the Divisional Court. The starting
point must be the language of the article. The thrust of this is to reflect the
sanctity which, particularly in Western eyes, attaches to life. The article protects
the right to life and prevents the deliberate taking of life save in very narrowly
defined circumstances. An article with that effect cannot be interpreted as
conferring a right to die or to enlist the aid of another in bringing about one's own
death. In his argument for Mrs Pretty, Mr Havers QC was at pains to limit his
argument to assisted suicide, accepting that the right claimed could not extend to
cover an intentional consensual killing (usually described in this context as
'voluntary euthanasia', but regarded in English law as murder). The right claimed
would be sufficient to cover Mrs Pretty's case and counsel's unwillingness to go
further is understandable. But there is in logic no justification for drawing a line
at this point. If art 2 does confer a right to self-determination in relation to life
and death, and if a person were so gravely disabled as to be unable to perform any

a act whatever to cause his or her own death, it would necessarily follow in logic that such a person would have a right to be killed at the hands of a third party without giving any help to the third party and the state would be in breach of the convention if it were to interfere with the exercise of that right. No such right can possibly be derived from an article having the object already defined.

[6] It is true that some of the guaranteed convention rights have been
b interpreted as conferring rights not to do that which is the antithesis of what there is an express right to do. Article 11, for example, confers a right not to join an association (*Young v UK* (1981) 4 EHRR 38), art 9 embraces a right to freedom from any compulsion to express thoughts or change an opinion or divulge convictions (Clayton and Tomlinson *The Law of Human Rights* (2000) p 974 (para 14.49)) and
c I would for my part be inclined to infer that art 12 confers a right not to marry (but see Clayton and Tomlinson p 913 (para 13.76)). It cannot, however, be suggested (to take some obvious examples) that arts 3, 4, 5 and 6 confer an implied right to do or experience the opposite of that which the articles guarantee. Whatever the benefits which, in the view of many, attach to voluntary euthanasia, suicide, physician-assisted suicide and suicide assisted without the intervention of a
d physician, these are not benefits which derive protection from an article framed to protect the sanctity of life.

[7] There is no convention authority to support Mrs Pretty's argument. To the extent that there is any relevant authority it is adverse to her. In *Osman v UK* (1998) 5 BHRC 293 the applicants complained of a failure by the United Kingdom
e to protect the right to life of the second applicant and his deceased father. The court said (at 321):

f '115. The court notes that the first sentence of art 2(1) enjoins the state not only to refrain from the intentional and unlawful taking of life, but also to take appropriate steps to safeguard the lives of those within its jurisdiction … It is common ground that the state's obligation in this respect extends beyond its primary duty to secure the right to life by putting in place effective criminal law provisions to deter the commission of offences against the person backed up by law enforcement machinery for the prevention, suppression and sanctioning of breaches of such provisions. It is thus
g accepted by those appearing before the court that art 2 of the convention may also imply in certain well-defined circumstances a positive obligation on the authorities to take preventive operational measures to protect an individual whose life is at risk from the criminal acts of another individual. The scope of this obligation is a matter of dispute between the parties.

h 116. For the court, and bearing in mind the difficulties involved in policing modern societies, the unpredictability of human conduct and the operational choices which must be made in terms of priorities and resources, such an obligation must be interpreted in a way which does not impose an impossible or disproportionate burden on the authorities. Accordingly, not
j every claimed risk to life can entail for the authorities a convention requirement to take operational measures to prevent that risk from materialising. Another relevant consideration is the need to ensure that the police exercise their powers to control and prevent crime in a manner which fully respects the due process and other guarantees which legitimately place restraints on the scope of their action to investigate crime and bring offenders to justice, including the guarantees contained in arts 5 and 8 of the convention.'

The context of that case was very different. Neither the second applicant nor his
father had had any wish to die. But the court's approach to art 2 was entirely *a*
consistent with the interpretation I have put upon it.

[8] *X v Germany* (1983) 7 EHRR 152 and *Keenan v UK* (2001) 10 BHRC 319 were
also decided in a factual context very different from the present. X, while in
prison, had gone on hunger strike and had been forcibly fed by the prison
authorities. His complaint was of maltreatment contrary to art 3 of the convention, *b*
considered below. The complaint was rejected and in the course of its reasoning
the European Commission of Human Rights held ((1983) 7 EHRR 152 at
153–154):

> 'In the opinion of the Commission forced feeding of a person does involve
> degrading elements which in certain circumstances may be regarded as *c*
> prohibited by Art. 3 of the Convention. Under the Convention the High
> Contracting Parties are, however, also obliged to secure to everyone the
> right to life as set out in Art. 2. Such an obligation should in certain
> circumstances call for positive action on the part of the Contracting Parties,
> in particular an active measure to save lives when the authorities have taken
> the person in question into their custody. When, as in the present case, a *d*
> detained person maintains a hunger strike this may inevitably lead to a
> conflict between an individual's right to physical integrity and the High
> Contracting Party's obligation under Art. 2 of the Convention—a conflict
> which is not solved by the Convention itself. The Commission recalls that
> under German law this conflict has been solved in that it is possible to *e*
> force-feed a detained person if this person, due to a hunger strike, would be
> subject to injuries of a permanent character, and the forced feeding is even
> obligatory if an obvious danger for the individual's life exists. The assessment
> of the above-mentioned conditions is left for the doctor in charge but an
> eventual decision to force-feed may only be carried out after judicial
> permission has been obtained ... The Commission is satisfied that the *f*
> authorities acted solely in the best interests of the applicant when choosing
> between either respect for the applicant's will not to accept nourishment of
> any kind and thereby incur the risk that he might be subject to lasting injuries
> or even die, or to take action with a view to securing his survival although
> such action might infringe the applicant's human dignity.' *g*

In *Keenan v UK* a young prisoner had committed suicide and his mother
complained of a failure by the prison authorities to protect his life. In the course
of its judgment rejecting the complaint under this article the court said ((2001)
10 BHRC 319 at 348–349):

> '90. In the context of prisoners, the court has had previous occasion to *h*
> emphasise that persons in custody are in a vulnerable position and that the
> authorities are under a duty to protect them. It is incumbent on the state to
> account for any injuries suffered in custody, which obligation is particularly
> stringent where that individual dies ... It may be noted that this need for
> scrutiny is acknowledged in the domestic law of England and Wales, where *j*
> inquests are automatically held concerning the deaths of persons in prison and
> where the domestic courts have imposed a duty of care on prison authorities
> in respect of those detained in their custody.'

Both these cases can be distinguished, since the conduct complained of took place
when the victim was in the custody of the state, which accordingly had a special

a responsibility for the victim's welfare. It may readily be accepted that the obligation of the state to safeguard the life of a potential victim is enhanced when the latter is in the custody of the state. To that extent these two cases are different from the present, since Mrs Pretty is not in the custody of the state. Thus the state's positive obligation to protect the life of Mrs Pretty is weaker than in such cases. It would, however, be a very large, and in my view quite impermissible,

b step to proceed from acceptance of that proposition to acceptance of the assertion that the state has a duty to recognise a right for Mrs Pretty to be assisted to take her own life.

[9] In the convention field the authority of domestic decisions is necessarily limited and, as already noted, Mrs Pretty bases her case on the convention. But it is worthy of note that her argument is inconsistent with two principles deeply

c embedded in English law. The first is a distinction between the taking of one's own life by one's own act and the taking of life through the intervention or with the help of a third party. The former has been permissible since suicide ceased to be a crime in 1961. The latter has continued to be proscribed. The distinction was very clearly expressed by Hoffmann LJ in *Airedale NHS Trust v Bland* [1993]

d 1 All ER 821 at 855, [1993] AC 789 at 831:

> *e* 'No one in this case is suggesting that Anthony Bland should be given a lethal injection. But there is concern about ceasing to supply food as against, for example, ceasing to treat an infection with antibiotics. Is there any real distinction? In order to come to terms with our intuitive feelings about whether there is a distinction, I must start by considering why most of us would be appalled if he was given a lethal injection. It is, I think, connected with our view that the sanctity of life entails its inviolability by an outsider. Subject to exceptions like self-defence, human life is inviolate even if the person in question has consented to its violation. That is why although suicide is not a crime, assisting someone to commit suicide is. It follows that,
> *f* even if we think Anthony Bland would have consented, we would not be entitled to end his life by a lethal injection.'

The second distinction is between the cessation of life-saving or life-prolonging treatment on the one hand and the taking of action lacking medical, therapeutic or palliative justification but intended solely to terminate life on the other. This

g distinction provided the rationale of the decisions in *Bland's* case. It was very succinctly expressed in the Court of Appeal in *Re J (a minor) (wardship: medical treatment)* [1990] 3 All ER 930, [1991] Fam 33, in which Lord Donaldson of Lymington MR said:

> *h* 'What doctors and the court have to decide is whether, in the best interests of the child patient, a particular decision as to medical treatment should be taken which *as a side effect* will render death more or less likely. This is not a matter of semantics. It is fundamental. At the other end of the age spectrum, the use of drugs to reduce pain will often be fully justified, notwithstanding that this will hasten the moment of death. What can never be justified is the
> *j* use of drugs or surgical procedures with the primary purpose of doing so.'
> (See [1990] 3 All ER 930 at 938, [1991] Fam 33 at 46.)

Similar observations were made by Balcombe and Taylor LJJ ([1990] 3 All ER 930 at 941–942, 943, [1991] Fam 33 at 51, 53 respectively). While these distinctions are in no way binding on the European Court of Human Rights there is nothing to suggest that they are inconsistent with the jurisprudence which has grown up

around the convention. It is not enough for Mrs Pretty to show that the United *a*
Kingdom would not be acting inconsistently with the convention if it were to
permit assisted suicide; she must go further and establish that the United
Kingdom is in breach of the convention by failing to permit it or would be in
breach of the convention if it did not permit it. Such a contention is in my opinion
untenable, as the Divisional Court rightly held.

b

Article 3 of the convention
  [10] Article 3 of the convention provides:

> '*Prohibition of torture*
> No one shall be subjected to torture or to inhuman or degrading treatment
> or punishment.'   *c*

This is one of the articles from which a member state may not derogate even in
time of war or other public emergency threatening the life of the nation (see
art 15). I shall for convenience use the expression 'proscribed treatment' to mean
'inhuman or degrading treatment' as that expression is used in the convention.
  [11] In brief summary the argument for Mrs Pretty proceeded by these steps. *d*
(1) Member states have an absolute and unqualified obligation not to inflict the
proscribed treatment and also to take positive action to prevent the subjection of
individuals to such treatment (see *A v UK* (1998) 5 BHRC 137, *Z v UK* [2001] 2 FCR
246 at 265 (para 73)). (2) Suffering attributable to the progression of a disease may
amount to such treatment if the state can prevent or ameliorate such suffering *e*
and does not do so (see *D v UK* (1997) 2 BHRC 273 at 283–285 (paras 46–54)).
(3) In denying Mrs Pretty the opportunity to bring her suffering to an end the
United Kingdom (by the Director) will subject her to the proscribed treatment.
The state can spare Mrs Pretty the suffering which she will otherwise endure
since, if the Director undertakes not to give his consent to prosecution, Mr Pretty
will assist his wife to commit suicide and so she will be spared much suffering. *f*
(4) Since, as the Divisional Court held, it is open to the United Kingdom under
the convention to refrain from prohibiting assisted suicide, the Director can
give the undertaking sought without breaking the United Kingdom's obligations
under the convention. (5) If the Director may not give the undertaking, s 2 of the
1961 Act is incompatible with the convention.
  [12] For the Secretary of State it was submitted that in the present case art 3 of *g*
the convention is not engaged at all but that if any of the rights protected by that
article are engaged they do not include a right to die. In support of the first of
these submissions it was argued that there is in the present case no breach of the
prohibition in the article. The negative prohibition in the article is absolute and
unqualified but the positive obligations which flow from it are not absolute (see *h*
Osman v UK (1998) 5 BHRC 293, *Rees v UK* (1986) 9 EHRR 56). While states may
be obliged to protect the life and health of a person in custody (as in the case of
Keenan v UK), and to ensure that individuals are not subjected to proscribed
treatment at the hands of private individuals other than state agents (as in *A v UK*),
and the state may not take direct action in relation to an individual which would *j*
inevitably involve the inflicting of proscribed treatment upon him (*D v UK*), none
of these obligations can be invoked by Mrs Pretty in the present case. In support
of the second submission it was argued that, far from suggesting that the state is
under a duty to provide medical care to ease her condition and prolong her life,
Mrs Pretty is arguing that the state is under a legal obligation to sanction a lawful
means for terminating her life. There is nothing, either in the wording of the

a convention or the Strasbourg jurisprudence, to suggest that any such duty exists by virtue of art 3. The decision how far the state should go in discharge of its positive obligation to protect individuals from proscribed treatment is one for member states, taking account of all relevant interests and considerations; such a decision, while not immune from review, must be accorded respect. The United Kingdom has reviewed these issues in depth and resolved to maintain the present

b position.

[13] Article 3 enshrines one of the fundamental values of democratic societies and its prohibition of the proscribed treatment is absolute (*D v UK* (1997) 2 BHRC 273 at 283 (para 47)). Article 3 is, as I think, complementary to art 2. As art 2 requires states to respect and safeguard the lives of individuals within their jurisdiction, so art 3 obliges them to respect the physical and human integrity of

c such individuals. There is in my opinion nothing in art 3 which bears on an individual's right to live or to choose not to live. That is not its sphere of application; indeed, as is clear from *X v Germany*, a state may on occasion be justified in inflicting treatment which would otherwise be in breach of art 3 in order to serve the ends of art 2. Moreover, the absolute and unqualified prohibition on a

d member state inflicting the proscribed treatment requires that 'treatment' should not be given an unrestricted or extravagant meaning. It cannot, in my opinion, be plausibly suggested that the Director or any other agent of the United Kingdom is inflicting the proscribed treatment on Mrs Pretty, whose suffering derives from her cruel disease.

e [14] The authority most helpful to Mrs Pretty is *D v UK*, which concerned the removal to St Kitts of a man in the later stages of AIDS. The convention challenge was to implementation of the removal decision having regard to the applicant's medical condition, the absence of facilities to provide adequate treatment, care or support in St Kitts and the disruption of a regime in the United Kingdom which had afforded him sophisticated treatment and medication in a compassionate

f environment. It was held that implementation of the decision to remove the applicant to St Kitts would amount in the circumstances to inhuman treatment by the United Kingdom in violation of art 3. In that case the state was proposing to take direct action against the applicant, the inevitable effect of which would be a severe increase in his suffering and a shortening of his life. The proposed deportation could fairly be regarded as 'treatment'. An analogy might be found

g in the present case if a public official had forbidden the provision to Mrs Pretty of pain-killing or palliative drugs. But here the proscribed treatment is said to be the Director's refusal of proleptic immunity from prosecution to Mr Pretty if he commits a crime. By no legitimate process of interpretation can that refusal be held to fall within the negative prohibition of art 3.

h [15] If it be assumed that art 3 is capable of being applied at all to a case such as the present, and also that on the facts there is no arguable breach of the negative prohibition in the article, the question arises whether the United Kingdom (by the Director) is in breach of its positive obligation to take action to prevent the subjection of individuals to proscribed treatment. In this context, the obligation

j of the state is not absolute and unqualified. So much appears from the passage quoted at [7] above from the judgment of the European Court of Human Rights in *Osman v UK*. The same principle was acknowledged by the court in *Rees v UK* (1986) 9 EHRR 56 at 63–64 where it said:

'37. As the Court pointed out in its abovementioned *Abdulaziz, Cabales and Balkandali* judgment (*Abdulaziz v UK* (1985) 7 EHRR 471) the notion of "respect" is not clear-cut, especially as far as those positive obligations are concerned: having regard to the diversity of the practices followed and the situations obtaining in the Contracting States, the notion's requirements will vary considerably from case to case. These observations are particularly relevant here. Several States have, through legislation or by means of legal interpretation or by administrative practice, given transsexuals the option of changing their personal status to fit their newly-gained identity. They have, however, made this option subject to conditions of varying strictness and retained a number of express reservations (for example, as to previously incurred obligations). In other States, such an option does not—or does not yet—exist. It would therefore be true to say that there is at present little common ground between the Contracting States in this area and that, generally speaking, the law appears to be in a transitional stage. Accordingly, this is an area in which the Contracting Parties enjoy a wide margin of appreciation. In determining whether or not a positive obligation exists, regard must be had to the fair balance that has to be struck between the general interest of the community and the interests of the individual, the search for which balance is inherent in the whole of the Convention. In striking this balance the aims mentioned in the second paragraph of Article 8 may be of a certain relevance, although this provision refers in terms only to "interferences" with the right protected by the first paragraph—in other words is concerned with the negative obligations flowing therefrom.'

That was an art 8 case, dealing with a very different subject matter from the present, but the court's observations were of more general import. It stands to reason that while states may be absolutely forbidden to inflict the proscribed treatment on individuals within their jurisdictions, the steps appropriate or necessary to discharge a positive obligation will be more judgmental, more prone to variation from state to state, more dependent on the opinions and beliefs of the people and less susceptible to any universal injunction. For reasons more fully given at [27] and [28] below, it could not in my view be said that the United Kingdom is under a positive obligation to ensure that a competent, terminally ill, person who wishes but is unable to take his or her own life should be entitled to seek the assistance of another without that other being exposed to the risk of prosecution.

Article 8 of the convention

[16] Article 8 of the convention provides:

'*Right to respect for private and family life*
1. Everyone has the right to respect for his private and family life, his home and his correspondence.
2. There shall be no interference by a public authority with the exercise of this right except such as is in accordance with the law and is necessary in a democratic society in the interests of national security, public safety or the economic well-being of the country, for the prevention of disorder or crime, for the protection of health or morals, or for the protection of the rights and freedoms of others.'

[17] Counsel for Mrs Pretty submitted that this article conferred a right to self-determination (see *X v Netherlands* (1985) 8 EHRR 235, *Rodriguez v A-G of Canada* [1994] 2 LRC 136, *Re A (children) (conjoined twins: surgical separation)* [2000] 4 All ER

a 961, [2001] Fam 147). This right embraces a right to choose when and how to die so that suffering and indignity can be avoided. Section 2(1) of the 1961 Act interferes with this right of self-determination: it is therefore for the United Kingdom to show that the interference meets the convention tests of legality, necessity, responsiveness to pressing social need and proportionality (see *R v A (No 2)* [2001] UKHL 25, [2001] 3 All ER 1, [2001] 2 WLR 1546, *Johansen v Norway*

b (1996) 23 EHRR 33, *R (P) v Secretary of State for the Home Dept, R (Q) v Secretary of State for the Home Dept* [2001] EWCA Civ 1151, [2001] 1 WLR 2002). Where the interference is with an intimate part of an individual's private life, there must be particularly serious reasons to justify the interference (*Smith v UK* (2000) 29 EHRR 493 at 530 (para 89)). The court must in this case rule whether it could be other than disproportionate for the Director to refuse to give the undertaking sought

c and, in the case of the Secretary of State, whether the interference with Mrs Pretty's right to self-determination is proportionate to whatever legitimate aim the prohibition on assisted suicide pursues. Counsel placed particular reliance on certain features of Mrs Pretty's case: her mental competence, the frightening prospect which faces her, her willingness to commit suicide if she

d were able, the imminence of death, the absence of harm to anyone else, the absence of far-reaching implications if her application were granted. Counsel suggested that the blanket prohibition in s 2(1), applied without taking account of particular cases, is wholly disproportionate, and the materials relied on do not justify it. Reference was made to *R v UK* (1983) 33 DR 270 and *Sanles v Spain* [2001] EHRLR 348.

e [18] The Secretary of State questioned whether Mrs Pretty's rights under art 8 were engaged at all, and gave a negative answer. He submitted that the right to private life under art 8 relates to the manner in which a person conducts his life, not the manner in which he departs from it. Any attempt to base a right to die on art 8 founders on exactly the same objection as the attempt based on art 2,

f namely, that the alleged right would extinguish the very benefit on which it is supposedly based. Article 8 protects the physical, moral and psychological integrity of the individual, including rights over the individual's own body, but there is nothing to suggest that it confers a right to decide when or how to die. The Secretary of State also submitted that, if it were necessary to do so, s 2(1) of the 1961 Act and the current application of it could be fully justified on the merits. He

g referred to the margin of judgment accorded to member states, the consideration which has been given to these questions in the United Kingdom and the broad consensus among convention countries. Attention was drawn to *Laskey v UK* (1997) 24 EHRR 39 in which the criminalisation of consensual acts of injury was held to be justified; it was suggested that the justification for criminalising acts of

h consensual killing or assisted suicide must be even stronger.

[19] The most detailed and erudite discussion known to me of the issues in the present appeal is to be found in the judgments of the Supreme Court of Canada in the *Rodriguez* case. The appellant in that case suffered from a disease legally indistinguishable from that which afflicts Mrs Pretty; she was similarly disabled;

j she sought an order which would allow a qualified medical practitioner to set up technological means by which she might, by her own hand but with that assistance from the practitioner, end her life at a time of her choosing. While suicide in Canada was not a crime, s 241(b) of the Criminal Code was in terms effectively identical to s 2(1) of the 1961 Act. The appellant based her claims on the Canadian Charter of Rights and Freedoms which, so far as relevant, included the following sections:

'1. The *Canadian Charter of Rights and Freedoms* guarantees the rights and
freedoms set out in it subject only to such reasonable limits prescribed by law *a*
as can be demonstrably justified in a free and democratic society …

7. Everyone has the right to life, liberty and security of the person and the
right not to be deprived thereof except in accordance with the principles of
fundamental justice …

12. Everyone has the right not to be subjected to any cruel and unusual *b*
treatment or punishment …

15.(1) Every individual is equal before and under the law and has the right
to the equal protection and equal benefit of the law without discrimination
and, in particular, without discrimination based on race, national or ethnic
origin, colour, religion, sex, age or mental or physical disability.'

c

The trial judge rejected Ms Rodriguez' claim, because (as his judgment was
summarised) 'it was the illness from which Ms Rodriguez suffers, not the state or
the justice system, which has impeded her ability to act on her wishes with
respect to the timing and manner of her death' ([1994] 2 LRC 136 at 144). He found
no breach of s 12 and said:

d

'To interpret s 7 so as to include a constitutionally guaranteed right to take
one's own life as an exercise in freedom of choice is inconsistent, in my
opinion, with life, liberty and the security of the person.'

He also held that s 241 did not discriminate against the physically disabled.

[20] The British Columbia Court of Appeal held by a majority that whilst the *e*
operation of s 241 did deprive Ms Rodriguez of her s 7 right to the security of her
person, it did not contravene the principles of fundamental justice ((1993) 76 BCLR
(2d) 145 at 171). McEachern CJ, dissenting, held (at 164) that there was a prima
facie violation of s 7 of the Canadian Charter when the state imposed prohibitions
that had the effect of prolonging the physical and psychological suffering of a
person, and that any provision that imposed an indeterminate period of senseless *f*
physical and psychological suffering on someone who was shortly to die anyway
could not conform with any principle of fundamental justice.

[21] In the Supreme Court opinion was again divided. The judgment of the
majority was given by Sopinka J, with La Forest, Gonthier, Iacobucci and Major JJ
concurring. In the course of his judgment Sopinka J said ([1994] 2 LRC 136 at 175): *g*

'As a threshold issue, I do not accept the submission that the appellant's
problems are due to her physical disabilities caused by her terminal illness,
and not by governmental action. There is no doubt that the prohibition in
s 241(b) will contribute to the appellant's distress if she is prevented from
managing her death in the circumstances which she fears will occur.' *h*

He continued:

'I find more merit in the argument that security of the person, by its nature,
cannot encompass a right to take action that will end one's life as security of
the person is intrinsically concerned with the well-being of the living person.' *j*

He then continued (at 177–178):

'There is no question, then, that personal autonomy, at least with respect
to the right to make choices concerning one's own body, control over one's
physical and psychological integrity, and basic human dignity are encompassed
within security of the person, at least to the extent of freedom from criminal

a prohibitions which interfere with these. The effect of the prohibition in s 241(b) is to prevent the appellant from having assistance to commit suicide when she is no longer able to do so on her own … In my view, these considerations lead to the conclusion that the prohibition in s 241(b) deprives the appellant of autonomy over her person and causes her physical pain and psychological stress in a manner which impinges on the security of her

b person. The appellant's security interest (considered in the context of the life and liberty interest) is therefore engaged, and it is necessary to determine whether there has been any deprivation thereof that is not in accordance with the principles of fundamental justice.'

He concluded (at 189):

c

> 'Given the concerns about abuse that have been expressed and the great difficulty in creating appropriate safeguards to prevent these, it can not be said that the blanket prohibition on assisted suicide is arbitrary or unfair, or that it is not reflective of fundamental values at play in our society.'

d With reference to s 1 of the Canadian Charter, Sopinka J said (at 192–193):

> 'As I have sought to demonstrate in my discussion of s 7, this protection is grounded on a substantial consensus among western countries, medical organisations and our own Law Reform Commission that in order to effectively protect life and those who are vulnerable in society, a prohibition

e without exception on the giving of assistance to commit suicide is the best approach. Attempts to fine-tune this approach by creating exceptions have been unsatisfactory and have tended to support the theory of the "slippery slope". The formulation of safeguards to prevent excesses has been unsatisfactory and has failed to allay fears that a relaxation of the clear

f standard set by the law will undermine the protection of life and will lead to abuses of the exception.'

He rejected the appellant's claims under ss 12 and 15 of the Canadian Charter.

[22] Lamer CJ dissented in favour of the appellant, but on grounds of discrimination under s 15 alone. McLachlin J (with whom L'Heureux-Dubé J

g concurred) found a violation not of s 15 but of s 7. She saw the case as one about the manner in which the state might limit the right of a person to make decisions about her body under s 7 of the charter (at 194). She said (at 195):

> 'In the present case, Parliament has put into force a legislative scheme

h which does not bar suicide but criminalises the act of assisting suicide. The effect of this is to deny to some people the choice of ending their lives solely because they are physically unable to do so. This deprives Sue Rodriguez of her security of the person (the right to make decisions concerning her own body, which affect only her own body) in a way that offends the principles of fundamental justice, thereby violating s 7 of the Charter … It is part of the

j persona and dignity of the human being that he or she have the autonomy to decided what is best for his or her body.'

She held (at 197):

> '… it does not accord with the principles of fundamental justice that Sue Rodriguez be disallowed what is available to others merely because it is

possible that other people, at some other time, may suffer, not what she
seeks, but an act of killing without true consent.'

Cory J also dissented, agreeing with Lamer CJ and also McLachlin J.

[23] It is evident that all save one of the judges of the Canadian Supreme Court
were willing to recognise s 7 of the Canadian Charter as conferring a right to
personal autonomy extending even to decisions on life and death. Mrs Pretty
understandably places reliance in particular on the judgment of McLachlin J, in
which two other members of the court concurred. But a majority of the court
regarded that right as outweighed on the facts by the principles of fundamental
justice. The judgments were moreover directed to a provision with no close
analogy in the convention. In the convention the right to liberty and security of
the person appears only in art 5(1), on which no reliance is or could be placed in the
present case. Article 8 contains no reference to personal liberty or security. It is
directed to the protection of privacy, including the protection of physical and
psychological integrity (*X v Netherlands*). But art 8 is expressed in terms directed
to protection of personal autonomy while individuals are living their lives, and
there is nothing to suggest that the article has reference to the choice to live no
longer.

[24] There is no Strasbourg jurisprudence to support the contention of
Mrs Pretty. In *R v UK* (1983) 33 DR 270 the applicant had been convicted and
sentenced to imprisonment for aiding and abetting suicide and conspiring to do
so. He complained that his conviction and sentence under s 2 of the 1961 Act
constituted a violation of his right to respect for his private life under art 8 and
also his right to free expression under art 10. The European Commission observed
(at 271–272):

'13. The Commission does not consider that the activity for which the
applicant was convicted, namely aiding and abetting suicide, can be described
as falling into the sphere of his private life in the manner elaborated above.
While it might be thought to touch directly on the private lives of those who
sought to commit suicide, it does not follow that the applicant's rights to
privacy are involved. On the contrary, the Commission is of the opinion that
the acts aiding, abetting, counselling or procuring suicide are excluded from
the concept of privacy by virtue of their trespass on the public interest of
protecting life, as reflected in the criminal provisions of the 1961 Act.'

This somewhat tentative expression of view is of some assistance to Mrs Pretty,
but with reference to the claim under art 10 the European Commission of Human
Rights continued (at 272):

'17. The Commission considers, that, in the circumstances of the case, there
has been an interference with the applicant's right to impart information.
However, the Commission must take account of the State's legitimate
interest in this area in taking measures to protect, against criminal behaviour,
the life of its citizens particularly those who belong to especially vulnerable
categories by reason of their age or infirmity. It recognises the right of the
State under the Convention to guard against the inevitable criminal abuses
that would occur, in the absence of legislation, against the aiding and
abetting of suicide. The fact that in the present case the applicant and his
associate appear to have been well intentioned does not, in the Commission's
view, alter the justification for the general policy.'

a   That conclusion cannot be reconciled with the suggestion that the prohibition of assisted suicide is inconsistent with the convention.

[25] *Sanles v Spain* arose from a factual situation similar to the present save that the victim of disabling disease had died and the case never culminated in a decision on the merits. The applicant was the sister-in-law of the deceased and was held not to be a victim and thus not to be directly affected by the alleged violations. It is of some interest that she based her claims on arts 2, 3, 5, 9 and 14 of the convention but not, it seems, on art 8.

b

[26] I would for my part accept the Secretary of State's submission that Mrs Pretty's rights under art 8 are not engaged at all. If, however, that conclusion is wrong, and the prohibition of assisted suicide in s 2 of the 1961 Act infringes her convention right under art 8, it is necessary to consider whether the infringement c   is shown by the Secretary of State to be justifiable under the terms of art 8(2). In considering that question I would adopt the test advocated by counsel for Mrs Pretty, which is clearly laid down in the authorities cited.

[27] Since suicide ceased to be a crime in 1961, the question whether assisted suicide also should be decriminalised has been reviewed on more than one d   occasion. The Criminal Law Revision Committee in its fourteenth report *Offences against the Person* (Cmnd 7844 (1980)) reported some divergence of opinion among its distinguished legal membership, and recognised a distinction between assisting a person who had formed a settled intention to kill himself and the more heinous case where one person persuaded another to commit suicide, but a majority was of the clear opinion that aiding and abetting suicide should remain e   an offence (pp 60–61 (para 135)).

[28] Following the decision in *Bland*'s case a much more broadly-constituted House of Lords Select Committee on Medical Ethics received extensive evidence and reported. The committee in its report (HL Paper (1993–94) 21–I) drew a distinction between assisted suicide and physician-assisted suicide (p 11 (para 26)) f   but its conclusion was unambiguous (p 54 (para 262)):

> 'As far as assisted suicide is concerned, we see no reason to recommend any change in the law. We identify no circumstances in which assisted suicide should be permitted, nor do we see any reason to distinguish between the act of a doctor or of any other person in this connection.'

g   The government in its response (*Government Response to the Report of the Select Committee on Medical Ethics* (Cm 2553 (1994))) accepted this recommendation:

> 'We agree with this recommendation. As the Government stated in its evidence to the Committee, the decriminalisation of attempted suicide in 1961 was accompanied by an unequivocal restatement of the prohibition of h   acts calculated to end the life of another person. The Government can see no basis for permitting assisted suicide. Such a change would be open to abuse and put the lives of the weak and vulnerable at risk.'

A similar approach is to be found in the Council of Europe's Recommendation j   1418 (1999) on the protection of the human rights and dignity of the terminally ill and the dying. This included the following passage (pp 2–4):

> '9. The Assembly therefore recommends that the Committee of Ministers encourage the member states of the Council of Europe to respect and protect the dignity of terminally ill or dying persons in all respects … c. by upholding the prohibition against intentionally taking the life of terminally ill or dying

persons, while: i. recognising that the right to life, especially with regard to a terminally ill or dying person, is guaranteed by the member states, in accordance with Article 2 of the European Convention on Human Rights which states that "no one shall be deprived of his life intentionally"; ii. recognising that a terminally ill or dying person's wish to die never constitutes any legal claim to die at the hand of another person; iii. recognising that a terminally ill or dying person's wish to die cannot of itself constitute a legal justification to carry out actions intended to bring about death.'

It would be by no means fatal to the legal validity of s 2(1) of the 1961 Act if the response of the United Kingdom to this problem of assisted suicide were shown to be unique, but it is shown to be in accordance with a very broad international consensus. Assisted suicide and consensual killing are unlawful in all convention countries except the Netherlands, but even if the Dutch Termination of Life on Request and Assisted Suicide (Review Procedures) Act 2001 and the Dutch Criminal Code were operative in this country it would not relieve Mr Pretty of liability under art 294 of the Dutch Criminal Code if he were to assist Mrs Pretty to take her own life as he would wish to do.

[29] On behalf of Mrs Pretty counsel disclaims any general attack on s 2(1) of the 1961 Act and seeks to restrict his claim to the particular facts of her case: that of a mentally competent adult who knows her own mind, is free from any pressure and has made a fully informed and voluntary decision. Whatever the need, he submits, to afford legal protection to the vulnerable, there is no justification for a blanket refusal to countenance an act of humanity in the case of someone who, like Mrs Pretty, is not vulnerable at all. Beguiling as that submission is, Dr Johnson gave two answers of enduring validity to it. First, 'Laws are not made for particular cases but for men in general'. Second, 'To permit a law to be modified at discretion is to leave the community without law. It is to withdraw the direction of that public wisdom by which the deficiencies of private understanding are to be supplied' (see Boswell's *Life of Johnson* (3rd edn, 1970) Oxford University Press, pp 735, 496). It is for member states to assess the risk and likely incidence of abuse if the prohibition on assisted suicide were relaxed, as the commission recognised in its decision in *R v UK* quoted above at [24]. But the risk is one which cannot be lightly discounted. The Criminal Law Revision Committee recognised how fine was the line between counselling and procuring on the one hand and aiding and abetting on the other (p 61 (para 135)). The House of Lords select committee recognised the undesirability of anything which could appear to encourage suicide (p 49 (para 239)):

'We are also concerned that vulnerable people—the elderly, lonely, sick or distressed—would feel pressure, whether real or imagined, to request early death. We accept that, for the most part, requests resulting from such pressure or from remediable depressive illness would be identified as such by doctors and managed appropriately. Nevertheless we believe that the message which society sends to vulnerable and disadvantaged people should not, however obliquely, encourage them to seek death, but should assure them of our care and support in life.'

It is not hard to imagine that an elderly person, in the absence of any pressure, might opt for a premature end to life if that were available, not from a desire to die or a willingness to stop living, but from a desire to stop being a burden to others.

a [30] If s 2(1) of the 1961 Act infringes any convention right of Mrs Pretty, and recognising the heavy burden which lies on a member state seeking to justify such an infringement, I conclude that the Secretary of State has shown ample grounds to justify the existing law and the current application of it. That is not to say that no other law or application would be consistent with the convention; it is simply to say that the present legislative and practical regime do not offend the
b convention.

Article 9 of the convention
[31] It is unnecessary to recite the terms of art 9 of the convention, to which very little argument was addressed. It is an article which protects freedom of thought, conscience and religion and the manifestation of religion or belief in
c worship, teaching, practice or observance. One may accept that Mrs Pretty has a sincere belief in the virtue of assisted suicide. She is free to hold and express that belief. But her belief cannot found a requirement that her husband should be absolved from the consequences of conduct which, although it would be consistent with her belief, is proscribed by the criminal law. And if she were able
d to establish an infringement of her right, the justification shown by the state in relation to art 8 would still defeat it.

Article 14 of the convention
[32] Article 14 of the convention provides:

e   'Prohibition of discrimination
The enjoyment of the rights and freedoms set forth in this Convention shall be secured without discrimination on any ground such as sex, race, colour, language, religion, political or other opinion, national or social origin, association with a national minority, property, birth or other status.'

f Mrs Pretty claims that s 2(1) of the 1961 Act discriminates against those who, like herself, cannot because of incapacity take their own lives without assistance. She relies on the judgment of the European Court of Human Rights in *Thlimmenos v Greece* (2000) 9 BHRC 12 at 22 where the court said:

'44. The court has so far considered that the right under art 14 not to be
g discriminated against in the enjoyment of the rights guaranteed under the convention is violated when states treat differently persons in analogous situations without providing an objective and reasonable justification … However, the court considers that this is not the only facet of the prohibition of discrimination in art 14. The right not to be discriminated against in the
h enjoyment of the rights guaranteed under the convention is also violated when states without an objective and reasonable justification fail to treat differently persons whose situations are significantly different.'

[33] The European Court of Human Rights has repeatedly held that art 14 is not autonomous but has effect only in relation to convention rights. As it was put
j in *Van Raalte v Netherlands* (1997) 24 EHRR 503 at 516–517:

'33. As the Court has consistently held, Article 14 of the Convention complements the other substantive provisions of the Convention and the Protocols. It has no independent existence since it has effect solely in relation to "the enjoyment of the rights and freedoms" safeguarded by those provisions. Although the application of Article 14 does not presuppose a

breach of those provisions—and to this extent it is autonomous—there can
be no room for its application unless the facts at issue fall within the ambit of   *a*
one or more of the latter.'

See also *Botta v Italy* (1998) 4 BHRC 81 at 90 (para 39).

[34] If, as I have concluded, none of the articles on which Mrs Pretty relies
gives her the right which she has claimed, it follows that art 14 would not avail
her even if she could establish that the operation of s 2(1) is discriminatory. A   *b*
claim under this article must fail on this ground.

[35] If, contrary to my opinion, Mrs Pretty's rights under one or other of the
articles are engaged, it would be necessary to examine whether s 2(1) of the 1961
Act is discriminatory. She contends that the section is discriminatory because it
prevents the disabled, but not the able-bodied, exercising their right to commit   *c*
suicide. This argument is in my opinion based on a misconception. The law
confers no right to commit suicide. Suicide was always, as a crime, anomalous,
since it was the only crime with which no defendant could ever be charged. The
main effect of the criminalisation of suicide was to penalise those who attempted
to take their own lives and failed, and secondary parties. Suicide itself (and with
it attempted suicide) was decriminalised because recognition of the common law   *d*
offence was not thought to act as a deterrent, because it cast an unwarranted
stigma on innocent members of the suicide's family and because it led to the
distasteful result that patients recovering in hospital from a failed suicide attempt
were prosecuted, in effect, for their lack of success. But while the 1961 Act
abrogated the rule of law whereby it was a crime for a person to commit (or   *e*
attempt to commit) suicide, it conferred no right on anyone to do so. Had that
been its object there would have been no justification for penalising by a
potentially very long term of imprisonment one who aided, abetted, counselled
or procured the exercise or attempted exercise by another of that right. The
policy of the law remained firmly adverse to suicide, as s 2(1) makes clear.

[36] The criminal law cannot in any event be criticised as objectionably   *f*
discriminatory because it applies to all. Although in some instances criminal
statutes recognise exceptions based on youth, the broad policy of the criminal law
is to apply offence-creating provisions to all and to give weight to personal
circumstances either at the stage of considering whether or not to prosecute or,
in the event of conviction, when penalty is to be considered. The criminal law   *g*
does not ordinarily distinguish between willing victims and others (*Laskey v UK*).
Provisions criminalising drunkenness or misuse of drugs or theft do not exempt
those addicted to alcohol or drugs, or the poor and hungry. 'Mercy killing', as it
is often called, is in law killing. If the criminal law sought to proscribe the conduct
of those who assisted the suicide of the vulnerable, but exonerated those who   *h*
assisted the suicide of the non-vulnerable, it could not be administered fairly and
in a way which would command respect.

[37] For these reasons, which are in all essentials those of the Divisional Court,
and in agreement with my noble and learned friends Lord Steyn and Lord Hope
of Craighead, I would hold that Mrs Pretty cannot establish any breach of any
convention right.   *j*

The claim against the Director

[38] That conclusion makes it strictly unnecessary to review the main ground
on which the Director resisted the claim made against him: that he had no power
to grant the undertaking which Mrs Pretty sought.

a [39] I would for my part question whether, as suggested on his behalf, the Director might not if so advised make a public statement on his prosecuting policy other than in the Code for Crown Prosecutors which he is obliged to issue by s 10 of the Prosecution of Offences Act 1985. Plainly such a step would call for careful consultation and extreme circumspection, and could be taken only under the superintendence of the Attorney General (by virtue of s 3 of the 1985 Act).

b The Lord Advocate has on occasion made such a statement in Scotland, and I am not persuaded that the Director has no such power. It is, however, unnecessary to explore or resolve that question, since whether or not the Director has the power to make such a statement he has no duty to do so, and in any event what was asked of the Director in this case was not a statement of prosecuting policy but a proleptic grant of immunity from prosecution. That, I am quite satisfied,

c the Director had no power to give. The power to dispense with and suspend laws and the execution of laws without the consent of Parliament was denied to the Crown and its servants by the Bill of Rights 1688. Even if, contrary to my opinion, the Director had power to give the undertaking sought, he would have been very wrong to do so in this case. If he had no reason for doubting, equally

d he had no means of investigating, the assertions made on behalf of Mrs Pretty. He received no information at all concerning the means proposed for ending Mrs Pretty's life. No medical supervision was proposed. The obvious risk existed that her condition might worsen to the point where she could herself do nothing to bring about her death. It would have been a gross dereliction of the Director's duty and a gross abuse of his power had he ventured to undertake that a crime

e yet to be committed would not lead to prosecution. The claim against him must fail on this ground alone.

[40] I would dismiss this appeal.

LORD STEYN.

f [41] My Lords, this is the first occasion on which the House of Lords has been asked to consider the question of assisted suicide by a terminally ill individual. She suffers from motor neurone disease and she has not long to live. The specific question before the House is whether the appellant is entitled to a declaration that the Director of Public Prosecutions (the Director) is obliged to undertake in advance that, if she is assisted by her husband in committing suicide, he will not

g be prosecuted under s 2(1) of the Suicide Act 1961. If Mrs Pretty is entitled to this relief, it follows that it may have to be granted to other terminally ill patients or patients suffering excruciating pain as a result of an incurable illness, who want to commit assisted suicide. Her case is squarely founded on the Human Rights Act 1998, which incorporated the European Convention for the Protection of

h Human Rights and Fundamental Freedoms (Rome, 4 November 1950; TS 71 (1953); Cmd 8969) (as set out in Sch 1 to that Act) into English law. For her to succeed it is not enough to show that the convention allows member states to legalise assisted suicide. She must establish that at least that part of s 2(1) of the 1961 Act which makes aiding or abetting suicide a crime is in conflict with her convention

j rights. In other words, she must persuade the House that the convention compels member states of the Council of Europe to legalise assisted suicide.

I. MOTOR NEURONE DISEASE AND ASSISTED SUICIDE

[42] Mrs Dianne Pretty is 42 years old and has been married for 25 years. She lives with her husband, daughter and granddaughter. In November 1999 she was diagnosed as having motor neurone disease, a progressive neuro-degenerative

disease of motor cells within the central nervous system. Its cause is unknown. No treatment can prevent the inevitable progression of this disease. It causes muscular weakness. Weakness of the arms and legs develop. It results in difficulty in swallowing and speaking. Eventually control of breathing deteriorates. Death usually occurs as a result of weakness of the breathing muscles in association with weakness of those muscles controlling speaking and swallowing leading to respiratory failure and pneumonia.

[43] In March 2000 Mrs Pretty became confined to a wheelchair. In December 2000 her speech and swallowing became affected. She is paralysed from the neck downwards. She has virtually no decipherable speech. The disease is now at an advanced stage. Her life expectancy is low. She has only months to live. Yet her intellect and her capacity to make decisions is unimpaired. She is able to give instructions to her lawyers and has done so.

[44] The suffering of Mrs Pretty is acute and she is frightened and distressed at her short but bleak future. She is in some physical pain but more importantly she is in constant dread of the day when she will no longer be able to swallow or breathe. She wishes to be spared the suffering and loss of dignity which is all that is left of life for her. She wishes to control when and how she dies. But for the disease she would be able to take her own life. The disease has, however, deprived her of the ability to commit suicide. Her solicitor explained in an affidavit that her wishes are that her husband should assist her in committing suicide. The agreed statement of facts and issues states:

'The disease prevents her from committing suicide unaided. Thus she wishes her husband to assist her and he has agreed, if the DPP will undertake not to prosecute him. This proviso arises because absent such undertaking the appellant's husband will be liable to prosecution and imprisonment for the offence of assisting suicide under s 2(1) of the Suicide Act 1961.'

There is, however, no information available as to how it is proposed that her husband would assist her suicide. Moreover, there is no medical evidence showing what Mrs Pretty herself can do to carry out her wish. It has, however, been emphasised on her behalf that the final act of suicide will be carried through by her.

[45] The 1961 Act provides as follows:

'1. The rule of law whereby it is a crime for a person to commit suicide is hereby abrogated.

2.—(1) A person who aids, abets, counsels or procures the suicide of another, or an attempt by another to commit suicide, shall be liable on conviction on indictment to imprisonment for a term not exceeding fourteen years.

(2) If on the trial of an indictment for murder or manslaughter it is proved that the accused aided, abetted, counselled or procured the suicide of the person in question, the jury may find him guilty of that offence ...

(4) No proceedings shall be instituted for an offence under this section except by or with the consent of the Director of Public Prosecutions.'

Counsel explained that the assistance to be given by Mr Pretty to his wife would amount to aiding and abetting within the meaning of s 2(1) but that Mr Pretty's conduct would not extend to counselling and procuring suicide.

[46] The legal officer of Liberty asked the Director of Public Prosecutions to give an undertaking not to prosecute Mr Pretty if he assists in the suicide of his

a wife. The letter described Mrs Pretty's condition and explained what she wanted to do and made a number of legal submissions. It ended by saying:

'We very much hope you can provide us with the undertaking we seek, in view of our client's illness and the distress she is suffering we would be grateful if you would let us have a reply within 7 days of the date of this letter.'

b

On 8 August 2001 the Director replied:

'I should like first to express my deepest sympathy to Mrs Pretty and to her family for the terrible suffering that she and they are having to bear. You have asked for an undertaking that the Director would not consent to a *c* prosecution of Mr Pretty under section 2 of the Suicide Act, 1961, were he to assist his wife to commit suicide. You have made a number of points in relation to the European Convention on Human Rights; the Human Rights Act, 1998; and the Code for Crown Prosecutors. I have read your comments with care. Successive Directors—and Attorneys General—have explained that *d* they will not grant immunities that condone, require, or purport to authorise or permit future commission of any criminal offence, no matter how exceptional the circumstances. I must therefore advise you that the Director cannot provide the undertaking that you seek. Whilst I believe that I have no choice but to refuse your request, I deeply regret any further suffering that this refusal may cause.'

e

Mrs Pretty issued an application for judicial review of the decision by the Director not to give the undertaking.

[47] The principal relief sought by Mrs Pretty was a declaration that the Director had acted unlawfully in refusing to give an undertaking that he would *f* not consent to a prosecution of her husband for an offence under s 2(1) of the 1961 Act if he should assist her in committing suicide. The Secretary of State was joined as an interested party because Mrs Pretty also sought in the alternative a declaration that s 2(1) of the 1961 Act is incompatible with s 4 of the 1998 Act.

II. THE JUDICIAL REVIEW PROCEEDINGS

g [48] Permission to apply for judicial review was granted. On 18 October 2001 the Divisional Court (Tuckey and Hale LJJ and Silber J) in a detailed judgment of the court dismissed the application ([2001] EWHC Admin 788, [2001] All ER (D) 251 (Oct)). The Divisional Court held: (i) the Director has no power to grant the undertaking sought; (ii) in any event, a decision of the Director to grant or refuse to grant the undertaking would not be amenable to judicial review; (iii) s 2(1) of *h* the 1961 Act is not incompatible with the convention.

[49] After giving judgment, the Divisional Court certified three points of general public importance:

'(1) Does the Director of Public Prosecutions have power under s 2(4) of *j* the Suicide Act 1961 or otherwise to undertake not to consent to prosecute in advance of the relevant events occurring? (2) If so, was he required in this case to undertake not to prosecute the appellant's husband, Mr Pretty, if he were to assist his wife to commit suicide having regard to her rights under arts 2, 3, 8, 9, and 14 of the convention and his obligation to act compatibly with the convention? (3) If not, is s 2(1) of the 1961 Act incompatible with arts 2, 3, 8, 9, and/or 14 of the convention?'

[50] An Appeal Committee granted leave to appeal. Given the circumstances *a* the appeal was expedited. Subject to three points the shape of the case is very much as it was presented to the Divisional Court. There has inevitably been some deterioration of Mrs Pretty's condition. Secondly, there was a dispute at the hearing of the appeal before the House as to whether Mrs Pretty can correctly be described as vulnerable. It is not possible for the House to express any view on this point. In the context of euthanasia and assisted suicide the report of the *b* House of Lords Select Committee on Medical Ethics (HL Paper (1993–94) 21-I) there is a relevant passage regarding the class of vulnerable people. Among its reasons for not recommending a relaxation of the existing law regarding euthanasia and assisted suicide, the select committee observed (p 49 (para 239)):

'We are also concerned that vulnerable people—the elderly, lonely, sick or *c* distressed—would feel pressure, whether real or imagined, to request early death. We accept that, for the most part, requests resulting from such pressure or from remediable depressive illness would be identified as such by doctors and managed appropriately. Nevertheless we believe that the message which society sends to vulnerable and disadvantaged people should not, *d* however obliquely, encourage them to seek death, but should assure them of our care and support in life.'

While Mrs Pretty may or may not be vulnerable, there is in the context of euthanasia and assisted suicide undoubtedly a class of vulnerable people to be *e* considered. This is important because the law must be stated for the generality of cases. The third point was a lack of agreement on what palliative care is available to Mrs Pretty. She apparently visits a hospice where she receives some medical and nursing care. In the final stages of the illness she will reside in the hospice and may, in the discretion of a consultant, be sedated. That is all we know. I will return to this point at the end of this judgment. *f*

[51] On the hearing of the appeal the House heard oral submissions on behalf of Mrs Pretty, the Director and the Home Secretary and received written submissions from a Roman Catholic Archbishop as well as the Medical Ethics Alliance, the Society for the Protection of Unborn Children and Alert. I wish to pay tribute to the quality of the arguments placed before the House. *g*

III. THE FRAMEWORK OF THE CASE

[52] It is necessary to explain two preliminary matters. First, terminally ill patients may sometimes be incompetent to take decisions. This is not such a case. Mrs Pretty is fully competent to take decisions about her personal autonomy and *h* in particular about the question whether she wants to commit suicide and when and how. Secondly, there is a distinction between voluntary euthanasia and assisted suicide. Glanville Williams *Textbook of Criminal Law* (2nd edn, 1983) p 580 illustrates the difference. If a doctor, to speed the dying of his patient, injects poison with the patient's consent, this is voluntary euthanasia and murder. If the *j* doctor places poison by the patient's side, and the patient takes it this will be assisted suicide and amount to the commission of the offence under s 2(1) of the 1961 Act. The arguments before the House are concerned with cases falling in the latter category. But to some extent the arguments about the two concepts are intertwined.

IV. THE SCHEME OF THIS JUDGMENT

a   [53] Reversing the order of considering the issues adopted by the Divisional Court, I will first examine whether Mrs Pretty has a right to die with the assistance of her husband (or anybody else) enforceable against the state under the convention. In other words, I will consider whether any of the articles of the convention relied on *require* the state to render lawful assisted suicide by a person b   in Mrs Pretty's position. It will, however, be necessary to sketch the contextual scene before I consider the specific articles. Thereafter, I will briefly consider the position of the Director in regard to requests for undertakings not to prosecute made in advance of the commission of the criminal act.

V. THE CONTEXTUAL SCENE

c

Controversial questions

[54] The subject of euthanasia and assisted suicide have been deeply controversial long before the adoption of the Universal Declaration of Human Rights in 1948 (Paris, 10 December 1948; UN TS 2 (1949); Cmd 7226), which was d   followed two years later by the convention. The arguments and counter-arguments have ranged widely. There is a conviction that human life is sacred and that the corollary is that euthanasia and assisted suicide are always wrong. This view is supported by the Roman Catholic Church, Islam and other religions. There is also a secular view, shared sometimes by atheists and agnostics, that human life is sacred. On the other side, there are many millions who do not hold these e   beliefs. For many the personal autonomy of individuals is predominant. They would argue that it is the moral right of individuals to have a say over the time and manner of their death. On the other hand, there are utilitarian arguments to the contrary effect. The terminally ill and those suffering great pain from incurable illnesses are often vulnerable. And not all families, whose interests are f   at stake, are wholly unselfish and loving. There is a risk that assisted suicide may be abused in the sense that such people may be persuaded that they want to die or that they ought to want to die. Another strand is that, when one knows the genuine wish of a terminally ill patient to die, they should not be forced against their will to endure a life they no longer wish to endure. Such views are countered by those who say it is a slippery slope or the thin end of the wedge. It g   is also argued that euthanasia and assisted suicide, under medical supervision, will undermine the trust between doctors and patients. It is said that protective safeguards are unworkable. The countervailing contentions of moral philosophers, medical experts and ordinary people are endless. The literature is vast: see for a sample of the range of views: Glanville Williams *The Sanctity of Life and the* h   *Criminal Law* (1958) ch 8, Ronald Dworkin *Life's Dominion: An Argument About Abortion and Euthanasia* (1993) ch 7, John Keown (ed) *Euthanasia Examined: Ethical, Clinical and Legal Perspectives* (1995), Otlowski *Voluntary Euthanasia and the Common Law* (1997) chs 5–8, Mary Warnock *An Intelligent Person's Guide to Ethics* (1998) ch 1. It is not for us, in this case, to express a view on these arguments. But j   it is of great importance to note that these are ancient questions on which millions in the past have taken diametrically opposite views and still do.

The relevance of existing English law

[55] Given the fact that Mrs Pretty's arguments are founded on the convention, the existing position under English law, even if in large measure very similar to

that under other European legal systems, cannot be decisive. But it demonstrates
how controversial the subject of the legalisation of euthanasia and assisted suicide   *a*
is in Europe. In outline the position in England is as follows. By virtue of
legislation suicide is no longer an offence and a suicide pact may result in a verdict
of manslaughter. Mercy killing in the form of euthanasia is murder and assisted
suicide is a statutory offence punishable by 14 years' imprisonment. A competent
patient cannot be compelled to undergo life-saving treatment (*St George's Healthcare*   *b*
NHS Trust v S, R v Collins, ex p S [1998] 3 All ER 673, [1999] Fam 26). Under the
double effect principle medical treatment may be administered to a terminally ill
person to alleviate pain although it may hasten death (*Airedale NHS Trust v Bland*
[1993] 1 All ER 821 at 868, [1993] AC 789 at 867 per Lord Goff of Chieveley). This
principle entails a distinction between foreseeing an outcome and intending it
(see also Anthony Arlidge 'The trial of Dr David Moor' [2000] Crim LR 31). The   *c*
case of *Bland* involved a further step: the House of Lords held that under judicial
control it was permissible to cease to take active steps to keep a person in a
permanent vegetative state alive. It involved the notion of a distinction between
doctors killing a patient and letting him die (see also *NHS Trust A v H* [2001] 2 FLR
501). These are at present the only inroads on the sanctity of life principle in   *d*
English law. In this corner of the law England is not an island on its own. It is
true that since the *Alkmaar* decision of the Supreme Court on 27 November 1984
(*Alkmaar NJ* (1984) No 106, 451) the Dutch courts, relying on the principle of
'noodtoestand' (necessity), relaxed the prohibition on euthanasia and assisted
suicide. The perceived necessity was the conflict between a doctor's respect for
life and his duty to assist a patient suffering unbearably. The Dutch courts   *e*
reasoned that it is necessary to be guided by responsible medical opinion. It is
important to note that this line of decisions is not based on the convention. See
also Otlowski pp 391–450. Earlier this year the Parliament of the Netherlands
enacted a statute, viz the Termination of Life on Request and Assisted Suicide
(Review Procedures) Act 2001, which formalises a relaxation of the law prohibiting   *f*
euthanasia and assisted suicide previously by judicial decision. Both the case law
and the 2001 statute only permit euthanasia and doctor-assisted suicide under a
regime of ascertaining the wishes of the patient and with considerable medical
supervision. It is to be noted, however, that the United Nations Human Rights
Committee in a report dated 27 August 2001 expressed serious concerns about
the operation of the system (CCPR/CO/72/NET, para 5: see also a review of   *g*
other concerns in Keown, ch 16). The other member states of the Council of
Europe have not legalised euthanasia or assisted suicide: compare, however, the
position in Switzerland (see Lesley Vickers 'Assisted dying and the laws of three
European countries' (1997) 147 NLJ 610). Furthermore, the Parliamentary Assembly
of the Council of Europe (the sponsoring body for the convention) has adopted   *h*
Recommendation 1418 (1999) on the protection of the human rights and dignity
of the terminally ill and the dying. In para 9(c), it recommended that the
Committee of Ministers should encourage the member states of the council to
respect and protect the dignity of terminally ill or dying persons in all respects, by
(among other things) 'upholding the prohibition against intentionally taking the   *j*
life of terminally ill or dying persons', while (at p 4):

> '... ii. recognising that a terminally ill or dying person's wish to die never
> constitutes any legal claim to die at the hands of another person;
>
>   iii. recognising that a terminally ill or dying person's wish to die cannot of
> itself constitute a legal justification to carry out actions intended to bring
> about death.'

a Paragraph 9(c)(iii) plainly covers assisted suicide. This recommendation is testimony of prevailing public opinion in member states. Given the fact that Mrs Pretty's case is based on the convention I have concentrated on European developments. It is, however, noteworthy that in the United States and Canada arguments similar to that of Mrs Pretty ultimately failed (*Vacco v Quill* (1997) 521 US 793, *Washington v Glucksberg* (1997) 521 US 702, *Rodriguez v A-G of Canada* [1994] 2 LRC
b 136).

The reach of human rights texts

[**56**] The human rights movement evolved to protect fundamental rights of individuals either universally or regionally. The theme of the declaration of 1948 was universal. It involved a common conception of human rights capable of
c commanding wide acceptance throughout the world despite huge differences between countries in culture, in religion, and in political systems (Johnson and Symonides *The Universal Declaration of Human Rights: A History of its Creation and Implementation: 1948-1998* (1998) p 39, Glendon *A World Made New: Eleanor Roosevelt and the Universal Declaration of Human Rights* (2001) p 176). Any proposal that the
d Universal Declaration should require states to guarantee a right to euthanasia or assisted suicide (as opposed to permitting states by democratic institutions so to provide) would have been doomed to failure. The aspirational text of the Universal Declaration was the point of departure and inspiration of the convention which opened for signature in 1950. It is to be noted, however, that the convention embodied in some respects a narrower view of human rights than
e the Universal Declaration. The framers of the convention required a shorter and uncontroversial text which would secure general acceptance among European nations. Thus the convention contains, unlike the Universal Declaration, no guarantees of economic, social and cultural rights. A further illustration relates to the guarantees of equality in the two texts. The guarantee in the Universal
f Declaration is free-standing and comprehensive (see art 7). In the convention the provision is parasitic: it is linked with other convention rights (art 14). The language of the convention is often open-textured. In 1950 the Lord Chancellor observed:

g 'Vague and indefinite terms have been used just because they were vague and indefinite, so that all parties, hoping and expecting that these terms will be construed according to their separate points of view, could be induced to sign them.' (See Cabinet Office memorandum CAB 130/64.)

Sir Hartley Shawcross QC, the Attorney General, attributed the lack of clarity in the drafting to a compromise to accommodate the different legal systems
h involved (see Geoffrey Marston 'The United Kingdom's Part in the Preparation of the European Convention on Human Rights' (1993) 42 ICLQ 796 at 818, 819). The generality of the language permits adaptation of the convention to modern conditions. It is also, however, necessary to take into account that in the field of fundamental beliefs the European Court of Human Rights does not readily adopt a creative role contrary to a European consensus, or virtual consensus. The fact is
j that among the 41 member states—north, south, east and west—there are deep cultural and religious differences in regard to euthanasia and assisted suicide. The legalisation of euthanasia and assisted suicide as adopted in the Netherlands would be unacceptable to predominantly Roman Catholic countries in Europe. The idea that the convention *requires* states to render lawful euthanasia and assisted suicide (as opposed to allowing democratically elected legislatures to adopt measures to that effect) must therefore be approached with scepticism.

That does not involve support for the proposition that one must go back to the *a* original intent of the convention. On the contrary, approaching the convention as a living instrument, the fact is that an interpretation *requiring* states to legalise euthanasia and assisted suicide would not only be enormously controversial but profoundly unacceptable to the peoples of many member states.

Policy grounds   *b*

[57] If s 2 of the 1961 Act is held to be incompatible with the convention, a right to commit assisted suicide would not be doctor-assisted and would not be subject to safeguards introduced in the Netherlands. In a valuable essay Professor Michael Freeman trenchantly observed: 'A repeal of Section 2 of the Suicide Act 1961, without more, would not be rational policy-making. We would need a *c* "Death with Dignity" Act to fill the lacuna.' (See 'Death, Dying and the Human Rights Act 1998' (1999) 52 CLP 218 at 237.) That must be right. In our parliamentary democracy, and I apprehend in many member states of the Council of Europe, such a fundamental change cannot be brought about by judicial creativity. If it is to be considered at all, it requires a detailed and effective regulatory proposal. In these circumstances it is difficult to see how a process of interpretation of convention *d* rights can yield a result with all the necessary in-built protections. Essentially, it must be a matter for democratic debate and decision-making by legislatures.

VI. THE SPECIFIC ARTICLES

[58] In combination the contextual factors which I have alluded to justify an *e* initial disbelief that any of the articles of the convention could possibly bear the strong meaning for which counsel for Mrs Pretty must argue. Despite his incisive arguments the position is in my opinion clear. None of the articles can bear the interpretation put forward.

Right to life   *f*

[59] Article 2 provides:

'1. Everyone's right to life shall be protected by law. No one shall be deprived of his life intentionally save in the execution of a sentence of a court following his conviction of a crime for which this penalty is provided by law. *g*

2. Deprivation of life shall not be regarded as inflicted in contravention of this Article when it results from the use of force which is no more than absolutely necessary: (a) in defence of any person from unlawful violence; (b) in order to effect a lawful arrest or to prevent the escape of a person lawfully detained; (c) in action lawfully taken for the purpose of quelling a *h* riot or insurrection.'

Counsel for Mrs Pretty argued that art 2 and in particular its first sentence acknowledges that it is for the individual to choose whether to live or die and that it protects her right of self-determination in relation to issues of life and death. This interpretation is not sustainable. The purpose of art 2(1) is clear. It *j* enunciates the principle of the sanctity of life and provides a guarantee that no individual 'shall be deprived of life' by means of intentional human intervention. The interpretation now put forward is the exact opposite, viz a right of Mrs Pretty to end her life by means of intentional human intervention. Nothing in the article or the jurisprudence of the European Court of Human Rights can assist Mrs Pretty's case on this article.

Prohibition of torture

a
   [60] Article 3 provides: 'No one shall be subjected to torture or to inhuman or degrading treatment or punishment.' The core of counsel's argument is that under art 3 the state's obligations are to take effective steps to ensure that no one shall be subjected to inhuman or degrading treatment. For my part art 3 is not engaged. The word 'treatment' must take its colour from the context in which it

b appears. While I would not wish to give a narrow interpretation to what may constitute degrading treatment, the concept appears singularly inapt to convey the idea that the state must guarantee to individuals a right to die with the deliberate assistance of third parties. So radical a step, infringing the sanctity of life principle, would have required far more explicit wording. But counsel argues that there is support for his argument to be found in the jurisprudence of the European

c Court of Human Rights on the 'positive obligations' of a state to render effective the protection of art 3. For this proposition he cites the decision of the European Court of Human Rights in *D v UK* (1997) 2 BHRC 273. The case concerned the intended deportation of an individual in the final stages of an incurable disease to St Kitts where there would not be adequate treatment for the disease. The

d European Court of Human Rights held that in the exceptional circumstances of the case the implementation of the decision to remove the individual to St Kitts would amount to inhuman treatment by the United Kingdom. Unlike *D v UK* the present case does not involve any positive action (comparable to the intended deportation) nor is there any risk of a failure to treat her properly. Instead the complaint is that the state is guilty of a failure to repeal s 2(1) of the 1961 Act. The

e present case plainly does not involve 'inhuman or degrading *treatment*'.

Right to respect for private life and family
   [61] Article 8 provides:

f   '1. Everyone has the right to respect for his private and family life, his home and his correspondence.
         2. There shall be no interference by a public authority with the exercise of this right except such as is in accordance with the law and is necessary in a democratic society in the interests of national security, public safety or the economic well-being of the country, for the prevention of disorder or crime,

g   for the protection of health or morals, or for the protection of the rights and freedoms of others.'

Counsel submitted that this article explicitly recognises the principle of the personal autonomy of every individual. He argues that this principle necessarily

h involves a guarantee as against the state of the right to choose when and how to die. None of the decisions cited in regard to art 8 assist this argument. It must fail on the ground that the guarantee under art 8 prohibits interference with the way in which an individual leads his life and it does not relate to the manner in which he wishes to die.

j   [62] If I had been of the view that art 8 was engaged, I would have held (in agreement with the Divisional Court) that the interference with the guarantee was justified. There was a submission to the contrary based on the argument that the scope of s 2(1) is disproportionate to its aim. This contention was founded on the supposition that Mrs Pretty and others in her position are not vulnerable. It is a sufficient answer that there is a broad class of persons presently protected by s 2 who are vulnerable. It was therefore well within the range of discretion of

Parliament to strike the balance between the interests of the community and the
rights of individuals in the way reflected in s 2(1).

a

Freedom of thought, conscience and religion
 [63] Article 9 provides:

> '1. Everyone has the right to freedom of thought, conscience and religion;
> this right includes freedom to change his religion or belief and freedom,
> either alone or in community with others and in public or private, to
> manifest his religion or belief, in worship, teaching, practice and observance.
> 2. Freedom to manifest one's religion or beliefs shall be subject only to
> such limitations as are prescribed by law and are necessary in a democratic
> society in the interests of public safety, for the protection of public order,
> health or morals, or for the protection of the rights and freedoms of others.'

b

c

Counsel submitted that Mrs Pretty is entitled to manifest her belief in assisted
suicide by committing it. This cannot be right. This article was never intended
to give individuals a right to perform any acts in pursuance of whatever beliefs
they may hold, e g to attack places where experiments are conducted on animals.
The article does not yield support for the specific proposition for which it is
invoked. In any event, for the reasons already discussed, s 2 is a legitimate,
rational and proportionate response to the wider problem of vulnerable people
who would otherwise feel compelled to commit suicide.

d

e

Prohibition of discrimination
 [64] Article 14 provides:

> 'The enjoyment of the rights and freedoms set forth in this Convention
> shall be secured without discrimination on any ground such as sex, race,
> colour, language, religion, political or other opinion, national or social
> origin, association with a national minority, property, birth or other status.'

f

Counsel submits that Mrs Pretty is in effect treated less favourably than those
who are physically capable of ending their lives. The Divisional Court held that
art 14 is not engaged. The alleged discrimination can only be established if the
facts of the case fall within arts 2, 3, 8 or 9 (*Botta v Italy* (1998) 4 BHRC 81 at 90
(para 39)). They do not. This is a sufficient reason to reject this argument. But there
is a more fundamental reason. The condition of terminally ill individuals, like
Mrs Pretty, will vary. The majority will be vulnerable. It is the vulnerability of the
class of persons which provides the rationale for making the aiding and abetting
of suicide an offence under s 2(1) of the 1961 Act. A class of individuals is
protected by s 2(1) because they are in need of protection. The statutory
provision does not therefore treat individuals in a discriminatory manner. There
is no unequal treatment before the law. In any event, for reasons already given,
s 2(1) is fully justified.

g

h

VII. THE POSITION OF THE DIRECTOR
 [65] This issue centres on the nature of the Director's discretion to grant or
refuse his consent to criminal proceedings under s 2(1) of the 1961 Act. This is a
provision of primary legislation. The discretion under s 2(4) is contained in a criminal
statute. It is concerned with the deep-rooted sanctity of life principle. In this
context it is plainly beyond the power conferred by s 2(4) for the Director to

j

a choose not to enforce s 2(1) or to disapply it. These propositions are self-evident and beyond reasonable challenge. The Director may not under s 2(4) exercise his discretion to stop all prosecutions under s 2(1). It follows that he may only exercise his discretion, for or against a prosecution, in relation to the circumstances of a specific prosecution. His discretion can therefore only be exercised in respect of past events giving rise to a suspicion that a crime under s 2(1) has been committed.
b And then the exercise of this discretion will take into account whether there is a realistic prospect of securing a conviction and whether a prosecution would be in the public interest. To hold that s 2(4) empowers the Director to give the undertaking sought in this case is not justified by the statutory language, and would be contrary to the manifest limited purpose of s 2(4). On this point I am in complete agreement with the careful judgment of the Divisional Court.
c
[**66**] It is, however, necessary to consider whether, apart from the terms of s 2(4) of the 1961 Act, the Director has any power to undertake in advance not to bring criminal proceedings in respect of a contemplated course of action. In agreement with the Divisional Court I would answer this question No. But I would qualify the thrust of the valuable judgment of the Divisional Court in one respect.
d The fact that there is a *duty* under s 10 of the Prosecution of Offences Act 1985 on the Director to issue a general code for Crown Prosecutors does not necessarily mean that he may not ever, in his absolute discretion, give guidance as to how the discretion will be exercised in regard to particular offences. It is important to bear in mind what is under consideration, viz the width of the powers of the
e Director. One should not be over-prescriptive on this subject. An example from Scotland was given of the Crown Agent stating that no proceedings for a contravention of s 6(1)(a) of the Road Traffic Act 1972 would be instituted on the basis of a breath alcohol reading of less than 40 mg. But I envisage that the occasions on which such statements would be appropriate and serve the public
f interest would be rare. Subject to this narrow qualification I would accept as sound the policy of the Director never to announce in advance, whether he will or will not bring criminal proceedings. Certainly, it is beyond his power to indicate, before the commission of a particular crime, that he will or will not prosecute if it is committed. But I regard this point as a diversion from the issues before the House. The response of the Director in this case cannot be faulted.
g
[**67**] There was some debate about the possibility of judicial review of a decision by the Director to refuse or grant consent to a prosecution. If the Director refuses consent, the only remedy is judicial review. On the other hand, if he grants consent a defendant can raise any complaint in the criminal trial or on appeal. Since satellite litigation should be avoided in such cases, I would stand by
h the rule in *R v DPP, ex p Kebeline, R v DPP, ex p Rechachi* [1999] 4 All ER 801, [2000] 2 AC 326, that, absent dishonesty, mala fides or an exceptional circumstance, judicial review is not available in such cases.

VIII. CONCLUSION

j [**68**] The logic of the convention does not justify the conclusion that the House must rule that a state is obliged to legalise assisted suicide. It does not require the state to repeal a provision such as s 2(1) of the 1961 Act. On the other hand, it is open to a democratic legislature to introduce such a measure. Our Parliament, if so minded, may therefore repeal s 2(1) and put in its place a regulated system for assisted suicide (presumably doctor-assisted) with appropriate safeguards.

IX. PALLIATIVE CARE

[69] The report of the House of Lords Select Committee on Medical Ethics stated *a* in 1994 that in the United Kingdom palliative care has been developed to a high standard by the hospice movement (p 49 (para 239)). The uncertainty in this case about the standard of palliative care which Mrs Pretty is receiving and will be entitled to receive in the last stages of her illness prompts me to express the hope that all is being done for her, and will be done, to make a little more tolerable *b* what remains of her life.

X. DISPOSAL

[70] In this sad case the Human Rights Act 1998 does not avail Mrs Pretty. For the reasons I have given, as well as the reasons given by Lord Bingham of Cornhill and Lord Hope of Craighead, the appeal must be dismissed.   *c*

LORD HOPE OF CRAIGHEAD.

[71] My Lords, Mrs Pretty is burdened with a misfortune which has attracted widespread sympathy. She is suffering from a terminal illness which she wishes to bring to an end at a time of her own choosing by committing suicide. But she is unable to commit that act as the same illness has deprived of her of the ability *d* to do it without help. The fact that her illness has driven her to contemplate suicide might be thought to indicate a lack of judgment on her part. But I believe that the decision which she has taken in such extreme circumstances ought not to be criticised. It has been stressed she is well able to make rational decisions as to her own future. I would accept her assurance that she has reached the *e* decision to end her life of her own free will and that she has not been subjected to outside pressure of any kind.

[72] Important questions of medical ethics and of morality have been raised by her request that her husband should be allowed to help her to end her own life. They are the subject of detailed comment in the helpful written submissions which have been submitted by the interveners in this appeal. They are of great *f* interest to society. But they are not the questions which have brought this matter before the court. The questions which your Lordships have to decide are questions of law. Mrs Pretty has invoked the Human Rights Act 1998. She is entitled to know where the law now stands on the issue of assisted suicide.

[73] The basic framework within which Mr Havers QC developed his arguments *g* is clear. The act of suicide itself, for long a common law crime in English law, is no longer criminal (see Blackstone *Commentaries on the Laws of England* (1769) vol 4, ch 14, p 189). Section 1 of the Suicide Act 1961 removed it from the criminal law. This means that a person who attempts to commit suicide but survives can no longer be prosecuted. But those who aid, abet, counsel or *h* procure the suicide of another, or an attempt by another, to commit suicide commit an offence. Section 2(1) of the 1961 Act provides that they shall be liable on conviction to imprisonment for a term not exceeding 14 years. That is the sanction which would confront Mr Pretty if in any way he were to help, or attempt to help, his wife to end her life.

[74] Proceedings for an offence under that section cannot be brought except *j* by or with the consent of the Director of Public Prosecutions (the Director) (s 2(4)). So Mrs Pretty has asked him to undertake that if Mr Pretty assists her to commit suicide he will not be prosecuted. The Director says that he is unable to give the undertaking which has been sought. The argument has therefore focused on Mrs Pretty's rights under the 1998 Act and on the powers of the Director. It proceeds in this way. Firstly, it is said that the Director has power to give the

a undertaking which has been sought. Second, there is the fact that s 6(1) of the 1998 Act makes it unlawful for a public authority to act in a way which is incompatible with a convention right. So the argument asserts that the Director is obliged to give the undertaking, because to withhold it would be incompatible with Mrs Pretty's convention rights. Third, it is said that if the Director does not have power to give the undertaking, s 2(1) of the 1961 Act is incompatible with *b* her convention rights as it imposes a blanket and indiscriminate ban on all assisted suicides.

Section 6(1) of the Human Rights Act 1998

[75] Had it not been for the 1998 Act, Mrs Pretty's case that the Director was obliged to give the undertaking would have been unarguable. Section 2(4) of the *c* 1961 Act leaves no room for doubt on this point. It leaves decisions as to whether or not a contravention of s 2(1) of that Act should be prosecuted to the discretion of the Director. But the Director is a public authority for the purposes of s 6(1) of the 1998 Act. It is unlawful for him to act in a way which is incompatible with a convention right. Section 6(6) provides that 'An act' for this purpose includes *d* a failure to act. A decision as to whether or not to prosecute has been held to be an act for the purposes of s 57(2) of the Scotland Act 1998 (*Brown v Stott (Procurator Fiscal, Dunfermline)* [2001] 2 All ER 97, [2001] 2 WLR 817). I see no reason why the word 'An act' in s 6(1) of the 1998 Act, which applies throughout the United Kingdom, should be construed differently. I would hold that a decision by the Director whether or not to prosecute is an act for the purposes of that subsection.

e [76] Mr Havers seeks to apply s 6(1) to the refusal of the Director to give an undertaking that he would not prosecute Mr Pretty. But in my opinion the words 'An act', construed with the benefit of s 6(6), do not require a public authority to do something which it has no power to do. A refusal by a public authority to do something which it has no power to do is not a failure to act. A public authority *f* can only act within its powers. Section 6(1) is concerned with acts which are otherwise lawful but are made unlawful by the 1998 Act on convention grounds. The Director cannot be held to have acted unlawfully within the meaning of s 6(1) of the 1998 Act when he declined to give the undertaking unless it can be demonstrated that the undertaking was one that he had power to give.

g [77] In *R v DPP, ex p Kebeline, R v DPP, ex p Rechachi* [1999] 4 All ER 801, [2000] 2 AC 326 it was held that a decision by the Director to consent to a prosecution was not amenable to judicial review, in the absence of dishonesty, mala fides or an exceptional circumstance. I would approach questions about a refusal by the Director to give an undertaking not to prosecute in the same way. But a sound rule must not be applied so rigidly that it becomes a denial of justice. It is *h* important to observe the assumptions on which the rule that was described in that case by Lord Steyn ([1999] 4 All ER 801 at 835, [2000] 2 AC 326 at 371) was based. They were that to allow challenges to be made by means of the judicial review process would open the door to delay in the conduct of criminal proceedings, and that the challenges could and should take place in the criminal trial or on *j* appeal.

[78] The argument in this case assumes that unless the undertaking is given Mr Pretty will not act to help Mrs Pretty to commit suicide. If the undertaking is not given there will be nothing to prosecute. We are not dealing in this case with the straightforward situation in which a person seeks an assurance after the event that he will not be prosecuted. So it is no answer for Mrs Pretty to be told that the matter should be dealt with at a criminal trial or on appeal. There will be no

criminal trial in which the issue as to whether the Director is acting compatibly
with Mrs Pretty's convention rights can be tested. In my opinion it is open to her   *a*
to raise the issue by judicial review in these exceptional circumstances.

The Director's powers

[79] The question whether or not a law officer (I include in that expression the
Director as well as the government law officers) should or should not consent to   *b*
a prosecution is one which the judiciary must approach with caution and with
due deference. Issues of policy may well be involved, and they should be left to
the government law officers to answer for in Parliament. The issues of fact will
be involved, and they may not be suitable for discussion in open court before trial.
In practice therefore our system of public prosecution depends to a large extent on the
integrity and judgment of the public prosecutor. He is likely to be in the best   *c*
position to judge what is in the public interest. His judgment must be respected
by the judiciary. It is against that background that I approach the question
whether the Director has power to give the undertaking which has been sought.

[80] It is important to identify precisely what it is that is being sought from the
Director. He is not being asked simply for a statement about the policy which he   *d*
will follow in cases of assisted suicide. If that was all that was being asked for,
I would not regard it as beyond his powers to make the statement. Mr Perry has
submitted that he has no such power, but I would not accept that argument. In
my opinion the Director is entitled to form a policy as to the criteria which he will
apply when he is exercising his discretion under s 2(4) of the 1961 Act. If he has   *e*
such a policy, it seems to me to follow that he is entitled to promulgate it. I would
hold that these matters lie entirely within the scope of the discretion which has
been given to him by the Act.

[81] Some guidance is to be found in the practice which is followed in Scotland
in the exercise of his common law powers by the Lord Advocate. A recent example,
following the decision of the Court of Session in *Law Hospital NHS Trust v Lord*   *f*
Advocate 1996 SLT 848, is to be found in his statement of policy regarding
prosecutions following the withdrawal of life sustaining treatment from patients
in a permanent or persistent vegetative state (at 860, 867). Another is the statement
issued in September 1983 by the Crown Agent on behalf of the Lord Advocate,
following a statement to the same effect issued on 25 March 1983 by the Home
Office (Home Office circular 46/1983), as to the policy which would be followed   *g*
in the prosecution of drivers for drink-driving offences based on evidence produced
by a breath testing machine (see *Lockhart v Deighan* 1985 SLT 549). The Lord
Advocate has not issued a statement as to his policy regarding the prosecution of
assisted suicide, which in Scotland is a common law crime. He would have
power to do so if he thought that in the public interest this was appropriate.   *h*

[82] But I do not see how the Director could be compelled to issue a statement
of policy. In Scotland the question whether such statements should be issued are
regarded as being entirely a matter for the Lord Advocate. It has never been
suggested that he could be ordered to do this by the court. But in any event it is
not as a statement of policy that the undertaking has been sought. What   *j*
Mrs Pretty seeks is an undertaking, before the event occurs, that if her husband
helps her to commit suicide he will not be prosecuted. I am not aware of any case
where the Lord Advocate has given an undertaking of that kind. It is not his
function to permit individuals to commit acts which the law treats as criminal.

[83] Mrs Pretty contends that the Director is obliged to give the undertaking
because, if he were to decline to give it, he would be acting incompatibly with her

a convention rights. As I see it, this argument raises two distinct issues. The first is whether any of Mrs Pretty's convention rights are engaged at all in this case. Unless it can be shown that the Director's refusal is incompatible with at least one of them, the argument that s 6(1) of the 1998 Act makes it unlawful for him to refuse the undertaking disappears. The second is whether, if Mrs Pretty's convention rights are engaged, the undertaking which she has sought is one which the Director is obliged to give to her. I have already indicated that this raises difficult

b issues of both fact and policy. I shall deal first with Mrs Pretty's convention rights.

The convention rights

[**84**] Mr Havers submitted that Mrs Pretty has a convention right to the assistance of her husband in committing suicide. He was at pains to point out that

c her case under the European Convention for the Protection of Human Rights and Fundamental Freedoms (Rome, 4 November 1950; TS 71 (1953); Cmd 8969) (as set out in Sch 1 to the 1998 Act) was not that it gave her a right to die. She was asserting a right to control how and when she died as part of her right to life, without being discriminated against on account of her physical disability. She

d was also asserting a right of self-determination. She had made up her own mind about the course which she wished to follow to end her life. She would, but for her disability, have intended to follow that course without seeking assistance from anybody.

[**85**] As I said earlier, it is not for us to form a judgment on the ethical or moral issues which these submissions have raised. That they have a part to play in the

e making of our laws is not in doubt (see the report of the House of Lords Select Committee on Medical Ethics (HL Paper (1993–94) 21-I)). The convention too is the product of a broad consensus of international opinion about the core values which demand respect for human life and human dignity. It is against that background that we must answer the question which she has raised, which is a

f question of law. It is whether the articles of the convention on which she relies confer the rights she needs to demonstrate if she is to make good her argument that the Director's refusal to give the undertaking is unlawful under s 6(1) of the 1998 Act. We must pay close attention to the words used in the convention and, where appropriate, to the jurisprudence of the European Court of Human Rights. Throughout, we must bear in mind that the rights which are in question

g are rights which the individual has against the state. They do not exist in the abstract. Their function is to control the actions of the state in its relationship with the individual.

(a) *Article 2*

h [**86**] The short point here is whether the Director's refusal to give the undertaking is incompatible with the first sentence of this article. It provides that everyone's right to life 'shall be protected by law'. The remaining parts of the article deal with the circumstances in which a person may be deprived of life. They plainly have nothing to do with Mrs Pretty's dispute with the Director.

j [**87**] It is important to observe both what the sentence says and what it does not say. The right to which it refers is the right to life. But it does not create a right to life. The right to life is assumed to be inherent in the human condition which we all share. Nor does it create a right to self-determination. It does not say that every person has the right to choose how or when to die. Nor does it say that the individual has a right to choose death rather than life. What the first sentence does—and all it does—is to state that the right to life must be protected

by law. This protection operates both negatively and positively. It enjoins the
state to refrain from the intentional and unlawful taking of life. It also enjoins the a
state to safeguard lives (*Osman v UK* (1998) 5 BHRC 293 at 321 (para 115)). But
the protection of human life is its sole object.

[88] The Director's refusal to give the undertaking has not disturbed or
interfered with Mrs Pretty's right to life. Nothing that he has done in response to
her request is contrary to any law which is designed to safeguard life. On the b
contrary, his act in declining to give the undertaking to enable Mr Pretty to assist
in his wife's suicide is compatible with the opening words of the second sentence
of the article. It provides that no one shall be deprived of his life intentionally. As
the Divisional Court pointed out ([2001] EWHC Admin 788 at [41], [2001] All ER
(D) 251 (Oct) at [41]), for a third person to take active steps deliberately to deprive
another of life, even with the consent of the person thus deprived, is forbidden by c
the article. The article is all about protecting life, not bringing it to an end. It is
not possible to read it as obliging the state to allow someone to assist another
person to commit suicide. I would hold that her claim does not engage any of her
rights under this article.

d

(b) *Article 3*

[89] The argument with regard to this article is that Mrs Pretty will inevitably
suffer inhuman or degrading treatment if the disease is allowed to run its course.
It is not suggested that the Director has done anything which is directly
prohibited by the article. The argument concentrates on its positive effects— e
what the state must do to ensure that the individual does not suffer treatment of
the kind that it prohibited. The terminal stages of motor neurone disease provide
the background. The inability to swallow leads to breathlessness and to the
sensation of choking, as muscle power in the mouth and throat degenerates. But
awareness and mental function is usually unimpaired. The patient can be
expected to suffer increasing anxiety and mental anguish, as she succumbs to the f
symptoms of the disease. Death usually results from respiratory failure and
pneumonia. Mrs Pretty says that by declining to give the undertaking the Director
has taken a decision which will subject her to these tragic consequences. She says
that he has subjected her to inhuman and degrading treatment within the
meaning of the article.

g

[90] The European Court of Human Rights has repeatedly said that art 3
prohibits torture or inhuman or degrading treatment or punishment in terms
which are absolute (*Chahal v UK* (1996) 1 BHRC 405 at 424 (para 79), *D v UK* (1997)
2 BHRC 273 at 283–284 (paras 47, 49)). From this proposition two things follow.
First, only serious ill treatment will be held to fall within the scope of the expression h
'inhuman or degrading treatment or punishment'. The court said in *A v UK* (1998)
5 BHRC 137 at 141 (para 20) that ill treatment must attain a minimum level of
severity if it is to fall within the scope of the article. It also said that the assessment
of this minimum is relative, as it depends on all the circumstances of the case such
as the nature and context of the treatment which is in issue. Second, although the
absolute prohibition is not capable of modification on grounds of proportionality, j
issues of proportionality will arise where a positive obligation is implied. The
jurisprudence of the European Court of Human Rights shows that where positive
obligations arise they are not absolute. In *Osman v UK* (1998) 5 BHRC 293 at 321
(para 116) the court recognised that such obligations must be interpreted in a way
which does not impose an impossible or disproportionate burden on the
authorities. This approach is consistent with that which the court takes where

a   other rights than those expressly stated are read into an article as implied rights
     (see *Brown v Stott* [2001] 2 All ER 97 at 129, [2001] 2 WLR 817 at 851). This makes
     it necessary to pay close attention to the question whether the act in question is
     one which is expressly prohibited or is based upon a positive obligation which is
     implied into the article.

     [91] As for the question whether the consequences of not giving the
b   undertaking will attain the required minimum level of severity, the facts must be
     seen in their whole context. Mrs Pretty cannot be forced to accept medical
     treatment for her condition as it reaches the terminal stages, but it is relevant to
     her case to see what is on offer. In its *Response to the Report of the Select Committee
     on Medical Ethics* (Cm 2553 (1994)) the government stated (at p 2), in its comment
c   on para 288 of the report of the select committee, that it would encourage the
     development of palliative care in all settings to ensure that patients received
     sensitive care and relief from pain and other distressing symptoms. Your Lordships
     were informed that nursing care and palliative treatment is already being provided
     to Mrs Pretty and that it will continue to be available. The use of drugs such as
     opiates in the form of morphine may be helpful in the terminal stages in relieving
d   the distress of breathlessness and the sensation of choking. It has not been possible
     in these proceedings to examine the facts in detail. But there is enough information
     available to us to cast serious doubt on the question whether the consequences of
     the refusal, taken as a whole in the context of the treatment which is available,
     attain the minimum level of inhuman or degrading treatment within the meaning
e   of the article.

     [92] Then there is the nature of the Director's act. It is clear that he is not
     directly responsible for the disease or for its consequences. Nothing has been
     identified that he has done and should be restrained from doing in order to
     remove or alleviate these consequences. I would conclude that we are not dealing
     here with a case with an act which is expressly prohibited. The argument is that
f   the article applies positively, as it requires the Director to do something to avoid
     the incompatibility. This raises the question whether the Director's refusal to
     give the undertaking is incompatible with art 3 because it is disproportionate.

     [93] Three matters fall to be considered where questions arise as to whether
     an interference with a convention right is proportionate. In *De Freitas v Permanent
g   Secretary of Ministry of Agriculture, Fisheries, Lands and Housing* [1999] 1 AC 69,
     [1998] 3 WLR 675, Lord Clyde adopted the analysis of Gubbay CJ in *Nyambirai v
     National Social Security Authority* [1996] 1 LRC 64 drawing on jurisprudence from
     South Africa and Canada (see also *Rodriguez v A-G of Canada* [1994] 2 LRC 136 at
     161 per Lamer CJ). The first is whether the objective which is sought to be
h   achieved is sufficiently important to justify limiting the fundamental right. The
     second is whether the means chosen are rational, fair and not arbitrary. The third
     is whether the means used impair the right as minimally as is reasonably possible.

     [94] As to these issues, the following points seem to me to point conclusively
     in favour of the Director. First, there is the objective. The Director is entitled to
j   regard the purpose of s 2(1) of the 1961 Act as being to protect the vulnerable
     from pressure to end their own lives. In its response to para 295 of the report of
     the select committee the government stated (at p 5) that it could see no basis for
     permitting assisted suicide as this would be open to abuse and would put the lives
     of the weak and vulnerable at risk. So the decriminalisation of attempted suicide
     in 1961 was accompanied by an unequivocal statement of the prohibition of acts
     calculated to end another person's life.

[95] Then there is the question whether the Director's refusal is rational, fair and not arbitrary. In my opinion he is entitled to take into account the nature of *a* the act which he was asked to sanction in this case. All he was told was that Mrs Pretty would be helped by her husband to commit suicide. Where, when and how this was to be done was not and probably cannot at this stage be specified. There is no suggestion that medical assistance will be available or that the act will be supervised by anybody. Sopinka J observed in *Rodriguez'* case (at 189) that the *b* official position of various medical associations, including the British Medical Association, is against decriminalising assisted suicide. It is common knowledge that most members of the medical profession are opposed to any involvement in this activity. A clear distinction is preserved between the withdrawal of treatment and palliative care on the one hand and acts on the other whose sole purpose is to destroy life. Moreover, the margin between assisting suicide and euthanasia is *c* so slender in Mrs Pretty's case as to be impossible to determine in the absence of a detailed account of the proposed act. All of this points to the conclusion that the Director is entitled to take the view that it is impracticable for him to give an undertaking in advance of the event that he will not prosecute.

[96] Then there is the third issue, which is whether the means used to achieve *d* the objective are proportionate. The object of s 2(1) of the 1961 Act is to avoid an abuse which would put the lives of the weak and vulnerable at risk. In this way it seeks to preserve life. I would be willing to give full weight to Mrs Pretty's assertion that she is not weak or vulnerable in this sense—that she has sufficient mental strength not to be vulnerable to pressure to commit suicide. I can appreciate her objection that vulnerability should not be imposed upon her simply because *e* her physical condition prevents her from doing so. But this does not meet the Director's argument. It is not unreasonable for him to think that, if he were to sanction one act of assisted suicide, this might lead to requests from others less well equipped to stand up to the unscrupulous. Separating out the good from the bad would be an impossible task for him, as he lacks the resources that would be *f* needed to conduct the exercise. He is entitled to think that the public interest is best served by holding the line against granting undertakings of this kind. In the present uncertain climate of public opinion, where there is no consensus in favour of assisted suicide and there are powerful religious and ethical arguments to the contrary, any change in the law which would make assisted suicide generally acceptable is best seen as a matter for Parliament. *g*

[97] I would hold therefore that the object which s 2(1) was designed to achieve struck the right balance between the interests of the individual and the public interest which seeks to protect the weak and vulnerable. Great weight must be attached to the state's interest in protecting the lives of its citizens. It was a proportionate response for Parliament to conclude that that interest could only *h* be met by a complete prohibition on assisted suicide. I would also hold that, although the effect of the Director's decision that he had no power to give the undertaking is likely to be to expose Mrs Pretty to acute distress as she succumbs to her illness, his act cannot be said to be unfair or arbitrary or to have impaired her convention right more than is reasonably necessary. It was not disproportionate *j* to the object of s 2(1).

(c) *Articles 8 and 9*

[98] I take these two articles together, as they are both invoked in support of the same argument. This is that they confer a right to self-determination through

a the right to private life and the right to freedom of expression which prohibits a blanket ban on assisted suicide. The object of these articles is to protect the individual against arbitrary interference by the public authorities. They compel the state to abstain from acts which are incompatible with the convention rights. But, in addition to the negative undertaking, here too positive obligations may be implied into them (see *X v Netherlands* (1985) 8 EHRR 235 at 239–240 (para 23)).

b [99] The first question is whether these articles are engaged at all by Mrs Pretty's claim that she is entitled to her husband's assistance in committing suicide. Can her claim be said to be based on her right to respect for her private and family life, her home and her correspondence in art 8? Can it be said to be based on her right to freedom of thought, conscience and religion in art 9?

c [100] No authority has been cited in support of either proposition. The wording of the articles does not help either. Respect for a person's 'private life', which is the only part of art 8(1) that is in play here, relates to the way a person lives. The way she chooses to pass the closing moments of her life is part of the act of living, and she has a right to ask that this too must be respected. In that respect Mrs Pretty has a right of self-determination. In that sense, her private life *d* is engaged even where in the face of a terminal illness she seeks to choose death rather than life. But it is an entirely different thing to imply into these words a positive obligation to give effect to her wish to end her own life by means of an assisted suicide. I think that to do so would be to stretch the meaning of the words too far.

e [101] A strained reading might have been appropriate if there was evidence of a consensus of international opinion in favour of assisted suicide. But there is none. As Sopinka J said in *Rodriguez'* case (at 176) no new consensus has emerged in society opposing the right of the state to regulate the involvement of others in exercising power over individuals ending their lives. The right to freedom of *f* thought, conscience and religion includes the right to manifest one's religion or beliefs without interference save as provided for in art 9(2). But here again it strains the wording of the article too far to say it gives the person a right to do whatever her beliefs allow her to do. Yet that precisely is her claim under this article.

[102] In any event, for the reasons already indicated, I would hold that the *g* Director's refusal to give the undertaking was not disproportionate to the object of s 2(1), which is to avoid abuse and to protect the weak and the vulnerable.

(d) *Article 14*

[103] This article prohibits discrimination in the enjoyment of the rights and *h* freedoms set forth in the convention. These rights are to be secured without discrimination on any ground such as sex, race, colour and the various other grounds which are expressly mentioned in the article. The European Court of Human Rights has held that the right not to be discriminated against in the enjoyment of the rights guaranteed under the convention is violated when states without an objective *j* and reasonable justification fail to treat differently persons whose situations are significantly different (*Thlimmenos v Greece* (2000) 9 BHRC 12 at 22 (para 44)).

[104] Two issues arise here. The first is whether the article is engaged at all. Does it extend to the ground of discrimination on which Mrs Pretty founds her claim? The second is whether, if it does, she can point to any right or freedom which is engaged by the convention to which art 14 can be attached.

[105] As to the first point, it is clear that the list of grounds for discrimination set out in the article is not closed. This is made clear by the words 'such as' which precede the list. I would hold that the article is capable of extending to discrimination in the enjoyment of the convention rights on the grounds of physical or mental capacity. Section 15(1) of the Canadian Charter of Rights and Freedoms recognises that discrimination on these grounds is contrary to fundamental rights. I see no difficulty in recognising that art 14 of the convention has that effect too. Mrs Pretty can reasonably claim that her physical situation is significantly different from that of others who wish to commit suicide, as she cannot take her own life without another person's assistance. The difficulty which she faces is that, for the reasons already stated, her case does not engage any of the other articles on which she relies. It was with reference to this second point that Mr Havers said that Mrs Pretty was entitled under art 14 not to be discriminated against in the exercise of what he described as her right under s 1 of the 1961 Act to commit suicide.

[106] The argument that art 14 prohibits discrimination in the enjoyment of a right to commit suicide would, if sound, have disturbing and far-reaching consequences. It would make it impracticable for the state to intervene to prevent people from taking their own lives, whether by removing them from places or equipment which could be used for the purpose or by rendering medical assistance to prevent death. But there is as yet no free-standing right under the convention not to be discriminated against. So I am far from being persuaded that s 1 provides a basis for invoking art 14. In any event I would reject the argument on a more fundamental ground. Section 1 of the 1961 Act did not create a right to commit suicide. All it did was to abrogate the rule of law which had previously made it a crime to commit suicide. The fact that it provided in s 2(1) that a person who aids or abets another to commit suicide points clearly to the conclusion that decriminalisation, not the creation of a right, was what was intended. There were good reasons for wishing to decriminalise the act itself. The removal of the fear of prosecution and of the stigma was likely to make it easier to deter those who were planning or attempting suicide. Broadly speaking, it was a measure in favour of saving life, with which the provisions of s 2 are entirely in sympathy. In my opinion the argument that art 14 is engaged by a right to commit suicide which is to be found in s 1 of the 1961 Act must be rejected.

Conclusion

[107] It has not been shown that any of the convention rights on which Mrs Pretty relies have been infringed by the Director's act when he said that he had no power to give the undertaking which she requested. So it cannot be said that his act was unlawful within the meaning of s 6(1) of the 1998 Act or that he was obliged by that Act to give the undertaking. Nor can it be said that the blanket ban which s 2(1) of the 1961 Act imposes on assisted suicide is incompatible with any of Mrs Pretty's convention rights.

[108] For these reasons and for those given by Lord Bingham of Cornhill and Lord Steyn I agree with the Divisional Court that the conclusions which it reached in this sad case are inescapable. I would dismiss the appeal.

LORD HOBHOUSE OF WOODBOROUGH.

[109] My Lords, this appeal concerns the sanctity of human life. The sanctity of human life is probably the most fundamental of the human social values. It is recognised in all civilised societies and their legal systems and by the

a internationally recognised statements of human rights. In English law it is given
effect to by the criminalisation of murder and manslaughter. In the European
Convention for the Protection of Human Rights and Fundamental Freedoms
(Rome, 4 November 1950; TS 71 (1953); Cmd 8969) (as set out in Sch 1 to the
Human Rights Act 1998) it is reflected by art 2, the right to life:

b '1. Everyone's right to life shall be protected by law. No one shall be
deprived of his life intentionally save in the execution of a sentence of a court
following his conviction of a crime for which this penalty is provided by law.'

The Parliamentary Assembly of the Council of Europe on 25 June 1999 adopted
a text which addressed the need to protect the dignity and quality of life of the
terminally ill and the dying and called upon states to respect and protect this
c dignity by providing palliative care, by protecting the terminally ill or dying
person's right to self-determination through the availability of truthful and
comprehensive information and respect for his expressed wishes as to the forms
of treatment he is willing to receive, provided that they do not violate human
dignity, and—

d 'by upholding the prohibition against intentionally taking the life of
terminally ill or dying persons, while: i. recognising that the right to life,
especially with regard to a terminally ill or dying person, is guaranteed by the
member states, in accordance with Article 2 of the European Convention on
Human Rights which states that "no one shall be deprived of his life
e intentionally"; ii. recognising that a terminally ill or dying person's wish to
die never constitutes any legal claim to die at the hand of another person;
iii. recognising that a terminally ill or dying person's wish to die cannot of
itself constitute a legal justification to carry out actions intended to bring
about death.' (See Recommendation 1418 (1999) on the protection of the
human rights and dignity of the terminally ill and the dying, p 4 (para 9(c)).)
f

In the Court of Appeal in *Airedale NHS Trust v Bland* [1993] 1 All ER 821 at 855,
[1993] AC 789 at 831, Hoffmann LJ said:

'... the sanctity of life entails its inviolability by an outsider. Subject to
exceptions like self-defence, human life is inviolate even if the person in
g question has consented to its violation. That is why although suicide is not
a crime, assisting someone to commit suicide is.'

[110] There are two salient features of these statements of principle. One is
that the consent of the deceased is no justification or defence to a charge of having
acted with the intention of causing the deceased's death. A similar principle has
h been recognised in certain other aspects of the criminal law where the protection
of the public order and the health of the society are considered to require it as, for
example, in relation to the criminal offence of inflicting of grievous bodily harm.
The consent of the injured person to an unlawful wounding is not a defence (*R v
Brown* [1993] 2 All ER 75, [1994] 1 AC 212, upheld by the European Court of
j Human Rights in *Laskey v UK* (1997) 24 EHRR 39). Assisted suicide and voluntary
euthanasia have the same criminality as murder notwithstanding the consent of
the deceased.

[111] The other feature is that the involvement of a second party in the
relevant conduct puts the conduct into a different category from conduct which
has involved the deceased alone. Joining in bringing about the intentional death
of another person is in principle the crime of murder. That the deceased wished

to die and was, so far as he was concerned, committing suicide did not prevent the other from being convicted as a principal or accessory to the crime of murder. *a* Thus, a party to a suicide pact, who was absent at the time the other party killed himself, could be convicted of murder as an accessory before the fact (see *R v Croft* [1944] 2 All ER 483, [1944] KB 295). In law, quite minor acts of encouragement can render a defendant liable to be convicted of murder as an accessory. (See for example *R v Giannetto* [1997] 1 Cr App R 1.) Where there was a suicide pact to *b* which the defendant was a party and which was to include his death, this consequence was mitigated by s 4 of the Homicide Act 1957 which reduced the offence, whether as principal or accessory, from murder to manslaughter. But, where there was no suicide pact, the crime of murder continued to apply. Where there is a joint purpose that the deceased's life should be ended and the deceased and the other person co-operate in achieving that end, the principle of joint *c* enterprise may apply so as to make the second person criminally liable for murder or manslaughter (see *R v Howe* [1987] 1 All ER 771, [1987] AC 417, overruling *R v Richards (Isabelle)* [1973] 3 All ER 1088, [1974] QB 776). Since the passing of the Suicide Act 1961, it has not been a criminal offence for a person to take his own life or attempt to do so (s 1). But the same Act preserved the criminality of the *d* conduct of the second person. Section 2(1) created the offence of aiding, abetting, counselling or procuring the suicide, or attempted suicide, of another with a maximum sentence of 14 years' imprisonment. The result is that the relevance of suicide as opposed to voluntary euthanasia is not that it negatives the criminality of the conduct of the defendant (the second person) but that it affects the gravity of the criminal offence committed—the s 2(1) offence, *e* manslaughter under s 4 of the 1957 Act, or murder. Assisted suicide inevitably offends against the principle of the sanctity of human life. The criminal law continues to reflect this. Assisted suicide will involve the commission of a criminal offence contrary to s 2(1) of the 1961 Act.

[112] Mr Havers QC, who appeared on behalf of the appellant and who *f* presented her argument with admirable objectivity and clarity, acknowledged, as he had to, that unless he could show that the appellant's human rights had been infringed contrary to the Human Rights Act 1998 he could not escape from the consequences of s 2(1) of the 1961 Act. For the reasons which they have given in their speeches, I agree with my noble and learned friends Lord Bingham of Cornhill, Lord Steyn and Lord Hope of Craighead that the appellant's human *g* rights are not being infringed and wish to add nothing in that regard to what they have said. This conclusion suffices to necessitate the dismissal of the appeal.

[113] But, like the Divisional Court ([2001] EWHC Admin 788, [2001] All ER (D) 251 (Oct)) and my noble and learned friend Lord Steyn and in agreement with them, I do not consider it right to leave this case without saying something about *h* the appellant's use of the remedy of judicial review to bring this matter before the court. The respondent to the application is the Director of Public Prosecutions (the Director) and the subject matter of her application is his negative response to a letter dated 27 July 2001 from the appellant's solicitor requesting a 'written undertaking' that he would not consent to a prosecution of Mr Pretty in the event *j* that Mr Pretty should aid, abet, counsel or procure the suicide of the appellant in a manner consistent with her wishes. She said that she wished to choose for herself the time when and the means by which she should die and, owing to her disabling illness, was unable to fulfil this wish unaided and wished that the necessary assistance be provided by her husband. The making of this request for an undertaking was said to be justified by the 1998 Act and the fact that any

a proceedings for an offence under s 2 or the 1961 Act may only be instituted by or
with the consent of the Director (s 2(4)). It thus raises again the considerations
discussed in the speeches of Lord Steyn and myself in *R v DPP, ex p Kebeline, R v
DPP, ex p Rechachi* [1999] 4 All ER 801, [2000] 2 AC 326.

[114] The office of Director is a statutory office with functions and powers
governed by statute, currently the Prosecution of Offences Act 1985 which
b introduced a radical restructuring of the management and conduct of criminal
prosecutions in England and Wales, bringing into existence the Crown Prosecution
Service and altering the role of the police. The functions of the Director are set
out in s 3 of the 1985 Act. They do not include the grant of dispensations from
the criminal law nor the grant of pardons; they primarily relate to the institution
and conduct of criminal proceedings. It is not part of his functions or duties to
c advise members of the public. He has a duty to issue a Code for Crown Prosecutors
giving them guidance on the general principles to be applied by them in deciding
when proceedings should be instituted or discontinued and what charges should
be preferred (s 10 of that Act). The undertaking which the appellant requested
was not one which the Director as the holder of the statutory office had the
authority or power to give and it would have been improper for him to give
d the undertaking whatever the merits of the appellant's solicitor's arguments.
Under s 2(4) of the 1961 Act his role is confined to giving his consent to the
institution of proceedings for an offence under s 2. This presupposes that an
alleged offence has been committed and that he can exercise his discretion under
s 2(4) in relation to all the circumstances disclosed by the evidence of what has
e occurred as the code issued under s 10 of the 1985 Act makes clear. The functions
of the Director do not include giving undertakings in advance of the event as to
how he would exercise that discretion on hypothetical facts. Even after the
event, the Director has no investigatory powers and is dependent upon evidence
supplied to him by others, normally the police.

f [115] The response of the Crown Prosecutor on behalf of the Director to the
letter of 27 July 2001 was:

'Successive Directors—and Attorneys General—have explained that they
will not grant immunities that condone, require, or purport to authorise or
permit the future commission of any criminal offence, no matter how
g exceptional the circumstances. I must therefore advise you that the Director
cannot provide the undertaking that you seek.'

This was a proper reply. Indeed, any other reply would almost certainly have
been improper.

h [116] In exceptional circumstances it may be proper for a member of the
public to bring proceedings against the Crown for a declaration that certain
proposed conduct is lawful and name the Attorney General as the formal
defendant to the claim. But that is not what occurred here and, even then, the
court would have a discretion which it would normally exercise to refuse to rule
upon hypothetical facts. Had the case raised by the appellant been one where it
j was appropriate to grant a declaration as to legality or compatibility, the court
would no doubt have adopted that approach. Indeed, the judgment of the
Divisional Court and the speeches of your Lordships on the human rights
questions will no doubt provide in practice the appropriate guidance to all those
concerned in this matter as to the correct understanding of the law.

[117] The request for the undertaking was a request for the grant of an
immunity from prosecution equivalent to the grant of a dispensation from the

operation of the criminal law or an anticipatory pardon. Even if there was a
power to grant a pardon, it could not be exercised in advance. As Lord Woolf said
in *A-G of Trinidad and Tobago v Phillip* [1995] 1 All ER 93 at 102, [1995] 1 AC 396 at
411:

> 'However, while a pardon can expunge past offences, a power to pardon
> cannot be used to dispense with criminal responsibility for an offence which
> has not yet been committed. This is a principle of general application which
> is of the greatest importance. The state cannot be allowed to use a power to
> pardon to enable the law to be set aside by permitting it to be contravened
> with impunity.'

Likewise any purported executive power to suspend or dispense with a law or the
execution of a law, save under an express statutory authority, has been unlawful
since at least 1688.

[118] The intentions stated in the solicitor's letter were wholly unparticularised,
save that the second person who was to assist was to be the appellant's husband
not any independent or medically-qualified person. This has remained the
position throughout these proceedings. The point was raised in a witness
statement dated 19 September filed on behalf of the Director. The Divisional
Court were told by Mr Havers ([2001] All ER (D) 251 (Oct) at [6]) that no further
information would be forthcoming and that they had been told all that they
needed to know. In the same context it was also stated that any non-availability
of appropriate palliative care was not part of the appellant's case. This lack of
detail demonstrates that even if he had had the power to do so the Director could
not properly have given any advance undertaking or assurance. He had not got
the information, let alone the evidence, which would be needed to make any
decision upon the question of consent in accordance with the s 10 code.

[119] But this lack of information illustrates two further points. The first is
that any undertaking or other advance assurance would inevitably give rise to the
need for a later investigation whether the death of the appellant had in truth been
by suicide and what, in the event, had been the actual participation of Mr Pretty
(in all probability, the sole surviving witness). It would then have to be decided
whether what had occurred had or had not been covered by the undertaking.
Further proceedings for judicial review would then no doubt ensue. This is a
wholly impractical and objectionable scenario. Issues of fact which should be left
to be tried in a criminal court on a criminal prosecution conducted in accordance
with the criminal law would be being raised in satellite litigation which would be
directly contrary to the guidance given in *Ex p Kebeline*.

[120] Secondly, it demonstrates the highly unsatisfactory character of the
approach adopted by the appellant and her advisors. If assisted suicide is to be
permitted, it is essential that the permission include suitable safeguards of an
appropriate rigour and specificity. The Dutch scheme includes an elaborate
medically supervised and executed procedure. The minority judgments in
Rodriguez v A-G of Canada [1994] 2 LRC 136 which favoured legalising assisted
suicide treated the formulation of satisfactory conditions as a necessary first step
and attempted to do so (see (1993) 76 BCLR (2d) 145 at 168–169 and [1994] 2 LRC
136 at 147–148). The reasoning of the majority decision included the view that
the proposed safeguards were inadequate and impractical. The conclusion is
inescapable that both the nature of the questions raised by assisted suicide and the
formulation of any new policies must under our system of Parliamentary
democracy be a matter for the legislature not the judiciary. For the time being,

a Parliament has spoken by including s 2 in the 1961 Act. Any amendment of that section and its terms would be a matter for Parliament.

[121] This leads on to a further matter, also covered by *Ex p Kebeline*. The Director is governed by the existing law. He must exercise his discretion in accordance with the law. If there are disputes as to what the law is he should, provided that they are real disputes, leave them to the criminal courts to decide.

b It is no part of the Director's function himself to decide arguable questions of law. Nor is it acceptable (save, perhaps, in the most exceptional circumstances which I cannot at present visualise) to seek to use an application for the judicial review of the Director's decision to prosecute as a means of challenging in advance some proposition of law upon which the prosecution will rely at the trial. The observations of my noble and learned friend Lord Steyn in *Ex p Kebeline* [1999]
c 4 All ER 801 at 835–836, [2000] 2 AC 326 at 371, from which he has already drawn in his speech on this appeal, are pertinent and their wisdom is further demonstrated by the present case.

[122] Some reliance was placed by the appellant, as has been noted by some of your Lordships, upon the fact that on some occasions the Director in England
d and the Lord Advocate in Scotland have made statements that in certain circumstances they would not authorise prosecutions. Upon examination, these have turned out to be examples of the application of the guidance given in the code or similar principles applicable in Scotland. The main example relied upon in relation to the Director (and replicated in Scotland) concerned breathalyser evidence using Home Office approved devices. The devices (or some of them) had been found to be unreliable below a certain level of breath alcohol. The
e effect of what the Director said, confirmed by the Home Office, was that in view of this unreliability, prosecutions would not be authorised where the evidence relied upon was unreliable, ie would fail the 'Evidential Test'. The instances referred to by the appellant thus provided no analogy for the present case nor any
f justification for the approach which her advisors adopted to the role of the Director.

[123] In conclusion therefore, in agreement with what my noble and learned friend Lord Steyn has said on this topic both in this case and in *Ex p Kebeline*, I would stress that the procedure of seeking to bypass the ordinary operation of our system of criminal justice by raising questions of law and applying for the
g judicial review of 'decisions' of the Director cannot be approved and should be firmly discouraged. It undermines the proper and fair management of our criminal justice system.

LORD SCOTT OF FOSCOTE.

h [124] My Lords, I have had the advantage of reading in advance the opinions of my noble and learned friends Lord Bingham of Cornhill, Lord Steyn and Lord Hope of Craighead. I am in complete agreement with them and, for the reasons they give, would dismiss the appeal in this sad case.

Appeal dismissed.

Dilys Tausz   Barrister.

Uratemp Ventures Ltd v Collins   a

[2001] UKHL 43

HOUSE OF LORDS

LORD IRVINE OF LAIRG LC, LORD BINGHAM OF CORNHILL, LORD STEYN, LORD HOBHOUSE   b
OF WOODBOROUGH AND LORD MILLETT

9 JULY, 11 OCTOBER 2001

Landlord and tenant – Assured tenancy – Tenancy under which a dwelling-house is let
as a separate dwelling – Whether cooking facilities prerequisite of dwelling-house –   c
Housing Act 1988, s 1(1).

The appellant, C, was a long-term resident of a room in a hotel owned by the
respondents. The room had a single bed, some furniture, a shower and a basin.
No cooking facilities were provided, although the room contained a power point.   d
C brought in some electrical equipment, including a pizza warmer and a toasted
sandwich maker, to enable him to make simple meals. In 1998 the hotel owners
served a notice terminating what they contended was C's licence to occupy the room,
and brought possession proceedings against him. Those proceedings were dismissed
by the judge who concluded that the room was a 'dwelling-house' let as a separate
'dwelling' within the meaning of s 1(1)[a] of the Housing Act 1988, and that accordingly   e
C held the room on an assured tenancy. The judge's decision was reversed by the
Court of Appeal which held, by a majority, that cooking facilities were a prerequisite
of a 'dwelling' and that C's room lacked the requisite facilities. C appealed to
the House of Lords.

f

Held – Cooking facilities were not an essential attribute of a 'dwelling-house' or
'dwelling' within the meaning of s 1(1) of the 1988 Act. The concept of a 'dwelling-
house' described a place where someone dwelt, lived or resided. In deciding in
any given case whether the subject matter of a letting fell within that description,
it was proper to have regard to the object of the legislation, directed as it was   g
to giving a measure of security to those who made their homes in rented
accommodation at the lower end of the housing market. It was not to be
expected that such accommodation would necessarily offer all of the amenities to
be found in more expensive accommodation. The legislative purpose was to
protect people in the occupation of their homes, not to encourage them to cook   h
their own meals. In the instant case, it was plain that the room was C's home, the
place where he lived, and that was so whether he had his meals out or warmed
up food to eat in his room or did a little rudimentary cooking or a bit of all three.
If the room had been let to C under a tenancy, it had clearly been let as a separate
dwelling house. Accordingly, the appeal would be allowed (see [1], [3], [5], [10],   j
[12], [13], [17], [19], [20], [57]–[59], [61], below).

    Dictum of Lord Templeman in *Westminster City Council v Clarke* [1992] 1 All ER
695 at 701 criticised.

a   Section 1, so far as material, is set out at [2], below

Notes

a For the meaning of 'dwelling-house', see 27(1) *Halsbury's Laws* (4th edn reissue) para 669.

For the Housing Act 1988, s 1, see 23 *Halsbury's Statutes* (4th edn) (1997 reissue) 1056.

b **Cases referred to in opinions**

Baker v Turner [1950] 1 All ER 834, [1950] AC 401, HL.

Barnett v Hickmott [1895] 1 QB 691.

Cole v Harris [1945] 2 All ER 146, [1945] KB 474, CA.

Curl v Angelo [1948] 2 All ER 189, CA.

c *Dunston v Paterson* (1858) 5 CB (NS) 267, 141 ER 106, CP.

Goodrich v Paisner [1956] 2 All ER 176, [1957] AC 65, [1956] 2 WLR 1053, HL.

Hayward v Marshall, Winchester v Sharpe [1952] 1 All ER 663, [1952] 2 QB 89, CA.

Kenyon v Walker, Stevenson v Kenyon [1946] 2 All ER 595, CA.

d *Marsh Ltd v Cooper* [1969] 2 All ER 498, [1969] 1 WLR 803, CA.

McCarthy v Preston [1951] NZLR 1091, NZ SC.

Metropolitan Properties Co (FCG) Ltd v Barder [1968] 1 All ER 536, [1968] 1 WLR 286, CA.

Monks v Dykes (1839) 4 M & W 567, 150 ER 1546.

Neale v Del Soto [1945] 1 All ER 191, [1945] KB 144, CA.

e *Palmer v McNamara* [1991] 1 EGLR 121, CA.

Parkins v Westminster City Council [1998] 1 EGLR 22, CA.

Powell v Guest (1864) 18 CB (NS) 72, 144 ER 367, CP.

Prout v Hunter [1924] 2 KB 736, [1924] All ER Rep 53, CA.

R v Ireland, R v Burstow [1997] 4 All ER 225, [1998] AC 147, [1997] 3 WLR 534, HL.

f *Stribling v Halse* (1885) 16 QBD 246, DC.

Thompson v Ward, Ellis v Burch (1871) LR 6 CP 327, DC.

Westminster City Council v Clarke [1992] 1 All ER 695, [1992] 2 AC 288, [1992] 2 WLR 229, HL.

Wimbush v Cibulia, Wimbush v Levinski [1949] 2 All ER 432, [1949] 2 KB 564, CA.

g *Winters v Dance* [1949] LJR 165, CA.

Wright v Howell (1947) 92 SJ 26, CA.

Appeal

The appellant, John Collins, appealed with permission of the Appeal Committee
h of the House of Lords given on 18 July 2000 from the decision of the Court of Appeal (Peter Gibson LJ and Moore-Bick J, Mance LJ dissenting in part) on 2 December 1999 ([2000] 1 EGLR 156) allowing an appeal by the respondents, Uratemp Ventures Ltd, from the order of Judge Cotran made in West London County Court on 29 January 1999 dismissing the proceedings brought by the respondents against Mr Collins
j for possession of room 403, The Viscount Hotel, 16 Prince of Wales Terrace, London W8 5PQ. The respondents took no part in the appeal to the House of Lords. The facts are set out in the opinion of Lord Millett.

Andrew Arden QC and *Richard Vain* (instructed by *Alan Edwards & Co*) for Mr Collins.
Michael Barnes QC (instructed by the *Treasury Solicitor*) as amicus curiae.

Their Lordships took time for consideration.

a

11 October 2001. The following opinions were delivered.

LORD IRVINE OF LAIRG LC.
[1] My Lords, I have had the advantage of reading in draft the comprehensive judgment of my noble and learned friend, Lord Millett. I adopt his analysis of the *b* facts, the relevant legislative histories and the authorities; and also the orders he proposes.
[2] This appeal concerns the words, 'a dwelling-house … let as a separate dwelling' in s 1 of the Housing Act 1988. A single room, as part of a house, may be a dwelling house; and on this appeal there is no issue of shared accommodation or facilities. The key issue is: whether the room which Mr Collins occupied, in the Viscount *c* Hotel, 16 Prince of Wales Terrace, Kensington, London W8 5PQ, when proceedings were brought, could in law qualify as a 'dwelling' only if cooking facilities were there available. Unless constrained to the contrary by authority, I would impose no such restrictive interpretation. Such a restrictive interpretation would both be unwarranted by the statutory language and an inappropriate gloss on provisions *d* designed to give some protection to tenants in modest rented accommodation under assured tenancies.
[3] 'Dwelling' is not a term of art, but a familiar word in the English language, which in my judgment in this context connotes a place where one lives, regarding and treating it as home. Such a place does not cease to be a 'dwelling' merely *e* because one takes all or some of one's meals out; or brings take-away food in to the exclusion of home cooking; or at times prepares some food for consumption on heating devices falling short of a full cooking facility.
[4] Decisions on the infinite factual variety of cases are for judges of trial and their decisions on the facts of individual cases should neither be treated nor cited as propositions of law. I would not myself, for example, regard a bed, any more *f* than cooking facilities, as an essential prerequisite of a 'dwelling': every case is for the judge of trial, but I would have no difficulty with a conclusion that one could live in a room, which is regarded and treated as home, although taking one's sleep, without the luxury of a bed, in an armchair, or in blankets on the floor.
[5] For these short reasons, along with those of Lord Bingham of Cornhill and *g* Lord Steyn, I too would allow the appeal and make the orders my noble friend, Lord Millett, proposes.

LORD BINGHAM OF CORNHILL.
[6] My Lords, I gratefully adopt the factual narrative given by my noble and *h* learned friend Lord Millett, and also his summary of the relevant legislation and authorities.
[7] Section 1 of the Housing Act 1988, which the House must construe, has a very long pedigree. For present purposes it poses two central questions. The first is whether the landlord has granted a tenancy of the premises in question or merely a licence to occupy them. That was a live question in the present case but *j* one which, if relevant when the second question had been answered, would have had to be remitted to the county court. The second question is whether, if a tenancy be assumed, the premises which were let are a dwelling house.
[8] Much of the case law on this section and its predecessors has been directed to the requirement that the premises be let as a 'separate' dwelling: see, in

a particular, *Neale v Del Soto* [1945] 1 All ER 191, [1945] KB 144, *Cole v Harris* [1945] 2 All ER 146, [1945] KB 474, *Kenyon v Walker, Stevenson v Kenyon* [1946] 2 All ER 595, *Winters v Dance* [1949] LJR 165, *Baker v Turner* [1950] 1 All ER 834, [1950] AC 401, *Hayward v Marshall, Winchester v Sharpe* [1952] 1 All ER 663, [1952] 2 QB 89, *Goodrich v Paisner* [1956] 2 All ER 176, [1957] AC 65, *Marsh Ltd v Cooper* [1969] 2 All ER 498, [1969] 1 WLR 803 and *Parkins v Westminster City Council* [1998] 1 EGLR 22.

b In these cases some space or facility was (or was said to be) enjoyed in common between the tenant and another or others, and the question was whether that which was enjoyed in common was of such a character or of such significance as to preclude description of what was let as a separate dwelling. In this context, distinctions were understandably and rightly drawn between living rooms, such as bedrooms and kitchens, and ancillary offices, such as bathrooms and lavatories:

c common enjoyment of the former but not the latter tended to weigh against recognition of the premises let as a separate dwelling.

[9] None of these problems arises here. It is accepted (rightly, on the long-standing authority of *Curl v Angelo* [1948] 2 All ER 189) that a single room may be a dwelling house. Mr Collins did not enjoy any space or facilities in common with

d other occupants. So the short question is whether room 403, the room let (as it is assumed) to Mr Collins, is a dwelling house.

[10] Save that a dwelling house may be a house or part of a house (s 45(1) of the 1988 Act), no statutory guidance is given on the meaning of this now rather old-fashioned expression. But the concept is clear enough: it describes a place

e where someone dwells, lives or resides. In deciding in any given case whether the subject matter of a letting falls within that description it is proper to have regard to the object of the legislation, directed as it is to giving a measure of security to those who make their homes in rented accommodation at the lower end of the housing market. It is not to be expected that such accommodation will

f necessarily offer all the amenities to be found in more expensive accommodation.

[11] The time at which it has to be judged whether premises are entitled to protection is when action is brought (see *Baker v Turner* [1950] 1 All ER 834 at 840, 842, [1950] AC 401 at 415, 419–420). At that stage it is necessary to consider the terms of the letting, the premises let and, in my opinion, the use made of them by the tenant: see s 1(1)(b) of the 1988 Act, which recognises that circumstances may

g change during the currency of a tenancy.

[12] It appears, in the present case, that Mr Collins habitually used some electrical devices to warm food in his room before eating it. The room was equipped with a power point which permitted that. I doubt if what he did could properly be described as cooking, but I do not think it matters. It is in my view

h plain on the evidence that this room was Mr Collins' home, the place where he lived, and this is so whether he had his meals out or warmed up food to eat in his room or did a little rudimentary cooking or a bit of all three. If a room were so small and cramped as to be unable to accommodate a bed, I should be inclined to doubt whether it would qualify to be called a dwelling house because, although

j sleeping in premises may not be enough to make them a dwelling house, premises will not ordinarily be a dwelling house unless the tenant sleeps there. But in my view the courts should be very wary of laying down inflexible rules which come to be mistaken for rules of law even though they are very largely conclusions of fact based on particular cases. That is what, as I think, has happened in this field, as Lord Millett has shown.

[13] I am of the clear opinion that room 403, if let to Mr Collins under a
tenancy, was let as a separate dwelling house. For these short reasons, as well as a
those given by Lord Irvine of Lairg LC, Lord Steyn and Lord Millett, I would
allow this appeal. For reasons given by Lord Millett it is now inappropriate to
remit the matter to the county court to determine whether there was a letting to
Mr Collins. On 25 September 2000 the landlord, Uratemp Ventures Ltd, withdrew
its opposition to this appeal. I agree with the costs order proposed by my noble b
and learned friend.

LORD STEYN.

[14] My Lords, the question is whether a modest room in the Viscount Hotel,
16 Prince of Wales Terrace, Kensington, London W8 5PQ, occupied by Mr Collins
is a dwelling house. It arises under s 1 of the Housing Act 1988 which speaks of c
'a dwelling-house ... let as a separate dwelling'. Since Mr Collins did not share
accommodation or facilities with other persons in the hotel the only issue before
the House is whether the room occupied by Mr Collins is a 'dwelling-house'
within the meaning of s 1. Part of a house may be a dwelling house (see s 45(1)).
And it is common ground that a bed-sitting room may be a dwelling house. But d
the majority in the Court of Appeal ([2000] 1 EGLR 156) held that the particular
room could not be a dwelling house because of the absence of cooking facilities.
They treated the presence of cooking facilities as an indispensable requirement for
a person's home being a 'dwelling-house' within the meaning of s 1. They thought
that an observation in the leading judgment of Lord Templeman in *Westminster
City Council v Clarke* [1992] 1 All ER 695 at 701, [1992] 2 AC 288 at 299, compelled e
this conclusion. On this question, 14 decisions, of which 11 were of the Court of
Appeal, were cited to the House. Acknowledging that such 'autopsies' have their
value at times, Cardozo J famously described such examinations as 'wearisome
and gruesome scenes'. In my view a resort to first principles points to a route
through this jungle of judicial glosses on the meaning of dwelling house. f

[15] The starting point must be that 'dwelling-house' is not a term of art. It is
an ordinary word in the English language. While I accept that dictionaries cannot
solve issues of interpretation, it nevertheless is helpful to bear in mind that
dwelling house has for centuries been a word of wide import. It is often used
interchangeably with lodging. It conveys the idea of a place where somebody
lives: see *Dr Johnson's Dictionary*, sv 'dwelling-house' and *Murray's Oxford English* g
Dictionary, sv 'dwelling-house' and 'lodging'. In ordinary parlance a bed-sitting
room where somebody habitually stays is therefore capable of being described as
a dwelling house. So much for generalities. The setting in which the word
appears in the statute is important. It is used in legislation which is intended to
afford a measure of protection to tenants under assured tenancies. This context h
makes it inappropriate for the court to place restrictive glosses on the word
'dwelling'. On the contrary, as counsel appearing as amicus curiae accepted, the
courts ought to interpret and apply the word 'dwelling-house' in s 1 the 1988 Act
in a reasonably generous fashion.

[16] The social phenomenon of the person 'Who friendless in a London lodging j
lives, Dines in a dingy chop-house' (*Oxford English Dictionary*, sv 'chop-house'
(1861)) goes back a very long time indeed. Dickens has described this world for
us in unforgettable scenes. It is to be contrasted with the world of ostentatious
dinner parties in smart houses mocked again and again by Trollope in many of
his novels. The world has changed. In recent years there have been great social
changes which reinforce the view that it is artificial to place on the word

a 'dwelling-house' the restrictive gloss that for a room or accommodation to qualify it must have cooking facilities. First, there are nowadays many more people who live alone. Specifically, a survey in the spring of 2000 recorded that three in ten households in Great Britain comprised one person living alone, more than two-and-a-half times the proportion in 1961 (Office for National Statistics *Social Trends 31* (2001 edn) p 41). Secondly, there has been an explosion in the
b growth of self-service cafeteria, sandwich shops, takeaway shops, home delivery services and other fast-food outlets. One only has to look under the entry 'FOOD & DRINK—DELIVERED' in the most recent edition of the Yellow Pages for Central London (2000/2001) to realise the scale of this development in the eating habits of large numbers of people of all ages. And it is necessary to interpret s 1 of the 1988 Act in the world of today (*R v Ireland, R v Burstow* [1997] 4 All ER 225 at 233,
c [1998] AC 147 at 158).

[17] The observation in *Westminster City Council v Clarke* [1992] 1 All ER 695 at 701, [1992] 2 AC 288 at 299 by Lord Templeman, that 'a bed-sitting room with cooking facilities may be a separate dwelling house even though bathroom and lavatory facilities might be elsewhere and shared with other people', was not part
d of the ratio decidendi of the case. The point was not in issue and the House heard no argument on it. Moreover, as Mance LJ convincingly demonstrated in the Court of Appeal in the present case, the observation was not justified by the earlier authorities. In my view the observation in *Westminster City Council v Clarke* was too restrictive. A bed-sitting room which a tenant occupies as his home may be a dwelling even if he brings in all his meals or goes out for all his meals. There
e is no authority binding on the House which precludes this construction. In these circumstances it follows that the room occupied by Mr Collins was his dwelling house.

[18] How such cases are approached by judges at the coal face is important. On this point I agree with the succinct statement of principles by Lord Bingham
f of Cornhill in paras [10] and [11] of his speech.

[19] For the reasons given by Lord Bingham and Lord Millett, as well as the brief reasons I have given, I would allow the appeal and make the orders proposed by Lord Bingham and Lord Millett.

LORD HOBHOUSE OF WOODBOROUGH.
g [20] My Lords, for the reasons already given and those to be given by my noble and learned friend Lord Millett whose speech I have the opportunity of reading in draft, I agree with the orders proposed. I will only add the further observation that the complications in the present case, as in some earlier cases, have arisen from treating factual decisions as if they involved the formulation of
h propositions of law. Consistency of approach is required from case to case. But that should not lead to the elaboration of a simple factual description with a supposed legal overlay preventing the language of the statute from being given effect to in each individual case in accordance with its ordinary meaning.

j **LORD MILLETT.**
[21] My Lords, this case calls upon your Lordships' House to consider, not for the first time, the familiar expression 'part of a house let as a separate dwelling'. This formula was the cornerstone of the Rent Acts and as such the daily fare of generations of county court and appellate judges for much of the last century. Yet this is the first time that that your Lordships have been called upon to decide the meaning of the word 'dwelling' which forms part of the statutory formula.

The question for decision is whether a part of a house can constitute a dwelling
if cooking facilities are not available or cooking is prohibited by the terms of the *a*
letting.

[22] In *Westminster City Council v Clarke* [1992] 1 All ER 695 at 700–701, [1992]
2 AC 288 at 298–299, Lord Templeman observed:

> 'Under the Rent Acts, in order to create a letting of part of a house as a *b*
> separate dwelling there must be an agreement by which the occupier has
> exclusive possession of essential living rooms of a separate dwelling house.
> Essential living rooms provide the necessary facilities for living, sleeping and
> cooking. Thus a bed-sitting room with cooking facilities may be a separate
> dwelling house even though bathroom and lavatory facilities might be
> elsewhere and shared with other people: see *Neale v Del Soto* [1945] 1 All ER *c*
> 191, [1945] KB 144, *Cole v Harris* [1945] 2 All ER 146, [1945] KB 474 and
> *Goodrich v Paisner* [1956] 2 All ER 176 at 179–180, [1957] AC 65 at 79.'

Following the guidance seemingly offered by this passage, the Court of Appeal in
the present case ([2000] 1 EGLR 156, Peter Gibson LJ and Moore-Bick J, Mance LJ *d*
dissenting) felt constrained to hold that the presence of cooking facilities was an
essential characteristic of a dwelling. The question for your Lordships is whether
the absence of such facilities prevents a person's home from being a 'dwelling'
within the meaning of the statutory formula and so precludes the occupier from
enjoying security of tenure.

e

The facts

[23] The respondents are the owners of the Viscount Hotel, 16 Prince of Wales
Terrace, Kensington, London W8 5PQ. The hotel has 58 rooms, 15 of which are
occupied by long-term residents. Mr Collins is one of them. He took up occupation
of room 510 in January 1985. The standard of accommodation was very modest. *f*
The room contained a bed and had a separate lavatory and a shower and wash
basin. Breakfast was available in the restaurant and was included in the rent.

[24] Mr Collins has changed rooms three times, first to room 501, paying the
same rent, and later to room 403, which he was still occupying when the Court
of Appeal gave judgment. He has since moved again. Breakfast ceased to be *g*
provided when the restaurant closed in 1988.

[25] Room 403 measures some 72 sq ft. It has a single bed, some furniture, a
shower and a basin. Except for an increase in the amount of the weekly rent the
terms of Mr Collins' occupation remained the same.

[26] No cooking facilities were provided in any of the rooms which Mr Collins *h*
occupied, although each of them contained at least one power point. Mr Collins
brought in some furniture of his own and electrical equipment to enable him to
prepare simple meals; a pizza warmer, a toasted sandwich maker, a warming plate,
a kettle, and what he described as 'an underlight'. He was not prohibited by the
terms of his occupation from bringing such equipment into his room. He took *j*
ready-cooked take-away meals into his room and ate them there.

[27] In 1993 the hotel published rules which on safety grounds prohibited
cooking in rooms otherwise than by the use of microwaves and kettles. Residents
were required to accept the rules by signing them, but Mr Collins never did so.
He maintained that the terms of his occupation never changed throughout the
period of his stay in the hotel.

The proceedings

a

[**28**] On 28 April 1998 the respondents served a notice terminating what they contended was Mr Collins' licence to occupy room 403. They brought proceedings for possession in the West London County Court. Judge Cotran dismissed the respondents' claim for possession and granted Mr Collins a declaration that he held the room on an assured tenancy within the meaning of s 1(1) of the Housing

b Act 1988, which employs the customary formula. It was not disputed that the room was part of a house. The respondents denied that it was let or, if it was, that it constituted a dwelling; though if it did it was a separate dwelling, since Mr Collins did not share accommodation or facilities with anyone else. The judge held that it was let as a separate dwelling and that Mr Collins' meagre

c culinary equipment satisfied any requirement that a dwelling should possess cooking facilities.

[**29**] The Court of Appeal considered that the judge had made inadequate findings in relation to the question whether Mr Collins' occupation was under a licence or a tenancy, and would if necessary have remitted the case to the county court for retrial of that issue. In the event they did not do so because, in the view

d of the majority, the absence of cooking facilities precluded a finding that room 403 was a dwelling. The room had been let furnished but without cooking facilities, and (it was said) a room did not have the necessary facilities for cooking merely because it had a power point. The position might be different if the room had been let unfurnished or it had been contemplated that the occupier would bring

e in his own cooking equipment. Mance LJ dissented. He held that the availability of cooking facilities was not an essential characteristic of a dwelling, and considered that it was artificial to draw a distinction between furnished and unfurnished lettings. On the footing that, contrary to his view, the presence of cooking facilities was essential, he would have remitted the case for retrial of the question

f whether the room constituted a dwelling, and in particular whether the terms on which Mr Collins occupied the room contemplated the use by him of his own cooking facilities.

The ordinary meaning of 'dwelling'

[**30**] The words 'dwell' and 'dwelling' are not terms of art with a specialised

g legal meaning. They are ordinary English words, even if they are perhaps no longer in common use. They mean the same as 'inhabit' and 'habitation' or more precisely 'abide' and 'abode', and refer to the place where one lives and makes one's home. They suggest a greater degree of settled occupation than 'reside' and 'residence', connoting the place where the occupier habitually sleeps and usually

h eats, but the idea that he must also cook his meals there is found only in the law reports. It finds no support in English literature. According to the Book of Common Prayer, 'the fir trees are a dwelling for the stork' (Psalm 104, v 17); while W S Gilbert condemned the billiard sharp 'to dwell in a dungeon cell' (where it will be remembered he plays with a twisted cue on a cloth untrue with elliptical

j billiard balls) (see The Mikado, Act II). It is hardly necessary to observe that Victorian prison cells did not possess cooking facilities. Of course, the word 'dwell' may owe its presence to the exigencies of the rhyme, but it does not strike the listener as incongruous. If faintly humorous, it is because the occupation of a prison cell is involuntary, not because of the absence of cooking facilities. As I shall show hereafter, Gilbert, who had qualified at the Bar, had got his law right. An earlier and greater poet wrote of Lucifer being hurled 'to bottomless perdition, there to dwell in adamantine chains and penal fire' (see Milton *Paradise Lost*, I.47).

 [31] In both ordinary and literary usage, residential accommodation is 'a dwelling' if it is the occupier's home (or one of his homes). It is the place where he lives and to which he returns and which forms the centre of his existence. Just what use he makes of it when living there, however, depends on his mode of life. No doubt he will sleep there and usually eat there; he will often prepare at least some of his meals there. But his home is not the less his home because he does not cook there but prefers to eat out or bring in ready-cooked meals. It has never been a legislative requirement that cooking facilities must be available for a premises to qualify as a dwelling. Nor is it at all evident what policy considerations dictate that a tenant who prepares his meals at home should enjoy security of tenure while a tenant who brings in all his meals ready-cooked should not. How, then, have the courts reached the conclusion that, as a matter of law, the presence of cooking facilities is an indispensable characteristic of 'a dwelling'?

The Parliamentary franchise

 [32] The first of the Rent Acts was the Increase of Rent and Mortgage Interest (War Restrictions) Act 1915. This applied to 'a house or a part of a house let as a separate dwelling' (see s 2(2)); and the formula was repeated in succeeding Rent Acts and has been carried over into the more recent Housing Acts. But its genesis was older, being derived from the formula which was employed in relation to the Parliamentary franchise.

 [33] The Reform Bill of 1832 (the Representation of the People Act 1832) extended the franchise to males over the age of 21 who satisfied a property qualification by occupying a house or other building in the constituency of a specified minimum annual value. The courts held that four elements must be present: tenement, value, occupation and estate. A difficulty was caused by the requirement that the tenement be 'a house or other building'. It was not doubted that a single room could constitute a separate house if there was a sufficient degree of structural separation from the rest of the building of which it formed part. The Representation of the People Act 1867 introduced the word 'dwelling house', but refrained from defining it except to provide (by s 61) that it should include 'any part of a house occupied as a separate dwelling, and separately rated to the relief of the poor'.

 [34] The meaning of this expression was explored in the great case of *Thompson v Ward, Ellis v Burch* (1871) LR 6 CP 327, in which a four-man court was divided on every issue and equally divided on the outcome. The court held (by a majority of three to one) that s 61 of the 1867 Act removed the requirement of structural separation by directing attention to the nature of the occupation rather than its subject matter. In the course of his judgment Bovill CJ (who was in the majority on this point) said (at 358):

  'It is quite clear that *part* of a house, even a single room, may properly and legally be considered and described as *a house* or *dwelling-house*. For instance, Lord Coke, in treating of burglary, in 3 Inst. 64–65, says: "A chamber or room, be it upper or lower, wherein any person doth inhabit or dwell, is domus mansionalis in law;" which Parke, B., explains, in *Monks* v. *Dykes* ((1839) 4 M & W 567, 150 ER 1546), to refer "to a chamber under certain circumstances, viz. when a house is divided into several chambers, with

a   separate outer doors." In that case Lord Abinger also makes the remark that
     "a room within a house may be a dwelling-house or it may not."'

In a passage of some significance for present purposes Bovill CJ proceeded (at 359)
to give examples of rooms which could properly be considered to be dwelling
houses:

b
     'The following may also be mentioned as familiar instances of parts of
     houses being considered houses, viz. chambers in the Albany, chambers in
     the Inns of Court, rooms in the colleges at the universities, shops in the
     Burlington Arcade, flats in Victoria Street, apartments in Hampton Court
     Palace.'
c
Whatever may have been the position in the case of the other examples given,
the inclusion of rooms in colleges at the universities is illuminating. Unmarried
fellows who lived in college in the nineteenth century did not prepare their own
meals or cook in their rooms. Their rooms not only lacked cooking facilities but
d   were without running water, and dons in residence, like the undergraduates, ate
in hall or had their meals brought to them from the college kitchens. At the most
they may have made tea in their rooms or toasted muffins over an open fire, but
the opportunity to engage in such minor activities can hardly be the distinctive
characteristic of a dwelling.

e   [35] There were limits, of course. Attempts to claim the franchise by persons
who were in gaol failed on the ground that a prison cell was not a dwelling. This
was not because it lacked cooking facilities, but because the residence was
compulsory and temporary and 'without any intention on the [occupier's] part of
remaining; but, on the contrary, with an intention ... of leaving it when she
could': *Dunston v Paterson* (1858) 5 CB (NS) 267 at 278, 141 ER 106 at 111 per
f   Willes J. In *Powell v Guest* (1864) 18 CB (NS) 72 at 80, 144 ER 367 at 370 Erle CJ
expressly approved a statement in a contemporary textbook which stated that the
occupant must have 'at the least a sleeping apartment'. He did not suggest that
this was insufficient.

     [36] The difficult case of *Stribling v Halse* (1885) 16 QBD 246 was a foretaste of
g   what was to come. A shop assistant had exclusive occupation of a furnished
bedroom in a dwelling house belonging to his employers. The house contained
other bedrooms and a dining room in which the residents took their meals in
common which were provided by their employers. It was doubted whether a
person could be said to occupy a bedroom as his dwelling when he dwelt partly
h   in the bedroom and partly in another room. In the mistaken belief that such
doubts had been removed by a decision of the Court of Appeal, the Divisional
Court held that the bedrooms were separately occupied as dwelling houses for
the purpose of the franchise. The decision was later doubted (see *Barnett v
Hickmott* [1895] 1 QB 691) but only because of the existence of the communal
j   dining room. No doubt was cast on the decision in so far as it involved a finding
that a bedroom which lacked cooking facilities was a dwelling. In *Barnett v
Hickmott* a policeman failed to obtain the franchise by virtue of his occupation of
a lock-up cubicle in a dormitory, but only because the cubicle was insufficiently
partitioned from the rest of the dormitory and the ventilation, atmosphere and
lighting were common to all the cubicles. He was not denied the vote because
he could neither cook nor eat in his cubicle.

The Rent Acts

[37] The Rent Acts adopted a similar formula but varied it slightly from 'occupied as a separate dwelling' to 'let as a separate dwelling', but nothing seems to have turned on this. The premises to which the Acts applied were necessarily let unfurnished or only sparsely furnished, since they did not apply where a substantial charge was made for the use of furniture. It was established very early that it was the state of things at the date when the proceedings were brought that mattered: *Prout v Hunter* [1924] 2 KB 736, [1924] All ER Rep 53 (a point which the majority judgments in the Court of Appeal in the present case appear to have overlooked) and the use to which the tenant put the premises once he had furnished them was taken to be indicative of their character and the purpose for which they were let. The Housing Acts have extended security of tenure (and the application of the statutory formula) to furnished lettings, but the question still has to be determined as at the date when proceedings are brought, by which time the premises will almost invariably have been furnished whether or not they were originally so let. Where the tenant has not installed cooking facilities of his own, no sensible distinction can be drawn between premises which were originally let unfurnished and premises which were let furnished but without such facilities.

[38] The object of the Rent Acts was to protect people from being evicted from their homes. Their legislative purpose was, therefore, very different from that of the Representation of the People Acts, and it could be dangerous to rely on the nineteenth century cases particularly in relation to the word 'separate'; but there is no reason to be chary of doing so in relation to the word 'dwelling'. Security of tenure, like the property qualification for the franchise, was given in respect of premises which constituted a person's home.

[39] Over the course of the twentieth century much judicial labour was expended on the statutory requirements that the premises must be 'let' (so that they must be occupied under a tenancy and not a mere licence) and that they must be let as a 'separate' dwelling (that is to say not shared with others). Shared accommodation or facilities presented a special problem, and it is convenient to deal first with the cases where this element was absent.

'Dwelling'

[40] There is only a handful of reported cases in which a single room has failed to qualify as a 'dwelling' for the purposes of the Rent Acts, and in none of them was this because it lacked cooking facilities. In *Wright v Howell* (1947) 92 SJ 26 the room had neither cooking facilities nor water supply at the date of the letting, though the tenant afterwards installed an electric cooker. After the tenant's wife had a baby, the family slept upstairs in a flat belonging to her parents. Scott LJ said that 'the word "dwelling"', on its true construction, included all the major activities of life, particularly sleeping, cooking and feeding' and that as one of those activities, sleeping, was not being carried on there, the room was not a dwelling and the tenancy was not protected. Given that the tenant did not sleep on the premises, the decision is unremarkable; it is not an authority for the proposition that the tenant must also be able to cook there, for at the date when the proceedings were brought he did. The case is simply one where at the relevant time the tenant did not dwell in his own flat, but partly there and partly in his parents-in-law's flat, so that his flat was not a dwelling but only part of a dwelling (see *McCarthy v Preston* [1951] NZLR 1091 at 1092–1093). This is how the case was explained by Lord Greene MR in *Curl v Angelo* [1948] 2 All ER 189 at 192,

a and it is in conformity with Lord Reid's explanation of the cases on shared accommodation in *Baker v Turner* [1950] 1 All ER 834 at 854, [1950] AC 401 at 437:

> 'If a tenant has to share with another person a living room which is not let to him, it is, in my view, impossible to find anything which is let to him as a separate dwelling. It cannot be the let rooms plus the right to use the other room, because that other room is not let to him at all—he is only a licensee
b there. And it cannot be the let rooms alone, because his having to share another room *shows that the let rooms are only a part of his dwelling place.*' (My emphasis.)

[41] In *Curl v Angelo* [1948] 2 All ER 189 two rooms were let to the proprietor of an adjoining hotel as additional accommodation for the hotel. They were used
c mainly for guests but occasionally for the tenant's family or staff. The tenant's claim for protection was rejected on the ground that the premises were not a dwelling. They were not 'the home of anybody; they were a mere annexe or overflow of the hotel'. But Lord Greene MR made it clear that a dwelling could consist of a single room. He said (at 190–191):

d > 'It must not be thought for a moment that I am throwing any doubt on the proposition that where there is a letting to a man of one room which is the only place where he moves and has his being, that circumstance will prevent the room being a "dwelling" within the meaning of the Act, but here one has the activities connected with the dwelling of all these people divided between two tenements. Their main activities of living are conducted in the
e > hotel. They go out to sleep in these rooms—sometimes the guests, sometimes the servants, and so on. Where is the "dwelling"? It seems to me clear that this annexe or accretion to the accommodation of the hotel cannot be regarded as a "dwelling," much less as a "separate dwelling."'

f Lord Greene MR explained *Wright v Howell* as another case where the tenant carried on only one of his home activities on the premises which were the subject of the letting while he carried on others in a different tenement altogether.

[42] In *Metropolitan Properties Co (FCG) Ltd v Barder* [1968] 1 All ER 536, [1968] 1 WLR 286 a protected tenant of a flat under a 12-year lease took a quarterly tenancy of a small single room on the opposite side of the corridor for use by an
g au pair. It was furnished as a bedroom with washbasin. It was held that 'this tiny room' was not let as 'a dwelling-house'. The basis of the decision is not entirely clear, but I have no doubt that it was correct. Even if the room could properly be regarded as the au pair's dwelling, she was not the tenant; and although the tenant was in occupation of the room by his servant it was not his dwelling but
h only part of his dwelling. Had it been possible to regard the arrangement as a mere extension of the original letting the result might have been different (see *Wimbush v Cibulia, Wimbush v Levinski* [1949] 2 All ER 432, [1949] 2 KB 564); but its terms showed it to be an entirely distinct letting. Edmund Davies LJ stressed ([1968] 1 All ER 536 at 542, [1968] 1 WLR 286 at 294) that the decision had no application to a case 'where a single room is let as the occupier's place of
j habitation for all purposes'.

[43] None of these cases turned on the absence of cooking facilities. All were cases where, on the facts, the subject matter of the letting constituted only a part of the tenant's dwelling.

[44] The question whether the landlord qualified as a 'residential landlord' for the purpose of s 12 of the Rent Act 1977 by occupying a bed-sitting room without cooking facilities arose in *Palmer v McNamara* [1991] 1 EGLR 121. The landlord

had never learned to cook, and either bought food which he did not need to cook
or ready-made take-away meals. It was argued that a room without a cooker
could not be described as a dwelling. This was rejected by the Court of Appeal,
which observed that the room occupied by the landlord contained everything
required to be his dwelling house except a cooker which he did not want. It was
his home and therefore his residence. I have no doubt that the case was rightly
decided. It did not, of course, turn on the statutory formula or the word
'dwelling'; but the decision of the majority of the Court of Appeal in the present
case ([2000] 1 EGLR 156) cannot stand with it. If the room was the landlord's
residence, it was his dwelling. The decision was explained by Moore-Bick J on the
basis that the landlord was in the same position as a tenant of an unfurnished
room who has the right to install a cooker if he wishes to do so: the fact that he
chooses not to do so cannot affect the nature of the premises themselves. But this
will not do. As I have already explained, the question has to be determined at the
date of the proceedings, not at the date of the original letting. At the relevant
time the premises were furnished but lacked a cooker. Either its absence was fatal
to the classification of the premises as a dwelling or it was not.

The sharing case

[45] The supposed requirement that cooking facilities must be available for
premises to qualify as a dwelling derives from cases directed to the question
whether the tenancy constituted a 'separate' dwelling when it included shared
accommodation or facilities. The conclusion which was reached was that a right to
share living accommodation put the tenancy outside the protection of the Acts,
whereas a right to make use of communal facilities such as a WC or bathroom
did not. For this purpose a kitchen was classified as a living room.

[46] The leading case was *Neale v Del Soto* [1945] 1 All ER 191, [1945] KB 144. The
tenant took a tenancy of two rooms together with the use, in common with the
landlord, of the garage, kitchen, bathroom, WC, coal house and conservatory. This
was held not to be a letting of the two rooms as a separate dwelling, but a sharing
of the house.

[47] *Neale v Del Soto* was explained and distinguished in *Cole v Harris* [1945]
2 All ER 146, [1945] KB 474 where the premises consisted of a bedroom, living
room and kitchen on the first floor of a dwelling house together with the use of
a bathroom and WC in common with the landlord and the tenant of the second
floor. The county court judge had understood *Neale v Del Soto* to lay down a rule
of law that—

> 'the sharing of any part of the accommodation included in the tenancy
> contract which is essential to the conception of a dwelling-house, according
> to ideas held at the present day, prevents the letting from being a letting of
> part of a house as a separate dwelling.' (See [1945] 2 All ER 146 at 148, [1945]
> KB 474 at 478–479.)

This test was accepted by Lawrence LJ in the Court of Appeal but was firmly
rejected by the majority, who said that *Neale v Del Soto* laid down no such
principle. They drew the line in a different place, between the sharing of living
accommodation, which took the case outside the Acts, and the use of shared
facilities such as a bathroom and WC, which did not. They agreed that a WC was
an essential part of the accommodation according to current modes of living, but
it was not a living room. Mackinnon LJ set out the test:

a   'It is, I think, difficult to formulate any principle of law which separates
what I have called the contrasted conceptions of (a) a demise of part of a
house as a separate dwelling, and (b) an agreement to share the use and
occupation of a house. But I think MORTON, L.J., provides the best formula
by saying that to create (a) there must be an agreement by which the
occupier has the exclusive use of the essential *living* rooms of a separate
b   dwelling-house. After all, a dwelling-house is that in which a person dwells
or lives, and it seems reasonable that a separate dwelling should be one
containing essential living rooms. A w.c. may be essential in modern days,
but I do not think it is a living room, whereas a kitchen, I think, is.' (See
[1945] 2 All ER 146 at 148, [1945] KB 474 at 479.)

c   This provides no support for the contention that the availability of cooking
facilities is an essential part of the concept of a dwelling house. Both the kitchen
and the WC were essential to ordinary living, but the one formed part of the
living accommodation and the other did not. Mackinnon LJ emphasised the word
'living', not the word 'essential'. Morton LJ did not even use the word 'essential'.
d   He said:

'I think that the true test, where the tenant has the exclusive use of some
rooms and shares certain accommodation with others, is as follows: there is
a letting of part of a house as a separate dwelling, within the meaning of the
relevant Acts if, and only if, the accommodation which is shared with others
e   does not comprise any of the rooms which may fairly be described as "living
rooms" or "dwelling rooms." To my mind a kitchen is fairly described as a
"living room," and thus nobody who shares a kitchen can be said to be tenant
of a part of a house let as a separate dwelling. In many households the
kitchen is the principal living room, where the occupants spend the greater
f   part of the day. Very often it is the warmest part of the house and the family
tend to congregate there for that reason. On the other hand, both the
bathroom and the w.c. are rooms which are only visited on occasions for a
specific purpose, and I think they may fairly be classed with such a room as
a box-room, though no doubt it is not visited so often.' (See [1945] 2 All ER
146 at 152, [1945] KB 474 at 485.)
g
This explains why the kitchen was classified as a living room. It was not because
it afforded the tenant the ability to cook his meals there, but because it was one
of the rooms in which he could fairly be said to live. A kitchenette measuring 7 ft
by 6 ft and containing inter alia a kitchen table was held to be a living room in
h   *Winters v Dance* [1949] LJR 165: but this is because it was treated as being merely
a small kitchen. In *Marsh Ltd v Cooper* [1969] 2 All ER 498, [1969] 1 WLR 803 an
even smaller room, probably no more than an alcove, which contained no
furniture and in which it was impossible to do anything except cook and wash up
(the tenant did not eat there), was held not to be a living room.

j   [48] These decisions lost much of their importance after the passing of s 8 of
the Landlord and Tenant (Rent Control) Act 1949. Henceforth the sharing of
accommodation did not preclude the application of the Rent Acts unless it was
shared with the landlord. The distinction was the key to the legislative policy
which lay behind the requirement that the dwelling be 'separate'. As later cases
explained, the right of a tenant to share his living accommodation was such an
invasion of the landlord's privacy that Parliament cannot be taken to have

intended that the tenant should have security of tenure. This was not so in the
case of a right to share the use of a bathroom or WC.

[49] Not every right to make use of the facilities of the kitchen was sufficient
to take the case out of the Rent Acts. In *Hayward v Marshall, Winchester v Sharpe*
[1952] 1 All ER 663, [1952] 2 QB 89 the tenant took a letting of three unfurnished
rooms together with a right to draw water in the kitchen and once a week to use
the gas stove in the kitchen to boil washing. These limited rights did not amount
to a right to use the kitchen as part of the living accommodation provided by the
tenancy, and the tenancy was held to be protected. Unfortunately in the course
of their judgments both Jenkins LJ and Evershed MR repeated the expression
'essential living accommodation' (without emphasising the word 'living'), and
this became something of a mantra in later cases. Evershed MR said:

> 'The distinction rests rather on the view that the ordinary uses and
> purposes of a kitchen are essential manifestations of living or residence, so
> that if a tenant of rooms has to rely on some licence for the exercise of those
> essential manifestations, he is not, as I have said, the tenant of a separate
> dwelling.' (See [1952] 1 All ER 663 at 669, [1952] 2 QB 89 at 99.)

This comes perilously close to reviving the test which was rejected in *Cole v Harris*.
Taken out of context and divorced from the reasoning in *Cole v Harris*, the use of
the word 'essential' is potentially misleading. The cases did not decide that a
kitchen is an essential part of a dwelling, so that premises which lack cooking
facilities are not a dwelling. What they decided was that the essential feature of
a dwelling is that it contains living accommodation, and that every room which
forms part of the tenant's living accommodation, including the kitchen if there is
one, forms part of his dwelling. It is fallacious to reason that, because a kitchen is
a living room and therefore part of any dwelling which possesses one, premises
which do not possess a kitchen are not a dwelling. Substitute the word 'sitting-
room' for 'kitchen' and the fallacy is exposed.

[50] I think that the word 'essential' is best omitted in this context. In
summarising the result of the cases in *Baker v Turner* [1950] 1 All ER 834, [1950] AC
401, none of the members of your Lordships' House found it necessary to use it to
qualify the words 'living rooms' or 'living accommodation'. Lord Porter ([1950]
1 All ER 834 at 839, [1950] AC 401 at 414) summarised the result of the decisions:

> '(i) A portion of a house which is let by a landlord to a tenant, even if in
> itself separate, ceases to be a separate dwelling or to be protected by the Acts
> if the terms of the letting contain a provision that the tenant shall have the
> right of using a living room belonging to the landlord: *Neale v. Del Soto*
> ([1945] 1 All ER 191, [1945] KB 144). (ii) To take away the protection of the
> Acts, the room over which rights are given must be a living room: a
> bathroom, lavatory or cupboard will not avail, but for this purpose a kitchen
> is a living room: see *Cole v. Harris* ([1945] 2 All ER 146, [1945] KB 474).'

Your Lordships were more forthright in *Goodrich v Paisner* [1956] 2 All ER 176,
[1957] AC 65. Lord Morton of Henryton considered the use of the word
'essential' in the present context to be 'not ... particularly appropriate'; while
Lord Radcliffe ([1956] 2 All ER 176 at 182, 187, [1957] AC 65 at 84, 91) regarded it
as a gloss on the statute which either begged the question or confused the issue.
Lord Radcliffe could see nothing more satisfying in the definition which had been
offered in the course of argument: 'a living room is a room wherein you cook,
eat, sleep and put your feet on the fender'. As he observed: 'Why ever should

a courts of law tie themselves down in this way?' He would have been astonished
at the idea that a room or set of rooms could not constitute a dwelling unless they
possessed facilities for cooking.

[51] The House confirmed the test laid down by the majority of the Court of
Appeal in *Cole v Harris* in the face of an attempt to revive the test which had been
adopted by the county court judge and Lawrence LJ in that case. It was argued
b that the question should be: 'Do the rooms so let in fact contain the essentials of
a separate dwelling, or is what is let a separate dwelling only if you include with
it the other rights or conveniences which the tenancy agreement confers?' This
was once again firmly rejected (see [1956] 2 All ER 176 at 183, [1957] AC 65 at 85
per Lord Morton (dissenting but not on this point)).

[52] In *Hayward v Marshall* counsel had suggested that there might be a distinction
c between a concurrent sharing and a consecutive sharing, only the former being
sufficient to take the tenancy out of the protection of the Rent Acts. This idea was
eventually taken up in *Goodrich v Paisner*, where the tenant's right to have the
occasional use of a bedroom in common with the landlord was held not to
exclude the application of the Rent Acts. It was assumed that the tenancy agreement
d did not contemplate simultaneous user; there would have had to be some further
arrangement by which there would be separate user at successive times. On this
footing, there was not such a sharing as would involve the invasion by the one
party of the privacy of the other sufficient to exclude the application of the Rent
Acts.

[53] So I can come to *Westminster City Council v Clarke* [1992] 1 All ER 695,
e [1992] 2 AC 288. The case concerned a hostel with 31 rooms, each with a bed and
limited cooking facilities. Accommodation was made available to vulnerable persons
by the local authority in the discharge of its social responsibilities. Mr Clarke
occupied one of the rooms as his only home. The question for decision was
whether he had exclusive possession of the room. If he did, he was a secure
f tenant. On the facts the House held that none of the occupants had exclusive
possession of his room. The restrictions placed on their use of the rooms, the
facts that they were not entitled to any particular room and might be required to
share a room, and above all the fact that the grant of exclusive possession would
be inconsistent with the social purpose for which the accommodation was
provided, all pointed to this conclusion.
g
[54] Lord Templeman gave the only reasoned speech. It is clear that the
passage which I have cited and on which the majority of the Court of Appeal
relied in the present case is not part of his reasoning. It is certainly not authority
for the proposition that a room is not a dwelling in the absence of cooking
facilities. In the first place, even a clear statement to that effect would have been
h obiter, since the room in question possessed them. In the second place, this was
not the issue: the question was whether Mr Clarke had exclusive possession of his
room, not whether it was a dwelling. In the third place, the authorities cited
(*Neale v Del Soto, Cole v Harris* and *Goodrich v Paisner*) lay down no such principle.
All are cases of shared accommodation which do not depend on the meaning of
j the word 'dwelling'; and the two last named are entirely inconsistent with the
proposition, which would seek to revive the test expressly rejected in each of
them.

[55] In *Parkins v Westminster City Council* [1998] 1 EGLR 22 the tenant occupied
a bedroom and shared the use of a common room, kitchen, bathroom and separate
WC. Chadwick LJ described the tenant as being faced with an unanswerable
dilemma. The premises as a whole were not let as a separate dwelling, since while

they provided cooking facilities the tenant did not have exclusive possession of *a*
them; nor was the bedroom alone let as a separate dwelling, since while he did
have exclusive possession of the room, it did not provide cooking facilities.
Whether the correct view was that the tenant was entitled to occupy the whole
of the premises or only the bedroom, there was no letting of a separate dwelling.

[56] I have no doubt that the decision was correct, but the distinction which
Chadwick LJ drew is an analytical not a factual one. The facts were capable of *b*
only one interpretation; the tenant was entitled to exclusive possession of the
bedroom and the shared use of two living rooms and other facilities. The
so-called dilemma is real enough, but is not that depicted by Chadwick LJ. It was
described by Lord Reid in *Baker v Turner* and does not depend on the presence or
absence of cooking facilities. The premises as a whole were not a separate
dwelling because the tenant did not have exclusive possession of them, and the *c*
bedroom alone was not the tenant's dwelling but only part of it. The absence of
cooking facilities in part of the house of which the tenant had exclusive possession
was not material.

[57] My Lords, in *Westminster City Council v Clarke* Lord Templeman was merely
summarising the result of the earlier cases. It was natural, but unfortunate, that in *d*
doing so he repeated ([1992] 1 All ER 695 at 701, [1992] 2 AC 288 at 299) the
expression 'essential living rooms', an expression which, as I have already
explained, is misleading when taken out of its original context. In agreeing with
him, the other members of the House cannot have intended to replace the
statutory language by a rigid test which makes the availability of cooking facilities
an essential precondition for security of tenure. This would place a gloss on the *e*
statute which is not justified by the language or purpose of the statute or the
decided cases; and once again revive the heresy, twice previously rejected, that a
room or set of rooms must possess 'all the features essential to the conception of
a dwelling house' in order to attract security of tenure. Moreover such a conclusion
would be productive of great difficulties in future cases. It would be necessary to *f*
consider just what is sufficient to constitute 'cooking facilities'. The Victorian
bedroom possessed an open grate; the modern one has a power point. What more
is required? And why should even this much be necessary to attract security of
tenure? The legislative purpose of the Rent and Housing Acts is to protect people
in the occupation of their homes, not to encourage them to cook their own
meals. *g*

[58] In my opinion the position is relatively straightforward. The first step is
to identify the subject matter of the tenancy agreement. If this is a house or part
of a house of which the tenant has exclusive possession with no element of
sharing, the only question is whether, at the date when the proceedings were
brought, it was the tenant's home. If so, it was his dwelling. (He must also *h*
occupy it as his only or principal home, but that is a separate requirement.) If the
tenancy agreement grants, in addition, the right to the shared use of other rooms,
the question is whether the room or rooms of which he has exclusive possession
are his dwelling place or only part of it. This depends on the nature and extent of
the right and the character of the other rooms. The right to occupy a living room *j*
in common with and at the same time as the landlord is such an invasion of his
privacy that Parliament cannot be taken to have intended that the tenant should
enjoy security of tenure. For this purpose a kitchen is a living room, at least if it
is possible to occupy it and not merely cook and wash up in it; so that a right to
occupy a kitchen (as distinct from a right to make some limited use of its facilities)
in common with the landlord will take the tenancy out of the Acts. The presence

a or absence of cooking facilities in the part of the premises of which the tenant has exclusive occupation is not relevant.

Conclusion

[59] In my opinion the appeal succeeds.

b [60] After leave was granted to bring the present appeal, and with the agreement of the respondents, Mr Collins vacated room 403 and moved to another room in their hotel. Accordingly there is no longer any lis between the parties and no remaining issue to be remitted to the county court for decision. On 25 September 2000 the respondents notified the judicial office that they did not intend to take any part in Mr Collins' appeal to the House, and their *c* Lordships are grateful to the amicus curiae for his careful and helpful argument.

[61] I would allow the appeal and set aside the orders of the Court of Appeal. I would direct that the respondents pay Mr Collins' costs in the Court of Appeal and of his appeal to this House up to and including 25 September 2000, and that there be no order for the costs of and incidental to the hearing in the West London County Court.

Appeal allowed.

Celia Fox   Barrister.

Sun Life Assurance plc v Thales
Tracs Ltd and another

a

[2001] EWCA Civ 704

COURT OF APPEAL, CIVIL DIVISION

b

WALLER, HALE AND DYSON LJJ

9, 10 MAY 2001

Landlord and Tenant – Business premises – Application for new tenancy – Request by tenant for new tenancy – Whether tenant of business premises required to have genuine intention to take up new tenancy when making request for such a tenancy – Landlord and Tenant Act 1954, ss 26(3), 37.

c

The defendants, two companies in the same group, were the tenants of business premises under two leases which were due to expire in December 1998. In the summer of 1996 the claimant landlord indicated to the tenants' agents that it *d* would require vacant possession of the premises at the end of the leases, and in January 1997 the landlord told the tenants that it would resist on redevelopment grounds any renewal of the tenancies. In November 1997 the tenants exchanged contracts for the purchase of an adjoining site which would enable them to replace the premises that they would have to give up. However, in March 1998 *e* the tenants served requests for new tenancies under s 26[a] of the Landlord and Tenant Act 1954. Section 26(3) provided that a tenant's 'request' for a new tenancy would not have effect unless, inter alia, it set out the tenant's 'proposals' as to the property to be comprised in the tenancy, the rent and the other terms. Although the landlord served counter-notices opposing the renewal of the leases, it subsequently offered to renew them and withdrew its ground of opposition. *f* The tenants rejected the offer, did not apply to the court for the grant of new tenancies and vacated the premises on the expiry of the leases. In subsequent proceedings brought by the landlord for breach of repairing covenants, the tenants counterclaimed for statutory compensation under s 37[b] of the 1954 Act. That counterclaim was sustainable only if the tenants had made valid requests for new tenancies under s 26. At trial, the judge held that 'proposals' in s 26(3) meant *g* 'genuine proposals', that accordingly a tenant making a request for a new tenancy under s 26 was required to have a genuine intention to take up such a tenancy when making the request, that the tenants had no such intention when serving their requests, that the proposals contained in the requests were therefore not genuine proposals and that accordingly the requests were invalid. In reaching *h* that conclusion, the judge reasoned that it was inherently unlikely that Parliament had intended that a tenant should be entitled to compensation by misrepresenting his intention as regards his desire for a new tenancy. The tenants appealed.

j

Held – A tenant of business premises was not required to have a genuine intention to take up a new tenancy when making a request for such a tenancy under s 26 of the 1954 Act. Such a conclusion gave effect to the ordinary meaning of the words

---

a   Section 26, so far as material, is set out at [10], below
b   Section 37, so far as material, is set out at [13], below

a 'request' and 'proposals' in s 26. A request was an act of asking for something and
   a proposal was something that had been put forward for consideration. As a
   matter of ordinary language, the fact that a request or a proposal had been put
   forward said nothing about the state of mind of the person who had made the
   request or proposal. The meaning of a request and proposal was judged objectively,
   and the state of mind of the person making them was irrelevant to their meaning.
b The words 'request' and 'proposals' in s 26 were to be given an unqualified
   objective meaning. That accorded with their ordinary meaning and was consistent
   with the law of contractual offers. Moreover, neither s 26 nor s 37 made any
   mention of the tenant's intentions, and where the Act required an intention, it
   expressly said so. Furthermore, the correct construction produced no results
   which it could safely be concluded could not have been intended by Parliament.
c The prospect of an inquiry into the tenant's state of mind was not contemplated
   by Parliament, and the inclusion of proposals in a s 26 request was a statutory
   formality which did not require the tenant to have any particular intention. It
   followed that evidence of a tenant's state of mind when he served a request was
   inadmissible. Accordingly, the appeal would be allowed (see [17], [18], [31], [41],
d [43]–[45], below).

   Sidney Bolsom Investment Trust Ltd v E Karmios & Co (London) Ltd [1956] 1 All ER
   536 applied.

   Cadogan v Morris [1999] 1 EGLR 59 distinguished.

   Notes
e
   For a tenant's request for a new tenancy, see 27(1) *Halsbury's Laws* (4th edn
   reissue) para 572.
   For the Landlord and Tenant Act 1954, ss 26, 37, see 23 *Halsbury's Statutes* (4th
   edn) (1997 reissue) 149, 164.

f **Cases referred to in judgments**
   Betty's Cafés Ltd v Phillips Furnishings Stores Ltd [1958] 1 All ER 607, [1959] AC 20,
      [1958] 2 WLR 513, HL.
   Bolsom (Sidney) Investment Trust Ltd v E Karmios & Co (London) Ltd [1956] 1 All ER
      536, [1956] 1 QB 529, [1956] 2 WLR 625, CA.
g *Cadogan v Morris* [1999] 1 EGLR 59, CA.
   Lloyds Bank Ltd v National Westminster Bank Ltd, Lloyds Bank Ltd v City of London Corp
      [1982] 1 EGLR 83; *affd* [1983] 1 All ER 92, [1983] 1 Ch 192, [1982] 3 WLR 1138,
      CA.
   Willingale v Globalgrange Ltd [2000] 2 EGLR 55, CA.
h
   Case also cited or referred to in skeleton arguments
   *Grafton Street (14), London W1, Re, De Havilland (Antiques) Ltd v Centrovincial Estates
   (Mayfair) Ltd* [1971] 2 All ER 1, [1971] Ch 935.

j **Appeal**
   By notice of appeal dated 24 January 2000, Thales Tracs Ltd and Thales Properties Ltd
   (Thales), the former tenants of commercial premises at 88 Bushey Road, Raynes
   Park, London SW20, appealed with permission of Mr Recorder Black QC from
   his decision, sitting in the Technology and Construction Court, on 1 December
   1999 ([2000] 1 EGLR 138) dismissing their counterclaim for compensation under
   s 37 of the Landlord and Tenant Act 1954 in proceedings for breach of repairing

covenants brought by the landlord of the premises, Sun Life Assurance plc (Sun Life). The facts are set out in the judgment of Dyson LJ.

Kim Lewison QC and *Malcolm Sheehan* (instructed by *Jean-Yves Haagen, Head of Legal Services for Thales Corporate Services Ltd*, Fleet) for Thales.
Hazel Williamson QC and *Mark Wonnacott* (instructed by *DLA*) for Sun Life.

WALLER LJ.

[1] I will ask Dyson LJ to deliver the first judgment.

DYSON LJ.

[2] This is an appeal by the defendants from the order of Mr Recorder Black QC, sitting as a deputy judge of the Technology and Construction Court ([2000] 1 EGLR 138). The single issued raised by the appeal is whether a tenant of business premises who makes a request for a new tenancy under s 26 of the Landlord and Tenant Act 1954 must have a genuine intention to take up a new tenancy at the time when he makes the request. The judge held that he must. On behalf of the defendants, Mr Lewison QC submits that he need not. The significance of the issue is that if the appeal succeeds the defendants will be entitled to compensation under s 37 of the 1954 Act. There is no authority directly on the point.

The facts

[3] The facts as found by the judge were as follows. Both defendants are companies in the Thales group of companies. They were previously known as the Racal group of companies. I shall refer to both defendants as 'Thales'. Thales was the tenant under two leases which were due to expire on 24 December 1998. One lease was held by the first defendant and the other by the second defendant. The claimant, Sun Life Assurance plc (Sun Life), was the landlord under both leases. In the summer of 1996 Sun Life indicated to Thales' agent that they would require vacant possession at the end of the leases. An adjoining site was on the market and both Sun Life and Thales were interested in acquiring it. In January 1997 Sun Life wrote to Thales saying that they would resist any renewal of the tenancies on redevelopment grounds. In September 1997 Thales held an internal meeting at which it was said that, on the basis that Sun Life would not renew the leases, the adjoining site would enable Thales to replace the premises which it would have to give up.

[4] In November 1997 Thales exchanged contracts for the purchase of the adjoining site. Completion was deferred until 1 April 1998. On 9 January 1998 Thales served two requests for a new tenancy under s 26 of the 1954 Act, one in respect of each lease. The validity of these requests was challenged by Sun Life on technical grounds which need not be mentioned here. Thales served further requests on 11 March. Sun Life served counter-notices to each request under s 26(6), stating that they would oppose a renewal of the leases on the grounds that they intended to redevelop. On 23 April 1998 Sun Life offered to renew the leases, but Thales replied that their plans were too far advanced to reconsider occupation of the buildings after December 1998. Nevertheless, the possibility of continued occupation after that date was discussed by Thales at an internal meeting on 18 June, but this option was rejected. By that time, Sun Life had withdrawn their ground of opposition.

a   [5] Thales did not apply to the court for the grant of new tenancies and vacated the buildings on 23 December 1998.

[6] The judge found that in September 1997 Thales had decided to move out if the adjoining site could be secured on acceptable terms and that the site had been secured on acceptable terms before the requests were served on 11 March 1998. He also found that this did not mean that Thales acted in bad faith. He
b accepted that Thales believed that, whether or not they genuinely wanted to renew the leases, they were entitled to compensation because they fulfilled the necessary statutory criteria.

[7] Having found that Thales had no intention of taking up new tenancies when they served their requests, the judge held that the proposals contained in the requests were not genuine proposals and that the requests were therefore
c invalid. I should say at once that there is no challenge by Thales to the finding of the judge that they had no intention of taking up new tenancies when they served their requests.

The statutory provisions
d   [8] Section 24(1) provides:

> 'A tenancy to which this Part of this Act applies shall not come to an end unless terminated in accordance with the provisions of this Part of this Act; and, subject to the provisions of section twenty-nine of this Act, the tenant under such a tenancy may apply to the court for a new tenancy—(a) if the
e   landlord has given notice under [s 25 of this Act] to terminate the tenancy, or (b) if the tenant has made a request for a new tenancy in accordance with section twenty-six of this Act.'

[9] Section 25 provides for the termination of a tenancy by the landlord.
[10] Section 26 provides for the termination of a tenancy by a tenant's request
f for a new tenancy. So far as material, it provides:

> '(3) A tenant's request for a new tenancy shall not have effect unless it is made by notice in the prescribed form given to the landlord and sets out the tenant's proposals as to the property to be comprised in the new tenancy (being either the whole or part of the property comprised in the current tenancy),
g   as to the rent to be payable under the new tenancy and as to the other terms of the new tenancy …
>   (5) Where the tenant makes a request for a new tenancy in accordance with the foregoing provisions of this section, the current tenancy shall, subject to the provisions of subsection (2) of section thirty-six of this Act and the provisions of Part IV of this Act as to the interim continuation of tenancies,
h   terminate immediately before the date specified in the request for the beginning of the new tenancy.
>   (6) Within two months of the making of a tenant's request for a new tenancy the landlord may give notice to the tenant that he will oppose an application to the court for the grant of a new tenancy, and any such notice
j   shall state on which of the grounds mentioned in section thirty of this Act the landlord will oppose the application.'

[11] The grounds of opposition mentioned in s 30(1) include para (f), which is in these terms:

> 'that on the termination of the current tenancy the landlord intends to demolish or reconstruct the premises comprised in the holding or a substantial

part of those premises or to carry out substantial work of construction on the
holding or part thereof and that he could not reasonably do so without *a*
obtaining possession of the holding ...'

[12] Section 29 provides for the grant of a new tenancy by order of the court.
Subsection (3) provides that no application for a new tenancy under s 24(1) shall
be entertained by the court unless it is made not less than two nor more than four
months after the making of the tenant's request for a new tenancy. *b*

[13] Section 37 provides for payment by the landlord to the tenant of
compensation where the court is precluded from granting a new tenancy on any
of the grounds specified in s 30(1)(e), (f) and (g) and no other grounds. It also
arises—

'where no other ground is specified in the landlord's notice under section *c*
25 of this Act or, as the case may be under section 26(6) thereof, than those
specified in the said paragraphs (e), (f) and (g) and either no application under
the said section 24 is made or such an application is withdrawn.'

The quoted words were introduced by amendment by s 11 of the Law of Property
Act 1969 so as to make it unnecessary for the tenant to press a doomed application *d*
for a new tenancy to the point of failure in order to obtain compensation. The
right to compensation now depends simply on whether the landlord has said that
he would oppose the grant of a new tenancy on one or more of the three specified
grounds.

e

The judge's reasoning
[14] The core of the judge's reasoning is to be found where he said:

'It seems inherently unlikely to me that the legislative intention of an Act,
said to enable tenants occupying property for business, professional or certain
other purposes to obtain new tenancies, was to allow compensation to *f*
outgoing tenants by misrepresenting their intentions concerning their desire
for a new tenancy. This would be a licence to any outgoing tenant to obtain
compensation merely on the service of a notice where he knows that the
landlord wishes, for example, to redevelop or occupy the premises himself.
I accept Mr Wonnacott's argument that the scheme of the 1954 Act is closely
analogous to that of the [Leasehold Reform, Housing and Urban Development *g*
Act 1993] and that the Court of Appeal's reasoning in the *Cadogan* case ought
to apply equally to the present. It seems to me that the 1954 Act is designed
to let each party know where he stands, to enable constructive discussion or
application to the court in default. I would therefore construe the reference
to "proposals" in section 26(3) to mean "genuine proposals".' (See [2000] *h*
1 EGLR 138 at 147.)

The reference to *Cadogan* was to *Cadogan v Morris* [1999] 1 EGLR 59, to which
I shall come later in this judgment. In response to the submission by Mr Sheehan
on behalf of Thales that there were commercial difficulties in Sun Life's
construction, the judge said that he thought that it would be a rare case in which *j*
a landlord could say that the tenant did not have a genuine intention when
serving his request. He added ([2000] 1 EGLR 138 at 148):

'It seems to me that it would not be enough to establish a misrepresentation
as to intention to show that a tenant was keeping his options open. It would
only be in comparatively rare cases, such as the present, where a landlord can

a show that the tenant has in fact taken steps to find alternative premises or where there is other proof that the tenant has taken a final decision not to renew before serving the notice, that the landlord would be able to succeed. That is perhaps why the experienced counsel in this case could find no direct authority on the issue, notwithstanding that the Act has been on the statute books for 45 years.'

b
Discussion

[15] It is common ground that, in a s 26 case, the right to compensation under s 37 depends on a s 26 request which is either valid or which the parties are estopped from contending is invalid. The appeal turns on the meaning of 'request' where it appears in s 26 and of 'the tenant's proposals' in s 26(3).

c [16] On behalf of Sun Life, Miss Williamson QC submits that it is an underlying assumption in s 26 that the tenant should be genuinely seeking the prospect of a new tenancy and proposing the terms of such a tenancy. The 1954 Act plainly intends that the tenant should set out genuine proposals as to the tenancy which the landlord is being invited to offer. A s 26 request is a mechanism whereby fixed *d* term business tenants can formalise the terms of the security of tenure granted to them by the 1954 Act after the termination of their contractual terms. It is not intended to be available for the tenant who does not wish to take advantage of such security. A tenant who does not want to have a new tenancy does not need to have recourse to s 26 in order to terminate the statutory continuation of an existing tenancy. He can achieve this objective by serving a notice under s 27. A *e* tenant who has decided not to take a new tenancy cannot request a new tenancy or make proposals in respect of a new tenancy because such a request and proposals would misrepresent his intention. The mental state that is a necessary condition of a valid request is that the tenant should either want a new tenancy on reasonable terms or at least be undecided as to whether he wants such a tenancy.

f [17] For the reasons that follow, I cannot accept these submissions. The words 'request' and 'proposal' are ordinary English words. A request is an act of asking for something. A proposal is something that is put forward for consideration. It may in some circumstances be an offer which, as a matter of law, is capable of being accepted so as to give rise to a binding contract. But it does not have to be. Both 'request' and 'proposal' are what Mr Lewison QC called 'performative *g* utterances'. They describe an act. They *do* something. It is not meaningful to ask whether a request or a proposal say anything about the state of mind of the person who makes the request or puts forward the proposal. The meaning of a request and a proposal is judged objectively. The state of mind of the person who makes the request and the proposal is irrelevant to their meaning. Nor is it *h* meaningful to consider whether they are true. On the other hand, there are different kinds of words that *do* say something about the *state of mind* of the person using them. Thus, for example, if a person says that he believes or intends something, he is undoubtedly saying something about his state of mind. It is meaningful, and may be relevant, to consider the truth of a statement of belief or *j* intention.

[18] I would, therefore, hold, as a matter of ordinary language, that the fact that a request is made or a proposal is put forward says nothing about the state of mind of the person making the request or proposal. A may make a proposal to B which he believes, and possibly even hopes, B will refuse. A may do this solely in order to show himself in a good light in the eyes of C, where he would be deeply unhappy if B were to accept the proposal. He does not wish or intend B to accept

the proposal but, as a matter of ordinary language, it is nevertheless a proposal. Take another example: suppose that A makes a proposal which he believes means X, but in fact it means Y, and, if he had understood that it meant Y, he would not have been willing to make it. Again, as a matter of ordinary language, what A puts forward is a 'proposal', notwithstanding his mistake. This is because whether something is a proposal is to be judged objectively and without regard to the state of mind of the proposer.

[19] This ordinary meaning of the word 'proposal' is reflected in the law. It is trite law that in the contractual context the existence and meaning of an offer has to be determined objectively. The law is not concerned with the subjective intention of the offeror.

[20] What about the context of s 26 of the 1954 Act?

[21] In my view, considerable light is shed by the decision of this court in *Sidney Bolsom Investment Trust Ltd v E Karmios & Co (London) Ltd* [1956] 1 All ER 536, [1956] 1 QB 529. The tenant requested a new tenancy under s 26. Its proposals did not specify a term of years; it did, however, propose a rent and other terms 'upon the terms of the current tenancy'. The term of the current tenancy was seven years. The tenant had intended to propose a new tenancy for a term of 14 years, but made a mistake in drafting the request. The landlord served a counter- notice saying that they would oppose the grant of a new tenancy. The tenant did not apply to the court for a new tenancy, but did not vacate the premises either. The landlord brought proceedings for possession. The tenant claimed that its own request was invalid because it did not state the duration proposed for the new tenancy.

[22] In this court it was held that the request did sufficiently set out the duration of the proposed new tenancy: the request impliedly proposed a duration of seven years. It was then argued on behalf of the tenant that the request was invalid because it was made under a mistake. The judge had admitted evidence of the mistake. It was held on appeal that this evidence was inadmissible. Denning LJ said:

'I do not think that that evidence was admissible. To my mind, this case falls within the general principle that parol evidence cannot be admitted to add to, vary or contradict the terms of a written document. Whatever his inmost state of mind, once a tenant has to all outward appearances made a valid request in the prescribed form setting out his proposals, then he cannot thereafter rely on his own mistake to say that it was a nullity or invalid, no matter how important the mistake was. The validity of the request must be judged by the true interpretation of it, without regard to what happened behind the scenes. It is a formal document with specific legal consequences and it must be treated as such. If the proposals had ripened into a contract, then the mistake might in some circumstances be a ground for setting the contract aside in equity, but it does not render the request invalid.' (See [1956] 1 All ER 536 at 538–539, [1956] 1 QB 529 at 539.)

[23] The judgment of Morris LJ is to similar effect. He said:

'The point has to be determined by reference to the document itself, looked at having regard to the provisions of the Act. When a request is made, then it is the document, in the form in which it was received by the recipient, which must to be looked at.' (See [1956] 1 All ER 536 at 540, [1956] 1 QB 529 at 542.)

a   [24] He said ([1956] 1 All ER 536 at 541, [1956] 1 QB 529 at 543): 'The request was, therefore, a good request for a new tenancy made in accordance with s. 26.'

[25] Harman J said ([1956] 1 All ER 536 at 542, [1956] 1 QB 529 at 545): 'What a man has written he has written, and, if what he has written be a request for a term of seven years, it does not become less his request because he did it by mistake.'

b   [26] The judge in the present case sought to distinguish the *Sidney Bolsom* case on two grounds, which Miss Williamson seeks to support. First, he said that it was a case of a tenant attacking the validity of his own notice that was formally valid, and there was no issue that the tenant wanted to renew. Miss Williamson says that it is a material distinction that in the *Sidney Bolsom* case the tenant wanted a new tenancy but was arguing for invalidity on the grounds of a mistake c   as to the detail of the proposals, whereas in the present case the tenant did not want a new tenancy at all. Secondly, he said that Denning LJ had already found that the notice complied with the 1954 Act. I agree with Mr Lewison that this authority cannot be distinguished in either respect. First, the observations of the court were quite general and did not depend on the fact that it was the tenant d   who was attacking the validity of its own notice or that there was no issue that the tenant wanted to renew. The essential part of the reasoning was that, as a matter of form, the request complied with the requirements of s 26 and was therefore valid. Validity involved simply looking at the form: evidence as to the state of mind of the tenant was inadmissible. Secondly, it is not right to say that the part of the judgment of Denning LJ which I cited was obiter. He was dealing e   explicitly with the question whether the mistake rendered the request invalid. The key words are: 'Whatever his inmost state of mind, once a tenant has *to all outward appearances* made a valid request' (see [1956] 1 All ER 536 at 539, [1956] 1 QB 529 at 539; my emphasis).

[27] I agree with Mr Lewison that, if the judge's approach in the present case f   were correct, then the decision in the *Sidney Bolsom* case would have gone the other way because, on the facts found by the trial judge, the s 26 request in that case did not contain the tenant's genuine proposals.

[28] Mr Lewison also relies on a passage in the judgment of Slade J in *Lloyds Bank Ltd v National Westminster Bank Ltd, Lloyds Bank Ltd v City of London Corp* [1982] g   1 EGLR 83. In that case the tenant sought leave to discontinue an application for a new tenancy under the 1954 Act on the grounds that it no longer wanted the tenancy in question. The landlord had opposed the grant of a new tenancy under s 30(1)(f) but then withdrew its opposition. It argued that leave to discontinue should only be granted on terms that the tenant gave an undertaking not to claim compensation under s 37. The judge refused to require such an undertaking as a h   condition of granting leave to discontinue. An appeal to this court was dismissed ([1983] 1 All ER 92, [1983] 1 Ch 192). Slade J said ([1982] 1 EGLR 83 at 86):

j   'I cannot, however, accept the wider submission that the legislature contemplated that the tenant should never get compensation if his motives for failing to press his possible rights to a new tenancy were merely that he did not want a new tenancy. Section 37(1), as amended, says nothing whatever about the motives which may prompt a tenant either to omit to apply for a new tenancy or to withdraw his application after it has been made. The motives prompting a tenant to take either of these courses, after he has received a landlord's notice under section 25 or section 26(6), relying on one or more of the grounds specified in paragraphs (e), (f) or (g) of section 30,

may be many and mixed. I cannot impute an intention to the legislature to
withhold compensation from a tenant who complies with all the other *a*
conditions in section 37(1) merely because his motives for omitting to apply
to the court, or for withdrawing an application when made, may be of a
particular nature. The rights to compensation given by the subsection, in
circumstances such as those of the plaintiffs in the present case, to a party
who withdraws his application and then vacates the premises, are in terms *b*
absolute, not qualified by reference to any considerations of motive.'

[29] Miss Williamson seeks to distinguish this case. She submits that it is
authority for the proposition that, once the procedure for terminating a tenancy
has been properly initiated, there should be no investigation of the tenant's motives
in the event of a subsequent failure to apply for a new tenancy or withdrawal of an *c*
application that has been made. But, she argues, it says nothing about the
conditions that are necessary for initiating the procedure in the first place. I agree
that the decision does not deal expressly with the question of what those
conditions are. But if the tenant's motives for failing to apply for a new tenancy
after receiving a landlord's notice under s 25 or s 26(6) are irrelevant to the right *d*
to compensation, it is difficult to see why Parliament should have intended that
his motives in serving a request for a new tenancy in the first place should be
relevant.

[30] Miss Williamson relies on *Betty's Cafés Ltd v Phillips Furnishings Stores Ltd*
[1958] 1 All ER 607, [1959] AC 20 in support of the proposition that notices given *e*
under the 1954 Act must be given honestly and truthfully. The issue in that case
was the validity of a landlord's counter-notice under s 26(6) which relied on
s 30(1)(f). In my judgment, it is not relevant to the issue that arises in the present
case. Section 30(1)(f) refers explicitly to the landlord's intention. A landlord can
only oppose an application for a new tenancy under that provision if he intends
to redevelop the premises. I derive no assistance from the *Betty's Cafés* case. *f*

[31] In my judgment, therefore, on the face of it the words 'request' and
'proposals' in s 26 should be given an unqualified objective meaning. That
accords with the ordinary meaning of the words and is consistent with the law of
contractual offers. It is consistent with the decision in the *Sidney Bolsom* case and
the observations of Slade J in the *Lloyds Bank* case. It is also worth pointing out *g*
that there is no mention of the tenant's intentions or motives in s 26 or s 37.
Where the Act requires an 'intention', it expressly says so (see, for example,
s 30(1)(f) and (g)). It would have been possible for the draftsman to require an
intention to take up a new tenancy as a condition of a valid request and/or as a
condition of the right to compensation under s 37. *h*

[32] The judge drew a distinction between a tenant having formed no intention
at all (which would not render the request invalid) and a tenant having positively
decided not to take a renewal in any circumstances (which would render the
request invalid). The judge was plainly concerned to minimise the implications
of his decision. It does not seem that this distinction was a necessary part of his *j*
reasoning, but in any event I have some difficulty in accepting it. If a person does
not know what his future plans are, how can he be said to intend to take up a new
tenancy? If the 1954 Act requires proposals to be realistic in the sense of being
genuinely intended, then surely the tenant who has not made up his mind as to
whether he wants a new tenancy is as precluded from making a request as is the
tenant who has firmly decided that he does not want one.

a   [33] Before I come to the wider considerations to see whether they cast any doubt on the conclusions that I have reached thus far, I need to refer to *Cadogan v Morris* [1999] 1 EGLR 59. That was a case which concerned the right of a tenant to purchase a long lease under the Leasehold Reform, Housing and Urban Development Act 1993. The tenant served a notice specifying a premium of £100. This was a formal nominal figure. A realistic figure lay between £100,000 and

b   £300,000. The question was whether the insertion of a purely nominal figure invalidated the notice. Section 42(3) of the Act provided that the notice 'must … (c) specify the premium which the tenant proposes to pay in respect of the grant of a new lease'. It will be seen at once that the words 'which the tenant proposes to pay' are very close to the words 'the tenant's proposals'. The Court of Appeal held that the tenant's notice was invalid. In giving the only substantive judgment,

c   Stuart-Smith LJ said (at 61):

'I do not consider it is necessary to read any words into section 42(3)(c). The tenant is required to specify the premium that he proposes to pay. He did not do so; he deliberately specified a figure that he did not propose to pay. I do not think the tenant is required to offer his final figure that he may be

d   prepared to go to, but he should, in my view, offer a realistic figure.'

[34] But as Mr Lewison points out, that case was concerned with a different Act and so was technically not binding. It was at best only an analogy. It was conceded in *Cadogan v Morris* that a notice served under a different part of the 1993 Act (s 13(3)(d)) did require a genuine proposal, and that concession clearly

e   influenced the court to some extent. Further, there were two particular factors which influenced the court in reaching its decision. The first was that, if the landlord failed to serve a counter-notice under the 1993 Act, it was arguable that the court was bound to order the grant of a new lease at the figure specified in the tenant's notice. That was understandably described as a 'very harsh result'. It has

f   since been held that what the court said was 'arguable' is in fact the correct construction (see *Willingale v Globalgrange Ltd* [2000] 2 EGLR 55). The second factor was that the sum proposed by the tenant by way of premium determined the amount of the deposit that was payable. It follows that, as Mr Lewison points out, there were two respects in which the premium proposed by the tenant under the 1993 Act had legal consequences of considerable significance. There are no

g   corresponding provisions in the 1954 Act. The tenant's request and proposals under s 26 have no legal consequences. They do not commit the tenant or the landlord to anything. They are merely the prelude to a possible new tenancy on terms to be agreed or determined by the court. The tenant is not obliged to pursue an application for a new tenancy. If he does make an application and the

h   court orders a new tenancy, the tenant may seek a revocation of the order under s 36(2). In my judgment, therefore, the decision in *Cadogan v Morris* is only of limited assistance in deciding the question of construction that arises in the present case.

[35] I turn, therefore, to consider whether there are any wider considerations

j   which cast doubt on what I have said so far as to the meaning of 'request' and 'tenant's proposals'. The question that arises is whether the meaning that I have ascribed to these words is inconsistent with the plain intent of the 1954 Act as a whole, or whether it involves absurdity or at least real commercial difficulty such that this meaning cannot have been intended by Parliament. In his judgment the judge did not point to any commercial or practical difficulty in Thales' interpretation. Rather, he reasoned ([2000] 1 EGLR 138 at 147) that it was 'inherently unlikely' that

Parliament intended that a tenant should be entitled to compensation by
misrepresenting his intention as regards his desire for a new tenancy. The judge
did not expand on this part of his reasoning. It seems that he treated it as a
self-evidently true proposition: so obvious that it went without saying. In my
judgment, he was wrong to do so.

[36] It is useful to consider some case examples.

[37] Case A: the tenant learns that his landlord intends to oppose the renewal of
a tenancy on the grounds of intention to redevelop. He learns of this 18 months
before the end of his current tenancy, ie before the earliest date on which he
could serve a request under s 26. The tenant then finds an ideal alternative site
which he takes. He would not have taken that site, and incurred all the expense
and disruption to his business entailed in a move, if he had not been told of the
landlord's intention to oppose the grant of a new tenancy. The tenant then serves
his request under s 26.

[38] Case B: the tenant finds alternative accommodation before the end of the
current tenancy and decides to move. He then discovers that the landlord would
oppose the grant of a new tenancy on the grounds of his intention to redevelop.
On learning this, the tenant serves a request under s 26.

[39] Case C: the facts are as in case B, except that shortly after the tenant serves
his request for a new tenancy the alternative accommodation is withdrawn from
the market. The tenant is desperate and decides that he wants a renewal of his
current tenancy after all. Moreover, he decides to contest the validity of the
landlord's ground of opposition, saying that the landlord's plans cannot be
implemented because they will not receive planning permission. At court, the
landlord proves his intention and the application for a new tenancy is dismissed.

[40] Case D: the tenant has the intention to take up a renewed tenancy at the
time when he serves his request. The landlord serves a counter-notice indicating
opposition on the grounds of intention to redevelop. The tenant then changes
his mind for reasons which are wholly unconnected with the landlord's response.

[41] These cases show that the construction rejected by the judge does not
produce results which it can safely be concluded could not have been intended by
Parliament. Take case A, which substantially reflects the facts in the present case.
I suggest that most people would say that it was unfair on the tenant that he
should be deprived of compensation under s 37 of the 1954 Act. There is no
question of a windfall in favour of the tenant. It might be said that, on the judge's
interpretation, case A yields a windfall to the landlord, since it is pure chance that
the tenant happens to find the alternative accommodation before he is able to
request a new tenancy. The statutory purpose that lies behind s 37 is that a tenant
should be compensated where he would be unable to renew his tenancy because
of opposition by the landlord on one of the grounds stated in s 30(1)(e), (f) or (g).
In case A, the tenant satisfies that purpose. The only reason why he secured
alternative accommodation was that he knew that an application for a new
tenancy under s 24 would fail on the ground stated in s 30(1)(f). It is true that case
B may be said to involve a windfall to the tenant. But what about case C? Is the
payment of compensation to the tenant in the circumstances of this example so
absurd, or even surprising, that one can safely say that Parliament cannot have
intended it? In my view, no. And then what about case D? In my view, it is
anomalous, if not perverse, to allow the tenant compensation if he happens to
want a new tenancy when he serves a request, even if he changes his mind
immediately afterwards, and yet to refuse compensation if the tenant does not
want a new tenancy at the date of his request, although he changes his mind on

a the following day. Far from casting doubt on the conclusion that I expressed earlier as to the meaning of 'request' and 'tenant's proposals', these examples support it. They certainly do not cast any doubt on it, and they lend no support to the judge's view that it is inherently unlikely that Parliament intended such a meaning.

b [42] Mr Lewison makes the further point that, if the procedure for terminating the tenancy is initiated by the landlord serving a notice under s 25, relying on grounds specified in s 30(1)(e), (f) or (g), the tenant is entitled to compensation irrespective of his intention. It would be anomalous for the entitlement to compensation to depend on who initiated the procedure. I agree. Miss Williamson submits that there is no anomaly: there is the important difference between a termination by notice under s 25 and by request under s 26 c that, if a landlord terminates under s 25, he controls the timing of the process. That is true to a certain extent, but it does not provide a rational explanation for requiring an investigation of the tenant's state of mind in the one case but not the other. In my view, this provides yet further support for the meaning that I have given to 'request' and 'tenant's proposals'.

d [43] To summarise, there is no justification for reading words into s 26(3) as the judge did. Words should be read into a statute only if there is some necessity to do so. The judge thought that it was necessary to do so because he believed that it was inherently unlikely that Parliament intended the words to be given their ordinary unqualified meaning. For the reasons that I have sought to give, I believe that he was wrong. The prospect of an inquiry into the tenant's state of e mind is not one that the 1954 Act contemplates. The inclusion of proposals in a s 26 request is a statutory formality and does not require the tenant to have any particular intention. It follows that evidence of the tenant's state of mind when he serves his request for a new tenancy is inadmissible because it is legally irrelevant. It should not have been admitted in the present case. I would allow f this appeal.

HALE LJ.
[44] I agree.

WALLER LJ.
[45] I also agree.

Appeal allowed. Permission to appeal refused.

Gillian Crew   Barrister.

Kalmneft JSC v Glencore International AG and another

QUEEN'S BENCH DIVISION (COMMERCIAL COURT)
COLMAN J
13 JUNE, 27 JULY 2001

Arbitration – Award – Setting aside award – Time limit for application – Relevant considerations when application for setting aside award made out of time – Arbitration Act 1996, ss 24(1)(d), 67, 68, 79, 80(5) – CPR 3.12.

The applicant, K, was an Russian oil company. In March 1998 K and the respondent company, G, entered into a prepayment agreement, together with a third party, B Ltd. Under the agreement K was to supply a substantial amount of crude oil to B Ltd under a separate supply contract. G further agreed to purchase certain quantities of crude oil from B Ltd at specified delivery dates. G claimed that it made substantial advances under the prepayment agreement to K and B Ltd, but that no oil was delivered in 1999 or subsequently. Notice of default was given by G to K by letter in March 1999 and to both K and B Ltd in November 1999. Clause 5.3 of the prepayment agreement provided that it was governed by the laws of England and any dispute would be submitted to arbitration in London under the Arbitration Act 1996. K asserted that it had been the victim of a fraud perpetrated by one of its directors, and claimed that it did not know that the director had entered into the prepayment agreement purportedly on its behalf. On that basis K claimed that it had never became a party to the agreement and was consequently not bound by the arbitration clause. In February 2000, after receiving no response to a letter suggesting arbitration, G applied to the court seeking the appointment of a sole arbitrator. K replied that the Russian local arbitration court had already held that the arbitration agreement was invalid, but in June 2000, on G's application, the court ordered the appointment of an arbitrator. In August 2000 the arbitrator gave directions as to the progress of the arbitration; in response K asserted, inter alia, that it had not received the prepayment and that B Ltd had failed to deliver any oil. After further correspondence the arbitrator, in the exercise of his powers under ss 30[a] and 31(4)[b] of the 1996 Act, ruled that he had jurisdiction on the ground that K's director did have authority to enter into the arbitration agreement and that agreement was therefore valid and binding on K. Some ten weeks later, K appointed English solicitors, who issued an application to have the arbitrator's ruling on jurisdiction set aside under s 67[c] of the 1996 Act, contending that the court should set aside the ruling on jurisdiction so that the arbitrator could at one and the same hearing determine the closely-related issues of whether K was bound by the prepayment agreement and whether it was bound by the arbitration agreement; alternatively, the court should adjourn the s 67 application but give directions as to the exchange of further evidence prior to a later hearing. Directions for the conduct of the substantive arbitration proceedings continued, but K also issued an application

a   Section 30 is set out at [7], below
b   Section 31(4) is set out at [7], below
c   Section 67, so far as is material, is set out at [7], below

a   under s 24(1)(d)^d of the 1996 Act to remove the arbitrator for having failed properly to conduct the proceedings, and then issued an application to set aside the ruling on the grounds of serious irregularity under s 68^e of the 1996 Act. As the applications under s 67 and s 68 were made out of time, K made secondary applications for extensions of the time limit set out in s 70(3)^f of the 1996 Act. G argued that it was only under s 79^g of the Act that K could obtain an extension
b   of time for compliance with the 28-day limit.

Held – The applications would be dismissed for the following reasons—

(1) The relevant provision in the 1996 Act with regard to extensions of time over the 28-day limit was s 80(5)^h, which provided that rules of the court relating to the reckoning of periods, the extending or abridging of periods, and the
c   consequences of not taking a step within a period prescribed by the rules, applied in relation to requirements under Pt I of the 1996 Act for an application or appeal to be made to the court within a specified time. Section 80(5) thereby incorporated CPR 3.12(a), which provided that except where the CPR provided otherwise, the court might extend or shorten the time for compliance with any
d   rule, practice direction or court order even if an extension was made after the time for compliance had expired. It followed that the effect of s 80(5) was to introduce the broad discretionary approach under CPR 3.12(a) into applications for the extension of the 28-day time limit under ss 67 to 69 of the 1996 Act. In determining the relative weight to be attached to discretionary criteria, the
e   starting point had to be the fact that the 1996 Act was founded on a philosophy which differed in important respects from that of the CPR: the twin principles of party autonomy and finality of awards which pervaded the 1996 Act tended to restrict the supervisory role of the court and to minimise the occasion for the court's interventions in arbitrations. Moreover, in approaching the identification of the applicable criteria, it was important to note that, on the one hand, English
f   jurisdiction was probably the most widely chosen jurisdiction in international arbitrations, and, on the other, that because of the wide international market for English arbitration, many of the parties might be located in remote jurisdictions and have little or no experience of English or international arbitration. Although each case turned on its own facts, the following considerations were likely to be material: (i) the length of the delay; (ii) whether, in permitting the time limit to
g   expire and the subsequent delay to occur, the party was acting reasonably in all the circumstances; (iii) whether the respondent to the application or the arbitrator caused or contributed to the delay; (iv) whether the respondent to the application would by reason of the delay suffer irremediable prejudice in addition to the mere loss of time if the application were permitted to proceed; (v) whether
h   the arbitration had continued during the period of delay and, if so, what impact on the progress of the arbitration or the costs incurred the determination of the application by the court might now have; (vi) the strength of the application; and

---

d   Section 24(1)(d), so far as is material, provides: 'A party to arbitral proceedings may ... apply to the
j   court to remove an arbitrator on any of the following grounds— ... that he has refused or failed—
     (i) properly to conduct the proceedings ... and that substantial injustice has been or will be caused
     to the applicant.'
e   Section 68, so far as is material, is set out at [7], below
f   Section 70, so far as is material, is set out at [7], below
g   Section 79, so far as is material, is set out at [45], below
h   Section 80(5) is set out at [44], below

(vii) whether, in the broadest sense, it would be unfair to the applicant for him to be denied the opportunity of having the application determined. The relative a weight to be given to those considerations was likely to be influenced by the general considerations relating to international arbitration. In the instant case, K had failed to show any reasonable excuse for its non-compliance with the statutory time limit: had it instructed solicitors at the outset, it would not have been ignorant of the time limits. That omission was not merely an understandable b consequence of its inexperience in international arbitration, but was totally unreasonable (see [48]–[51], [57]–[60], [65], below).

(2) The function of an application under s 67 was not to challenge a decision taken under s 31(4), which permitted an arbitrator to rule on his own jurisdiction in an award on jurisdiction or to postpone a decision until his award on the merits, but to challenge the arbitrator's ruling as to his jurisdiction or to challenge c his ruling on the merits on the ground that he did not have jurisdiction. Once an arbitrator had decided under s 31(4) to rule on his own jurisdiction, the only function of an application under s 67 was to challenge the arbitrator's conclusion either that he had jurisdiction or that he did not. The court had no power to set aside a ruling that the arbitrator had jurisdiction on the grounds that it would be d better if he reconsidered the matter in the light of more evidence that might be available at a hearing on the merits. In the instant case, K's application under s 67 had been bound to fail and its attempt to use the s 67 jurisdiction to challenge the arbitrator's underlying decision to rule on his own jurisdiction under s 30(1)(a) was a misuse of that jurisdiction (see [69]–[71], below).

(3) The claimant's explanation for its failure to make the application under s 68 e at the same time as that made under s 67 was incomprehensible and there was therefore no more to explain the delay under the s 68 application than there was to explain the delay under the s 67 application. It followed that the claimant had not acted reasonably in allowing the time period to elapse or the subsequent delay to occur. Moreover, even if there were to be an extension of time, there f would be no realistic prospect of either the s 68 application or the s 24 application succeeding (see [63], [65], [75], [76], [93], [98], below).

Notes

For statutory extension of time, see 2 *Halsbury's Laws* (4th edn reissue) para 651.

For the Arbitration Act 1996, ss 24, 30, 31, 67, 68, 79, 80, see respectively g 2 *Halsbury's Statutes* (4th edn) (1999 reissue) 582, 585, 586, 607, 608, 616, 617.

Cases referred to in judgment

Azov Shipping Co v Baltic Shipping Co (No 3) [1999] 2 All ER (Comm) 453.

Edwards (Inspector of Taxes) v Bairstow [1955] 3 All ER 48, [1956] AC 14, [1955] h 3 WLR 410, HL.

Harbour and General Works Ltd v Environment Agency [1999] 1 All ER (Comm) 953; *affd* [1999] 2 All ER (Comm) 686, CA.

Pioneer Shipping Ltd v BTP Tioxide Ltd, The Nema [1981] 2 All ER 1030, [1982] AC 724, [1981] 3 WLR 292, HL. j

Applications

The applicant Russian company, Kalmneft JSC, applied by application notice dated 12 March 2001 to have a ruling of the sole arbitrator (Mr Andrew Berkeley) (the second respondent) dated 24 November 2000 on his substantive jurisdiction *a* set aside under s 67 of the Arbitration Act 1996 on the ground that the arbitrator had no jurisdiction. By application notice dated 27 March 2001, Kalmneft applied under s 24(1)(d) of the 1996 Act to remove the arbitrator on the ground that he had failed properly to conduct the proceedings, and by application notice dated 4 April 2001 Kalmneft applied under s 68 of the Act to set aside the ruling on the ground of serious irregularity. Kalmneft further applied for extensions of the *b* time limit set out in s 70(3) of the 1996 Act for the bringing of the applications under ss 67 and 68. The claim in the arbitration was brought by the first respondent, Glencore International AG. The facts are set out in the judgment.

Simon Crookenden QC (instructed by *Peter Levine*, Leeds) for Kalmneft.
Steven Berry (instructed by *Baker & McKenzie*) for Glencore.
c The arbitrator did not appear.

Cur adv vult

27 July 2001. The following judgment was delivered.

d COLMAN J.

Introduction
[1] There are three primary applications before the court. They arise in circumstances which are frequently encountered in international arbitrations and *e* which raise important issues as to the appropriate policy of this court in relation to the operation of the Arbitration Act 1996 where foreign parties are involved.
[2] The three applications are made in relation to a 'Ruling on Substantive Jurisdiction', dated 24 November 2000 by a sole arbitrator, Mr Andrew Berkeley.
[3] By application notice dated 12 March 2001 the applicants (Kalmneft) apply to have the ruling set aside under s 67 of the 1996 Act on the ground that the *f* arbitrator had no jurisdiction. In substance it is submitted that there is evidence to suggest that there was no binding agreement to arbitrate as between the respondent (Glencore) and Kalmneft.
[4] By application notice dated 27 March 2001 Kalmneft apply to remove the arbitrator under s 24(1)(d) of the 1996 Act on the ground that he failed *g* properly to conduct the proceedings.
[5] By application notice dated 4 April 2001 Kalmneft apply under s 68 of the 1996 Act to set aside the ruling on the grounds of serious irregularity affecting the proceedings and the ruling which has caused substantial injustice to Kalmneft. In substance, it is said that there was a failure to comply with s 33(1)(a) (general *h* duty of the tribunal) in as much as the arbitrator failed to act fairly and impartially as between the parties because he did not give Kalmneft a reasonable opportunity of putting its case or dealing with that of its opponent.
[6] There are also secondary applications for extensions of the time limit set out in s 70(3) for the bringing of the s 67 and s 68 applications, in each case 28 days from the date of the award.
j [7] The relevant statutory provisions are as follows. Section 24:

'(1) A party to arbitral proceedings may (upon notice to the other parties, to the arbitrator concerned and to any other arbitrator) apply to the court to remove an arbitrator on any of the following grounds ... (d) that he has refused or failed—(i) properly to conduct the proceedings, or (ii) to use all reasonable despatch in conducting the proceedings or making an award, and that substantial injustice has been or will be caused to the applicant.'

Section 30:

'(1) Unless otherwise agreed by the parties, the arbitral tribunal may rule on its own substantive jurisdiction, that is, as to—(a) whether there is a valid arbitration agreement, (b) whether the tribunal is properly constituted, and (c) what matters have been submitted to arbitration in accordance with the arbitration agreement.

(2) Any such ruling may be challenged by any available arbitral process of appeal or review or in accordance with the provisions of this Part.'

Section 31:

'(4) Where an objection is duly taken to the tribunal's substantive jurisdiction and the tribunal has power to rule on its own jurisdiction, it may—(a) rule on the matter in an award as to jurisdiction, or (b) deal with the objection in its award on the merits.'

Section 67:

'(1) A party to arbitral proceedings may (upon notice to the other parties and to the tribunal) apply to the court—(a) challenging any award of the arbitral tribunal as to its substantive jurisdiction; or (b) for an order declaring an award made by the tribunal on the merits to be of no effect, in whole or in part, because the tribunal did not have substantive jurisdiction.

A party may lose the right to object (see section 73) and the right to apply is subject to the restrictions in section 70(2) and (3).

(2) The arbitral tribunal may continue the arbitral proceedings and make a further award while an application to the court under this section is pending in relation to an award as to jurisdiction.

(3) On an application under this section challenging an award of the arbitral tribunal as to its substantive jurisdiction, the court may by order—(a) confirm the award, (b) vary the award, or (c) set aside the award in whole or in part.'

Section 68:

'(1) A party to arbitral proceedings may (upon notice to the other parties and to the tribunal) apply to the court challenging an award in the proceedings on the ground of serious irregularity affecting the tribunal, the proceedings or the award.

A party may lose the right to object (see section 73) and the right to apply is subject to the restrictions in section 70(2) and (3).

(2) Serious irregularity means an irregularity of one or more of the following kinds which the court considers has caused or will cause substantial injustice to the applicant—(a) failure by the tribunal to comply with section 33 (general duty of tribunal) ...'

Section 33:

'(1) The tribunal shall—(a) act fairly and impartially as between the parties, giving each party a reasonable opportunity of putting his case and dealing with that of his opponent, and (b) adopt procedures suitable to the circumstances of the particular case, avoiding unnecessary delay or expense, a   so as to provide a fair means for the resolution of the matters falling to be determined.

(2) The tribunal shall comply with that general duty in conducting the arbitral proceedings, in its decisions on matters of procedure and evidence and in the exercise of all other powers conferred on it.'

Section 70:

b   '(1) The following provisions apply to an application or appeal under section 67, 68 or 69 ...

(3) Any application or appeal must be brought within 28 days of the date of the award or, if there has been any arbitral process of appeal or review, of the date when the applicant or appellant was notified of the result of that

c   process.'

Section 73:

'(1) If a party to arbitral proceedings takes part, or continues to take part, in the proceedings without making, either forthwith or within such time as

d   is allowed by the arbitration agreement or the tribunal or by any provision of this Part, any objection—(a) that the tribunal lacks substantive jurisdiction, (b) that the proceedings have been improperly conducted, (c) that there has been a failure to comply with the arbitration agreement or with any provision of this Part, or (d) that there has been any other irregularity affecting the

e   tribunal or the proceedings, he may not raise that objection later, before the tribunal or the court, unless he shows that, at the time he took part or continued to take part in the proceedings, he did not know and could not with reasonable diligence have discovered the grounds for the objection.

(2) Where the arbitral tribunal rules that it has substantive jurisdiction and a party to arbitral proceedings who could have questioned that

f   ruling—(a) by any available arbitral process of appeal or review, or (b) by challenging the award, does not do so, or does not do so within the time allowed by the arbitration agreement or any provision of this Part, he may not object later to the tribunal's substantive jurisdiction on any ground which was the subject of that ruling.'

g   *The underlying dispute*

[8] Kalmneft is an oil production company carrying on business in the Republic of Kalmykia, an autonomous republic of the Russian Federation located in the Caucasus. Glencore is an oil trading company based in Switzerland.

[9] The claim in the arbitration is brought by Glencore for moneys due under

h   a prepayment agreement dated 19 March 1998 entered into between Glencore and Kalmneft and a company incorporated in the Republic of Ireland called Briarwise International Ltd (Briarwise). In substance, Kalmneft was to supply a substantial amount of crude oil to Briarwise under a separate supply contract dated 10 March 1998. Under an agreement dated 19 March Glencore agreed to

j   purchase certain quantities of crude oil from Briarwise at specified delivery dates.

[10] Under the prepayment agreement Glencore was to pay by way of advance to Kalmneft and Briarwise $US 10m. That was to be a prepayment in respect of the price of the oil to be delivered to Glencore under the supply contract of 19 March. By cl 1.2 of the prepayment agreement it was provided that the prepayment would be made in two amounts. Up to $7m was to be made in cash into Briarwise's bank account and the balance of $3m was to be made

available by way of the supply of equipment by or procured by Glencore. Interest was to be payable to Glencore until delivery of the oil to it.   *a*

[11] Pursuant to an equipment supply agreement of 3 April 1998 Glencore's subsidiary, Glencore Oil Products AG, supplied equipment to and carried out work for Kalmneft and Briarwise relating to Kalmneft's Kurganoy field. It was agreed that the invoice value of such equipment and works should be treated as a prepayment by Glencore under the prepayment agreement.   *b*

[12] Glencore claims that it made prepayments totalling $US 8,506,329·79 including $7m in cash.

[13] By cl 3 of the prepayment agreement it was provided that oil to the value of at least $US 420,000 per month would be delivered to Glencore during the period from January 1999 to December 2000. Clause 3.3 provided that Kalmneft and Briarwise unconditionally undertook that the oil cargoes would be delivered   *c* in full according to the Briarwise/Glencore contract by 31 December 2000. If any prepayment and/or interest was still outstanding on that date, that is to say sufficient oil had not been delivered to offset the prepayment and interest, Kalmneft and Briarwise were to pay the balance in cash to Glencore. Clause 4 provided that the prepayment would become immediately repayable in full   *d* together with accrued interest and all other moneys payable if at any time either Kalmneft or Briarwise were to be in breach of the prepayment agreement or of any other agreement with Glencore.

[14] It is alleged that no oil was delivered to Glencore in January or February 1999. Notice of default was given by Glencore to Kalmneft by letter dated 10 March 1999 and to both Kalmneft and Briarwise by letters dated 19 November   *e* 1999. By 30 September 2000 interest had accrued to the extent of $US 3,702,728·29, increasing at the rate of $US 6,100·05 per day. No deliveries of oil were made during 1999 or subsequently.

[15] The prepayment agreement provided by cl 5.3:

'This Agreement shall be governed by the laws of England and any dispute   *f* or matter arising directly or indirectly under or relating to this Agreement shall be submitted to arbitration in London under the Arbitration Acts.'

[16] The prepayment agreement was signed over the official corporate stamp of Kalmneft by the then first deputy general director of Kalmneft, Mr Daginov. He held a power of attorney signed by the general director of Kalmneft, one   *g* Kourneyev. This empowered Daginov to enter into and sign contracts on behalf of Kalmneft.

[17] Kalmneft asserts that it has been the victim of a fraud perpetrated by Daginov. It claims to have known about the contract to supply oil to Briarwise and to have known that the oil was being ultimately supplied to Glencore but not   *h* to have known that Daginov had entered into the prepayment agreement, purportedly on behalf of Kalmneft. It is said that Kalmneft believed that Briarwise was Glencore's associated company. It is therefore contended that Kalmneft never became a party to the prepayment agreement and is accordingly not bound by the arbitration clause. Not only is it not liable for amounts due under that   *j* agreement, but it is not obliged to take part in the arbitration.

The arbitration proceedings

[18] On 13 January 2000 Glencore sent letters to Kalmneft and Briarwise alleging the breaches of the prepayment agreement which I have described. They called on those parties to join with them in appointing an arbitrator within 28 days failing which they would apply to the High Court in London under s 16

a of the 1996 Act for such appointment to be made. At the same time they proposed that Mr Berkeley be jointly appointed as sole arbitrator. This letter was ignored.

[19] Glencore then applied to the court. The proceedings were served on Kalmneft but by their letter of 24 April 2000 Kalmneft stated that the Arbitration Court of Kalmykia had already held that the agreement was invalid on the ground

b that the arbitration agreement contained 'numerous flaws', that Briarwise had ceased to be registered in Ireland, that criminal proceedings had been commenced against Daginov by the Ministry of Internal Affairs of Kalmykia and that the arbitration proceedings in London should be terminated because the Kalmykia State Court had already ruled on the validity of the agreement and no award of a foreign tribunal would be recognised or enforced.

c
[20] By order of Longmore J on 9 June 2000 Mr Berkeley was appointed sole arbitrator.

[21] On 25 August 2000 Mr Berkeley gave the following directions as to the progress of the arbitration.

d [22] Glencore was to serve its statement of case and supporting documents on the respondents with a copy to the arbitrator not later than 25 September 2000. Upon such service on the respondents they were to have 30 days from the date of service to serve defences and supporting documents with copies to the arbitrator. Glencore was then to have 30 days either to serve its reply and supporting documents or to notify the respondents and arbitrator that it did not wish to do

e so. Disclosure of documents beyond those disclosed with the pleadings was to be dispensed with. Paragraph 5 provided:

'The Arbitrator shall hold an oral hearing if so requested by any of the parties. Such request must be made within 15 days of the service of the Reply or of the Claimant's notice that no Reply will be served. Any such hearing

f shall be held as soon as convenient, in London. If no such request is made, then the Arbitrator shall make an award based on the Pleadings and the documents provided therewith as soon as possible.'

[23] The order further stated that the directions were to be varied and/or

g amplified at the discretion of the arbitrator.

[24] Kalmneft responded immediately to this order. By letter sent on 1 September 2000 it referred to various proceedings before the Arbitration Court of Kalmykia by which it had been concluded that the prepayment agreement was invalid and then to an appeal before the Arbitration Court of the Russian Federation and asserted in substance that Kalmneft had not received the

h prepayment and that Briarwise had failed to deliver any oil and that it was for Briarwise and not Kalmneft to repay the money to Glencore. The letter went on to assert that the English 'court' had no jurisdiction because the events took place in Russia. In any event, if the respondents did not participate in the arbitration, the award would not be 'in accordance with international requirements'. There

j is then an opaque reference to execution of the court only in Russia.

[25] On 25 September 2000 the arbitrator sent a letter to all parties. He made it clear that there would be no question of his receiving communications from one side which were not communicated to the other parties and stated that all communications to him must be simultaneously copied to the other parties. Glencore was given until 9 October to comment on Kalmneft's 1 September letter. The letter continued:

'It is clear that Kalmneft is submitting that I have no jurisdiction in this matter. I have power to rule on the question of my jurisdiction under section 30 of the *a* Arbitration Act 1996. In the event that I should decide that it would be desirable to make such a ruling, I would remind Kalmneft of its right to take legal advice and, in addition to considering any submissions which it may make directly to me. I would therefore be happy to consider submissions by its legal advisers. Kalmneft, or its lawyer, may make further written *b* submissions relating to my jurisdiction not later than 9 October 2000.'

[26] On 30 September 2000 Baker & McKenzie (B&M) submitted Glencore's statement of case as to its substantive claim. Whereas it referred to the arbitration agreement in cl 5.3 of the prepayment agreement, it did not direct itself specifically to the points raised by Kalmneft in its 1 September letter. However, by their *c* letter of 9 October B&M submitted a paragraph by paragraph response to Kalmneft's points. They explained that although the Arbitration Court of Kalmykia had found that the prepayment agreement was invalid and that this decision had been upheld on appeal, it was arrived at without reference to any evidence or the relevant procedural laws. Glencore's legal representative had *d* appeared solely to protest the jurisdiction. Glencore's further appeal to the Federal Arbitration Court, North Caucasus District was allowed but Kalmneft was understood to have appealed yet again to the Supreme Arbitration Court in Moscow. B&M made the point that any challenge to the jurisdiction of the arbitrator could only be determined by the arbitrator under s 30 of the 1996 Act or by the English court under s 32. They further maintained that Kalmneft's *e* argument against the jurisdiction of any English court was without foundation.

[27] On 11 October 2000 the arbitrator wrote to the parties stating that, although Kalmneft had said that it had evidence and explanations as to its case on jurisdiction, it had so far produced neither documents nor evidence nor had it produced any coherent legal argument as to want of jurisdiction. He had *f* concluded that it was his duty under the 1996 Act to give Kalmneft an opportunity to make its case on jurisdiction and for him to rule on jurisdiction in exercise of his powers under ss 30 and 31(4) of that Act. He thereupon made the following orders:

'(1) Kalmneft shall, not later than Friday, 27 October 2000, submit to me *g* and to the other parties in writing its arguments concerning my jurisdiction in this arbitration and it shall annexe true notarially certified copies of all documents upon which it relies. The claimant shall have until Friday, 10 November 2000 to reply in writing to such arguments, annexing notarially certified copies of any documents on which it relies. *h*

(2) In addition to the submission of written evidence and argument, either party may request a hearing limited to the question of jurisdiction. Oral testimony may be given at such hearing. If the arbitrator shall grant such request, he may do so upon such conditions, including time limits within which hearings may be held and venue, as he thinks just and convenient. *j*

(3) Pending the award of the arbitrator on his jurisdiction, proceedings on the merits of the case shall be suspended.

(4) If Kalmneft does not present written argument and evidence as required by para 1 above within the time limit therein laid down, the arbitrator shall nevertheless proceed forthwith to issue an award on jurisdiction under his powers in s 41(4) of the Arbitration Act 1996.'

a

[28] By a letter dated 28 October 2000 Kalmneft made the following main points. (i) The Arbitration Court of Kalmykia had already decided that Briarwise should pay $US 7,189,504 to Kalmneft and that the Kalmneft/Briarwise contract should be cancelled. (ii) Given that Briarwise had ceased to exist, there was no ground for London jurisdiction. (iii) Daginov's conduct in signing the prepayment agreement without submitting it for the approval of the board of directors of

b

Kalmneft bore the marks of criminality and criminal proceedings had been started against him and against Mr Pyataev, the former director general of Kalmneft, who had already been imprisoned pending investigation into the theft of $US 100,000 from that company. (iv) The prepayment agreement did not contain an arbitration clause requiring all disputes to be resolved on an ad hoc basis. (v) Russian law governed the question whether a Russian company was

c

bound by a contract not submitted for the approval of the board of directors, irrespective of the fact that an arbitration clause was included. Accordingly, the prepayment agreement was invalid under Kalmneft's statutes and the Federal Joint Stock Companies Act.

[29] The latter concluded by stating that Kalmneft placed its trust in the

d

impartiality and expertise that the arbitrator would bring to bear in reaching a final decision. It contained no request for an oral hearing and was accompanied by neither evidence nor documents.

[30] It is to be observed that Kalmneft's challenge to the arbitrator's jurisdiction was at least in part based on the assertion that the prepayment agreement, and therefore the agreement to arbitrate in cl 5.3, was not binding on

e

Kalmneft. This is an increasingly prevalent situation in jurisdictional challenges to arbitration encountered in this court. On the preliminary issue of jurisdiction the arbitrator or the court, as the case may be, is called upon to decide whether any contract exists between the parties and, if there is found to be no such contract, the claim may necessarily fail. In such cases the whole issue of liability

f

may therefore be decided by the determination of the issue on jurisdiction.

[31] On 20 November 2000 B&M sent Glencore's submissions in reply on the jurisdiction issue to the arbitrator and to Kalmneft. In summary, their submissions in so far as material were that: (i) in as much as cl 5.3 of the prepayment agreement contained an express choice of law provision, the agreement to arbitrate was governed by English law; (ii) the validity of that agreement to arbitrate was by

g

English conflicts rules governed by the law by which such agreement would have been governed if it were binding; (iii) therefore its validity in this case was to be governed by English law; (iv) the receipt or otherwise of the prepayment by Kalmneft was irrelevant to the jurisdiction issue; (v) s 36 of the Companies Act 1985 as modified by the Foreign Companies (Execution of Documents) Regulations 1994, SI 1994/950 provided that a company incorporated outside

h

Great Britain could have a contract made on its behalf by any person who, in accordance with the laws of that territory of incorporation, was acting under the authority express or implied of that company; (vi) Daginov had express or implied authority to enter into the prepayment agreement by reason of the company's power of attorney, Kalmneft's articles of association and certain

j

provisions of the Russian Civil Code, in particular art 182(1) governing the effect of powers of attorney; (vii) alternatively Daginov had ostensible authority to bind Kalmneft by reason of his position as a director of Kalmneft and of the power of attorney; and (viii) alternatively Kalmneft ratified his authority by part performance in as much as they went ahead and accepted equipment and services which were supplied by or on behalf of Glencore as the non-cash element of the prepayment.

[32] That letter contained no request for an oral hearing.

[33] The arbitrator then proceeded directly to his ruling on jurisdiction which he issued on 24 November 2000. In an impressive and carefully reasoned analysis he concluded that he had jurisdiction because Daginov did have authority to enter into the arbitration agreement and that agreement was therefore valid and binding on Kalmneft. At the same time the arbitrator issued directions for service of a defence in the substantive dispute by 15 December 2000.

[34] By a letter dated 13 December 2000 Kalmneft rejected the arbitrator's ruling and repeated that any award he might make in the absence of Kalmneft and Briarwise could not be enforceable in Russia. The letter did not state that Kalmneft had expected to be permitted to make reply submissions or adduce more written evidence or to attend an oral hearing on the jurisdiction issue.

[35] On 18 December 2000 the arbitrator issued a peremptory order under s 41 of the 1996 Act that Kalmneft and Briarwise must serve a defence within 14 days of service on them of an affidavit to be produced by Glencore verifying the matters relied on in its statement of case. If a defence were not served the arbitrator would proceed to his award under his powers under s 41(4) of the 1996 Act.

[36] On 12 January 2001 Glencore served its affidavit on Kalmneft.

[37] On 17 January 2001 the arbitrator, in response to Kalmneft's request, ordered that a 'meeting' of the parties with him should take place on 19 and 20 February 2001. He suspended the operation of his peremptory order until after 2 March 2001. This had the effect of extending Kalmneft's time for service of a defence.

[38] At this point, for the first time since the dispute began, Kalmneft on 5 February 2001 appointed English solicitors, over ten weeks after the arbitrator had issued his ruling on jurisdiction. The meeting was postponed until 20 March 2001. Messrs Peter Levine of Leeds then made contact with the arbitrator. They asked whether, in view of his ruling on jurisdiction, it was still open to Kalmneft to contend that it was not bound by the prepayment agreement. They further stated that Kalmneft would be asking for an order for disclosure of Glencore's documents before defence. The letter contained no objection to the jurisdiction of the arbitrator.

[39] On 12 March 2001 Kalmneft's solicitors issued its application to have the arbitrator's ruling on jurisdiction set aside under s 67 of the 1996 Act.

[40] Following a hearing on 20 March 2001 at which Kalmneft was represented by leading counsel the arbitrator issued further directions for the service of a defence by 30 April, disclosure of documents and exchange of witness statements.

[41] Meanwhile, on 27 March 2001 Kalmneft issued its application to remove the arbitrator for having failed properly to conduct the proceedings and on 4 April it issued its application to set aside the ruling on the grounds of serious irregularity.

[42] Finally, on 11 May 2001, Kalmneft served its defence on the merits of the underlying claim, but in which it expressly declined to accept that the arbitrator had jurisdiction.

Extensions of time under the 1996 Act

[43] Each of the applications under ss 67 and 68 of the 1996 Act was brought long out of time. Section 70(3) imposes a time limit of 28 days from the date of the award. Therefore, the applications should have been issued by 22 December 2001. The s 67 application was issued over 11 weeks beyond the time limit and the s 68 application was issued over 14 weeks out of time.

a   [44] The relevant provision in the 1996 Act with regard to extensions of time in respect of the 28-day limit is s 80(5). This provides:

> '(5) Where any provision of this Part requires an application or appeal to be made to the court within a specified time, the rules of court relating to the reckoning of periods, the extending or abridging of periods, and the consequences of not taking a step within the period prescribed by the rules,
b   > apply in relation to that requirement.'

[45] Mr Steven Berry has submitted on behalf of Glencore that it is only under s 79 of the 1996 Act that Kalmneft can obtain an extension of time for compliance with the 28-day time limit. Section 79 provides:

c   > '(1) Unless the parties otherwise agree, the court may by order extend any time limit agreed by them in relation to any matter relating to the arbitral proceedings or specified in any provision of this Part having effect in default of such agreement.
> This section does not apply to a time limit to which section 12 applies (power or court to extend time for beginning arbitral proceedings, &c).
d   > (2) An application for an order may be made—(a) by any party to the arbitral proceedings (upon notice to the other parties and to the tribunal), or (b) by the arbitral tribunal (upon notice to the parties).
> (3) The court shall not exercise its power to extend a time limit unless it is satisfied—(a) that any available recourse to the tribunal, or to any arbitral
e   > or other institution or person vested by the parties with power in that regard, has first been exhausted, and (b) that a substantial injustice would otherwise be done.'

[46] The 28-day time limit under s 70(3) is not a time limit specified by a provision of Pt I of the 1996 Act in default of a time limit agreed by the parties: it
f   is simply a provision of Pt I requiring an application or appeal to be made to the court within a specified time. In the course of argument Mr Simon Crookenden QC, on behalf of Kalmneft, did not challenge Mr Berry's reliance on s 79. Indeed, he positively submitted that, if time were not extended, his clients would suffer a substantial injustice for the purposes of s 79(3)(b). However, s 79 does not apply to the extension of time unless, as, for example, under s 16, the 1996 Act lays
g   down time limits in default of agreement.

[47] Both counsel appear to have overlooked s 80(5). This provision incorporates into the 1996 Act the rules of court relating to extending periods of time under the rules and makes them applicable to the statutory time limits. At the time when the 1996 Act became law, the relevant rule was RSC Ord 3, r 5. Now, under
h   the new regime, it is CPR 3.1(2), which provides:

> 'Except where these Rules provide otherwise, the court may—(a) extend or shorten the time for compliance with any rule, practice direction or court order even if an application for extension is made after the time for
j   > compliance has expired.'

[48] The effect of s 80(5) is to introduce the broad discretionary approach under this rule into applications for the extension of the 28-day time limit under ss 67, 68 and 69 of the 1996 Act.

[49] It is therefore necessary to identify the criteria applicable to such applications under the 1996 Act, for they may differ from those applicable under the CPR.

[50] In determining the relative weight that should be attached to discretionary criteria the starting point must be to take into account the fact that the 1996 Act is founded on a philosophy which differs in important respects from that of the CPR.

[51] Thus, the twin principles of party autonomy and finality of awards which pervade the 1996 Act tend to restrict the supervisory role of the court and to minimise the occasion for the court's intervention in the conduct of arbitrations. Nowhere is this more clearly demonstrated than in s 68 itself where there was superimposed upon the availability of a remedy for what used to be called 'misconduct' by the arbitrator and was redefined as 'serious irregularity' a requirement that it had caused or would cause substantial injustice to the applicant. No longer was it enough to demonstrate failure by the arbitrator scrupulously to adhere to the audi alterem partem rule.

[52] Section 12 also reflects this general approach by redefining the circumstances in which the court will extend the time for the commencement of arbitration fixed by the arbitration agreement: as explained in *Harbour and General Works Ltd v Environment Agency* [1999] 1 All ER (Comm) 953 at 961. Further, the relatively short period of time for making an application for relief under ss 67, 68 and 69 also reflects the principle of finality. Once an award has been made the parties have to live with it unless they move with great expedition. Were it otherwise, the old mischief of over-long unenforceability of awards due to the pendency of supervisory proceedings would be encouraged.

[53] At this point it is necessary to have in mind the general principles set out in s 1 of the 1996 Act:

'(1) The provisions of this Part are founded on the following principles, and shall be construed accordingly—(a) the object of arbitration is to obtain the fair resolution of disputes by an impartial tribunal without unnecessary delay or expense; (b) the parties should be free to agree how their disputes are resolved, subject only to such safeguards as are necessary in the public interest; (c) in matters governed by this Part the court should not intervene except as provided by this Part.'

[54] The reference to unnecessary delay is pertinent to identifying the relevant discretionary criteria.

[55] The need for expedition in proceedings before the court is reflected in paras 9 and 12 of App 19 of the *Commercial Court Guide*. This states under the heading 'Arbitration Matters: Related Practice':

'Progress—
(9) In arbitration matters it is the particular duty of the Court to see that court proceedings are not a cause of delay.
(10) A hearing date must (where applicable) be applied for promptly after the issue of the required practice form (whether serving as an arbitration claim form or an application notice) or after obtaining permission to appeal under the Arbitration Acts 1979 and 1996.
(12) A failure to act with all deliberate speed founds the Court's discretion to strike out. When it comes to the attention of the Court that delay is occurring, the Court may itself direct that the matter be listed for hearing.'

[56] It is, however, also to be remembered that the threshold requirement set out in s 79(3)(b) for extension of time limits to which s 79 relates—'that a substantial injustice would otherwise be done' —is not expressed to be applicable

a to extensions of time under s 80(5). In that respect, therefore, a lower unfairness threshold must be presumed to have been intended.

[57] In approaching the identification of the applicable criteria it is also important to take into account the fact that, at least in international arbitrations, English arbitration is probably the most widely chosen jurisdiction of all. It is chosen because of the ready availability of highly skilled and experienced

b arbitrators operating under a well-defined regime of legal and procedural principles in what is often a neutral forum. Supervisory intervention by the courts is minimal and well defined and the opportunities for a respondent with a weak case to delay the making of an award or to interfere with its status of finality are very restricted. Accordingly, much weight has to be attached to the avoidance of delay at all stages of an arbitration, both before and after an interim

c or final award. If the English courts were seen by foreign commercial institutions to be over-indulgent in the face of unjustifiable non-compliance with time limits, those institutions might well be deterred from using references to English arbitration in their contracts. This is a distinct public policy factor which has to be given due weight in the discretionary balance.

d [58] On the other hand it has to be recognised that because of the extremely wide international nature of the market for English arbitration many of the parties may be located in remote jurisdictions and may have little or no previous experience of international or English arbitration. When these relatively unsophisticated parties find themselves involved in such an arbitration, it is only

e to be expected that they move somewhat more tentatively than would an international trading house well experienced in this field. It would therefore be wrong to fail to make at least some allowance for this factor in evaluating the element of fault in failing to comply with time limits.

[59] Accordingly, although each case turns on its own facts, the following considerations are, in my judgment, likely to be material: (i) the length of the

f delay; (ii) whether, in permitting the time limit to expire and the subsequent delay to occur, the party was acting reasonably in all the circumstances; (iii) whether the respondent to the application or the arbitrator caused or contributed to the delay; (iv) whether the respondent to the application would by reason of the delay suffer irremediable prejudice in addition to the mere loss of

g time if the application were permitted to proceed; (v) whether the arbitration has continued during the period of delay and, if so, what impact on the progress of the arbitration or the costs incurred the determination of the application by the court might now have; (vi) the strength of the application; and (vii) whether in the broadest sense it would be unfair to the applicant for him to be denied the

h opportunity of having the application determined.

[60] The relative weight to be given to these considerations in the discretionary balance in any given case is likely to be influenced by the general considerations relating to international arbitration to which I have already referred.

j *Application of the relevant principles on extension of time*

[61] The delay has to be counted from the date of the award. In the case of the s 67 application this was over 11 weeks after the 28 days, nearly three times longer than the permitted period. In the case of the s 68 application it was 14 weeks after the 28 days.

[62] It is to be said at the outset that these are very considerable periods of delay. It is therefore necessary to investigate whether the applicant has put forward any

reasonable excuse for such a substantial departure from the requirements of the 1996 Act.

[63] There can be no doubt that one of the main reasons for Kalmneft's failure to act within the time limits was its failure to take advice on English arbitration law. It did not consult solicitors until 5 February 2001. As early as 24 May 2000 B&M had advised Kalmneft to instruct English solicitors to advise them. That was at the stage of Glencore's application to this court for the appointment of a sole arbitrator. Yet that suggestion was ignored for a period of over seven months. The arbitrator gave similar advice in his letter of 25 September 2000. No satisfactory explanation has been provided by Kalmneft for ignoring that advice. It seems to have been assumed that it would be better to present its own case on the issue as to jurisdiction, starting from the basis that there was no jurisdiction because the prepayment agreement had been entered into by Daginov without authority and that the Russian courts had or would ultimately reach this conclusion and that any award from England would be unenforceable in Kalmykia.

[64] It is of course always open to a foreign corporation to ignore an English arbitration if it takes the position that the arbitrator has no jurisdiction, leaving it to the other party to proceed unilaterally to an award and then to attempt to enforce it in the foreign jurisdiction. In the enforcement proceedings it would normally be open to a party who had taken no part in the arbitration amounting to submission to the arbitrators to assert that it was not bound by the award. However, if a foreign respondent is to take advantage of English procedural facilities for testing the arbitrators' jurisdiction, it is incumbent upon it to comply to the best of its ability with the requirements of that procedure. It is not permitted to adopt an exploratory foray into those procedural facilities in the course of which it ignores the procedural requirements.

[65] Kalmneft has, in my judgment, failed to show any reasonable excuse for its non-compliance with the statutory time limit. Had it instructed solicitors at the outset it would not have been ignorant of the time limits. Its omission to take professional advice on English law from the outset (June 1999) or, failing that, from the time of the arbitrator's letter of 25 September 2000 or from when the arbitrator made his directions as to the jurisdiction issue (October 2000) or, even at the last minute, on receiving the ruling on jurisdiction (November 2000) was not merely an understandable consequence of inexperience in international arbitration: it was totally unreasonable. However inexperienced a foreign corporation was as to how to conduct an arbitration, it should have been quite obvious to it on reading Glencore's submission on jurisdiction that it urgently needed advice on English law.

[66] Solicitors first having been instructed on 5 February 2001, they had to obtain instructions from relatively inaccessible clients and had to familiarise themselves with the facts and issues giving rise to the arbitration. As soon as they had been informed that Kalmneft challenged jurisdiction in the face of the arbitrator's ruling, they should have appreciated that there was a time limit relevant to any further challenge and should have moved with maximum urgency. As it is, it was over a month before they contacted the arbitrator to enquire about the implications of his ruling on the arbitration as to the merits. Only after receiving his reply (9 March 2001) did they issue their application under s 67. In the circumstances I find their approach somewhat leisurely in spite of the points relied on in para 6 of Mr Levine's second witness statement and in the other witness statements.

a
[67] It is at this point that it is necessary to examine the s 67 application. The witness statement of Peter Levine set out the main events in the arbitration, stating (para 10) that the arbitrator had not given Kalmneft an opportunity to reply to B&M's submissions before making his ruling. It summarised the ruling, quoting what it described as the correct statement of the doctrine of severability and stating that by his finding that Daginov had authority to

b
enter into the arbitration agreement he had made findings that went both to the validity of the arbitration agreement and to that of the prepayment agreement itself. The statement then went on as follows:

'Kalmneft seek no declaration at this stage as to the validity or otherwise of the arbitration agreement. This issue is inextricably mixed up with the basic issues in the dispute as to the validity of the prepayment agreement itself.

c
Kalmneft simply seek the setting aside of the Ruling on Jurisdiction in so far as it concerns the validity of the arbitration agreement so that this issue can be dealt with by the Arbitrator at the same time as his award on the merits of the claim. Kalmneft have arguable defences to Glencore's claim though they are not yet in a position to plead those defences in full. The position is

d
set out in the letter dated 9 March 2001 from my firm to the Arbitrator. It is Kalmneft's case that there is ample evidence to show that Kalmneft have been the victim of an actual or at least attempted fraud. It is also Kalmneft's case that there is evidence at least sufficient to justify further investigation as to whether there was any involvement of Glencore in the fraud. Justice

e
requires that Kalmneft be given a proper opportunity to make their investigations and to plead such defences as may be available to them both as regards the merits of the dispute and as to the Arbitrator's jurisdiction. Even if the evidence eventually obtained would not justify a plea of fraud against Glencore, Kalmneft would still have arguable defences based on the authority of Mr Daginov to enter into the prepayment agreement on behalf

f
of Kalmneft. Such defences would go both to the validity of the prepayment agreement itself and also to the validity of the arbitration agreement contained within it.'

[68] In opening this application Mr Crookenden QC explained that he was inviting the court to set aside the ruling on jurisdiction so that the arbitrator could

g
at one and the same hearing determine the closely related issues of whether Kalmneft was bound by the prepayment agreement and whether it was bound by the arbitration agreement. Alternatively, if the court could not take that course, it should adjourn the s 67 application but giving directions as to the exchange of further evidence prior to a later hearing by the court. He submitted that there

h
was on the evidence so far adduced at least an arguable case that Kalmneft was not bound by the arbitration agreement due to the fraud of Daginov. Kalmneft was prepared to give up the proceedings in Russia—leaving the issue of jurisdiction to be determined in accordance with the 1996 Act.

[69] The course taken by the applicants is, in my judgment, a misuse of the

j
s 67 jurisdiction.

[70] Firstly, Kalmneft is attempting to use that jurisdiction to challenge, not the arbitrator's conclusion on jurisdiction, but his underlying decision to rule on his own jurisdiction under s 30(1)(a) and by way of a preliminary award. It was open to the arbitrator under s 31(4) either to rule on the matter in an award on jurisdiction or to postpone a decision until his award on the merits. He chose the former course, no doubt because he considered that it would be a more

cost-efficient and speedier way of resolving the dispute. This was not a surprising course. At the time when, on 11 October 2000, he decided to deal with ^{a} jurisdiction as a preliminary issue it was open to him sensibly to take the view that in spite of the overlapping issues of fact and law relating to Daginov's authority to enter into the agreement to arbitrate and the prepayment agreement it would be of advantage to the parties to know where they stood on jurisdiction as early as possible. ^{b}

[71] The function of s 67 is not to challenge a decision as to what course to take under s 31(4) but to challenge the arbitrator's ruling as to his jurisdiction or to challenge his award on the merits on the ground that he did not have jurisdiction. Once an arbitrator has decided under his powers under s 31(4) to rule on his own jurisdiction, the only function of s 67 is to challenge the arbitrator's conclusion either that he had jurisdiction or that he did not. Above ^{c} all the court has no power to set aside a ruling that the arbitrator has jurisdiction on the grounds that it would be better if he reconsidered the matter in the light of more evidence that might be available at a hearing on the merits.

[72] It is to be observed that the evidence filed in support of the s 67 application at no point suggests that the court should forthwith set aside the arbitrator's ^{d} ruling because it was wrong. Nor does it suggest that the court should first give directions relating to the evidence to be adduced at a subsequent hearing by the court of a challenge to jurisdiction. Indeed, para 13 of Mr Levine's affidavit is wholly inconsistent with that intention.

[73] For these reasons, the application issued on 12 March 2001 was bound to fail on the evidence on which it was based. Had it been brought within time it ^{e} would have been open to the court to strike it out.

[74] Accordingly, it is unnecessary to investigate any other considerations relevant to the exercise of the court's discretion to extend time. On the grounds already considered, namely the extent and the absence of a reasonable excuse for the delay and the intrinsic weakness of the application, the application for extension ^{f} of time must be refused, for these grounds necessarily outweigh or dispose of all other criteria.

[75] I turn now to the application to extend time for the s 68 application. This was issued three weeks later than the s 67 application. In para (iv) of the grounds of application set out in the arbitration application there is set out the following explanation, not for the whole delay since 22 December, but for the failure to ^{g} make the application under s 68 at the same time as that under s 67. That explanation is as follows:

'(iv) This application was not made at the same time as the application under s.67 of the Arbitration Act since, there being no requirement for leave ^{h} under s.67, it was not thought necessary to apply also under s.68. On consideration it was thought appropriate to apply also under s.68 since the evidence to support such an application is already before the court and it is appropriate for the court to have available to it all relevant powers under the Arbitration Act.'

^{j}
[76] I regret to say that I have found this explanation incomprehensible. It goes nowhere to explaining why a further period of delay after 12 March 2000 was allowed to elapse. There is therefore no more to explain the delay than there is in relation to the s 67 application in Mr Levine's first and second witness statements and the other witness statements. In particular the meeting with the arbitrator which he convened on 20 March had no bearing whatever on the

a substance of the application. The only relevant serious irregularity could be that which had occurred in relation to the arbitrator's ruling on jurisdiction four months earlier.

[77] I therefore conclude that Kalmneft had not acted reasonably in allowing the 28-day time period to elapse or the subsequent delay of 14 weeks to occur.

[78] The grounds of relief relied upon in the arbitration application are that—

b '(i) In breach of s.33 of the Arbitration Act 1996 the arbitrator failed to give the applicant any or any adequate opportunity to lead evidence in support of their challenge to the arbitrator's jurisdiction.

(ii) In further breach of s.33 of the Arbitration Act 1996 the arbitrator failed to give the applicant any opportunity to reply to the submissions made
c on behalf of the Respondent in a letter from Baker & McKenzie dated 20 November 2000.'

[79] The evidence relied upon is said to be that contained in the witness statements deployed for the s 67 application and the witness statement of Peter Levine deployed in support of the application of 27 March to remove the
d arbitrator under s 24 of the 1996 Act.

[80] Essentially, two main points are relied on as amounting to a serious irregularity: (i) the arbitrator's decision to determine his own jurisdiction as a preliminary point notwithstanding that it involved deciding whether Kalmneft gave express or implied or ostensible authority to Daginov to bind it to the agreement to arbitrate, an issue extremely closely related to the issue whether
e Daginov was authorised to bind it to the prepayment agreement; and (ii) proceeding to his ruling without giving Kalmneft a reasonable opportunity to put forward submissions or adduce evidence in response to B&M's submissions on behalf of Glencore in their letter of 20 November 2000, having previously failed to make it clear that Kalmneft's response to his letter of 10 October 2000
f was to be its only opportunity to put forward its case on jurisdiction.

[81] As to (i), it is submitted that the arbitrator should have taken one of three courses:

'(i) Left over any issues that related both to his jurisdiction and to the merits for decision in an award on the merits; or (ii) Identified those issues
g that related both to his jurisdiction and to the merits and determined those issues as preliminary issues having given both parties a full and proper opportunity to lead evidence and make submissions on those issues; or (iii) Suggest that the issue of Jurisdiction be submitted to the Court under s.32 of the Arbitration Act 1996.'

h [82] It is said that his failure to do so amounted to a serious irregularity in as much as it was contrary to the arbitrator's duty under s 33(1)(b), namely to adopt procedures suitable to the circumstances of the particular case, avoiding unnecessary delay or expense, so as to provide a fair means for the resolution of the matters falling to be determined. It is said that this decision has caused
j substantial injustice to Kalmneft by forcing it to pursue as a preliminary point its whole case that Daginov acted without its authority.

[83] As indicated earlier in this judgment, it is commonplace in international arbitration for jurisdiction and liability both to be disputed on the ground that there was no binding contract or agreement to arbitrate between the parties. When an arbitrator is confronted by this situation, his duty is to consider how his duty under s 33(1)(b) should be complied with. That decision must necessarily

take into account not only all the factual circumstances, such as the nature of the
evidence likely to be relevant and what procedure would be best suited to it in *a*
the interests of both parties, but also the availability of recourse to the court
by the party against whom he decided the jurisdiction issue by reason of the right
to challenge either a preliminary ruling on jurisdiction or a final award on the
merits which involved the assumption of jurisdiction where it was said that none
existed. In deciding what procedure is suitable so as to provide for a fair *b*
resolution of the dispute he must have regard to cost-efficiency and the need to
avoid unnecessary delay. In this connection two observations are relevant:
(i) there is nothing in the 1996 Act to suggest that a preliminary ruling on
jurisdiction should involve a less comprehensive investigation of evidence than
determination of the merits by a final award; and (ii) the very availability of the
s 67(1)(a) jurisdiction which necessarily involves the arbitrator already having *c*
decided to determine jurisdiction as a preliminary issue necessarily recognises
that a decision to take that course may, in some cases, be consistent with his duty
under s 33(1)(b). In other words, at least the mere fact that the arbitrator adopts
a course which may involve the issue of his jurisdiction being first determined by
him and then all over again by the court cannot without more be used as a basis *d*
for an allegation of breach of his duty under s 33(1)(b).

[84] It is thus perfectly clear that an arbitrator may be entitled to take the view
that it would be more efficient in time and cost to rule on his own jurisdiction at
the outset, even if that involves deciding whether there was a binding contract to
arbitrate and even if his decision on that matter gives rise to a conclusion in
respect of a major issue on the merits of the underlying claim in the arbitration. *e*
The suggestion that in all those cases where those issues are or nearly are
co-extensive the arbitrator should be shut out from determining his own
jurisdiction is, in my judgment, quite unsustainable. Provided that he has
satisfied himself that such a course is time-efficient and cost-efficient and fair to
all parties, the arbitrator should not be deterred from taking that course simply *f*
because the issues on jurisdiction and liability are co-extensive.

[85] Further, intervention under s 68 should be invoked only in a clear case of
serious irregularity. The court's powers to interfere with an arbitrator's
discretionary decision as to how he should exercise his jurisdiction under s 30(1)
should not be engaged unless it is clear that in exercising his discretion he has
failed to have regard to the relevant facts and to his duty under s 33. Unless he *g*
has arrived at a conclusion which no reasonable arbitrator could have arrived at
in the case in question having regard to his duties under s 33, it cannot be said that
his decision is capable of being characterised as a serious irregularity. This
threshold for intervention by the court has long been recognised in the field of the
courts' supervisory jurisdiction as appropriately preserving the finality of awards *h*
and party autonomy. Thus in *Pioneer Shipping Ltd v BTP Tioxide Ltd, The Nema*
[1981] 2 All ER 1030 at 1039 and 1041, [1982] AC 724 at 742 and 744, Lord Diplock
adopted the *Edwards v Bairstow* test (see *Edwards (Inspector of Taxes) v Bairstow* [1955]
3 All ER 48, [1956] AC 14) for the purposes of decisions of the courts as to leave to
appeal against an arbitrator's conclusion on whether the facts were such as to *j*
frustrate the commercial purpose of the contract. Where the matter in issue is
the exercise of an arbitrator's discretion as to how to exercise his jurisdiction
under s 30(1) there is obviously an even stronger case for the irrationality test.

[86] The arbitrator's letter of 11 October 2000 does not explain in terms of cost-
efficiency or the avoidance of unnecessary delay why he decided to determine
jurisdiction as a preliminary issue. However, there were clearly grounds upon

a
which it was open to him to do so. First, there was, at the time when his decision was made, much to be said for resolving that issue separately from overall liability. Thus, it might not necessarily follow that under the applicable law, if Daginov had authority to bind Kalmneft to the arbitration agreement, he also had authority to bind it to the substantive terms of the prepayment agreement. Secondly, there might be real issues in addition to that of whether the
b prepayment agreement was binding, such as whether the reimbursement provision had been triggered and quantum. If so, there might be much to be said for resolving at the outset whether he had jurisdiction so that costs were not needlessly incurred on issues that might never arise. Further, if he decided at the outset that the arbitration agreement was binding, the parties might be persuaded to negotiate a settlement of the claim in the belief that he would
c ultimately hold that the prepayment agreement was also binding.

[87] Having regard to these considerations, it is not arguable that no reasonable arbitrator acting with due regard to his duty under s 33 would have arrived at the same decision as Mr Berkeley.

[88] The second matter said to amount to a serious irregularity relates to the
d opportunity given by the arbitrator to Kalmneft to present its case on the jurisdiction issue. In particular, it is said that the order of 11 October did not give Kalmneft a reasonable time to put its case and did not make it clear that the arbitrator would proceed to his award immediately after receiving Glencore's submission in reply.

[89] In response to that order Kalmneft could have asked for more time to assemble its evidence and get documents translated or notarially attested if that
e time was needed. Further, it could have requested a hearing limited to the question of jurisdiction, as envisaged by para 2 of the order, to enable oral testimony to be given. It is, in my judgment, quite clear that it was open to either party to request an oral hearing when they put in their written submissions and that if neither of them did so, that would be the end of the presentation of their
f respective cases prior to an award. The argument advanced on behalf of Kalmneft that, following the submission of Glencore's reply submissions, if it had not requested an oral hearing, there would be an open-ended period before the issue of an award during which it was to be open to Kalmneft to request an oral hearing or to reply in writing is, in my judgment, quite unsustainable. The order obviously means that, if a party wants an oral hearing, it has to request it when it
g sends in its written submissions.

[90] Accordingly, the argument that the arbitrator was guilty of any serious irregularity in the conduct of the proceedings is confronted by what are, in my judgment, insurmountable obstacles.

[91] There is, however, an even more insurmountable obstacle to success on
h the s 68 application. The applicant has to show that if there has been serious irregularity it has caused substantial injustice to that party. In order to make good that element of the grounds for relief, it has to be shown that the applicant has been prejudiced by the lack of the just conduct of the arbitration. If he relies on being deprived of the opportunity of making further submissions, he cannot
j merely complain that the opportunity was not provided; he has to go on to say how he would probably have used it. If he had no further material submissions to make and no further material evidence to present, he will hardly be able to establish substantial injustice. Further, the substantiality of any injustice on that account has to be tested against the availability of the facility for challenging the ruling on jurisdiction under s 67. Even if an arbitrator makes a ruling on the basis of incomplete evidence, it is always open to the losing party to challenge that

ruling in court, for which purpose he can adduce additional evidence and
arguments: see for example, *Azov Shipping Co v Baltic Shipping Co (No 3)* [1999] *a*
2 All ER (Comm) 453. Consequently, even if evidence has been shut out before
the arbitrator, any prejudice to the losing party is ameliorated by his opportunity
to adduce that evidence under s 67 in the course of challenging the arbitrator's
ruling. Although there might be cases where serious prejudice was suffered in
spite of the opportunities under s 67, where, for example, a key witness had died, *b*
these cases are likely to be uncommon.

[92] In the present case there is no evidence as to whether or how Kalmneft
would have availed itself of a further opportunity to put forward further
submissions or further evidence or whether it would have requested an oral
hearing. Indeed, following its receipt of the arbitrator's ruling, it never
complained that it had been deprived of any further opportunity to do so. There *c*
is thus simply no case at all on substantial injustice attributable to the lack of
opportunity for further evidence or an oral hearing. Nor is there any evidence of
substantial injustice due to the alleged failure of the arbitrator to perform his
duties under s 33(1)(b).

[93] I therefore conclude that, even if there were an extension of time in this *d*
case, there is no realistic prospect of the s 68 application succeeding. Accordingly,
taking into account the extent of the delay, the lack of a satisfactory explanation
for it and the intrinsic weakness of the application, time should not be extended
in this case. The other criteria are incapable of outweighing these considerations.

The application to remove the arbitrator   *e*
[94] This application is based on the submission that the arbitrator has failed
to conduct the proceedings properly and that as a result substantial injustice has
been or will be caused to Kalmneft. The 1996 Act does not impose a 28-day time
limit for such applications and there is therefore no application for an extension
of time.   *f*
[95] The 1996 Act does not define failure 'properly to conduct the proceedings',
but the clear intent of the provision must involve at least some form of serious
irregularity under s 68. The evidence relied upon in support of the application is
the same as that relied upon in support of the s 68 application. As to that I have
already concluded that there is no realistic case on serious irregularity in any of
the respects complained of.   *g*
[96] Indeed, even if it were established that serious irregularity had been made
out on any other grounds relied upon, I should not have ordered the removal of
the arbitrator. This is a step which should be taken only if the serious irregularity
is such that it may reasonably be concluded that there is a serious risk that the
arbitrator's future conduct of the proceedings will not be in accordance with his *h*
duties under s 33. That must be the test in cases such as this where there is no
reliance on s 24(1)(a) ('that circumstances exist that give rise to justifiable doubts
as to his impartiality').
[97] In the present case the evidence goes nowhere near showing that there
would be a serious risk of the arbitrator failing to comply in future with his duties
under s 33 or that substantial injustice would thereby be caused to Kalmneft.   *j*
[98] The application under s 24 therefore also fails.

Applications dismissed.

James Wilson   Barrister (NZ).

a   # Director General of Fair Trading v First National Bank plc
    ## [2001] UKHL 52

b   HOUSE OF LORDS
    LORD BINGHAM OF CORNHILL, LORD STEYN, LORD HOPE OF CRAIGHEAD, LORD MILLETT
    AND LORD RODGER OF EARLSFERRY
    2, 3, 25 OCTOBER 2001

    Consumer credit – Agreement – Form and content of agreement – Standard form
c   *agreement – Unfair terms – Good faith – Bank making loans to consumers under*
    standard form regulated credit agreement – Agreement requiring borrower to pay
    interest after judgment at contractual rate – Whether provision for post-judgment
    interest subject to assessment as to fairness – Whether provision unfair – Unfair Terms
    in Consumer Contracts Regulations 1994, regs 3(2), 4(1).

d   *Contract – Consumer contracts – Unfair terms – Bank making loans to consumers under*
    standard form regulated credit agreement – Agreement requiring borrower to pay
    interest after judgment at contractual rate – Whether provision for post-judgment
    interest subject to assessment as to fairness – Whether provision unfair – Unfair Terms
    in Consumer Contracts Regulations 1994, regs 3(2), 4(1).

e   The appellant, a bank licensed to carry on consumer credit business, lent money
    under a standard form credit agreement regulated by the Consumer Credit Act
    1974. Under condition 8 of the agreement, the bank was entitled, on default of
    an instalment, to demand payment of the balance and interest outstanding.
    Condition 8 further provided that interest on the amount that became payable
f   would be charged at the contractual rate until payment, after as well as before any
    judgment, and that such obligation was to be independent of and not to merge
    with the judgment (the interest provision). In the absence of such a provision, a
    lender seeking to enforce a regulated credit agreement in the county court, which
    had exclusive jurisdiction in such proceedings, would have been unable to
g   recover post-judgment interest since the ordinary contractual obligation to pay
    interest would merge in the judgment and the county court was precluded by the
    County Courts (Interest on Judgments Debts) Order 1991 from awarding statutory
    interest on a money judgment in such proceedings. As a result of the interest
    provision, however, a judgment debtor who had fully complied with an order to
h   pay the debt by instalments under s 71[a] of the County Courts Act 1984 could find
    himself facing a continuing liability to the bank in respect of post-judgment
    contractual interest. The Director General of Fair Trading therefore applied for
    an injunction restraining use of, or reliance on, the interest provision on the
    ground that it was an 'unfair term' within the meaning of reg 4(1)[b] of the Unfair
    Terms in Consumer Contracts Regulations 1994, which implemented Council
j   Directive (EEC) 93/13. Regulation 4(1) defined unfair term as any term which,
    contrary to the requirement of good faith, caused a significant imbalance in the

    a   Section 71, so far as material, provides: '(1) Where a judgment is given or an order is made by a
        county court under which a sum of money of any amount is payable ... the court may, as it thinks
        fit, order the money to be paid ... by such instalments payable at such time as the court may fix ...'
    b   Regulation 4 is set out at [13], below

parties' rights and obligations under the contract to the detriment of the
consumer. In determining whether a term satisfied the requirement of good a
faith, the court was required to have regard to the matters specified in Sch 2^c to
the regulations, including the strength of the parties' bargaining position and the
extent to which the seller or supplier had dealt fairly and equitably with the
consumer. On the application, the bank relied, inter alia, on reg 3(2)(b)^d which
provided that, in so far as it was in plain, intelligible language, a term which b
concerned the adequacy of the price or remuneration, as against the goods or
services sold or supplied, was not to be assessed as to its fairness. The judge
rejected the bank's contention that the interest provision fell within reg 3(2)(b),
but concluded that it was not unfair within the meaning of reg 4(1). On the
Director General's appeal, the Court of Appeal agreed with the judge that the
interest provision fell outside reg 3(2)(b), but differed from him on the question c
of unfairness, holding that the provision was unfair to the extent that it enabled
the bank to obtain an order for payment by instalments under s 71 of 1984 Act
without the court considering whether to make a time order under s 129^e of the
1974 Act or, if it did make such an order, whether also to make an order to reduce
the contractual interest under s 136^f of that Act. Accordingly, the appeal was d
allowed, but the court did not grant the Director General an injunction. Instead,
it accepted an undertaking from the bank (subject to appeal) that it would draw
the attention of borrowers to the court's powers under ss 129 and 136 of the 1974
Act, and would not enforce a claim to post-judgment contractual interest after
the court had made an instalment order unless the court had considered whether
to exercise those powers. On its appeal to the House of Lords, the bank again e
relied on reg 3(2)(b) of the 1994 regulations while submitting that the interest
provision was, in any event, fair. For his part, the Director General contended
that the provision was unfair on a ground wider than that found by the Court of
Appeal, namely that it denied the borrower the protection afforded by the 1991
order in relation to post-judgment interest. f

Held – (1) Regulation 3(2)(b) of the 1994 regulations did not apply to the interest
provision. The object of the regulations and the directive was to protect
consumers against the inclusion of unfair and prejudicial terms in standard form
contracts into which they entered, and that object would plainly be frustrated if
reg 3(2)(b) were so broadly interpreted as to cover any terms other than those g
falling squarely within it. The interest provision, as part of a provision prescribing
the consequences of default, plainly did not fall within it. It did not concern the
adequacy of the interest earned by the bank as its remuneration but was designed
to ensure that its entitlement to interest did not come to an end on the entry of
judgment. It was an ancillary provision, not one concerned with the adequacy of h
the bank's remuneration as against the services supplied. Accordingly, it was
necessary to consider the fairness of the interest provision (see [12], [34], [40], [42],
[43], [53], [62], below).

   (2) The interest provision was not unfair within the meaning of reg 4(1) of the
1994 regulations. Whether a given term was or was not unfair depended on j
whether it caused a significant imbalance in the parties' rights and obligations

---

c   Schedule 2 is set out at [13], below
d   Regulation 3(2) is set out at [9], below
e   Section 129, so far as material, is set out at [7], below
f   Section 136 is set out at [7], below

a under the contract. That involved looking at the contract as a whole, considering the position of typical parties when it was made. The requirement of good faith in that context was one of fair and open dealing. Openness required that the terms should be expressed fully, clearly and legibly, containing no concealed pitfalls or traps. Appropriate prominence should be given to terms which might operate disadvantageously to the customer. Fair dealing required that a supplier *b* should not, whether deliberately or unconsciously, take advantage of the consumer's necessity, indigence, lack of experience, unfamiliarity with the subject matter of the contract, weak bargaining position or any other factor listed in or analogous to those listed in Sch 2 to the regulations. The interest provision could not be said to cause a significant imbalance in the parties' rights and obligations under the contract to the detriment of the consumer in a manner or *c* to an extent which was contrary to the requirement of good faith. The essential bargain was that the bank would make funds available to the borrower which the latter would repay, over a period, with interest. Neither party could suppose that the bank would willingly forgo any part of its principal or interest. If the bank thought that outcome at all likely, it would not lend. If there were any room for *d* doubt about the borrower's obligation to repay the principal in full with interest, that obligation was very clearly and unambiguously expressed in the conditions of the contract. There was nothing unbalanced or detrimental to the consumer in that obligation, and the interest provision could not be stigmatised as unfair on the ground that it violated or undermined a statutory regime enacted for the protection of consumers. The 1974 Act did not prohibit terms providing for *e* post-judgment interest, and such a prohibition would doubtless have been enacted if it had been recognised as a desirable form of protection. Nor did the 1974 Act require notice to be given of the effects of ss 129 and 136. Regulation 4 was directed to the unfairness of a contract term, not the use which a supplier might make of a term which was in itself fair. Accordingly, the appeal would be *f* allowed (see [17], [20], [22], [24], [25], [36], [38]–[40], [45], [46], [53], [57], [62], [66], below).

Decision of the Court of Appeal [2000] 2 All ER 759 reversed.

Notes
For unfair terms in consumer contracts, see 9(1) *Halsbury's Laws* (4th edn reissue) *g* paras 790–796.

For the Consumer Credit Act 1974, ss 129, 136, see 11 *Halsbury's Statutes* (4th edn) (2000 reissue) 109, 113.

For the County Courts Act 1984, s 71, see 11 *Halsbury's Statutes* (4th edn) (2000 reissue) 745.

h For the County Courts (Interest on Judgment Debts) Order 1991, see 3 *Halsbury's Statutory Instruments* (2001 issue) 661.

As from 1 October 1999, the Unfair Terms in Consumer Contracts Regulations 1994 were revoked and replaced by the Unfair Terms in Consumer Contracts Regulations 1999.

j
Cases referred to in opinions
Arnott v Redfern (1826) 3 Bing 353.
Bank of Scotland v Davis 1982 SLT 20, Ct of Sess.
Bank of Scotland v Forsyth 1969 SLT (Sh Ct) 15, Sh Ct.
Ealing LBC v El Isaac [1980] 2 All ER 548, [1980] 1 WLR 932, CA.
Economic Life Assurance Society v Usborne [1902] AC 147, HL.

Forward Trust Ltd v Whymark [1989] 3 All ER 915, [1990] 2 QB 670, [1989] 3 WLR
1229, CA.

Interfoto Picture Library Ltd v Stiletto Visual Programmes Ltd [1988] 1 All ER 348,
[1989] QB 433, [1988] 2 WLR 615, CA.

Sneyd, Re, ex p Fewings (1883) 25 Ch D 338, CA.

Southern and District Finance plc v Barnes [1996] 1 FCR 679, CA.

Appeal

First National Bank plc appealed with permission of the Appeal Committee of the
House of Lords given on 29 November 2000 from the decision of the Court of
Appeal (Peter Gibson, Waller and Buxton LJJ) on 3 February 2000 ([2000] 2 All ER
759, [2000] QB 672) allowing an appeal by the respondent, the Director General
of Fair Trading, from the order of Evans-Lombe J on 30 July 1999 ([2000] 1 All ER
240, [2000] 1 WLR 98) dismissing the Director General's application for an
injunction restraining the bank from (i) including in any agreement with a
consumer any contractual term or provision having the object or effect of
(a) making interest payable on the amount of any judgment obtained by the bank
for sums owing by a consumer under an agreement regulated by the Consumer
Credit Act 1974, or (b) making interest payable upon interest; (ii) enforcing or
seeking to enforce any such term which had already been included in any existing
agreement with a consumer to which the Unfair Terms in Consumer Contracts
Regulations 1994 applied; (iii) otherwise using or seeking to use any similar term,
or term having like effect; and (iv) recommending the use of any similar term, or
term having like effect. The facts are set out in the opinion of Lord Bingham of
Cornhill.

Lord Goodhart QC, Malcolm Waters QC and *Frederick Philpott* (instructed by *Davis &
Co*) for the bank.

Jonathan Crow and *John McCaughran* (instructed by the *Treasury Solicitor*) for the
Director General.

Their Lordships took time for consideration.

25 October 2001. The following opinions were delivered.

LORD BINGHAM OF CORNHILL.

[1] My Lords, First National Bank plc (the bank) is licensed to carry on
consumer credit business. It is a major lender in the market and has lent large
sums to borrowers under credit agreements regulated under the Consumer
Credit Act 1974. Such agreements are made on its printed form which contains
a number of standard terms. The Director General of Fair Trading (the Director),
in exercising powers conferred on him by reg 8 of the Unfair Terms in Consumer
Contracts Regulations 1994, SI 1994/3159 (the regulations), sought an injunction
to restrain use of or reliance on one such standard term on the ground that it was
unfair. The bank resisted the Director's application on two grounds. The first,
rejected by Evans-Lombe J at first instance ([2000] 1 All ER 240, [2000] 1 WLR 98)
and the Court of Appeal (Peter Gibson, Waller and Buxton LJJ ([2000] 2 All ER
759, [2000] QB 672)), was that the fairness provisions of the regulations did not
apply to the term in question. The second, accepted by the judge but partially
rejected by the Court of Appeal, was that the term in question was not unfair. In
this appeal to the House the bank again relies on both these arguments. The

a   Director seeks to uphold the decision of the Court of Appeal but contends that the term was more fundamentally unfair than the Court of Appeal held it to be. Thus there are two broad questions before the House: (1) Do the fairness provisions of the regulations apply to the term in question? (2) If so, is the term unfair and, if it is, on what ground?

[2] By its standard form of regulated credit agreement the bank agrees to
b   make a sum of money available to the borrower for a specified period in consideration of the borrower's agreement to repay that sum by specified instalments on specified dates with interest at a specified rate. Condition 4 of the bank's standard form provided:

c   'The rate of interest will be charged on a day to day basis on the outstanding balance and will be debited to the Customer's account monthly in arrears ...'

and provided that the rate of interest might be varied. Condition 8 of the agreement was in these terms:

d   'Time is of the essence for making all repayments to FNB as they fall due. If any repayment instalment is unpaid for more than 7 days after it became due, FNB may serve a notice on the Customer requiring payment before a specified date not less than 7 days later. If the repayment instalment is not paid in full by that date, FNB will be entitled to demand payment of the balance on the Customer's account and interest then outstanding together
e   with all reasonable legal and other costs charges and expenses claimed or incurred by FNB in trying to obtain the repayment of the unpaid instalment of such balance and interest. *Interest on the amount which becomes payable shall be charged in accordance with Condition 4, at the rate stated in para D overleaf (subject to variation) until payment after as well as before any judgement (such
f   obligation to be independent of and not to merge with the judgement).'*

Emphasis has been added to the last sentence of this condition, since it is to that sentence alone that the Director's objection relates. I shall refer to this sentence as 'the term'.

[3] The bank's stipulation that interest shall be charged until payment after as
g   well as before any judgment, such obligation to be independent of and not to merge with the judgment, is readily explicable. At any rate since *Re Sneyd, ex p Fewings* (1883) 25 Ch D 338, not challenged but accepted without demur by the House of Lords in *Economic Life Assurance Society v Usborne* [1902] AC 147, the understanding of lawyers in England has been as accurately summarised by the
h   Court of Appeal of the judgment under appeal:

        'It is trite law in England that once a judgment is obtained under a loan agreement for a principal sum and judgment is entered, the contract merges in the judgment and the principal becomes owed under the judgment and not under the contract. If under the contract interest on any principal sum is
j   due, absent special provisions the contract is considered ancillary to the covenant to pay the principal, with the result that if judgment is obtained for the principal, the covenant to pay interest merges in the judgment. Parties to a contract may agree that a covenant to pay interest will not merge in any judgment for the principal sum due, and in that event interest may be charged under the contract on the principal sum due even after judgment for that sum.' (See [2000] 2 All ER 759 at 765, [2000] QB 672 at 682.)

[4] To ensure that they were able to recover not only the full sum of principal
outstanding but also any interest accruing on that sum after judgment as well as   a
before, it became the practice for lenders to include in their credit agreements a
term to the effect of the term here in issue. If such a provision had not been
included, a lender seeking to enforce a loan agreement against a borrower in the
High Court would suffer prejudice only to the extent that the statutory rate of
interest on judgment debts at the material time is lower than the contractual   b
interest rate, because the High Court has, since 1838, had power to award
statutory interest on a judgment debt until payment.

[5] But a lender seeking to enforce a regulated credit agreement is in a different
position. He is obliged by s 141 of the 1974 Act to sue in the county court. Until
the Lord Chancellor, exercising his power under s 74 of the County Courts Act
1984, made the County Courts (Interest on Judgment Debts) Order 1991, SI   c
1991/1184, the county court lacked power to award statutory interest on any
judgment debt and, when such a general power was conferred by the order,
judgments given in proceedings to recover money due under agreements
regulated by the 1974 Act were expressly excluded from its scope. It was further
provided in the order: d

'3. Where under the terms of the relevant judgment payment of a
judgment debt—(a) is not required to be made until a specified date, or (b) is
to be made by instalments, interest shall not accrue under this Order—(i) until
that date, or (ii) on the amount of any instalment, until it falls due, as the case
may be.'   e

[6] Thus a lender under a regulated credit agreement who obtains judgment
against a defaulting borrower in the county court will be entitled to recover the
principal outstanding at the date of judgment and interest accrued up to that date
but will not be entitled to an order for statutory interest after that date, and even
if the court had power to award statutory post-judgment interest it could not do   f
so, in any case where an instalment order had been made, unless there had been
a default in the due payment of any instalment. The lender may recover
post-judgment interest only if he has the benefit of an independent covenant by
the borrower entitling him to recover such interest. There is nothing to preclude
inclusion of such a covenant in a regulated credit agreement, unless it falls foul of   g
the fairness requirement in the regulations.

[7] Section 71 of the 1984 Act conferred a general power on the county court,
where any judgment was given or order made for payment of a money sum, to
order that the money might be paid 'by such instalments payable at such times as
the court may fix'. The 1974 Act also conferred on the county court three powers   h
relevant for present purposes. First, the court was empowered to make a time
order. Sections 129 and 130 of the Act, so far as relevant, provided:

'129.—(1) If it appears to the court just to do so ... (c) in an action brought
by a creditor or owner to enforce a regulated agreement or any security, or
recover possession of any goods or land to which a regulated agreement   j
relates, the court may make an order under this section (a "time order").

(2) A time order shall provide for one or both of the following, as the court
considers just—(a) the payment by the debtor or hirer or any surety of any
sum owed under a regulated agreement or a security by such instalments,
payable at such times, as the court, having regard to the means of the debtor
or hirer and any surety, considers reasonable ...

a
130.—(1) Where in accordance with rules of court an offer to pay any sum by instalments is made by the debtor or hirer and accepted by the creditor or owner, the court may in accordance with rules of court make a time order under section 129(2)(a) giving effect to the offer without hearing evidence of means ...'

b
Secondly, s 136 provided:

'The court may in an order made by it under this Act include such provision as it considers just for amending any agreement or security in consequence of a term of the order.'

c
Thirdly, by ss 137, 138 and 139 of the Act the county court was given power to reopen credit agreements 'so as to do justice between the parties' if it found a credit bargain to be 'extortionate'. A credit bargain was defined as extortionate if it—

d
'(a) requires the debtor or a relative of his to make payments (whether unconditionally, or on certain contingencies) which are grossly exorbitant, or (b) otherwise grossly contravenes ordinary principles of fair dealing.' (Section 138.)

In determining whether a credit bargain was extortionate regard was to be had to such evidence as might be adduced concerning interest rates prevailing at the time the bargain was made, a number of factors relating to the debtor and the circumstances of the transaction and 'any other relevant considerations'.

e
[8] The provisions of the regulations directly at issue in these proceedings must be considered in more detail below. It should, however, be noted that the regulations were made to give effect in the United Kingdom to Council Directive (EEC) 93/13 on unfair terms in consumer contracts (OJ 1993 L95 p 29). (They were superseded by further regulations in 1999 (Unfair Terms in Consumer Contracts Regulations 1999, SI 1999/2083), but these are to very much the same effect, do not govern this case and need not be further considered.) It is common ground that the regulations should be construed so as to give effect to the directive, to which resort may properly be made for purposes of construction. Regulation 5, giving effect to art 6 of the directive, provides:

f

g
'(1) An unfair term in a contract concluded with a consumer by a seller or supplier shall not be binding on the consumer.
(2) The contract shall continue to bind the parties if it is capable of continuing in existence without the unfair term.'

h
Thus the Director's challenge, although addressed only to the bank's use of and reliance on the term, if upheld, may well invalidate any similar term in any other regulated agreement made by any other lender with any borrower. The questions at issue are accordingly of general public importance.

j
(1) The applicability of the regulations
[9] Regulation 3(2) of the regulations provides:

'In so far as it is in plain, intelligible language, no assessment shall be made of the fairness of any term which—(a) defines the main subject matter of the contract, or (b) concerns the adequacy of the price or remuneration, as against the goods or services sold or supplied.'

This gives effect, almost word for word, to art 4(2) of the directive, although
some light may be shed on its meaning by the nineteenth recital to the directive: a

> 'Whereas, for the purposes of this Directive, assessment of unfair character
> shall not be made of terms which describe the main subject matter of the
> contract nor the quality/price ratio of the goods or services supplied;
> whereas the main subject matter of the contract and the price/quality ratio
> may nevertheless be taken into account in assessing the fairness of other   b
> terms; whereas it follows, inter alia, that in insurance contracts, the terms
> which clearly define or circumscribe the insured risk and the insurer's
> liability shall not be subject to such assessment since these restrictions are
> taken into account in calculating the premium paid by the consumer ...'

[10] In reliance on reg 3(2)(b) Lord Goodhart QC, on behalf of the bank,   c
submitted that no assessment might be made of the fairness of the term because
it concerns the adequacy of the bank's remuneration as against the services supplied,
namely the loan of money. A bank's remuneration under a credit agreement is
the receipt of interest. The term, by entitling the bank to post-judgment interest,
concerns the quantum and thus the adequacy of that remuneration. This was the   d
more obviously true if, as Lord Goodhart submitted, the merger rule as
commonly understood is unsound. Where judgment is given for outstanding
principal payable under a loan agreement and interest accrued up to the date of
judgment, those claims (he accepted) are merged in the judgment. That is a
conventional application of the principle of res judicata. But no claim for future
interest has been the subject of adjudication by the court and such a claim cannot e
be barred as res judicata. The borrower's covenant to pay interest on any part of
the principal loan outstanding thus survives such a judgment, and *Ex p Fewings*
(1883) 25 Ch D 338 was wrong to lay down any contrary principle. Lord Goodhart
adopted the observation of Templeman LJ in *Ealing LBC v El Isaac* [1980] 2 All ER
548 at 551, [1980] 1 WLR 932 at 937:   f

> 'I do not for myself understand how a debt payable with interest until
> actual repayment can be merged in a judgment without interest or with a
> different rate of interest payable thereafter.'

[11] To this submission Mr Crow, representing the Director, gave two short
answers. First, condition 8, of which the term forms part, is a default provision.   g
Its purpose, and its only purpose, is to prescribe the consequences of a default by
the borrower. It does not lay down the rate of interest which the bank is entitled
to receive and the borrower bound to pay. It is an ancillary term, well outside the
bounds of reg 3(2)(b). Secondly, there is no merger 'rule' but only a rule of
construction. It is a question of construction of any given agreement whether the   h
borrower's covenant to pay interest is or is not to be understood as intended to
continue after judgment. But whatever the correct approach to merger, it is an
irrelevance. Even if a bank's borrower's covenant to pay interest is ordinarily to
be taken, as in Scotland (see *Bank of Scotland v Davis* 1982 SLT 20), to continue
until the full sum of principal is repaid, after as before judgment, the term remains   j
part of a default provision and not one falling within the provisions of reg 3(2)(b).
[12] In agreement with the judge and the Court of Appeal, I do not accept the
bank's submission on this issue. The regulations, as Professor Sir Guenter Treitel
QC has aptly observed (*The Law of Contract* (10th edn, 1999) p 248), 'are not
intended to operate as a mechanism of quality or price control' and reg 3(2) is of
'crucial importance in recognising the parties' freedom of contract with respect

a to the essential features of their bargain' (see p 249). But there is an important 'distinction between the term or terms which express the substance of the bargain and "incidental" (if important) terms which surround them' (*Chitty on Contracts* (28th edn, 1999) p 747 (para 15-025), 'Unfair Terms in Consumer Contracts'). The object of the regulations and the directive is to protect consumers against the inclusion of unfair and prejudicial terms in standard form b contracts into which they enter, and that object would plainly be frustrated if reg 3(2)(b) were so broadly interpreted as to cover any terms other than those falling squarely within it. In my opinion the term, as part of a provision prescribing the consequences of default, plainly does not fall within it. It does not concern the adequacy of the interest earned by the bank as its remuneration but is designed to ensure that the bank's entitlement to interest does not come to an end on the c entry of judgment. I do not think the bank's argument on merger advances its case. It appears that some judges in the past have been readier than I would be to infer that a borrower's covenant to pay interest was not intended to extend beyond the entry of judgment. But even if a borrower's obligation were ordinarily understood to extend beyond judgment even in the absence of an d independent covenant, it would not alter my view of the term as an ancillary provision and not one concerned with the adequacy of the bank's remuneration as against the services supplied. It is therefore necessary to address the second question.

(2) Unfairness

e [13] Regulation 4 of the regulations is entitled 'Unfair terms' and provides:

'(1) In these Regulations, subject to paragraphs (2) and (3) below, "unfair term" means any term which contrary to the requirement of good faith causes a significant imbalance in the parties' rights and obligations under the contract to the detriment of the consumer.

f (2) An assessment of the unfair nature of a term shall be made taking into account the nature of the goods or services for which the contract was concluded and referring, as at the time of the conclusion of the contract, to all circumstances attending the conclusion of the contract and to all the other terms of the contract or of another contract on which it is dependent.

g (3) In determining whether a term satisfies the requirement of good faith, regard shall be had in particular to the matters specified in Schedule 2 to these Regulations.

(4) Schedule 3 to these Regulations contains an indicative and non-exhaustive list of the terms which may be regarded as unfair.'

h Schedule 2 to the regulations provides:

'In making an assessment of good faith, regard shall be had in particular to—(a) the strength of the bargaining positions of the parties; (b) whether the consumer had an inducement to agree to the term; (c) whether the goods or services were sold or supplied to the special order of the consumer, and j (d) the extent to which the seller or supplier has dealt fairly and equitably with the consumer.'

Each of (a), (b) and (c) also appear in Sch 2 to the Unfair Contract Terms Act 1977 among the guidelines for application of the reasonableness test laid down by that statute, suggesting that some similarity of approach in applying the two tests may be appropriate. In a case such as the present, where the fairness of a term is

challenged in the absence of any individual consumer, little attention need be
paid to (b) and (c). It may, however, be assumed that any borrower is in a much *a*
weaker bargaining position than a large bank contracting on its own standard
form. (d) applies a general test of fair and equitable dealing between supplier and
consumer. Schedule 3 contains a list of indicative and illustrative terms which
may because of their object or effect be regarded as unfair. Examples are terms
which have the object or effect of '(e) requiring any consumer who fails to fulfil his *b*
obligation to pay a disproportionately high sum in compensation', '(i) irrevocably
binding the consumer to terms with which he had no real opportunity of
becoming acquainted before the conclusion of the contract', or '(k) enabling the
seller or supplier to alter unilaterally without a valid reason any characteristics of
the product or service to be provided'. It is not suggested that the term falls
within any specific entry in the list. It is common ground that fairness must be *c*
judged as at the date the contract is made, although account may properly be
taken of the likely effect of any term which is then agreed and said to be unfair.

[14] The fifteenth and sixteenth recitals to the directive are relevant. They
provide:

'Whereas it is necessary to fix in a general way the criteria for assessing the *d*
unfair character of contract terms;
Whereas the assessment, according to the general criteria chosen, of the
unfair character of terms, in particular in sale or supply activities of a public
nature providing collective services which take account of solidarity among
users, must be supplemented by a means of making an overall evaluation of *e*
the different interests involved; whereas this constitutes the requirement of
good faith; whereas, in making an assessment of good faith, particular regard
shall be had to the strength of the bargaining positions of the parties, whether
the consumer had an inducement to agree to the term and whether the
goods or services were sold or supplied to the special order of the consumer; *f*
whereas the requirement of good faith may be satisfied by the seller or
supplier where he deals fairly and equitably with the other party whose
legitimate interests he has to take into account ...'

Article 3(1) of the directive is the counterpart of reg 4(1), and is in terms which
are for present purposes indistinguishable. The directive has no annex to the *g*
effect of Sch 2 to the regulations, but has an annex in terms identical to those of
Sch 3.

[15] The trial judge first asked himself whether the term was inherently unfair
and concluded that it was not because a borrower, to whom the effect of the term
had been fully explained, would not have regarded it as unfair that he would be *h*
obliged, in the event of his default, to pay interest on the full sum owed to the
lender until complete repayment, even if the court permitted him to pay by
instalments extending over a substantial period ([2000] 1 All ER 240 at 249–250,
[2000] 1 WLR 98 at 108). The judge then considered whether the term was unfair
because a defaulting borrower would not expect to bear an interest charge over
and above any instalments ordered by the court, and whether the term deprived *j*
the consumer of a benefit or advantage which he might reasonably expect to
receive. The judge resolved these issues in favour of the bank ([2000] 1 All ER 240
at 250–253, [2000] 1 WLR 98 at 108–111), observing that—

'if the provisions of ss 129 and 136 of the 1974 Act are correctly used by the
courts the inclusion of the provisions of cl 8 need not operate to impose on

a   a borrower post-judgment interest where it would not be appropriate and
     just to do so.' (See [2000] 1 All ER 240 at 253, [2000] 1 WLR 98 at 111.)

[16] The Court of Appeal differed from the judge on the question of
unfairness. In the judgment of the court it was said:

b   'In our judgment the relevant term is unfair within the meaning of the
          regulations to the extent that it enables the bank to obtain judgment against
          a debtor under a regulated agreement and an instalment order under s 71 of
          the Act of 1984 without the court considering whether to make a time order,
          or, if it does and makes a time order, whether also to make an order under
          s 136 to reduce the contractual interest rate. The bank, with its strong
c   bargaining position as against the relatively weak position of the consumer,
          has not adequately considered the consumer's interests in this respect. In
          our view the relevant term in that respect does create unfair surprise and so
          does not satisfy the test of good faith, it does cause a significant imbalance in
          the rights and obligations of the parties by allowing the bank to obtain
          interest after judgment in circumstances when it would not obtain interest
d   under the Act of 1984 and the 1991 order and no specific benefit to
          compensate the borrower is provided, and it operates to the detriment of
          that consumer who has to pay the interest.' (See [2000] 2 All ER 759 at 770,
          [2000] QB 672 at 688.)

e   The Court of Appeal did not grant an injunction but instead accepted
     undertakings offered by the bank (subject to appeal) which would bring to the
     borrower's attention the powers of the court under ss 129 and 136 of the 1974 Act
     and ensure that a claim to post-judgment contractual interest would not be
     enforced by the bank after the court had made an instalment order unless the
     court's attention had previously been drawn to its powers under ss 129 and 136
f   and it had considered whether to exercise those powers.
     [17] The test laid down by reg 4(1), deriving as it does from art 3(1) of the
     directive, has understandably attracted much discussion in academic and
     professional circles and helpful submissions were made to the House on it. It is
     plain from the recitals to the directive that one of its objectives was partially to
     harmonise the law in this important field among all member states of the
g   European Union. The member states have no common concept of fairness or
     good faith, and the directive does not purport to state the law of any single
     member state. It lays down a test to be applied, whatever their pre-existing law,
     by all member states. If the meaning of the test were doubtful, or vulnerable to
     the possibility of differing interpretations in differing member states, it might be
h   desirable or necessary to seek a ruling from the European Court of Justice on its
     interpretation. But the language used in expressing the test, so far as applicable
     in this case, is in my opinion clear and not reasonably capable of differing
     interpretations. A term falling within the scope of the regulations is unfair if it
     causes a significant imbalance in the parties' rights and obligations under the
j   contract to the detriment of the consumer in a manner or to an extent which is
     contrary to the requirement of good faith. The requirement of significant
     imbalance is met if a term is so weighted in favour of the supplier as to tilt the
     parties' rights and obligations under the contract significantly in his favour. This
     may be by the granting to the supplier of a beneficial option or discretion or
     power, or by the imposing on the consumer of a disadvantageous burden or risk
     or duty. The illustrative terms set out in Sch 3 to the regulations provide very

good examples of terms which may be regarded as unfair; whether a given term is or is not to be so regarded depends on whether it causes a significant imbalance *a* in the parties' rights and obligations under the contract. This involves looking at the contract as a whole. But the imbalance must be to the detriment of the consumer; a significant imbalance to the detriment of the supplier, assumed to be the stronger party, is not a mischief which the regulations seek to address. The requirement of good faith in this context is one of fair and open dealing. *b* Openness requires that the terms should be expressed fully, clearly and legibly, containing no concealed pitfalls or traps. Appropriate prominence should be given to terms which might operate disadvantageously to the customer. Fair dealing requires that a supplier should not, whether deliberately or unconsciously, take advantage of the consumer's necessity, indigence, lack of experience, unfamiliarity with the subject matter of the contract, weak bargaining position or any other *c* factor listed in or analogous to those listed in Sch 2 of the regulations. Good faith in this context is not an artificial or technical concept; nor, since Lord Mansfield was its champion, is it a concept wholly unfamiliar to British lawyers. It looks to good standards of commercial morality and practice. Regulation 4(1) lays down a composite test, covering both the making and the substance of the contract, and *d* must be applied bearing clearly in mind the objective which the regulations are designed to promote.

[18] In support of his contention that the term is unfair the Director adduced evidence of complaints made to him by a number of borrowers. Some of these disclose a very highly unsatisfactory state of affairs. In one case a husband and wife borrowed £3,000 plus £443·70 for insurance to finance improvements to *e* their home. The principal was repayable over a five-year term by instalments of £84·89 plus £8·98 insurance. The borrowers fell into arrear and judgment was given for £3,953·11. The court ordered this sum to be paid by monthly instalments of £4·18, at which rate (it was calculated) the judgment debt would take 78 years to clear. Meanwhile, under the contract, interest would continue to accrue even if *f* the instalments were fully and punctually paid. The bank's deponent described these borrowers as—

> 'a good example of customers who demonstrated an ability easily to pay the instalments for home improvements when the credit was granted but thereafter appeared to have undertaken many other financial commitments *g* which seriously prejudiced their ability to pay [the bank].'

A financial statement prepared on these borrowers some months before the county court judgment is consistent with that assertion.

[19] For the Director, reliance was placed on the provisions in the 1991 order which denied the court power to order payment of statutory interest on money *h* judgments given under regulated agreements and precluded entitlement to interest in any case where payment by instalments had been ordered and the instalments had been fully and punctually paid. It was argued that the term was unfair because it denied the borrower the protection which those provisions afforded. It was argued, in the alternative, that the term was unfair for the more *j* limited reason upheld by the Court of Appeal.

[20] In judging the fairness of the term it is necessary to consider the position of typical parties when the contract is made. The borrower wants to borrow a sum of money, often quite a modest sum, often for purposes of improving his home. He discloses an income sufficient to finance repayment by instalments over the contract term. If he cannot do that, the bank will be unwilling to lend.

a The essential bargain is that the bank will make funds available to the borrower which the borrower will repay, over a period, with interest. Neither party could suppose that the bank would willingly forgo any part of its principal or interest. If the bank thought that outcome at all likely, it would not lend. If there were any room for doubt about the borrower's obligation to repay the principal in full with interest, that obligation is very clearly and unambiguously expressed in the *b* conditions of contract. There is nothing unbalanced or detrimental to the consumer in that obligation; the absence of such a term would unbalance the contract to the detriment of the lender.

[**21**] It seems clear, as the judge pointed out ([2000] 1 All ER 240 at 253, [2000] 1 WLR 98 at 111), that a secured lender who does not obtain a money judgment but instead proceeds for possession and sale under the mortgage may obtain *c* interest at the contract rate provided for in the mortgage down to the date when he is actually repaid, and in my opinion there is nothing unbalanced or detrimental to the consumer in that result either.

[**22**] Should it then be said that the provisions of the 1991 order render the term unfair, providing as it does for a continuing obligation to pay interest after *d* judgment notwithstanding the payment of instalments by the borrower in accordance with a court order? It is, I think, pertinent that the 1974 Act, which laid down a number of stipulations with which regulated agreements must comply, did not prohibit terms providing for post-judgment interest even though it required claims to enforce regulated agreements to be brought in the county court which could not at the time award statutory interest in any circumstances. *e* The 1974 Act was passed to protect consumers and such a prohibition would no doubt have been enacted had it been recognised as a necessary or desirable form of protection. The Crowther Committee, on whose report (Cmnd 4596) (1971) the Act was based, did not recommend such a prohibition; indeed, it contemplated the recovery of contractual interest (see paras 5.4.3, 6.6.33, *f* 6.6.44(iv) and 6.7.16). It is also pertinent that judgments based on regulated agreements appear to have been excluded from the scope of the county court's power to award statutory interest in response to observations of Lord Donaldson MR in *Forward Trust Ltd* v *Whymark* [1989] 3 All ER 915 at 921, [1990] 2 QB 670 at 681: but that was a case based on a flat rate agreement, in which the judgment in default would include a sum for future interest not yet accrued, in contrast with *g* a simple rate agreement of the present kind (see [2000] 1 All ER 240 at 252–253, [2000] 1 WLR 98 at 110–111 (Evans-Lombe J); [2000] 2 All ER 759 at 762, [2000] QB 672 at 679 (Court of Appeal)); the logic underpinning exclusion of statutory interest in the one case would not apply, at any rate with the same force, in the other. It is understandable that when a court is exercising a statutory power to *h* order payment by instalments it should not also be empowered to order payment of statutory interest if the instalments are duly paid, but the term is directed to the recovery of contractual and not statutory interest. I do not think that the term can be stigmatised as unfair on the ground that it violates or undermines a statutory regime enacted for the protection of consumers.

j [**23**] It is of course foreseeable that a borrower, no matter how honourable and realistic his intentions when entering into a credit agreement, may fall on hard times and find himself unable to honour his obligations. The bank's standard conditions recognise that possibility by providing for the contingency of default. The 1974 Act even more fully recognises that possibility, by providing for time orders to be made and providing that when a time order is made the terms of the underlying agreement may also be amended. These provisions are

clearly framed for the relief not of the borrower who, having the means to meet
his contractual obligations, chooses not to do so, but for the relief of those who
cannot pay or cannot pay without more time. Properly applied, these provisions
enable the undeserving borrower to be distinguished from the deserving and for
the contractual obligations of the deserving to be re-drawn in terms which
reasonably reflect such ability, if any, as he may then have to repay within a
reasonable period. Where problems arise in practice, it appears to be because
borrowers do not know of the effect of ss 129 and 136; neither the procedure for
giving notice of default to the borrower nor the prescribed county court forms
draw attention to them; and judgments will routinely be entered in the county
court without the court considering whether to exercise its power under the
sections.

[24] I have no hesitation in accepting the proposition, inherent in the
Director's submissions, that this situation is unacceptable. I have much greater
difficulty in deciding whether the difficulties derive, as the Court of Appeal
concluded, from the unfairness of the term or from the absence of procedural
safeguards for the consumer at the stage of default. When the contract is made,
default is a foreseeable contingency, not an expected outcome. It is not customary,
even in consumer contracts, for notice to be given to the consumer of statutory
reliefs open to him if he defaults. The 1974 Act does not require that notice of the
effect of ss 129 and 136 be given. The evidence contains examples of clauses used
by over 30 other lenders providing for the payment of interest after judgment,
and none alerts the borrower to these potential grounds of relief. Regulation 4 is
directed to the unfairness of a contract term, not the use which a supplier may
make of a term which is in itself fair. It is readily understandable that a borrower
may be disagreeably surprised if he finds that his contractual interest obligation
continues to mount despite his duly paying the instalments ordered by the court,
but it appears that the bank seeks to prevent that surprise by sending what is
described in the evidence as a standard form of letter:

'You need only pay the amount ordered by the Court under the terms of
the judgment but you should be aware that under the terms of the
agreement interest continues to accrue on your account. It is therefore in
your interest to increase the instalment paid as soon as possible otherwise a
much greater balance than the judgment debt may quickly build up.'

On balance, I do not consider that the term can properly be said to cause a
significant imbalance in the parties' rights and obligations under the contract to
the detriment of the consumer in a manner or to an extent which is contrary to
the requirement of good faith.

[25] I do not think that the issues raised in this appeal raise any question on
which the House requires a ruling from the European Court of Justice to enable
it to give judgment and I would not accordingly order a reference to be made.

[26] For the reasons I have given, and those given by each of my noble and
learned friends, I would allow the bank's appeal with costs in the House and the
Court of Appeal and restore the order of the judge.

[27] In conclusion, I would add a footnote on ss 129 and 136 of the 1974 Act.
In the course of argument the House was referred to the decision of the Court of
Appeal in *Southern and District Finance plc v Barnes* [1996] 1 FCR 679 and two
related appeals. The effect and interaction of ss 129 and 136 were there
considered.

[28] Of s 129 the court said (at 686):

a
'When a time order is made, it should normally be made for a stipulated period on account of temporary financial difficulty. If, despite the giving of time, the debtor is unlikely to be able to resume repayment of the total indebtedness by at least the amount of the contractual instalments, no time order should be made. In such circumstances it will be more equitable to allow the regulated agreement to be enforced.'

b
I would in general agree that time orders extending over very long periods of time are usually better avoided. But I note that the court dismissed an appeal against a judge who had rescheduled payments over a period of 15 years ('Though the Judge's methods were robust and his reasoning economical, his instincts were sound and his order just' ([1996] 1 FCR 679 at 689)), and the broad
c language of s 129 should be so construed as to permit the county court to make such order as seems to it just in all the circumstances.

[29] Of s 136 the court said (at 686):

'The court may include in a time order any amendment of the agreement, which it considers just to both parties, and which is a consequence of the
d term of the order.'

In the case already referred to the judge had ordered that no additional interest should be payable beyond that which had already accrued, and the Court of Appeal upheld his decision. It was right to do so: provided the amendment is a consequence of a term of the time order, the court should be ready to include in
e a time order any provision amending the agreement which it considers just to both parties.

LORD STEYN.

[30] My Lords, this is the first occasion on which the House has had the
f opportunity to examine an important branch of consumer law. It is therefore appropriate to consider the framework in which the questions before the House must be considered.

[31] As between the directive and the domestic implementing regulations, the former is the dominant text. Fortunately, the Unfair Terms in Consumer Contracts Regulations 1994, SI 1994/3159 (the regulations), and even more so the
g Unfair Terms in Consumer Contracts Regulations 1999, SI 1999/2083, appear to have implemented Council Directive (EEC) 93/13 (OJ 1993 L95 p 29) in domestic law in a manner which ought not to cause serious difficulty. The purpose of the directive is twofold, viz the promotion of fair standard contract forms to improve the functioning of the European market place and the protection of consumers
h throughout the European Community. The directive is aimed at contracts of adhesion, viz 'take it or leave it' contracts. It treats consumers as presumptively weaker parties and therefore fit for protection from abuses by stronger contracting parties. This is an objective which must throughout guide the interpretation of the directive as well as the implementing regulations. If contracting parties were able to
j avoid the application of the directive and regulations by exclusionary stipulations the regulatory scheme would be ineffective. The conclusion that the directive and regulations are mandatory is inescapable.

[32] The directive is not an altogether harmonious text. It reflects the pragmatic compromises which were necessary to arrive at practical solutions between member states with divergent legal systems. But, despite some inelegance and untidiness in the text, the general principle that the construction must be

adopted which promotes the effectiveness and practical value of the system
ought to overcome difficulties. And the concepts of the directive must be given   *a*
autonomous meanings so that there will be uniform application of the directive
so far as is possible.

[33] The directive made provision for a dual system of *ex casu* challenges and
pre-emptive or collective challenges by appropriate bodies (see art 7). This
system was domestically enacted in the regulations, with the Director General of   *b*
Fair Trading as the administering official to investigate and take action on
complaints (see reg 8). The 1999 regulations extended the system of enforcement
by including other bodies as qualified to undertake pre-emptive challenges. The
system of pre-emptive challenges is a more effective way of preventing the
continuing use of unfair terms and changing contracting practice than *ex casu*
actions (see Susan Bright 'Winning the battle against unfair contract terms' (2000)   *c*
20 LS 331, at 333–338). It is, however, to be noted that in a pre-emptive challenge
there is not a direct *lis* between the consumer and the other contracting party.
The directive and the regulations do not always distinguish between the two
situations. This point is illustrated by the emphasis in art 4(1) of the directive and
reg 4(2) on the relevance of particular circumstances affecting a contractual   *d*
relationship. The directive and the regulations must be made to work sensibly
and effectively and this can only be done by taking into account the effects of
contemplated or typical relationships between the contracting parties. Inevitably,
the primary focus of such a pre-emptive challenge is on issues of substantive
unfairness.
                                                                                           e
[34] Under the regulations, a term in a standard form contract that is unfair is
not binding on the consumer. But certain provisions, sometimes called core terms,
have been excepted from the regulatory regime. Regulation 3(2) so provides:

'In so far as it is in plain, intelligible language, no assessment shall be made
of the fairness of any term which—(a) defines the main subject matter of the   *f*
contract, or (b) concerns the adequacy of the price or remuneration, as
against the goods or services sold or supplied.'

Condition 8 of the contract, the only provision in dispute, is a default provision.
It prescribes remedies which only become available to the lender upon the default
of the consumer. For this reason the escape route of reg 3(2) is not available to the   *g*
bank. So far as the description of terms covered by reg 3(2) as core terms is
helpful at all, I would say that condition 8 of the contract is a subsidiary term. In
any event, reg 3(2) must be given a restrictive interpretation. Unless that is done
reg 3(2)(a) will enable the main purpose of the scheme to be frustrated by endless
formalistic arguments as to whether a provision is a definitional or an   *h*
exclusionary provision. Similarly, reg 3(2)(b) dealing with 'the adequacy of the
price of remuneration' must be given a restrictive interpretation. After all, in a
broad sense all terms of the contract are in some way related to the price or
remuneration. That is not what is intended. Even price escalation clauses have
been treated by the Director as subject to the fairness provision (see (2000) 20 LS   *j*
333, at 345 and 349). It would be a gaping hole in the system if such clauses were
not subject to the fairness requirement. For these further reasons I would reject
the argument of the bank that reg 3(2), and in particular 3(2)(b), take condition 8
outside the scope of the regulations.

[35] Given these conclusions the attack on the merger principle mounted by
the bank was misplaced. In any event, I am not willing to uphold criticism by the

a bank of the well-tried and tested principle of merger. I would therefore reject the bank's submissions under this heading.

[36] It is now necessary to refer to the provisions which prescribe how it should be determined whether a term is unfair. Implementing art 3(1) of the directive, reg 4(1) provides:

b '... "unfair term" means any term which contrary to the requirement of good faith causes a significant imbalance in the parties' rights and obligations under the contract to the detriment of the consumer.'

There are three independent requirements. But the element of detriment to the consumer may not add much. But it serves to make clear that the directive is aimed at significant imbalance against the consumer, rather than the seller or c supplier. The twin requirements of good faith and significant imbalance will in practice be determinative. Schedule 2 to the regulations, which explains the concept of good faith, provides that regard must be had, amongst other things, to the extent to which the seller or supplier has dealt fairly and equitably with the consumer. It is an objective criterion. Good faith imports, as Lord Bingham of d Cornhill has observed in his opinion, the notion of open and fair dealing (see also *Interfoto Picture Library Ltd v Stiletto Visual Programmes Ltd* [1988] 1 All ER 348, [1989] QB 433). And helpfully the commentary to the 2000 edition of Lando and Beale *Principles of European Contract Law* Pts I and II (combined and revised), prepared by the Commission of European Contract Law, explains that the purpose of the provision of good faith and fair dealing is 'to enforce community e standards of fairness and reasonableness in commercial transactions' (see p 113); a fortiori that is true of consumer transactions. Schedule 3 to the regulations (which corresponds to the annex to the directive) is best regarded as a checklist of terms which must be regarded as potentially vulnerable. The examples given in Sch 3 convincingly demonstrate that the argument of the bank that good faith is f predominantly concerned with procedural defects in negotiating procedures cannot be sustained. Any purely procedural or even predominantly procedural interpretation of the requirement of good faith must be rejected.

[37] That brings me to the element of significant imbalance. It has been pointed out by Hugh Collins that the test 'of a significant imbalance of the obligations obviously directs attention to the substantive unfairness of the g contract' (see 'Good Faith in European Contract Law' (1994) 14 OJLS 229 at 249). It is, however, also right to say that there is a large area of overlap between the concepts of good faith and significant imbalance.

[38] It is now necessary to turn to the application of these requirements to the facts of the present case. The point is a relatively narrow one. I agree that the h starting point is that a lender ought to be able to recover interest at the contractual rate until the date of payment, and this applies both before and after judgment. On the other hand, counsel for the Director advanced a contrary argument. Adopting the test of asking what the position of a consumer is in the contract under consideration with or without condition 8, he said that the j consumer is in a significantly worse position than he would have been if there had been no such provision. Certainly, the consumer is worse off. The difficulty facing counsel, however, is that this disadvantage to the consumer appears to be the consequence not of condition 8 but of the County Courts (Interest on Judgment Debts) Order 1991, SI 1991/1184. Under this order no statutory interest is payable on a county court judgment given in proceedings to recover money due under a regulated agreement (see reg 2). Counsel said that for policy

reasons it was decided that in such a case no interest may be recovered after
judgment. He said that it is not open to the House to criticise directly or *a*
indirectly this legal context. In these circumstances he submitted that it is not
legitimate for a court to conclude that fairness requires that a lender must be able
to insist on a stipulation designed to avoid the statutory regime under the 1991
order. Initially I was inclined to uphold this policy argument. On reflection,
however, I have been persuaded that this argument cannot prevail in circumstances *b*
where the legislature has neither expressly nor by necessary implication barred a
stipulation that interest may continue to accrue after judgment until payment in
full.

[39] For these reasons as well as the reasons given by Lord Bingham I agree
that condition 8 is not unfair and I would also make the order which Lord
Bingham proposes. *c*

LORD HOPE OF CRAIGHEAD.
[40] My Lords, I have had the advantage of reading in draft the speech of my
noble and learned friend Lord Bingham of Cornhill. I agree with it, and for
reasons which he has given I too would allow the appeal. I also agree with my *d*
noble and learned friend Lord Millett that the real source of the problem revealed
by this case remains to be tackled. It is with that point particularly in mind that I
wish to add these observations.

[41] The term to which the Director has taken objection is to be found in the
last sentence of condition 8 of the bank's standard form. It seeks to do three
things. Firstly, it provides that interest on the amount which becomes payable *e*
under that condition is to be payable in accordance with condition 4. Second, it
provides that interest is to be payable on that amount until payment after as well
as before any judgment. Third, it makes it clear that the obligation to pay interest
is to be independent of and not to merge with the judgment. The amount on
which the interest is to be charged is described in the preceding sentence. It *f*
consists of (a) the balance on the customer's account, (b) interest outstanding at
the specified date and (c) other costs, charges and expenses incurred in trying to
obtain the repayment of the unpaid instalment of such balance and interest.
Mr Crow for the Director made it clear that no objection was taken to the
provision in the first part of the sentence that interest was to be payable on that
amount. He accepted that this part of the sentence cannot be regarded as unfair. *g*
The contractual term which he says is unfair is to be found in the other parts of
the sentence, which provide that interest on the amount referred to in the first
part of it is to be payable after as well as before any judgment and that the
obligation to do so is to be independent of and not to merge with the judgment.

[42] Regulation 3(2)(b) of the Unfair Terms in Consumer Contracts Regulations *h*
1994, SI 1994/3159, provides that no assessment is to be made of the fairness of
any term which concerns the adequacy of the price or remuneration as against
the goods or services supplied. This is the provision on which Lord Goodhart QC
relied when he said that the fairness provisions did not apply in this case. But it
seems to me to be plain that the last sentence of condition 8 is not concerned with *j*
the adequacy of the remuneration which the bank is to receive for making its
money available to the borrower.

[43] As the nineteenth recital to Council Directive (EEC) 93/13 (OJ 1993 L95
p 29) indicates, reg 3(2) applies only to terms which describe the main subject
matter of the contract or are directly related to the adequacy of the price charged
for the goods or services. The last sentence of condition 8 is concerned with

a neither of these two things. The obligation to pay interest on the outstanding balance is set out in condition 4. It is there that the provisions are to be found that concern the adequacy of the price charged for the loan. Condition 8 is a default provision. The last sentence of it is designed to enable interest to be recovered on the whole of the amount due on default. That amount includes legal and other costs, charges and expenses, so it is not confined to the outstanding balance

b due by the borrower. I do not think that it can be said to be directly related to the price charged for the loan or to its adequacy. It is concerned instead with the consequences of the borrower's breach of contract. It sets out what is to happen if he fails to make the repayments to the bank as they fall due. I agree that reg 3(2)(b) does not apply to it, and that its fairness as defined in reg 4(1) of the regulations must be assessed.

c [44] The primary reason which the Director has given for maintaining that the term is unfair is the uncertainty, confusion and hardship which has been shown to result from the bank's practice of claiming contractual interest from its borrowers after judgment has been given for the principal. Particular unfairness is said to arise where an order is made to pay the debt by instalments, whether

d under s 71 of the County Courts Act 1984 or a time order under s 129 of the Consumer Credit Act 1974, and where no consideration has been given to making an order under s 136 of the 1974 Act to amend the agreement so as to prevent the accrual of contractual interest on instalments which are paid when they fall due. The fact that it is commonplace for no consideration to be given to the use of s 136 when payment by instalments is being ordered is not in dispute.

e So it is not surprising that borrowers, on finding that they are liable for further amounts in addition to the instalments provided for in judgments obtained against them by the bank, have complained to the Director.

[45] I am not persuaded that, despite these consequences, the term is unfair. The meaning to be given to the word 'unfair' in this context is laid down in

f reg 4(1) of the regulations. Guidance as to how the words used in that paragraph are to be understood is to be found in the sixteenth recital to the directive. The recital explains what 'constitutes the requirement of good faith'. It states that an assessment of the unfair character of unfair terms must be supplemented by an overall evaluation of the different interests involved. Regulation 4(2) indicates the wide range of circumstances to be taken into account in the assessment. It

g provides that the assessment is to be done as at the time of the conclusion of the contract. But an appreciation of how the term will affect each party when the contract is put into effect must clearly form part of the exercise. It has been pointed out that there are considerable differences between the legal systems of the member states as to how extensive and how powerful the penetration has

h been of the principle of good faith and fair dealing (see Lando and Beale *Principles of European Contract Law* Pts I and II (2000, combined and revised) p 116). But in the present context there is no need to explore this topic in any depth. The directive provides all the guidance that it needed as to its application.

[46] Following this approach, it does not seem to me that there is a significant

j imbalance to the detriment of the borrower in the stipulation that the interest which is payable in terms of the first part of the last sentence is to be charged after as well as before any judgment and that this obligation is not to merge in the judgment. The primary obligation in condition 4 is to pay interest on the outstanding balance due to the bank. The plain fact is that, in the event of a default by the borrower, the bank will not have recovered all of its money until the entire balance on the borrower's account has been paid. The main purpose

of the last sentence is to ensure that the borrower does not enjoy the benefit of the
outstanding balance after judgment without fulfilling the corresponding obligation   *a*
which he has undertaken to pay interest on it as provided for in the contract.
While the working out of that purpose may give rise to uncertainty in practice,
the term itself does not seem to me to be unfair.

[47] There is, however, an underlying problem, and it is not difficult to
identify. It is not possible for a lender who seeks to enforce a regulated agreement   *b*
in England and Wales to obtain from the court an order for interest to be paid on
the judgment debt. Section 141 of the 1974 Act provides that the county court is
to have jurisdiction to hear and determine such actions and that they shall not be
brought in any other court. The County Courts (Interest on Judgment Debts)
Order 1991, SI 1991/1184 enables the county court to award statutory interest,
but it excludes regulated agreements from that power. It also provides that   *c*
where payment of a judgment debt is to be made by instalments interest is not to
accrue under that order on the amount of any instalment until it falls due. Where
there is an independent covenant to pay interest which does not merge in the
judgment, contractual interest will continue nevertheless to accrue and remain
payable. It is not unreasonable to think that the problem would be greatly   *d*
reduced, and perhaps removed entirely, if it were possible for the lender to obtain
an order from the county court which included post-judgment contractual
interest when judgment was being given for the principal. If that were possible,
separate proceedings to recover post-judgment contractual interest would be
unnecessary. It would also enable the court to take account of the borrower's
liability for post-judgment contractual interest when it is considering whether to   *e*
make an order for the amount due to be paid by instalments.

[48] This is an English appeal, so the practice of the Scottish courts as regards
the making of orders for the payment of contractual interest is not directly
relevant. But the 1974 Act extends to the whole of the United Kingdom, and the
bank uses the same standard form when it is entering into transactions with   *f*
Scottish borrowers. In Scotland, actions to enforce regulated agreements must
be brought in the sheriff court (s 141(3) of the 1974 Act). It appears never to have
been doubted that post-judgment interest may be awarded on a money claim in
the sheriff court, although a sheriff does not have power to order the payment of
interest on the sum awarded in any decree unless it has been asked for expressly
in the sum sued for (see Dobie *Sheriff Court Practice* (1952) p 104; Macphail *Sheriff*   *g*
Court Practice (2nd edn, 1998) (para 9.93)). The rate at which interest may be
recovered on a judgment in that court is regulated by s 9 of the Sheriff Courts
(Scotland) Extracts Act 1892 as amended from time to time by various Acts of
Sederunt. It provides that where interest is included in a decree or extract it shall
be deemed to be at the prescribed rate (currently 8%) 'unless otherwise stated'.   *h*

[49] The question whether it was competent for post-judgment interest to be
ordered at the contractual rate was the subject of competing decisions in the
sheriff court. But doubts on this point were removed by the decision of the Inner
House in *Bank of Scotland v Davis* 1982 SLT 20. It was held in that case that there
was no good reason why the court should refuse to grant a decree for payment
of interest in terms of the parties' contract. The Lord Justice-Clerk (Wheatley)   *j*
referred with approval to observations by Sheriff Sir Allan G Walker QC in *Bank
of Scotland v Forsyth* 1969 SLT (Sh Ct) 15. I think that it is worth quoting the
following passage (at 16) from the sheriff's note in that case:

'When an obligation to pay is created for the first time by a decree of court,
as in an action of damages for negligence, it is clearly desirable that interest

a from the date of the decree until payment should be at the customary rate which at present is 5 per cent. No doubt this customary rate is susceptible of change, but until it is deliberately changed by the courts, it will be allowed automatically on all such decrees. I can see no reason, however, why this customary rate should be applied when the parties themselves have, by their own contract, fixed the rate of interest which is to be paid ... it seems clearly

b inequitable that the bank should be denied the right to obtain the agreed interest on the money lent because, from the date of the decree onwards, the court absolves the defender from paying interest in excess of 5 per cent. The view has been expressed that when pursuers obtain the advantages and sanctions of the law by constituting their debt by action, they must be content with interest at the rate of 5 per cent. I cannot myself understand,

c however, why it should be regarded as just that a contracting party must be denied the aid of the court in enforcing a contract, unless he is prepared, as the price of obtaining that aid, to surrender his right to receive the rate of interest which the other party contracted to pay.'

d [50] As the sheriff's use of the phrase 'constituting their debt by action' indicates, a similar rule is followed in Scotland to that which applies in England under the merger rule. When the court pronounces decree for a principal sum due under a contract, the obligation to pay that sum is then owed under the court's decree and not under the contract. This principle has been recognised by the Prescription and Limitation (Scotland) Act 1973, which provides that the

e five-year prescription which applies to any obligation to pay a sum of money does not apply to an obligation to obtemper a decree of court (para 2(a) of Sch 1). The sheriff's discussion of the application of the principle appears also to assume—consistent with the merger rule—that, if the court is unable to award post-judgment interest on the principal sum at the rate provided for in the contract, the right to recover interest thereafter at the contractual rate would be

f lost.

[51] The question whether the court will enforce a term that interest at the contractual rate may be charged on the principal sum due after as well as before any judgment does not seem to have been tested in Scotland. But it has been rendered academic by the decision in *Davis'* case that post-judgment interest at

g the contractual rate may be awarded in the sheriff court. In contrast to the position which applies in England under the 1991 order, s 1(7) of the Debtors (Scotland) Act 1987 provides that interest may be recovered on a time to pay order pronounced in the sheriff court if the creditor has given notice to the debtor of his intention to claim interest: see also the Act of Sederunt (Summary Applications, Statutory Applications and Appeals etc Rules) 1999 (SI 1999/929) which

h prescribes the form of notice which is to be used. There is no provision which excludes regulated agreements from this power.

[52] As Lord Millett has observed, the Scottish practice of awarding post-judgment interest at the contractual rate in the sheriff court avoids the uncertainty, confusion and hardship which would otherwise arise if the borrower

j were to be exposed to further proceedings to satisfy the bank's claim for interest at the contractual rate. Like him, I do not think that it would be right to express a view in this case as to whether the Scottish practice could be followed under existing law and practice in England in the county court. But I suggest that consideration should now be given to the question whether the present constraints on the awarding of interest in the county court should be relaxed to enable this to be done. Any such relaxation could be combined with the making

of rules, similar to those in the 1999 Act of Sederunt, designed to ensure that a
borrower against whom proceedings were brought is made fully aware at the *a*
outset of the powers which the county court has under the relevant statutes to
prevent hardship.

LORD MILLETT.

[53] My Lords, I have had the advantage of reading in draft the speech of my *b*
noble and learned friend Lord Bingham of Cornhill. I agree with it, and for the
reasons he gives I too would allow the appeal. Because of the importance of the
case, and because the real source of the problem remains to be tackled, I propose
to add a few brief observations of my own.

[54] A contractual term in a consumer contract is unfair if 'contrary to the *c*
requirement of good faith [it] causes a significant imbalance in the parties' rights
and obligations under the contract to the detriment of the consumer' (reg 4(1) of
the Unfair Terms in Consumer Contracts Regulations 1994, SI 1994/3159). There
can be no one single test of this. It is obviously useful to assess the impact of an
impugned term on the parties' rights and obligations by comparing the effect of
the contract with the term and the effect it would have without it. But the inquiry *d*
cannot stop there. It may also be necessary to consider the effect of the inclusion
of the term on the substance or core of the transaction; whether if it were drawn
to his attention the consumer would be likely to be surprised by it; whether the
term is a standard term, not merely in similar non-negotiable consumer
contracts, but in commercial contracts freely negotiated between parties acting *e*
on level terms and at arms' length; and whether, in such cases, the party adversely
affected by the inclusion of the term or his lawyer might reasonably be expected
to object to its inclusion and press for its deletion. The list is not necessarily
exhaustive; other approaches may sometimes be more appropriate.

[55] The substance of the transaction in the present case is self-evident. It is a *f*
loan repayable by instalments with interest on the balance from time to time
outstanding until the whole of the principal is repaid. The borrower would have
no difficulty in understanding this. Nor would he think it unfair. If his attention
were drawn to the impugned term, i e that interest should continue to be paid on
the outstanding balance after as well as before judgment, he might well be
surprised at the need to spell this out, but he would surely not be at all surprised *g*
by the fact. It is what he would expect. The term does not affect the substance of
the transaction, which is that the borrower should continue to pay interest on the
principal from time to time outstanding, nor does it impose any further or
unexpected liability upon him not inherent in the basic transaction. It is included
only to protect the lender from the (to modern eyes artificial) meaning placed on *h*
a covenant to pay interest by the Court of Appeal in *Re Sneyd, ex p Fewings* (1883)
25 Ch D 338, where a covenant to pay interest on the balance of the principal sum
from time to time remaining unpaid was construed as meaning remaining due
under the covenant, so that it fell when the covenant was subsumed in the
judgment.   *j*

[56] The term is not only a standard term in non-negotiable loans to
consumers, but in commercial loans freely negotiated between parties on equal
terms and acting with professional advice. I venture to think that no lawyer
advising a commercial borrower would dream of objecting to the inclusion of
such a term, which merely reinforces and carries into effect what the parties
themselves would regard as the essence of the transaction.

a [57] I am satisfied, therefore, that the term is not unfair. It does not cause an imbalance in the parties' rights and obligations; and the lender did not act in bad faith by taking advantage of the borrower's weakness of bargaining power or lack of professional advice to insist upon a term which would otherwise have been omitted.

b [58] This is not to say that the many complaints which the Director General has received from borrowers are without substance. These are borrowers who have failed to keep up the instalments and suffered a judgment in consequence. Asked to suggest terms on which they can satisfy the judgment, they offer to pay it off by instalments. They are advised to offer as much as they can afford. They do so; their offer is accepted; and they duly pay all the instalments required of them. Despite having done so, they find that they have not discharged their c contractual obligations but are still liable in respect of interest which has accrued since judgment and which was not covered by the instalment agreement. Where the agreed instalments are insufficient to keep interest down, the amount still outstanding when all the instalments have been paid is greater than the amount for which judgment was given.

d [59] Despite the fact that lenders draw attention to these consequences when inviting borrowers to agree terms of repayment, they must still come as a nasty shock to many of them. I think that they have a legitimate grievance. A man who breaks his contract, suffers a judgment, makes an offer which is accepted to satisfy the judgment by instalments, and duly pays all the instalments required of him, would expect to be discharged from all further liability. The reason that this is not e the case is that the amount for which judgment is given is not co-extensive with the amount for which the borrower is contractually liable. The practice in England and Wales is for the court to give judgment for the amount of principal and interest outstanding at the date of judgment, without reference to the borrower's continuing liability to pay interest on the outstanding balance of the f principal sum after judgment. This has the unfortunate (though not I think the inevitable) consequence that the parties subsequently agree terms of repayment of the judgment debt rather than of the borrower's greater contractual liability.

[60] This does not happen in Scotland, where I understand the courts give judgment for the arrears of principal and interest at the date of judgment together with interest at the contractual rate on the arrears of principal until payment. If g the judgment were in that form, then the borrower's compliance with a repayment schedule designed to satisfy the judgment debt would automatically discharge his contractual obligations. This would avoid the unfairness that occurs where a borrower who could not afford the instalments necessary to discharge his contractual obligations is induced to offer the smaller or fewer instalments h sufficient to satisfy the judgment, and (because he can afford them) refrains from applying for relief while leaving himself exposed to further proceedings.

[61] But this unfairness does not arise from any inherent unfairness of the term. It is due to the limited nature of the judgment and the fact that it does not cover the whole of the borrower's indebtedness to the lender. I am not myself convinced that an English court could not make an order in the same form as the j Scottish courts do; and there is old authority that it could do so (see *Arnott v Redfern* (1826) 3 Bing 353). Counsel were unable to identify any persuasive reason why it cannot. But we have heard no argument on the question, and it would be wrong to express any concluded view on so important a matter without full argument. In the meantime I would hope either (i) that lenders would invite borrowers to agree instalment terms to discharge the contractual indebtedness

and not merely the judgment debt or (ii) that administrative arrangements could
be made so that instalment agreements which left an outstanding contractual ___a___
liability were automatically referred to the district judge for consideration.

LORD RODGER OF EARLSFERRY.

[62] My Lords, I have had the opportunity of reading the speech of my noble
and learned friend Lord Bingham of Cornhill in draft and, for the reasons which ___b___
he gives, I too would allow the appeal. I add two short observations.

[63] On behalf of the appellants Lord Goodhart QC submitted that the last
sentence in condition 8 fell within reg 3(2)(b) of the Unfair Terms in Consumer
Contracts Regulations 1994, SI 1994/3159, which provides:

'In so far as it is in plain, intelligible language, no assessment shall be made ___c___
of the fairness of any term which ... (b) concerns the adequacy of the price
or remuneration, as against the goods or services sold or supplied.'

This is a transposition of part of art 4(2) of Council Directive (EEC) 93/13 (OJ 1993
L95 p 29):

'Assessment of the unfair nature of the terms shall relate neither to the ___d___
definition of the main subject matter of the contract nor to the adequacy of
the price and remuneration, on the one hand, as against the services or goods
supplied in exchange, on the other, in so far as these terms are in plain
intelligible language.'

It is common ground, of course, that the domestic regulation requires to be read ___e___
in conformity with the meaning of the directive.

[64] At first sight the language of both the regulation and the directive is
somewhat strange since it might seem to suggest that the court is not to consider
the fairness of a term which concerns 'the adequacy', in its usual sense of 'the
sufficiency', of the price or remuneration as against the goods or services sold or ___f___
supplied. But it is obvious from the context that this cannot be what is intended.
In his opinion Evans-Lombe J ([2000] 1 All ER 240 at 248, [2000] 1 WLR 98 at 107)
accepted a submission to the effect that 'adequacy' must be read 'as meaning the
equivalent of "the extent of ... the remuneration"'. That interpretation seems to
me to risk watering down what the directive may have intended. While the point ___g___
was not explored before us and I therefore express no concluded view on it, I note
that the French text of the directive uses the word 'adéquation' and the German
text the word 'Angemessenheit'. Both may suggest that what is in issue is the
'appropriateness' of the price or remuneration as compared with the services or
goods—in other words whether there is an equivalence between the services
or goods and the consideration for them. This would seem to be consistent with ___h___
the reference to 'the price/quality ratio' in the nineteenth recital. It may
therefore be that 'adequacy' in both the directive and the regulations should be
interpreted in that spirit. Which is indeed how I understand your Lordships to
have approached the matter.

[65] The appeal reveals that, under the system that prevails in England and ___j___
Wales, a borrower may punctually pay all the instalments required of him under
a time order and still find, to his dismay, that he owes money to the bank because
post-judgment interest has been accruing and has not been factored into the
instalments. I share the general view that this is a highly unsatisfactory state of
affairs. Basing himself on this unsatisfactory position, in one part of his argument
the Director General suggested that the final sentence of condition 8, which

a ensures that post-judgment interest is recoverable, is unfair because the bank do not draw attention to the borrower's rights under s 129 of the Consumer Credit Act 1974 to apply for a time order and, more particularly perhaps, under s 136 to ask the court making a time order to amend the loan agreement. The suggestion was that, if the borrower were made aware of the powers and drew attention to it, the county court judge might use s 136 to adjust the rate of post-judgment interest so as to ensure that the borrower who duly paid the required instalments

b thereby discharged the whole of his liability to the bank.

[66] I agree with your Lordships that condition 8 cannot be regarded as unfair simply because the bank do not draw the borrower's attention to the remedies that may be available under the 1974 Act. The Act itself does not require that the borrower should be alerted to the effect of ss 129 and 136. But if the Director

c General thinks that the borrower's attention should be drawn to this matter at the time when the agreement is made, then he has powers under the Act to deal with the situation. The form and content of documents embodying regulated agreements, such as the agreement in this case, are prescribed by regulations made by the Secretary of State under s 60(1) of the 1974 Act. In terms of para (c)

d of that subsection the Secretary of State may make such provisions as appear to him appropriate with a view to ensuring that the debtor is made aware of the protection and remedies available to him under the Act. It would therefore be open to the Secretary of State to amend the relevant regulations so as to require the prescribed form of agreement to include a reference to the borrower's remedies under ss 129 and 136. This is a matter as to the working of the

e regulations on which the Director General could advise the Secretary of State, in the exercise of his general duty under s 1(2)(b) of the Act.

Appeal allowed.

Celia Fox   Barrister.

Secretary of State for the Home *a*
Department v Rehman
[2001] UKHL 47

HOUSE OF LORDS   *b*

LORD SLYNN OF HADLEY, LORD STEYN, LORD HOFFMANN, LORD CLYDE AND LORD
HUTTON

2, 3 MAY, 11 OCTOBER 2001

Immigration – Appeal – Deportation – Appeal against deportation on grounds of national *c*
security – Secretary of State concluding that Pakistani national supporting terrorist
organisation abroad and deciding to deport him on grounds of national security –
Appeals commission not being satisfied of truth of factual allegations on high civil
balance of probabilities – Whether activities capable of being threat to national security
if not targeted at United Kingdom or its citizens – Whether appeals commission applying
correct approach to standard of proof.   *d*

R, a Pakistani national with temporary leave to stay in the United Kingdom,
applied for indefinite leave to remain. An assessment by the security service
concluded that R was involved with an Islamic terrorist organisation, and that,
whilst it was unlikely that he and his followers would carry out any acts of *e*
violence in the United Kingdom, his activities were intended to further the cause
of a terrorist organisation abroad. On the basis of that information, the Secretary
of State refused R's application and instead certified that his departure from the
United Kingdom would be conducive to the public good in the interests of
national security. R appealed to the Special Immigration Appeals Commission.
The commission allowed the appeal, holding that conduct could only constitute *f*
a threat to national security if it were targeted at the United Kingdom, its citizens
or its system of government, and concluding that the Secretary of State had failed
to prove to a 'high civil balance of probabilities' the acts which were said to have
endangered national security. On the Secretary of State's appeal, the Court of
Appeal held that the commission had taken too narrow a view of what constituted
a threat to national security, that the 'high civil balance of probabilities' test applied *g*
by the commission was incorrect and that it was necessary instead to ask
whether, viewing the case as a whole, the individual was a danger to national
security, taking into account the executive's policy with regard to that matter.
Accordingly, the appeal was allowed, and R appealed to the House of Lords.
                                                                           h
Held – (1) Although a deportation in the interests of national security could only
be justified by the existence of some possibility of risk or danger to the well-being
of the nation which the Secretary of State considered made it desirable for the
public good that the individual should be deported, that risk did not have to be
the result of a direct threat to the United Kingdom, and the interests of national *j*
security were not limited to action by an individual which could be said to be
targeted at the United Kingdom, its system of government or its people. In
contemporary world conditions, action against a foreign state might be capable
indirectly of affecting the security of the United Kingdom. The means open to
terrorists, both in attacking another state and attacking international or global
activity by the community of nations, whatever the objectives of the terrorist,

a might well be capable of reflecting on the safety and well-being of the United Kingdom or its citizens. The sophistication of means available, the speed of movement of persons and goods, and the speed of modern communication were all factors which might have to be taken into account in deciding whether there was a real possibility that the national security of the United Kingdom might immediately or subsequently be put at risk by the actions of others. To require

b the matters in question to be capable of resulting directly in a threat to national security limited too tightly the discretion of the executive in deciding how the interests of the state, including not merely military defence but democracy and the legal and constitutional systems of the state, needed to be protected. The reciprocal co-operation between the United Kingdom and other states in combating

c international terrorism was capable of promoting the country's national security, and such co-operation was itself capable of fostering such security by, inter alia, the United Kingdom taking action against supporters within the United Kingdom of terrorism directed against other states. That involved a very large element of policy which was primarily for the Secretary of State, and was an area where he could claim that a preventative or precautionary action was justified. If an act

d was capable of creating indirectly a real possibility of harm to national security, the state did not have to wait until action had been taken which had a direct effect against the United Kingdom. Accordingly, the Court of Appeal had been correct to hold that the interests of national security were not to be confined in the way accepted by the commission (see [15]–[17], [20], [27], [32], [49], [63], [64], below).

e (2) In determining whether there was a real possibility of activities harmful to national security, the Secretary of State did not have to be satisfied, or show on appeal, that all the material before him was proved, and that his conclusion was justified, to a high civil degree of probability. Although fairness required that specific past acts, relied on as grounds for the deportation of an individual, should be proved to the civil standard of proof, that was not the whole exercise. In

f deciding whether it was conducive to the public good that a person should be deported, the Secretary of State was entitled to have regard to all the information in his possession about the actual and potential activities and the connections of the person concerned. He was entitled to have regard to the precautionary and preventative principles rather than to wait until directly harmful activities had

g taken place, the individual in the meantime remaining in the United Kingdom. In doing so, he was not merely finding facts but forming an executive judgment or assessment. There had to be material on which, proportionately and reasonably, the Secretary of State could conclude that there was a real possibility of activities harmful to national security, but establishing a degree of probability did not seem

h relevant to the reaching of a conclusion on whether there should be a deportation in the public good. That approach did not confuse proof of facts with the exercise of discretion. Specific acts had to be proved and an assessment made of the whole picture. The discretion then had to be exercised as to whether there should be a decision to deport. Although the commission had powers of review both of fact

j and of the exercise of discretion, it had to give due weight to the assessment and conclusions of the Secretary of State in the light, at any particular time, of his responsibilities, or of government policy and the means at his disposal of being informed of, and understanding, the problems involved. He was undoubtedly in the best position to judge what national security required, and the assessment of what was needed in the light of changing circumstances was primarily for him. Accordingly, the Court of Appeal had also been correct on the second point, and the appeal would therefore be dismissed (see [22], [23], [25]–[27], [32], [49], [61], [63]–[66], below).

Decision of the Court of Appeal [2000] 3 All ER 778 affirmed.

Notes
For liability for deportation, see 4(2) *Halsbury's Laws* (4th edn reissue) para 121.

Cases referred to in opinions
Chahal v UK (1996) 23 EHRR 413, ECt HR.
Chandler v DPP [1962] 3 All ER 142, [1964] AC 763, [1962] 3 WLR 694, HL.
Council of Civil Service Unions v Minister for the Civil Service [1984] 3 All ER 935, [1985] AC 374, [1984] 3 WLR 1174, HL.
H (minors) (sexual abuse: standard of proof), Re [1996] 1 All ER 1, [1996] AC 563, [1996] 2 WLR 8, HL.
Johnston v Chief Constable of the Royal Ulster Constabulary Case 222/84 [1986] 3 All ER 135, [1987] QB 129, [1986] 3 WLR 1038, [1986] ECR 1651, ECJ.
R (on the application of Alconbury Developments Ltd) v Secretary of State for the Environment, Transport and the Regions [2001] UKHL 23, [2001] 2 All ER 929, [2001] 2 WLR 1389.
R v Ministry of Defence, ex p Smith [1996] 1 All ER 257, [1996] QB 517, [1996] 2 WLR 305, CA.
R v Secretary of State for the Home Dept, ex p Hosenball [1977] 3 All ER 452, [1977] 1 WLR 766, CA.
R v Secretary of State for the Home Dept, ex p Chahal [1995] 1 All ER 658, [1995] 1 WLR 526, CA.
R v Secretary of State for the Home Dept, ex p McQuillan [1995] 4 All ER 400.
Smith and Grady v UK (2000) 29 EHRR 493, ECt HR.
Tinnelly & Sons Ltd v UK (1998) 27 EHRR 249, ECt HR.

Appeal
The appellant, Shafiq Ur Rehman, appealed from the decision of the Court of Appeal (Lord Woolf MR, Laws LJ and Harrison J) on 23 May 2000 ([2000] 3 All ER 778, [2000] 3 WLR 1240) allowing an appeal by the respondent, the Secretary of State for the Home Department, from the decision of the Special Immigration Appeals Commission (Potts J, Judge Pearl and Sir Brian Barder) on 7 September 1999 ([1999] INLR 517) allowing an appeal by Mr Rehman against the Secretary of State's decision, communicated in a letter dated 9 December 1998, to deport him from the United Kingdom on the grounds that his deportation would be conducive to the public good in the interests of national security. Permission to appeal was granted in respect of one ground of appeal by the Court of Appeal on 23 May 2000 and in respect of another ground of appeal by the Appeal Committee of the House of Lords on 4 October 2000. The two petitions of appeal were consolidated by order of 6 November 2000. The facts are set out in the opinion of Lord Slynn of Hadley.

Sibghat Kadri QC, Arthur Blake and *Adrian Berry* (instructed by *Bhatti & Co,* Manchester) for Mr Rehman.
Philip Sales and *Robin Tam* (instructed by the *Treasury Solicitor*) for the Secretary of State.

a Their Lordships took time for consideration.

11 October 2001. The following opinions were delivered.

LORD SLYNN OF HADLEY.

[1] My Lords, Mr Rehman, the appellant, is a Pakistani national, born in June
b 1971 in Pakistan. He was educated and subsequently, after obtaining a Master's
degree in Islamic studies, taught at Jamid Salfiah in Islamabad until January
1993. On 17 January 1993 he was given an entry clearance to enable him to work
as a minister of religion with the Jamait Ahle-e-Hadith in Oldham. His father is
such a minister in Halifax and both his parents are British citizens. He arrived here
c on 9 February 1993 and was subsequently given leave to stay until 9 February 1997
to allow him to complete four years as a minister. He married and has two
children born in the United Kingdom. In October 1997 he was given leave to stay
until 7 January 1998 to enable him to take his family to Pakistan from which he
returned on 4 December 1997. He applied for indefinite leave to remain in the
United Kingdom but that was refused on 9 December 1998. In his letter of refusal
d the Secretary of State said:

> '... the Secretary of State is satisfied, on the basis of the information he has
> received from confidential sources, that you are involved with an Islamic
> terrorist organisation Markaz Dawa Al Irshad (MDI). He is satisfied that in
> the light of your association with the MDI it is undesirable to permit you to
e > remain and that your continued presence in this country represents a danger
> to national security. In these circumstances, the Secretary of State has decided
> to refuse your application for indefinite leave to remain in accordance with
> paragraph 322(5) of the Immigration Rules (HC395). By virtue of section
> 2(1)(b) of the Special Immigration Appeals Commission Act 1997 you are
f > entitled to appeal against the Secretary of State's decision as he has personally
> certified that [sic] your departure from the United Kingdom to be conducive
> to the public good in the interests of national security.'

The Secretary of State added that his deportation from the United Kingdom
would be conducive to the public good 'in the interests of national security
g because of your association with Islamic terrorist groups'. Mr Rehman was told
that he was entitled to appeal, which he did, to the Special Immigration Appeals
Commission by virtue of s 2(1)(c) of the Special Immigration Appeals Commission
Act 1997. The Special Immigration Appeals Commission (Procedure) Rules 1998,
SI 1998/1881 allowed the Secretary of State to make both an open statement and
a closed statement, only the former being disclosed to Mr Rehman. The Secretary
h of State in his open statement said:

> 'The Security Service assesses that while Ur Rehman and his United
> Kingdom-based followers are unlikely to carry out any acts of violence in this
> country, his activities directly support terrorism in the Indian subcontinent
j > and are likely to continue unless he is deported. Ur Rehman has also been
> partly responsible for an increase in the number of Muslims in the United
> Kingdom who have undergone some form of militant training, including
> indoctrination into extremist beliefs and at least some basic weapons
> training. The Security Service is concerned that the presence of returned
> jihad trainees in the United Kingdom may encourage the radicalisation of the

British Muslim community. His activities in the United Kingdom are intended to further the cause of a terrorist organisation abroad. For this reason, the Secretary of State considers both that Ur Rehman poses a threat to national security and that he should be deported from the United Kingdom on [the] grounds that his presence here is not conducive to the public good for reasons of national security.'

[2] The appeal was heard both in open and in closed sessions. The commission in its decision of 20 August 1999 held ([1999] INLR 517 at 528):

'That the expression "national security" should be construed narrowly, rather than in the wider sense contended for by the Secretary of State and identified in the passages from Mr Sales' written submissions cited above. We recognise that there is no statutory definition of the term or legal authority directly on the point. However, we derive assistance from the passages in the authorities cited to us by Mr Kadri, namely (*Council of Civil Service Unions v Minister for the Civil Service* [1984] 3 All ER 935 at 950, [1985] AC 374 at 410 per Lord Diplock and *R v Secretary of State for the Home Dept, ex p Hosenball* [1977] 3 All ER 452 at 456–457, 461, [1977] 1 WLR 766 at 778, 783 per Lord Denning MR), and note the doubts expressed by Staughton LJ in [*R v Secretary of State for the Home Dept, ex p Chahal* [1995] 1 All ER 658 at 663–664, [1995] 1 WLR 526 at 531]. Moreover, whilst we recognise the terms of the Security Service Act 1989 are in no way decisive in the issue, we have derived assistance from the general approach contended for by Mr Nicholas Blake [special advocate before the commission]. We have found the passage cited by him from Professor Grahl-Madsen's book [*The Status of Refugees in International Law* (1966)] to be particularly helpful. In the circumstances, and for the purposes of this case, we adopt the position that a person may be said to offend against national security if he engages in, promotes, or encourages violent activity which is targeted at the UK, its system of government or its people. This includes activities directed against the overthrow or destabilisation of a foreign government if that foreign government is likely to take reprisals against the UK which affect the security of the UK or of its nationals. National security extends also to situations where UK citizens are targeted, wherever they may be. This is the definition of national security which should be applied to the issues of fact raised by this appeal.'

[3] They then considered the allegations of fact and they said (at 528–529):

'... we have asked ourselves whether the Secretary of State has satisfied us to a high civil balance of probabilities that the deportation of this appellant, a lawful resident of the UK, is made out on public good grounds because he has engaged in conduct that endangers the national security of the UK and, unless deported, is likely to continue to do so. In answering this question we have to consider the material, open, closed, and restricted, the oral evidence of witnesses called by the respondent, and the evidence of the appellant produced before us. We are satisfied that this material and evidence enables us properly to reach a decision in this appeal (r 3 of the 1998 rules).'

[4] The commission declined to set out in detail their analysis of the 'open', 'restricted' and 'closed' evidence on the basis that this would be capable of

a creating a serious injustice and they confined themselves to stating (at 530–531) their conclusions, namely:

'(1) Recruitment. We are not satisfied that the appellant has been shown to have recruited British Muslims to undergo militant training as alleged.

(2) We are not satisfied that the appellant has been shown to have engaged in fund-raising for the LT [Lashkar Tayyaba] as alleged.

b (3) We are not satisfied that the appellant has been shown to have knowingly sponsored individuals for militant training camps as alleged.

(4) We are not satisfied that the evidence demonstrates the existence in the UK of returnees, originally recruited by the appellant, who during the course of that training overseas have been indoctrinated with extremist

c beliefs or given weapons training, and who as a result allow them to create a threat to the UK's national security in the future.'

[5] They added (at 531):

'We have reached all these conclusions while recognising that it is not disputed that the appellant has provided sponsorship, information and

d advice to persons going to Pakistan for the forms of training which may have included militant or extremist training. Whether the appellant knew of the militant content of such training has not, in our opinion, been satisfactorily established to the required standard by the evidence. Nor have we overlooked the appellant's statement that he sympathised with the aims of the LT insofar

e as that organisation confronted what he regarded as illegal violence in Kashmir. But, in our opinion, these sentiments do not justify the conclusion contended for by the respondent. It follows, from these conclusions of fact, that the respondent has not established that the appellant was, is, and is likely to be a threat to national security. In our view, that would be the case whether the wider or narrower definition of that term, as identified above, is

f taken as the test. Accordingly, we consider that the respondent's decisions in question were not in accordance with the law or the Immigration Rules (para 364 of HC 395) and thus we allow these appeals.'

[6] The Secretary of State appealed. The Court of Appeal ([2000] 3 All ER 778, [2000] 3 WLR 1240) considered that the commission had taken too narrow a view

g of what could constitute a threat to national security in so far as it required the conduct relied on by the Secretary of State to be targeted at this country or its citizens. The Court of Appeal also considered ([2000] 3 All ER 778 at 791, [2000] 3 WLR 1240 at 1254) that the test was not whether it had been shown 'to a high degree of probability' that the individual was a danger to national security but

h that a global approach should be adopted 'taking into account the executive's policy with regard to national security'. Accordingly they allowed the appeal and remitted the matter to the commission for redetermination applying the approach indicated in their judgment.

[7] The Court of Appeal in its judgment has fully analysed in detail the

j provisions of the Immigration Act 1971, the 1997 Act and the 1998 rules. I adopt what the court has said and can accordingly confine my references to the legislation which is directly in issue on this appeal to your Lordships' House.

[8] The 1971 Act contemplates first a decision by the Secretary of State to make a deportation order under s 3(5) of that Act, in the present case in respect of a person who is not a British citizen '(b) if the Secretary of State deems his

deportation to be conducive to the public good'. There is no definition or
limitation of what can be 'conducive to the public good' and the matter is plainly   a
in the first instance and primarily one for the discretion of the Secretary of State.
The decision of the Secretary of State to make a deportation order is subject to
appeal by s 15(1)(a) of the 1971 Act save that by virtue of s 15(3)—

> 'A person shall not be entitled to appeal against a decision to make   b
> a deportation order against him if the ground of the decision was that his
> deportation is conducive to the public good as being in the interests of
> national security or of the relations between the United Kingdom and any
> other country or for other reasons of a political nature.'

[9] Despite this prohibition there was set up an advisory procedure to   c
promote a consideration of the Secretary of State's decision under that Act. This,
however, was held by the European Court of Human Rights in *Chahal v UK* (1996)
23 EHRR 413 not to provide an effective remedy within art 13 of the European
Convention for the Protection of Human Rights and Fundamental Freedoms
(Rome, 4 November 1950; TS 71 (1953) (Cmd 8969) (the convention). Accordingly
the commission was set up by the 1997 Act and by s 2(1)(c) a person was given a   d
right to appeal to the commission against—

> 'any matter in relation to which he would be entitled to appeal under
> subsection (1)(a) of section 15 of [the 1971 Act] (appeal to an adjudicator or
> the Appeal Tribunal against a decision to make a deportation order), but for
> subsection (3) of that section (deportation conducive to public good).'   e

The exclusion of the right of appeal if the decision to deport was on the ground
that deportation was conducive to the public good on the basis that it was in the
interests of national security or of the relations between the United Kingdom and
any other country or for any other reasons of a political nature was thus removed.   f
[10] Section 4 of the 1997 Act provides that the commission—

> '(a) shall allow the appeal if it considers—(i) that the decision or action
> against which the appeal is brought was not in accordance with the law or
> with any immigration rules applicable to the case, or (ii) where the decision
> or action involved the exercise of a discretion by the Secretary of State or an   g
> officer, that the discretion should have been exercised differently, and (b) in
> any other case, shall dismiss the appeal.'

[11] It seems to me that on this language and in accordance with the purpose
of the legislation to ensure an 'effective remedy', within the meaning of art 13 of
the convention, that the commission was empowered to review the Secretary of   h
State's decision on the law and also to review his findings of fact. It was also given
the power to review the question whether the discretion should have been
exercised differently. Whether the question should have been exercised differently
will normally depend on whether on the facts found the steps taken by the
Secretary of State were disproportionate to the need to protect national security.   j
[12] From the commission's decision there is a further appeal to the Court of
Appeal on 'any question of law material to' the commission's determination
(s 7(1)).
[13] The two main points of law which arose before the Court of Appeal are
now for consideration by your Lordships' House. Mr Kadri QC has forcefully
argued that the Court of Appeal was wrong on both points.

a [14] As to the meaning of 'national security' he contends that the interests of national security do not include matters which have no direct bearing on the United Kingdom, its people or its system of government. 'National security' has the same scope as 'defence of the realm'. For that he relies on what was said by Lord Diplock in *Council of Civil Service Unions v Minister for the Civil Service* [1984] 3 All ER 935 at 950, [1985] AC 374 at 410, and on the use of the phrases in a
b number of international conventions. Moreover he says that since the Secretary of State based his decision on a recommendation of the Security Services it can only be on matters within their purview and that their function, by s 1(2) of the Security Service Act 1989, was—

c 'the protection of national security and, in particular, its protection against threats from espionage, terrorism and sabotage, from the activities of agents of foreign powers and from actions intended to overthrow or undermine parliamentary democracy by political, industrial or violent means.'

He relies moreover on statements by groups of experts in international law, the Johannesburg Principles on National Security, Freedom of Expression and Access
d to Information, as approved on 1 October 1995 in Johannesburg which stressed as:

'Principle 2: Legitimate National Security Interest
(a) A restriction sought to be justified on the ground of national security is not legitimate unless its genuine purpose and demonstrable effect is to protect a country's existence or its territorial integrity against the use or threat
e of force, or its capacity to respond to the use or threat of force, whether from an external source, such as a military threat, or an internal source, such as incitement to violent overthrow of the government.

(b) In particular, a restriction sought to be justified on the ground of national security is not legitimate if its genuine purpose or demonstrable effect
f is to protect interests unrelated to national security, including, for example, to protect a government from embarrassment or exposure of wrongdoing, or to conceal information about the functioning of its public institutions, or to entrench a particular ideology, or to suppress industrial unrest.'

[15] It seems to me that Mr Rehman is entitled to say that 'the interests of
g national security' cannot be used to justify any reason the Secretary of State has for wishing to deport an individual from the United Kingdom. There must be some possibility of risk or danger to the security or well-being of the nation which the Secretary of State considers makes it desirable for the public good that the individual should be deported. But I do not accept that this risk has to be the result
h of 'a direct threat' to the United Kingdom as Mr Kadri has argued. Nor do I accept that the interests of national security are limited to action by an individual which can be said to be 'targeted at' the United Kingdom, its system of government or its people as the commission considered. The commission agreed ([1999] INLR 517 at 528) that this limitation is not to be taken literally since they accepted that such
j targeting—

'includes activities directed against the overthrow or destabilisation of a foreign government if that foreign government is likely to take reprisals against the UK which affect the security of the UK or of its nationals.'

[16] I accept as far as it goes a statement by Professor Grahl-Madsen in *The Status of Refugees in International Law* (1966):

'A person may be said to offend against national security if he engages in activities directed at the overthrow by external or internal force or other *a* illegal means of the government of the country concerned or in activities which are directed against a foreign government which as a result threaten the former government with intervention of a serious nature.'

That was adopted by the commission but I for my part do not accept that these *b* are the only examples of action which makes it in the interests of national security to deport a person. It seems to me that, in contemporary world conditions, action against a foreign state may be capable indirectly of affecting the security of the United Kingdom. The means open to terrorists both in attacking another state and attacking international or global activity by the community of nations, whatever the objectives of the terrorist, may well be capable of reflecting on the *c* safety and well-being of the United Kingdom or its citizens. The sophistication of means available, the speed of movement of persons and goods, the speed of modern communication, are all factors which may have to be taken into account in deciding whether there is a real possibility that the national security of the United Kingdom may immediately or subsequently be put at risk by the actions *d* of others. To require the matters in question to be capable of resulting 'directly' in a threat to national security limits too tightly the discretion of the executive in deciding how the interests of the state, including not merely military defence but democracy, the legal and constitutional systems of the state need to be protected. I accept that there must be a real possibility of an adverse affect on the United *e* Kingdom for what is done by the individual under inquiry but I do not accept that it has to be direct or immediate. Whether there is such a real possibility is a matter which has to be weighed up by the Secretary of State and balanced against the possible injustice to that individual if a deportation order is made.

[17] In his written case Mr Kadri appears to accept (contrary it seems to me to his argument in the Court of Appeal that they were mutually exclusive and to be *f* read disjunctively) that the three matters referred to in s 15(3) of the 1971 Act, namely 'national security', 'the relations between the United Kingdom and any other country' or 'for other reasons of a political nature' may overlap but only if action which falls in one or more categories amounts to a direct threat. I do not consider that these three categories are to be kept wholly distinct even if they are *g* expressed as alternatives. As the commission itself accepted, reprisals by a foreign state due to action by the United Kingdom may lead to a threat to national security even though this is action such as to affect 'relations between the United Kingdom and any other country' or to be 'of a political nature'. The Secretary of State does not have to pin his colours to one mast and be bound by his choice. At *h* the end of the day the question is whether the deportation is conducive to the public good. I would accept the Secretary of State's submission that the reciprocal co-operation between the United Kingdom and other states in combating international terrorism is capable of promoting the United Kingdom's national security, and that such co-operation itself is capable of fostering such security 'by, *j* inter alia, the United Kingdom taking action against supporters within the United Kingdom of terrorism directed against other states'. There is a very large element of policy in this which is, as I have said, primarily for the Secretary of State. This is an area where it seems to me particularly that the Secretary of State can claim that a preventative or precautionary action is justified. If an act is capable of creating indirectly a real possibility of harm to national security it is in principle

a wrong to say that the state must wait until action is taken which has a direct effect against the United Kingdom.

[18] National security and defence of the realm may cover the same ground though I tend to think that the latter is capable of a wider meaning. But if they are the same then I would accept that defence of the realm may justify action to prevent indirect and subsequent threats to the safety of the realm.

b [19] The United Kingdom is not obliged to harbour a terrorist who is currently taking action against some other state (or even in relation to a contested area of land claimed by another state) if that other state could realistically be seen by the Secretary of State as likely to take action against the United Kingdom and its citizens.

[20] I therefore agree with the Court of Appeal that the interests of national
c security are not to be confined in the way which the commission accepted.

[21] Mr Kadri's second main point is that the Court of Appeal were in error when rejecting the commission's ruling that the Secretary of State had to satisfy them, 'to a high civil balance of probabilities', that the deportation of this appellant, a lawful resident of the United Kingdom, was made out on public good
d grounds because he had engaged in conduct that endangered the national security of the United Kingdom and, unless deported, was likely to continue to do so. The Court of Appeal said:

'However, in any national security case the Secretary of State is entitled to make a decision to deport not only on the basis that the individual has
e in fact endangered national security but that he is a *danger* to national security. When the case is being put in this way, it is necessary not to look only at the individual allegations and ask whether they have been proved. It is also necessary to examine the case as a whole against an individual and then ask whether on a global approach that individual is a danger to national security, taking into account the executive's policy with regard to
f national security. When this is done, the cumulative effect may establish that the individual is to be treated as a danger, although it cannot be proved to a high degree of probability that he has performed any individual act which would justify this conclusion.' (See [2000] 3 All ER 778 at 791, [2000] 3 WLR 1240 at 1254.)

g
[22] Here the liberty of the person and the practice of his family to remain in this country is at stake and when specific acts which have already occurred are relied on, fairness requires that they should be proved to the civil standard of proof. But that is not the whole exercise. The Secretary of State, in deciding whether it is conducive to the public good that a person should be deported, is
h entitled to have regard to all the information in his possession about the actual and potential activities and the connections of the person concerned. He is entitled to have regard to the precautionary and preventative principles rather than to wait until directly harmful activities have taken place, the individual in the meantime remaining in this country. In doing so he is not merely finding facts
j but forming an executive judgment or assessment. There must be material on which proportionately and reasonably he can conclude that there is a real possibility of activities harmful to national security but he does not have to be satisfied, nor on appeal to show, that all the material before him is proved, and his conclusion is justified, to a 'high civil degree of probability'. Establishing a degree of probability does not seem relevant to the reaching of a conclusion on whether there should be a deportation for the public good.

[23] Contrary to Mr Kadri's argument this approach is not confusing proof of facts with the exercise of discretion—specific acts must be proved, and an assessment made of the whole picture and then the discretion exercised as to whether there should be a decision to deport and a deportation order made.

[24] If of course it is said that the decision to deport was not based on grounds of national security and there is an issue as to that matter then 'the government is under an obligation to produce evidence that the decision was in fact based on grounds of national security' (see *Council of Civil Service Unions v Minister for the Civil Service* [1984] 3 All ER 935 at 944, [1985] AC 374 at 402). That however is not the issue in the present case.

[25] On the second point I am wholly in agreement with the decision of the Court of Appeal.

[26] In conclusion even though the commission has powers of review both of fact and of the exercise of the discretion, the commission must give due weight to the assessment and conclusions of the Secretary of State in the light at any particular time of his responsibilities, or of government policy and the means at his disposal of being informed of and understanding the problems involved. He is undoubtedly in the best position to judge what national security requires even if his decision is open to review. The assessment of what is needed in the light of changing circumstances is primarily for him. On an appeal the Court of Appeal and your Lordships' House no doubt will give due weight to the conclusions of the commission, constituted as it is of distinguished and experienced members, and knowing as it did, and as usually the court will not know, of the contents of the 'closed' evidence and hearing. If any of the reasoning of the commission shows errors in its approach to the principles to be followed, then the courts can intervene. In the present case I consider that the Court of Appeal was right in its decision on both of the points which arose and in its decision to remit the matters to the commission for redetermination in accordance with the principles which the Court of Appeal and now your Lordships have laid down. I would accordingly dismiss the appeal.

LORD STEYN.

[27] My Lords, I am in agreement with the reasons given by Lord Slynn of Hadley in his opinion and I would also dismiss the appeal. I can therefore deal with the matter quite shortly.

[28] Section 15(3) of the Immigration Act 1971 contemplated deportation of a person in three situations, viz where—

'his deportation is conducive to the public good as being in the interests of national security or of the relations between the United Kingdom and any other country or for other reasons of a political nature.'

The commission ([1999] INLR 517) thought that s 15(3) should be interpreted disjunctively. In the Court of Appeal Lord Woolf MR explained ([2000] 3 All ER 778 at 790, [2000] 3 WLR 1240 at 1253) that while it is correct that these situations are alternatives 'there is clearly room for there to be an overlap'. I agree. Addressing directly the issue whether the conduct must be targeted against the security of this country, Lord Woolf MR observed:

'Whatever may have been the position in the past, increasingly the security of one country is dependent upon the security of other countries. That is why this country has entered into numerous alliances. They acknowledge a the extent to which this country's security is dependent upon the security of other countries. The establishment of NATO is but a reflection of this reality. An attack on an ally can undermine the security of this country.' (See [2000] 3 All ER 778 at 788–789, [2000] 3 WLR 1240 at 1251.)

b Later in his judgment ([2000] 3 All ER 778 at 790, [2000] 3 WLR 1240 at 1253–1254) Lord Woolf MR said that the government 'is perfectly entitled to treat any undermining of its policy to protect this country from international terrorism as being contrary to the security interests of this country'. I respectfully agree. Even democracies are entitled to protect themselves, and the executive is the best judge of the need for international co-operation to combat terrorism and counter-terrorist strategies. This broader context is the backcloth of the Secretary

c of State's statutory power of deportation in the interests of national security.

[29] That brings me to the next issue. Counsel for Mr Rehman submitted that the civil standard of proof is applicable to the Secretary of State and to the commission. This argument necessarily involves the proposition that even if the Secretary of State is fully entitled to be satisfied on the materials before him that the person concerned *may* be a real threat to national security, the Secretary of State

d may not deport him. That cannot be right. The task of the Secretary of State is to evaluate risks in respect of the interests of national security. Lord Woolf MR expressed the point with precision as follows:

e '... in any national security case the Secretary of State is entitled to make a decision to deport not only on the basis that the individual has in fact endangered national security but that he is a *danger* to national security. When the case is being put in this way, it is necessary not to look only at the individual allegations and ask whether they have been proved. It is also necessary to examine the case as a whole against an individual and then ask whether on a global approach that individual is a danger to

f national security, taking into account the executive's policy with regard to national security. When this is done, the cumulative effect may establish that the individual is to be treated as a danger, although it cannot be proved to a high degree of probability that he has performed any individual act which would justify this conclusion. Here it is important to remember that the individual is still subject to immigration control. He is not in the same

g position as a British citizen. He has not been charged with a specific criminal offence. It is the danger which he constitutes to national security which is to be balanced against his own personal interests.' (See [2000] 3 All ER 778 at 791, [2000] 3 WLR 1240 at 1254.)

h The dynamics of the role of the Secretary of State, charged with the power and duty to consider deportation on grounds of national security, irresistibly supports this analysis. While I came to this conclusion by the end of the hearing of the appeal, the tragic events of 11 September 2001 in New York reinforce compellingly that no other approach is possible.

j [30] The interpretation of s 4 of the Special Immigration Appeals Commission Act 1997 was not explored in any depth on the appeal to the House. Section 4 so far as relevant reads:

'(1) The Special Immigration Appeals Commission on an appeal to it under this Act—(a) shall allow the appeal if it considers—(i) that the decision or action against which the appeal is brought was not in accordance with the law or with any immigration rules applicable to the case, or (ii) where the

decision or action involved the exercise of a discretion by the Secretary of
State or an officer, that the discretion should have been exercised differently, *a*
and (b) in any other case, shall dismiss the appeal.

(2) Where an appeal is allowed, the Commission shall give such directions
for giving effect to the determination as it thinks requisite, and may also
make recommendations with respect to any other action which it considers
should be taken in the case under the Immigration Act 1971; and it shall be *b*
the duty of the Secretary of State and of any officer to whom directions are
given under this subsection to comply with them.'

In the light of the observations of the European Court of Human Rights in
Chahal v UK (1996) 23 EHRR 413 Parliament has provided for a high-powered
commission, consisting of a member who holds or has held high judicial office, *c*
an immigration judge, and a third member, who will apparently be someone
with experience of national security matters (see s 1 of and Sch 1 to the 1997 Act
and per Lord Woolf MR [2000] 3 All ER 778 at 782, 783, [2000] 3 WLR 1240 at
1245, 1246). Lord Woolf MR observed ([2000] 3 All ER 778 at 791, [2000] 3 WLR
1240 at 1254) that the commission were correct to regard it as their responsibility *d*
to determine questions of fact and law. He added:

'The fact that Parliament has given SIAC [the Special Immigration Appeals
Commission] responsibility of reviewing the manner in which the Secretary
of State has exercised his discretion, inevitably leads to this conclusion.
Without statutory intervention, this is not a role which a court readily adopts. *e*
But SIAC's membership meant that it was more appropriate for SIAC to
perform this role.'

I respectfully agree. Not only the make-up of the commission but also the
procedures of the commission serve to protect the interests of national security:
Special Immigration Appeals Commission (Procedure) Rules 1998, SI 1998/1881; *f*
see also the discussion of the new procedure in (1998) 12 INLP 67–70.

[31] Moreover the expression 'in accordance with the law' in s 4 of the 1997 Act
comprehends also since 2 October 2000 convention rights under the Human Rights
Act 1998. Thus art 8 (right of respect for family life), art 10 (freedom of
expression) and art 11 (freedom of assembly and association) all permit such *g*
derogations as are prescribed by law and are necessary in a democratic society in
the interests of national security. While a national court must accord appropriate
deference to the executive, it may have to address the questions: Does the
interference serve a legitimate objective? Is it necessary in a democratic society?
In *Tinnelly & Sons Ltd v UK* (1998) 27 EHRR 249 the European Court of Human *h*
Rights had to consider public interest immunity certificates involving national
security considerations issued by the Secretary of State in discrimination
proceedings. The court observed (at 290 (para 77)):

'... the conclusive nature of the section 42 [Fair Employment (Northern
Ireland) Act 1976] certificates had the effect of preventing a judicial *j*
determination on the merits of the applicants' complaints that they were
victims of unlawful discrimination. The Court would observe that such a
complaint can properly be submitted for an independent judicial determination
even if national security considerations are present and constitute a highly
material aspect of the case. The right guaranteed to an applicant under
Article 6(1) of the Convention to submit a dispute to a court or tribunal in

a order to have a determination on questions of both fact and law cannot be displaced by the *ipse dixit* of the executive.'

It is well established in the case law that issues of national security do not fall beyond the competence of the courts: see, for example, *Johnston v Chief Constable of the Royal Ulster Constabulary* Case 222/84 [1986] 3 All ER 135, [1987] QB 129, [1986] ECR 1651; *R v Secretary of State for the Home Dept, ex p McQuillan* [1995] 4 All
b ER 400; *R v Ministry of Defence, ex p Smith* [1996] 1 All ER 257, [1996] QB 517 and *Smith and Grady v UK* (2000) 29 EHRR 493; compare also the extensive review of the jurisprudence on expulsion and deportation in van Dijk and van Hoof *Theory and Practice of the European Convention on Human Rights* (3rd edn, 1998) pp 515–521. It is, however, self-evidently right that national courts must give great weight to
c the views of the executive on matters of national security. But not all the observations in *Chandler v DPP* [1962] 3 All ER 142, [1964] AC 763 can be regarded as authoritative in respect of the new statutory system.

[**32**] For the reasons given by Lord Woolf MR, the reasons given by Lord Slynn, and my brief reasons, I would dismiss the appeal.

d **LORD HOFFMANN.**

The decision to deport

[**33**] My Lords, Mr Shafiq Ur Rehman is a Pakistani national. He came to this country in 1993 and was given limited leave to enter and to work as a minister of
e religion. In 1997 he applied for indefinite leave to remain. On 9 December 1998 the Home Secretary refused the application. His letter said that he was satisfied, on the basis of information from confidential sources, that Mr Rehman was involved with an Islamic terrorist organisation called Markaz Dawa Al Irshad (MDI) and that his continued presence in this country was a danger to national
f security. The Home Secretary also gave notice of his intention to make a deportation order under s 3(5)(b) of the Immigration Act 1971 on the ground that for the same reasons his deportation would be conducive to the public good.

The right of appeal

[**34**] Until 1998 Mr Rehman would have had no right of appeal against the
g Home Secretary's decision to deport him. Ordinarily there is a right of appeal to an immigration adjudicator against a decision of the Secretary of State to make a deportation order under s 3(5) (see s 15(1)). The adjudicator hearing the appeal is required by s 19(1) to allow the appeal if he considers that the decision was 'not in accordance with the law or with any immigration rules applicable to the case'
h or, where the decision involved the exercise of a discretion by the Secretary of State, 'that the discretion should have been exercised differently'. Otherwise, the appeal must be dismissed.

[**35**] But this general right of appeal is excluded by s 15(3) if the ground of the decision to make the deportation order—

j 'was that his deportation is conducive to the public good as being in the interests of national security or of the relations between the United Kingdom and any other country or for other reasons of a political nature.'

Parliament took the view that the need to preserve the confidentiality of the material taken into account by the Home Secretary in making a deportation order on one or other of these grounds made it impossible to allow an effective

right of appeal. All that could be permitted was the right to make representations
to an extra-statutory panel appointed by the Home Secretary to advise him.

[36] In *Chahal v UK* (1996) 23 EHRR 413 the European Court of Human Rights
decided that this procedure was inadequate to safeguard two of the deportee's
convention rights. First, he was entitled under art 13 to an effective remedy from
an independent tribunal to protect his right under art 3 not to be deported to a
country where there was a serious risk that he would suffer torture or inhuman
or degrading treatment. Secondly, if he was detained pending deportation, he was
entitled under art 5(4) to the determination of an independent tribunal as to
whether his detention was lawful. The European court rejected the United
Kingdom government's argument that considerations of national security or
international relations made it impossible to accord such a right of appeal. The
court (at 469 (para 131)) commended the procedure established by the Canadian
Immigration Act 1976, under which the confidentiality of secret sources could be
maintained by disclosing it only to a special security-cleared advocate appointed
to represent the deportee who could cross-examine witnesses in the absence of
the appellant (see 472 (para 144)).

[37] The European Court also considered the argument that decisions on
national security were essentially a matter for the executive and that it would be
contrary to principle to allow an independent tribunal to substitute its own
decision on such matters for that of the responsible minister. It acknowledged
(at 468 (para 127)) that art 5(4)—

> 'does not guarantee a right to judicial review of such breadth as to
> empower the court, on all aspects of the case including questions of pure
> expediency, to substitute its own discretion for that of the decision-making
> authority. The review should, however, be wide enough to bear on those
> conditions which are essential for the "lawful" detention of a person
> according to Article 5(1).'

The term 'question of expediency' is regularly used by the European Court to
describe what English lawyers would call a question of policy (see the discussion
of the European cases in the recent case of *R (on the application of Alconbury
Developments Ltd) v Secretary of State for the Environment, Transport and the Regions*
[2001] UKHL 23, [2001] 2 All ER 929, [2001] 2 WLR 1389).

[38] This was the background to the passing of the Special Immigration
Appeals Commission Act 1997, under which Mr Rehman was able to appeal. The
Act was intended to enable the United Kingdom to comply with the convention
as interpreted by the court in *Chahal's* case. It established a Special Immigration
Appeals Commission (the commission) with jurisdiction to hear various categories
of appeals, including (under s 2(1)(c)) those excluded from the jurisdiction of the
adjudicator by s 15(3) of the 1971 Act. Section 4(1) gave the commission power
to deal with such appeals in the same terms as the power conferred upon the
adjudicator by s 19(1) of the 1971 Act. The 1997 Act enabled the Lord Chancellor
to make procedural rules for the commission and pursuant to this power he
made the Special Immigration Appeals Commission (Procedure) Rules 1998,
SI 1998/1881. This follows the Canadian model in allowing part of the
proceedings to be conducted at a private hearing from which the appellant may
be excluded but represented by a special advocate.

The Home Secretary's reasons

a

[**39**] Pursuant to r 10(1)(a), the Home Secretary provided the commission with a summary of the facts relating to his decision and the reasons for the decision. It said that Mr Rehman was the United Kingdom point of contact for MDI, an 'extremist organisation' whose mujahidin fighters were known as Lashkar Tayyaba (LT). Mr Rehman was said to have been involved on MDI's behalf in
b the recruitment of British Muslims to undergo military training and in fund raising for LT. He was a personal contact of Mohammed Saeed, the worldwide leader of MDI and LT. The Security Service assessed that his activities directly supported a terrorist organisation.

[**40**] The grounds upon which these activities were seen as a threat to national
c security was that, while Mr Rehman and his followers were unlikely to carry out acts of violence in the United Kingdom, his activities directly supported terrorism in the Indian subcontinent. Mr Peter Wrench, head of the Home Office Terrorism and Protection Unit, told the commission that the defence of United Kingdom national security against terrorist groups depended upon international reciprocity and co-operation. It was therefore in the security interests of the
d United Kingdom to co-operate with other nations, including India, to repress terrorism anywhere in the world.

[**41**] An additional reason was that Mr Rehman had been responsible for an increase in the number of Muslims in the United Kingdom who had undergone some form of militant training and that the presence of returned trainees in the
e United Kingdom might encourage the radicalisation of the British Muslim community.

The commission's decision

[**42**] The commission ([1999] INLR 517) said that the appeal raised two issues.
f The first was whether Mr Rehman was engaged in the activities alleged by the Home Secretary. The second was whether his activities, so far as the commission found them proved, were against the interests of the security of the United Kingdom. The view taken by the commission was that the Home Secretary's allegations had to be established 'to a high civil balance of probabilities'. The commission went through each of the principal allegations: (1) involvement in
g recruitment of British Muslims to go to Pakistan for terrorist training; (2) fund-raising for LT; (3) sponsorship of individuals for militant training camps; and (4) creation of a group of returnees who had been given weapons training or been indoctrinated with extremist beliefs so as to create a threat to the security of the United Kingdom. In each case it said that it was not satisfied to the necessary
h standard of proof that the allegation had been made out.

[**43**] On the question of whether Mr Rehman's activities, so far as proved, constituted a threat to national security, the commission rejected the argument that the question of what could constitute a threat to national security was a matter for the Home Secretary to decide. It said that the definition of national
j security was a question of law which it had jurisdiction to decide. It examined various authorities and came to the conclusion (at 528) that a person 'may be said to offend against national security if he engages in, promotes, or encourages violent activity which is targeted at the UK, its system of government or its people'. It included within this definition activities against a foreign government 'if that foreign government is likely to take reprisals against the UK which affect the security of the UK or of its nationals'.

[44] Finally, the commission said that the various grounds of decision which s
15(3) of the 1971 Act excluded from the jurisdiction of the adjudicator (and which
consequently fell within the jurisdiction of the commission) were to be read
disjunctively:

> 'Once the Secretary of State identified "the public good" as being "the
> interests of national security" as the basis of his decision, he cannot broaden
> his grounds to avoid difficulties which he may encounter in proving his case.'

The Court of Appeal's decision
[45] The Secretary of State appealed to the Court of Appeal ([2000] 3 All ER
778, [2000] 2 WLR 1240) under s 7 of the 1997 Act on the ground that the
commission had erred in law. The court (Lord Woolf MR, Laws LJ and Harrison J)
allowed the appeal and remitted the appeal to the commission for reconsideration
in accordance with its judgment. Against that decision Mr Rehman appeals to
your Lordships' House.
[46] The Court of Appeal identified three errors of law. First, it considered
that the commission had given too narrow an interpretation to the concept of
national security. It did not think that a threat to national security had to be
'targeted' against this country and it accepted Mr Wrench's evidence of the need
for international co-operation against terrorism as a legitimate point of view.
It was sufficient that there was a real possibility of adverse repercussions on the
security of the United Kingdom, its system of government or its people.
[47] Secondly, the commission should not have treated national security,
international relations and other political reasons as separate compartments.
Conduct which adversely affected international relations, for example, could
thereby have adverse repercussions on security.
[48] Thirdly, it was wrong to treat the Home Secretary's reasons as counts in
an indictment and to ask whether each had been established to an appropriate
standard of proof. The question was not simply what Mr Rehman had done but
whether the Home Secretary was entitled to consider, on the basis of the case
against him as a whole, that his presence in the United Kingdom was a danger to
national security. When one is concerned simply with a fact-finding exercise
concerning past conduct such as might be undertaken by a jury, the notion of a
standard of proof is appropriate. But the Home Secretary and the commission do
not only have to form a view about what the appellant has been doing. The final
decision is evaluative, looking at the evidence as a whole, and predictive, looking
to future danger. As Lord Woolf MR said:

> '... the cumulative effect may establish that the individual is to be treated
> as a danger, although it cannot be proved to a high degree of probability that
> he has performed any individual act which would justify this conclusion.'
> (See [2000] 3 All ER 778 at 791, [2000] 2 WLR 1240 at 1254.)

[49] My Lords, I will say at once that I think that on each of these points the
Court of Appeal were right. In my opinion the fundamental flaw in the reasoning
of the commission was that although they correctly said that s 4(1) gave them full
jurisdiction to decide questions of fact and law, they did not make sufficient
allowance for certain inherent limitations, first, in the powers of the judicial
branch of government and secondly, within the judicial function, in the appellate
process. First, the limitations on the judicial power. These arise from the principle
of the separation of powers. The commission is a court, a member of the judicial

a branch of government. It was created as such to comply with art 6 of the convention. However broad the jurisdiction of a court or tribunal, whether at first instance or on appeal, it is exercising a judicial function and the exercise of that function must recognise the constitutional boundaries between judicial, executive and legislative power. Secondly, the limitations on the appellate process. They arise from the need, in matters of judgment and evaluation of evidence, to

b show proper deference to the primary decision-maker.

The separation of powers

[50] I shall deal first with the separation of powers. Section 15(3) of the 1971 Act specifies 'the interests of national security' as a ground on which the Home Secretary may consider a deportation conducive to the public good. What is

c meant by 'national security' is a question of construction and therefore a question of law within the jurisdiction of the commission, subject to appeal. But there is no difficulty about what 'national security' means. It is the security of the United Kingdom and its people. On the other hand, the question of whether something is 'in the interests' of national security is not a question of law. It is a matter of

d judgment and policy. Under the constitution of the United Kingdom and most other countries, decisions as to whether something is or is not in the interests of national security are not a matter for judicial decision. They are entrusted to the executive.

[51] In *Chandler v DPP* [1962] 3 All ER 142, [1964] AC 763 the appellants, campaigners for nuclear disarmament, had been convicted of conspiring to commit

e an offence under s 1 of the Official Secrets Act 1911, namely, for a purpose prejudicial to the safety or interests of the state to have entered a RAF station at Wethersfield. They claimed that their purpose was to prevent nuclear bombers from taking off and wanted the judge or jury to decide that stopping the bombers was not at all prejudicial to the safety or interests of the state. They said

f that, on the contrary, the state would be much safer without them. But the House ruled that whether having nuclear bombers was conducive to the safety of the state was a matter for the decision of the executive. A court could not question it.

[52] Mr Kadri QC, who appeared for Mr Rehman, emphasised that s 4(1) of the 1997 Act gave the commission the same full appellate jurisdiction as adjudicators had under the 1971 Act. But the question is not the extent of the

g commission's appellate jurisdiction. It is whether the particular issue can properly be decided by a judicial tribunal at all. The criminal and appellate courts in *Chandler*'s case had full jurisdiction over questions of fact and law in the same way as the commission. The refusal of the House to re-examine the executive's decision that having nuclear bombers was conducive to the safety of the state was

h based purely upon the separation of powers. Lord Radcliffe said:

'... we are dealing with a matter of the defence of the realm and with an Act designed to protect state secrets and the instruments of the state's defence. If the methods of arming the defence forces and the disposition of those forces are at the decision of Her Majesty's ministers for the time being,

j as we know that they are, it is not within the competence of a court of law to try the issue whether it would be better for the country that that armament or those dispositions should be different.' (See [1962] 3 All ER 142 at 151, [1964] AC 763 at 798.)

[53] Accordingly it seems to me that the commission is not entitled to differ from the opinion of the Secretary of State on the question of whether, for

example, the promotion of terrorism in a foreign country by a United Kingdom
resident would be contrary to the interests of national security. Mr Kadri rightly *a*
said that one man's terrorist was another man's freedom fighter. The decision as
to whether support for a particular movement in a foreign country would be
prejudicial to our national security may involve delicate questions of foreign
policy. And, as I shall later explain, I agree with the Court of Appeal that it is
artificial to try to segregate national security from foreign policy. They are all *b*
within the competence of responsible ministers and not the courts. The commission
was intended to act judicially and not, as the European Court recognised in
Chahal v UK (1996) 23 EHRR 413 at 468 (para 127), to substitute its own opinion
for that of the decision-maker on 'questions of pure expediency'

[54] This does not mean that the whole decision on whether deportation
would be in the interests of national security is surrendered to the Home *c*
Secretary, so as to 'defeat the purpose for which the commission was set up' (see
the commission's decision [1999] INLR 517 at 528). It is important neither to blur
nor to exaggerate the area of responsibility entrusted to the executive. The
precise boundaries were analysed by Lord Scarman, by reference to *Chandler's*
case in his speech in *Council of Civil Service Unions v Minister for the Civil Service* *d*
[1984] 3 All ER 935 at 947–948, [1985] AC 374 at 406. His analysis shows that the
commission serves at least three important functions which were shown to be
necessary by the decision in *Chahal's* case. First, the factual basis for the
executive's opinion that deportation would be in the interests of national security
must be established by evidence. It is therefore open to the commission to say
that there was no factual basis for the Home Secretary's opinion that Mr Rehman *e*
was actively supporting terrorism in Kashmir. In this respect the commission's
ability to differ from the Home Secretary's evaluation may be limited, as I shall
explain, by considerations inherent in an appellate process but not by the
principle of the separation of powers. The effect of the latter principle is only,
subject to the next point, to prevent the commission from saying that although the *f*
Home Secretary's opinion that Mr Rehman was actively supporting terrorism in
Kashmir had a proper factual basis, it does not accept that this was contrary to the
interests of national security. Secondly, the commission may reject the Home
Secretary's opinion on the ground that it was 'one which no reasonable minister
advising the Crown could in the circumstances reasonably have held'. Thirdly,
an appeal to the commission may turn upon issues which at no point lie within *g*
the exclusive province of the executive. A good example is the question, which
arose in *Chahal's* case itself, as to whether deporting someone would infringe his
rights under art 3 of the convention because there was a substantial risk that he
would suffer torture or inhuman or degrading treatment. The European
jurisprudence makes it clear that whether deportation is in the interests of *h*
national security is irrelevant to rights under art 3. If there is a danger of torture,
the government must find some other way of dealing with a threat to national
security. Whether a sufficient risk exists is a question of evaluation and
prediction based on evidence. In answering such a question, the executive enjoys
no constitutional prerogative. *j*

The standard of proof

[55] I turn next to the commission's views on the standard of proof. By way
of preliminary I feel bound to say that I think that a 'high civil balance of
probabilities' is an unfortunate mixed metaphor. The civil standard of proof
always means more likely than not. The only higher degree of probability

a required by the law is the criminal standard. But, as Lord Nicholls of Birkenhead explained in Re H (minors) (sexual abuse: standard of proof) [1996] 1 All ER 1 at 16, [1996] AC 563 at 586, some things are inherently more likely than others. It would need more cogent evidence to satisfy one that the creature seen walking in Regent's Park was more likely than not to have been a lioness than to be satisfied to the same standard of probability that it was an Alsatian. In this basis, cogent

b evidence is generally required to satisfy a civil tribunal that a person has been fraudulent or behaved in some other reprehensible manner. But the question is always whether the tribunal thinks it more probable than not.

[56] In any case, I agree with the Court of Appeal that the whole concept of a standard of proof is not particularly helpful in a case such as the present. In a criminal or civil trial in which the issue is whether a given event happened, it is

c sensible to say that one is sure that it did, or that one thinks it more likely than not that it did. But the question in the present case is not whether a given event happened but the extent of future risk. This depends upon an evaluation of the evidence of the appellant's conduct against a broad range of facts with which they may interact. The question of whether the risk to national security is sufficient

d to justify the appellant's deportation cannot be answered by taking each allegation seriatim and deciding whether it has been established to some standard of proof. It is a question of evaluation and judgment, in which it is necessary to take into account not only the degree of probability of prejudice to national security but also the importance of the security interest at stake and the serious consequences of deportation for the deportee.

e

Limitations of the appellate process

[57] This brings me to the limitations inherent in the appellate process. First, the commission is not the primary decision-maker. Not only is the decision entrusted to the Home Secretary but he also has the advantage of a wide range of

f advice from people with day-to-day involvement in security matters which the commission, despite its specialist membership, cannot match. Secondly, as I have just been saying, the question at issue in this case does not involve a Yes or No answer as to whether it is more likely than not that someone has done something but an evaluation of risk. In such questions an appellate body traditionally allows a considerable margin to the primary decision-maker. Even if the appellate body

g prefers a different view, it should not ordinarily interfere with a case in which it considers that the view of the Home Secretary is one which could reasonably be entertained. Such restraint may not be necessary in relation to every issue which the commission has to decide. As I have mentioned, the approach to whether the rights of an appellant under art 3 are likely to be infringed may be very different.

h But I think it is required in relation to the question of whether a deportation is in the interests of national security.

[58] I emphasise that the need for restraint is not based upon any limit to the commission's appellate jurisdiction. The amplitude of that jurisdiction is emphasised by the express power to reverse the exercise of a discretion. The need for

j restraint flows from a commonsense recognition of the nature of the issue and the differences in the decision-making processes and responsibilities of the Home Secretary and the commission.

Section 15(3) of the 1971 Act

[59] Finally I come to the construction of s 15(3) of the 1971 Act, which excludes certain cases from the jurisdiction of the adjudicator and by the same definition

brings them within the jurisdiction of the commission under s 2(1)(c) of the 1997
Act. For the purpose of deciding whether an appeal is excluded by s 15(3), it is a
necessary only to decide that the Home Secretary's reasons fall into one or more
of the specified categories. If his reasons could be said to relate to national
security or foreign relations or possibly both, it is unnecessary to allocate them to
one class or the other. The categories, with their sweeping-up words 'or for other
reasons of a political nature', do not create separate classes of reasons but a single b
composite class. In my opinion the other side of the coin, conferring jurisdiction
on the commission, operates in the same way. The Home Secretary does not
have to commit himself to whether his reasons can be described as relating to
national security, foreign relations or some other political category. The
commission has jurisdiction if they come under any head of the composite class.

[60] In my view, therefore, the commission was wrong to say that s 15(3) c
should be 'read disjunctively'. All that is necessary is that the appellant should be
given fair notice of the case which he has to meet, in accordance with r 10(1) of
the 1998 rules. It is unnecessary to engage in what may be a barren dispute over
whether those reasons can be said to concern national security or foreign
relations or be otherwise political, provided that they fall within the composite d
class of reasons which gives the commission jurisdiction. What matters is not
how the reasons are categorised but the reasons themselves and the facts relied
upon to support them.

[61] I would therefore dismiss the appeal. The case should be remitted to the
commission to hear and determine in accordance with the principles stated by the
House. e

Postscript

[62] I wrote this speech some three months before the recent events in New
York and Washington. They are a reminder that in matters of national security,
the cost of failure can be high. This seems to me to underline the need for the f
judicial arm of government to respect the decisions of ministers of the Crown on
the question of whether support for terrorist activities in a foreign country
constitutes a threat to national security. It is not only that the executive has
access to special information and expertise in these matters. It is also that such
decisions, with serious potential results for the community, require a legitimacy
which can be conferred only by entrusting them to persons responsible to the g
community through the democratic process. If the people are to accept the
consequences of such decisions, they must be made by persons whom the people
have elected and whom they can remove.

LORD CLYDE. h

[63] My Lords, I have had the advantage of reading a draft of the speech of my
noble and learned friend Lord Hoffmann. For the reasons he has given I too
would dismiss this appeal.

LORD HUTTON. j

[64] My Lords, I have had the advantage of reading in draft the speeches of my
noble and learned friends Lord Slynn of Hadley, Lord Steyn and Lord Hoffmann.
I agree with them that the appeal should be dismissed on two grounds. The first is
that the commission fell into error in holding that for a person to constitute a
threat against national security he must engage in, promote, or encourage violent
activity—

a 'which is targeted at the United Kingdom, its system of government or its people. This includes activities directed against the overthrow or destabilisation of a foreign government if that foreign government is likely to take reprisals against the United Kingdom which affect the security of the United Kingdom or of its nationals.' (See [1999] INLR 517 at 528.)

b In my opinion the Court of Appeal ([2000] 3 All ER 778, [2000] 3 WLR 1240) was right to hold that the promotion of terrorism against any state is capable of being a threat to the security of the United Kingdom, and that there can be an overlap between the three situations referred to in s 15(3) of the Immigration Act 1971.

[65] Secondly, I agree with my noble and learned friends that the Court of Appeal was right to hold that the Secretary of State was concerned to assess the *c* extent of future risk and that he was entitled to make a decision to deport on the ground that an individual is a danger to national security, viewing the case against him as a whole, although it cannot be proved to a high degree of probability that he has carried out any individual act which would justify the conclusion that he is a danger.

[66] I would dismiss the appeal.

d

Appeal dismissed.

Kate O'Hanlon   Barrister.

Burman v Mount Cook Land Ltd   *a*
[2001] EWCA Civ 1712

COURT OF APPEAL, CIVIL DIVISION

CHADWICK LJ AND SIR MURRAY STUART-SMITH

11 OCTOBER, 20 NOVEMBER 2001

b

Landlord and tenant – Leasehold enfranchisement – Landlord's counter-notice – Tenant serving notice on landlord claiming new lease of flat – Landlord purporting to serve counter-notice – Counter-notice not stating whether tenant's claim admitted or not admitted and which if any of tenant's proposals accepted – Whether counter-notice valid – Leasehold Reform, Housing and Urban Development Act 1993, s 45.   *c*

The claimant tenant had the right, under the provisions of the Leasehold Reform, Housing and Urban Development Act 1993, to acquire a new lease of her flat on payment of a premium. She gave notice to the defendant landlord under s 42 of *d* the 1993 Act claiming to exercise that right. In compliance with s 42, the notice set out the premium which the tenant proposed to pay for a new lease; the terms which she proposed in respect of it; and the date by which the landlord was required to give a counter-notice under s 45(2)[a]. Section 45(2) required that the counter-notice should (a) state that the landlord admitted that the tenant had on the relevant date the right to acquire a new lease to the flat; or (b) state that, for *e* reasons specified, the landlord did not admit that the tenant had such a right on that date. Section 45(3) provided that if a counter-notice complied with the requirements in s 45(2)(a), it had additionally to state which (if any) of the proposals contained in the tenant's notice were accepted or not accepted by the landlord, and specify, in relation to each proposal which was not accepted, the landlord's *f* counter-proposal. The landlord gave the tenant a written notice, described in the heading as a landlord's counter-notice under s 45, containing a statement that the landlord did not accept the tenant's proposal as to premium and specifying the landlord's counter-proposal in relation to it, but failing to contain a statement that the landlord did or did not admit that the tenant had on the relevant date the right to acquire a new lease of the flat, or a statement as to which (if any) of the *g* proposals contained in the tenant's notice were accepted by the landlord. The tenant took the view that the landlord's notice was not a valid counter-notice under s 45(2), and accordingly made an application to the county court under s 49 of the Act for an order determining the terms of the acquisition in accordance with the proposals contained in her notice. On the application, the judge asked *h* himself whether a reasonable tenant could have been misled into thinking that the landlord's counter-notice did not admit the right to a new lease. He held that such a tenant would not have been so misled because (i) the landlord's counter-proposal as to premium would have been inconsistent with its not having admitted the tenant's right and (ii) the counter-notice could not be a *j* notice under s 45(2)(b) since it contained no reasons why the tenant's right had not been admitted. On that basis, the judge concluded that the landlord's notice was an effective counter-notice under s 45(2)(a). Accordingly, he dismissed the application, and the tenant appealed.

---

a   Section 45, so far as material, is set out at [2], below

a **Held** – In order to comply with s 45(2)(a) and (3) of the 1993 Act, a landlord's counter-notice had to state (i) that the landlord admitted that the tenant had on the relevant date the right to acquire a new lease of his flat, and (ii) which (if any) of the proposals contained in the tenant's notice had been accepted by the landlord, specifying the landlord's counter-proposal in relation to each proposal which was not accepted. Such a conclusion was consistent with the proper

b working of the statutory scheme which required the tenant to be left in no doubt as to what the landlord admitted, how far the tenant's proposals were accepted and what (if any) were the landlord's counter-proposals. It followed in the instant case that the judge had asked himself the wrong question. The correct question was whether the counter-notice served by the landlord stated that it admitted that the tenant had on the relevant date the right to acquire a new lease of the flat.

c If that question was answered in the affirmative, there was a further question, namely whether the counter-notice stated which (if any) of the proposals contained in the tenant's notice had been accepted by the landlord and which (if any) of those proposals had not been accepted. The answer to both those questions was No. The counter-notice had plainly not contained, in terms, either

d of the requisite statements and there was no permissible process of construction which could lead to the conclusion that it had contained such statements. The fact that the notice could not be a valid notice under s 45(2)(b) did not demand or justify the response that it had to be a valid notice under s 45(2)(a). That might have been a legitimate response if it were accepted that the notice had to be valid under one of the paragraphs of s 45(2), but the notice was not valid under s 45

e simply because it purported, by its heading, to have been given under that section. Furthermore, the fact that the statement that the landlord did not accept the premium proposed by the tenant was consistent with a notice under s 45(2)(a) did not lead to the conclusion that the notice had to be a notice under that paragraph, or that the notice had to be construed as if it contained an admission

f of the tenant's right. If the notice were otherwise an invalid notice, the inclusion of some of the information which a valid notice contained did not alter that position. The true effect of the landlord's counter-notice was that it informed the tenant that the landlord had not decided whether to admit, or not admit, the tenant's right to acquire a new lease—or had chosen not to disclose to the tenant whether the right was admitted or not admitted—and had not decided (or not

g chosen to disclose) whether, if there were to be a new lease, it accepted, or did not accept, that the terms were to be the same as those proposed in the tenant's notice. So construed, the counter-notice did not comply with the requirements of s 45(2). Accordingly, the appeal would be allowed (see [15], [16], [19], [28], [29], [31]–[34], below).

h *Carradine Properties Ltd v Aslam* [1976] 1 All ER 573 and *Mannai Investment Co Ltd v Eagle Star Life Assurance Co Ltd* [1997] 3 All ER 352 distinguished.

Notes

For landlord's counter-notice, see 27(2) *Halsbury's Laws* (4th edn reissue) para 1543.

j For the Leasehold Reform, Housing and Urban Development Act 1993, s 45, see 23 *Halsbury's Statutes* (4th edn) (1997 reissue) 576.

Cases referred to in judgments

Andrews v Brewer [1997] EGCS 19, CA.
Carradine Properties Ltd v Aslam [1976] 1 All ER 573, [1976] 1 WLR 442.
John Lyon Grammar School (Keepers and Governors) v Secchi [1999] 3 EGLR 49, CA.

Lewis v MTC (Cars) Ltd [1974] 3 All ER 423, [1974] 1 WLR 1499; *affd* [1975] 1 All ER
874, [1975] 1 WLR 457, CA.   a
Mannai Investment Co Ltd v Eagle Star Life Assurance Co Ltd [1997] 3 All ER 352,
[1997] AC 749, [1997] 2 WLR 945, HL.
Panayi v Roberts [1993] 2 EGLR 51, CA.
Speedwell Estates Ltd v Dalziel [2001] EWCA Civ 1277, [2001] All ER (D) 454 (Jul).
Willingale v Globalgrange Ltd [2000] 2 EGLR 55, CA.   b
York v Casey [1998] 2 EGLR 25, CA.

Appeal
The appellant, Meera Burman, the tenant of flat 4, Rossetti House, 106–110 Hallam
Street, London W1 (the flat), appealed with permission of Judge Knight QC from   c
his order made in Central London County Court on 20 November 2000
dismissing her application under s 49 of the Leasehold Reform, Housing and
Urban Development Act 1993 for an order determining the terms of the
acquisition of the flat in accordance with the proposals contained in a notice
served by her on the respondent landlord, Mount Cook Land Ltd, under s 42 of
the 1993 Act. The facts are set out in the judgment of Chadwick LJ.   d

Edwin Prince (instructed by *Wallace & Partners*) for the appellant.
Anthony Radevsky (instructed by *Speechly Bircham*) for the respondent.

Cur adv vult
e

20 November 2001. The following judgments were delivered.

CHADWICK LJ.
[1] This is an appeal against an order made in the Central London County
Court on 20 November 2000 by Judge Knight QC in proceedings for a new lease f
brought by the appellant under the Leasehold Reform, Housing and Urban
Development Act 1993.
[2] Chapter II in Pt I of the 1993 Act confers on the tenant of a flat held under
a long lease at a low rent, in the circumstances mentioned in s 39(2), the right
(exercisable subject to and in accordance with the provisions in that Chapter) to
acquire a new lease of the flat on payment of a premium. A claim by a tenant to g
exercise the right is made by the giving of notice under s 42 of the Act. Section
45 of the Act provides for the landlord to give a counter-notice to the tenant.
Subsection (2) of that section requires that—

'The counter-notice must comply with one of the following requirements— h
(a) state that the landlord admits that the tenant had on the relevant date the
right to acquire a new lease of his flat; (b) state that, for such reasons as are
specified in the counter-notice, the landlord does not admit that the tenant
had such a right on that date; (c) contain such a statement as is mentioned in
paragraph (a) or (b) above but state that the landlord intends to make an
application for an order under section 47(1) on the grounds that he intends j
to redevelop any premises in which the flat is contained.'

In that context 'the relevant date' is the date on which notice of the tenant's claim
is given to the landlord under s 42 (see s 39(8) of the Act). Section 45(3) of the
1993 Act is in these terms:

a
'If the counter-notice complies with the requirement set out in subsection (2)(a), it must in addition—(a) state which (if any) of the proposals contained in the tenant's notice are accepted by the landlord and which (if any) of those proposals are not so accepted; and (b) specify, in relation to each proposal which is not accepted, the landlord's counter-proposal.'

b
The question in the present case is whether a notice which does not state, in terms, that the landlord does, or does not, admit that the tenant had on the relevant date the right to acquire a new lease of her flat—and which does not state, in terms, which (if any) of the proposals contained in the tenant's notice are accepted by the landlord—is a valid counter-notice under s 45 of the 1993 Act.

[3] The appellant, Ms Meera Burman, is tenant of a flat known as 4 Rossetti

c House, 105–110 Hallam Street, London W1. The respondent, Mount Cook Land Ltd, is the landlord in relation to that lease for the purposes of the provisions in Ch II of Pt I of the 1993 Act. It is not in dispute that the appellant holds the flat under a long lease at a low rent; and that, accordingly, she is a 'qualifying tenant' for the purposes of those provisions. Nor is it in dispute that she had occupied the flat as her only or principal home for a period in excess of three years in the ten years

d before the relevant date; so that she was a qualifying tenant who had the right to acquire a new lease (see s 39(2) and (2B) of the Act).

[4] On 19 October 1999 the appellant gave notice to the respondent under s 42 of the 1993 Act. That notice complied with the requirements of that section; in particular, it set out the matters required by s 42(3)(b). Those matters include:

e (i) the premium which the tenant proposes to pay in respect of the grant of a new lease; (ii) the terms which the tenant proposes should be contained in any such lease; and (iii) the date by which the landlord must respond to the notice by giving a counter-notice under s 45 of the Act. In the present case the premium which the appellant proposed to pay for a new lease was £110,000; the terms which she

f proposed in respect of the new lease were that it should be a—

'lease at a peppercorn for a term expiring 90 years after the term date of the existing lease and otherwise on the same terms as the existing lease subject to any amendments required by Sections 56 and 57 of the Act'

and the date by which the respondent was required to give a counter-notice was

g 25 December 1999.

[5] On 23 December 1999 the respondent, by its solicitors, gave written notice to the appellant. The notice was headed with the description:

'LEASEHOLD REFORM, HOUSING AND URBAN DEVELOPMENT ACT 1993

h   Section 45
                        Landlord's Counter-Notice'

After setting out the names and respective addresses of the appellant and the respondent, the notice continued in these terms:

j   'TAKE NOTE THAT
          1. We have received your notice dated 19 October 1999 claiming a new lease for Flat 4 Rossetti House 106–110 Hallam Street London W1 ("the Notice").
          2. The Landlord does not accept the premium proposed by the Tenant.
          3. The Landlord's counter-proposal to the premium proposed is £175,000.

4. The address in England and Wales at which the Landlord may be given
Notice under Part 1 Chapter 2 of the Act is Speechly Bircham 6 St Andrews a
Street London EC4A 3LX.'

[6] The notice of 23 December 1999 does not contain a statement that the
landlord does, or does not, admit that the tenant had on the relevant date the
right to acquire a new lease of the flat. Nor does it contain a statement as to
which (if any) of the proposals contained in the tenant's notice are accepted by b
the landlord; in particular it does not state whether the landlord accepts the
tenant's proposal that the terms of the new lease—other than the rent (a
peppercorn) and the duration and commencement of the term (90 years from the
term date of the existing lease), which are prescribed by s 56(1) of the 1993
Act—should be the same terms as the existing lease; as to which, see s 57 of the Act. c
On the other hand, the notice does contain a statement that the landlord does not
accept the tenant's proposal as to premium; and does specify the landlord's
counter-proposal in relation to premium.

[7] The appellant took the view that the notice of 23 December 1999 was not
a valid counter-notice under s 45 of the 1993 Act. Accordingly, she made
application to the Central London County Court on 19 May 2000 for an order d
under s 49 of that Act. Section 49(1) is in these terms (so far as material):

'Where the tenant's notice has been given in accordance with section 42
but—(a) the landlord has failed to give the tenant a counter-notice in
accordance with section 45(1), or (b) if required to give a further counter-
notice to the tenant by or by virtue of section 46(4) or section 47(4) or (5), the e
landlord has failed to comply with that requirement, the court may, on the
application of the tenant, make an order determining, *in accordance with the
proposals contained in the tenant's notice*, the terms of acquisition.' (My emphasis.)

The effect of the words that I have emphasised is to limit the power of the court,
when determining the terms upon which the tenant is to acquire a new tenancy f
on an application under s 49(1), to the proposals contained in the tenant's notice
(see the decision of this court in *Willingale v Globalgrange Ltd* [2000] 2 EGLR 55).

[8] The respondent denied that the appellant was entitled to an order under
s 49 of the 1993 Act; and, by counterclaim in the proceedings, sought a
declaration that the notice of 23 December 1999 was a valid counter-notice. That g
issue came before Judge Knight QC. He dismissed the appellant's claim and
made a declaration that the notice of 23 December 1993 was 'a valid and effective
Counter-Notice under Section 45(2)(a) of the [1993] Act'. He gave the appellant
permission to appeal against that order.

[9] The reasons which led the judge to the conclusion that he reached appear h
from para 7 of the written judgment which he handed down:

'I have, therefore, to ask myself the question whether a reasonable tenant
could be misled into thinking that the landlord's counter-notice did not
admit the right to a new lease? I must determine this question objectively.
In my judgment a reasonable tenant would not be so misled. In reaching this j
conclusion I have taken into account that a reasonable tenant would have a
degree of familiarity with the scheme of Ch II of the Act, in particular the
notice and counter-notice provision. Subsections (2) and (3) of s 45 have to
be read together. Paragraphs 2 and 3 of the counter-notice comply with
s 45(3), which are applicable to a s 45(2)(a) counter-notice. These paragraphs
have no application to a s 45(2)(b) counter-notice, which must state reasons

a   why the landlord does not admit the tenant's right to a new lease. The counter-notice contains no such reasons. In my view the only reasonable conclusion which a reasonable tenant could come to is that the landlord did admit the tenant's right, but did not accept the proposed premium, as to which there was a counter-proposal. Such a counter-proposal would be inconsistent with the landlord not admitting the tenant's right. The statutory

b   scheme does not cater for a hybrid counter-notice, ie one which does not admit a tenant's right to a new lease, while at the same time specifying a landlord's counter-proposal. In my judgment a reasonable tenant on receipt of this counter-notice would reasonably conclude that the presence of the landlord's counter-proposal to the tenant's proposed premium, and the absence of any reasons for not admitting the tenant's right to a new tenancy,

c   that the tenant's right to a new tenancy was admitted.'

[10] The first question for decision on this appeal, as it seems to me, is whether the judge was right to pose the question which, as he thought, he had to decide in the terms that he did: 'whether a reasonable tenant could be misled into thinking that the landlord's counter-notice did not admit the right to a new lease?'

d   Implicit in the question posed by the judge is the assumption that a notice served by a landlord in response to a tenant's notice under s 42 of the Act is capable of being a valid counter-notice under s 45 provided that a reasonable tenant, on receipt of the notice, could not be misled into thinking that the right to a new lease was not admitted. To put the point another way, is it right to assume—as

e   the judge did assume—that s 45(2)(a) of the Act requires the landlord's notice to do more than bring home to a reasonable tenant, having a degree of familiarity with the scheme of Ch II, Pt I, that the landlord does not deny the right to a new lease? Or does s 45(2)(a) of the Act require, as a literal construction of the statutory language would suggest, that the landlord's notice must state that the landlord admits that the tenant had on the relevant date the right to acquire a new

f   lease of his flat?

[11] The answer to that question is not to be found in the terms of the landlord's notice. The relevant inquiry is what does the statutory language require. The task is to construe the words which Parliament has used in the context of the statutory scheme. It is only when the court has informed itself of

g   the true nature of the statutory requirement that it can sensibly address the second question: does the notice in this case meet that requirement?

[12] I turn, therefore, to consider the statutory scheme, of which s 45 is a part. As I have said, s 42 of the 1993 Act provides that a claim by a qualifying tenant to exercise the right to acquire a new lease is made by the giving of a notice to the

h   landlord. Section 45 provides for the landlord to give a counter-notice in response to the tenant's notice. The counter-notice may contain a statement that the landlord does not admit that the tenant had on the relevant date the right to acquire a new lease of the flat (see paras (b) and (c) of s 45(2)). In such a case the landlord may apply to the court, within two months of the date of the giving of

j   the counter-notice, for a declaration to that effect (see s 46 of the Act). But, if the landlord does not make an application under s 46 within that period of two months—or subsequently withdraws an application made under that section— the position is as if no counter-notice has been given; and s 49 of the Act applies (see s 46(2) of the Act).

[13] Where a landlord who has given a counter-notice which contains a statement that the tenant's right to acquire a new lease is not admitted makes,

and does not withdraw, an application to the court under s 46 of the Act, the court
may make the declaration sought. In such a case the tenant's notice ceases to
have effect on the order becoming final (see s 46(3) of the Act). Or the court may
refuse the declaration and dismiss the application. In such a case—save where the
counter-notice has contained a statement (under s 45(2)(c) of the Act) that the
landlord intends to apply for an order under s 47(1) on the grounds that he
intends to redevelop any premises in which the flat is contained—the counter-
notice must be declared to be of no effect, and the court must require the landlord
to give a further counter-notice to the tenant within such time as is specified in
the order (see s 46(4) of the Act). Where, under s 46(4), the court requires a
further counter-notice to be given, the counter-notice must comply with
requirements of s 45(3) of the Act—that is to say, it must state which (if any) of
the proposals contained are accepted by the landlord and which (if any) of those
proposals are not so accepted, and must specify, in relation to each proposal
which is not accepted, the landlord's counter-proposal 'as if [the further
counter-notice] were a counter-notice under [s 45] complying with the requirement
set out in subsection (2)(a) of that section' (see s 46(6) of the Act). It is, I think,
implicit in s 46(6) that the further counter-notice is not required to state that the
landlord admits the tenant's right to acquire a new lease; so as actually to comply
with s 45(2)(a) of the Act. That question having been determined by the court on
the application under s 46, no such statement is needed.

[14] Section 47 of the 1993 Act is directed to the case where a landlord has
given a counter-notice under s 45 which contains a statement of intention to
redevelop—that is to say, which complies with the requirement set out in
s 45(2)(c). In such a case the landlord may apply to the court within two months
for an order declaring that the right to acquire a new lease shall not be exercisable
by reason of the landlord's intention to redevelop. If no application is made
within the two-month period—or is made and subsequently withdrawn—the
landlord must give a further counter-notice to the tenant—see s 47(5). If an
application is made and the court makes the order sought, the tenant's notice
ceases to have effect. But, if the application is dismissed, then—as in the case of
an application under s 46 of the Act—the counter-notice must be declared of no
effect and the court must require the landlord to give a further counter-notice to
the tenant within such time as is specified in the order—see s 47(4) of the Act.
And, again, where, under s 47(4) or (5), a further counter-notice has to be given,
the counter-notice must comply with requirements of s 45(3) of the Act 'as if it
were a counter-notice under [s 45] complying with the requirement set out in
subsection (2)(a) of that section' (see s 47(8) of the Act). There are provisions
which have the effect of deferring consideration of an application under s 47 of
the Act until after the determination of an application (if any) under s 46, but it is
unnecessary to describe those provisions in detail.

[15] Section 48(1) of the 1993 Act is in these terms:

'Where the landlord has given the tenant—(a) a counter-notice under
section 45 which complies with the requirement set out in subsection (2)(a)
of that section, or (b) the further counter-notice required by or by virtue of
section 46(4) or section 47(4) or (5), but any of the terms of acquisition
remain in dispute at the end of the period of two months beginning with the
date when the counter-notice or further counter-notice was so given, a
leasehold valuation tribunal may, on the application of either the tenant or
the landlord, determine the matters in dispute.'

a   Section 48(2) requires that an application under sub-s (1) for the determination of matters in dispute must be made not later than the end of the period of six months beginning with the date on which the counter-notice or further counter-notice was given to the tenant. Section 48(3) provides that where the landlord has given to the tenant such a counter-notice or further counter-notice as is mentioned in paras (a) or (b) of s 48(1) and all the terms of acquisition have either

b   been agreed or determined by a leasehold valuation tribunal, either party may apply to the court for an order for the performance or discharge of any obligations arising out of the tenant's notice. If no application is made under s 48(1) for the determination of matters in dispute, or if no lease is entered into and no application is made under s 48(3) for an order for the performance of the obligations arising out of the tenant's notice, within the time periods respectively

c   prescribed, the tenant's notice is deemed to have been withdrawn (see s 53(1) of the Act).

[16] With these provisions in mind, the statutory scheme—following service by the tenant of a notice which complies with s 42 of the Act—may be summarised as follows. (1) A landlord who intends to contest the tenant's right to acquire a

d   new lease must (a) serve a counter-notice which states that the landlord does not admit that right, (b) specify in the counter-notice the reasons why the right is not admitted, and (c) make application to the court within two months of the counter-notice for a declaration that the tenant does not have the right claimed. Failure to take those steps will enable the tenant to apply to the court, under

e   s 49(1), for an order determining that the terms of acquisition shall be in accordance with the proposals contained in the tenant's notice. (2) A landlord who intends to admit the tenant's right to acquire a new lease, but who wishes to advance counter-proposals as to the terms of acquisition, must serve a counter-notice which (a) states that the landlord does admit the right, (b) states which of the proposals contained in the tenant's notice are accepted by the landlord,

f   (c) states which of the proposals contained in the tenant's notice are not accepted by the landlord, and (d) specifies, in relation to each proposal which is not accepted, the landlord's counter-proposal. Again, failure to take those steps will enable the tenant to apply to the court, under s 49(1), for an order determining that the terms of acquisition shall be in accordance with the proposals contained in the tenant's notice. (3) A landlord who intends to resist the acquisition of a new

g   lease on the grounds that he intends to redevelop the premises in which the flat is contained (whether or not he admits the tenant's right to acquire a new lease) must (a) serve a counter-notice which states that the landlord does, or does not, admit (as the case may be) the tenant's right to acquire a new lease and states that the landlord intends to make an application for an order under s 47(1) on the grounds that he intends to redevelop and (b) make an application to the court

h   within two months of the counter-notice for a declaration that the tenant's right to acquire a new lease shall not be exercisable by the tenant by reason of the landlord's intention to redevelop. Failure to take the first of those steps will enable the tenant to apply to the court, under s 49(1) of the Act, for an order

j   determining that the terms of acquisition shall be in accordance with the proposals contained in the tenant's notice. Failure to apply for an order under s 47(1) within the prescribed period of two months leads—in a case where there has been no application for an order under s 46(1) of the Act—to the requirement to serve a further counter-notice which complies with s 45(3). Failure to comply with that requirement leads, once again, to the position in which the tenant can apply to the court for an order under s 49(1) of the Act. (4) A landlord who has

served a counter-notice in the appropriate form and who has applied to the court
(under s 46(1) of the Act) for a declaration that the tenant had no right to acquire   *a*
a new lease, or (under s 47(1) of the Act) for a declaration that the right to
acquire a new lease shall not be exercisable, or for each of those declarations, but
whose applications have been dismissed, must give a further counter-notice
which complies with s 45(3) of the Act. Failure to do so leads, once again, to the
position in which the tenant can apply to the court for an order under s 49(1) of   *b*
the Act. (5) It is only where the landlord has served a counter-notice which
complies with the requirement set out in s 45(2)(a) (that is to say, a counter-notice
which states that the landlord admits that the tenant had on the relevant date the
right to acquire a new lease of the flat)—or which is served following the
determination by the court that the tenant did have that right or was entitled to
exercise that right—that the procedure for the determination by a leasehold   *c*
valuation tribunal of matters in dispute in relation to the terms of acquisition can
be invoked under s 48(1) of the Act. And, in any such case, the counter-notice
must comply with the requirements set out in s 45(3) of the Act—thereby
ensuring that the matters in dispute are identified and defined.

[17] It can be seen that the landlord's counter-notice is integral to the proper   *d*
working of the statutory scheme. The scheme requires that the tenant must
know, by the date specified in his own notice (under s 42(3)(f) of the Act),
whether the landlord has given a counter-notice in accordance with s 45(1).
Absent a counter-notice in accordance with s 45(1), the period of six months
within which the tenant can apply for an order under s 49(1) begins to run from
that date. Further, if the landlord does give a counter-notice by the date specified   *e*
in the tenant's notice under s 42, the scheme requires that the tenant must know,
from that counter-notice, whether the landlord does, or does not, admit that the
tenant had on the relevant date the right to acquire a new lease; and (whether or
not the landlord admits that right) must know whether the landlord intends to
apply for an order under s 47 of the Act. If the landlord admits the right to acquire   *f*
a new lease, and does not intend to apply for an order under s 47, the period of
six months during which the tenant can apply to a leasehold valuation tribunal
under s 48(1) for the determination of any terms of acquisition which may be in
dispute begins to run from the date on which the counter-notice was given. If the
landlord does not admit the right to acquire a new tenancy—or (whether or not
he admits the right) states his intention to apply for an order under s 47 of the   *g*
Act—the period of two months during which the landlord can apply to the court
under ss 46(1) or 47(1) (as the case may be) begins to run from the date on which
the counter-notice was given; and the tenant needs to know that, because the
landlord's failure to make an application before the end of that period of two
months will, itself, be an event which determines the period during which the   *h*
tenant can apply for an order under s 49(1) (see ss 46(2), 47(3) and (5) and 49(3) of
the Act).

[18] The importance of the landlord's counter-notice to the proper working of
the statutory scheme is reflected in the language of s 45(2) and (3) of the Act. The
counter-notice *must comply* with the requirements in one or other of paras (a), (b)   *j*
or (c) in sub-s (2). It *must state* whether the landlord admits, or does not admit,
that the tenant had the right to acquire a new lease. If the counter-notice complies
with the requirement in sub-s (2)(a)—that is to say, if it does state that the
landlord admits the right—sub-s (3)(a) requires that it *must* in addition *state* which
(if any) of the proposals contained in the tenant's notice are accepted by the
landlord and which are not so accepted; and sub-s (3)(b) requires that it *must*

a *specify*, in relation to each proposal which is not accepted, the landlord's counter-proposal. The words which I have emphasised are mandatory and specific. There is good reason why they should be. The proper working of the statutory scheme requires that the tenant is left in no doubt as to what the landlord admits, how far the tenant's proposals are accepted, and what (if any) are the landlord's counter-proposals. Further, the importance of the statement which

b sub-s (2)(a) requires, *as an admission*, is emphasised by sub-s (5) of s 45 of the Act.

[19] In my view the answer to the question 'what does s 45(2)(a) of the 1993 Act require?' is not open to doubt. If a notice is to comply with the requirement under that paragraph it must state that the landlord admits that the tenant had on the relevant date the right to acquire a new lease of his flat. Further, the notice must state which (if any) of the proposals contained in the tenant's notice are

c accepted by the landlord, as well as stating which of those proposals are not accepted and specifying, in relation to each proposal which is not accepted, the landlord's counter-proposal. Section 45(2)(a) must be read in conjunction with s 45(3) of the Act.

[20] The question which the judge posed for decision—'whether a reasonable

d tenant could be misled into thinking that the landlord's counter-notice did not admit the right to a new lease?'—is, I think, derived from the test applied by Goulding J in *Carradine Properties Ltd v Aslam* [1976] 1 All ER 573 at 576, [1976] 1 WLR 442 at 444—and approved in the House of Lords in *Mannai Investment Co Ltd v Eagle Star Life Assurance Co Ltd* [1997] 3 All ER 352, [1997] AC 749 by Lord Steyn, by Lord Hoffmann and by Lord Clyde ([1997] 3 All ER 352 at 373, 381, 382, [1997]

e AC 749 at 772, 780, 782 respectively). In each of those cases the notice in question was given under break clause in a lease. In the *Carradine* case the lease could be determined by either party if it (the landlord) or he (the tenant)—

'shall desire to determine the present demise at the expiration of the first seven or 14 years of the said term and shall give 12 months notice in writing

f   of such its or his desire ...'

In the *Mannai* case the break clause—cl 7(13)—was in these terms (so far as material):

'The tenant may by serving not less than six month's notice in writing on

g   the landlord or its solicitors such notice to expire on the third anniversary of the term commencement date determine this lease ...'

In each case the notice contained an error. In the *Carradine* case the error was obvious on the face of the notice. The notice, served by the landlord's solicitors and dated 6 September 1974, purported to determine the lease on 17 September

h 1973—a date already in the past. Goulding J held that the tenant must have seen that there was a mistake; and must have appreciated that the notice was given for termination in September 1975. In the *Mannai* case the term of the lease had commenced on 13 January 1992. The tenant gave notice to determine the lease 'on 12 January 1995'. The third anniversary of the term commencement date was

j 13 January 1995. The House of Lords held (Lord Goff of Chieveley and Lord Jauncey of Tullichettle dissenting) that what the lease required was a notice sufficient to communicate to the landlord the tenant's desire to terminate the lease on the third anniversary of the commencement of the term; and that (although the date specified in the notice was not the date of the third anniversary of the commencement date) the notice given by the tenant fulfilled that function. But it is important to appreciate that, in neither of those cases, did the break

clause in the lease require the notice to be given in any particular form. The *a*
relevant question was whether the notice was sufficient to leave the recipient in
no doubt as to the information which the giver of the notice wished to
communicate. The point is made by Lord Hoffmann in the *Mannai* case [1997]
3 All ER 352 at 377, [1997] AC 749 at 776:

> 'If the clause had said that the notice had to be on blue paper, it would have *b*
> been no good serving a notice on pink paper, however clear it might have
> been that the tenant wanted to terminate the lease. But the condition in
> cl 7(13) related solely to the meaning which the notice had to communicate
> to the landlord.'

Observations to the same effect are found in the speech of Lord Steyn ('This is not *c*
a case of a contractual right to determine which prescribes as an indispensable
condition for its effective exercise that the notice must contain specific
information' (see [1997] 3 All ER 352 at 368, [1997] AC 749 at 767)) and in the
speech of Lord Clyde ('But it is not required that the notice should include
mention of the date of the intended determination of the lease' (see [1997] 3 All ER
352 at 382, [1997] AC 749 at 781)).   *d*

[21] The principles reviewed and restated in the *Mannai* case were applied to
the contents of a statutory notice by this court in *York v Casey* [1998] 2 EGLR 25.
The notice was to be served under s 20(1)(c) of the Housing Act 1988, in advance
of the creation of a tenancy, with the object of ensuring that the tenancy should
be an assured shorthold tenancy. Section 20(2) of the 1988 Act required that the *e*
notice was in the prescribed form; was served before the tenancy was entered
into; was served by the person who was to be the landlord on the person who was
to be the tenant; and contained a statement that the assured tenancy to which it
related was to be a shorthold tenancy. Regulation 2 of the Assured Tenancy and
Agricultural Occupancies (Forms) Regulations 1988, SI 1988/2203 prescribed that
form no 7 in Sch 1 to the regulations 'or a form substantially to the like effect' *f*
should be used. The prescribed form contained a statement, for completion as
appropriate: 'You are proposing to take a tenancy of the dwelling known as [   ]
from [   ] to [   ].' In completing the form the landlord's agents inserted in
that statement a commencement date of 28 September 1996 (which was correct)
and a termination date of 6 September 1996. The latter was an obvious error, *g*
being the date of the notice itself and a date before the commencement date. The
notice had been sent under cover of a letter which set out the true position;
namely that the tenancy was to be for a period of six months from 28 September
1996. Peter Gibson LJ (with whose judgment Bennett J agreed) said this (at 27):

> '... what the court must do is to see whether the error in the notice was *h*
> obvious or evident and, second, whether notwithstanding that error the
> notice read in its context is sufficiently clear to leave a reasonable recipient in
> no reasonable doubt as to the terms of the notice.'

The court held that it was plain, reading the notice and the letter together, that *j*
the intended termination date was 27 March 1997.

[22] It is of interest to note the two other cases on notices under s 20(1)(c) of
the 1988 Act to which reference is made in the judgment in *York's* case. In the one,
Panayi v Roberts [1993] 2 EGLR 51, the decision went the other way. On the facts,
this court (Mann and Ralph Gibson LJJ) found that the mistake in the termination
date was not obvious. Mann LJ observed (at 52):

a   'The narrow issue is whether a notice which gives a wrong date (here a termination) is "substantially to the same effect" as one which gives the correct date. Authority and an evident error apart, I find it difficult to say that it was.'

In the other case, *Andrews v Brewer* [1997] EGCS 19, Auld LJ (with whom Morland J agreed) found that there was an obvious error—in that the termination date in
b   respect of a tenancy for one year commencing on 29 May 1993 was expressed to be 28 May 1993. As Peter Gibson LJ pointed out in *York's* case, those cases illustrate the application of the principle to different facts.

[**23**] I have said that it is important to appreciate that in neither of the two cases on notices served under break clauses to which I have referred—the
c   *Carradine* case and the *Mannai* case—did the break clause in the lease require the notice to be given in any particular form. Had the break clause required the notice to be in a particular form, the result would have been different. The point was recognised by Peter Gibson LJ in *York's* case [1998] 2 EGLR 25 at 27:

'It is of course right, as [counsel] for the defendants, has submitted, that one
d   should bear in mind that in a statutory context there may be requirements which have to be observed and without which a notice will be invalid. But the same may be true in the case of a contractual notice. For my part, I can see no material distinction between the approach in a case such as the present and the approach which the House of Lords has said [in *Mannai*] should be adopted in the case of a notice in a contractual setting.'
e

[**24**] The validity of a tenant's notice under s 42 of the 1993 Act was considered by this court in *John Lyon Grammar School (Keepers and Governors) v Secchi* [1999] 3 EGLR 49. Section 42(3)(f) of the 1993 Act requires a tenant's notice to specify the date by which the landlord must respond by giving a counter-notice; and
f   s 42(5) requires that that date must be a date falling not less than two months after the date of the giving of the notice. Notices dated 11 February 1997 specified 11 April 1997 as the date by which the landlord was required to serve a counter-notice. One notice was served on the landlord on 12 February 1997; the other notice was served on a third party—who had entered into covenants in the lease to repair and insure the premises—on 23 April 1997. The court held that the
g   notices were invalid. After referring to the relevant passages in the *Mannai* case, and to *York's* case, Aldous LJ (with whose judgment Beldam LJ and Tuckey LJ agreed) said this (at 51–52):

'[Counsel for the appellant landlord] drew attention to the speeches of Lord Steyn and Lord Hoffmann, which, he submitted, made it clear that the
h   conclusion sought to be reached could only be achieved if the error in the notice was obvious and, also, was sufficiently clear to leave the reasonable recipient in no reasonable doubt as to its terms. In the present case the date was chosen by the tenants to set the time for the counternotices. The landlord could not know when the notices had been given to the third party
j   and therefore had to rely upon the date in the notices. As it turned out, the third party was not given notice until 23 April. It followed that the date for the service of the counternotices could not have been 12 April, as was suggested to be the obvious date to be inferred by the landlord when he received the notices. There was no way in which the notices could be construed as requiring the date for the counternotices to be no later than 23 June. It followed that, even applying the principles set out by the House

of Lords in the *Mannai* case, these notices cannot be saved. I agree with those
submissions. It is quite clear, and I think was really conceded by [counsel for
the tenant], that if the time for service of the counternotices started to run
from the later of the dates upon which notice was given to the landlord and
the third party then the principles in *Mannai* could not be applied. Even if
the date for the counternotices only ran from the date of the notices that had
been given to the landlord, I do not believe that the notices could have been
saved by construing them according to the principles set out in the speeches
in the House of Lords. I see no reason why the date of 12 April would be
evident as opposed to some other date after 12 April.'

[25] We were referred, also, to the decision of this court in *Speedwell Estates Ltd v
Dalziel* [2001] EWCA Civ 1277, [2001] All ER (D) 454 (Jul). The notices, in that
case, were notices of the tenants' desire to have the freehold under Pt I of the
Leasehold Reform Act 1967. Paragraph 6 in Pt II of Sch 3 to the 1967 Act required
such a notice to be given in a prescribed form; and set out the particulars which
it should contain. At the relevant date the form prescribed was Form 1 in the
schedule to the Leasehold Reform (Notices) Regulations 1997, SI 1997/640. The
schedule to Form 1 contained nine paragraphs directed to the provision by the
tenant of various information. The deficiencies in the forms, as completed by the
tenants, included failure to identify the instruments creating the tenancies, failure
to provide any information as to the rateable values of the houses on the
appropriate day sufficient to show that the rent was a low rent, and failure to
provide particulars as to the tenants' occupation of the houses. The court held
that the failure to provide particulars as to the tenants' occupation, and the failure
to provide information as to rateable value, was fatal to the validity of the notices.

[26] Rimer J (with whose judgment the other members of the court, Pill and
May LJJ, agreed), after referring to the speeches in the House of Lords in the
Mannai case, pointed out (at [17]) that it was important—

'to emphasise that the House of Lords was not saying that anything less
than proper compliance with the terms of a contractual break clause would
be sufficient to effect the break.'

He referred, also, to the passage in the judgment of Peter Gibson LJ in *York v
Casey* [1998] 2 EGLR 25 at 27 which I have already set out. He went on (at [22])
to say this:

'... I consider that the better approach is to look at the particular statutory
provisions pursuant to which the notice is given and to identify what its
requirements are. Having done so, it should then be possible to arrive at a
conclusion as to whether or not the notice served under it adequately
complies with those requirements. If anything in the notice contains what
appears to be an error on its face, then it may be that there will be scope for
the application of the *Mannai* approach, although this may depend on the
particular statutory provisions in question. The key question will always be:
is the notice a valid one for the purpose of satisfying the relevant statutory
provision.'

In my view, that passage encapsulates, succinctly and accurately, the correct
approach. I may add that I think that that is the approach to be adopted not only
in relation to notices served under statute but also to notices served under
contractual provisions such as those commonly found in leases.

a   [27] I should add that, following completion of oral argument on this appeal, we were referred by counsel to the decision of Templeman J in *Lewis v MTC (Cars) Ltd* [1974] 3 All ER 423, [1974] 1 WLR 1499. The case turned on the validity of a notice served by a headlandlord under Pt II of the Landlord and Tenant Act 1954. Section 25 of that Act enables a landlord to determine a business tenancy to which Pt II applies by the service of a notice in the prescribed form. Subsection (6)
b   provides that a notice under that section shall not have effect unless it states whether the landlord would oppose an application to the court for the grant of a new tenancy; and, if so, also states on which of the grounds mentioned in s 30 of the Act he would do so. Paragraph 3 of the prescribed form contained two sentences. The first was in these terms: 'I would not oppose an application to the court under Part II of the Act for the grant of a new tenancy ...' The second
c   sentence, to be used in the alternative, read: 'I would oppose an application to the court ... under Part II of the Act for the grant of a new tenancy on the grounds that ...' The landlord failed to strike out either sentence; but in the space following the second sentence—which, as Templeman LJ found, was provided so that the statutory grounds of opposition could be set out—the landlord had
d   included the following:

'(a) You ought not to be granted a new tenancy in view of the state of repair of the holding, being a state resulting from your failure to comply with the repairing covenant in your sub-underlease. (b) On the termination of the current tenancy I intend to demolish or reconstruct the premises comprised
e   in the holding and that I cannot reasonably do so without obtaining possession thereof.'

As Templeman J observed:

'No one reading that notice can be in the slightest doubt; the landlord
f   accidentally failed to strike out the first sentence and intended to oppose an application to the court for the reasons set forth in the notice.' (See [1974] 3 All ER 423 at 426, [1974] 1 WLR 1499 at 1501.)

He went on:

g   'In the present case it would be perverse to turn a blind eye to the clear intention of the landlord as expressed in the notice, with the result that the notice does, in my judgment, on a true construction, state that which s 25(6) requires to be stated.' (See [1974] 3 All ER 423 at 426, [1974] 1 WLR 1499 at 1502.)

h   It is clear that Templeman J's approach was to ask, first, what did s 25(6) of the 1954 Act require to be stated; and then to ask whether, as a matter of construction, the notice did state that which the section required to be stated. That approach is wholly consistent with the later authorities.
    [28] I return, therefore, to the question posed by the judge in the present case:
j   'whether a reasonable tenant could be misled into thinking that the landlord's counter-notice did not admit the right to a new lease?' In my view that was not the correct question. The correct question is: 'does the counter-notice served by the landlord state that the landlord admits that the tenant had on the relevant date the right to acquire a new lease of his flat?' And, if that question is answered in the affirmative, there is the further question: 'does the counter-notice served by the landlord state which (if any) of the proposals contained in the tenant's

notice are accepted by the landlord and which (if any) of those proposals are not
so accepted?'

[29] I would hold that the answer to the first of those questions is that the
notice served by the landlord in the present case does not state that the landlord
admits that the tenant had on the relevant date the right to acquire a new lease of
his flat. I would also hold that the answer to the second of those questions (if it
arose) was that the notice does not state which (if any) of the proposals for a new
lease contained in the tenant's notice are accepted by the landlord. Plainly, the
notice does not, in terms, contain either of those statements. I accept, of course,
that it would be enough if, upon a true construction of the notice, it could be
found to contain such a statement or statements. But I am satisfied that there is
no permissible process of construction which leads to that conclusion.

[30] The judge held that 'the only reasonable conclusion which a reasonable
tenant would come to is that the landlord did admit the tenant's right'. He
reached that view for the two reasons which he gave in the passage at para 7 of
his judgment which I have already set out. First, the inclusion of a statement that
the landlord did not accept the premium proposed by the tenant, and the
landlord's counter-proposal in respect of premium, were consistent with an intention
to serve a notice which satisfied the requirement under s 45(2)(a); would have had
no relevance to a notice which did not admit the tenant's right; and would be
inconsistent with an intention not to admit that right. Second, a notice which did
not admit the tenant's right ought to have contained reasons why the right was
not admitted (see s 45(2)(b) of the Act). The notice contained no such reasons and
so could not be a notice under para (b); so it must be a notice under para (a) of the
subsection.

[31] I am not persuaded that the reasons given by the judge lead to the
conclusion that, on a true construction, the notice in the present case states that
the landlord admits the tenant's right to acquire a new lease. The fact that the
notice could not be a valid notice under s 45(2)(b) of the Act—nor, as is the case,
a valid notice under s 45(2)(c)—does not demand or justify the response that it
must be a valid notice under s 45(2)(a). That might be legitimate response if it
were accepted that the notice had to be valid under one of the paragraphs in
s 45(2) of the Act; but to accept that is to beg the question. The notice is not a
valid notice under s 45 of the Act simply because it purports, by its heading, to be
given under that section. Further, it does not follow from the fact that the
statement that the landlord does not accept the premium proposed by the tenant
is consistent with a notice under para (a) of s 45(2) that the notice must be a notice
under that paragraph; nor that the notice must be construed as if it contained an
admission of the tenant's right. If the notice is otherwise an invalid notice, the
inclusion of some of the information which a valid notice would contain does not
alter that position.

[32] On a true construction, the effect of the notice, as it seems to me, is that
it informs the recipient that the landlord has not decided whether to admit, or not
to admit, the tenant's right to acquire a new lease; or has chosen not to disclose
to the tenant whether the right is admitted or not admitted; and has not decided
(or not chosen to disclose) whether—if there is to be a new lease—it accepts, or
does not accept, that the terms (other than those as to rent and duration
prescribed by s 56(1) of the 1993 Act) are to be the same as those of the existing
lease, as proposed in the schedule to the tenant's notice. So construed, the notice
does not comply with the requirements of s 45(2) of the Act. It is not permissible,

a in my view, to read into the notice as served admissions which are not there in
   order to treat it as a valid notice.
   [33] For those reasons I would allow this appeal.

SIR MURRAY STUART-SMITH.
   [34] I agree.

Appeal allowed. Permission to appeal refused.

                                        Kate O'Hanlon   Barrister.

Practice Note

COURT OF APPEAL, CIVIL DIVISION
LORD PHILLIPS OF WORTH MATRAVERS MR
19 DECEMBER 2001

Court of Appeal – Practice – Civil Division – Reserved judgments – Arrangements to be made for handing down of judgments.

LORD PHILLIPS OF WORTH MATRAVERS MR gave the following direction at the sitting of the court.

1. Where judgment is to be reserved the presiding judge may, at the conclusion of the hearing, seek the views of the parties' advocates as to the arrangements to be made for the handing down of the judgment. Where the result of the appeal need attract no special degree of confidentiality or sensitivity the following arrangements will usually apply.

2. A copy of the judgment will be supplied to the parties' legal advisers two clear working days, or such other period as the court may direct, before the judgment is to be pronounced and handed down. This can be shown, in confidence, to the parties but only for the purpose of obtaining instructions and on the strict understanding that the judgment, or its effect, is not to be disclosed to any other person. A working day is any day on which the Civil Appeals Office is open for business.

3. The appeal will be listed for judgment in the cause list, and the judgment handed down at the appointed time.

4. Where any consequential orders are agreed there will be no obligation on the parties to be represented by their advocates on the occasion of the handing down of the judgment. Draft orders should be (a) faxed to the clerk to the presiding judge (together with any proposed corrections or amendments to the draft judgment) *and* (b) four copies filed in the Civil Appeals Office, no later than 12.00 noon on the working day before hand down, bearing the Court of Appeal case reference, the date of hand down and the name of the presiding judge. Where the court considers that there has been attendance at hand down which was not necessary the costs of such attendance may be disallowed. Where the parties do not indicate their intention of attending, the judgment may be handed down by a single member of the court.

5. Where a party wishes to apply for permission to appeal to the House of Lords pursuant to s 1 of the Administration of Justice (Appeals) Act 1934 the court will be prepared, if all parties agree, to deal with the application on the basis of written submissions made by all parties to the appeal as to why such permission should, or should not, be granted. These submissions should likewise be faxed to the clerk to the Presiding Judge and four copies filed in the Civil Appeals Office, no later than 12.00 noon on the working day before hand down, bearing the Court of Appeal case reference, the date of hand down and the name of the presiding judge.

6. Any proposed correction to the draft judgment should, as at present, be sent to the clerk to the judge who prepared the draft, with a copy to any other party.

7. These arrangements will take effect in respect of judgments which are reserved from the date of this Practice Note.

Kate O'Hanlon   Barrister.

R v Sargent

[2001] UKHL 54

HOUSE OF LORDS

LORD NICHOLLS OF BIRKENHEAD, LORD STEYN, LORD HOPE OF CRAIGHEAD, LORD
HUTTON AND LORD HOBHOUSE OF WOODBOROUGH

16, 17 JULY, 25 OCTOBER 2001

*Criminal evidence – Interception of communications – Telephone intercepts – Interception
by person engaged in the running of a public telecommunications system – Employee of
telephone company using company equipment at workplace to intercept telephone call
for private purposes – Whether employee a person 'engaged in' the running of a public
telecommunication system when making intercept – Interception of Communications
Act 1985, ss 1, 9.*

The defendant, S, was suspected by his mistress's former husband, P, of having
set fire to his car in the driveway of his house. P worked as a telephone engineer
with a telephone company. His job included making use of equipment at his
workplace which enabled him to monitor and record telephone calls, but his
authority to use that equipment was strictly limited and did not allow him to use
it for any private purpose. P nevertheless used the equipment to listen to a
telephone conversation between his former wife and S in which he believed they
were talking about the burning of his car. In intercepting the call, P was
committing an offence contrary to s 1[a] of the Interception of Communications
Act 1985. He recorded the conversation, made a transcript of what he thought
were the incriminating parts and gave the tape recording and the transcript to the
police. As a result, S was arrested and questioned. He initially denied any
involvement, but after learning of the existence of the tape recording he admitted
that he had paid another man to burn P's car. S was charged with conspiracy to
commit arson being reckless as to whether P's life would be endangered. At trial,
P gave evidence of the interception of the call and the making of the tape and the
transcript, while a police officer gave evidence of what S had said in the interview.
S was convicted and sentenced to three years' imprisonment. He appealed,
contending that, at the time of the interception, P was a person 'engaged in' the
running of a public telecommunications system within the meaning of s 9(2)(c)[b]
of the 1985 Act, and that accordingly evidence of the interception should have
been excluded under s 9(1), which provided that in any proceedings before a
court no evidence was to be adduced that tended to suggest that an offence had
been committed under s 1 by any of the persons mentioned in s 9(2). The Court
of Appeal dismissed the appeal, holding that s 9(2) referred to a person engaged
in the running of a public telecommunications system acting as such, and that
accordingly a person acting for his own private purposes, like P, was not engaged
in the running of such a system. S appealed.

Held – Where a public telecommunications employee intercepted a communication
contrary to s 1 of the 1985 Act, he was a person engaged in the running of a public

---

a   Section 1, so far as material, provides: '(1) … a person who intentionally intercepts a communication
    … by means of a public telecommunications system shall be guilty of an offence …'
b   Section 9 is set out at [27], below

telecommunications system within the meaning of s 9(2)(c) of the Act even if he *a* were acting for his own private purposes. Section 9(2) presupposed that a person in one of the categories to which it referred had, or might have, committed an offence under s 1, ie that, where a public telecommunications employee was concerned, his purpose was not connected with the services which his employer provided. It was in that context that s 9(2)(c) had to be construed. The Court of Appeal's interpretation would have the effect of confining that paragraph to *b* authorised acts of the employee done in the interests of the employer. That focus upon the act or conduct of the person conflicted with the drafting of s 9(2) which was concerned with categorising the person. The words 'engaged in' denoted the person's employment at the relevant time, and not whether he was acting within his authority. Sections 1 and 9 clearly contemplated and covered the misuse of an employee's position. Further, the clear and express intent of s 9(1) was to *c* exclude evidence which touched upon whether the person concerned was acting lawfully or not, ie whether he was acting with lawful authority or not. The interpretation put upon s 9(2) by the Court of Appeal would require the court to inquire into the lawfulness of the interceptor's conduct before deciding whether he was a person who came within s 9(2), and such an inquiry would expressly *d* conflict with s 9(1). In the instant case, P was at the material time a person engaged in the business of running a public telecommunications system. He had taken advantage of the opportunity it gave to intercept S's communication with his former wife contrary to s 1. The evidence of his having done so and the fruits of his interception were accordingly inadmissible under s 9(1), and the statute required that they should have been excluded from the evidence adduced at the trial. *e* S had accordingly been convicted in part on inadmissible evidence. If the intercept evidence had been excluded, the case against S would still have been strong on the basis of the admissions that he had made in the police interview. It was possible, however, that the exclusion of the evidence would have enabled P's case to be put more convincingly and might have enabled the defence to raise a doubt *f* in the minds of the jury as to whether the confession was genuine. In those circumstances, the conviction was unsafe. Accordingly, the appeal would be allowed and the conviction set aside (see [1], [2], [9], [10], [13], [14], [20]–[22], [31]–[33], [37], [38], below).

Notes   *g*
For exclusion of evidence relating to interception of communications, see 11(2) *Halsbury's Laws* (4th edn reissue) para 1165.

For the Interception of Communications Act 1985, ss 1, 9, see 45 *Halsbury's Statutes* (4th edn) (1999 reissue) 289, 298.

h

Cases referred to in opinions
A-G's Ref (No 3 of 1999) [2001] 1 All ER 577, [2001] 2 AC 91, [2001] 2 WLR 56, HL.
Fox v Chief Constable of Gwent [1985] 3 All ER 392, [1986] AC 281, [1985] 1 WLR 1126, HL.
Jasper v UK (2000) 30 EHRR 441, ECt HR.   *j*
Khan v UK (2000) 8 BHRC 310, ECt HR.
Morgans v DPP [2000] 2 All ER 522, [2001] 1 AC 315, [2000] 2 WLR 386, HL.
R v Effik (1992) 95 Cr App R 427, CA; *affd* [1994] 3 All ER 458, [1995] 1 AC 309, [1994] 3 WLR 583, HL.
R v Khan (Sultan) [1996] 3 All ER 289, [1997] AC 558, [1996] 3 WLR 162, HL.
R v Owen [1999] 1 WLR 949, CA.

a
R v P [2001] 2 All ER 58, [2001] 2 WLR 463, HL.
R v Preston [1993] 4 All ER 638, [1994] 2 AC 130, [1993] 3 WLR 891, HL.
R v Rasool [1997] 4 All ER 439, [1997] 1 WLR 1092, CA.
R v Sang [1979] 2 All ER 1222, [1980] AC 402, [1979] 3 WLR 263, HL

Appeal
b Ian Michael Sargent appealed with leave of the Appeal Committee of the House
of Lords given on 12 February 2001 from the order of the Court of Appeal
(Lord Bingham of Cornhill CJ, Ian Kennedy and Jackson JJ) on 18 January 1999
dismissing his appeal against his conviction in the Crown Court at Manchester on
24 March 1998 on a count of conspiracy to commit arson following a trial before
Judge Lewis and a jury. The Court of Appeal certified that two points of law of
c public importance, set out at [23], below, were involved in its decision. The facts
are set out in the opinion of Lord Hobhouse of Woodborough.

Ben Emmerson QC, John McClure and *Danny Friedman* (instructed by *Widdows,
Pilling & Co*, Walkden) for the appellant.
d *Bruce Houlder QC* and *David Perry* (instructed by the *Crown Prosecution Service*) for
the Crown.

Their Lordships took time for consideration.

e 25 October 2001. The following opinions were delivered.

LORD NICHOLLS OF BIRKENHEAD.
[1] My Lords, I have had the advantage of reading a draft of the speeches of
my noble and learned friends Lord Hope of Craighead and Lord Hobhouse
of Woodborough. For the reasons they give, and with which I agree, I would
f allow this appeal.

LORD STEYN.
[2] My Lords, I have read the opinions of my noble and learned friends Lord
Hope of Craighead and Lord Hobhouse of Woodborough. For the reasons they
g give, I would also allow the appeal and set aside the conviction.

LORD HOPE OF CRAIGHEAD.
[3] My Lords, I have had the advantage of reading in draft the speech of my
noble and learned friend, Lord Hobhouse of Woodborough. I gratefully adopt
his narrative of the facts of the case and the statutory background. I would like
h however to add two points by way of further explanation as to the background.
[4] The first is that Mr Emmerson QC for the appellant did not seek to
maintain the argument which was submitted to but rejected by the Court of Appeal
that there had been a breach of the appellant's right to privacy under art 8 of the
European Convention for the Protection of Human Rights and Fundamental
j Freedoms (Rome, 4 November 1950; TS 71 (1953); Cmd 8969) which in itself
rendered the resulting evidence inadmissible. He directed his principal argument
to the proposition that ss 1 and 9 of the Interception of Communications Act 1985
rendered both the fact that there had been an interception and the material which
had been obtained by means of it inadmissible in evidence. The second is that his
submission with regard to the second certified question was that the effect of ss 1
and 9 was that it was unlawful for the police to make any use whatever of the

intercept when the appellant was being interviewed. It was this unlawfulness
rather than the inadmissibility of the intercept in evidence which, according to his *a*
argument, made the confession which resulted from its use at the interview
inadmissible.

[5] The context for these submissions can best be appreciated by noting the
following exchange which took place in the course of Det Con Hussey's interview
of the appellant at Eccles police station on 2 August 1997, as recorded on p 21 of *b*
the transcript:

'A. He's illegally taped something has he?
Q. I'm going to come to that in a minute mate. Do you know who he
works for?
A. Nynex. *c*
Q. Right. Have there been any problems at all between Christine and
Nynex or Neil and Nynex about his previous actions or ...
A. There's has been a lot of er things going on for the past nine or ten
months about him er making malicious phone calls to her and Nynex aren't
doing anything about it.'
d

[6] Det Con Hussey showed the appellant a tape, which he said was a tape of a
conversation which had taken place between himself and Christine Page at 10.15 am
on the same day that Neil Page's car was set alight in the early hours. He also
showed him a transcript of the conversation which he said had been prepared by
Neil Page, and he told him that apart from the odd spelling mistake it was an
accurate record. He asked the appellant whether, before he went through the *e*
transcript, he wished to change what he had said in answer to his previous
questions as to what he knew about the car being set alight. It was only then that
the appellant began to make the admissions about his involvement which
provided the basis in evidence for his conviction. Such was the effect of the
production of these items however that the appellant had already made a full *f*
confession before Det Con Hussey went through the transcript and the details of
the conversation which had been recorded on the tape were put to him. It is plain
that the appellant already knew that Neil Page worked for Nynex Cable Co, the
public telecommunications operator from whom Christine Page rented her
telephone line, and that Mr Page had the opportunity, if so minded, to tape
her telephone conversations illegally. *g*

Section 9(2) of the 1985 Act

[7] It was accepted at the trial that, in carrying out the intercept, Neil Page had
committed an offence contrary to s 1(1) of the 1985 Act. The crucial question
therefore as to the admissibility of the evidence of the intercept was whether he *h*
was at that time a person 'engaged in the running of a public telecommunication
system' within the meaning of s 9(2)(c) of the Act. As Lord Bingham of Cornhill CJ
said in the Court of Appeal, while Mr Page was working for a public
telecommunications operator, he was plainly not acting in the course of his
employment or for the purposes of his employer when he intercepted the telephone *j*
conversation. As Lord Bingham CJ put it, Mr Page was acting entirely off his own
bat for his own private purposes. But does this mean, as the Court of Appeal held,
that he was not 'engaged in' the running of a public telecommunication system?

[8] The words 'engaged in' which appear in both s 9(2)(b)—'engaged in the
business of the Post Office'—and in s 9(2)(c)—'engaged in the running of a public
telecommunication system'—are capable of two meanings. On one view, the

a words are used simply to indicate the person's office, status or position within the relevant organisation. On this view, it would be enough to show that the person was an employee or other agent of that organisation when he carried out the intercept. The other view is that the words are used to indicate that at the time the person was embarked upon a particular activity. On this view, it would be necessary to examine what he was doing at the time and to determine whether

b or not it was within the scope of his duties or his instructions. The admissibility of the intercept would depend not on whether he was employed by the organisation but on whether he was acting within the scope of his employment or on his instructions at the time of the interception.

[9] It is plain that the second of these two alternatives would require more detailed investigation than the first to determine whether the intercept was

c inadmissible under s 9(1) of the 1985 Act or was admissible. Indeed, it is hard to see how an investigation into the person's activities at the time of the intercept could be conducted without entering into what was described by Steyn LJ in *R v Effik* (1992) 95 Cr App R 427 at 432 as the 'forbidden territory'. Section 9(1)(a) provides that no evidence shall be adduced and no question asked in cross-

d examination which tends to suggest that an offence under s 1 of the 1985 Act has been committed by the person who carried out the intercept or whether a warrant has been or is to be issued to him. The underlying purpose, as Lord Mustill said in *R v Preston* [1993] 4 All ER 638 at 667, [1994] 2 AC 130 at 167, is to protect information as to the authorisation and carrying out of official intercepts. But the prohibition extends to unauthorised as well as to authorised activity. It reflects

e the public interest that the circumstances in which the activities of those involved in serious crime came to the knowledge of the police should not be capable of being explored at a trial.

[10] Questions as to the scope of the person's duties, the extent of his authority and the instructions which he had been given would be hard to avoid if

f the decision as to admissibility were to depend on evidence as to whether he was acting within the scope of his employment at the time when the interception was carried out. They would be almost certainly crucial to the issue of admissibility if the intercept was carried out, as it was in this case, at the person's place of work using his employer's equipment within normal working hours. They indicate the difficulties which the prohibition in s 9(1) would create in the conduct of such an

g investigation. These difficulties suggest quite strongly that the first alternative meaning of the phrase is the one which it bears in the present context.

[11] This impression is confirmed by other provisions in s 9. First on the list of persons mentioned in s 9(2) is any person 'holding office under the Crown' (see s 9(2)(a)). No inquiry into the person's authority or instructions is necessary in his

h case. All that is needed to determine inadmissibility is evidence of the person's status. This suggests that the same exercise is appropriate in the case of the persons mentioned in s 9(2)(b) and (2)(c).

[12] Then there is the list of relevant offences in s 9(4)(a) to which, by s 9(3)(a), s 9(1) does not apply. Included in this list is s 45 of the Telecommunications Act

j 1984. Section 45(1) provides that a person engaged in the running of a public telecommunication system who 'otherwise than in the course of his duty' intentionally intercepts a message sent by means of that system or, where a message so sent has been intercepted, intentionally discloses to any person the contents of that message shall be guilty of an offence. The phrase 'otherwise than in the course of his duty' appears also in s 45(2), which makes it an offence for a person engaged in the running of a public telecommunication system to disclose to any

person the contents of any statement of account specifying the telecommunication
services provided to another person by means of that system. These provisions
contemplate that a person may be 'engaged in' the running of a telecommunication
system and yet at the same time be acting 'otherwise that in the course of his
duty'. All the offences mentioned in s 9(4)(a) of the 1985 Act involve unlawful
acts by persons referred to in s 9(2) which are outwith or contrary to their duty or
their instructions. Unless the context requires otherwise, the words 'engaged in'
ought to be given the same meaning in s 9(2) as they have for the purposes of
s 9(4)(a).

[13] Then there is the prohibition in s 9(1)(a) of the 1985 Act. It extends to
evidence or cross-examination tending to suggest that an offence under s 1 has
been committed by any of the persons mentioned in s 9(2). In *Morgans v DPP*
[2000] 2 All ER 522 at 542, [2001] 1 AC 315 at 337 it was recognised that it would
be an extraordinary and unacceptable anomaly if the position were to be that
evidence obtained by any of the persons mentioned in s 9(2) by the interception
of communications for which a warrant had been issued under s 2 was inadmissible
but evidence which they had obtained by an interception for which a warrant was
required but had not been issued was admissible. An anomaly of the same
magnitude would result if the words 'engaged in' were to be read in such a way
as to confine the persons mentioned in s 9(2)(b) and (2)(c) to persons who were
acting within the scope of their instructions or their employment. This would
mean that a person's departure from the scope of his authority or the instructions
given to him by the Post Office or the telecommunications operator, such as
where he carried out the intercept for his own private purposes or those of a third
party by whom he had been threatened or been bribed, would render admissible
evidence which, if it had been obtained within his authority or instructions,
would have been inadmissible. The scheme of the 1985 Act suggests strongly that
no use of the intercept should be permissible irrespective of the question whether
it was lawful or had been authorised or instructed by the telecommunications
operator.

[14] I would hold therefore that the Court of Appeal were wrong to find that
there was nothing in the 1985 Act to preclude the introduction into evidence of
the interception of the appellant's telephone call and of the contents of the
intercept. In my opinion the effect of s 9(1) of that Act is that this evidence was
inadmissible.

Whether the confession was admissible

[15] Mr Emmerson submitted that the effect of ss 1 and 9 of the 1985 Act,
taken together, was to prohibit the use at interview of an intercept which would
be inadmissible in evidence at trial. He said that there was an implied statutory
prohibition against its use in these circumstances. Alternatively he submitted that
it would have been wrong for the trial judge, had he appreciated that the
intercept was inadmissible, to have admitted the confession evidence in view of
the fact that the transcript of the intercept was inadmissible. He made it clear that
he was not seeking to suggest as a general proposition that material which was
inadmissible in evidence could not be used when a person was being interviewed.
There is ample authority to the contrary. In *Fox v Chief Constable of Gwent* [1985]
3 All ER 392 at 396, [1986] AC 281 at 292 Lord Fraser of Tullybelton referred to
the well-established rule, recognised in *R v Sang* [1979] 2 All ER 1222, [1980] AC
402, that apart from confessions, to which special considerations apply, any
evidence which is relevant is admissible even if it has been obtained illegally. If

a   that rule is applied, the fact that the appellant was confronted with the intercept in the course of his interview would not of itself render his confession inadmissible.

[16] Section 9 of the 1985 Act does not in terms prohibit the use at a person's interview of an inadmissible intercept. Mr Emmerson said that the prohibition was to be found by necessary implication from ss 1 and 9 of the Act, read alone
b   or in conjunction with art 6 of the convention. His proposition was that, as the intercept evidence was rendered inadmissible, it necessarily followed that it was unlawful to deploy it in a person's interview for the purpose of eliciting a confession which was to be used against him in evidence at his trial. The basis for this proposition lay in the rules about disclosure which were established in *R v Preston* and *Morgans v DPP*. The duty to give complete disclosure of unused
c   materials does not extend to any material obtained by means of an interception which has been withheld from the prosecutor, whether or not it was obtained under a warrant or was obtained consensually. He said that the use of such material in an interview would put the defence at an unfair disadvantage, as the police would be free to put unfavourable material to the accused without being
d   under any corresponding obligation to disclose any favourable interception material. This was inconsistent both with the concept of fairness at common law and with the principle of equality of arms between the prosecution and the defence which is inherent in the requirement of fairness under art 6(1) of the convention (see *Jasper v UK* (2000) 30 EHRR 441).

e   [17] I am not persuaded that these considerations demonstrate by necessary implication that the effect of ss 1 and 9 of the 1985 Act is that an inadmissible intercept can never be used by the police at interview. Three factors seem to me to indicate the contrary. The first is the general rule that the test of admissibility is whether the evidence is relevant. The fact that it was obtained illegally does not render it inadmissible if the evidence is relevant. From this it follows that the
f   use at a person's interview of illegally obtained material does not of itself render evidence of what was said at that interview inadmissible. It is well established that the police can put to a suspect at interview information available to them, such as the contents of a confession by another suspect, which would not be admissible against him in evidence. The second is the fact that Mr Emmerson's proposition,
g   if sound, would extend to cases where there had been a frank and full disclosure not only of the fact of the intercept but also of all the intercepted material. The present is indeed such a case. It is plain from the passage which I quoted at the outset that the appellant knew that Mr Page was in a position to intercept the contents of his telephone conversations with Christine Page illegally. He was shown a full and accurate transcript of the conversation which was said to be
h   incriminating. There is no suggestion that any trick or improper pressure was brought to bear upon him, that he was misled or that his confession when he was shown the tape and the transcript was other than voluntary. There was no inequality of arms here, as nothing was withheld from him. The better view therefore is to approach each case on its own facts as to the question whether or not the use of
j   the intercept at the interview was unfair. The third is that s 78(1) of the Police and Criminal Evidence Act 1984 provides the essential safeguard that is needed to ensure that the accused receives a fair trial. Section 78(1) provides:

'In any proceedings the court may refuse to allow evidence on which the prosecution proposes to rely to be given if it appears to the court that, having regard to all the circumstances, including the circumstances in which the evidence was obtained, the admission of the evidence would have such an adverse effect on the fairness of the proceedings that the court ought not to admit it.'

The scope of this discretionary power is plainly wide enough to enable the trial judge to take into account any disadvantage that may result from the rules about the non-disclosure of intercepts.

[18] There are other considerations too which seem to me to indicate clearly that an absolute rule against the use of inadmissible intercepts in a police interview is not to be read into s 9 of the 1985 Act. As Lord Steyn said in *A-G's Ref (No 3 of 1999)* [2001] 1 All ER 577 at 584, [2001] 2 AC 91 at 118, the purpose of the criminal law is to permit everyone to go about their daily lives without fear or harm to person or property. It is in the interests of everyone that serious crime should be effectively investigated and prosecuted. There must, of course, be fairness to all sides. But in the context of the criminal law the interests of the victim and the public interest must be taken into account as well as that of the accused. A rigid rule which excluded the use in all cases of all inadmissible intercepts at a person's interview would go further than was necessary to protect the accused. It could create an imbalance in his favour which would operate against the public interest, and that of the victim, when an alleged crime was being investigated. I do not think that a rule in such absolute terms can be justified.

Whether the conviction was unsafe

[19] It was crucial to the success of the prosecution case that the appellant's confession was accepted by the jury as genuine. The other facts and circumstances of the case, while indicating motive, had no direct bearing on this issue. But, once the intercept was admitted into evidence and the full text of the interview was presented to the jury unedited, the whole case against him fell into place. Powerful support for the proposition that the confession was genuine was afforded by the appellant's reaction as soon as he was made aware of the intercept. He confessed without waiting for the contents of the transcript of his telephone conversation with Christine Page to be put to him. By the time the contents were put to him it was all over. The contents were used simply to confirm what he had already said. The question is, as Mr Houlder QC for the Crown accepted, whether the jury would inevitably have convicted if the transcript of the interview had been edited so as to exclude all mention of the intercept and the transcript of the intercept itself had been withheld from them.

[20] I am unable to say that this high test is satisfied in this case. It is always a matter for concern when an accused is convicted solely on the basis of a confession which he has given to the police. In the interests of fairness to the accused it is right that one should look for some other factor in the evidence before the jury that indicates that the confession was genuine. For the reasons which I have just given, I consider that that other factor was before the jury when they were told about the fact and contents of the intercept and were able to observe its effect on the appellant when he was being interviewed. But once that element is stripped out of the case the position is far less clear and, in my opinion, quite uncertain. All one is left with is the progress of the interview from its initial stage when the appellant made no admissions to the later stage when, necessarily without explanation, he changed his position and began to admit his part in the offence. Coupled with that admission however were remarks from which it might be inferred that he was intent on sheltering Christine. In the absence of evidence about the intercept the jury might have had at least some doubt as to whether his

a confession was genuine. This leads to the inevitable conclusion that the conviction
was unsafe.

Conclusion
   [21] For these reasons, and those given by my noble and learned friend,
Lord Hobhouse, with which I agree, I would allow the appeal and set aside the
b conviction.

LORD HUTTON.
   [22] My Lords, I have had the advantage of reading in draft the opinions of my
noble and learned friends Lord Hope of Craighead and Lord Hobhouse of
Woodborough. For the reasons which they give I also would allow this appeal.
c

LORD HOBHOUSE OF WOODBOROUGH.
   [23] My Lords, on 24 March 1998 after a trial in the Crown Court at Manchester
before Judge Lewis and a jury, Ian Sargent, the appellant, was convicted of
conspiracy to commit arson being reckless as to whether the life of Neil Page
d would thereby be endangered contrary to s 1(1) of the Criminal Law Act 1977 and
was sentenced to three years imprisonment. He appealed to the Court of Appeal
(Lord Bingham of Cornhill CJ, Kennedy and Jackson JJ) who dismissed his appeal
but certified two points of law as being of general public importance. These are:

e   'Is it the law that material obtained illegally through the public
      telecommunications system by means of an unauthorised telephone tap by
      a person committing an offence under section 1 of the Interception of
      Communications Act 1985 is admissible in evidence?'

   And:

f   'Where material has been obtained in contravention of a statutory
      prohibition on interception and such material is inadmissible in evidence but
      the material is used by the Police in an interview to obtain a confession,
      should the Judge exercise his discretion at Common Law or under section 78
      of the Police and Criminal Evidence Act 1984 to exclude that confession?'

g The relevance of these questions turns primarily upon the application of s 9 of the
1985 Act to the particular facts of this case.
   [24] Neil Page was the former husband of Christine Page. The appellant was
a lover of Christine Page. There was continuing ill will between Neil and
Christine Page with the appellant taking the part of Christine. In the early hours
of 29 July 1997, someone set fire to the car belonging to Neil Page which was
h standing close to the garage door of his house. The police were on the scene
almost at once and the fire brigade were called and were able to put the fire out
quickly. The house was damaged but not seriously. By chance, Neil Page was
away in Blackpool that night so his life was never in fact at risk. He returned the
next morning and discovered what had happened. He suspected that Christine
j and the appellant may have had something to do with it. Neil worked as a
telephone engineer with a telephone company called Nynex Cable Co (Nynex).
At his workplace his job included making use of equipment there to check
telephone lines and their use and it enabled him to monitor and record telephone
calls. He knew that Christine had a telephone line supplied by Nynex. His
authority to use the equipment was strictly limited and did not allow him to use
it for any private purpose. He had got into trouble previously for misusing the

equipment. Notwithstanding this, he took the opportunity that morning to put *a* a 'tester' on Christine's telephone line so that if any calls were made on the line that morning he would be able to overhear what was said. He wanted to discover whether Christine had anything to do with the burning of his car. When, in mid-morning, a call was made on the line, he connected the headphones and listened in on the conversation. He recognised the voices of Christine and the appellant and things which they said led him to believe that they were talking *b* about the burning of his car. He connected the line to record and recorded the conversation on a tape and later made a transcript of what he thought were the relevant and incriminating parts. He later gave the tape and partial transcript to Det Con Hussey who was handling the investigation. This led to Christine and the appellant being arrested and questioned.

[25] In interview the appellant initially denied any involvement or knowledge *c* of how the car came to be burnt. But when he learnt of the existence of the tape recording made by Neil Page and was shown it, he began to make admissions. The gist of the admissions was that he had paid a man £100 to burn the car on the driveway of the house in order to frighten Neil and get back at him for the way he had treated Christine. After he had made these admissions Det Con Hussey *d* took him through the partial transcript and obtained his confirmation of what had been said. He throughout clearly appreciated that the tape had been unlawfully made. He showed a concern to shield Christine from any responsibility for what had happened. The appellant was charged and in due course committed for trial. It seems that Christine was not charged. At the appellant's trial evidence was given by Neil of the interception of the call and the making of the tape and *e* the transcript, both of which he produced and were made exhibits in the case. Det Con Hussey gave evidence of what the appellant had said in interview and a transcript of the material parts of the interview was given to the jury. It was the evidence of Neil and Det Con Hussey which provided the incriminating link between the appellant and the burning of the car. The appellant elected not to *f* give evidence. Christine was not called as a witness by either side. After a summing up which is not criticised and a retirement of two hours including the midday adjournment, the jury returned a unanimous verdict of guilty.

[26] It is not in dispute that Neil Page had committed an offence under s 1 of the Interception of Communications Act 1985 when he intercepted the call on Christine's telephone line. Section 1 makes it an offence to intercept a communication *g* in the course of its transmission on a public telecommunication system intentionally unless it is done in obedience to a warrant or in belief that one of the parties has consented. There is a general exclusion for communications 'intercepted for purposes connected with the provision of … public telecommunication services' (see s 1(3)(a)). Neil could not have said that his interception was for any such *h* purpose. His purposes were purely private and he had no warrant or other justification. With the consent of the Director of Public Prosecutions he could have been prosecuted but he was not and was simply cautioned.

[27] For present purposes the important section is s 9:

j

'*Exclusion of evidence.*—(1) In any proceedings before any court or tribunal no evidence shall be adduced and no question in cross-examination shall be asked which (in either case) tends to suggest—(a) that an offence under section 1 above has been or is to be committed by any of the persons mentioned in subsection (2) below; or (b) that a warrant has been or is to be issued to any of those persons.

a (2) The persons referred to in subsection (1) above are—(a) any person holding office under the Crown; (b) the Post Office and any person engaged in the business of the Post Office; and (c) any public telecommunications operator and any person engaged in the running of a public telecommunication system.

b (3) Subsection (1) above does not apply—(a) in relation to proceedings for a relevant offence or proceedings before the Tribunal [established under the Act]; or (b) where the evidence is adduced or the question in cross-examination is asked for the purpose of establishing the fairness or unfairness of a dismissal on grounds of an offence under section 1 above or of conduct from which such an offence might be inferred; and paragraph (a) of that subsection does not apply where a person has been convicted of the offence

c under that section.

(4) In this section "relevant offence" means—(a) an offence under section 1 above or under section 45 of the Telegraph Act 1863, section 20 of the Telegraph Act 1868, section 58 of the Post Office Act 1953 or section 45 of the 1984 Act [the Telecommunications Act 1984]; (b) an offence under section 1 or

d 2 of the Official Secrets Act 1911 relating to any sketch, plan, model, article, note, document or information which tends to suggest as mentioned in subsection (1) above; (bb) an offence under section 4 of the Official Secrets Act 1989 relating to any such information, document or article as is mentioned in subsection (3)(a) of that section; (c) perjury committed in the course of proceedings for a relevant offence; (d) attempting or conspiring to

e commit, or aiding, abetting, counselling or procuring the commission of, an offence falling within any of the preceding paragraphs; and (e) contempt of court committed in the course of, or in relation to, proceedings for a relevant offence.'

f [28] This is a statutory provision which has the effect of excluding evidence which would otherwise be admissible under the principle in R v Sang [1979] 2 All ER 1222, [1980] AC 402. It reflects the statutory policy of preserving secrecy identified in R v Preston [1993] 4 All ER 638, [1994] 2 AC 130 and later cases (eg R v P [2001] 2 All ER 58, [2001] 2 WLR 463). As Lord Mustill put it in R v Preston [1993] 4 All ER 638 at 670, [1994] 2 AC 130 at 170: 'Parliament has grasped the nettle and put the

g interests of secrecy first.' It also has the indirect consequence of necessitating the exclusion of evidence of the results of the interception (Morgans v DPP [2000] 2 All ER 522, [2001] 1 AC 315 overruling R v Rasool [1997] 4 All ER 439, [1997] 1 WLR 1092 and R v Owen [1999] 1 WLR 949). In Morgans v DPP, Lord Hope of Craighead, giving the leading speech, referred to the fact that the exclusions

h in s 9 and the necessity for a fair trial provided a strong indication that it had not been the intention of Parliament that evidence obtained by unlawful interceptions should be admissible. He said:

'... evidence of material obtained by the interception by the persons mentioned in s 9(2) of the 1985 Act of communications of the kind described

j in s 1(1) of that Act, except for the purposes described in s 1(3), will always be inadmissible. It is not possible to say that s 9(1) of the 1985 Act provides this in express language. But, in the context of the 1985 Act as a whole, the prohibitions which it contains lead inexorably to that result. So I would hold that it has that effect by necessary implication.' (See [2000] 2 All ER 522 at 543, [2001] 1 AC 315 at 338.)

[29] Therefore, unless the present case can be brought within one of the
limitations to the operation of s 9(1), the evidence of Neil Page's telephone tap had to *a*
be excluded. The exclusion in s 9(1) is limited by the provisions of sub-ss (2) and (3).
Under sub-s (3) the exclusion does not apply to the giving of evidence in
proceedings under s 1 of the 1985 Act or under a number of similar statutory
provisions listed in sub-s (4) nor to proceedings before the statutory tribunal
constituted under s 7. Similarly, once a person has been convicted of the offence *b*
under s 1, the prohibition ceases to apply presumably because that means that the
relevant facts have entered the public domain. These limitations do not apply to
the present case because the prosecution of the appellant was for an offence
unrelated to any interception and because Neil had never been prosecuted for his
offence under s 1, merely cautioned. That leaves sub-s (2). This restricts the
persons to whose involvement in the interception s 9(1) applies. The person has *c*
to fall within one of the three classes set out in s 9(2). Neil was not an office
holder under the Crown nor was he employed by or engaged in the business of
the Post Office. The question is therefore whether he was a person engaged in the
running of a public telecommunication system. It is not in dispute that Nynex's
system was a public telecommunication system. It is also not in dispute that the *d*
question whether he was so engaged must be answered by reference to the time
when he was committing the offence under s 1, ie intercepting the telephone call
between the appellant and Christine.

[30] The Court of Appeal held that what Neil did did fall outside s 9. Differing
from the trial judge, Lord Bingham CJ delivering the judgment of the court said: *e*

> 'It is argued by Mr McClure [counsel for the appellant] that Mr Page fell
> within s 9(2), not as a telecommunications operator but as a person engaged
> in the running of a public telecommunication system. In our judgment that
> is not a sound argument, although the judge accepted it, because, as we
> construe the section, it is plain that sub-s (2)(c) must refer to a person engaged
> in the running of a public telecommunication system *acting as such*. It has no *f*
> reference, as we read the subsection, to a person like Mr Page acting entirely
> off his own bat for his own private purposes. Accordingly, on our reading of
> s 9, there is nothing to preclude the introduction into evidence of the product
> of an interception such as this.' (My emphasis.)

This approach adopts a criterion similar to scope of employment and the *g*
inclusion of the phrase 'acting as such' (which I have emphasised) confirms this.

[31] There is a reference to the purpose for which the interception has been
made in s 1(3)(a) already referred to. If the call had been intercepted for a purpose
connected with the provision of a public telecommunication service, it would
have not come within s 1 and no offence under that section would have been *h*
committed. The question in the present case under s 9 only arises because the
intercept was for an alien purpose. Section 9(2) is concerned with defining the
three categories of persons to whom s 9(1) refers. It already presupposes that
they have (or may have) committed an offence under s 1, ie that, where a public
telecommunications employee is concerned, his purpose was not connected with *j*
the services which his employers provided. It is in this context that s 9(2)(b) and
(c) have to be construed. The effect of the Court of Appeal's interpretation would
be to confine these paragraphs to authorised acts of the employee done in the
interests of his employer. This focus upon the act or conduct of the person both
detracts from the force of s 1(3)(a) and conflicts with the drafting of s 9(2) which
is concerned with categorising the person. The words 'engaged in' denote the

a person's employment at the relevant time not whether he was acting within his authority.

[32] On the facts of the present case, on the morning of 28 July, Neil was at his place of work, engaged on doing his job, using his employer's equipment and having access there to the Nynex lines. There is no suggestion that what he did in putting a tester on to Christine's line and then monitoring it was not the same
b as or similar to the acts which he was ordinarily employed to do for his employers nor that they did not ordinarily form part of acts incidental to the provision of a public telecommunication system. What distinguished what he did that morning from what he did on other mornings was not what he did but his purpose in doing it; the acts were done for an unlawful and unauthorised purpose. But this does not alter the fact that he was that morning a person engaged in the running of a
c public telecommunication system. Sections 1 and 9 clearly contemplate and cover the misuse of an employee's position. Further the clear and express intent of s 9(1) is to exclude evidence which touches upon whether the person concerned was acting lawfully or not, that is to say, whether he was acting with lawful authority or not. The interpretation put on s 9(2) by the Court of Appeal would
d require the court to inquire into the lawfulness of the interceptor's conduct before deciding whether he was a person who came within s 9(2). Such an inquiry would expressly conflict with s 9(1). The interpretation adopted by the Court of Appeal cannot stand.

[33] On the facts of this case Neil was at the material time a person engaged in the business of running a public telecommunication system. He took advantage
e of the opportunity it gave to intercept the appellant's communication with Christine contrary to s 1. The evidence of his having done so and the fruits of his interception were accordingly inadmissible under s 9(1) and the statute required that they be excluded from the evidence adduced at the trial. The appellant was convicted in part on inadmissible evidence.

f [34] At the trial the defence moved to exclude both the intercept evidence and the confessions in interview. Judge Lewis held that Neil was a person falling within s 9(2)(c). He did not have the advantage of the decision in *Morgans v DPP*. He therefore held that the exclusion of evidence did not extend to the fruits of the interception. There was nothing which made the interview confessions inadmissible. He considered the fairness of admitting the evidence and decided, in the exercise
g of his discretion under s 78 of the Police and Criminal Evidence Act 1984, to allow the intercept and confession evidence to be given. In his summing up, the judge reminded the jury of this evidence.

[35] In the Court of Appeal, the question under s 9 was, as I have stated, decided in favour of the Crown. The remaining question for the Court of Appeal
h was therefore whether the evidence should be excluded on the ground of some rule of policy to be derived from the 1985 Act or human rights law or the common law or under s 78. The Court of Appeal upheld the judge's ruling that it was fair to admit the evidence.

[36] Before your Lordships' House the appellant has argued that the Court of
j Appeal was wrong on both of the issues before it—both the narrower question under s 9 and the broader question of the exclusion of evidence on one or more of the grounds mentioned. The evidence upon which the appellant was convicted included both the intercept and the interview. If the exclusion of the intercept should have led to the exclusion of the interview, or at least the incriminating parts of the interview, there would be no sufficient evidence to support the conviction of the appellant and his appeal should clearly be allowed. It is

therefore appropriate to refer briefly to the hypothetical situation of what the   *a*
judge should have done about the interview evidence if he had ruled (as he
should have done) that the intercept evidence was inadmissible. The interview
transcript would have had to be edited so as to remove the direct and indirect
references to the intercept. This could have been done. In my judgment what
was then left could have been properly put before the jury. Det Con Hussey
conducted the interview in essentially three sections. First he obtained the   *b*
appellant's accounts of his movements and his blanket denials of any involvement
saying that he had known nothing of the incident until he had driven past Neil's
house the following morning on his way to work and seen the burnt out car.
Secondly, he told the appellant of the arrest of Christine and the existence of the
taped conversation and questioned the appellant more closely as to his involvement   *c*
in the incident, the appellant making detailed and incriminating admissions.
Finally, he took the appellant through the transcript of the taped conversation
obtaining confirmation of what the appellant had said earlier in the interview. The
incriminating admissions made during the second part of the interview were
free-standing, although no doubt motivated by the appellant's knowledge that he
had incriminated himself during the telephone conversation. To exclude all   *d*
reference to the telephone conversation would in no way have been adverse to
the appellant. There was no entrapment, oppression or deceit of the appellant.
No problem of non-disclosure arose. The appellant clearly understood what had
happened, that Neil had acted illegally and that the tape contained, as it did, a
recording of the bulk of his telephone conversation the following morning with   *e*
Christine. His case at the trial was that he had made the admissions to
Det Con Hussey which he did because he was seeking to shield Christine not
because they were true. Therefore, had the judge appreciated that he must
exclude the evidence of the intercept, he could have required the transcript of the
interview to be edited accordingly and the oral evidence of Neil and Det Con Hussey
to be similarly limited. In my judgment a fair trial would have been possible on   *f*
that basis. The judge was not required to exclude the evidence of the confessions
made in interview.

[37] However that was not what occurred. The inadmissible evidence was
admitted. The jury were therefore left with an almost unanswerable case against
the appellant. He had incriminated himself twice, once in the telephone conversation
and a second time in interview. He could try to explain away what he said in   *g*
interview by suggesting that he was trying to shield Christine but this provided
no explanation for what he had said during the telephone conversation. The
comment made by the judge during his summing up was inevitable:

> 'Or, alternatively, as the prosecution say, as soon as the police revealed   *h*
> their knowledge of his telephone call with Christine Page and revealed the
> fact that it had been tape recorded, did he then realise, in effect, that the game
> was up and made admissions in the light of that knowledge?'

If the intercept evidence had been excluded, the jury would have heard of only
one set of admissions, those made during the second part of the interview. The   *j*
case against him would have still been strong and, it may be thought, would have
been likely to have led to his conviction. But it is far from impossible that the
exclusion of the intercept evidence would have enabled the defence case to be put
more convincingly, perhaps with evidence from the appellant himself, and might
have enabled the defence to raise a doubt in the minds of the jury. In my
judgment the evidence which was wrongly admitted was relevant and cogent.

a The statute required that it be excluded. The appellant's trial cannot be said to have been in accordance with the law nor can it be said that his conviction was in the circumstances safe.

[38] It follows that the appellant's appeal should be allowed and his conviction set aside. The answers to the certified questions have in substance been provided by earlier decisions of your Lordships' House. The exclusion of evidence required

b by s 9 of the 1985 Act extend to the fruits of the interception as well as to the interception itself (see *Morgans v DPP* [2000] 2 All ER 522, [2001] 1 AC 315). The fact that an interception was unlawful does not itself preclude the use of the material so obtained; the criteria to be applied are those contained in s 78 of the 1984 Act (see *R v Khan (Sultan)* [1996] 3 All ER 289, [1997] AC 558 and the same case in the European Court of Human Rights, *Khan v UK* (2000) 8 BHRC 310 and

c *R v P* [2001] 2 All ER 58, [2001] 2 WLR 463).

[39] I have had the advantage of reading the speech of my noble and learned friend Lord Hope in which he gives his reasons for agreeing that the appeal should be allowed. I agree with what he says. As regards the submission of counsel for the appellant that the unlawfulness of the intercept itself, ipso facto,

d meant that evidence could not have been given of the police interview, the submission was clearly unsound and contrary to established authority. Cases such as *R v Sang* and *R v Khan* decide that the use of illegally obtained material in the course of the investigation of a suspected crime does not, without more, render any evidence obtained as a result of such use inadmissible. As previously stated,

e s 78 of the 1984 Act (which has been upheld by the European Court) provides the criterion for deciding whether to exclude such evidence. It requires the trial judge to assess the fairness of admitting it 'having regard to all the circumstances, including the circumstances in which the evidence was obtained'. Neither the inadmissibility of the intercept evidence nor the fact that it was obtained unlawfully would necessitate the exclusion of the interview evidence provided that its

f admission would not have such an adverse effect on the fairness of the proceedings that the judge ought not to admit it. This is the point I have discussed at [36] above.

Appeal allowed.

Kate O'Hanlon   Barrister.

Mohamed v Hammersmith and Fulham   a
London Borough Council
[2001] UKHL 57

HOUSE OF LORDS   b
LORD SLYNN OF HADLEY, LORD STEYN, LORD HOFFMANN, LORD HUTTON AND LORD
HOBHOUSE OF WOODBOROUGH

2 JULY, 1 NOVEMBER 2001

Housing – Homeless person – Duty of housing authority to provide accommodation –   c
Decision by local housing authority to refer applicant to another authority on grounds
of 'local connection'– Material date for determining whether applicant having local
connection – Relevance of occupation of interim accommodation for establishment of
local connection – Scope of review of local housing authority's decision to refer applicant
to another authority – Housing Act 1996, ss 184, 198, 199.

d

The respondent, M, came to England at the end of January 1998 and lived with a
friend in the district of the appellant local housing authority. In that month, M's
wife, who had come to England in 1994, also began living with a friend in the
authority's district, but until then she had lived most of the time in the district of
another authority. On 16 April 1998 M and his wife jointly asked the appellant   e
authority for accommodation and were given temporary accommodation. On
11 May they made a formal application for assistance to the authority under the
Housing Act 1996 on the basis that they were homeless. Under s 184[a] of the 1996
Act, the authority was required to inquire whether the applicants were eligible
for assistance and, if so, whether any duty was owed to them under other
provisions of the Act. Section 184(2) provided that the authority could also make   f
inquiries as to whether an applicant 'has a local connection' with the district of
another local authority. By virtue of s 198(2)[b], a case could be referred to another
authority if, inter alia, neither the applicant nor any person who might reasonably
be expected to reside with him 'has a local connection' with the district of the
authority to which the application had been made, and the applicant or such
other person 'has a local connection' with the district of the other authority.   g
Under s 199(1)(a)[c], a person 'has a local connection' with the district of a local
housing authority if he had a connection with it because 'he is, or in the past was,
normally resident there, and that residence is or was of his own choice'.
Although the authority decided that it had a duty to arrange accommodation for
M's wife, it also concluded that she had no local connection with it but did have   h
such a connection with the authority in whose district she had previously lived.
It therefore referred the applications to the other authority. A formal application
was made for a review of that decision, but in September 1998 the reviewing

a   Section 184, so far as material, provides: '(1) If the local housing authority have reason to believe   j
    that an applicant may be homeless or threatened with homelessness, they shall make such inquiries
    as are necessary to satisfy themselves—(a) whether he is eligible for assistance, and (b) if so,
    whether any duty, and if so what duty, is owed to him under the following provisions of this Part.
        (2) They may also make inquiries whether he has a local connection with the district of another
    local housing authority ...'
b   Section 198, so far as material, is set out at [5], below
c   Section 199, so far as material, is set out at [6], below

a officer upheld the decision to refer, concluding that neither M nor his wife had a local connection with the authority. An appeal to the county court was dismissed by the judge who held that it was wrong to take into account on the review the period between the original decision and the date of review. His decision was reversed by the Court of Appeal which held that the material date for considering whether an applicant had a local connection was the date of the review, and that
b interim accommodation provided by the authority pending decision and review could constitute normal residence of choice. On the authority's appeal to the House of Lords, their Lordships were therefore required to determine (i) whether the occupation of interim accommodation pending a decision of an application for assistance could be 'normal residence' for the purposes of s 199(1)(a) of the 1996 Act; (ii) whether the correct date to decide if a person had a local connection
c was the date of his application rather than the date of the decision or any subsequent review; and (iii) whether the reviewing officer might look at facts which had come into existence after the original decision had been made.

Held – (1) The occupation of interim accommodation pending a decision of an
d application for assistance could be 'normal residence' for the purposes of s 199(1)(a) of the 1996 Act. Although words such as 'ordinary residence' and 'normal residence' might take their precise meaning from the context of the legislation in which they appeared, the prima facie meaning of normal residence was a place where at the relevant time the person in fact resided. Accordingly, it was not appropriate to consider whether in a general or abstract sense such a place would
e be considered an ordinary or normal residence. So long as the place where he ate and slept was voluntarily accepted by him, the reason why he was there rather than somewhere else did not prevent that place from being his normal residence. Thus where a person was given interim accommodation by a local housing authority, that accommodation was the place where, for the time being, he was
f normally resident. The fact that it was provided subject to statutory duty did not prevent it from being such. That conclusion did not defeat the purpose intended by the 1996 Act. While there was a redistributive purpose to the Act, it had to be read with the other statutory purpose of providing for people to stay in a borough with which they had established a local connection. There was no overriding reason or principle why interim accommodation should not count as normal
g residence for that purpose. It followed that the occupation of interim accommodation could be taken into account in determining whether a local connection existed (see [18], [21], [22], [30]–[33], below).

(2) The correct date for deciding whether a person had a local connection was the date of the decision or the review, not the date of the making of the application. The
h question for the local housing authority under s 198(2) of the 1996 Act was whether the applicant 'has a local connection', and that had to mean such a connection at the date of the decision or review (see [23], [30]–[33], below).

(3) The reviewing officer was required to take into account all the circumstances at the time of the review. There was nothing in the statutory language which
j required the review to be confined to the date of the initial application or determination. In requiring the authority to inquire whether the applicant 'has' a local connection, the natural meaning of the language in s 184(2) of the 1996 Act was that the authority should consider that at the date of the review decision. The process at that stage was an administrative one, and there could be no justification for the final administrative decision of the reviewing officer to be limited to the circumstances existing at the date of the initial decision. Moreover,

the decision of the reviewing officer was at large both as to whether all the
conditions in s 198(2) of the Act were satisfied and as to the exercise of the   *a*
discretion to refer. He was not simply considering whether the initial decision
was right on the material before the authority at the date it was made. He could
therefore have regard to information relevant to the period before the first
decision, but only obtained thereafter, and to matters occurring after the initial
decision. Accordingly, the appeal would be dismissed (see [25], [26], [29],   *b*
[30]–[33], below).
    Decision of the Court of Appeal [2000] 2 All ER 597 affirmed.

Notes

For referrals to another local housing authority and for reviews, see 22 *Halsbury's*
Laws (4th edn reissue) paras 261, 263.   *c*
    For the Housing Act 1996, ss 184, 198, 199, see 21 *Halsbury's Statutes* (4th edn)
(1997 reissue) 892, 906, 907.

Cases referred to in opinions

Eastleigh BC v Betts [1983] 2 All ER 1111, [1983] 2 AC 613, [1983] 3 WLR 397, HL.   *d*
R v Southwark London BC, ex p Hughes (1998) 30 HLR 1082.
Shah v Barnet London BC [1983] 1 All ER 226, [1983] 2 AC 309, [1983] 2 WLR 16, HL.

Appeal

The appellant local housing authority, Hammersmith and Fulham London Borough   *e*
Council, appealed with permission of the Appeal Committee of the House of
Lords given on 20 November 2000 from the decision of the Court of Appeal
(Henry and Potter LJJ) on 21 January 2000 ([2000] 2 All ER 597, [2001] QB 97)
allowing an appeal by the respondent, Abdulrahman Mohamed, from the
decision of Judge Richard Walker at West London County Court on 17 June 1999
dismissing the respondent's appeal from the authority's decision on 23 September   *f*
1998 affirming, on a review under s 202 of the Housing Act 1996, its decision on
23 July 1998 to transfer to Ealing London Borough Council the respondent's
application for accommodation under Pt VII of the 1996 Act. The facts are set out
in the opinion of Lord Slynn of Hadley.

Andrew Arden QC and *Robert Levy* (instructed by *Michael Cogher*) for the appellant   *g*
    authority.
Jan Luba QC and *Stephen Knafler* (instructed by the *Hammersmith & Fulham*
    Community Law Centre) for the respondent.

    h
Their Lordships took time for consideration.

1 November 2001. The following opinions were delivered.

LORD SLYNN OF HADLEY.   *j*

    [1] My Lords, this appeal raises questions under the Housing Act 1996 which
Henry LJ in the Court of Appeal below ([2000] 2 All ER 597 at 598, [2001] QB 97
at 101 (para 1)) said frequently arose but had not then been resolved by that court.
The answers to those questions have important consequences for those who are
homeless and who have priority needs; they are no less important for those
authorities who are said to be responsible for providing accommodation and who

a may have applicants with competing needs but insufficient accommodation or finances to provide for all who apply for somewhere to live.

[2] The statutory provisions can be summarised shortly. A person who contends that he is homeless with priority needs and eligible for assistance may apply to a local housing authority. The authority receiving such an application must by virtue of s 184 of the Act inquire as to the applicant's eligibility for assistance and *b* must inquire as to what, if any, duty is owed to that person. The authority may then decide or refuse to provide accommodation but it has also the option of inquiring whether the applicant has a local connection with the district of another housing authority. If they consider that he has but has no connection with its own authority then that authority may refer the application to the other authority.

[3] By s 193, if after inquiry the local housing authority 'are satisfied that an *c* applicant is homeless, eligible for assistance and has a priority need, and are not satisfied that he became homeless intentionally' they must 'secure that accommodation is available for occupation by the applicant' for a minimum period of two years unless they 'refer the application to another local housing authority'.

d [4] If a local housing authority would be liable to provide accommodation but consider that the conditions are met for referral of the case to another local housing authority they may notify that other authority of their opinion (s 198).

[5] The relevant conditions by virtue of s 198 are that:

e '... (a) neither the applicant nor any person who might reasonably be expected to reside with him has a local connection with the district of the authority to whom his application was made, (b) the applicant or a person who might reasonably be expected to reside with him has a local connection with the district of that other authority ...'

[6] By s 199(1):

f 'A person has a local connection with the district of a local housing authority if he has a connection with it—(a) because he is, or in the past was, normally resident there, and that residence is or was of his own choice, (b) because he is employed there, (c) because of family associations, or (d) because of special circumstances.'

g [7] The authority's decision to notify another authority that conditions are met for a referral to the latter authority is subject to review by virtue of s 202(1) and regulations may be made under s 203 of the Act to provide for the procedure to be followed on such a review.

[8] By virtue of the Allocation of Housing and Homelessness (Review Procedures *h* and Amendment) Regulations 1996, SI 1996/3122, in force at the time, it was provided that the review should be conducted by an officer senior to the one who took the decision and that it should be carried out 'on the basis of facts known to them at the date of the review' (reg 8): the latter was deleted from the 1999 regulations, the Allocation of Housing and Homelessness (Review Procedures) *j* Regulations 1999, SI 1999/71.

[9] By s 204 of the 1996 Act an applicant dissatisfied with the decision on the review may appeal to the county court on a point of law and the county court may confirm, quash or vary the decision.

[10] Although Mr Mohamed is the respondent he is not the only person concerned by the appeal. His wife, Mrs Farah, and two sons left Somalia during the civil war in 1992 and went to Kenya. In 1994 Mrs Farah came to England

though without their sons. She lived most of the time in flats in Ealing until in
January 1998 she moved to live with a friend at an address in the appellant a
authority's district. The respondent came to England on 31 January 1998 and
although in contact with his wife he lived with a friend in the authority's district.
On 16 April 1998 they jointly asked the appellant authority for accommodation
and were given temporary accommodation first in an hotel and then in a flat in
the authority's district. On 11 May they made their formal application as being b
homeless under the provisions of the Act to which I have referred. On 23 July 1998
the authority told Mrs Farah that they accepted a duty to arrange accommodation
for her but that, although she had a local connection with Ealing where she had
lived, she had no connection with the appellant authority and on 27 July the
applications of both the respondent and his wife were referred to Ealing London
Borough Council on the basis that they appeared to have a local connection with c
Ealing but not with the appellant authority's district. Representations were made
to the appellant authority on behalf of both applicants against this decision and a
formal application was made for a review of the decision to refer the matter to
Ealing.

[11] The reviewing officer by letter of 23 September 1998 said that having d
considered all the matters set out in letters sent on behalf of the applicants during
August and in the light of the outcome of the council's inquiries prior to the
decision under review he was satisfied to uphold the decision to refer. He said:

'... I am satisfied to uphold the decision to refer as I am satisfied that
neither Mr Mohamed nor Ms Farah have a local connection with this e
authority, that Ms Farah has a local connection with LB Ealing via her
lengthy previous normal residence there, that neither would be at risk of
domestic or other violence in that area and that there are no grounds on
which the Council could exercise our discretionary power not to refer the
application.'

f

[12] He did not consider that the respondent's residence in the borough between
31 January and 17 April 1998 was sufficient to give rise to 'a local connection in
real terms'. He did not accept that the existence of relatives in the borough or the
need for medical treatment in these two cases established a local connection in
view of the proximity of the two boroughs and the ease of passing from one to
the other to visit a hospital. g

[13] He concluded:

'I have also considered the cumulative effect of all of these various factors
but I am not satisfied that the households stated need to live in this borough
is an essential compassionate, social or support need or that this is a significant h
factor to the households medical well being sufficient to give rise to a local
connection with this authority in real terms. I have also considered whether
there are any grounds on which this authority could exercise our residual
power of discretion not to maintain the referral to Ealing but, for the same
reasons as set out in this letter and taking into account the competing
demands for the Council's limited housing resources including the housing j
needs of other households accepted for a s193 duty who have a local
connection with ourselves, I am satisfied that there are no grounds on which
to exercise our discretion not to refer.'

[14] There was then an appeal to the West London County Court which
dismissed the appeal on 17 June 1999. It was Judge Richard Walker's view that

a the reviewing officer had not erred in law. His reference to there having to be a local connection 'in real terms' did not set too high a standard. There had to be a real local connection rather than an artificial or fanciful one. The judge took the view that 'the duty of the review is to give fresh consideration to the original application' and that it was wrong to take into account on the review the period between the original decision and the date of the review though on the review

b there could be taken into account facts relevant to the original decision but not known at that time. The judge said:

> 'If it were to be decided that the very act of providing ex gratia housing of homeless people, pending the processes of review and appeal, had the effect in law of strengthening the hand of the applicant for housing, it could have
> *c* the effect of inducing housing authorities to refuse to provide interim housing in such circumstances in order to prevent applicants from gaining such advantage. The consequent putting on to the streets of those who are potentially among the most vulnerable in our society cannot be in accordance with the essential purpose of the legislation under review.
> *d* I therefore conclude that either the reviewing officer made no error of law in taking into account only those facts known to him to have existed at the date of the original decision, or that if I am wrong about this I should not, for this reason, quash the decision, since no new relevant fact had come into being by the time of the review which should have led to a different decision.'

e [15] As to the facts existing at the date of the original decision he concluded that the fact that Mrs Farah's sister had lived for two months in the appellant authority's district was not significant and the fact that the respondent had lived in the borough from 31 January 1998 to 16 April 1998 did not establish the necessary connection. He therefore dismissed the appeal.

[16] The Court of the Appeal were firmly of the view that the material date
f for considering whether an applicant had a local connection was the date the authority reviewed its decision. It was the facts established at that stage which the authority should take into account on its review. A local connection developed during the period between the initial decision and the review could compatibly with the purposes of the legislation be taken into account. They also held that interim accommodation provided by the authority pending decision and review

g could constitute normal residence 'of his choice'.

[17] Thus on this appeal it is accepted that the respondent was homeless, was eligible for assistance, had a privileged need and was not intentionally homeless. The question is accordingly whether it can be said that he had no local connection with the district of the appellant authority and in that regard the principal

h question is whether it can be said that he is, or in the past was, normally resident in the district of that authority. The authority's principle argument is that the occupation of interim accommodation pending a decision of his application under the Act is not (ie cannot be) 'normal residence' for the purposes of s 199(1)(a) of the 1996 Act. The respondent has lost his normal residence and has asked for

j and was given only temporary shelter until replacement accommodation is provided. At the relevant time accordingly he had no normal residence so that he could not establish a local connection on the ground of residence. For that purpose 'normally resident' is to be given the same meaning as ordinarily resident. In *Shah v Barnet London BC* [1983] 1 All ER 226 at 235, [1983] 2 AC 309 at 343 which was concerned with ordinary residence it was said that that phrase referred to—

'a man's abode in a particular place or country which he has adopted
voluntarily and for settled purposes as part of the regular order of his life for   *a*
the time being, whether of short or of long duration.'

[18] It is clear that words like 'ordinary residence' and 'normal residence' may
take their precise meaning from the context of the legislation in which they
appear but it seems to me that the prima facie meaning of normal residence is a   *b*
place where at the relevant time the person in fact resides. That therefore is the
question to be asked and it is not appropriate to consider whether in a general or
abstract sense such a place would be considered an ordinary or normal residence.
So long as that place where he eats and sleeps is voluntarily accepted by him, the
reason why he is there rather than somewhere else does not prevent that place
from being his normal residence. He may not like it, he may prefer some other   *c*
place, but that place is for the relevant time the place where he normally resides.
If a person, having no other accommodation, takes his few belongings and moves
into a barn for a period to work on a farm that is where during that period he is
normally resident, however much he might prefer some more permanent or
better accommodation. In a sense it is 'shelter' but it is also where he resides.
Where he is given interim accommodation by a local housing authority even   *d*
more clearly is that the place where for the time being he is normally resident.
The fact that it is provided subject to statutory duty does not, contrary to the
appellant authority's argument, prevent it from being such.

[19] Although the point is not conclusive, counsel for the respondent are
entitled as they do to point to the fact that Parliament has specifically provided in   *e*
s 199 that residence due to service in the armed forces or through detention
under statutory powers is not 'of choice' and the Secretary of State may specify
other circumstances in which residence in a district is not to be treated as of a
person's own choice, but nothing has been done to exclude residence under the
homelessness provisions with which this appeal is concerned as not being of a   *f*
person's own choice. If it had been intended to exclude such accommodation it
would have been easy to have done so in the section or by the exercise of powers
by the Secretary of State under s 119(5) of the 1996 Act.

[20] The appellant authority contends that interim accommodation cannot
lead to the creation of a local connection attributable to normal residence even 'if
a person is in interim accommodation for an extensive period, e g years' though   *g*
it recognises that local connection through other factors specified (e g special
circumstances) can arise during the occupation of interim accommodation. The
authority says that to allow such interim accommodation to count as normal
residence defeats the purpose intended by the Act. Such accommodation was not
intended to give an applicant the chance to build up a local connection; to take   *h*
such interim accommodation into account benefits those whose cases demand
long inquiry to the disadvantage of those whose cases can be dealt with quickly.

[21] I agree with Henry LJ [2000] 2 All ER 597 at 606, [2001] QB 97 at 109
(para 45) that although there is a redistributive purpose to the Act, it has to be
read with the other statutory purpose of providing for people to stay in a borough   *j*
with which they have established a local connection and that there is no
overriding reason or principle why interim accommodation should not count as
normal residence for that purpose.

[22] In *Eastleigh BC v Betts* [1983] 2 All ER 1111 at 1120, [1983] 2 AC 613 at 628
Lord Brightman stressed that 'the real exercise will be to decide whether the
normal residence has been such as to establish a subsisting local connection'. In

a my opinion the occupation of interim accommodation can be taken into account in deciding whether such a local connection exists.

[23] A second question which has been raised is whether the correct date to decide whether a person has a local connection is the date of the making of his application or the date of the decision or, if there is a review, the date of the review. It seems to me plain that since the question for the local housing *b* authority is whether the applicant 'has a local connection' that must mean such a connection at the date of decision or review, whether in the meantime the applicant has acquired or lost (by moving away) his local connection.

[24] A linked question which arises is as to the material which may be looked at on the review. The appellant authority contends that the reviewing officer may look at facts known to the original decision-maker and those which existed before *c* the time of the original decision but were not known to the original decision-maker but he may not look at facts which have come into existence subsequently. The respondent on the other hand says that the reviewing officer can and should look at all the circumstances at the time of the review. In *R v Southwark London BC, ex p Hughes* (1998) 30 HLR 1082 at 1089, in a case decided under the Housing Act *d* 1985, before a statutory right of review was given, Turner J said:

> 'It may be thought therefore that there are compelling reasons why the circumstances of an individual, at the time the inquiry is carried out and the decision is made, must be the circumstances which the housing authority is required to investigate for the purposes of coming to their decision whether *e* or not the applicant is homeless ...'

[25] The present case is not concerned with whether the applicant tenants were homeless but whether there was a connection with Hammersmith or whether the applicants had a connection with Ealing and not with Hammersmith. It seems to me, however, plain that the approach should be as stated by Turner J and *f* perhaps with more force since there is now a statutory right of review. I find nothing in the statutory language which requires the review to be confined to the date of the initial application or determination. The natural meaning of the language in s 184(2) of the 1996 Act in requiring the local housing authority to inquire whether the applicant 'has' a local connection is that they should consider that at the date of the review decision. It is to be remembered that the process *g* is an administrative one at this stage and there can be no justification for the final administrative decision of the reviewing officer to be limited to the circumstances existing at the date of the initial decision.

[26] The decision of the reviewing officer is at large both as to the facts (i e as to whether the three conditions in s 198(2) of the Act are satisfied) and as to the *h* exercise of the discretion to refer. He is not simply considering whether the initial decision was right on the material before it at the date it was made. He may have regard to information relevant to the period before the first decision but only obtained thereafter and to matters occurring after the initial decision.

[27] As already shown the reviewing officer took into account in his letter *j* whether there had been an essential compassionate, social or support need. The Court of Appeal held that this was a clear misdirection in law. Requiring that the applicant must show an essential compassionate, social or support need to live in the district was putting the test for local connection too high.

[28] The appellant authority contends that this was not a separate test but an overall review of all the other matters which had been considered as to whether local connection by reference to special circumstances had been shown and that

accordingly there was no misdirection. There is some force in this but it seems
to me that the reviewing officer was using this additional test as part of his *a*
consideration as to whether there was a local connection by reason of special
circumstances. On that basis as I understand it the appellant authority accepts
that there was a misdirection as the Court of Appeal held. I agree with the Court
of Appeal on this matter.

[29] I would accordingly dismiss the appeal.   *b*

LORD STEYN.

[30] My Lords, I have read the opinion of my noble and learned friend, Lord
Slynn of Hadley. For the reasons he gives I would also dismiss the appeal.

LORD HOFFMANN.   *c*

[31] My Lords, I have had the advantage of reading in draft the speech of my
noble and learned friend, Lord Slynn of Hadley. For the reasons he gives I would
also dismiss the appeal.

LORD HUTTON.   *d*

[32] My Lords, I have had the advantage of reading in draft the speech of my
noble and learned friend, Lord Slynn of Hadley. For the reasons he gives, and
with which I agree, I would also dismiss this appeal.

LORD HOBHOUSE OF WOODBOROUGH.

[33] My Lords, for the reasons given by my noble and learned friend, Lord
Slynn of Hadley, I agree that this appeal should be dismissed.

Appeal dismissed.

Dilys Tausz   Barrister.

a # Harris v Harris
[2001] EWCA Civ 1645

COURT OF APPEAL, CIVIL DIVISION
THORPE, WALLER AND MANTELL LJJ
b 27 SEPTEMBER, 8 NOVEMBER 2001

Contempt of court – Release of contemnor – Application for release of contemnor – Whether court having jurisdiction to impose suspended sentence in respect of unserved balance of prison sentence when ordering contemnor's release.

c The appellant, H, was sentenced to ten months' imprisonment for contempt of court involving various breaches of injunctions. After two unsuccessful applications to purge his contempt, H made a third application, seeking either immediate release or release on the basis that the remaining part of his sentence should be suspended. Under RSC Ord 52, r 7(1)ᵃ (as scheduled to the CPR), the court *d* making an order of committal had power to direct that execution of the sentence be suspended, but there was no provision for a suspended sentence on an application to purge contempt. The judge nevertheless acceded to the application on the alternative basis, ordering H's release forthwith on terms that the execution of the remaining part of his sentence (just over seven months) be suspended for nine months, on condition that until then P complied with the terms of the injunctions. *e* On appeal, H challenged the judge's jurisdiction to make such an order, contending that an application to purge contempt could only have three possible outcomes, namely immediate release, deferred release at a stated future date or the refusal of the application. Counsel instructed as amicus curiae argued that, apart from limited statutory restrictions, the powers exercised by the judge were unbounded *f* common law powers and that, in the absence of direct authority, it was permissible and indeed praiseworthy for a judge to evolve the common law imaginatively to increase the flexibility and sophistication of the court's powers.

Held – Where, on an application to purge contempt, the court ordered the release of the contemnor, it had no jurisdiction to impose a suspended sentence *g* in respect of the unserved balance of the prison sentence. On such an application, which was rooted in quasi-religious concepts of purification, expiation and atonement, the judge could only say 'yes', 'no' or 'not yet'. It was of great importance that the powers of the court and the rights of the contemnor should be as clear and as certain as was consistent with the need to design orders that did justice and *h* reflected the infinite variety of fact and circumstance displayed by individual cases. Whilst the power to create, sometime after the imposition of the original sentence, a sentence partly immediate and partly suspended would arguably be a useful refinement, the gain would be outweighed by the introduction of complications to a contemnor's judgment as to whether or not to apply to purge, and could risk an *j* increase of litigation in an already over-burdened field. Moreover, it could not be said with any certainty that the order made by the judge in the instant case represented a variation of the original sentence rather than the imposition of a fresh penalty. The only power to suspend was the power to suspend the execution of the first order of imprisonment. The court's choice was only between a warrant

---

a   Rule 7(1) is set out at [14], below

to be immediately executed or a warrant to be suspended. That choice was made a at the sentencing hearing and did not recur. Furthermore, even if the judge's order could be accepted as a variation of the original order committing H to prison, it was by no means clear that it was a variation by way of amelioration in view of the imposition of the Damoclean sword throughout a period of future liberty. The principle that variation had to be by way of amelioration was important, and the amelioration had to be self-evident and almost irrefutable. It b followed that the judge had lacked jurisdiction to make the order as drawn. Since he had clearly been satisfied that there had been a measure of atonement, the only realistic disposal was to substitute an order for unconditional release in place of the conditional order made by the judge. Accordingly, the appeal would be allowed (see [21]–[23], [25], [28]).

Delaney v Delaney [1996] 1 All ER 367 considered. c

Notes

For discharge of a contemnor by court order, see 9(1) Halsbury's Laws (4th edn reissue) para 522.

d

Cases referred to in judgments

Delaney v Delaney [1996] 1 All ER 367, [1996] QB 837, [1996] 2 WLR 74, CA.
Villiers v Villiers [1994] 2 All ER 149, [1994] 1 WLR 493, CA.

Appeal

e

Mark Dean Harris, a litigant who had been sentenced on 23 March 2001 to ten months' imprisonment for contempt of court, appealed with permission of the Court of Appeal granted on 2 July 2001 from the order of Munby J on 14 June 2001, for which reasons were given on 21 June 2001 ([2001] 3 WLR 765), ordering his release from prison on terms that the execution of the remaining part of the sentence of imprisonment be suspended for nine months until 14 March 2002. f The facts are set out in the judgment of Thorpe LJ.

Mark Twomey (instructed by Thornleys, Plymstock) for Mr Harris.
Richard Ritchie (instructed by the Treasury Solicitor) as amicus curiae.

Cur adv vult g

8 November 2001. The following judgments were delivered.

THORPE LJ.

[1] For about the last three years Mr Harris has been an embattled litigant in h the family justice system. With the passage of time the battle has intensified. Very considerable sums of public money have been spent, principally on the issue of contact. Many judges of the Family Division have had a hand in the case. On many occasions orders have been made restricting Mr Harris' ordinary rights in order to protect either his former wife or his children. Self-evidently Mr Harris j has never accepted the court's authority and there have been numerous breaches leading to regular applications for committal. The last Family Division judge to deal with the case was Munby J. He delivered a comprehensive judgment reviewing the whole history of the proceedings on 22 March 2001. On the following day for various breaches of injunctions he imposed sentences, including a sentence of ten months imprisonment.

a [2] Many of the judges of this court have also dealt with the case and on 2 May 2001 Waller LJ presided in a constitution that dismissed Mr Harris' appeal against that prison sentence. In the interim Mr Harris had made two unsuccessful applications to Munby J to purge his contempt. Mr Harris applied for permission to appeal other orders made by the judge on 22 or 23 March and that application was refused by another constitution of this court on 2 July.

b [3] However on 14 June Mr Harris made his third application to Munby J to purge his contempt. In letters written to the judge Mr Harris had sought immediate release, alternatively release on the basis that the remaining part of his sentence should be suspended. Munby J, who has particular expertise in this field, recognised that an application for conditional release under a suspended sentence of imprisonment raised a difficult point of law and accordingly invited the Attorney c General to instruct counsel on the application as a friend of the court. Thus on 14 June the judge heard from Mr Harris in person and Mr Richard Ritchie instructed by the Attorney General.

[4] After hearing submissions the judge acceded to Mr Harris' alternative application. The order dated 14 June and perfected on 19 June reads in its essential d paragraph:

e 'It is ordered that the applicant having today conditionally purged his contempt be released forthwith today (14 June 2001) from prison on terms that and it is further ordered that execution of the remaining part of the said sentence of imprisonment be suspended for nine months until 14 March 2002 when this order and the committal order shall cease to have effect on condition that until 14 March 2002 the applicant complies with the following terms namely that the applicant obeys the terms of the injunctions contained in the injunction order.'

f [5] The judgment explaining the judge's reasons for finding jurisdiction to make and for making that order were subsequently handed down on 21 June 2001 ([2001] 3 WLR 765). On 2 July this court, whilst refusing all other applications for permission to appeal, granted permission to appeal the order of 14 June, if permission were required. Subsequently the Attorney General was asked to instruct Mr Ritchie to repeat his assistance to the court on the point of law. Fortunately Mr Harris g has received legal aid for this hearing and his case has been exceptionally well put by Mr Twomey. Mr Ritchie has equally performed his function in exemplary fashion in presenting the arguments for and the arguments against the conclusion that the order of Munby J rests on a secure legal foundation. There has been no challenge to the judge's exercise of discretion. Mr Twomey conceded that if the h judge had the power to make the order it was plainly within the discretionary range.

[6] Thus this appeal raises the short point: can a court releasing a contemnor on his application to purge his contempt impose a suspended sentence in respect of the unserved balance of the prison sentence and, if yes, for what period can the j court order the suspension to run.

[7] As I understand it Mr Harris' original complaint was that the suspended sentence which he had invited should not have been made to run beyond 22 August (the realistic date of his release from the sentence imposed on 23 March) or certainly beyond 22 January 2002 (the theoretical date of his release). However Mr Twomey attacked the judge's conclusion root and branch. His first and simple submission is that a contemnor applying to purge his contempt faces only

three possible outcomes: (i) immediate release, (ii) deferred release at a stated
future date, and (iii) the refusal of his application.

[8] If the outcome is either (ii) or (iii) above, then the order giving effect to
that conclusion will clearly state his continuing right to reapply to purge. Whilst
Mr Twomey accepts that the court has power to renew orders for protection,
make fresh orders for protection or require undertakings from the applicant in
acceding to the application to purge, he submits it has no power to vary the
original sentence, other than in the manner indicated above, and has no power to
impose a fresh sentence.

[9] His second submission is that in the event that the court did have such
jurisdiction, it did not permit the suspension of the sentence beyond the period
that the contemnor would actually have spent in prison had he served his sentence,
alternatively, beyond the length of the original sentence as formally declared.
Mr Twomey's third submission was that the elaboration devised by the judge
was impermissible since the original order of committal of 23 March 2001 simply
stated, in a short paragraph following the sentencing paragraphs, 'And the
contemnor Mark Dean Harris can apply to the judge to purge his contempt and ask
for release.' That simple statement supported the submission that on an application
to purge the judge's options were matchingly simple.

[10] Mr Ritchie directed his written argument to points raised in Mr Twomey's
second ground. However in his oral submissions he dealt with Mr Twomey's
fundamental attack on jurisdiction stressing that, apart from limited statutory
restrictions, the powers exercised by the judge were unbounded common law
powers and in the absence of direct authority it was permissible, and indeed
praiseworthy for a judge to evolve the common law imaginatively to increase the
flexibility and sophistication of the court's powers. Having set out with great
fairness the arguments for and against the appeal Mr Ritchie sought to uphold the
judge simply because we received the contrary argument from Mr Twomey.

[11] Before coming to my conclusions I will record the relevant statutory
provisions and rules of court. I will then briefly consider relevant authorities.

[12] The principal statutory restriction on common law powers of the court is
to be found in s 14(1) of the Contempt of Court Act 1981 which provides:

'In any case where a court has power to commit a person to prison for
contempt of court and (apart from this provision) no limitation applies to the
period of committal, the committal shall (without prejudice to the power of
the court to order his earlier discharge) be for a fixed term, and that term
shall not on any occasion exceed two years in case of committal by a superior
court ...'

[13] The other relevant statutory provision is s 45 of the Criminal Justice Act
1991 which provides essentially that once a contemnor—

'has served the appropriate proportion of his term, that is to say—(a) one-half,
in the case of a person committed for a term of less than 12 months ... it shall be
the duty of the Secretary of State to release him unconditionally.'

[14] The relevant Supreme Court rule is RSC Ord 52 (as scheduled to the
CPR). Rule 7(1) provides:

'The court by whom an order of committal is made may by order direct
that the execution of the order of committal shall be suspended for such
period or on such terms or conditions as it may specify.'

a **[15]** Rule 8(1) provides more simply: 'The court may, on the application of any person committed to prison for any contempt of court, discharge him.'

[16] A number of cases were cited to us in argument but, since it was common ground that the point for decision is not covered by any direct authority, I will be selective in my references. The case of *Villiers v Villiers* [1994] 2 All ER 149 at 152, [1994] 1 WLR 493 at 497 illustrates passingly within its history a judge abstracting *b* an undertaking from an applicant on granting his application to purge, in the instance an undertaking to consult a psychiatrist.

[17] Of greater moment is the decision of this court in *Delaney v Delaney* [1996] 1 All ER 367, [1996] QB 837. The problem presented to this court by that appeal was that the judge had sought to remand the contemnor in custody for reports in order to guide him in the sentencing exercise on an adjourned hearing. This *c* court held that he had no power so to do. However, Bingham MR adopted a solution advanced by Mr Munby, on that occasion instructed by the Official Solicitor as friend of the court. Bingham MR said:

'In reliance on those authorities Mr Munby accordingly submitted that *d* where the sentencing judge was uncertain as to what sentence he should impose, he could impose a sentence at the top end of the appropriate bracket whilst at the same time directing that the matter be restored for further hearing at the end of a suitable period. At that hearing the judge would in effect have three options. One would be to affirm the original order and leave the contemnor in prison, subject always to his right to make further *e* applications to purge; secondly, the judge could order the immediate release of the contemnor; or thirdly, the judge could indicate a future date at which the contemnor would be released subject, as I repeat again, to the right of the contemnor to make further application in the interim. That submission appears to me to be soundly based on the authorities to which reference has been made and it resolves the concerns the court felt on 16 October about *f* the practicalities of handling situations of this kind.' (See [1996] 1 All ER 367 at 377, [1996] QB 837 at 400–401.)

[18] Mr Twomey has pointed out that parliament swiftly provided a power to remand in the case of occupation orders and non-molestation orders. *g* Section 47(7)(b) of the Family Law Act 1996 provides a general power to remand and s 48 provides a specific power to remand for medical examination and report. However, that statutory enlargement is only available in family cases and then only in those involving breach of occupation orders or non-molestation orders made under that statute.

h **[19]** Certainly the case of *Delaney v Delaney* illustrates the court's jurisdiction to use the common law power flexibly and imaginatively in order to meet a particular practical problem, albeit one which does not commonly arise. In the generality of cases at the stage where the judge is faced with the responsibility of imposing a custodial sentence he will have gained extensive knowledge of and insight into the parties to the proceedings. But plainly the common law power is *j* not unlimited, quite apart from statutory restrictions. Certainly the sentence first imposed is mutable either by the judge of his own motion or as a consequence of an application by the contemnor to purge. However, no one is liable to be sentenced twice for the same contempt nor can the original sentence be varied by way of increase. Much of the argument before us has turned upon whether the judge's order of 14 June constituted a variation of an existing sentence or the

imposition of a fresh sentence and whether, if a variation, it was a variation by
way of amelioration. Equally it was argued on the one hand that the order of *a*
14 June was a demonstration of the living common law adapting flexibly to do
better justice and on the other hand that the result produced by the order was
uncertain and difficult to implement. For what was meant by 'the remaining part
of the said sentence of imprisonment'? In the event of breach, what term would
be served and how would s 45 of the 1991 Act operate?   *b*

[20] Although the arguments on both sides are skilfully presented and finally
balanced I am of the clear opinion that the judge did not have jurisdiction to make
the order as drawn for two principal reasons.

[21] First I accept Mr Twomey's submission that the application to purge is
rooted in quasi-religious concepts of purification, expiation and atonement. On such
an application the judge may only say 'yes', 'no' or 'not yet'. In family proceedings *c*
imprisonment for civil contempt has proved a complex field generating much
work in the courts of trial and a significant number of appeals. In my opinion it
is of great importance that the powers of the court and the rights of the contemnor
should be as clear and as certain as is consistent with the need to design orders
that do justice and reflect the infinite variety of fact and circumstance displayed *d*
by individual cases. Whilst arguably the power to create, sometime after the
imposition of the original custodial sentence, a sentence partly immediate and
partly suspended would be a useful refinement, in my opinion the gain would be
outweighed by the introduction of complications which would certainly complicate
a contemnor's judgment as to whether or not to apply to purge and which would
arguably risk an increase of litigation in this already over-burdened field.   *e*

[22] Second it cannot in my opinion be said with any certainty that the order
represents a variation of the original sentence rather the imposition of a fresh penalty.
Certainly the RSC as presently framed suggest to me that the only power to
suspend is the power to suspend the execution of the first order of imprisonment.
The court's choice is only between a warrant to be immediately executed or a *f*
warrant to be suspended. That choice is made at the sentencing hearing and does
not recur. Furthermore even if the order of 14 June could be accepted as a
variation of the order of 23 March I am by no means clear that it is a variation by
way of amelioration. Whilst on the one hand I recognise the argument that a
reduction of two months and eight days on a sentence of five months must be
counted a significant amelioration (and Mr Harris must so have regarded it since *g*
that was what he sought in the alternative) a balance still has to be struck between
the element of amelioration and the price paid by imposition of the Damoclean
sword throughout a period of future liberty. The principle that variation must be
by way of amelioration is important and in my judgment amelioration should be
self-evident and almost irrefutable. Of course it would be possible to contrast *h*
extremes such as an immediate release ordered early into a long sentence
balanced by a suspended sentence of brief duration for a limited period and an
immediate release well into the original sentence balanced by a suspension for
an indefinite period. Although Mr Harris in this case was not in doubt as to his
preference, it is easy to postulate the hypothetical contemnor who would prefer *j*
to serve his term in order to achieve unconditional liberty.

[23] It has of course been pointed out that if Mr Harris succeeds in his appeal
he strikes down one of the objectives for which he contended on 14 June and risks
a return to prison for a period of two months and eight days. However, that
would not in my opinion be the right conclusion. Munby J was clearly satisfied
that there had been a measure of atonement, otherwise he would have dismissed

a this application like its two predecessors. In my opinion the only realistic disposal is to substitute an order for unconditional release for the conditional order made by the judge.

[24] Finally I would like to pay tribute to the most learned judgment handed down by Munby J on 21 June. I express some diffidence at disagreeing with him in an area of the law of which he has such evident command. I only make the
b obvious point that on 14 June Munby J acceded to an application, in the alternative, advanced by an unrepresented contemnor. Furthermore Mr Ritchie's argument did not seek to deter him but only to marshal the finely balanced arguments for and against. We have had the same helpful presentation from Mr Ritchie but by contrast the skilful attack on the judgment below marshalled by Mr Twomey.

c **WALLER LJ.**

[25] I agree and would merely add the following point. In my view it actually adds very little to the armoury of the court to allow someone to 'conditionally purge' with the remainder of a sentence placed in suspense. Even on an unconditional release, it must be clear to Mr Harris that if he commits a further breach of the
d orders, the court will in assessing sentence take account of the fact that by his previous promises of good behaviour he was released part way through his ten month sentence. The court is likely to start from the position that he should at least serve that unserved part plus some further period for the contempts committed in breach of those promises, all subject to the overall limit of two years.

[26] If Munby J's order were maintained, the court which had to deal with any
e further breaches of the order (presuming those breaches occurred within the period of suspension) would have to give effect to Munby J's order. It would then impose a further sentence for the further contempts again restrained so far as totality was concerned by the two-year limit.

[27] I am not sure that I see any real difference between the two exercises.
f The exercise which a court would have to do if Mr Harris were to break the promises he has given not to breach the orders in the future will in practical terms be the same whether the remainder of his present sentence is suspended or whether he is unconditionally released with the warning of the consequences which will follow if he commits further contempts.

MANTELL LJ.

[28] I also agree.

Appeal allowed.

Kate O'Hanlon   Barrister.

Cachia v Faluyi   *a*

[2001] EWCA Civ 998

COURT OF APPEAL, CIVIL DIVISION

LORD PHILLIPS OF WORTH MATRAVERS MR, HENRY AND BROOKE LJJ

25, 27 JUNE 2001   *b*

Fatal accident – Action – Limitation to one action only – Claimant's wife being killed in accident – Claimant issuing writ claiming damages on behalf of deceased's dependants but not serving writ – Claimant issuing fresh writ within limitation period claiming damages for three of deceased's children – Judge striking out claim because of *c* *statutory provision restricting fatal accident claim to one 'action' – Whether 'action' to be interpreted as 'served process' in order to give effect to children's right of access to court under human rights convention – Fatal Accidents Act 1976, s 2(3) – Human Rights Act 1998, s 3(1), Sch 1, Pt I, art 6(1).*

The wife of the claimant, C, was killed after being struck by a car driven by the *d* defendant, F. C subsequently issued a writ against F under the Fatal Accidents Act 1976, claiming damages, inter alia, on behalf of the deceased's dependants who included three of her children. That writ was never served, but some years later, when the children's claims were still within the limitation period, C issued a fresh writ under the 1976 Act. After the second writ was served, F applied to *e* strike out the children's claims. The judge granted the application, holding that the children's claims were barred by s 2(3)[a] of the Act, which provided that not more than one 'action' was to lie for and in respect of the same subject matter of complaint. C appealed, contending, inter alia, that the word 'action' in s 2(3) meant 'served process'. On the appeal, the court considered whether, if such a *f* construction was impermissible on normal principles of construction, s 2(3) could be so construed in order to give effect to the children's right of access to the court under art 6(1)[b] of the European Convention for the Protection of Human Rights and Fundamental Freedoms 1950 (as set out in Sch 1 to the Human Rights Act 1998). Section 3(1)[c] of the 1998 Act required the court, so far as it was possible to do so, to read and give effect to legislation in a way that was compatible with *g* convention rights.

Held – Although an action naturally began when the initiating process was issued rather than when it was served, it was possible to interpret the word 'action' in s 2(3) of the 1976 Act as meaning 'served process' in order to give effect to the *h* children's convention rights. Restrictions on the right of access to the court under art 6(1) of the convention were required to have a legitimate aim. In cases where a writ had never been served and a new writ had been issued within the primary limitation period, the fortuitous effect of s 2(3) could not have any such aim. It was merely a procedural quirk, brought about by the chance that Parliament had never considered that particular problem, and because traditional English *j*

---

a   Section 2(3) is set out at [2], below
b   Article 6, so far as material, provides: '(1) In the determination of his civil rights ... everyone is entitled to a fair and public hearing within a reasonable time ... '
c   Section 3, so far as material, provides: '(1) So far as it is possible to do so, primary legislation ... must be read and given effect in way which is compatible with the Convention rights ... '

a   methods of interpreting statutes could not correct an obvious injustice. It followed that s 2(3) presented no artificial bar to the children's claims, and accordingly the appeal would be allowed (see [12], [18]–[24], below).

Notes

For the right of access to a court and for the restriction of claims for dependencies
b   to one action, see respectively 8(2) *Halsbury's Laws* (4th edn reissue) para 141 and 33 *Halsbury's Laws* (4th edn reissue) para 626.

For the Fatal Accidents Act 1976, s 2, see 31 *Halsbury's Statutes* (4th edn) (2000 reissue) 482.

For the Human Rights Act 1998, s 3, Sch 1, Pt I, art 6, see 7 *Halsbury's Statutes* (4th edn) (1999 reissue) 502, 523.
c

Cases referred to in judgments

Ashingdane v UK (1985) 7 EHRR 528, [1985] ECHR 8225/78, ECt HR.
Avery v London and North Eastern Rly Co [1938] 2 All ER 592, [1938] AC 606, HL.
Berry (Herbert) Associates Ltd v IRC [1978] 1 All ER 161, [1977] 1 WLR 1437, HL.
d   *Cooper v Williams* [1963] 2 All ER 282, [1963] 2 QB 567, [1963] 2 WLR 913, CA.
Farrell v Alexander [1976] 2 All ER 721, [1977] AC 59, [1976] 3 WLR 145, HL.
Stubbings v UK (1996) 23 EHRR 213, [1996] ECHR 22083/93, ECt HR.

Cases also cited or referred to in skeleton arguments

De Freitas v Permanent Secretary of Ministry of Agriculture, Fisheries, Lands and Housing
e   [1999] 1 AC 69, [1998] 3 WLR 675, PC.
Golder v UK (1975) 1 EHRR 524, [1975] ECHR 4451/70, ECt HR.
J A Pye (Oxford) Ltd v Graham [2001] EWCA Civ 117, [2001] 2 WLR 1293.
Kammins Ballrooms Co Ltd v Zenith Investments (Torquay) Ltd [1970] 2 All ER 871, [1971] AC 850, HL.
f   *R v A* [2001] UKHL 25, [2001] 3 All ER 1, [2001] 2 WLR 1546, HL.
R v Governor of Brockhill Prison, ex p Evans (No 2) [1998] 4 All ER 933, [1999] QB 1043, CA.
Wilson v First County Trust Ltd [2001] EWCA Civ 633, [2001] 3 All ER 229, [2001] 3 WLR 42.

g   **Appeal**

By notice filed on 10 November 2000, the claimant, Michael Cachia, appealed with permission of Judge Charles Harris QC, sitting as a judge of the High Court, from his order on 31 October 2000 striking out claims for damages under the Fatal Accidents Act 1976 brought against the defendant, Francis Ola Faluyi, by the
h   claimant, as administrator of the estate of his late wife, on behalf of three of her children. The facts are set out in the judgment of Brooke LJ.

Patrick Lawrence (instructed by *Glazer Delmar*) for the claimant.
Francis Treasure (instructed by *Burrells*) for the defendant.

j

BROOKE LJ (giving the first judgment at the invitation of Lord Phillips of Worth Matravers MR).

[1] This is an appeal by the claimant Michael Cachia against an order of Judge Harris QC, sitting as a judge of the High Court, dated 31 October 2000 whereby he directed that his claim in this action be struck out. The judge said that the application by the defendant to have the claim struck out raised an unusual point,

on which there was no previous authority. He granted permission to appeal, *a* commenting that the point at issue was a matter of some importance. Although in the events that have occurred in this court the defendant eventually conceded that the appeal should be allowed, the issue is of some general importance. I am therefore delivering this judgment to explain why we are taking the course of allowing this appeal.

[2] Put shortly, the issue was this. Section 2(3) of the Fatal Accidents Act 1976 *b* provides: 'Not more than one action shall lie for and in respect of the same subject matter of complaint.' Did this mean that if a writ was issued in a 1976 Act claim brought on behalf of a deceased's dependants but never served, this automatically precluded the bringing of a new action some years later?

[3] The facts of the case are simple. On 6 October 1988 Mrs Cachia was riding *c* her bicycle in a road in South-East London when she was hit by a car driven by the defendant. She died 12 days later. Liability for the accident has never been admitted. The defendant claims that she caused the accident by veering in front of him. She left a husband and four children, who were aged 13, 11, 8 and 4 at the date of her death.

[4] On 16 October 1991, just before the three-year limitation period expired, a *d* firm of solicitors issued a writ in her husband's name claiming damages both on behalf of the estate and on behalf of her dependants under the 1976 Act. This writ was never served. There was evidence before the judge that this firm of solicitors represented the claimant up to the end of 1992, and after their last letter to the defendant's representatives on 10 December 1992 Mr Cachia had some direct *e* contact with them himself, although this contact came to nothing.

[5] On 18 April 1997 a new firm of solicitors appeared on the scene on behalf of the claimant. On 10 June 1997 they issued a new writ, which was served ten days later. By this time the Cachias' eldest daughter had reached the age of 21: the claims of the other three children were not statute-barred by any primary *f* limitation period. The statement of claim was served on 2 July 1997, and the defence on 11 July 1997. On 1 August 1997 the defendant's solicitors issued a summons, presumably in support of the pleas of limitation in paras 1 to 3 of the defence, which did not at that time include any reliance on s 2(3). The claimant's solicitors, however, asked them to take no action on this summons pending the resolution of a claim they were pursuing against their client's former solicitors. It *g* appears that liability was eventually conceded in relation to the claims made on behalf of the estate and the 1976 Act claims brought on behalf of the claimant and the couple's eldest daughter, but not in respect of the dependency claims of the three younger children.

[6] On 17 May 2000 the claimant's solicitors issued an application for a *h* declaration to the effect that the three younger children had the right to pursue their claim against the defendant despite the issue of the earlier writ. The defendant's solicitors riposted four months later with an application for an order that the claim be struck out, alternatively for such order limiting the defendant's exposure on liability and quantum as might be just. When Judge Harris heard the *j* matter in October 2000, he was concerned only with the question whether proceedings on the 1997 writ were barred pursuant to the effect of s 2(3) of the 1976 Act. He said he did not propose to go on to consider the alternative application to strike out for want of prosecution or delay, although it seemed to him not unlikely that there must be some strength in the defendant's argument that it would not be possible at this length of time to have a fair trial.

a   [7] I have set out the wording of s 2(3) at para [2], above. The language of this provision has remained the same since it was first enacted as s 3 of the Fatal Accidents Act 1846, except that at that time the section read:

> 'Provided always, and be it enacted, That *not more than One Action shall lie for and in respect of the same Subject Matter of Complaint*; and that every such Action shall be commenced within Twelve Calendar Months after the Death of such deceased Person.' (My emphasis.)

b

[8] By the time the fatal accidents legislation was consolidated in 1976, the limitation provision had been siphoned off into other legislation. Most recently, the Limitation Act 1975 had introduced a revised code making new provision for personal injuries litigation. This code adopted the phraseology 'an action ... shall

c   not be brought' when indicating that a primary limitation period had fully run.

[9] On this appeal, before the introduction of a point on the European Convention for the Protection of Human Rights and Fundamental Freedoms 1950 (as set out in Sch 1 to the Human Rights Act 1998), the defendant adopted the argument which found favour with the judge. The judge held that although

d   it was certainly one of the aims of those who framed the 1846 legislation to ensure that all the dependants joined in a single action, the language of the Act was clear. An action had been brought on behalf of these dependants in 1991 and was allowed to die. It was not permissible in these circumstances to bring another action now. In this context he accepted the concession by counsel for the claimant to the effect that the words 'shall lie' were the equivalent in modern

e   language of the words 'shall be brought' (see, for example, *Avery v London and North Eastern Rly Co* [1938] 2 All ER 592 at 595, [1938] AC 606 at 613 per Lord Atkin: 'One action alone can be brought, and the persons who stand out stand out for ever.'). He also referred to a dictum of Lord Simon of Glaisdale in *Herbert Berry Associates Ltd v IRC* [1978] 1 All ER 161 at 170, [1977] 1 WLR 1437 at 1446 to the

f   effect that: 'The primary sense of "action" as a term of legal art is the invocation of the jurisdiction of a court by writ ...'

[10] Mr Lawrence originally submitted that it was unlikely that Parliament intended that dependants should be without a remedy in circumstances such as have arisen in this case. He suggested three possible routes by which justice might be done.

g   [11] The first involved interpreting the word 'action' as meaning 'served process' in this context. He said that the fact that the word 'action' in other contexts might refer to unserved proceedings was nothing to the point: this statute must be construed by reference to its purpose.

[12] In my judgment, this route was not open to us. Although the House of

h   Lords has said that if the words of a consolidating statute are clear, one should not go backwards into the legislative history of the words used in it (*Farrell v Alexander* [1976] 2 All ER 721, [1977] AC 59), an action naturally begins when initiating process is issued and a court thereby acquires jurisdiction to make orders against the defendant, notwithstanding that he has not yet been served with process. If

j   there was any lack of clarity there, recourse to the 1846 Act would show that it was inconceivable that Parliament intended the word 'action' to have two different meanings in a single short section.

[13] Mr Lawrence's second route involved withdrawing the concession made in the court below about the meaning of the words 'not more than one action shall lie'. He now sought to argue, notwithstanding Lord Atkin's dictum, that they should mean that there was only one cause of action, which would merge in

any judgment given in any action, and which would be disposed of by any
settlement. He conceded that this construction did not wholly deal with all the
practical problems that might arise, since it was possible (see *Cooper v Williams*
[1963] 2 All ER 282, [1963] 2 QB 567) for one dependant to be prejudiced by the
settlement of (or entry of judgment in) an action brought by another. He suggested,
however, that this interpretation did provide a defendant with appropriate
protection, in that if a defendant settles a claim, or if a claim goes to judgment,
that defendant cannot be troubled by any further proceedings.

[14] In my judgment, this route was equally illegitimate. If Parliament had
wanted to give legislative effect to this concept it would have been easy for it to
have found the appropriate language to give effect to its wish. The fact of the
matter is that this provision had remained on the statute book for 130 years prior
to 1976 without giving rise to any particular difficulty, and it may be that it was
only the advent of extended limitation periods for minors, unaccompanied by
any similar extension of the period of validity of an unserved writ, that gave rise
to the problem that has surfaced in the present case. We must not turn ourselves
into legislators if the language used by Parliament simply does not permit it.

[15] Mr Lawrence's third route was slightly more promising. He suggested
that we might be willing to interpret the words of the subsection as meaning that
no action should be maintained. If it simply withered away because a protective
writ was not served and the defendant had never been troubled with it, it would
be a misuse of language to say it had ever been maintained (or had ever 'lain' in
any real sense of the word). I might have been tempted down that imaginative
route of statutory construction to right an obvious injustice to these children if a
more orthodox route was not now provided by the 1998 Act.

[16] Mr Lawrence raised a human rights point for the first time on the Friday
before we were due to hear the appeal the following Monday. When we first
heard the appeal we gave him permission to amend the notice of appeal to take
the point, since the court would in any event have been obliged to consider it
pursuant to our duty under s 6(1) of the 1998 Act. He opened the appeal on this
extended basis, and we heard Mr Treasure's reply on the non-convention points.
We then adjourned the hearing for two days to enable Mr Treasure to prepare his
response on the convention point. In the event, he conceded that it was a good
one, and that the appeal should be allowed on this basis.

[17] The point arises in this way. The convention gives these three children a
right of access to a court to claim compensation for their loss of dependency
following the death of their mother. Although the European Court of Human
Rights recognises that the enactment of limitation periods represents the pursuit
of a legitimate aim (see *Stubbings v UK* (1996) 23 EHRR 213 at 227 (paras 53–55)),
these claims were not statute-barred when this writ was issued in 1997.

[18] The European Court of Human Rights has also recognised the legitimacy
of other restrictions on the right of access to a court that have been drawn to its
attention from time to time. Cases involving vexatious litigants, persons under
disability, and the striking out of actions for want of prosecution are obvious
examples. A fuller list can be found in standard text-books on art 6(1): see, for
example, Clayton and Tomlinson *The Law of Human Rights* (2000) vol 1, pp 640–641,
para 11.191. The governing test, set out in the judgment of the European Court
of Human Rights in *Ashingdane v UK* (1985) 7 EHRR 528 at 546 (para 57), and
repeated often in later cases, is that such restrictions must not impair the essence
of the right of access; they must have a legitimate aim, and the means used must
be reasonably proportionate to the aim sought to be achieved.

a   [19] In my judgment, Mr Treasure was right not to seek to argue that the
fortuitous effect of s 2(3) of the 1976 Act in a case where a writ has never been
served and a new writ has been issued within the primary limitation period could
have any legitimate aim. It was just a procedural quirk, brought about by the
chance that Parliament had never considered this particular problem, and
because our traditional English methods of interpreting statutes could not right
b   an obvious injustice. He was also right to place no reliance on the words 'within
a reasonable time' in art 6(1) when Parliament permitted children an extended
period in which to exercise their right of access to a court. Mr Treasure was also
wise to accept, on reflection, that the right to rely on a procedural quirk as a bar
to these children's right of access to a court could not possibly amount to a
'possession' within the meaning of art 1 of the First Protocol of the convention.
c   [20] Since 2 October 2000 we have been under a duty not to act in a way which
is incompatible with a convention right (s 6(1) of the 1998 Act), and so far as it is
possible to do so, primary legislation must be read and given effect in a way which
is compatible with the convention rights (s 3(1)). It is certainly possible to
interpret the word 'action' as meaning 'served process' in order to give effect to
d   the convention rights of these three children. Until the present writ was served
in July 1997, no process had been served which asserted a claim to compensation
by these children for their mother's death. Section 2(3) of the 1976 Act therefore
presents no artificial bar to this claim.
    [21] This is a very good example of the way in which the enactment of the
1998 Act now enables English judges to do justice in a way which was not
e   previously open to us.
    [22] The appeal must therefore be allowed, and the matter remitted to the
High Court so that a judge can consider the other issues arising on the
defendant's application.

f   **HENRY LJ.**
    [23] I agree.

LORD PHILLIPS OF WORTH MATRAVERS MR.
    [24] I also agree.

Appeal allowed.

                                        Gillian Crew   Barrister.

National Westminster Bank plc v Somer International (UK) Ltd

[2001] EWCA Civ 970

COURT OF APPEAL, CIVIL DIVISION

PETER GIBSON, POTTER AND CLARKE LJJ

9 APRIL, 22 JUNE 2001

Estoppel – Representation – Mistake – Payment of money – Bank making payment to customer by mistake and representing that money was customer's – Customer suffering financial detriment as a result but in a sum much smaller than amount of overpayment – Whether estoppel by representation providing complete defence to claim for recovery of money paid by mistake.

The defendant company, which exported computer equipment, was a customer of the claimant bank. From time to time, the company received payments in dollars from foreign purchasers by sums paid to the credit of a dollar account maintained at the bank. In April 1997 the company informed the bank that it expected receipt of a payment of between $US 70,000 and 78,000 from a customer, M. Later that month, as a result of an error within the bank, a sum of $US 76,708·57 received by the bank, and intended for the account of another of its customers with a name similar to that of the company, was credited to the company's dollar account. The bank then notified the company that the expected dollar payment had been received into its dollar account. In the belief that, by such payment, M had reduced the balance of its trading account with the company, the latter despatched to M two shipments of goods to a total value of £13,180·57. In February 1998 the bank notified the company that the dollar payment made in April 1997 had been made in error and requested repayment. By then, M had ceased to trade from its former premises and had effectively disappeared as a trading entity. The bank subsequently brought proceedings to recover the dollar payment from the company. At trial, the company relied on the defence of estoppel by representation in respect of the entirety of the sum transferred. The judge found that the money had been paid by mistake; that, at the same time, the bank had made a representation that the money was due to the company and that it could treat the money as its own; and that the company had acted on that representation to its detriment by shipping the goods to M. He nevertheless held that the company was entitled to rely on the estoppel to which those facts gave rise only to the extent of the detrimental reliance, and rejected the company's contention that it had lost the opportunity to recover other moneys from M. The judge therefore ordered the company to repay the amount of the dollar payment less the value of the goods that had been despatched to M. The company appealed, contending that, on the facts found by the judge, he should have held that the bank was estopped from claiming repayment of any part of the payment made, because estoppel by representation could not operate pro tanto, but rather normally served to provide a complete defence to a claim for money had and received since it was a rule of evidence that precluded the representor from averring facts contrary to the representation.

a **Held** – Although estoppel by representation was a rule of evidence which, ordinarily, provided that a more than de minimis degree of detriment was definitive of the transferee's right to retain the entirety of a mistaken payment, there remained scope for the operation of equity to alleviate the position on grounds of unfairness or unconscionability. Indeed, the doctrine of estoppel by representation stemmed from and was governed by considerations of justice and *b* equity. That being so, it was difficult to see why equity should, as between the parties, be powerless in an appropriate case or category of case to require a person relying upon the defence of estoppel by representation to rely upon it only to the extent of any detriment suffered. In the instant case, the judge had been fully entitled to hold that the payment sought by the bank was of such a size that it bore no relation to the detriment which the company could possibly have *c* suffered, and that it would be unconscionable for the company to retain the balance over and above the value of the goods shipped. Accordingly, the appeal would be dismissed (see [40], [43], [48]–[50], [59], [60], [62], [67]–[69], below).

Scottish Equitable plc v Derby [2001] 3 All ER 818 followed.

Avon CC v Howlett [1983] 1 All ER 1073 considered.

d
Notes

For estoppel as a defence to a restitutionary claim, see 9(1) *Halsbury's Laws* (4th edn reissue) para 1167.

Cases referred to in judgments
e *Allied Maples Group Ltd v Simmons & Simmons (a firm)* [1995] 4 All ER 907, [1995] 1 WLR 1602, CA.
Amalgamated Investment and Property Co Ltd (in liq) v Texas Commerce International Bank Ltd [1981] 3 All ER 577, [1982] QB 84, [1981] 3 WLR 565, CA.
Avon CC v Howlett [1983] 1 All ER 1073, [1983] 1 WLR 605, CA.
f *Canada and Dominion Sugar Co Ltd v Canadian National (West Indies) Steamships Ltd* [1947] AC 46, PC.
Crabb v Arun DC [1975] 3 All ER 865, [1976] Ch 179, [1975] 3 WLR 847, CA.
David Securities Pty Ltd v Commonwealth Bank of Australia (1992) 175 CLR 353, Aust HC.
Empire Life Insurance Co v Neufeld Estate (24 April 1998, unreported), BC Sup Ct.
Evans v Bartlam [1937] 2 All ER 646, [1937] AC 473, HL.
g *First National Bank plc v Thompson* [1996] 1 All ER 140, [1996] Ch 231, [1996] 2 WLR 293, CA.
Greenwood v Martins Bank Ltd [1932] 1 KB 371; *affd* [1933] AC 51, [1932] All ER Rep 318, HL.
Grundt v Great Boulder Pty Gold Mines Ltd (1937) 59 CLR 641, Aust HC.
h *Holt v Markham* [1923] 1 KB 504, [1922] All ER Rep 134, CA.
Indian Endurance (No 2), The, Republic of India v India Steamship Co Ltd [1997] 4 All ER 380, [1998] AC 878, [1997] 3 WLR 818, HL.
Johnson v Gore Wood & Co (a firm) [2001] 1 All ER 481, [2001] 2 WLR 72, HL.
Jones (R E) Ltd v Waring & Gillow Ltd [1926] AC 670, [1926] All ER Rep 36, HL.
j *Jorden v Money* (1854) 5 HL Cas 185, [1843–60] All ER Rep 350, 10 ER 868.
Kleinwort Benson Ltd v Lincoln City Council [1998] 4 All ER 513, [1999] 2 AC 349, [1998] 3 WLR 1095, HL.
Kleinwort Benson Ltd v South Tyneside Metropolitan BC [1994] 4 All ER 972.
Lipkin Gorman (a firm) v Karpnale Ltd [1992] 4 All ER 512, [1991] 2 AC 548, [1991] 3 WLR 10, HL.
Lloyds Bank Ltd v Brooks (1950) 6 Legal Decisions Affecting Bankers 161.

London Joint Stock Bank Ltd v Macmillan [1918] AC 777, [1918–19] All ER Rep 30, HL.

Low v Bouverie [1891] 3 Ch 82, [1891–4] All ER Rep 348, CA.

Moorgate Mercantile Co Ltd v Twitchings [1975] 3 All ER 314, [1976] QB 225, [1975] 3 WLR 286, CA; *rvsd* [1976] 2 All ER 641, [1977] AC 890, [1976] 3 WLR 66, HL.

Moses v Macferlan (1760) 2 Burr 1005, [1558–1774] All ER Rep 581, 97 ER 676.

Nippon Menkwa Kabushiki Kaisha (Japan Cotton Trading Co Ltd) v Dawsons Bank Ltd (1935) 51 Ll L Rep 147, PC.

Ogilvie v West Australian Mortgage and Agency Corp Ltd [1896] AC 257, PC.

Philip Collins Ltd v Davis [2000] 3 All ER 808.

RBC Dominion Securities Inc v Dawson (1994) 111 DLR (4th) 230, Nfld CA.

Scottish Equitable plc v Derby [2000] 3 All ER 793; *affd* [2001] EWCA Civ 369, [2001] 3 All ER 818.

Skyring v Greenwood (1825) 4 B & C 281, [1824–34] All ER Rep 104, 107 ER 1064, KBD.

South Tyneside Metropolitan BC v Svenska International plc [1995] 1 All ER 545.

Case also cited or referred to in skeleton arguments

Young v Bristol Aeroplane Co Ltd [1944] 2 All ER 293, [1944] KB 718, CA; *affd* [1946] 1 All ER 98, [1946] AC 163, HL.

Appeal

The defendant, Somer International (UK) Ltd (Somer), appealed with permission of Judge Neligan from his decision at Bristol County Court on 18 February 2000 requiring it to repay to the claimant, National Westminster Bank plc (NatWest), the sum of £38,688·02 including interest mistakenly paid to it by NatWest. The facts are set out in the judgment of Potter LJ.

John Virgo (instructed by *Thatcher & Hallam*, Midsomer Norton) for Somer.

Dominic Chambers (instructed by *William Enderby*) for NatWest.

Cur adv vult

22 June 2001. The following judgments were delivered.

POTTER LJ (giving the first judgment at the invitation of Peter Gibson LJ).

INTRODUCTION

[1] This is an appeal by the defendants Somer International (UK) Ltd (Somer) from the judgment dated 18 February 2000 of Judge Neligan in the Bristol County Court whereby he ordered Somer to repay to the claimant National Westminster Bank plc (NatWest) the sum of £38,688·02 inclusive of interest previously transferred by mistake by NatWest into the account of Somer. The amount ordered to be repaid was the amount of the original transfer made in error, namely $US 76,708·57 less $US 21,616·14, that latter sum being the value of goods despatched by Somer to one of its customers on the basis of the transfer before the error was discovered. The judge held that, despite the plea of estoppel by representation raised by Somer in respect of the entirety of the sum transferred, Somer was entitled to rely upon such representation only to the extent that it acted to its detriment in reliance upon it.

[2] In deciding as he did, the judge followed the decision of Harrison J in *Scottish Equitable plc v Derby* [2000] 3 All ER 793, since affirmed by this court on 16 March 2001 ([2001] EWCA Civ 369, [2001] 3 All ER 818). On this appeal, Somer

a has argued that the judge was wrong to follow the *Scottish Equitable* decision, being bound to follow the previous decision of this court in *Avon CC v Howlett* [1983] 1 All ER 1073, [1983] 1 WLR 605, in which it was stated that estoppel cannot operate pro tanto. NatWest, on the other hand, seek to uphold the decision of the judge. They further argue that this court should if necessary depart from the principle stated in the *Avon CC* case, applying instead the more limited defence b of 'change of position' recognised by the House of Lords in *Lipkin Gorman (a firm) v Karpnale Ltd* [1992] 4 All ER 512, [1991] 2 AC 548, by which the defence of 'change of position' was held to be a defence to a restitutionary claim for repayment of money paid under a mistake of fact to the extent that it would be an injustice if the payee were called upon to repay or to repay in full (see [1992] 4 All ER 512 at 533–534, [1991] 2 AC 548 at 579–580 per Lord Goff of Chieveley).

c   [3] NatWest also appeal by way of respondent's notice, as to which see further at [33] below.

THE FACTS

      [4] Somer, which carried on business exporting computer equipment, was at d all material times the customer of NatWest and from time to time received payment in dollars from foreign purchasers by sums paid to the credit of a dollar account maintained at NatWest. In summer 1996, Somer began trading with an African based company called Mentor, supplying computer equipment to Mentor for on-sale to African end users. Dealing in round figures, by 1997 Mentor owed Somer £166,000 in relation to such supplies. In April 1997 Mentor remitted £100,000 e to Somer and indicated shortly afterwards that a further payment of between $US 70,000 and $US 78,000 would be forwarded shortly. Somer were in touch with NatWest about the prospective receipt of such payment.

      [5] On 28 April 1997, as a result of an error within NatWest a sum of $US 76,708·57 received by NatWest from a company called Moffett Engineering Ltd and intended f for the account of another NatWest client called Somer Sundstrand Ltd, was credited to Somer's dollar account. On or about the same date NatWest notified Somer that the further dollar moneys which they were expecting had been received into that account. In the belief that, by such payment, Mentor had reduced the balance of its trading account with Somer, on 30 April 1997 Somer despatched goods to Mentor to the value of £5,221·99, and on 30 May 1997, in the g same belief, made a further shipment of goods to the value of £7,958·58.

      [6] On 24 February 1998, the bank notified Somer that the dollar payment made on 28 April 1997 had been made in error and requested repayment. By this date, Mentor had ceased to trade from its former premises in Africa and had effectively disappeared as a trading entity. The bank thereafter brought proceedings h to recover the dollar payment of $US 76,708·57.

THE DECISION BELOW

      [7] The case for Somer depended upon the evidence of Mr Richardson, its managing director with overall responsibility for finance and accounts. In his j witness statement he said that towards the end of April 1997 he made inquiry of a lady who rang him from the bank's international business department to advise him on another matter, whether the expected sum of $US 70,000–78,000 had yet arrived from Mentor in a dollar account. He was told it had not. However, a few days later he received another telephone call from another female employee in which he was told that the payment he had been expecting had been received and that the sum of $US 76,708·57 had arrived and been credited to the account. He

said it was possible that he was told that the funds had arrived from Moffett
Engineering, but this would have meant nothing to him as such payments were a
often received from customers of Somer's African clients by way of payment on
their behalf. He said that, after receiving notification from NatWest he had
informed Mentor over the telephone that Somer had received the expected
moneys, to which he received the reply 'Have you? OK'. He stated that he had
no suspicion that the credit of the dollar payment to Somer was other than b
money which Somer was owed by Mentor. Mr Richardson's evidence was fully
tested in cross-examination and, in particular, the bank relied upon a credit advice
of payments received by Somer from the bank within a week after the payment
had been made which made clear that the sum had been received from Moffett
Engineering and was intended for 'Somer Sundstrand Ltd' not 'Somer c
International Ltd', which NatWest contended put Somer on notice of the error.

[8] The judge made no finding in terms upon the nature or content of any
representation made by the bank. However, he found that Mr Richardson was
an honest and reliable witness and accepted his evidence that he honestly
believed that the dollar payment came from Mentor and was money to which d
Somer was lawfully entitled. His findings can only sensibly be taken as reflecting
and amounting to an acceptance of Mr Richardson's evidence that he was told by
the bank on or about 28 April 1997 that the expected dollar payment from Mentor
had now been received and was standing to the credit of Somer's dollar account
at NatWest. e

[9] The judge went on to find that:

'... in the belief that the dollar payment had been paid by Mentor, which
thereby reduced its debt to Somer, Somer released goods on 30 April to the
value of £5,221·99 and on 30 May 1997 to the value of £7,958·58 ... making a
total of £13,180·57 and thereby changed its position because of the mistaken f
credit of the dollar payment to its account on 28 April.'

Thus, the judge found that the reason and cause of the detriment to Somer was
the representation of the bank that the expected dollar payment from Mentor had
now arrived. g

[10] The judge went on to state that he was not prepared to find, as Somer had
argued, that Somer lost the value of an opportunity thereafter to recover other
moneys owed by Somer. He said:

'In the first case I am not satisfied that the causal link exists between receipt h
of the dollar payment and the [loss of the] chance to pursue Mentor
successfully for payment of all or a substantial part of Mentor's liability to
Somer. Secondly, the evaluation of that chance is nil in my judgment which
again gives rise to a totally different situation than that which arose in *Allied
Maples Group Ltd v Simmons & Simmons (a firm)* [1995] 4 All ER 907, [1995] j
1 WLR 1602. The result therefore of my findings and conclusions is that
having found that Somer had changed its position in reliance upon the dollar
payment to the extent £13,180·57 there will consequently be a set-off of that
sum or the dollar equivalent against the dollar payment of $US76,708·57 in
accordance with the principles adopted by Harrison J in *Scottish Equitable plc v
Derby* [2000] 3 All ER 793.'

THE LAW

a [11] In the *Lipkin Gorman* case, the House of Lords in 1991 recognised 'change of position' as a general defence to all restitutionary claims: see the review of the authorities and the conclusion of Lord Goff ([1992] 4 All ER 512 at 532–534, [1991] 2 AC 548 at 577–581). Lord Goff stated:

b 'Historically, despite broad statements of Lord Mansfield CJ to the effect that an action for money had and received will only lie where it is inequitable for the defendant to retain the money (see in particular *Moses v Macferlan* (1760) 2 Burr 1005, [1558–1774] All ER Rep 581), the defence has received at most only partial recognition in English law … Instead, where change of position has been relied upon by the defendant, it has been usual to approach *c* the problem as one of estoppel: see e g *R E Jones Ltd v Waring & Gillow Ltd* [1926] AC 670, [1926] All ER Rep 36 and *Avon CC v Howlett* [1983] 1 All ER 1073, [1983] 1 WLR 605. But it is difficult to see the justification for such a rationalisation. First, estoppel normally depends upon the existence of a representation by one party, in reliance upon which the representee has so *d* changed his position that it is inequitable for the representor to go back upon his representation. But, in cases of restitution, the requirement of a representation appears to be unnecessary. It is true that, in cases where the plaintiff has paid money directly to the defendant, it has been argued (though with difficulty) that the plaintiff has represented to the defendant that he is entitled to money; but in a case such as the present, in which the money is *e* paid to an innocent donee by a thief, the true owner has made no representation whatever to the defendant. Again, it was held by the Court of Appeal in *Avon CC v Howlett* that estoppel cannot operate pro tanto, with the effect that if, for example, the defendant has innocently changed his position by disposing of part of the money, a defence of estoppel would *f* provide him with a defence to the whole of the claim. Considerations such as these provide a strong indication that, in many cases, estoppel is not an appropriate concept to deal with the problem … It is not however appropriate in the present case to attempt to identify all those actions in restitution to which change of position may be a defence. A prominent example will, no doubt, be found in those cases where the plaintiff is seeking repayment of *g* money paid under a mistake of fact; but I can see no reason why the defence should not also be available in principle in a case such as the present, where the plaintiff's money has been paid by a thief to an innocent donee, and the plaintiff then seeks repayment from the donee in an action for money had and received. At present I do not wish to state the principle any less broadly *h* than this: that the defence is available to a person whose position has so changed that it would be inequitable in all the circumstances to require him to make restitution, or alternatively to make restitution in full. I wish to stress, however, that the mere fact that the defendant has spent the money, in whole or in part, does not of itself render it inequitable that he should be *j* called upon to repay, because the expenditure might in any event have been incurred by him in the ordinary course of things. I fear that the mistaken assumption that mere expenditure of money may be regarded as amounting to a change of position for present purposes has led in the past to opposition by some to recognition of a defence which in fact is likely to be available only on comparatively rare occasions.' (See [1992] 4 All ER 512 at 532–533, 534, [1991] 2 AC 548 at 578, 579, 580.)

[12] Prior to the *Lipkin Gorman* case, as pointed out by Lord Goff, in order to establish a defence of change of position in respect of money paid under a mistake a of fact, it was necessary for the defendant to spell an estoppel out of the circumstances surrounding the mistake of fact on the basis of which the plaintiff asserted his right to recover in a claim for money had and received. That was not always easy and, in the case of a bank making a mistaken transfer or credit entry in the account of a customer, a degree of inventiveness might sometimes prove b necessary. However, it is plain that, in the passage from his speech quoted above, Lord Goff did not attack the reasoning of the Court of Appeal in the *Avon CC* case.

[13] In *Avon CC v Howlett* [1983] 1 All ER 1073, [1983] 1 WLR 605, the terms of the defendant's contract of employment with the plaintiffs and the manner in which the plaintiffs controlled the assessment of the defendant's pay rendered the plaintiffs under a duty to determine his entitlement and not to misrepresent it. c Thus, the court held that in making over payments in error to him from time to time, the plaintiffs represented to the defendant that the sums paid were indeed his entitlement. The defendant pleaded that, in reliance upon the plaintiffs' representation, he incurred expenditure which he would not otherwise have incurred had he appreciated that his income was lower than that represented by d the sums paid to him. The trial judge held that the defendant could retain any of those sums he had spent in reliance on the plaintiffs' representations. Slade LJ stated as follows in relation to the defence of estoppel:

'The following general propositions of law are to be found set out in Goff and Jones's *Law of Restitution* (2nd edn, 1978) pp 554–555 (though I do not e quote them verbatim). A plaintiff will be estopped from asserting his claim to restitution if the following conditions are satisfied: (a) the plaintiff must generally have made a representation of fact which led the defendant to believe that he was entitled to treat the money as his own; (b) the defendant must have, bona fide and without notice of the plaintiff's claim, consequently f changed his position; (c) the payment must not have been primarily caused by the fault of the defendant. In my opinion these propositions are entirely consistent both with the general principles which govern the doctrine of estoppel and with the authorities which have been cited to this court, illustrating the relevance of estoppel as a defence to claims to restitution. Examples of the more important of such authorities are *Skyring v Greenwood* g (1825) 4 B & C 281, [1824–34] All ER Rep 104, *Holt v Markham* [1923] 1 KB 504, [1922] All ER Rep 134 and *Lloyds Bank Ltd v Brooks* (1950) 6 Legal Decisions Affecting Bankers 161.' (See [1983] 1 All ER 1073 at 1085, [1983] 1 WLR 605 at 620.)

[14] Later, he said: h

'The judge considered that the defence of estoppel was in fact capable of being applied pro tanto, in the sense that a payer who has overpaid a payee, even in circumstances where all of conditions (a), (b) and (c) above are satisfied, will be precluded from claiming restitution only to the extent that j it would be inequitable to require the payee to repay the relevant sums or part of the relevant sums in question. The judge clearly regarded the doctrine of estoppel as being a flexible doctrine, as indeed Lord Denning MR so described it in *Amalgamated Investment and Property Co Ltd (in liq) v Texas Commerce International Bank Ltd* [1981] 3 All ER 577 at 584, [1982] QB 84 at 122. If I may respectfully say so, I feel some sympathy with the judge's point

a
of view. I also initially found unattractive the submission, placed before and rejected by him, that, if the defendant be treated as having spent in reliance on the plaintiffs' representations some £546·61 of the £1,007 received, the plaintiffs could not recover the balance of £460·39 even if it were still sitting untouched in some deposit account. At first sight such a conclusion would seem to leave the defendant unjustly enriched.' (See [1983] 1 All ER 1073 at

b
1086, [1983] 1 WLR 605 at 621.)

[15] None the less, Slade LJ went on to state that the conclusion of the judge involved the proposition that, if the defendant was successfully to resist a claim for repayment of a particular sum, the onus fell on him to prove specifically that the pecuniary amount of the prejudice suffered by him as a result of relying

c
on the plaintiffs' representation equalled or exceeded that sum and pointed out the difficulties of doing so in a situation where the defendant, as in the instant case, had relied on a representation by ordering his general mode of living or undertaking commitments which it would be difficult for him subsequently to recall and identify in detail. He stated:

d
'... though extreme hypothetical cases can be envisaged, and indeed were canvassed in argument, in which broad considerations of equity and justice might appear to require the barring of a plaintiff's claim only pro tanto, if this were legally possible, I would not expect many such cases to arise in practice. In any event I do not consider the present case to be one of them, even on

e
the basis of the facts as pleaded. I prefer to approach it simply by what I regard as the established legal principles governing the doctrine of estoppel.' (See [1983] 1 All ER 1073 at 1086–1087, [1983] 1 WLR 605 at 622.)

[16] He pointed out that estoppel by representation is a rule of evidence, the consequence of which is simply to preclude the representor from averring facts contrary to his own representation. That being so, a party entitled to rely on an

f
estoppel might in some cases recover more than the actual damage suffered by him as a result of the representation which gave rise to it. He went on to refer to a number of authorities which demonstrated that in cases where estoppel by representation was available as a defence to money had and received the courts do not treat the operation of the estoppel as being restricted to the precise

g
amount of the detriment which the representee proves he has suffered in reliance on the representation. He stated:

'If it were in every case possible for the doctrine of estoppel by representation to operate merely pro tanto in cases where it is being involved as a defence to an action for money had and received, I think that the Court of King's

h
Bench in *Skyring v Greenwood*, and the Court of Appeal in *Holt v Markham*, and indeed Lynskey J in *Lloyds Bank Ltd v Brooks*, would have been bound to conduct a much more exact process of quantification of the alteration of the financial position of the recipients, which had occurred by reason of the representations. The courts, however, in those cases, manifestly regarded

j
any such process as irrelevant and inappropriate. All the relevant conditions for the operation of an estoppel being satisfied in those cases, the plea operated as a rule of evidence which precluded the payers from recovering any part of the money mistakenly overpaid or from retaining any part of the moneys mistakenly overcredited. I think that no authority has been cited, other than the judgment of the judge, which directly supports the proposition that estoppel is capable of operating merely pro tanto in a case

such as the present, where it is otherwise capable of being invoked as a
complete defence to an action for money had and received. For the reasons
which I have given, I conclude that such a proposition is contrary to principle
and authority.' (See [1983] 1 All ER 1073 at 1088, [1983] 1 WLR 605 at 624.)

[17] None the less, Slade LJ went on to observe:

'I recognise that in some circumstances the doctrine of estoppel could be
said to give rise to injustice if it operated so as to defeat in its entirety an
action which would otherwise lie for money had and received. This might
be the case for example where the sums sought to be recovered were so large
as to bear no relation to any detriment which the recipient could possibly
have suffered. I would for my part prefer to leave open the question whether
in such a case the court would have jurisdiction, in the exercise of its
discretion, to exact an undertaking of the nature referred to by Viscount
Cave LC, if it was not voluntarily proffered by the defendant.' (See [1983]
1 All ER 1073 at 1089, [1983] 1 WLR 605 at 624–625.)

[18] The undertaking referred to was a reference to the observations of
Viscount Cave LC in *R E Jones Ltd v Waring & Gillow Ltd* [1926] AC 670 at 685,
[1926] All ER Rep 36 at 42 in which, in the course of his dissent (with which Lord
Atkinson agreed), he would have required the recital in the order made on the
appeal of an undertaking by the defendants in that case which reflected their offer
to repay to the plaintiffs any part of the sum received which they ought not to be
entitled to keep on the basis that it would have represented a profit to them.

[19] For his part, Cumming-Bruce LJ in the *Avon CC* case expressed the view
that—

'it is not easy to determine whether and when the court will restrict the
effect of an estoppel if to apply it with the full rigour will clearly produce
injustice. Viscount Cave LC in *R E Jones Ltd v Waring & Gillow Ltd* ... evidently
thought that the court should find a way of preventing a party so using
estoppel as to make a profit, but Lord Denning MR thought that estoppel
was a flexible doctrine: see *Amalgamated Investment and Property Co Ltd (in liq) v
Texas Commerce International Bank Ltd* ... I do not consider that the decision
of this court in the instant appeal is authority for the proposition that, where
on the facts it would be clearly inequitable to allow a party to make a profit
by pleading estoppel, the court will necessarily be powerless to prevent it.'
(See [1983] 1 All ER 1073 at 1075–1076, [1983] 1 WLR 605 at 608.)

[20] Finally, Eveleigh LJ said:

'However, I am far from saying that, whenever the recipient of money paid
under a mistake has been led to think that it is his, then he will be entitled to
retain the whole by demonstrating that he has spent part of it. The payment
may involve no representation, as where a debtor presents an account to the
creditor. Then while there might have been a representation there may be
circumstances which would render it unconscionable for the defendant to
retain a balance in his hands. There may also be circumstances which would
make it unfair to allow the plaintiff to recover.' (See [1983] 1 All ER 1073 at
1078, [1983] 1 WLR 605 at 611–612.)

[21] In *Scottish Equitable plc v Derby*, the claimant insurance company had
overstated the amount of a pension fund available to the defendant, as a result of

a which he received a substantial overpayment, the company having overlooked the fact that he had previously exercised an option to take an early retirement benefit. The result of the benefits accruing to the defendant were, in broad terms, that he received an overpayment of some £172,500, while incurring expenditure of some £9,600 in making modest improvements to his lifestyle in reliance on the overstatement received. At first instance, Harrison J ([2000] 3 All ER 793 at 805),

b in referring to the *Avon CC* case, cited the reservations contained in the individual judgments which we have quoted and said as follows:

'On the face of it, therefore, *Avon CC v Howlett* provides strong support for the defendant's submission that, some detriment having been shown, estoppel should operate as a complete defence. However, it is important to

c bear in mind two matters. Firstly, the reservations expressed by the Court of Appeal as to the ambit of the decision in that case, and, secondly, the fact that that case was decided before the House of Lords recognised the defence of change of position in the *Lipkin Gorman* case (*Lipkin Gorman (a firm) v Karpnale Ltd* [1992] 4 All ER 512, [1991] 2 AC 548).'

d [**22**] He went on to say (at 806):

'In my judgment, it would be unconscionable, or clearly inequitable, to allow the defendant to keep the whole of the overpayment of £172,451 when his detriment is limited to £9,662 of that amount. In those circumstances, and having regard to the dicta of the Court of Appeal, which I have just

e quoted, I do not consider that I am bound by *Avon CC v Howlett* to hold, in the circumstances of this case, that estoppel must operate as a complete defence. Secondly, there is the fact, as I have mentioned, that the case was decided before the House of Lords recognised the defence of change of position in the *Lipkin Gorman* case. In the latter case Lord Goff remarked that previously these kind of cases have been dealt with on the basis of estoppel.'

f [**23**] Before turning to the decision on appeal in the *Scottish Equitable* case, I pause to make reference to the decision of Jonathan Parker J in *Philip Collins Ltd v Davis* [2000] 3 All ER 808, in which he was concerned with a change of position defence in a situation where he did not regard the making of the payments sought to be repaid as amounting to a representation for the purposes of estoppel by

g representation. In so holding, he made the following observation (at 826):

'In any event, as I read the relevant authorities, the law has now developed to the point where a defence of estoppel by representation is no longer apt in restitutionary claims where the most flexible defence of change of position is

h in principle available (see the *Lipkin Gorman* case [1992] 4 All ER 512 at 534, [1991] 2 AC 548 at 580, Goff and Jones *The Law of Restitution* (5th edn, 1998) pp 828-829, *Scottish Equitable plc v Derby* [2000] 3 All ER 793 and *Avon CC v Howlett* [1983] 1 All ER 1073, [1983] 1 WLR 605).'

[**24**] He then went on to find that the ingredients of the defence of change of

j position had been established in respect of half the overpayment claimed.

[**25**] In his leading judgment in the Court of Appeal, affirming the decision of Harrison J in the *Scottish Equitable* case, Robert Walker LJ asked three questions, the second and third of which were how far the defence of change of position assisted the payee in the circumstances of the case and what part (if any) had estoppel to play now that the defence of change of position has been recognised. So far as change of position was concerned, he referred to the view of Andrew

Burrows *The Law of Restitution* (1993) pp 425–428, that there is a narrow and a wide version of the defence. Robert Walker LJ stated ([2001] 3 All ER 818 at [30]): *a*

'The narrow view treats the defence as "the same as estoppel minus the representation" (so that detrimental reliance is still a necessary ingredient). The wide view looks to a change of position, causally linked to the mistaken receipt, which makes it inequitable for the recipient to be required to make *b* restitution. In many cases either test produces the same result, but the wide view extends protection to (for instance) an innocent recipient of a payment which is later stolen from him (see *Goff and Jones* p 822, also favouring the wide view).'

He went on ([2001] 3 All ER 818 at [31]): *c*

'In this court Mr Stephen Moriarty QC ... for Scottish Equitable ... did not argue against the correctness of the wide view, provided that the need for a sufficient causal link is clearly recognised. The fact that the recipient may have suffered some misfortune (such as a breakdown in his health, or the loss of his job) is not a defence unless the misfortune is causally linked (at least on *d* a "but for" test) with a mistaken receipt. In my view Mr Moriarty was right to make that concession. Taking a wide view of the scope of the defence facilitates "a more generous approach ... to the recognition of the right to restitution" (Lord Goff in the *Lipkin Gorman* case [1992] 4 All ER 512 at 534, [1991] 2 AC 848 at 581; and compare Lord Goff's observations in *Kleinwort* *e* *Benson Ltd v Lincoln City Council* [1998] 4 All ER 513 at 541, [1999] 2 AC 349 at 385).'

[26] Having referred to the particular submissions of counsel as to the nature of the decisions which the payee may make and put into effect in reliance on the mistaken overpayment and the degree to which such decisions may properly be *f* regarded as involving a change of position for the purposes of the defence, Robert Walker LJ observed ([2001] 3 All ER 818 at [33]):

'I would readily accept that the defence is not limited (as it is, apparently, in Canada and some states of the United States: see *David Securities Pty Ltd v Commonwealth Bank of Australia* (1992) 175 CLR 353 at 385, noted in *Goff and* *g* *Jones* p 819) to specific identifiable items of expenditure. I would also accept that it may be right for the court not to apply too demanding a standard of proof when an honest defendant says that he has spent an overpayment by improving his lifestyle, but cannot produce any detailed accounting: see the observations of Jonathan Parker J in *Philip Collins Ltd v Davis* [2000] 3 All ER *h* 808 at 827, with which I respectfully agree.'

He added, however ([2001] 3 All ER 818 at [34], [35]):

'But the court must proceed on the basis of principle, not sympathy, in *j* order that the defence of change of position should not (as *Burrows* puts it at p 426) "disintegrate into a case by case discretionary analysis of the justice of individual facts, far removed from principle" ... In general it is not a detriment to pay off a debt which will have to be paid off sooner or later: *RBC Dominion Securities Inc v Dawson* (1994) 111 DLR (4th) 230. It might be if there were a long-term loan on advantageous terms, but it was not suggested that that was the case here ...'

a [27] So far as estoppel was concerned Robert Walker LJ referred to Lord Goff's observation in *Lipkin Gorman (a firm) v Karpnale Ltd* [1992] 4 All ER 512, [1991] 2 AC 548 quoted above to the effect that estoppel is not an appropriate concept to deal with mistakes of this kind, partly because of its 'all or nothing' operation. He observed that the same view has been widely expressed both by academic writers and in the courts. However, on the basis of the finding of Harrison J that

b the claimant had made a representation to the defendant that he really was entitled to the payment he had received, Robert Walker LJ proceeded to consider the decision in *Avon CC v Howlett* [1983] 1 All ER 1073, [1983] 1 WLR 605 in detail. Having referred to various of the passages which I have already quoted, he said in relation to the facts of the case before him ([2001] 3 All ER 818 at [44]):

c   'I would be content to follow the judge in refraining from attempting any general statement of principle and treating this case as comfortably within the exception recognised by all three members of this court in *Avon CC*. We cannot overrule that case but we can note that it was not seen, even by the court which decided it, as a wholly satisfactory authority, because of its fictional element.'

d [28] He then proceeded to record a novel argument addressed to the court by counsel for the claimant that, since the *Lipkin Gorman* case, the defence of change of position pre-empts and disables the defence of estoppel by negating detriment in the following sense. As stated by Dixon J in *Grundt v Great Boulder Pty Gold Mines Ltd* (1937) 59 CLR 641 at 674:

e

f   '... the basal purpose of the doctrine [of estoppel in pais] ... is to avoid or prevent a detriment to the party asserting the estoppel by compelling the opposite party to adhere to the assumption upon which the former acted or abstained from acting ... the real detriment or harm from which the law seeks to give protection is that which would flow from the change of position if the assumption were deserted that led to it. So long as the assumption is adhered to, the party who altered his situation upon the faith of it cannot complain. His complaint is that when afterwards the other party makes a different state of affairs the basis of an assertion of right against him then, if it allowed, his own original change of position will operate as a detriment.'

g [29] That being so, in a situation where A mistakenly transfers to B, or recognises his entitlement to a sum of money and B spends or loses some of it in a bad investment, but places the balance in the bank, if A then sues B but limits his claim to that balance, no detriment is demonstrable by B. Robert Walker LJ stated that he found this argument, which appeared not to have been considered by

h commentators interested in this area of law, to be not only ingenious but convincing. However, he placed his decision upon the basis that recovery was in this case consistent with the decision in the *Avon CC* case. He concluded his judgment by predicting 'with some confidence' that with the emergence of the defence of change of position the court would no longer feel constrained to find

j that a representation has been made, in a borderline case, in order to avoid an unjust result, as appeared historically to be the position. He also predicted that the development of the law on a case by case basis would have the effect of enlarging rather than narrowing the exception recognised in the *Avon CC* case. Finally, he observed ([2001] 3 All ER 818 at [48]):

      'That process might be hastened (or simply overtaken) if the House of Lords were to move away from the evidential origin of estoppel by representation

towards a more unified doctrine of estoppel, since proprietary estoppel is a
highly flexible doctrine which, so far from operating as "all or nothing", aims   *a*
at "the minimum equity to do justice" (*Crabb v Arun DC* [1975] 3 All ER 865
at 880, [1976] Ch 179 at 198).'

[30] It seems to me that the facts of this case are such that, assuming the judge
was correct in holding that a representation had been made by NatWest upon
which Somer acted to its detriment in consigning further goods to Mentor to the   *b*
value of some £13,000 but in no further respect, it involves this court in facing
directly the questions raised by Robert Walker LJ. In the *Scottish Equitable* case
the actual detriment found by the court, and which Scottish Equitable conceded
it would not seek to recover, was some £9,660 out of a total overpayment of
£172,451, a ratio of 1:17, giving rise to an overpayment of £162,790. While it   *c*
could not be said that the detriment to Mr Derby was de minimis, it could readily
be held that it was unconscionable and inequitable to allow him to retain the vast
bulk of the overpayment, when his real detriment was limited to such a small
proportion, and hence within the exception to the 'all or nothing' rule recognised
in the *Avon CC* case. The instant case is, by reason of the sums involved, a
somewhat less glaring illustration of an unjustifiable windfall to the defendant.   *d*
That said, however, in cases of payments made under a mistake of fact, it is
difficult to see why principles of equity and unconscionability should not apply to
cover any case in which it appears a substantial windfall would otherwise be
incurred by the transferee at the expense of the mistaken transferor.

e

THE GROUNDS OF APPEAL

Somer International (UK) Ltd
[31] For Somer Mr Virgo has submitted that the judge was wrong to rely upon
the reservations expressed by the Court of Appeal in *Avon CC v Howlett* [1983]
1 All ER 1073, [1983] 1 WLR 605 and to adopt the same process of reasoning as   *f*
Harrison J in *Scottish Equitable plc v Derby* [2000] 3 All ER 793. He submits that,
having accepted and found that the bank mistakenly made the dollar payment to
Somer, representing at the time that the moneys were due to Somer and that it
might treat them as its own, and that Somer had thereafter acted on such
representation to its detriment, he ought to have held that the bank was estopped   *g*
from claiming repayment of any part of the payment made in accordance with
the general principle upheld and applied in the *Avon CC* case. He submits that the
exception to the principle recognised in the *Avon CC* case and applied in the *Scottish
Equitable* case should only be applied 'where the sums sought to be recovered
were so large as to bear no relation to any detriment which the recipient would
possibly have suffered' (see per Slade LJ at [17] above). In the present case, he   *h*
submits that the sum sought by the bank was not in that category. Mr Virgo also
relies upon the observation of Slade LJ in the *Avon CC* case that, if the pecuniary
amount of a defendant's prejudice has to be precisely quantified, he may be faced
with obvious difficulties of proof where he has either altered his general mode of
living or (as in this case) proceeded to conduct his business on the assumption   *j*
that the representation is correct.
[32] In this connection, he submits that, but for the bank's representation,
Somer would have refused to ship further goods unless it received payment of its
outstanding account and thus there was a chance that the outstanding sums due
to Somer would have been paid. He points out that the evidence given by Somer
was that Mentor had always (eventually) paid in the past and that the sub-purchasers,

a   upon whose creditworthiness Mentor's ability to pay depended, were substantial
     concerns. He submits that, having received an assurance from Mentor that it was
     shortly to make further payment of $US70,000–78,000, there is no reason to think
     that this did not reflect a realistic level of receipts in hand from subpurchasers.
     However, when, as a result of the bank's error, Mr Richardson indicated to
     Mentor that the expected moneys had been received, this enabled Mentor to take
b   advantage of the situation by accepting the suggestion that the moneys had been
     paid. If the inference is to be drawn that Mentor were dishonest, then the bank's
     error facilitated the very fraud which was then committed. Further, if Somer had
     pressed for payment there was no reason to suppose that Mentor would not have
     passed on, rather than dissipated elsewhere, moneys received from its sub-purchasers.
     The very difficulty of valuing Somer's lost opportunity in that respect was itself a
c   reason for holding NatWest to the representation which it made without any
     form of restitution.

NatWest Bank plc

     [33] There is an extensive respondent's notice in this case, largely directed to
d   the factual findings of the judge. First it is contended that there was no sufficient
     evidence of a representation by the bank. Second that, Somer failed to adduce
     sufficient evidence for the judge to be satisfied even that further goods had been
     shipped in reliance upon the representation. Third, that the judge failed to take
     proper account of the inequity to the bank in allowing Somer to retain any part
     of the money paid to it by mistake. I do not propose to deal with the matters
e   advanced in any detail. Suffice it to say, that it seems clear to me that there was
     before the judge evidence which entitled him to come to all his main conclusions
     as I have stated them.

     [34] So far as the law is concerned, the respondent's notice summarises
     NatWest's submissions in law (without reference to authority) as follows. First,
f   it states that the defence of estoppel by representation cannot operate so as to
     defeat a claim for restitution of money paid by mistake when the detriment said
     to have been suffered as a result can be accurately assessed to the court's
     satisfaction in money's worth and is less than the amount received in error. In
     such a case, equity requires only that the recipient be entitled to retain an amount
     sufficient to compensate him for his detriment; accordingly, in such circumstances,
g   only the defence of change of position is available to the recipient and he must
     account to the payor for the balance of the money received by him in error.
     Secondly, it is submitted that in any event the defence of estoppel by representation
     should not be allowed to defeat a claim for restitution of money paid by mistake
     unless the unintended recipient can show that the value of the detriment suffered
h   by him in reliance on the representation founding the estoppel was substantial
     when compared to the amount of money received.

DISCUSSION

     [35] It is unattractive that, in a case of moneys paid over under a mistake of fact
j   and sought to be recovered on the basis of unjust enrichment, the extent of the
     recovery should depend on whether or not, at the time of the transfer of the moneys,
     the transferor represented by words or conduct that the transferee was entitled
     to such payment. When the mistake occurs, particularly in the context of a
     banker/customer relationship, whether or not an actual representation as to
     entitlement was made or can be spelt out is largely fortuitous and ex hypothesi
     the result of accident rather than deliberate conduct. It also seems clear that,

where there has been such a representation, the only substantial hurdle standing
in the way of recovery, subject to an appropriate equitable adjustment in relation   *a*
to the actual 'detriment' suffered, is the view that the historical origin and
technical status of estoppel by representation as a rule of evidence dictates an 'all
or nothing' solution the effect of which is that, once the representation has been
acted on to the detriment of the transferee the contrary may not be asserted. This
differs from the position in the case of so-called 'equitable' or 'promissory'   *b*
estoppel in respect of which a specific promise to waive or refrain from enforcing
rights may be withdrawn on reasonable notice and, in 'proprietary' estoppel,
where when giving effect to the interest or right in property which the party
raising the estoppel asserts, the court assumes a wide discretion as to the terms
on which such relief is granted. In this respect estoppel by representation also
differs in nature from the defence of 'change of position' which is only permitted   *c*
to prevail to the extent that it would be inequitable to require the transferee to
return the money.

[36] There is no doubt that the preponderance of legal authority and judicial
dicta at the highest level favours the view that estoppel by representation is a rule
of evidence rather than of substantive law: see *Low v Bouverie* [1891] 3 Ch 82 at   *d*
105, [1891–4] All ER Rep 348 at 355 per Bowen LJ:

'Estoppel is only a rule of evidence; you cannot found an action upon
estoppel ... [It] ... is only important as being one step in the progress towards
relief on the hypothesis that the defendant is estopped from denying the
truth of something which he has said.'   *e*

And see to similar effect *Nippon Menkwa Kabushiki Kaisha (Japan Cotton Trading
Co Ltd) v Dawsons Bank Ltd* (1935) 51 Ll L Rep 147 at 150 per Lord Russell of
Killowen, see also *London Joint Stock Bank Ltd v Macmillan* [1918] AC 777 at 818,
[1918–19] All ER Rep 30 at 50 per Viscount Haldane: '... it is hardly a rule of what
is called substantive law in the sense of declaring an immediate right or claim. It   *f*
is rather a rule of evidence, capable not the less on that account of affecting
gravely substantive rights.' Finally in *Evans v Bartlam* [1937] 2 All ER 646 at 653,
[1937] AC 473 at 484 per Lord Wright: '... estoppel is a rule of evidence that
prevents the person estopped from denying the existence of a fact ...'

[37] None the less, because of the decisive impact which estoppel by representation   *g*
may have upon the outcome of any individual case, whether as a step on the way
to establishing a cause of action, or as defeating a prima facie valid claim based on
facts which (absent the representation) would entitle the claimant to recover,
such estoppel undoubtedly gives rise to substantive legal consequences. As Lord
Wright later observed in *Canada and Dominion Sugar Co Ltd v Canadian National*   *h*
(West Indies) Steamships Ltd [1947] AC 46 at 56:

'Estoppel is a complex legal notion, involving a combination of several
essential elements, the statement to be acted on, action on the face of it,
resulting detriment to the actor. Estoppel is often described as a rule of
evidence, as, indeed, it may be so described. But the whole concept is more   *j*
correctly viewed as a substantive rule of law.'

It seems that the only judicial statement in unqualified form which classifies
estoppel by representation as a rule of substantive law rather than a rule of
evidence is the observation of Lord Denning MR in *Moorgate Mercantile Co Ltd v
Twitchings* [1975] 3 All ER 314 at 323, [1976] QB 225 at 241:

a

'Estoppel is not a rule of evidence. It is not a cause of action. It is a principle of justice and of equity. It comes to this. When a man, by his words or conduct, has led another to believe in a particular state of affairs, he will not be allowed to go back on it when it would be unjust or inequitable for him to do so.'

b

In the light of the state of the authorities and the clear statement in *Avon CC v Howlett* [1983] 1 All ER 1073, [1983] 1 WLR 605 on a matter integral to the court's decision, it does not seem to me that it is open to this court at least to depart from the traditional classification of estoppel by representation as a rule of evidence.

[38] I would only add in this connection that there are various dicta in terms which support the view that a single purpose underlies all forms of estoppel on

c   the basis that all aspects of the rules developed are examples of general principle applied so as to prevent A from refusing to recognise, or seeking unjustly to deny or avoid, an assumption or belief which he has induced, permitted or encouraged in B and on the basis of which B has acted or regulated his affairs: see for instance the *Moorgate Mercantile* case [1975] 3 All ER 314 at 323–324, [1976] QB 225 at

d   241–242, see also the observations of Scarman LJ in *Crabb v Arun DC* [1975] 3 All ER 865 at 875, [1976] Ch 179 at 193 in relation to the distinction between promissory and proprietary estoppel. However, various particular difficulties in the manner in which, and the limitations subject to which, the various types of estoppel have been developed, have so far prevented a rationalisation of this kind. As stated by Millett LJ in *First National Bank plc v Thompson* [1996] 1 All ER 140 at 144, [1996]

e   Ch 231 at 236:

'[An attempt] to demonstrate that all estoppels other than estoppel by record are now subsumed in the single and all-embracing estoppel by representation and that they are all governed by the same requirements has never won general acceptance. Historically unsound, it has been repudiated by

f   academic writers and is unsupported by authority.'

[39] Despite some advances in this direction made in Commonwealth jurisdictions, it seems to me that the position remains unchanged in this country to date. Thus, faced with an invitation to formulate a single general principle to cover two types of estoppel with which he was called upon to deal in *The Indian

g   Endurance (No 2), Republic of India v India Steamship Co Ltd* [1997] 4 All ER 380 at 392, [1998] AC 878 at 914, Lord Steyn observed:

'The question was debated whether estoppel by convention and estoppel by acquiescence are but aspects of one overarching principle. I do not underestimate the importance in the continuing development of the law of

h   the search for simplicity. I, also, accept that at a high level of abstraction such an overarching principle could be formulated. But ... to restate the law in terms of an overarching principle might tend to blur the necessarily separate requirements, and distinct terrain of application, of the two kinds of estoppel.'

j

[40] That said, and accepting estoppel by representation to be a rule of evidence, which *ordinarily* requires that a more than de minimis degree of detriment is definitive of the transferee's right to retain the entirety of a mistaken payment, it is plain that the court in the *Avon CC* case, and subsequently in the *Scottish Equitable* case, considered that there yet remained scope for the operation of equity to alleviate the position on grounds of unfairness or unconscionability, although in

the latter case it failed to elucidate that conclusion by reference to authority other
than the *Avon CC* case which in turn quoted no authority to that effect. It seems
to me that authority in the form of a clear statement as to the underlying
principles being those of equity is none the less available, whatever the appropriate
juridical classification of estoppel by representation.

[41] Although the doctrine of estoppel by representation was developed in the
field of commercial transactions by the common law in the early nineteenth
century as a principle of broad application it had its origins in cases concerning
the negotiation of marriage settlements which were principally heard in the
Courts of Equity (see generally Cooke *The Modern Law of Estoppel* (2000)
pp 19–22). In *Jorden v Money* (1854) 5 HL Cas 185 at 210, [1843–60] All ER Rep 350
at 354 estoppel by representation was described by Lord Cranworth LC as 'a
principle well known in the law, founded upon good faith and equity, a principle
equally of law and of equity'.

[42] Later he stated:

'The whole doctrine was very much considered at law, for it is a doctrine
not confined to cases in equity, but one that prevails at law also; and there
are, in fact, more cases upon the subject at law than in equity.' (See (1854)
5 HL Cas 185 at 212–213, [1843–60] All ER Rep 350 at 355.)

[43] Thus, whether or not the dicta of Lord Denning MR in the *Moorgate
Mercantile* case (see [37] above) be correct in terms of classification, it is clear that
the doctrine of estoppel by representation stems from and is governed by
considerations of justice and equity. That being so, it is difficult to see why equity
should, as between the parties, be impotent in an appropriate case or category of
case to require a person relying upon the defence of estoppel by representation
to rely upon it only to the extent of any detriment suffered.

[44] In the *Avon CC* case the court cited three cases which suggested that,
where estoppel by representation is raised as a defence to a claim for money had
and received, the courts do not treat the operation of estoppel as being restricted
to the precise amount of the detriment which the representee proves he has
suffered in reliance on the representation: *Skyring v Greenwood* (1825) 4 B & C 281
at 289, [1824–34] All ER Rep 104 at 106, citing a passage from the judgment of
Abbott CJ, *Holt v Markham* [1923] 1 KB 504, [1922] All ER Rep 134, and *Lloyds
Bank Ltd v Brooks* (1950) 6 Legal Decisions Affecting Bankers 161. The court also
cited *Ogilvie v West Australian Mortgage and Agency Corp Ltd* [1896] AC 257 and
Greenwood v Martins Bank Ltd [1932] 1 KB 371 (affirmed in the House of Lords
[1933] AC 51, [1932] All ER Rep 318) as demonstrating that a claimant who, as a
result of being able to rely on estoppel, succeeds on a cause of action on which,
without being able to rely on it, he would necessarily have failed, may be able to
recover more than the actual damage suffered by him as a result of the
representation which gave rise to it.

[45] It is difficult to see how the last two cases support the principle for which
they were cited. In each case a bank customer discovered that cheques drawn on
his account had been forged, but failed to inform the bank until a substantial
period had elapsed. In each case it was held that there was no need to investigate
whether the bank could in fact have recovered money from the forger had it
acted immediately. The banks had not received benefit, but had suffered loss of
any opportunity for recovery elsewhere, as to which the uncertainty of such
recovery was resolved in favour of the representee. That point is made in Goff
and Jones *The Law of Restitution* (5th edn, 1998) p 832.

a [46] Similarly, the point is made that, albeit in *Skyring v Greenwood* and *Holt v Markham* there was no exact inquiry into the degree to which each defendant had altered his financial position, there was equally no judicial statement that estoppel by representation could not operate pro tanto in an appropriate case. In *Skyring v Greenwood*, indeed, it is not clear that there was evidence of any detrimental reliance, the court simply assuming that it had taken place. In *Holt v*
b *Markham*, while it is clear from the judgment of Warrington LJ ([1923] 1 KB 504 at 512, [1922] All ER Rep 134 at 140) that not all the money had been spent, there is no indication whether the balance which remained was substantial and it is clear that, in addition to mere spending, the defendant had parted with his war savings certificates (see [1923] 1 KB 504 at 511, [1922] All ER Rep 134 at 139 per Bankes LJ). It seems to me that those cases do no more than establish that the
c court will generally think it appropriate to treat the matter broadly and will not require the defendant to demonstrate in detail the precise degree or value of the detriment which he has suffered in circumstances where, as Slade LJ pointed out (*Avon CC v Howlett* [1983] 1 All ER 1073 at 1086, [1983] 1 WLR 605 at 622), he may find it difficult subsequently to recall and identify retrospectively the nature and
d extent of commitments undertaken or expenditure incurred as a result of an alteration in his general mode of living. However, it is open to the court, acting on equitable principles, to take the view that some restitution is necessary, albeit the burden upon the defendant of proving the precise extent of his detriment should be a light one. In these circumstances, the court may well have broad regard to, without being bound to follow, the developing lines of the courts'
e approach in 'change of position' cases. However, the two defences will remain distinct, unless or until the House of Lords rules otherwise.

[47] There may indeed be good reasons why this should be so and why the issue is not simply one of jurisprudential 'tidiness'. First, in considering the equities between the parties, there are plainly arguments for holding that the fact that a
f representation was made (albeit mistakenly) may in particular circumstances affect the court's view as to whether and how far, detriment having been established, it should order a restitutionary payment. Second, as pointed out by Fung and Ho in their article 'Change of Position and Estoppel' (2001) 117 LQR 14 at 17, the defence of 'change of position' only protects actual reduction of the transferee's assets following receipt. A transferee who, in reliance upon a receipt, forgoes a
g realistic and quantifiable opportunity to increase his assets is not apparently protected. It has also been held in *South Tyneside Metropolitan BC v Svenska International plc* [1995] 1 All ER 545, following Hobhouse J in *Kleinwort Benson Ltd v South Tyneside Metropolitan BC* [1994] 4 All ER 972 that, in order to be successful, a change of position defence must be based on a change *after* the receipt of the
h mistaken payment, the facts of *Lipkin Gorman (a firm) v Karpnale Ltd* [1992] 4 All ER 512, [1991] 2 AC 548 having been exceptional. The *South Tyneside* decision has been the subject of some criticism (see *Goff and Jones* pp 822–824). However, assuming its correctness (and we have heard no submissions in that regard), it marks a further difference between the defence of 'change of position' and of
j estoppel in any case where a representation as to the entitlement of the payee has been communicated to him and relied on in anticipation of actual receipt.

[48] Thus, the question to be decided on this appeal is whether, in the light the judge's findings that Somer had suffered detriment and/or changed its position only to the extent of £13,180·57, it should be obliged to repay the balance of the sum received from NatWest on the basis of the exception recognised in the *Avon CC* case. This was a case where the mistake of the bank would have been detected

early had Somer kept close account of its dealings with Mentor. Although the
judge found that Mr Richardson had continued to rely upon the information first
communicated to him that the payment from Mentor had now been received,
NatWest shortly afterwards forwarded a credit advice which made the position
clear at a time when Somer had forwarded goods worth only £5,221·99. The
judge rejected the case for Somer that it had incurred any detriment other than
despatch of goods worth £13,180·57 in reliance upon the representation, being
satisfied that Somer's chance of pursuing Mentor successfully for payment was
nil. In those circumstances, it seems to me that the judge was fully entitled to
hold that the payment sought was of such a size that it bore no relation to the
detriment which Somer could possibly have suffered and that it would be
unconscionable for Somer to retain the balance over and above the value of the
goods shipped.

CONCLUSION
[49] For the reasons above stated, I would dismiss this appeal.

CLARKE LJ.
[50] I agree that this appeal should be dismissed for the reasons given by Peter
Gibson and Potter LJJ, whose judgments I have seen in draft.
[51] The decision in *Scottish Equitable plc v Derby* [2001] EWCA Civ 369, [2001]
3 All ER 818, and the argument in this case have again demonstrated some of the
problems which surround the doctrine of estoppel by representation. In particular
there are two problems which it seems to me should if possible be considered by
the House of Lords in an appropriate case. The first is the extent, if at all, to which
estoppel by representation can operate pro tanto and the second is the
relationship between such an estoppel and the defence of change of position.
I agree that it is not open to this court either to hold that there is no room for
estoppel where the defence of change of position is available or to depart from
Avon CC v Howlett [1983] 1 All ER 1073, [1983] 1 WLR 605.
[52] I do not wish to say anything about the defence of change of position, but
only to consider briefly the principles which seem to me to apply to the application
of the doctrine of estoppel by representation as matters stand at present and
absent any definitive consideration by the House of Lords. I do so in part because
this is an estoppel case on the facts and because it seems to me that, even if the
House of Lords were to hold that there is no longer any room for the operation
of estoppel where a defence of change of position is available, there are likely to
remain cases where a defendant who has acted on a promise that he is to receive
money will properly wish to plead an estoppel.
[53] In order to consider the law as it stands at present, it seems to me that it
is necessary to identify the propositions of law for which the *Avon CC* case is
authority. To my mind it is authority for two propositions and there is a tension
between them. The first is that estoppel by representation is a rule of evidence,
the consequence of which is to preclude the representor from averring facts
contrary to his own representation (see [1983] 1 All ER 1073 at 1087, [1983] 1
WLR 605 at 622 per Slade LJ). Slade LJ discussed ([1983] 1 All ER 1073 at
1087–1088, [1983] 1 WLR 605 at 622–624) the operation of the doctrine in a
number of classes of case and concluded:

'All the relevant conditions for the operation of an estoppel being satisfied
in those cases, the plea operated as a rule of evidence which precluded the
payers from recovering any part of the money mistakenly overpaid or from

a retaining any part of the moneys mistakenly overcredited. I think that no authority has been cited, other than the judgment of the judge, which directly supports the proposition that estoppel is capable of operating merely pro tanto in a case such as the present, where it is otherwise capable of being invoked as a complete defence to an action for money had and received.' (See [1983] 1 All ER 1073 at 1088, [1983] 1 WLR 605 at 624.)

b
[54] In the interesting article by Fung and Ho on 'Change of Position and Estoppel' (2001) 117 LQR 14 which is referred to by Potter LJ, the authors criticise that approach and say (at p 19) that it is high time that estoppel was regarded as a substantive (as opposed to an evidential) defence and that it can operate pro tanto. There seems to me to be much to be said for that point of view, but I do c not think that it is open to this court to develop the law in that way in the light of the decisions in the *Avon CC* case and the *Scottish Equitable* case. However, as I see it, much the same result has been achieved by an application of the second proposition to be derived from the *Avon CC* case.

[55] All three members of the court in the *Avon CC* case recognised that the d application of the first proposition might lead to injustice. So they concluded that there was or might be an exception to it, although they did not all express the exception in the same terms. Potter LJ has quoted the relevant passages from the judgments. Slade LJ gave as an example ([1983] 1 All ER 1073 at 1089, [1983] 1 WLR 605 at 625) a case where the sums sought to be recovered were so large as to bear no relation to any detriment which the recipient could possibly have e suffered. Cumming-Bruce LJ, who was particularly concerned by the hypothetical nature of the exercise upon which (as Peter Gibson LJ explains) the court was engaged, said ([1983] 1 All ER 1073 at 1076, [1983] 1 WLR 605 at 608) that he did not consider the decision as authority for the proposition that where, on the facts, it would be clearly inequitable to allow a party to make a profit by pleading f estoppel, the court will necessarily be powerless to prevent it.

[56] Eveleigh LJ to my mind most clearly pointed the way to the future. He said:

'However, I am far from saying that, whenever the recipient of money paid under a mistake has been led to think that it is his, then he will be entitled to g retain the whole by demonstrating that he has spent part of it. The payment may involve no representation, as where a debtor presents an account to a creditor. Then while there might have been a representation there may be circumstances which would render it unconscionable for the defendant to retain a balance in his hands. There may also be circumstances which would h make it unfair to allow the plaintiff to recover.' (See [1983] 1 All ER 1073 at 1078, [1983] 1 WLR 605 at 611–612.)

Eveleigh LJ thus appears to have regarded a relevant test, if not the relevant test, as unconscionability.

j [57] The exception was further considered in the *Scottish Equitable* case [2001] 3 All ER 818, although the court did not attempt to formulate the nature of the exception. Robert Walker LJ, who gave the leading judgment, did not attempt a formulation of his own but (at [43]) was content to adopt the view of the judge that the case was 'just the sort of situation that the Court of Appeal must have had in mind in … *Avon CC v Howlett* when expressing reservations about the ambit of the decision'. He added ([2001] 3 All ER 818 at [44]) that it can be predicted (albeit with some reservation) that development of the law on a case by case basis will have the effect of enlarging rather than narrowing the exception.

[58] It seems to me that the exception recognised in both the *Avon CC* case and the *Scottish Equitable* case can best be formulated as suggested by Cumming-Bruce and Eveleigh LJJ, namely that the estoppel should not operate in full where it would be clearly inequitable or unconscionable for the defendant to retain a balance in his hands. Whether it would or not of course depends upon all the circumstances of the particular case, which may include the nature of the representation and (as Peter Gibson LJ observes) will certainly include the steps taken by the recipient in reliance upon the representation.

[59] I recognise that there is a tension between the first proposition in the *Avon CC* case and the exception because, as I see it, even after making all allowances in favour of the recipient, it will very often be unconscionable to permit him to keep the whole of the sums paid to him. However, I do not think that it is appropriate to allow a defendant to rely upon an estoppel, whether at common law or in equity, to achieve a result which can fairly be regarded as unconscionable. I am conscious of recent cases in which it has been said that it is not appropriate to try to identify a common principle applicable to all estoppels. However, I observe that in *Johnson v Gore Wood & Co (a firm)* [2001] 1 All ER 481, [2001] 2 WLR 72, which was admittedly not concerned with estoppel by representation, Lord Goff of Chieveley said:

> 'In the end, I am inclined to think that the many circumstances capable of giving rise to an estoppel cannot be accommodated within a single formula, and that it is unconscionability which provides the link between them.' (See [2001] 1 All ER 481 at 508, [2001] 2 WLR 72 at 100.)

[60] This is perhaps an example of the principles of equity being employed to mitigate the rigours of the common law. However that may be, it seems to me to follow from the *Avon CC* case and the *Scottish Equitable* case that there are exceptions to the strict rule of evidence that an estoppel by representation cannot operate pro tanto and that those exceptions are or include cases where it would be unconscionable or wholly inequitable to permit the recipient of money to retain the whole of it.

[61] I am not sure that this approach is markedly different from that described by Robert Walker LJ in the *Scottish Equitable* case [2001] 3 All ER 818 at [45]–[47] and referred to as a 'novel and ingenious point'. If, as Dixon J put it in *Grundt v Great Boulder Pty Gold Mines Ltd* (1937) 59 CLR 641 at 674, and as Robert Walker LJ said was correct ([2001] 3 All ER 818 at [45]), detriment must be judged when the representee seeks to go back on his representation, the recipient will not have acted to his detriment if he is entitled to keep the part of the money that he has spent but not the rest. Provided that he is entitled to keep the amount spent, it is likely (subject to the circumstances of the particular case) to be unconscionable to allow him to keep the rest, in which event he should not in principle be entitled to do so. As I see it, the application of what may be called the unconscionability test does not involve the exercise of a discretion but provides a principled approach to the problem in a case of this kind.

[62] For the reasons given by both Peter Gibson and Potter LJJ I agree that on the facts found by the judge it would be unconscionable and inequitable for Somer International (UK) Ltd to be permitted to retain the balance paid to it in error by National Westminster Bank plc. It follows that I too would dismiss the appeal.

PETER GIBSON LJ.

a   [63] The consequences of the recognition by the House of Lords in the landmark decision in *Lipkin Gorman (a firm) v Karpnale Ltd* [1992] 4 All ER 512, [1991] 2 AC 548 of the defence of change of position to a claim in restitution based on unjust enrichment are still being worked out by the English courts. The Law Commission in its report, *Restitution: mistakes of law and ultra vires public authority*
b   *receipts and payments* (Law Com No 227) (1994), considered this area of the law but recommended no legislative intervention (para 5.14). It reported that the majority of persons consulted by the commission favoured retaining estoppel by representation as a defence as well as the defence of change of position, but it thought that the precise relationship between those defences should be worked out by the common law. It continued (para 5.17): 'We believe that the
c   importance of estoppel will diminish as a result of the introduction of a broad defence of change of position, but it is premature to regard it as redundant.'

    [64] Mr Virgo for Somer International (UK) Ltd (Somer) submits that the two defences are recognised as distinct and necessary parts of English law, estoppel being a defence of general availability apt to be invoked against the assertion of
d   any kind of right, whereas the defence of change of position may be available in circumstances where the defence of estoppel could not be established, for example where there is no representation accompanying the mistaken payment. He relies on *Avon CC v Howlett* [1983] 1 All ER 1073, [1983] 1 WLR 605 as authority binding this court that the operation of the defence of estoppel is not restricted to the precise amount which the recipient may prove he has suffered in reliance on the
e   representation.

    [65] Mr Chambers for the bank submits that the defence of estoppel is no longer available in a case such as the present where the defence of change of position is available to the defendant. There are Canadian authorities which hold that estoppel is no longer an appropriate way of dealing with the problem, the
f   defence of change of position most fairly balancing the equities (see *RBC Dominion Securities Inc v Dawson* (1994) 111 DLR (4th) 230, a decision of the Newfoundland Court of Appeal, applied in *Empire Life Insurance Co v Neufeld Estate* (24 April 1998, unreported), a decision of Lowry J in the Supreme Court of British Columbia). In this country Jonathan Parker J in *Philip Collins Ltd v Davis* [2000] 3 All ER 808 at 826 has suggested that a defence of estoppel is no longer apt in
g   restitutionary claims where the defence of change of position is available. Mr Chambers argues that we should not follow the *Avon CC* case on the basis that it cannot now stand with the decision of the House of Lords in the *Lipkin Gorman* case. Alternatively, he submits that the present case plainly falls within an exception recognised in the *Avon CC* case to the 'all or nothing' application of the
h   estoppel defence.

    [66] The *Avon CC* case is a procedural oddity. The trial judge found as a fact that the defendant had spent all the money overpaid to him but decided the case on the artificial basis pleaded in the defence that he had only spent a little over half the money overpaid. The judge held that the payers were entitled to recover
j   the balance, but they undertook not to execute the judgment without leave of the court. The defendant appealed, although, as Cumming-Bruce LJ put it ([1983] 1 All ER 1073, [1983] 1 WLR 605 at 608), he had no practical reason for objecting to the order, and the appeal was brought in order to obtain the decision of this court upon a purely hypothetical question of detriment in its relevance to the law of estoppel. It was decided at a time when the defence of change of position was not recognised. But it was not expressly overruled by the House of Lords in the

Lipkin Gorman case. In Goff and Jones *The Law of Restitution* (5th edn, 1998) p 829, it is said that 'the House of Lords may conclude that *Avon County Court v. Howlett* ***a*** cannot stand with *Lipkin Gorman (a firm) v. Karpnale Ltd* and should be overruled'. The caution of the editor should be noted: he is suggesting the possibility that the *Avon CC* case will be overruled by the House of Lords. I doubt if this court is free to treat the *Avon CC* case as overruled.

[67] In my judgment in the present case this court should follow the approach ***b*** adopted in *Scottish Equitable plc v Derby*, both by Harrison J at first instance ([2000] 3 All ER 793) and by this court on appeal from him ([2001] EWCA Civ 369, [2001] 3 All ER 818), and should consider whether the circumstances are such that the case falls within the exception recognised as a possibility by each of the members of this court in the *Avon CC* case (see [1983] 1 All ER 1073 at 1076, 1078, 1089, [1983] 1 WLR 605 at 608–609, 611–612, 624–625 per Cumming-Bruce, Eveleigh ***c*** and Slade LJJ respectively). (See also *Chitty on Contracts* (28th edn, 1999) vol 1, p 1527 (para 30-113).) When Slade LJ posited the case where the sums sought to be recovered were so large as to bear no relation to any detriment which the recipient could possibly have suffered, he did so expressly by way of an example of circumstances where the doctrine of estoppel could be said to give rise to ***d*** injustice were it to defeat in its entirety an action in restitution. The test is whether it would be unconscionable and inequitable for the recipient of the moneys mistakenly paid to retain the moneys having regard to what the recipient did in reliance on the representation made to him.

[68] I fully accept that the court, when assessing detriment, should not apply too demanding a standard of proof because of the practical difficulties faced by a ***e*** defendant conducting a business who has been led to believe that the moneys paid by mistake are his (see the remarks of Slade LJ in the *Avon CC* case [1983] 1 All ER 1073 at 1086–1087, [1983] 1 WLR 605 at 621–622). But in view of the clear findings of fact made by the judge as to the extent of the detriment suffered by Somer and in particular his outright rejection of the argument that Somer was ***f*** induced to forgo the opportunity to pursue Mentor for payment, I am not able to accede to Mr Virgo's submission that this is a case where it would be unjust not to give full effect to the estoppel. On the contrary, the circumstances here, as found by the judge, are such that the disparity between the $US 76,708·57 mistakenly credited to Somer and £13,180·57, being the value of the goods despatched by Somer in reliance on the bank's representation, makes it unconscionable and ***g*** inequitable for Somer to retain the balance.

[69] For these as well as the reasons given by Potter LJ I would dismiss the appeal. I also agree with him in rejecting the bank's challenges by the respondent's notice to the judge's findings of fact.

Appeal dismissed.

Kate O'Hanlon   Barrister.

a # Bland v Ingram's Estates Ltd and others

COURT OF APPEAL, CIVIL DIVISION
NOURSE, CHADWICK AND HALE LJJ
10, 11 OCTOBER, 21 DECEMBER 2000

b
Landlord and tenant – Relief against forfeiture – Right to apply for relief – Equitable chargee – Claimant having equitable charge over lease – Landlord forfeiting lease for non-payment of rent – Tenants failing to claim relief from forfeiture – Whether equitable chargee of lease having right to claim indirect relief from forefeiture for c *non-payment of rent under High Court's inherent jurisdiction.*

The claimant, B, was the tenant of business premises held under a lease granted by the defendant landlord. She sold the premises, together with trade fixtures and fittings, for a sum payable by instalments. Shortly afterwards, the landlord granted the purchasers a lease of the premises. The purchasers failed to pay d certain of the instalments due to B under the sale agreement, and she obtained two summary judgments against them. In order to secure the judgment debts, the court granted B charging orders over the purchasers' interests in various properties, including the premises comprised in the lease. Those orders, which rendered B an equitable chargee of the legal estate in the lease, were registered at the Land Charges Registry, pursuant to the provisions of the Land Charges Act e 1972. The purchasers had also fallen into arrears of rent, and the landlord, who had received actual notice that B had a charging order over the purchasers' lease, subsequently forfeited the lease by peaceable re-entry. A few days later, the landlord granted a lease of the premises to new tenants who took it with constructive notice of the purchasers' right to claim relief against forfeiture. In f the event, the purchasers did not exercise that right. Instead, B brought an action against the landlord and the new tenants, relying on her equitable charge to ground a claim, under the inherent jurisdiction of the High Court, for direct relief from forfeiture, ie relief in the form of an order vesting in B a new lease. The judge dismissed the action, and B appealed. On the appeal, the issue arose whether, if an equitable chargee of a lease could not claim direct relief under the g inherent jurisdiction, he was nevertheless entitled to make a claim for indirect relief, ie to claim, in the shoes of the tenant, relief in a form which restored or revived the tenant's lease.

Held – Where a lease had been forfeited for non-payment of rent and the tenant h had not sought relief against forfeiture, an equitable chargee of the lease could claim indirect relief, in the shoes of the tenant, under the inherent jurisdiction of the High Court. Such a chargee (per Nourse and Chadwick LJJ) could not make a claim for direct relief since the inherent jurisdiction to grant such relief from forfeiture for non-payment of rent was confined to cases in which the person j claiming relief was entitled to possession of the land or, at any rate, had a legal estate or equitable interest in it. An equitable chargee, unlike an equitable mortgagee, had no equitable interest and no right to possession. There was, however, an implied obligation on the chargor to take reasonable steps to preserve the chargee's security, and where the security was a lease which had been forfeited for non-payment of rent, such steps, as a general rule, included initiating and pursuing an application for relief against the forfeiture. Only in that

way could the security be preserved from annihilation. The position was
analogous to that as between a beneficiary under a trust and a trustee who failed *a*
or neglected, in the performance of a duty owed by him to the beneficiary, to
protect the trust estate or the beneficiary's interest therein. In such a case, the
beneficiary could join the trustee as defendant and sue in right of the trust and in
the shoes of the trustee. There was no distinction in principle between a case
where the obligation arose under the law of trusts and one where it arose in *b*
contract. It followed that in the instant case B could join the purchasers as
defendants to the action for relief against forfeiture and claim in their shoes.
Moreover, she was entitled, in principle, to relief in a form which restored or
revived the purchasers' lease. Accordingly, the appeal would be allowed, but
there would be an adjournment for further consideration of the terms on which
relief would be granted (see p 227 *j*, p 230 *h* to p 231 *a c d f* to *h*, p 232 *g*, p 235 *d e*, *c*
p 239 *d g* to p 240 *a c* to *e g* to *j*, p 241 *f* and p 242 *e* to *g*, below); *Ladup Ltd v Williams
& Glyn's Bank plc* [1985] 2 All ER 577 and *Croydon (Unique) Ltd v Wright (Crombie
intervening)* [1999] 4 All ER 257 considered.

Per Chadwick and Hale LJJ. Where a lessor has enforced against a lessee, by
re-entry without action, a right of re-entry or forfeiture for non-payment of rent, *d*
a county court judge has jurisdiction under s 139(2)[a] of the County Courts Act
1984 to grant an application for relief from forfeiture by an equitable chargee of
the lease (see p 238 *a* to *c e* to *h*, and p 243 *b c*, below).

Notes

For equitable charges and for the right to relief against forfeiture for non-payment *e*
of rent, see respectively 4(1) *Halsbury's Laws* (4th edn reissue) para 610 and 27(1)
Halsbury's Laws (4th edn reissue) para 522.

Cases referred to in judgments

Abbey National Building Society v Maybeech Ltd [1984] 3 All ER 262, [1985] Ch 190, *f*
    [1984] 3 WLR 793.
BICC plc v Burndy Corp [1985] 1 All ER 417, [1985] Ch 232, [1985] 2 WLR 132, CA.
Bowser v Colby (1841) 1 Hare 109, [1835–42] All ER Rep 478, V-C Ct.
Carreras Rothmans Ltd v Freeman Mathews Treasure Ltd (in liq) [1985] 1 All ER 155,
    [1985] Ch 207, [1984] 3 WLR 1016.
Clark v Chief Land Registrar, Chancery plc v Ketteringham [1994] 4 All ER 96, [1994] *g*
    Ch 370, [1994] 3 WLR 593, CA.
Cosslett (Contractors) Ltd, Re [1997] 4 All ER 115, [1998] Ch 495, [1998] 2 WLR 131,
    CA.
Croydon (Unique) Ltd v Wright (Crombie intervening) [1999] 4 All ER 257, [2001] Ch 318,
    [2000] 2 WLR 683, CA.   *h*
Cummins v Perkins [1899] 1 Ch 16, CA.
Dendy v Evans [1910] 1 KB 263, [1908–10] All ER Rep 589, CA.
Faith Panton Property Plan Ltd v Hodgetts [1981] 2 All ER 877, [1981] 1 WLR 927, CA.
Gill v Lewis [1956] 1 All ER 844, [1956] 2 QB 1, [1956] 2 WLR 962, CA.
Harmer v Armstrong [1934] Ch 65, [1933] All ER Rep 778, CA.   *j*
Hayim v Citibank NA [1987] AC 730, [1987] 3 WLR 83, PC.
Howard v Fanshawe [1895] 2 Ch 581, [1895–9] All ER Rep 855.
King v Smith (1843) 2 Hare 239.
Ladup Ltd v Williams & Glyn's Bank plc [1985] 2 All ER 577, [1985] 1 WLR 851.

---

a   Section 139, so far as material, is set out at p 237 *h j*, below

a *Newbolt v Bingham* (1895) 72 LT 852, CA.
Scandinavian Trading Tanker Co AB v Flota Petrolera Ecuatoriana, The Scaptrade [1983] 2 All ER 763, [1983] 2 AC 694, [1983] 3 WLR 203, HL.
Shiloh Spinners Ltd v Harding [1973] 1 All ER 90, [1973] AC 691, [1973] 2 WLR 28, HL.
Sport International Bussum BV v Inter-Footwear Ltd [1984] 2 All ER 321, [1984] 1 WLR 776, HL.

b **Cases also cited or referred to in skeleton arguments**
Bank of Credit and Commerce International SA (No 8), Re [1997] 4 All ER 568, [1998] AC 214, HL.
Bank of Ireland Home Mortgages v South Lodge Developments [1996] 1 EGLR 91.
Billson v Residential Apartments Ltd [1992] 1 All ER 141, [1992] 1 AC 494, HL.
c *Borzak v Ahmed* [1965] 1 All ER 808, [1965] 2 QB 320.
Brompton Securities Ltd (No 2), Re [1988] 3 All ER 677.
Chandless-Chandless v Nicholson [1942] 2 All ER 315, [1942] 2 KB 321, CA.
Doe d Whitfield v Roe (1811) 3 Taun 402.
Driscoll v Church Comrs for England [1956] 3 All ER 802, [1957] 1 QB 330, CA.
d *Fuller v Judy Properties Ltd* [1992] 1 EGLR 75, CA.
Good's Lease, Re, Good v Wood [1954] 1 All ER 275, [1954] 1 WLR 309.
Lovelock v Margo [1963] 2 All ER 13, [1963] 2 QB 786, CA.
Meadows v Clerical, Medical and General Life Assurance Society [1980] 1 All ER 454, [1981] Ch 70.
e *Midland Bank plc v Pike* [1988] 2 All ER 434.
On Demand Information plc v Michael Gerson (Finance) plc [1999] 2 All ER 811; *affd* [2000] 4 All ER 734, [2001] 1 WLR 155, CA.
Perry v Phoenix Assurance plc [1988] 3 All ER 60, [1988] 1 WLR 940.
Swiss Bank Corp v Lloyds Bank Ltd [1979] 2 All ER 853, [1979] Ch 548; *varied* [1980] 2 All ER 419, [1982] AC 584, CA; *affd* [1981] 2 All ER 449, [1982] AC 584, HL.
f *Tickner v Buzzacott* [1965] 1 All ER 131, [1965] Ch 426.
Transag Haulage v Leyland DAF Finance plc [1994] 2 BCLC 88.
Webber v Smith (1689) 2 Vern 103.

Appeals
g By notice dated 10 May 1999, Davinia Patricia Bland, the claimant in proceedings brought against the defendants, Ingram's Estates Ltd (Ingrams), the landlord of business premises known as 54/56 The Parade, Bourne End, Buckinghamshire, and Fogir Uddin and his wife, Ripon Chowdhery Fogir, the tenants of the premises, appealed with permission of Nourse LJ granted on 30 July 1999 from
h the decision of Peter Leaver QC, sitting as a deputy judge of the High Court, on 13 April 1999 ([1999] 2 EGLR 49) dismissing Mrs Bland's claim for relief from forfeiture of a lease of the premises granted by Ingrams to Franco and Caroline Beer on 12 May 1994 and over which Mrs Bland held charging orders as security for judgments obtained against the Beers. Mr Uddin, as defendant to proceedings brought by the Beers in respect of fixtures and fittings in the premises, appealed
j from the refusal of the judge, in the same decision, to make an award of damages against Mrs Bland in respect of a cross-undertaking in damages given by her, as claimant in interpleader proceedings, on the renewal, on 18 June 1996, of an injunction granted to the Beers by Judge Hull QC at High Wycombe County Court on 16 May 1996 restraining Mr Uddin from dismantling or taking away the fixtures and fittings or from damaging and/or otherwise using them generally or as part of his own business. The facts are set out in the judgment of Nourse LJ.

Robert Denman (instructed by *Joseph Aaron & Co*, Ilford) for Mrs Bland.
Timothy Fancourt (instructed by *Collyer-Bristow*) for Ingrams.
Justin Althaus (instructed by *Armstrong & Co*) for the Uddins.

Cur adv vult

21 December 2000. The following judgments were delivered.

NOURSE LJ.
2. The principal question on these appeals is whether an equitable chargee of a lease which has been forfeited for non-payment of rent can, where the tenant himself does not seek relief, claim relief against the forfeiture under the inherent jurisdiction of the High Court, either directly or indirectly in the shoes of the tenant.

The facts
3. The premises affected are 54/56, The Parade, Bourne End in Buckinghamshire, which, before the events that must now be described, had been used as a café. The freehold owners of the premises were Ingram's Estates Ltd (Ingrams). In May 1989 they granted to Davinia Patricia Bland and her husband, John Colin Bland, a lease of the premises (the Bland lease) for a term of 16 years from 25 March 1988 at an annual rent, subject to review, of £10,000. That was double the rent paid by the previous tenants, whose lease, when surrendered, had about 18 months to run and to whom Mr and Mrs Bland paid £100,000 in order to obtain possession. In 1990 and 1991, at a further cost of about £100,000, they extended the premises and turned them into an Italian restaurant which opened towards the end of 1991.
4. In 1992 a bankruptcy order was made against Mr Bland. His trustee having disclaimed his interest under the Bland lease, Ingrams permitted Mrs Bland to remain in possession as the sole tenant. By an agreement dated 4 May 1994 she sold the premises, together with the trade fixtures and fittings, to Franco Beer and his wife, Caroline, for £172,500 payable by instalments over a period ending on 25 June 1996. It may not be clear whether the Bland lease was surrendered or forfeited by peaceable re-entry. In any event, on 12 May 1994 Ingrams granted to Mr and Mrs Beer a lease of the premises (the Beer lease) for a term of 16 years from 25 March 1994 at an annual rent, subject to review, of £14,000.
5. Mr and Mrs Beer were soon in financial difficulties. They paid a number of instalments of the purchase price to Mrs Bland and drew three postdated cheques in favour of her solicitors in the aggregate amount of £24,000 which were dishonoured on presentation. On 30 November 1995 Mrs Bland obtained summary judgment against them in the Queen's Bench Division for £24,000 together with interest of £354·83 and costs. On the same day the master made a charging order nisi against Mr and Mrs Beer's interests in four different properties, one of which was the premises. So far as material, the order provided:

'IT IS ORDERED … that unless sufficient cause to the contrary be shown … on the 20th day of December 1995 … the Defendants interests in the said assets shall, and IT IS ORDERED THAT in the meantime do, stand charged with the payment of £24,354·83p and costs to be taxed due on the said judgment and interest thereon at the statutory rate together with the costs of this application.'

6. It is clear that the effect of the order nisi was to create a defeasible charge on the legal estate in the Beer lease, as well as on Mr and Mrs Beer's beneficial

a interests therein (cf *Clark v Chief Land Registrar, Chancery plc v Ketteringham* [1994] 4 All ER 96 at 102–103, [1994] Ch 370 at 380–381). On 20 December 1995 the master made an order absolute in the case of Mrs Beer only and directed that as against Mr Beer the hearing be adjourned. That order provided that 'the interests of the Second Defendant Caroline Beer in the assets specified in the Schedule hereto stand charged with the payment of £24,354·83 etc'. On 10 January 1996

b the master made an order against Mr Beer in similar terms.

7. There was some debate in argument as to the effect of the two orders absolute in regard to the legal estate in the Beer lease. It is clear, and it was not disputed, that they rendered absolute and indefeasible the charges on the respective beneficial interests of Mr and Mrs Beer. But it was argued that they had in some way brought to an end the defeasible charge on the legal estate. I am

c unable to see how they could have had that effect. What the order nisi said was that unless sufficient cause to the contrary was shown on 20 December 1995 (or, by implication, at any adjourned hearing) Mr and Mrs Beers' interests in the specified assets should, and in the meantime did, stand charged with payment. A literal reading of those words might suggest that, since sufficient cause to the

d contrary was not shown either on 20 December 1995 or on 10 January 1996, the charge on the legal estate became absolute and indefeasible on the latter date. However, since no order absolute was made against Mr and Mrs Beer jointly, it seems unlikely that that could be a correct view of the position. But that is not an end of the point. In my view it is difficult, indeed impossible, to see how the defeasible charge on the legal estate could have been brought to an end. In my

e view that charge continued. By virtue of s 3(4) of the Charging Orders Act 1979 it has the like effect and is enforceable in the same courts and in the same manner as an equitable charge created by the debtor by writing under his hand. I therefore proceed on the footing that Mrs Bland was at all material times an equitable chargee of the legal estate in the Beer lease.

f 8. On 9 February 1996 Mrs Bland obtained a further summary judgment against Mr and Mrs Beer in the Queen's Bench Division, this time for £72,500, together with interest of £360·55 and costs. Shortly afterwards a bankruptcy order was made against Mr Beer. On 4 March 1996 the master made a charging order absolute against Mrs Beer in respect of the judgment for £72,860·55. All three orders absolute were registered at the Land Charges Registry pursuant to the provisions of the

g Land Charges Act 1972.

9. Mr and Mrs Beer were in debt not only to Mrs Bland. By the end of February 1996 there were arrears of rent owing to Ingrams under the Beer lease of between £11,000 and £12,000. There were discussions between Ingrams' solicitors and Mr and Mrs Beer's solicitors about a replacement tenant to be

h found by the Beers, the transaction to be carried out either by a surrender or by forfeiture by peaceable re-entry, followed in either case by the grant of a new lease to the new tenant. By the end of the first week of March Ingrams' solicitors were in correspondence with solicitors acting for Fogir Uddin and his wife, Ripon Chowdhery Fogir, as to the terms of a new lease.

j 10. On 29 April 1996 Ingrams granted to Mr and Mrs Uddin a lease of the premises (the Uddin lease) for a term of 24 years from 25 March 1996 at a premium of £12,000 and an annual rent, subject to review, of £14,000. On the view I take of the case and by reason of a concession made by Mr Althaus on behalf of Mr and Mrs Uddin, it is unnecessary to examine in any great depth the circumstances in which the Uddin lease came to be granted. It is enough to record, first, that, at a time while the Beer lease was still subsisting, Ingrams

received actual notice that Mrs Bland had a charging order over it; secondly, that
the Beer lease was forfeited by peaceable re-entry on Friday 26 April; thirdly, that *a*
on Monday 29 April at 12·41 pm Ingrams' solicitors received a faxed letter from
Mr and Mrs Beer's solicitors stating that they would be applying for relief against
the forfeiture of the Beer lease (that information was not passed on to Mr and
Mrs Uddin); fourthly, that it was not until 1·38 pm on that day, nearly an hour
later, that the Uddin lease was granted; fifthly, that, before it was granted, Mr and *b*
Mrs Uddin had actual notice that the Beer lease had been forfeited. It was the fifth
of these points that was conceded by Mr Althaus, without doubt correctly on the
facts. It necessarily follows that, before the Uddin lease was granted, Mr and
Mrs Uddin had constructive notice of Mr and Mrs Beer's right to claim relief
against the forfeiture of the Beer lease.

11. Mr and Mrs Beer did not, as their solicitors had intimated they would, *c*
apply for relief against the forfeiture of the Beer lease. Instead, on or about
15 May 1996, they commenced an action in the High Wycombe County Court
(the chattels action) against Mr Uddin, claiming ownership of the fixtures and
fittings in the premises, the return thereof and damages. I will return to that
action, in which there is a subsidiary question for our decision, in due course. *d*
Our main concern is with a second action (the forfeiture action), which was
brought by Mrs Bland against Ingrams and Mr and Mrs Uddin, also in the High
Wycombe County Court, on 26 August 1996. In it she claimed relief against the
forfeiture of the Beer lease. Ultimately, both actions were tried together in the
Chancery Division.

e

The forfeiture action

12. The forfeiture action first came before Judge Hull QC at Epsom. In his
judgment delivered on 17 September 1998, the judge recorded that Mrs Bland,
relying on her equitable charge of the Beer lease in order to give her the necessary
locus standi, claimed relief against its forfeiture under s 146(4) of the Law of *f*
Property Act 1925 and, further or alternatively, s 139 of the County Courts Act
1984. He held that he had no jurisdiction to grant relief under either of those
provisions. However, recognising that the High Court, unlike the county court,
has power to grant relief under the inherent jurisdiction, he did not dismiss the
action but transferred it to the Chancery Division pursuant to s 44(2) of the 1984
Act. *g*

13. The forfeiture action came on again in March 1999 before Mr Peter
Leaver QC, sitting as a deputy judge of the Chancery Division. He gave
Mrs Bland leave to re-re-amend her statement of claim in order to rely on the
inherent jurisdiction of the court. In a reserved judgment delivered on 13 April
1999 ([1999] 2 EGLR 49), the judge rejected Mrs Bland's claim for relief and *h*
dismissed the action. He refused an application by her for permission to appeal
to this court. On 30 July 1999 permission was granted by myself on
consideration of the documents.

14. One point can be disposed of straightaway. In the court below, Mr Denman,
for Mrs Bland, sought to contend that it was open to her to claim relief not only *j*
under the inherent jurisdiction but also under s 146(4) of the 1925 Act. The
learned deputy judge ruled, correctly, that it was not open to her to rely on that
provision and that, in the absence of any appeal against it, the judgment of Judge
Hull was decisive on that question. Mr Leaver based his ruling on estoppel by
record, but I think it would be more accurate to say that, within and for the
purposes of the forfeiture action, it had already been disposed of at first instance.

a   Mr Denman sought to reopen it before us. Since it is a question of pure law, we could, had there been anything in it, have given Mrs Bland leave to appeal against Judge Hull's decision out of time. But it is plain that the question is unarguable. Section 146(4), as both Judge Hull and Mr Leaver observed, only allows an application for relief to be made by 'any person claiming as under-lessee'. Whatever else may or may not be said about the interest or status of an equitable
b   chargee of a lease (see below), it cannot be said that he claims as an underlessee.

15. In the circumstances, relief against the forfeiture of the Beer lease can only be granted to Mrs Bland, if at all, under the inherent jurisdiction of the court. In the court below and in the early stages of the argument in this court her case proceeded on the footing that, where the tenant himself does not seek relief, an equitable chargee of a lease has a direct right to claim relief against its forfeiture.
c   However, as a result of exchanges between the court and Mr Denman, and while the claim for direct relief was not abandoned, Mrs Bland's case came to be based primarily on the proposition that the equitable chargee can claim relief in the shoes of the tenant.

d   *The claim for direct relief*

16. The convenient course is to start with the claim for direct relief. Recently, such a claim was successful in *Croydon (Unique) Ltd v Wright (Crombie intervening)* [1999] 4 All ER 257, [2001] Ch 318, where it was held by a majority of this court that an equitable chargee of a lease, being 'a person with an interest under a lease of the land derived (whether immediately or otherwise) from the lessee's interest
e   therein' within s 138(9C) of the 1984 Act, was entitled to apply to the court for relief against forfeiture under s 138(9A). That decision, having been based on the particular wording of s 138(9C), is not an authority on the inherent jurisdiction. However, each member of the court referred to, and the majority to an extent relied on, *Ladup Ltd v Williams & Glyn's Bank plc* [1985] 2 All ER 577, [1985] 1 WLR
f   851, a decision under the inherent jurisdiction, on which Mr Denman has also relied and to which I will return presently.

17. It is necessary to start by defining the attributes of an equitable charge. In *Carreras Rothmans Ltd v Freeman Mathews Treasure Ltd (in liq)* [1985] 1 All ER 155 at 169, [1985] Ch 207 at 227, Peter Gibson J said:

g   'Such a charge is created by an appropriation of specific property to the discharge of some debt or other obligation without there being any change in ownership either at law or in equity, and it confers on the chargee rights to apply to the court for an order for sale or for the appointment of a receiver, but no right to foreclosure (so as to make the property his own) or [to] take
h   possession.'

18. In *Re Cosslett (Contractors) Ltd* [1997] 4 All ER 115 at 126, [1998] Ch 495 at 508, Millett LJ, in distinguishing between a mortgage and an equitable charge, said: 'The difference between them is that a mortgage involves a transfer of legal or equitable ownership to the creditor, whereas an equitable charge does not.'

j   19. As applied to land, those observations emphasise, correctly in my judgment, that the creation of an equitable charge, unlike an equitable mortgage, does not give the chargee an equitable interest in the land. A fortiori it gives him no right to possession. Nevertheless, his right to protect or realise his security by applying to the court for the appointment of a receiver or an order for sale does give him an interest of a sort. This has been variously described in the authorities, most frequently, it appears, as a proprietary interest. In so far as the appointment of a

receiver or an order for sale enables the chargee to appropriate, in the first case
the rents and profits of the land and in the second its proceeds of sale, to the
discharge of his debt, I do not quarrel with that description. But it is important
to bear in mind that the interest, though registrable against the chargor, remains
inchoate and ineffectual until an order of the court is made.

20. Such being the attributes of an equitable charge, can the chargee of a lease
which has been forfeited for non-payment of rent, where the tenant himself does
not seek relief, claim relief against the forfeiture? If the question could be
considered simply as between the chargee and the tenant, everything would
point to its being answered in the affirmative. After all, by asking the court to
reinstate his security he seeks relief preliminary to, and of the same character as,
an order for the appointment of a receiver or sale. Clearly, however, the question
is not as simple as that. The grant of relief necessarily creates a relationship,
which did not exist before, between the chargee and the landlord. While the case
of a sub-tenant demonstrates that that in itself is not necessarily an objection, the
position of someone who has never had a legal estate or equitable interest in the
land is clearly distinguishable.

21. The inherent jurisdiction of the court was developed by the old Court of
Chancery, whose practice and the effect of whose decrees are described by
Wigram V-C in *Bowser v Colby* (1841) 1 Hare 109 at 126, 130, [1835–42] All ER Rep
478 at 484, 485–486 and by Cozens-Hardy MR and Farwell LJ in *Dendy v Evans*
[1910] 1 KB 263 at 266–267, 270, [1908–10] All ER Rep 589 at 590–591, 592–593.
In *Shiloh Spinners Ltd v Harding* [1973] 1 All ER 90 at 104, [1973] AC 691 at 726,
Lord Simon of Glaisdale spoke thus of the jurisdiction:

'The last 100 years have seen many examples of relaxation of the stance of
regarding contractual rights and obligations as sacrosanct and exclusive of
other considerations: although these examples do not compel equity to
follow—certainly not to the extent of overturning established authorities—
they do at least invite a more liberal and extensively based attitude on the
part of courts which are not bound by those authorities. I would therefore
myself hold that equity has an unlimited and unfettered jurisdiction to
relieve against contractual forfeitures and penalties. What have sometimes
been regarded as fetters to the jurisdiction are, in my view, more properly to
be seen as considerations which the court will weigh in deciding how to
exercise an unfettered jurisdiction.'

22. That broad view was not shared by Lord Wilberforce, with whose speech
Viscount Dilhorne, Lord Pearson and Lord Kilbrandon agreed. Further, the
tendency of subsequent authorities relied on by Mr Fancourt, for Ingrams,
(though none of them was concerned with land) has been against the broader
view (see *Scandinavian Trading Tanker Co AB v Flota Petrolera Ecuatoriana, The
Scaptrade* [1983] 2 All ER 763, [1983] 2 AC 694, *Sport International Bussum BV v
Inter-Footwear Ltd* [1984] 2 All ER 321, [1984] 1 WLR 776 and *BICC plc v Burndy
Corp* [1985] 1 All ER 417, [1985] Ch 232).

23. The only authority cited which is directly in point is *Ladup Ltd v Williams &
Glyn's Bank plc* [1985] 2 All ER 577, [1985] 1 WLR 851, whose facts were very like
those of the present case. The plaintiff (Ladup) obtained a charging order
absolute over a lease of a flat in Westminster. Subsequently, the landlord, having
obtained judgment for forfeiture of the lease for non-payment of rent, recovered
possession of the flat. Shortly afterwards Ladup issued an originating summons
in the Chancery Division claiming relief against the forfeiture under both statute

a and the inherent jurisdiction of the court. The landlord applied for an order that the summons be struck out as disclosing no reasonable cause of action or as an abuse of the process of the court. The landlord's application was dismissed.

24. At the hearing it was conceded on behalf of Ladup that the claim for relief could only be made, if it could be made at all, under the inherent jurisdiction of the court. The essential contention of counsel for the landlord (Miss Hazel

b Williamson) was that the originating summons was misconceived because an equitable chargee was not within the category of persons who could claim, as against the landlord, relief against forfeiture for non-payment of rent. She did not take any point based on Ladup's omission to join the tenant as a party or to explain his absence; as to these three matters see [1985] 2 All ER 577 at 579, [1985] 1 WLR 851 at 854.

c 25. In a reserved judgment, Warner J, having started by considering s 3(4) of the 1979 Act and the attributes of an equitable charge, referred to s 90 of the Law of Property Act 1925, whose effect, so far as material, is to enable the court to create and vest in an equitable chargee a legal term of years absolute, so as to enable him to carry out a sale as if the charge had been created by deed by way of

d legal mortgage. He then proceeded to consider the arguments of counsel for the landlord in relation to the inherent jurisdiction. Having done that, he said ([1985] 2 All ER 577 at 583, [1985] 1 WLR 851 at 859) that he did not find that the statutory provisions relied on or the cases cited by counsel pointed to any clear conclusion on the question whether an equitable chargee of a lease was a person in whose favour the court might, in the exercise of its inherent equitable jurisdiction, grant

e relief against forfeiture for non-payment of rent. He accordingly had to approach that question as one of principle.

26. Warner J then turned to the arguments of counsel for Ladup, who relied primarily on Lord Simon's dictum in the *Shiloh Spinners* case. Having referred to Lord Wilberforce's narrower view, the judge said that it was in his speech that

f guidance must be looked for. He summarised the crucial points in it by saying that there was not and never had been any fetter on the jurisdiction of courts of equity to relieve against forfeiture where the object of the insertion of the right to forfeit was essentially to secure the payment of money, as in the case of the right to forfeit a lease for non-payment of rent. However, as counsel for the landlord had pointed out, Lord Wilberforce did not deal with the question in

g whose favour the equitable jurisdiction might be exercised, being a question which remained free from authority.

27. The judge summarised the submission made by counsel for the landlord:

h '[Miss Williamson], for her part, submits that relief against forfeiture imports that someone should remain in, or assume, possession of the demised property in right of the lease, who will be, in consequence, under a continuing liability to the landlord for the rent and for compliance with the other covenants in the lease, and that that someone cannot be a person such as an equitable chargee who is not entitled to possession.' (See [1985] 2 All ER

j 577 at 584, [1985] 1 WLR 851 at 860.)

28. Though he felt the force of that submission, the judge thought that the submission made on behalf of Ladup had greater force. He said:

'It may be that because of difficulties of the kind suggested by [Miss Williamson], there will be cases where the court will be unable to exercise its jurisdiction to grant relief to an equitable chargee where it would have been able to grant relief to an applicant with a right to possession. I do not think, *a* however, that such possible difficulties constitute a compelling reason for holding that the court has no jurisdiction at all to entertain an application for relief made by an equitable chargee. It seems to me that the fact that the court has power, at the suit of an equitable chargee, to order the sale of the property subject to his charge, coupled with the fact that, in the case of land, it has the powers conferred by s 90 of the Law of Property Act 1925, should *b* enable the difficulties in question to be overcome in most or at least many cases. At all events, I am certainly not persuaded that it is plain and obvious that as a matter of law this court has no jurisdiction to entertain Ladup's application. I therefore propose to dismiss the motion to strike it out.' (See [1985] 2 All ER 577 at 584, [1985] 1 WLR 851 at 860–861.)

c

29. It would be quite wrong to discount the value of Warner J's view of this question simply because it was expressed in the context of an application to strike out. Clearly, it was the product of a careful process of reasoning. Moreover, the judge had to examine the application of an equitable jurisdiction to a species of security which, as he pointed out, it is probable was comparatively rare at the time *d* that the jurisdiction was first assumed (see [1985] 2 All ER 577 at 581, [1985] 1 WLR 851 at 857). There being no authority to the contrary, it was not unnatural that he should feel that the jurisdiction ought to extend to the case of an equitable charge; see also the observation of Butler-Sloss LJ in *Croydon (Unique) Ltd v Wright (Crombie intervening)* [1999] 4 All ER 257 at 273, [2001] Ch 318 at 336:

e

'It seems to me astonishing that the holder of a charging order over a lease is said to be unable to be heard in forfeiture proceedings and powerless to obtain any relief or protection of the asset, which is the object of the charging order.'

f

30. It has not been suggested that the case against the grant of relief to an equitable chargee can be put higher or better than it was put by Miss Williamson in the *Ladup* case. The culmination of her submission was that relief cannot be granted to someone who is not entitled to possession. If we were exercising a truly discretionary jurisdiction, I would see no great magic in that requirement. I would think that the more important requirement was that identified earlier in *g* the submission, namely that someone should remain in, or assume possession of, the demised property in right of the lease, who will in consequence be under a continuing liability to the landlord for the rent and for compliance with the other covenants in the lease. And I would see no reason why an equitable chargee should be incapable of assuming that role simply because he was not entitled to *h* possession.

31. While I sympathise with the feelings of Warner J and Butler-Sloss LJ, I do not think it is open to us to give them effect. A jurisdiction does not become discretionary just because it is both inherent and equitable. The authorities show that the cases in which the inherent jurisdiction to grant relief against forfeiture *j* for non-payment of rent has been exercised have been restricted to those in which the person claiming relief is entitled to possession of the land or at any rate, which is not necessarily the same thing, has a legal estate or equitable interest in it. Now that so much of the jurisdiction has been overtaken by statute, any legitimate basis for its extension has disappeared. Admittedly and notoriously, there are gaps and anomalies in the statutory framework. But it is not for the courts to fill

a the gaps and cure the anomalies in purported reliance on a jurisdiction which has never existed. In the circumstances, I would reject the claim for direct relief.

The claim for indirect relief

32. I turn to the claim for relief in the shoes of the tenant. The basis of this claim is an implied obligation on the chargor under an equitable charge to take
b reasonable steps to preserve the chargee's security. Mr Fancourt and Mr Althaus suggested that no such obligation exists. In support of that suggestion Mr Fancourt referred us to *King v Smith* (1843) 2 Hare 239, in which Wigram V-C held that the court would not, on the application of a mortgagee out of possession, restrain the mortgagor from felling timber growing on the mortgaged property, unless the security was insufficient. However, Mr Fancourt recognised that that
c was really a decision on voluntary waste, a doctrine far removed, both in time and space, from the obligations which ought to be implied in an equitable charge deemed by statute to have been created by a debtor by writing under his hand in 1979 or later. If the law did not imply an obligation on the chargor to take reasonable steps to preserve the security, my astonishment would be at least as
d great as Butler-Sloss LJ's. No other relevant authority having been cited, I hold that it does. Moreover, where the security is a lease which has been forfeited for non-payment of rent, reasonable steps must, as a general rule, include initiating and pursuing an application for relief against the forfeiture. Only in that way can the security be preserved from annihilation.

e 33. In an attempt to defeat that seemingly self-evident proposition, Mr Althaus directed our attention to cases where the preservation of the security would involve the taking of steps other than the payment of money, for example the carrying out of repairs to the demised premises. I say nothing at all about such cases, nor about what steps might or might not be regarded as reasonable in relation thereto. I confine myself to cases of forfeiture for non-payment of rent.

f 34. On this footing, the position as between an equitable chargee of a lease which has been forfeited for non-payment of rent and a tenant who does not himself seek relief is analogous to the position as between a beneficiary under a trust and a trustee who fails or neglects, in the performance of a duty owed by him to the beneficiary, to protect the trust estate or the interests of the beneficiary
g therein; see the judgment of the Privy Council delivered by Lord Templeman in *Hayim v Citibank NA* [1987] AC 730, [1987] 3 WLR 83, in which the previous authorities are reviewed. In such a case the beneficiary may join the trustee as a defendant to the action and sue in right of the trust and in the shoes of the trustee. I can see no distinction in principle between a case where the obligation arises under the law of trusts and one where it arises in contract. So here Mrs Bland
h may join Mr and Mrs Beer as defendants to the forfeiture action and claim relief in their shoes.

35. I would therefore hold that Mrs Bland's claim for indirect relief is one which the court can entertain. The present position in regard to Mr and Mrs Beer appears from a passage in the judgment of Mr Leaver:

j
'During the course of the trial, an issue arose as to whether the proceedings were properly constituted in the absence of Mr and Mrs Beer. I indicated that, in my judgment, it would be necessary to have the Beers as parties to the action: alternatively, as Nicholls J suggested in *Abbey National Building Society v Maybeech Ltd* ([1984] 3 All ER 262, [1985] Ch 190), the Beers should be notified of the proceedings and should consent to the court granting relief

against forfeiture, if the court so ordered. This they did, on Mrs Bland's
undertaking to assume their responsibilities under the Beer lease, if it were   *a*
revived. In addition, Mr Beer's trustee in bankruptcy stated that he would
disclaim the Beer lease if relief were granted to Mrs Bland. On that basis,
I allowed the proceedings to continue as constituted before me.' (See [1999]
2 EGLR 49 at 50.)

36. From that it is clear that Mr and Mrs Beer's consent to the court granting   *b*
relief against forfeiture, if the court so ordered, was on the basis of the direct
claim. If this court should decide that relief ought to be granted on the basis of
the indirect claim, then a further approach will have to be made to Mr and
Mrs Beer (and the trustee in bankruptcy) and they will in any event have to be
made parties to the order for relief.   *c*

Relief—discretion

37. In the court below Mr Leaver, having rejected Mrs Bland's entitlement to
claim direct relief, nevertheless, in case he was wrong in that conclusion, went on
to ask himself (at 51–52) whether she ought, as a matter of discretion, to be granted   *d*
relief. He answered that question in the negative. However, his examination of it
was necessarily in the context of the claim for direct relief. To the claim for indirect
relief, which was not advanced before him, different considerations apply. The
question of discretion must therefore be examined afresh.

38. Because the claim for indirect relief emerged only during Mr Denman's   *e*
opening of the appeal, counsel were not in a position, as it appeared to me, fully
to argue the question of discretion in relation thereto. They must be given a
further opportunity to do so after consideration of our judgments. However,
three points are in my view clear. First, as all counsel accepted, if relief is granted,
the Uddin lease will take effect as a demise of the premises subject to the Beer
lease, with the consequence that, as from 29 April 1996, the rent reserved by the   *f*
Beer lease will be payable to Mr and Mrs Uddin and not to Ingrams. Secondly,
since Mr and Mrs Uddin had constructive notice, before the Uddin lease was
granted, of Mr and Mrs Beer's right to claim relief against the forfeiture of the
Beer lease, they are in no better a position to resist the claim for indirect relief
than Ingrams itself. Thirdly, the claim for indirect relief ought in principle to   *g*
succeed, on terms that Mrs Bland makes payment to Ingrams and Mr and
Mrs Uddin respectively of all arrears of rent payable under the Beer lease and
costs.

39. As to the third of the above points, it was suggested in argument that the
court ought to adopt a broad approach to the question of discretion, taking into   *h*
account the conduct of the parties. I reject that suggestion. The correct approach
appears from the following passage in the judgment of Jenkins LJ in *Gill v Lewis*
[1956] 1 All ER 844 at 852, [1956] 2 QB 1 at 13:

'... as the conclusion of the whole matter, the function of the court in
exercising this equitable jurisdiction is, save in exceptional circumstances, to   *j*
grant relief when all that is due for rent and costs has been paid, and (in
general) to disregard any other causes of complaint that the landlord may
have against the tenant. The question is whether, provided all is paid up, the
landlord will not have been fully compensated; and the view taken by the
court is that if he gets the whole of his rent and costs, then he has got all he

a   is entitled to so far as rent is concerned, and extraneous matters of breach of covenant are, generally speaking, irrelevant.'

40. Mr Fancourt and Mr Althaus nevertheless argued that Mrs Bland ought to be denied relief on a number of grounds, including her omission to commence the forfeiture action until nearly four months after the forfeiture, her failure to join Mr and Mrs Beer or to notify them of it until she was required to do so at the
b   trial in March 1999 and her failure to advance the claim for indirect relief until the hearing in this court. Mr Althaus added that Mr and Mrs Uddin had been prejudiced by Mrs Bland's not having taken those steps when she ought to have done. I do not think that there is anything of substance in any of these points. The important considerations are, first, that in a letter of 8 May 1996 Mrs Bland's
c   solicitors informed Mr and Mrs Uddin's solicitors of her charging order and that her right to enforce it against the premises was reserved and, secondly, that by the end of August 1996 Mr and Mrs Uddin knew that Mrs Bland was seeking relief against the forfeiture of the Beer lease. The capacity in which she did so and the constitution of the forfeiture action were matters of form rather than of substance.

41. Two further points must be made in regard to Mrs Bland's entitlement to
d   relief in principle. First, in a witness statement signed shortly after the hearing before Judge Hull in 1998 Mrs Bland's son, Mr Errol Bland, who described himself as a director and part-owner of an electrical installation company, confirmed that, if she was required to pay the arrears of rent under the Beer lease as a condition of obtaining relief, then he was able and willing to provide her with
e   the necessary sum for that purpose. In that connection he stated his understanding to be that the arrears of rent at the time of the forfeiture were in the region of £15,000. (We were told that the exact figure was £15,217·16.) It was suggested that that evidence came too late and, further, that, since the arrears and costs would now considerably exceed £15,000, it was inadequate for the purpose of showing that Mrs Bland would be able to put up the sum necessary to obtain
f   relief. However, while that eventuality may prevent her from obtaining relief, it is not a reason for holding that she is not entitled to it in principle.

42. Secondly, it was said that Mrs Bland had not established that the Beer lease, if revived, would have any premium value in the open market. That point was considered by Mr Leaver, who said:

g   'Furthermore, there is no evidence that I can accept that Mrs Bland would obtain any substantial value for the lease if she were to be granted relief and then immediately sell it.' (See [1999] 2 EGLR 49 at 52.)

43. The judge referred to valuation evidence put in on behalf of Mrs Bland,
h   which he described as confused and confusing. However, it is not in general necessary for someone claiming relief against forfeiture to establish that the lease, if revived, would be a valuable asset. Except where the evidence establishes that the claim is frivolous or vexatious, the court should entertain it. It cannot be said, on the evidence that was before the judge, that Mrs Bland's claim is either frivolous or vexatious.

j   44. Having held that Mrs Bland is entitled to relief in principle, I refer to the particular feature of this case which may make it inappropriate for it to be granted simply on terms that she makes payment to Ingrams and Mr and Mrs Uddin respectively of all arrears of rent payable under the Beer lease and costs. That feature consists in the cross-claims between the parties, actual or potential, to which a revival of the Beer lease will give rise. Though some of them were

discussed in argument, they were not enumerated nor were their implications
fully addressed. Mr Fancourt's position was that it would be either impossible or   *a*
impracticable to dispose of all the cross-claims in these proceedings. That may
prove to be the case. But the first step should be for the parties to identify the
cross-claims they wish to make, so that the position can be considered after
judgment and directions given for any further hearing that may be necessary. We
will also consider the further approach which must now be made to Mr and   *b*
Mrs Beer and Mr Beer's trustee in bankruptcy.

The chattels action

45. The progress of the chattels action up to the beginning of September 1996
(when the fixtures and fittings were removed from the premises by Mrs Bland) is
described in Mr Leaver's judgment (at 52–53) under the heading 'Claim on the   *c*
cross-undertaking'. It need not be repeated. The central event for present
purposes was Mrs Bland's giving of the usual cross-undertaking in damages in
favour of Mr Uddin on the 'renewal', on 18 June 1996, of the injunction which
had been granted against him, at the suit of Mr and Mrs Beer, on 16 May 1996.
The injunction restrained Mr Uddin from dismantling or taking away the fixtures   *d*
and fittings at the premises or 'from damaging and/or otherwise using the
fixtures and fittings generally or as part of his own business'. Mrs Bland's
cross-undertaking was 'to be responsible for any loss or damage which [Mr Uddin]
might suffer by reason of the injunction in the event that it should not have been
granted'.

46. In the court below Mr Uddin claimed both that the injunction should not   *e*
have been granted and, because it had prevented him from trading from the
premises until 23 September 1996, that he had suffered loss and damage by reason
of it. Mr Leaver did not think that it would be right for him to act as an appellate
court in respect of the injunction and therefore proceeded on the basis that it was
rightly granted (see 53). Although it made no difference in the result, it was not   *f*
correct to say that the judge was being asked to act as an appellate court. He was
the trial judge who was being asked, once the facts had been found, to decide
whether an injunction granted at an interlocutory stage, when the facts had not
been found, had or had not been rightly granted. However, the judge went on to
consider the merits of Mr Uddin's claim and concluded that the loss and damage
alleged was not such as should fairly and reasonably be regarded as having been   *g*
in the contemplation of the parties at the time that the undertaking was given;
still less was it something that was in the actual contemplation of the parties
(see 53). He therefore dismissed it.

47. In response to Mr Uddin's appeal against the dismissal of his claim,
Mr Denman has adopted the judge's view as Mrs Bland's second line of defence.   *h*
Her primary defence is that it was not the injunction which prevented Mr Uddin
from trading, but his taking possession of premises containing fixtures and fittings
which did not belong to him. Mr Denman submitted that the 14-odd weeks
needed to sort out the chattels between 18 June and 23 September 1996 were the
consequence of Mr Uddin's own actions, not of the injunction.   *j*

48. Since I am satisfied, on one ground or another, that Mr Leaver's decision
to dismiss Mr Uddin's claim on the cross-undertaking ought to be affirmed,
I propose to deal with the matter relatively briefly. I agree with the judge that the
first question to be determined is whether the injunction granted to Mrs Bland on
18 June 1996 was or was not rightly granted. In this respect Mr Denman pointed
to Mr Uddin's application to discharge it, on which, on 2 July 1996, no order was

a   made, save that Mr Uddin was ordered to pay the costs of Mr and Mrs Beer and Mrs Bland (see 53). However, that was simply a further interlocutory application, on which the rights of the parties could not be finally determined. The crucial event was an order made in interpleader proceedings between Mrs Bland and Mr and Mrs Beer on 28 April 1998, by which it was determined that Mrs Bland was the owner of the fixtures and fittings. Thus it was established that the injunction had been rightly granted to her on 18 June 1996.

b   49. Mr Althaus contested that proposition, primarily on the ground that Mr and Mrs Uddin had not been parties to the interpleader proceedings. To that I would answer that, since they did not themselves claim ownership, that was hardly surprising. However, since the question whether the injunction was or was not rightly granted was not fully argued, it would not be right to base the

c   decision on the view expressed in the preceding paragraph. It can be based either on the judge's view that the loss and damage claimed by Mr Uddin was too remote or on Mr Denman's primary submission that the claim fails on causation. My own preference is for the latter of these. It was not satisfactorily established on the evidence that, if the injunction had not been granted, Mr Uddin would have

d   succeeded in sorting out his self-induced problems over the chattels in such a way as to enable him to start trading from the premises before 23 September 1996.

Conclusion

  50. I would allow Mrs Bland's appeal in the forfeiture action and adjourn further consideration of the terms on which relief ought to be granted to her.

e   I would dismiss Mr Uddin's appeal in the chattels action.

CHADWICK LJ.

The appeal against the refusal to grant relief from forfeiture

f   53. Section 3(4) of the Charging Orders Act 1979 provides that a charge imposed by a charging order—

> 'shall have the like effect and shall be enforceable in the same courts and in the same manner as an equitable charge created by the debtor by writing under his hand.'

g

That is the effect that must be given to the charging order made on 30 November 1995 in the proceedings brought by Mrs Bland against Mr and Mrs Beer. The order imposed a charge over the leasehold interest of Mr and Mrs Beer in the property known as 54/56 The Parade, Bourne End. It is immaterial that that order was an

h   order nisi; so that the charge which it imposed was defeasible. Nothing has occurred which can have had the effect of defeating the charge.

  54. Mr and Mrs Beer held the property under a lease granted on 12 May 1994 by Ingram's Estates Ltd (Ingram's Estates) for a term of 16 years from 25 March 1994. The lease contained the usual proviso for re-entry in the event of

j   non-payment of rent. On 26 April 1996 the amount unpaid in respect of rent due under the lease was £15,217. It is not in dispute that the landlord was entitled to, and did, forfeit the lease by peaceable re-entry on that day.

  55. The power to re-enter and forfeit a lease for non-payment of rent has long been regarded in equity as a security for the rent: see *Howard v Fanshawe* [1895] 2 Ch 581 at 588, [1895–9] All ER Rep 855 at 859 and *Newbolt v Bingham* (1895) 72 LT 852 at 854. In the latter case Rigby LJ referred to 'the settled practice of a

court of equity to grant relief against forfeiture for nonpayment of rent on payment of all rent in arrear and costs'. He went on:

'Of course, the court was not absolutely bound by its practice where it would not do justice, and if some new interest had been created before the application, the court would refuse to interfere. That was not done to put the landlord in a better position, but because the rights of third parties had intervened.'

56. In the present case, in the circumstances to which Nourse LJ has referred, it is accepted that—notwithstanding the grant of a new lease on 29 April 1996 to Mr Fogir Uddin and his wife—there was no reason why the court should depart from its settled practice and refuse to grant relief from forfeiture on an application by Mr and Mrs Beer. In particular, it was accepted (i) that there would be no inequity in the grant of relief from forfeiture against the landlord, Ingram's Estates, because the landlord's solicitors knew, before the grant of the new lease on 29 April 1996, that Mr and Mrs Beer intended to apply for that relief, and (ii) that there would be no inequity in an order which had the effect that the new lease granted to Mr and Mrs Uddin was made subject to the (revived) 1994 lease, because, at the time of the grant of the new lease on 29 April 1996, Mr and Mrs Uddin had constructive notice of Mr and Mrs Beer's right to seek such relief (see s 199(1)(ii)(b) of the Law of Property Act 1925).

57. The issue in the present case arises because the application for relief from forfeiture is made, not by Mr and Mrs Beer, as tenants (or former tenants) under the 1994 lease, but by Mrs Bland, as a person having an equitable charge over that lease. In *Croydon (Unique) Ltd v Wright (Crombie intervening)* [1999] 4 All ER 257 at 273, [2001] Ch 318 at 336 Butler-Sloss LJ observed that it seemed—

'astonishing that the holder of a charging order over a lease is said to be unable to be heard in forfeiture proceedings and powerless to obtain any relief or protection of the asset, which is the object of the charging order.'

I agree. I agree, also, with the view expressed by Sir Christopher Staughton on that appeal ([1999] 4 All ER 257 at 267, [2001] Ch 318 at 330) that it would usually 'be manifestly unjust to deprive the holder of a charging order … of any right to apply for relief from forfeiture'. But that is, of course, subject to the proviso that relief, if granted, will be granted upon terms which restores the landlord to the position that he would have been in if the breach which gave rise to the right of re-entry had not occurred.

58. In the *Croydon (Unique) Ltd* case the issue arose in circumstances in which the landlord had obtained an order for possession against the tenant in the county court. The creditors, having a charging order on the tenant's interest in the lease, sought to intervene in those proceedings and obtain relief from forfeiture. The question before the court was whether the creditors were persons 'with an interest under [the] lease of the land derived (whether immediately or otherwise) from the lessee's interest therein' so as to enable them to make application under s 138(9C) of the County Courts Act 1984 (as amended by the Administration of Justice Act 1985). The county court judge (who was, by coincidence, Judge Hull QC) held that they were not. This court (Butler-Sloss LJ and Sir Christopher Staughton, Pill LJ dissenting) held that they were. That led to consideration of the relief that could be granted under s 138(9C) of the 1984 Act.

59. Section 138(9C) of the 1984 Act empowered the court to make an order which—

a
'vests the land in [the applicant], as lessee of the lessor, for the remainder of the term of the lease under which he has any such interest as aforesaid, or for any lesser term.'

The grant of a new lease to an applicant under s 138(9C) was in contrast to the position where the lessee had applied under s 138(9A). In the latter case, if relief

b were granted, the lessee was to hold the land 'according to the lease [meaning the lease which had been forfeited] without any new lease' (see s 138(9B)). Sir Christopher Staughton asked himself ([1999] 4 All ER 257 at 267, [2001] Ch 318 at 329) whether the only remedy available to the holder of a charging order (assuming that his case fell within s 138(9C)) was to acquire a lease which he never had before, and to impose on the landlord a new tenant. In answer to that

c question he said this:

'First, I do not think that an applicant under sub-s (9C) is confined to the relief mentioned under that section. Subsection (9C) begins: "An application under subsection (9A) may be made by a person." If so made, it is still an application under sub-s (9A); and the words "on any such application" in

d sub-s (9A) consequently apply. Nor do I think that relief under sub-ss (9A) or (9C) is confined by sub-s (9B). Accordingly it seems to me that, on an application by the holder of a charging order, the court could if it thought fit *restore the original lease* for the purpose merely of enabling the applicant to apply for an order for sale, and on condition that he do so. The second

e answer amounts, in practice, to much the same thing. One should not be shocked if the effect of sub-s (9C) is that the holder of a charging order can obtain a lease, which he never had before, and can thrust upon the landlord himself as a new tenant. Similar relief is provided in the Law of Property Act 1925 itself at s 90 ...' (See [1999] 4 All ER 257 at 267, [2001] Ch 318 at 329–330.)

f   60. The present case is not one in which the landlord was ever proceeding *by action* to enforce a right of re-entry. It had effected a peaceable re-entry without recourse to the court. Accordingly, the application made by Mrs Bland to the county court, in the present case, was not made under s 138 of the County Courts Act 1984. But it was made under s 139 of that Act; as well as under s 146(4) of the

g 1925 Act. Judge Hull held, correctly in my view, that s 146(4) of the 1925 Act was of no assistance to Mrs Bland. As Nourse LJ has pointed out, whatever else may be said as to the position of a person entitled to an equitable charge over a leasehold interest, he or she is not a person 'claiming as underlessee any estate or interest in the property comprised in the lease'. But Judge Hull held, also, that he had no jurisdiction to grant relief under s 139 of the 1984 Act. For my part, I am

h not at all sure that he was right to take that view.

61. Section 139(2) and (3) of the 1984 Act are in these terms:

'(2) Where a lessor has enforced against a lessee, by re-entry without action, a right of re-entry or forfeiture as respects any land for non-payment of rent, the lessee may ... at any time within six months from the date on

j which the lessor re-entered apply to the county court for relief, and on any such application the court may, if it thinks fit, grant to the lessee such relief as the High Court could have granted.

(3) Subsections (9B) and (9C) of section 138 shall have effect in relation to an application under subsection (2) of this section as they have effect in relation to an application under subsection (9A) of that section.'

62. Judge Hull delivered judgment in the present case on 17 September 1998, some three months before his judgment in the *Croydon (Unique) Ltd* case (18 December 1998). In his judgment in the present case he held that 'lessee' for the purposes of s 139(2) of the 1984 Act—even giving that expression the extended meaning provided by s 140 of the Act—did not include a person claiming as equitable chargee. He did not address s 139(3) of the Act; which, as it seems to me, enables an application under s 139(2) to be made by a person who *b* could have made an application (in a case to which s 138 applied) under s 138(9C)—that is to say, a person 'with an interest under the lease of the land derived ... from the lessee's interest'. If he had done, there is no reason to think that he would have not have reached the same conclusion as he did reach, some three months later, in the *Croydon (Unique) Ltd* case—that Mrs Bland was not a person with an interest under the lease derived from the lessee's interest. But, as *c* this court held on appeal from his later decision, that conclusion would have been wrong.

63. Judge Hull remitted the matter to the High Court in order that Mrs Bland should have the opportunity (if she could) of invoking the inherent jurisdiction to relieve from forfeiture. That was a jurisdiction which could be exercised by the *d* High Court; but which, in 1998, could not be exercised in the county court. It was the exercise of the inherent jurisdiction which was for consideration before Mr Peter Leaver QC, sitting as a deputy judge of the High Court (see his observations at [1999] 2 EGLR 49 at 50). It would not have been open to the deputy judge to revisit the question whether there had been jurisdiction in the *e* county court to grant relief under s 139 of the 1984 Act—and he was not asked to do so.

64. It would have been open to Mrs Bland to seek leave to appeal, out of time, against the decision of Judge Hull that he had no jurisdiction under s 139(2) of the 1984 Act—read with ss 139(3) and 138(9C) of that Act—to grant her the relief from forfeiture which she sought. If such an application had been made, the *f* reasoning of the majority of this court in the *Croydon (Unique) Ltd* case would, as it seems to me, have been directly in point. For my part, I have little doubt (at present) that, had such an application been made, I would have taken the view that it would have been right to hear an appeal out of time against Judge Hull's decision on the s 139(2) point; and to allow that appeal. But no such application *g* has been made; and so we have not heard argument on the question whether the decision of this court in the *Croydon (Unique) Ltd* case is determinative in favour of holding that s 139(2) does confer jurisdiction on the county court to grant relief to an equitable chargee of an interest under a lease. In those circumstances, notwithstanding my strong pre-disposition to hold that the section does have that *h* effect, I think that it would be wrong to determine this appeal on that ground. The question before us, on the appeal from the deputy judge, is whether relief can be granted under the inherent jurisdiction of the High Court.

65. But, even if the reasoning of this court in the *Croydon (Unique) Ltd* case is of no direct assistance on that question, it is, I think, of help: (i) in identifying the *j* conceptual distinction between relief from forfeiture in a form which restores, or revives, the pre-existing lease and relief in a form which vests a new lease in the applicant and thereby 'thrusts upon the landlord [the applicant] as a new tenant'; and (ii) in demonstrating that, in practice, whether the pre-existing lease is restored or a new lease is vested in the applicant, the end result is likely to be much the same. That is because s 90 of the 1925 Act provides:

a
'Where an order for sale is made by the court in reference to an equitable mortgage on land (not secured by a legal term of years absolute or by a charge by way of legal mortgage) the court may, in favour of a purchaser, make a vesting order conveying the land or may appoint a person to convey the land or create and vest in the mortgagee a legal term of years absolute to enable him to carry out the sale, as the case may require, in like manner as if

b
the mortgage had been created by deed by way of legal mortgage ...'

66. So, in practice, if the pre-existing lease is restored, the court has ample power, under s 90 of the 1925 Act, to make a further order which enables that lease to be sold; there is no need to create a new lease vested in the chargee for that purpose—and, even if there were, that could be done under s 90 of the 1925 Act.

c
67. The reasoning of this court in the *Croydon (Unique) Ltd* case is of assistance, also, in identifying the two distinct questions (i) who can apply for relief from forfeiture, and (ii) what form should the relief take. In particular, it demonstrates that the answer to the first of those questions does not, necessarily, dictate the answer to the second. There is no reason, in principle, to assume that, on an

d
application by an equitable chargee (if such an application can be entertained), the only order that could be made is an order vesting a new lease in the applicant. There is no reason in principle why, on an application by an equitable chargee, the court should not make an order which restores the pre-existing lease—with the consequence that the former lessee remains liable under the covenants in that lease—if that is an appropriate order to make in the circumstances. It is, as it

e
seems to me, unlikely that that will be an appropriate order unless the applicant is able to offer satisfactory indemnities to the lessee against the lessee's continuing liability under the restored lease—and, perhaps, to assume some liability to the landlord as surety for the performance of those covenants—but that goes to the exercise of the jurisdiction, not to its existence. Those considerations provide a

f
good reason why, as Sir Christopher Staughton observed in the *Croydon (Unique)* *Ltd* case in the passage ([1999] 4 All ER 257 at 267, [2001] Ch 318 at 330) to which I have already referred, the court should restore the pre-existing lease on an application by the holder of a charging order for the purpose merely of enabling the applicant to apply for an order for sale and on condition that he do so.

g
68. Nourse LJ has drawn a distinction between the claim for direct relief and the claim for indirect relief. As I understand that distinction it is between a claim for relief in the form of an order vesting in the applicant a new lease (for a term equal to or less than the residue of the term of the pre-existing lease) (direct relief) and a claim for relief in a form which restores or revives the pre-existing lease,

h
under which the former lessee remains tenant (indirect relief). In the latter case, the applicant claims to be entitled to make the application for relief which the lessee could have made; and to have relief in the form that would be granted on an application by the lessee. It is in that sense that the applicant claims to stand in the shoes of the lessee. The applicant does not claim a right to become tenant of the property under the restored lease.

j
69. I respectfully agree that the authorities do not sanction, or lend any support to, an extension of the inherent jurisdiction of the court so as to recognise a claim for direct relief by an applicant who has no legal estate or equitable interest in the land and no right to be in possession. But I see no difficulty in recognising an inherent jurisdiction—in so far as it is still required, having regard to what I would regard as the true effect of s 139(2) of the 1984 Act—in relation

to a claim for indirect relief. That does not, as it seems to me, require any
extension of well-established principles.   *a*

70. It is well established that equity will grant relief from forfeiture of a lease
for non-payment of rent; on the grounds that the power to forfeit is properly to
be regarded as security for the payment of the rent. It is well established, also,
that equity will preserve and protect a fund which is held as security for the
discharge of a liability; for example, by the appointment of a receiver (see   *b*
Cummins v Perkins [1899] 1 Ch 16 at 19, and *Faith Panton Property Plan Ltd v Hodgetts*
[1981] 2 All ER 877 at 881, 884, [1981] 1 WLR 927 at 931–932, 935–936). I agree
with Nourse LJ that it would be astonishing if equity would not intervene, in an
appropriate case, to preserve and protect for the benefit of an equitable chargee
a leasehold interest which was the subject of the charge. For example, it would
be remarkable if a court of equity were to refuse to preserve a leasehold interest   *c*
from forfeiture by appointing a receiver to pay the rent out of funds provided by
an applicant whose interest was as chargee; or to compel the lessee to apply funds
provided by the applicant for the same purpose. It would, I think, be equally
remarkable if the court could not require a former lessee to seek relief from
forfeiture (against a suitable indemnity from the chargee) where the leasehold   *d*
interest has been forfeited on the grounds of non-payment of rent. As Nourse LJ
has observed, the proposition seems self evident.

71. If, as I would hold, there is equitable jurisdiction, on the application of a
chargee of a leasehold interest which has been forfeited on the grounds of
non-payment of rent, to require the former lessee to apply for relief from
forfeiture, then I can see no reason why the two applications should not be made   *e*
together, in proceedings brought by the chargee to which both the former lessee
and the landlord are party. I find confirmation that that is the correct approach
in the judgments of this court in *Harmer v Armstrong* [1934] Ch 65, [1933] All ER
Rep 778. Lawrence LJ said this:

> 'Whenever a party under a contract, at the date when he enters into it is   *f*
> (or thereafter constitutes himself) a trustee for a third party that party has a
> right conferred upon him by way of property to sue on the contract ... and
> can, according to well settled principles, enforce that right in equity, joining
> the trustee as a defendant to the action. The right of a beneficiary in such a
> case as the present, however is to enforce the agreement according to its   *g*
> tenor, that is to say in favour of the [trustee], and not in favour of the plaintiff
> [beneficiary].' (See [1934] Ch 65 at 88, [1933] All ER Rep 778 at 785.)

72. In the present case, the effect of the charging order was to impose upon
Mr and Mrs Beer equitable obligations, enforceable by Mrs Bland, in respect of
the lease subject to the charge. Those obligations included, in my view, the   *h*
obligation to apply for relief from forfeiture of the lease (against a sufficient
indemnity from Mrs Bland). The right to apply for relief from forfeiture is a right
in equity which Mr and Mrs Beer, as former lessees, were obliged to exercise, if
Mrs Bland so required, for the protection of her interest as chargee. The principle
recognised in *Harmer*'s case enables her to enforce, in the same proceedings, both *j*
her right against Mr and Mrs Beer and their right, as former lessees, against the
landlord, Ingram's Estates.

73. It will be clear that I take the view that Mr and Mrs Beer are necessary
parties to proceedings brought by Mrs Bland to obtain relief from forfeiture
under the inherent jurisdiction. But it has not been suggested that, in the absence
of Mr and Mrs Beer as parties, the present proceedings ought to be struck out.

a The reason lies in the passage in the judgment of the deputy judge ([1999] 2 EGLR 49 at 50), to which Nourse LJ has already referred. It seems to me that the terms in which consent has already been obtained from Mr and Mrs Beer may well cover the grant of what has been described above as indirect relief—that is to say, relief which takes the form of restoring or reviving the pre-existing lease—but I agree with Nourse LJ that the position should be put beyond doubt by joining
b them (and, perhaps, Mr Beer's trustee in bankruptcy) as parties to these proceedings so that they will be formally bound by the order for relief.

74. I agree, also, that, if relief from forfeiture is to be granted, then, in principle, the grant must be on terms that Mrs Bland pays all arrears of rent and the costs of re-entry. But, as Nourse LJ has pointed out, the way in which effect should be given to that principle is not free from difficulty in the present case. It seems clear
c (i) that Ingram's Estates is the person entitled to arrears of rent under the 1994 lease, up to the date upon which the 1996 lease was granted (29 April 1996), and (ii) that Mr and Mrs Uddin are the persons entitled to arrears of rent under the 1994 lease from 29 April 1996. That is because the effect of the 1996 lease is that Mr and Mrs Uddin became the immediate landlords entitled to receive rent under
d the 1994 lease, to which their lease was subject. But (a) Ingram's Estates may have a claim for unpaid rent due from Mr and Mrs Uddin under the 1996 lease; (b) Mr and Mrs Uddin may have a claim against Ingram's Estates on the covenant for quiet enjoyment in the 1996 lease; (c) Mr and Mrs Uddin may have a claim against Ingram's Estates in respect of the premium which they paid in consideration for the grant of the 1996 lease; and (d) Mrs Bland may have a claim
e against Mr and Mrs Uddin for mesne profits in respect of their occupation of the property since 29 April 1996. The list is intended to be illustrative rather than exhaustive. The point which it is intended to illustrate is that it may well not be just, in the circumstances of the present case, when granting relief, to impose terms which require Mrs Bland to make substantial payments to both Ingram's
f Estates and Mr and Mrs Uddin. It may well be necessary, first, to consider the extent to which the potential claims and cross-claims (if established) should be set off against each other. I agree that further consideration will have to be given to the terms upon which relief should be granted when the parties have had the opportunity to make representations in the light of this judgment.

g *The appeal in the chattels action*

75. I turn, now, to the appeal against the refusal to award damages on the cross-undertaking given by Mrs Bland in the chattels action.

76. The injunction granted on 16 May 1996 on the application ex parte by Mr and Mrs Beer, and continued on 18 June 1996 on the application of Mrs Bland,
h restrained Mr Uddin from dismantling or taking away fixtures or fittings at the property (listed in the schedule to the particulars of claim) and from damaging or using the fixtures and fittings generally or as part of his business.

77. The chattels action was commenced by Mr and Mrs Beer (and one other) against Mr Uddin. But the real dispute was between Mr and Mrs Beer on the one hand and Mrs Bland on the other hand; each claiming ownership of the chattels.
j Mr Uddin interpleaded. Mrs Bland was joined in the action on 18 June 1996 in order to be claimant in the interpleader proceedings. She gave a cross-undertaking in the chattels action 'to be responsible for any loss or damage which the defendant [Mr Uddin] might suffer by reason of the injunction in the event that it should not have been granted'. Eventually, on 25 March 1998, Mrs Bland obtained judgment against Mr and Mrs Beer in the interpleader proceedings.

78. The disputed chattels remained at 54/56 The Parade, Bourne End, until
the end of August 1996, when they were removed to storage or sold. Mr Uddin's   *a*
claim, under the cross-undertaking, is based on the assertion that, because the
chattels remained on the premises until the end of August 1996, he was unable to
commence trading until 23 September 1996. He claims loss of profits over the
period of 18 weeks from June to September 1996.

79. I agree with Nourse LJ that the short answer to the claim under the   *b*
cross-undertaking is that it was never established that the loss which Mr Uddin
claims to have suffered was caused by the grant of the injunction on 18 June 1996.
He had chosen to go into possession, on 29 April 1996, of premises which had
been the subject of a peaceable re-entry in circumstances in which the former
tenants were asserting a right to relief from forfeiture and in which there were
chattels which (on any view) were not the landlord's fixtures and which had not   *c*
been removed by the owner. By going into possession under the 1996 lease at a
time when the premises contained fixtures and fittings which were not the
subject of that lease, he became bailee of those chattels until he could deliver
them to the owner. He could not dispose of them. In the circumstances that the
ownership of the chattels was in dispute, there was a difficulty in obtaining a   *d*
receipt. It was to meet that difficulty that Mr Uddin interpleaded in the proceedings
which the Beers had commenced against him. But it was that difficulty, rather
than the injunction, which was the primary cause of his inability to commence
trading at the premises. Unless he could show that, but for the injunction, that
difficulty could have been removed earlier than it was, his claim that he suffered
loss or damage 'by reason of the injunction' must fail. In the event he did not   *e*
establish the necessary causal link.

Conclusion

80. For the reasons which I have set out, as well as for the reasons given by
Nourse LJ, with which I agree, I, too, would allow Mrs Bland's appeal against the   *f*
refusal to grant relief from forfeiture and adjourn further consideration of the
terms upon which relief should be granted. I would dismiss Mr Uddin's appeal in
the chattels action.

HALE LJ.

82. I agree that relief against forfeiture is available and should be granted in   *g*
this case in the form of the restoration or revival of the 1994 lease. The advantages
of that course and the reasons why it is available in this case have been fully
explained by Chadwick LJ. The appropriate financial consequences of that will,
as Nourse and Chadwick LJJ have explained, require further consideration.

83. In reaching that conclusion, however, I would not wish to express any   *h*
opinion upon whether the inherent jurisdiction is available to the holder of a
charging order in the alternative form of 'thrusting upon the landlord a new
tenant'. I accept, of course, that there is no precedent for such a claim. The cases
which explore the extent of the right to claim relief against forfeiture do refer to
'proprietary or possessory rights' (see *Scandinavian Trading Tanker Co AB v Flota*   *j*
Petrolera Ecuatoriana, The Scaptrade [1983] 2 All ER 763 at 767, [1983] 2 AC 694 at
702; *Sport International Bussum BV v Inter-Footwear Ltd* [1984] 2 All ER 321 at 325,
[1984] 1 WLR 776 at 794; and *BICC plc v Burndy Corp* [1985] 1 All ER 417, [1985]
Ch 232). The nature of an equitable charge, and the difference between such a
charge and a mortgage, were explained in *Carreras Rothmans Ltd v Freeman*
Mathews Treasure Ltd (in liq) [1985] 1 All ER 155 at 169, [1985] Ch 207 at 227 and

a   in *Re Cosslett (Contractors) Ltd* [1997] 4 All ER 115 at 126, [1998] Ch 495 at 508, both cases relating to chattels. It does not necessarily follow, it seems to me, that the holder of a charging order over a lease of land does not have such a proprietary interest in the lease as would entitle him to seek relief from forfeiture of the lease. There is a distinction between a proprietary interest and a right to possession.

84. It is likely, however, that the point is an entirely academic one. I cannot
b   immediately see any answer to the point raised for the first time in this case in the judgment of Chadwick LJ. Section 139(3) of the County Courts Act 1984 clearly applies s 138(9B) and (9C) to applications for relief after re-entry without action as they apply to applications for relief after recovery of possession by action. This court held, in *Croydon (Unique) Ltd v Wright (Crombie intervening)* [1999] 4 All ER 257, [2001] Ch 318, that the holder of a charging order was 'a person with an
c   interest under a lease of the land derived (whether immediately or otherwise) from the lessee's interest therein' for the purpose of s 138(9C). This enables the court to grant relief in either of the forms contemplated by s 128(9C).

85. If so, this will in future avoid any need for further discussion of whether the holder of a charging order who has an 'interest' for that purpose does or does
d   not have a proprietary interest either in the land or in the lease for the purpose of the inherent jurisdiction.

Mrs Bland's appeal allowed, but consideration of terms on which relief should be granted adjourned. Mr Uddin's appeal dismissed.

Victoria Parkin   Barrister.

Bland v Ingram's Estates Ltd and others (No 2) *a*

[2001] EWCA Civ 1088

COURT OF APPEAL, CIVIL DIVISION
CHADWICK AND HALE LJJ
b
16 MAY, 11 JULY 2001

Landlord and tenant – Relief against forfeiture – Arrears of rent – Terms of relief – Whether lessor having to give credit for benefits accruing from exercise of right of re-entry when determining price to be paid by lessee for obtaining relief. *c*

Where a lease has been forfeited for non-payment of rent by exercise of a right of re-entry, the benefits obtained by the lessor as a consequence of the re-entry have to be taken into account when determining the sum to be paid by the lessee as the price of obtaining relief from forfeiture. The foundation of the equitable jurisdiction to grant such relief is that the right of re-entry reserved by the lease *d* in the event of non-payment of rent is regarded as a security for the rent. It is inconsistent with that principle to grant relief from forfeiture on terms which enable the lessor to profit from the exercise of the right of re-entry. The lessor is entitled to be restored to the position in which he would have been if the default giving rise to the exercise of the right of re-entry had not occurred. That, *e* however, leads to the conclusion that he should give credit for benefits which he has enjoyed as a consequence of the re-entry. In so far as those are benefits which he would not have enjoyed if he had not re-entered, he should bring them into account (see [23], [26], [39], below).

Notes *f*
For the right to relief against forfeiture for non-payment of rent, see 27(1) *Halsbury's Laws* (4th edn reissue) para 522.

Cases referred to in judgments
Abbey National Building Society v Maybeech Ltd [1984] 3 All ER 262, [1985] Ch 190, *g* [1984] 3 WLR 793.
Barton Thompson & Co Ltd v Stapling Machines Co [1966] 2 All ER 222, [1966] Ch 499, [1966] 2 WLR 1429.
Dendy v Evans [1910] 1 KB 263, [1908–10] All ER Rep 589, CA.
Driscoll v Church Comrs for England [1956] 3 All ER 802, [1957] 1 QB 330, [1956] *h* 3 WLR 996, CA.
Egerton v Jones [1939] 3 All ER 889, [1939] 2 KB 702, CA.
Gill v Lewis [1956] 1 All ER 844, [1956] 2 QB 1, [1956] 2 WLR 962, CA.
Howard v Fanshawe [1895] 2 Ch 581, [1895–9] All ER Rep 855.
King, Re, Robinson v Gray [1963] 1 All ER 781, [1963] Ch 459, [1963] 2 WLR 629, CA. *j*
London and County (A & D) Ltd v Wilfred Sportsman Ltd [1970] 2 All ER 600, [1971] Ch 764, [1970] 3 WLR 418, CA.
Marriott v Anchor Reversionary Co Ltd (1861) 3 De GF & J 177.
Newbolt v Bingham (1895) 72 LT 852, CA.
Soteri v Psylides [1991] 1 EGLR 138, CA.
Wilson v Burne (1888) 24 LR Ir 14, DC and CA.

a Cases also cited or referred to in skeleton arguments
Bank of Ireland Home Mortgages v South Lodge Developments [1996] 1 EGLR 91.
Bilson v Residential Apartments Ltd [1992] 1 All ER 141, [1992] 1 AC 494, HL.
Croydon (Unique) Ltd v Wright (Crombie intervening) [1999] 4 All ER 257, [2001] Ch 318, CA.
Factors (Sundries) Ltd v Miller [1952] 2 All ER 630, CA.
b *Fuller v Judy Properties Ltd* [1992] 1 EGLR 75, CA.
Hertfordshire Investments v Bubb [2000] 1 WLR 2318, CA.
Ladd v Marshall [1954] 3 All ER 745, [1954] 1 WLR 1489, CA.
Ladup Ltd v Williams & Glyn's Bank plc [1985] 2 All ER 577, [1985] 1 WLR 851.
Lovelock v Margo [1963] 2 All ER 13, [1963] 2 QB 786, CA.
c *Quilter v Mapleson* (1882) 9 QBD 672, CA.
Silverman v AFCO (UK) Ltd [1988] 1 EGLR 51, CA.
Wadman v Calcraft (1804) 10 Ves 67.
Williams v Burrell (1845) 1 CB 402.

Adjourned appeal
d On 21 December 2000 the Court of Appeal (Nourse, Chadwick and Hale LJJ) ([2002] 1 All ER 221, [2001] 2 WLR 1638) allowed an appeal by Davinia Patricia Bland from the decision of Peter Leaver QC, sitting as a deputy judge of the High Court, on 13 April 1999 ([1999] 2 EGLR 49) dismissing her claim against the respondents, Ingram's Estates Ltd, Fogir Uddin and his wife, Ripon Chowdhery Fogir, for relief from forfeiture of a lease of business premises known as 54/56
e The Parade, Bourne End, Buckinghamshire, granted by Ingram's Estates to Franco and Caroline Beer on 12 May 1994 and over which Mrs Bland held charging orders as security for judgments obtained against the Beers. The court held that Mrs Bland was entitled in principle to relief, but adjourned for further consideration of the terms on which relief would be granted. The facts are set out
f in the judgment of Chadwick LJ.

Robert Denman (instructed by *Joseph Aaron & Co,* Ilford) for Mrs Bland.
Timothy Fancourt (instructed by *Collyer-Bristow*) for Ingram's Estates.
Justin Althaus (instructed by *Armstrong & Co*) for the Uddins.
g
Cur adv vult

11 July 2001. The following judgments were delivered.

CHADWICK LJ.
h [1] This appeal came before the court (Nourse, Hale LJJ and myself) at the end of last year. In judgments which we handed down on 21 December 2000 ([2002] 1 All ER 221, [2001] 2 WLR 1638) we indicated that the appeal would be allowed and that we were minded to grant the appellant the relief from forfeiture which she sought; but that further consideration needed to be given to the terms upon
j which that relief should be ordered. Hale LJ and I have now heard full argument as to the terms for relief. This judgment is directed to that question.

The underlying facts
[2] The first-named respondent, Ingram's Estates Ltd, is the freehold owner of premises known as 54/56, The Parade, Bourne End. On 12 May 1994 Ingram's Estates granted a lease of those premises to Mr Franco Beer and his wife,

Mrs Caroline Beer, for a term of 16 years from 25 March 1994 at an annual rent, subject to review, of £14,000. The lease contained the usual proviso for re-entry in the event of non-payment of rent.

[3] On 30 November 1995 the appellant, Mrs Davinia Bland, obtained summary judgment against Mr and Mrs Beer in the Queen's Bench Division in an amount of £24,000, together with interest and costs. On the same day she obtained a charging order nisi over the Beers' interest under the 1994 lease. The charging order took effect as an equitable charge created by the debtors.

[4] By the end of April 1996 there were substantial arrears of rent due from the Beers under the 1994 lease. It is not in dispute that, on 26 April 1996, Ingram's Estates was entitled to, and did, forfeit the 1994 lease by peaceable re-entry. Three days later, on 29 April 1996, Ingram's Estates granted a new lease of the premises to the second and third respondents, Mr Fogir Uddin and his wife, Mrs Ripon Chowdhery Fogir. The 1996 lease was for a term of 24 years from 25 March 1996 at an annual rent, subject to review, of £14,000. The lease was granted in consideration of the payment by the Uddins to Ingram's Estates of a premium of £12,000. It is common ground that, before they took the 1996 lease, the Uddins had actual notice of the 1994 lease and of the circumstances in which it had been forfeited by re-entry. It follows that they had constructive notice of the Beers' right to claim relief from forfeiture; and so took subject to that right.

These proceedings

[5] The present proceedings were commenced by Mrs Bland on 26 August 1996. By a summons issued in the High Wycombe County Court she claimed relief from forfeiture of the 1994 lease. The action came before His Honour Judge Hull QC, sitting at Epsom, on 17 September 1998. He held that he had no jurisdiction to grant relief from forfeiture at the suit of Mrs Bland either under s 146(4) of the Law of Property Act 1925 or under s 139 of the County Courts Act 1984. But he did not dismiss the claim. He took the view that the action should be transferred to the High Court. The purpose of that transfer was to enable the High Court to consider whether relief should be granted under the inherent jurisdiction of that court; that is to say under an inherent jurisdiction which lies in the High Court but not in the county court.

[6] The action came before Mr Peter Leaver QC, sitting as a deputy judge of the High Court in the Chancery Division. His judgment, delivered on 13 April 1999, is reported at [1999] 2 EGLR 49. He rejected Mrs Bland's claim for relief from forfeiture and dismissed the action. On 30 July 1999 Mrs Bland obtained permission to appeal to this court.

[7] As I have said, the judgments in this court were handed down on 21 December 2000. The only question then before us for decision was whether the deputy judge had been right to hold that he had no inherent jurisdiction to grant relief from forfeiture at the suit of a claimant who neither had, nor had had, any estate in the land or any interest other than as equitable chargee of the former lease. For the reasons which we gave, we held that his conclusion was wrong. But, in the course of my judgment, I expressed the view (with which Hale LJ agreed) that, upon a true analysis of the position, it had never been necessary to invoke the inherent jurisdiction. Relief could have been granted in the county court under s 139(2) of the 1984 Act—read in conjunction with ss 139(3) and 138(9C). If that had been recognised at an earlier stage, the very considerable costs that have been incurred in the High Court and in this court in relation to the claim under the inherent jurisdiction could have been avoided.

a [8] The basis of our decision on 21 December 2000 was that there was inherent jurisdiction, at the suit of an equitable chargee and in proceedings to which the former lessees and the landlord are parties, to grant relief from forfeiture by restoring the former leasehold interest which had been the subject of the charge. We rejected the submission, so far as it was pursued, that there was any inherent jurisdiction to grant relief by vesting a new lease in the claimant; b although (i) there would be jurisdiction to make such an order under s 138(9C) of the 1984 Act and (ii) if relief were granted by the restoration of the former lease, there would be jurisdiction under s 90 of the 1925 Act to vest a new lease in the chargee for the purpose of enabling the property to be sold.

[9] Following delivery of our judgments on 21 December 2000, the further hearing of the appeal was adjourned so that consideration could be given to c joining the Beers (and, if appropriate, Mr Beer's trustee in bankruptcy) as parties to the proceedings; and, after hearing such submissions (if any) as they might wish to make and the further submissions of the existing parties, to the terms upon which relief from forfeiture should be granted in this case. That further hearing has now taken place.

d [10] It is clear from the correspondence and attendance notes now before us that Mr and Mrs Beer were given notice of the further hearing; and were given notice that the court was minded to join them as parties to these proceedings. They have not appeared, either in person or through legal representatives. They were invited, by the appellant's solicitors in a letter dated 4 May 2001, to put in writing any observations to which they wished the attention of the court to be e drawn. Their response, in a letter dated 14 May 2001, does not suggest that they have any objection to being joined as parties. In those circumstances we indicated that we would treat them as parties and would make an order that they be joined. I would propose that they be given a short time—say, 14 days after service of the order upon them—to make such application (if any) to vary the order that we will f make today as they may be advised is necessary in order to protect their interests.

[11] It is clear, also, that Mr Beer's trustee in bankruptcy has been kept informed of the position. He does not appear today. By a letter dated 31 April 2001 he informed the appellant's solicitors that he held signed notices of intended disclaimer which he proposed to serve on 'the landlord, mortgagee and your client' as soon as he heard that the appellant had been granted relief from g forfeiture. It is not at all clear (at least to me) to whom the trustee intends to refer by the expression 'the mortgagee' unless it is the appellant herself, as chargee. Nor is it clear why the trustee takes the view that he is in a position to disclaim the leasehold estate; as distinct from Mr Beer's beneficial interest under the trust for sale upon which the lease was (and would be, if restored) held by Mr and h Mrs Beer. Prima facie, at least, the leasehold estate did not vest in the trustee in bankruptcy upon appointment under s 306(1) of the Insolvency Act 1986. It was property which Mr Beer held upon trust for himself and another (Mrs Beer); and so it did not form part of the bankrupt's estate (see s 283(3) of that Act). In those circumstances we have not thought it necessary to treat Mr Beer's trustee as a j party to this appeal. We do not order him to be joined; but, for my part, I would think it right to give him the same opportunity to apply for a variation of the order which we will make today as that which is to be given to Mr and Mrs Beer.

The principles applicable to relief from forfeiture

[12] I turn now to the terms upon which relief from forfeiture should be granted. The principles are not, I think, in doubt. First, the proviso for re-entry

on non-payment of rent is treated in equity as a security for the rent (see *Howard v Fanshawe* [1895] 2 Ch 581 at 588, [1895–9] All ER Rep 855 at 859). Accordingly, relief will normally be granted upon terms that the arrears of rent and any costs properly associated with the re-entry are discharged (see *Newbolt v Bingham* (1895) 72 LT 852 at 854). Jenkins LJ put the point in these terms, in *Gill v Lewis* [1956] 1 All ER 844 at 852, [1956] 2 QB 1 at 13:

'... the function of the court in exercising this equitable jurisdiction is, save in exceptional circumstances, to grant relief when all that is due for rent and costs has been paid up, and (in general) to disregard any other causes of complaint that the landlord may have against the tenant. The question is whether, provided all is paid up, the landlord will not have been fully compensated; and the view taken by the court is that if he gets the whole of his rent and costs, then he had got all he is entitled to so far as rent is concerned, and extraneous matters of breach of covenant are, generally speaking, irrelevant.'

See, also, the observations of Pennycuick J in *Barton Thompson & Co Ltd v Stapling Machines Co* [1966] 2 All ER 222 at 225, [1966] Ch 499 at 510:

'It is an invariable condition of relief from forfeiture for non-payment of rent that the arrears, if not already available to the lessor, shall be paid within a time specified by the court. The precise length of time is a matter of discretion ... but the imposition of the condition is not a matter of discretion; it is a requirement of law rooted in the principle on which relief is granted.'

[13] Second, the effect of an order granting relief from forfeiture is to restore the lease for all purposes; the original lease continues as if there had been no interruption by re-entry (see *Dendy v Evans* [1910] 1 KB 263 at 269, 270, [1908–10] All ER Rep 589 at 592–593, and *Driscoll v Church Comrs for England* [1956] 3 All ER 802 at 806, 809, 811–812, [1957] 1 QB 330 at 340, 344, 348). The consequence, in the present case, of the grant of relief from the forfeiture of the 1994 lease will be that the 1996 lease takes effect as a lease of the reversion. As from 29 April 1996 Mr and Mrs Uddin will have been the persons immediately entitled in reversion on the determination of the 1994 lease. They will have been interposed as intermediate landlord between Mr and Mrs Beer and Ingram's Estates.

[14] Third, the object of the court when granting relief is to put the lessor (as well as the lessee) back in the position in which he would have been if there had been no forfeiture (see *Egerton v Jones* [1939] 3 All ER 889 at 892, [1939] 2 KB 702 at 706). It is this principle which underlies the practice of requiring the applicant, as a term of relief, to pay the costs properly incurred by the lessor in connection with the re-entry and the proceedings for relief. Accordingly, the applicant will normally be required to pay the lessor's costs of the forfeiture proceedings, save in so far as those costs have been increased by the lessor's opposition to the grant of relief, upon appropriate terms (see *Howard's* case [1895] 2 Ch 581 at 592, [1895–9] All ER Rep 855 at 860, and *Abbey National Building Society v Maybeech Ltd* [1984] 3 All ER 262 at 271, [1985] Ch 190 at 206). Prima facie, the costs which the applicant will be required to pay to the lessor as a term of obtaining relief will be assessed on an indemnity basis; if it were otherwise the lessor would not obtain the indemnity against proper expenses to which he is entitled (see *Egerton's* case [1939] 3 All ER 889 at 894, [1939] 2 KB 702 at 710). But, to the extent that costs have been increased by the lessor's unnecessary opposition to the grant of relief, the normal rules apply: the lessor will normally be ordered to pay the applicant's

a costs on the standard basis, and the applicant will be able to set those costs off against what he would otherwise be required to pay to the lessor as a term of obtaining relief from forfeiture.

[15] Fourth—and by way of further application of the principles (i) that, on relief being granted, the lease is restored for all purposes and (ii) that the object of the court is to put the lessor back into the position in which he would have been *b* if there had been no forfeiture—the court must take into account the fact (if it be so) that the lease contains a provision for rent review at a date between the date of forfeiture and the date of relief. The lessor is not to be denied the benefit of any increased rent which would have resulted from the operation of the rent review provisions during the period prior to the grant of relief from forfeiture *c* (see *Soteri v Psylides* [1991] 1 EGLR 138 at 140).

The issues to be decided

[16] The starting point, therefore, is that the applicants in the present case—that is to say, Mr and Mrs Beer and Mrs Bland collectively—should have the relief from forfeiture which they seek upon payment to the respondents— *d* that is to say, Ingram's Estates and Mr and Mrs Uddin collectively (as the persons from time to time entitled as immediate landlords)—of an amount equal to (i) the arrears of rent down to the date of payment and (ii) the respondents' costs of these proceedings, save in so far as those costs have been increased by unnecessary opposition to the grant of relief. To that must be added (iii) interest on arrears of *e* rent—itself recoverable as rent in arrears under the provisions in cl 3(2) of the 1994 lease—at the contractual rate there provided. And some provision must be made to take account of any increased rent that will or may become payable on the rent review which was due, under cl 5 of the 1994 lease, on 25 March 1998.

[17] The amount of the arrears of rent as at 26 April 1996 (£15,217·16) is not in *f* dispute; nor is there any dispute as to the amount of interest which had accrued on those arrears of rent as at 26 April 1996 (£1,314·91). The costs of effecting forfeiture are agreed at £310·39. Interest on the amount of arrears up to 26 April 1996 has been agreed at £1,314·91 and interest from 26 April 1996 on those arrears, the amount of rent which would, but for the forfeiture, have been due to be paid between 26 and 29 April 1996 (agreed at £76·72) and the costs of effecting *g* forfeiture, has been agreed at £5,280·72, giving a total sum for interest on these items as at 16 May 2001 of £6,495·63. Those figures will require some adjustment to carry the position down to the date of payment under any order which we shall make and to cover the three days between 26 and 29 April 1996. But, subject to that necessary adjustment, the terms upon which relief from forfeiture can be *h* granted to the applicants must include payment (or credit) to the respondents of an amount equal to the aggregate of those amounts—that is to say, £23,023·18. Further, there must be added to that amount of £23,000-odd—at least prima facie—(i) rent at the rate of £14,000 pa from 29 April 1996 to the date of payment (an amount in excess of £70,000), (ii) interest at the contractual rate on arrears of *j* rent accruing after 29 April 1996 from the due dates for payment, and (iii) such part of the respondents' costs of these proceedings as the applicants ought to pay as a term of obtaining relief from forfeiture. But there must be deducted from the aggregate amount which the applicants would otherwise be required to pay as the price for relief such part of the applicants' costs of these proceedings (or, more precisely, Mrs Bland's costs—as there is no reason to think that the Beers have incurred any costs in these proceedings) as are properly attributable to the

respondents' unnecessary opposition to relief and which the respondents ought to pay.

[18] The issues which this court now needs to decide are: (i) whether the respondents should be required to give credit against the rent from 29 April 1996 (including any increase in that rent that will or may be payable as the result of the rent review due on 25 March 1998) and the interest on that rent in order to take account of the fact that the Uddins have been in actual occupation of the property since 29 April 1996 for the purposes of the restaurant business which they have carried on there; and (ii) what provision in respect of costs should be reflected in the terms for relief. There is a further (but subsidiary) issue: whether the court should make an order under s 90 of the 1925 Act vesting a new lease in Mrs Bland, as chargee, for the purpose of enabling the property to be sold.

Issue (i): Should the respondents be required to give credit in respect of their actual occupation of the property since 29 April 1996?

[19] Since 29 April 1996 the Uddins have been entitled to possession of the property, as against Ingram's Estates, under the 1996 lease. They have been in actual occupation of the property, and have carried on business there. They have, of course, paid rent (or been liable to pay rent) to Ingram's Estates. There is no doubt that, if the applicants are required to pay the arrears of rent and interest which have accrued under the 1994 lease since 29 April 1996 as a condition of relief from forfeiture, it will be the Uddins (rather than Ingram's Estates) who will be entitled to receive such payment. Indeed, it is, in my view, now plain that it is Mr and Mrs Uddin (rather than Ingram's Estates) who, on relief from forfeiture being granted, would be entitled to any payment which the applicants are required to make in respect of arrears of rent and interest which accrued under the 1994 lease before 29 April 1996—see s 141 of the 1925 Act and the observations of this court in *Re King, Robinson v Gray* [1963] 1 All ER 781, [1963] Ch 459 and *London and County (A & D) Ltd v Wilfred Sportsman Ltd* [1970] 2 All ER 600, [1971] Ch 764. The question is whether, in determining what payment should be made to the Uddins as a condition of relief from forfeiture, it is right to bring into account the benefits they have enjoyed as the persons in actual occupation during the period (or part of the period) in respect of which that payment is made.

[20] It is said on behalf of the respondents that nothing need be brought into account against the payment in respect of arrears of rent (and, in this case, interest on such arrears) which equity requires as the price of relief from forfeiture. It is said that if relief from forfeiture is granted upon terms that the applicants pay all the arrears of rent and interest—and, if they comply with those terms—then the Beers, as the persons who, following relief from forfeiture, will be treated as if they had been entitled to possession under the 1994 lease throughout (under the principle of relation back), will have an action against the Uddins as trespassers in which they may expect to recover damages or mesne profits. But, it is said, before such an action could be brought, the applicants must first obtain relief from forfeiture. Absent relief, there is no basis upon which Mr and Mrs Beer could bring an action in trespass. And, even if relief were obtained, there could be no basis upon which Mrs Bland could bring an action for trespass; for she would have no right to possession. But, in order to obtain relief from forfeiture, the applicants must comply with the terms for relief; and those terms must require payment of all arrears of rent and interest.

a
[21] It might be thought that there was some unnecessary circuity in requiring the applicants to pay to the Uddins a sum representing all arrears of rent and interest in respect of the period from 29 April 1996 in order to put the Beers in a position where they could bring proceedings in trespass against the Uddins to which there would be no defence and in which the Beers would recover mesne profits which—prima facie at least—would be likely to equal the market rent and

b
interest under statute. But, of course, the reason why the Uddins urge the court to adopt that circuitous approach lies in the figures. The amount to be paid in respect of all arrears of rent and interest (if no credit can be taken for the benefits enjoyed by the Uddins as the persons in actual occupation since 29 April 1996) is likely to be well in excess of £100,000. Substantial costs are sought in addition. Plainly, the respondents take the view that Mrs Bland (who brings these proceedings

c
with the assistance of the Legal Services Commission) can have no prospect of finding that amount. So, if the court can be persuaded to grant relief on those terms, she will be forced to abandon her claim. The proceedings which she commenced nearly five years ago in the High Wycombe County Court will have proved fruitless.

d
[22] I do not find that an attractive result. I find it doubly unattractive in the circumstances that, for the reasons that I sought to explain in my earlier judgment, this is a case in which relief from forfeiture could and should have been granted in the county court under s 139(2) of the 1984 Act with the minimum of delay and expense. If the respondents were correct in their contention that equity requires the applicants first to pay the whole of the arrears of rent and interest

e
(without bringing into account the benefits which the Uddins have enjoyed from their actual occupation) before the Beers can be in a position to claim mesne profits at law in respect of that occupation, the applicants' claim for relief in these proceedings (which this court has upheld) will have proved illusory; the relief to which this court has held them entitled will have been frustrated by the course

f
which the proceedings have taken.

[23] I am satisfied that that result is not merely unattractive; it is based on an approach which is wrong in principle. The respondents are not correct in their contention that equity requires payment by the lessee of the whole of the arrears of rent and interest (without bringing into account the benefits enjoyed by the lessor) as the price of relief from forfeiture. It is important to keep in mind that

g
the foundation of the equitable jurisdiction to relieve from forfeiture on non-payment of rent is that the right of re-entry reserved by the lease in the event of non-payment of the rent is regarded as a security for the rent (see *Howard v Fanshawe* [1895] 2 Ch 581 at 588, [1895–9] All ER Rep 855 at 859). It would be inconsistent with that principle to grant relief from forfeiture on terms which

h
enabled the lessor to profit from the exercise of the right of re-entry. The lessor is entitled to be restored to the position in which he would have been if the default which gave rise to the exercise of the right of re-entry had not occurred; but that leads to the conclusion that he should give credit for benefits which he has enjoyed as a consequence of the re-entry. In so far as those are benefits which

j
he would not have enjoyed if he had not re-entered, he should bring them into account.

[24] The need to bring into account benefits enjoyed by the lessor as a consequence of the re-entry when determining the sum to be paid by the lessee as the price of relief from forfeiture was treated by the Divisional Court in Ireland, in *Wilson v Burne* (1888) 24 LR Ir 14, as so well established as to be beyond doubt. The facts provide a convenient illustration of the principles upon which equity

acts in these cases. Property was held by the lessee on a lease for an unexpired
term of years at a reserved rent of £205 p a payable half-yearly. The rent due on   *a*
25 March 1887 was not paid. On 23 August 1887 the lessor re-entered and
remained in possession until 27 September 1887. It was found as a fact that, if the
lessee had claimed an account of mesne profits in respect of that period, the lessor
would have been chargeable with the sum of £34—attributable to the grazing,
meadowing and cropping of the land which he had carried out during those five   *b*
weeks. On 27 September 1887 the lessee paid the arrears of rent due as at
25 March 1887, without claiming an account of mesne profits in respect of the
period between 23 August and 27 September 1887, and went back into possession.
In a subsequent action by the lessor to recover possession on the grounds of
non-payment of the following year's rent, due on 25 March 1888, the lessee
sought to set off the £34 in reduction of the rent due. The importance of the   *c*
point, in context, was that, under the statute applicable in Ireland at the time, the
lessor could not proceed to ejectment unless a year's rent were in arrear; and so,
it was said, the set-off of £34 in respect of the period between 23 August and
27 September 1887 would reduce the outstanding rent to an amount which was
below that threshold. That argument failed. But the reason why it failed was that   *d*
the lessee's right to have the lessor's mesne profits taken into account in
determining what the lessee should pay in an action for relief from forfeiture—or
a redemption action as it is described in the judgments in that case—was not
capable of being advanced as a separate claim. It was a right which could only
arise in the context of the taking of the account which equity required in order to   *e*
determine the terms upon which relief from forfeiture should be granted. That
the right to set-off the lessor's mesne profits did arise in that context was
unquestioned.

[25] In *Wilson's* case Johnson J explained the practice applicable to these cases
in nineteenth century Ireland. He said (at 28–29):   *f*

> 'Under the Landlord and Tenant Act, 1860, sections 70, 71, the application
> for redemption is now made in a summary manner to the Division in which
> the ejectment is brought, and the lessee or tenant is by writ of restitution
> restored to the possession of the premises and given such relief "as a Court
> of Equity might have given": this, in substance, is that the lessee or tenant on   *g*
> his part shall account for the rent and costs in the ejectment, and for all rent
> which subsequently became due up to the day of the report of the Master to
> whom the Court refers the account, *and that the lessor or landlord on his part
> shall account for the profits, without wilful default, during his possession*; that a
> balance shall be struck on foot of these two accounts, and the party against   *h*
> whom the balance is found shall pay that balance to the other party ... By
> redemption ... the interest of the lessee or tenant which was divested by the
> execution of the *habere* is revested in the lessee or tenant, and continued as
> of his former estate, the inchoate forfeiture (as it is termed in some of the
> cases) being wiped out; by the redemption he is restored to the possession,   *j*
> as if he had not been dispossessed, on terms not only of payment of rent and
> costs in the ejectment, but also that he is liable for and bound to pay all rent
> accruing after the rent in the ejectment, *and is also given an account against the
> lessor or landlord for the rents and profits*. The landlord's possession under the
> judgment in the ejectment and the *habere* is lawful, and is given by statute on
> the tenant's default. If the tenant redeems, the rent is not suspended, and *the*

a   *only liability of the lessor or landlord to the lessee or tenant on redemption is to account for the rents and profits during his possession.'* (Emphasis added.)

There are passages to the like effect in the judgment of O'Brien J (at 18, 21), and in the judgment of Gibson J (at 32, 34), the other two members of the Divisional Court. It is, of course, true that the court was concerned with the position under

b   a statute applicable only to Ireland—the Landlord and Tenant Law Amendment (Ireland) Act 1860—but nothing turns on that. There were similar statutory provisions in force here. The statute was essentially procedural; it empowered the court in which the ejectment was brought to give such relief 'as a Court of Equity might have given'. In that context there was no relevant distinction between the equitable principles applicable in Ireland and those applicable in

c   England and Wales. Nor is there any reason why those principles should not remain applicable today.

[26] The reasoning and the decision in *Wilson's* case provides the answer not only to the question whether the lessor had to bring into account the benefits which he has derived from his occupation of the land during the period of

d   'inchoate forfeiture', but also to the question whether the lessee should be left to bring an action in trespass after the lease has been restored. There can be no such action, for the reason that, during the period of inchoate forfeiture, the lessor's possession of the land is lawful. The appropriate way of dealing with mesne profits during the period of inchoate forfeiture is by bringing them into account

e   in determining the amount which the lessee should pay as the price of relief from forfeiture.

[27] If, as I would hold, the Uddins must give credit in respect of their actual occupation of the property since 29 April 1996, the question arises: 'in what amount?'. In my view, it is pertinent to consider, by way of analogy, the position

f   of a mortgagee who goes into possession of mortgaged property. It is unnecessary to hold that the lessor should account on the basis of wilful default (and I do not do so); it is enough to hold (as I do) that, as in the case of a mortgagee who goes into possession of mortgaged property for his own benefit, a lessor who uses the property for his own business during a period of inchoate forfeiture should be charged with a full occupation rent (see the observations of

g   Turner LJ in *Marriott v Anchor Reversionary Co Ltd* (1861) 3 De GF & J 177 at 193).

[28] In the present case, I am satisfied that there is sufficient material before this court to enable us to reach the conclusion that a full occupation rent during the period from 29 April 1996 until 25 March 1998 (the rent review date under the 1994 lease) was not less than £14,000 p a. That was the rent reserved over the first

h   four years of the 1994 lease; and that was the initial rent reserved under the 1996 lease, for which the Uddins were willing to pay a premium of £12,000. Further, I think it appropriate to assume that a full occupation rent since 25 March 1998 will have been not less than the 'market rent' to which the rent under the 1994 lease would be reviewed under the provisions of cl 5 of the 1994 lease. Accordingly, I

j   would hold that the respondents should bring into account an amount in respect of mesne profits equal to the amount which would otherwise be payable by the applicants in respect of rent (and any revised rent payable on a review under cl 5 of the 1994 lease) for the period since 29 April 1996. Further, the respondents should bring into account in respect of mesne profits an additional amount equal to the interest which would otherwise be payable by the applicants on rent accruing since that date. The interest payable under the 1994 lease is treated as additional rent and, as it seems to me, mesne profits should be assessed on a similar basis.

[29] The effect of assessing the amount to be brought into account in respect of mesne profits on the basis which I have indicated is that, subject to the question of costs (to which I am about to turn), the amount to be paid by the applicants as a term of the grant of relief from forfeiture is limited to the figure of £23,000-odd (subject to adjustment) to which I have referred earlier in this judgment. The amount that would otherwise be payable by the applicants in respect of rent and interest since 29 April 1996 is matched by the amount for which the respondents must give credit in respect of mesne profits.

Issue (ii): what provision in respect of costs should be reflected in the terms for relief?

[30] The costs incurred in these proceedings have been substantial. It is convenient to set out the figures with which we have been provided; whilst recognising, of course, that they have not yet been subject to taxation or detailed assessment. Mrs Bland's costs are put at £90,808; of which £23,043 is attributable to the county court hearing, £20,204 to the hearing in the High Court and £47,561 to the hearing in this court. The respondents' costs (taken together) amount to £100,009; of which £31,524 is attributable to the county court hearing, £21,196 to the hearing in the High Court and £47,289 to the hearing in this court. Ingram's Estates (on the one hand) and Mr and Mrs Uddin (on the other hand) were separately represented throughout; with the result that the respondents have incurred two sets of costs between them.

[31] The proceedings were commenced on 22 August 1996. The claim was for relief from forfeiture under s 146(4) of the 1925 Act. Thereafter the following dates are said to be of significance: (i) 16 September 1998, the first day of the hearing before Judge Hull QC in the county court, when Mrs Bland amended her claim to seek relief, in the alternative, under s 139(2) of the 1984 Act; (ii) 27 October 1998, when Mrs Bland (who was bringing her claim under a legal aid certificate) provided evidence that the arrears of rent would be paid by her son; (iii) 17 March 1999, the second day of the hearing before Mr Leaver QC, when Mrs Bland produced consents from Mrs Beer and from Mr Beer's trustee in bankruptcy to the relief from forfeiture which she sought; (iv) 12 October 2000, when, on opening the appeal in this court, counsel for Mrs Bland sought to rely (it is said for the first time) on the charging order nisi (as distinct from the two separate charging orders absolute) and on her right, as equitable chargee, to claim through the Beers. On the basis of that chronology the respondents submit that it was not until 10 October 2000 that Mrs Bland was in a position to persuade a court to grant the relief which she sought. Accordingly, they submit, she should pay all the costs incurred before that date; and, in particular, that it should be a term of relief from forfeiture that she does so.

[32] There would be greater force in those submissions if it were not for three factors which they ignore. First, it is impossible to avoid the conclusion that Mrs Bland's claim for relief from forfeiture would not have been resisted with the tenacity which has been a feature of this litigation if it had not been for the fact that, within three days of re-entry, a new lease of the property had been granted to the Uddins. It is important to keep in mind that that step was taken by Ingram's Estates in the knowledge that the Beers were asserting an intention to apply for relief from forfeiture; and that the Uddins took the 1996 lease with constructive notice of the Beer's right to such relief. It is, to my mind, beyond argument that the circumstances in which re-entry took place and the new lease was granted, over the period of three days between 26 and 29 April 1996, were

a intended (at least by Ingram's Estates) to impede or frustrate any claim to relief from forfeiture by or on behalf of the Beers; and that, the new lease having been granted in those circumstances, the commercial need to maintain the Uddins in occupation under the new lease has dictated the respondents' conduct of the litigation thereafter. But for the grant of the 1996 lease, there is no reason to think that Mrs Bland's claim to relief from forfeiture would have been resisted by

b Ingram's Estates; and, of course, the Uddins would have had no interest in the matter. Either Mrs Bland could pay the arrears of rent and costs which, following forfeiture on 26 April 1996, would, plainly, have been payable as a condition of relief; or she could not. If she could pay, Ingram's Estates had no reason (absent the new lease) to oppose relief on the usual terms—it being plain that, as a term of relief, Mrs Bland would be required to sell the 1994 lease and that, on such a

c sale, the assignee would be a person in respect of whom Ingram's Estates (acting reasonably) would have the right to withhold consent under the usual covenant against assignment without consent which the 1994 lease contained. If she could not pay, Ingram's Estates could enter into a new lease with impunity. It was the attempt to impede or frustrate a legitimate claim to relief from forfeiture which

d has led to this extensive litigation.

[33] Second, for the reasons which I have given in my earlier judgment, I remain of the view that the county court had jurisdiction, under s 139(2) of the 1984 Act read in conjunction with ss 139(3) and 138(9C), to grant the relief which Mrs Bland sought. The hearing in the High Court seems to me to have been the cause of unnecessary expense and delay. And, in any event, this court has reversed

e the decision in the High Court.

[34] Third, I can see no reason why it was necessary for the respondents to incur two sets of separate costs in relation to the claim to relief from forfeiture. Given that the 1996 lease had been granted, the effective defendants to the claim to relief from forfeiture were the Uddins as the immediate lessors. There is no

f reason, as it seems to me, why the applicants should be required to make any payment to Ingram's Estates as a condition for the grant of relief—see s 141 of the 1925 Act and the cases to which I have already referred, Re King [1963] 1 All ER 781, [1963] Ch 459 and the London and County (A & D) Ltd case [1970] 2 All ER 600, [1971] Ch 764. For Ingram's Estates to choose to expend in excess of £68,000 in defending a claim to relief from forfeiture in relation to a lease in which it does

g not appear to have any direct commercial or financial interest may seem bizarre. More pertinently, there is no good reason why Mrs Bland should be required to reimburse that expenditure.

[35] In my view, it would be right for Mrs Bland to have her costs in this court (such costs to include the whole costs of counsel's appearance at the hearing of

h the appeal). I would make a joint and several order to that effect; but I would direct that, as between Ingram's Estates and the Uddins the burden of those costs should be borne equally. I do not think that it would be right to make an order requiring the respondents to pay any costs incurred by Mrs Bland before 10 October 2000 other than those directly attributable to the issues actually

j argued at the hearing of the appeal. In reaching that conclusion, I have had in mind (i) that there has been no appeal against the decision of Judge Hull to refuse relief under s 139 of the 1984 Act, (ii) that, in my view, the High Court proceedings could have been avoided if there had been an appeal against the decision in the county court, (iii) that the arguments presented to the High Court were different from those which succeeded in this court, and (iv) that there is some force in the point that it was not until the appeal was opened in this court that Mrs Bland was formally in a position to obtain the relief which she claimed.

[36] It does not follow, in the circumstances of this case, that the respondents
should have all their costs of the proceedings prior to 10 October 2000. For the *a*
reasons which I have sought to explain, I can see no reason why Ingram's Estates
should have any costs in relation to the claim to relief from forfeiture. There was
no need for Ingram's Estates to take any active role in resisting that claim. Further,
I am satisfied that the defence of this litigation has been dictated by an ill-considered
attempt, in April 1996, to which the Uddins (through their advisors) were party, to *b*
impede and frustrate a legitimate claim to relief from forfeiture. The litigation has
taken the course which it has because the Uddins have sought to defend the
position which arose from their over-hasty entry into the 1996 lease at a time when
the Beers had given notice of their intention to seek relief from forfeiture. It would
be appropriate to require the applicants to pay the costs that would have been
incurred on a short and unopposed application to the county court for relief from *c*
forfeiture; but it would not be appropriate to require the applicants to pay the costs
which flow from the respondents' attempt to defend the indefensible.

Section 90 of the 1925 Act
[37] Section 90 of the 1925 Act enables the court, where it has made an order for *d*
sale of property subject to an equitable charge, to vest in the chargee a legal term of
years absolute so as to enable him (or her) to carry out the sale in like manner as if
the charge had been created by deed by way of legal mortgage pursuant to s 87 of
the Act. The effect of such an order, in the present case, would be that Mrs Bland
could, herself, transfer the interest under the 1994 lease to a purchaser (see s 89(1)
of that Act). If relief from forfeiture is granted it will be on terms that the 1994 lease *e*
is sold; but—prima facie, at least—the transfer on sale can be effected by the Beers,
with the consent of Mrs Bland, without the need for an order under s 90 of the 1925
Act. I am not persuaded that there is any reason to make such an order at this stage.
I would give liberty to apply in case some difficulty arises in the future.

f
Conclusion
[38] For the reasons which I have set out, I would grant relief from forfeiture on
terms that Mrs Bland pays to Mr and Mrs Uddin a sum equal to the aggregate of
(i) the £23,000-odd to which I have referred (adjusted to take account of the period
between 26 and 29 April 1996 and to carry the interest down to the date of payment)
in respect of rent accruing before 29 April 1996, the costs of effecting re-entry and *g*
interest thereon to the date of payment and (ii) an amount in respect of their costs
equal to the amount of costs that would have been incurred on an unopposed
application for relief in the county court, but after deduction of (iii) one half of her
costs in this court. For the avoidance of doubt I should make it clear that, if (as may
be the case) the amount to be deducted under (iii) exceeds the aggregate of the *h*
amounts under (i) and (ii), then no sum will be payable. If the parties are unable to
agree the amount to be paid (if any) the matter should be remitted to the county
court for an account to be taken.

HALE LJ.
[39] I agree.   *j*

Order accordingly.

                                        Melanie Martyn   Barrister.

a
R v Kansal (No 2)
[2001] UKHL 62

HOUSE OF LORDS

LORD SLYNN OF HADLEY, LORD LLOYD OF BERWICK, LORD STEYN, LORD HOPE OF
b CRAIGHEAD AND LORD HUTTON

8–11, 15 OCTOBER, 29 NOVEMBER 2001

*Criminal law – Appeal – Appeal against conviction – Whether person convicted of
offence before implementation of human rights legislation entitled to rely on convention
rights in post-implementation appeal – Human Rights Act 1998, ss 7(1)(b), (6), 22(4).*
c

*Precedent – House of Lords – Freedom to depart from own decisions – Recent decision –
Whether appropriate for House of Lords to depart from recent decision of the House.*

In 1992 the defendant was convicted of various offences after a trial in which the
d Crown had relied on answers given by him, under statutory compulsion, in the
course of an examination by the Official Receiver during bankruptcy proceedings.
In 1998 and 2000 the Criminal Cases Review Commission referred those
convictions to the Court of Appeal on the ground, inter alia, that there was a real
possibility that the court would find that the admission of testimony obtained
under compulsion was contrary to art 6 of the European Convention for the
e Protection of Human Rights and Fundamental Freedoms 1950 (as set out in Sch 1
to the Human Rights Act 1998) and that the convictions were unsafe as a result.
On the appeal, which was heard after the incorporation of the convention into
domestic law by the implementation of the 1998 Act, the Court of Appeal held
that s 22(4)[a] of the Act entitled the defendant to rely retrospectively on art 6 of the
f convention. It further held that art 6 had been breached by the admission of the
answers in evidence, that they had therefore been wrongly admitted and that
accordingly the convictions were unsafe. The defendant's appeal was therefore
allowed. Shortly afterwards, in July 2001, a five-member panel of the House of
Lords delivered opinions in another case (the July decision), holding by a majority
that the retrospective effect of s 22(4), read together with s 7(1)(b)[b] and (6) of the
g Act, was confined to the trial of proceedings brought by public authorities, and
that accordingly an appellant, convicted before the implementation of the Act,
could not rely on convention rights on an appeal against that conviction heard
after the implementation of the Act. The Crown relied on that decision in
bringing an appeal to the House of Lords against the Court of Appeal's decision
h in the defendant's case. On the appeal, which was also heard by a five-member
panel, their Lordships considered whether the reasoning of the July decision was
erroneous and, if so, whether it was appropriate to depart from such a recent
decision of the House.

j **Held** – Although (Lord Slynn and Lord Hutton dissenting) the reasoning of the
July decision was erroneous, it would be wrong (Lord Hope dissenting) to depart
from so recent a decision, bearing in mind that it represented a possible view, that
it had not been shown to be unworkable and that the issue related only to a

---

a   Section 22(4) is set out at [13], below
b   Section 7, so far as material, is set out at [13], below

transitional provision rather than the entire future of the 1998 Act. Since the July
decision could not be distinguished, its reasoning precluded the defendant from *a*
relying on the retrospective effect of s 22(4) of the Act. Accordingly (Lord Hope
concurring on other grounds), the appeal would be allowed (see [9]–[12], [17],
[21], [22], [24], [26]–[28], [65], [72], [74], [99], [100], [110]–[112], below).

R v Lambert [2001] 3 All ER 577 criticised but followed.

b

Notes
For circumstances in which the House of Lords will depart from one of its
previous decisions, see 10 *Halsbury's Laws* (4th edn) para 745.

For the Human Rights Act 1998, ss 7, 22, see 7 *Halsbury's Statutes* (4th edn)
(1999 reissue) 505, 521.

c

Cases referred to in opinions
Aston Cantlow and Wilmcote with Billesley Parochial Church Council v Wallbank
[2001] EWCA Civ 713, [2001] 3 All ER 393.
Brown v Stott (Procurator Fiscal, Dunfermline) [2001] 2 All ER 97, [2001] 2 WLR 817,
PC.   *d*
Courtauld v Legh (1869) LR 4 Exch 126.
Fitzleet Estates Ltd v Cherry (Inspector of Taxes) [1977] 3 All ER 996, [1977] 1 WLR
1345, HL.
*Jones v Secretary of State for Social Services, Hudson v Secretary of State for Social
Services* [1972] 1 All ER 145, [1972] AC 944, [1972] 2 WLR 210, HL.
Knuller (Publishing, Printing and Promotions) Ltd v DPP [1972] 2 All ER 898, [1973] *e*
AC 435, [1972] 3 WLR 143, HL.
Lewis v A-G of Jamaica [2001] 2 AC 50, [2000] 3 WLR 1785, PC.
Mills v HM Advocate (No 2) 2001 SLT 1359, HC of Just.
Minto v Police [1990–92] 1 NZBORR 208, NZ HC.
Mitchell v WT Grant & Co (1974) 416 US 600, US SC.   *f*
Montgomery v HM Advocate, Coulter v HM Advocate [2001] 2 WLR 779, PC.
Planned Parenthood of Southeastern Pennsylvania v Casey (1992) 505 US 833, US SC.
Practice Statement (Judicial Precedent) [1966] 3 All ER 77, [1966] 1 WLR 1234.
Preiss v General Dental Council [2001] UKPC 36, [2001] 1 WLR 1926.
R v Benjafield [2001] 2 All ER 609, [2001] 3 WLR 75, CA.
R v Campbell [1997] 1 Cr App R 199, CA.   *g*
R v DPP, ex p Kebeline, R v DPP, ex p Rechachi [1999] 4 All ER 801, [2000] 2 AC 326,
[1999] 3 WLR 972, HL.
R v Lambert [2001] UKHL 37, [2001] 3 All ER 577, [2001] 3 WLR 206.
R v Mitchell [1977] 2 All ER 168, [1977] 1 WLR 753, CA.
R v Preddy [1996] 3 All ER 481, [1996] AC 815, [1996] 3 WLR 255, HL.   *h*
R v Staines [1997] 1 Cr App R 426, CA.
Saunders v UK (1997) 2 BHRC 358, ECt HR.
Shaw v DPP [1961] 2 All ER 446, [1962] AC 220, [1961] 2 WLR 897, HL.
Sirros v Moore [1974] 3 All ER 776, [1975] QB 118, [1974] 3 WLR 459, CA.

j

Appeal
The Crown appealed with leave from the order of the Court of Appeal (Rose LJ,
Rougier and McCombe JJ) on 24 May 2001 ([2001] 3 WLR 751) allowing, on a
referral from the Criminal Cases Review Commission, an appeal by the respondent,
Yash Pal Kansal, against his conviction in the Crown Court at Snaresbrook on
18 February 1992, after a trial before Judge Rucker and a jury, of two counts of

a obtaining property by deception contrary to s 15(1) of the Theft Act 1968, one count of, being a bankrupt, removing property contrary to s 354(2) of the Insolvency Act 1986 and one count of, being a bankrupt, failing to account for property contrary to s 354(3) of the 1986 Act. The court certified that a point of law of general public importance, set out at [5], below, was involved in its decision. Isidore Jack Lyons, Gerald Maurice Ronson and Anthony Keith Parnes were
b given leave to intervene on the appeal. The facts are set out in the opinion of Lord Slynn of Hadley.

John McGuinness QC and *James Eadie* (instructed by *David Nissen*, Head of Legal Services, Department of Trade and Industry) for the Crown.
Ivan Krolick and *Lindsay Weinstein* (instructed by *Campbell Chambers*) for the
c respondent.
Ben Emmerson QC, Murray Hunt and *Piers Gardner* (instructed by *Stephenson Harwood*) for Mr Lyons, (instructed by *Mishcon de Reya*) for Mr Ronson and (instructed by *Peters & Peters*) for Mr Parnes.

d Their Lordships took time for consideration.

29 November 2001. The following opinions were delivered.

LORD SLYNN OF HADLEY.
e   [1] My Lords, on 18 February 1992 the respondent was convicted of two counts of obtaining property by deception contrary to s 15 of the Theft Act 1968. He was also convicted of two counts under the Insolvency Act 1986, namely that being a bankrupt (a) he removed property which he was required to deliver up to the Official Receiver or his trustee, contrary to s 354(2); and (b) he failed without reasonable excuse to account for the loss of a substantial part of his property or
f to give a satisfactory explanation of the manner of the loss, contrary to s 354(3). Large sums were involved—he obtained from the Halifax Building Society £150,000 and £116,250 on a false representation as to his income and that he was not bankrupt and that he did not have any judgment or proceedings for debt outstanding. Prior to these advances on 11 March 1998 a bankruptcy order was made against him. On 23 March 1988 his wife collected from his solicitor £104,000
g in cash, part of the moneys advanced by the building society, and took it in a bin liner to India.
   [2] At his trial in 1992 the prosecution, pursuant to s 433 of the 1986 Act brought evidence of answers given by him under compulsion in his bankruptcy proceedings and the trial judge ruled that these answers were not rendered
h inadmissible by virtue of s 31 of the 1968 Act but were admissible under s 433. The Court of Appeal [1992] 3 All ER 844, [1993] QB 244 upheld the judge's ruling on 12 May 1992.
   [3] On 27 April 1998 the Criminal Cases Review Commission (the CCRC) referred the respondent's conviction on the counts of obtaining property by
j deception to the Court of Appeal (Criminal Division) on the basis that there was a real possibility that the court would find the convictions on those counts unsafe in the light of the decision in *R v Preddy* [1996] 3 All ER 481, [1996] AC 815. On 30 June 2000 the commission also referred the convictions on the counts under the 1986 Act to the Court of Appeal on the ground that subsequent to the decision of the European Court of Human Rights in *Saunders v UK* (1997) 2 BHRC 358 and the passing of the Human Rights Act 1998 that there was a real possibility that the

court would find the admission of the respondent's testimony obtained under
compulsion to have been in breach of art 6 of the European Convention for the *a*
Protection of Human Rights and Fundamental Freedoms 1950 (as set out in Sch 1
to the Human Rights Act 1998) (the convention) and that the convictions which
resulted from the trial were therefore unsafe.

[4] The Court of Appeal ([2001] EWCA Crim 1260 at [23], [2001] 3 WLR 751)
in the light of what had been said in *R v DPP, ex p Kebeline, R v DPP, ex p Rechachi* *b*
[1999] 4 All ER 801, [2000] 2 AC 326 ruled that—

> '(i) the CCRC, subject to the proper exercise of the discretion conferred by
> section 9 of the Criminal Appeal Act, can refer to this court a conviction
> following a trial whenever it took place; (ii) this court, once such a reference
> has been made, has no option, however old the case, but to declare the *c*
> conviction unsafe if that is the result either of the admission of evidence
> obtained in breach of article 6 or of a change in the common law, which is
> deemed always to have been that which it is authoritatively declared to be,
> as, for example, by reason of *R v Preddy* ...'

—a conclusion which they reached with no enthusiasm whatever. *d*

[5] They accordingly held that the convictions could not be regarded as safe
because of the inadmissibility of the answers. The court certified the following
question:

> 'Following a reference to the Court of Appeal, Criminal Division, by the
> Criminal Cases Review Commission, is a defendant whose trial took place *e*
> before the coming into force of ss 6(1) and 7(1)(b) of the Human Rights Act
> 1998 entitled, after they come into force, to rely on an alleged breach of his
> convention rights whenever the alleged breach took place?'

[6] The Crown has now appealed in the light of the decision in the House in
R v Lambert [2001] UKHL 37, [2001] 3 All ER 577, [2001] 3 WLR 206 by a majority *f*
(Lord Steyn dissenting) on the basis that the appellant could not rely on the
provisions of Sch 1 to the 1998 Act in a national court in respect of a conviction
before the 1998 Act came into force and in particular could not rely on the 1998
Act to challenge the judge's direction to the jury. See my opinion ([2001] 3 All ER
577 at [14], [18]); Lord Hope of Craighead: *g*

> 'I would therefore answer the question whether an accused whose trial
> took place before the coming into force of the 1998 Act is entitled to rely in
> an appeal after the coming into force of that Act on an alleged breach of his
> convention rights by the trial court in the negative.' (See [2001] 3 All ER 577
> at [116].) *h*

Lord Clyde:

> 'In my view the intention is that s 22(4) should not extend to the other kind
> of "legal proceedings" mentioned in s 7(6), namely an appeal. I am not
> persuaded that s 22(4) can avail the appellant.' (See [2001] 3 All ER 577 at *j*
> [140].)

Lord Hutton:

> '... s 7(6) provides: "In subsection (1)(b) 'legal proceedings' includes—
> (a) proceedings brought by or at the instigation of a public authority; and
> (b) an appeal against the decision of a court or tribunal." The subsection

a   therefore distinguishes between "proceedings brought by or at the
instigation of a public authority" and "an appeal against the decision of a
court or tribunal". Accordingly when s 22(4) refers, in identical words to the
words of s 7(6)(a), to "proceedings brought by or at the instigation of a public
authority", the retrospective operation permitted by that subsection does
not apply to an appeal against the decision of the Crown Court in this case.'
b   (See [2001] 3 All ER 577 at [172].)

[7] There are really three issues. The first is whether the majority in R v Lambert
were wrong in their decision of 5 July 2001 as to whether criminal convictions,
unimpeachable when made, can now be reconsidered since the passing of the
1998 Act. The second is whether in any event R v Lambert can be distinguished,
c   since what is involved here is the act of the prosecution in seeking to put in and
putting in the evidence, rather than that of the judge and the Court of Appeal in
ruling that it was admissible. The third is whether in any event the court should
in accordance with its usual practice follow a recent decision of the House when
the point was clearly in issue to be decided.

d   [8] I am not persuaded that the decision of the House in R v Lambert was
wrong. Briefly and without going into the detailed arguments which are set out
in R v Lambert it seems to me that the combined effect of ss 22(4), 7(6) and 7(1)(b)
is that for the purposes of deciding retrospectivity, a distinction is drawn between
'proceedings brought by or at the instigation of a public authority' (the language
used in both ss 22(4) and 7(6)) and an appeal even though in ordinary parlance an
e   appeal would be considered as part of legal proceedings. If Parliament had
intended to allow convictions valid when made before the 1998 Act came into force
to be reopened on the basis of rights conferred by the 1998 Act when that
came into force, it would have said so clearly and used language more clear and
direct in this context than that in s 22(4). Nor do I consider that the filter provided
f   by the commission's role in looking at old cases, nor the opportunity for the court to
control the flow of late applications, requires or indicates the opposite interpretation.

[9] Nor do I think that R v Lambert can be distinguished in any of the ways
advanced in argument but in particular by the distinction which is sought to be
drawn between acts of the judiciary and acts of the prosecutor. That is not only
g   artificial in a case like the present but also likely to lead to infinite arguments as
to the application of the distinction. Nor do I see any valid distinction between
acts whether of the court or of the prosecutor which are mandatory and those
which are discretionary.

[10] I would however allow this appeal on the ground that the issue was
h   resolved in R v Lambert after detailed argument. In that case unlike in Ex p Kebeline
it was the central issue in the decision and it was a decision deliberately come to.
As Lord Steyn has written in his speech we are dealing 'only with a transitional
provision on which the House has very recently given a clear-cut decision' and
I do not think it right because there is one change in the composition of the
Appellate Committee, and despite the skilled arguments on behalf of the
j   intervenors, for the House to depart from the decision in R v Lambert.

[11] I would therefore follow that decision in relation to this point.

[12] I would accordingly allow the appeal from the decision of the Court of
Appeal on this issue and, since the reference is to be treated as an appeal pursuant
to s 9(2) of the Criminal Appeal Act 1995, I would dismiss the appeal of the
respondent against his conviction.

LORD LLOYD OF BERWICK.

[13] My Lords, to what extent can a person rely on a breach of his convention rights in respect of an act which took place before the relevant provisions of the Human Rights Act 1998 came into force? The answer depends on the inter-relation of ss 6(1), 6(2), 7(1), 7(6) and 22(4) of the 1998 Act. For convenience I set them out:

'**6.**—(1) It is unlawful for a public authority to act in a way which is incompatible with a Convention right.

(2) Subsection (1) does not apply to an act if—(a) as the result of one or more provisions of primary legislation, the authority could not have acted differently; or (b) …

7.—(1) A person who claims that a public authority has acted … in a way which is made unlawful by section 6(1) may—(a) bring proceedings against the authority under this Act in the appropriate court or tribunal, or (b) rely on the Convention right or rights concerned in any legal proceedings, but only if he is … a victim of the unlawful act …

(6) In subsection (1)(b) "legal proceedings" includes—(a) proceedings brought by or at the instigation of a public authority; and (b) an appeal against the decision of a court or tribunal …

22.—(4) Paragraph (b) of subsection (1) of section 7 applies to proceedings brought by or at the instigation of a public authority whenever the act in question took place; but otherwise that subsection does not apply to an act taking place before the coming into force of that section.'

[14] The very same question was considered and answered by the House in *R v Lambert* [2001] UKHL 37, [2001] 3 All ER 577, [2001] 3 WLR 206. The Appellate Committee on that occasion consisted of the same five members of your Lordships' House, save that I have taken the place of Lord Clyde. In the ordinary way, the only question for decision would be whether the present case can be distinguished on the facts. There can be no doubt what *R v Lambert* actually decided. It was that the 1998 Act is retrospective in respect of proceedings brought by or at the instigation of a public authority, but not in respect of appeals in those proceedings. This distinction was founded on the language of s 7(6) of the 1998 Act, which was held by the majority to draw a contrast between (a) proceedings brought by or at the instigation of a public authority and (b) an appeal against the decision of a court or tribunal. The distinction could, it was said, be justified on the policy ground that convictions prior to the coming into force of the 1998 Act should not be disturbed.

[15] I confess that from the start of the hearing in the present appeal, I have had grave doubts whether the majority decision in *R v Lambert* could be supported. Had I been a party to the hearing in *R v Lambert*, I would have found myself in the embarrassing position of not agreeing with anyone, even though three different views were expressed. I should not have been able to agree with the majority, since to my mind the language of s 7(6) is not sufficiently clear to exclude by implication appeals in proceedings brought by or at the instigation of a public authority from the retrospective operation of s 22(4). I should not have been able to agree with Lord Steyn, because on his reading of s 6(1), s 22(4) would be deprived of all effect. I should have agreed with almost all of Lord Hope of Craighead's reasoning, but not with the last step in which he drew a distinction between the act of a court and the act of the prosecuting authority, and pointed

a out that the court is not a party to any proceedings, and is not therefore a public
authority by or at the instigation of which proceedings are brought.

[16] I might have held that it was unnecessary to decide the retrospective
question in *R v Lambert* because the act of the judge in summing up on the burden
of proof was not in any event unlawful within the meaning of s 6(1) of the 1998
Act, since he could not have 'acted differently' within the meaning of s 6(2)(a).
b He was compelled to sum up as he did by virtue of the provisions of ss 5(3) and 28
of the Misuse of Drugs Act 1971. I say I might have so decided. But I doubt
whether I would, since the point was never argued on behalf of the Crown.

[17] None of these considerations would have been worth mentioning if your
Lordships were all of the view (i) that the principle stated in *R v Lambert* is binding
on the House and (ii) that the facts are indistinguishable. But unfortunately two
c of your Lordships have given further reasons for supporting the decision in *R v
Lambert*, and two of your Lordships have held that the reasoning in *R v Lambert* is
erroneous. In those circumstances it would not have been right for me to sit on
the fence. I must express a view on the merits. We have heard full argument on
the point, perhaps fuller than the argument in *R v Lambert*. At the end of the
d argument I was even more convinced than I was at the beginning that the
decision in *R v Lambert* is erroneous, and if it be necessary to say so, plainly
erroneous. My reasons are the same as those set out at length in the speech of
Lord Hope, which I would respectfully adopt, and more shortly in the speech
of Lord Steyn. It does not matter that the actual decision in *R v Lambert* could
have been supported on some other ground. If the reasoning in *R v Lambert*
e covers the facts of the present case, then we are bound to follow it, whatever our
own views may be, unless we are going to apply the *Practice Statement (Judicial
Precedent)* [1966] 3 All ER 77, [1966] 1 WLR 1234. This seems to me to be the point
of major importance in the case.

[18] Lord Hope is of the view that we can depart from *R v Lambert* on the
f ground that we are here in a developing field of jurisprudence, and therefore the
sooner any mistakes are corrected the better. Moreover, the decision in *R v
Lambert* was itself inconsistent with a previous majority decision of the House of
Lords in *R v DPP, ex p Kebeline, R v DPP, ex p Rechachi* [1999] 4 All ER 801, [2000]
2 AC 326, to which Lord Slynn of Hadley, Lord Steyn and Lord Hope were all
party, and which was given as recently as October 1999 less than two years before
g *R v Lambert*. In the Divisional Court in *Ex p Kebeline* Lord Bingham of Cornhill CJ
took it for granted that a defendant would be entitled to rely on s 22(4) at the
hearing of an appeal against his conviction: (see [1999] 4 All ER 801 at 812–813,
[2000] 2 AC 326 at 341). Laws LJ was of the same view ([1999] 4 All ER 801 at 823,
[2000] 2 AC 326 at 352). In *R v Benjafield* [2001] 2 All ER 609 at 625, [2001] 3 WLR
h 75 at 92 (para 51) Lord Woolf MR said that where the original proceedings are
brought by a public authority, an appeal is part of those proceedings to which
s 22(4) applies. I respectfully agree with Lord Hope that these are all very
weighty considerations. They cannot be brushed aside. But they lead me to
a different conclusion.

j [19] In my opinion the only satisfactory way of resolving the present conflict
of judicial opinion at the highest level would be to require the present appeal to
be reargued before a panel of seven Law Lords. That is the traditional way in
which problems of this kind are dealt with. In addition to the unsatisfactory
features to which Lord Hope has drawn attention, I am especially concerned that
the decision in the present case will affect other cases in the pipeline, and in
particular the so called 'Guinness appellants', whose appeals are currently

pending in the Court of Appeal. Justice to them requires that the present appeal
be reheard, and the conflict finally resolved. But it seems that a rehearing before   *a*
a panel of seven Law Lords cannot be arranged in time. So the conflict remains
unresolved, and the only question is whether, as a panel of five, we should depart
from the decision in *R v Lambert*. I am quite clear that we should not.

[20] In *Lewis v A-G of Jamaica* [2001] 2 AC 50, [2000] 3 WLR 1785, an appeal to
the Privy Council from the Court of Appeal of Jamaica, the board took a different   *b*
view on three questions which had been considered and answered in three recent
decisions of the board. In a dissenting judgment, Lord Hoffmann drew attention
to the evils which would follow if the power to overrule previous decisions of the
Privy Council were exercised too readily. It is worth quoting again two passages
which Lord Hoffmann quoted from recent decisions of the Supreme Court of the
United States. In *Planned Parenthood of Southeastern Pennsylvania v Casey* (1992) 505   *c*
US 833 at 854, O'Connor, Kennedy and Souter JJ, speaking for the court, said:

> '... no judicial system could do society's work if it eyed each issue afresh in
> every case that raised it ... Indeed, the very concept of the rule of law
> underlying our own Constitution requires such continuity over time that a
> respect for precedent is, by definition, indispensable.'   *d*

In *Mitchell v WT Grant & Co* (1974) 416 US 600 at 636, Stewart J said:

> 'A basic change in the law upon a ground no firmer than a change in our
> membership invites the popular misconception that this institution is little
> different from the two political branches of the government. No misconception   *e*
> could do more lasting injury to this court and to the system of law which it
> is our abiding mission to serve.'

Lord Hoffmann ([2001] 2 AC 50 at 90, [2000] 3 WLR 1785 at 1816) went on to
point out that the observations of Stewart J apply with even greater force in our
own jurisdiction, where the Privy Council and the House of Lords customarily   *f*
sit in panels of five, and not in banc.

[21] I find that I share Lord Hoffmann's concern. The reasons given by
Lord Hope for departing from *R v Lambert* justify, and justify in full, a rehearing
of the present appeal before a panel of seven Law Lords. That is the course which
I would advocate. But those reasons fall short of the sort of compelling considerations
necessary to justify your Lordships departing from so recent a decision. The   *g*
reasoning in *R v Lambert* represents a possible view. Of that there can be no
doubt. It has not been shown to be unworkable. In my view it should be
followed. If we were to depart from *R v Lambert* today, who is to say that a
differently constituted Appellate Committee, presented with fresh arguments,
might not depart from our decision tomorrow?   *h*

[22] There remains the question whether the present case can be distinguished
from *R v Lambert* on the facts. There are, of course, factual differences. In the
present case we are concerned with the act of the prosecuting authority, whereas
in *R v Lambert* we were concerned with the act of the trial judge. There is much
to be said for the argument put forward on behalf of the interveners that whereas   *j*
the judge in *R v Lambert* was compelled by primary legislation to act as he did, the
prosecuting authority in the present case had a discretion whether to introduce
the evidence obtained in accordance with s 433 of the Insolvency Act 1986. I am
not at present persuaded that the discretionary act of the prosecution in
introducing the challenged evidence is saved from being unlawful by the
provisions of s 6(2)(b) in the way that the mandatory obligation of the judge in

a *R v Lambert* might have been saved by the provisions of s 6(2)(a), if the point had been taken. In any event it would not be satisfactory to decide the point without fuller argument; and even if we were so to decide it would not help the respondent. It is the reasoning in *R v Lambert* which binds, not the bare decision.

[23] There is nothing in the suggested distinction that this is not an ordinary appeal, but proceedings brought by or at the instigation of the Criminal Cases
b Review Commission.

[24] For the above reasons, I consider that the reasoning in *R v Lambert* prohibits the respondent from relying on the retrospective effect of s 22(4) of the 1998 Act. Accordingly, I would allow the appeal.

c **LORD STEYN.**

[25] My Lords, the question is whether the House should depart from the decision in *R v Lambert* [2001] UKHL 37, [2001] 3 All ER 577, [2001] 3 WLR 206 which was announced in July this year.

[26] In *R v Lambert* the House by a majority held that s 22(4) of the Human Rights Act 1998, read with s 7(6), draws a distinction between criminal trials and
d appeals, and does not permit a defendant in proceedings brought by or at the instigation of a public authority to rely on convention rights after 2 October 2000 where the trial took place before that date but the appeal after that date. In the light of the arguments now before the House I am satisfied that the majority in *R v Lambert* were mistaken. Three points stand out. First, the word 'proceedings'
e cover both trials and appeals. Section 7(6) does not require a different approach. Indeed s 7(6)(a) and (b) are not mutually exclusive, e g an appeal to the Divisional Court on a case stated by the Crown falls under both. Secondly, the rationale of s 22(4) was not appreciated in *R v Lambert*. We now know that 'proceedings brought by or at the instigation of a public authority' in s 22(4) were singled out for special treatment in recognition of the United Kingdom's international
f obligations under the European Convention for the Protection of Human Rights and Fundamental Freedoms 1950 (as set out in Sch 1 to the Human Rights Act 1998) (the convention) from the date of ratification by the United Kingdom in 1951 or the date of conferment of the right of petition in 1966. This rationale does not support the artificial distinction between criminal trials and appeals. Thirdly,
g in *R v Lambert* the majority was strongly influenced by the view that the contrary interpretation would lead to the challenging of old convictions. It is now clear that there is a perfectly effective filter by way of the discretion of the Court of Appeal to refuse to extend time for leave to appeal in such cases. Moreover, a similar filter is applicable to the decision of the Criminal Cases Review Commission. For these briefly expressed reasons I am of the opinion that the
h holding of the majority in *R v Lambert* was mistaken.

[27] It does not, however, follow that we must now depart from that decision. In *Knuller (Publishing, Printing and Promotions) Ltd v DPP* [1972] 2 All ER 898, [1973] AC 435 Lord Reid faced a similar problem. He observed:

j   'It was decided by this House in *Shaw v Director of Public Prosecutions* that conspiracy to corrupt public morals is a crime known to the law of England. So if the appellants are to succeed on this count, either this House must reverse that decision or there must be sufficient grounds for distinguishing this case. The appellants' main argument is that we should reconsider that decision; alternatively they submit that it can and should be distinguished. I dissented in *Shaw*'s case ([1961] 2 All ER 446, [1962] AC 220). On reconsideration I still think that the decision was wrong and I see no reason to alter anything which I said in my speech. But it does not follow that *a* I should now support a motion to reconsider the decision. I have said more than once in recent cases that our change of practice in no longer regarding previous decisions of this House as absolutely binding does not mean that whenever we think that a previous decision was wrong we should reverse it. In the general interest of certainty in the law we must be sure that there is *b* some very good reason before we so act ... I think that however wrong or anomalous the decision may be it must stand and apply to cases reasonably analogous unless or until it is altered by Parliament.' (See [1972] 2 All ER 898 at 902–903, [1973] AC 435 at 455.)

Taking into account that we are not dealing with the entire future of the 1998 Act, *c* but only with a transitional provision on which the House has very recently given a clear-cut decision, I am persuaded that it would be wrong now to depart from the ratio decidendi of *R v Lambert*. I reject the principal and alternative submissions advanced on behalf of the respondent.

[28] For these reasons I would also make the order which Lord Slynn of *d* Hadley proposes.

LORD HOPE OF CRAIGHEAD.

[29] My Lords, when I first circulated a draft judgment in this case I hoped that it might have been possible for your Lordships to agree that we should depart *e* from the view of the majority in *R v Lambert* [2001] UKHL 37, [2001] 3 All ER 577, [2001] 3 WLR 206. My noble and learned friend, Lord Lloyd of Berwick has suggested as an alternative that the question whether it should be departed from should be referred to a panel of seven Law Lords. It is now clear that there is no majority in favour of either of these two solutions.

[30] Much of what I have written about at such length may now seem to be *f* pointless, as a clear majority has emerged in this case in favour of adhering to the majority view in *R v Lambert*. It has occurred to me that I should then, out of loyalty to the view of the majority, simply withdraw my draft judgment. On balance I have decided that I ought to adhere to it, in case it may still be necessary in some future case to consider the question whether the benefit of retrospectivity *g* under s 22(4) of the Human Rights Act 1998 is available in an appeal. What follows, with only a few changes, is my judgment as originally circulated.

[31] The first question raised by this appeal is whether, following a reference to the Court of Appeal (Criminal Division) by the Criminal Cases Review Commission, a defendant whose trial took place before the coming into force of *h* ss 6(1) and 7(1)(b) of the 1998 Act is entitled, after the coming into force of these provisions, to rely as a ground of appeal against his conviction on an alleged breach of his convention rights at the trial by the prosecutor. Unless it was open to the respondent in his appeal to rely on those provisions retrospectively, the appeal must be allowed. It would plainly not have been open to the Court of *j* Appeal [2001] EWCA Crim 1260, [2001] 3 WLR 751 to apply s 22(4) of the 1998 Act and quash the convictions. But if the question is answered in the affirmative, it will be necessary to consider a further question which was dealt with for the most part in written submissions put in after the end of the oral argument. This is whether the prosecutor's act in relying at the trial under s 433 of the Insolvency Act 1986 on compulsory questioning evidence was an unlawful act for the

a purposes of s 7(1)(b). If it was not, that too would be a ground for allowing the appeal.

[32] In R v Lambert the issues in the certificate which was given by the Court of Appeal under s 33(2) of the Criminal Appeal Act 1968 included the following question:

b   'Is a defendant whose trial took place before the coming into force of ss 6 and 7(1)(b) of the Human Rights Act 1998 entitled, after they come into force, to rely, in the course of an appeal, on an alleged breach of his convention rights by the trial court or an investigating or prosecuting authority?'

c Your Lordships held by a majority, Lord Steyn dissenting, that it was not open to an appellant whose trial took place before the coming into force of the 1998 Act to impugn decisions of courts or tribunals under s 6 of that Act on the ground that the court or tribunal had acted in way that was incompatible with a convention right.

[33] Lord Hutton, who was the only one of your Lordships to indicate in
d terms how he would answer the question in that case, said that he would answer it No in relation to an alleged breach of his rights 'by the trial court' (see [2001] 3 All ER 577 at [203]). I said ([2001] 3 All ER 577 at [116]) that I, too, was of the view that the question should be answered in the negative in regard to an alleged breach of the appellant's convention rights by the trial court. Lord Clyde said
e ([2001] 3 All ER 577 at [148]), that it was not open to the appellant to invoke the provisions of the 1998 Act 'in the present appeal'. There was thus a majority for the view that it was appropriate to express the decision in that case in terms which did not extend to a breach of convention rights by an investigating or prosecuting authority.

[34] But there is no doubt that the reasons which three of your Lordships gave
f for that decision were not so confined. Lord Slynn of Hadley said ([2001] 3 All ER 577 at [18]), that he would dismiss the appeal on the broader ground that the appellant could not rely on convention rights in a national court 'in respect of a conviction' before the 1998 Act came into force. He said ([2001] 3 All ER 577 at [9]) that s 22(4) of the 1998 Act, which extends the application of s 7(1)(b) only where proceedings are brought by a public authority, appeared to indicate that an appeal
g by an unsuccessful defendant was not to be treated as a proceeding brought by or at the instigation of a public authority. Lord Clyde ([2001] 3 All ER 577 at [140]), also said that in his view the intention was that s 22(4) should not extend to an appeal. Lord Hutton expressed the same view ([2001] 3 All ER 577 at [172]). I reached my decision by a different route, as I said ([2001] 3 All ER 577 at [107])
h that an accused whose trial took place before the Act came into force was entitled to rely in an appeal after it was in force on an alleged breach of his convention rights by the prosecuting authority. But Lord Slynn's line of reasoning was supported by a majority of their Lordships in that appeal. That view, which I shall call 'the majority view', was the ratio for the decision of the majority.

j [35] On its facts the present case differs from R v Lambert in two respects. In the first place, the respondent's appeal against his conviction in the Crown Court on 18 February 1992 was dismissed by the Court of Appeal (Criminal Division) on 12 May 1992. But his conviction has now been referred back to the Court of Appeal by the Criminal Cases Review Commission. The reference has been made under s 9 of the Criminal Appeal Act 1995 on the ground that, following the judgment of the European Court of Human Rights in Saunders v UK (1997)

2 BHRC 358 and the coming into effect of the 1998 Act, there is a real possibility
that the conviction was unsafe. In the second place, the breach of the respondent's
convention rights in this case is said to have been an act of the prosecutor, not an
act by the trial court. The act which was alleged in *R v Lambert* to be incompatible
with the appellant's convention rights was a direction given to the jury by the trial
judge that the appellant required to establish his defence to a charge of possession
of a class A controlled drug with intent to supply contrary to s 5(3) of the Misuse
of Drugs Act 1971 under s 28 of that Act on the balance of probabilities. Your
Lordships held that this direction was not compatible with art 6(2) of the
European Convention for the Protection of Human Rights and Fundamental
Freedoms 1950 (as set out in Sch 1 to the Human Rights Act 1998) (the convention).
As the direction was given by the trial judge it was regarded as an act on the part
of the trial court, not an act of the prosecutor.

[36] I shall return later to the question whether the fact that the appeal in this
case follows upon a reference by the Criminal Cases Review Commission is a
ground for saying that the decision in *R v Lambert* does not apply to it. It is the
second ground for distinguishing that case on its facts that sets the scene for the
point which lies at the centre of this case. This is whether the majority view
expressed in *R v Lambert* has foreclosed the argument that the respondent is
entitled to take advantage in this appeal of the retrospective application of
s 7(1)(b) of the 1998 Act in terms of s 22(4) of that Act as he was the victim of a
breach of his convention rights at his trial by the prosecutor.

THE FACTS

[37] The respondent came to this country from India in 1967. He qualified in
1973 as a pharmacist. He later formed a company which operated 20 chemist
shops. In about 1983, with the assistance of a large mortgage, he bought a house
in joint names with his wife. In 1986 he and his company began to encounter
financial problems. In February 1987 the company went into liquidation. On
20 May 1987 a bankruptcy petition was presented against him, and on 11 March
1988 a bankruptcy order was made. On 16 and 23 March 1988 he obtained a
substantial sum of money from the Halifax Building Society. He had deceived the
building society into making advances to him by making false representations in
his application form. On 23 March 1988 his wife took possession of £104,000 in
cash, which was part of the amount advanced to the respondent by the building
society, and took it in a bin liner to India. On 16 March 1988 the respondent was
interviewed by an examiner at the Official Receiver's office. He was further
interviewed there on 20 May 1988. These interviews were conducted under s 291
of the Insolvency Act 1986, which imposes a duty on the bankrupt to answer
questions put to him by the Official Receiver. On 17 June 1988 the respondent was
ordered to lodge a cash account relating to his estate. He was publicly examined
on 29 July 1988. He failed to account for or give a satisfactory explanation of the
loss of his property prior to his bankruptcy.

[38] On 18 February 1992 the respondent was found guilty in the Crown
Court at Snaresbrook of two counts of obtaining property by deception contrary
to s 15(1) of the Theft Act 1968 (counts 1 and 2) of, being a bankrupt, removing
property contrary to s 354(2) of the 1986 Act (count 4) and of, being a bankrupt,
failing to account for the loss of his property contrary to s 354(3) of the 1986 Act
(count 5). The prosecution led evidence against him at his trial of answers which
he had given under compulsion when he was examined on oath in the bankruptcy
proceedings. Section 433 of the 1986 Act provides that statements made by a

a person in response to a requirement imposed by the Act or rules made under it may be used in evidence in proceedings against him. A submission on his behalf that, notwithstanding s 433 of that Act, the transcript of his public examination in the bankruptcy proceedings was inadmissible by virtue of s 31 of the 1968 Act was rejected by the trial judge.

[39] The respondent was sentenced to 15 months' imprisonment on counts 1 and
b 2 concurrently and to three months' imprisonment on counts 4 and 5 concurrently with each other and with the 15 months' imprisonment on counts 1 and 2. He appealed to the Court of Appeal (Criminal Division) on the ground that the trial judge erred in law in ruling that the answers which he had given during his examination on oath in the bankruptcy proceedings were admissible under s 433 of the 1986 Act and were not rendered inadmissible by s 31 of the 1968 Act. On
c 12 May 1992 the Court of Appeal dismissed his appeal.

[40] On 27 April 1998 the Criminal Cases Review Commission referred the respondent's convictions on counts 1 and 2 only to the Court of Appeal (Criminal Division) under s 9(1) of the Criminal Appeal Act 1995. It did so on the ground that there was a real possibility that the court would find his conviction on those
d counts unsafe in the light of the decision in R v Preddy [1996] 3 All ER 481, [1996] AC 815. On 20 June 2000, following further representations on behalf of the respondent, the commission referred his convictions on counts 4 and 5 also to the Court of Appeal (Criminal Division): see s 9(4) of the 1995 Act. This was done on the ground, among others, that there was a real possibility, following the judgment of the European Court of Human Rights in Saunders v UK and the
e passing of the 1998 Act, that the court would find that the admission of the respondents' answers under compulsion at his trial was in breach of art 6 of the convention and that his convictions on counts 4 and 5, as well as his convictions on counts 1 and 2, were unsafe.

[41] In the meantime, on 28 October 1999, your Lordships gave judgment in
f R v DPP, ex p Kebeline, R v DPP, ex p Rechachi [1999] 4 All ER 801, [2000] 2 AC 326. One of the issues in that case was whether the 1998 Act gave rise to a legitimate expectation that, prior to its taking full effect, the Director would exercise his discretion to consent to a prosecution under the Prevention of Terrorism (Temporary Provisions) Act 1989 in accordance with art 6(2) of the convention which guarantees the presumption of innocence. The applicants' argument in
g the Divisional Court was summarised by Lord Bingham of Cornhill CJ ([1999] 4 All ER 801 at 810–811, [2000] 2 AC 326 at 338–339):

'The applicants point out, quite correctly, that s 22(4) introduces an element of retrospectivity on which victims of acts made unlawful by the
h convention may rely when s 7(1)(b) is brought into force. Thus they submit that if the applicants are tried and convicted before the central provisions of the 1998 Act come into force, but their appeal against conviction is heard after those provisions come into force, they will then be entitled on appeal to rely on any ground open to them under the convention as a ground for quashing the conviction. This, they contend, founds a legitimate expectation
j that the Director will, before the central provisions come into force, exercise his prosecutorial discretion so as to refuse consent to any prosecution which would, after the provisions come into force, be held unsafe on any convention ground.'

The applicants' argument failed in the Divisional Court on other grounds. But that part of it which relied on the effect of s 22(4) as to their right to rely on the convention in an appeal was accepted (see [1999] 4 All ER 801 at 812–813 and 823, [2000] 2 AC 326 at 341 and 352 per Lord Bingham of Cornhill CJ and Laws LJ respectively). 	*a*

[42] The same point formed part of the applicants' argument in this House (see [2000] 2 AC 326 at 360). Lord Hobhouse of Woodborough said ([1999] 4 All ER 801 at 856, [2000] 2 AC 326 at 395), that it was the cornerstone of their argument. The Director presented a contrary argument. Lord Steyn said ([1999] 4 All ER 801 at 832, [2000] 2 AC 326 at 368): 	*b*

'On appeal to the House, but not in the Divisional Court, Mr Pannick argued that s 22(4), read with s 7(1)(b), is apt only to extend to the trial. It was an argument of some technicality. The language of the statute does not compel its adoption and a construction which treats the trial and the appeal as parts of one process is more in keeping with the purpose of the convention and the 1998 Act. It is the sensible and just construction. I would reject the argument advanced on behalf of the DPP on this point.' 	*c*

Lord Slynn of Hadley ([1999] 4 All ER 801 at 362, [2000] 2 AC 326 at 362), agreed 	*d* with Lord Steyn. Lord Cooke of Thorndon too said ([1999] 4 All ER 801 at 836, [2000] 2 AC 326 at 372), that he was in general agreement with Lord Steyn. I said ([1999] 4 All ER 801 at 839, [2000] 2 AC 326 at 375) that if the Act were in force, the appropriate remedy would be to raise the issue of incompatibility with the convention right at trial or on appeal. 	*e*

[43] On 24 May 2001 the Court of Appeal (Criminal Division) (Rose LJ, Rougier and McCombe JJ) [2001] EWCA Crim 1260, [2001] 3 WLR 751 allowed the appeal. The court held that, as a matter of construction, the consequences of the absence from the 1995 Act of any time limit for references by the Criminal Cases Review Commission and of s 22(4) of the 1998 Act as interpreted in *Ex p Kebeline* were (1) that it was open to the commission to refer a conviction 	*f* following a trial whenever it took place and (2) that the court had no option but to declare the conviction unsafe if that was the result either of the admission of evidence obtained in breach of art 6 of the convention or of a change in the common law: [2001] EWCA Crim 1260 at [23], [2001] 3 WLR 751 at [23]. As for the challenge to the safety of the respondent's conviction on all four counts 	*g* because of the use made at the trial under s 433 of the Insolvency Act 1986 of his answers in the bankruptcy proceedings before the Official Receiver which were compelled by s 291 of that Act, the court held that the convictions on those counts could not be regarded as safe in the light of the inadmissibility, as it must now be held to be, of those answers and the judge's direction to the jury as to the 	*h* potential significance of the transcript of those proceedings. The appeal was allowed and the convictions on all counts were quashed.

[44] The Crown asked for and were granted permission to appeal. A certificate was granted under s 33(2) of the Criminal Appeal Act 1968 that the following point of law of general public importance was involved in the decision: 	*j*

'Following a reference to the Court of Appeal, Criminal Division, by the Criminal Cases Review Commission, is a defendant whose trial took place before the coming into force of ss 6(1) and 7(1)(b) of the Human Rights Act 1998 entitled after they come into force to rely on an alleged breach of his convention rights whenever the alleged breach took place?'

THE ISSUES IN THIS APPEAL

a [45] The parties are agreed that the issue in this appeal turns on whether there is any material distinction between the facts in R v Lambert [2001] 3 All ER 577 and the facts in this case. The Crown submits that no such distinction can be drawn, that the reasons given by the majority in that case should be applied here also and that in any event, having regard to the provisions of s 6 of the 1998 Act read with b s 7(1)(b), the two cases are indistinguishable. The respondent submits that his case is to be distinguished from R v Lambert and that the House is not bound by the reasons given in that case by the majority.

[46] Shortly before the hearing of the appeal the Guinness appellants sought leave to intervene and were granted leave to present submissions both orally and c in writing. They are parties to two sets of proceedings which raise issues substantially similar to those in the present case and are likely therefore to be affected directly by its outcome. These are their pending appeals before the Court of Appeal (Criminal Division) following references of their cases to that court by the Criminal Cases Review Commission and the Crown's pending application for judicial review of the Commission's reference of their case to the Court of d Appeal. Your Lordships have had the benefit of detailed and carefully presented submissions by Mr Emmerson QC for the interveners on a number of matters which were not dealt with at the hearing of the appeals in Ex p Kebeline and R v Lambert.

[47] On one view of the decision in R v Lambert, all that was decided was that e decisions of courts and tribunals made before 2 October 2000 cannot be impugned after that date on the ground that the court or tribunal acted incompatibly with a convention right as the retrospective application of s 7(1)(b) provided for in s 22(4) does not apply to the acts of courts or tribunals. That interpretation of the decision is consistent with the views which I expressed in f that case as to the meaning and effect of these provisions in the 1998 Act. As I have explained, it is consistent also with the views expressed by both Lord Clyde and Lord Hutton as to how the question in that case should be answered. That also is how Lord Cooke of Thorndon understood the position to be when he was giving the judgment of the board in Preiss v General Dental Council [2001] UKPC 36 at [21], [2001] 1 WLR 1926. But the Crown maintains that it was decided in R v g Lambert that all appeals by an unsuccessful defendant are excluded from the retrospective application of s 7(1)(b) whether or not the act made unlawful by s 6(1) was that of the court or the prosecutor.

[48] If the Crown is right on this point, it will be necessary to deal with two further arguments. The respondent submits that references made to the Court h of Appeal by the Criminal Cases Review Commission, and appeals from decisions made on those references, are themselves proceedings brought by or at the instigation of a public authority within the meaning of s 7(6)(a). He also submits that appeals by the Crown or any other public authority in any proceedings, including this appeal to your Lordships' House, are proceedings brought by or at j the instigation of a public authority within the meaning of that paragraph. The Crown says in its reply that neither of these propositions assists the respondent. It submits that references by the commission and appeals which follow after a conviction are to be seen, not as separate proceedings, but as part of the criminal proceedings brought by the Crown with a view to obtaining a conviction. But, as they are appeals, s 7(6)(b) applies to them. So they are not proceedings brought by or at the instigation of a public authority for the purposes of s 22(4).

[49] I propose therefore to approach this case in five stages. The first is to *a* revisit the provisions of ss 7(1) and 7(6) of the 1998 Act in order to see whether the reasons given by the majority in *R v Lambert* can now be regarded as tenable in the light of the further consideration which has been given to the effect of these provisions in this case. The second is to examine and assess the various practical objections which have been advanced both by the respondent and the interveners to a reading of them which would exclude all appeals against any decisions made *b* before 2 October 2000 from the retrospective effect which is given to s 7(1)(b) by s 22(4). The third is to set out my conclusion on the difficult question whether or not the majority view in *R v Lambert* should now be departed from if it can no longer be regarded as tenable. The fourth is to examine a ground for the dealing with the point raised in *R v Lambert* which would appear to avoid the difficulty and then to consider how that reasoning should be applied in this case. I shall deal *c* finally with the respondent's arguments that references by the Criminal Cases Review Commission and appeals by the Crown or other public authority are proceedings by or at the instigation of a public authority to which retrospectivity is given by s 22(4).

MUST WE ADHERE TO THE MAJORITY VIEW?

[50] I should like to say something at the outset about the test which I think should be applied as to whether it is open to your Lordships to depart from the majority view in *R v Lambert* on the question whether the effect of s 22(4) read together with ss 7(1)(b) and 7(6) of the 1998 Act is to exclude all appeals from retrospectivity. I do so because I am conscious of the fact that your Lordships, for *e* various reasons, do not agree with me that it is open to us to depart from the majority view in this case. I must explain why I have reached a different opinion on this point.

[51] As Lord Wilberforce observed in *Fitzleet Estates Ltd v Cherry (Inspector of Taxes)* [1977] 3 All ER 996 at 999, [1977] 1 WLR 1345 at 1349, the best way to *f* resolve a question as to which there are two eminently possible views is by the considered majority opinion of the ultimate tribunal, and much more than mere doubts as to the correctness of that opinion are needed to justify departing from it. But the development of our jurisprudence on the 1998 Act has only just begun. New problems are being revealed every week, if not every day. I believe that the interests of human rights law would not be well served if the House was to regard *g* itself as bound by views expressed by the majority in a previous case about the meaning of provisions in that Act, if to adhere to those reasons would produce serious anomalies or other results which are plainly unsatisfactory: see *Jones v Secretary of State for Social Services, Hudson v Secretary of State for Social Services* [1972] 1 All ER 145 at 149, 171, [1972] AC 944 at 966, 993 per Lord Reid and *h* Viscount Dilhorne respectively. Furthermore, as I shall attempt to show, I do not think that this is case where each of the two competing views on the critical question can be described, in Lord Wilberforce's words, as 'eminently possible'. With great respect, I consider that the view of the majority in *R v Lambert* was a mistaken one. If a mistake was indeed made, I believe that it would be better to *j* face up to that fact now and to correct it as soon as possible.

[52] There are four other important factors which I think ought to be taken into account. The first is that views contrary to those of the majority in *R v Lambert* were expressed by a majority of your Lordships in *Ex p Kebeline*. The majority view in *Ex p Kebeline* was referred to and applied by the Court of Appeal in this case: [2001] EWCA Crim 1260 at [15] and [20], [2001] 3 WLR 751 at [15]

a   and [20]. It was also followed by the Court of Appeal in *R v Benjafield* [2001] 2 All ER
     609 at 624–625, [2001] 3 WLR 75 at 92–93). Lord Woolf CJ, giving the judgment
     of the court, added these observations (*R v Benjafield* [2001] 2 All ER 609 at 625,
     [2001] 3 WLR 75 at 93):

         'In our judgment, where the original proceedings are brought by, or at the
b   instigation of, a public authority, as is the case with a prosecution, an appeal
         by the defendant is part of the proceedings to which s 22(4) applies. There
         cannot be a different position on an appeal from that of the trial so far as the
         issue of retrospectivity of the 1998 Act is concerned. Any other construction
         would mean that in criminal cases, the Court of Appeal could not give the
         required protection to the individual (who would clearly be a victim of any
c   unlawful act) so that there would be a need for an otherwise unnecessary but
         time-consuming and expensive trip to Strasbourg. In addition, otherwise
         s 7(1)(b) will apply where the appeal is by a public authority, but not when
         the appeal is made by the defendant.'

     The fact that the majority view in *Ex p Kebeline* was consistent with the view
d   expressed by Lord Bingham of Cornhill CJ in the Divisional Court in that case and
     was endorsed by Lord Woolf CJ in *R v Benjafield* is significant. It is not easy to
     dismiss that view as a mistake. It seems to me that this is one of those rare cases
     which are bound to occur from time to time in a jurisdiction such as ours,
     however well organised, where the court of last instance has arrived at different
     conclusions in different cases on the same point. On the other hand I would
e   attach no importance to what was said in *Preiss v General Dental Council* [2001]
     UKPC 36, [2001] 1 WLR 1926. Judgment was not given in *R v Lambert* until after
     the hearing of that appeal, so the effect of that judgment was not explored at all
     during the argument.
         [53] The second factor is that the House has not been asked by either party in
f   this case to apply the *Practice Statement (Judicial Precedent)* [1966] 3 All ER 77,
     [1966] 1 WLR 1234 and depart from the bare decision in *R v Lambert*. I think that
     this helps to show that the situation is different from that contemplated by Lord
     Hoffmann in his dissenting judgment in *Lewis v A-G of Jamaica* [2001] 2 AC 50,
     [2000] 3 WLR 1785. As he explained (2 AC 50 at 88, [2000] 3 WLR 1785 at 1814),
g   all three questions raised by that case had already been considered and answered
     in three recent decisions of the board and he did not think that there was any
     justification for departing from any of them. I do not think that we are presented
     in this case with the same difficulty. We are dealing here with a question as to
     the meaning of a statute, not judge-made law or broad issues of principle. As I said
     at the outset of this judgment, I think that the decision in *R v Lambert* can be
h   regarded as having been confined by Lord Clyde, Lord Hutton and myself to an
     alleged breach of convention rights by the trial court—deliberately so, as that was
     the only point about the effect of s 22(4) that had to be decided in that case. The
     question is how the reasoning of the majority about the meaning of the relevant
     provisions in the 1998 Act is to be applied to different facts and circumstances.
j   Experience tells us that it is not always possible at a stroke to solve all the
     problems which may arise as to the meaning of a statute. I agree that we should
     try to speak with one voice and to achieve consistency. There are obvious dangers
     in departing from a line of reasoning in a previous case which had the support of
     a majority. But we are not infallible. Looking to the wider public interest, it
     seems to me that in the present context correction is more desirable than
     consistency.

[54] The third factor is that the majority view has still not been tested in a civil case. As I shall mention later, one of the principal concerns of the majority was the effect of retrospectivity on past convictions. I agree that this a matter of legitimate concern. But if Parliament had wished to preserve past convictions it could have done so by providing expressly that s 22(4) did not extend to an appeal against conviction. As it is, it is plain that the words in s 7(6)(b) on which the majority view relies extend to all appeals, whether civil or criminal. It would be unsatisfactory if the majority view were to be regarded as having pre-empted the question whether s 22(4) applies to civil appeals, to which the concern about past convictions does not apply.

[55] The fourth factor is the context in which the question which is before the House in this case has been raised. The United Kingdom is required by its treaty obligations to comply with art 13 of the European Convention for the Protection of Human Rights and Fundamental Freedoms 1950 (as set out in Sch 1 to the Human Rights Act 1998) (the convention), which provides:

'Everyone whose rights and freedoms as set forth in this Convention are violated shall have an effective remedy before a national authority notwithstanding that the violation has been committed by persons acting in an official capacity.'

The United Kingdom has also undertaken under art 46 of the convention to accept the jurisdiction of the European Court of Human Rights in all matters concerning the interpretation and application of the convention. These obligations have been binding on the United Kingdom in international law since ratification in 1951. Since 1966 the right of individual petition against the state under art 25 has been available. The purpose of ss 7 to 9 of the 1998 Act is to provide a structure within which effect can be given to these obligations in domestic law. The extent to which the 1998 Act gives retrospective effect to its provisions needs to be seen in that context. This is an exercise which was absent from the discussion which took place in *R v Lambert*.

[56] The effect of s 22(4) has been explained in the annotations to the 1998 Act in *Current Law Statutes*, to which the late Peter Duffy QC contributed, as being to enable the Act to be used defensively against public authorities with retrospective effect but not, it appears, offensively. The example is given of a person charged with an offence under subordinate legislation pre-dating the 1998 Act's entry into force who would be entitled to rely on the convention to show that the legislation was invalid but not to bring an application for judicial review for a declaration that it was invalid. There remain however a number of difficult issues in regard to retrospectivity which s 22(4) does not address directly and on which no view has been expressed in the commentary. They include the question whether its effect is to permit a defendant in proceedings brought by or at the instigation of a public authority to rely on his convention rights where the proceedings at first instance took place before the Act came into force and the point is raised for the first time on appeal. A further question is whether, in criminal cases, it makes any difference whether the breach was brought about by an act of the prosecutor or by a judicial act and, if judicial acts (or at least some judicial acts) are to be treated differently, what it is that enables these acts to be distinguished from acts of the prosecutor.

DOES s 22(4) EXCLUDE APPEALS?

[57] Section 22(4) provides that s 7(1)(b) applies 'to proceedings brought by or at the instigation of a public authority' whenever the act in question took place,

a but that otherwise that subsection does not apply to an act taking place before the coming into force of that section. The word 'proceedings' is not, as such, defined anywhere in the 1998 Act. At first sight this provision extends to proceedings of any kind in any court or tribunal, whether at first instance or on appeal. In any event it must be taken to apply to proceedings in every kind of case, whether civil or criminal. Nevertheless, in order to understand fully the scope which is to be
b given to the word in its context, it is necessary to examine the provisions in s 7 to which s 22(4) refers.

(a) *Section 7(1)(a)*

[**58**] Section 7, as indicated by its side-note, deals with 'proceedings'. Subsection (1) provides that a person who claims that a public authority has acted,
c or proposes to act, in a way which is made unlawful by s 6(1) may do one or other of two things. He may bring proceedings against the authority under the 1998 Act in the appropriate court or tribunal: s 7(1)(a). Or he may rely on the convention right or rights concerned in any legal proceedings: s 7(1)(b). Section 22(4) gives retrospective effect only to s 7(1)(b). As retrospective effect is given only to
d proceedings brought by or at the instigation of a public authority, it would not have been appropriate for s 22(4) to have referred also to s 7(1)(a). That provision refers only to proceedings brought by the victim against the authority whose act is made unlawful by s 6(1).

[**59**] Lord Clyde referred in *R v Lambert* [2001] 3 All ER 577 at [139] to the fact that, in so far as the act for the purposes of s 7(1)(a) is a judicial act, the
e proceedings must be one or other of those set out in s 9(1). The first of these is by exercising a right of appeal: s 9(1)(a). He said that it did not appear likely that there should be a retrospectivity under s 7(1)(b) in respect of an appeal against a decision given prior to 2 October 2000 if there was none under s 7(1)(a). This was one of the two reasons which he gave for his view that s 22(4) did not extend
f retrospectivity to appeals. I have looked more closely at this point in the light of the more detailed argument which we have had in this case. With great respect, I do not think that it bears the weight which Lord Clyde would wish to attach to it.

[**60**] Section 7(1)(a) and s 7(1)(b) are designed to provide two quite different remedies. Section 7(1)(a) enables the victim of the unlawful act to bring proceedings
g under the 1998 Act against the authority. It is intended to cater for free-standing claims made under the 1998 Act where there are no other proceedings in which the claim can be made. This provision also differs from that in s 7(1)(b), in that claims made under it are subject to the time limit prescribed by s 7(5). This subsection provides that proceedings under s 7(1)(a) must be brought before the
h end of the period of one year beginning with the date on which the act complained of took place or such longer period as the court or tribunal considers equitable, but subject to any rule imposing a stricter time limit in relation to the procedure in question. Among the remedies that may be obtained by this means against the public authority is that of damages: see s 8. Section 8(2) provides that
j damages may be awarded only by a court which has power to award damages, or to order the payment of compensation, in civil proceedings. The purpose of this provision is to ensure that a claim for damages as a result of a criminal prosecution is brought in a civil court.

[**61**] The Lord Chancellor's Consultation Paper, *Human Rights Act 1998: Rules and Practice Directions*, CP5/00, March 2000, proposed in para 12 that what it described as 'a free-standing case under section 7(1)(a) of the Act' should be brought (a) by using the existing judicial review procedures, (b) in the county

court or in the High Court where a claim of damages is made or (c) in the county
court or the High Court following a finding of unlawfulness under s 7(1)(b) in ^{a}
some other court or tribunal which does not have the power to award damages
or compensation—where, for example, damages are claimed arising out of a
ruling by a magistrates' court or the Crown Court that the prosecution had acted
unlawfully. In para 15 reference was made to proposals designed to ensure that
issues of art 5(5) damages were determined in the appropriate court. The Civil ^{b}
Procedure (Amendment No 4) Rules 2000, SI 2000/2092, which made the
appropriate amendments to the Civil Procedure Rules 1998, came into force on
2 October 2000. Among the new rules is CPR 7.11(1), which provides that a claim
under s 7(1)(a) in respect of a judicial act may be brought only in the High Court;
see also r 19.4A(3) and r 33.9.

[62] Article 5(5) of the convention provides that everyone who has been the ^{c}
victim of arrest or detention in contravention of that article shall have an enforceable
right to compensation. But under English law, there was prior to the 1998 Act,
no right to compensation where the detention took place following the issue of a
warrant by a court. The prison governor was protected by the court's warrant,
and the judge was protected by his immunity from liability in a civil action for ^{d}
damages in respect of acts done in his judicial capacity: *Sirros v Moore* [1974] 3 All ER
776, [1975] QB 118; see also the Justices of the Peace Act 1997, ss 51 and 52 as
regards magistrates. Section 9 of the 1998 Act preserves judicial immunity except
to the extent required by art 5(5). Section 9(1) provides that proceedings under
s 7(1)(a) in respect of a judicial act may be brought only by exercising a right of
appeal, on an application for judicial review or in such other forum as may be ^{e}
prescribed by rules. Section 9(3) provides that in proceedings under the 1998 Act
in respect of a judicial act done in good faith, damages may not be awarded
otherwise than to compensate a person to the extent required by art 5(5) of the
convention, and s 9(4) provides that any award of damages under s 9(3) is to be
made against the Crown. ^{f}

[63] Thus the purpose of s 7(1)(a) is to enable the victim to bring free-standing
proceedings against the public authority whose act was unlawful under s 6(1).
Section 7(2) provides that the reference in s 7(1)(a) to 'appropriate court or
tribunal' means such court or tribunal as may be determined in accordance with
rules. The rules make it clear that these proceedings are civil proceedings, and
that they cannot be brought in a criminal court. The reference in s 9(1)(a) to ^{g}
exercising a right of appeal is intended to describe one of the means by which a
s 7(1)(a) claim may be brought in civil court under the special procedures which
apply where the act complained of is a judicial act.

[64] Section 7(1)(a) does not apply where the victim wishes to rely on his
convention rights in his capacity as the defendant in proceedings which have been ^{h}
brought against him by a public authority. His remedy in those proceedings is
that provided by s 7(1)(b). The reference in s 9(1)(a) to exercising a right of appeal
is intended to describe one of the means by which a s 7(1)(a) claim may be
brought in a civil court where the act complained of is a judicial act and where
such a right of appeal is available. These provisions are not concerned with the ^{j}
situation where a person claiming to be a victim of a violation wishes to rely on
his convention rights in existing proceedings brought against him by a public
authority.

[65] For these reasons I think that the fact that s 22(4) does not give
retrospective effect to s 7(1)(a)—and thus to proceedings under that provision in
respect of a judicial act which are brought by exercising a right of appeal, as

a   s 9(1)(a) provides—has no bearing on the meaning to be given to the word 'proceedings' in s 7(1)(b) as applied retrospectively by s 22(4). The remedy by way of an appeal to which s 9(1) refers is an entirely different remedy from that provided by s 7(1)(b).

(b) *Section 7(6)*

b   [66] The second reason which Lord Clyde gave for his view that s 22(4) did not apply retrospectively to appeals is the same as that given by Lord Slynn ([2001] 3 All ER 577 at [9]) and Lord Hutton ([2001] 3 All ER 577 at [172]). It is based on the wording of s 7(6), which provides:

c   'In subsection (1)(b) "legal proceedings" includes—(a) proceedings brought by or at the instigation of a public authority; and (b) an appeal against the decision of a court or tribunal.'

[67] The words used in s 7(1)(b) to describe the proceedings in which the victim may rely on his convention rights are 'any legal proceedings'. The words 'legal proceedings' are the subject of the definition in s 7(6) which I have just d   quoted. It is said to distinguish between (a) proceedings brought by or at the instigation of a public authority on the one hand and (b) an appeal against the decision of a court or tribunal on the other. Attention is then drawn to the fact that the words used in s 22(4) to describe the proceedings in which the victim has the benefit of retrospectivity are 'proceedings brought by or at the instigation of a public authority'. Section 22(4) uses the same words as those which form the e   first part of the definition in s 7(6), and it does not mention an appeal. This is said to indicate that the retrospective provision does not extend to appeals. In other words, the benefit of s 22(4) is available only in proceedings at first instance.

[68] The Crown do not dispute that the word 'proceedings' is capable of including an appeal against a decision at first instance in the same action. As Lord f   Slynn said in *R v Lambert* [2001] 3 All ER 577 at [9] an appeal may be considered as part of the proceedings initiated by a particular party. The same point was made by Lord Steyn in *R v DPP, ex p Kebeline, R v DPP, ex p Rechachi* [1999] 4 All ER 801 at 832, [2000] 2 AC 326 at 368 and by Lord Woolf CJ in *R v Benjafield* [2001] 2 All ER 609 at 625, [2001] 3 WLR 75 at 93 (para 51). Indeed Mr McGuinness QC for the Crown put much emphasis on the point that an appeal remains part of g   the original criminal proceedings brought by the prosecuting authority when he was submitting that neither a reference by the Criminal Cases Review Commission nor an appeal by the Crown were separate proceedings for the purposes of s 22(4).

[69] If the intention was to restrict the meaning of the word in this context to h   proceedings at first instance only, one would have expected this to have been made clear in s 22(4). For example, the Legal Aid Act 1988 is careful to define the courts and tribunals in which legal aid is available, with the result that proceedings in each court or tribunal are separate proceedings for the purposes of legal aid: see ss 14(1) and 19(1). There is no indication in s 22(4) that it was j   seeking to make that kind of distinction. It does not distinguish between proceedings according to whether they are civil or criminal or restrict them to those before any particular court or tribunal. Nor does it restrict the benefit of retrospectivity to proceedings which were commenced after s 7(1)(b) was brought into force.

[70] The only point of distinction to which s 22(4) refers relates to the person by whom or at whose instigation the proceedings are brought. It applies only to

proceedings brought by or at the instigation of a public authority. Why then did
the provision take this form? In my opinion the answer is not hard to seek. The
purpose of the provision was to give effect in domestic law to art 13 of the
convention, which sets out everyone's right to an effective remedy for a violation
of his convention rights notwithstanding that the violation has been committed
by persons acting in an official capacity. As I said in *Brown v Stott (Procurator Fiscal,
Dunfermline)* [2001] 2 All ER 97 at 125, [2001] 2 WLR 817 at 847, ss 7 to 9 were
intended to lay down a remedial structure for giving effect to the convention rights
as defined by s 1(1) of the Act. Section 22(4), in so far as it gives retrospectivity to
s 7(1)(b), is part of that structure. This fact suggests that, although the provision is
limited to proceedings brought by or at the instigation of a public authority, it
was not the intention to restrict its effect to any particular stage in those
proceedings. It is not possible to identify any good reason, consistent with the
principles which underpin convention rights, for preventing the state from taking
advantage of its pre-commencement breach in proceedings at first instance but
allowing it do so on appeal.

[71] The majority view that s 22(4) does not extend to appeals depends
entirely on the words used in s 7(6). The first thing to notice about this provision
is that the word which it uses to introduce the definition is the word 'includes'.
The definition does not pretend to be a restrictive or an exhaustive one. It seeks
instead, by stating what is to be *included* in the words 'legal proceedings', to put
the two matters with which it deals beyond doubt. The second thing to notice
about it is that the two matters which are dealt with in it are each directed to
different questions. The matters with which it deals are not mutually exclusive.
The first question is whether the expression 'legal proceedings' includes proceedings
brought by or at the instigation of a public authority. The second question is
whether the expression includes an appeal against the decision of a court or
tribunal. The definition seeks to clarify the circumstances in which the victim of
an act of a public authority made unlawful by s 6(1) may exercise the remedy in
s 7(1)(b), bearing in mind the fact that s 6(3)(a) provides that a court or tribunal is
included in the expression 'public authority'. The word 'proceedings' in s 7(6)(a)
appears simply to be a shorthand way of referring back to the words 'legal
proceedings' in s 7(1)(b). On this view, the reference to an appeal in s 7(6)(b) is
available to explain what is meant by 'proceedings' in s 7(6)(a). The effect of
s 7(6)(b) is that the word 'proceedings' in s 7(6)(a) includes an appeal in those
proceedings.

[72] For these reasons it seems to me that it does not follow from the fact that
s 7(6)(b) mentions an appeal against the decision of a court or tribunal that
appeals against decisions taken in proceedings brought by or at the instigation of
a public authority are excluded from s 7(6)(a). I consider, with great respect, that
the balance of the argument is quite plainly the other way. In any event I regard
the position favoured by the majority in *R v Lambert* as unclear, in the absence of
an express provision in s 22(4) which limits the retrospective effect of s 7(1)(b) to
decisions taken at first instance. In this situation it is necessary to examine the
consequences of a reading of s 22(4) which would limit its effect in this way by
implication.

ANOMALIES

[73] There are a number of points which arise under this heading.

(a) A prosecution appeal by way of case stated under s 28 of the Supreme
Court Act 1981 against an acquittal in the magistrates' court is a proceeding by a

a public authority. Although it is described as an appeal, the Crown accepts that it
is also a separate proceeding by the public authority which is brought in the High
Court. This means that a person can rely on a violation of his convention rights
at a trial which took place before 2 October 2000 if the prosecution appeals by
way of case stated against his acquittal. But if the majority view is right, he cannot
do so if he was convicted and he wishes to appeal by way of case stated on the
b ground that there was a violation of his convention rights at his trial against his
conviction. This is because s 22(4) does not extend to an appeal, and the
proceeding which the defendant brings by way of case stated is not by or at the
instigation of a public authority.

(b) A reference by the Attorney General to the Court of Appeal under s 36 of
the Criminal Justice Act 1988 for review of a sentence pronounced in the Crown
c Court prior to 2 October 2000 which he considers to be unduly lenient is a
separate proceeding by a public authority. Here again the person against whom
the sentence was passed can rely on his convention rights in those proceedings so
far as they may be relevant to the question whether his sentence was unduly
lenient. But if the majority view is right, he cannot do so if he wishes to appeal
d against his sentence under s 9 of the Criminal Appeal Act 1968 on the ground that
it was imposed in violation of his convention rights. The Crown says that there
is no anomaly here, as no examples can be envisaged in the case of a s 36 reference
which would engage a possible incompatibility with convention rights. I do not
agree. Sections 36(1)(b)(i) and (ii) make it clear that if the original sentence is
quashed the whole sentencing process is re-opened. Articles 3, 5, 7 and 14 all have
e potential relevance to sentencing exercises carried out by any court.

(c) If the majority view is right, a person would not be able to rely on a
violation of his convention rights as a ground of appeal against a conviction at a
trial which took place before 2 October 2000. The Court of Appeal would not be
able to quash the conviction and order a retrial on this ground, as the defendant
f would not be entitled to ask the Court of Appeal to take account of the violation
when it was considering whether the appeal should be allowed and whether or
not there should be a retrial. The Crown says that if he was successful in his
appeal against his conviction on other grounds and a retrial was ordered, he
would be able to rely at the retrial on the same violation of his convention rights.
I agree. But it seems to me that difficult questions may arise as to whether the
g Court of Appeal can have regard to the violation when it is deciding whether
or not there should be a retrial, bearing in mind that it was not open to it to have
regard to the violation when it was considering whether the conviction is unsafe.
It would not be satisfactory to have to wait for the retrial if the question whether
or not there was a violation which would make a conviction in that trial unsafe
h could be decided before the appeal was disposed of.

(d) If the majority view is right, a defendant in civil proceedings brought
against him by or at the instance of a public authority based upon a pre-
commencement act which he says was a violation of his convention rights would
not be able to use this as ground of appeal retrospectively against a decision
j which went against him at first instance. Examples of appeals in civil proceedings
to which this proposition would apply which are likely to raise issues about
convention rights are where the appeal was against a committal order, a refusal
to grant habeas corpus or the making of a secure accommodation order under
s 25 of the Children Act 1989; see also *Aston Cantlow and Wilmcote with Billesley
Parochial Church Council v Wallbank* [2001] EWCA Civ 713, [2001] 3 All ER 393,
where the right to peaceful enjoyment of possessions was said to have been

breached by a repair notice. Nor would he be able to rely on the violation if the decision was in his favour and an appeal was taken against that decision after *a* 2 October 2000 by the public authority. This is because, on the majority view, s 22(4) does not apply to an appeal.

[74] It seems to me that these four examples suggest that serious anomalies could result if the majority view is right. They would disappear if the word 'proceedings' is given the wider meaning which it is capable of bearing so as to *b* include appeals in the same proceedings. To give it that wider meaning would be consistent with what I understand to have been the purpose of s 22(4), namely to give effect to the state's treaty obligation under art 13 to provide an effective remedy in domestic law in proceedings brought by or at the instigation of a public authority. The underlying policy is that the state should no longer be able to take *c* advantage in those proceedings of its breach of its obligation not to act incompatibly with the convention rights. On the majority view, the remedy provided by s 22(4) would be effective against violations of convention rights at first instance in some situations, but not in others. The situations in which it would be effective against those violations would appear, at least in some cases, to depend upon initiatives taken by the public authority which was alleged to have acted unlawfully. It is *d* hard to believe that the framers of the Act, who must have been aware of basic convention rights principles such as those which require that there be equality of arms between the defendant and the prosecutor and that the victim is afforded an effective remedy, intended this to be so.

[75] For these reasons I would, with great respect, depart from the majority *e* view in *R v Lambert* on this point. I would hold that a defendant whose trial took place before the date of the coming into force of s 7(1)(b) is entitled to rely in an appeal after that date on an alleged breach of his convention rights at the trial by the prosecutor.

[76] I should add that I have considered whether it might be possible to *f* confine the majority view to criminal cases only, as *R v Lambert* was a criminal case and one of the principal concerns of the majority was about the effect of retrospectivity on past convictions: see [2001] 3 All ER 577 at [10], [147], [173] per Lord Slynn, Lord Clyde and Lord Hutton respectively. The question, as it has been put to us in this case, is once again confined to criminal cases. So once again was the argument, as the speeches of my noble and learned friends Lord Slynn *g* and Lord Hutton demonstrate. But the reference in s 7(6)(b) to an appeal is unqualified. It extends to any appeal against a decision by a court or tribunal, whether criminal or civil. So the majority view is not capable of being applied to an appeal of one kind only and not to others. It embraces all appeals of whatever kind from decisions at first instance in any kind of case, whether civil or criminal, *h* by any tribunal and by any court. I do not believe that the implications of this result were fully explored in *R v Lambert*, and they do not appear to have been addressed by Parliament. That is why I think that it would be right for your Lordships now to depart from that reasoning.

[77] As I do not feel able to decide this case by following the majority view in *j* *R v Lambert*, I must now turn to the reasons which I gave for agreeing with the majority that on the facts of that case the appellant, whose trial took place before 2 October 2000, was not entitled to rely on an alleged breach of his convention rights by the trial court. The arguments which I shall now consider were dealt with only briefly in the oral argument. But they have been dealt with fully in written submissions which were put in afterwards. The question is whether the

a decision in *R v Lambert* can still be supported, albeit for different reasons than those given by the majority.

JUDICIAL ACTS

[78] As I explained in *R v Lambert* [2001] 3 All ER 577 at [109] I based my decision on the view that a court or tribunal is not a party to the proceedings which are brought before it in its judicial capacity and that, for this reason, the *b* words used in s 7(1)(b) are not capable of being applied to a judicial act in the course of those proceedings. But I would be the first to recognise, after hearing further argument, that this approach gives rise to a number of problems and that it is not satisfactory.

[79] The first point which I would at once accept is that all three branches of *c* government, including the judiciary, are bound by the treaty obligations which have been assumed by the state under the convention. This suggests that it is not possible in the context of ss 7 to 9 of the 1998 Act, which are designed to give effect to the state's obligations under art 13 where a person claims that a public authority has acted in a way which is incompatible with a convention right, to *d* maintain a rigid distinction between acts of a court or tribunal on the one hand and acts of the prosecutor on the other. Furthermore, all public authorities are dealt with in the same way by s 6.

[80] In the context of the Scotland Act 1998 the position is different, for the reasons which I gave in *Montgomery v HM Advocate, Coulter v HM Advocate* [2001] 2 WLR 779 at 796–798 and *Brown v Stott (Procurator Fiscal, Dunfermline)* [2001] *e* 2 All ER 97, [2001] 2 WLR 817 at 846–848. The system which the legislation provides ensures that the state's obligations are respected both by the Scottish Parliament and the Scottish Executive by limiting their competence. The Lord Advocate is a member of the Scottish Executive and all those who prosecute in his name or under his authority have no power to do anything that is incompatible *f* with any of the convention rights: s 57(2). But these limits on competence do not apply to the court, which is a separate branch of government from the Scottish Executive. The limits on the court's competence are to be found in s 6(1) of the Human Rights Act 1998. But the relevant provisions of that Act came into force on a different date from the relevant provisions of the Scotland Act 1998, and there are important differences between the systems laid down by these two Acts *g* with regard to the provision of an effective remedy. As Lord Coulsfield said in *Mills v HM Advocate (No 2)* 2001 SLT 1359 at 1365 (para 20), intriguing issues may arise as to the interrelationship between the duty imposed on the court under the convention—which does not raise any kind of devolution issue—and the duty or duties imposed by the devolution legislation on the Lord Advocate. In that *h* context the drawing of a distinction between acts of the court and acts of the prosecutor may be inevitable. But that is not so in cases to which the special features of the devolution legislation do not apply.

[81] I would accept also that the character of things that a court may do which are incompatible with a person's right to a fair trial under art 6 of the convention *j* may be indistinguishable from that of things done by a prosecutor. Some of the things which a court does may be regarded as judicial acts. Decisions made in the course of a trial by the trial judge as to whether to admit evidence and the directions which he is required to give in his summing up are judicial acts. But other things that a court does which may affect the conduct of the proceedings, perhaps through its officials, are administrative in character. If they are incompatible with a convention right, they should be treated in the same way as acts of the

same kind by the prosecutor which are incompatible with the defendant's right
to a fair trial.   *a*

[82] On the other hand, as Mr Emmerson for the interveners pointed out,
there is room for the view that some judicial acts may be distinguished from
others on the ground that, as a result of one or more provisions of primary
legislation, the public authority could not have acted differently: see s 6(2)(a) of
the 1998 Act. Acts to which that subsection applies are not made unlawful by   *b*
s 6(1). I would prefer not to develop this point in any detail as it was not argued
in *R v Lambert* and your Lordships would decide this case on other grounds. But
I think that it can be said that, as the direction by the trial judge which was under
challenge in that case was in accordance with the meaning and effect of ss 5(3)
and 28 of the Misuse of Drugs Act 1971 as it was understood at the time when he
gave the direction, no element of discretion was involved in what he did. As the   *c*
law stood at that time, in terms of s 6(2)(a), he 'could not have acted differently'.
On this approach his act was not made unlawful by s 6(1), so the appellant could
not say that he was the victim of an unlawful act for the purposes of s 7(1)(b).
I should add that it was not contended in *R v Lambert* that what occurred in that
case was due to any act on the part of the prosecutor.   *d*

[83] It would be possible therefore by this route to confine the decision in *R v
Lambert* to its own facts. Decisions of courts or tribunals made before 2 October
2000 which they were required to make by primary legislation are not affected by
s 22(4) of the 1998 Act. Section 22(4) requires s 7(1)(b) to be read together with
s 6(1), as it presumes that acts of a public authority may be made unlawful by that
subsection whenever the act took place. But the Act does not say that effect must   *e*
be given retrospectively to s 3(1). As I indicated in *R v Lambert* [2001] 3 All ER 577
at [115], I would hold that the interpretative obligation in s 3(1) cannot be applied
so as to change retrospectively the meaning which was previously given to a
provision in primary legislation. It does not make unlawful acts of courts or
tribunals or other public authorities which, as a result of provisions in primary   *f*
legislation, could not at the time when the acts were done have been done
differently: see s 6(2)(a).

[84] I do not overlook the fact that in *R v Benjafield* [2001] 2 All ER 609 at 624,
[2001] 3 WLR 75 at 92 (para 48) Lord Woolf CJ said that s 3(1) cannot be considered
in isolation, and that he concluded ([2001] 2 All ER 609 at 625, [2001] 3 WLR 75 at
94 (para 53)) that it has retrospective effect if ss 22(4) and 7(1)(b) apply. In my opinion   *g*
however the usual presumption that statutes are not intended to be retrospective in
effect applies to s 3(1). The fact that s 22(4) gives limited retrospectivity only to
s 7(1)(b) supports the application of the presumption elsewhere in the Act. Of
course, s 7(1)(b) requires to be read with s 6 when it is applied retrospectively to
pre-commencement acts. his is because the purpose of the subsection is to enable   *h*
a person to rely on a pre-commencement act by a public authority which is made
unlawful by s 6(1). But I do not find anything either in s 7(1)(b) or in ss 6(1) and
(2) which requires retrospective effect to be given to s 3(1). If that were to be
done, the result could be that legislation which at the time of the
pre-commencement act was being applied correctly according to the traditional   *j*
rules of statutory interpretation must now for the purposes of s 7(1)(b) be given
a different meaning which best accords with convention rights. Such a result
could have profound consequences. It would not be consistent with the general
principle on which primary legislation depends, which is legal certainty. So
I would not extend retrospectivity to s 3(1), in the absence of an express provision
to that effect.

SECTION 6(2)(b)

a [85] In the present case the Crown says that the trial judge could not have acted differently, as he was duty bound to admit the compulsory questioning evidence. This is because, according to the traditional rules of construction, it was lawful for that evidence to be used at the trial: see s 6(2)(a). It also says, applying the same rules of construction, that the prosecutor was giving effect to *b* s 433 of the Insolvency Act 1986 when he was leading and relying on that evidence: see s 6(2)(b) of the Human Rights Act 1998.

[86] I agree that, applying those rules, the judge's act was not unlawful within the meaning of s 6(1), read together with s 6(2)(a), as he had no discretion to refuse to allow the prosecutor to adduce that evidence. To do otherwise would have amounted to a repeal, or at least to a substantial repeal, of legislation *c* enacted by Parliament which authorised the use of that evidence: see *R v Staines* [1997] 1 Cr App R 426 at 442–443 per Lord Bingham of Cornhill CJ. But I think that there is force in the point developed in written submissions by the Crown that the prosecutor's act also was not unlawful on the ground, reading s 6(1) with s 6(2)(b), that what the prosecutor was doing was 'acting so as to give effect to' *d* s 433 of the 1986 Act.

[87] The respondent and the interveners say that this is not so, as the prosecutor was entitled to make his own choice as to the evidence which was to be led at the trial. They point to the fact that in February 1998 the Attorney General circulated a guidance note to prosecutors on the use by the prosecution of answers obtained under compulsory powers in criminal proceedings which *e* illustrates this point. It took account of the judgment of the European Court of Human Rights in *Saunders v UK* (1997) 2 BHRC 358. In para 3 of his note the Attorney General said that the prosecution should not normally use in evidence as part of its case or in cross-examination answers obtained under compulsory powers. In para 4 he said that there was a discretion for such answers to be used *f* in evidence in particular circumstances, as where the defendant who provided the answers himself introduced them in evidence or where he was being prosecuted for a failure or refusal to answer. So, it is said, s 433 of the 1986 Act could be given effect to according to traditional rules of construction by the prosecutor in a way that was compatible with convention rights.

[88] In my opinion however the question whether or not the prosecutor was *g* giving effect to s 433 of the 1986 Act within the meaning of s 6(2)(b) does not depend on whether he had a discretion as to whether or not to use these answers in evidence. The question is whether, having decided to use the answers and invite the judge to hold them to be admissible, he was doing what he was authorised to do by s 433. It seems to me that there can be only one answer to *h* this question. According to the traditional rules of construction by reference to which at the time that provision was to be interpreted, s 433 authorised him to lead and to rely on that evidence. He was entitled also to give effect to s 433 by asking the judge to hold that in terms of that section the evidence was admissible. In this respect I would hold that this case is indistinguishable from *R v Lambert* and *j* that it too can be decided by applying the provisions of s 6(2). I would hold that there was no act made unlawful by s 6(1) on which the respondent can rely in this appeal under s 7(1)(b).

CRIMINAL CASES REVIEW COMMISSION

[89] Mr Krolick for the respondent submitted that, if he was wrong on his main argument about retrospectivity, the respondent was nevertheless entitled

to the benefit of s 22(4) in this case because it had come before the Court of *a*
Appeal on a reference by the Criminal Cases Review Commission, which is a
public authority. He maintained that, that being so, these were proceedings
brought or instigated by a public authority within the meaning of s 7(6)(a) and
s 22(4) of the Human Rights Act 1998.

[90] As I am in his favour on the main argument but against him on the
question whether there was an unlawful act I do not need to deal with this point *b*
at any length. I am not persuaded that it is right to regard a reference under s 9
of the Criminal Appeal Act 1995 as a proceeding by the commission. Section 9(2)
states that the reference, once made, shall be treated for all purposes as an appeal
by the person under s 1 of the Criminal Appeal Act 1968. The commission takes
no part in the appeal itself, the conduct of which is entirely in the hands of the
person whose conviction is under review. Nor do I think that it is right to regard *c*
the appeal as having been instigated by the commission. The commission has
power to make a reference without an application having been made to it by the
person to whom it relates: see s 14(1) of the 1995 Act. But that is not what
happened in this case. The reference was made in response to an application
which was made by the respondent. He took the initiative, so it would be more *d*
accurate to say that it was he rather than the commission who instigated it.

PROSECUTION APPEALS

[91] Mr Krolick also submitted that, if he was wrong on the previous argument,
the respondent was nevertheless entitled to the benefit of retrospectivity because
the appeal to your Lordships' House was an appeal by the prosecutor and as such *e*
was to be regarded as a proceeding by a public authority within the meaning of
s 7(6)(a) and s 22(4) of the Human Rights Act 1998. He said that the respondent
was entitled for this reason to rely on the violation of his convention right in
response to this appeal.

[92] Here again I do not need to deal with the point at any length. It is *f*
sufficient to say that I would reject this argument on the ground that, for reasons
already given, the reference to the Court of Appeal and the appeal to this House
must both be regarded as part of the criminal proceedings which were initiated at
first instance by the prosecutor.

CONCLUSION   *g*

[93] For these reasons I would hold that the Court of Appeal were right to find
that the respondent was entitled to rely on the retrospectivity provision in s 22(4)
of the Human Rights Act 1998 in his appeal. But I think that they were wrong to
declare his convictions unsafe on the ground that they were obtained as the result
of the admission of evidence obtained in breach of art 6 of the convention. *h*
I consider that the act of the prosecutor was not made unlawful by s 6(1) as he
was acting so as to give effect to a provision in primary legislation which, at the
time when the act was done, could not have been read differently. I would allow
the appeal.

LORD HUTTON.   *j*

[94] My Lords, the respondent was convicted nine years ago in February 1992
by a Crown Court of two offences of obtaining property by deception and two
offences contrary to s 354 of the Insolvency Act 1986. He appealed against his
convictions and his appeal was dismissed by the Court of Appeal on 12 May 1992.
It is clear that at the time of his convictions and at the time of the dismissal of his

a appeal his convictions were lawful and safe in accordance with the law of England. The admission at his trial of answers which the respondent was obliged to give in his examination by the Official Receiver (which admission is now claimed by him to have constituted a breach of art 6 of the European Convention for the Protection of Human Rights and Fundamental Freedoms 1950 (as set out in Sch 1 to the Human Rights Act 1998) (the convention)) was expressly

b sanctioned by Parliament in s 433 of the 1986 Act which provided:

'In any proceedings (whether or not under this Act)—(a) a statement of affairs prepared for the purposes of any provision of this Act which is derived from the Insolvency Act 1985, and (b) any other statement made in pursuance of a requirement imposed by or under any such provision or by

c   or under rules made under this Act, may be used in evidence against any person making or concurring in making the statement.'

[95] Subsequently in 1998 two of his convictions were referred to the Court of Appeal by the Criminal Cases Review Commission and in 2000 the remaining two convictions were also referred and the appeal was heard by the Court of

d Appeal in April 2001. The Court of Appeal ([2001] EWCA Crim 1260, [2001] 3 WLR 751) allowed the appeal and quashed the convictions on the ground that the admission in evidence at the trial of the answers given in the examination by the Official Receiver constituted a violation of art 6 of the convention and were accordingly wrongly admitted in evidence so that the convictions were unsafe.

e [96] The judgment of the Court of Appeal was delivered before the decision of this House in *R v Lambert* [2001] UKHL 37, [2001] 3 All ER 577, [2001] 3 WLR 206 and the Court of Appeal was of the opinion that, in the light of the authorities which were then before it, s 22(4) of the Human Rights Act 1998 applied to appeals, so that if evidence had been admitted in breach of art 6 of the European Convention in a criminal trial prior to 2 October 2000 when the 1998 Act came

f into operation, convictions resulting from the admission of that evidence must be held to be unsafe, notwithstanding that the evidence had been properly admitted in accordance with the domestic law which was then applicable. Therefore, 'with no enthusiasm whatever' (see [2001] 3 All ER 577 at [24]) the Court of Appeal allowed the appeal and quashed the convictions. On the application of the Crown the Court of Appeal then certified the following point of law of general

g public importance:

'Following a reference to the Court of Appeal, Criminal Division, by the Criminal Cases Review Commission, is a defendant whose trial took place before the coming into force of ss 6(1) and 7(1)(b) of the Human Rights Act 1998 entitled, after they come into force, to rely on an alleged breach of his

h   convention rights whenever the alleged breach took place?'

[97] On this appeal by the Crown against the decision of the Court of Appeal two principal questions arise. The first question is whether the decision of the House in *R v Lambert* can be distinguished. If it cannot be distinguished, the

j second question is whether the House should depart from the decision in *R v Lambert*.

Can the decision in R v Lambert be distinguished?
[98] Mr Krolick, on behalf of the respondent, and Mr Emmerson QC, on behalf of the interveners, submitted that *R v Lambert* can be distinguished on the

ground that in that appeal the case made on behalf of the appellant was that it was
the trial judge who had violated his convention rights under art 6 by directing the   *a*
jury (as he was obliged to do under domestic law) that the onus of proof rested
upon him to prove lack of knowledge that the bag he was carrying contained
drugs, whereas in the present case the respondent claims that it was the
prosecutor who violated his convention right against self-incrimination under
art 6 by putting in evidence before the jury, in exercise of a discretion, the   *b*
answers which he had been compelled to give in his examination before the
Official Receiver.

[99] I am unable to accept this submission. Whilst in *R v Lambert* the House
was considering a claim that the trial judge had acted in violation of art 6, the ratio
of the decision given by Lord Slynn of Hadley, Lord Clyde and myself was that   *c*
on an appeal after 2 October 2000 s 22(4) of the 1998 Act did not operate so as to
permit a convicted person to rely on a violation of a convention right occurring
in a trial before 2 October 2000. Lord Slynn stated:

'It is to be noted that s 7(6) distinguishes between proceedings brought by
a public authority and "an appeal against the decision of a court" whereas   *d*
s 22(4) extends the application of s 7(1)(b) only where proceedings are
brought by a public authority. This appears to indicate that an appeal by an
unsuccessful defendant is not to be treated as a proceeding brought by or at
the instigation of a public authority albeit in other contexts an appeal may be
considered to be part of the proceedings initiated by a particular party.' (See   *e*
[2001] 3 All ER 577 at [9].)

Lord Clyde, referring to s 7(1)(b) stated:

'That subsection applies to "legal proceedings" as defined in s 7(6), that is
both "proceedings brought by or at the instigation of a public authority" and   *f*
an appeal. But the provision admitting reliance on earlier acts in s 22(4) is
limited to "proceedings brought by or at the instigation of a public
authority". The use of the same language as was used in s 7(6) is significant.
In my view the intention is that s 22(4) should not extend to the other kind
of "legal proceedings" mentioned in s 7(6), namely an appeal. I am not   *g*
persuaded that s 22(4) can avail the appellant.' (See [2001] 3 All ER 577 at [140].)

And, referring to s 7(6), I stated:

'The subsection therefore distinguishes between "proceedings brought by
or at the instigation of a public authority" and "an appeal against the decision   *h*
of a court or tribunal". Accordingly when s 22(4) refers, in identical words to
the words of s 7(6)(a), to "proceedings brought by or at the instigation of a
public authority", the retrospective operation permitted by that subsection
does not apply to an appeal against the decision of the Crown Court in this
case.' (See [2001] 3 All ER 577 at [172].)   *j*

[100] It is clear, in my opinion, that this ratio governs a case where the
violation of the convention right was caused by the act of the prosecutor
(whether or not acting in the exercise of a discretion) as well as a case where the
violation was caused by the act of the judge.

Should the House depart from the decision in R v Lambert?

a [101] It is clear that there is a division of judicial opinion on the correctness of the decision of the majority in *R v Lambert* that the words in s 22(4) 'proceedings brought by or at the instigation of a public authority' do not include 'an appeal against the decision of a court or tribunal'. I recognise that an argument of considerable force can be advanced in support of the view that the decision in *R v*
b *Lambert* was erroneous. This argument includes the points that the term 'proceedings' usually includes an appeal from the court of first instance and that s 7(6) is not a definition section and does not purport to give exclusive meanings to 'proceedings' in sub-cl (a) and 'an appeal' in sub-cl (b).

[102] Nevertheless having considered the matter afresh I remain, with respect, of the opinion that the contrary argument is a stronger one and that the decision
c of the majority in *R v Lambert* is correct. I think that when Parliament in s 7(6) refers separately to 'proceedings brought by or at the instigation of a public authority' and to 'an appeal against the decision of a court or tribunal', and then uses only one of those phrases in s 22(4) (which relates directly to s 7) it is clear that s 22(4) does not relate to an appeal. Having separated the two subsets of
d 'legal proceedings' in s 7(6) into 'proceedings brought by or at the instigation of a public authority' and 'an appeal against the decision of a court or tribunal', if Parliament had intended s 22(4) to apply to an appeal it would not have referred in that subsection to the first subset only. It is a well established principle that when Parliament uses words in a statute those words should be given a similar meaning in other parts of the statute unless there is some reason to give them a
e different meaning: see *Courtauld v Legh* (1869) LR 4 Exch 126 at 130 per Cleasby B.

Policy considerations

[103] I also think that there is an additional ground to that based on a consideration of the wording of s 7(6) and s 22(4) which supports the decision in
f *R v Lambert*. This ground relates to the policy to which Parliament was giving effect in enacting s 22(4). Mr Emmerson submitted in the present appeal before the House that the policy of Parliament in relation to s 22(4) was to ensure that if a public authority (including a prosecutor) brought proceedings against a citizen and prior to, or in the course of, those proceedings violated one of his convention rights, he should be able to defend himself by relying on his convention right
g even if the public authority's action in violating it had taken place before the Human Rights Act 1998 came into operation, and this policy required that this defence should be available in an appeal as well as in a trial at first instance. In my opinion Parliament did intend that a citizen whose convention rights had been violated before the date on which the Human Rights Act 1998 came into
h operation and was then a defendant in a trial after that date should be able to rely on his convention rights at that trial. However, there are strong reasons of policy, grounded in the need for certainty in the law and finality in litigation, why a conviction which was valid and lawful at the time it took place should not be set aside because of a change in the substantive law brought about by legislation.
j [104] In *R v Mitchell* [1977] 2 All ER 168 at 171, [1977] 1 WLR 753 at 757 Geoffrey Lane LJ stated:

'This is an application for an extension of time in which to appeal against conviction. It should be clearly understood, and this court wants to make it even more abundantly clear, that the fact that there has been an apparent change in the law or, to put it more precisely, that previous misconceptions about the meaning of a statute have been put right, does not afford a proper ground for allowing an extension of time in which to appeal against conviction.'   *a*

And in *R v Campbell* [1997] 1 Cr App R 199 at 206 Lord Bingham of Cornhill CJ stated: 'It would be quite contrary to the general practice of this Court to permit convictions to be reopened because the law has changed since the date of conviction.' In *Minto v Police* [1990–92] 1 NZBORR 208 (cited by Lord Clyde in   *b* his speech in *R v Lambert* [2001] 3 All ER 577 at [147]) the appellants had been convicted of obstructing a police officer in the execution of his duty. The Bill of Rights Act 1990 in New Zealand came into force four months after the convictions of the appellants. On the appeal by the defendants Robertson J described the argument advanced by counsel on their behalf as follows: *c*

'He argued that s 16 (which guarantees freedom of peaceful assembly) altered the test for determining the lawfulness of police instructions by now requiring the police to do anything else which is reasonably possible to prevent a breach of the peace before interfering with a protester's s 16 right. Further, he submitted that the Court should give the Bill of Rights Act   *d* retrospective effect, and decide that even if the police instruction was reasonable, and therefore lawful at the time it was given, s 16 retroactively made it unlawful. Counsel's thesis was that the police must prove beyond reasonable doubt that there was no other reasonable way of averting a breach of the peace before the request could be upheld as lawful. He argued that the "beneficial" effect of such a retrospective interpretation should   *e* overwhelm the presumption against the retrospective effect of statutes.'

Robertson J rejected this argument and stated ([1990–92] 1 NZBORR 208 at 214):

'Certainly, it would be beneficial from his clients' point of view to have their misdemeanour undone in this fashion. But I do not accept that it would   *f* be "beneficial" for the law or society at large if a Court were to declare invalid that which was valid at the time it was done.'

Therefore I do not consider that in enacting s 22(4) Parliament intended that a conviction which was validly and lawfully imposed should be quashed on an appeal perhaps many years later.   *g*

[105] Mr Emmerson sought to answer this objection by submitting that appeals in respect of old convictions could be filtered out of the system by the Court of Appeal exercising its discretion to refuse leave to appeal out of time, or by the Criminal Cases Review Commission deciding, in the exercise of its discretion, not to refer old convictions to the Court of Appeal. I am unable to   *h* accept this submission. If it were to be established by a decision of this House, reversing the decision in *R v Lambert*, that s 22(4) applied to appeals to the Court of Appeal as well as to trials at first instance, I consider that where a person had been convicted before the Human Rights Act 1998 came into operation in a manner which violated his convention rights he would have a strong argument that he should be able to rely on that violation in an appeal to the Court of   *j* Appeal. He would be able to contend that it would be an improper exercise of the Court of Appeal's discretion to refuse him leave to appeal out of time having regard to the consideration that s 22(4) applies 'whenever the act in question [ie the breach of the convention right] took place'. Where an applicant claimed that he had been convicted before 2 October 2000 in breach of a convention right

a it would be difficult, in my opinion, for the Court of Appeal to formulate a principle which would permit some of those appeals to proceed out of time but which would exclude other appeals on the ground that the convictions were too old.

[106] Section 9 of the Criminal Appeal Act 1995 provides:

b   '(1) Where a person has been convicted of an offence on indictment in England and Wales, the [Criminal Cases Review] Commission—(a) may at any time refer the conviction to the Court of Appeal ...

(2) A reference under subsection (1) of a person's conviction shall be treated for all purposes as an appeal by the person under section 1 of the 1968 Act against the conviction.'

c
The argument that the commission should exercise its discretion to filter out old convictions, notwithstanding that the manner in which they were obtained might well have constituted violations of convention rights is, in my opinion, even less persuasive than the similar argument in respect of the Court of Appeal when one considers the reasons given by the commission for referring the case of *d* the intervenors to the Court of Appeal. After the commission had referred their case to the Court of Appeal in the exercise of its discretion under s 9(1) the Director of the Serious Fraud Office brought an application for judicial review against the commission and the nature of the application was set out in the papers as follows:

e   '1. The claimant [the Director of the Serious Fraud Office] submits that the Commission should have exercised its discretion not to refer the convictions of Mr Lyons and others to the Court of Appeal. In particular, it is submitted that the Statement of Reasons does not show whether the Commission had regard to the consistent practice of the Court of Appeal *f* when refusing leave to appeal out of time on the basis of a change in the law. Further the Commission did not consider whether it would be desirable to leave the appellants to apply for leave out of time. The Claimant also submits that the Commission should have referred a question for the opinion of the Court before making a reference of the convictions'.

g [107] The grounds which the commission gave for contesting the Director's application were as follows:

'4. In each of these cases, the Commission determined, having regard to argument not previously raised concerning the coming into force of the Human Rights Act 1998 and the fairness of the trial, that there was a real *h* possibility that the Court of Appeal would not uphold the convictions. The Commission decided to refer the convictions under s 9 of the Act and, in accordance with s 14(4) of the Act, Statements of Reasons by the Commission were given to the Court and to the parties ...

15. ... In the case of Mr Lyons and others, the Commission concluded— *j* and it is not challenged by the Claimant—that there is a real possibility that the Court of Appeal would find their convictions unsafe because their right to a fair trial had been undermined by the admission of evidence obtained under compulsion. The Commission decided not to exercise its discretion not to refer. Indeed, the Commission submits that to have gone on to conclude in such circumstances that the Commission should not refer the

convictions—on the ground that no substantial injustice had occurred— *a*
would itself have been irrational and open to challenge.

16. The effect of the Claimant's argument is that, while there is a real
possibility that there has been a breach of the applicants' human rights so as
to affect the safety of their convictions, there has been no concomitant
substantial injustice which justifies the Commission referring their case to
the Court. This is an argument that can neither be sustained in law nor *b*
common sense.'

[108] It would not be appropriate for me to express a concluded opinion on
the validity of the reasons given by the commission, but I consider that they show
the serious obstacles to an argument that, if s 22(4) applies to appeals, the
commission should not exercise its discretion to refer a conviction to the Court *c*
of Appeal where there has been or may have been a breach of a convention right
in the obtaining of a conviction a considerable number of years before the
Human Rights Act 1998 came into operation.

[109] In my opinion Parliament did intend that valid convictions should not
be quashed years later by the Court of Appeal, but it gave effect to this intention, *d*
not by leaving it to the uncertain exercise of the discretion of the Court of Appeal
or the Criminal Cases Review Commission to filter out appeals in respect of old
convictions, but by wording s 22(4) so that it applied to proceedings at first
instance and not to appeals. Accordingly, for the reasons which I have given,
I consider that the decision of the majority in *R v Lambert* was correct. *e*

[110] I would add that if I had considered after the further argument in the
present appeal that, on balance, the decision in *R v Lambert* was erroneous,
I would nevertheless have been of the opinion that the decision should be
followed. In *Fitzleet Estates Ltd v Cherry (Inspector of Taxes)* [1977] 3 All ER 996 at
999, [1977] 1 WLR 1345 at 1349 Lord Wilberforce stated:
f

'There is therefore nothing left to the taxpayer but to contend, as it frankly
does, that the 1966 decision is wrong. This contention means, when
interpreted, that three or more of your Lordships ought to take the view
which appealed then to the minority. My Lords, in my firm opinion, the
1966 Practice Statement (*Practice Statement (Judicial Precedent)* [1966] 3 All ER *g*
77, [1966] 1 WLR 1234) was never intended to allow and should not be
considered to allow such a course. Nothing could be more undesirable, in
fact, than to permit litigants, after a decision has been given by this House
with all appearance of finality, to return to this House in the hope that a
differently constituted committee might be persuaded to take the view *h*
which its predecessors rejected. True that the earlier decision was by
majority: I say nothing as to its correctness or as to the validity of the
reasoning by which it was supported. That there were two eminently
possible views is shown by the support for each by at any rate two members
of the House. But doubtful issues have to be resolved and the law knows no
better way of resolving them than by the considered majority opinion of the *j*
ultimate tribunal. It requires much more than doubts as to the correctness
of such opinion to justify departing from it.'

[111] In my opinion the view of the majority in *R v Lambert* was an eminently
possible one and should be followed for the reason stated by Lord Wilberforce.

a [112] Accordingly I would answer the certified question in the negative and would allow the appeal by the Crown and would set aside the order of the Court of Appeal and restore the conviction of the respondent.

Appeal allowed.

Kate O'Hanlon   Barrister.

Smith (Administrator of Cosslett (Contractors) Ltd) v Bridgend County Borough Council

[2001] UKHL 58

a

b

HOUSE OF LORDS

LORD BINGHAM OF CORNHILL, LORD BROWNE-WILKINSON, LORD HOFFMANN, LORD SCOTT OF FOSCOTE AND LORD RODGER OF EARLSFERRY

8–10 OCTOBER, 8 NOVEMBER 2001

c

Company – Charge – Floating charge – Company in administration – Effect of non-registration of charge – Engineering contract giving employer right to sell contractor's on-site plant in event of default in satisfaction of sums due from contractor – Whether right constituting floating charge – Whether unregistered floating charge void against company in administration or only against administrator – Companies Act 1985, s 395(1) – Institution of Civil Engineers Conditions of Contract (5th edn), cl 63.

d

The predecessor of the respondent local authority entered into an engineering contract with C Ltd. Under the contract, which was made on the Institution of Civil Engineers Conditions of Contract (the ICE conditions), C Ltd agreed to carry out land reclamation works for the authority involving the processing of coal-bearing shale. For the purposes of the works, C Ltd purchased, with the benefit of an advance of £1·8m from the authority, two coal-washing plants which were installed on the site. Under cl 53 of the ICE conditions, all plant owned by the contractor were deemed to be the property of the employer when on site, but in accordance with an amendment made by the parties the washing plant was at all times owned by C Ltd. Clause 63 gave the employer the right, in various circumstances of default by the contractor (including the abandonment of the contract), to enter the site, expel the contractor, complete the works themselves or employ another contractor to do so, use the plant for that purpose, sell it and apply the proceeds of sale towards the satisfaction of any sums due to the employer from the contractor under the contract. After two years, C Ltd fell into financial difficulties and abandoned the contract. The authority then entered the site and reached a provisional agreement with another contractor under which the latter started work using C Ltd's washing plant. Shortly afterwards, C Ltd went into administration. In subsequent summary proceedings brought by the administrator against the authority under s 234 of the Insolvency Act 1986 for delivery up of the washing plant, the administrator contended that cl 63 was an unregistered floating charge over the company's property. He therefore sought to rely on s 395(1)[a] of the Companies Act 1985 which provided that such a charge was 'void against the liquidator or adminstrator'. While the s 234 proceedings were pending, the authority entered into another agreement with the new contractor. By one of its terms, the new contractor would, on completion of the

e

f

g

h

j

---

a   Section 395, so far as material, provides: '(1) ... a charge created by a company registered in England and Wales and being a charge to which this section applies is, so far as any security on the company's property or undertaking is conferred by the charge, void against the liquidator or administrator ... unless the prescribed particulars of the charge together with the instrument (if any) by which the charge is created or evidenced, are delivered to or received by the registrar of companies for registration in the manner required ... within 21 days after the charge's creation ...'

a   works, become owners of the washing plant and could remove and dispose of it.
Three years later, the s 234 proceedings reached the Court of Appeal. By that
time, the works had been completed and the new contractor had either removed
the washing plant from the site or was just about to remove them, eventually
selling them directly to a third party. However, in the absence of any clear
information to the contrary, the Court of Appeal dealt with the case on the basis

b   that the authority was still exercising its right to use the plant under cl 63.
The court held that that right could not be a charge and therefore dismissed the
appeal. It nevertheless expressed the view that the power of sale in cl 63 was a
floating charge and that it was therefore void against the administrator under
s 395(1) of the 1985 Act for want of registration. Accordingly, on discovering that
the plant had been sold, the administrator brought proceedings for conversion

c   against the authority and applied for summary judgment. The judge granted the
application, but his decision was reversed, and the proceedings struck out, by the
Court of Appeal which held that s 395(1) made the floating charge void against
the administrator rather than against the company in administration, that the
right to sue for conversion (unlike s 234 proceedings) was vested in the company

d   rather than its adminstrator, that accordingly the power of sale in cl 63 remained
valid against C Ltd and that it therefore provided an answer to the claim for
conversion. The administrator appealed to the House of Lords, challenging the
Court of Appeal's view of the effect of s 395(1). On the appeal, the authority
contended that the power of sale was not a charge at all, or, if it was, that it was
a fixed rather than a floating charge and therefore fell outside the scope of s 395(1).

e   If that was wrong and, contrary to the Court of Appeal's view, the charge was
void against C Ltd itself, the authority submitted that it was entitled to an
equitable set-off. Finally, the authority contended that, in any event, it had not
done any act which could be regarded as conversion of the plant since it had been
entitled to possession of the plant when it had entered into the agreement giving

f   the new contractor the right to remove the plant on completion of the works.

Held – (1) Clause 63 of the ICE conditions constituted a floating charge,
registrable under s 395 of the 1985 Act, in so far as it allowed the employer, in
various situations of default by the contractor, to sell the contractor's plant and
equipment and apply the proceeds in discharge of its obligations. A right to sell

g   an asset belonging to a debtor and appropriate the proceeds to payment of the
debt could not be anything other than a charge. It was a floating charge because
the property subject to cl 63 was a fluctuating body of assets which could be
consumed or removed from the site in the ordinary course of the contractor's
business (see [1], [2], [41], [58], [64], [81], below).

h   (2) On the true construction of s 395(1) of the 1985 Act, an unregistered floating
charge on a company's property was void against the company in administration,
ie it was void against the company when acting by its administrator. Such a
charge was void against a company in liquidation, and s 395 operated in relation
to a company in administration in exactly the same way as it did in relation to a
company in liquidation. Its purpose was to protect the interests of the company

j   in administration and, if it should subsequently go into liquidation, the interests
of creditors. If, on the other hand, the company emerged solvent from the
administration, the secured creditor would by definition obtain payment of its debt
without recourse to the avoided security. In the instant case, the administrator
had ample power to cause C Ltd to bring an action against the authority for
converting its property. If the defence to such a claim was a charge that was
avoided by s 395(1), C Ltd would be entitled to rely upon that provision. Nor did

the authority have any right of equitable set-off. Such a set-off depended upon
showing some equitable reason for protection against the claimant's demand. A
defendant could not, in the absence of a lien or other security, claim to retain an
asset belonging to a claimant by way of set-off against a monetary cross-claim. If
that were not so, everyone would in effect have a lien over any property of his
debtor which happened to be in his possession. It followed that he could not
improve his security in equity by wrongfully converting the debtor's property.
To allow an equitable set-off would be to allow the authority to exercise the very
right which it could have exercised if the charge had been registered but which
s 395 was intended to avoid. Moreover, the authority had consented to the removal
of the plant by the new contractor in violation of C Ltd's right to possession. The
fact that it had given such consent in advance, at a time when C Ltd was not
entitled to possession, could make no difference. The consent remained effective
until the moment when the new contractor took the plant. That was sufficient
to amount to a conversion. Accordingly, the appeal would be allowed (see [1],
[2], [21], [29], [31], [33], [36], [39], [41], [45],[67], [68], [70], [73]–[76], [78], [80], [81],
below).

Notes
For floating charges and the effect of non-registration, see 7(2) *Halsbury's Laws*
(4th edn reissue) paras 1260, 1299.
  For the Companies Act 1985, s 395, see 8 *Halsbury's Statutes* (4th edn) (1999
reissue) 454.

Cases referred to in opinions
Agnew v Comr of Inland Revenue [2001] UKPC 28, [2001] 2 BCLC 189, [2001] 2 AC 710,
  [2001] 3 WLR 454.
Ayala Holdings Ltd, Re (No 2) [1996] 1 BCLC 467.
Cuckmere Brick Co Ltd v Mutual Finance Ltd [1971] 2 All ER 633, [1971] Ch 949,
  [1971] 2 WLR 1207, CA.
Dimond v Lovell [2000] 2 All ER 897, [2000] 2 WLR 1121, HL.
Evans v Rival Granite Quarries Ltd [1910] 2 KB 979, CA.
Governments Stock and Other Securities Investment Co Ltd v Manila Rly Co Ltd [1897]
  AC 81, HL.
Hanak v Green [1958] 2 All ER 141, [1958] 2 QB 9, [1958] 2 WLR 755, CA.
Independent Automatic Sales Ltd v Knowles & Foster [1962] 3 All ER 27, [1962] 1 WLR 974.
Manson v Smith (liquidator of Thomas Christy Ltd) [1997] 2 BCLC 161, CA.
Monolithic Building Co, Re, Tacon v Monolithic Building Co [1915] 1 Ch 643, [1914–15]
  All ER Rep 249, Ch D and CA.
Newitt, Ex p, re Garrud (1881) 16 Ch D 522, [1881–5] All ER Rep 1039, CA.
Orakpo v Manson Investments Ltd [1977] 3 All ER 1, [1978] AC 95, [1977] 3 WLR
  229, HL.
Tse Kwong Lam v Wong Chit Sen [1983] 3 All ER 54, [1983] 1 WLR 1349, PC.
Winter Garden Theatre (London) Ltd v Millenium Productions Ltd [1947] 2 All ER 331,
  [1948] AC 173, HL.

Appeal
The claimant, Gerald Clifford Smith, the administrator of Cosslett (Contractors) Ltd
(the company), appealed with permission of the Appeal Committee of the House
of Lords given on 24 July 2000 from the order of the Court of Appeal (Lord
Woolf MR, Ward and Laws LJJ) on 19 January 2000 ([2000] 1 BCLC 775), as
amended on 15 February 2000, whereby it (i) allowed an appeal by the defendant,

a Bridgend County Borough Council, from the order of Judge Toulmin QC perfected
on 8 September 1998 giving effect to his decision on 9 July 1998 granting an
application by the then administrator of the company, Ian Clark, for summary
judgment against the council in proceedings for conversion of certain plant
owned by the company, and (ii) struck out those proceedings. The facts are set
out in the opinion of Lord Hoffmann.

b
Richard Wilmot-Smith QC and *Alan Maclean* (instructed by *Hammond Suddards
Edge*, Manchester) for the administrator.
Gabriel Moss QC and *Peter Arden* (instructed by *Edwards Geldard*, Cardiff) for
the council.

c Their Lordships took time for consideration.

8 November 2001. The following opinions were delivered.

LORD BINGHAM OF CORNHILL.
d [1] My Lords, I have had the advantage of reading in draft the opinion of my
noble and learned friend Lord Hoffmann. I am in full agreement with it and for
the reasons which he gives I would allow the appeal and make the order which
he proposes.

e ### LORD BROWNE-WILKINSON.
[2] My Lords, I have had the advantage of considering the speech of my noble
and learned friend, Lord Hoffmann, in draft. I agree with it and for the reasons
he gives I too would allow the appeal.

LORD HOFFMANN.
f [3] My Lords, this appeal raises two questions of general importance. The first
is whether a standard condition in the Institution of Civil Engineers (ICE) form
of contract which allows the employer, in various situations of default by the
contractor, to sell his plant and equipment and apply the proceeds in discharge of
his obligations, is a floating charge which should be registered under s 395 of the
g Companies Act 1985 (the 1985 Act). The second is the effect of a failure to register
when the contractor has gone into administration but the employer has nevertheless
purported to exercise the power of sale.
[4] The contract, dated 28 January 1991, was for engineering works to rehabilitate
an area of 141 hectares of the upper Garw valley which had been disfigured by
h derelict coal dumps. The employer was the Mid-Glamorgan County Council, which
disappeared on a reorganisation of Welsh local government and was succeeded
for this purpose by the Bridgend County Borough Council. I shall refer to both
as 'the council'. The contractor was Cosslett (Contractors) Ltd, which I shall call
'the company'.
[5] The largest items of equipment brought on site by the contractor were two
j coal-washing plants which were used to separate usable coal from residue. The
council had advanced about £1·8m to the company to enable it to buy the washing
plants and the contract provided for repayment by way of deduction from the
sums which would periodically become payable to the company over the term of
the contract, which was expected to last about four years.
[6] Clause 53(1) of the standard ICE conditions has a definition of 'plant' and
cl 53(2) provides that all plant, goods and materials owned by the contractor 'shall

when on the site be deemed to be the property of the employer'. In this case,
however, the parties had amended the definition of plant to include a specific *a*
reference to the coal-washing plant:

'For the purpose of this clause ... the expression "Plant" shall mean any
constructional plant coal washing plant temporary works and material for
temporary works but shall exclude any vehicles engaged in transporting any *b*
labour, plant or material to or from the Site.'

'Constructional plant' has its own definition in cl 1(1)(o): '"Constructional Plant"
means all appliances or things of whatsoever nature required in or about the
construction completion and maintenance of the Works ...' That seems easily
wide enough to accommodate the washing plant and so it is not clear why they *c*
needed a special mention in cl 53(1). Perhaps the draftsman of the amendments
did not notice that constructional plant was a defined expression. In any event,
I do not think that it made any difference.

[7] Clause 53(2), which, as I have said, provided that the contractor's plant goods
and materials should, when on site, 'be deemed to be the property of the employer',
was amended to add 'The washing plant must be owned by the Contractor or by *d*
a company in which the Contractor has a controlling interest'. This condition
was observed. The washing plant was at all times owned by the company.

[8] Also relevant are cl 53(6) and (7):

'(6) No Plant (except hired Plant) goods or materials or any part thereof
shall be removed from the Site without the written consent of the Engineer *e*
which consent shall not be unreasonably withheld where the same are no
longer immediately required for the purposes of the completion of the
Works ... (7) Upon the removal of any such Plant goods or materials as have
been deemed to have become the property of the Employer under
sub-clause (2) of this Clause with the consent as aforesaid the property *f*
therein shall be deemed to revest in the Contractor ...'

[9] Thus the status of being deemed to be property of the employer attached to
plant etc when it was brought onto the site and ceased to attach when, subject
to the consent of the engineer, it was removed from the site.

[10] The condition which gives rise to the present dispute is cl 63(1):   *g*

'If the Contractor shall become bankrupt ... or (being a corporation) shall
go into liquidation ... or if the Engineer shall certify in writing to the
Employer that in his opinion the Contractor ... has abandoned the Contract
... then the Employer may after giving 7 days' notice in writing to the
Contractor enter upon the Site and the Works and expel the Contractor *h*
therefrom ... and may himself complete the Works or may employ any
other contractor to complete the Works and the Employer or such other
contractor may use for such completion so much of the Constructional Plant
Temporary Works goods and materials which have been deemed to become
the property of the Employer under [clause 53] ... as he or they may think *j*
proper and the Employer may at any time sell any of the said Constructional
Plant Temporary Works and unused goods and materials and apply the
proceeds of sale in or towards the satisfaction of any sums due or which may
become due to him from the Contractor under the Contract.'

[11] After about two years of operating the contract the company found that
selling the recovered coal was not as profitable as it had expected. In the summer

a of 1993 it told the council that it appeared to be heading for insolvency and would not be able to carry on with the contract. On 4 August 1993 it abandoned the site and on 6 August the engineer gave a certificate to that effect in accordance with cl 63. On 12 August the council gave seven days' notice of its intention to enter upon the site. It found another contractor, Burrows Bros (Sales) Ltd (Burrows) and entered into a provisional agreement under which they started work at the

b end of August, using the company's washing plant.

[12] On 8 September 1993 the company went into administration. Mr Ian Clark was appointed administrator. He demanded the immediate return of the plant or payment of a substantial hire fee for its use. When the council replied that it was entitled under cl 63 to use the plant, Mr Clark said that the condition was an unregistered floating charge and void against him under s 395(1) of the 1985 Act.

c On 22 November 1993 he commenced summary proceedings under s 234 of the Insolvency Act 1986 for delivery up of the washing plant.

[13] On a date in January 1994, while the proceedings under s 234 were pending, the council replaced the provisional arrangements under which Burrows had been employed with a 'continuation contract' for the completion of the works.

d One of the terms of that agreement was that when the works had been completed, Burrows would become owners of the washing plant and could remove and dispose of it.

[14] The administrator's application came before the court in December 1995, when Burrows was using the plant under the continuation contract. The council's first line of defence was that the provision in cl 53 by which the plant, when on

e site, was 'deemed to be the property of the employer' meant that it actually became their property. The company lost all title. The judge rejected this argument (see [1996] 4 All ER 46, [1997] Ch 23). He said that cl 63 created a charge over the company's property. But he held that the charge was fixed, not floating. In his opinion cl 53(6) gave the employer an absolute right to refuse to allow any plant

f to be removed from site and therefore from the scope of the charge if it was immediately required to complete the works and a right to refuse in any other circumstances if it was not unreasonable to do so. This meant that the contractor did not have that freedom to deal with the assets until crystallisation which was the badge of a floating charge. As a fixed charge, it did not need to be registered. On that ground, he dismissed the application.

g [15] The administrator appealed. By the time the case got to the Court of Appeal in July 1997, the works had been completed and Burrows had either removed or were just about to remove the washing plants from the site. In fact they sold them to a third party for their own account. The administrator does not appear to have had much information about what was happening and the Court

h of Appeal was invited to deal with the appeal on the basis that the council was still exercising its right to use the plant but, for the avoidance of further litigation, to express a view about what the position would be if the council exercised the power of sale.

[16] The Court of Appeal (Evans and Millett LJJ and Sir Ralph Gibson) ([1997]

j 4 All ER 115, [1998] Ch 495) said that one had to distinguish between the two rights which cl 63 conferred upon the employer. The right to use the plant to finish the works could not be a charge. It was simply a contractual right which continued to be exercisable whether the company was in administration or not. On that ground, the court dismissed the appeal. On the other hand, they agreed with the judge that the right to sell the plant and apply the proceeds to discharge any debt from the company to the council was a charge. But they did not agree that it was a fixed charge. Millett LJ, with whom the other two judges agreed,

pointed out that power to refuse consent to the removal of the plant, which
the judge had treated as vested in the employer, was actually conferred upon the *a*
engineer. This suggested that the discretion was to be exercised independently
on operational grounds and not as a method of enforcing the employer's security
for the payment of money. It therefore did not give the employer such control
over the plant as to create a fixed charge in advance of crystallisation.

[17] The result was that the power of sale was void against the administrator *b*
under s 395(1) of the 1985 Act. In the course of discussion after judgments had
been handed down, counsel told the court that according to their information,
the plant had been sold. Millett LJ remarked that 'on our judgment, as it stands
at the moment, you would be entitled to an RSC Ord 14 judgment'.

[18] The administrator took the judge at his word and issued a fresh writ
claiming damages for conversion of its plant, followed by an application for *c*
judgment under RSC Ord 14. Judge Toulmin QC gave judgment for damages to
be assessed and an interim payment of £389,000. The council appealed and the
Court of Appeal (Lord Woolf MR, Ward and Laws LJJ) ([2000] 1 BCLC 2000) set
aside the judgment on entirely new grounds. Laws LJ (with whom the other judges
agreed) said that s 395(1) made the floating charge void against the administrator but *d*
not against the company. This meant that in cases in which the administrator
had a personal cause of action (such as to recover the company's property in specie
by summary proceedings under s 234 of the 1986 Act) he could disregard the charge.
But the right to sue for conversion of its property vested in the company, not the
administrator. The power of sale remained valid against the company and was an
answer to the claim for conversion. The Court of Appeal therefore allowed the *e*
appeal and struck out the action. Against that order the administrator appeals to
your Lordships' House.

[19] My Lords, I shall first address the grounds upon which the Court of Appeal
decided the case. They are in my view startling and unorthodox. Section 395 of
the 1985 Act, which can be traced back to the Companies Act 1900 was intended *f*
for the protection of the creditors of an insolvent company. It was intended to
give persons dealing with a company the opportunity to discover, by consulting
the register, whether its assets were burdened by floating and certain fixed
charges which would reduce the amount available for unsecured creditors in a
liquidation. Whether this was a realistic form of protection and whether the
choice of registrable charges was entirely logical is not presently relevant. The *g*
plain intention of the legislature was that property subject to a registrable but
unregistered charge should be available to the general body of creditors (or a
secured creditor ranking after the unregistered charge) as if no such charge
existed.

[20] When a winding-up order is made and a liquidator appointed, there is no *h*
divesting of the company's assets. The liquidator acquires no interest, whether
beneficially or as trustee. The assets continue to belong to the company but the
liquidator is able to exercise the company's right to collect them for the purposes
of the liquidation.

[21] It must in my opinion follow that when s 395 says that the charge shall be *j*
'void against the liquidator', it means void against a company acting by its liquidator,
that is to say, a company in liquidation. In *Re Monolithic Building Co, Tacon v
Monolithic Building Co* [1915] 1 Ch 643 at 667–668, [1914–15] All ER Rep 249 at 254
Phillimore LJ said of a predecessor of s 395:

'It makes void a security; not the debt, not the cause of action, but the
security, and not as against everybody, not as against the company grantor,

a   but against the liquidator, and against any creditor, and it leaves the security
to stand as against the company while it is a going concern. It does not make
the security binding on the liquidator as successor of the company.'

The last sentence shows some degree of confusion because of course the liquidator
is not a successor of the company. But Phillimore LJ was quite right in saying that
b   s 395 does not invalidate a charge against a company while it is a going concern,
that is to say, when it is not in liquidation. On the other hand, once the company
is in liquidation and can act only by its liquidator, there seems to me little value
in a distinction between whether the charge is void against the liquidator or void
against the company. It is void against the company in liquidation.

[22] In *Independent Automatic Sales Ltd v Knowles & Foster* [1962] 3 All ER 27,
c   [1962] 1 WLR 974 a company in liquidation which had sold machines on hire
purchase brought an action against a finance company to recover hire-purchase
agreements and other securities which it had charged to secure the repayment of
advances. When the finance company relied upon the charge, the plaintiff replied
that it was void because it should have been registered as a charge over book debts
under a predecessor of s 395. The plaintiff named in the writ was the company.
d   Mr Arthur Bagnall QC for the defendant took the preliminary point that as the
liquidator was claiming that the charges were void as against him, he should have
been the plaintiff. Buckley J agreed but allowed an amendment to join the
liquidator as an additional plaintiff and the action proceeded.

[23] As everyone knew that the company was in liquidation and suing by its
e   liquidator, it is hard to see what the point of this manoeuvre was, unless the
defendants had omitted or been unable to obtain an order for security for costs
and hoped to be able to make the liquidator personally liable. (In the event they
lost, so it did not matter.) But I respectfully think that Buckley J was wrong. The
cause of action was vested in the company. It owned the hire-purchase agreements.
It should therefore have been the plaintiff. The liquidator was causing it to sue for
f   the purpose of realising assets to be distributed in the liquidation. The fact that he
relied upon the statute to invalidate what would otherwise be a defence open to
the holder of the assets does not alter the nature of the proceedings or provide a
reason why he should have to expose himself to personal liability for costs.

[24] I express no view on the related question, which came before Knox J in
g   *Re Ayala Holdings Ltd (No 2)* [1996] 1 BCLC 467 as to whether a liquidator (or
administrator) can assign the company's right to recover property free from a
charge avoided by s 395. Even if I am right in thinking that the proceedings in the
Independent Automatic Sales case were properly brought in the name of the company,
the decision of Knox J against such an assignment can be upheld on the ground
h   that the right of avoidance under s 395 is not in itself an assignable item of
property and can be claimed only by the company acting by its liquidator or
administrator.

[25] This brings me to s 234 of the 1986 Act, which Laws LJ treated as the only
situation in which the administrator would be able to sue in his own name and
therefore be able to rely upon the fact that the charge was void against him. This
j   section can be traced back to s 100 of the Companies Act 1862. Originally it was
confined to applications against contributories and any 'Trustee, Receiver, Banker,
or Agent, or Officer of the Company'. It provided a summary procedure by which
they could be required to 'pay, deliver, convey, surrender, or transfer' to the
liquidator 'any Sum or Balance, Books, Papers, Estate, or Effects which happen
to be in his Hands for the Time being, and to which the Company is *primâ facie*
entitled'.

[26] In its original form, such an application was not an originating process. It was an application in the liquidation, invoking the summary jurisdiction of the *a* Companies Court against certain persons connected with the company and in possession of its money or property. Its purpose was to enable the liquidator to carry out his statutory functions. It did not necessarily involve a determination of title. If, for example, the liquidator appeared on affidavit evidence to be prima facie entitled to property, books or records which he needed to proceed with the *b* liquidation, the court could in its discretion order the person in possession to hand over the property and argue about ownership later.

[27] Plainly, therefore, when the 1900 Act said that an unregistered charge should be void against the liquidator, it was not intending to confine the scope of that provision to cases in which the liquidator was making a summary application under s 100 of the 1862 Act. The registration provisions would have had little value *c* if they applied only to charges in favour of the persons subject to the summary jurisdiction. It is to be observed that the *Independent Automatic Sales* case was an ordinary action commenced by writ.

[28] The scope of the summary procedure was enlarged by provisions of the Insolvency Act 1985 which are now contained in s 234 of the 1986 Act. It is now *d* available against any person who has in his control 'any property, books, papers or records to which the company appears to be entitled'. It remains, however, a summary discretionary remedy, obtainable by a liquidator or other office-holder for the purpose of enabling him to carry out his functions and which does not necessarily involve any determination of title. *e*

[29] When administration was introduced by the Insolvency Act, s 395 of the 1985 Act was amended simply by adding the words 'or administrator' after the word 'liquidator'. This seems to me to indicate that the section was to operate in relation to a company in administration exactly as it had in relation to a company in liquidation. An administration order did not vest any of the company's property in the administrator any more than a winding-up order vested it in the *f* liquidator. Instead, s 14 of the 1986 Act gave the administrator powers in many respects similar to those of a liquidator over the company's property:

'(1) The administrator of a company—(a) may do all such things as may be necessary for the management of the affairs, business and property of the *g* company, and (b) without prejudice to the generality of paragraph (a), has the powers specified in Schedule 1 to this Act ...'

[30] Paragraph 1 of Sch 1 to the 1986 Act gives the administrator power to 'take possession of, collect and get in the property of the company and, for that *h* purpose, to take such proceedings as may seem to him expedient' and para 5 confers power to bring any action in the name and on behalf of the company.

[31] Ordinarily, therefore, an action brought by an administrator to assert a claim on behalf of the company should be in the name of the company. The title to the claim will be vested in the company. In the present case, for example, s 14(1) and the Schedule gave the administrator ample power to cause the company *j* to bring an action against the council for converting its property. If the defence to such a claim is a charge which is avoided by s 395 of the 1985 Act, the company will be entitled to rely upon the section. As in the case of liquidation, I consider that 'void against the administrator' means void against the company in administration or (another way of saying the same thing) against the company when acting by its administrator.

a [32] In fact, the title given to the writ in the proceedings under appeal was headed 'Between: Ian Clark, the Administrator of Cosslett (Contractors) Ltd and Bridgend County Borough Council'. In my view, the proper heading should have been 'Between: Cosslett (Contractors) Ltd (in administration) and Bridgend County Borough Council'. But no one was misled about the nature of the proceedings because the statement of claim endorsed on the writ made it clear
b that the claim was for loss and damage suffered by the company on account of the conversion of its property. So I do not think that any amendment was necessary. On the other hand, the earlier proceedings under s 234 were at first headed 'In the matter of Cosslett (Contractors) Ltd and in the matter of the Insolvency Act 1986, between Cosslett (Contractors) Ltd, applicant, and Mid-Glamorgan County Council, respondent'. Later the title was amended to substitute the name of the administrator
c for that of the company as applicant. In this case I think that second thoughts were correct.

[33] Laws LJ described ([2000] 1 BCLC 775 at 791) the effect of s 395 of the 1985 Act as being to confer upon the administrator 'a purely adventitious potential claim in specie to recover or retain the plant' and the right to 'take advantage' of
d the ineffectiveness of the floating charge as 'nothing but statutory serendipity'. I see no reason to impute such whimsical intentions to the legislature. The purpose of s 395 as originally enacted was to protect the interests of the general body of creditors. The purpose of s 395 as extended to administrators is to protect the interests of the company in administration and, if it should subsequently go into liquidation, the interests of creditors. If, on the other hand, the company emerges
e solvent from the administration, the secured creditor will by definition obtain payment of his debt without recourse to the avoided security.

[34] In giving s 395 a narrow and arbitrary construction, Laws LJ appears to have been influenced by what he regarded as the merits of the case. He thought it was unfair that the council should lose its security over the plant when it had a
f cross-claim greatly exceeding the value of that security, part of which arose from the advances which had enabled the company to buy the plant in the first place. He said that if there had been no charge created by cl 63, any claim by the company for damages for conversion would 'plainly' have been met by a set-off, either in equity or under r 4.90 of the Insolvency Rules 1986, SI 1986/1925, raising the council's cross-claim. There would in his judgment have been 'no answer' to
g such a set-off. Why should the council be in a worse position because it had taken an unregistered charge?

[35] If there was indeed such a right of set-off, the argument would be a strong one. And, encouraged by the judge's remarks, Mr Moss QC, who appeared for the council, submitted that even if the charge was void not merely against the
h administrator personally but against the company in administration, he could still rely upon an equitable set-off. But in my opinion neither equitable set-off nor (if the company were to go into liquidation) set-off under r 4.90 would be available. The position under r 4.90, which provides for a set-off arising out of 'mutual credits, mutual debts or other mutual dealings between the company and any
j creditor', was expressly considered by Millett LJ in *Manson v Smith (liquidator of Thomas Christy Ltd)* [1997] 2 BCLC 161. There a director who had been held liable for misappropriating funds belonging to an insolvent company attempted to invoke r 4.90 to set off his liability against what the company owed him on loan account. Millett LJ said 'a misappropriation of assets is not a dealing'. Nor is a conversion of the company's property.

[36] Similarly, equitable set-off depends upon showing some equitable reason for protection against the plaintiff's demand (see *Hanak v Green* [1958] 2 All ER

141, [1958] 2 QB 9). In my opinion a defendant could not, in the absence of a lien
or other security, claim to retain an asset belonging to a plaintiff by way of set-off
against a monetary cross-claim. If this were not the case, everyone would in effect
have a lien over any property of his debtor which happened to be in his possession.
It follows, in my opinion, that he cannot improve his security in equity by
wrongfully converting the debtor's property. As Lord Uthwatt said in *Winter
Garden Theatre (London) Ltd v Millenium Productions Ltd* [1947] 2 All ER 331 at 343,
[1948] AC 173 at 203: 'In a court of equity, wrongful acts are no passport to
favour.' To allow an equitable set-off would be to allow the council to exercise
the very right which it could have exercised if the charge had been registered but
which s 395 was intended to avoid.

[37] Mr Moss next submitted that the council had not done any act which
could be regarded as a conversion of the plant. Conversion is a tort against a
person entitled to possession and when the council entered into the continuation
contract which gave Burrows the right to take away the plant on completion of
the works, the company had no right to possession. The council was entitled, as the
first Court of Appeal held, to retain possession for the purpose of completing
the works. When the works were completed and the company became entitled
to possession, the council did not do anything to interfere with that right.
Burrows simply removed the plant. If anyone converted the plant, Burrows did.

[38] These arguments were presented to the Court of Appeal and tentatively
rejected by Laws LJ. He said that if he thought on other grounds that the
company should have a remedy, he—

'would have been prepared to hold that as between A, B and C, A converts
B's goods when he (A) gives possession and purported title in the goods to C,
notwithstanding that A's obligation to C to do so had been undertaken at a
time when B had no right to immediate possession.' (See [2000] 1 BCLC 775
at 787.)

[39] I agree. The council consented to the removal of the plant by Burrows in
violation of the company's right to possession. The fact that they gave such consent
in advance, at a time when the company was not entitled to possession, can make
no difference. The consent remained effective until the moment when Burrows
took the plant. This was sufficient to amount to a conversion.

[40] My Lords, in my opinion Millett LJ was therefore right in saying that on
the basis of the first Court of Appeal judgment, there could be no answer to the
company's claim for damages for conversion. But, in addition to attempting to
support the second Court of Appeal's grounds for differing from this view, Mr Moss
also challenged the original decision that cl 63 created a floating charge. He said
that it was not a charge and that if it was, it was fixed and not floating.

[41] On these points I can be brief because I agree with Millett LJ for the
reasons which he gave. I do not see how a right to sell an asset belonging to a
debtor and appropriate the proceeds to payment of the debt can be anything
other than a charge. And because the property subject to cl 63 (constructional
plant, temporary works, goods and materials on the site) was a fluctuating body
of assets which could be consumed or (subject to the approval of the engineer)
removed from the site in the ordinary course of the contractor's business, it was
a floating charge (see *Agnew v Comr of Inland Revenue* [2001] UKPC 28, [2001]
2 BCLC 189 at 199, [2001] 2 AC 710 at 724).

[42] Mr Moss submitted that in the many years during which cl 63 had been in
use, no one had imagined that it created a floating charge. A requirement of

a   registration might ruin the credit of contractors when a search revealed the existence of such charges or cause them to be in breach of covenants with lenders which prohibited the granting of charges to third parties. The parties cannot therefore be supposed to have intended to create such a charge. But the intentions of the parties, as expressed in the ICE form of contract, are relevant only to establish their mutual rights and obligations. Whether such rights and obligations

b   are characterised as a floating charge is a question of law (see *Agnew's* case [2001] 2 BCLC 189 at 191, [2001] 2 AC 710 at 716). The answer to this question may come as a surprise to the parties but that is no reason for adopting a different characterisation.

[43] I would also observe that the first Court of Appeal decision was reported more than four years ago and we were shown nothing to suggest that it has been

c   the cause of any difficulties in the building or engineering industries.

[44] Mr Moss also submitted that while cl 63 might create a floating charge over materials and small items of plant which were more obviously likely to come and go during the course of a four-year contract, it should be construed as a fixed charge over the washing plant, which was unlikely to be removed and

d   received a separate mention in cl 53(1) as amended. As I said at the beginning of this speech, it is not easy to guess why the washing plant was treated separately in cl 53(1). But it receives no separate treatment in cl 63, where it falls within the charge simply as an item of constructional plant. It is in my opinion impossible to construe the latter condition as creating a charge over the washing plant different in nature from that which it created over the other plant and materials

e   brought on site. Although the washing plant was very large, it was not inconceivable that during the contract, just as it was found necessary to acquire a second plant, it might be found advantageous to replace one or both by a more efficient machine. In that case the contractor would have been entitled to withdraw the old machine from the site and the charge.

f   [45] Finally, Mr Moss submitted that even if he was not entitled to raise an equitable set-off, any claim for conversion should be stayed pending the determination of its cross-claim. For my part, I can see no reason why there should be such a stay. It is agreed that the company is insolvent. But for the existence of these proceedings, it would no doubt have been wound up long ago. The council will be entitled to prove in the liquidation. But the claim for

g   conversion is an asset which the administrator is entitled now to recover in due course of administration. In my opinion the judgment and interim order of Judge Toulmin should be restored.

LORD SCOTT OF FOSCOTE.

h   [46] My Lords, there are, in my opinion, four main issues to be decided on this appeal. (1) Did the terms of the Institution of Civil Engineers Conditions of Contract (the ICE conditions) entered into between Cosslett (Contractors) Ltd (Cosslett) and the council on 28 January 1991 entitle the council, in the events which happened, to a security interest in the two coal-washing plants? (2) If so, did that security constitute a charge that was registrable pursuant to s 395 of the Companies

j   Act 1985 (the 1985 Act)? (3) If so, and having regard to the fact that the charge was never registered but that nevertheless the two plants were sold by the council to Burrows Bros (Sale) Ltd (Burrows) under the continuation contract entered into between them in January 1994, did the terms of the continuation contract constitute the tort of conversion? If so, can Cosslett's administrator sue on that tort in his own name? And on what basis should the damages for conversion be calculated? (4) On the footing that the council's security interest in the coal-washing

plants was void against Cosslett's administrator as a result of the failure to register
it pursuant to s 395, can the council set-off against the conversion damages for a
which the council is liable to Cosslett the contractual damages for breach of the
28 January 1991 contract for which Cosslett is liable to the council?

[47] The essential background facts relating to these issues have been set out
by my noble and learned friend Lord Hoffmann and I gratefully adopt them.

[48] It is, in my view, essential to keep in mind that at all material times Cosslett b
was the legal owner of the coal-washing plants. It was so decided by Jonathan
Parker J ([1996] 4 All ER 46, [1997] Ch 23) and the Court of Appeal ([1997] 4 All ER
115, [1998] Ch 495) in the first set of proceedings regarding the coal-washing plants.

[49] It is also essential to bear in mind the nature of the ICE conditions. The
contract between the council and Cosslett was a commercial contract in a form
used widely within the construction industry. Mr Moss QC, who appeared for c
the council before your Lordships, stressed the importance of keeping in mind the
commercial character and purpose of the ICE conditions when construing their
terms and considering their effect. I agree with him about that importance.

(1) Did the council have a security interest in the coal-washing plants? d

[50] In my opinion it plainly did. The coal-washing plants were items falling
within the definition in the ICE conditions of 'constructional plant'. No one has
argued the contrary. Clause 63(1) of the ICE conditions gave rights and remedies
to 'the employer' ie in this case, the council, in a number of specified events, one of
which was that the 'Contractor ... (a) has abandoned the Contract'. That is what e
happened in the present case. Cosslett abandoned the contract on 4 August 1993.
The contractual rights and remedies given to the employer are triggered by the
service on the contractor of a seven-day notice. The council, presumably for belt-
and-braces reasons, gave two such notices. No one has suggested a valid notice
was not given. The rights and remedies that follow the service of a valid seven-
day notice fall into three groups. (i) The employer may enter the site, expel the f
contractor from it, and take possession of the 'constructional plant' and materials
on the site. (ii) The employer may itself complete the works, or may engage some
substitute contractor to do so, and the employer, or the substitute contractor,
may use any items of 'constructional plant' and any of the materials for that
purpose. (iii) The employer may—
g

> 'at any time sell any of the said Constructional Plant ... and unused goods
> and materials and apply the proceeds of sale in or towards satisfaction of any
> sums due or which may become due to him from the Contractor under the
> Contract.'

[51] As to (i), the right to enter and expel is a necessary preliminary both to the h
exercise of the right to use the constructional plant, and to the exercise of the right
to sell it. As to (ii), the right to use the plant is not a security right. It was so
decided by the Court of Appeal. Millett LJ said:

> '... this right of the council in the present case ... does not constitute any j
> kind of security interest, since it is not given to the council by way of security.
> It does not secure the performance of the contract by the company, but
> merely enables the council to perform the contract in its place.' (See [1997]
> 4 All ER 115 at 125, [1998] Ch 495 at 508; see also [1997] 4 All ER 115 at 123,
> [1998] Ch 495 at 505 per Evans LJ.)

[52] But, as to (iii), the Court of Appeal held that:

a   'By contrast the council's power to sell the plant and apply the proceeds in
or towards discharge of whatever sums might be or become due from the
company by reason of its failure to complete the works clearly is a security
interest.' (See [1997] 4 All ER 115 at 125, [1998] Ch 495 at 508 per Millett LJ.)

[53] In the second hearing before the Court of Appeal ([2000] 1 BCLC 775),
which culminated in the judgment now under appeal before your Lordships, the
b security character of the employer's cl 63(1) right to sell the plant and apply the
proceeds in discharge of sums due to it from the contractor seems to have been
accepted (see at 783–784 (paras 15, 16) of Laws LJ's judgment). But before your
Lordships Mr Moss challenged the proposition. He submitted that the purpose
of the power of sale was to enable the council to clear the site by disposing of
c plant and materials when they were no longer needed for completion of the
engineering works and that the council's right to apply the proceeds of sale in or
towards satisfaction of any sum owing by Cosslett was simply a contractual right
of set-off and not intended to constitute equitable security. I do not agree. The
power to sell was not only for the purpose of enabling the council to clear the site
of plant and materials no longer needed but was, plainly, also for the purpose of
d enabling the council to bring into existence a fund that it could appropriate
towards any debt owing to it by Cosslett. In my opinion, a contractual right
enabling a creditor to sell his debtor's goods and apply the proceeds in or towards
satisfaction of the debt is a right of a security character. The conclusion does not
depend on the parties' intention to create a security. Their intention, objectively
ascertained, is relevant to the construction of their contract. But once contractual
e rights have, by the process of construction, been ascertained, the question
whether they constitute security rights is a question of law that is not dependent
on their intentions (see *Agnew v Comr of Inland Revenue* [2001] UKPC 28, [2001]
2 BCLC 189 at 200, [2001] 2 AC 710 at 725–726 per Lord Millett).

[54] The classification of the council's rights under cl 63(1) as a security right
f is, in my opinion, supported by the decision of the Court of Appeal in *Ex p Newitt*,
re Garrud (1881) 16 Ch D 522, [1881–5] All ER Rep 1039. That case arose out of a
building agreement between a landowner and a builder. The agreement entitled
the landowner, in the event of default by the builder, to re-enter the building site
and expel the builder. It provided that:

g   '... on such re-entry all such buildings, erections, constructions, materials,
and things then in and about the said premises shall be forfeited to and
become the property of the said lessor, as and for liquidated and settled
damages ...'

h [55] The issue for decision was whether the agreement should have been
registered as a bill of sale. The landowner argued that although the agreement
did grant 'a licence to take possession of personal chattels', the licence was not
granted 'as security for a debt' (see s 7 of the Bills of Exchange Act 1854). The
court agreed. James LJ said (at 530): 'It was no doubt "an authority or licence to
take possession of personal chattels," but not as security for a debt' and Brett LJ
j explained (at 532): '... the chattels were taken, not as security for, but in discharge
of the debt'.

[56] Clause 63(1), however, has the features that the *Ex p Newitt* argument
lacked. First, despite the index and the side heading, which refer to 'forfeiture',
the subclause is not a forfeiture provision. The employer does not take the proceeds
of sale in satisfaction for sums due by the contractor, but on account of sums due.
If there were a deficiency, the contractor would still owe the amount of the

deficiency. If there were a surplus, the employer would have to account for it to the contractor.

[57] Moreover, an employer exercising a cl 63(1) power of sale would, in my opinion, have to take reasonable care to obtain a proper price (cf *Cuckmere Brick Co Ltd v Mutual Finance Ltd* [1971] 2 All ER 633, [1971] Ch 949) and would not be entitled to sell to himself (cf *Tse Kwong Lam v Wong Chit Sen* [1983] 3 All ER 54, [1983] 1 WLR 1349). These obligations are not expressed in cl 63(1) but, in my opinion, have to be implied in order to provide proper protection for the contractor's interest in the items being sold and are all indicia of a security interest.

[58] Accordingly, in my opinion, the council's rights under cl 63(1) included security rights over the plant and materials that were on the site when the council entered into possession after the expiry of the seven day notice and over the proceeds of sale of any items of plant or materials that were sold.

(2) *Did the council's security rights under cl 63(1) constitute a charge registrable under s 395?*

[59] Section 396(1) of the 1985 Act specifies the types of charge that are registrable under s 395. Subparagraph (f) specifies 'a floating charge on the Company's undertaking or property'. Subparagraph (c) specifies 'a charge created or evidenced by an instrument which, if executed by an individual, would require registration as a bill of sale'. The argument before your Lordships concentrated on the question whether the council's security constituted a floating, as opposed to a fixed, charge. After argument had concluded the parties were given leave to make supplemental written submissions on the bills of sale point.

[60] In the first Court of Appeal hearing the court held that the security constituted a floating charge. The reasons were given by Millett LJ (see [1997] 4 All ER 115 at 127, [1998] Ch 495 at 510). He described the essential difference between a floating charge and a fixed charge in the following passage:

'The essence of a floating charge is that it is a charge, not on any particular asset, but on a fluctuating body of assets which remain under the management and control of the chargor, and which the chargor has the right to withdraw from the security despite the existence of the charge. The essence of a fixed charge is that the charge is on a particular asset or class of assets which the chargor cannot deal with free from the charge without the consent of the chargee. The question is not whether the chargor has complete freedom to carry on his business as he chooses, but whether the chargee is in control of the charged assets.'

He then held that the provisions of cl 53 of the ICE conditions enabled Cosslett to remove items of plant or materials from the site provided the removal would not prejudice or delay the completion of the works. This ability, he concluded, justified categorising the council's security as a floating charge. This conclusion does not seem to have been challenged in the second Court of Appeal hearing. Laws LJ described the categorisation of the council's security as a floating charge as 'uncontentious' (see [2000] 1 BCLC 775 at 784 (para 16)). The conclusion has, however, been firmly challenged before your Lordships by Mr Moss. He submitted that if he was wrong in contending that the ICE conditions did not create a charge at all, as I in common with all of your Lordships think that he was, the charge did not come into existence until a valid seven-day notice had been given under cl 63(1) and then came into existence as a fixed charge over all the plant and materials then on the site.

a   [61] Up to a point I agree with Mr Moss' analysis, but I am not sure that it makes any difference. A charge expressed to be granted over all the assets of a company but with liberty for the company until the occurrence of some specified future event to deal with the assets in the ordinary course of its business would be a classic floating charge (see Lord McNaghten in *Governments Stock and Other Securities Investment Co Ltd v Manila Rly Co Ltd* [1897] AC 81 at 86). The grant would vest in the grantee an

b   equitable security interest in the assets of the company for the time being; but the interest, although existing, would remain dormant until the requisite event happened. Contrast a charge expressed to come into existence on a specified future event and then to attach to assets then owned by the company. Such a grant would not, in my opinion, vest in the grantee any immediate equitable interest in the company's assets for the time being. Mr Moss would categorise such a grant as a

c   grant creating a future fixed charge over the assets in question, rather than as a floating charge over the company's assets for the time being. I agree with Mr Moss that a grant of the sort described would not create a traditional floating charge. And if parties want to create future charges over assets that cannot be identified until the future event happens, I do not see why, unless there be some public policy objection,

d   they should not be free to do so.

     [62] However, there has never been any statutory definition of 'floating charge'. The definitions are all judicial ones and, in most cases, expressed in order to distinguish floating charges from fixed charges. Buckley LJ in *Evans v Rival Granite Quarries Ltd* [1910] 2 KB 979 at 999 said: 'A floating security is not a future security; it is a present security, which presently affects all the assets of the company expressed to

e   be included in it.' This language, I think, assists Mr Moss. It suggests that a future security lacks something of the character of a floating charge. In the present case, over the period between the date of the contract, 28 January 1991, and the date of one or other of the seven-day notices given in August 1993 was there a 'present' security that 'presently' affected the coal- washing plants? To put the point another way, did the

f   council have any equitable interest in the coal-washing plants until the service of a seven day notice? In my opinion, it did not. Its rights over constructional plant and materials during the pre-seven-day notice period were contractual operational right, not property rights. Its security rights were dependent on the occurrence of one or other of the future events specified in cl 63(1).

     [63] I do not think, however, that this analysis bars the cl 63(1) future security

g   rights from constituting a floating charge for s 395 registration purposes. In my opinion, a charge expressed to come into existence on the occurrence of an uncertain future event and then to apply to a class of assets that cannot be identified until the event has happened would, if otherwise valid, qualify for registration as a floating charge. The future charge would have the essential characteristic of floating, remaining dormant, until the occurrence of the specified event. It would, I think,

h   come within the mischief sought to be dealt with by the s 395 requirement of registration of floating charges. For the same reasons, it would also, in my view, constitute a floating charge for Insolvency Act 1986 purposes (see eg ss 15(3) and 245).

     [64] The conclusion that the council's security was registrable as a floating charge makes it unnecessary to decide whether it might also have been registrable as a bill of

j   sale; as to which see ss 4 and 8 of the Bills of Sale Act 1878 and ss 3, 4 and 8 of the Bills of Sale Act (1878) Amendment Act 1882.

(3) In disposing of the coal-washing plants to Burrows under the continuation contract of January 1994 did the council commit the tort of conversion?

     [65] The failure to register the charge under s 395(1) of the 1985 Act made the charge 'void against the liquidator or administrator and any creditor of the company'.

It has been suggested that this language leaves an unregistered charge valid against
the grantor company, that the cl 63(1) charge was accordingly valid as against Cosslett
notwithstanding that it was void against the administrator, and that consequently the
disposition by the council of the coal-washing plants did not constitute the tort of
conversion. In *Re Monolithic Building Co, Tacon v Monolithic Building Co* [1915] 1 Ch 643
at 667, [1914–15] All ER Rep 249 at 253 Lord Cozens-Hardy MR said this of an
unregistered charge: 'It is a perfectly good deed against the company so long as it is a
going concern.' And Phillimore LJ said:

> 'We have to construe s. 93 of the statute. It makes void a security; not the debt,
> not the cause of action, but the security, and not as against everybody, not as
> against the company grantor, but against the liquidator, and against any creditor,
> and it leaves the security to stand as against the company while it is a going
> concern.' (See [1915] 1 Ch 643 at 667, [1914–15] All ER Rep 249 at 254.)

[66] The words 'or administrator' were inserted into s 395(1) by the Insolvency
Act 1985 (see s 109(1) and Sch 6, para 10). The previous language 'void as against the
liquidator and any creditor' may have been derived from the Bills of Sale Acts. Under
s 8 of the 1878 Act the consequence of failure to register was that the bill of sale
became void 'as against all trustees or assignees of [the grantor of the bill of sale] and
against [any creditor levying execution]'—I have endeavoured to summarise the
rather turgid language of the section. Section 8 did not make the unregistered bill of
sale void against the grantor. But, on a bankruptcy or assignment for the benefit of
creditors, the grantor's title to his assets would have left the grantor and passed to his
trustee or assignee. The references in *Re Monolithic Building Co* to the unregistered
security remaining enforceable while the grantor company was a going concern
produce the same effect for companies pre-liquidation as s 8 of the 1878 Act produced
for individuals pre-bankruptcy. Until bankruptcy intervened the unregistered bill of
sale was enforceable against the grantor. Thereafter it was not. Until a liquidation
or administration intervenes, the unregistered charge is enforceable against the
grantor company. Thereafter, or until the liquidation or administration comes to
an end, it is not.

[67] I am, therefore, in full agreement with my noble and learned friend Lord
Hoffmann that for as long as an unregistered charge is void under s 395(1) against a
liquidator or administrator the charge is, for the reasons he gives, void against the
grantor company in liquidation or in administration.

[68] It follows, in my opinion, that the council's security rights under cl 63(1),
being unregistered, have been void against Cosslett since 8 September 1993 when the
administration order was made.

[69] In *Clerk & Lindsell on Torts* (18th edn, 2000), conversion is described as 'a wide
tort, covering the deliberate taking, receipt, purchase, sale, disposal or consumption
of another's property' (p 726 (para 14-03)). Paragraph 14-08 (p 729) says that 'The
essence of the wrong [is] the unauthorised dealing with the claimant's chattel so as to
question or deny his title to it'.

[70] Under the continuation contract between the council and Burrows the
council purported to dispose of the coal-washing plants to Burrows. But since
Cosslett was the owner of the plants and the council's power of sale under cl 63(1) was
void as against Cosslett in administration, the disposal was, in my opinion, a clear act
of conversion.

[71] I would add that even if the cl 63(1) power of sale had been valid as against
Cosslett, I do not think the disposal to Burrows would have been franked by the
power. A sale is a disposition of property for a price. The obligation of a chargee with

a a power of sale is to obtain the best price reasonably obtainable. Under the
continuation contract, only parts of which were available to your Lordships, it seems
that the council disposed of the plants to Burrows on the footing that Burrows would
be allowed a credit of £100,000 for each against its tender price for completion of the
engineering works. But by a letter to the council dated 13 October 1993 Burrows
estimated the residual value of the plants to be £500,000 and stated that 'The £200,000

b credit quoted in our tender is after making allowance for the cost of expected barren
earthworks'. On this evidence it seems to me impossible for the council to contend
that it made a proper exercise of its cl 63(1) power of sale. If the cl 63(1) power had
been valid as against Cosslett in administration, I think the position would be that the
council had become a mortgagee in possession on entry on the site and, accordingly,
accountable to Cosslett on the footing of wilful default for the proper value of the

c coal-washing plants.

[72] Mr Moss contended that conversion was a wrongful interference with the
right of possession, that the council was entitled to retain possession of the coal-
washing plants in order to complete the engineering works and that the purported
disposal to Burrows at a time when the works had not been completed and Cosslett

d did not have a right to possession could not have constituted a conversion. He argued
that the eventual removal of the plants by Burrows after the works had been
completed, although done pursuant to the continuation contract, did not constitute a
conversion by the council for it was not done by the council.

[73] I am unable to accept these submissions. The continuation contract, being a
purported disposal of the plants by the council, was a wrongful interference with

e Cosslett's title to the plants. It was repudiatory in character and, had it been relied on
in the first set of proceedings between the parties, might well have enabled Cosslett
to succeed in its claim to immediate possession of the plants. The details of the
continuation contract were not, however, then known and the right of the council to
retain the plant pending completion of the works became res judicata as between the

f council and Cosslett.

[74] Both the coal-washing plants were removed from the site in or about June
1997. By that time they were no longer needed for completion of the works and were
removed by Burrows, acting in reliance on the continuation contract.

[75] In these circumstances, in my opinion, the fact that at the date of the
continuation contract Cosslett did not have an immediate right to possession did not

g deprive the continuation contract of its effect as constituting a conversion by the
council of the coal-washing plants. What it did do was to postpone the date at which,
for measure of damages purposes, the value of the converted plants had to be
assessed. Cosslett was, and in my opinion is, entitled to damages for conversion
representing the value of the plants at the date of the conversion, that is to say,

h January 1994. But the plants were, at that date, subject to the cl 63(1) rights of user
that were binding on Cosslett. So the value should be adjusted accordingly. In
practice, I imagine that the value of the plants subject to the rights of user will be
equivalent to the value of the plants in their used state at the completion of the works.

(4) Set-off

j [76] Can the council, even if its cl 63(1) rights do constitute a security that was
unregistered and therefore void, claim the benefit of equitable set-off so as to set off
its contractual damages claim against Cosslett's conversion damages claim? In my
opinion, clearly not. This is a case in which the parties, in cl 63(1) of their contract,
have provided the council with a contractual right of set-off that, for failure to comply
with applicable statutory provisions, is void against Cosslett in administration. Why
should equity intervene and protect the council from its failure to comply with the

statutory provisions? Similar questions arose in *Orakpo v Manson Investments Ltd* [1977] 3 All ER 1, [1978] AC 95 and in *Dimond v Lovell* [2000] 2 All ER 897, [2000] 2 WLR 1121. *Orakpo*'s case was a moneylending case. The defendants were licensed moneylenders but, in respect of loans to the plaintiff with which the plaintiff had purchased properties, had failed to comply with the requirements of the Moneylenders Act 1927. The consequence was that the loan agreements were unenforceable and so were the mortgages granted by the plaintiff to secure the repayment of the loans. The defendants claimed to be entitled by subrogation to the benefit of the vendors' liens. This House rejected the claim and Lord Salmon commented ([1977] 3 All ER 1 at 13, [1978] AC 95 at 111) that he could not think 'that it would be proper to apply an equitable doctrine for the purpose of enabling a moneylender to escape from the consequences of his breach of the statute'. Lord Edmund-Davies, in answer to the question whether a court of equity should grant relief to a moneylender who was in breach of the Act, said that he felt compelled to answer in the negative: '... for to answer affirmatively would be to enable the court to express a policy of its own in regard to moneylending transactions which would be in direct conflict with the policy of the 1927 Act itself.' (See [1977] 3 All ER 1 at 16, [1978] AC 95 at 115.)

[77] In *Dimond v Lovell* a regulated consumer credit agreement relating to the hire of a car was unenforceable for failure to comply with the requirements of the Consumer Credit Act 1974. It was argued for the car hire company that it should have an unjust enrichment remedy. The argument was rejected by this House. Lord Hoffmann, citing *Orakpo*'s case, said:

'Parliament intended that if a consumer credit agreement was improperly executed, then ... the debtor should not have to pay. This meant that Parliament contemplated that he might be enriched and I do not see how it is open to the court to say that this consequence is unjust and should be reversed by a remedy at common law ...' (See [2000] 2 All ER 897 at 906, [2000] 2 WLR 1121 at 1131.)

[78] Similar reasoning applies here. If the council's cl 63(1) security is barred by s 395(1) from being enforceable against Cosslett in administration, it is no part of equity to provide, via equitable set-off, an alternative security.

(5) *Title to sue in conversion*

[79] I respectfully agree that the plaintiff/claimant in Cosslett's conversion action ought to have been 'Cosslett (Contractors) Ltd (in administration)' and have nothing to add on this point to what Lord Hoffmann has already said.

[80] For all these reasons I agree that the appeal should be allowed and the judgment and interim order of Judge Toulmin QC restored.

LORD RODGER OF EARLSFERRY.

[81] My Lords, I have had the advantage of considering the speech of my noble and learned friend, Lord Hoffmann, in draft. I agree with it and for the reasons he gives I too would allow the appeal.

Appeal allowed.

Celia Fox   Barrister.

a

Bellinger v Bellinger
[2001] EWCA Civ 1140

COURT OF APPEAL, CIVIL DIVISION

DAME ELIZABETH BUTLER-SLOSS P, THORPE AND ROBERT WALKER LJJ

b 23, 24 MAY, 17 JULY 2001

Marriage – Validity – Declaration – Marriage void if parties not male and female – Appellant correctly registered at birth as male but undergoing sex-change operation – Appellant marrying man and seeking declaration that marriage was valid – Whether
c *gender of person fixed immutably at birth for purposes of marriage – Matrimonial Causes Act 1973, s 11(c).*

The appellant, B, was correctly classified at birth as male, but underwent gender reassignment surgery which was completed in 1981. That year B went through a ceremony of marriage with a man who was at all times aware of her
d background and was entirely supportive of her. The couple had thereafter lived together as husband and wife, although s 11(c)ᵃ of the Matrimonial Causes Act 1973 provided that a marriage was void if the parties were not respectively male and female. B subsequently petitioned the court for a declaration, opposed by the Attorney General but not by her husband, that the marriage was valid at its
e inception and was subsisting. The judge refused to grant the declaration, holding that B was male at the time of the marriage ceremony and remained so. In so concluding, the judge followed a long-standing first instance authority which had held that chromosomal, gonadal and genital criteria determined whether a person was a woman in the context of marriage; that those biological criteria were fixed at birth; and that accordingly, if congruent, they determined a person's
f sex for the purpose of marriage regardless of any subsequent operative intervention. B appealed, contending that it was no longer the case that the biological constitution of a person was fixed at birth. The Court of Appeal was therefore required to determine at what point, if any, a court could hold that a person had changed his gender status.

g
Held – (Thorpe LJ dissenting) Although it was for the court to determine whether a person was male or female by assessing the facts of the individual case against a clear statutory framework, it was for Parliament to determine the point at which it would be consistent with public policy to recognise that a person should be treated for all purposes, including marriage, as a person of the sex
h opposite to that which had been correctly assigned to that person at birth. The legal recognition of marriage, like divorce, was a matter of status and was not for the spouses alone to decide. It affected society and was a question of public policy. For that reason, even if for no other, marriage was in a special position and was different from the change of gender on a driving licence, social security
j payments book and so on. Birth, adoption, marriage, divorce or nullity and death had to be registered. Each child born had to be placed into one of two categories for the purpose of registration, and the chromosomal, gonadal and genital criteria remained the only basis for determining the gender of a child at birth. Status was

---

a   Section 11(c) re-enacted s 1(c) of the Nullity of Marriage Act 1971. Section 1(c) is set out at [16], below.

not conferred only by a person upon himself. It had to be recognised by society. *a*
The propriety of requiring pre-conditions for recognition of acquired gender was
a matter for public policy and public consultation, not a matter for imposition by
the courts on the public. When considering social issues in particular, judges were
not to substitute their own views to fill gaps in the legislation. Accordingly, the
appeal would be dismissed (see [43], [97], [99], [105], [106], [108], below).

Corbett v Corbett (otherwise Ashley) [1970] 2 All ER 33 applied.   *b*

Notes

For the requirement for a marriage to be between a male and a female, see 29(3)
Halsbury's Laws (4th edn reissue) paras 34, 378.

For the Matrimonial Causes Act 1973, s 11, see 27 *Halsbury's Statutes* (4th edn)
(2000 reissue) 942.   *c*

Cases referred to in judgment

A-G v Otahuhu Family Court [1995] 1 NZLR 603, NZ HC.
B v France [1993] 2 FCR 145, (1992) 16 EHRR 1, ECt HR.
Corbett v Corbett (otherwise Ashley) [1970] 2 All ER 33, [1971] P 83, [1970] 2 WLR *d*
1306.
Cossey v UK [1993] 2 FCR 97, (1990) 13 EHRR 622, ECt HR.
Cowan v Cowan [2001] 2 FCR 331, CA.
Dart v Dart [1997] 1 FCR 21, CA.
F (in utero), Re [1988] 2 All ER 193, [1988] Fam 122, [1988] 2 WLR 1288, CA.
Fitzpatrick v Sterling Housing Association Ltd [1999] 4 All ER 705, [2001] 1 AC 27, *e*
[1999] 3 WLR 1113, HL.
Hyde v Hyde and Woodmansee (1866) LR 1 P & D 130, [1861–73] All ER Rep 175,
Con Ct.
Lindo v Belisario (1795) 1 Hag Con 216, [1775–1802] All ER Rep 293, Con Ct.
Littleton v Prange (1999) 9 SW 3d 223, Tex CA.   *f*
M v M (marriage: transsexuals) [1991] NZFLR 337, NZ Fam Ct.
MT v JT (1976) 355 A 2d 204, NJ SC (AD).
P v S Case C-13/94 [1996] All ER (EC) 397, [1996] ECR I-2143, ECJ.
R v Registrar General, ex p P and G [1996] 2 FCR 588.
R v Tan [1983] 2 All ER 12, [1983] QB 1053, [1983] 3 WLR 361, CA.
Rees v UK [1993] 2 FCR 49, (1986) 9 EHRR 56, ECt HR.   *g*
Royal College of Nursing of the UK v Dept of Health and Social Security [1981] 1 All ER
545, [1981] AC 800, [1981] 2 WLR 279, QBD, CA and HL.
S-T (formerly J) v J [1998] 1 All ER 431, [1998] Fam 103, [1997] 3 WLR 1287 CA.
S v S (otherwise W) (No 2) [1962] 3 All ER 55; sub nom SY v SY (otherwise W) [1963]
P 37, [1962] 3 WLR 526, CA.   *h*
Sheffield v UK (1998) 5 BHRC 83, ECt HR.
Van Oosterwijck (D) v Belgium (1980) 3 EHRR 557, E Com HR.
W v W (physical inter-sex) [2001] Fam 111, [2001] 2 WLR 674.

Appeal   *j*

Elizabeth Ann Bellinger appealed with permission of the Court of Appeal from the
decision of Johnson J on 2 November 2000 ([2000] 3 FCR 733) dismissing her petition
under s 55 of the Family Law Act 1986 for a declaration that the marriage celebrated
between her and the respondent to the petition, Michael Jeffrey Bellinger, on 2 May
1981 was valid at its inception and was subsisting. Mr Bellinger had not opposed the
petition, but it had been opposed by the respondent to the appeal, the Attorney

a General, who had intervened in the proceedings under s 59(2) of the 1986 Act. The facts are set out in the judgment of Dame Elizabeth Butler-Sloss P and Robert Walker LJ.

Laura Cox QC and Ashley Bayston (instructed by Law for All) for the appellant.
Andrew Moylan QC and Timothy Amos (instructed by the Treasury Solicitor) for the
b Attorney General.

Cur adv vult

17 July 2001. The following judgments were delivered.

c **DAME ELIZABETH BUTLER-SLOSS P** AND **ROBERT WALKER LJ.**
[1] This is an appeal, with leave of the Court of Appeal, by the appellant, Mrs Bellinger, from the refusal of Johnson J on 2 November 2000 ([2000] 3 FCR 733) to grant her petition for a declaration that the marriage celebrated between Mr Bellinger and herself was valid at its inception and is subsisting. The reason for the judge's refusal to grant the declaration was that the appellant was at the
d time of the marriage ceremony, and still remains, male. Mr Bellinger was the respondent to the petition, which he did not oppose. The Attorney General intervened, filed an answer and opposed the granting of the declaration.
[2] Behind those bare facts lies a human problem, which deeply affects a small minority of the population. In considering the difficult medical and legal issues facing this court, admirably encapsulated in the written and oral submissions of
e Mrs Cox QC for the appellant and Mr Moylan QC for the Attorney General, we are very much aware of the plight of those who, like the appellant, are locked into the medical condition of transsexualism, within the group described as gender dysphoria or gender identity disorder.

f THE HISTORY
[3] The appellant was born on 7 September 1946 and was at birth correctly classified as male. However, from as long as she could remember, she felt more inclined to be female. Despite her inclinations, and under some pressure, at the age of 21 she married a woman. The marriage broke down and they divorced in
g 1971. After the divorce she began to dress as and live as a woman. She went through the various stages of treatment, and finally underwent gender reassignment surgery which was completed in 1981. On 2 May 1981 she went through a ceremony of marriage with Mr Bellinger, a widower. He was at all times aware of the appellant's background and was entirely supportive of her. The appellant was described on her marriage certificate as a spinster but apart from that she was not asked by the
h Registrar of Marriages, nor did she volunteer any information, about her gender status. The couple have lived together ever since as husband and wife. The appellant petitioned for the declaration under s 55 of the Family Law Act 1986. The Attorney General intervened under the provisions of s 59(2) of the Act.

j MEDICAL CONDITION OF THE APPELLANT
[4] There is no suggestion now that the appellant was incorrectly assigned to be male at birth, nor that she falls within the group described as inter-sexed. From the medical evidence it is clear that the appellant was correctly assigned at birth as male. The appellant felt an increasing urge to live as a woman rather than as a man. She first consulted Dr Randall, a consultant psychiatrist at the Charing Cross Hospital, with special expertise in this area of medicine. She had a long

course of counselling and hormonal treatment and, in February 1981, she
underwent reconstruction surgery, which involved the removal of her testicles   *a*
and penis and, as Johnson J expressed it ([2000] 3 FCR 733 at 735)—

> 'the creation of an orifice which can be described as an artificial vagina but
> she was still without uterus or ovaries or any other biological
> characteristics of a woman.'
                                                                                   b

[5] The report on a chromosomal test, dated 8 April 1999, showed her to have
a Karyotype 46 XY pattern, an apparently normal male Karyotype. She clearly
comes within the diagnosis of gender disorder and she is a transsexual. She has
completed the four stages of change from male to female.

[6] The background to the issue raised by the appellant is the current
understanding of the meaning of 'marriage'. Lord Penzance, in *Hyde v Hyde*   *c*
(1866) LR 1 P & D 130 at 133, [1861–73] All ER Rep 175 at 177, gave the classic
definition of a Christian marriage:

> 'I conceive that marriage, as understood in Christendom, may for this
> purpose be defined as the voluntary union for life of one man and one
> woman, to the exclusion of all others.'   *d*

[7] Although that definition can no longer be taken as correct in all particulars,
since those married can now bring their marriages to an end during their lifetime,
Ormrod J in *Corbett v Corbett (otherwise Ashley)* [1970] 2 All ER 33 at 48, [1971] P 83
at 105 said that sex was an essential determinant of marriage, because 'it is and   *e*
always has been recognised as the union of man and woman'.

[8] In refusing to make the declaration sought by the appellant, Johnson J
considered extensive written medical evidence from three distinguished experts
in the field of gender identity disorder. They were largely in agreement and no
oral evidence was given. The judge accepted that, since *Corbett*'s case in 1970,
there has been a marked change in social attitudes to problems of those in the   *f*
situation of the appellant. He concluded:

> 'There is now a distinct possibility that were it possible to do so, examination
> of the brain of a living individual would reveal further indications of gender.
> But that is not yet possible and the practical reality is that whatever may
> ultimately emerge from advances in medical science, the only criteria for   *g*
> determining the gender of an individual remain those identified in *Corbett*'s
> case.' (See [2000] 3 FCR 733 at 747.)

[9] He therefore decided that the medical criteria, set out by Ormrod J in
Corbett's case, remained equally valid today, and that under those criteria the   *h*
appellant was unable to marry Mr Bellinger. He dismissed her petition.

Corbett's case
[10] The facts in *Corbett*'s case have some similarities to the present case. The
respondent had been registered at birth in 1935 as male, and had served in the
merchant navy, which he left after taking an overdose of tablets. After taking   *j*
hormonal treatment for some years and working as a female impersonator, he
underwent, in 1960 in Casablanca, reconstruction surgery, and thereafter changed
his name and lived as a woman. In September 1963, the respondent went through
a ceremony of marriage with the petitioner, a man, who knew the respondent's
background. The 'marriage' was not a success, and in December 1963, the

a petitioner petitioned for nullity based on the ground that the respondent was male. The judge granted a decree of nullity.

[11] Nine medical experts gave evidence at the hearing and the judge said:

b 'All the medical witnesses accept that there are, at least, four criteria for assessing the sexual condition of an individual. These are—(i) Chromosomal factors. (ii) Gonadal factors (ie presence or absence of testes or ovaries). (iii) Genital factors (including internal sex organs). (iv) Psychological factors. Some of the witnesses would add—(v) Hormonal factors or secondary sexual characteristics (such as distribution of hair, breast development, physique etc., which are thought to reflect the balance between the male and female sex hormones in the body). It is important to note that these criteria have *c* been evolved by doctors for the purposes of systematising medical knowledge, and assisting in the difficult task of deciding the best way of managing the unfortunate patients who suffer, either physically or psychologically, from sexual abnormalities. As Professor Dewhurst observed "We do not determine sex—in medicine we determine the sex in which it is best for the individual to live". These criteria are, of course, relevant to, but do not necessarily *d* decide, the legal basis of sex determination.' (See [1970] 2 All ER 33 at 44, [1971] P 83 at 100.)

[12] Earlier in his judgment, Ormrod J considered the aetiology of transsexualism and he referred to:

e 'The alternative view is that there may be an organic basis for the condition. This hypothesis is based on experimental work ... which suggests that the copulatory behaviour of the adult animals may be affected by the influence of certain sex hormones on particular cells in the hypothalamus ... At present the application of this work to the human being is purely hypothetical and speculative ... The use of such phrases as "male or female *f* brain" in this connection is apt to mislead owing to the ambiguity of the word "brain" ... In my judgment, these theories have nothing to contribute to the solution of the present case.' (See [1970] 2 All ER 33 at 43–44, [1971] P 83 at 99–100.)

[13] He said:

g 'It is common ground between all the medical witnesses that the biological sexual constitution of an individual is fixed at birth (at the latest), and cannot be changed, either by the natural development of organs of the opposite sex, or by medical or surgical means. The respondent's operation, therefore, cannot affect her true sex. The only cases where the term "change of sex" is *h* appropriate are those in which a mistake as to sex is made at birth and subsequently revealed by further medical investigation.' (See [1970] 2 All ER 33 at 47, [1971] P 83 at 104.)

[14] The finding by Ormrod J that the biological sexual constitution of an *j* individual was fixed at birth is said by Mrs Cox no longer to reflect the true position.

[15] Ormrod J concluded:

'Since marriage is essentially a relationship between man and woman, the validity of the marriage in this case depends, in my judgment, on whether the respondent is or is not a woman. I think, with respect, that this is a more

precise way of formulating the question than that adopted in para 2 of the
petition, in which it is alleged that the respondent is a male. The greater, of *a*
course, includes the less, but the distinction may not be without importance,
at any rate in some cases. The question then becomes what is meant by the
word "woman" in the context of a marriage, for I am not concerned to
determine the "legal sex" of the respondent at large. Having regard to the
essentially heterosexual character of the relationship which is called *b*
marriage, the criteria must, in my judgment, be biological, for even the most
extreme degree of transsexualism in a male or the most severe hormonal
imbalance which can exist in a person with male chromosomes, male gonads
and male genitalia cannot reproduce a person who is naturally capable of
performing the essential role of a woman in marriage. In other words, the
law should adopt, in the first place, the first three of the doctors' criteria, ie *c*
the chromosomal, gonadal and genital tests, and, if all three are congruent,
determine the sex for the purpose of marriage accordingly, and ignore any
operative intervention. The real difficulties, of course, will occur if these
three criteria are not congruent. This question does not arise in the present
case and I must not anticipate, but it would seem to me to follow from what *d*
I have said that greater weight would probably be given to the genital criteria
than to the other two. This problem and, in particular, the question of the
effect of surgical operations in such cases of physical inter-sex, must be left
until it comes for decision. My conclusion, therefore, is that the respondent
is not a woman for the purposes of marriage but is a biological male and has
been so since birth. It follows that the so-called marriage of 10th September *e*
1963 is void.' (See [1970] 2 All ER 33 at 48–49, [1971] P 83 at 106.)

THE LEGISLATION

[16] The judgment of Ormrod J was not appealed and its conclusions were put
on a statutory basis in the Nullity of Marriage Act 1971, s 1 of which stated: *f*

> 'A marriage which takes place after the commencement of this Act shall be
> void on the following grounds only, that is to say … (c) that the parties are
> not respectively male and female.'

[17] Section 1(c) was re-enacted in s 11(c) of the Matrimonial Causes Act 1973,
which applies to the present proceedings. *g*

Male and female—gender

[18] The words 'male and female' have not been interpreted either in the
statute or in subsequent decisions of the courts. Mrs Cox at one stage suggested
that the words 'male' and 'female' were deliberately left undefined so that they *h*
were capable of being interpreted more broadly than 'man' and 'woman', and
'female' might, therefore, encompass the position of the appellant. There was
some slight support for that proposition in the judgments of Ward LJ and
Sir Brian Neill in *S-T (formerly J) v J* [1998] 1 All ER 431, [1998] Fam 103. Ward LJ
said: *j*

> 'It is suggested that the Act has made a subtle but perhaps important
> change to the terminology. What governed Ormrod J's decision in *Corbett v
> Corbett*, based as it was on ecclesiastical principles, was whether the parties
> were "a man and a woman". It may be—but I express no view about it—that
> the choice of the words "male and female" has left the way open for a future
> court, relying on the developments of medical knowledge, to place greater

a   emphasis on gender than on sex in deciding whether a person is to be regarded as male or female. There is a body of very respectable academic opinion making that point: see, for example, Cretney and Masson *Principles of Family Law* (5th edn, 1990) pp 46–48, Sebastian Poulter "'The Definition of Marriage in English Law" (1979) 42 MLR 409, 421–425 and Anthony Bradney "'Transsexuals and the Law" [1987] Fam Law 350.' (See [1998] 1 All ER 431 at

b   449–450, [1998] Fam 103 at 124.)

[19] Sir Brian Neill said:

'It is not necessary for the purpose of this appeal to consider whether the decision of Ormrod J in *Corbett v Corbett* ... requires re-examination in the

c   light of modern medical advances and in the light of decisions in other jurisdictions, or whether it is distinguishable because the words used in s 11 of the 1973 Act are "male and female" which, I suppose it might be argued, indicate a test of gender rather than sex.' (See [1998] 1 All ER 431 at 476, [1998] Fam 103 at 153.)

d   [20] Allowing for the possibility of some ambiguity in the use of the words 'male' and 'female' in s 1(c), both Johnson J and this court were invited to look at the relevant extract from Hansard during the passage of the Nullity of Marriage Bill through the House of Commons (814 HC Official Report (5th series) cols 1827–1854, 2 April 1971). This did not seem to us to elucidate the meaning of the words, but it did demonstrate that the decision to include the issue of

e   gender within the law governing nullity, rather than to provide for it by way of a declaration as to status, was a humane one designed to provide for the possibility of applications for financial relief by either party to the nullity decree. This approach was of some significance in the light of the definition in Jackson *The Formation and Annulment of Marriage* (2nd edn, 1969) p 131:

f   'If two persons of the same sex contrive to go through a ceremony of marriage, the ceremony is not matrimonial at all: it is certainly not a void marriage, and matrimonial principles have no application to such an "union" ...'

g   [21] The requirement that the issue, as to whether a person was male or female, was to be decided within the framework of the law of nullity was made crystal clear by s 58(5)(a) of the Family Law Act 1986, which stated that no court may make a declaration 'that a marriage was at its inception void'.

[22] The words 'male' and 'female' are obviously broader than 'man' and 'woman', since they encompass the entire animal world. Among humans, it

h   includes those who are not yet adults. It does not, however, appear to us necessary to delve deeper into the extended meaning of 'male and female' in this judgment, since Mrs Cox does not now seek to rely strongly upon it.

[23] The words 'sex' and 'gender' are sometimes used interchangeably, but today more frequently denote a difference. Mrs Cox submitted that gender was

j   broader than sex. Her suggested definition was that 'gender' related to culturally and socially specific expectations of behaviour and attitude, mapped on to men and women by society. It included self-definition, that is to say, what a person recognised himself to be. See also Sir Brian Neill in *S-T (formerly J) v J* [1998] 1 All ER 431 at 476, [1998] Fam 103 at 153). It would seem from the definition proposed by Mrs Cox, with which we would not disagree, that it would be impossible to identify gender at the moment of the birth of a child.

THE MEDICAL EVIDENCE

[24] The aetiology of the condition of transsexualism appears to be uncertain. *a*
Professor Green, consultant psychiatrist and Research Director of the Gender
Identity Clinic at the Charing Cross Hospital, identified transsexualism as follows:

'Gender dysphoria is discontent with being a person of the sex to which one
was born and discontent with living in the gender role consistent with that birth
sex. Gender dysphoria when profound is popularly known as transsexualism. *b*
In the current version of the American Psychiatric Association's Diagnostic and
Statistical Manual of Mental Disorders IV, this condition is known as gender
identity disorder.'

[25] Ormrod J in *Corbett's* case described the condition: *c*

'The transsexual ... has an extremely powerful urge to become a member
of the opposite sex to the fullest extent which is possible ... This goes on
until they come to think of themselves as females imprisoned in male bodies,
or vice versa ...' (See [1970] 2 All ER 33 at 42, [1971] P 83 at 98.)

[26] Three eminent consultants provided reports to the court, Professor *d*
Gooren, Professor Green and Mr Terry.

Professor Gooren

[27] The evidence of Professor Gooren, Professor of Endocrinology at the Free
University Hospital, Amsterdam, was provided in a report on transsexualism, dated *e*
20 June 1999, an undated affidavit, a medical report on the appellant dated
18 February 2000 and a subsequent letter of 11 October 2000. He was clear that
transsexualism was a medical condition:

'Traditionally it is assumed that sexual differentiation, the process of
becoming man or woman is completed with the formation of the external *f*
genitalia, the criterion used to assign a new-born child to the male or female
sex. From the beginning of this century it became clear in laboratory animals
that this is not the endpoint of the sexual differentiation process but that the
brain undergoes a sexual differentiation process into male and female,
largely predicting/correlating with future sexual and non-sexual behaviour. *g*
The process of sexual differentiation takes place in distinct steps, first the
chromosomal configuration is established, next gonadal differentiation, next
differentiation of the internal and external genitalia and finally the differentiation
of the brain into male or female. Normally all steps in the process of sexual
differentiation are concordant (in men an XY chromosomal pattern, testis,
male internal and external genitalia and a male brain differentiation being the *h*
substrate of male-type behaviour; in women an XX chromosomal pattern,
ovary, female internal and external genitalia and a female brain
differentiation being the substrate of female-type behaviour). Nature is not
free of errors and the process of sexual differentiation is no exception. There
are human beings in which not all the traditional criteria of sex are *j*
concordant. They may have some biological characteristics of one sex and
some of the others, a condition known as inter-sexed. The human condition
requires that new-born children be assigned to one sex or the other. The
social and legal systems have left no room for inter-sexed subjects. If a
new-born child presents with an inter-sexed condition a medical decision
must be made to assign this baby to the male or female sex. It is now a

a generally accepted medical practice to assign an inter-sexed new-born child to that sex in which the unlucky creature, on the basis of medical expertise and reasonable expectation, will function best. It is of note that biological characteristics are not imperative in this decision process. The decision is based on prognosticated future sexual and non-sexual functioning. The legal system registers these new-born children in accordance with the medical

b decision. So it is no longer tenable to claim the genetic or gonadal criterion determines one's status as male or female. Some of our fellow human beings live lives of women with a male-type XY chromosomal pattern or testis or vice versa ... Sexual and non-sexual brain differentiation is now accepted as part of the process of becoming male or female of the mammalian species to which humans belong. In animal experimentation it is easily possible to

c induce a female type of sexual and non-sexual behaviour in animals that have, up to that final stage of sexual differentiation, a completely male pattern and vice versa. Depending on the type of manipulation applied in the animal experiment, in-between types of behaviour can also be observed. On the basis of the findings of these experiments it has been hypothesised that in

d human subjects with gender identity problems the sexual differentiation of their brains has not followed the pattern predicted by their earlier steps in the sexual differentiation process (such as chromosomes, gonadal, genitalia) but has followed a pattern typical of the opposite sex in the final stage of that differentiation process; as indicated above, a situation that can be induced in laboratory animals by experimental manipulation ... The validity of

e extrapolation of the sexual differentiation process of the brain in other mammals to the human has been corroborated by findings of anatomical and functional brain differences between males and females, including the human species.'

f [28] Professor Gooren said that the findings based on research into the human brain structure carried out post mortem showed that a biological structure in the brain distinguished male-to-female transsexuals from men (see Zhou, Hofman, Gooren and Swaab 'A Sex Difference in the Human Brain and its Relation to Transsexuality' (1995) 378 *Nature* 68, 2 November):

g 'In conclusion: there is now reason to believe that transsexualism is a disorder of sexual differentiation, the process of becoming man or woman as we conventionally understand it. Like other subjects afflicted with errors in this process, these subjects need to be medically rehabilitated so that they can live acceptable lives as men or women. This decision is not essentially different from the one made in inter-sexed children where assignment takes

h place to the sex in which they in all likelihood will function best. In them the decision most of the times takes place shortly after birth ... similarly it is the case in transsexualism, since there is evidence that the sexual differentiation of the brain in humans occurs (also) after birth. As such it is unavoidable that in subjects with errors of the sexual differentiation of the brain, sex

j reassignment takes place after birth, sometimes much later in their lives since it requires a large amount of life experience to discover the predicament of being born in the wrong sex, in other words having sexual and non-sexual brain patterns that are in contradiction with the other sex characteristics. The established diagnostic and therapeutical approach to transsexuals is that it is a stepwise procedure: the decision to treat hormonally is contingent upon the outcome of the psycho-diagnostic process, the decision to recommend

surgery is contingent upon the successful outcome of hormone treatment
and the real life test. If both appear to resolve the subject's gender problems,   *a*
it is imperative to recommend sex reassignment surgery.'

[29] In his paper he made it clear that there are significant health risks in
refusal of sex reassignment to those who qualify for it as a result of careful and
thorough psycho-diagnostic process. The risks include suicide as not uncommon.
[30] In his letter of 11 October, Professor Gooren said: *b*

'The process of becoming man or woman is not complete with the
formation of the external genitalia, the common criterion to label someone
male or female is extremely expeditious in that regard. But the brain is also
sex-dimorphic, and is an organ that becomes sex-dimorphic in the course of
normal female/male development. Both the paper in *Nature* and *Journal of*   *c*
Clinical Endocrinology substantiate the hypothesis that transsexuals are inter-
sexed at brain level and deserve the same medical care as other inter-sexed
patients ...'

Professor Green   *d*
[31] Professor Green made a report to the Treasury Solicitor of 5 October
1999, followed by letters of 12 October and 2 November 1999 and a further report
of 20 December 2000.
[32] In his 5 October report he said:

'Over the past four decades, gender identity disorder, or transsexualism, has   *e*
been acknowledged as a psychiatric disorder requiring unique therapeutic
interventions. Severe gender dysphoria cannot be alleviated by any conventional
psychiatric treatment, whether it be psycho-analytic therapy, eclectic psychiatric
treatment, aversion treatment, or by any standard psychiatric drugs.
Consequently, the strategies of therapeutic intervention include, firstly,   *f*
clinical exploration of the extent of the patient's gender dysphoria. When it
is considered that a transition to living in the other sex and gender role could
result in a better psychological, psychosocial and psychosexual functioning,
an extended trial transition period is initiated. Treatment stages include
reversible steps before those that are irreversible. Thus, early on, there may
be name change, and clothing style change. This is followed by cross-sex   *g*
hormone administration. If during the next one to two years the individual
can demonstrate to self and health care professionals that life is more successful
in the new gender role, consideration can be given for referral for sex
reassignment surgical intervention ... The onset of gender dysphoria is
typically dated by patients to the earliest years of life. It is reported to have   *h*
begun "as far back as I can remember" ... The criteria for designating a
person as male or female are complex. They are not simply an outcome of
chromosomal configuration, genital configuration, or gonadal.'

[33] He set out a number of situations in which the patient's chromosomal
pattern did not fit the gender assignment given to the patient. This applied both   *j*
to those within the male grouping and female grouping. In such cases the criteria
set out in *Corbett*'s case are not concordant with their designation. Such patients
are inter-sexed. Professor Green instanced the condition of androgen insensitive
syndrome. Those with that condition are psychologically female and appear to be
normal women, but two of their three sexual criteria under *Corbett*'s case are male.

a
[34] Professor Green then said:

'The *Corbett* criteria are too reductionistic to serve as a viable set of criteria to determine sex. They also ignore the compelling significance of the psychological status of the person as a man or a woman.'

[35] Mrs Cox placed great reliance on that passage as showing that the
b advances in medical knowledge made the *Corbett* criteria dated and inadequate. Mr Moylan, however, pointed to the previous passages of Professor Green's report which were dealing with those who came within the definition of inter-sexed and not transsexuals.

[36] Professor Green referred to the research relied upon by Professor Gooren:

c   'In recent years there has been a widely publicized finding from the Netherlands indicating, in a small series of male-female transsexuals studied post-mortem, that the bed nucleus of the stria terminalis region of the brain was similar in size to that of typical females and different in size from typical male. The interpretation of this finding is that it provides evidence of a biological central nervous system basis for male transsexualism. Because of
d   the difficulties in replicating such a study which must be conducted after death this report remains neither refuted nor confirmed.'

[37] In his letter of 12 October, Professor Green agreed that the Zhou et al paper on sexual differentiation of the brain should not be considered a preliminary report but he underlined that the research was conducted on a small sample of
e male transsexuals. In his letter of 2 November 1999, Professor Green wrote in a reply to a request to consider the *Corbett* criteria:

'The four criteria, even the potential fifth criterion of hormonal factors or secondary sexual characteristics, noted by medical experts nearly thirty years
f   ago, are derived from the landmark studies of the anatomically inter-sexed, the work of Dr John Money and additionally Drs John and Joan Hampson in the 1950s at The John Hopkins Hospital. There has been no substantive alteration in considering these criteria during the intervening years. There are medical experts who would value the psychological factor as the most important criterion particularly when psychological factors, or the person's
g   gender identity, is at variance with any of the other factors. In fact, in the pioneering studies of the anatomically inter-sexed the psychological factor was most commonly the overriding one in determining psychosexual development of the individual.'

[38] In his final report of 20 December 2000, he answered specific questions
h asked by the Treasury Solicitor. He set out the criteria applied to determine the sex of a child at birth and the problems in assigning the sex of an inter-sexed individual. He said:

'Psychological factors cannot be considered at birth because they do not yet manifest. They may become an overriding consideration subsequently
j   as the individual develops. Physical differences in the brain are as yet not measurable at birth, if at all later in life. They may ultimately override all other criteria. Thus, though not apparent at birth, this would influence the ultimate developmental outcome with respect to a new-born.'

[39] In the management of those who are born inter-sexed he said:

'... there is considerable sentiment for delaying any surgical modification
of the genitalia which had been thought to help pre-set the evolving gender
identity. Now there is more of a wait and see approach until the individual
is old enough to express its own wishes ... There is growing acceptance of
findings of sexual differences in the brain that are determined prenatally.
They are seen as influencing sex-typed and sexual behaviours. I do not know
how much of an international consensus there is on this or just what a
reasonable body of medical opinion would constitute here. However, there
is a growing momentum in that direction.'

[40] He was asked how the sex of the petitioner's brain could be determined
during her lifetime:

'At present there is probably no method within neuroscience to make such
a determination. Rather it may be best to abide by the person's gender
identity, which is the psychological manifestation as mediated by the brain
... If a biological sexual condition of an individual is conceptualised to
include psychological sex, perhaps reflective of brain sex differentiation, this
status does not express itself until several years postnatally. Therefore it is
not possible to say that the biological sexual condition of an individual is
fixed at birth in that not all of the bases of the biological sexual condition can
be determined at birth ... As a psychiatrist I am biased towards psychological
factors. I would argue that with a transsexual the psychological sex has been
contrary to other somatic factors for many years, if not the great majority of
the person's life. Taking that position gender reassignment treatment and
surgery would align the somatic features with the psychological features ...
By the standards applied at the time of the patient's birth it would be
considered that the infant was male. However, current considerations with
respect to determining the correct sex of an individual at birth, such as
psychological and brain sex, might render that designation less certain ... the
hormonal sex and genital sex have been changed by medico-surgical
intervention. Gonadal factors have been modified in that they have been
eliminated. Chromosomal factors have not been altered so far as XX or XY
is concerned, but within the chromosomes there may be genes that
determine that the petitioner was psychologically female. At present the
patient is functioning as a woman, not as a man. From that perspective the
petitioner's sex could be judged to have changed.'

Mr Terry

[41] Mr Terry, consultant urological surgeon at the Leicester University
Hospitals, which have a gender identity disorder group, provided a report dated
21 October 1999 to the Treasury Solicitor and a letter of 14 March 2000 to
Professor Green. He supported the reports of Professor Gooren and Professor
Green. He referred to the *Harry Benjamin International Gender Dysphoria Association's
Standards of Care for Gender Identity Disorders* (5th version, 1998), which classified
gender identity disorder either under the ICD-10 (*The International Classification
of Diseases-10*) or the DSM-IV (*Diagnostic and Statistical Manual of Mental Disorders*
(4th edn)). He set out the required stages before a patient was accepted for genital
reconstructive surgery: the patient had to be over 18, having had 12 months of
continuous hormonal therapy, 12 months of successful, continuous full-time real
life experience, and full understanding of the consequences of surgery and the

a possibilities available. He was aware of the study of the interaction between the
developing brain and sex hormones in Zhou et al. He said:

'This study, although composed of small numbers of patients, shows a
significant difference in the size of the central subdivision of the bed nucleus
of the stria terminalis between groups of men and women and male to
b   female transsexuals. This paper therefore lends credence to the view that the
formation of external genitalia which is currently the criteria to assign a
new-born child to the female or male sex is not the end point of sexual
differentiation and that sexual differentiation of the brain may be more
important in predicting or correlating future sexual and non sexual behaviour
… With further research into the neuro-anatomy/neuro-pharmacology of
c   brains of transsexual patients the pathogenesis of transsexualism may become
more clearly understood.'

[42] In an addendum to his report he said:

'The psychological profile of male to female transsexuals is female by
d   medical definition. The only biological factor which has not changed in such
individuals is their chromosomal makeup. The paper reported in *Nature* in
1995 would suggest this in itself may be irrelevant in the sexual development
of transsexuals. Accepting that transsexualism is a medically recognised
condition and that such patients undergo appropriate medical and surgical
treatment to achieve their chosen sexual orientation it seems to me
e   irrelevant to consider the chromosome makeup of an individual as the
critical factor when determining the rights of that individual in the society in
which he/she lives.'

Conclusions on the medical evidence

f   [43] In our judgment the gender assignment at birth of a transsexual in
accordance with the *Corbett* criteria cannot be challenged. There are at present
no other criteria that can be applied to a new-born child.

[44] The next question is whether the assignment made at birth is immutable,
other than for those with uncertain sexual characteristics, or whether there is a
point at which it can be said that the gender which was correct at birth is no
g   longer applicable.

[45] The significant difference between the three consultants, despite their
general agreement, was their approach to the classification of the diagnosis of
transsexualism. Professor Gooren was clear that it was a medical condition with
an organic basis, 'a disorder of sexual differentiation' and, based upon the
h   research described in the paper of Zhou et al, went so far as to say that the research
substantiated 'the hypothesis that transsexuals are inter-sexed at brain level'.

[46] Both Professor Green and Mr Terry considered that the Zhou et al
research was important, but based upon a small sample, and its findings could not
at present be refuted nor confirmed—it has not been so far widely accepted.
j   Professor Green placed transsexualism within the category of psychiatric
disorder, as did Mr Terry who referred to its categorisation by the Harry
Benjamin International Gender Dysphoria Association, within the manual of
mental disorders.

[47] Transsexualism is, therefore, according to the present accepted medical
knowledge, recognised as a psychiatric condition, coming within gender dysphoria
or gender identity disorder. There is the possibility that it is a medical condition

with a biological basis by reason of sexual differentiation of the brain after birth.
Another disorder within the same group is the condition called inter-sex, which *a*
has certain similarities to transsexualism but is recognised as a distinct disorder.
An inter-sexed person is someone whose biological criteria at birth are not
congruent, and is, therefore, of uncertain sex and, as Professor Gooren and
Professor Green described, would be assigned to the sex the medical profession
considered most appropriate for psychological reasons rather than biological reasons. *b*
By contrast the transsexual would be born with congruent biological criteria and
would be appropriately assigned to one sex, but would become seriously
discontented with that 'label' as he/she grew up. At some stage a transsexual
would be likely to seek medical advice. As Professor Gooren said, it would be a
stepwise procedure.

[48] The identification and treatment of transsexualism can be divided into *c*
four stages: (a) psychiatric assessment; (b) hormone treatment; (c) a period of the
real life test (living as a member of the opposite sex); and, in suitable cases,
(d) gender reassignment surgery.

[49] After diagnosis, the purpose of the treatment is to deal as effectively as
possible with the psychological problems of being born into the gender with *d*
which the person is profoundly unhappy. The diagnosis, as Mr Moylan pointed
out, is based upon the correct assignment at birth, determined by the existing
biological criteria which subsequently turns out to be psychologically incorrect.

[50] The three possible additional factors not taken into account by Ormrod J
in *Corbett's* case are: (a) psychological; (b) secondary sexual characteristics; and
(c) brain differentiation. *e*

(a) Psychological

[51] Ormrod J, of course, recognised the psychological factor and disregarded
it for the purpose of assignment of the biological sex of the baby. If he was correct
that assignment of sex has to be fixed at birth for all whose biological criteria are *f*
congruent, then the psychological factor has to be disregarded. For those who
are inter-sexed, since the assignment is uncertain, provision is made for
redefinition, e g *W v W (physical inter-sex)* [2001] Fam 111, [2001] 2 WLR 674.
Professor Green considered that psychological factors might become an
overriding consideration as the individual developed. Those factors would clearly
have to be recognised at a later stage in the life of the individual. *g*

(b) Secondary sexual characteristics

[52] None of the medical evidence suggested that the secondary criteria
should be a primary factor in assignment or reassignment.
  h

(c) Brain differentiation

[53] Professor Gooren's evidence on the recent research on animals, and
post-mortem on the brains of transsexuals, shows the developments in medical
science since this hypothesis was dismissed by Ormrod J in *Corbett's* case. The
size of the brain in men is significantly larger than in women and in the group of *j*
post-mortems on transsexual male to females the size of the brain corresponded
to the gender assumed. The research may potentially be of great significance in
guiding the medical profession and the courts in a reassessment of the correct
gender of transsexuals.

[54] There are however, at present, a number of formidable obstacles. The
research is on a limited basis. It has not yet been generally accepted, and clearly

a   more research will have to be carried out to demonstrate that the biological
factor which causes brain sexual differentiation in men and women is to be found
congruent with the transsexual's preferred gender.

[55] A much larger obstacle is the present impossibility of recognition of brain
differentiation in living people. The possible psychological or other signs of such
brain differentiation are at such an early stage that, in our judgment, a court could
b   not accept them as clear indications. No one in this case has asked us to do so.
Consequently, the work on brain sexual differentiation, which may become of
great significance in the future, cannot at present be one of the relevant criteria
for the purpose of assignment of the sex of a transsexual in court.

[56] There was no medical evidence, other than the psychological, upon
c   which the court could come to a conclusion different from the criteria set out by
Ormrod J. Although the psychological factor was strongly relied upon by
Professor Green, he did not suggest a clear point at which the psychological
changes had reached a stage, with or without hormonal treatment and
reassignment surgery, at which a person should be seen to have become a
member of the sex into which he/she was not born.

d

THE CASE LAW

[57] There has been no decision, since *Corbett's* case, on the validity of the
marriage between a transsexual and a person of the same sex as that in which
he/she was assigned at birth. *Corbett's* case was a decision of first instance and this
e   court is not, therefore, bound by its conclusions, but it undoubtedly has much
persuasive authority. There are only a few English cases which can throw any
light upon the modern position. None of them departs to any marked extent
from the approach of Ormrod J in *Corbett's* case.

[58] In *R v Tan* [1983] 2 All ER 12 at 19, [1983] QB 1053 at 1064, the criteria in
Corbett's case were applied to the criminal law. The Court of Appeal rejected a
f   submission that if a person had become philosophically or psychologically or
socially female, that person should be held not to be a man. In the judgment of
the court, Parker J said:

'In our judgment, both common sense and the desirability of certainty and
g   consistency demand that the decision in *Corbett v Corbett* should apply for the
purpose, not only of marriage, but also for a charge under s 30 of the Sexual
Offences Act 1956 or s 5 of the Sexual Offences Act 1967.'

[59] In *S-T (formerly J) v J* [1998] 1 All ER 431, [1998] Fam 103 the defendant was
born female but lived as a male. He underwent reconstructive surgery. He met
h   and married the plaintiff without informing her of his history. Upon discovering
the truth, the plaintiff obtained a decree of nullity and, upon the defendant
applying for ancillary relief, she challenged his right to do so upon the ground of
public policy, in that the defendant had committed an offence under the Perjury
Act 1911. Hollis J dismissed the defendant's claim.

j   [60] In this court, Ward LJ reviewed the position of transsexuals and the
matrimonial law. He considered decisions from other jurisdictions, and was
impressed by the reasoning of Judge Aubin in the New Zealand Family Court in
M v M (marriage: transsexuals) [1991] NZFLR 337, and of Ellis J in the High Court
of New Zealand in *A-G v Otahuhu Family Court* [1995] 1 NZLR 603, neither of
whom followed the criteria in *Corbett's* case. Each held that there was no
lawful impediment to the marriage of a transsexual. Ward LJ said:

'Hollis J did not find this "persuasive authority". For my part, I find myself
unable lightly to dismiss it. Taken with the new insight into the aetiology of
transsexualism, it may be that *Corbett v Corbett* would bear re-examination at
some appropriate time.' (See [1998] 1 All ER 431 at 447, [1998] Fam 103 at
122.)

[61] He pointed out, however, that the correctness of the decision in *Corbett's*
case had not been challenged in the Court of Appeal (see also Sir Brian Neill
[1998] 1 All ER 431 at 476, [1998] Fam 103 at 153). In our view, this court in
S-T's case raised the question as to whether the developments in medical
knowledge provided the basis for a reconsideration of the criteria in *Corbett's* case.
We agree with them that it is appropriate to review those criteria, but are not
persuaded that the judgments of Ward LJ and Sir Brian Neill did more than put
down a marker for a future court to reconsider the whole issue as we are now
doing.

[62] In *W v W (physical inter-sex)* [2001] Fam 111, [2001] 2 WLR 674, Charles J
had to decide whether the respondent was male or female at the date of the
marriage on a petition for nullity by the petitioner. It is clear from the tragic facts
that the respondent's sex at birth was uncertain, and that the parents chose to
register her as a boy.

[63] As a child and a young woman she dressed as, appeared as, and acted as
female. At 17, she finally ran permanently away from home and thereafter lived
as a woman. Charles J held that he was not concerned with a transsexual. He was
concerned with a case in which the biological test set and applied in *Corbett's* case
was not satisfied, and did not provide the answer to the question as to whether
the respondent was a female for the purposes of marriage. The judge found that
there was a correct diagnosis of the respondent of partial androgen insensitivity,
with ambiguous external genitalia, and came within the convenient shorthand
definition of physical inter-sex.

[64] He held that she was a female for the purposes of her marriage to the
petitioner. He said ([2001] Fam 111 at 145, [2001] 2 WLR 674 at 708) that, on the
true construction of the 1973 Act, greater emphasis could be placed on gender
rather than sex. Although we respectfully agree with the judgment in *W v W*,
Charles J made it entirely clear that he was dealing with a different disorder
within gender dysphoria, and not with a transsexual.

[65] Mrs Cox argued that the appellant and Mrs W were, after surgery,
physiologically the same. That similarity does not change the essential fact that
Mrs W was, at birth, of uncertain sex, and assigned by the choice of her parents
to male, whereas the appellant was indisputably male at birth. We cannot see
how *W v W* helps the appellant's case.

[66] In *Fitzpatrick v Sterling Housing Association Ltd* [1999] 4 All ER 705, [2001]
1 AC 27 the House of Lords grappled with the consequences of the death of one
partner in a longstanding homosexual relationship, upon the right of succession
to a statutory tenancy under Sch 1 to the Rent Act 1977. The House of Lords held
that the extended meaning of the word 'spouse' in para 2(2) of Sch 1 did not apply
to same sex partners. By a majority the House held that a same sex partner was
capable of being a member of the original tenant's family for the purpose of
para 3 of the same Schedule. The House of Lords was, therefore, considering a
situation, which was in all respects entirely different from the present question
before this court. None the less, Mrs Cox relies on observations made by

a   Lord Slynn of Hadley in his speech, and seeks to apply them by analogy. One
    passage is relevant to the broader issue faced by this court. Lord Slynn said:

    'It has been suggested that for your Lordships to decide this appeal in
    favour of the appellant would be to usurp the function of Parliament. It is
    trite that that is something the courts must not do. When considering social
b   issues in particular judges must not substitute their own views to fill gaps.
    They must consider whether the new facts "fall within the parliamentary
    intention" (see *Royal College of Nursing of the UK v Dept of Health and Social
    Security* [1981] 1 All ER 545 at 565, [1981] AC 800 at 822 per Lord Wilberforce).
    Thus in the present context if, for example, it was explicit or clear that
    Parliament intended the word "family" to have a narrow meaning for all
c   time, it would be a court's duty to give effect to it whatever changes in social
    attitudes a court might think ought to be reflected in the legislation.
    Similarly, if it were explicit or clear that the word must be given a very wide
    meaning so as to cover relationships for which a court, conscious of the
    traditional views of society might disapprove, the court's duty would be to
    give effect to it. It is, however, for the court in the first place to interpret each
d   phrase in its statutory context. To do so is not to usurp Parliament's function;
    not to do so would be to abdicate the judicial function. If Parliament takes the
    view that the result is not what is wanted it will change the legislation.' (See
    [1999] 4 All ER 705 at 710, [2001] 1 AC 27 at 33.)

e   [67] In *Fitzpatrick*'s case the House of Lords gave a broad interpretation to the
    word 'family'. In the present case, no help seems to be gained from the context
    of s 11 of the 1973 Act. We have to look at the medical evidence and see whether
    the present state of the medical knowledge, in the absence of statutory
    interpretation, permits the court to give the word 'female' the meaning advanced
    by Mrs Cox. The decisions in the English cases have not, so far, proceeded
f   beyond the decision in *Corbett*'s case, other than to recognise the unsatisfactory
    present situation and the need for reconsideration of the legal position of a
    transsexual.

    Overseas authorities
g   [68] In their well-researched submissions counsel referred not only to English
    authorities but also to some decisions of the European Court of Human Rights
    and to other cases in which the legal position of transsexuals has been considered
    by foreign courts. In view of the Human Rights Act 1998 it is the Strasbourg
    decisions which call for the fullest treatment. But it is convenient to take all the
    overseas authorities in chronological order, since many of the cases emphasise
h   the need for the law to respond to developments in scientific knowledge and in
    society's attitudes.
    [69] The earliest overseas authority referred to in counsel's submissions was
    the decision of the Appellate Division of the Superior Court of New Jersey in
    MT v JT (1976) 355 A 2d 204. That decision, and a decision in 1978 of the West
j   German Federal Constitutional Court (Bundesverfassungsgericht) 49 BVerfGE
    286 were summarised in the dissenting judgment of Judge Martens in *Cossey v UK*
    [1993] 2 FCR 97 at 114, (1990) 13 EHRR 622 at 647:

    'Both judgments—and their similarity is the more striking because they
    come from different legal traditions—make the same essential points. Both
    judgments may be summarized as taking the view that the change of sexual

identity which results from successful reassignment surgery should be deemed a change of sex for legal purposes.'   *a*

[70] The German decision led to a change of law in West Germany in 1980, following changes in Sweden and Denmark in 1972 and 1975 respectively. There have been more recent changes in many other member states of the Council of Europe.

[71] The earliest Strasbourg decision which calls for mention is *Van Oosterwijck*   *b*
(D) v Belgium (1980) 3 EHRR 557. The case was brought by a Belgian female-to-male post-operative transsexual who wished to have his birth certificate altered. This case failed before the European Court of Human Rights on the ground of failure to exhaust local remedies, but the European Commission on Human Rights took the view that there had been a violation of both art 8 and art 12 of the   *c*
European Convention for the Protection of Human Rights and Fundamental Freedoms 1950 (as now set out in Sch 1 to the Human Rights Act 1998). The commission's report is discussed at some length in Lord Reed's paper 'Splitting the Difference: Transsexuals and Human Rights Law' (presented to the Anglo-German Family Law Judicial Conference in Edinburgh in September 2000). In relation to art 8 the commission regarded the concept of respect for   *d*
private life as going beyond the right to privacy and as approximating to self-determination under the German basic law. The commission was much more divided about art 12. Lord Reed has commented:

'The diversity of views in relation to art 12, and the greater reluctance to find a definite right to marry on the part of transsexuals, has remained a   *e*
feature of the case law under the convention.'

[72] *Rees v UK* [1993] 2 FCR 49, (1986) 9 EHRR 56 was a complaint under arts 8 and 12 by a female-to-male post-operative transsexual (whose medical and surgical treatment had been provided by the National Health Service). In 1980, six years after the gender reassignment surgery, the applicant's solicitor applied   *f*
to the Registrar General under s 29(3) of the Births and Deaths Registration Act 1953 for alteration of his birth certificate on the ground of mistake. The court recognised in its majority judgment that the United Kingdom did not require citizens to have identity cards, and that a transsexual could readily obtain a driving licence and a passport with a new gender prefix. But birth certificates   *g*
were regarded as records of historical facts.

[73] The court recognised that although the essential purpose of art 8 is to protect the individual against arbitrary interference by the state, the requirement of respect for private life may also impose positive obligations on the state. But in relation to the rights of transsexuals there was a marked lack of uniformity   *h*
between member states:

'It would, therefore, be true to say that there is at present little common ground between the Contracting States in this area and that, generally speaking, the law appears to be in a transitional stage. Accordingly, this is an area in which the Contracting Parties enjoy a wide margin of appreciation.'   *j*
(See [1993] 2 FCR 49 at 58, (1986) 9 EHRR 56 at 64 (para 37).)

[74] The court considered the complex issues which would have to be covered by amending legislation in the United Kingdom. It concluded:

'Having regard to the wide margin of appreciation to be afforded to the State in this area and to the relevance of protecting the interests of others in a   striking the requisite balance, the positive obligations arising from Article 8 cannot be held to extend that far.' (See [1993] 2 FCR 49 at 60–61, (1986) 9 EHRR 56 at 67 (para 44).)

[75] The court dealt with art 12 much more shortly and simply, concluding that the right to marry guaranteed by the article 'refers to the traditional marriage between persons of opposite biological sex'. The decision on art 12 was
b   unanimous. The decision on art 8 was reached by a majority of twelve to three. The views of the minority appear from the joint dissenting opinion:

c   'There is obviously no question of *correcting* the registers by concealing the historical truth or of claiming that Mr. Rees has *changed sex* in the biological sense of the term. The idea is merely (as already happens in the United Kingdom in other cases—for example, with adoption) to mention a development in the person's status due to changes in his apparent sex—what we have called his sexual identity—and to give him the opportunity to obtain a short certificate which does not disclose his previous status. This would better reflect the real situation and to that extent would even be in the public interest.' (See [1993]
d   2 FCR 49 at 63, (1986) 9 EHRR 56 at 70.)

[76] Four years later in *Cossey v UK* [1993] 2 FCR 97, (1990) 13 EHRR 622 the European Court of Human Rights reached the same conclusions, but only by majorities of ten to eight in relation to art 8, and 14 to four in relation to art 12. The applicant was a male-to-female transsexual who had received reassignment
e   surgery in 1974. In 1984 she complained of the Registrar General's refusal to alter her birth certificate. While the complaint was pending she went through a marriage ceremony at a London synagogue in 1989 but she later obtained a decree that the marriage was void. The commission concluded, surprisingly in view of *Rees*'s case, that there had been no violation of art 8 but that there had been a violation of art 12.
f   [77] The court, in its majority judgment, asked itself whether it should follow *Rees*'s case. Its general practice was to follow precedent, but a departure might be warranted to reflect scientific and societal developments. But there was no evidence of significant scientific advances and (despite some changes in the laws of member states of the Council of Europe) this was still an area in which there
g   was a wide margin of appreciation. Nevertheless the court—

'is conscious of the seriousness of the problems facing transsexuals and the distress they suffer. Since the Convention always has to be interpreted and applied in the light of current circumstances, it is important that the need for appropriate legal measures in this area should be kept under review.' (See
h   [1993] 2 FCR 97 at 109, (1990) 13 EHRR 622 at 641 (para 42).)

[78] Again, the majority judgment dealt quite shortly with art 12 (despite the contrary view taken by the commission).
[79] In *Cossey*'s case there were several dissenting opinions, most notably the long and eloquent opinion of Judge Martens. The whole opinion merits study,
j   but its central thesis appears from para 2.7 ([1993] 2 FCR 97 at 114, (1990) 13 EHRR 622 at 648):

'The principle which is basic in human rights and which underlies the various specific rights spelled out in the Convention is respect for human dignity and human freedom. Human dignity and human freedom imply that a man should be free to shape himself and his fate in the way that he deems

best fits his personality. A transsexual does use those very fundamental
rights. He is prepared to shape himself and his fate. In doing so he goes   a
through long, dangerous and painful medical treatment to have his sexual
organs, as far as is humanly possible, adapted to the sex he is convinced he
belongs to. After these ordeals, as a post-operative transsexual, he turns to
the law and asks it to recognize the *fait accompli* he has created. He demands
to be recognised and to be treated by law as a member of the sex he has won;   b
he demands to be treated without discrimination, on the same footing as all
other females or, as the case may be, males. This is a request which the law
should refuse to grant only if it truly has compelling reasons ...'

[80] *Rees* and *Cossey*'s cases were distinguished in *B v France* [1993] 2 FCR 145,
(1992) 16 EHRR 1, in which the only complaint was under art 8. The applicant, c
a French national born in Algeria, was a male-to-female post-operative
transsexual who complained of the French court's refusal to make an order
rectifying her birth certificate or declaring that she should bear female forenames.
Although it was argued that in *Cossey*'s case the court had erred in discounting
scientific and societal developments, the decision in *B v France* seems to have
turned on the different functions and importance (as between the United   d
Kingdom and France) of civil registration.

[81] The next case in chronological sequence is a decision of the High Court
of New Zealand, *A-G v Otahuhu Family Court* [1995] 1 NZLR 603. In applying s 23
of the New Zealand Marriage Act 1955 Ellis J declined to follow *Corbett*'s case and
preferred the reasoning in the New Jersey decision in *MT v JT* and the New   e
Zealand decision in *M v M (marriage: transsexuals)* [1991] NZFLR 337. The
essential point of the decision appears at [1995] 1 NZLR 603 at 606:

'Some persons have a compelling desire to be recognised and be able to
behave as persons of the opposite sex. If society allows such persons to
undergo therapy and surgery in order to fulfil that desire, then it ought also   f
to allow such persons to function as fully as possible in their reassigned sex,
and this must include the capacity to marry. Where two persons present
themselves as having the apparent genitals of a man or a woman, they should
not have to establish that each can function sexually ... There is no social
advantage in the law not recognising the validity of the marriage of a
transsexual in the sex of reassignment. It would merely confirm the factual   g
reality.'

[82] *P v S* Case C-13/94 [1996] All ER (EC) 397, ECR-I 2143 is a decision of the
Court of Justice of the European Communities on a reference by the Truro
Industrial Tribunal raising a question on the Equal Treatment Council Directive h
(76/207/EEC). P was a manager employed by the county council at an educational
establishment. In 1992 P told S, the principal of the establishment, of her
intention to undergo male-to-female reassignment surgery. At first S was
supportive, but while P was on sick leave after the surgery she was dismissed.
The question referred by the industrial tribunal was whether the directive's
prohibition of sex discrimination extended to dismissal of a transsexual on   j
account of gender reassignment. The Court of Justice answered that question in
the affirmative:

'Such discrimination is based, essentially if not exclusively, on the sex of the
person concerned. Where a person is dismissed on the ground that he or she
intends to undergo, or has undergone, gender reassignment, he or she is

a   treated unfavourably by comparison with persons of the sex to which he or she was deemed to belong before undergoing gender reassignment. To tolerate such discrimination would be tantamount, as regards such a person, to a failure to respect the dignity and freedom to which he or she is entitled, and which the court has a duty to safeguard.' (See [1996] All ER (EC) 397 at 410 (paras 21–22).)

b   [83] *P v S* led to the Sex Discrimination (Gender Reassignment) Regulations 1999, SI 1999/1102, enacted under s 2(2) of the European Communities Act 1972. These regulations have amended the Sex Discrimination Act 1975.

[84] The most recent of the line of cases in the European Court of Human Rights is *Sheffield v UK* (1998) 5 BHRC 83. The two applicants were both male-to-
c female transsexuals who had undergone surgery for gender reassignment. Miss Sheffield put forward detailed evidence of the embarrassment which she had suffered, especially in connection with legal proceedings, in having to disclose her original gender. Miss Horsham described herself as living in exile in the Netherlands because she could not (if domiciled in England) marry her male
d partner in any jurisdiction.

[85] The court held, by a majority of eleven to nine, that there had been no violation of art 8; and by a majority of eighteen to two, that there had been no violation of art 12. As to art 8, the main majority judgment noted the applicants' contention that there was new scientific evidence, especially in the work of Professor Gooren (although his thesis does not seem to have been
e correctly summarised in para 43 of the judgment). It also referred to *P v S* and to what the pressure group Liberty called 'an unmistakably clear trend in the Member States of the Council of Europe towards giving full recognition to gender reassignment'. But the court regarded the scientific evidence as inconclusive and noted that Liberty's survey—

f   'does not indicate that there is yet any common approach as to how to address the repercussions which the legal recognition of a change of sex may entail for other areas of law such as marriage, filiation, privacy or data protection, or the circumstances in which a transsexual may be compelled by law to reveal his or her pre-operative gender.' (See (1998) 5 BHRC 83 at 95
g   (para 57).)

[86] Nevertheless the majority noted that the United Kingdom had failed to legislate in this area, despite previous observations by the court, and it repeated the same warning in stronger language:

h   'Even if there have been no significant scientific developments since the date of the *Cossey* judgment which make it possible to reach a firm conclusion on the aetiology of transsexualism, it is nevertheless the case that there is an increased social acceptance of transsexualism and an increased recognition of the problems which post-operative transsexuals encounter. Even if it finds no breach of art 8 in this case, the court reiterates that this area
j   needs to be kept under review by contracting states.' (See (1998) 5 BHRC 83 at 96 (para 60).)

[87] On art 12 the majority did not move perceptibly from *Rees* and *Cossey*. The concurring opinion of the United Kingdom judge, Sir John Freeland, said (at 100) that he had concurred in the vote on art 8 only 'after much hesitation and even with some reluctance'. Of the various dissenting opinions, the most notable

is that of Judge Van Dijk which follows on from that of his predecessor, Judge
Martens. He too emphasised that the individual's right of self-determination is an   *a*
important part of the content of the rights enjoyed under art 8.

[88] The most recent overseas decision cited to the court is the decision of the
Court of Appeals of Texas in *Littleton v Prange* (1999) 9 SW 3d 223, in which a
transsexual who had gone through a marriage ceremony was held not to be the
deceased partner's surviving spouse for the purpose of a wrongful death and   *b*
survival statute. The majority judgment referred to *MT v JT*, *Corbett*'s case and
the New Zealand case of *M v M*. It decided the issue as essentially one of statutory
construction, commenting (at 231) that 'courts are wise not to wander too far
into the misty fields of sociological philosophy'.

[89] The dissenting judgment of Lopez J pointed out that gender was
determined at birth in a summary and not always accurate manner: *c*

> 'This declaration [of the obstetrician or midwife after a quick visual
> inspection] is then memorialized by a certificate of birth, without an
> examination of the child's chromosomes or an inquiry about how the child
> feels about its sexual identity.'
      d

[90] In the European Court of Human Rights the United Kingdom government
is more severely criticised for its failure to respond to earlier criticisms of its
approach to potential breaches of art 8 than of art 12, but there is a momentum
for change increasingly recognised in the court at Strasbourg and articulated in
judgments critical of the whole approach of the English law to the present
position of transsexuals. Decisions of other countries show a marked divergence   *e*
of opinion over the proper treatment of transsexuals in the law.

THE REPORT OF THE INTER-DEPARTMENTAL WORKING GROUP ON TRANSSEXUAL
PEOPLE
[91] As a result, no doubt, of the criticisms made by members of the European   *f*
Court of Human Rights in the cases referred to above, the Home Secretary set up
an Inter-Departmental Working Group with the terms of reference—

> 'to consider, with particular reference to birth certificates, the need for
> appropriate legal measures to address the problems experienced by
> transsexual people, having due regard to scientific and societal developments,   *g*
> and measures undertaken in other countries to deal with this issue.'

[92] The report of the working group was completed and presented to
ministers in April 2000. It is a careful and comprehensive review of the medical
condition, current practice in other countries, the present state of English law in
all aspects of the life of an individual including marriage, the position with regard   *h*
to birth certificates. It contains various annexes, including details of the practice
in common law states and European countries.

[93] In its conclusions the working group identified three options for the
future: (a) to leave the current situation unchanged; (b) to issue birth certificates
showing the new name and, possibly, gender; and (c) to grant full legal   *j*
recognition of the new gender subject to certain criteria and procedures.

[94] The working group concluded: 'We suggest that before taking a view on
these options the government may wish to put the issues out to public
consultation.'

[95] The report was published in April 2000. We inquired of Mr Moylan, on
behalf of the Attorney General, what steps were being taken by any government

a department, to take forward any of the recommendations of the report, or to prepare a consultation paper for public discussion.

[96] To our dismay, we were informed that no steps whatsoever have been, or to the knowledge of Mr Moylan were intended to be, taken to carry this matter forward. It appears, therefore, that the commissioning and completion of the report is the sum of the activity on the problems identified both by the Home

b Secretary in his terms of reference, and by the conclusions of the members of the working party. That would seem to us to be a failure to recognise the increasing concerns and changing attitudes across Western Europe which have been set out so clearly and strongly in judgments of members of the European Court at Strasbourg, and which in our view need to be addressed by the United Kingdom.

c GENERAL CONCLUSIONS

[97] It is clear that the three criteria relied upon by Ormrod J in *Corbett's* case remain the only basis upon which to decide the gender of a child at birth. It is, as Professor Gooren and others have pointed out, necessary to choose the gender of a child immediately. There are obvious reasons for assigning the sex of the child

d and among those reasons is the matter of status. Other than in the case of a person who is inter-sexed, the biological criteria point at that stage conclusively to a decision whether the child is male or female. At birth therefore the *Corbett* criteria remain valid today.

[98] Mrs Cox suggested that there was no reason to fix the gender of a person immutably at birth. On the present state of medical knowledge the only possible

e criterion to be added to the existing three criteria would be the psychological factor. The possibility of brain sexual differentiation is, for reasons already set out above, not yet possible to take into account. The medical evidence in this case show the enormously increased recognition of, and reliance upon, the psychological factor in the assessment of a person diagnosed as suffering from

f gender disorder. There is, in informed medical circles, a growing momentum for recognition of transsexuals for every purpose and in a manner similar to those who are inter-sexed. The current approach recognises changes in social attitudes as well as advances in medical research. Those social changes are well exemplified in the recent judgments of the Court at Strasbourg and in the lecture given by Lord Reed. They cannot be ignored.

g [99] How are the social changes to be given legal recognition? In matters other than marriage, the report of the working party sets out steps which have been taken. This court is not concerned with the question whether those steps meet the criticisms levelled by members of the European Court at Strasbourg. We are however concerned with legal recognition of marriage which, like

h divorce, is a matter of status and is not for the spouses alone to decide. It affects society and is a question of public policy. For that reason, even if for no other reason, marriage is in a special position and is different from the change of gender on a driving licence, social security payments book and so on. Birth, adoption, marriage, divorce or nullity and death have to be registered. Each child born has

j to be placed into one of two categories for the purpose of registration. Status is not conferred only by a person upon himself; it has to be recognised by society. In the absence of legislation, at what point can the court hold that a person has changed his gender status?

[100] The point at which a change of gender should be recognised is not easily to be ascertained. The line could be drawn at a number of different points from the initial diagnosis of gender disorder to the completion of reconstructive

surgery. It is clear from the report of the working party that the point at which
people feel they have achieved their change of gender varies enormously. From   *a*
the research it can be seen how much more difficult it is to undergo successful
female-to-male reconstructive surgery than male-to-female but the self-identification
in the preferred male gender can be as strong as in a post-operative male to female
transsexual.

[101] Mrs Cox submitted that, since the surgery at the fourth stage was   *b*
irreversible unlike the previous stages, it would be correct to recognise the
appellant as reassigned to the opposite sex once she became a post-operative male
to female transsexual, or presumably vice versa. Mr Moylan asked why the court
should arbitrarily choose the point of completion of the fourth stage of treatment
by successful gender reconstruction surgery.

[102] We agree with Mr Moylan that the fourth stage, although irreversible,   *c*
is the completion of the last stage of the treatment. The diagnosis of gender
disorder is not revised after the successful completion of any part of the
treatment. The successful completion of all stages of the treatment permits the
transsexual to live in his/her preferred gender role. To choose, however, to
recognise a change of gender as a change of status would require some certainty   *d*
and it would be necessary to lay down some pre-conditions which would
inevitably be arbitrary. So, on Mrs Cox's hypothesis, for instance, if a patient
started but failed to complete such surgery for whatever reason, he/she would
remain in the birth-registered gender, whereas further surgery would permit
him/her to be recognised for the purposes of s 11(c) as having changed his/her   *e*
gender.

[103] Annex 3 of the report of the working party sets out with clarity the
problems of gender re-registration. The German approach, for example, in its
legislation provides for recognition by a court of acquired gender under certain
conditions. The requirements are: (i) a person has lived for three years as
belonging to the sex the person feels he or she belongs to; (ii) the person is   *f*
unmarried; (iii) of age; (iv) permanently sterile; and (v) has undergone an
operation by which clear resemblance to the other sex has been achieved.

[104] The propriety of requiring pre-conditions, such as these, are matters for
public policy and, no doubt, public consultation, not for imposition by the courts
on the public. The absence of pre-conditions would leave the applicability of the   *g*
law to an individual diagnosed as suffering from gender disorder in complete
confusion.

[105] It seems to us that two questions arise. The first question is for the
court. What is the status of the appellant? Is she male or female? That question
should, in our judgment, be answered by assessing the facts of an individual case   *h*
against a clear statutory framework. The second question is for Parliament. At
what point would it be consistent with public policy to recognise that a person
should be treated for all purposes, including marriage, as a person of the opposite
sex to that to which he/she was correctly assigned at birth? The second question
cannot properly be decided by the court.   *j*

[106] As Lord Slynn said in *Fitzpatrick v Sterling Housing Association Ltd* [1999]
4 All ER 705 at 710, [2001] 1 AC 27 at 33, when considering social issues in
particular, judges must not substitute their own views to fill gaps. In *Re F (in
utero)* [1988] 2 All ER 193, [1988] Fam 122 the Court of Appeal (in a wholly
different context), had to consider the legal position of the foetus in a wardship
application designed to make the unborn child a ward of court. Balcombe LJ said:

a   'If the law is to be extended in this manner, so as to impose control over
the mother of an unborn child, where such control may be necessary for the
benefit of that child, then under our system of parliamentary democracy it is
for Parliament to decide whether such controls can be imposed and, if so,
subject to what limitations or conditions.' (See [1988] 2 All ER 193 at 200,
[1988] Fam 122 at 144.)

b
    [107] Those observations, we would respectfully suggest, are equally apposite
to the present appeal.

    [108] We would therefore dismiss the appeal.

    [109] We would add, however, with the strictures of the European Court on
Human Rights well in mind, that there is no doubt that the profoundly
c   unsatisfactory nature of the present position and the plight of transsexuals
requires careful consideration. The recommendation of the Inter-Departmental
Working Party for public consultation merits action by the government
departments involved in these issues. The problems will not go away and may
well come again before the European Court sooner rather than later.

d
THORPE LJ.

The judgment below
    [110] I have had the advantage of the judgment in draft of Dame Elizabeth
Butler-Sloss P and Robert Walker LJ. Although I differ from them in my
e   conclusion I gratefully adopt their summary of the relevant facts.

    [111] Two criticisms are made of the judgment below, the first of which is in
my opinion insubstantial. Johnson J ([2000] 3 FCR 733 at 739) seems to conclude
that the decree in *Corbett v Corbett (otherwise Ashley)* [1970] 2 All ER 33, [1971] P 83
was pronounced under s 1 of the Nullity of Marriage Act 1971 rather than under
f   the common law. But that is a chronological confusion of no importance.

    [112] However of more significance is his erroneous citation of Professor Green
at the conclusion of his judgment (at 747) to support the proposition that the
three *Corbett* factors remain 'the only criteria for determining the gender of an
individual'. The words that Johnson J relied on were not a statement of opinion
but only the summary of a question for his opinion posed by the Treasury
g   Solicitor in his letter of 29 October. In reality Professor Green's position was that
the three *Corbett* factors were in present times 'too reductionistic'. Despite
Johnson J's skilful summary of the expert evidence in his judgment (at 737–738),
his ultimate conclusion that the medical opinion that guided Ormrod J remained
unchanged might be said to erode the validity of the conclusion.

h   [113] However overall Johnson J's judgment is characteristically careful and
understanding. In my opinion the key to this appeal lies not so much in a scrutiny
of his judgment as in a fresh appraisal of the extent to which the passage of
30 years requires the revision of the propositions of law, of medical science and
of social policy upon which Ormrod J founded his judgment in *Corbett*'s case.

j   [114] The decision of Charles J in *W v W (physical inter-sex)* [2001] Fam 111,
[2001] 2 WLR 674 coincidentally emerged during the hearing before Johnson J.
In those circumstances it is not surprising that it did not receive much attention,
particularly since counsel before Johnson J agreed that it had no bearing on his
decision. However since the issues considered in these judgments are so
inter-related I have found it helpful to reflect on both judgments in attempting to
resolve the difficult issues raised by this appeal.

[115] Although Johnson J found support from my judgment in *Dart v Dart* [1997] 1 FCR 21 for his conclusion that the issues raised by the petitioner were better left to Parliament, I differ from him on this issue for reasons which I will explain later in this judgment.

The expert evidence

[116] Since the expert evidence at the trial was all agreed none of the three experts was called to give oral evidence. It follows that this court is in as good a position as the trial judge to assess its impact. Clearly the parties sought advice from experts of the greatest distinction. Dr Louis Gooren is Professor of Endocrinology at the Free University Hospital of Amsterdam. His unit serves 95% of a Dutch population of 15 million. His experience extends over 23 years. Over this period his clinic has treated an average of 150 new patients per annum, approximately 60% of whom proceed through the various stages of treatment to genital reassignment. Professor Richard Green is the Research Director of the Gender Identity Clinic at the Charing Cross Hospital. It is perhaps the largest such clinic in the world. As well as offering treatment it conducts research into the origins of transsexualism. Mr TR Terry is consultant urological surgeon at Leicester University Hospitals where he specialises in the surgical treatment of male to female gender dysphoric patients. Since each of these three experts agreed with the written opinions offered by the others and since some provided supplemental answers to specific questions raised by the lawyers, their attendance at trial became unnecessary. I would therefore draw from their reports the opinions and conclusions which I have found particularly influential.

(i) There are various stages in the development of the sex of the human being, some pre-natal and some post-natal. As Professor Gooren put it:

'The process of sexual differentiation takes place in distinct steps, first the chromosomal configuration is established, next gonadal differentiation, next differentiation of the internal and external genitalia and finally the differentiation of the brain into male or female ... this process of brain sexual differentiation takes place after birth ... one brain structure, that is different between men and women, becomes only sex-dimorphic between the ages of two and four years ...'

To the same effect is Professor Green who wrote:

'If a biological sexual condition of an individual is conceptualised to include psychological sex, perhaps reflective of brain sex differentiation, this status does not express itself until several years post-natally. Therefore it is not possible to say that the biological sexual condition of an individual is fixed at birth ...'

(ii) Since 1970 there has been some research into brain differentiation. Professor Gooren was co-author of a paper published in 1995 (see Zhou, Hofman, Gooren and Swaab 'A Sex Difference in the Human Brain and its Relation to Transsexuality' (1995) 378 *Nature* 68, 2 November) that demonstrated that in one of the human brain structures that is different between men and women, a totally female pattern was encountered in six male-to-female transsexuals. In Professor Gooren's words: 'These findings showed that a biological structure in the brain distinguishes the male-to-female transsexuals from men.' I also cite Professor Green's evaluation of this research. He says: 'The interpretation of this finding is that it provides evidence of a biological central nervous system basis for male a transsexualism.' Because the finding is based upon a small sample and because research can only be conducted post mortem the finding remains neither confirmed nor refuted. A subsequent publication in April 2000, of which Professor Gooren was again a co-author, provided only slight corroboration since it relied largely on the original sample. Because of the obvious difficulties in examining the brain for differentiation Professor Green has conducted research

b on four proxies which might reflect pre-natal biological influences associated with transsexualism. The research has shown significant differences which Professor Green evaluates tentatively:

c   'These indirect measures may reflect differences in pre-natal brain organisation leading to manifestations of gender dysphoria beginning in early childhood and culminating in the need for sex reassignment surgery.'

Whilst scientific proof for the theory is far from complete, Professor Green's assessment is that there is a growing acceptance of findings of sexual differences in the brain that are determined pre-natally. Mr Terry in his commentary on Professor Green's opinion said:

d   'Although the current scientific literature arguing for a biological causation in the development of gender dysphoria is not irrefutable, it is certainly compelling to my mind.'

(iii) It follows from the preceding paragraph that medical opinion no longer
e accepts the three *Corbett* factors for the determination of sex. Professor Gooren states: 'It is no longer tenable to claim that the genetic or gonadal criterion determines one's status as male or female.' More specifically, Professor Green rejects the *Corbett* criteria, stating:

f   'The *Corbett* criteria are too reductionistic to serve as a viable set of criteria to determine sex. They also ignore the compelling significance of the psychological status of the person as a man or as a woman.'

He also states:

g   'The criteria for designating a person as male or female are complex. They are not simply an outcome of chromosomal configuration, genital configuration, or gonadal configuration.'

(iv) The essential limitation of the *Corbett* criteria lies in the exclusion of psychological factors, whether or not further research will prove such factors to be mediated by brain differentiation. As Professor Green put it:
h
'Psychological factors cannot be considered at birth because they do not yet manifest. They may become an overriding consideration subsequently as the individual develops.'

j Later in his opinion Professor Green succinctly expresses his position:

'As a psychiatrist I am biased towards psychological factors. I would argue that with a transsexual the psychological sex has been contrary to other somatic factors for many years, if not the great majority of the person's life. Taking that position, gender reassignment treatment and surgery would align these somatic features with the psychological element. The correct designation of sex would be the outcome.'

Professor Green also shows that these psychological factors cannot be averted by psychoanalytic or other therapies. Nor can outcomes be achieved by consistent psychological socialisation as male or female from very early childhood. He therefore states in relation to inter-sex patients:

    'More evidence is available for a pre-natally determined biological bias towards maleness or femaleness in gender identity that may overrule efforts at contrary socialisation as female or male. There is considerable current sentiment for delaying any surgical modification of the genitalia which had earlier been thought to help pre-set the evolving gender identity. Now there is more of a wait and see approach until the individual is old enough to express its own wishes.'

(v) The three experts reflect their huge understanding of transsexualism in their compassionate feelings for transsexuals. Professor Gooren wrote:

    'One of the serious obstacles to understanding gender dysphoria is that it is an unimaginable and inconceivable problem to those who do not have it. This distinguishes it from other forms of human suffering for which it is much easier to generate empathy and sympathy.'

More specifically on the issue raised by this appeal Mr Terry speaks for these experts when he writes:

    'To argue that in the case of a male to female gender dysphoric patient who has undergone rigorous psychological and psychiatric counselling, prolonged hormone treatment and usually several major surgical procedures and who has successfully adapted to a female existence both socially and professionally should not be allowed a legal marriage seems to me brutally insensitive and is diametrically opposed to what we as clinicians, who manage gender dysphoria, are trying to achieve.'

The law

[117] In my opinion the focus must be upon the development of our domestic law. The decisions of the Strasbourg Court and of judges in other jurisdictions have been comprehensively reviewed by Dame Elizabeth Butler-Sloss P and Robert Walker LJ in their judgment. As far as the Strasbourg decisions are concerned, all the evolution has been in the appraisal of the rights under art 8 of the European Convention for the Protection of Human Rights and Fundamental Freedoms 1950 (as now set out in Sch 1 to the Human Rights Act 1998). I accept Mr Moylan's submission that, since the right to marry is the very subject of art 12, it is impermissible to introduce the right to marry as an ingredient of art 8 rights. The consistent judgments of the court in relation to art 12 do not demonstrate the same evolution in approach as do the judgments in relation to art 8. Member states are accorded a wide latitude in defining the right to marriage and it remains permissible for states to restrict the definition to the conventional union between man and woman. In my opinion the judgments in the Strasbourg cases only assist the appellant to the extent that they may demonstrate shifts in social attitudes and values.

[118] In domestic law the landmark decision is, of course, the judgment of Ormrod J in *Corbett v Corbett (otherwise Ashley)* [1970] 2 All ER 33, [1971] P 83. Few judgments in family law have had a longer reign. It defined the common law. It informed the subsequent statutory codification of the law of nullity. The statutory

a provision has since been consistently interpreted and applied in accordance with the decision in *Corbett's* case. It has been followed in allied fields: see *R v Tan* [1983] 2 All ER 12, [1983] QB 1053 and *R v Registrar General, ex p P and G* [1996] 2 FCR 588. However recently judicial comments have questioned its continuing legitimacy. Thus a fundamental question raised by this appeal is whether this court in 2001 should approve and apply the reasoning in *Corbett's* case. To answer

b the question it is first necessary to analyse the propositions on which Ormrod J founded his conclusion. I will therefore emphasise those passages of his judgment that seem to me to be critical to the question. Note first that in his review of the phenomenon of transsexuality Ormrod J describes sex reassignment surgery at what now seems a comparatively early stage of development (see [1970] 2 All ER 33 at 42–43, [1971] P 83 at 98–99). Equally his summary of the expert evidence as

c to the aetiology or causation of transsexualism reveals the comparatively significant extent to which medical knowledge has progressed in the last 30 years (see [1970] 2 All ER 33 at 43–44, [1971] P 83 at 99–100). However all the experts were agreed that there were:

d '... at least four criteria for assessing the sexual condition of an individual. These are: (i) chromosomal factors; (ii) gonadal factors (ie presence or absence of testes or ovaries); (iii) genital factors (including internal sex organs); and (iv) psychological factors.'

[119] Of these Ormrod J held at the conclusion of the following paragraph:
e 'These criteria are, of course, relevant to, but do not necessarily decide, the *legal* basis of sex determination.' (My emphasis.)

[120] Another area of expert agreement was recorded:

'It is common ground between all the medical witnesses that the biological sexual constitution of an individual is fixed at birth (at the latest), and cannot

f be changed, either by the natural development of organs of the opposite sex, or by medical or surgical means.' (See [1970] 2 All ER 33 at 47, [1971] P 83 at 104.)

[121] The essential rationale for Ormrod J's conclusion is where he said:

g 'The fundamental purpose of law is the regulation of the relations between persons, and between persons and the State or community. For the limited purposes of this case, legal relations can be classified into those in which the sex of the individuals concerned is either irrelevant, relevant or an essential determinant of the nature of the relationship ... On the other hand, sex is clearly an essential determinant of the relationship called marriage, because

h it is and always has been recognised as the union of man and woman. It is the institution on which the family is built, and in which the capacity for natural heterosexual intercourse is an essential element. It has, of course, many other characteristics, of which companionship and mutual support is an important one, but the characteristics which distinguish it from all other

j relationships can only be met by two persons of opposite sex ... Since marriage is essentially a relationship between man and woman, the validity of the marriage in this case depends, in my judgment, on whether the respondent is or is not a woman. I think, with respect, that this is a more precise way of formulating the question than that adopted in para 2 of the petition, in which it is alleged that the respondent is a male. The greater, of course, includes the less, but the distinction may not be without importance,

at any rate in some cases. The question then becomes what is meant by the
word "woman" in the context of a marriage, for I am not concerned to
determine the "legal sex" of the respondent at large. Having regard to the
essentially heterosexual character of the relationship which is called
marriage, the criteria must, in my judgment, be biological, for even the most
extreme degree of transsexualism in a male or the most severe hormonal
imbalance which can exist in a person with male chromosomes, male gonads
and male genitalia cannot reproduce a person who is naturally capable of
performing the essential role of a woman in marriage. In other words, the
law should adopt, in the first place, the first three of the doctors' criteria, i e
the chromosomal, gonadal and genital tests, and, if all three are congruent,
determine the sex for the purpose of marriage accordingly, and ignore any
operative intervention.' (See [1970] 2 All ER 33 at 48, [1971] P 83 at 105–106.)

[122] In this rationale it is to be noted that Ormrod J rejected the last of the
four criteria agreed by all the experts to determine sex medically, namely
psychological factors.
[123] In rejecting submissions on behalf of the respondent he enunciated
another proposition thus:

'I have dealt, by implication, with the submission that, because the
respondent is treated by society for many purposes as a woman, it is illogical
to refuse to treat her as a woman for the purpose of marriage. The illogicality
would only arise if marriage were substantially similar in character to national
insurance and other social situations, but the differences are obviously
fundamental. These submissions, in effect, confuse sex with gender. Marriage
is a relationship which depends on sex and not on gender.' (See [1970] 2 All ER
33 at 49, [1971] P 83 at 106–107.)

[124] So let me question each of the four following propositions drawn from
the passages that I have cited: (i) 'The biological sexual constitution of an
individual is fixed at birth (at the latest)'; (ii) 'The relationship called marriage ...
is and always has been recognised as the union of man and woman'; (iii) 'The law
should adopt ... the first three of the doctors' criteria ... and ... determine the sex
for the purposes of marriage accordingly'; and (iv) 'Marriage is a relationship
which depends on sex and not on gender'.
[125] The first is a scientific proposition then agreed by all the experts but
which, 30 years on, is rejected by the three experts in the present case (see my
review of the expert evidence at [116], above).
[126] The second is an echo of eighteenth and nineteenth-century authority.
In *Lindo v Belisario* [1795] 1 Hag Con 216 at 230, [1775–1802] All ER Rep 293 at
296 Sir William Scott rejected the classification of marriage as either a civil or a
sacred contract, holding:

'It is a contract according to the law of nature, antecedent to civil
institution, which may take place to all intents and purposes wherever two
persons of different sexes engage, by mutual contracts, to live together.'

[127] In the second half of the nineteenth century in *Hyde v Hyde and Woodmansee*
(1866) LR 1 P & D 130 at 133, [1861–73] All ER Rep 175 at 177 the Judge Ordinary,
later Lord Penzance, said:

'The position or status of "husband" and "wife" is a recognised one
throughout Christendom. The laws of all Christian nations throw about that

a status a variety of legal incidents during the lives of the parties, and induce definite rights upon their offspring. What, then, is the nature of this institution as understood in Christendom? Its incidents vary in different nations, but what are its essential elements and invariable features? If it be of common acceptance and existence, it must needs (however varied in different countries in its minor incidents) have some pervading identity and universal

b basis. I conceive that marriage, as understood in Christendom, may for this purpose be defined as the voluntary union for life of one man and one woman, to the exclusion of all others.'

[128] But the world that engendered those classic definitions has long since gone. We live in a multi-racial, multi-faith society. The intervening 130 years

c have seen huge social and scientific changes. Adults live longer, infant mortality has been largely conquered, effective contraception is available to men and women as is sterilisation for men and women within marriage. Illegitimacy with its stigma has been legislated away: gone is any social condemnation of cohabitation in advance of or in place of marriage. Then marriage was terminated

d by death: for the vast majority of the population divorce was not an option. For those within whose reach it lay, it carried a considerable social stigma that did not evaporate until relatively recent times. Now more marriages are terminated by divorce than death. Divorce could be said without undue cynicism to be available on demand. These last changes are all reflected in the statistics

e establishing the relative decline in marriage and consequentially in the number of children born within marriage. Marriage has become a state into which and from which people choose to enter and exit. Thus I would now redefine marriage as a contract for which the parties elect but which is regulated by the state, both in its formation and in its termination by divorce, because it affects status upon which depend a variety of entitlements, benefits and obligations.

f [129] Of course the changes which I trace are most dramatically drawn by a contrast between the age of high Victorian moral confidence and our uncertain present. But even in the last 30 years there has been some shift in the status of marriage within our society that has some relevance to the question of whether a minority group should be denied the election to marry.

g [130] Because of its close relationship to the second proposition it is convenient to consider next the fourth, namely marriage depends on sex not gender. The proposition seems to me to be now of very doubtful validity. The scientific changes to which I have referred have diminished the once cardinal role of procreative sex. The reluctance of Ormrod J to acknowledge the validity of the

h sexual relationship between a man and a post-operative male-to-female transsexual is at odds with the decision of this court in *S v S (otherwise W) (No 2)* [1962] 3 All ER 55, [1963] P 37 which Ormrod J avoided on the grounds that the most relevant passages were obiter. Within any marriage there may be physical factors on either or both sides that require acknowledgment and accommodation in the

j sexual relationship of the parties. But that accommodation does not rob the result of its essential characteristic, namely the sexual dimension of the couple's relationship. Acknowledging that it is a dimension of cardinal importance, I would nevertheless conclude that in cases such as the present it is sufficiently fulfilled. Beside the question of whether the post-operative male-to-female has the legal capacity to consummate, gender rather than sex has steadily increased as a defining characteristic of an individual's core since its first recognition in the

1950s. The *Oxford English Dictionary* notes under the use of the word 'gender' as
an alternative to 'sex', a second and modern usage thus:
a

> 'A euphemism for the sex of a human being, often intended to emphasise
> the social and cultural, as opposed to the biological, distinction between the
> sexes.'

[131] The first usage in this sense is recorded in 1963. So does Ormrod J's   *b*
rejection of the developing concept of gender hold good 30 years on? In my
opinion, plainly not.

[132] Perhaps the third proposition has the most direct bearing on the
outcome of the appeal. Can the legal definition of what constitutes a female
person be determined by only three of the criteria which medical experts apply?
Are judges entitled to leave out of account psychological factors? For me the   *c*
answers do not depend on scientific certainty as to whether or not there are areas
of brain development differentiating the male from the female. In my opinion
the test that is confined to physiological factors, whilst attractive for its simplicity
and apparent certainty of outcome, is manifestly incomplete. There is no logic or
principle in excluding one vital component of personality, the psyche. That its   *d*
admission imports the difficulties of application that may lead to less certainty of
outcome is an inevitable consequence. But we should prefer complexity to
superficiality in that the psychological self is the product of an extremely complex
process, although not fully understood. It is self-evident that the process draws
on a variety of experiences, environmental factors and influences throughout the
individual's development particularly from birth to adolescence, but also beyond.   *e*

[133] In summary, therefore, the foundations of Ormrod J's judgment are no
longer secure. It remains as a monument to his mastery of complex scientific
evidence and to his clarity of thought and lucidity of expression. It served its time
well but its time has passed. Recently it has been criticised, particularly by
commentators in other jurisdictions, for the insensitivity of its language. That   *f*
criticism risks injustice to a judge of exceptional humanity and understanding.
The language reflects the era in which it was written rather than the writer. But
his judgment does not bind us and, for reasons upon which I will endeavour to
expand later, should not in my opinion now be followed.

[134] However I would first like to consider in some detail the recent decision
of Charles J in *W v W (physical inter-sex)* [2001] Fam 111, [2001] 2 WLR 674.   *g*
Although not directly in point, since the case deals with an inter-sex male-to-
female and not a male-to-female transsexual, there are obviously such clear areas
of common ground that it is important to consider the modern approach in that
territory. I will focus on the essential conclusions but it is necessary first to note
the judge's findings as to the respondent, who contested her husband's nullity   *h*
petition in which he asserted that at the date of the marriage she had not been
female (see [2001] Fam 111 at 120–121, [2001] 2 WLR 674 at 683). Whilst finding
that Mrs W was correctly labelled 'physical inter-sex', he found that at birth:
(i) her chromosomal sex was male; (ii) her gonadal sex was male; (iii) her genital
sex was ambiguous, but more male than female; but that subsequently (iv) her   *j*
psychological development was female.

[135] Although different medical labels are attached to Mrs W and Mrs Bellinger,
their subsequent state post-operatively is remarkably similar. It is principally in
the detail and degree of surgery that their paths to that state have differed.

[136] On those findings Charles J ruled that Mrs W was female at the date of
marriage. In reaching that conclusion he applied six factors, namely:

a
'(i) chromosomal factors; (ii) gonadal factors (ie presence or absence of testes or ovaries); (iii) genital factors (including internal sex organs); (iv) psychological factors; (v) hormonal factors, and (vi) secondary sexual characteristics (such as distribution of hair, breast development, physique etc). Dr Conway had regard to all these factors. Another way of putting this is that the decision as to whether the person is male or female for the purposes of marriage can be

b
made with the benefit of hindsight looking back from the date of the marriage or if earlier the date when the decision is made.' (See [2001] Fam 111 at 146, [2001] 2 WLR 674 at 709.)

[137] This last consideration he had amplified in the preceding paragraph, when he said:

c
'As Dr Conway explained, and I accept, people with partial androgen insensitivity can develop physically and socially in a range of ways. Their assignment to a sex or gender in which they are to be brought up and live is a difficult one and it seems to me that in such cases (and in other cases where

d
a decision as to the sex or gender in which a child should be brought up falls to be made by doctors and others) there is considerable force in the argument that it would be best to "wait and see". How long it would be appropriate to wait, and what tests would be appropriate, would vary from case to case.'

e
[138] It is also relevant to note his finding that Mrs W post-operatively had the capacity to consummate the marriage as a female and that that was 'a factor (although not a decisive factor) in considering whether that person is male or female for the purposes of marriage'.

[139] These findings and conclusions are in my opinion sound and are
f
relevant in the sense that it would be hard to justify a significantly different approach and outcome for the post-operative physical inter-sex male-to-female and the post-operative male-to-female transsexual.

[140] Those being the most relevant decisions in the Family Division, it remains to consider the statutory provisions and their development. The Marriage Act 1949 established the prohibited degrees within which a marriage is
g
void, the minimum age which the parties must have attained in order to contract a valid marriage and what constitutes a valid ceremony. The Supreme Court of Judicature (Consolidation) Act 1925 had established three other grounds of nullity: (i) prior existing marriage; (ii) insanity at the time of marriage; and (iii) lack of consent.

h
[141] That was the state of the statutory provisions in relation to void marriages at the date that the Law Commission issued for consultation its working paper of 14 June 1968. The view of the Law Commission expressed in the working paper was that there was no case for extending those grounds. However in its subsequent 1970 report *Family Law: Report on Nullity of Marriage*
j
(Law Com No 33) the Law Commission considered two possible additional grounds of nullity in the light of the responses which it had received to the working paper. The first was parties of the same sex. However again the Law Commission concluded that that would be an unnecessary addition. Impliedly rejecting Ormrod J's preference for a decree of nullity rather than a declaration as to status, the commission considered that the only consequence of the decision would be to allow or to bar applications for financial relief. It left to Parliament

the decision as to whether the draft bill proffered with the report should be *a* extended to include same sex parties as a ground of annulment.

[142] An amendment to add as a ground of annulment 'that the parties are not respectively male and female' was moved by Mr Lyon MP, the promoter of the bill. He did not propose any statutory definition of 'male' or 'female'. In Hansard's report of the debate on 2 April 1971 (814 HC Official Report (5th series) cols 1827–1854) Mr Lyon is recorded as follows: *b*

'The way that a judge decides the sex of a particular person is and always will remain a question of fact. It will be a question of fact which will change with the change in medical opinion which will ensue in the coming years. If medical opinion were that the mere sex change operation was enough to change a person from a man to a woman or a woman to a man, that would *c* be the end of the case; but because the medical evidence is not so clear cut the judge in the *Corbett* case took the view which he did and courts will continue to take the course which he took. I urge upon those who have written to me and are concerned about the matter to appreciate that this is not a matter about which Parliament can legislate. In the final analysis it must depend upon the state of medical opinion. If in the end medical opinion *d* is able to state with greater certainty who is male and who is female on tests which were not applied in the *Corbett* case then some new court can apply those tests because the evidence will have changed and the question of fact, therefore, will also have changed. If the amendment is accepted we shall not be making a rule about how one determines who is male and who is female. *e* All we are saying is that once one has come to the conclusion that the parties are not respectively male and female, then one can grant a decree of nullity.'

[143] Thus emerged s 1(c) of the Nullity of Marriage Act 1971, subsequently consolidated as s 11(c) of the Matrimonial Causes Act 1973.

f

Conclusions

[144] The arguments for the Attorney General might be summarised into three principal propositions. (i) Expert medical evidence does not demonstrate that Mrs Bellinger is and always was female or that her medical treatment has changed her from male to female. (ii) The complexity of the issues surrounding transsexualism demand that the legislature bears the responsibility for introducing *g* change rather than the judges. (iii) To accede to this petition would create enormous difficulties, even in the context of the transsexual's right to marry.

[145] I will begin to express my conclusions on the present appeal by reviewing those three propositions.

[146] The first may only be made good if regard is restricted to biological *h* factors and physiological criteria. But in my view such a restricted approach is no longer permissible in the light of scientific, medical and social change. Leaving aside the possibility that one area of the appellant's brain may not be congruent with the other three biological factors that established her original sex, there can be no doubt that she suffered from gender identity disorder (within the DSM-IV *j* and ICD-10 classifications) and has for many years been a psychological female. Her only remaining male feature is chromosomal. Post-operatively she has functioned sexually as a female having the capacity to consummate within the definition of sexual intercourse established by this court in *S v S*. My approach reflects the views expressed in the sections above devoted to the expert evidence and the judgment of Ormrod J.

a [147] The second proposition demands a fuller response both because I have not touched on the point in earlier sections of this judgment and because it is in any event a point of real substance.

[148] Of course judges must not usurp the function of Parliament. Johnson J when citing from my judgment in *Dart v Dart* [1997] 1 FCR 21 at 37 acknowledged that my words were written in a very different context. But the context is all
b important in deciding on which side of the boundary line that divides the permissible from the impermissible a particular development of law falls. In *Dart*'s case, and more recently in *Cowan v Cowan* [2001] 2 FCR 331, I acknowledged that new mechanisms for redistribution of assets could not be introduced by judicial reinterpretation of s 25 of the 1973 Act. But here we are asked to construe s 11(c), not previously construed (and so untrammelled by previous judicial
c effort) and to be construed in the light of moral, ethical and societal values as they are now rather than as they were at the date of first enactment or subsequent consolidation. Indeed the case rests on the construction of the single word 'female'. That Parliament intended some judicial licence seems clear to me from the absence of any definition within the statute and from the preceding debate,
d particularly the passage cited at [142], above. (In my opinion nothing turns on the fact that Parliament adopted the words 'male' and ' female' instead of 'man' and 'woman' which the common law applied.)

[149] The role, and indeed the responsibility, of the court in the construction of a word or phrase in a way that is reactive to or reflective of change is very clearly stated by Lord Slynn of Hadley in *Fitzpatrick v Sterling Housing Association Ltd* [1999]
e 4 All ER 705 at 710, [2001] 1 AC 27 at 33:

'It has been suggested that for your Lordships to decide this appeal in favour of the appellant would be to usurp the function of Parliament. It is trite that that is something the courts must not do. When considering social issues in particular judges must not substitute their own views to fill gaps.
f They must consider whether the new facts "fall within the parliamentary intention" (see *Royal College of Nursing of the UK v Dept of Health and Social Security* [1981] 1 All ER 545 at 565, [1981] AC 800 at 822 per Lord Wilberforce). Thus in the present context if, for example, it was explicit or clear that Parliament intended the word "family" to have a narrow meaning for all
g time, it would be a court's duty to give effect to it whatever changes in social attitudes a court might think ought to be reflected in the legislation. Similarly, if it were explicit or clear that the word must be given a very wide meaning so as to cover relationships for which a court, conscious of the traditional views of society might disapprove, the court's duty would be to give effect to it. It is, however, for the court in the first place to interpret each
h phrase in its statutory context. To do so is not to usurp Parliament's function; not to do so would be to abdicate the judicial function. If Parliament takes the view that the result is not what is wanted it will change the legislation.'

j [150] I did not take any encouragement from Mr Moylan's response to questions from the court. I surmise, I think not unfairly, that the Inter-Departmental Working Group set up in April 1999 was convened in reaction to mounting pressure from the Strasbourg Court. After all criticism reached its culmination in the judgment of the court in *Sheffield v UK* (1998) 5 BHRC 83 delivered on 30 July 1998. Furthermore the focus of the Inter-Departmental Working Group was not on the right of transsexuals to marry but upon their right to re-register (see terms of reference: 'To consider, with particular reference to birth certificates, the need for appropriate legal measures ...'). The report when delivered in April 2000 identified (at para 5.5) three options for the future: (a) no change, (b) reissue birth certificates with new name and gender, (c) full legal recognition of the new gender) and continued: 'We suggest that before taking a view on these options the government may wish to put the issues out to public consultation.'

[151] However although the report has been made available by publication, Mr Moylan said that there has since been no public consultation. Furthermore when asked whether the government had any present intention of initiating public consultation or any other process in preparation for a parliamentary bill, Mr Moylan said that he had no instructions. Nor did he have any instructions as to whether the government intended to legislate. My experience over the last ten years suggests how hard it is for any department to gain a slot for family law reform by primary legislation. These circumstances reinforce my view that it is not only open to the court but it is its duty to construe s 11(c), either strictly, alternatively liberally, as the evidence and submissions in this case justify.

[152] I turn to Mr Moylan's third proposition, namely that any relaxation of the present clear-cut boundary would produce enormous practical and legal difficulties. I grant at once that to give full legal recognition to the transsexual's right to acquire (perhaps not irreversibly) his or her psychological gender gives rise to many wide-ranging problems, some profoundly difficult. That territory is surveyed by the Inter-Departmental Working Group in their report as well as in a most distinguished paper written by Lord Reed 'Splitting the Difference: Transsexuals and Human Rights Law' (subsequently presented to the Anglo-German Family Law Judicial Conference in Edinburgh in September 2000). Indeed in reality such a development would almost certainly throw up additional problems as yet unforeseen. But we are not contemplating or empowered to contemplate such a fundamental development. That indeed can only be for Parliament. All we consider is whether the recognition of marriage should be denied to a post-operative male-to-female transsexual applying the decision in *Corbett's* case. In that context difficulties are much reduced. We need concern ourselves only with those that arise from recognising marriages already celebrated and permitting the future celebration of marriages between parties one of whom is a transsexual seeking to satisfy the requirements of s 11(c) in his or her post-operative gender. The principal difficulty seems to me to stem from the emphasis that such a person will inevitably place on his or her psychological gender. If that, the fourth factor in the *Corbett* classification, is admitted to the decision making process, does it immediately become the trump factor? If so, why does it not operate immediately and without the reinforcement of medical treatment? Whilst conceding that any line can be said to be arbitrarily drawn and to lack logic, I would contend that spectral difficulties are manageable and acceptable if the right is confined by a construction of s 11(c) to cases of fully achieved post-operative transsexuals such as the present appellant. In assessing how formidable are the difficulties postulated by Mr Moylan, we can surely take some comfort from the knowledge that within wider Europe many states have recognised the transsexual's right to marry in the acquired gender. Although different jurisdictions have adopted a widely differing range of responses (as to which see Lord Reed's paper at pp 18–20) there seems to be no evidence that they have encountered undue difficulty in applying liberalised provisions. Furthermore we have the example of a common law jurisdiction, New Zealand, which has

often legislated innovatively in the family law field. In his judgment in *A-G v*
a *Otahuhu Family Court* [1995] 1 NZLR 603, Ellis J confined the right of marriage in
the acquired gender to a transsexual who 'has undergone surgical and medical
procedures that have effectively given that person the physical conformation of a
person of a specified sex'. He continued (at 608):

b   'Submissions were directed to the *practical aspects* of any declaration, when
the Registrar may be in doubt. In such cases a medical examination can be
arranged and opinions obtained to enable the Registrar to reach his own
conclusion.'

[153] In our family justice system declarations as to existing marriages would
c be the subject of the existing statutory procedures provided by ss 55 and 59 of the
Family Law Act 1986. In the case of an intended marriage, if the registrar were
not satisfied on the medical evidence submitted by the parties, then an
application would have to be issued in the Family Division in advance of the
ceremony for a declaration that the transition had been fully achieved by all
available medical treatments.
d   [154] My responses to Mr Moylan's submissions partially express my
conclusion that this appeal should be allowed. But in view of the importance of
the appeal, not only to the appellant but also to the minority in similar
circumstances, I wish to amplify the reasons for my conclusion.

[155] Ormrod J's monumental judgment in *Corbett's* case was undoubtedly
e right when given on 2 February 1970. It is only subsequent developments, both
medical and social, that render it wrong in 2001. The major relevant medical
developments are as follows. (i) In 1980 DSM-III introduced the diagnosis of
transsexualism for gender dysphoric individuals who demonstrated at least two
years of continuous interest in removing their sexual anatomy and transforming
their bodies and social roles. In 1994 the DSM-IV committee replaced the
f diagnosis of transsexualism with gender identity disorder, denoting those with a
strong and persistent cross-gender identification and a persistent discomfort with
his or her sex or a sense of inappropriateness in the gender role of that sex. A
similar classification is to be found in ICD-10. Gender identity disorder is a mental
disorder, that is to say a behavioural pattern resulting in a significant adaptive
g disadvantage to the person causing personal mental suffering. The use of the
formal diagnosis is an important step in offering relief, providing health insurance
coverage, and generating research to provide more effective future treatments.
All the above is derived from, and in the main directly quotes, the *Harry Benjamin*
International Gender Dysphoria Association's Standards of Care for Gender Identity
Disorders (fifth version, 1998) and provided for us in the Attorney General's
h bundle. (ii) The research of Professor Louis Gooren published in 1995 and 2000
suggests that gender dysphoria is not a purely psychological condition. His
research suggests, but does not prove, that gender dysphoria has a physiological
basis in the structure of the brain. The expert evidence in the present case
suggests that support for the premise is growing in specialist medical circles.
j Mr Terry in his report says of the 1995 *Nature* study:

    'In my opinion this medical report diminishes the view that chromosomal
makeup is the critical factor in determining the sexual orientation/behaviour
for any individual … Accepting that transsexualism is a medically recognised
condition and that such patients undergo appropriate medical and surgical
treatment to achieve their chosen sexual orientation it seems to me

irrelevant to consider the chromosome make-up of an individual as the
critical factor when determining the rights of that individual in the society in   *a*
which he/she lives.'

To make the chromosomal factor conclusive, or even dominant, seems to me
particularly questionable in the context of marriage. For it is an invisible feature
of an individual, incapable of perception or registration other than by scientific   *b*
test. It makes no contribution to the physiological or psychological self. Indeed
in the context of the institution of marriage as it is today it seems to me right as a
matter of principle and logic to give predominance to psychological factors just
as it seems right to carry out the essential assessment of gender at or shortly
before the time of marriage rather than at the time of birth.   *c*

[156] The major relevant social developments are—(i) For the purposes of
this appeal we consider only gender identity disorder within the context of the
right to marry. Accordingly it is necessary to recognise changes to the institution
of marriage over the last 30 years. I have addressed that issue at [126]–[129],
above. (ii) There have been highly significant developments throughout Europe   *d*
since the year 1970. Sweden led the way in 1972 by legislation enabling
transsexuals to change their legal sex and to marry a person of their former sex.
In the mid-1970s Denmark followed suit followed by West Germany in 1980,
Italy in 1982 and the Netherlands in 1985. Of course the legislative provisions
varied from state to state. In other jurisdictions similar results were achieved
through administrative or court practice. The transsexual's right to legal   *e*
recognition to some extent had been achieved in at least 23 of the member states
of the Council of Europe, according to the judgment of the court in the most
recent case of *Sheffield v UK* (1998) 5 BHRC 83. In the same judgment it is also
said that the only member states whose legal systems do not recognise a change
of gender are the United Kingdom, Ireland, Andorra and Albania. Furthermore   *f*
in 1989 the Parliamentary Assembly of the Council of Europe and the European
Parliament adopted resolutions recommending that reclassification of the sex of
a post-operative transsexual be made legally possible. In 1998 we introduced the
European Convention for the Protection of Human Rights and Fundamental
Freedoms into our law. The convention is founded upon the concepts of human   *g*
dignity and human freedom. Human dignity and human freedom are not
properly recognised unless the individual is free to shape himself and his life in
accordance with his personality, providing that his choice does not interfere with
the public interest. In 1990 Judge Martens, in his dissenting judgment in *Cossey v
UK* [1993] 2 FCR 97 at 123–124, (1990) 13 EHRR 622 at 660 (para 5.5), expressed   *h*
social developments as he then saw them in these words:

'There is an ever growing awareness of the essential importance of
everyone's identity and of recognising the manifold differences between
individuals that flow therefrom. With that goes a growing tolerance for, and   *j*
even comprehension of, modes of human existence which differ from what
is considered "normal". With that also goes a markedly increased recognition
of the importance of privacy, in the sense of being left alone and having the
possibility of living one's own life as one chooses. The tendencies are
certainly not new, but I have a feeling that they have come more into the
open especially in recent years.'

a [157] Of course social developments are scarcely capable of proof but judges must be sensitive to these developments and must reflect them in their opinions, particularly in family proceedings, if the law is to meet the needs of society. It is also, in my opinion, important that in this field law and medicine should move together in recognising and responding to disorder. In 1990, in his dissenting judgment in *Cossey*'s case, Judge Martens summarised medical perception in these words:

b

'... medical experts in this field have time and again stated that for a transsexual the "rebirth" he seeks to achieve with the assistance of medical science is only successfully completed when his newly acquired sexual identity is fully and in all respects recognized by law. This urge for *full legal*

c *recognition* is part of the transsexual's plight.' (See [1993] 2 FCR 97 at 112–113, 13 EHRR 622 at 645 (para 2.4).)

[158] Is there not inconsistency in the state which through its health services provides full treatment for gender identity disorder but by its legal system denies the desired recognition? As Judge Van Diijk pointed out in his dissenting

d judgment in *Sheffield v UK* (1998) 5 BHRC 83 at 106:

'Among the member states of the Council of Europe which allow the surgical re-assignment of sex to be performed on their territories, the United Kingdom appears to be the only state that does not recognise the legal implications of the result to which the treatment leads.'

e [159] I would like to conclude by adopting this passage from Lord Reed's paper. I could not equal its clarity of thought and language:

'In those societies which do permit it, it seems to me to be difficult to justify a refusal to recognise that successful gender reassignment treatment has had any legal consequences for the patient's sexual identity, although the context

f in which, and conditions under which, a change of sexual identity should be recognised is a complex question. But for the law to ignore transsexualism, either on the basis that it is an aberration which should be disregarded, or on the basis that sex roles should be regarded as legally irrelevant, is not an option. The law needs to respond to society as it is. Transsexuals exist in our

g society, and that society is divided on the basis of sex. If a society accepts that transsexualism is a serious and distressing medical problem, and allows those who suffer from it to undergo drastic treatment in order to adopt a new gender and thereby improve their quality of life, then reason and common humanity alike suggest that it should allow such persons to function as fully

h as possible in their new gender. The key words are "as fully as possible": what is possible has to be decided having regard to the interests of others (so far as they are affected) and of society as a whole (so far as that is engaged), and considering whether there are compelling reasons, in the particular context in question, for setting limits to the legal recognition of the new gender.'

j
[160] That citation formulates and clarifies the essential issue for decision in this appeal. The range of rights claimed by transsexuals falls across the divisions of our justice systems. The present claim lies most evidently in the territory of the family justice system. That system must always be sufficiently flexible to accommodate social change. It must also be humane and swift to recognise the right to human dignity and to freedom of choice in the individual's private life.

One of the objectives of statute law reform in this field must be to ensure that the law reacts to and reflects social change. That must also be an objective of the *a* judges in this field in the construction of existing statutory provisions. I am strongly of the opinion that there are not sufficiently compelling reasons, having regard to the interests of others affected or, more relevantly, the interests of society as a whole, to deny this appellant legal recognition of her marriage. I would have allowed this appeal.

Appeal dismissed. Permission to appeal refused.

Kate O'Hanlon   Barrister.

a

Practice Direction

SUPREME COURT

LORD WOOLF CJ

14 JANUARY 2002

b

Judgment – Numbering of judgments – Neutral citation – Extension of neutral citation to all parts of High Court.

LORD WOOLF CJ gave the following direction at the sitting of the court.

c   This practice direction is made with the concurrence of Lord Phillips of Worth Matravers MR, Dame Elizabeth Butler-Sloss P and Sir Andrew Morritt V-C. It covers the extension of the neutral citation arrangements announced in the *Practice Note* (*judgments: neutral citation*), issued on 11 January 2001 ([2001] 1 All ER 193, [2001] 1 WLR 194), as foreshadowed in para 2.6 of that Practice Direction.

1. With effect from 14 January 2002 the practice of neutral citation is being *d* extended to all judgments given by judges in the High Court in London. A unique number will be furnished to every such High Court judgment from a register kept at the High Court. A unique number will also be furnished, on request (see below) to High Court judgments delivered by judges outside London.

2. The judgments will be numbered in the following way:

e
Chancery Division	EWHC *number* (Ch)
Patents Court	EWHC *number* (Pat)
Queen's Bench Division	EWHC *number* (QB)
Administrative Court	EWHC *number* (Admin)
Commercial Court	EWHC *number* (Comm)
f Admiralty Court	EWHC *number* (Admlty)
Technology & Construction Court	EWHC *number* (TCC)
Family Division	EWHC *number* (Fam)

For example, [2002] EWHC 123 (Fam), or [2002] EWHC 124 (QB), or [2002] EWHC 125 (Ch).

g
3. Under these arrangements, it will be unnecessary to include the descriptive word in brackets when citing the paragraph number of a judgment. Thus para 59 in *Smith v Jones* [2002] EWHC 124 (QB) would be cited: *Smith v Jones* [2002] EWHC 124 at [59].

4. There is to be no alteration to the arrangements for the neutral citation of *h* judgments given in the two divisions of the Court of Appeal, where the official shorthand writers will continue to provide the number for the neutral citation.

As indicated above, neutral citations will not be automatically assigned to judgments delivered by judges in the High Court outside London, because they appear much less frequently in published reports. The Mechanical Recording *j* Department, Royal Courts of Justice, Strand, London WC2A 2LL (tel no: 020 7947 7771) will supply a citation for such a judgment to anyone wishing to include it in a published report.

5. Apart from the changes set out above, the rules set out in section 2 of the earlier Practice Direction are still applicable. Brooke LJ, the judge in charge of modernisation, is still responsible for advising the Judges' Council on these matters. Paragraph 4.1 of that Practice Direction remains unchanged.

6. Although the judges cannot dictate the form in which law publishers
reproduce the judgments of the court, this form of citation contains the official   *a*
number given to each judgment which they hope will be reproduced wherever
the judgment is republished, in addition to the reference given in any particular
series of reports.

Kate O'Hanlon   Barrister.

a AIB Group (UK) plc (formerly Allied Irish Banks plc and AIB Finance Ltd) v Martin and another

[2001] UKHL 63

b

HOUSE OF LORDS

LORD IRVINE OF LAIRG LC, LORD HUTTON, LORD MILLETT, LORD SCOTT OF FOSCOTE
AND LORD RODGER OF EARLSFERRY

25 OCTOBER, 13 DECEMBER 2001

c

Mortgage – Debt – Repayment – Joint and several liability – Bank making advances to defendants jointly and to one of them solely – Defendants covenanting as 'mortgagor' in standard form mortgage to pay all sums advanced to 'mortgagor' – Mortgage defining 'mortgagor' as referring to all or any of the mortgagors when there was more than one – Mortgage declaring obligations of all such persons to be joint and several –
d *Whether payment covenant rendering joint mortgagor liable for advances made solely to other joint mortgagor.*

The defendants, M and G, formed a business partnership to acquire and develop properties. In order to pursue that enterprise, they jointly borrowed money from companies in the claimant banking group (the bank). M also acquired development
e properties on his own account and borrowed from the bank for that purpose. As part of a restructuring both of their joint borrowings and M's sole borrowings, each of the defendants entered into individual mortgages with the bank in its standard form. Under those mortgages, each covenanted to pay his own liabilities to the bank, whether due from him alone or jointly, and charged his own
f separately-owned properties with payment of those liabilities. At the same time, the defendants also granted the bank a joint mortgage, again in the latter's standard form, which described them together as 'the mortgagor' and which charged their jointly-owned properties with payment of the moneys that were subject to the payment covenant in cl 2 of the mortgage. Under that clause, 'the
g mortgagor' covenanted with the bank to pay or discharge on demand all sums advanced to 'the mortgagor' by the bank and all other indebtedness of 'the mortgagor' to the bank. Clause 1 provided that, where there was more than one 'mortgagor', that term was to be construed as referring to all and/or any one of those persons and 'the obligations of such persons hereunder shall be joint and several'. The bank eventually called in the loans, and later brought proceedings
h to enforce the payment covenant in cl 2 of the joint mortgage, contending that the defendants had thereby agreed to pay or discharge the indebtedness to the bank not only of the two of them jointly but also of each of them separately. The judge gave judgment for the bank, but on his appeal G contended that he was not liable to repay sums advanced to M alone. In so contending, he submitted that
j 'the mortgagor' in cl 2 should be construed as referring first to both M and G, next to one of them and then to the other (the distributive construction). The Court of Appeal rejected that contention and accordingly dismissed the appeal. G appealed to the House of Lords, contending that the distributive construction was to be preferred to the bank's construction since the factual matrix supplied no reason why G should have been expected to undertake personal liability for M's debts.

Held – On its true construction, cl 2 of the mortgage made G liable to repay not *a*
only the sums that the bank had advanced to him, whether jointly or solely, but
also the sums that had been advanced by the bank solely to M. Such a construction
gave effect to the unambiguous meaning of cl 2 which constituted a covenant by
the defendants to pay their joint debts to the bank, to pay M's debts to the bank
and to pay G's debts to the bank. Clause 2 started with a joint covenant by G and
M. It was not three separate covenants, one of them jointly and one by each of *b*
them individually. It was a single joint covenant, and their liability under it was
declared to be joint and several. That dealt with the effect of their joint covenant.
It did not turn a single covenant into three covenants. The defendants had
covenanted to pay all sums of money advanced by the bank to the two of them
and/or to each of them. No process of construction could avoid the conclusion
that they had covenanted to pay the sums advanced by the bank to M alone as *c*
well as the sums advanced by the bank to them jointly. Similarly, they had
covenanted to pay or discharge the indebtedness of M to the bank as well as their
joint indebtedness to the bank. Accordingly, the appeal would be dismissed (see
[1], [3], [6], [22], [27], [39]–[41], [43], [45], [46], below).

Decision of the Court of Appeal [2000] 2 All ER (Comm) 686 affirmed. *d*

Notes
For liability where there are several mortgagors, see 32 *Halsbury's Laws* (4th edn
reissue) para 827.

Cases referred to in opinions *e*
Mallan v May (1844) 13 M & W 511, 153 ER 213, Exch.
Wright v Tennent Caledonian Breweries Ltd 1991 SLT 823, Ct of Sess (IH).

Appeal
The second defendant, Alan Clive Gold, appealed with permission of the Appeal
Committee of the House of Lords given on 1 February 2001 from the order of the *f*
Court of Appeal (Morritt, Sedley LJJ and Sir Christopher Slade) on 27 June 2000
([2000] 2 All ER (Comm) 686) dismissing his appeal from the order of Jacob J on
26 April 1999 that judgment be entered for the claimant, AIB Group (UK) plc (the
bank), against Mr Gold and the first defendant, David Martin, and each of them
in the sum of £3,143,944·51, being the liability of the defendants under the *g*
payment covenant in a mortgage granted by them to the bank's predecessors,
Allied Irish Banks plc and AIB Finance Ltd, on 22 July 1993. Mr Martin took no
part in the proceedings before the Court of Appeal and the House of Lords. The
facts are set out in the opinion of Lord Scott of Foscote.

Nicholas Davidson QC and *Howard Smith* (instructed by *Beveridge Milton*) for *h*
Mr Gold.
Michael Briggs QC, Jeremy Cousins QC and *John Brennan* (instructed by *Moran &
Co*, Tamworth) for the bank.

Their Lordships took time for consideration. *j*

13 December 2001. The following opinions were delivered.

LORD IRVINE OF LAIRG LC.
[1] My Lords, I have had the advantage of reading in draft the speeches of Lord
Scott of Foscote and Lord Millett. I would have contented myself with deciding

a that this appeal should be dismissed for the reasons given by the former, but for
the fact that, unlike my Lord, I found attractive both prior to the appeal, and in
the course of argument, the 'distributive construction' fully elucidated by Lord
Millett. None the less, I have on balance concluded that the better view is that
favoured by Lord Scott of Foscote. I too therefore agree that the appeal should
be dismissed.

b
LORD HUTTON.

[2] My Lords, I have had the advantage of reading in draft the speeches of my
noble and learned friends Lord Millett, Lord Scott of Foscote and Lord Rodger of
Earlsferry. It is not in dispute that the relevant provisions in the mortgage can be
construed, as they were by the Court of Appeal ([2000] 2 All ER (Comm) 686), as
c imposing an obligation on Mr Alan Gold jointly with Mr Martin, but also severally,
to pay to the bank not only moneys advanced to the two of them jointly, but also
moneys advanced to Mr Martin alone for purposes which had no connection
with Mr Gold.

[3] Lord Millett has set out in his speech the reasons why a distributive
d construction could be adopted but for the reasons stated by Lord Scott and Lord
Rodger I consider that the construction adopted by the Court of Appeal was
correct and should be upheld.

[4] I would add one further observation. It is a general rule in the construction
of deeds that the intention of the parties is to be ascertained from the words used
in the deed and that, with certain limited exceptions, extrinsic evidence cannot be
e given to show the real intention of the parties. On occasions this rule may lead
to the actual intention of the parties being defeated but the rule is applied to
ensure certainty in legal affairs. In *Mallan v May* (1844) 13 M & W 511 at 517, 153
ER 213 at 216 Pollock CB stated:

f   'We must apply the ordinary rules of construction to this instrument; and
though, by so doing, we may, in some instances, probably in this, defeat the
real intention of the parties, such a course tends to establish a greater degree
of certainty in the administration of the law.'

[5] However, whilst in the present case it would not have been permissible in
construing the mortgage deed to take into account extrinsic evidence of the
g intention of the parties, I note with some satisfaction that it is apparent that the
construction given to the mortgage by Lord Scott and Lord Rodger does not
defeat the real intention of the parties. It is clear from the passage in the judgment
of Jacob J on the non est factum point set out by Lord Scott in his speech that
Mr Howard Gold, Mr Alan Gold's solicitor upon whom he entirely relied, fully
h understood that the deed had the effect for which the bank contends and Jacob J
added: 'He [Howard] had even ensured that such a clause did not apply when he
and Alan gave supporting security for Mr Martin's nursing home project.'

[6] Accordingly I would dismiss the appeal.

j **LORD MILLETT.**

[7] My Lords, your Lordships are concerned with the application of an
interpretation clause contained in a standard form. Both features are significant.
A standard form is designed for use in a wide variety of different circumstances.
It is not context-specific. Its value would be much diminished if it could not be
relied upon as having the same meaning on all occasions. Accordingly the
relevance of the factual background of a particular case to its interpretation is

necessarily limited. The danger, of course, is that a standard form may be
employed in circumstances for which it was not designed. Unless the context in *a*
a particular case shows that this has happened, however, the interpretation of the
form ought not to be affected by the factual background.

[8] The fact that the question concerns the application of an interpretation
clause is also significant. The purpose of such a clause is twofold. It shortens the
drafting and avoids unnecessary repetition; and it enables the form to be used in *b*
a variety of different situations. It is not the purpose of such a clause to enlarge
the parties' rights and obligations beyond those provided by the operative
provisions by imposing, for example, a secondary liability as surety in addition to
a primary liability as principal debtor. The application of such a clause is not
merely a question of construction. If it is capable of being applied to the operative
provisions in more than one way, it should be applied in a way which serves its *c*
purpose rather than in a way which extends the parties' obligations beyond those
contemplated by the operative provisions. Of course, an interpretation clause
may have this effect; but if so it should do so plainly and unambiguously.

[9] The form which your Lordships are called upon to construe ('the joint
mortgage') is drafted for the case of a single mortgagor and employs an interpretation *d*
clause to adapt it for use where there are two or more mortgagors. It is commonly
used in cases where the mortgagors are husband and wife who are mortgaging
the matrimonial home, where it is unlikely to give rise to difficulty; but it may be
used in other cases also where its use is more problematical. In the present case
the mortgagors were partners who carried on a business in partnership together
and each of whom also carried on his own separate business. The bank advanced *e*
money to the mortgagors jointly, and also to each of them separately. By the
joint mortgage the mortgagors personally covenanted to repay the bank's
advances and charged their jointly-owned properties by way of security. By
separate deeds entered into at the same time each of them also covenanted to pay
and charged his own separately-owned property with payment of his own *f*
liabilities to the bank, whether due from him alone or jointly with any other
person and whether as principal or surety.

[10] It is beyond dispute that the mortgagors thereby undertook a joint and
several liability for the joint debts and charged the jointly-owned properties to
secure their repayment. It is also beyond dispute that each of them also undertook
a personal obligation to repay not only the joint debts but also his own separate *g*
debts, and charged his own separate properties to secure the repayment of all
such debts. The question is whether each of them also covenanted by way of
guarantee to pay the debts of the other and charged his separate properties with
such payment. None of the documents contains an express guarantee. If there is
such a guarantee, it derives exclusively from the way in which the interpretation *h*
clause in the joint mortgage is applied to the operative provisions.

[11] The relevant operative clause is cl 2(1) of the joint mortgage. So far as
material this reads: 'The Mortgagor hereby covenants with ... the Bank ... that it
will on demand pay or discharge to the Bank ... all sums of money ... advanced
to the Mortgagor by the Bank ...' When used by a single mortgagor there is no *j*
room for any surety liability. There is complete identity between the covenantor
and the subject matter of the covenant. The covenantor undertakes a personal
obligation as principal debtor to repay money advanced to himself.

[12] In the present case, however, 'the Mortgagor' is defined as 'Mr Martin
and Mr Gold'. Substituting these names for 'the Mortgagor' in the relevant clause
produces the following: 'Mr Martin and Mr Gold hereby covenant with ... the

a Bank ... that they will on demand pay or discharge to the Bank ... all sums of money ... advanced to Mr Martin and Mr Gold by the Bank ...' There is still no room for any surety liability. The identity between the covenantors and the subject matter of the covenant, indicated by the repetition of the words 'the Mortgagor', is retained. The two covenantors are jointly liable for money advanced to them jointly. They undertake a personal obligation as principal
b debtors.

[13] The interpretation clause, however, contains an expanded definition to adapt the form for use where the expression 'the Mortgagor' includes more than one person. In such a case, it provides that the expression 'shall be construed as referring to all and/or any one of those persons and the obligations of such persons hereunder shall be joint and several'. Applying this to the words 'the
c Mortgagor' where they first appear in cl 2(1) has the effect of modifying the covenant but not its subject matter. As modified the clause reads:

> 'Mr Martin and Mr Gold hereby jointly and severally covenant and each of them hereby severally covenants with ... the Bank ... that they will on demand pay or discharge to the Bank ... all sums of money ... advanced to
d > Mr Martin and Mr Gold ...'

There is some duplication, but the effect is to produce three distinct covenants and three distinct obligations; a joint and several covenant by both Mr Martin and Mr Gold and a separate covenant by each of them. Each of the covenants is a covenant to repay the money advanced to them jointly, so there is still no room
e for any surety liability. The identity between the covenantors and the subject matter of the covenants indicated by the repetition of the words 'the Mortgagors' is retained. They undertake joint and several obligations as principal debtors.

[14] Applying the interpretation clause to the expression 'the Mortgagor' where it secondly appears in cl 2(1), however, modifies the subject matter of the
f covenant and extends the covenantors' liability. The only question is: how far? If the interpretation clause is applied literally and comprehensively, cl 2(1) reads:

> 'Mr Martin and Mr Gold and each of them hereby jointly and severally covenant with ... the Bank ... that they and each of them will on demand pay or discharge to the Bank ... all sums of money ... advanced to Mr Martin and
g > Mr Gold or either of them by the Bank ...'

This produces no fewer than nine covenants: three joint and several covenants on the part of Mr Martin and Mr Gold to pay (i) their joint debts, (ii) Mr Martin's debts, and (iii) Mr Gold's debts; three similar covenants by Mr Martin alone; and three similar covenants by Mr Gold alone. Each of the covenantors undertakes a
h personal liability both jointly with the other of them and separately to pay the moneys advanced (i) to both of them, (ii) to himself, and (iii) to the other of them. The inclusion of (iii) breaks the identity between the covenantor and the subject matter of the covenant indicated by the repetition of the words 'the Mortgagor' and introduces for the first time a secondary liability as surety.

j [15] If this were the only possible way of applying the interpretation clause, it would have to be adopted. But it is not. It is perfectly possible to apply the clause distributively so as to avoid both unnecessary duplication and the introduction of secondary liability. A distributive construction is commonly adopted when a plural subject is followed by a plural predicate and the plurals are broken down into their component singulars. An example from everyday speech would be to say: 'A and B took their children to school'. Prima facie the word 'their' means 'belonging to both of them'. But this is not its only possible meaning, and if A and B are not married it is obviously not its meaning. In that case the word 'their' means 'of each of them'. But this means that A and B took *their respective* children to school, not each other's children. The children are distributed to the relevant parent. And it goes further than that. Although the word 'school' is in the singular, it may conceal a plural. If necessary, the sentence means that A and B took the children to their respective schools.

[16] This is a well-established principle of construction. It often, and perhaps usually, gives the words their most natural meaning. It parades under a Latin name, reddendo singula singulis. This simply means that, when plurals are broken down, each singular component must be attributed to its respective singular and not to every other possible singular. It is a broad and general principle which departs from the literal and grammatical meaning and does not depend upon minutiae of language.

[17] In the present case the principle would operate in two ways. It would apply the interpretation clause to cl 2(1) by attributing the obligation to repay the moneys advanced to Mr Martin and Mr Gold jointly to their joint and several covenant, thereby removing the unnecessary duplication resulting from the attribution of the same obligation to their individual covenants. This reading preserves the identity between the covenantor and the subject matter of the covenant, and makes no difference to the effect of the joint mortgage. It is the most natural way to read the operative clause and ought not to be controversial. Mr Martin and Mr Gold thereby jointly and severally covenant to pay the joint debts and each of them separately covenants to pay the separate debts.

[18] Critically, however, a distributive application of the interpretation clause would not stop there. It would also attribute the obligation to repay the separate debts of 'the Mortgagor', not to each member of the class, but to the relevant member who owed them. This is a perfectly legitimate, and in my opinion the more natural, way to apply the interpretation clause. It treats a covenant by two or more persons (in so far as it means by each of them) to discharge their debts (in so far as it means the debts of each of them) as a covenant by each of them to discharge his own debts and not the debts of the other or others. Put shortly, it treats the obligation of two or more persons to pay their debts as an obligation to pay their respective debts.

[19] This is 'an intellectually respectable way' (see the judgment of Sedley LJ in the Court of Appeal ([2000] 2 All ER (Comm) 686)) of reaching the conclusion which the Court of Appeal clearly wanted but felt unable to reach. It is not clear to me why they refused to apply the interpretation clause distributively. They seem to have done so because it produces a result at variance with that produced by applying it comprehensively. But that is necessarily the case. The Court of Appeal assumed that the question was one of construing cl 2(1) after the interpretation clause has been applied to it. But the real question is concerned with the proper way of applying the interpretation clause to cl 2(1). The Court of Appeal assumed that there was only one way to apply the clause, and did not consider whether a distributive application was the more appropriate way.

[20] If legitimate, a distributive application of the interpretation clause in the present case is clearly appropriate. It gives full effect to every word of the interpretation clause and its purpose in adapting the form to the case where there are two or more mortgagors, while retaining the identity between the covenantors and the subject matter of their respective covenants. It avoids the creation of a secondary liability not contemplated by the wording of the operative clause,

a which on its face creates one (or more) obligations of one (or more) principal
debtors but no secondary liability.

[21] In my opinion invoking cl 2(3) begs the question. Mr Martin and Mr Gold
jointly and severally undertook to discharge the costs of the bank in relation to the
joint mortgage. Since the joint mortgage effected a charge on their jointly-owned
properties, it was appropriate to charge the bank's costs in relation to the taking
b and realisation of the security to each of the mortgagors. Assuming, without
deciding, that such costs would also extend to the costs of proceedings to enforce
the personal covenants in cl 2(1), the question whether either of them is liable
under cl 2(3) to pay the costs of proceedings against the other depends on the true
construction of cl 2(1). Whether or not the interpretation clause is applied
distributively to cl 2(1), the liability for costs is co-extensive with the substantive
c obligation.

[22] At the conclusion of argument I was persuaded that a distributive
application of the interpretation clause is both legitimate and appropriate. Your
Lordships, however, are unanimously of the opinion that it is not legitimate, and
I am not prepared to dissent from that view. Accordingly, with the same reluctance
d as was displayed by the Court of Appeal, I agree that the appeal should be
dismissed.

LORD SCOTT OF FOSCOTE.

[23] My Lords, the appeal before your Lordships raises a short point of
construction of a mortgage. The mortgage is in the standard form that at the date
e of the mortgage, 22 July 1993, was used by lenders in the Allied Irish Banks group
of companies for taking security from their borrowers.

[24] There are two mortgagors, Mr Gold, who is the appellant and second
defendant, and Mr Martin. In the description of the parties in the opening lines
of the mortgage Mr Gold and Mr Martin are together described as 'the Mortgagor'.
f Clause 1 of the mortgage is an interpretation clause. It defines the term 'the
Mortgagor' as 'the Mortgagor named as such on page 1 hereof' ie Mr Gold and
Mr Martin. The last sentence of cl 1 says that:

> 'If the expression "the Mortgagor" includes more than one person it shall
> be construed as referring to all and/or any one of those persons and the
g   obligations of such persons hereunder shall be joint and several.'

[25] In cl 3(1) of the mortgage:

> 'The Mortgagor as beneficial owner hereby charges by way of legal
> mortgage all and singular the property or properties described or referred to
h   in the Schedule hereto as a continuing security with payment to the Bank
> and the Company of all monies covenanted to be paid under Clause 2
> hereof.'

Fourteen properties were specified in the schedule. Each was jointly owned by
Mr Gold and Mr Martin.
j [26] Clause 2 of the mortgage, which contains the payment covenant, is the
clause that has led to the problem. I will set it out in full:

> 'The Mortgagor hereby covenants with each of the Bank and the Company
> that it will on demand pay or discharge to the Bank and the Company:—
> (1) all sums of money which have been or are now or may hereafter at any
> time or from time to time be advanced to the Mortgagor by the Bank or the

Company (as the case may be); (2) all other indebtedness and/or liabilities
whatsoever of the Mortgagor to the Bank or the Company (as the case may *a*
be) present, future, actual and/or contingent and whether on any banking or
other account or otherwise in any manner whatsoever including such
indebtedness and/or liabilities due under the terms hereof (whether alone or
jointly with any other person and in whatever style, name or form and
whether as principal or surety); (3) all costs and expenses incurred by the *b*
Bank or the Company in relation to this Legal Mortgage and/or any such
advances, indebtedness and/or liabilities on a full indemnity basis; (4) the
amount of any acceptance or other credits and any cheques, notes or bills
from time to time given or assumed by the Bank or the Company and all
commission, discount and banking charges; and (5) interest and charges
upon or relating to all such advances, indebtedness, liabilities, unpaid *c*
interest, costs, and expenses, acceptance credits, cheques, notes, bills,
commission, discount and banking charges, until demand at such rate or
rates as have been or may from time to time be agreed between the
Mortgagor and the Bank or the Mortgagor and the Company (as the case
may be), or in default of any agreed rate or rates and in any event from and *d*
after demand until full discharge (as well after as before judgment) at the
Specified Rate of interest.'

[27] The issue is whether the cl 2 covenant makes Mr Gold liable to the bank
for Mr Martin's indebtedness to the bank arising out of advances to Mr Martin
which had nothing to do with Mr Gold. The trial judge, Jacob J, and the Court of *e*
Appeal ([2000] 2 All ER (Comm) 686) thought that it clearly did. But, with the
leave of the House, Mr Gold has appealed.

[28] Before outlining the way in which the argument has been put, a little
background needs to be mentioned.

[29] Mr Gold is a dentist but formed a business partnership with Mr Martin, a *f*
property dealer, to acquire and develop properties. In order to pursue this
enterprise they borrowed money from companies in the Allied Irish Banks group.
For convenience and simplicity I shall use the expression 'the bank' to refer
indiscriminately to the lender company, whichever company in the group it may
have been, and to the respondent to this appeal. Mr Martin also acquired *g*
development properties on his own account and borrowed from the bank for that
purpose.

[30] In 1993 the bank decided to re-structure both the joint borrowings of
Mr Gold and Mr Martin and the sole borrowings of Mr Martin. Facility letters
dated 11 February 1993 were sent to the borrowers. The letter to Mr Gold and *h*
Mr Martin offered them a joint facility of £1,710,000 to be secured on 46 specified
properties. Some of these properties were owned by the borrowers jointly,
28 were owned by Mr Martin alone and two by Mr Gold alone. The letter to
Mr Martin offered him a facility of £591,000 to be secured on the 28 specified
properties owned by Mr Martin alone and intended also as security for the joint *j*
facility.

[31] The acceptance by the borrowers of the facilities offered by these letters
led not only to the mortgage by Mr Gold and Mr Martin jointly, the construction
of cl 2 of which is in issue, but also to a mortgage by Mr Gold of his two properties
and a mortgage by Mr Martin of his 28 properties. Each of these individual
mortgages was, of course, in the bank's same standard form. The payment

a covenant in each of these would catch any indebtedness or liability of the mortgagor under the joint mortgage.

[32] For the purposes of these arrangements with the bank Mr Gold was represented by a firm of solicitors, Mincoff Science and Gold. The partner in the firm who dealt with the matter on Mr Gold's behalf was Mr Howard Gold, his brother. Mr Howard Gold knew the level of Mr Martin's personal indebtedness
b to the bank as well as the amount of the joint indebtedness. The second defendant Mr Gold signed the joint mortgage and his individual mortgage on Mr Howard Gold's advice.

[33] Later, and for reasons that are not material, the bank called in the loans. The sale by the bank of the properties comprised in its security has been completed but has left a substantial shortfall. So the bank is attempting to enforce
c the cl 2 covenant for payment in the joint mortgage contending that Mr Gold and Martin thereby agreed to pay or discharge the indebtedness to the bank not only of the two of them jointly but also of each of them separately.

[34] Before Jacob J, it seems to have been accepted that cl 2 on its true construction did have the effect contended for by the bank. The second defendant sought to
d escape by relying on a non est factum point. In dealing with, and rejecting, this point, Jacob J referred to Mr Howard Gold's knowledge of the mortgage and its effect:

e 'There is no doubt that Howard saw the final deed, including the "frightening" provisions. Nor is there any doubt that he knew what their effect was. He had been concerned with similar clauses in the past, including for Alan ... Howard also knew that the provisions were not theoretical in that Mr Martin undoubtedly did have debts owed to the bank.'

The 'frightening' provisions to which the judge referred were sub-cll (1) and (2)
f of cl 2. The judge concluded:

'I cannot see any room for non est factum here. Alan signed without reading the document. He never read any documents approved by Howard. Howard was his appointed agent. That is really the end of the case.'

g [35] The construction point that has been advanced before your Lordships was raised for the first time in the Court of Appeal. The construction contended for has been described, as a form of convenient shorthand, as a 'distributive' construction. It is contended that because 'the Mortgagor', as defined, includes more than one person, ie Mr Gold and Mr Martin, it should be construed as
h referring first to the two of them, next to one of them, and then to the other of them. This distributive construction requires, it is said, that cl 2 be interpreted thus:

j 'A. Mr Gold and Mr Martin jointly and severally covenant to pay (1) all sums of money which have been advanced to them, Mr Gold and Mr Martin jointly, and (2) all other indebtedness and/or liabilities whatsoever of them, Mr Gold and Mr Martin, whether together or jointly with any other person and

B. Mr Gold hereby covenants to pay ... (1) all sums of money which have been advanced to Mr Gold, and (2) all other indebtedness and/or liabilities whatsoever of Mr Gold whether alone or jointly with any other person and

C. Mr Martin hereby covenants to pay (1) all sums of money which have
been advanced to Mr Martin (2) all other indebtedness and/or liabilities   *a*
whatsoever of Mr Martin whether alone or jointly with any other person.'

[36] This is the so-called distributive construction. If it were right, Mr Gold
would not be liable to repay sums advanced to Mr Martin alone. The Court of
Appeal did not accept this construction. Morritt LJ, who gave the leading   *b*
judgment, said ([2000] 2 All ER (Comm) 686 at 691):

'Once it is recognised that each reference to "Mortgagor" includes
Mr Martin and Mr Gold jointly, and Mr Martin and Mr Gold severally and in
isolation from the others, then both the obligation to pay and the liability
which that obligation extends to is a several obligation of Mr Gold in relation   *c*
to a several liability of Mr Martin, as well as the other way round ...'

[37] Mr Davidson QC, counsel for Mr Gold, protests that this passage, while
it plainly rejects the distributive construction contended for, does not explain
why it does so.
[38] Mr Davidson accepts that the construction contended for by the bank,   *d*
and accepted by the Court of Appeal, is a legitimate construction but argues that
the distributive construction, too, is legitimate and that the court, in choosing
which of two legitimate constructions to adopt, should choose that which is more
appropriate having regard to the factual matrix. The factual matrix, he says,
supplies no reason why Mr Gold should have been expected to undertake
personal liability for Mr Martin's debts and that the distributive construction is,   *e*
therefore, to be preferred.
[39] I am afraid that I do not find Mr Davidson's submissions in the least
compelling or cl 2 in the least ambiguous. The clause starts with a joint covenant
by Mr Gold and Mr Martin. It is not three separate covenants, one by them
jointly and one by each of them individually. It is a single joint covenant. Their   *f*
liability under this joint covenant is declared to be joint and several. This deals
with the effect of their joint covenant. It does not turn a single covenant into
three covenants.
[40] But the critical issue is not whether Mr Gold and Mr Martin, as well as
jointly covenanting to pay, have severally covenanted to pay. The critical issue
is *what* have they covenanted to pay? Under sub-cl (1) they have covenanted to   *g*
pay 'all sums of money ... advanced to the Mortgagor by the Bank'. The
mortgagor means the two of them and/or each of them. So they have
covenanted to pay all sums of money advanced by the bank to the two of them
and/or to each of them. I do not understand how any process of construction can
avoid the conclusion that they have covenanted to pay the sums advanced by the   *h*
bank to Mr Martin alone as well as the sums advanced by the bank to them
jointly.
[41] The point is the same under sub-cl (2). Mr Gold and Mr Martin have
covenanted to pay or discharge 'all other indebtedness and/or liabilities
whatsoever of the Mortgagor to the Bank' ie 'of the two of them and/or each of   *j*
them'. So they have covenanted to pay or discharge the indebtedness of Mr Martin
to the bank as well as their joint indebtedness to the bank.
[42] The distributive construction, which treats the single joint covenant as
three separate covenants, makes no sense of sub-cl (3). Mr Gold and Mr Martin
covenant to pay 'all costs and expenses incurred by the Bank ... in relation to this
Legal Mortgage'. This would cover the costs of proceedings taken by the bank to

a enforce payment of the indebtedness of Mr Martin alone as well as the cost of proceedings to enforce payment of any joint indebtedness. There is no reference in sub-cl (3) to 'the Mortgagor' and no distributive construction can exclude Mr Gold's liability to pay all costs and expenses caught by the subclause, whether incurred in connection with the recovery of indebtedness for which Mr Martin is primarily liable or of any joint indebtedness. A construction that excludes

b Mr Gold from liability in respect of advances to Mr Martin alone but leaves him liable to pay the bank's costs of proceedings to recover those advances does not produce a result that could sensibly, or reasonably, have been intended.

[43] In my opinion, there are no real difficulties of construction arising out of the reference to 'the Mortgagor' in cl 2. As was succinctly put by Mr Cousins QC, following for the bank, cl 2 constitutes a covenant by Mr Gold and Mr Martin to

c pay their joint debts to the bank, to pay Mr Martin's debts to the bank and to pay Mr Gold's debts to the bank.

[44] This simple construction may leave Mr Gold under obligations that he had not foreseen and had not intended at the time he signed the joint mortgage. But he has already succeeded in an action for negligence against the firm of

d solicitors who acted for him and, as I understand it, this appeal is being funded by their insurers.

[45] In my opinion the Court of Appeal came to the correct conclusion for the correct reasons. I would dismiss the appeal.

LORD RODGER OF EARLSFERRY.

e [46] My Lords, I have had the privilege of reading in draft the speeches of both my noble and learned friends, Lord Millett and Lord Scott of Foscote. Despite Lord Millett's reservations I have come to the view that the relevant provisions should be construed as Lord Scott proposes.

[47] There is, of course, no doubt about the value of the canon of interpretation

f which Lord Millett invokes. It occurs in a number of slightly different forms, all of them still—happily—in concise and precise Latin. Like any other rule of interpretation, it is there to help to ascertain the objective meaning of the document in question. Like all such rules, it must be used with discrimination. In this case I am by no means satisfied that applying it in the manner suggested would truly bring out the intended effect of cl 2(1).

g [48] As Lord Scott points out, the covenant in cl 2(1) is a single covenant by the mortgagor which, by reason of the definition of 'the Mortgagor' in cl 1, is 'joint and several'. Prima facie—and without reading any further—the use of these words indicates that Mr Martin and Mr Gold are jointly and severally liable for any obligations to be specified in cl 2(1). In other words, each of them

h is liable to pay the whole or any part of the sums specified, as opposed to being liable simply to pay a pro rata (half) share of those sums.

[49] It is necessary, however, to go further into cl 2(1) to discover for what sums Mr Martin and Mr Gold are to be liable. As Lord Millett explains, if parsed out, cl 2(1) provides:

j   'Mr Martin and Mr Gold and each of them hereby jointly and severally covenant with ... the Bank ... that they and each of them will on demand pay or discharge to the Bank ... all sums of money ... advanced to Mr Martin and Mr Gold or either of them by the Bank ...'

It is common ground that this provision can indeed be construed as imposing an obligation on Mr Gold, jointly with Mr Martin but also severally, to pay not only

all sums of money advanced by the bank to Mr Martin and Mr Gold but also all
sums advanced by the bank to either of them as an individual. In other words, *a*
Mr Gold is to be jointly and severally liable, inter alia, to pay the sums advanced
by the bank to Mr Martin. Both Jacob J and the Court of Appeal ([2000] 2 All ER
(Comm) 686) interpreted the provision in this way. The suggestion is, however,
that it would be preferable to interpret it reddendo singula singulis so that liability
for the separate debts of the individuals making up 'the Mortgagor' would be *b*
attributed only to the individual who incurred the debt in question. The result is
then that there is in effect a joint and several liability on Mr Martin and Mr Gold
to pay the joint debts and a several liability on each of them to pay his separate
debts. On that footing Mr Gold is liable to pay his own separate debts to the bank
but not Mr Martin's.

[50] I accept, of course, that the rule of construction, reddendo singula *c*
singulis, could be applied to a document containing obligations on the part of two
debtors. So, for instance, a mortgage deed in which A and B covenanted to pay
'their debts' might be interpreted, reddendo singula singulis, as meaning that
each of them undertook to pay his own debts. I am not persuaded, however, that
in the present case the single covenant, for joint and several liability, should in *d*
effect be divided up so as to withdraw the separate debts of the individuals from
the joint and several liability and then to subject them to a separate, several
liability of the relevant individual. I do not question the intellectual respectability
of the proposed way of reaching that result; I simply do not believe that the result
reflects the intention of the parties to this particular agreement.

[51] In part, at least, I have difficulty in accepting the second defendant's *e*
construction because Mr Davidson acknowledged on his behalf that provisions
making one of two debtors liable for the debts of the other are frequently found
in documents used by banks and lending institutions. This can be seen from a
number of specimens which the bank produced. For instance, in the case of the
Royal Bank of Scotland, condition 12.2—also dealing with interpretation— *f*
provides that, where two or more persons are included in the expression
'Mortgagor', each of them is to be 'primarily liable by way of indemnity for the
liabilities to the Bank of the other or others of them'. Counsel accepted that
explicit provisions of this kind are indeed intended to make one debtor liable for
the debts of the other and that they are valid. Against that background I do not
find the result produced by the straightforward interpretation of the wording of *g*
cl 2(1) surprising.

[52] In the circumstances the second defendant's argument had really to rest
on the form of the provisions in this case. In effect, counsel argued that definition
clauses should not be interpreted so as to produce what are, in effect, important
substantive effects on the obligations of the debtors concerned. As is apparent, *h*
however, from the Royal Bank of Scotland and other examples shown to the
House, interpretation clauses of this kind are by no means unusual. In the
absence of reported cases to the contrary, it must be assumed that they are given
effect.

[53] More positively, I note that in *Wright v Tennent Caledonian Breweries Ltd* *j*
1991 SLT 823—to which the House was not referred—the First Division of the
Court of Session had to deal with a deed of variation of a loan agreement where
'the borrower' was defined in a somewhat similar manner to 'the Mortgagor' in
this case. In particular, in the case of two or more individuals, the obligations and
conditions affecting the borrower were to be binding on the individuals 'jointly
and severally'. Despite this, one of the debtors submitted that her liability under

a the loan agreement was only pro rata, because it would have required clear provisions in the deed of variation to incorporate the joint and several liability into the loan agreement. The court rejected that argument. In his opinion, with which Lord Allanbridge and Lord Sutherland concurred, Lord President Hope said (at 827):

b 'In my opinion the statement in cl. 1.03 of the deed of variation that the obligations and conditions affecting the borrower shall be binding on two or more persons jointly and severally goes beyond a mere definition of the expression "the Borrower". It is concerned not with the question who is to be taken to be the borrower—that is to say, with the person or persons to whom that expression extends—but with the measure of the obligations c undertaken by those persons in that capacity.'

He went on to say that the whole structure of the loan agreement as varied 'including the use of the expression "the Borrower" in the singular at the outset to describe the two persons who are to receive the loan' confirmed his view that the debtors' liability under the agreement was joint and several (as opposed to d pro rata).

[54] In much the same way, the definition of 'the Mortgagor' in the agreement in this case was not concerned simply with the question of who was to be taken to be the mortgagor: it dealt with the measure of the obligations which Mr Martin and Mr Gold undertook. It must be treated accordingly. There may be various reasons why the draftsman of the bank's standard form agreement e chose to draft it in this particular way. I need not go as far as the First Division and draw a positive inference from the use of the singular 'the Mortgagor'. It is sufficient that I find nothing in the chosen form of drafting which would, of itself, justify the House in adopting the second defendant's preferred interpretation of cl 2(1).

Appeal dismissed.

Celia Fox   Barrister.

R v Smith (David)
[2001] UKHL 68

a

HOUSE OF LORDS

LORD BINGHAM OF CORNHILL, LORD NOLAN, LORD HOFFMANN, LORD HUTTON, LORD
RODGER OF EARLSFERRY

b

19 NOVEMBER, 13 DECEMBER 2001

*Sentence – Confiscation order – Fraudulent evasion of excise duty – Pecuniary
advantage – Defendant fraudulently evading excise duty on imported goods – Customs
officers seizing goods before sale – Whether defendant obtaining pecuniary advantage*   *c*
from failure to pay duty – Criminal Justice Act 1988, ss 71, 74.

The defendant and others sailed into the Humber estuary in a motor vessel laden
with cigarettes purchased in Heligoland. They passed two customs houses, and
then travelled up river to a point where the boat was stopped and searched by
customs officers. The officers found the cigarettes and seized them. The excise   *d*
duty on those cigarettes, which had become payable when the vessel had passed
the customs posts, would have been £130,666.40. The defendant and his co-accused
were charged with, and pleaded guilty to, an offence of fraudulent evasion of
excise duty. The sentencing judge imposed a confiscation order on the defendant.
Section 71[a] of the Criminal Justice Act 1988 required the court, when the possibility   *e*
of making such an order arose, to determine first whether the offender had
benefited from any relevant criminal conduct. Under s 71(4), a person benefited
from an offence if he obtained property as a result of or in connection with its
commission, and his benefit was the value of the property so obtained. Section 71(5)
provided that where a person derived a 'pecuniary advantage' as a result of or in
connection with the commission of an offence, he was to be treated as if he had   *f*
obtained as a result or in connection with the commission of the offence a sum of
money equal to the value of the pecuniary advantage. By virtue of s 74(5)[b],
references to the value at any time of any property obtained by a person as a
result of or in connection with the commission of an offence were references to
the value of the property to him when he obtained it or, if it were greater, the   *g*
value at the subsequent material time. On the defendant's appeal against the
confiscation order, the Court of Appeal held that the defendant had not derived
any pecuniary advantage, within the meaning of s 71(5), from evading payment
of the duty because the seizure of the cigarettes had prevented him from selling
them, and that accordingly he had not benefited, in terms of s 71(4), from the
evasion of duty. The defendant's appeal was therefore allowed, and the Crown   *h*
appealed to the House of Lords.

Held – Where a person had evaded excise duty on imported goods through not
paying the required duty at the point of importation, he had derived, for the
purposes of s 71(5) of the 1988 Act, a pecuniary advantage from the evasion at the   *j*
moment of importation even though he had been unable to realise the value of
the goods because they had been forfeited by customs officers. A conclusion to
the contrary would go a long way to making the confiscation provisions

---

a   Section 71, so far as material, is set out at [11], below
b   Section 74, so far as material, is set out at [22], below

a ineffective against smugglers, but fortunately the terms of the legislation did not lead to that result. The ordinary and natural meaning of 'pecuniary advantage' included the evasion or deferral of a debt, and s 71(4) and (5) of the Act had the effect of treating an offender who had derived such an advantage from his offence as a person who had obtained 'property' as a result of or in connection with the commission of the offence, the 'property' in question being a sum of money equal

b to the value of the pecuniary advantage. Under s 74(5), the value of the property was its value to the offender when he obtained it save where the actual property obtained by the offender had subsequently increased in value. It therefore made no difference if, after he obtained it, the property was destroyed or damaged in a fire or was seized by customs officers: subsequent events were to be ignored. The same general approach applied in the case of a pecuniary advantage. Such a

c scheme had the merit of simplicity. If in some circumstances it could operate in a penal or even a draconian manner, that might not be out of place in a scheme for stripping criminals of the benefits of their crimes. That was a matter for the judgment of the legislature, which had adopted a similar approach in enacting legislation for the confiscation of the proceeds of drug trafficking. It followed in

d the instant case that the defendant had, by evading the duty, derived a pecuniary advantage at the moment when he imported the cigarettes; that the sum equalling that advantage was to be treated as the property obtained by the defendant at that moment; that its value was therefore to be determined at that moment, disregarding the seizure of the cigarettes by the customs officers; and that accordingly the defendant had derived a pecuniary advantage to the value of

e £130,666.40. The appeal would therefore be allowed (see [1]–[4], [18], [19], [21], [23], [26], [27], [29], [30], below).

R v Dimsey, R v Allen [2000] 2 All ER 142 approved.

Notes

f For confiscation orders, see 11(2) *Halsbury's Laws* (4th edn reissue) paras 1284–1285.

For the Criminal Justice Act 1988, ss 71, 74, see 12 *Halsbury's Statutes* (4th edn) (1997 reissue) 1025, 1034.

g **Cases referred to in opinions**

DPP v Turner [1973] 3 All ER 124, [1974] AC 357, [1973] 3 WLR 352, HL.

R v Banks [1997] 2 Cr App R (S) 110, CA.

R v Dimsey, R v Allen [2000] 2 All ER 142, CA.

R v Smith (Ian) [1989] 2 All ER 948, [1989] 1 WLR 765, CA.

h

Appeal

The Crown appealed with leave of the Appeal Committee of the House of Lords given on 21 June 2001 from the decision of the Court of Appeal (Mance LJ, Newman and Burton JJ) on 16 June 2000 ((2000) 164 JP 575) allowing an appeal

j by the respondent, David Cadman Smith, from a confiscation order in the sum of £46,250 imposed on him by Judge Moore in the Crown Court at Sheffield on 22 July 1999 following his conviction on 2 October 1998, on a plea of guilty, of fraudulently evading excise duty contrary to s 170(2) of the Taxes Management Act 1979. The Court of Appeal certified that a point of law of general public importance, set out at [9], below, was involved in its decision. The facts are set out in the opinion of Lord Rodger of Earlsferry.

Andrew Mitchell QC and *Kennedy Talbot* (instructed by the *Solicitor for Customs and Excise*) for the Crown.

Ben Emmerson QC and *Peter Weatherby* (instructed by *Howells*, Sheffield) for the respondent.

Their Lordships took time for consideration.

13 December 2001. The following opinions were delivered.

LORD BINGHAM OF CORNHILL.
[1] My Lords, for reasons given by my noble and learned friend Lord Rodger of Earlsferry, which I have had the opportunity to read in draft and with which I am in complete agreement, I would allow this appeal and restore the order of the Crown Court.

LORD NOLAN.
[2] My Lords, I have had the opportunity of reading in draft the speech of my noble and learned friend, Lord Rodger of Earlsferry. For the reasons which he has given, I would allow this appeal and restore the order of the Crown Court.

LORD HOFFMANN.
[3] My Lords, I have had the opportunity of reading in draft the speech of my noble and learned friend, Lord Rodger of Earlsferry. For the reasons which he has given, I would allow this appeal and restore the order of the Crown Court.

LORD HUTTON.
[4] My Lords, I have had the advantage of reading in draft the speech of my noble and learned friend Lord Rodger of Earlsferry and for the reasons which he gives, with which I am in full agreement, I would allow this appeal and restore the order of the Crown Court.

LORD RODGER OF EARLSFERRY.
[5] My Lords, on 2 October 1998 at the Crown Court at Sheffield David Cadman Smith (the respondent) pled guilty to count 3 of an indictment alleging fraudulent evasion of excise duty contrary to s 170(2) of the Customs and Excise Management Act 1979. His co-accused, John Anthony Marriott, pled guilty to the same charge. The respondent was sentenced to 21 months' imprisonment and a confiscation order was made in the sum of £46,250. The respondent appealed against the confiscation order. On 16 June 2000 the Court of Appeal (Criminal Division) (Mance LJ, Newman and Burton JJ) ((2000) 164 JP 575) allowed the appeal and quashed the order.

[6] By letter dated 26 June 2000 the administrator of the chambers of counsel for Her Majesty's Customs and Excise served on the registrar of the Court of Appeal an application for leave to appeal to this House. The terms of the letter indicated that counsel would be content for the Court of Appeal to deal with the application without an oral hearing. The papers were passed to the members of the Court of Appeal who considered the matter and, on 28 July 2000, certified that the appeal involved a point of general public importance but refused leave to appeal. This decision was incorporated into an order dated 31 July 2000 but the order was not despatched or notified to the legal representative of either party until it was sent by second class post on 9 August 2000. The notice was not

a received by Customs and Excise. On 21 August their solicitors telephoned the Court of Appeal office to ask about the position in regard to their application. The office sent a copy of the order. On the basis that the Court of Appeal had reached their decision on 28 July, the 14-day period for applying to this House for leave expired on 10 August, the day after the second class letter was posted. Because they had not received the order by 10 August, the Crown were unable

b to exercise their right to apply to this House for leave to appeal.

[7] The matter was relisted before the Court of Appeal on 27 November. Despite the opposition of junior counsel for the respondent, on 20 December the Court of Appeal decided that they had power in the interests of justice to issue a fresh certificate so that the Crown could ask the House for leave to appeal. The Court of Appeal accordingly certified that the case raised the same point of law of

c public importance as they had previously certified and again refused the Crown leave to appeal against their decision of 16 June. In due course, on report from an oral appeal committee, the House gave leave to appeal.

[8] In his written case the respondent argued that the appeal raised the question whether the Court of Appeal had had jurisdiction to hear a 'renewed'

d application for leave to appeal in these circumstances. At the start of the hearing, however, Mr Emmerson QC, who appeared for the respondent, explained that he did not propose to argue that matter. He pointed out that the Court of Appeal had not certified the question as one of public importance. Moreover, in their opinion of 20 December, delivered by Mance LJ, the Court of Appeal had indicated that the court intended to adopt a different procedure which was designed to

e prevent a similar difficulty occurring in future. In these circumstances, understandably, counsel felt unable to argue that this procedural point was of general importance and therefore one that the House should consider. He was accordingly content for us simply to deal with the question certified by the Court of Appeal. On behalf of the Crown Mr Mitchell QC adopted a similar position.

f In these circumstances, your Lordships decided that it would indeed be appropriate to proceed simply on the basis that, in their order of 20 December 2000, the Court of Appeal had certified a point of public importance on which the House had then granted leave to appeal.

[9] The point of public importance which the Court of Appeal certified is in these terms:

g
> 'Whether an importer of uncustomed goods, who intends not to enter them for customs purposes and not pay any duty on them, derives a benefit under s 74 of the Criminal Justice Act 1988 through not paying the required duty at the point of importation, where the goods are forfeited by HM Customs

h following importation, before their value can be realised by the importer.'

The relevant facts which give rise to that issue can be stated fairly briefly.

[10] Between June and November 1997 John Marriott made a number of trips abroad on his own boat to smuggle cigarettes and, on one occasion, spirits into the United Kingdom. In November 1997 he was arrested and made a full

j admission. His boat was confiscated but he was granted bail. While on bail, he approached the respondent and, it appears, put up £55,000 with which the respondent bought a motor vessel, the Vertine. In the words of the judge when imposing sentence, the respondent allowed himself to be used as Marriott's shipowner and captain. The Crown did not argue that the respondent himself had put up any of the money to buy the boat. The boat was used in April 1998 on a run to Heligoland to buy cigarettes and to smuggle them into this country without paying duty. On 8 May 1998 the respondent, Marriott and another man, David Russell, set sail once more for Heligoland. Two days later, on 10 May, they *a* sailed the Vertine, laden with cigarettes, into the Humber estuary, past the customs houses at Immingham and Hull and so on for some 50 miles up the River Ouse until she reached Ocean Lock at the entrance to Goole. There is no customs house at this point. When the boat arrived at Goole, customs officers stopped and searched her. They found 1·25m cigarettes on board. The excise duty *b* payable on that quantity of cigarettes would have been £130,666·40.

[11] Pt VI of the Criminal Justice Act 1988, as amended by the Criminal Justice Act 1993 and the Proceeds of Crime Act 1995, contains the statutory provisions dealing with the confiscation of the proceeds of an offence. When the possibility of making a confiscation order arises, the court must first determine 'whether the offender has benefited from any relevant criminal conduct' (s 71(1A)). Subsections (4) *c* and (5) of s 71 provide:

'(4) For the purposes of this Part of this Act a person benefits from an offence if he obtains property as a result of or in connection with its commission and his benefit is the value of the property so obtained.

(5) Where a person derives a pecuniary advantage as a result of or in *d* connection with the commission of an offence, he is to be treated for the purposes of this Part of this Act as if he had obtained as a result of or in connection with the commission of the offence a sum of money equal to the value of the pecuniary advantage.'

In terms of s 102(1) 'property' includes 'money'. *e*

[12] When making the confiscation order against the respondent, the sentencing judge proceeded on the basis that, by evading the duty payable on the cigarettes, the respondent had derived a pecuniary advantage. In terms of sub-s (5) he was therefore to be treated as if he had obtained, as a result of the commission of the offence, a sum of money equal to the duty evaded, viz £130,666·40. In addition, *f* the judge held that, in terms of sub-s (4), the respondent had obtained the Vertine, worth £55,000, in connection with the commission of the offence. The judge therefore calculated that, for the purposes of Pt VI of the Act, the respondent had benefited to the extent of £185,666·40. The respondent's 'realisable property' (s 74(1)) was limited, however, to an apparent equity in his matrimonial home and the value of another boat which he owned, amounting in total to £46,250. *g* Applying s 71(6) the judge therefore made a confiscation order for the sum of £46,250.

[13] In the Court of Appeal counsel for the respondent argued that the judge had erred in holding that the appellant had actually evaded payment of the excise duty. Counsel contended that, since the respondent had smuggled the cigarettes *h* and had not made entry of them, duty had not been payable on them in terms of s 43 of the 1979 Act. The Court of Appeal rightly rejected this argument by observing that under reg 4(1) and (5) of the Excise Goods (Holding, Movement, Warehousing and REDS) Regulations 1992, SI 1992/3135, the excise duty point was the time when the cigarettes were charged with duty at importation and the duty became *j* payable at that point in terms of reg 6(1). The respondent did not cross-appeal against that determination. While rejecting the respondent's argument, the Court of Appeal proceeded to allow the appeal on the basis of an argument that had not been advanced to them. They held that, even though he had evaded payment of the duty, the respondent had not derived any pecuniary advantage from doing so and so had not benefited, in terms of s 71(4) of the 1988 Act, from evading the

a duty. The Crown's appeal to this House against that decision was argued on the
agreed basis that, when the Vertine passed the customs posts at Hull and
Immingham, the excise duty on the cigarettes had become payable and the
respondent had not paid it when the boat reached Goole and the customs officers
boarded it.

[14] A number of other matters are not in dispute. The customs officers at
b Goole seized both the cigarettes and the Vertine which were forfeited to the
Crown. The respondent has never paid the duty on the cigarettes. He remains
liable to pay it, however, even though he has been imprisoned for the fraudulent
evasion of the duty and even if a confiscation order is made against him.

[15] The nub of the decision of the Court of Appeal, so far as it relates to the
evasion of the excise duty, is to be found in paras 34 and 35 of the judgment
c delivered by Burton J. Having referred to the decision of the Court of Appeal
(Criminal Division) in *R v Dimsey, R v Allen* [2000] 2 All ER 142, Burton J said
((2000) 164 JP 575 at 583–584):

> '[34.] It appears to us that the position in this case is very different. It is
> true to say that the liability for duty on the cigarettes was incurred, in the
d > light of our conclusions, and was evaded, and indeed is still due because,
> although the cigarette[s] themselves were forfeited, the appellant remains
> liable to the duty on those forfeited cigarettes. But there was, and is, in the
> view of this court no benefit to the appellant as a result of that deferment.
> He has never had or sold on the cigarettes; he has not retained any sum from
e > which he could be said to have benefited and indeed he now remains liable
> for the duty. Insofar as he has not paid over a sum to the Customs and Excise
> as yet (for which he remains liable), it is, in the view of this court, difficult to
> say that there has been a benefit in connection with the commission of the
> offence, and the unpaid duty certainly could not be said, as Laws LJ so
> persuasively said in *R. v. Dimsey and Allen* in relation to the monies that the
f > appellant retained, to have been the proceeds of the offence.
> [35.] In those circumstances, we are satisfied that the position is that if the
> cigarettes had been retained by the appellant, then the duty payable would
> have been part of the profit that he made as a result of selling on the
> cigarettes. Given that the cigarettes were immediately forfeited, there remained
g > the liability for duty, but the liability which remains can neither be said to be
> the proceeds of the crime nor indeed a benefit which arises to him in
> connection with the commission of the crime.'

[16] In essence, the court held that the respondent had not derived any
pecuniary benefit, in terms of s 71(5) of the 1988 Act, from evading the payment
h of duty since he remained liable to pay the duty, but had 'never had or sold on'
the cigarettes because they had been seized by the customs officers when they
boarded the boat. The position would have been different if the respondent had
been able to sell the cigarettes, since then the duty evaded would have been part
of the profit on that sale.

j [17] The reasoning of the Court of Appeal involves a consideration of the fate
of the cigarettes: since they were taken from the respondent before he could do
anything with them, he could not be said to have derived a pecuniary advantage
from evading payment of the duty on them. That is not, however, by any means
the only possible analysis of the situation.

[18] Suppose that a captain had sailed his boat laden with cigarettes into the
Humber and had stopped at Hull to pay the excise duty before going on to Goole

where, before the cigarettes could be unloaded, the boat sank, making the *a*
waterlogged cigarettes unsellable. The captain would not only have lost the
cigarettes but would have paid the duty, which would not be recoverable.
Suppose, on the other hand, that, undetected by any customs officers, the captain
had sailed past the customs posts without paying the duty and had gone on to
Goole where the ship sank and the cigarettes were ruined. All that he would have
lost would have been the cigarettes. So, even though the cigarettes were *b*
subsequently destroyed, by evading payment of the duty, the captain would be
better off, or less badly off, than if had paid the duty. I would respectfully adopt
the view of Laws LJ in *R v Dimsey* [2000] 2 All ER 142 at 145, that 'The ordinary
and natural meaning of pecuniary advantage must surely include the case where
a debt is evaded or deferred'. In the example which I have given, therefore, the
captain would have derived a pecuniary advantage from evading payment of *c*
the excise duty, even though the cigarettes were subsequently spoiled.

[19] In the same way, it can be said that the respondent derived a pecuniary
advantage when he evaded payment of the excise duty on the cigarettes at the
customs posts. This remains the case even though the cigarettes were seized by
the customs officers when they boarded the boat at Goole. In my view, this *d*
analysis of the circumstances in which a smuggler derives a 'pecuniary advantage'
in terms of s 71(5) is to be preferred to that of the Court of Appeal.

[20] Laws LJ's interpretation of 'pecuniary advantage' as including the case
where a debt is evaded or deferred was based on his view of the ordinary and
natural meaning of the words. He went on to find support for that view in the
observations of Lord Reid in *DPP v Turner* [1973] 3 All ER 124, [1974] AC 357 on *e*
the meaning of the same words where they appeared in s 16(2)(a) of the Theft Act
1968. Mr Emmerson analysed the history of that provision in considerable detail,
in order to show why the observations of Lord Reid in *DPP v Turner* should be
regarded as an unsafe guide to the meaning of the phrase in the 1988 Act. On the
other hand, Mr Mitchell for the Crown did not cite *DPP v Turner* in support of his *f*
argument. Since, like Laws LJ, I consider that evading or deferring a debt falls
within the scope of the ordinary and natural meaning of deriving a 'pecuniary
advantage', I find it unnecessary to consider *DPP v Turner* when interpreting the
words in this case.

[21] When considering whether to make a confiscation order, the court must *g*
first determine whether the offender has benefited from any relevant criminal
conduct (s 71(1A) of the 1988 Act). Subsections (4) and (5) of s 71, which are
closely linked, show how the court is to go about this task. Subsection (4) is the
general provision which explains when, for the purposes of sub-s (1A), a person
benefits from an offence. He benefits if he obtains 'property' as a result of, or in
connection with, the commission of the offence. The measure of his benefit is the *h*
value of the property so obtained. Since 'property' includes 'money' (s 102(1)),
sub-s (4) covers the case where the offender obtains money as a result of, or in
connection with, the commission of an offence. Subsection (5), on the other
hand, deals with the situation where the offender derives a 'pecuniary advantage'
as a result of or in connection with the commission of an offence. Under sub-s (5), *j*
such a person is to be treated as if he had obtained a sum of money equal to the
value of the pecuniary advantage. Since 'a sum of money' is 'property', he is in
effect treated as having obtained 'property' and, for that reason, in terms of
sub-s (4), he has benefited from the offence: the benefit is the sum of money that
is equal to the value of the pecuniary advantage. By treating persons who derive
a pecuniary advantage as persons who have obtained property, Parliament has

a indicated that, for the purposes of confiscation orders, the same approach is to be applied to both types of offender.

[**22**] In terms of sub-s (4) the measure of the offender's benefit is the value of the property which he obtains. Section 74(5) and (6) provide:

b '(5) References in this Part of this Act to the value at any time (referred to in subsection (6) below as "the material time") of any property obtained by a person as a result of or in connection with the commission of an offence are references to—(a) the value of the property to him when he obtained it adjusted to take account of subsequent changes in the value of money; or (b) where subsection (6) below applies, the value there mentioned, whichever is the greater.

c (6) If at the material time he holds—(a) the property which he obtained (not being cash); or (b) property which, in whole or in part, directly or indirectly represents in his hands the property which he obtained, the value referred to in subsection (5)(b) above is the value to him at the material time of the property mentioned in paragraph (a) above or, as the case may be, of *d* the property mentioned in paragraph (b) above, so far as it so represents the property which he obtained, but disregarding any charging order.'

[**23**] These provisions show that, when considering the measure of the benefit obtained by an offender in terms of s 71(4), the court is concerned simply with the value of the property to him at the time when he obtained it or, if it is greater, at *e* the material time. In particular, where the offender has property representing in his hands the property which he obtained, the value to be considered is the value of the substitute property 'but disregarding any charging order'. Except, therefore, where the actual property obtained by the offender has subsequently increased in value, the court is simply concerned with its value to the offender 'when he obtained it'. It therefore makes no difference if, after he obtains it, the property *f* is destroyed or damaged in a fire or is seized by customs officers: for confiscation order purposes the relevant value is still the value of the property to the offender when he obtained it. Subsequent events are to be ignored, in just the same way as any charging order is to be ignored under sub-s (6) of s 74. Such a scheme has the merit of simplicity. If in some circumstances it can operate in a penal or even *g* a draconian manner, then that may not be out of place in a scheme for stripping criminals of the benefits of their crimes. That is a matter for the judgment of the legislature, which has adopted a similar approach in enacting legislation for the confiscation of the proceeds of drug trafficking. In that context the courts have consistently held that 'payments' received in connection with drug trafficking *h* mean gross payments rather than net profit and that the 'proceeds' of drug trafficking mean the gross sale proceeds, rather than the net profit after deducting the cost of the drug trafficking operation. I give two examples by way of illustration.

[**24**] *R v Smith (Ian)* [1989] 2 All ER 948, [1989] 1 WLR 765 concerned a confiscation order under the Drug Trafficking Offences Act 1986. The Court of *j* Appeal had to consider what was meant by 'payments or other rewards' received by the appellant in connection with drug trafficking (s 2(1) of that Act). Lord Lane CJ said:

'The words "any payments" are on the face of them clear. They must mean, indeed it is clear from the wording, any payment in money or in kind. It does not mean, in the judgment of this court, net profit derived from the

payment after the deduction of expenses, whether the expenses are those of
purchase, travelling, entertainment or otherwise. The same consideration
applies to the words "other rewards". They also have to be valued. If for
example the receiver of the drugs had rewarded the appellant by providing
him with an expensive holiday or an expensive motor car, it would not, we
think, [be] legitimate to construe the words "value of the rewards" as
meaning the value of the holiday or motor car less the business expenses
involved in earning the reward. It seems to us that the section is deliberately
worded so as to avoid the necessity, which the appellant's construction of the
section would involve, of having to carry out an accountancy exercise, which
would be quite impossible in the circumstances of this case. It may be that
the wording is draconian, and that it produces a draconian result. But it
seems to us that, if that is the case, it was a result intended by those who
framed the Act.' (See [1989] 2 All ER 948 at 951, [1989] 1 WLR 765 at 769.)

[25] In *R v Banks* [1997] 2 Cr App R (S) 110 the applicant submitted that the
sentencer had been wrong to assess the value of the proceeds of his drug
trafficking on the basis of his gross receipts as opposed to his actual profits.
Giving the judgment of the Court of Appeal and rejecting that argument, Lord
Bingham of Cornhill CJ said (at 116):

'All these provisions are in our judgment directed to trying to stamp on the
transfer of funds which have been used for the purposes of financing drug
trafficking. It would in our judgment reduce those provisions to absurdity if
the expression "proceeds" were to be read as applying only to profits made
from drug trafficking and to leave parties free to bank or transfer or conceal
or disguise sums which are the product of drug trafficking but which do not
represent profits.'

[26] If, then, the value of property obtained as a result of or in connection with
the commission of an offence is simply the value of the property to the offender
when he obtained it, even if it is subsequently destroyed, damaged or forfeited,
one would expect the same general approach to apply in the case of a pecuniary
advantage. And indeed sub-ss (4) and (5) of s 71 of the 1988 Act produce that result.
As I have already noted, the combined effect of those subsections is that the
offender who has derived a pecuniary advantage from his offence is treated as a
person who has obtained 'property' as a result of or in connection with the
commission of the offence, the 'property' in question being a sum of money equal
to the value of the pecuniary advantage. Under s 74(5) for the purposes of making
a confiscation order the value of the property is its value to the offender when he
obtained it. In this case the respondent derived a pecuniary advantage by evading
the duty at the moment when he imported the cigarettes. The sum equalling that
pecuniary advantage is treated as property obtained by the respondent at that
moment. In terms of s 74(5), its value must therefore be determined at that moment,
disregarding the fact that, soon after, the customs officers seized the cigarettes at
Goole.

[27] That being so, the fact that the respondent and his co-accused were unable
to realise the value of the contraband cigarettes is irrelevant to the question of
whether they derived a pecuniary advantage from fraudulently evading the
excise duty on them. If the cigarettes had not been seized and the respondent and
his co-accused had been able to sell them, then the money which they received
from selling them would have been 'property' in terms of s 71(4). In that situation,

a they would not only have derived a pecuniary advantage in terms of s 71(5) from evading the duty but would also have obtained property in terms of s 71(4) in the form of the sales receipts. Their benefit from the commission of the offence would have been made up of these two elements.

[**28**] Mr Emmerson sought to support the approach of the Court of Appeal to the application of s 71(5) by arguing that the question of whether an offender had *b* derived a pecuniary advantage from his offence was a question of fact, to be determined in the particular circumstances of each case. In some cases—for example, where the contraband goods were sold—the position would be clear. The same might apply where someone smuggled in a Cartier watch and subsequently wore it for some months. In this case, however, where the customs officers had forfeited the cigarettes as soon as the boat reached Goole, it was *c* impossible to say that the respondent had derived any pecuniary advantage whatever from evading the duty. Apart from all the other difficulties, this approach introduces a degree of uncertainty that is out of place in the application of a penal provision of this kind. This was highlighted by counsel's understandable reluctance to indicate how long the respondent would have had to have the *d* cigarettes after evading payment of the duty before he could be said to have derived a pecuniary advantage from his offence. Would a day have been enough? Or a week? The test to be applied in answering such a question is altogether obscure. For this reason alone, the approach advocated by Mr Emmerson would be unworkable and must be rejected.

[**29**] I am accordingly satisfied that the decision of the Court of Appeal on this *e* point was wrong. It is worth adding that, if adopted, their interpretation would go a long way to making the confiscation provisions ineffective against smugglers. After all, there will be few, if any, cases where customs officers will fail to seize contraband goods which they find in the hands of smugglers. The decision of the Court of Appeal would mean that in any such case, for the purposes of s 71(5), *f* the smugglers would derive no pecuniary benefit from evading the excise duty and so no confiscation order could be made against them. Fortunately, the terms of the legislation do not lead to that result.

[**30**] I would accordingly allow the appeal of the Crown and hold that the respondent derived a pecuniary advantage to the value of £130,666·40 as a result of fraudulently evading the excise duty on the cigarettes. On that basis I would *g* restore the order of the Crown Court dated 22 July 1999 making a confiscation order in the sum of £46,250.

[**31**] In their judgment the Court of Appeal touched only briefly on a further issue which 'was hardly pursued' by counsel for the Crown in the proceedings before them. This related to the value of the Vertine which had been purchased *h* in the respondent's name with moneys provided by Marriott. The argument for the Crown was that this was property which the respondent had obtained in connection with the commission of the offence. The Court of Appeal held that, even if the respondent had obtained any such benefit, he no longer had it at the date of the confiscation order since the Vertine had been forfeited. Mr Emmerson *j* did not seek to support this aspect of the reasoning of the Court of Appeal, which is plainly inconsistent with the terms of ss 71(4) and 74(5). Not surprisingly, in view of the lack of prominence given to the issue before them, the Court of Appeal did not certify it as one of public importance and the House did not give leave to appeal in respect of it.

[**32**] None the less during the hearing Mr Mitchell argued that the respondent had obtained the boat in connection with the commission of the offence and that

he had accordingly benefited to the extent of its value. Since I would allow the
appeal and restore the confiscation order for £46,250, which exhausts the respondent's
realisable assets, this point is entirely academic. In these circumstances I would
say only this. Even on the Crown approach, it was not entirely clear, on the
available evidence, what the value of the boat would have been to the respondent
at the time when he obtained it (s 74(5)). For that reason I should not be taken as
necessarily accepting the Crown's submission that the respondent had obtained
property worth £55,000 to him by virtue of the transaction involving the Vertine.

Appeal allowed.

Kate O'Hanlon   Barrister.

a
Ashworth Frazer Ltd v Gloucester City Council
[2001] UKHL 59

b
HOUSE OF LORDS
LORD BINGHAM OF CORNHILL, LORD BROWNE-WILKINSON, LORD HOFFMANN, LORD
SCOTT OF FOSCOTE AND LORD RODGER OF EARLSFERRY
10, 11 OCTOBER, 8 NOVEMBER 2001

Landlord and tenant – Assignment of lease – Consent not to be unreasonably withheld –
c *Landlord refusing consent to assignment on ground that prospective assignee's proposed*
use of premises would breach covenant restricting use of premises – Whether covenant
restricting use of premises – Whether landlord's refusal to consent to assignment
necessarily unreasonable if based solely on belief that proposed assignee intended to breach
user covenant.

d
The claimant was the tenant of premises partly occupied by a building which had
been erected in accordance with cl 2(iii)(a) of a development lease granted by the
predecessor in title of the defendant landlord. Clause 2(iii)(a) required the lessee
to erect within five years a building development for uses within Use Classes III,
IV or X of the Town and Country Planning (Use Classes) Order 1963. By cl 2(viii)
e of the lease, the lessee covenanted not to assign the lease without the landlord's
previous consent in writing, such consent not to be unreasonably withheld. The
tenant wished to assign the lease to M Ltd, a company which had been granted
planning permission for use of the premises for metal recycling. It therefore
sought the landlord's consent to the assignment. Such consent was refused on the
f ground that M Ltd's proposed use of the site was contrary to cl 2(iii)(a) of the lease.
In subsequent proceedings, the tenant sought a declaration that the landlord was
not entitled to refuse its consent to the assignment. The deputy judge accepted
the landlord's contention that cl 2(iii)(a) included a negative covenant that the
building would not be used for uses falling outside the specified use classes, and his
decision on that point was upheld on the tenant's appeal by the Court of Appeal.
g That court further held, however, that if the only objection to the use proposed by
the prospective assignee was that it would, or might, be a breach of the lease, it
was unreasonable for the landlord to refuse consent to an assignment. The
tenant's appeal was therefore allowed, and the landlord appealed to the House of
Lords. The tenant cross-appealed against the Court of Appeal's decision on the
h construction of cl 2(iii)(a). In the event of the cross-appeal succeeding, the landlord
accepted that it would have to consent to the assignment since the only ground on
which it had refused consent was that the proposed use would be in breach of
cl 2(iii)(a).

Held – (Lord Bingham and Lord Rodger dissenting) On its true construction,
j cl 2(iii)(a) of the lease did not restrict the uses to which the building development
could be put. The purpose of the whole of cl 2(iii) was to describe what the lessee
had positively covenanted to do, and sub-para (a) described the buildings he was
to erect. The subject matter of the whole clause was altogether different from
restrictions on the use of the premises. Those were contained in other provisions
of the lease. It followed that the user proposed by M Ltd would not have been in
breach of covenant, and it was therefore not necessary to decide whether a refusal

of consent to such use would be unreasonable. Accordingly, the tenant's
cross-appeal would be allowed (see [11], [13], [16], [21], [28], [29], [31], [32], below).   *a*

Per curiam. There is no rule of law that the belief of a landlord, however
reasonable, that the proposed assignee intends to use the demised premises for a
purpose which would give rise to a breach of a user covenant cannot, of itself, be
a ground for withholding consent to the assignment. Rather, the correct approach
is to consider what the reasonable landlord would do when asked to consent in the   *b*
particular circumstances. A reasonable landlord, faced with the prospect that the
assignment of the lease is likely to result in a breach of a user covenant, may well
decide to withhold consent. Reasonable landlords need not confine their
consideration to what will necessarily happen, and they can have regard to what
will probably happen. Although the landlord would have exactly the same powers
to prevent a breach of covenant by an assignee as by an existing tenant, a   *c*
reasonable landlord may well look at the matter more broadly and see that his
position would be significantly altered by the assignment. He may face the
prospect of becoming embroiled in legal proceedings, and a reasonable landlord is
entitled to take that prospect into account when asked to consent to the
assignment of a lease (see [1], [6], [12], [21], [26], [68]–[71], [73], [74], below); *Killick v*   *d*
Second Covent Garden Property Co Ltd [1973] 2 All ER 337 disapproved.

Notes
For unreasonable withholding of consent to an assignment and grounds of refusal
of consent, see 27(1) *Halsbury's Laws* (4th edn reissue) paras 397, 401.
                                                                                          e

Cases referred to in opinions
Ashworth Frazer Ltd v Gloucester City Council [1997] 1 EGLR 104, CA.
Bates v Donaldson [1896] 2 QB 241, [1895–9] All ER Rep 170, CA.
Bickel v Duke of Westminster [1976] 3 All ER 801, [1977] QB 517, [1976] 3 WLR 805, CA.
Blunt v Blunt [1943] 2 All ER 76, [1943] AC 517, HL.
Gibbs & Houlder Brothers & Co Ltd's Lease, Re, Houlder Brothers & Co Ltd v Gibbs   *f*
    [1925] Ch 575, [1925] All ER Rep 128, CA.
Granada TV Network Ltd v Great Universal Stores Ltd (1963) 187 EG 391.
International Drilling Fluids Ltd v Louisville Investments (Uxbridge) Ltd [1986] 1 All ER
    321, [1986] Ch 513, [1986] 2 WLR 581, CA.
Killick v Second Covent Garden Property Co Ltd [1973] 2 All ER 337, [1973] 1 WLR   *g*
    658, CA.
LTSS Print and Supply Services Ltd v Hackney LB [1976] 1 All ER 311, [1976] QB 663,
    [1976] 2 WLR 253, CA.
Packaging Centre Ltd v Poland Street Estate Ltd (1961) 178 EG 189, CA.
Pimms Ltd v Tallow Chandlers Co in the City of London [1964] 2 All ER 145, [1964]   *h*
    2 QB 547, [1964] 2 WLR 1129, CA.
Tredegar (Viscount) v Harwood [1929] AC 72, [1928] All ER Rep 11, HL.
Ward v James [1965] 1 All ER 563, [1966] 1 QB 273, [1965] 2 WLR 455, CA.
West Layton Ltd v Ford [1979] 2 All ER 657, [1979] QB 593, [1979] 3 WLR 14, CA.

Appeal   *j*
The defendant, Gloucester City Council, the landlord of premises comprising part
of land adjacent to the Cattle Market, St Oswald's Road, Gloucester, appealed
with permission of the Appeal Committee of the House of Lords given on
28 November 2000 from the order of the Court of Appeal (Waller and
Chadwick LJJ) on 21 December 1999 ((1999) 80 P & CR 11) (i) declaring that it was
unreasonable for the landlord to refuse consent to the assignment of the premises

a by the claimant tenant, Ashworth Frazer Ltd, to Mountstar Metal Corp Ltd (Mountstar) if the only objection to the use proposed by Mountstar was that it would or might be a breach of the lease under which the premises were held, and (ii) allowing to that extent the tenant's appeal from the order of David Donaldson QC, sitting as a deputy judge of the High Court, on 24 February 1999 whereby he varied an order made by Master Bowman on 9 November 1998 in

b proceedings brought by the tenant for a declaration that the landlord was not entitled to refuse its consent to the assignment. The tenant cross-appealed from the Court of Appeal's decision upholding a declaration granted by Mr Donaldson that the only uses permitted by the lease were those set out in Classes III, IV and X of the Town and Country Planning (Use Classes) Order 1963 and subject to the user restrictions contained in cl 2(vi) of the lease. The facts are set out in opinion

c of Lord Rodger of Earlsferry.

Christopher Pymont QC and *Andrew Westwood* (instructed by *Sharpe Pritchard*) for the landlord.
Kim Lewison QC and *Edward Peters* (instructed by *Rowe & Maw*) for the tenant.

d Their Lordships took time for consideration.

8 November 2001. The following opinions were delivered.

e **LORD BINGHAM OF CORNHILL.**
[1] My Lords, there are before the House an appeal by the Gloucester City Council (the landlord) and a cross-appeal by Ashworth Frazer Ltd (the tenant). On the issues arising in both the appeal and the cross-appeal I am in complete agreement with the opinion of my noble and learned friend Lord Rodger of Earlsferry, whose account of the facts and background I gratefully adopt.

f

The landlord's appeal
[2] The combined effect of cl 2(viii) of the lease and s 1 of the Landlord and Tenant Act 1988 is in my opinion clear. The tenant covenants not to assign the demised land or any part thereof (other than to a subsidiary of the tenant). But the covenant is not absolute. The tenant may assign with the previous consent in

g writing of the landlord. The landlord's consent is not to be unreasonably withheld in the case of a respectable and responsible assignee being proposed. Where the tenant makes written application for consent the landlord owes the tenant a duty within a reasonable time to give consent, or give consent subject to notified conditions, or refuse consent for notified reasons. If the reasonableness of any

h condition imposed by the landlord or the reasonableness of the landlord's withholding of consent is questioned, the landlord must show that the condition or the withholding was reasonable.
[3] When a difference is to be resolved between landlord and tenant following

j the imposition of a condition (an event which need not be separately considered) or a withholding of consent, effect must be given to three overriding principles. The first, as expressed by Balcombe LJ in *International Drilling Fluids Ltd v Louisville Investments (Uxbridge) Ltd* [1986] 1 All ER 321 at 325, [1986] Ch 513 at 520 is that—

'a landlord is not entitled to refuse his consent to an assignment on grounds which have nothing whatever to do with the relationship of landlord and tenant in regard to the subject matter of the lease.'

The same principle was earlier expressed by Sargant LJ in *Re Gibbs & Houlder Brothers & Co Ltd's Lease, Houlder Brothers & Co Ltd v Gibbs* [1925] Ch 575 at 587, [1925] All ER Rep 128 at 134:

> '... in a case of this kind the reason must be something affecting the subject matter of the contract which forms the relationship between the landlord and the tenant, and ... it must not be something wholly extraneous and completely dissociated from the subject matter of the contract.'

While difficult borderline questions are bound to arise, the principle to be applied is clear.

[4] Secondly, in any case where the requirements of the first principle are met, the question whether the landlord's conduct was reasonable or unreasonable will be one of fact to be decided by the tribunal of fact. There are many reported cases. In some the landlord's withholding of consent has been held to be reasonable (as, for example, in *Pimms Ltd v Tallow Chandlers Co in the City of London* [1964] 2 All ER 145, [1964] 2 QB 547 and *Bickel v Duke of Westminster* [1976] 3 All ER 801, [1977] QB 517), in others unreasonable (as, for example, in *Bates v Donaldson* [1896] 2 QB 241, [1895–9] All ER Rep 170, *Re Gibbs & Houlder Brothers & Co Ltd's Lease* and the *International Drilling* case). These cases are of illustrative value. But in each the decision rested on the facts of the particular case and care must be taken not to elevate a decision made on the facts of a particular case into a principle of law. The correct approach was very clearly laid down by Lord Denning MR in *Bickel's* case [1976] 3 All ER 801 at 804–805, [1977] QB 517 at 524.

[5] Thirdly, the landlord's obligation is to show that his conduct was reasonable, not that it was right or justifiable. As Danckwerts LJ held in the *Pimms'* case [1964] 2 All ER 145 at 151, [1964] 2 QB 547 at 564:

> '... it is not necessary for the landlords to prove that the conclusions which led them to refuse consent were justified, if they were conclusions which might be reached by a reasonable man in the circumstances ...'

Subject always to the first principle outlined above, I would respectfully endorse the observation of Viscount Dunedin in *Viscount Tredegar v Harwood* [1929] AC 72 at 78, [1928] All ER Rep 11 at 14 that one 'should read reasonableness in the general sense'. There are few expressions more routinely used by British lawyers than 'reasonable', and the expression should be given a broad, commonsense meaning in this context as in others.

[6] The Court of Appeal held itself to be precluded by *Killick v Second Covent Garden Property Co Ltd* [1973] 2 All ER 337, [1973] 1 WLR 658 from holding on the facts of this case that the belief of the landlord, however reasonable, that the proposed assignee intended to use the demised premises for a purpose which would give rise to a breach of the user covenant was of itself a ground for withholding consent to assignment (see (1999) 80 P & CR 11 at 23, per Chadwick LJ). Lord Rodger has fully analysed that decision. I would myself criticise it on three grounds. First, it purported to treat as a question of law what was in truth a question of fact. Secondly, in holding that the landlord's withholding of consent was unreasonable because the outcome which he wished to avoid was not a necessary consequence of the assignment (which was, it seems clear, based on the landlord's contention (see [1973] 2 All ER 337 at 339, [1973] 1 WLR 658 at 660, 661)) the court accepted much too high a test. A reasonable landlord may seek to avoid not only an undesirable outcome which must occur but also one which he reasonably fears may well occur, not least where that involves the prospect of

a unwelcome litigation. Thirdly, the decision as expressed gave quite inadequate weight to the user covenant in a lease. The lease is, after all, the contract between landlord and tenant, a contract with special characteristics and subject to special rules but a contract all the same. It records what the parties respectively agree to do and not to do. Unless a term is discharged or consensually varied or revoked, a party is ordinarily bound by what he has agreed, even if (with the benefit of *b* hindsight) he regrets his bargain. The contract is, as civil lawyers put it, the law between the parties, and it would rarely be right to hold that a landlord was unreasonable in withholding consent to an assignment which in his reasonable judgment would or might well lead to a breach of covenant. *Killick's* case should no longer be treated as authoritative.

[7] The reasoning of the deputy judge was in my view correct on this issue. *c* The Court of Appeal's decision was vitiated by its reliance on *Killick's* case. I would restore the decision of the judge.

The tenant's cross-appeal

[8] The tenant's cross-appeal turns on a short question of construction: are the *d* words 'for uses within Use Classes III IV or X of the Town and Country (Use Classes) Order 1963' in cl 2(iii)(a) of the lease to be understood as restricting the uses to which the building development described by the clause might be put? On this question I have the misfortune to disagree with the majority of the House but the consolation of agreeing with the deputy judge, both members of the Court of Appeal and my noble and learned friend Lord Rodger.

e [9] By cl 2(iii)(a) the tenant covenants to commence and complete a building development. Such building development must among other things be—

'in conformity with all licences permissions and consents required by bye-laws regulations planning provisions orders and statutes and in conformity with detailed plans elevations sections and specifications as shall previously be *f* approved by the City Architect.'

Since the landlord is the local planning authority, it thus has full control over the physical design, size, appearance, layout and location of the development. The use classes in the Town and Country (Use Classes) Order 1963, SI 1963/708 do not describe buildings. They describe uses. There can have been no conceivable *g* purpose in making reference to those use classes other than for the purpose of restricting the permitted user to those classes, expressed as they are in terms which will be as readily intelligible at the end of the lease as at the beginning. It is idle to speculate what use might be made of buildings other than those comprised in the development to which cl 2(iii)(a) applies in the absence of evidence to suggest that *h* the site will accommodate any significant buildings once the building development described in cl 2(iii)(a) has been completed. The inclusion and terms of cl 2(vi) have been fully explained by the landlord's earlier grant of leases to tenants carrying on the miscellaneous activities there specified and its desire to protect those tenants against competition. Clause 2(xiii) does not in my opinion throw light on the construction of cl 2(iii)(a). If the reference to the use classes in cl *j* 2(iii)(a) does not apply to the user of the building development it is entirely otiose.

[10] I would for my part dismiss the tenant's cross-appeal.

LORD BROWNE-WILKINSON.

[11] My Lords, for the reasons given in the speeches to be delivered by my noble and learned friends, Lord Hoffmann and Lord Scott of Foscote, that the cross-appeal should be allowed.

[12] As to the appeal, I agree with the speeches of all your Lordships that if, contrary to my view, cl 2(iii)(a) of the lease contains a restriction on user, the city council would not necessarily have acted unreasonably in refusing their consent to a proposed assignment on the grounds that the assignee proposed to commit a breach of such restriction.

LORD HOFFMANN.

[13] My Lords, there are two issues in this appeal. The first is whether the use of the premises for metal recycling would be a breach of covenant. The second question is whether a refusal of consent on that ground would be unreasonable.

[14] Since the first question turns entirely upon the construction of the language of the lease and raises no question of general public importance, I can be brief in my reasons. I gratefully adopt the recital of the facts and relevant provisions of the lease set out in the speech of my noble and learned friend Lord Rodger of Earlsferry.

[15] The provision relied upon as prohibiting the intended use is a phrase in cl 2(iii)(a):

'The Lessee hereby covenants with the Corporation ... to complete ... the erection on the demised land [of] ... a building development for uses within Use Classes III IV or X of the Town and Country (Use Classes) Order 1963 together with all necessary roads [etc] ... (hereinafter called "the works" ...'

[16] The landlord contends that the words 'a building development for uses within Use Classes III IV or X' means not, or not only, that the building must be suitable for such uses but that during the term of the lease it may be used only for such uses. But I find it impossible to construe cl 2(iii)(a) as having any application to the use which may be made of the premises. The purpose of the whole of cl 2(iii) is to describe what the tenant has positively covenanted to do. Subparagraph (a) describes the buildings he is to erect, (b) the road and cattle grid he is to build, (c) the materials he is to use (d) the use to be made of the earth, clay, gravel and sand displaced by the construction, (e) the disposal of antiquities he may find and (f) the fences to be built and maintained. The subject matter of the whole clause is altogether different from restrictions on the use of the premises. They are contained in cll 2(v), (vi) and (xi).

[17] The argument that a restriction on user has been embedded in the description of the premises to be constructed is based upon the argument that the lease is badly drafted. But that seems to me to beg the question. It is only badly drafted if one assumes that cl 2(iii)(a) was intended to restrict the use of the premises. To slip a rather ambiguous user clause into the middle of a description of the buildings would indeed be poor drafting. On the other hand, if one assumes that the parties intended in orthodox fashion to describe the buildings to be erected in one clause and the restrictions on the use of the premises in another, there is nothing particularly bad about the drafting. Clause 2(iii)(a) may be somewhat prolix or even contain redundant material. But few leases could escape that reproach.

[18] The argument from redundancy is that since cl 2(iii)(a) provides that the plans for the buildings must have been approved by the city architect, there was no reason why it should go on to stipulate that they should be suitable for any particular use. The city architect would in any case have had full control over the kind of buildings which could be erected.

[19] Even if this were true, I would be more inclined to accept some degree of redundancy rather than assume that the draftsman had muddled up the question

a of what the tenant had to build within five years (which was part of the consideration for the lease) with the question of what use could be made of the premises during its 114-year term. But I am far from satisfied that it is true. We have very little evidence of the factual background against which the lease was executed. The parties may already have had some mutual understanding about the buildings to be erected but we have no idea of how far this had gone. The city

b architect could not unreasonably withhold approval of the plans. Perhaps the reference to the use classes was intended to pre-empt argument over whether it would be reasonable to object to buildings which were not suitable for those uses. These matters are entirely speculative. So I do not think that the argument from redundancy has enough weight to displace an interpretation based on the conventional structure of the clauses.

c   [20] There are other factors which point against cl 2(iii)(a) containing a user clause. First, it is common ground that it would apply only to the buildings erected pursuant to the covenant. But those buildings did not cover the entire 14.5 acre site. There was room for new ones and no covenant against new buildings. What would be the commercial purpose of prohibiting a use of the old buildings when

d a new one erected on vacant land could be used for that purpose? Secondly, it seems odd to define permissible user in a 114-year lease by reference to use classes in a 1963 statutory instrument. Such a description of the buildings makes perfectly good sense in a covenant which was intended to be spent within five years. But was it contemplated that the parties in 2080 would have to research mid-twentieth century planning law to discover the permissible user? Although it is fair to say

e that this might be necessary if the premises had to be reinstated after a fire under cl 2(xiii). Thirdly, the covenant is absolute. The landlord is under no obligation to consent to a change, whether this would be reasonable or not. The tenant's only escape is through the very limited jurisdiction of the court to vary such covenants under s 84 of the Law of Property Act 1925. Would the parties have been likely to

f intend such restrictions to endure for over a century? Fourthly, the landlord was the planning authority. In that capacity, it could prevent any use which was undesirable on planning grounds. This control was supplemented by cl 2(vi), which contained prohibitions to protect existing tenants against competition, which could probably not have been justified on planning grounds. In combination, planning control and cl 2(vi) constitute a rational system for controlling the use of

g the premises.
    [21] For these reasons I would allow the tenant's cross-appeal. I also agree that the appeal should be allowed for the reasons given in the opinions of my noble learned friends Lord Bingham of Cornhill and Lord Rodger of Earlsferry.

h **LORD SCOTT OF FOSCOTE.**
    [22] My Lords, I have had the advantage of reading in draft the opinion of my noble and learned friend, Lord Rodger of Earlsferry and gratefully adopt his recital of the relevant facts. As is made plain in his opinion there are two issues which arise on this appeal. One is a short issue of construction of one of the lessee's

j covenants in the lease dated 28 April 1969 under which Gloucester City Council demised a site consisting of 14.5 acres of industrial development land to a developer for a term of 114 years from 25 December 1968. Clause 2(iii)(a) of the lease is expressed as a positive covenant requiring the lessee within five years to commence and complete the development of the site by erecting industrial buildings in conformity with plans to be approved by the city architect. The subclause describes the required development as 'a building development for uses within Use Classes III IV or X of the Town and Country (Use Classes) Order 1963'.

Class III in the Town and Country (Use Classes) Order 1963, SI 1963/708 was 'Use
as a light industrial building', Class IV was 'Use as a general industrial building' and   a
Class X was 'Use as a wholesale warehouse or repository'. The issue of
construction is whether cl 2(iii)(a), although in form a positive covenant requiring
the lessee to construct a particular type of building development, contains also, by
implication, a negative covenant by the lessee not to use the buildings for any use
other than a use falling within one or other of the three specified use classes. At   b
first instance the deputy judge, Mr Donaldson QC and, on appeal, the Court of
Appeal ((1999) 80 P & CR 11) decided that cl 2(iii)(a) did impose this negative user
covenant. Had that been the only issue in the case I am sure that leave to appeal
to this House would not have been granted. But the second issue raises an
important point of general principle.

[23] In *Killick v Second Covent Garden Property Co Ltd* [1973] 2 All ER 337 at 339,   c
[1973] 1 WLR 658 at 661 (per Stamp LJ), the Court of Appeal agreed that 'a
landlord may reasonably refuse consent to an assignment if the assignment would
necessarily involve a breach of covenant' but did not agree that, if the proposed
assignment went ahead, 'there would as a necessary consequence be a breach of
the user covenant' and held that, in the circumstances, the landlord had   d
unreasonably withheld consent to the assignment.

[24] In the Court of Appeal in the present case Chadwick LJ said ((1999) 80
P & CR 11 at 23):

> 'In my view the decision in the *Killick* case precludes this court from holding
> that the belief of the landlord, however reasonable, that the proposed   e
> assignee intends to use the demised premises for a purpose which would give
> rise to a breach of a user covenant is, of itself, a ground for withholding
> consent to assignment.'

[25] The second issue, therefore, is whether, if that is indeed what *Killick's* case
decided, *Killick's* case was rightly decided and, if it was not, whether the council   f
had unreasonably refused its consent to the proposed assignment by Ashworth
Frazer Ltd to Mountstar Metal Corp Ltd. It was this issue that led to leave to
appeal to this House being granted.

The second issue

[26] On this issue I am in respectful and complete agreement with what Lord   g
Rodger has said in paras [29] to [43] of his opinion. I concur in his conclusions,
expressed in para [41], and in his reasons for reaching them. I agree also with the
reasons given by my noble and learned friend, Lord Bingham of Cornhill, for
reaching the same conclusions. Those conclusions would lead to this appeal being
allowed if, but not unless, the first issue, the issue of construction, had been   h
correctly decided in the council's favour. To that issue I now turn.

The construction issue

[27] The issue is a short one. It does not involve any point of principle and is
not assisted by reference to any authorities. The lease was a building development
lease for a term of 114 years. It was a lease which, over the first five years, was   j
going to involve the lessee in the expenditure of a considerable capital sum in
carrying out the proposed development. The rent for the first seven years of the
term was nil, a peppercorn; for the period from 1970 to 1989 the yearly rent was
£9,425 and thereafter it was to be either the £9,425 or 8% of the rack-rents
receivable by the lessee from the developed site, whichever were higher. The
relevance of these rental provisions is that they demonstrate that both parties had

a   a commercial interest in the lessee being able to develop the site and sublet, or
    assign, the developed plots to the best financial advantage. User restrictions would
    naturally be important in that they would restrict the types of business that could
    be carried on on the various plots forming part of the development.

    [28] It is obvious, and hardly worth saying, that the ability of the lessee to
    exploit the developed site, or of any sublessee or assignee to exploit any of the
b   individual plots, to its best commercial advantage would depend not only on the
    user covenants in the lease but also on the user permitted under the applicable
    planning law. It is very usual to find in a lease a tenant's covenant not to use the
    property in a manner in breach of planning law. In a development lease granted
    by a private lessor it would be very surprising not to find such a covenant. In this
    lease, however, there is no such covenant. But this is not surprising. The council,
c   the lessor, was the planning authority. It was able, wearing its planning authority
    hat, to exercise control over the use to which the various plots on the site could be
    put. In cl 2(vi), the lease imposed specific user restraints on the lessee. These
    restraints had nothing to do with planning law but were imposed in order, it seems
    fairly clear, to protect from competition existing businesses located in the vicinity
d   of the 14.5 acres. In my opinion, a development lessee, taking a 114-year lease in
    the form of the lease with which your Lordships are concerned, would be entitled
    to suppose that, provided the user restrictions in cl 2(vi) were observed, the
    industrial buildings he erected could be used for any use from time to time
    permitted under the planning law.

    [29] It is argued that unless the reference in cl 2(iii)(a) is construed so as to
e   impose a negative user covenant, additional to that in cl 2(vi) and restricting the
    permitted user to user within Use Classes III, IV or X, no sensible purpose could
    be attributed to the reference in the subclause to those use classes. I am in
    respectful disagreement both with the premise to this argument and with the
    conclusion. The use classes describe the type of building development that the
f   lessee is to commence and complete within the five years. The requirement that
    the city architect's approval to the lessee's building plans is not to be unreasonably
    withheld is thereby given a degree of definition that would otherwise be lacking.
    His refusal to approve plans that did not relate to a development consistent with
    those uses could not be challenged on unreasonableness grounds. If the references
    to the three use classes had not been included the lessee might have proposed a
g   more profitable development involving uses outside the three use classes and then
    sought to categorise as unreasonable the city architect's refusal to approve the
    plans. So there is, in my opinion, no cogency in the premise that there was no
    sensible commercial purpose in the reference to the three use classes other than
    the imposition of an unexpressed negative user covenant. But even if, contrary to
h   my view, the premise had been sound, the conclusion that a negative user
    covenant should be implied does not, in my opinion, follow. The implied negative
    covenant is not necessary to give business efficacy to the subclause. If the
    subclause is accorded its literal meaning and read simply as a positive covenant to
    build, it lacks nothing in efficacy. Nor is the proposed implied term one that can
    be justified by the 'Oh of course the parties must have intended it' test. I would,
j   for my part, find it easier to give an 'Oh of course' answer if asked whether the
    parties intended the user restrictions to be confined to those found in sub-cl (vi).

    [30] In my opinion, however, the strongest argument against the proposed
    implied term is that to imply into the lease an unexpressed user covenant would
    be thoroughly unfair to Ashworth Frazer Ltd, the assignee of a part of the
    developed site, who can reasonably have supposed that the subclauses in cl 2
    meant what they said, that the building obligations in sub-cl (iii) were spent (unless

rebuilding after a fire became necessary) and that the user restrictions were to be found in sub-cl (vi). If the council wanted additional contractual user restrictions to bolster the planning control that they could anyway exercise they should, in my opinion, have included the restrictions in their lease. They did not do so expressly and, in my opinion, cannot cure their failure by contending for an implied user restriction.

[31] In my opinion, for the reasons I have given, the user proposed by Mountstar would not have been in breach of any covenant contained in the lease. Nor would it have been in breach of the planning law. Whether in the circumstances the council's refusal of leave to assign was unreasonable or whether the council can excuse their refusal on the ground that they were proceeding on a genuine and reasonable, although mistaken, view as to the effect of cl 2(iii)(a) is an issue of fact which has yet to be decided.

[32] I would allow the council's appeal on the *Killick* point, allow Ashworth Frazer Ltd's cross-appeal on the construction point and set aside the declarations made by the first instance judge and by the Court of Appeal. I would make a declaration that cl 2(iii)(a) of the lease does not constitute a covenant by the lessee not to use the premises for any use other than those set out in Classes III, IV and X of the 1963 Order and remit to the Chancery Division the question whether in all the circumstances the council's refusal to consent to the assignment to Mountstar was unreasonable and, if so, what, if any consequences as to damages should follow.

LORD RODGER OF EARLSFERRY.

The facts

[33] My Lords, by a lease dated 28 April 1969 the Mayor, Aldermen and Citizens of the City of Gloucester, the predecessors of the appellants, Gloucester City Council (the council), demised to Mackenzie Hill Ltd 14.5 acres of land at the Cattle Market, St Oswald's Road, Gloucester. The lease was to run for 114 years from 25 December 1968. No premium was payable and until 28 April 1970 the lessee was to pay only a peppercorn rent. From then until 25 December 1989 the lessee was to pay a yearly rent of £9,425, after which the rent was to be determined in accordance with the rent review provisions in cl 4. As the absence of a premium and the low level of the initial rent suggest, the lease was a development lease under which, in terms of sub-cl 2(iii)(a), the lessee required to begin erecting a building development on the demised land within a year and to complete the development within five years. Although it was apparently envisaged that the lessee would sublet the development to various subtenants, this did not happen. Rather, the development was severed. In particular, in 1973 Mackenzie Hill Ltd transferred 0.45 hectares of the property in the lease (the premises) to Kentron Plastics Ltd. Part of the premises is occupied by a building erected in terms of the lessee's obligation under sub-cl 2(iii)(a). On 24 March 1993 Kentron Plastics transferred the premises to Ashworth Frazer Ltd (the respondents).

[34] By cl 2(viii) the lessee covenants with the council not—

'to assign the demised land or any part thereof (other than to a subsidiary of the Lessee) to any person without the previous consent in writing of the Corporation such consent not to be unreasonably withheld in the case of a respectable and responsible assignee being proposed ...'

[35] At some time before November 1996 Mountstar Metal Corp Ltd (Mountstar), who were not, of course, tenants under the lease, applied to the council as

a planning authority for planning permission to use the premises, described as 'the former Kentron Plastics site', for metal recycling. The council refused that application in November 1996 but on 26 February 1997 Mountstar submitted an amended application and on 13 May 1997 the council granted planning permission for the 'use of land and building for metal recycling and erection of boundary fencing and storage bay enclosures'. To judge from the correspondence between

b Mountstar's agents and the planning department, while the two applications were being considered, the council's planning officials, at least, must have been given a considerable amount of information about Mountstar's proposed operations on the premises.

[36] Two months later, on 16 July 1997, solicitors acting on behalf of the respondents, as lessee, wrote to the council saying:

c

> 'Our client wishes to assign the Lease to Mountstar Metal Corporation Limited and accordingly we are applying to you for consent to the assignment.'

Counsel referred to only one other letter dealing with the matter at this time. It is

d from Mr David Hook, the council's senior surveyor and valuer, to the solicitors and is dated 16 September 1997. Mr Hook refers to a previous letter dated 12 September and continues:

> 'The City Secretary and Solicitor having regard to the User Clause in the Lease is of the opinion that Mountstar Metal's proposed use for the site is

e > contrary to the existing User Clause and therefore he is not prepared to exercise delegated authority to approve an assignment which would be in breach of the User Clause. Gloucester City Council as landlords will not therefore be approving your request.'

In the present proceedings against the council the respondents seek a declaration

f that the council are not entitled to refuse their consent to the assignment, a second declaration that the respondents are entitled to assign the lease to Mountstar without the further consent of the council and damages. It is agreed that Mountstar are a respectable and responsible company.

g *The issues*
[37] Before this House and the Court of Appeal ((1999) 80 P & CR 11) there were two main issues in dispute between the parties. As Mr Hook made clear in his letter, the council refused to approve the respondents' application for consent to assign the lease of the premises to Mountstar because they considered that Mountstar's proposed use was 'contrary to the existing User Clause'. It is common

h ground that Mr Hook was referring to sub-cl 2(iii)(a):

> 'The Lessee hereby covenants with the Corporation as follows:-
> (iii)(a) to commence within a period of One year from the date hereof and within the period of five years from the date hereof to complete the erection on the demised land fit for immediate occupation and use in a substantial and

j > workmanlike manner with good quality materials and in conformity with all licences permissions and consents required by bye-laws regulations planning provisions orders and statutes and in conformity with detailed plans elevations sections and specifications as shall previously be approved by the City Architect (such approval not to be unreasonably withheld and be given within one month of the submission of the said plans and specifications) a building development for uses within Use Classes III IV or X of the Town and

Country (Use Classes) Order 1963 together with all necessary roads amenity
areas cattle grids fences drains and sewers (hereinafter called "the works"   a
which expression shall also be deemed to mean any work which may from
time to time be necessary for the replacement maintenance alterations or
repair of such buildings erections or constructions) …'

The council contend that this covenant includes a negative covenant that the   b
buildings erected in terms of this obligation will not be used for uses falling outside
Use Classes III, IV or X of the Town and Country Planning (Use Classes) Order
1963, SI 1963/708. For their part the respondents submit that the subclause simply
imposes an obligation to erect buildings of a certain kind and contains no negative
covenant restricting their use. The only restrictions on use, they contend, are to be
found in cl 2(v) and (vi). On the basis of their own preferred interpretation of   c
sub-cl 2(iii)(a), however, the council refused consent to the respondents' application
to assign the lease to Mountstar because they considered that Mountstar's
proposed use of the premises for recycling scrap metal was not one of the uses
permitted under sub-cl 2(iii)(a) and so would be in breach of the covenant in that
subclause. The respondents contend that, in terms of cl 2(viii), it was unreasonable   d
of the council to withhold consent on this ground alone.

[38] Mr David Donaldson QC, sitting as a deputy judge, found in favour of the
council on the interpretation of the covenant in sub-cl 2(iii)(a). He also made a
declaration that, even if the user proposed by Mountstar would constitute a breach
of the lease, that does not of itself render unreasonable the council's objection to
the proposed assignment to Mountstar. The respondents appealed and the   e
decision of the Court of Appeal is reported as *Ashworth Frazer Ltd v Gloucester City
Council* (1999) 80 P & CR 11. The Court of Appeal (Waller and Chadwick LJJ)
agreed with the deputy judge on the interpretation point and therefore left
undisturbed his first declaration that the only uses permitted by the lease are those
set out in the relevant use classes and subject to the user restrictions in cl 2(vi). As   f
Chadwick LJ noted (at 24–25), the particular point on which the deputy judge had
focused in the second of his declarations was not argued before the Court of
Appeal where the contention for the respondents was simply that, if the only
objection to the use proposed by Mountstar is that it would, or might, be a breach
of the lease, it is unreasonable for the council to refuse consent to an assignment
to Mountstar on that ground alone. In those circumstances, since it had not been   g
challenged, the Court of Appeal were content to leave the deputy judge's second
declaration standing. But on the consent point, as argued before them, the Court
of Appeal held in favour of the respondents. They therefore allowed the appeal
and added a third declaration to the effect that, if the only objection to the use
proposed by the prospective assignee is that it would, or might, be a breach of the   h
lease, it is unreasonable for the landlord to refuse consent to an assignment on that
ground alone. The council have appealed against the order of the Court of Appeal
in respect of this third declaration while the respondents have cross-appealed in
respect of the deputy judge's first declaration which the Court of Appeal left
undisturbed. The point in the second of the deputy judge's declarations was not   j
reopened before this House.

[39] The council accept that, if the respondents succeed in their cross-appeal,
the council will have to give consent to the assignment since the only ground on
which they refused consent was that the proposed use would be in breach of
sub-cl 2(iii)(a). On the other hand Mr Pymont QC emphasised that this concession
did not imply any further concession that, in refusing consent on the basis of their
interpretation of the subclause, the council had acted unreasonably for the

a purposes of the respondents' claim for damages for breach of duty under s 4 of the Landlord and Tenant Act 1988.

[40] I turn to the point of interpretation raised in the cross-appeal since, logically, it arises first.

Interpretation of sub-cl 2(iii)(a)

b [41] No one could pretend that the lease is well drafted. It comes as no surprise to find that the rent review clause was indeed the subject of earlier proceedings between the same parties in the Court of Appeal and that the judges were divided as to the proper interpretation (see *Ashworth Frazer Ltd v Gloucester City Council* [1997] 1 EGLR 104). History repeats itself, for it is my misfortune to find that I indeed differ from the majority of your Lordships as to the interpretation of the
c terms now in question. Because of the drafting, there is a risk that, whatever interpretation is adopted of a particular provision, there may be unsatisfactory aspects when the terms of the lease as a whole are considered. I therefore prefer to begin by concentrating on the terms of sub-cl 2(iii)(a) before considering how the subclause fits into the overall scheme of the lease.

d [42] Subclause 2(iii)(a) embodies what is perhaps the principal obligation of the lessee, to complete within five years—

> 'the erection on the demised land fit for immediate occupation and use ... a building development for uses within Use Classes III IV or X ... together with all necessary roads amenity areas cattle grids fences drains and sewers ...'

e If stripped down in this way the covenant is remarkably vague since it does not spell out the scale of the building development. It does not specify, for instance, how many buildings are to be constructed or how they are to be laid out on the demised land. But, of course—even though there is no evidence on the point—it can safely be said that the developers could hardly have entered into the lease
f unless these matters had been explored with the council so that the developers knew what their financial and other obligations under the lease would be. The subclause contains provisions which would in practice have resulted in these matters being clarified. First, it envisages that the development will be 'in conformity with all licences permissions and consents required by bye-laws regulations planning provisions orders and statutes'. In other words it must
g comply with all the public law requirements that apply to it. Since the council were also the local planning authority, they would be responsible, with that hat, for considering any planning applications relating to the development. And, obviously, the finalised detailed planning consent would deal with various aspects not only of the siting of the buildings making up the development but also of the
h design, including the height and appearance, of those buildings. The subclause next envisages that the development will be built to detailed plans approved by the city architect. And again that provision would mean that, through their architect, the council would have control over the design, including the detailed design, of the buildings to be erected. Taken together, these provisions would in my view constitute a more than sufficient mechanism for specifying the form of the
j building development that was to be erected.

[43] The contention for the respondents is, however, that when the parties agreed that the development was to be fit for immediate occupation and use 'for uses within Use Classes III IV or X of the Town and Country (Use Classes) Order 1963' they were simply concerned to give some (further) indication of the type of building to be erected, rather than to specify the uses to which the buildings were to be put after completion. In other words the parties were doing no more than

agreeing that the buildings comprising the development were to be of a form that
would be suitable for the uses permitted under those use classes. So, once the   *a*
buildings were up, any lessee or sublessee could immediately proceed to use them
for any purpose whatever, provided only that they could obtain the necessary
planning and other consents.

[44] Confining myself, for the moment, to the terms of sub-cl (iii)(a), in
agreement with the deputy judge and the Court of Appeal, I find the respondents'   *b*
construction unpersuasive. The covenant is concerned with the development as
a whole: the lessee's obligation is to complete a building development which will
be fit for immediate occupation and use for the uses in the relevant use classes.
Given the provisions which the covenant already contains about planning
permission and the city architect's consent, it is hard to see why the parties should
have considered it necessary to insert yet another provision dealing with the   *c*
design of the buildings. But, even supposing that they had wished to do so, a
requirement that the development was to be fit 'for uses' in these use classes
would add nothing, so far as design was concerned, to the immediately preceding
provisions in the same subclause. At best, therefore, it would be superfluous. This
is only to be expected because, under the planning system, use classes are   *d*
concerned with the use, not with the form of buildings. Their whole purpose is
indeed to describe a range within which the use of premises can be changed
without the need to make a fresh application for planning permission. The
descriptions are couched accordingly. In the 1963 Order, Class III was 'Use as a
light industrial building for any purpose', Class IV 'Use as a general industrial
building for any purpose' and Class X 'Use as a wholesale warehouse or repository   *e*
for any purpose'. Under the lease these broad descriptions would indicate
satisfactorily the uses to which the buildings in the development were to be put.
But in themselves they would tell the parties nothing about the form of the
buildings to be erected and certainly nothing that would add to what would be
specified by the council planning officials and the city architect. The respondents'   *f*
construction therefore robs the words in question of all real practical effect. For
that very reason I regard it as unsatisfactory.

[45] Looking at the covenant in sub-cl 2(iii)(a) in isolation, therefore, I prefer
what I regard as, in any event, the more natural construction of the wording. On
that approach the words 'fit for immediate occupation and use ... for uses within
Use Classes III, IV or X' are intended to set out the uses to which the building   *g*
development—which is ex hypothesi designed to meet the council's planning
requirements and based on plans approved by the city architect—is to be put. The
buildings can be used for light industry or general industry or as warehouses or
repositories—and, therefore, for no other purpose. While Mr Pymont QC did not
argue that the words in sub-cl (iii)(a) imposed a positive covenant on the lessee to   *h*
occupy the buildings for the specified uses, he did submit that the covenant against
other uses was an express covenant. In my view, however, any covenant against
other uses must be derived by implication from the positive specification of the
uses for which the development is to be fit.

[46] So far I have proceeded simply on the basis of the words in sub-cl 2(iii)(a).
But the subclause has, of course, to be considered within the wider context of the   *j*
lease as a whole. As Mr Lewison QC emphasised, sub-cl (iii)(a) is found in that part
of cl 2 which is concerned with the lessee's obligations in relation to the erection
of the building development 'together with all necessary roads amenity areas
cattle grids fences drains and sewers'—taken together, they are called 'the works'.
The remaining subclauses of cl 2(iii) all deal with matters, of a somewhat physical
nature, which may arise while the works are being carried out within the five-year

a period allowed for their completion. The only exception is the obligation in sub-cl (f) 'as soon as practicable to erect construct and thereafter maintain on the boundaries of the demised land good and sufficient stock proof fences in all respects to the reasonable satisfaction of the city architect' where the obligation to 'maintain' the fences would continue beyond the five-year period. Even allowing for that limited exception, cl 2(iii) as a whole is concerned with the lessee's
b obligations to carry out the development within the five-year period.

[47] If the developers completed the development within five years by constructing the various buildings as specified in the planning and other consents and in the plans approved by the city architect, then they would have complied with the covenant in sub-cl 2(iii)(a). It is apparent, however, that the parties recognised that buildings other than those to be built under sub-cl 2(iii)(a) might
c be erected on the demised land. This emerges, for instance, from cl 2(ix) with its obligation to repair and keep in good tenantable repair 'the demised land and every part thereof and all additions thereto and all other buildings *now or hereafter to be erected thereon* (my emphasis), as well as from the differing words to the same effect to be found in cl 2(x), (xi) and (xii). Similarly, by cl 2(xiii) the lessee
d undertakes inter alia—

'as often as all or any buildings erection or structure of any part of the same *now or hereafter erected* on the demised land shall be destroyed or damaged by fire forthwith to rebuild and reinstate the same under the surveillance and to the reasonable satisfaction of the City Architect and in all respects in
e accordance with the provisions of Clause 2(iii) of this Lease as if those requirements had mutatis mutandis been herein repeated in full ...' (My emphasis.)

[48] Although it is impossible on the evidence to tell what scope there would
f actually have been for further building, the fact that the parties specifically envisage that the lessee may erect other buildings at some future date has two related consequences for the construction of the lease. First, since those other buildings will not be erected in terms of the lessee's obligation under sub-cl 2(iii)(a), the provisions of that subclause will not apply to them. As Mr Pymont accepted, this means that, even on his construction, the lessee may
g erect buildings on the demised land that will not be subject to any user restriction contained in sub-cl (iii)(a). Secondly and conversely, the covenants of general application in the other subclauses of cl 2 will apply not only to the buildings erected under sub-cl 2(iii)(a) but to any other building that the lessee may put up on the demised land. Indeed, cl 2(v), for instance, has an even wider effect since
h the lessee's obligation not to create or permit a nuisance must apply to things done anywhere on the demised land and not simply to operations carried out in any buildings erected on it.

[49] Among the covenants which apply to all buildings, whether forming part of the original development or built later, is cl 2(xiii) which deals with the situation where a building is burned down or damaged by fire. It is to be rebuilt and
j reinstated under the surveillance of the city architect and 'in all respects in accordance with the provisions of clause 2(iii) of this Lease as if those requirements had mutatis mutandis been herein repeated in full'. While it is difficult to work out precisely what the parties intended should happen in some situations, it seems clear that, in the case of a building which had been constructed as part of the original development, it would have to be rebuilt so as to be fit for immediate occupation and use for uses within the use classes specified in sub-cl (iii)(a). Like

the Court of Appeal, I find it hard to see why that obligation should have been *a*
imposed on the lessee if, before the fire, the building could have been used for any
purpose whatever. While I would not attach great weight to it, that consideration
tends to confirm the interpretation of sub-cl (iii)(a) which I prefer.

[50] Mr Lewison argued, however, that this interpretation was incompatible
with the overall structure of the lease. His first and more general submission was
that you would not expect to find a continuing restriction on the use of the *b*
premises in sub-cl 2(iii)(a) which deals with the lessee's obligation to build and
complete the development within five years. As a general observation that may
well be true. But, in any given case, the content of the obligations to be found in
any part of a lease depends on what the draftsman has provided. In this case it
depends on the wording of sub-cl 2(iii)(a). For the reasons that I have given, I
consider that, despite its position, the wording of that provision is apt to impose a *c*
continuing restriction on the use of the premises.

[51] Mr Lewison went on to reinforce his general submission by pointing out
that the lease does in fact contain express provisions which impose restrictions on
the use of the premises. These are to be found in cl 2(v) and (vi):
d

'(v) not to do or permit to be done any act or thing which in the reasonable
opinion of the Corporation may be or become a nuisance or annoyance or
cause damage or inconvenience to the Corporation or any lessees tenants or
occupiers of any adjoining or neighbouring land or premises

(vi) not to use the demised land for the purposes of a garage and filling *e*
station café restaurant public house abattoir the storage of meat except as a
small part of a cash and carry or wholesale grocers or the sale of fuel oils
lubricants or inflammable liquids provided that nothing in this clause shall
prohibit the storage of fuel oils lubricants or inflammable liquids in properly
constructed containers for the lessee['s] or its sublessee's own use.'
f

He argued that these provisions constituted the only restrictions on the
permissible use of the premises and that, where the parties had dealt with the
matter expressly, a court should be slow to read an implied use restriction into
sub-cl 2(iii)(a), especially when the lease made perfectly good business sense
without it. In particular, it seemed unlikely that, when drawing up a lease to run *g*
for 114 years, the parties would have wanted to limit the possible use of the
premises by reference to use classes which might have been appropriate in
planning terms in 1969 but which, as the city developed and commerce changed,
would almost inevitably become outmoded long before the lease expired.

[52] The argument—that the parties would have been unlikely to include a *h*
negative user covenant in sub-cl (iii)(a), when they had inserted specific provisions
restricting use in cl 2(vi)—would obviously be extremely powerful if the only
buildings to which cl 2(vi) could apply were buildings erected under sub-cl (iii)(a).
The argument appears to me to lose all or much of its force, however, once it is
realised that the restrictions in cl 2(vi) apply more widely. There is nothing
particularly surprising in the idea that the parties may have agreed a special *j*
restriction on the use of the buildings comprising the original development. The
purpose may have been, for instance, to encourage the growth of industry as the
core of the development. However that may be, a special restriction of this kind
is quite consistent with the imposition of other restrictions that will apply to all the
buildings erected on the demised land—whether comprising the original
development or not. In these circumstances I do not regard the existence of the

a non-user provisions in cl 2(vi) as a reason in itself to conclude that no restriction on the use of premises would be found in sub-cl 2(iii)(a).

[53] I therefore find nothing in the mere existence of the use restriction in cl 2(vi) which would affect my interpretation of sub-cl 2(iii)(a).

[54] The respondents go further, however. They draw attention not merely to the existence of cl 2(vi) but to the express provisions which it contains. It spells out

b what appear to be a ragbag of uses to which the demised land is not to be put. These include use as a café, restaurant or public house and use for the storage of meat 'except as a small part of a cash and carry or wholesale grocers'. The argument is that use as a café or restaurant, for instance, would in any event fall outside the scope of Use Classes III, IV or X and so there would have been no need to exclude those uses specifically in cl 2(vi) if sub-cl (iii)(a) had been intended to

c prevent the buildings being used for any purpose outside those use classes. The respondents back this argument up with a slightly different point. Use as a cash and carry, it is said, would not have fallen within any of the relevant use classes (*LTSS Print and Supply Services Ltd v Hackney LB* [1976] 1 All ER 311, [1976] QB 663) and so would not have been permissible if sub-cl (iii)(a) contained a restriction.

d Therefore, since cl 2(vi) envisages that premises could be used for storing meat as a small part of a cash and carry or wholesale grocers, the parties cannot have intended, by referring to the use classes in sub-cl (iii)(a), to prevent the buildings being used as a cash and carry or wholesale grocers. It follows, so runs the argument, that sub-cl (iii)(a) contains no bar on the use of the buildings for a purpose that would fall outside the relevant use classes.

e [55] It may well be, as the council submit, that the somewhat eclectic list of forbidden uses in cl 2(vi) is to be explained by a desire on the part of the council to give a measure of protection to other traders who had already leased premises from the council on land bordering the development. I am also prepared to assume, without deciding and without examining the *LTSS* case, that use as a cash

f and carry would not have been use in accordance with any of the relevant use classes.

[56] Whatever the precise position may be on these matters, the important point remains that cl 2(vi) applies not simply to the original development under sub-cl 2(iii)(a) but to the demised land as a whole. In other words cl 2(vi) applies to *any* buildings or structures erected during the currency of the lease. The sphere

g of application of the two provisions is therefore different, with cl 2(vi) being wider. That being so, it is scarcely surprising to find that cl 2(vi) bans various uses which would not have been permitted under any of the relevant use classes and which would therefore not have been permitted under sub-cl (iii)(a). The overlap to which the respondents point is not an indication of inconsistency

h between the two provisions. Nor does it show that sub-cl (iii)(a) contains no restriction on the use of the original development.

[57] The respondents' cash and carry argument is also unconvincing. Clause 2(vi) applies, inter alia, to buildings which are not subject to the restrictions in sub-cl 2(iii)(a). So, other things being equal, those buildings could be used as a cash and carry or wholesale grocers. An exception in cl 2(vi), allowing meat storage as

j a small part of a cash and carry or wholesale grocers, is therefore not inconsistent with the existence of a use restriction in sub-cl (iii)(a) applying to the original development.

[58] In these circumstances I find nothing in the specific terms of cl 2(vi) that is incompatible with the interpretation of sub-cl (iii)(a) which I prefer.

[59] Finally, as I have noted, the respondents argued that the restriction on the use of the buildings in the development to uses in accordance with the particular

use classes would make little sense in a lease of this length. In the absence of
evidence it is dangerous to travel beyond the agreed terms and to speculate as to
the intentions of those who entered into this lease more than 30 years ago and as
to what would have seemed sensible to them at that time. But I have already
suggested that the landlord may have wanted to encourage industry in this area of
Gloucester. If so, that would not be an outlandish aim, even in the long term, for
a landlord which was also the local council. The respondents argued that, if the
council had wished to restrict the use of the premises in this or any other way, they
could have done so without having a restriction in the lease since they could have
taken appropriate steps in their role as the local planning authority. But that
argument proves too much. It would, after all, apply equally—or a fortiori—to the
respondents' preferred construction of the relevant words in sub-cl (iii)(a) as
dealing simply with the form of the development: that matter also could be dealt
with by the council as planning authority when giving the permissions that are
specifically mentioned in the subclause.

[60] For all these reasons I agree with the interpretation of sub-cl 2(iii)(a)
favoured by the Court of Appeal. I would therefore dismiss the cross-appeal. In
that situation it is necessary to consider the council's appeal against the Court of
Appeal's declaration that it was unreasonable of them to refuse consent to the
respondents' application to assign the lease to Mountstar.

Did the council withhold consent unreasonably?

[61] The covenant in cl 2(viii), providing that the demised land is not to be
assigned without the previous consent of the council, 'such consent not to be
unreasonably withheld in the case of a respectable and responsible assignee', is of
a familiar kind. Its purpose is well settled. In *Bates v Donaldson* [1896] 2 QB 241,
[1895–9] All ER Rep 170, AL Smith LJ rejected any suggestion that a similar clause
had been inserted so as to allow the landlord to regain possession of the premises
before the expiry of the lease. He went on:

'It was in my judgment inserted alio intuitu altogether, and in order to
protect the lessor from having his premises used or occupied in an undesirable
way or by an undesirable tenant or assignee ...' (See [1896] 2 QB 241 at 247,
[1895–9] All ER Rep 170 at 174.)

The clause must be interpreted and applied so as to give effect to this purpose. It
is equally well settled that, under such a clause—

'a landlord is not entitled to refuse his consent to an assignment on grounds
which have nothing whatever to do with the relationship of landlord and
tenant in regard to the subject matter of the lease' (See *International Drilling
Fluids Ltd v Louisville Investments (Uxbridge) Ltd* [1986] 1 All ER 321 at 325,
[1986] Ch 513 at 520 per Balcombe LJ.)

[62] Here the council's refusal of consent relates to the likely use of the
premises for a purpose which they consider to be in breach of the non-user
covenant in sub-cl 2(iii)(a). The respondents contend that, even so, consent is
'unreasonably withheld' in terms of the clause if it is withheld simply because the
prospective assignee is likely to wish to use the premises for a purpose that the
landlord considers would be in breach of one of the terms of the lease.
Mr Lewison outlined the situation in the present case in this way. Mountstar
considered that sub-cl 2(iii)(a) did not restrict the use of the premises. If
Mountstar were right on that point, then the council accepted that they would
have to give consent to the assignment. But even if Mountstar were wrong on that

a   point, there would be an issue as to whether the proposed use was indeed in contravention of the restriction in sub-cl (iii)(a). Finally, if the proposed use did indeed fall foul of the restriction, then an application might be made to the Lands Tribunal to vary the terms of the covenant. All these were legitimate points for Mountstar to take and there was no question of them acting unlawfully in breach of the covenant. In that situation it was unreasonable for the council to withhold *b*   consent to the proposed assignment to them.

[63] While counsel was, rightly, at pains to place the legal issue within the proper factual context, the respondents' submission does not depend on the facts of the case. Their fundamental contention is that, as a matter of law, the words 'unreasonably withheld' in the subclause must be interpreted as meaning that the council *cannot* withhold consent simply on the ground that the prospective *c*   assignee is unwilling to comply with the terms of the lease. So, even if it appeared likely that the prospective assignee would actually breach the terms of the lease, it would nevertheless be unreasonable for the landlord to withhold consent. It was by persuading the court to apply this reasoning that the respondents secured victory in the Court of Appeal.

d   [64] Uninstructed by the case law on this matter, I confess that I should have found the respondents' proposition startling. It derives support, however, from the decision of the Court of Appeal in *Killick v Second Covent Garden Property Co Ltd* [1973] 2 All ER 337, [1973] 1 WLR 658. The case involved a lease of premises in the City of London. The lease contained a user covenant preventing the premises being used—
e

'for any other purpose than the trade or business of a printer nor have or permit any sale by auction in or upon the demised premises or any part thereof without [the landlords'] written consent which shall not be unreasonably withheld.'

f   The underlessee had indeed used the premises for their trade or business as printers but, as Stamp LJ observed:

'It is … common ground that, owing to the situation of the premises, in the City, and for reasons which I need not specify, that trade or business can no longer be profitably carried on there.' (See [1973] 2 All ER 337 at 339, [1973] *g*   1 WLR 658 at 661.)

In the circumstances the lessee and sublessee applied for the landlord's consent to assign their leases to Primaplex, a company who were not printers and who proposed to apply for planning permission to use the premises as offices and to do the necessary works to convert them for that purpose. The landlords did not give *h*   the necessary consent and the lessee and underlessee applied for a declaration that the landlords had unreasonably withheld their consent to the assignments. The judge at the Mayor's and City of London Court made the declaration and the Court of Appeal refused the landlords' appeal.

[65] Stamp LJ records that the ground on which the landlords sought to justify *j*   their refusal of consent as not being unreasonable was 'simply that it will be a necessary consequence that there will be a breach of the user covenant'. In advancing that view the landlords interpreted the covenant as absolute while the other parties argued that it was qualified. The critical passage in the judgment of Stamp LJ then follows:

'Counsel for the landlords submitted that a landlord may reasonably refuse consent to an assignment if the assignment would necessarily involve a breach of covenant, and I will accept that submission as being well-founded. But whatever view one takes as to the construction of the user covenant, I *a* cannot accept that, if the landlords ... did consent to the proposed assignments, there would as a necessary consequence be a breach of the user covenant. As a result of the assignments Primaplex Ltd would step into the shoes of the lessee and underlessees and would thereupon become subject to the user covenant. The landlords would be in the same position, neither *b* better nor worse, to enforce the user covenant as would be the case if the present underlessees ... were themselves proposing to seek planning permission for use of the premises as offices and proposed so to use them. On that short ground I would hold that the landlords' withholding of consent is unreasonable.' (See [1973] 2 All ER 337 at 339, [1973] 1 WLR 658 at 661.)

c

In the present case Chadwick LJ, with whom Waller LJ agreed, considered that the Court of Appeal was bound by the decision in *Killick's* case and on that basis they allowed the respondents' appeal and made the third declaration. Chadwick LJ ((1999) 80 P & CR 11 at 23–24) put the matter in this way:

'In my view the decision in the *Killick* case precludes this court from holding *d* that the belief of the landlord, however reasonable, that the proposed assignee intends to use the demised premises for a purpose which would give rise to a breach of a user covenant is, of itself, a ground for withholding consent to assignment. Provided that, when giving consent to the assignment, the landlord does not disable himself, necessarily and inevitably *e* (by waiver, estoppel, or otherwise), from continuing to insist on due observance of the user covenant by the assignee, he is in no worse a position, following assignment, than he would have been if the assignor had himself proposed to use the demised premises for that purpose. This is not a case in which the giving of consent (coupled, if the Council thinks fit, with notice to Mountstar that it intends to enforce the restrictions as to user contained in *f* sub-clause 2(iii)(a) of the 1969 lease) will disable the Council from continuing to insist on due observance of those restrictions. It is not inevitable that, following assignment, there will be a breach of the user restrictions. Mountstar may succeed in its present contention that the use proposed by its planning application is within Use Class IV of the 1963 Order. Mountstar will apply, successfully, to the Land Tribunal for a discharge or modification of the *g* restriction—see s 84(12) of the Law of Property Act 1925. The Council is not entitled, by refusing consent, to compel the appellant to accept its interpretation of the user covenant. Nor is it entitled, as it seems to me, to refuse consent to assignment on the grounds that the proposed assignee may wish to exercise the rights which the law allows to a tenant under this lease.' *h*

[66] As one part of his argument Mr Pymont submitted that too much had been read into the passage in the judgment of Stamp LJ in *Killick's* case. As he pointed out, it appears that, perhaps because of the particular circumstances to which Stamp LJ alluded, counsel for the landlords had chosen to pitch his *j* submission at the highest level: he had contended that a breach of the user covenant would be 'a necessary consequence' of an assignment to Primaplex. All that the Court of Appeal decided was that, on the facts, a breach of the covenant was not a necessary consequence and, for that reason, they rejected the landlords' submission. While that is indeed a possible interpretation of the case, it is plain, not least from the decision in the Court of Appeal in the present case, that *Killick's* case has been treated as laying down law which has to be applied in interpreting

a covenants of this kind. In the course of a somewhat chequered career the decision has even won the accolade of being 'the refuge of the desperate' (J Gaunt, 'Principle and Pretext: The rules governing landlords' consent' (1987) 284 EG 1371). But that is only an additional reason why, when the point has been fully argued, the House should consider the principle that it has been thought to enshrine.

b [67] The test of reasonableness is to be found in many areas of the law and the concept has been found useful precisely because it prevents the law becoming unduly rigid. In effect, it allows the law to respond appropriately to different situations as they arise. This has to be remembered when a court is considering whether a landlord has 'unreasonably withheld' consent to the assignment of a lease. In this context I would follow Viscount Dunedin's advice in *Viscount* c *Tredegar v Harwood* [1929] AC 72 at 78, [1928] All ER Rep 11 at 14 that one 'should read reasonableness in the general sense'. I have derived the greatest assistance, however, from the comments of Lord Denning MR in a passage in *Bickel v Duke of Westminster* [1976] 3 All ER 801, [1977] QB 517. The Grosvenor Belgravia Estate had refused to consent to the assignment of the head lease of a house in Burton d Mews off Chester Square to a lady who, if she had become tenant under the head lease and had remained so for five years, would have been entitled to buy the freehold from the Estate. Having referred to a number of earlier cases, Lord Denning said this:

e 'If those cases can properly be regarded as laying down propositions of law, I would agree that we ought to hold the landlords' refusal to be unreasonable. But I do not think they do lay down any propositions of law, and for this reason. The words of the contract are perfectly clear English words: "such licence shall not be unreasonably withheld". When those words come to be applied in any particular case, I do not think the court can, or should, f determine by strict rules the grounds on which a landlord may, or may not, reasonably refuse his consent. He is not limited by the contract to any particular grounds. Nor should the courts limit him. Not even under the guise of construing the words. The landlord has to exercise his judgment in all sorts of circumstances. It is impossible for him, or for the courts, to envisage them all. When this lease was granted in 1947 no one could have g foreseen that 20 years later Parliament would give a tenant a right to buy up the freehold. Seeing that the circumstances are infinitely various, it is impossible to formulate strict rules as to how a landlord should exercise his power of refusal. The utmost that the courts can do is to give guidance to those who have to consider the problem. As one decision follows another, h people will get to know the likely result in any given set of circumstances. But no one decision will be a binding precedent as a strict rule of law. The reasons given by the judges are to be treated as propositions of good sense—in relation to the particular case—rather than propositions of law applicable to all cases. It is rather like the cases where a statute gives the court a discretion. j It has always been held that this discretion is not to be fettered by strict rules: and that all that can be properly done is to indicate the chief considerations which help to arrive at a just conclusion: see *Blunt v Blunt* ([1943] 2 All ER 76 at 78, [1943] AC 517 at 525) and *Ward v James* ([1965] 1 All ER 563 at 571, [1966] 1 QB 273 at 295).' (See [1976] 3 All ER 801 at 804–805, [1977] QB 517 at 524.)

That statement of the general approach to be taken was endorsed by Roskill and Lawton LJJ, with whom Megaw LJ concurred, in *West Layton Ltd v Ford* [1979] 2

All ER 657 at 663, 664, [1979] QB 593 at 604, 606. I would respectfully adopt it. In the *International Drilling* case [1986] 1 All ER 321, [1986] Ch 513 Balcombe LJ distilled a number of propositions from the earlier authorities on covenants of this kind but then, under reference to *Bickel's* case [1976] 3 All ER 801, [1977] QB 517 and *West Layton Ltd v Ford* [1979] 2 All ER 657, [1979] QB 593, added:

> 'Subject to the propositions set out above, it is, in each case, a question of fact, depending on all the circumstances, whether the landlord's consent to an assignment is being unreasonably withheld ...' (See [1986] 1 All ER 321 at 326, [1986] Ch 513 at 521.)

[68] Approaching the matter in this way, I am satisfied that it cannot be said, as a matter of law, that the belief of a landlord, however reasonable, that the proposed assignee intends to use the demised premises for a purpose which would give rise to a breach of a user covenant cannot, of itself, be a reasonable ground for withholding consent to the assignment.

[69] I accept that, as Mr Lewison stressed, in proceedings such as the present the court is not concerned with whether or not the terms of the contract are reasonable as between the parties. The court is concerned only with the assignment and with whether or not it is reasonable for the landlord to withhold consent to that assignment. But in determining that matter, as *Bickel's* case shows, the correct approach is to consider what the reasonable landlord would do when asked to consent in the particular circumstances. The rule of law derived from *Killick's* case introduces a rigidity which makes it impossible to apply that approach. It should, for that very reason, be rejected.

[70] Indeed the reasoning in *Killick's* case requires the landlord to proceed in a way in which, it appears to me, no reasonable landlord would actually proceed. It is accepted, by analogy with the position where a landlord is asked to consent to a sublease, that a landlord may act reasonably if he refuses consent where the assignment of the lease will necessarily result in a breach of a user covenant (see *Packaging Centre Ltd v Poland Street Estate Ltd* (1961) 178 EG 189 and *Granada TV Network Ltd v Great Universal Stores Ltd* (1963) 187 EG 391; *Killick v Second Covent Garden Property Co Ltd* [1973] 2 All ER 337 at 339, [1973] 1 WLR 658 at 661–662). And one can easily see that a reasonable landlord faced with such a prospect could well decide to withhold consent. But one can equally easily see that a reasonable landlord, faced with the prospect that the assignment of the lease is likely to result in a breach of a user covenant, could well reach precisely the same decision. After all, a landlord considering whether to accept a tenant in the first place would almost certainly reject a person who would probably, even if not necessarily, use the premises in breach of a covenant in the lease. His decision to do so would be both rational and reasonable. In my view it may be equally rational and reasonable for a landlord to withhold consent to an assignment to a prospective assignee who will probably, even though not necessarily, breach the covenant. In deciding whether to withhold consent to an assignment reasonable landlords need not confine their consideration to what will necessarily happen; like everyone else taking an important decision, they may have regard to what will probably happen.

[71] The central plank in the reasoning of the court in *Killick's* case seems to be that it would be unreasonable for the landlord to withhold consent because the assignment does not change the legal relationship between the landlord and the tenant. So the landlord would have exactly the same powers to prevent a breach of covenant by the assignee as by the existing tenant. The landlord would therefore be in the same position, neither better nor worse, to enforce the user

a covenant. As an analysis of the landlord's legal position that is undoubtedly correct. But the reality is that a reasonable landlord could well look at the matter more broadly and see that his position would be significantly altered by the assignment. It is one thing to have a tenant who complies with the user covenant in the lease and against whom there is no need to take steps to enforce the covenant. It is quite another to have a new tenant who does not comply with, or
b who challenges the interpretation of, the user covenant and against whom the landlord might need to take steps to enforce it or to contest the tenant's interpretation, with all the inconvenience and potential cost involved. It is also a different thing to have a new tenant who intends to apply to the Lands Tribunal under s 84 of the Law of Property Act 1925 to discharge or modify the user covenant. Again the landlord would face the prospect of becoming embroiled in
c legal proceedings. If they occurred, all or any of these matters would make a huge practical difference to the landlord. So the prospect that one or other of them will probably happen is one which a reasonable landlord must be entitled at least to take into account when asked to consent to the assignment of a lease. It is therefore in my view wholly unrealistic to suggest, as *Killick*'s case does, that no
d reasonable landlord, faced with the probability of real changes of these kinds, would withhold consent to an assignment simply because, technically, his legal position and his legal remedies would remain the same. I accordingly reject the central strand of the reasoning on which the decision in *Killick*'s case depends.

[72] Mr Lewison submitted that, if the council were permitted to withhold consent in a case like the present, they would in effect have the power to impose
e their interpretation of the user covenant and the tenant would have no real interest to pursue the matter. So far as the tenant's interest is concerned, the history of the present proceedings, where the respondents have pursued a point of interpretation all the way to this House, would seem in itself to show that the argument cannot be pressed too far. For the rest, it is simply not the case that the
f landlord would have power to impose his particular interpretation of a user covenant. On the contrary, a tenant who is faced with a refusal of consent based on a particular interpretation may always apply to the county court for a declaration as to the proper interpretation. If the ruling shows that the landlord's interpretation is wrong, then it would plainly be unreasonable for the landlord to continue to withhold consent on that basis.

g [73] For these reasons I would reject the supposed rule of law that the Court of Appeal derived from *Killick*'s case. In so far as *Killick*'s case is thought to lay down any such rule, it should be overruled. Since the decision of the Court of Appeal to make the third declaration was based solely on an application of *Killick*, it follows that the council's appeal against that part of the court's order must be allowed.

h [74] It is important not to exaggerate the effect of overruling *Killick*'s case. In particular, it does not establish any contrary rule of law that it will always be reasonable for a landlord to withhold consent to an assignment simply on the ground that the proposed assignee intends to use the premises for a purpose which would give rise to a breach of a user covenant. While that will usually be a
j reasonable ground for withholding consent, there may be circumstances where refusal of consent on this ground alone would be unreasonable. As Lord Denning stressed, it will depend on the circumstances of the particular case.

[75] I would add this. In the course of his submissions Mr Lewison referred to the Landlord and Tenant 1988 and in particular to s 1(3) and (6)(c):

> (3) Where there is served on the person who may consent to a proposed transaction a written application by the tenant for consent to the transaction,

he owes a duty to the tenant within a reasonable time—(a) to give consent, except in a case where it is reasonable not to give consent, (b) to serve on the tenant written notice of his decision whether or not to give consent specifying in addition—(i) if the consent is given subject to conditions, the conditions, (ii) if the consent is withheld, the reasons for withholding it ...
    (6) It is for the person who owed any duty under subsection (3) above ... (c) if he did not give consent and the question arises whether it was reasonable for him not to do so, to show that it was reasonable, and, if the question arises whether he served notice under that subsection within a reasonable time, to show that he did.'

Mr Lewison commented on the succinct reply which the council official, Mr Hook, had sent to the respondents' agents on 16 September 1997 and appeared to suggest that it might somehow limit the range of evidence or argument which the council could deploy in seeking to show that it had been reasonable for the council not to give consent on the ground set out in the letter. I would deprecate any such suggestion. As my noble and learned friend Lord Scott pointed out in the course of argument, the degree of detail contained in such a letter is likely to depend to a large extent on what is said by the tenant in the application to which the landlord is responding. In practice a dialogue may develop. Here, to judge from the terms of the letter from the respondents' solicitors on 16 July, the application for consent was brief and contained no elaboration. In those circumstances an equally succinct reply was to be expected. Had the respondents continued the correspondence and elaborated their application in the light of the council's reply, then the council might well have developed their thinking in more detail. Of course, once the landlord has stated in writing the ground on which he refuses consent, he cannot later rely on any other ground. But that does not mean to say that, when seeking to show that it was reasonable for him not to consent on the stated ground, he is confined to what he has said in his letter. Section 1(6)(c) contains no such restriction. And rightly so. Otherwise, instead of being a straightforward practical document, the notice containing the landlord's reasons for withholding consent would soon become a battleground for litigants and an increasingly sophisticated playground for conveyancers. Such cannot have been the intention of Parliament in enacting the legislation.
    [76] In summary, for the reasons that I have given I would allow the council's appeal and refuse the respondents' cross-appeal.

Cross-appeal allowed.

Kate O'Hanlon   Barrister.

a

Nasser v United Bank of Kuwait
[2001] EWCA Civ 556

COURT OF APPEAL, CIVIL DIVISION
SIMON BROWN AND MANCE LJJ

b 4, 11 APRIL 2001

*Costs – Security for costs – Claimant ordinarily resident out of the jurisdiction –
Claimant resident in United States – Rules of procedure empowering court to order
security for costs against such a claimant or appellant – Whether rules capable of being
c discriminatory for purposes of human rights convention – Guidance on exercise of
discretion – Human Rights Act 1998, Sch 1, Pt I, arts 6, 14 – CPR 25.13, 25.15.*

The claimant, N, was resident in the United States of America, and accordingly
was not a person against whom a claim could be enforced under the Brussels and
d Lugano Conventions on the Jurisdiction and Enforcement of Judgments in Civil
and Commercial Matters (as set out in the Schedules to the Civil Jurisdiction and
Judgments Act 1982) (the enforcement conventions). She brought proceedings in
England against the defendant bank, but they were struck out by the judge, and she
was given permission to appeal. After the appeal was listed, the bank applied to a
single judge of the Court of Appeal for an order under CPR 25.15[a], requiring N,
e who was apparently impecunious, to provide the bank with security for its costs of
the appeal. Rule 25.15(1) empowered the court to order security for costs against
an appellant on the same grounds as it might order security against a claimant.
Under r 25.13(1)[b], the court could make an order for security for costs against a
claimant if it were satisfied, having regard to all the circumstances of the case, that
it was just to make an order, and one or more of the conditions in r 25.13(2)
f applied. Those conditions included, at para (2)(a), that the claimant was an
individual who was ordinarily resident out of the jurisdiction and was not a
person against whom a claim could be enforced under the enforcement
conventions. The single judge ordered N to pay security of £17,500, and she
applied to a two-judge Court of Appeal to have the order discharged or varied.
g On the application, issues arose as to (i) whether the limitation of the power to
order security for costs to those resident outside the contracting states of the
enforcement conventions was or could be discriminatory for the purposes of
art 14[c] of the European Convention for the Protection of Human Rights and
Fundamental Freedoms 1950 (as set out in Sch 1 to the Human Rights Act 1998),
h and (ii) if so, the basis on which that power could properly be exercised. Article 14
provided that the enjoyment of convention rights—which included the right of
access to a court under art 6[d] of the convention—was to be 'secured without
discrimination on any ground such as ... national ... origin'.

j **Held** – The discretion, under CPR 25.13 and 25.15, to award security for costs
against an individual claimant or appellant not resident in a contracting state of
the enforcement conventions was to be exercised only on objectively justified

---

a   Rule 25.15 is set out at [33], below
b   Rule 25.13, so far as material, is set out at [34], below
c   Article 14 is set out at [47], below
d   Article 6, so far as material, is set out at [37], below

grounds relating to obstacles to, or the burden of, enforcement in the context of
the particular individual or country concerned. It would be both discriminatory   *a*
and unjustifiable if the mere fact of residence outside a contracting state of the
enforcement conventions could justify the exercise of the discretion to make
orders for security for costs with the purpose or effect of protecting defendants or
respondents to appeals against risks to which they would equally be subject, and
in relation to which they would have no protection, if the claim or appeal had   *b*
been brought by a resident of a contracting state of the enforcement conventions.
Potential difficulties or burdens of enforcement in states not party to those
conventions were the rationale for the existence of the discretion, and it should
be exercised in a manner reflecting its rationale.   It could not be used to
discriminate against individuals resident in such states on grounds unrelated to
enforcement. In that connection, there could be no inflexible assumption that   *c*
any such person should provide security for costs.   Enforcement was not
necessarily more difficult merely because a person was not resident in England or
another contracting state of the enforcement conventions. In so far as
impecuniosity might have a continuing relevance, it was not on the ground that
the claimant lacked apparent means to satisfy any judgment—that principle could   *d*
not survive in an era which no longer permitted discrimination in access to justice
on grounds of national origin—but on the ground (where it applied) that the
effect of impecuniosity would either preclude or hinder or add to the burden of
enforcement abroad against such assets as did exist abroad, or, as a practical
matter, make it more likely that the claimant would take advantage of any   *e*
available opportunity to avoid or hinder such enforcement abroad. The court
should, however, take notice of obvious realities without formal evidence. There
were some parts of the world where the natural assumption would be that
enforcement would be impossible, but in other cases it might be incumbent on
an applicant to show some basis for concluding that enforcement would face any
substantial obstacle or extra burden, meriting the protection of an order for   *f*
security for costs. Even then, the court should consider tailoring the order for
security to the particular circumstances. If there were likely to be no obstacle to,
or difficulty about, enforcement, but simply an extra burden in the form of costs
or moderate delay, the appropriate course would be to limit the amount of the
security ordered by reference to that potential burden. Moreover, the mere   *g*
absence of reciprocal arrangements or legislation providing for enforcement of
foreign judgments could not of itself justify an inference that enforcement would
not be possible. In the instant case, the court could infer that steps taken to
enforce any English judgment for costs in the United States would be likely to
involve a significantly greater burden in terms of costs and delay than an   *h*
enforcement of a costs order against an unsuccessful claimant or appellant
resident in England or another contracting state of the enforcement conventions.
However, the amount of security ordered by the single judge was excessive. His
order would be set aside, and N would instead be required to provide security of
£5,000 (see [58], [59], [61]–[67], [74], [76]–[78], below).

 Tolstoy Miloslavsky v UK (1995) 20 EHRR 442 and *Fitzgerald v Williams, O'Regan v* *j*
Williams [1996] 2 All ER 171 considered.

Notes

For the right of access to a court and the prohibition of discrimination in the
enjoyment of convention rights, see 8(2) *Halsbury's Laws* (4th edn reissue) paras 141,

a   164, and for security for costs, see 37 *Halsbury's Laws* (4th edn reissue) paras 834–850.

For the Human Rights Act 1998, Sch 1, Pt I, arts 6, 14, see 7 *Halsbury's Statutes* (4th edn) (1999 reissue) 523, 525.

Cases referred to in judgments

b   *Belgian Linguistics Case (No 2)* (1968) 1 EHRR 252, [1968] ECHR 1474/62, ECt HR.
Federal Bank of the Middle East v Hadkinson, Hadkinson v Saab [2000] 1 Costs LR 94, CA.
Fitzgerald v Williams, O'Regan v Williams [1996] 2 All ER 171, [1996] QB 657, [1996] 2 WLR 447, CA.

c   *Golder v UK* (1975) 1 EHRR 524, [1975] ECHR 4451/70, ECt HR.
Gulf Azov Shipping Co Ltd v Idisi [2000] CA Transcript 2316.
Mund & Fester v Hatrex International Transport Case C-398/92 [1994] ECR I-467.
Pordéa v Times Newpapers [2000] IL Pr 763, Cour de Cassation de France.
Rasmussen v Denmark (1984) 7 EHRR 371, [1984] ECHR 8777/79, ECt HR.

d   *Sporrong v Sweden* (1982) 5 EHRR 35, [1982] ECHR 7151/75, ECt HR.
Stubbings v UK (1996) 23 EHRR 213, [1996] ECHR 22083/93, ECt HR.
Thune v London Properties Ltd [1990] 1 All ER 972, [1990] 1 WLR 562, CA.
Tolstoy Miloslavsky v UK (1995) 20 EHRR 442, [1995] ECHR 18139/91, ECt HR.
Yorke (M V) Motors (a firm) v Edwards [1982] 1 All ER 1024, [1982] 1 WLR 444, HL.

e   **Application**

The claimant, Amy Nasser, applied for the discharge or variation of the order of Judge LJ, sitting as a single judge of the Court of Appeal, on 10 October 2000 requiring her to pay into court the sum of £17,500 as security for the costs of the defendants, United Bank of Kuwait, on her appeal against the decision of Ian Kennedy J on 26
f   October 1999 striking out her action against the defendants for want of prosecution. The facts are set out in the judgment of Mance LJ.

Simon Edwards (instructed by *Charles Khan*, Slough) for the claimant.
Peter Irvin (instructed by *Wedlake Bell*) for the defendants.

g   *Cur adv vult*

11 April 2001. The following judgments were delivered.

h   **MANCE LJ** (giving the first judgment at the invitation of Simon Brown LJ).

INTRODUCTION
[1] This application arises from an immediate factual background of some intricacy and difficulty for the claimant. But, assuming that the claimant can overcome her difficulties in this respect, it raises a point of general interest as to
j   the Court of Appeal's approach to applications for security for the costs of an appeal under the CPR, bearing in mind the restriction since 2 May 2000 of the jurisdiction to make such orders, effected by CPR 25.15, read with r 25.13(2)(a) and arts 6(1) and 14 of the European Convention for the Protection of Human Rights and Fundamental Freedoms 1950 (as set out in Sch 1 to the Human Rights Act 1998) (the European Convention on Human Rights) as incorporated into English law since 2 October 2000 by the 1998 Act.

HISTORY OF THE PROCEEDINGS

[2] These proceedings go back to early 1993 when the claimant asserted that jewellery and other items worth some £900,000 had been stolen from her deposit box with the defendants, and on 15 April 1993 issued a writ. I do not need to go into the long procedural history, save to note that on 18 February 1994 the claimant (by then resident in the United States) was ordered to pay into court within 14 days £10,000 as security for the defendants' costs, which was done.

[3] In January 1996 the claimant returned from the United States and obtained legal aid. A trial date was fixed for April 1996. Progress towards it was then effectively halted on 26 February 1996 following a decision of Master Foster ordering the claimant give further security for costs in the sum of £25,000. The master was, unfortunately, not reminded, by the junior counsel who attended, of the principle that orders for security for costs should not generally be made if they would stifle genuine proceedings. Much later Mr Ross-Munro QC, the claimant's leading counsel, learnt of the position, and advised an application to appeal out of time. Leave to appeal was granted on 14 November 1997, and the appeal was successfully pursued before Curtis J on 22 June 1998. Curtis J held that the mere fact that the claimant was on legal aid did not necessarily exclude any order for security for costs, but that in the particular circumstances there should be no order, because, as he put it: 'I consider that if I made any order of any substance, i e anything more than a nominal order, the plaintiff's action would be snuffed out and consequently it would not be right to make the order.'

[4] However, as Mr Irvin for the defendants points out, Curtis J expressed concern about aspects of the claimant's evidence regarding lack of means and appears to have placed some weight on the Legal Aid Board's investigation and satisfaction as to her eligibility.

[5] After the hearing before Curtis J, the claimant's legal aid was withdrawn and regranted on numerous occasions, some further pleadings were exchanged and a case management conference was fixed for the end of October 1999, at which it was intended to seek directions leading to a trial date estimated to last five to seven days. But on 20 October 1999 the defendants applied to strike the action out for want of prosecution under CPR 3.4. The application was granted by Ian Kennedy J on 26 October 1999. Permission to appeal against his decision was granted by Latham LJ on 4 May 2000, together with permission to rely on the appeal on new evidence identifying the alleged address of a witness, Lena Sabbagh, who the defendants had said was untraceable. In the meantime in or about December 1999 the claimant's legal aid certificate was discharged. Her present solicitors are acting on a contingency fee basis, without uplift, which extends, we are told, to any hearing of the appeal against Ian Kennedy J's decision. In contrast, counsel, Mr Simon Edwards, who appeared before us for the claimant, was, he told us, instructed for a brief fee of £1,500 funded by a loan from a taxi-driver friend of the claimant, who attended the hearing before us with the claimant.

[6] The appeal against Ian Kennedy J's decision was due for a three hour hearing on 2 or 3 November 2000. On 27 June 2000 the defendants wrote seeking £15,000 security for their costs of the appeal. Chasers of 4 and 14 July led only to holding responses, the second of which said that instructions were anticipated by 24 July; a further chaser of 28 July went unanswered. On 1 September 2000 the defendants issued an application for £19,000 security, supported by witness statement of Mr Hewitt, a partner in their solicitors, Wedlake Bell, producing a costs draughtsman's skeleton bill said to show likely costs of £19,694·93.

a [7] The Civil Appeals Office (the Office) wrote on 2 October 2000 giving
notice that the hearing of the application would take place on 17 October 2000.
From the statements and documents (not all of them available to Judge LJ) it is
possible to piece together a complicated jigsaw as follows. On 4 October 2000,
Wedlake Bell faxed a copy of this notice to the claimant's solicitors, Charles Khan
of Slough, Berkshire, together with a copy of a reply from Wedlake Bell to the
b Office asking whether the hearing of the application could be advanced. Mr Shah
of Charles Khan produced through counsel before us attendance notes and
telephone messages for the period 5 to 9 October 2000. They show that he saw
the Office's letter on his return to his office on 5 October, and that at or after
4.15 pm he spoke to Mr Ross- Munro's clerk, Paul Dennison, to request him to
make to the listing department of the Office the (unrealistic) suggestion that the
c application for security be listed with the appeal to which it related, in order that
both might be argued by Mr Ross-Munro who had appeared before Ian
Kennedy J but was in Australia on holiday until 31 October.
    [8] A second attendance note dated 6 October at 4.30 pm records Mr Ross-Munro's
clerk as ringing back to say that he had spoken to Julie Whittam (ie Julie Witham,
d a listing assistant in the Office)—

    'to have matter listed with substantive hearing and she has asked for our
    reasons in writing—told Paul I will fax a letter to that effect to Julie Whittam
    (fax no 0207 947 6621)—I will also send him a copy. Told him I will try to see
    if Mr Rashid [junior counsel in another set of chambers] available for
e   17 October 2000 otherwise get back to him for replacement counsel.'

    [9] It seems that Miss Witham also mentioned to the clerk 'that she had been
requested to see if [the matter] could be listed before 17 October by Wedlake Bell',
an obvious reference to Wedlake Bell's letter dated 4 October, of which Mr Shah
anyway had a copy. At 5.15 pm a third attendance note records that Mr Shah had
f a 17 minute conversation with Mr Rashid discussing the matter with him, reserving
him for 17 October if the application was not relisted, and booking a conference
with him for 5.00 pm on Wednesday 11 October.
    [10] Wedlake Bell's request for an earlier listing date was, according to the
Office's records, referred to Judge LJ on 5 October. His judgment dated 10 October
2000 records that he asked the Office to see 'whether arrangements could be made
g for the hearing of these applications to take place' on 10 October 2000. On Friday,
6 October 2000, Miss Avis Jones, deputy listing officer of the Office, telephoned
Charles Khan, and, as she has recorded, was told that there was no one there with
whom a message could be left. She then spoke to Mr Ross-Munro's clerk, Paul
Dennison, to inform him, as she puts it, 'of the date of the rearranged hearing'.
h Inferentially, this call must have been after the clerk's two conversations with
Mr Shah at 4.15 pm and 4.30 pm which I have already recounted, since otherwise
the clerk would have told Mr Shah during one of these conversations about
Miss Jones' call. The clerk, according to his fax dated 9 October 2000, tried to
speak again to Mr Shah, but was told that he was no longer available, having, it
j may well be, left for the weekend.
    [11] Before leaving for the weekend, Mr Shah dictated a letter to the Office
seeking to have the application relisted for 2/3 November, as he had told Mr Ross-
Munro's clerk that he would. But he failed to ensure that it was despatched and
it remained in draft until eventually sent, still unsigned, by his assistant, Mr Khan
junior, on the morning of 10 October. He also started to prepare but left in draft
a further witness statement updating the position in relation to the claimant's lack

of assets. I cannot infer that he did this because of any awareness that the hearing *a* date was being brought forward from 17 October. This witness statement (with some additions to reflect the fact of the hearing and order by Judge LJ on 10 October 2000) was eventually signed on 15 October. It records that Mr Shah was away from his office on both Monday 9 and Tuesday 10 October, and, in another letter dated 10 October, Mr Khan says that this was due to illness.

[12] On Friday 6 October, the clerk to Mr Irvin for the defendants was informed *b* (probably direct by the Office) that the application was being brought forward to 10 October 2000. The two clerks spoke, and Mr Ross-Munro's clerk said that his side were objecting to the new hearing date, in view of Mr Ross-Munro's unavailability, and would be applying to defer the date from 17 October.

[13] On Monday 9 October, Mr Ross-Munro's clerk made repeated attempts to contact Charles Khan, to no avail, until, finally at 6.08 pm, he addressed to *c* Mr Shah at Charles Khan a fax as follows:

> 'I write further to our conversation on Friday afternoon concerning the Security for Costs Application by the other side. When we spoke on Friday it was your intention to write to the Court of Appeal requesting that the application be heard when the main substantive hearing is listed, and *d* furthermore you were going to forward me copy correspondence. Since speaking to you on Friday I have left numerous messages informing you that the Court of Appeal have brought the other side's application from the 17th October to Tuesday 10th October (tomorrow). Given that my calls remain unanswered I will not pursue this matter any further and treat it that we are *e* without instructions in respect of the above hearing. I am obliged for your assistance.'

[14] By that time, according to Mr Shah's statement, Charles Khan's office had closed. The only record within Charles Khan of the earlier calls appears to consist of two telephone pad messages for Mr Shah asking him to call Mr Ross-Munro's *f* clerk in relation to this case, without any indication of the reason. But it seems to me inconceivable that the clerk would not have left (as he says in his fax that he left) an indication as to the reason. Mr Shah has not in any evidence addressed this aspect, though Mr Khan junior's long letter of 10 October asserts the efficiency of Charles Khan's systems for receiving and responding to messages. I cannot accept this assertion. It is evident that, at the least, Charles Khan lacked *g* any proper system for handling outstanding court matters in Mr Shah's absence and for responding promptly to any development. I add that, even on the next day, 10 October, Miss Avis Jones' note of events records her inability to obtain any prompt reaction on the matter despite urgent calls.

[15] An attendance note made by Wedlake Bell records the following as *h* occurring on the morning of 10 October:

> 'Subsequently ringing Charles Khan. Having introduced myself and asked for Mr Shah, there was a pause and the switchboard operator came back to say that Mr Shah had stepped out of the office. I said that the matter was urgent and Mr Shah must be told immediately that we were going ahead *j* with our application to the Court of Appeal which was listed not before 12 this morning. I was then put through to a Mr Khan who told me that he was Mr Shah's assistant. I gave him the same message.'

[16] The switchboard operator's statement to Wedlake Bell that 'Mr Shah had stepped out of the office' contrasts with Mr Khan's letter of the same morning,

a saying that Mr Shah was ill and Mr Shah's statement dated 7 November 2000, saying that he was away from the office. Here, as at some other points, there may be room for suspicion, but we must, I think, proceed on the basis that this was a mere gloss. It would be disproportionate to attempt to investigate such a point further. There is on any view nothing to justify any suspicion in this regard affecting the applicant herself, as distinct from the firm of solicitors instructed by her.

b [17] Also on the morning of 10 October an unidentified member of the staff of Charles Khan, probably Mr Khan junior, saw the fax sent by Mr Ross-Munro's clerk the previous evening. By letter faxed to the Office he said that the clerk's fax had been received after office hours and had just come to his attention, and that Mr Shah was away ill, Mr Ross-Munro away in Australia and junior counsel *c* engaged on another trial. He enclosed the letter that Mr Shah had dictated on Friday 6 October and repeated the request for an adjournment of the application.

[18] Judge LJ ordered the matter to be put back to 3.00 pm, so that the Office could contact Charles Khan and give them the opportunity to make further representations on the claimant's behalf. Mr Trott of the Office spoke to Charles *d* Khan. All that was then forthcoming was Mr Khan's long letter faxed at 2.42 pm. After saying that Charles Khan had no prior knowledge of any hearing date on 10 October, Mr Khan indicated that he had now spoken to Blackstone Chambers, who had no counsel available who could attend that afternoon, and said:

e 'It obviously appears that there has been some administrative oversight or confusion at the Court of Appeal in listing the matter and not informing us, as we were in the procedure [sic] of making representations and having this matter listed together with the Substantive Hearing of the 2nd and 3rd November 2000.'

[19] After referring once again to the suggested relevance of Curtis J's decision, *f* the letter concluded:

'We would respectfully submit that the matter be adjourned to be heard with the Substantive Hearing. We assure the Court that no disrespect is intended for our non-appearance today, which is purely due to not having been informed of today's hearing.'

g [20] I have set out the full position as it now emerges from close examination of all the available material. The material produced after Judge LJ's decision on 10 October, particularly Mr Shah's statement of 7 November 2000 and its enclosures and now the attendance notes and telephone message notes demonstrates (a) that Mr Shah did not on 6 October know that there had been a definite change of *h* hearing date, as opposed to a proposal or request concerning a possible change, (b) the likelihood, however unsatisfactory from an office management viewpoint, that Mr Shah was away on 9 and 10 October, and that no one within Charles Khan appreciated until the morning of 10 October that the hearing date had been advanced to 10 October, and (c) the likelihood that, once this was appreciated, *j* Mr Shah's assistant did at least seek, in open correspondence with Wedlake Bell and the court, and by making inquiries of counsel's chambers, to address the problem.

[21] It follows from (a) that I see no fault on the part of Mr Shah or Charles Khan before the weekend, save in so far as (i) the whole handling of the security application appears to have been dilatory—any witness statement from Mr Shah in response to an application made in early September should have been prepared

long before October, (ii) there was no one in Charles Khan's office who could take a message from Miss Jones—but, at a relatively late hour on a Friday afternoon, this failure seems to me venial, and (iii) Mr Shah failed to fax the Office and send Mr Ross-Munro's clerk a copy as he had told the clerk that he would—but this failure is unrelated to any attempt by the Office to bring forward the previously announced hearing date of 17 October.

[22] As to (b), Charles Khan are in my judgment open to justifiable criticism for not having proper procedures for receiving and responding to messages and developments on outstanding court matters in Mr Shah's absence. However, it is right to add that, even if there had been a due response to Mr Ross-Munro's clerk's messages on Monday 9 October, and counsel had been instructed to attend on 10 October, there is room for some doubt whether the matter could have proceeded then in Mr Shah's absence and without his witness statement having yet been signed or served.

[23] As to (c), once Tuesday 10 October had come, I find it understandable that Mr Khan junior did not attend himself from Slough. But it is less easy to accept that he could not have arranged counsel's attendance from some chambers. However, at that stage this would almost certainly have been pointless, save as a matter of politeness to the court, since counsel could not have familiarised himself with the matter in any way that would have assisted either the claimant or the court. The letters Mr Khan junior wrote were inaccurate regarding the efficiency of the firm's systems for receiving and acting on messages, but they do indicate genuine attempts to deal with an urgent and unexpected matter that had only just come to the attention of an assistant in the absence of his partner.

[24] With hindsight, at least, it is also clear that it would have been better, if the Office—having sent out an original written notice giving 17 October as the hearing date—had, during Friday 6 or (at very latest) Monday 9 October given, by fax, a further written notice bringing forward that date to 10 October. Even in Mr Shah's absence, I do not think that one can exclude the possibility that such a notice would have reached Mr Khan junior's attention and led him to act on Monday 9 October. However, as Mr Shah's own attendance notes acknowledge, such matters are commonly dealt with by contact between counsel's clerk and listing. It was incumbent on Charles Khan to have an efficient internal system for handling outstanding matters in Mr Shah's absence.

JUDGE LJ'S DECISION OF 10 OCTOBER 2000

[25] On the material before Judge LJ, it is not difficult to understand why he refused the suggestion of an adjournment. Nor, in the light of all the material now available, can Charles Khan be excused from blame in the respects that I have identified. On the other hand, any failings undoubtedly look more limited and much less blatant now than they would have done before Judge LJ; and the claimant, whose appeal has been dismissed, was clearly not involved and not to blame in any way, at least during the critical period of 5 October onwards. In the circumstances, I consider it appropriate to look at the wider position and address (a) the question whether there is any procedural basis for revisiting Judge LJ's decision on security, (b) if there is, whether there is any substantive basis for the claimant's submission that no or only much less security should be ordered.

[26] Judge LJ dealt in his judgment with the substantive application for security, quite shortly, as follows:

'10. I have read all the relevant papers. The applicants, the United Bank, are respondents to this appeal which is brought by Amy Nasser against the a   decision of Ian Kennedy J striking out her claim against the bank on grounds of delay. That word sufficiently encompasses the basis on which the judge made his order. Leave has been granted for this appeal to be brought, hence the present application for security.

11. The appellant as she now is, is a citizen of the United States of America. She resides there. There were previous orders for security, the last only

b   discharged when the claimant was granted legal aid in this country. She no longer enjoys the benefit of a legal aid certificate. Those orders were, however, made a long time ago and I have decided that I should examine this application on the basis of more recent events and the facts known to me as they now stand. The evidence suggests that she has no assets at all in this jurisdiction. If her appeal is unsuccessful the respondents will have, putting

c   it neutrally, considerable difficulty in recovering the costs of successfully contesting the appeal. Efforts have been made, and I have seen the correspondence both in June and again in July, to persuade the solicitors for the claimant to provide some security so as to avoid an application. Apart from what could be described as standard courtesies, effectively, there never

d   was any response to those letters. I understood from Mr Irvin this morning, but I am open to correction, that his solicitors have continued to write to the solicitors for the other side trying to encourage rather more activity than the negative responses that were received to the June and July letters.

12. Be that as it may, having stood back from the facts of this case, I am satisfied that the application is justified. I have looked at the figures, there is

e   no one to contend that they are unreasonable, the figures are now approaching something just under £20,000. It seems to me that the appropriate order should be less than that. I shall make it in the sum of £17,500.'

[27] The order drawn up after Judge LJ's decision read as follows:

f   'IT IS ORDERED
1. That the claimant's application contained in letters dated 10 October 2000 to adjourn the hearing of this application be refused. 2. That the claimant provide security for the defendant's costs of the appeal herein by paying the sum of £17,500·00 into court by 4 pm on Tuesday 24 October 2000 and in default of such security being furnished as directed and on the

g   solicitor for the defendant notifying the Civil Appeals Office of such default the said appeal shall stand dismissed with costs without further order ... 6. There be permission to both parties to apply.'

It was stamped 11 October and faxed to Charles Khan on the same date.

h   THE PRESENT APPLICATION
[28] Charles Khan have, in a letter dated 24 October 2000, referred to a copy of a letter dated 11 October 2000 supposedly sent to the listings department of the Court of Appeal, under the permission to apply contained in para 6 of the order, seeking to have the order discharged and/or varied. The Office has not located

j   any original, and Mr Shah's statement does not deal with the matter at all. Suffice it to say, that, even assuming such an original to have been sent and even assuming that the permission to apply could properly be invoked by letter, it cannot assist. Permission to apply is appropriate to enable an order to be worked out, or varied so as to be worked out differently, e g by extending the time for compliance. Here, what is intended is quite different. It is revocation of the whole order for security, or variation of the amount ordered.

[29] The present application was not made until 25 October 2000, after the date
for putting up security had passed. Nevertheless, CPR 3.1(7) and 23.11 confer a
discretion wide enough to cover it. They read:

'3.1 ...
(7) A power of the court under these Rules to make an order includes a
power to vary or revoke the order ...
23.11 ...
(1) Where the applicant or any respondent fails to attend the hearing of an
application, the court may proceed in his absence.
(2) Where—(a) the applicant or any respondent fails to attend the hearing
of an application; and (b) the court makes an order at the hearing, the court
may, on application or of its own initiative, re-list the application.'

[30] These are new and wider powers than previously available (cf the note to
r 23.11). They need to be exercised cautiously in relation to hearings of which a
party has received appropriate notice. But that procedural power exists to set aside
Judge LJ's order regarding security is clear and was in the event accepted before us.

THE MERITS OF THE ISSUE WHETHER AN ORDER FOR SECURITY SHOULD HAVE BEEN
MADE

[31] I turn therefore to the merits of the issue whether the order for security
should have been made and whether it should, in the light of the further evidence
and submissions now before the court, stand. We have invited and heard submissions
on aspects of the matter that neither side had, it appears, previously considered.
This case highlights an important change in the practice of this court as regards
security for the costs of appeals. The change appears from a comparison of the
new CPR 25.15, read with r 25.13(2)(a) with the old RSC Ord 59, r 10(5). It is
discussed in the notes at para 25.15.1 of the 2001 White Book.

[32] Formerly, the court had a discretion to order security 'in special
circumstances', and it was 'settled practice' that impecuniosity constituted, of itself,
such a circumstance (see notes at para 59/10/20 in the 1999 and prior White
Books). That was, however, counterbalanced in an extreme case, by the
consideration mentioned earlier in this judgment, that a genuine claim, at least
one with apparent prospects, should not be stifled by a requirement to put up
security that an appellant could not provide. In this connection, it was
well-established that it was for an appellant to show not only that he could not
raise the money from his own resources, but also (and the onus was on him on
this issue too) that he could not raise the money from other sources, e g friends
or supporters (see the note at para 59/10/39 in the 1999 White Book, referring to
M V Yorke Motors (a firm) v Edwards [1982] 1 All ER 1024, [1982] 1 WLR 444).

[33] In contrast, since 2 May 2000, r 25.15 provides:

'25.15 Security for costs of an appeal
(1) The court may order security for costs of an appeal against—(a) an
appellant; (b) a respondent who also appeals, on the same grounds as it may
order security for costs against a claimant under this Part.
(2) The court may also make an order under paragraph (1) where the
appellant, or the respondent who also appeals, is a limited company and
there is reason to believe it will be unable to pay the costs of the other parties
to the appeal should its appeal be unsuccessful.'

a   **[34]** The court may now, therefore, only order security for the costs of an appeal 'against … an appellant … on the same grounds as it may order security for costs against a claimant under this Part'. Impecuniosity is no longer of itself a ground. The only potentially applicable ground in the present case is found in r 25.13(1) and (2)(a). I set this out in context:

b   '(1) The court may make an order for security for costs under rule 25.12 if—(a) it is satisfied, having regard to all the circumstances of the case, that it is just to make such an order; and (b) (i) one or more of the conditions in paragraph (2) applies, or (ii) an enactment permits the court to require security for costs.

(2) The conditions are—(a) the claimant is an individual—(i) who is ordinarily
c   resident out of the jurisdiction; and (ii) is not a person against whom a claim can be enforced under the Brussels Conventions or the Lugano Convention, as defined by section 1(1) of the Civil Jurisdiction and Judgments Act 1982; (b) the claimant is a company or other incorporated body—(i) which is ordinarily resident out of the jurisdiction; and (ii) is not a body against whom
d   a claim can be enforced under the Brussels Conventions or the Lugano Convention; (c) the claimant is a company or other body (whether incorporated inside or outside Great Britain) and there is reason to believe that it will be unable to pay the defendant's costs if ordered to do so …'

[35] Rule 25.13(2)(a)(i) and (b)(i) mirror a ground for ordering a plaintiff to
e   give security for costs at first instance under the previous rules. In that connection there was clear authority, indicating that, although foreign residence was a precondition to the making of such an order, once that precondition was satisfied, the court could have regard not merely to matters related directly to the foreign residence, but also to matters intrinsic to the plaintiff wherever he or she might
f   be, such as impecuniosity (see *Thune v London Properties Ltd* [1990] 1 All ER 972, [1990] 1 WLR 562).

[36] One aspect of the rationale of the change now made to the rules relating to security for costs of an appeal is found in the precondition under CPR to any appeal, that permission to appeal should have been obtained. Once it has been obtained, then in the normal case, it follows that there must be a 'real prospect'
g   of the appeal succeeding. But that cannot represent the only aspect to the change, since the existence of a 'real prospect' of a successful appeal was not an automatic bar to an order for security for the costs of an appeal under the old rules.

[37] The other aspect must in my judgment lie in recognition that, for those with a real prospect of success, ease of access to appellate justice should be given
h   greater priority than hitherto. That is consistent both with one important aim of the new CPR generally and with art 6 of the European Convention on Human Rights, which provides:

'*Article 6*
Right to a fair trial
j   1. In the determination of his civil rights and obligations … everyone is entitled to a fair and public hearing within a reasonable time by an independent and impartial tribunal established by law.'

[38] Since 2 October 2000, English courts are obliged to act compatibly with the European Convention on Human Rights and, when determining any question which has arisen in connection with a convention right, to take into account decisions of the European Court of Human Rights (ss 2(1), 6(1) and (3) of the Human Rights Act 1998). *a*

[39] I start by noting the approach of the European Court to orders for security for costs of an appeal made under the old rules. In *Tolstoy Miloslavsky v UK* (1995) 20 EHRR 442, the European Court had to consider an order that security for costs of an appeal be provided in the sum of £124,900 within 14 days. The court's starting point (at 475 (para 59)) was that 'a Contracting State which sets up an *b* appeal system is required to ensure that persons within its jurisdiction enjoy before appellate courts the fundamental guarantees in Article 6'.

[40] 'However', it went on (at 475–476):

'2. *Compliance of Article 6(1)*

59. The Court reiterates that the right of access to the courts secured by *c* Article 6(1) may be subject to limitations in the form of regulation by the State. In this respect the State enjoys a certain margin of appreciation. However, the Court must be satisfied, firstly, that the limitations applied do not restrict or reduce the access left to the individual in such a way or to such an extent that the very essence of the right is impaired. Secondly, a restriction *d* must pursue a legitimate aim and there must be a reasonable relationship of proportionality between the means employed and the aim sought to be achieved. It follows from established case law that Article 6(1) does not guarantee a right of appeal. Nevertheless, a Contracting State which sets up an appeal system is required to ensure that persons within its jurisdiction enjoy before appellate courts the fundamental guarantees in Article 6. *e* However, the manner of application of Article 6 to proceedings before such courts depends on the special features of the proceedings involved; account must be taken of the entirety of the proceedings in the domestic legal order and of the role of the appellate court therein. The Court's task is not to substitute itself for the competent British authorities in determining the most *f* appropriate policy for regulating access to the Court of Appeal in libel cases, nor to assess the facts which led that court to adopt one decision rather than another. The Court's role is to review under the Convention the decisions that those authorities have taken in the exercise of their power of appreciation.'

[41] After a careful examination of the course of the proceedings between *g* Lord Aldington and Count Tolstoy, the court (at 476 (para 62)) rejected Count Tolstoy's submission that the order impaired the 'very essence of the right of access to court and was disproportionate for the purposes of Article 6'. But it is its reasons for doing so that are most relevant here. They appear from paras 63–67 (at 477–478): *h*

'63. In the first place, the case had been heard for some 40 days at first instance before the High Court, in the course of which Lord Aldington gave evidence for more than six days and was cross-examined, the applicant gave evidence for more than five days and a number of witnesses were called. It is undisputed that the applicant enjoyed full access to court in those *j* proceedings. It is true that he initially complained about their lack of fairness. However, that complaint was declared inadmissible by the Commission as being manifestly ill-founded. The Court attaches great weight to the above considerations in its assessment of the compatibility with Article 6 of the restrictions on the applicant's access to the Court of Appeal. Indeed, as indicated earlier, the entirety of the proceedings must be taken into account.

64. Admittedly, the sum required—£124,900—was very substantial and
the time-limit—14 days—for providing the money was relatively short.
However, there is nothing to suggest that the figure was an unreasonable
estimate of Lord Aldington's costs before the Court of Appeal or that the
applicant would have been able to raise the money had he been given more
time.

65. According to the relevant practice in the Court of Appeal, impecuniosity
was a ground for awarding security for costs of an appeal to that court, but
only on certain conditions. In exercising its discretion as to whether to grant
an application for such an order, the Court of Appeal would consider
whether the measure would amount to a denial of justice to the defendant,
in particular having regard to the merits of the appeal. If it had reasonable
prospects of success, the Court of Appeal would be reluctant to order
security for costs. The disagreement between the applicant and Lord
Aldington in the security for costs proceedings concerned the merits or lack
of merits of the appeal. The Registrar of the Court of Appeal, with hesitation,
decided that the appeal had just enough strength to allow the applicant to
proceed without furnishing security for costs. This decision was subsequently
reversed by the Court of Appeal because the applicant had failed to show real
and substantial grounds for his appeal, both on liability and on damages. On
the point of damages, the Court of Appeal observed, *inter alia*, that the
applicant was not so interested in that issue as in the question of liability and
that he had declined to accept Lord Aldington's offer to settle for £300,000.
Therefore, an appeal on damages only would have been no more than an
academic exercise. The Court does not find that the justification given by the
Court of Appeal for ordering security for costs disclosed any arbitrariness.

66. Moreover, the security for costs issue was first examined by the
Registrar of the Court of Appeal and then heard by the court for six days.
The Court of Appeal's decision was thus based on a full and thorough
evaluation of the relevant factors.

67. In the light of the foregoing, the Court does not find that the national
authorities overstepped their margin of appreciation in setting the conditions
which they did for the applicant to pursue his appeal in the Court of Appeal.
It cannot be said that those conditions impaired the essence of the applicant's
right of access to court or were disproportionate for the purposes of Article 6(1).'

[42] It is evident that the European Court attached great weight to (a) the fact
that there had been a full hearing on the merits of the libel case, (b) the fact that
there had been full hearings of the security for costs application, (c) the Court of
Appeal's conclusion on the hearing for security that the appellant had no real or
substantial grounds for his appeal on liability or damages (that appeal being
brought as of right under the then procedure), (d) the reasonableness of the
estimate of costs, (e) Count Tolstoy's ability to raise the money required, at least
if given an extension of time, and (f) on the evidence before the European Court
(at 477 (para 65)), the Court of Appeal's reluctance to order security for costs,
against an appellant with reasonable prospects of success and its readiness to
consider in the context of any application for an extension of time, whether
refusal 'would amount to a denial of justice to the defendant, in particular having
regard to the merits of the appeal'.

[43] A cautionary warning that there may be unexpected implications in
orders for security for costs that have the effect that no hearing occurs is also

found in the Cour de Cassation decision in the case of *Pordéa v Times Newpapers* [2000] IL Pr 763. Mr Pordéa had had his claim for libel in the English High Court dismissed in 1988, following his non-compliance with an order to put up security for costs in the sum of £25,000. Judgment was entered against him for The Times' costs of the action in a sum taxed, later in 1988, at £20,078. The Cour de Cassation refused to enforce this judgment against Mr Pordéa, taking the view under art 27(1) of the Brussels Convention on Jurisdiction and Enforcement of Judgments in Civil and Commercial Matters (as set out in Sch 1 to the Civil Jurisdiction and Judgments Act 1982 as amended) (the Brussels Convention) that it was contrary to public policy, in that the security for costs order made against Mr Pordéa had infringed art 6(1) of the European Convention on Human Rights. The order for security in *Pordéa*'s case was made long before the Court of Appeal's decision in *Fitzgerald v Williams, O'Regan v Williams* [1996] 2 All ER 171, [1996] QB 657 precluded the making of such orders against persons domiciled and resident in another member state of the European Union (and so party to the Brussels Convention), because so to order would be covertly discrimatory. This has been overlooked by French commentators writing, somewhat caustically, about English practice in the light of *Pordéa*'s case (see e g Georges A L Droz 'Variations Pordéa (À propos de l'arrêt de la Cour de cassation; 1re Chambre Civile, du 16 Mars 1999)' (2000) 89(2) Rev crit dr intl priv 181). But the incorporation of art 6(1) into English domestic law means that the decision retains some general interest.

[44] Following the introduction of the general requirement of permission to appeal, but before the introduction of the new rule relating to security, r 25.15, and the incorporation of the convention, this court considered the impact of *Tolstoy Miloslavsky v UK* on an order for security for the costs of an appeal in *Federal Bank of the Middle East v Hadkinson, Hadkinson v Saab* [2000] 1 Costs LR 94. Morritt LJ as the single judge pointed out that the European Convention on Human Rights was not then in force and that the effects of the order he proposed would expire before it came into force. The full court upholding his order said that it did not breach art 6 because it had 'not been demonstrated that the appeal would be stifled by making the order'.

[45] With the introduction of r 25.15, the grant of permission to appeal achieves a wider significance. A personal litigant with permission to appeal is equated with a personal claimant. Impecuniosity has been abandoned as a ground for ordering security for the costs of an appeal. The grant of permission denotes at the least a real prospect of success or some other compelling reason for an appeal. In this context, the policy adopted has been to restrict the grounds on which security may be ordered, and so to ease access to an appellate court for those with a real prospect of success or some other compelling reason for an appeal.

[46] What remains as one ground on which security may be ordered is foreign residence—except in cases involving the 'single legal market' to which the Brussels Convention and the Lugano Convention on Jurisdiction and the Enforcement of Judgments in Civil and Commercial Matters (as set out in Sch 3C to the 1982 Act as inserted by s 1(3) and Sch 1 to the Civil Jurisdiction and Judgments Act 1991) (the Lugano Convention) aspire in matters of enforcement and recognition. The rationale of the discretion to order security on that ground is that enforcement of an order for security for costs abroad may be more difficult or costly than elsewhere (cf Sir Jeffery Bowman's 1997 Review (paras 33–37)). The single legal market of the Brussels and Lugano Conventions means that 'abroad' in this context now means not merely outside England or the United

a Kingdom, but outside the jurisdictions of the states party to those conventions. It is however important that rr 25.15(1) and 25.13(1) involve a discretion.

[47] I turn now to consider whether and to what extent these rules raise any issue of discrimination. It is at this point that art 14 of the European Convention on Human Rights, now incorporated, has potential significance. It reads:

b
'*Article 14*
Prohibition of discrimination
The enjoyment of the rights and freedoms set forth in this Convention shall be secured without discrimination on any ground such as sex, race, colour, language, religion, political or other opinion, national or social origin, association with a national minority, property, birth or other status.'

c
[48] The ambit of art 14 in the light of its express terms has been considered by the European Court. The following principles are put forward by Mr Irvin for the defendants and not challenged by Mr Edwards for the claimant:

'(a) Article 14 applies to the "enjoyment" of convention rights. This
d means that even if there is no actual *breach* of a convention right there can still be an art 14 claim if the conduct complained of comes within the *ambit* of the right, ie its subject matter is linked to the exercise of the right concerned (*Belgian Linguistics Case (No 2)* (1968) 1 EHRR 252) ... (b) Therefore, as long as it is established that orders for security for costs fall within the *ambit* of the right to a fair trial in art 6, the United Kingdom is obliged to exercise its
e discretion in granting orders in a way which does not discriminate under art 14. (c) A claim falls within the ambit of art 6 if the conduct is linked to one of the rights inherent in art 6, which includes *effective access to the courts* in the determination of a civil right or obligation (or a criminal charge) (*Golder v UK* (1975) 1 EHRR 524). (d) An applicant next has to show that he or she is
f treated less favourably than other people who are in a *relevantly similar or analogous situation* (*Stubbings v UK* (1996) 23 EHRR 213). (e) Article 14 then prohibits discrimination between those people on a "prohibited ground", which includes those listed in art 14 and others. (f) Conduct which would otherwise be unlawful will not breach art 14 if it is *objectively justified*, ie it pursues a legitimate aim (the *Belgian Linguistics Case*). (g) The conduct must
g also be a *proportionate* means of achieving the legitimate aim. Proportionality under the convention involves striking a fair balance between the protection of the interest of the community and a respect for the rights and freedoms safeguarded by the convention (*Sporrong v Sweden* (1982) 5 EHRR 35). (h) Finally, contracting states enjoy a *margin of appreciation* (ie a discretion) in
h relation to the question of justification, which depends on all the circumstances, subject matter and background of the case (*Rasmussen v Denmark* (1984) 7 EHRR 371).'

[49] The last principle is, however, applicable rather at the level of the European Court in Strasbourg than before us. We have to make up our own
j minds what, in the English domestic context, is a justifiable and proportionate exercise of discretion.

[50] Mr Irvin accepts, realistically, that the rules relating to the provision of security for costs fall within the ambit of the right of access to courts under art 6. The reasoning in *Tolstoy Miloslavsky v UK* indicates this, likewise that in the *Federal Bank* case. I took the same view, after the incorporation of the convention, sitting as a single judge of this court in *Gulf Azov Shipping Co Ltd v Idisi* [2000] CA

Transcript 2316. My reasoning there (in the context of applications made under both the old and the new rules, though the application under the new rules failed for the special reason that the appeal related to a finding of contempt) depended on clear evidence that there would, in the light of the defendant's conduct in the action so far and influence and conduct in Nigeria, be very substantial difficulty in enforcing any judgment for costs against him in Nigeria. That made it appropriate to order security on the first application by reference to the full amount of the costs likely to be incurred in the Court of Appeal.

[51] Whilst, in *Tolstoy Miloslavsky v UK*, the European Court has considered and accepted an application for security for costs made on the ground of impecuniosity in the context of the old rules, the new rules, with their distinction between residents inside and outside Brussels and Lugano Convention states, raise a potential issue of discrimination that could not have arisen under the old rules. The European Court pointed out in *Belgian Linguistics Case (No 2)* (1968) 1 EHRR 252 at 283 (para 9), giving the example of a right of appeal, that a state may not be obliged to have a particular procedure, but that, if it does have it, then the procedure must not involve undue discrimination. The question can therefore arise whether the limitation of the right to order security for costs to those resident outside Brussels/Lugano states is or may be discriminatory.

[52] It is instructive to look more closely at *Fitzgerald v Williams, O'Regan v Williams* [1996] 2 All ER 171, [1996] QB 657 to which I have already made passing reference. The argument there turned on art 6 of the EC Treaty (now art 12 EC), which provided: 'Within the scope of application of this Treaty, and without prejudice to any special provisions contained therein, any discrimination on grounds of nationality shall be prohibited.'

[53] The Court of Appeal in *Fitzgerald v Williams* referred to the European Court's decision in *Mund & Fester v Hatrex International Transport* Case C-398/92 [1994] ECR I-467 as establishing that any automatic provision for security for costs against a person resident in another member state of the European Union would be covertly discriminatory on grounds of nationality. The *Mund* case concerned such a provision (under German law). The former English rule, which *Fitzgerald v Williams* concerned, was different. It contained no explicit presumption that a judgment would be more difficult to enforce abroad, and it conferred a discretionary power. The Court of Appeal concluded however that a modification of English law or practice was required in the light of the *Mund* decision:

> 'The answer compelled by *Mund* in my view is: the English court should never exercise its discretion under the rule to order security to be given by an individual plaintiff who is a national of and resident in another member state party to the convention [ie the Brussels Convention], at any rate in the absence of very cogent evidence of substantial difficulty in enforcing a judgment in that other member state.' (See [1996] 2 All ER 171 at 183, [1996] QB 657 at 675 per Bingham MR.)

[54] There was no suggestion in *Fitzgerald v Williams* that the traditional practice of the English court required any modification where a plaintiff was ordinarily resident in a country not a member of the European Union. But the introduction of r 25.15, the incorporation into English law of the European Convention on Human Rights and the provisions of s 6(1) and (3)(a) of the 1998 Act making it unlawful for the court as a public authority to act in a way which is incompatible with a convention right, require us to address the possibility that it now is.

a   [55] Although the precise phraseology of art 14 of the European Convention on Human Rights is different to that of art 6 of the EC Treaty (which speaks simply of 'nationality'), I do not think that the two articles can sensibly be distinguished as regards the protection that they may afford in respect of orders against foreign residents for security for costs. And the national origin of the great majority of foreign residents affected by orders for security for costs under
b   (now) r 25.15(1) read with r 25.13(2)(a) is likely to be in states not party to the Brussels or Lugano Conventions: compare the *Mund* case and *Fitzgerald v Williams*, where the fact that the great majority of persons resident abroad against whom enforcement abroad would take place would be foreign nationals led to the conclusion that there was illegitimate discrimination. However, there is the distinction that in *Fitzgerald v Williams* the discrimination was between those
c   resident in the United Kingdom and those resident in other European Union states party to the Brussels Convention. The existence of the Brussels Convention was a central element in the reasoning in both the *Mund* case and *Fitzgerald v Williams*.

[56] Mr Irvin submits on this basis that r 25.13(2)(a)(i) and (b)(i) do not treat
d   the claimant differently from anyone 'in an analogous or relevantly similar situation', a phrase taken from *Stubbings v UK* (1996) 23 EHRR 213. The European Court there upheld the distinction drawn by the English Limitation Act 1980 between cases of intentionally and negligently inflicted harm (the former subject to a strict six-year time limit running from the age of majority, which could operate more restrictively than the latter, based on a time limit of three years
e   running from the date of knowledge with provisions for discretionary extension under s 33 of the 1980 Act). The European Court (at 238–239 (para 71)) accepted that English law could legitimately regard these cases as falling within different categories (pointing out that it may be more readily apparent to the victims of deliberate wrongdoing that they have a cause of action). It went on (at 239
f   (para 72)) that, even if a comparison could properly be drawn between the two groups, 'the difference in treatment may be reasonably and objectively justified, again by reference to their distinctive characteristics'. It is, thus, evident that there is a close relationship between the questions whether two groups are to be regarded as falling within different categories and whether, if so, any difference in their treatment is reasonable and objectively justified; the two questions tend to
g   merge into each other.

[57] Mr Irvin's submission here is that the claimant is in an analogous or relevantly similar position to all other foreign residents in states not party to the Brussels or Lugano Conventions, and that she is treated alike with them. That submission depends upon the level at which the class is identified, and this may,
h   in my view, also depend upon the context in which the analogy is drawn or the similarity is said to be 'relevant'. At one most obvious level, all personal claimants (or appellants) before the English courts fall into one category. But the rules draw a distinction at another level, between claimants resident within and outside Brussels and Lugano states. This distinction serves simply to identify *when* a
j   discretion exists to order security for a defendant's or respondent's costs. In that context, the distinction between residents within and outside Brussels and Lugano states cannot be regarded as unduly discriminatory, since, first, it can be said that the recognition of separate categories makes sense as a broad rule of thumb, defining when any question of discretion can arise (rather than how it will be exercised); and, secondly and in any event, the distinction drawn is in that context reasonable and objectively justifiable. The single legal market of the

Brussels and Lugano Conventions is a significant achievement on the road to easy *a* and automatic recognition and enforcement of judgments, as recognised by the decision in the *Mund* case.

[58] The exercise of the discretion conferred by r 25.13(1), (2)(a)(i) and (b)(i) raises, in my judgment, different considerations. That discretion must itself be exercised by the courts in a manner which is not discriminatory. In this context, at least, I consider that all personal claimants (or appellants) before the English *b* courts must be regarded as the relevant class. It would be both discriminatory and unjustifiable if the mere fact of residence outside any Brussels/Lugano member state could justify the exercise of discretion to make orders for security for costs with the purpose or effect of protecting defendants or respondents to appeals against risks, to which they would equally be subject and in relation to which they would have no protection if the claim or appeal were being brought *c* by a resident of a Brussels or Lugano state. Potential difficulties or burdens of enforcement in states not party to the Brussels or Lugano Conventions are the rationale for the existence of any discretion. The discretion should be exercised in a manner reflecting its rationale, not so as to put residents outside the Brussels/Lugano sphere at a disadvantage compared with residents within. The distinction *d* in the rules based on considerations of enforcement cannot be used to discriminate against those whose national origin is outside any Brussels and Lugano state on grounds unrelated to enforcement.

[59] In this connection, I do not consider that one can start with any inflexible assumption that any person not resident in a Brussels or Lugano state should provide security for costs. Merely because a person is not resident in England or *e* another Brussels or Lugano state does not *necessarily* mean that enforcement will be more difficult. The modern European equivalent of the Queen's writ may not run. But the entire rest of the world cannot be regarded as beyond the legal pale. For example, the United Kingdom has reciprocal arrangements for recognition and enforcement with many Commonwealth and common law countries which *f* have introduced legislation equivalent to Pt I of the Foreign Judgments (Reciprocal Enforcement) Act 1933 (or Pt II of the Administration of Justice Act 1920), and which have highly sophisticated and respected legal systems. Many other countries have well-established procedures for recognising English judgments. The exercise of the discretion on grounds of foreign residence should not be either automatic *g* or inflexible.

[60] I would interpose at this point that, even where a claimant or appellant is resident abroad, there may of course be special factors indicating that any order for costs will be satisfied in some other fashion. The interesting possibility was raised before us that a claimant or appellant who has insured against liability for the defendants' costs in the event of the action or appeal failing might be able to *h* rely on the existence of such insurance as sufficient security in itself. I comment on this possibility only to the extent of saying that I would think that defendants would, at the least, be entitled to some assurance as to the scope of the cover, that it was not liable to be avoided for misrepresentation or non-disclosure (it may be that such policies have anti-avoidance provisions) and that its proceeds could not *j* be diverted elsewhere. The new arrangements for the funding of litigation certainly appear capable of throwing up possible imbalance, in so far as they permit contingency fee arrangements with uplifts potentially recoverable from losing defendants, but enable claimants to pursue litigation without insuring or securing the defendants' fees. The claimant's contingency fee arrangement in the present case is, however, without uplift.

a [61] Returning to rr 25.15(1), 25.13(1), (2)(a) and (b), if the discretion to order security is to be exercised, it should therefore be on objectively justified grounds relating to obstacles to or the burden of enforcement in the context of the particular foreign claimant or country concerned. The former principle was that, once the power to order security arose because of foreign residence, impecuniosity became one along with other material factors (see the case of *Thune v London*
b *Properties Ltd* [1990] 1 All ER 972, [1990] 1 WLR 562). This principle cannot in my judgment survive, in an era which no longer permits discrimination in access to justice on grounds of national origin. Impecuniosity of an individual claimant resident within the jurisdiction or in a Brussels or Lugano state is not a basis for seeking security. Insolvent or impecunious companies present a different situation, since the power under r 25.13(2)(c) applies to companies wherever incorporated
c and resident, and is not discriminatory.

[62] The justification for the discretion under rr 25.13(2)(a), (b) and 25.15(1) in relation to individuals and companies ordinarily resident abroad is that in some, it may well be many, cases there are likely to be substantial obstacles to or a substantial extra burden (e g of costs or delay) in enforcing an English judgment,
d significantly greater than there would be as regards a party resident in England or in a Brussels or Lugano state. In so far as impecuniosity may have a continuing relevance, it is not on the ground that the claimant lacks apparent means to satisfy any judgment, but on the ground (where this applies) that the effect of the impecuniosity would be either (i) to preclude or hinder or add to the burden of
e enforcement abroad against such assets as *do* exist abroad, or (ii) as a practical matter, to make it more likely that the claimant would take advantage of any available opportunity to avoid or hinder such enforcement abroad.

[63] It also follows, I consider, that there can be no inflexible assumption that there will in every case be substantial obstacles to enforcement against a foreign resident claimant in his or her (or, in the case of a company, its) country of foreign
f residence or wherever his, her or its assets may be. If the discretion under rr 25.13(2)(a) or (b) or 25.15(1) is to be exercised, there must be a proper basis for considering that such obstacles may exist, or that enforcement may be encumbered by some extra burden (such as costs or the burden of an irrecoverable contingency fee or simply delay).

g [64] The courts may and should, however, take notice of obvious realities without formal evidence. There are some parts of the world where the natural assumption would be without more that there would not just be substantial obstacles but complete impossibility of enforcement; and there are many cases where the natural assumption would be that enforcement would be cumbersome
h and involve a substantial extra burden of costs or delay. But in other cases—particularly other common law countries which introduced in relation to English judgments legislation equivalent to Pt I of the 1933 Act (or Pt II of the 1920 Act)—it may be incumbent on an applicant to show some basis for concluding that enforcement would face any substantial obstacle or extra burden, meriting
j the protection of an order for security for costs. Even then, it seems to me that the court should consider tailoring the order for security to the particular circumstances. If, for example, there is likely at the end of the day to be no obstacle to or difficulty about enforcement, but simply an extra burden in the form of costs (or an irrecoverable contingency fee) or moderate delay, the appropriate course could well be to limit the amount of the security ordered by reference to that potential burden.

[65] I also consider that the mere absence of reciprocal arrangements or legislation providing for enforcement of foreign judgments cannot *of itself* justify an inference that enforcement will not be possible. The present case illustrates this. It is a remarkable fact that no country has ever entered into any treaty providing for recognition and enforcement of judgments with the United States of America. But the reason is concern about the breadth of American jurisdiction, the corollary of which has been a willingness on the United States part to recognise and enforce foreign judgments by action on a similarly liberal and flexible basis (see e g Kevin M Clermont 'Jurisdictional Salvation and the Hague Treaty' (1999) 85 Cornell L Rev 89 at 97–98). I am not aware that anyone has ever suggested that access to justice or to the means of executing justice is an American problem. Certainly no evidence has been put before us to suggest that the defendants would, or even could, face any real obstacle or difficulty of legal principle in enforcing in the United States any English judgment for costs against this claimant.

[66] There is also no express suggestion in any evidence in this case that the defendants would face any extra burden in taking any such enforcement action against the claimant for costs. But we can, I think, infer without more that it would in the case of this particular claimant resident in Milwaukee. First, the defendants would have to bring an action on any English judgment for costs, before proceeding to any enforcement steps that United States law or the law of Wisconsin permits. Second, the claimant's impecuniosity has collateral relevance, in so far as it is likely that the defendants would have to investigate whether it is as real and great as she asserts, and this is likely to be more expensive to undertake abroad than it would be if she was resident in the United Kingdom or a Brussels/Lugano state. Third, the course of the present litigation to date suggests that the claimant is a determined litigant who can be relied upon by one means or another to take every conceivable step she can to defend what she asserts to be her rights, but whose very lack of means to fund the appropriate conduct of litigation appears prone to add to the difficulty faced by the defendants. Fourth, there would be likely to be delay in enforcement, by reason of each of the first three points. Viewing the matter both in the light of these factors and as a matter of general common sense, I consider that it is open to us to infer that steps taken to enforce any English judgment for costs in the United States would thus be likely to involve a significantly greater burden in terms of costs and delay than enforcement of a costs order made against an unsuccessful domestic or Brussels/Lugano claimant or appellant. It is possible that an irrecoverable costs burden (or an irrecoverable contingency fee) would also be involved, even if the claimant proved to have sufficient assets to satisfy any judgment, but I do not think that this can be assumed without evidence.

[67] The risk against which the present defendants are entitled to protection is, thus, not that the claimant will not have the assets to pay the costs, and not that the law of her state of residence will not recognise and enforce any judgment against her for costs. It is that the steps taken to enforce any such judgment in the United States will involve an extra burden in terms of costs and delay, compared with any equivalent steps that could be taken here or in any other Brussels/Lugano state. Any order for security for costs in this case should be tailored in amount to reflect the nature and size of the risk against which it is designed to protect.

[68] When the matter came before Judge LJ, in the absence of the claimant, these matters were not considered. They had not been raised in any skeleton or

a submission put before him on either side. Further, they arise from the need to interpret a new rule, and in doing so to take into account the principles of the newly incorporated European Convention on Human Rights. Now that they have been considered, the position looks very different. But, before attempting to quantify the level of any security, it is appropriate to deal with two other objections to the order made by Judge LJ.

b
OTHER OBJECTIONS TO THE ORDER FOR SECURITY

(a) *'Stifling' the claim*
[69] Even under the old principles, although impecuniosity was a ground for an order for security, impecuniosity so severe that an order for security would
c stifle a genuine appeal provided a basis for resisting an order, although the force of the objection was commonly related to the strength of the prospects of the appeal. In the present case, the claimant must be taken to have a real prospect of success. No conditions were imposed on the permission granted. Latham LJ did not give reasons for the grant of permission. But the skeletons before him indicate that the challenge to Ian Kennedy J's order striking out the whole proceedings for
d want of prosecution is based very substantially on submissions (borne out by his judgment) that Ian Kennedy J nowhere referred to the principles of CPR (as distinct from those applicable under the old rules) and that the result he reached was disproportionate in depriving the claimant of any trial at all on the basis of no more than about two years inexcusable delay; it was also said that a witness who
e Ian Kennedy J thought could not be traced was in fact readily traceable and has been traced (although that is in issue).
[70] Here, furthermore, the claimant has not only not had any trial of her original action, but the order for security has now meant that she has not had heard any appeal against the decision that there should be no such trial. In both these respects the present case contrasts starkly with factors on which the European
f Court placed emphasis in *Tolstoy Miloslavsky v UK* (1995) 20 EHRR 442. Further, the European Court in *Tolstoy Miloslavsky v UK* underlined that there was no suggestion there that Count Tolstoy could not have provided the security ordered, or that his access to justice was thereby denied, and also recorded its understanding that the English court of appeal would be reluctant to order
g security for the costs of any appeal with reasonable prospects of success.
[71] We have not been invited to revisit the material put before Curtis J concerning the claimant's assets and her relatives' and friends' unwillingness to lend her further financial support. The claimant relies on Curtis J's conclusion in 1998 that anything more than a nominal order would 'snuff out' the claimant's action and that consequently it would not be right to make an order. That
h conclusion is, as I have pointed out, weakened by its reliance on the Legal Aid Board's investigations leading to the grant of legal aid that was later withdrawn. The withdrawal appears not to have related to the sum of £40,000 transferred from an account in the claimant's name said to belong to her sister, which troubled Curtis J, but to another withdrawal in December 1997 of further
j moneys (c $US9,000) from a 'Firstar' account in the claimant's name said to belong to her husband.
[72] Mr Shah's witness statement prepared in draft on 6 October and signed on 15 October 2000 is aimed at updating the claimant's financial position and reinforcing a conclusion that she continues to lack both funds and the means to raise any funds. The claimant has separated from her husband (it is said due to disagreement over her obsession with this litigation). The unusual separation

agreement made through lawyers with her husband on 13 November 1995
provided, it seems, originally for her to receive a roof over her head, $US100 a
week and one return airfare to England each year. But she later moved out to live
with her sister, who does not charge her rent or for food or other bills. Her
husband still gives her $US100 a week and one return airfare to England each
year. Curtis J was not prepared to accept that this agreement was some sort of
device, and this suggestion was not repeated before us. The claimant is said to
have no other income or assets and to have debts of £18,000.

[73] Before us, however, it emerged that (unlike her solicitors) counsel was
not operating on a contingency fee basis, so that the claimant has been able to
raise a further loan for £1,500. In addition, we were told of (unsuccessful) attempts
to take out insurance to cover her exposure to the defendants' costs of this action.
They too suggest some ability to raise funds to pay a premium. It was not suggested
that the solicitors were proposing to lend her the premium. So I for my part
remained unconvinced that the claimant is absolutely without funds or the ability
to raise them. The history of two accounts in her name, said on each occasion to
belong to someone else, generates concern, but I do not feel able to reject out of
hand and without cross-examination her explanations. Accepting her separation
as genuine, I am prepared also to accept that she is short of money and indeed
owes substantial sums. But, on the material available at this point in time, I
conclude that she is still able to raise, at the least, modest sums.

(b) *The amount of security sought*

[74] The second objection relates to the amount of security sought and
ordered. This, it is submitted, was and is excessive. I need not go into the matter
in great detail. I agree with the submission, though not to its full extent which
was that the security claimed could on no account exceed £2,500. It is the fact,
however, that the application to strike out was fully prepared and was argued by
counsel below, and that its course will be largely repeated on appeal. The draft
bill of costs submitted by Wedlake Bell's costs draughtsman includes figures that
I cannot accept as justifiable or proportionate on an appeal of this nature. The
partner in charge (costed at £270 per hour) is recorded as having spent two hours
on the matter in conference with counsel and, since the hearing below, a further
nine and a half hours on 'Perusal, consideration and preparation of documents,
reviewing notice of appeal, application notices and witness statements, perusing
transcript of judgment, [and] drafting instructions to counsel', in addition to five
and a half hours spent under the same heading by a trainee solicitor, costed at £80
per hour. The reference to application notices no doubt embraces the successful
application to adduce fresh evidence, but that was very limited in scope and, even
assuming that the work described should be read as covering some approach to
check whether the right Lena Sabbagh had been identified, this can hardly have
involved much partner time. Yet, it is said that the partner would before the
hearing of the appeal (fixed at that date for early November 2000) have needed to
have a further one hour conference and spend a further 19 hours with the trainee
spending a further eight hours on—

> 'Preparation for hearing of appeal, considering draft index, preparation of
> bundle for counsel's use, perusing counsel's skeleton arguments, preparation
> for conference, reviewing in detail judgment and relevant documentation,
> briefing counsel, attendance upon defendant, claimant, court and counsel to
> include time for routine telephone attendances and letters written.'

a Assuming that a partner could spend so much time on such activities at the rate suggested, I cannot accept that it would be proportionate or reasonable to do so (cf CPR 44.5(1)). The brief fee for junior counsel (1972 call) of £7,500 on a three hour appeal in a matter that he had argued below also seems to me disproportionate. Even if it were appropriate to measure any order for security by reference to the full amount of the costs likely to be ordered against the claimant if her appeal

b failed, I would not for my part contemplate a figure of more than half that claimed by the defendants' bill of costs, say £9,000 to £10,000.

CONCLUSIONS

[75] For all these reasons, I consider that we should now accede to the claimant's application to relist the application for security under CPR 23.11 and

c reconsider the order made by Judge LJ. The points of principle relating to the circumstances in which and extent to which security for an appeal should be ordered under r 25.15(1) were not before him. The extent of the change worked by the change in rules and the incorporation of the European Convention on Human Rights was not identified before him. The claimant's updated financial

d position was not before him, and the consideration that an appeal with a real prospect of success should not be stifled was not argued before him. The conduct of the claimant's solicitors, which led directly to the application going unopposed, was inefficient, but nothing like as blatant as it must have seemed to Judge LJ. Further, Charles Khan have accepted personal responsibility for costs thrown away by the abortive hearing on 10 October 2000, subject to assessment, if the

e court considers, as I for my part do, that their fault was a cause of its being abortive. In any event, it is clear that the claimant was in no way involved in her solicitors' failures or aware of what was going on at all in early October 2000. Yet it is on her that the consequences would fall, subject only to the prospect of yet further litigation against Charles Khan; and this would occur, in circumstances

f where the claimant has never had (a) a trial on the merits of her action against the present defendants, or (b) a hearing of her appeal against the dismissal of her action without a trial on the merits, or (c) a hearing at which her interests were represented of the application for an order for security for the costs of that appeal, which led to her appeal being dismissed. I do not think that it would be proportionate to allow the undoubted failures of her solicitors to lead to these

g consequences. The case is on any view an advertisement for the wisdom of the recent reforms, that should ensure that orders striking out for want of prosecution become of merely historical interest. Now that these matters have all been considered, the position looks very different to the position as it appeared before Judge LJ.

h [76] I consider however that this is an appeal in respect of which an order for limited security is in principle justified by the claimant's residence in the United States, where any assets (if any) that she has are likely to be and where any steps towards enforcement of an order against her for costs would be likely to be taken. I have concluded that (1) any costs would on assessment not exceed £10,000,

j (2) any order should be related to the probable extra burden (in terms of costs and delay) of taking enforcement steps in the United States against the claimant, compared with enforcement steps in the United Kingdom or another Brussels/ Lugano state, and (3) the claimant is likely to be able to raise, at the least, modest further sums to secure any order. I consider that a fair assessment of a figure likely to cover the burden identified in (2) would be £5,000, and that this would be within the claimant's ability under (3). For completeness, I add that we are of course only concerned with the amount of security appropriate in respect of the costs of appeal against Ian Kennedy J's order striking out the claim. We have not been concerned on this application with what might be the position in any respect with regard to the trial that would take place if that appeal succeeds.

[77] I would therefore set aside Judge LJ's order, order that the claimant should put up security for the costs of the appeal in the sum of £5,000 within a time and on terms on which I consider that we should hear counsel, and order the claimant's appeal against the decision of Ian Kennedy J made on 26 October 1999 to be restored to the list, for hearing as soon as can be.

SIMON BROWN LJ.
[78] I agree.

Order accordingly.

Dilys Tausz   Barrister.

a

South Bucks District Council v Porter
Chichester District Council v Searle and others
Wrexham County Borough Council v Berry
b # Hertsmere Borough Council v Harty and others
[2001] EWCA Civ 1549

COURT OF APPEAL, CIVIL DIVISION

c SIMON BROWN, PETER GIBSON AND TUCKEY LJJ

4–6 SEPTEMBER, 12 OCTOBER 2001

Town and country planning – Enforcement of planning control – Unauthorised development of land – Power of court to grant injunction restraining breach of planning *d* *control – Whether court required to exercise independent judgment on planning issues and hardship when considering whether to grant injunction – Guidance on exercise of power – Town and Country Planning Act 1990, s 187B – Human Rights Act 1998, Sch 1, Pt I, art 8.*

In four appeals raising issues on the proper approach to the exercise of the court's *e* power, under s 187B[a] of the Town and Country Planning Act 1990, to restrain breaches of planning control, the appellants were gipsies living in mobile homes on land occupied in breach of planning control. In each case, planning permission had been refused and enforcement notices issued. Following non-compliance with those notices, the respondent local planning authorities applied for injunctions under s 187B of the 1990 Act. By s 187B(1), a local planning authority could make *f* such an application where it considered it necessary or expedient for any actual or apprehended breach of planning control to be restrained by injunction. Section 187B(2) provided that, on such an application, the court 'may' grant such an injunction as it thought appropriate for the purpose of restraining the breach. In all four cases the court granted an injunction requiring the appellants to move off *g* site. On their appeals, the Court of Appeal considered the extent to which a judge was required to exercise an independent judgment in deciding whether to grant an injunction, having regard to the right to respect for a person's private life, family life and home under art 8(1)[b] of the European Convention for the Protection of Human Rights and Fundamental Freedoms 1950 (as set out in Sch 1 *h* to the Human Rights Act 1998) and the prohibition, in art 8(2), on interference with that right by a public authority except such as was in accordance with the law and necessary in a democratic society for the protection of the rights of others. In particular, the Court of Appeal considered the extent to which the judge should exercise an independent judgment in respect of issues of planning policy involved in the decision to refuse permission and of hardship if the gipsy *j*

---

a   Section 187B, so far as material, is set out at [1], below
b   Article 8 provides: '1. Everyone has the right to respect for his private and family life, his home and correspondence.
    2. There shall be no interference by a public authority with the exercise of this right except such as is in accordance with the law and is necessary in a democractic society … for the protection of the rights … of others.'

were to be removed, and the degree of deference, if any, that he should show a
towards the planning judgment of the local planning authority.

Held – Although a judge was not entitled to reach his own independent view of
the planning merits of the case when exercising his power under s 187B of the
1990 Act, he should not grant injunctive relief unless he would be prepared if
necessary to contemplate committing the defendant to prison for breach of the b
order, and he would not be of that mind unless he had considered for himself all
questions of hardship for the defendant and his family if they were required to
move, including the availability of suitable alternative sites. Questions of the
family's health and education would inevitably be of relevance, as would
countervailing considerations, such as the need to enforce planning control in the
general interest and the planning history of the site. The degree and flagrancy of c
the postulated breach of planning control might well prove critical. If
conventional enforcement measures had failed over a prolonged period of time
to remedy the breach, then the judge would obviously be readier to use his own,
more coercive powers. Conversely, he might well be reluctant to use his powers
in a case where enforcement action had never been taken. On the other hand, d
there might be some urgency in the situation sufficient to justify the pre-emptive
avoidance of an anticipated breach of planning control. Considerations of health
and safety might arise. Previous planning decisions would always be relevant,
though the degree of relevance would inevitably depend on a variety of matters,
including how recent they were, the extent to which considerations of hardship
and availability of alternative sites were taken into account, the strength of e
the conclusions reached on land use and environmental issues, and whether the
defendant had, and properly took, the opportunity to make his case for at least a
temporary personal planning permission. Relevant too would be the authority's
decision under s 187B(1) to seek injunctive relief as they were the
democratically-elected and accountable body principally responsible for planning f
control in their area. Again, however, the relevance and weight of their decision
would depend above all on the extent to which they could be shown to have had
regard to all the material considerations and to have properly posed and
approached the art 8(2) questions as to necessity and proportionality. Whilst it
was not for the judge to question the correctness of the existing planning status
of the land, in deciding whether or not to grant an injunction (and, if so, whether g
and for how long to suspend it) he was bound to come to some broad view as to
the degree of environmental damage resulting from the breach and the urgency
or otherwise of bringing it to an end. In that regard, the judge was not required
to shut his mind to the possibility of the planning authority itself coming to reach
a different planning judgment in the case. It was true that once the planning h
decision was taken as final, the legitimate aim of preserving the environment was
only achievable by removing the gipsies from the site. However, the judge did
not always have to accept that the achievement of that aim outweighed whatever
countervailing rights the gipsies might have. Still less was he bound to grant
injunctive relief. Rather, the court's discretion was absolute and injunctive relief j
was unlikely unless properly thought to be proportionate. Proportionality
required not only that the injunction be appropriate and necessary for the
attainment of the public interest objective sought, but also that it did not impose
an excessive burden on the individual whose private interests were at stake. The
judge, therefore, had to strike the necessary balance between the competing
interests. Provided that he did so in a structured and articulate way, the

a appropriate conclusion should emerge. On that approach, the court had misdirected itself in the first three cases under appeal, and the appeals in those cases would therefore be allowed. However, the fourth appeal would be dismissed (see [38]–[44], [49], [57], [59]–[61], below).

Hambleton DC v Bird [1995] 3 PLR 8 disapproved.
Chapman v UK (2001) 10 BHRC 48 considered.

b
Notes
For the right to respect for private life, family life and home, see 8(2) *Halsbury's Laws* (4th edn reissue) paras 149–151, and for injunctions restraining breaches of planning control, see 46 *Halsbury's Laws* (4th edn reissue) para 684.

c For the Town and Country Planning Act 1990, s 187B, see 46 *Halsbury's Statutes* (4th edn) (1998 reissue) 698.

For the Human Rights Act 1998, Sch 1, Pt I, art 8, see 7 *Halsbury's Statutes* (4th edn) (1999 reissue) 524.

Cases referred to in judgments

d *Associated Provincial Picture Houses Ltd v Wednesbury Corp* [1947] 2 All ER 680, [1948] 1 KB 223, CA.
Aylesbury Vale DC v Miller (30 July 1999, unreported), QBD.
Buckley v UK (1996) 23 EHRR 101, [1996] ECHR 20348/92, ECt HR.
Chapman v UK (2001) 10 BHRC 48, ECt HR.
Guildford BC v Smith (1994) JPL 734, CA.
e *Hambleton DC v Bird* [1995] 3 PLR 8, CA.
Mole Valley DC v Smith, Reigate and Banstead BC v Brown [1992] 3 PLR 22, CA.
Pioneer Aggregates (UK) Ltd v Secretary of State for the Environment [1984] 2 All ER 358, [1985] AC 132, [1984] 3 WLR 32, HL.
R (on the application of Alconbury Developments Ltd) v Secretary of State for the
f *Environment, Transport and the Regions* [2001] UKHL 23, [2001] 2 All ER 929, [2001] 2 WLR 1389.
R v Beard [1997] 1 PLR 64, CA.
R v Kerrier DC, ex p Uzell (1996) 71 P & CR 566.
R v Lincolnshire CC, ex p Atkinson [1997] JPL 65.
g *R v Secretary of State for the Home Dept, ex p Daly* [2001] UKHL 26, [2001] 3 All ER 433, [2001] 2 WLR 1622.
Tandridge DC v Delaney [2000] 1 PLR 11.

Cases also cited or referred to in skeleton arguments
Ashingdane v UK (1985) 7 EHRR 528, [1985] ECHR 8225/78, ECt HR.
h *B v Secretary of State for the Home Dept* [2000] Imm AR 478, CA.
Brind v Secretary of State for the Home Dept [1991] 1 All ER 720, sub nom *R v Secretary of State for the Home Dept, ex p Brind* [1991] 1 AC 696, HL.
Brown v Stott (Procurator Fiscal, Dunfermline) [2001] 2 All ER 97, [2001] 2 WLR 817, PC.
Bryan v UK (1995) 21 EHRR 342, [1995] ECHR 19178/91, ECt HR.
j *Buckland v Secretary of State for the Environment, Transport and Regions, Smith v Secretary of State for the Environment, Transport and Regions, Evans v Secretary of State for the Environment, Transport and Regions, Wychavon DC v Smith* [2001] EWHC Admin 524.
Connors v Reigate and Banstead BC [2000] JPL 1178, CA.
Coster v UK [2001] ECHR 24876/94, ECt HR.
Cremieux v France (1993) 16 EHRR 357, [1993] ECHR 11471/85, ECt HR.

Croydon LBC v Gladden [1994] 1 PLR 30, CA.
De Freitas v Permanent Secretary of Ministry of Agriculture, Fisheries, Lands and Housing [1999] 1 AC 69, [1998] 3 WLR 675, PC.
Dudgeon v UK (1981) 4 EHRR 149, [1981] ECHR 7525/76, ECt HR.
ISKCON v UK (1994) 76A DR 90, E Com HR.
Johansen v Norway (1996) 23 EHRR 33, [1996] ECHR 17383/90, ECt HR.
Johnson (B) & Co (Builders) Ltd v Minister of Health [1947] 2 All ER 395, CA.
Lee v UK [2001] ECHR 25289/94, ECt HR.
Malone v UK (1984) 7 EHRR 14, [1984] 8691/79, ECt HR.
Mayor and Burgesses of the London Borough of Lambeth v Howard [2001] EWCA Civ 468, (2001) 33 HLR 58.
Miles v Secretary of State for the Environment [2000] JPL 192, CA.
Poplar Housing and Regeneration Community Association Ltd v Donoghue [2001] EWCA Civ 595, [2001] 4 All ER 604, [2001] 3 WLR 183.
Pye (J A) (Oxford) Ltd v Graham [2001] EWCA Civ 117, [2001] 2 WLR 1293.
R (on the application of Johns) v Bracknell Forest DC (2001) 33 HLR 45.
R (on the application of Mahmood) v Secretary of State for the Home Dept [2001] 1 WLR 840, CA.
R (on the application of Samaroo) v Secretary of State for the Home Dept, R (on the application of Sezek) v Secretary of State for the Home Dept [2001] EWCA Civ 1139, [2001] UKHRR 1150.
R v A [2001] UKHL 25, [2001] 3 All ER 1, [2001] 2 WLR 1546.
R v Basildon DC, ex p Clarke [1996] JPL 866.
R v Beard [2001] ECHR 24882/94, ECt HR.
R v DPP, ex p Kebeline, R v DPP, ex p Rechachi [1999] 4 All ER 801, [2000] 2 AC 326, [1999] 3 WLR 972, HL.
R v Durham CC, ex p Huddlestone [2000] 3 WLR 1484, CA.
R v North and East Devon Health Authority, ex p Coughlan (Secretary of State for Health intervening) [2000] 3 All ER 850, [2001] QB 213, CA.
R v X, R v Y, R v Z [2000] TLR 405, CA; *affd sub nom R v P* [2001] 2 All ER 58, [2001] 2 WLR 463, HL.
Runnymede BC v Harwood [1994] 1 PLR 22, CA.
Silver v UK (1983) 5 EHRR 347, [1983] ECHR 5947/72, ECt HR.
Smith v UK (1999) 29 EHRR 493, [1999] ECHR 25154/94, ECt HR.
Soering v UK (1989) 11 EHRR 439, [1989] ECHR 14038/88, ECt HR.
Tinnelly & Sons Ltd v UK [1998] 4 BHRC 393, ECt HR.
Varey v UK App No 26662/95 (21 December 2000, unreported), ECt HR.
W and B (children) (care plan), Re, Re W (children) (care plan) [2001] EWCA Civ 757, [2001] 2 FCR 450.
Wilson v Dagnall [1972] 2 All ER 44, [1972] 1 QB 509, CA.
Zumtobel v Austria (1993) 17 EHRR 116, [1993] ECHR 12235/86, ECt HR.

Appeals

South Bucks DC v Porter

The appellant, Linda Porter, appealed with permission of Sedley LJ granted on 18 March 2001 from the decision of Burton J on 27 January 2000 granting the respondent, South Bucks District Council, an injunction under s 187B of the Town and Country Planning Act 1990 requiring the appellant within one year to cease using land at Willow Tree Farm, Iver, Buckinghamshire for stationing caravans and storage and business purposes, to demolish various outbuildings

a and to remove the hardstanding. The facts are set out in the judgment of Simon
   Brown LJ.

Chichester DC v Searle and ors

   The appellants, Darren Searle, Danny Keet and Kim Searle, appealed with
   permission of Sedley LJ granted on 18 March 2001 from the decision of Judge
b Barratt QC at the Chichester County Court on 30 June 2000 granting the
   respondent, Chichester District Council, an injunction under s 187B of the Town
   and Country Planning Act 1990 prohibiting the residential use of certain land by
   the appellants and requiring them within 28 days to remove mobile homes,
   certain other structures and the hardcore base. The facts are set out in the
c judgment of Simon Brown LJ.

Wrexham County BC v Berry

   The appellant, Michael Berry, appealed with permission of Sedley LJ granted on
   18 May 2001 from the decision of McCombe J on 12 February 2001 granting the
d respondent, Wrexham County Borough Council, an injunction under s 187B of
   the Town and Country Planning Act 1990 requiring the appellant to remove all
   caravans and vehicles off land lying within the Green Barrier near Wrexham. The
   facts are set out in the judgment of Simon Brown LJ.

Hertsmere BC v Harty and ors

e The appellants, Patrick Casey and Aaron Jones, appealed with permission of
   Sedley LJ granted on 3 April 2001 from the decision of Judge Brunning QC, sitting
   as a judge of the High Court, on 13 March 2001 granting the respondent,
   Hertsmere Borough Council, an injunction under s 187B of the Town and
   Country Planning Act 1990 requiring the appellants to cease using land at the
f Pylon Site, Barnet Road, Potters Bar, Hertfordshire, as a caravan or mobile home
   site, and to remove from it all caravans, mobile homes and vehicles by 5 April
   2001. The two other parties to the proceedings, Dominic Harty and Tom Smith,
   took no part in the appeal. The facts are set out in the judgment of Simon Brown LJ.

   Charles George QC and *Stephen Cottle* (instructed by *Christopher Johnson*, Community
g   Law Partnership, Birmingham) for Mrs Porter.
   Timothy Straker QC and *Ian Albutt* (instructed by *Sharpe Pritchard* as agents for
      Lynne Reardon, Slough) for South Bucks.
   David Watkinson (instructed by *Christopher Johnson*, Community Law Partnership,
      Birmingham) for the appellants in the Searle appeal.
h *Timothy Straker QC* and *Robin Green* (instructed by *Sharpe Pritchard* as agents for
      Mr M Kelley, Chichester) for Chichester.
   Richard Drabble QC and *Stephen Cottle* (instructed by *Christopher Johnson*, Community
      Law Partnership, Birmingham) for Mr Berry.
   Timothy Straker QC and *Robin Green* (instructed by *Sharpe Pritchard* as agents for
j   *Berwyn Edwards*, Wrexham) for Wrexham.
   Richard Drabble QC and *Murray Hunt* (instructed by *Bramwell, Brown & O'Dedra*,
      Chesham) for the appellants in the Harty appeal.
   Robert McCracken and *Gregory Jones* (instructed by *Sharpe Pritchard* as agents for
      Beryl Foster, Borehamwood) for Hertsmere.

                                                              Cur adv vult

12 October 2001. The following judgments were delivered.

a

SIMON BROWN LJ.

[1] These four appeals raise difficult questions of some general application as to how a court should approach the exercise of its power under s 187B of the Town and Country Planning Act 1990, the power on application by a local planning authority to grant an injunction to restrain a breach of planning control. *b* Section 187B provides by sub-ss (1) and (2):

'(1) Where a local planning authority consider it necessary or expedient for any actual or apprehended breach of planning control to be restrained by injunction, they may apply to the court for an injunction, whether or not they have exercised or are proposing to exercise any of their other powers *c* under this Part.

(2) On an application under subsection (1) the court may grant such an injunction as the court thinks appropriate for the purpose of restraining the breach.'

[2] The appellants in each case are gipsies, living in mobile homes on land *d* which they occupy in breach of planning control. In all four cases the court granted injunctive relief requiring them (whether immediately or otherwise) to move off site. At the heart of these appeals lies art 8 of the European Convention for the Protection of Human Rights and Fundamental Freedoms 1950 (as set out in Sch 1 to the Human Rights Act 1998). It is not disputed that such removals constitute an interference with the gipsies' right to respect for their private life, *e* family life and home within the meaning of art 8(1). But nor is it in dispute that the interference is 'in accordance with the law' and is pursued 'for the protection of the rights ... of others' within the meaning of art 8(2), namely through the preservation of the environment.

[3] The question ultimately arising in these cases is, therefore, whether the *f* interference is 'necessary in a democratic society', ie whether it answers to a 'pressing social need' and in particular is proportionate to the legitimate aim pursued. That, however, as all parties agree, is not in these cases a question for us: rather the question for us is whether the judges below correctly directed themselves. If they did, the appeals fail. If they did not, then, whether or not injunctions should properly be granted will have to be decided afresh at first *g* instance on up-to-date facts.

[4] The central issue for determination on the appeals is the extent to which the court itself on a s 187B application should exercise an independent judgment in deciding whether or not to grant an injunction. Five different counsel addressed us on the point. Their contentions as to the correct approach spanned a very wide *h* spectrum. At one extreme Mr Watkinson submits that the court is bound to consider afresh all facts and matters including, indeed, all issues of policy as to whether planning permission should be granted and all questions of hardship were the gipsy to be removed. At the opposite end of the spectrum Mr Straker QC, for three of the respondent authorities, contends that, providing only that the *j* planning authority has considered and struck the balance between the interests of the gipsy and those of the wider community and not reached a manifestly erroneous conclusion, an injunction should be granted unless there has been a material change in circumstances since the application was made. That, however, is not the approach contended for by Mr McCracken on behalf of the other respondent authority; such an approach, indeed, he himself describes as

a 'uncompromising'. But nor is Mr Watkinson's approach that contended for by Mr George QC and Mr Drabble QC on behalf of the other appellants; rather they accept that some deference must be paid to the planning judgments arrived at by the local planning authorities although, they submit, very considerably less deference than has hitherto been thought appropriate. Two of the judgments under appeal were given before the 1998 Act came into force on 2 October 2000,
b two after that date. It is not now contended by the respondent authorities, however, that anything (save perhaps as to costs) should turn on that distinction. The question, therefore, arises in all four cases as to whether the hitherto established approach to s 187B is compliant with the 1998 Act. Mr Straker QC submits that it is. The appellants submit the contrary; indeed, they submit that even before the 1998 Act came into play the courts were taking too narrow a view
c of their discretion to withhold relief under the section.

[5] Against that background it will readily be seen that the detailed facts of these cases are of secondary importance only on the appeals. True, '[i]n law context is everything,' as Lord Steyn said in *R v Secretary of State for the Home Dept, ex p Daly* [2001] UKHL 26 at [28], [2001] 3 All ER 433 at [28], [2001] 2 WLR 1622.
d Whereas, however, the substantive decision whether to grant injunctive relief against these individual appellants will certainly depend upon their particular facts, the question whether the judges below directed themselves correctly upon the approach to the exercise of their discretion does not. The following very brief summary of the circumstance of each case will, therefore, suffice.

e SOUTH BUCKS DC v PORTER

[6] Mr and Mrs Porter live in a caravan on a site known as Willow Tree Farm lying within the Green Belt at Iver in Buckinghamshire. The site was purchased by Mrs Porter in 1985 and since then has been occupied and used in breach of planning control. Mr Porter uses the land for horse dealing and breeding. Enforcement
f notices were first served in 1987. Planning permission for a detached dwelling house was refused in 1988. In November 1988 the appellant pleaded guilty to non-compliance with the enforcement notices and was fined £600. In 1992 planning permission for retention of a mobile home was refused and an appeal to the Secretary of State withdrawn. In 1993 planning permission for change of use from agricultural to mixed use including use as a private gipsy caravan site for five
g mobile homes was refused and again an appeal to the Secretary of State was withdrawn. Further enforcement notices were served in September 1993 requiring the destruction of various outbuildings and in July 1994 the appeal against these was dismissed although the inspector allowed 12 months for compliance. A fourth application for residential use of the site including retention of the mobile home
h and buildings was refused in November 1997 and in October 1998 the appeal against that refusal was dismissed by the inspector. A yet further application for planning permission was refused and the appeal against that refusal was due to be heard in September this year. The appellants' principal arguments for remaining on the land include the impossibility of finding suitable alternative accommodation,
j the suitability (as they contend) of horse-breeding for countryside use, and Mrs Porter's health problems: chronic asthma, severe generalised osteoarthritis and chronic urinary tract infection.

[7] On 27 January 2000 Burton J granted the respondent council injunctive relief requiring the appellants within one year to cease using the land for stationing caravans and storage and business purposes, to demolish the relevant outbuildings, and to remove the hardstanding.

CHICHESTER DC v SEARLE

[8] This is the only one of the four appeal sites not in the Green Belt. It is, *a* however, in an area of countryside where development is closely controlled. In May 2000 the appellants purchased the plot for £14,000 from a Mrs Collins, her prior application for outline planning permission for a detached bungalow and garage having been refused and her appeal against that refusal dismissed by the inspector in June 1999. Shortly after acquiring the land the appellants were *b* advised by two of the respondent's enforcement officers that planning permission was needed to move a mobile home onto the land. The appellants agreed not to do this without permission and later repeated their assurance. These assurances notwithstanding, the appellants in mid-June 2000 brought two double unit mobile homes onto the land and took up residence. Within days the respondent's Area Development Control Committee resolved to apply for injunctive relief *c* under s 187B(1) of the 1990 Act. On 30 June 2000 Judge Barratt QC granted an injunction with immediate effect prohibiting the residential use of the land and ordering within 28 days the removal of the mobile homes, certain other structures and the hardcore base.

WREXHAM COUNTY BC v BERRY   *d*

[9] The appellant is a traditional gipsy traveller living with his wife and six children (variously aged between 4 and 20) in mobile caravans. For some years the family lived in poor conditions on an unofficial site owned by the respondent council at Croessnewydd but in September 1999 that site was closed and they were evicted. They then reluctantly moved to another site owned by the respondent *e* at Ruthin Road. Meantime, in August 1994, the appellant had acquired the appeal site, land lying within the Green Barrier (the Welsh equivalent of the Green Belt) near Wrexham, and had applied for planning permission to put a residential caravan on it. That application was refused by the council in October 1994 as was a second such application in December 1995 and a third in July 1999. In September 2000, however, notwithstanding those earlier refusals of planning permission, the *f* appellant left the council's Ruthin Road site and moved his caravans and vehicles onto the appeal site. He did this because of a number of incidents of violence suffered by his family at the hands of other residents at the Ruthin Road site. In October 2000 the respondent authority resolved both to issue an enforcement notice and to apply for injunctive relief against the appellant under s 187B. In the *g* event, no enforcement notice was issued until 31 July 2001. The s 187B application, however, was made immediately following the October resolution albeit its hearing was stayed by Astill J in November 2000 pending the decision of the European Court of Human Rights in *Chapman v UK* (2001) 10 BHRC 48 (an authority to which I shall come later). The judgment in *Chapman v UK* having *h* been delivered on 18 January 2001, the application came before McCombe J on 12 February 2001 when an injunction was given requiring the appellant to remove all caravans and vehicles off the land by 20 April 2001.

HERTSMERE BC v HARTY

[10] The appellants are two of a group comprising six related gipsy families *j* whose wish is to settle down rather than lead a travelling life so that their children can benefit from a conventional education. Many of the children attend local schools. In addition, several of the family group have health problems. The land they occupy is known as the Pylon Site within the Green Belt bordering Barnet Road at Potters Bar in Hertfordshire. The site has a long planning history. In 1990 enforcement notices were served against previous occupiers for changing its use

a   to a caravan site and the appeals against those notices were dismissed by an inspector
in December 1991 although the period for compliance was extended to 12 months.
The site was then vacated. In 1994 the site was acquired by Mr Harty and again
occupied, this time by families within the appellant group. After service upon
Mr Harty of a fresh enforcement notice and a stop notice to prevent further
operations including the removal of soil and the laying of hardcore, the site was
b   again vacated. In January 1995 the site was reoccupied by the appellant families
notwithstanding that planning permission for its use as a gipsy caravan site for six
families had been refused in November 1994. Following the prosecution of
Mr Harty under s 179(2) of the 1990 Act for breach of the enforcement notice and
a s 187B application for injunctive relief against the other appellants, a consent
order was made on 28 June 1995 whereby the appellants undertook that in the
c   event of Mr Harty's outstanding appeal against the refusal of planning permission
being dismissed they would within 28 days of such dismissal remove all caravans,
mobile homes and vehicles and would not return to the site. The appeal against
the refusal of planning permission was dismissed on 18 September 1995 and the
site was once again vacated. However, despite the appellants' undertaking not to
d   return, they yet again reoccupied the site, arriving in stages between about August
and October 2000. On 21 September 2000 an application was made for planning
permission for change of use of the site to residential use for six mobile homes
(each measuring 36 ft by 20 ft) and six touring caravans (for use while travelling).
It was refused by the respondent authority on 13 February 2001 and the appellants'
appeal against that refusal, due to have been heard by an inspector on 6 June 2001,
e   was withdrawn. On 24 October 2000 the respondents had resolved to seek an
injunction subject to counsel's advice about the implications of the 1998 Act.
On 28 February 2001, following the respondent's refusal of planning permission,
the s 187B application was made. On 13 March 2001 Judge Brunning ordered the
appellants to cease using the land as a caravan or mobile home site and to remove
f   from it all caravans, mobile homes and vehicles by 5 April 2001.
[11] Against that broad factual background I now turn to the court's injunctive
power under s 187B. The section was introduced into the 1990 Act by
amendment in 1991. This followed a 1989 report by Mr Robert Carnwath QC (as
he then was) entitled *Enforcing Planning Control* which recommended a new power
to grant injunctions against planning offenders as 'a useful back-up to the
g   statutory system in difficult cases', not least given the doubts then existing as to
the circumstances in which injunctive relief was available under s 222 of the Local
Government Act 1972.
[12] It is convenient at this stage to see how the courts approached the exercise
of these injunctive powers before the 1998 Act was enacted. This approach is to
h   be found in three decisions of the Court of Appeal. I start with *Mole Valley DC v
Smith, Reigate and Banstead BC v Brown* [1992] 3 PLR 22 which concerned the grant
of injunctions against gipsies under s 222 of the 1972 Act and addressed the respective
powers and duties of planning authorities and the courts. Lord Donaldson MR
(at 31) quoted with approval Hoffmann J's judgment in the court below:

j   'There can be no doubt that requiring [the appellants] to leave the site
would cause considerable hardship. This court, however, is not entrusted
with a general jurisdiction to solve social problems. The striking of a balance
between the requirements of planning policy and the needs of these defendants
is a matter which, in my view, has been entrusted to other authorities.'

[13] Lord Donaldson MR then observed:

'No doubt there are potential disadvantages for the public in moving the appellants off their existing sites if no other site is available, but where the balance of the public interest lies is for the respondent councils to determine and not for this court.'

[14] Noting the submission that the injunction should be refused on the ground that the councils were themselves in breach of their duty under s 6 of the Caravan Sites Act 1968 to provide adequate sites for gipsies residing in or resorting to their area (since repealed and replaced by a series of government circulars strongly encouraging local planning authorities to help meet the need for gipsy accommodation) Lord Donaldson MR said (at 32): 'Suffice it to say that it is not for the courts to usurp the policy decision-making functions of the Secretary of State as it were by a side wind.'

[15] Balcombe LJ agreed, adding (at 33):

'The argument is that no injunction should be granted, or the operation of any injunction granted should be suspended, until the county council provides sufficient caravan sites for the use of gipsies. This is equivalent to saying that the appellants should be granted temporary planning permission for the use of their land pending the availability of sufficient authorised sites. That is a policy decision for the planning authorities and … even temporary planning permission was considered and rejected by the Secretary of State. Thus, the court is being asked to reverse the decisions of the authorities to whom Parliament has entrusted the relevant decision, not on grounds of illegality, but on grounds of policy. This is not something which, in my judgment, the court should do.'

[16] The next case was *Guildford BC v Smith* (1994) JPL 734 in which the court rejected Mr Straker's invitation on behalf of the planning authority to overturn Sedley J's refusal to make even a suspended committal order against gipsies for breach of a s 187B injunction requiring them to cease the unlawful use of land as a residential caravan site. Having noted that the gipsies were in contempt, albeit a contempt brought about by the council's failure to fulfil its duty to provide sufficient sites for gipsies, Staughton LJ said (at 739) (the case is reported in indirect speech):

'There were three possible solutions which the law might provide in such a case. The first would be to refuse any injunction; the second to grant an injunction but impose no penalty if it is broken; and the third to grant an injunction and if it were broken to impose a penalty of imprisonment, perhaps suspended for a time. As to the first solution to refuse an injunction altogether it was his view that the court should not make orders which it did not contemplate enforcing. In the rules of nursery and discipline, "No" means "No" and was usually followed by sanctions if disobeyed. Those who make orders but do not enforce them may tend to be regarded with contempt, not an inappropriate word in this context. But the case of *Mole Valley D.C. v. Smith* ([1992] 3 PLR 22), shows that it would have been wrong to take that course. It was not for the courts to refuse an injunction because there were no other sites available. We were bound by that decision. Furthermore, there had been no application to discharge the injunction, and no appeal against the order granting it. The second possible solution was to grant an injunction but impose no penalty if it was broken. That was a poor substitute. The order had been broken. It would remain in force and would a presumably continue to be broken, and no sanctions will be imposed unless circumstances change. That was a position which the law ought to avoid if it could. The third solution was that the court was required to grant an injunction and required to enforce it by imprisonment without regard to the personal circumstances of the defendants (whoever they may be) or to any other circumstances of the case. That, it seems is even worse than the second

b solution.'

The court adopted the second solution.

[17] I come next to what for some years has been regarded as the leading authority on the correct approach to s 187B of the 1990 Act, *Hambleton DC v Bird* [1995] 3 PLR 8, another case concerned with unlawfully stationed gipsy caravans.

c Pill LJ, having cited at length from the *Mole Valley* case, said (at 15):

'The granting of an injunction in any particular case is dependent on the court's discretion. This does not however entitle a judge in the present context to act as a court of appeal against a planning decision or to base a refusal to grant an injunction upon his view of the overall public interest.

d While disclaiming any such role it is, in my view, clear from his reasoning that the learned judge assumed it. The judge referred to the rehousing that would follow an injunction and he referred to public interest in a general way, weighing the considerations that affect this family alone and to the lack, as he saw it, of public benefit which would result from an injunction. To take upon himself the role of assessing the benefits and disbenefits to the public as

e a whole was erroneous. The learned judge was taking upon himself the policy function of the planning authorities and housing authorities and their powers and duties. The existence of the court's discretion to refuse to enforce an injunction by imprisonment was confirmed by this court in *Guildford Borough Council v Smith* [1994] JPL 734. It does not empower a court to

f approach an application for an injunction in the way the judge did.'

[18] Finally under this head I must consider two first instance decisions given within days of each other, respectively by Burton J on 30 July 1999 in *Aylesbury Vale DC v Miller* (30 July 1999, unreported) and by Mr Robin Purchas QC sitting as a deputy judge of the Queen's Bench Division on 3 August 1999 in *Tandridge DC v*

g *Delaney* [2000] 1 PLR 11. Two arguments were advanced on behalf of the defendant gipsies in the *Aylesbury Vale* case: first, that the council's decision to seek a s 187B injunction was unlawful on a *Wednesbury* basis (see *Associated Provincial Picture Houses Ltd v Wednesbury Corp* [1947] 2 All ER 680, [1948] 1 KB 223); secondly, that there is in any event a residual discretion in the court not to make an order.

h It is that second argument with which we are now concerned. Burton J recorded and rejected the submission as follows:

'The submission is that the court can, and should, even though upholding the lawfulness and the validity of the council's decisions, nevertheless reintroduce and reconsider questions of hardship at the injunction stage.

j This submission is, in my view, entirely foreclosed by two Court of Appeal authorities which are binding upon me. [These were the *Mole Valley* and *Hambleton* cases, from both of which the judge then cited yet more extensively than I have done.] It is quite clear both from *Guildford BC v Smith* (1994) JPL 734 and from the way the *Hambleton* case deals with it that the decision on whether to enforce the injunction by imprisonment is an entirely separate question from whether to grant an injunction to start with … The

effect thus appears to be that s 187B of the 1990 Act certainly allows for a
challenge to the decision made by the claimant, including the decision to
seek an injunction, and it may be that evidence of hardship falling for
consideration on such an application to the court will be so strong that it
could support a case ... that the decision by the council is *Wednesbury*
unreasonable, as indeed is the primary submission in this case ... It is plain
that questions of hardship, questions of policy, questions of alternative
accommodation, are all matters which are previously considered by the
council, at least if they are not acting *Wednesbury* unreasonably, and do not
fall for reconsideration by the court.'

[19] In the *Tandridge* case Mr Purchas too cited from Pill LJ's judgment in the
Hambleton case and expressly accepted and applied those principles. He then set out
([2000] 1 PLR 11 at 24–25) the approach he believed should be taken and the
considerations he considered to be particularly relevant:

'1. The starting point must be the existence and the nature of the breach
or breaches to be restrained. It is not for this court to reassess or act as a court
of appeal from the decisions that have already been made on the part of the
authorities through the relevant planning procedures in determining
whether or not planning permission should be granted or the enforcement
notices confirmed: see *Hambleton District Council v Bird* ([1995] 3 PLR 8), *per*
Pill LJ (at 15).
2. The defendants' rights under Article 8 of the Convention are a highly
material consideration. Those rights are not, however, unqualified. Again,
it seems to me that it is not for this court to act as a reviewing chamber for
the decisions that have been made in the planning process as to the
appropriate balance to be struck between those private rights and the public
necessity: see *Buckley v United Kingdom* ((1996) 23 EHRR 101) and *R v Beard*
([1997] 1 PLR 64) *per* Hobhouse LJ (as he then was) at p 72.
3. The same approach applies to the consideration of other humanitarian
aspects affecting the personal circumstances of the defendants, as referred to
by Sedley J (as he then was) in *ex parte Atkinson* (*R v Lincolnshire CC, ex p
Atkinson* [1997] JPL 65) and Latham J in *ex parte Uzell* (*R v Kerrier DC, ex p Uzell*
(1996) 71 P & CR 566).
4. However, in respect of both the last two considerations, it is for this
court carefully to examine any change in circumstances since the matter was
previously considered as part of the planning process, not to revisit the
decisions then taken but to see what effect any changes may have on the
conclusions then reached.
5. Finally, to reach a conclusion whether, in all the circumstances, the
grant of an injunction would be just and proportionate.'

[20] It should be noted that in the *Tandridge* case, although not in the *Aylesbury
Vale* case, the art 8 point was taken—both cases, of course, being decided in the
period between the enactment and the coming into full force of the 1998 Act.
Buckley v UK (1996) 23 EHRR 101, one of the two cases mentioned in para 2 of
Mr Purchas' analysis, was the first of these gipsy cases to be considered by the
European Court of Human Rights. These appeals, however, have focused much
more closely on the more recent decision of the European Court in *Chapman v UK*
(2001) 10 BHRC 48, and I shall not therefore consider *Buckley v UK* further. *R v
Beard* [1997] 1 PLR 64, I should observe, the other case mentioned in para 2, was

a a decision of the Criminal Division of the Court of Appeal dismissing a gipsy's appeal against his conviction for failing to comply with an enforcement notice contrary to s 179 of the 1990 Act. Hobhouse LJ (at 72–73), having referred to *Buckley v UK* and *Guildford BC v Smith* (1994) JPL 734, said:

b 'There is no inconsistency between the scheme of the United Kingdom planning legislation and the convention. The legislative scheme allows for the legitimate rights and expectations of gipsies to be taken into account at the appropriate stages of the procedure, including at the stage of deciding whether or not an enforcement notice should be upheld. Once an appropriate decision has been made in accordance with the law to uphold the enforcement notice, its enforcement involves no conflict with article 8. The subject-
c matter of section 179 is failure to comply with a lawful enforcement notice. There is no ambiguity, the resolution of which requires recourse to the convention ...'

[21] Let me indicate briefly at this stage the importance of those earlier decisions when it comes to determining the present four appeals. Eventually I
d shall have to return to the judgments in rather more detail. For present purposes, however, it is sufficient to note the following. (i) Burton J, deciding *South Bucks DC v Porter* on 22 January 2000, simply applied his own earlier decision in the *Aylesbury Vale* case. Although on this occasion art 8 of the convention was touched on, he remarked that it was not yet 'enshrined in English law' and that it
e did not enable him to reconsider the decisions of the Court of Appeal in the *Mole Valley* case or the *Hambleton* case. (ii) Judge Barratt QC, giving judgment in *Chichester DC v Searle* on 30 June 2000, directed himself substantially in accordance with the *Hambleton* case (in which he had acted as counsel for the successful appellant authority). He was not persuaded to a different approach by the European Court's judgment in *Buckley v UK*. (iii) McCombe J, deciding *Wrexham*
f *County BC v Berry* on 12 February 2001, appears to have regarded the European Court's judgment in *Chapman v UK* (2001) 10 BHRC 48 as decisive of the application before him. (iv) Judge Brunning's judgment, given on 13 March 2001, gives rise to greater difficulty in determining just what approach he took to the application before him, the form of his judgment appearing to be to some extent
g dictated by the need to deal with the submissions which the appellants then advanced but which are put somewhat differently before us. Certainly, however, he was provided with a press release issued by the registrar of the European Court of the court's judgment in *Chapman*'s case (decided together with four other gipsy cases against the United Kingdom on 18 January 2001) which summarised the decision of the majority of the court on art 8 as follows:
h

j 'In all five cases, the Court considered that the applicants' occupation of their caravans was an integral part of their ethnic identity as gipsies and that the enforcement measures and planning decisions in each case interfered with the applicants' rights to respect for their private and family life. However, the Court found that the measures were "in accordance with the law" and pursued the legitimate aim of protecting the "rights of others" through preservation of the environment. As regards the necessity of the measures taken in pursuit of that legitimate aim, the Court considered that a wide margin of appreciation had to be accorded to the domestic authorities who were far better placed to reach decisions concerning the planning considerations attaching to a particular site. In these cases, the Court found that the planning inspectors had identified strong environmental objections *a* to the applicants' use of their land which outweighed the applicants' individual interests. The Court also noted that gipsies were at liberty to camp on any caravan site with planning permission. Although there were insufficient sites which gipsies found acceptable and affordable and on which they could lawfully place their caravans, the Court was not persuaded that there were no alternatives available to the applicants besides occupying land *b* without planning permission, in some cases on a Green Belt or Special Landscape area. The Court did not accept that, because statistically the number of gipsies was greater than the number of places available in authorised gipsy sites, decisions not to allow the applicants to occupy land where they wished to install their caravans constituted a violation of Article 8. Neither was the Court convinced that Article 8 could be interpreted *c* to impose on the United Kingdom, as on all the other Contracting States to the European Convention on Human Rights, an obligation to make available to the gipsy community an adequate number of suitably equipped sites. Article 8 did not give a right to be provided with a home, nor did any of the Court's jurisprudence acknowledge such a right. Whether the State provided *d* funds to enable everyone to have a home was a matter for political not judicial decision. *Finding: no violation.*'

[22] Having been taken in very considerable detail through much of the court's long judgment in *Chapman*'s case (including several passages in the dissenting minority judgment), I would say that that summary by the court *e* registrar seems to me both entirely accurate and for present purposes in large part sufficient.

[23] Both sides in these appeals seek to rely on *Chapman*'s case. The appellants point to the court's reference, in para 73 of the majority judgment ((2001) 10 BHRC 48 at 67), to the 'applicant's occupation of her caravan [as] an integral part *f* of her ethnic identity as a gipsy' (and that notwithstanding that 'many gipsies no longer live a wholly nomadic existence and increasingly settle for long periods in one place in order to facilitate, for example, the education of their children'). Similarly they stress the 'positive obligation imposed ... [by] art 8 to facilitate the gipsy way of life' referred to in para 96 of the judgment (at 71), and the court's recognition in para 103 (at 73) that it is a consideration relevant to the question of *g* proportionality 'if no alternative accommodation is available' because 'the interference is more serious than where such accommodation is available'.

[24] The respondents for their part draw attention to para 99 of the judgment (at 72) which recalls that art 8 does not in terms give a right to be provided with a home, and para 102 on which they place particular emphasis: *h*

'When considering whether a requirement that the individual leave his or her home is proportionate to the legitimate aim pursued, it is highly relevant whether or not the home was established unlawfully. If the home was lawfully established, this factor would self-evidently be something which *j* would weigh against the legitimacy of requiring the individual to move. Conversely, if the establishment of a home in a particular place was unlawful, the position of the individual objecting to an order to move is less strong. The court will be slow to grant protection to those who, in conscious defiance of the prohibitions of the law, establish a home on an environmentally protected site. For the court to do otherwise would be to encourage illegal *a* action to the detriment of the protection of the environmental rights of other people in the community.'

[25] Important though all these various points are when it comes to deciding whether or not gipsies should in the first place be granted planning permission and, if not, whether they should be removed from the site, the real point to make about *Chapman*'s case is that it is a decision by an international court which by its *b* nature is exercising a supervisory and supranational jurisdiction. To my mind it casts very little light on the relatively narrow point now arising as to the extent of the court's discretion on a s 187B application for coercive relief.

[26] Paragraph 92 of the court's judgment (at 70–71) reads:

c   'The judgment in any particular case by the national authorities that there are legitimate planning objections to a particular use of a site is one which the court is not well equipped to challenge. It cannot visit each site to assess the impact of a particular proposal on a particular area in terms of impact on beauty, traffic conditions, sewerage and water facilities, educational facilities, medical facilities, employment opportunities and so on. Because planning *d*   inspectors visit the site, hear the arguments on all sides and allow examination of witnesses, they are better situated than the court to weigh the arguments. Hence, as the court observed in *Buckley v UK* ((1996) 23 EHRR 101 at 129 (para 75)) "in so far as the exercise of discretion involving a multitude of local factors is inherent in the choice and implementation of planning policies, the national authorities in principle enjoy a wide margin of appreciation", although *e*   it remains open to the court to conclude that there has been a manifest error of appreciation by the national authorities. In these circumstances, the procedural safeguards available to the individual applicant will be especially material in determining whether the respondent state has, when fixing the regulatory framework, remained within its margin of appreciation. In *f*   particular, it must examine whether the decision-making process leading to measures of interference was fair and such as to afford due respect to the interests safeguarded to the individual by art 8 (see *Buckley v UK* at 129–130 (paras 76–77)).'

g [27] The essential contrast being struck there is between the European Court and 'the national authorities', not between the domestic planning authorities and the domestic courts. True, para 92 stresses the opportunities enjoyed by planning inspectors in 'the choice and implementation of planning policies' which is why the European Court's role is confined principally to examining the domestic 'procedural safeguards' and deciding whether there has been 'a manifest error of *h* appreciation'. Whilst, however, this approach clearly supports the view that the recent House of Lords' decision in *R (on the application of Alconbury Developments Ltd) v Secretary of State for the Environment, Transport and the Regions* [2001] UKHL 23, [2001] 2 All ER 929, [2001] 2 WLR 1389, rejecting art 6 of the convention challenges to the legislative scheme for statutory appeals and applications in *j* planning cases which affords the court only a limited review jurisdiction over inspectors' decisions, applies equally in art 8 cases—see, indeed, the reference to *Chapman*'s case in Lord Nolan's speech in the *Alconbury Developments* case [2001] 2 All ER 929 at [63]—to my mind it cannot resolve the present issue arising under s 187B. *Chapman*'s case, be it noted, was concerned with enforcement action and failed appeals rather than with the grant of an injunction. True, in *R v Beard* (one of the four linked cases), the gipsies had vacated the land pursuant to a suspended three month committal order imposed for breach of a s 187B injunction. The court did not, however, address the question as to what, if any, deference should *a* be shown by the judge to the views of the planning authorities in deciding whether to grant an injunction.

[28] Let me, therefore, now turn directly to this issue. Counsel's arguments upon it ranged far and wide and encompassed a large number of authorities. Joining together four separate appeals brings with it, I fear, real problems of manageability. *b* The principal submissions, however, I understood to be these.

THE APPELLANTS' CASE

[29] Section 187B(2) of the 1990 Act affords the judge a clear discretion: the court 'may', not must, grant an injunction, even though by definition it will be concerned with an actual or apprehended breach of planning control. True it is *c* that in para 10.3 of his report Mr Carnwath said:

'What is required is its recognition [i e the recognition of injunctive relief] in the Act as a normal back-up to the other remedies, and acceptance that it is for the authority to judge (subject to the ordinary judicial review criteria of reasonableness) when its use is appropriate.' *d*

Circular 21/91, however, which explained the new powers being introduced into the 1990 Act, said (in para 7 of annexe 4):

'The decision whether to grant an injunction is always solely a matter for the Court, in its absolute discretion in the circumstances of any case. *e* Nevertheless, it is unlikely that the Court will grant an injunction unless all the following criteria are satisfied: ... (3) injunctive relief is a commensurate remedy in the circumstances of the particular case ...'

[30] It is further to be noted that Mr Carnwath's recommendation, in the case of residential caravans, for the repeal of the provision that stop notices cannot *f* issue to prohibit the use of any building as a dwellinghouse, was rejected.

[31] Injunctions are likely to prove the most effective way of remedying breaches of planning control because they are attended by the most severe sanctions, including imprisonment. Breaches of enforcement notices, by contrast, are punishable only by fines. By the same token, submit the appellants, this more *g* draconian remedy should only be granted when plainly appropriate and when, moreover, the court granting it is prepared to contemplate that its breach should attract these severe penalties. If the court is unwilling to commit it should be unwilling to enjoin. As already indicated, the appellants contend that even before art 8 fell to be considered, the courts took too narrow a view of their discretion: Staughton LJ's evident preference for the first of the three possible solutions he *h* identified in *Guildford BC v Smith* (1994) JPL 734 was to be preferred to the approach earlier dictated by *Mole Valley DC v Smith, Reigate and Banstead BC v Brown* [1992] 3 PLR 22 and later reaffirmed in *Hambleton DC v Bird* [1995] 3 PLR 8. Courts should not grant injunctions unless they propose to enforce them if necessary by imprisonment. On this approach, of course, the court would only *j* be prepared to grant injunctive relief in cases which the court itself regarded as clear, cases where it was quite satisfied first that the planning authority (whether the district council or the Secretary of State/inspector on appeal) had properly reached a final conclusion that the gipsies' continuing occupation of the site could no longer be tolerated in the public interest, and secondly that it was appropriate to enforce their removal by injunction even though, in a case where no alternative

a sites were available, that would drive the gipsies either onto the roads, into homelessness accommodation (see *Chapman v UK* (2001) 10 BHRC 48 at 62–63 (para 54)) or, on non-compliance with the injunction, into prison.

[32] Section 187B does not confer on the court merely a review power. Rather the court is exercising an original jurisdiction. Whatever may have been the position before the 1998 Act came into force, moreover, now certainly it is for the court b itself to address the issues arising under art 8(2) and it must accordingly reach its own decision upon whether the gipsies' removal from site is proportionate to the public interest in preserving the environment. The court must decide that removal on pain of imprisonment is necessary for that end and that this would not impose an excessive burden on the gipsy. In all these gipsy cases, submit the appellants, the court should ask itself whether an immediate (or even, indeed, a postponed) c order dispossessing them is really necessary to protect the environment. May it not be preferable to allow the breach of planning control to continue and, certainly for the present, to await the outcome of the more conventional enforcement process—the service of an enforcement notice and, if necessary, prosecution for its breach?

d [33] That is not to say, however, Mr George and Mr Drabble (if not Mr Watkinson) accept, that the judge will pay no heed to decisions taken by the planning authorities in the case. On the contrary, counsel recognise that the issue as to whether or not planning permission should be granted is exclusively a matter for them and that the planning history of the site, and in particular any recent decisions about it, will be highly relevant. Decisions by the Secretary of State and e his inspectors are, of course, independent and so carry particular weight. Even decisions taken by the local planning authority, whether with regard to planning permission or enforcement, are taken by them as a democratically accountable body and, provided they approach the matter correctly, are on that account to be accorded respect. But in either case, of course, it would be necessary for the f planning authority on a s 187B application to show that the gipsy's art 8 rights were properly considered and, in the case of pre-1998 Act decisions, that would be unlikely to be so.

[34] As stated, the appellants' principal argument is that the court is itself making the primary decision under s 187B(2) rather merely than reviewing the local authority's decision under s 187B(1) to apply for injunctive relief. But, they g submit, even assuming that to be wrong, it would nevertheless still be for the court to reach its own independent conclusion on the proportionality of the relief sought to the object to be obtained. In this regard the appellants point particularly to the decision of the House of Lords in *R v Secretary of State for the Home Dept, ex p Daly* [2001] 3 All ER 433, [2001] 2 WLR 1622, where Lord Bingham of Cornhill h said (at [23]):

'Now, following the incorporation of the convention by the Human Rights Act 1998 and the bringing of that Act fully into force, domestic courts must themselves form a judgment whether a convention right has been breached (conducting such inquiry as is necessary to form that judgment) and, so far j as permissible under the Act, grant an effective remedy.'

THE RESPONDENTS' CASE

[35] The essential argument put by Mr Straker—and, I think he recognises, the argument that must prevail if all three of the respondent authorities he represents are successfully to resist these appeals—is that the judge exercising his s 187B jurisdiction is more or less bound to grant an injunction unless the local

planning authority's application can be shown to be flawed on *Wednesbury* grounds. This, he submits, was always how the section fell to be applied and it *a* remains so today. The exercise of the power, he submits, is 'a public law exercise'. Section 187B was deliberately inserted by Parliament into the Town and Country Planning Act 1990 and that Act was itself described by Lord Scarman in *Pioneer Aggregates (UK) Ltd v Secretary of State for the Environment* [1984] 2 All ER 358 at 363, [1985] AC 132 at 141 as providing 'a comprehensive code imposed in the public *b* interest'. Mr Straker relies on various passages in Mr Carnwath's report (including para 10.3 to which I have already referred) to contend that the court's function is essentially supervisory only. He suggests that as a matter of interpretation the words 'such an injunction as the court thinks appropriate for the purpose of restraining the breach' themselves demonstrate that the power should be used in support of planning control. The *Mole Valley* and *Hambleton* cases, he submits, *c* were correctly decided. It is not until the committal stage is reached (for breach of the injunction) that the court steps outside the planning code and is entitled to reach an independent view on proportionality. At the injunction stage itself the court is to consider only whether the gipsies should leave the site, not whether they should suffer serious penalty if they fail to do so. Nor, runs the argument, is *d* any of this affected by the 1998 Act. In this regard Mr Straker relies heavily upon the *Alconbury Developments* case, there being many passages in the speeches to which he drew our attention.

[36] Those, I repeat, are arguments which Mr McCracken on behalf of Hertsmere Borough Council does not adopt. He accepts that s 187B(2) of the 1990 Act gives the court a discretion whether or not to grant an injunction and accepts too that *e* the judge should do so only on the basis of a preparedness to fine or if necessary imprison the defendant gipsy on breach. He does, however, submit that the court in exercising its discretion should not arrogate to itself the power to decide whether or not planning permission should be granted, that question being exclusively one for the planning authorities subject only to ss 288 and 289 of the *f* 1990 Act. He further submits that, the planning status of the land having already been determined, the judge must therefore recognise, when he comes to carry out the proportionality test, that no lesser interference with the gipsies' rights than their removal from site will achieve the legitimate aim of preserving the environment.

[37] I propose now to state first my conclusions on the general point arising— *g* the proper approach to the exercise of the court's power under s 187B—and secondly, how in my judgment that conclusion falls to be applied in each of the four appeals before us.

THE APPROACH TO s 187B *h*

[38] I would unhesitatingly reject the more extreme submissions made on either side. It seems to me perfectly clear that the judge on a s 187B application is not required, nor even entitled, to reach his own independent view of the planning merits of the case. These he is required to take as decided within the planning process, the actual or anticipated breach of planning control being a given when he comes *j* to exercise his discretion. But it seems to me no less plain that the judge should not grant injunctive relief unless he would be prepared if necessary to contemplate committing the defendant to prison for breach of the order, and that he would not be of this mind unless he had considered for himself all questions of hardship for the defendant and his family if required to move, necessarily including, therefore, the availability of suitable alternative sites. I cannot accept

a   that the consideration of those matters is, as Burton J suggested was the case in the pre-1998 Act era, 'entirely foreclosed' at the injunction stage. Questions of the family's health and education will inevitably be of relevance. But so too, of course, will countervailing considerations such as the need to enforce planning control in the general interest and, importantly therefore, the planning history of the site. The degree and flagrancy of the postulated breach of planning control

b   may well prove critical. If conventional enforcement measures have failed over a prolonged period of time to remedy the breach, then the court would obviously be the readier to use its own, more coercive powers. Conversely, however, the court might well be reluctant to use its powers in a case where enforcement action had never been taken. On the other hand, there might be some urgency in the situation sufficient to justify the pre-emptive avoidance of an anticipated

c   breach of planning control. Considerations of health and safety might arise. Preventing a gipsy moving onto the site might, indeed, involve him in less hardship than moving him out after a long period of occupation. Previous planning decisions will always be relevant; how relevant, however, will inevitably depend on a variety of matters, including not least how recent they are,

d   the extent to which considerations of hardship and availability of alternative sites were taken into account, the strength of the conclusions reached on land use and environmental issues, and whether the defendant had and properly took the opportunity to make his case for at least a temporary personal planning permission.

     [39] Relevant too will be the local authority's decision under s 187B(1) to seek

e   injunctive relief. They, after all, are the democratically-elected and accountable body principally responsible for planning control in their area. Again, however, the relevance and weight of their decision will depend above all on the extent to which they can be shown to have had regard to all the material considerations and to have properly posed and approached the art 8(2) questions as to necessity

f   and proportionality.

     [40] Whilst it is not for the court to question the correctness of the existing planning status of the land, the court in deciding whether or not to grant an injunction (and, if so, whether and for how long to suspend it) is bound to come to some broad view as to the degree of environmental damage resulting from the breach and the urgency or otherwise of bringing it to an end. In this regard the

g   court need not shut its mind to the possibility of the planning authority itself coming to reach a different planning judgment in the case.

     [41] True it is, as Mr McCracken points out, that, once the planning decision is taken as final, the legitimate aim of preserving the environment is only achievable by removing the gipsies from site. That is not to say, however, that the achievement

h   of that aim must always be accepted by the court to outweigh whatever countervailing rights the gipsies may have, still less that the court is bound to grant injunctive (least of all immediate injunctive) relief. Rather I prefer the approach suggested by the 1991 circular: the court's discretion is absolute and injunctive relief is unlikely unless properly thought to be 'commensurate'—in

j   today's language, proportionate. The *Hambleton* approach seems to me difficult to reconcile with that circular. However, whatever view one takes of the correctness of the *Hambleton* approach in the period prior to the coming into force of the 1998 Act, to my mind it cannot be thought consistent with the court's duty under s 6(1) to act compatibly with convention rights. Proportionality requires not only that the injunction be appropriate and necessary for the attainment of the public interest objective sought—here the safeguarding of the environment—

but also that it does not impose an excessive burden on the individual whose
private interests—here the gipsy's private life and home and the retention of his *a*
ethnic identity—are at stake.

[42] I do not pretend that it will always be easy in any particular case to strike
the necessary balance between these competing interests, interests of so different
a character that weighing one against the other must inevitably be problematic.
This, however, is the task to be undertaken by the court and, provided it is *b*
undertaken in a structured and articulated way, the appropriate conclusion
should emerge.

THE FOUR APPEALS

(1) *South Bucks DC v Porter*   *c*
[43] This decision plainly cannot stand following the coming into force of the
1998 Act. Burton J may well have been right to regard all questions of hardship
as 'entirely foreclosed' by the decisions in *Mole Valley DC v Smith, Reigate and
Banstead BC v Brown* [1992] 3 PLR 22 and *Hambleton DC v Bird* [1995] 3 PLR 8.
That, for present purposes, it is unnecessary to decide. Such an approach, *d*
however, is no longer open to the court.

(2) *Chichester DC v Searle*
[44] This decision too seems to me unsustainable. Judge Barratt QC referred
to the decisions in the *Mole Valley* and *Hambleton* cases and decided that he 'should
apply the law as it currently is'. Ultimately, in the determinative passages of his *e*
judgment, he made it plain that his essential concern was with the legality of the
respondent council's decision to seek injunctive relief. He expressed himself
'satisfied in all the circumstances that the council were entitled to reach the
decision that they did' and said that he could 'find no other factors in this case
such that justify me in taking an exceptional course having regard to the planning *f*
policies applicable to this site'. I recognise that he referred also to 'the particular
personal needs of the defendants'. Taking the judgment as a whole, however, he
appears to have regarded himself as having only the barest residual discretion to
withhold relief. The main part of the injunction, that for the removal of the
mobile homes, was not even suspended.

                                                                                       g
(3) *Wrexham County BC v Berry*
[45] McCombe J's very full judgment in this case extends to 25 pages of
transcript and addresses the European Court's judgment in *Chapman v UK* (2001)
10 BHRC 48 in considerable detail. Having noted the appellant's submission, in
part based on *Tandridge DC v Delaney* [2000] 1 PLR 11, that 'the court can no *h*
longer adopt ... a "hands-off approach" to the underlying planning considerations',
the judge said:

    'On this issue, I do not think I have to decide the extent to which in any
    individual case the court may have to investigate planning considerations in
    deciding whether a proper approach to art 8 has been adopted. For my part, *j*
    I believe that the case on this issue can adequately be resolved by the decision
    in *Chapman v UK* itself, where the facts were not at all dissimilar to those, in
    my view, in issue here ... It must, of course, be noticed that other relevant
    considerations have to be taken into account by the national authorities, and
    those include the availability or otherwise of alternative accommodation. [The
    appellant] urges upon me that in reality there is no alternative accommodation

a   because of the Berry family's difficulty at the Ruthin Road site. In my view, however, *Chapman v UK* also provides an answer to this point by reference to its own facts, which again are not dissimilar to those which confront me in the present matter.'

[46] The judge then quoted at length from the judgment in *Chapman v UK*
b   (2001) 10 BHRC 48 including this passage (at 74 (para 113)): 'The court is therefore not persuaded that there were no alternatives available to the applicant besides remaining in occupation on land without planning permission in a Green Belt area.'

[47] McCombe J then continued:

c   'In my view, those statements apply equally to this case. I am not persuaded that there is any material distinction in the factor that in *Chapman*'s case the planning issues had been considered by a planning inspector. Mr Berry has had ample opportunity to invoke the appeal processes open to him under the law to contest the previous decisions of the planning authority and he has
d   chosen not to take them. Neither has he made any further application for permission since September 2000. He cannot, in my view, now be heard to contend that this court should itself now undertake a planning review which Mr Berry has consciously eschewed on more than one previous occasion and seems disinclined to seek in any proper way even now.'

e   [48] The appellant advances two main criticisms of that paragraph. First and most importantly he points out that, unlike in *Chapman*'s case where in terms the court expressed itself unsatisfied that there were no alternative sites available, here the judge appears to have accepted that the appellant was in effect forced off the Ruthin Road site and unable to return there, there being no other gipsy caravan sites provided by the council. Secondly it is submitted that the judge was
f   too critical of the appellant's failure to appeal the respondent's earlier refusals of planning permission: these planning applications, Mr Drabble points out, had been made at a time when the appellant was not resident on the site and when, accordingly, the humanitarian considerations which arose when he was forced to leave the Ruthin Road site were lacking. Finally, in contrasting the facts of this
g   case with those of *Chapman*'s case, Mr Drabble points to the protracted enforcement process in *Chapman*'s case, including a 15-month period for compliance given by the inspector hearing the second enforcement notice appeal, whereas the respondent council here immediately adopted the s 187B route as a deliberate alternative to enforcement action, thereby precluding any right of appeal to an independent
h   inspector against the enforcement notice.

[49] In my judgment there is substance in these arguments and I am persuaded that the judge erred in regarding *Chapman*'s case as effectively determinative of the application before him.

j   (4) *Hertsmere BC v Harty*

[50] The two main authorities by which Judge Brunning appears to have directed himself were the *Tandridge* case and *Chapman v UK*. *Chapman*'s case in particular looms large in the judgment where it is accurately summarised save for a reference to the wide margin of appreciation left to 'local authorities' (instead of 'national authorities'). As to the local authority's approach in that case, the judge considered in some detail the council officers' report to the planning

committee on 13 February 2001, the report which led the committee to refuse
even a temporary planning permission, and continued:

a

'The whole tenor of the considerations put before the local authority
therefore was that there had to be a balance between the various needs of the
defendants as applicants for planning permission and the various planning
considerations that were set out ... [The judgment then explained that the
appellants were represented by an experienced firm of solicitors who had
been able to put all the relevant considerations before the council.] It may
well be that there are circumstances which arise where a local authority will
not satisfactorily have carried out a balancing exercise by reason of its failure
to make factual enquiries. This, however, was not such a case. Accordingly,
I am satisfied that this local authority did carry out the process which the law
requires it to carry out and has demonstrated in striking the balance it did
that it has given full weight to the considerations it is required to give under
the Human Rights Act 1998 ... I am aware of the needs of the individuals
concerned and some of the particularly difficult circumstances that prevail.
On the other hand, I am required in the exercise of discretion to strike a
balance, and whilst I have those humanitarian matters in mind, I must at the
same time look at the wider picture and other interests. I am satisfied that
this is an appropriate case for an injunction. It is [the fourth unlawful
occupation of this site over a period of some years] ... which in its own way
is of some significance when coming to consider the exercise of discretion.'

b

c

d

[51] Mr Drabble criticises those conclusions from two standpoints in particular:
first, by reference to the officers' report to the planning committee, and second
on the basis that, by directing himself in accordance with the *Tandridge* approach,
the judge failed to recognise the proper width of his discretion.

e

[52] As to the officers' report, although much of it is relevant I shall confine
myself to three paragraphs only:

'2 ... Members may recall that they passed a resolution on the 24th
October last year for the Council to apply for injunctive relief following the
occupation of the site. Instructions have been given and the papers settled
but proceedings have not been issued in order that the members have the
opportunity to consider all of the arguments now put forward on behalf of
the applicants for this development. In the event that the members were to
refuse planning permission proceedings would be issued forthwith for
interim and full injunctive relief ...

f

g

6.21 It is legitimate ... for Members to balance Green Belt and other land
use objectives against the rights in article 8. In the absence of any compelling
case of "very special circumstances", it is clear that the proposal would be
inappropriate development which, by definition, is harmful to the Green
Belt. The applicant's agent acknowledges the *Buckley* case. He also argues
that the applicant and the other families have no alternative site and that to
refuse planning permission in this instance would be a breach of their rights
under article 8. He adds that the site is of poor landscape quality and that the
applicant is prepared to landscape the site, in collaboration with the local
planning authority.

h

j

6.22 The need for the protection of the Green Belt is a serious public
interest and objections in this respect cannot be overcome by the use of
conditions on a planning permission. The public interest can therefore only

a be protected by the refusal of planning permission. It is considered that the
refusal of planning permission is necessary having regard to the important
and legitimate aim of protecting the Green Belt. It is considered that such a
decision would not place a disproportionate burden on the appellants and
would not result in a violation of their rights under article 8 of the
Convention.'

b [53] The minutes of the committee meeting on 13 February record:

'Some Members of Committee were minded to support the grant of a
temporary permission for one year only. However, the Officers reported
that if the sub-committee was minded to reverse the Officers' recommendation
and to grant such a permission the application would have to be reported to
c the environment committee as a departure from the local plan. The sub-
committee would also have to be satisfied that very special circumstances
existed even if the application to be granted was a temporary one. As stated
in their report, the Officers were of the opinion that those very special
circumstances did not exist.'

d [54] Mr Drabble's criticism of para 6.22 of the report was finally formulated in
writing as follows:

'The basic approach at para 6.22 cannot be regarded as a proper exercise
that recognises the need to protect the gipsies' particular rights under art 8
e unless the environmental harm *in the individual case* justifies the interference.
Its logic is that protection of the Green Belt is "a serious public interest";
conditions do not avoid conflict; "the public interest can therefore only be
protected by the refusal of planning permission". This approach could be
repeated, in identical words, whether the damage to the Green Belt is great
or small and whether the humanitarian considerations, including abandonment
f of the traditional lifestyle, are great or small.'

[55] Mr Drabble further criticises the council's approach of applying forthwith
for injunctive relief upon the refusal of planning permission (as foreshadowed in
para 2 of the report) without, therefore, awaiting any appeal against the refusal.
[56] As to the judge's reliance on the *Tandridge* case, Mr Drabble argues that,
g on true analysis, the *Hambleton* case is central to the *Tandridge* case and that
although para 5 of Mr Purchas' summary suggests that the court itself should
reach 'a conclusion whether, in all the circumstances, the grant of an injunction
would be just and proportionate', this is required to be done on the basis of the
balance between the interests of the gipsies and those of the public previously
h struck by the planning authority.
[57] My views on this fourth appeal have, I confess, shifted more than once
during the course of the hearing. At various stages I was inclined to accept
Mr Drabble's criticisms of the all-important officers' report and of the council's
decision in reliance upon it not merely to refuse planning permission but immediately
j to apply for an injunction. The critical question, however, is whether in the end
the judge when granting injunctive relief deferred excessively to the respondent's
own views as to how the balance between the competing interests fell to be
struck. Looking at that question as a matter of substance rather than form I am
not ultimately persuaded that he did. Rather I have reached the conclusion that
he recognised the true width of his discretion and exercised his own independent
judgment in deciding that the time had finally come to bring the unlawful use of

this site to an end. That was, I have to say, an entirely understandable judgment given the quite remarkable planning history of this site.

[58] There are, of course, factors even in the first three cases which will undoubtedly present the appellants with real difficulty if and when the respondent authorities seek fresh injunctive relief. Such difficulties, however, are for the future. Our judgments today merely indicate how courts should henceforth approach the exercise of their s 187B power.

[59] In the result I would allow the appeals in the first three cases but dismiss that of Mr Harty and others against Hertsmere Borough Council in the fourth case.

PETER GIBSON LJ.

[60] I agree.

TUCKEY LJ.

[61] I also agree.

The Porter, Searle and Berry appeals allowed. The Harty appeal dismissed.

Dilys Tausz   Barrister.

a

A v B (a company) and another

QUEEN'S BENCH DIVISION

JACK J

24, 25 MAY, 4 JUNE, 10 SEPTEMBER 2001

b

Confidential information – Injunction against disclosure of information – Newspaper intending to publish articles relating to claimant's extra-marital affairs – Whether law affording protection of confidentiality to facts concerning sexual relations outside marriage – Human Rights Act 1998, s 12, Sch 1, Pt I, art 10.

c

The claimant, A, was a professional footballer and a married man with a family. He had extra-marital affairs with two women, C and D, who sold their stories to the defendant newspaper. After learning that the newspaper intended to publish articles relating to his sexual relationships with the two women—including salacious descriptions of the sexual activity—A applied for an interim injunction

d restraining publication on the ground, inter alia, of breach of confidence. The judge granted the injunction, but the newspaper subsequently applied to have it discharged. At the hearing, the issue arose as to whether sexual matters occurring between two persons were subject to a duty of confidence in the absence of any express agreement between them that they keep such matters confidential. The

e court also considered the effect of s 12ᵃ of the Human Rights Act 1998. Section 12 applied when the court was considering whether to grant any relief which, if granted, might affect the exercise of the right to freedom of expression under art 10ᵇ of the European Convention for the Protection of Human Rights and Fundamental Freedoms 1950 (as set out in Sch 1 to the Human Rights Act 1998) —a right that was subject, by virtue of art 10(2), to such restrictions as were

f prescribed by law and were necessary in a democratic society for, inter alia, the protection of the rights of others and preventing the disclosure of information received in confidence. Section 12(3) provided that no relief affecting the convention right to freedom of expression was to be granted so as to restrain publication before trial unless the court was satisfied that the applicant was likely to establish that publication should not be allowed. Section 12(4) required the court to have

g particular regard to that right and, where the proceedings related to journalistic material, to the extent to which it would be in the public interest for the material to be published.

Held – The law afforded the protection of confidentiality to facts concerning

h sexual relations both within and outside marriage. As regards the ambit of that protection, two questions arose, namely what was to be protected by preventing communication, and to whom was communication to be prevented. There could be no absolute answer to those questions, and each case would depend on its circumstances. In the instant case the answer was straightforward. There had

j been communication to the newspaper not just of the facts of the relationships but of the details of the sexual conduct that had occurred. The newspaper had no interest in simply publishing the fact of the relationships alone. It intended to publish the whole, and needed the detail to interest its readers. It had been a

---

a   Section 12, so far as material, is set out at [17], below
b   Article 10 is set out at [26], below

breach of confidence for C and D to provide the information which they had to
the newspaper or to anyone else with a view to its publication in the media. It
would be a breach of confidence for the newspaper to publish it. That publication
could be restrained by injunction. Nor was there any public interest in the
publication of the articles and the information which they contained. Although
A's conduct was to be condemned by any moral standard, that did not provide a
public interest in the publication of the information about the two extra-marital
affairs. In so far as A had established himself as a public figure, it was simply as a
professional footballer. It was not suggested that he was someone who had
courted publicity and who had laid open his private life to public scrutiny
by courting publicity. In that situation, A should succeed in the balancing
operation required by s 12 of the 1998 Act and art 10 of the convention, and it was
therefore likely that he would satisfy at trial the burden of showing that his right
to confidence should prevail over the newspaper's right to freedom of expression.
Accordingly, an injunction would be granted (i) prohibiting publication and
disclosure by the newspaper of information concerning the facts that A was
having sexual relationships with C and D, and facts relating to the sexual intercourse
and other sexual conduct which had occurred with C and D, and (ii) prohibiting
disclosure of that information by C and D to anyone with a view to publication
in the media (see [56]–[59], [67]–[71], [74], below).

Venables v News Group Newspapers Ltd [2001] 1 All ER 908 and Douglas v Hello! Ltd
[2001] 2 All ER 289 considered.

Notes
For the convention right to freedom of expression, see 8(2) Halsbury's Laws (4th
edn reissue) para 159.

For the Human Rights Act 1998, s 12, Sch 1, Pt I, art 10, see 7 Halsbury's Statutes
(4th edn) (1999 reissue) 510, 524.

Cases referred to in judgment
A-G v Guardian Newspapers Ltd (No 2) [1988] 3 All ER 545, [1990] 1 AC 109, [1988]
    2 WLR 805, CA; affd [1988] 3 All ER 545, [1990] 1 AC 109, [1988] 3 WLR 776, HL.
American Cyanamid Co v Ethicon Ltd [1975] 1 All ER 504, [1975] AC 396, [1975]
    2 WLR 316, HL.
Argyll (Duchess of) v Duke of Argyll [1965] 1 All ER 611, [1967] Ch 302, [1965] 2 WLR 790.
Barrymore v News Group Newspapers Ltd [1997] FSR 600.
Bladet Tromsø v Norway (1999) 29 EHRR 125, ECt HR.
Coco v AN Clark (Engineers) Ltd [1969] RPC 41.
Douglas v Hello! Ltd [2001] 2 All ER 289, [2001] QB 967, [2001] 2 WLR 992, CA.
Kaye v Robertson [1991] FSR 62, CA.
Spencer (Earl) v UK (1998) 25 EHRR CD 105, E Com HR.
Stephens v Avery [1988] 2 All ER 477, [1988] Ch 449, [1988] 2 WLR 1280.
Venables v News Group Newspapers Ltd [2001] 1 All ER 908, [2001] Fam 430, [2001]
    2 WLR 1038.
X and Y v The Netherlands (1985) EHRR 235, ECt HR.

Application
The first defendant, a newspaper publishing company, applied for the discharge
of an injunction granted by Jack J on 30 April 2001 restraining it and the second
defendant, C, until trial or further order from using, disclosing or publishing any
personal information of and/or information about (i) the private life of the

a claimant, A, arising out of the matters referred to in the witness statements in the action or any other information concerning A's relationships with C and another woman, D, and (ii) any other matters concerning A's sexual life. The case was heard and judgment given in private, and the judgment is reported on the basis that the anonymity of all parties would be preserved. The facts are set out in the judgment.

b
Richard Spearman QC and *Victoria Sharp QC* for the newspaper.
Alastair Wilson QC and *Stephen Bate* for A.
C did not appear and was not represented.

Cur adv vult

c
10 September 2001. The following judgment was delivered.

JACK J.

d *Introduction*

[1] This judgment rules on one of the two grounds on which the defendant newspaper based its application to set aside the restraining order made by me on 30 April 2001. The two grounds of the application can be identified as the merits of the claimant's case for an order and alleged non-disclosure by the claimant. I ruled on the second in a judgment delivered on 20 June 2001, in which I held that

e the order should be set aside for non-disclosure. For the reasons given in the judgment I did not deal on an alternative basis with the newspaper's case as to the merits. Immediately following the delivery of that judgment and before any order had been drawn up the claimant provided further evidence and further submissions were made on his behalf. In a further judgment delivered on 5 July 2001

f I took the exceptional course of reconsidering my judgment of 20 June and I rejected the newspaper's case that the order of 30 April should be set aside for non-disclosure. That left outstanding the newspaper's case that the order should be set aside on the merits, and it is to that that this judgment relates.

[2] The further paragraphs of this introduction and those relating to the facts are taken from my judgment of 20 June 2001, with some small modifications.

g
[3] On Sunday 29 April 2001 the defendant newspaper publishers intended to publish an article relating to the claimant, a successful professional footballer, who is a married man with a family. It would have concerned his sexual relations with two women, one of whom, C, is the second defendant. It was probably C who had initially gone to the newspaper with her story. It was what is popularly

h called a 'kiss and tell' situation. I will refer to the second woman as D. Both C and D have sold their stories to the newspaper. D is not a party to the action.

[4] The claimant learnt of the intended publication. In consequence an application came before me as judge in chambers at 2pm on Friday, 27 April 2001. It was made without the service of a formal notice of application, but both defendants

j had been notified of it. The newspaper appeared before me, represented by leading counsel. C did not appear and was not represented. She had, however, provided a statement to the newspaper to be used at the hearing. I heard the application over three hours and gave my decision that I would grant an injunction restraining publication. I reserved giving my reasons until Monday 30 April when I delivered them and heard further argument as to the form of the order which I had made, which was in consequence amended. I also granted permission to the newspaper to appeal—that permission has not been taken up. After discussion the injunction *a* was granted until trial or further order. The order provided that the defendants might apply to vary or discharge it.

[5] On 17 May the newspaper issued an application that the injunction should be discharged. This came before me on 24 May. I heard the submissions of Mr Richard Spearman QC for the newspaper and Mr Alastair Wilson QC for the claimant on that day and the day following, and on 4 June. Further witness *b* statements were adduced on both sides including a second statement from B and one from D, which were responded to in a second statement from A. Extracts from the mobile telephone bills of the claimant, and of C and of D were also put in evidence to show the communications between them by either telephone text messages or oral telephone.

[6] I heard both the original application in April and subsequent applications *c* in private. The action is titled to prevent the identification of the parties, and this judgment and my previous judgments are phrased to preserve that anonymity. The order made on 30 April forbids the defendants from disclosing the existence of the action.

[7] The claimant founded his claim to restrain publication of the proposed *d* article on three grounds: first, breach of confidence; second, breach of privacy; and third, breach of copyright. The last relates to telephone text messages sent by the claimant to C and also a card. It is of minor importance.

The facts

[8] It is common ground that the claimant had affairs with C and D. It is *e* common ground that they were seen in public together at restaurants and clubs. Some incidents are not in dispute between the claimant and C or D: others are. Likewise some details. I am not in a position to resolve these differences.

[9] The summaries of the claimant's relations with C and D, which follow, are based on the common ground which emerges from the various statements which *f* are now before the court.

[10] The claimant and C first met in late January 2001 at a bar and later the same night at a club. There is a dispute as to who then got in touch with whom. That resulted in his taking her out for a drink at one, or perhaps two, establishments on 29 January. On 1 February he took her out to lunch. There is a dispute as to *g* whether he met her mother and brother. On 8 February he went to her house. On 9 February he sent her a telephone text message in which he told her that, contrary to what he had said before, he was married. On 10 February they spent the night together at a hotel. They did not have sexual intercourse. This meeting was omitted from the claimant's first statement, in which he said that they did not meet on 10 February and did not meet again until 17 February. On 14 February, *h* Valentine's Day, they met and he gave her presents. On 15 February they had lunch together. On 17 February they spent the night together at a hotel and had intercourse for the first time. On 25 February they met and possibly had lunch together, certainly dinner. She says that they had sexual intercourse: he is silent as to that. They met on 1 March. She asserts that on 8 March he picked her *j* up from a gym and they had intercourse at her house after some lunch: he denies that this occurred. On 10 March they went to a club and spent the night at her house and they had intercourse. She alleges that on various occasions he had promised to marry her and to move in with her. By the end of March she says that she was angry that he had lied so much. On 31 March she therefore posted through the door of his parents house a transcript of the text message which he

a had sent saying that he was married, which she had kept. She said that he should show it to his wife and referred to photographs of him at the second hotel at which they had stayed. No such photographs have been exhibited. A photograph has been referred to. This brought their relationship to an end.

[11] On learning of the envelope delivered to his parents' house, the claimant telephoned C. He alleges that C then tried to blackmail him by requesting £3,000
b to finance breast surgery, saying that she had already spoken to two newspapers. He says that he put the phone down on her. She denies that this occurred. In late April he had a telephone call from D who told him that her name had been given to the newspaper by C. The claimant then made a complaint about C to the police. He asserts that he complained that she had tried to blackmail him. It is difficult to see why else he might have contacted the police about her. It is disputed
c by the newspaper that the complainant did make a formal complaint and that the police are pursuing it. The evidence before me does not enable me to form a view on this very serious matter. As I did for the purpose of my judgment delivered on 30 April, I must put it on one side. I do not accept Mr Spearman's submission that I should conclude from the evidence before me that there is
d nothing in the allegation of blackmail.

[12] An analysis of telephone bills shows that between 31 January and 21 April 2001 the claimant called C 438 times. It is likely that the great number of these were text messages. She called him of the order of 300 times. The first calls are shown as being in the small hours of 31 January. If this reflects that they first met earlier that night on 30 January—as it may well, then the summary which I have
e set out cannot be correct for the period prior to 9 February. That part of the summary originates from C's recollection. Because a long message has to be sent as several short messages, the number of calls may be thereby substantially increased and the total may give an exaggerated picture of the real number of communications.

f [13] In his witness statement of 26 April the claimant had simply said of D 'I had a brief affair with [her]' by way of introduction to her telephone conversation with him on about 21 April to which I will come. The newspaper has now put in a full statement from D, to which the claimant has responded.

[14] D works as a lap dancer in a bar. The claimant came into the bar in
g November 1999 and she danced for him. He came into the bar again on 15 December 1999. There is a dispute whether they arranged to meet later in a club or whether they met there by coincidence. At that club there was some kissing between them. It is disputed whether this was in a public area or not. They next met on 21 December 1999 when they went out for a drink and then back to her flat. While they were talking she says that he said that they should not advertise their
h relationship as he was a footballer and she a lap dancer and they would not want the story to end in the papers. He gave her presents for Christmas. They next met on 30 December at her flat where they had sexual intercourse for the first time. He came to her flat again on 4 January 2000, when it seems that they again had intercourse. They met at a club on 7 January. D asserts that on 17 January
j she found out the claimant was married. He says that she already knew. There is a dispute as to what he told her about the state of his marriage. They met on 5 February and after going out spent the night together in a hotel. At her request he bought her presents for Valentine's day. They did not properly meet again until June. The details of the meeting are in dispute though it is agreed that they spent the night together in a hotel. She has given a lurid account of their intimacies, the detail of which he denies. They did not meet again until 21 November,

when he stayed the night at her flat. The next event of importance was the telephone conversation between them in late April 2001 concerning the newspaper's involvement and C. The details of the conversation are disputed. D accepts that she suggested that he give her £5,000 for her story, but says she said it in anger at what he was saying about C.

[15] This summary of their few meetings over a year does not, however, present the whole picture. For they were in frequent contact by telephone or telephone text message from 23 December 1999 to 11 April 2001 as recorded on their telephone bills. She called him on one or more occasions on 106 days between 23 December 1999 and June 2000. Likewise on nine days between July and October 2000, on 18 days in November 2000 including every day from 14 November, on 26 days in December 2000, and on seven days in January 2000. He called her 712 times in all, including some 250 times in December 1999 to January 2000 and 86 times in November 2000 and 91 times in December 2000. The same point arises as with C as to multiple calls required to communicate what is really one message.

[16] The newspaper has introduced in evidence drafts of two articles which it had proposed to publish. One concerns the claimant's relations with C, and one concerns his relations with D. Much of each is concerned with salacious description of the sexual activity between the claimant and C or D. They are intended for the prurient.

The legal framework

[17] The context in which the claimant's application for interim relief must be decided is provided by s 12 of the Human Rights Act 1998 which applies because the grant of relief affects the newspaper's right to freedom of expression provided by art 10 of the European Convention for the Protection of Human Rights and Fundamental Freedoms 1950 (as set out in Sch 1 to the 1998 Act). Subsections (3) and (4) provide:

'(3) No such relief is to be granted so as to restrain publication before trial unless the court is satisfied that the applicant is likely to establish that publication should not be allowed.

(4) The court must have particular regard to the importance of the Convention right to freedom of expression and, where the proceedings relate to material which the respondent claims, or which appears to the court, to be journalistic, literary or artistic material (or to conduct connected with such material), to—(a) the extent to which—(i) the material has, or is about to, become available to the public; or (ii) it is, or would be, in the public interest for the material to be published; (b) any relevant privacy code.'

[18] The effect of s 12(3) was considered by the Court of Appeal in *Douglas v Hello! Ltd* [2001] 2 All ER 289, [2001] QB 967. In para 150 (with which Brooke and Sedley LJJ expressed agreement) Keene LJ stated of s 12(3):

'It requires the court to look at the merits of the case and not merely to apply the test [in *American Cyanamid Co v Ethicon Ltd* [1975] 1 All ER 504, [1975] AC 396]. Thus the court has to look ahead to the ultimate stage and to be satisfied that the scales are likely to come down in the applicant's favour.' (See [2001] 2 All ER 289 at 326, [2001] QB 967 at 1008.)

[19] So here, before the claimant can be given the interim relief that he seeks, he must satisfy me that at the trial of the action he is likely to succeed against the newspaper in restraining publication.

a   **[20]** Section 12(4) is applicable generally, that is, both to interim applications and to decisions made at trial. Particular regard must be had to the art 10 right to freedom of expression. Because the material which is the subject matter of the claim is 'journalistic'—at least as between the newspaper and the claimant, particular regard is to be had to the extent to which it is already available to the public, and to the extent to which it would be in the public interest for it to be *b* published. Likewise particular regard must be had to a relevant privacy code.

   [21] The reference to a privacy code shows that the section intends that privacy considerations may be weighed against the right to freedom of expression. So in appropriate cases there will be a balancing exercise between the two.

   [22] The Press Complaints Commission Code of Practice is a relevant code. Clause 3 is titled 'Privacy'. Clause 3(1) provides:
c

   'Everyone is entitled to respect for his or her private and family life, home, health and correspondence. A publication will be expected to justify intrusions into any individual's private life without consent.'

d   **[23]** This is a clause which is marked as 'subject to exception' where the exception can be demonstrated to be in the public interest. Under the heading of 'The public interest' the code provides:

   '1. The public interest includes: (i) Detecting or exposing crime or a serious misdemeanour. (ii) Protecting public health and safety. (iii) Preventing the public from being misled by some statement or action of an individual or *e* organisation.

   2. In any case where the public interest is invoked, the Press Complaints Commission will require a full explanation by the editor demonstrating how the public interest was served.

   3. There is a public interest in freedom of expression itself. The Commission *f* will therefore have regard to the extent to which material has, or is about to, become available to the public.'

Paragraph 4 relates to children and is not relevant.

   [24] In his judgment in *Douglas'* case [2001] 2 All ER 289 at 313–314, [2001] QB 967 at 994 (para 94) Brooke LJ stated:
g

   'It appears to me that the existence of these statutory provisions [he was referring to s 12] coupled with the current wording of the relevant privacy code, mean that in any case where the court is concerned with issues of freedom of expression in a journalistic, literary or artistic context, it is bound *h* to pay particular regard to any breach of the rules set out in cl 3 of the code, especially where none of the public interest claims set out in the preamble to the code is asserted. A newspaper which flouts cl 3 of the code is likely in those circumstances to have its claim to an entitlement to freedom of expression trumped by art 10(2) considerations of privacy. Unlike the court in *Kaye v Robertson* [1991] FSR 62, Parliament recognised that it had to *j* acknowledge the importance of the art 8(1) respect for private life, and it was able to do so untrammelled by any concerns that the law of confidence might not stretch to every aspect of private life.'

   [25] In para 136 of his judgment Sedley LJ expressly agreed with this paragraph ([2001] 2 All ER 289 at 323, [2001] QB 967 at 1004). Brooke LJ continued in para 95:

'It follows that on the present occasion it is not necessary to go beyond s 12 of the [1998 Act] and cl 3 of the code to find the ground rules by which we should weigh the competing considerations of freedom of expression on the one hand and privacy on the other.' (See [2001] 2 All ER 289 at 314, [2001] QB 967 at 994–995.)

[26] It is convenient next to set out art 10 of the convention. It is titled 'Freedom of expression'. The first paragraph provides the right of freedom of expression. The second provides for limitations to it:

'1. Everyone has the right to freedom of expression. This right shall include freedom to hold opinions and to receive and impart information and ideas without interference by public authority and regardless of frontiers. This Article shall not prevent States from requiring the licensing of broadcasting, television or cinema enterprises.

2. The exercise of these freedoms, since it carries with it duties and responsibilities, may be subject to such formalities, conditions, restrictions or penalties as are prescribed by law and are necessary in a democratic society, in the interests of national security, territorial integrity or public safety, for the prevention of disorder or crime, for the protection of health or morals, for the protection of the reputation or rights of others, for preventing the disclosure of information received in confidence, or for maintaining the authority and impartiality of the judiciary.'

[27] A provision of English law which may be applied to protect an individual's private life or privacy, such as the law relating to breach of confidence, may be a restriction on the right to freedom of expression prescribed by law falling within art 10(2). Where that may occur the balancing process provided for by s 12 of the Act must take place, with the possible outcome considered by Brooke LJ in para 94 of his judgment in *Douglas'* case quoted above.

[28] Mr Spearman referred me to a number of authorities which emphasise the importance of the freedom of expression and that part of it which is called the freedom of the press. He appeared at times almost to be suggesting on behalf of the newspaper that the right to freedom of expression must always prevail. If such a submission had been made, it would have ignored art 10(2) and s 12. It would also have been contrary to the judgments in *Douglas'* case and that of Dame Elizabeth Butler-Sloss P in *Venables v News Group Newspapers Ltd* [2001] 1 All ER 908 at 922, [2001] Fam 430 at 451, para 42 in particular. In para 44 of her judgment in that case following a review of authority which I need not repeat, Butler-Sloss P stated her conclusion on this aspect as follows:

'The onus of proving the case that freedom of expression must be restricted is firmly upon the applicant seeking relief. The restrictions sought must, in the circumstances of the present case, be shown to be in accordance with the law, justifiable as necessary to satisfy a strong and pressing social need, convincingly demonstrated, to restrain the press in order to protect the rights of the claimants to confidentiality, and proportionate to the legitimate aim pursued. The right to confidence is, however, a recognised exception within art 10(2) ...' (See [2001] 1 All ER 908 at 922, [2001] Fam 430 at 451.)

[29] *Venables'* case was a case where there was at least arguably a strong public interest in knowing the new identities of the two applicants as the authors of a horrific murder. That had to be balanced against the risk to their persons and lives

a if they were identified. And, I would add, there was a public interest in their being rehabilitated into society.

[30] It is worth here quoting two paragraphs from the judgment of the European Court in *Bladet Tromsø v Norway* (1999) 29 EHRR 125 at 166–167:

b '58. According to the Court's well-established case law, the test of "necessity in a democratic society" requires the Court to determine whether the "interference" complained of corresponded to a "pressing social need", whether it was proportionate to the legitimate aim pursued and whether the reasons given by the national authorities to justify it are relevant and sufficient. In assessing whether such a "need" exists and what measures should be adopted to deal with it, the national authorities are left a certain

c margin of appreciation. This power of appreciation is not, however, unlimited but goes hand in hand with a European supervision by the Court, whose task it is to give a final ruling on whether a restriction is reconcilable with freedom expression as protected by Article 10.

d 59. One factor of particular importance for the Court's determination in the present case is the essential function the press fulfils in a democratic society. Although the press must not overstep certain bounds, in particular in respect of the reputation and rights of others and the need to prevent disclosure of confidential information, its duty is nevertheless to impart—in a manner consistent with its obligations and responsibilities—information and ideas on all matters of public interest. In addition, the Court is mindful

e of the fact that journalistic freedom also covers possible recourse to a degree of exaggeration, or even provocation. In cases such as the present one the national margin of appreciation is circumscribed by the interest of democratic society in enabling the press to exercise its vital role of "public watchdog" in imparting information of serious public concern.'

f [31] In my judgment it follows as a matter of logic, and is consistent with the structure of art 10 in two paragraphs, that where the public interest, the public benefit, in the publication of a matter is great, any justification for suppressing that publication must be very strong in order to prevail. Conversely, where the public interest in publication is very slight, or non-existent, a lesser justification may be sufficient. This is consistent with s 12 and in particular circumstances may

g have the outcome foreseen by Brooke LJ in para 94 of his judgment in *Douglas'* case [2001] 2 All ER 289, [2001] QB 967. But the court must not drop its guard. It must be cautious in restricting freedom of expression in any circumstances. For the danger is that a restriction permitted at one time, perhaps to restrain what is then seen as an abuse of freedom of expression by the press, or by a section of it,

h may at a later time be sought to be used for wider purposes.

[32] Next I should set out art 8 of the convention. It is titled 'Right to respect for private and family life', and provides:

j '1. Everyone has the right to respect for his private and family life, his home and his correspondence.

2. There shall be no interference by a public authority with the exercise of this right except such as is in accordance with the law and is necessary in a democratic society in the interests of national security, public safety or the economic well-being of the country, for the prevention of disorder or crime, for the protection of health or morals, or for the protection of the rights and freedoms of others.'

[33] In *X and Y v The Netherlands* (1985) EHRR 235 at 239–240 (para 23) the European Court stated in its judgment:

'The Court recalls that although the object of Article 8 is essentially that of protecting the individual against arbitrary interference by the public authorities, it does not merely compel the State to abstain from such interference: in addition to this primarily negative undertaking, there may be positive obligations inherent in an effective respect for family life. These obligations may involve the adoption of measures designed to secure respect for private life even in the sphere of the relations of individuals between themselves.'

[34] This passage was cited by Brooke and Sedley LJJ in *Douglas'* case and by Dame Elizabeth Butler-Sloss P in *Venables'* case.

[35] A right provided under national law which supports the right to respect for a person's private life may be a right to be considered in conjunction with art 10(2).

[36] In her judgment in *Venables'* case Dame Elizabeth Butler-Sloss P considered the court's duty in the application of the convention. She stated ([2001] 1 All ER 908 at 918, [2001] Fam 430 at 446):

'26. In the light of the judgments in *Douglas'* case, I am satisfied that I have to apply art 10 directly to the present case.

27. That obligation on the court does not seem to me to encompass the creation of a free-standing cause of action based directly upon the articles of the convention, although that proposition is advanced by [counsel for Venables] as a fall-back position, if all else fails. The duty on the court, in my view, is to act compatibly with convention rights in adjudicating upon existing common law causes of action, and that includes a positive as well as a negative obligation.'

[37] That is the approach I intend to adopt, which makes it unnecessary to consider certain questions as to the interpretation of the convention and the Act, which were touched on in *Douglas'* case but were not decided.

[38] Lastly, I should quote para 127 of the judgment of Sedley LJ in *Douglas'* case [2001] 2 All ER 289 at 320, [2001] QB 967 at 1001:

'It is relevant, finally, to note that no Strasbourg jurisprudence contra-indicates, much less countermands, the establishment in national legal systems of a qualified right of privacy; and that the courts of France and Germany, to take two other signatories of the convention, have both in recent years developed long-gestated laws for the qualified protection of privacy against both state and non-state invasion (see Etienne Picard, "The right to privacy in French law" in *Protecting Privacy*, ed Basil Markesinis (1999); Basil Markesinis *The German Law of Torts: A Comparative Introduction* (3rd edn, 1994) pp 63–66).'

[39] It would be interesting to know what answers French and German law would give in the present situation.

The law of breach of confidence

[40] As in particular *Douglas'* and *Venables'* cases show, the law relating to breach of confidence is in a state of growth.

a   **[41]** The important question to which this case gives rise is whether sexual matters occurring between two persons are subject to a duty of confidence in the absence of any express agreement between them that they keep such matters confidential. An essential aspect of that is the ambit or scope of any such duty. There is but little authority.

   [42] The injunction obtained in *Duchess of Argyll v Duke of Argyll* [1965] 1 All ER
b   611, [1967] Ch 302 was to prevent the publication of secrets relating to her private life communicated by the Duchess to the Duke during their marriage. The court recognised that the information which was the object of its order was in its nature confidential and held that it was the policy of the law to protect that confidentiality with the object of preserving the marital relationship. It does not seem that the information concerned the relations of the parties between themselves.

c   **[43]** In *Stephens v Avery* [1988] 2 All ER 477, [1988] Ch 449 the application before the court was to strike out the claim as disclosing no reasonable cause of action. It failed. The claimant alleged that she had communicated to the first defendant information concerning her lesbian relationship with a married third party. She alleged that she had done so in confidence, and this was assumed for
d   the purpose of the application. It was held that the information was not outside the law's protection because it concerned immorality, and that it was confidential information which the law would protect. Browne-Wilkinson V-C approached the case in accordance with the three requirements stated by Megarry J in *Coco v AN Clark (Engineers) Ltd* [1969] RPC 41 at 47, that the information must have the necessary quality of confidence about it, that it must have been imparted in
e   circumstances importing an obligation of confidence, and that there must be an unauthorised use of it. In the course of his judgment he stated:

> 'Next, I consider the submission that because in all cases of sexual conduct both parties are aware of the facts, information relating to those facts cannot in law be confidential. In my judgment this submission is wholly misconceived.
f   > It is based on the premise that as between unmarried sexual partners there is no duty of confidentiality. Therefore, both parties are free to discuss the matter with the whole world. I will assume that submission to be correct, but without expressing any view on its correctness in law. Even on that assumption, the fact that the other partner to a sexual relationship *may*
g   > disclose what has happened does not mean that he or she has done so. To most people the details of their sexual lives are high on their list of those matters which they regard as confidential. The mere fact that two people know a secret does not mean that it is not confidential. If in fact information is secret, then in my judgment it is capable of being kept secret by the
h   > imposition of a duty of confidence on any person to whom it is communicated. Information only ceases to be capable of protection as confidential when it is in fact known to a substantial number of people.' (See [1988] 2 All ER 477 at 481, [1988] Ch 449 at 454.)

   [44] Browne-Wilkinson V-C went on to cite from the judgments in the
j   *Spycatcher* case in the Court of Appeal (*A-G v Guardian Newspapers Ltd (No 2)* [1988] 3 All ER 545, [1990] 1 AC 109) to the effect that information generally available to the relevant public would not be protected.

   [45] In the *Spycatcher* case, in the House of Lords, Lord Goff of Chieveley stated in the course of his judgment:

> 'The first limiting principle ... is that the principle of confidentiality only applies to information to the extent that it is confidential. In particular, once

it has entered what is usually called the public domain (which means no
more than that the information in question is so generally accessible that, in
all the circumstances, it cannot be regarded as confidential) then, as a general
rule, the principle of confidentiality can have no application to it.' (See [1988]
3 All ER 545 at 659, [1990] 1 AC 109 at 282.)

[46] *Barrymore v News Group Newspapers Ltd* [1997] FSR 600 is the case nearest
on its facts to the present. The application was for an interim injunction, and was
heard as a matter of urgency. The claimant, a married man, had had a
homosexual relationship with the second defendant, who provided information
concerning it to the first defendant for publication in the Sun newspaper. The
claimant and the second defendant had entered a trust and confidence agreement
which was relied on to impose a duty of confidence. As there was doubt as to the
application of the agreement, Jacob J proceeded without reliance on it. He held
(at 602):

'However, irrespective of this agreement, I think that there is a strongly
arguable case that the details of the relationship between Mr Barrymore and
the second defendant, Mr Wincott, should be treated as confidential. I say
that because, first, common sense dictates that, when people enter into a
personal relationship of this nature, they do not do so for the purpose of it
subsequently being published in *The Sun*, or any other newspaper. The
information about the relationship is for the relationship and not for a wider
purpose. It is well established that in many cases the law will spell out a duty
of confidence when information is given for a limited purpose.'

[47] It might be that in this last sentence Jacob J is equating the knowledge that
the participants to sexual relations have concerning those relations to information
given for a limited purpose. The headnote to the report refers to an 'article about
the first plaintiff and his homosexual relationship with the second defendant on
the basis of details received from the second defendant'. A further passage from
the judgment suggests that at least some of the information which was sought to
be injuncted was what Mr Barrymore had told Mr Wincott concerning his wife
and similar matters: I refer to the last passage to be quoted below. Two further
passages require quotation, the first (at 603):

'The information presented in *The Sun* newspaper's article today was not
known to a substantial number of people ... That was why *The Sun* claimed
the whole story as "an exclusive".'

[48] The second is a longer passage from later on that page:

'Of course, if something is expressly said to be confidential, then it is much
more likely to be so held by the courts, but it by no means follows that
something that is not so expressly stated to be confidential is not confidential.
The whole question turns on the relationship between the parties. The fact
is that when people kiss and later one of them tells, that second person is
almost certainly breaking a confidential arrangement. It all depends on
precisely what they do. If they merely indicate that there has been a
relationship, that may not amount to a breach of confidence and that may
well be the case here, because Mr Barrymore had already disclosed that he
was homosexual, and merely to disclose that he had had a particular partner
would be to add nothing new.'

a   [49] It seems to me, with due respect, that the naming of a partner—which amounts to a statement that two persons have had sexual relations, may well add substantially to knowledge that the persons in question are heterosexual or knowledge that they are homosexual. Jacob J continued (at 603):

b   'However, when one goes into detail (as in *The Sun* article), about what Mr Barrymore said about his relationship with his wife and so on, one has crossed the line into breach of confidence. I think that there is a very strongly arguable case of breach of confidence and I grant an injunction ...'

[50] *Earl Spencer v UK* (1998) 25 EHRR CD 105 concerned a complaint to the European Commission on Human Rights as to the publication of a telephoto photograph taken of Lady Spencer in the grounds of a clinic where she was
c receiving treatment. In reliance on *Kaye v Robertson* [1991] FSR 62, where it was held (or at least assumed) by the Court of Appeal that there was no right of privacy in English law, no claim was pursued in the English courts. It was argued before the Commission on behalf of the United Kingdom government, and accepted by the Commission, that English law provided a potentially satisfactory
d remedy in an action for breach of confidence. In my view that envisaged a substantial extension to the law as established by the outcome of decided cases. It would impose a duty of confidence where there was no relationship between the parties other than the taking of the intrusive photograph.

[51] In *Douglas'* case [2001] 2 All ER 289, [2001] QB 967 the Court of Appeal was concerned with an application to prevent the publication in a magazine of
e photographs of a private wedding. A contract had been entered into with a rival magazine giving the latter the exclusive right to publish photographs of the wedding. There were extensive measures taken to prevent those present at it from taking unauthorised photographs. The court declined to exercise its discretion in favour of the grant of an injunction and left the claimants to their financial
f remedies.

[52] In his judgment Brooke LJ concluded that where parties make clear that no photographs are to be taken on some private occasion, all those present would be bound by the obligation of confidence created by their actual or imputed knowledge of the restriction (see [2001] 2 All ER 289 at 307, [2001] QB 967 at 988
g (para 71)). He stated that English law had not yet recognised that an obligation of confidence might be relied on to preclude an intrusion into people's privacy when those conditions did not exist. He stated that in the circumstances of the wedding in question the claim to privacy was not a strong one (see [2001] 2 All ER 289 at 314, [2001] QB 967 at 995 (para 95)). He concluded that the claimants were likely to establish that the publication should not be allowed on confidentiality
h grounds (see [2001] 2 All ER 289 at 314, [2001] QB 967 at 995 (para 96)). That then left the question of discretion.

[53] Sedley LJ stated in his judgment that if the photographer was a guest then the received law of confidence was probably all the defendants needed, but if he was an intruder a right to breach of privacy might need to be established (see
j [2001] 2 All ER 289 at 317, [2001] QB 967 at 998 (para 112)). He concluded that English law could now recognise privacy itself as a legal principle (see [2001] 2 All ER 289 at 320, [2001] QB 967 at 1001 (para 126)).

[54] In his judgment Keene LJ concluded that whether a liability was described as being for breach of confidence or for a breach of a right to privacy might be little more than deciding what label was to be attached to the cause of action (see [2001] 2 All ER 289 at 330, [2001] QB 967 at 1012 (para 166)).

[55] In *Venables v News Group Newspapers Ltd* [2001] 1 All ER 908, [2001] Fam 430 the claimants, who were notorious as the young and brutal murderers of a toddler, sought to prevent the defendant newspapers from disclosing information as to them and their lives following release from custody. It was held that the risk to the claimants' lives and their right to life established by art 2 required that the right to confidence protecting the disclosure of their new identities should be placed above the right of the media to freedom of expression. Dame Elizabeth Butler-Sloss P concluded in her judgment that 'taking into account the effect of the convention on our law, the law of confidence can extend to cover the injunctions sought in this case' (see [2001] 1 All ER 908 at 932, [2001] Fam 430 at 461 (para 80)).

[56] In my judgment the law should afford the protection of confidentiality to facts concerning sexual relations within marriage (which is surely straightforward) and, in the context of modern sexual relations, it should be no different with relationships outside marriage. As was said by Browne-Wilkinson V-C in *Stephens v Avery* [1988] 2 All ER 477 at 481, [1988] Ch 449 at 454, quoted above, 'To most people the details of their sexual lives are high on their list of those matters which they regard as confidential.'

[57] The more difficult question is the ambit of any protection which the law may provide. This was a matter on which Mr Spearman laid considerable emphasis. He submitted that there could be no satisfactory line drawn between what could properly be protected and what could not. He pointed out that the law applicable to C and D also applied to the claimant, and submitted in particular that the wide terms of the injunction as presently drawn, if applied to the claimant, would prevent him telling his wife what he had done.

[58] In my view the problem has two aspects, namely what is to be protected by preventing communication of it, and to whom communication of it is to be prevented. On the first aspect, is the mere fact of the relationship to be protected, or is it what happened in the bedroom that should be protected? On the second aspect, is communication to any one including relations and friends to be prohibited, or, at the other extreme, is only communication to the media to be prohibited.

[59] I do not think that these questions can be given an absolute answer, nor should they be. Each case depends on its circumstances. I should consider the circumstances before me, leaving other situations to be considered as and when they arise. What we have here is communication to a newspaper not just of the fact of the relationships but of the details of the sexual conduct that occurred. The newspaper has no interest in simply publishing the fact of the relationships alone: it intends to publish the whole: to interest its readers it needs the detail. The answer in the present case is therefore straightforward. It was a breach of confidence for C and D to provide the information which they have to the newspaper or to anyone else with a view to its publication in the media. It would be a breach of confidence for the paper to publish it. That publication may be restrained by injunction. The issue here is not whether C or D are entitled to talk to their friends about their relationship with the claimant. Nor is it whether the claimant would be entitled to talk to his wife.

[60] Mr Spearman submitted that there was no distinction between communication of information to an individual and communication to the press for publication. In my view there is likely to be, and here is, a substantial distinction.

The law of privacy

[61] In my judgment delivered on 30 April I briefly considered whether a right of privacy might now be part of English law having emerged from the shadow of

a confidentiality. I concluded that it was likely that the claimant would establish such a right at a trial. I have now been able to consider the judgment of Dame Elizabeth Butler-Sloss P in *Venables'* case. In the light of that judgment and my conclusion as to breach of confidence I think it better to express no view.

Breach of copyright

b [62] This minor matter was uncontested.

Is the information in the public domain?

[63] Mr Spearman submitted that the relationships had been conducted publicly and were known to a number of people, and were therefore outside the protection of the law of confidence. It is true that the claimant met with C and with D in

c places of public entertainment where they were seen by their companions and by others. On occasions they may have been seen kissing. Neither C nor D says that anyone knew that they were having an affair in the sense of sexual relations including sexual intercourse. I exclude from that hotel staff. Nor are the details of that intercourse known to anyone save the participants. None of this information

d is in the public domain. It is capable of protection.

The application of s 12(4) and regard to art 10

[64] Section 12(4) requires the court to have particular regard to the importance of the convention right to freedom of expression, and by s 12(4)(a)(ii) the extent to which it would be in the public interest for the material to be published. I take

e these together, because the right to freedom of expression is, certainly in a media context, the more important where there is a public interest in publication, as I have previously considered.

[65] By art 10(2) the right to freedom of expression may be subject to restrictions prescribed by law. The law relating to breach of confidence is covered by that. Any

f such restriction must also be necessary in a democratic society, inter alia, for the protection of the rights of others, or for preventing the disclosure of information received in confidence. Here the claimant has a right to respect for his private life. It is that that he seeks to protect. As to 'the disclosure of information received in confidence' (the wording of art 10), although the information that C and D have was not in a literal sense 'received' by them, in my view, giving the words a

g purposive construction, they are to be treated as having received it as the events occurred. It is subject to a duty of confidence to the extent that I have outlined.

[66] Article 10(2) also refers to a pressing social need. As art 8 shows, there is a pressing social need for respect for a person's private life.

[67] In my judgment there is no public interest in the publication of the articles

h and the information which they contain. I refer to public interest in the sense of being in the interests of the public, and approximating to public benefit. It was suggested that as a successful professional footballer, the claimant is held as a role model, in particular for young people, and that it is in the public interest that the truth about him as an adulterer be known. This was supported by the flimsiest material. The claimant's conduct is to be condemned by any moral standard: but

j that does not provide a public interest in the publication of the information about these two extra-matrimonial affairs. I should make clear that in so far as the claimant has established himself as a public figure it is simply as a professional footballer. It is not suggested that he is someone who has courted publicity and who has laid open his private life to public scrutiny by his courting of publicity.

[68] In this situation para 94 of the judgment of Brooke LJ in *Douglas'* case [2001] 2 All ER 289 at 313–314, [2001] QB 967 at 994 quoted above suggests that

the claimant should succeed in the balancing operation which s 12 and art 10
require. I am satisfied that in the circumstances here the claimant is likely at a
trial to satisfy the burden of showing that his right to confidence (or in plainer
terms, right to privacy for his private life) should here prevail over the newspaper's
right to freedom of expression. He is likely to establish, in the words of the
judgment in *Bladet Tromsø v Norway* (1999) 29 EHRR 125, that the interference
with the right to freedom of expression is proportionate to the legitimate aim
pursued.

An injunction and its terms
[69] I conclude that at trial the claimant is likely to succeed in establishing that
the facts as to the existence of his affairs with C and D, and as to the sexual acts
which occurred between them privately, are confidential in that they should not
be communicated for the purpose of publication in the media, nor published in
the media by an entity which has received them in breach of confidence.
[70] I am satisfied also that it is likely at a trial that the application of s 12(4) of
the Act will favour the claimant.
[71] It is therefore open to me to consider whether in the exercise of my
discretion the newspaper should be restrained in appropriate terms from publication.
Having reached this position, it is plain that the discretion should be exercised to
grant an injunction. To deprive the claimant of an injunction at this stage, would
render his action largely futile.
[72] The present order restrains the newspaper from using, disclosing or
publishing any of the defined information. The defined information is—

'any personal information of and/or information about—(i) the private life
of A [the claimant] arising out of the matters referred to in the witness
statements in this action or any other information concerning the
relationship between A and [C] or between A and [D]; (ii) any other matters
concerning the sexual life of A.'

[73] One reason why the order took this form was uncertainty whether the
newspaper had obtained other information about the claimant. It has since been
made clear that it has not.
[74] I am satisfied that the order is in wider terms than is appropriate. The
order should relate to information concerning the facts that the claimant was
having sexual relationships with C and D, and facts relating to the sexual
intercourse and other sexual conduct which occurred with C and with D. It
should prohibit publication by the newspaper and disclosure by the newspaper.
It should prohibit disclosure by C or D to anyone with a view to such information
being published in the media.

Order accordingly.

Dilys Tausz   Barrister.

a

Porter and another v Magill
[2001] UKHL 67

HOUSE OF LORDS

LORD BINGHAM OF CORNHILL, LORD STEYN, LORD HOPE OF CRAIGHEAD, LORD

b HOBHOUSE OF WOODBOROUGH AND LORD SCOTT OF FOSCOTE

5, 6, 7, 8, 12 NOVEMBER, 13 DECEMBER 2001

Local government – Audit – Surcharge – Ruling party on local authority formulating and implementing new policy on sale of authority's properties designed to increase
c *party's voting base in key wards – Auditor finding authority's leader and deputy leader guilty of wilful misconduct which had caused authority loss – Whether auditor correct – Whether auditor's calculation of loss correct – Local Government Finance Act 1982, s 20.*

Natural justice – Judge – Bias – Test for determining apparent bias.
d

In the 1986 local government elections the ruling Conservative party on Westminster City Council was returned with a narrow and much-reduced majority. At that time, the respondents, P and W, were respectively the Conservative leader and deputy leader of the council. With a view to achieving greater success in the 1990 elections, a group chaired by P (P's group) developed
e a new policy on the sale of council-owned properties in exercise of the council's powers of disposal under s 32 of the Housing Act 1985. A major element in that policy—based on the belief that owner-occupiers were more likely to vote Conservative—was a plan to increase designated sales of such properties in eight key marginal wards to at least 250 per annum. The council's solicitor was
f consulted on whether a 100% designation for sale in those wards would conflict with the council's statutory duties. He warned of legal difficulties and advised seeking the advice of counsel. The latter advised that the council could not lawfully sell 250 properties per annum in the marginal wards alone, that properties had to be designated for proper reasons across the whole of the council's area and that the choice had to be made without reference to anything
g but the proper criteria. Subsequently, P's group resolved to extend the programme of designated sales to 500 sales per annum city-wide in order to achieve the target of 250 in the eight key wards. Shortly afterwards, in July 1987, the council's Conservative-controlled housing committee resolved to designate a number of specific properties which were expected to produce 500 sales per annum. Of the
h eligible dwellings in the key wards, 74% were designated for sale. In other wards only 28% of all such properties were designated. In 1989 a number of local government electors made written objections about the policy, and an auditor was appointed under the Local Government Finance Act 1982. Acting under powers contained in that Act, the auditor conducted an inquiry in which he
j perused large quantities of documents and accepted representations from the respondents. In January 1994 the auditor held a press conference in which he stated his provisional view as to the culpability of the respondents. In 1996, after holding an audit hearing at the request of the council, the auditor made his final decision, concluding that the designated-sales policy was unlawful, that the respondents had been responsible for determining the policy's direction and content, that they had known that it was unlawful, that accordingly they had

been guilty of wilful misconduct and that that misconduct had caused the council financial loss. He therefore certified under s 20(1)[a] of the 1982 Act that the respondents were liable to make good that loss, including a sum of £15.47m which represented the difference between the open market value with vacant possession of the properties sold under the policy and the discounted prices for which they had actually been sold. The respondents appealed to the Divisional Court under s 20(3) of the 1982 Act. Such an appeal could take the form of a rehearing on the merits. After conducting such a rehearing, the court upheld the auditor's decision, and therefore dismissed the respondents' appeal, in December 1997. That decision was reversed by the Court of Appeal which quashed the auditor's certificate. On the auditor's appeal to the House of Lords, the respondents, relying on the judgments in the Court of Appeal, contended that councillors could not be expected to be oblivious to considerations of party political advantage, and that their conduct could not be impugned provided that their reasons for taking action were not purely partisan political reasons. They also contended, inter alia, that the auditor's statement in January 1994 had given rise to the appearance of bias, infringing their common law right to an unbiased judge. Their Lordships were therefore required to consider the correct test for bias at common law. A further issue arose in respect of quantum, namely whether, as the respondents contended, there was no loss arising from the discounted prices since the properties would have been sold at that those prices irrespective of the lawfulness of the policy.

Held – (1) Although an authority could dispose of land under s 32 of the 1985 Act to promote any public purpose for which such power was conferred, it could not lawfully do so for the purpose of promoting the electoral advantage of any party represented on the council. In the instant case, the council's policy was unlawful because it was directed to the pursuit of electoral advantage and not the achievement of proper housing objectives. Further, the respondents had been parties to the adoption and implementation of the unlawful policy, and they had both known that they were acting unlawfully in adopting and implementing it. There had been a deliberate, blatant and dishonest use of of public power (see [17], [25], [31], [48], [59], [60], [131], [142], [144], [148], [164], below).

(2) In determining whether there had been apparent bias on the part of a tribunal, the court should no longer simply ask itself whether, having regard to all the relevant circumstances, there was a real danger of bias. Rather, the test was whether the relevant circumstances, as ascertained by the court, would lead a fair-minded and informed observer to conclude that there was a real possibility that the tribunal had been biased In the instant case, the auditor had made an error of judgment when he decided to make his statement in public at a press conference. The main impression which that would have conveyed to the fair-minded observer was that the purpose of the exercise was to attract publicity to the auditor. It was an exercise in self-promotion in which he should not have indulged, but it was quite another matter to conclude from that exercise that there was a real possibility that he was biased. The auditor's conduct had to be seen in the context of the investigation which he was carrying out. It had generated a great deal of public interest, and a statement as to his progress would not have been inappropriate. His error was to make it at a press conference. That created the risk of unfair reporting,

---

a   Section 20, so far as material, is set out at [69], [70], below

a but there was nothing in the words he used to indicate that there was a real
possibility that he was biased. Looking at the matter objectively, it had not been
demonstrated that there was a real possibility that he was biased (see [57], [59],
[102], [103], [105], [131], [161], below); dictum of Lord Goff of Chieveley in *R v
Gough* [1993] 2 All ER 724 at 737–738 modified.

(3) The principle underlying the certification of loss under s 20(1) of the 1982
b Act was one of compensation, namely to put the body that had suffered loss or
deficiency through the wilful misconduct of any person in the same position that
it would have been in but for that misconduct. In the instant case the wilful
misconduct of the respondents had caused the sale of some of the council's
properties pursuant to an unlawful policy, and the council had lost the difference
between the full market value of the properties and the discounted prices
c received. It was not open to those responsible to contend that if the properties
had been sold under a lawful policy they would have been sold at equally
discounted prices. If the policy had been lawful, the council might never have
sold the properties at all, and in any event it was a matter for the owner of an asset
to decide whether he would exploit its value to the maximum extent or not. It
d followed that the auditor's calculation was correct, and accordingly the appeal
would be allowed (see [54], [55], [58]–[60], [126], [130], [131], [139], [158], [163],
[164], below).

Notes
For apparent bias and audits of public bodies, see respectively 1(1) *Halsbury's Laws*
e (4th edn reissue) para 99 and 29(1) *Halsbury's Laws* (4th edn reissue) paras 662–683.

The Local Government Finance Act 1982, s 20, has been repealed by the Audit
Commission Act 1998, s 54(3), Sch 5, but substantially re-enacted as s 18 of the
1998 Act. For s 18, see 25 *Halsbury's Statutes* (4th edn) (2001 reissue) 1392. Section
18 itself has been prospectively repealed by the Local Government Act 2000,
f s 90(1), (3), Sch 6.

Cases referred to in opinions
A-G ex rel Rea v Belfast Corp (1855) 4 Ir Ch R 119.
A-G v Wilson (1840) Cr & Ph 1.
AP, MP and TP v Switzerland (1997) 26 EHRR 541, ECt HR.
g *Ausiello v Italy* (1996) 24 EHRR 568, ECt HR.
Bell v DPP of Jamaica [1985] 2 All ER 585, [1985] AC 937, [1985] 3 WLR 73, PC.
Bradford v McLeod 1986 SLT 244, HC of Justiciary.
Brown v Stott (Procurator Fiscal, Dunfermline) [2001] 2 All ER 97, [2001] 2 WLR 817, PC.
Bryan v UK (1995) 21 EHRR 342, ECt HR.
h *Charitable Corp v Sutton* (1742) 2 Atk 400.
Credit Suisse v Allerdale BC [1996] 4 All ER 129, [1997] QB 306, [1996] 3 WLR 894, CA.
Crummock (Scotland) Ltd v HM Advocate 2000 SLT 677, HC of Justiciary.
Darmalingum v State [2001] 1 WLR 2303, PC.
DC, HS and AD v UK [2000] BCC 710, ECt HR.
j *De Cubber v Belgium* (1984) 7 EHRR 236, ECt HR.
Demicoli v Malta (1991) 14 EHRR 47, ECt HR.
Deweer v Belgium (1980) 2 EHRR 439, ECt HR.
DPP v Tokai [1996] AC 856, [1996] 3 WLR 149, PC.
Engel v Netherlands (1976) 1 EHRR 647, ECt HR.
Findlay v UK (1997) 24 EHRR 221, ECt HR.

Flowers v R [2000] 1 WLR 2396, PC.

Graham v Teesdale (1981) 81 LGR 117.

Hauschildt v Denmark (1989) 12 EHRR 266, ECt HR.

Jones v Swansea City Council [1989] 3 All ER 162, [1990] 1 WLR 54, CA; *rvsd* [1990] 3 All ER 737, [1990] 1 WLR 1453, HL.

Kingsley v UK (7 November 2000, unreported), ECt HR.

König v Federal Republic of Germany (1978) 2 EHHR 170, ECt HR.

Law v Chartered Institute of Patent Agents [1919] 2 Ch 276, [1918–19] All ER Rep Ext 1237.

Lloyd v McMahon [1987] 1 All ER 1118, [1987] AC 625, [1987] 2 WLR 821, CA and HL.

Locabail (UK) Ltd v Bayfield Properties Ltd, Locabail (UK) Ltd v Waldorf Investment Corp, Timmins v Gormley, Williams v HM Inspector of Taxes, R v Bristol Betting and Gaming Licensing Committee, ex p O'Callaghan [2000] 1 All ER 65, [2000] QB 451, [2000] WLR 870, CA.

Lutz v Germany (1987) 10 EHRR 182, ECt HR.

McIntosh v Lord Advocate [2001] UKPC D1, [2001] 2 All ER 638, [2001] 3 WLR 107.

Medicaments and Related Classes of Goods (No 2), In re [2001] 1 WLR 700, CA.

Millar v Dickson 2001 SLT 988, PC.

Padfield v Minister of Agriculture, Fisheries and Food [1968] 1 All ER 694, [1968] AC 997, [1968] 2 WLR 924, HL.

Phillips v UK (2001) 11 BHRC 280, ECt HR.

Piersack v Belgium (1982) 5 EHRR 169, ECt HR.

Pullar v UK (1996) 22 EHRR 391, ECt HR.

R (on the application of Alconbury Developments Ltd) v Secretary of State for the Environment, Transport and the Regions [2001] UKHL 23, [2001] 2 All ER 929, [2001] 2 WLR 1389.

R (on the application of Pretty) v DPP [2001] UKHL 61, [2002] 1 All ER 1, [2001] 3 WLR 1598.

R v Board of Education [1910] 2 KB 165, CA.

R v Bow Street Metropolitan Stipendiary Magistrate, ex p Pinochet Ugarte (No 2) [1999] 1 All ER 577, [2000] 1 AC 119, [1999] 2 WLR 272, HL.

R v Bradford City Metropolitan Council, ex p Wilson [1989] 3 All ER 140, [1990] 2 QB 375n, [1990] 2 WLR 255, DC.

R v Gough [1993] 2 All ER 724, [1993] AC 646, [1993] 2 WLR 883, HL.

R v Kansal (No 2) [2001] UKHL 62, [2002] 1 All ER 257, [2001] 3 WLR 1562.

R v Lambert [2001] UKHL 37, [2001] 3 All ER 577, [2001] 3 WLR 206.

R v Local Comr for Administration in North and North East of England, ex p Liverpool City Council [2001] 1 All ER 462, CA.

R v Port Talbot BC, ex p Jones [1988] 2 All ER 207.

R v Sheffield City Council, ex p Chadwick (1985) 84 LGR 563.

R v Waltham Forest LBC, ex p Baxter [1987] 3 All ER 671, [1988] QB 419, [1988] 2 WLR 257, CA.

Royal Brunei Airlines Sdn Bhd v Tan [1995] 3 All ER 97, [1995] 2 AC 378, [1995] 3 WLR 64, PC.

Tan v Cameron [1993] 2 All ER 493, [1992] 2 AC 205, [1992] 3 WLR 249, PC.

Tower Hamlets LBC v Chetnik Developments Ltd [1988] 1 All ER 961, [1988] AC 858, [1988] 2 WLR 654, HL.

Webb v R (1994) 181 CLR 41, Aust HC.

Appeal

a The appellant auditor, John Magill, appealed with permission of the Court of Appeal from its decision (Kennedy and Schiemann LJJ, Robert Walker LJ dissenting) on 30 April 1999 ([2000] 2 WLR 1420) allowing an appeal by the respondents, Dame Shirley Porter and David Weeks, from the decision of the Divisional Court (Rose LJ, Latham and Keene JJ) on 19 December 1997 ((1997) 96 LGR 157)

b dismissing their appeal from the auditor's certificate, given on 9 May 1996 under s 20 of the Local Government Finance Act 1982, that they had caused through wilful misconduct a loss to Westminster City Council of £27,023,376 (amended to £26,462,621 on 12 January 1998). The facts are set out in the opinions of Lord Bingham of Cornhill and Lord Hope of Craighead.

c *John Howell QC* and *Karen McHugh* (instructed by *Rowe & Maw*) for the auditor.
Jeremy McMullen QC, Stuart Cakebread and *Clare Roberts* (instructed by *Nicholson Graham Jones*) for Dame Shirley Porter.
Stuart Cakebread and *Clare Roberts* (instructed by *Nicholson Graham Jones*) for Mr Weeks.

d
Their Lordships took time for consideration.

13 December 2001. The following opinions were delivered.

e **LORD BINGHAM OF CORNHILL.**
   [1] My Lords, the issue in this appeal is whether the auditor should have certified any sum to be due to the Westminster City Council from Dame Shirley Porter and Mr David Weeks and, if so, in what amount.
   [2] The appellant, Mr John Magill, is the auditor. He was appointed by the Audit Commission under s 13 of the Local Government Finance Act 1982 to audit

f the accounts of Westminster City Council for the years 1987–1988 to 1994–1995. He conducted a very lengthy and detailed audit and certified under s 20 of the Act that three councillors and three officers had, by wilful misconduct, jointly and severally caused a loss of approximately £31m to the council which they were liable to make good. All three of the councillors and two of the officers pursued appeals against the auditor's decision to the Queen's Bench Divisional Court

g (Rose LJ, Latham and Keene JJ) ((1997) 96 LGR 157). The councillors were Dame Shirley Porter, who was leader of the council at all material times, Mr David Weeks, who was deputy leader, and Mr Hartley, who from June 1987 was chairman of the council's Housing Committee. The two officers were Mr England, who was the council's director of housing, and Mr Phillips, who was managing

h director of the council. The Divisional Court upheld the auditor's finding that Dame Shirley Porter and Mr Weeks were liable, although it reduced the sum certified; it allowed the appeals of Mr Hartley and the two officers and quashed the auditor's certificate in relation to them. On further appeal by Dame Shirley Porter and Mr Weeks, the Court of Appeal ([2000] 2 WLR 1420) by a majority

j (Kennedy and Schiemann LJJ, Robert Walker LJ dissenting) upheld both appeals on liability. Robert Walker LJ, although in favour of dismissing both appeals against liability, would have reduced the sum of the auditor's certificate (see [2000] 2 WLR 1420 at 1504). On this quantum issue Kennedy LJ (at 1429) agreed with him and Schiemann LJ (at 1447) expressed no opinion. The auditor now appeals to this House seeking to reinstate the certificate issued against Dame Shirley Porter and Mr Weeks in the sum certified by the Divisional Court. Mr Hartley

and the two officers are no longer directly involved in the proceedings. It is
necessary to decide whether the Court of Appeal was right to quash the certificate *a*
issued against Dame Shirley Porter and Mr Weeks and, if not, in what sum that
certificate should have been issued.

[3] My Lords, the facts giving rise to this appeal and much of the evidence
have been summarised at some length by the Divisional Court ((1997) 96 LGR
157 at 164–166, 175–203) and by the Court of Appeal ([2000] 2 WLR 1420 at *b*
1431–1432, 1463–1482) and are the subject of a lengthy statement of facts agreed
between the parties for purposes of this appeal. The facts and the evidence are
crucial to the appeal, but it is unnecessary to repeat the detailed summaries
already made. It is enough, for present purposes, to highlight some of the key
events in the narrative, which I take from the agreed statement of facts.

[4] The council comprised 60 councillors elected to represent 23 wards. As a *c*
result of the local government elections in May 1986, the overall Conservative
Party majority was reduced from 26 to 4. The close results of those elections
prompted leading members of the council to consider how council policies could
be developed in order to advance the electoral prospects of the Conservative
Party in the next local government election to be held in 1990. Dame Shirley *d*
Porter was determined that the Conservative Party would have a greater
majority at the 1990 elections than that which it had narrowly achieved in 1986.
With this end in view, she reorganised the party's administrative and
decision-making structure and herself chaired a group of committee chairmen.
This body comprised herself as leader, Mr Weeks, the deputy leader, the majority
party's chief whip and the chairmen of the council's committees. It was not a *e*
committee or sub-committee appointed by the council. It met on a regular basis,
sometimes with officers in attendance. It developed and promoted policy. One
of these concerned the designation of council-owned properties for sale.

[5] The council first introduced a policy of designated sales in 1972. Under this
policy, blocks of council dwellings were designated and, when a dwelling in a *f*
designated block became vacant, it was not re-let but offered for sale to an
approved applicant with the intention that all dwellings in designated blocks
would become owner-occupied. Under the scheme as it was in July 1987, 10 to
20 sales per annum were generated from the 300 dwellings then designated.
With a view to achieving greater success in the 1990 elections, the chairmen's
group formulated a policy entitled 'Building Stable Communities' (known for *g*
short as 'BSC'). This included targets for increasing the numbers of Conservative
voters in each of eight key wards, the target voter figures for those wards adding
up to a total of 2,200. The eight most marginal wards in the election of May 1986
from the Conservative Party's point of view were Bayswater, Cavendish,
Hamilton Terrace, Little Venice, Millbank, St James's, Victoria and West End. *h*
Those eight wards were chosen in mid-February 1987 by some members of the
majority party on the council (including Dame Shirley Porter and Cllr Weeks),
and were known as the 'key wards'. Both the eight key wards and the target voter
figures (which envisaged an overall increase of 2,200 Conservative supporters in
the eight key wards) were identified to officers in February 1987. The target voter *j*
figures remained the same thereafter and the achievement of those figures
(including the contribution of designated sales to them) was monitored by
leading members and officers. The references in contemporary documents to
'new residents', 'more electors' and 'new electors' in many instances were
euphemisms for 'more potential Conservative voters', particularly in marginal
wards. A major element of BSC was to increase designated sales of council

a properties in the eight key wards to potential owner-occupiers. It was believed that owner-occupiers would be more likely to vote Conservative. In some of the key wards there was very little council housing and few or no designated properties. But, even in respect of those wards, designated sales appeared on monitoring charts recording the progress towards the targets in the eight key wards. From July 1986, if not before, concentrating on marginal wards was
b majority party policy. The intention of the majority party was to develop council policies which would target marginal wards, including such housing policies as could affect the make-up of the electorate in those wards.

[6] Very soon after the 1986 local government elections, the first suggestions for disposing of council housing, including increased designation, were made. On 19 May 1986, Mr England informed the then chairman of the Housing
c Committee that it would be virtually impossible for the council to meet its statutory obligations if a policy of wholesale disposal of council housing were to be adopted. On 3 June 1986 the chairmen's group decided that major policy initiatives should come down from it (and from the Policy and Resources Committee) and it discussed marginal wards. On 5 June 1986 the chairman of the
d Housing Committee responded to Dame Shirley Porter's request for a note on 'balancing the social mix' by identifying a number of factors contributing to the drop in the Conservative Party's 'natural support' and suggesting various options for increasing home ownership, including increased designated sales which would, however, lessen the council's 'already stretched ability to meet our statutory requirements'. On 24 June 1986 Dame Shirley Porter and Mr Weeks
e attended the chief officers' board when the officers were told that the focus of attention would be on winning the next election, and there was discussion of the majority party's objective of 'social engineering including housing'. On 30 June 1986 a working lunch, attended by Dame Shirley Porter and others, was held to discuss a prospective planning study: Mr England made a note of the discussion
f which included references such as 'economic justification for Gmander on Hsg', 'who is a Tory Voter?', 'Gentrification' and 'will company lets vote Tory'. On 29 July 1986 Dame Shirley Porter had a discussion with Mr Phillips concerning properties in key wards, voting records and decanting and she asked Mr England for information in respect of key wards. By the beginning of September 1986 the council's policy unit had prepared a paper on 'homelessness/gentrification'. It
g stated that 'homelessness is reaching crisis proportions' and described 'gentrification' as—

'ensuring that the right people live in the right areas. The areas are relatively easy to define: target wards identified on the basis of electoral
h trends and results. Defining "people" is much more difficult and not strictly Council business ... the housing/planning study should be used to define which initiatives are likely to produce the desired results, and in which areas.'

On 1 September 1986 Mr England produced a paper for Mr Weeks on 'Gentrification' in which he identified the major constraints on initiatives to increase home
j ownership as the duties to the homeless and other high priority rehousing requirements.

[7] Dame Shirley Porter wrote a paper setting out her 'Strategy to 1990' in which she gave top priority to winning the 1990 elections. Two of the key issues identified in the 'Strategy to 1990' in relation to electoral success were 'homelessness/gentrification' and how best to use the study about to be commissioned from consultants. The paper prepared by the policy unit on

'homelessness/gentrification' formed part of Dame Shirley Porter's paper. Her
'Strategy to 1990' was agreed by the chairmen's group on 2 September 1986 and *a*
on 3 September was circulated by the head of the policy unit to all chief officers.
Officers recommended that the consultants' study should be used to establish the
key wards and the need for increased home ownership in them. At a meeting on
15 September 1986 with representatives of the consultants, attended by Dame
Shirley Porter and Mr Weeks, there was a discussion of a strategy—   *b*

> 'to push labour voters out of marginal wards. Housing Dept can't say
> privatise/gentrify council blocks in marginal wards—400 in B & B but we
> could say—preserve economic base—need to boot out these blocks.'

Reference was also made to an aim to 'preserve local communities—but boot out *c*
certain categories' and to community groups which 'don't vote Tory'. Dame
Shirley Porter told the consultants 'we want the right answers'. In January 1987
a paper on home ownership was written at Dame Shirley Porter's request by the
then vice-chairman of the Housing Committee, Mr Segal. That paper, written in
advance of the consultants' report, identified the short-term objective as being—
d
> 'to target the marginal wards and, as a matter of the utmost urgency,
> redress the imbalance by encouraging a pattern of tenure which is more
> likely to translate into Conservative votes.'

The paper assumed that owner-occupiers were more inclined to vote
Conservative and drew attention to the low proportion of owner-occupiers in *e*
Westminster relative to the national average. It called for the council to
reappraise its designation policy and to 'identify far more blocks particularly in
key marginal wards'. The paper was submitted to, and generally endorsed, by the
chairmen's group at its meeting on 27 January 1987. Further work on designated
sales in marginal wards followed. At least from the time of this paper in January *f*
1987, targeting designated sales in marginal wards was firm political policy. The
chairmen's group decided on 24 March 1987 to adopt a target of 250 designated
sales per annum in the marginal wards. At that meeting, attended by Dame
Shirley Porter and Mr Weeks, she stated: 'need a peg in the [consultants'] report'.
The chairmen's group also considered a draft report. Dame Shirley Porter
indicated that she did not want the report to go into detail because it exposed the *g*
other sales policies for discussion, notwithstanding that the report had been
prepared, according to Mr England, to give members a 'smokescreen' to identify
the designated area for growth. Mr England explained to the managing director
in a memorandum dated 26 March 1987 that the intention was to plant a question
at the Housing Committee on 1 April 1987 in order to obtain authority for officers *h*
to provide a report on how to increase designated sales to at least 250 p a, and that
he intended to report back 'once we have [the consultants'] steer on 250 in certain
wards'.

[8] By this stage legal concerns were beginning to surface. On 20 March 1987
the deputy city solicitor advised the then chairman of the Housing Committee on *j*
the need to have sufficient justification for a major change in policy on designated
sales, reinforcing (as he put it) the notes of caution that had already been
expressed. On 24 March 1987 one of Dame Shirley Porter's aides (Mr Greenman)
addressed certain questions to the director of housing and the city solicitor. In
response to the first question addressed to him, namely, whether the council's
new policy on 100% designation for sale in the eight target wards would conflict

a with the council's statutory obligations, the city solicitor replied on 24 March 1987 to Dame Shirley Porter that:

'If the policy is to be introduced then as a matter of law the reasons for its introduction have got to be carefully argued. The needs of the homeless and the impact of a decision to sell accommodation which might otherwise be available for them is a highly relevant consideration which will have to
b be balanced against the advantages of selling. It is fundamental that the arguments in favour of selling be soundly based and properly argued. Anything which smacks of political machinations will be viewed with great suspicion by the courts.'

A further question was addressed: 'Is there any possibility that this policy will lay
c the council open to (a) judicial review of its policy or (b) surcharging for illegality etc'. To this question the city solicitor replied:

'(a) Yes. The way to avoid successful challenge is to devise legitimate arguments and to ensure that all possible ramifications have been considered by those taking the decision. If this is done judicial review may be
d successfully resisted unless it can be demonstrated that the decision takers have acted irrationally or relied on an irrelevant consideration.

(b) ... The possibility of surcharge exists but it will be necessary for those challenging to demonstrate that the loss flowed from the act of wilful misconduct. This re-emphasises the need for a good argument to be
e constructed in favour of sale.'

In response to a further question the city solicitor said:

'It is crucial that any report should critically examine a proposal to designate for sale. The advantages of sale have to be considered not from any ulterior motive but from the standpoint of what is right in view of the
f council's role as a housing authority. A general policy of disposal is much more likely to be susceptible of challenge than decisions taken in respect of each block or each property. It might be sensible to go forward in stages rather than offer a broad target. Lawyers should be involved in consideration of any reports at the earliest possible stage. Since a general policy will
g inevitably draw fire the advice of counsel should be sought at an early stage so that if judicial review is commenced the prospects of successful challenge can be minimised.'

[9] The consultants' report was received by the council on about 10 April 1987. The Divisional Court found that Dame Shirley Porter plainly hoped and
h was deeply interested in the possibility that the report would provide a peg on which to hang the policy of increasing designated sales in marginal wards. Both she and Mr Weeks knew that, without the consultants' support, the officers could not provide professional justification for designation only in the eight wards. In fact, the consultants' report gave no such support. The report did not identify the
j eight key wards. Of the five 'stress' wards it considered, only two were among the eight key wards. On its face the report gave no support for any increase in designated sales. It recommended that the council should exercise its powers with a view to 'making available a supply of low and medium priced rented housing'.

[10] Before receipt of this report, on 17 March 1987, a memorandum from the director of housing to the chairmen's group advised that, with the scale of

designation then proposed, namely of all council properties in the eight key
wards (490 sales per annum), the council might find it impossible to meet its
statutory obligations to a number of homeless households; that it was not
possible in professional terms to justify a designation of all properties in the eight
key wards given the impact on the homeless and other priority cases; that the 'key
ward analysis' would have to be provided by the forthcoming consultants' study;
and that members should seek legal advice on the reasonableness of the proposed
course of action. In a further memorandum on the following day, the director of
housing advised Dame Shirley Porter in addition that it was necessary to consider
providing additional properties for the homeless and 'non-statutory groups' in
non-key wards but that the time required for such provision might conflict 'with
the objective of achieving the number of sales within the three year period'.
A later discussion paper on designated sales, prepared in the housing department
and presented to Dame Shirley Porter and the chairmen's group on 5 May 1987,
stated that the Housing Committee would need to set the number of designated
sales per annum to be achieved and select the relevant properties for designation.
It recorded that the city solicitor and secretary had advised that it was imperative
that counsel's advice should be obtained on the final shape of the committee
report and that there were four further matters for decision by the committee.
The fourth of these was:

> 'Given the inevitable impact on rented supply ... should the Council's target
> be 250 per annum or will this have an impact on the Council's re-housing
> abilities which could not be justified? The [consultants'] report suggests a
> need to supplement the rented supply. There is nothing in the [consultants']
> report which at the moment would justify a designated sales programme on
> the scale presently proposed.'

Having read this discussion paper, Dame Shirley Porter summoned its author and
the deputy city solicitor to her office at 9.45 am on 5 May 1987. She told the
author that the paper was not what was required; that the policy was clear; and
that the note needed to spell out how it was to be achieved, not give options. She
told the deputy city solicitor to obtain leading counsel's advice. She also required
that a revised note be prepared for the chairmen's group meeting that evening.

[11] That afternoon, Mr Jeremy Sullivan QC saw the deputy city solicitor,
Mr England and the author of the discussion paper in consultation. He was
informed that the majority group wished to target sales in marginal wards for
electoral advantage. He advised that the council could not lawfully sell 250
properties per annum in the marginal wards alone. He advised that properties
had to be designated for proper reasons, across the whole of the city and not in
particular wards and that, in identifying properties to be designated, the same
criteria had to be applied across the whole city and, ultimately, choice made
without reference to anything other than those proper criteria. He also advised
on a number of other matters, including the legality of a scheme of capital grants
which was not ultimately adopted. Following this consultation, Mr England
wrote a note to Dame Shirley Porter suggesting action in relation to the matters
identified in the discussion paper. The note was relayed to the chairmen's group
at its meeting on the evening of 5 May 1987. That meeting was attended (among
others) by Dame Shirley Porter, Mr Weeks and Mr Hartley. In interview on
5 November 1992, in his affidavit and in cross-examination Mr England accepted
that Mr Sullivan had not advised that marginality of a ward was a proper factor
when designating for sale. In the course of his note Mr England stated:

'The Housing Committee has already decided that the designated sales target should be "at least 250" ... Counsel advises that designated estates should be identified in both marginal and non-marginal wards in order to protect the Council. The Group will, therefore, need to decide whether the 250 target applies across the City or whether in fact 250 sales in marginal wards are required in which case following Counsel's advice, somewhere in the region of 300–350 properties will need to be sold across the City. This will clearly exacerbate the problems of dealing with housing demand ... The target set by the Housing Committee is "at least 250". Counsel advises that this cannot be targeted solely in key wards, therefore, the Group will have to decide whether the final target is 250 or some greater figure which would yield 250 in the marginal wards. Counsel also advises that reference to affordable housing contained in the [consultants'] study should be included in the report. This report has now been released to the opposition. The Housing Committee has set a target of at least 250. If the Group wishes to go for a larger global target in order to achieve 250 in the marginal wards, this will require a decision by the Committee. Counsel confirms that the report should be considered at the same meeting.'

On the evening of 5 May 1987, the chairmen's group agreed to target designated sales city-wide in order to produce the agreed number of designated sales in marginal wards. The group decided to adopt the course described in Mr England's note of increasing the number of designated sales so as to be able to achieve the policy objective of 250 sales per annum in the marginal wards.

[12] On 13 May 1987, Dame Shirley Porter was re-elected leader and Mr Weeks deputy leader of the majority party. Dame Shirley Porter appointed Mr Weeks as lead chairman for BSC with responsibility for ensuring that its performance met timescales. She appointed Mr Hartley to be chairman of the Housing Committee.

[13] The chairmen's group met on 13–14 June 1987. In a note by Dame Shirley Porter presented to the meeting it was stated that:

'We face a tremendous challenge. The electoral register for the 1990 elections will be compiled in just over 2 years' time. Some very ambitious policies must be implemented by then: providing a great deal of affordable housing in key areas; protecting the electoral base in other areas ... There is very little time to achieve these radical policy objectives ...'

In a note by Dame Shirley Porter on BSC the key elements of the policy were summarised. One of these was the targeting of key areas, under which heading the voter targets for the eight marginal wards, in the total of 2,200 voters already mentioned, were listed. The note said that:

'A key element in BSC must be to attract homeowners into Westminster. This means finding innovative ways of ensuring that the right sort of housing is available to the right sort of buyer or tenant. And it must be available by October 1989.'

October 1989 was the qualifying date for inclusion in the electoral register for the 1990 local government elections. At this meeting the chairmen's group endorsed the target of 500 sales per annum across the council area in order to produce the number of sales desired in the marginal wards. Mr Hartley, the new chairman of the Housing Committee, knew that the policy for designated sales which he had to carry forward was to produce 250 sales in the marginal wards, in order to

improve the Conservative vote in those wards. The target of 500 was passed on
to officers, and members agreed that they would select at the Housing Committee   *a*
the estates they wished to see designated for sale. A meeting was held on 6 July
1987, two days before the Housing Committee was to meet, attended by Dame
Shirley Porter, Mr Weeks, Mr Hartley and others to discuss how to monitor the
impact of BSC policies on each key ward in the context of electoral considerations
and to monitor targets for such policies including designated sales. It was   *b*
recorded that 'the Leader reaffirmed the agreed BSC programme of action as
agreed by chairmen as an all embracing strategic Council policy with priorities for
BSC initiatives' and that both she and Mr Hartley 'felt that the City Council had
an agreed plan of action which could be clearly understood and implemented by
officers'.

[14] At the meeting of the Housing Committee on 8 July 1987, Mr Hartley   *c*
presented a joint report in which option 3, designation of sufficient properties to
produce 500 sales per annum, was the majority party's preferred option. That
option was placed before the committee because Dame Shirley Porter and
Mr Weeks hoped to increase the Conservative vote in marginal wards by selling
each year 250 council properties in those wards. They knew, or had every reason   *d*
to believe, that as adoption of option 3 was Conservative policy, promulgated by
Mr Hartley as chairman of the committee, it would become council policy.
There was no instance of the Housing Committee, at this time, not adopting the
majority party's policy. Mr Hartley knew that he was promoting this policy in
order to produce 250 sales per annum in the eight marginal wards in order to   *e*
increase the number of Conservative Party voters in them. He also knew that, in
supporting this policy, it would be adopted by the Housing Committee. The
committee resolved to designate a number of specific properties for sale which
were expected to produce 500 sales per annum. The committee further resolved
to introduce a scheme of capital grants. 20,697 properties had been identified in
the joint report to the committee as eligible for designation. Of these, 5,912   *f*
dwellings (29%) were in the eight key wards, 13,633 dwellings (66%) were in the
other 15 wards and there were in addition 1,152 scattered miscellaneous
properties. The list of properties to be designated was not recommended by
officers; it was presented by the chairman of the Housing Committee. 9,360
dwellings were designated, including all the scattered miscellaneous properties.   *g*
74% of all eligible dwellings in the eight key wards were designated; only 28% of
all eligible properties in the other wards were designated.

[15] There were seven Conservative Party members who voted at the
meeting of the Housing Committee: Cllrs Hartley, Dutt, Warner, Bianco, Buxton,
Evans and Hooper. Councillors Hartley, Dutt, Evans, Hooper and Bianco were   *h*
appointed to be members of the Housing Committee by Dame Shirley Porter
acting as the chairman of the Policy and Resources Committee. For five of these
members (Cllrs Hartley, Dutt, Evans, Buxton and Hooper) it was the first
meeting of the Housing Committee they had attended as voting members.
There were five members of the committee who were members of the Labour   *j*
Party. Designated sales was the seventh of eighteen items on the agenda. The
committee adopted the list proposed by Cllr Hartley by seven votes to five. The
Conservative members voted in favour; the opposition members voted against.

[16] At a meeting on 29 July 1987 the council received a report from the
Housing Committee. The city solicitor informed the council that a report on
designated sales had been prepared following a consultation with leading counsel

a and that it had been seen and approved by leading counsel before it went to the Housing Committee. The council voted to receive the report.

[17] The achievement of the electoral targets set out in the BSC campaign 'plan for action', including those for designated sales, was monitored by the chairmen's group and by members' and officers' steering groups. On 14 September 1987, the chairmen's group decided that the managing director of b the council should produce a BSC monitoring report to every other of its meetings, and confidential BSC monitoring reports were produced to such meetings on a number of dates thereafter. The reports considered what progress was being made in each of the eight key wards towards the sales target for that ward in 1987–1988. Two reports which were presented to the Policy and Resources Committee of the council, in October 1987 and May 1988, referred to c BSC but did not refer to the key wards, the targets established for them or the system established to secure the achievement of those targets. Documents which were intended for public consumption did 'not speak to key wards'. In 1988, opposition members of the council raised questions about why the key/marginal wards were being monitored. There were deliberate attempts by officers to d conceal the system of monitoring which had been established by giving deliberately misleading answers to proper questions from members of the minority party on the council. Under this pressure from the opposition, the BSC members' steering group (which Mr Weeks chaired) sought, but was unable to find, a rationale (other than their electoral marginality) for the selection of the eight key wards. On 12 April 1988 the chairmen's group, with Dame Shirley e Porter and Mr Weeks in attendance, were informed that the BSC members' steering group would consider a BSC monitoring report (in the form requested by the chairmen) and a 'rationale for key wards' at its meeting on 28 April 1988. Item 3 on the agenda for that meeting was 'Rationale for Key Wards'. This took the form of a paper by an officer, which did not provide any rationale for the f selection of the eight key wards. The minutes recorded that 'the paper looked at ways of going public on targeted wards. It was agreed that no such paper should be a formal document; each ward should be taken individually'. Mr England's note of the meeting, under 'area approach' recorded 'Minority Party interest ... not easy to confirm just the 8 ... Keep on Dodging???' Subsequent attempts were made to find a rationale (other than their electoral marginality) for the eight key g wards. On 25 July 1988 Mr England met with Dr Dutt and discussed (among other things) 'explanation for eight wards', 'public audit ... can we justify why eight were chosen' and 'why did we pick them? Members will ask us', and Mr England's action list as a result of the meeting included 'key wards—find defence of 8 wards'. In a memorandum dated 24 August 1988, the city solicitor h asked why the eight wards were chosen, by whom they were chosen and why they were regarded as key, but those questions were never answered.

[18] On 19 July 1989 the BBC transmitted a 'Panorama' programme on the designated sales policy in Westminster. Charts presented to the BSC members' steering group after 28 July 1989 recorded rights to buy and designated sales in all j 23 wards in the city, not just the eight key wards. The auditor was appointed following objections made by a number of local government electors in letters dated 18 July, 20 July and 8 November 1989.

The underlying legal principles

[19] The legal principles which underlie the auditor's findings against Dame Shirley Porter and Mr Weeks are not in the main controversial, but since they are

the bedrock of his decision they should be briefly summarised. (1) *Powers conferred on a local authority may be exercised for the public purpose for which the powers were conferred and not otherwise.* A very clear statement of this principle is to be found in Wade and Forsyth *Administrative Law* (8th edn, 2000) pp 356–357. The corresponding passage in an earlier edition of that work was expressly approved by Lord Bridge of Harwich in *Tower Hamlets LBC v Chetnik Developments Ltd* [1988] 1 All ER 961 at 966, [1988] AC 858 at 872:

> 'Statutory power conferred for public purposes is conferred as it were upon trust, not absolutely—that is to say, it can validly be used only in the right and proper way which Parliament when conferring it is presumed to have intended ...'

The principle is routinely applied, as by Neill LJ in *Credit Suisse v Allerdale BC* [1996] 4 All ER 129 at 150, [1997] QB 306 at 333 who described it as 'a general principle of public law'. (2) *Such powers are exercised by or on the delegation of councillors. It is misconduct in a councillor to exercise or be party to the exercise of such powers otherwise than for the public purpose for which the powers were conferred.* Where public powers are conferred on a council, it is the body of elected councillors who must exercise those powers save to the extent that such exercise is lawfully delegated to groups of councillors or to officers. All will act in the name or on behalf of the council. It follows from the proposition that public powers are conferred as if upon trust that those who exercise powers in a manner inconsistent with the public purpose for which the powers were conferred betray that trust and so misconduct themselves. This is an old and very important principle. It was clearly expressed by the Lord Chancellor of Ireland in *A-G ex rel Rea v Belfast Corp* (1855) 4 Ir Ch R 119 at 160-161:

> 'Municipal Corporations would cease to be tangible bodies for any purpose of redress on account of a breach of trust, if the individuals who constitute its executive, and by whom the injury has been committed, cannot be made responsible. They are a collection of persons doing acts that, when done, are the acts of the Corporation, but which are induced by the individuals who recommend and support them; and this Court holds that persons who withdraw themselves from the duties of their office may be rendered equally answerable for the acts of those whom they allow, by their absence, to have exclusive dominion over the corporate property ... As the trustees of the corporate estate, nominated by the Legislature, and appointed by their fellow-citizens, it is their duty to attend to the interests of the Corporation, conduct themselves honestly and uprightly, and to see that every one acts for the interests of the trust over which he and they are placed.'

(3) *If the councillors misconduct themselves knowingly or recklessly it is regarded by the law as wilful misconduct.* The auditor's power to surcharge councillors under s 20(1)(b) of the 1982 Act is dependent on a finding of wilful misconduct. That expression was defined by Webster J in *Graham v Teesdale* (1981) 81 LGR 117 at 123 to mean 'deliberately doing something which is wrong knowing it to be wrong or with reckless indifference as to whether it is wrong or not'. That definition was approved by the Court of Appeal in *Lloyd v McMahon* [1987] 1 All ER 1118 at 1130, 1137, 1151, [1987] AC 625 at 646–647, 655 and 674 and by the House of Lords ([1987] 1 All ER 1118 at 1157, 1160, [1987] AC 625 at 697 and 702). It was adopted by the Divisional Court in the present case ((1997) 96 LGR 157 at 167–168). It was also accepted by the Court of Appeal (see [2000] 2 WLR 1420 at

1443). There was no challenge to this definition before the House and I would
a accept it as representing the intention of Parliament when using this expression.
(4) *If the wilful misconduct of a councillor is found to have caused loss to a local authority
the councillor is liable to make good such loss to the council.* This is the rule now laid
down in s 20(1) of the 1982 Act. But it is not a new rule. A similar provision was
expressed in s 247(7) of the Public Health Act 1875, s 228(1)(d) of the Local
b Government Act 1933 and in s 161(4) of the Local Government Act 1972 (although
in the two earlier sections the reference was to 'negligence or misconduct' and
not to 'wilful misconduct'). Even before these statutory provisions the law had
been declared in clear terms. One such statement may be found in *A-G v Wilson*
(1840) Cr & Ph 1 at 23, 26–27 where Lord Cottenham LC said:

c   'The true way of viewing this is to consider the members of the governing
        body of the corporation as its agents, bound to exercise its functions for the
        purposes for which they were given, and to protect its interests and property;
        and if such agents exercise those functions for the purposes of injuring its
        interests and alienating its property, shall the corporations be estopped in
        this Court from complaining because the act done was ostensibly an act of
d   the corporation? ... As members of the governing body, it was their duty
        as the corporation, whose trustees and agents they, in that respect, were, to
        preserve and protect the property confided to them; instead of which, having
        previously, as they supposed, placed the property, by the deeds of the 30th
        May 1835, in a convenient position for that purpose, they take measures for
e   alienating that property, with the avowed design of depriving the
        corporation of it; and, with this view, they procure trusts to be declared, and
        transfers of part of the property to be made to the several other Defendants
        in this cause, for purposes in no manner connected with the purposes to
        which the funds were devoted, and for which it was their duty to protect and
        preserve them. This was not only a breach of trust and a violation of duty
f   towards the corporation, whose agents and trustees they were, but an act of
        spoliation against all the inhabitants of *Leeds* liable to the borough rate; every
        individual of whom had an interest in the fund, for his exoneration, *pro tanto*,
        from the borough rate. If any other agent or trustee had so dealt with
        property over which the owner had given him control, can there be any
g   doubt but that such agent or trustee would, in this Court, be made
        responsible for so much of the alienated property as could not be recovered
        in specie? But if Lord *Hardwicke* was right in [*Charitable Corp v Sutton* (1742)
        2 Atk 400], and I am right in this case, in considering the authors of the wrong
        as agents or trustees of the corporation, then the two cases are identical.
h   I cannot doubt, therefore, that the Plaintiffs are entitled to redress against the
        three trustees and those members of the governing body who were
        instrumental in carrying into effect the acts complained of; and it is proved
        that the five Defendants fall under that description.'

(5) *Powers conferred on a local authority may not lawfully be exercised to promote the
j   electoral advantage of a political party.* Support for this principle may be found in
R v Board of Education [1910] 2 KB 165 at 181 where Farwell LJ said:

        'If this means that the Board were hampered by political considerations,
        I can only say that such considerations are pre-eminently extraneous, and
        that no political consequence can justify the Board in allowing their
        judgment and discretion to be influenced thereby.'

This passage was accepted by Lord Upjohn in *Padfield v Minister of Agriculture, Fisheries and Food* [1968] 1 All ER 694 at 717, 718, [1968] AC 997 at 1058, 1061. In *R v Port Talbot BC, ex p Jones* [1988] 2 All ER 207 at 214, where council accommodation had been allocated to an applicant in order that she should be the better able to fight an election, Nolan J regarded that decision as based on irrelevant considerations.

[20] Counsel for Dame Shirley Porter and Mr Weeks urged upon the House what were said to be the realities of party politics. Councillors elected as members of a political party and forming part of that party group on the council could not be expected to be oblivious to considerations of party political advantage. So long as they had reasons for taking action other than purely partisan political reasons their conduct could not be impugned. Reliance was placed on observations of Kennedy LJ in the Court of Appeal:

'Some of the submissions advanced on behalf of the auditor have been framed in such a way as to suggest that any councillor who allows the possibility of electoral advantage even to cross his mind before he decides upon a course of action is guilty of misconduct. That seems to me to be unreal. In local, as in national, politics many if not most decisions carry an electoral price tag, and all politicians are aware of it. In most cases they cannot seriously be expected to disregard it, but they know that if the action which they take is to withstand scrutiny (to be "judge-proof") there must be sound local government reasons, not just excuses, on which they can rely.' (See [2000] 2 WLR 1420 at 1444.)

Schiemann LJ (at 1448, 1449) spoke to similar effect:

'Whether or not the decision of the housing committee was unlawful depends, in the circumstances of this case, on the motivation of the committee at the time of the vote. If its motive was purely to secure electoral advantage for the Conservative Party then the decision was unlawful. If purely Housing Act considerations were its motivation then its decision would be lawful ... There is a complication. Frequently individual persons act from mixed motives. Further, group decisions may have multiple motivations—in part because there are many votes cast and in part because each voter may himself have several motivations ... It is legitimate for councillors to desire that their party should win the next election. Our political system works on the basis that they desire that because they think that the policies to which their party is wedded are in the public interest and will require years to be achieved. There is nothing disgraceful or unlawful in councillors having that desire. For this court to hold otherwise would depart from our theory of democracy and current reality.'

[21] Whatever the difficulties of application which may arise in a borderline case, I do not consider the overriding principle to be in doubt. Elected politicians of course wish to act in a manner which will commend them and their party (when, as is now usual, they belong to one) to the electorate. Such an ambition is the life blood of democracy and a potent spur to responsible decision-taking and administration. Councillors do not act improperly or unlawfully if, exercising public powers for a public purpose for which such powers were conferred, they hope that such exercise will earn the gratitude and support of the electorate and thus strengthen their electoral position. The law would indeed part company with the realities of party politics if it were to hold otherwise. But a public power

a is not exercised lawfully if it is exercised not for a public purpose for which the power was conferred but in order to promote the electoral advantage of a political party. The power at issue in the present case is s 32 of the Housing Act 1985, which conferred power on local authorities to dispose of land held by them subject to conditions specified in the Act. Thus a local authority could dispose of its property, subject to the provisions of the Act, to promote any public purpose

b for which such power was conferred, but could not lawfully do so for the purpose of promoting the electoral advantage of any party represented on the council.

[22] The House was referred to a number of cases in which the part which political allegiance may properly play in local government has been explored: *R v Sheffield City Council, ex p Chadwick* (1985) 84 LGR 563; *R v Waltham Forest LBC, ex p Baxter* [1987] 3 All ER 671, [1988] QB 419; *Jones v Swansea City Council* [1989]

c 3 All ER 162, [1990] 1 WLR 54; *R v Bradford City Metropolitan Council, ex p Wilson* [1989] 3 All ER 140, [1990] 2 QB 375n; *R v Local Comr for Administration in North and North East of England, ex p Liverpool City Council* [2001] 1 All ER 462. These cases show that while councillors may lawfully support a policy adopted by their party they must not abdicate their responsibility and duty of exercising personal

d judgment. There is nothing in these cases to suggest that a councillor may support a policy not for valid local government reasons but with the object of obtaining an electoral advantage.

The findings made against Dame Shirley Porter and Mr Weeks

e [23] Reference has already been made to the detailed and protracted investigation conducted by the auditor. Details are given in the judgment of the Divisional Court (see (1997) 96 LGR 157 at 161–162). He made very lengthy findings. The Divisional Court in its turn received a mass of written material, heard evidence from Dame Shirley Porter and Mr Weeks and conducted a hearing extending over 23 sitting days. The decision of the auditor and the

f Divisional Court adverse to Dame Shirley Porter and Mr Weeks rested on four main findings.

[24] The first of these findings was that the Westminster City Council adopted a policy the object of which was to achieve a specified annual level of sales of properties owned by the council in the eight marginal wards with the intention that the properties thus vacated should be sold to new residents who, as

g owner-occupiers, might reasonably be expected to vote conservative and so increase the electoral strength of the Conservative Party in those wards in the 1990 council elections. The auditor put his conclusions on this point in a number of different ways. It is enough to quote para 53(2)(d)(v) of his summary of his findings and views:

h
'... both the decision to increase the number of designated sales and the selection of the properties designated for sale were influenced by an irrelevant consideration, namely the electoral advantage of the majority party. I have found that the electoral advantage of the majority party was the driving force behind the policy of increased designated sales and that that

j consideration was the predominant consideration which influenced both the decision to increase designated sales by 500 per annum and the selection of properties designated for sale. My view is that the Council was engaged in gerrymandering, which I have found is a disgraceful and improper purpose, and not a purpose for which a local authority may act.'

The Divisional Court accepted this conclusion (at 164–165):

'In the 1986 local government elections the Conservative Party on the
council were returned with a very small majority. With a view to greater
success in the 1990 elections, the party formulated a policy of "building stable
communities". A major element in this policy was to increase designated
sales of council properties in eight key marginal wards to potential
owner-occupiers. It was believed that owner-occupiers would be more
likely to vote Conservative ... On 8 July 1987 the housing committee, having
received a much amended joint report from council officials, resolved to
extend the programme of designated sales so as to produce 500 sales per
annum city-wide and introduced a scheme for capital grants of £15,000 to
encourage tenants to move. On 29 July 1987 the council refused to overturn
the committee's decision. Thereafter, the progress of the policy in marginal
wards was monitored.'

In the Court of Appeal Robert Walker LJ could see no reason why that court,
which had not heard the witnesses, could or should depart from the Divisional
Court's findings, which there was ample documentary evidence to confirm and
virtually no evidence to contradict. These conclusions are clearly accepted in the
agreed findings briefly summarised in [4]–[18] above.

[25] Nothing that the House has heard gives any ground for doubting the
correctness of the conclusion of the auditor and the Divisional Court on this
point. It follows from the legal principles already summarised that the council's
policy was unlawful because directed to the pursuit of electoral advantage and
not the achievement of proper housing objectives.

[26] The decision of the auditor and the Divisional Court adverse to Dame
Shirley Porter and Mr Weeks was based, secondly, on the conclusion that they
were both party to the adoption and implementation of this unlawful policy.

[27] With regard to Dame Shirley Porter the auditor found (p 417 (para 1147)):

'I find as a fact that Councillor Lady Porter was one of the Members
responsible for determining the direction and content of the policy of the
majority group on the Council. She formulated the "*Strategy to 1990*" which
aimed to give top priority in the development of Council policies to electoral
success. I find that, after the local government elections in May 1986, her top
priority was to secure that the Conservative Party was successful in the local
government elections for the Council in 1990 and she ensured that the
policies of the Council on matters such as home ownership and homelessness
were directed to that end. I find as a fact that she was concerned to secure
an increase in the number of home owners and a reduction in the number of
homeless households accommodated in marginal (or key) wards by 1990, in
order to increase the number of likely Conservative voters in those wards in
the 1990 local government elections. For her, the designated sales policy was
a means to that end.'

The auditor made similar findings concerning Mr Weeks (p 578):

'1579. I have found that Councillor Weeks was one of the Members
responsible for determining the direction and content of the policy of the
majority group on the Council. He was aware of, and supported, the Leader's
"*Strategy to 1990*" which aimed to give top priority in the development of
Council policies to electoral success. He was aware of, and supported, the
initial housing strategy, evolved after the May 1986 local government
elections, which involved concentration of activity in marginal wards to help

a the Conservative party to win the 1990 local government elections, including increased designated sales. I have found as a fact that he was concerned to secure an increase in the number of home owners and a reduction in the number of homeless households accommodated in marginal (or key) wards by 1990, in order to increase the number of likely Conservative voters in those wards in the 1990 local government elections.

b For him, the designated sales policy was a means to that end. 1580. I have found that thereafter, Councillor Weeks promoted and supported the Leader's "*Strategy to 1990*" and a policy of targeting designated sales and other Council policies in marginal wards in order to secure electoral advantage for the Conservative Party.'

c The Divisional Court reached similar conclusions ((1997) 96 LGR 157 at 175, 176 and 183):

'[Dame Shirley Porter] was by title leader of the majority party and by personality a leader not a follower. Targeting marginal wards was, probably from the end of July 1986 at the latest, central to her political objectives, as a

d succession of contemporaneous documents makes plain ... [Mr Weeks] said that the idea of targeting designated sales in marginal wards had "not got to a detailed stage by March 1987": it was still "pretty loose" and remained so, even after 5 May. Although he was the lead BSC chairman monitoring the performance of other chairmen, he said he had no direct responsibility for designated sales policy which was a matter "wholly within the purview of

e the housing committee". We reject this. As we have said, one of [Dame Shirley Porter's] central objectives from July 1986 was targeting marginal wards and we accept [Mr England's] evidence that, at least from the time of the Segal paper in January 1987, targeting designated sales in marginal wards was firm political policy. As deputy leader and, as he admitted, one who

f worked closely with the leader and was "the details man", [Mr Weeks] was well aware of [Dame Shirley Porter's] objectives and determination and we find that one of his roles was to ensure by supervision that the housing committee fulfilled the objectives of the leader and the majority party, particularly in targeting designated sales in marginal wards. Whereas in his affidavit he said that key wards were not selected because of their

g marginality, in his oral evidence he said that marginality was the reason for their selection ... We find that designated sales in marginal wards was, as [Mr Hartley] put it, very much [Dame Shirley Porter's] "baby" and it was embraced by the chairmen's group including [Mr Weeks]. We have no hesitation in finding that the eight wards were identified in early 1987 by

h members of the majority party *because* they were marginal, albeit that there were also particular problems to be addressed in some of them, such as those in the central activity zone.'

In the Court of Appeal Robert Walker LJ summarised the facts at considerable length, but expressed his conclusion briefly:

j

'The overall impression throughout, from mid-1986 to mid-1989, is that the most influential members of the Conservative group on the city council, led by Dame Shirley and Mr. Weeks, had electoral advantage as the overriding objective in formulating their housing policy, securing its adoption by the council, and implementing it with high priority given to the marginal wards.' (See [2000] 2 WLR 1420 at 1485.)

[28] These findings again are clearly accepted in the agreed findings already *a*
summarised. There is no reason to doubt their correctness.

[29] The third finding crucial to the decision against Dame Shirley Porter and
Mr Weeks is that they both knew the designated sales policy targeted on marginal
wards to be unlawful. The auditor found (p 500):

'1363. I find as a fact that Councillor Lady Porter knew that Council *b*
facilities could not lawfully be used for party political purposes and that the
Council was not entitled to exercise its powers or expend its resources to
promote the electoral advantage of her party. As she told Councillor Peter
Bradley, in answer to a question from him at a meeting of the Council on
10 June 1987: *"As the member well knows, Council facilities must not be used for
party political purposes"*. *c*

1364. I find as a fact that although Councillor Lady Porter may have
believed that Leading Counsel had advised that the Council could lawfully
extend its programme of designated sales on the basis of the Joint Report
without acting inconsistently with its statutory duties to the homeless,
Councillor Lady Porter knew that it was unlawful and wrong for the Council
to exercise its powers to secure an electoral advantage for any political party *d*
or to gerrymander or, in pursuit of such advantage for her party, she was at
least recklessly indifferent as to whether it was right or wrong.'

Save for the reference to Dame Shirley Porter's answer to Cllr Peter Bradley, the
auditor made identical findings in relation to Mr Weeks (p 584 (paras 1597–1598)). *e*

[30] The Divisional Court made a number of findings on this point:

'[Dame Shirley Porter] failed to explain to us why and by whom the eight
wards were identified. In our judgment, this failure is explicable not by the
effect of the subsequent passage of time on recollection but by the realisation
on her part that the more knowledge of detail which she admitted the more *f*
closely she would become identified with a policy of targeting designated
sales to enhance Conservative prospects in marginal wards which she knew
in 1987 and knows now was unlawful ... From March 1987 when [Dame
Shirley Porter] saw [the city solicitor's] answer to the Greenman questions
she knew, as she asserts in her affidavit, that the advantages of sale had to "be
considered not from any ulterior motive but from the standpoint of what is *g*
right in view of the council's role as a housing authority". She told us that
she was not surprised by that advice and that she did not understand
counsel's advice on 5 May to be any different. If this is true, [Dame Shirley
Porter] cannot have thought that the suggestion of increasing the numbers
city-wide came from Sullivan, because this would have left untouched the *h*
continuing ulterior motive in relation to marginal wards which [the city
solicitor] had advised against. Clearly there was nothing in Sullivan's advice,
as reported by [Mr England], which legitimated designated sales targeted in
marginal wards. Indeed, on 10 June [Dame Shirley Porter] answered a
question at a council meeting in these terms: "Council facilities must not be *j*
used for party political purposes". As all members and officers of the council
well knew, council properties could not be sold for these purposes. [The city
solicitor's] view expressed to the auditor, was that "everyone in the
Conservative Party in Westminster would have known that they could not
take party political advantage into account in deciding this policy" ...
Because [Dame Shirley Porter] and [Mr Weeks] knew the targeting policy
was unlawful they were content, without further inquiry of Sullivan,

a
[Mr England], [the deputy city solicitor] or anyone else, to adopt the suggestion in [Mr England's] note that it be dressed up in city-wide clothes: neither claims this was a proper course. Their purpose throughout was to achieve unlawful electoral advantage. Knowledge of the unlawfulness and such deliberate dressing-up both inevitably point to, and we find, wilful misconduct on behalf of each of them.' (See (1997) 96 LGR 157 at 184–185.)

b
In the Court of Appeal Robert Walker LJ concluded (at 1488) that Dame Shirley Porter cannot at any stage have believed that targeting marginal wards for electoral advantage was a lawful use of council resources, and that the position was similar but even clearer in relation to Mr Weeks.

[31] Both Dame Shirley Porter and Mr Weeks, in their respective printed
c cases, accept that they knew that the council could not use its powers for electoral advantage. They plainly did know that. It follows, subject to the points discussed below, that in adopting and implementing the designated sales policy both acted in a way they knew to be unlawful.

[32] Fourthly, it was found that the designated sales policy promoted and
d implemented by Dame Shirley Porter and Mr Weeks caused financial loss to the council. The auditor's conclusion was as follows (p 499 (para 1361)):

'The fact that Councillor Lady Porter was not present at the meeting of the Housing Committee on 8 July 1987 or at the meetings of the Appointed Members' Panels on 4 September 1987, and did not, at those meetings, vote
e for the extended designated sales policy, which she had sought to procure, does not mean that she was not responsible for the consequences of those decisions. Without Councillor Lady Porter's promotion and support there would have been no proposal put to the Housing Committee for an increased programme of designated sales, targeted in the key/marginal wards and on the scale proposed. I find as a fact that she was one of those
f responsible for the decisions taken and the consequences which ensued. The resulting financial consequences were caused, in my view, by her misconduct.'

An identical finding was made in relation to Mr Weeks (p 583 (para 1595)). The Divisional Court found that such loss as resulted to the council from the decisions taken by the Housing Committee and the council in July 1987 was caused by the
g wilful misconduct of Dame Shirley Porter and Mr Weeks ((1997) 96 LGR 157 at 204). In the Court of Appeal Robert Walker LJ accepted that conclusion ([2000] 2 WLR 1420 at 1496). But Dame Shirley Porter and Mr Weeks have raised an issue on causation which it is necessary to consider in more detail below.

[33] In argument before the House, counsel for Dame Shirley Porter and
h Mr Weeks raised a large number of points in resistance to the auditor's appeal. The three most substantial of these arguments are considered in the sections which follow.

Reliance on legal advice
j [34] On behalf of Dame Shirley Porter and Mr Weeks it was argued before the House that whatever the lawfulness or unlawfulness of the designated sales policy they acted, in promoting it after 5 May 1987, in accordance with what they believed to be legal advice given to the council and were accordingly not guilty of wilful misconduct.

[35] The auditor's findings on this matter in relation to Dame Shirley Porter were set out in his decision (pp 499–500):

'1362. I find as a fact that Councillor Lady Porter did not act reasonably or in the belief that any expenditure resulting from the decisions of the Housing Committee and the Appointed Members' Panels, was authorised by law. Councillor Lady Porter did not receive any legal advice which could have led her to believe that it was open to the Council to engage in gerrymandering or to exercise its powers to secure an electoral advantage for the Conservative Party. She does not claim that the Council was engaged in gerrymandering or in exercising its powers to secure an electoral advantage for the Conservative Party. She does not claim that she received legal advice that it was lawful for the Council to engage in gerrymandering or to exercise its powers to secure an electoral advantage for the Conservative Party. On the contrary, she received legal advice from the City Solicitor that the Council was not entitled to exercise its powers for an ulterior purpose. Neither this advice nor the advice from Mr Sullivan QC gave any support for targeting designation in the key/marginal wards to promote the electoral advantage of the Conservative Party. As Councillor Lady Porter was aware, that could not lawfully be done ...

1366. I am further strengthened in my conclusion by the evasive, false and misleading evidence given to me by Councillor Lady Porter in interview as to the reason for the selection of the 8 key wards, the nature of the targets adopted and the monitoring which took place against those targets and by the misleading answers she gave in response to questions at Council meetings. Councillor Lady Porter did not admit that the designated sales policy was introduced for the purpose of securing electoral advantage for the Conservative Party in the 1990 local government elections in the City of Westminster. If Councillor Lady Porter had believed that the policy of adopting an extended programme of designated sales in order to secure electoral advantage for the Conservative Party was legally acceptable and supported by legal advice, she had ample opportunity to tell me that this was what the Council was doing and that she had received legal advice that it was lawful for the Council so to do.'

In relation to Mr Weeks, very similar findings were made in paras 1596 and 1600 (pp 583–585).

[36] The Divisional Court found as follows:

'The position of [Dame Shirley Porter] in relation to legal advice was initially, as reflected in the opening skeleton argument on her behalf, that she never sought or received advice which could have led her to believe that it was open to the council to exercise its powers to secure an electoral advantage for the majority party. In her affidavit she said her duty as a councillor was "to decide matters in council only upon considerations relevant to local government factors identified by officers" ... She also said that [the city solicitor's] advice that there must not be any ulterior motive came as no surprise in the light of her experience and she did not understand leading counsel's advice on 5 May to have differed from that of [the city solicitor]. In the light of this evidence, although we accept that [Dame Shirley Porter] was always anxious to obtain and follow legal advice, it is, in our judgment, impossible for [Dame Shirley Porter] to contend that she believed at any stage that targeting marginal wards for electoral advantage was legally permissible.' (See (1997) 96 LGR 157 at 179.)

a The Divisional Court then, in relation to Mr Weeks, found (at 179):

'[Mr Weeks'] evidence in cross-examination was that, as a result of
counsel's advice on 5 May it was clear "that you could not just designate for
250 in the marginal wards" and that he greeted that advice "with some relief"
because a major aspect of contentiousness could be removed. He said that,
following counsel's advice, he and other members "immediately abandoned"
b talk of designating blocks in marginal wards and the lists produced "after
5 May were constructed on other grounds". Whether that evidence is
credible we shall consider later. But it provides no basis whatever for
suggesting that, if [Mr Weeks] continued to be party to a scheme for
targeting designated sales in marginal wards for electoral advantage, he did
so in reliance on legal advice.'

c
[37] In the Court of Appeal Robert Walker LJ, in a passage to part of which
reference has already been made, said:

'The way in which Dame Shirley's case has been presented has varied from
time to time. Only in this court, I think, has much emphasis been placed on
d her reliance on legal advice. In her oral evidence she said that she was well
aware that local authority resources must not be used for party political ends,
and that the legal advice which she received came as no surprise to her. She
also said that it never occurred to her to ask to see Mr. Sullivan's advice in
writing. She did not contend, either in her oral evidence or through her
counsel (apart from drawing attention to [the city solicitor's] unfortunate
e references to devising or constructing arguments), that she was relying on
any legal advice to the effect that an unlawful policy could be made lawful
by camouflage. On the basis of Mr. England's "Note to Leader" it seems
likely that Mr. Sullivan's unambiguous advice was distorted in the course of
transmission to Dame Shirley, although in the absence of any minutes of the
f meeting of the chairmen's group on the evening of 5 May 1987 (at which
Mr. England was present) it is impossible to gauge the degree of distortion.
But as the Divisional Court found, she cannot at any stage have believed
(either in reliance on legal advice or otherwise) that targeting marginal wards
for electoral advantage was a lawful use of council resources.' (See [2000]
2 WLR 1420 at 1488.)

g
As already noted, Robert Walker LJ considered the position of Mr Weeks to be
similar but if anything even clearer.

[38] Counsel for Dame Shirley Porter and Mr Weeks naturally placed much
reliance on the contrary views expressed by the majority in the Court of Appeal.
h In the course of his judgment Kennedy LJ said (at 1445–1446):

'I remind myself that the Divisional Court had the advantage of seeing the
two appellants, as well as others, when they gave evidence, and clearly that
court was not particularly impressed by these two appellants, but what
I cannot follow is how the court was able to find these appellants guilty of
j wilful misconduct having regard to its conclusions in relation to those
important factual issues which I set out at the beginning of this section of this
judgment, conclusions which led the court to conclude that three out of five
appeals must be allowed. I recognise that long before 5 May 1987 Dame
Shirley, but not Mr. Weeks, had received legal advice from [the city
solicitor], but on 5 May 1987 the possibility of targeting sales in marginal
wards for political gain was put to leading counsel of considerable standing.

Mr. England, who received and reported upon counsel's advice, was led to
believe that designating city-wide would not be unlawful merely because it   *a*
met Dame Shirley's objective of 250 in marginal wards. The judgment of the
Divisional Court simply does not explain why the advice of leading counsel
did not affect Dame Shirley and Mr. Weeks as it affected Mr. England, and
for that matter Mr. Hartley and Mr. Phillips, and I cannot make good the
omission because there seems to have been no reason to make any   *b*
distinction. The Divisional Court said that the purpose of the appellants
throughout was "to achieve unlawful electoral advantage." The use of the
word "unlawful" begs the question. Their submission is that having taken
legal advice they, like the others, believed that electoral advantage could
lawfully be pursued by the route envisaged in Mr. England's report of his
consultation with Mr. Sullivan, and thereafter the route chosen was, they   *c*
believed, entirely legitimate ... I recognise, of course, that in the Divisional
Court the appellants contended that the great increase in the number of
designated properties was not promoted in order to achieve 250 sales per
annum in marginal wards, and that the Divisional Court held otherwise, but
in all essential matters the records speak for themselves. On 5 May 1987   *d*
counsel and the officers who attended on him knew all there was to know
about Dame Shirley's ambition as to sales in marginal wards. The Divisional
Court was critical of both appellants for saying that, in the light of
Mr. Sullivan's advice, the policy was abandoned. The court said, 96 L.G.R.
157, 185, that they "lied," but on any view option 3 was not the proposal
which Mr. Sullivan was asked to consider. It was only formulated as a result   *e*
of his advice. As Mr. McMullen pointed out, those who wish to offend
against the law do not usually consult lawyers of good reputation, give them
access to all relevant information, and then act in accordance with their
understanding of the lawyer's advice, arranging for further advice to be
obtained as events progress. In most cases where a breach of section 20 has   *f*
been found proved, the evidence shows an unwillingness to obtain or a
defiance of legal advice. That is not this case.'

Schiemann LJ said (at 1453):

'As the division of opinion in this court shows, there is no doubt that the   *g*
borderline between what is permissible and what is not permissible in the
context of what Dame Shirley was trying to achieve is not easily perceived
by lawyers and even less easily perceived by laymen. It is clear to me that
Dame Shirley was seeking to avoid doing anything illegal and that this was
the reason why she laid bare her hopes to her legal advisers and asked for
legal advice.'   *h*

[39] The issue of inconsistency of findings is one which I consider separately
below. The issue here is whether the majority of the Court of Appeal had any
sustainable grounds for rejecting the very clear conclusions reached by the
primary fact-finders, the auditor and the Divisional Court. Before the auditor   *j*
Dame Shirley Porter and Mr Weeks did not contend that they had pursued the
designated sales policy on legal advice. At that stage they were seeking to
distance themselves from the policy. In the Divisional Court they contended that
the policy had been abandoned after 5 May 1987, a contention found by that court
to be dishonest and untrue. Only in the Court of Appeal was the case made that
reliance had been placed on legal advice, as Robert Walker LJ pointed out in the

a passage quoted in para [37] above. It is not clear to me how the Court of Appeal majority felt able to reject the very clear findings of the auditor and the Divisional Court, which in my opinion are entitled to stand. But I draw attention to two particular, in my view fatal, weaknesses in the majority reasoning. First, it is simply not true that Mr Sullivan was given access to all relevant information or that Dame Shirley laid bare her hopes to her legal advisors. Mr Sullivan received

b no written instructions and gave no written advice. There were two questions which the council should have put to him. The first was whether it was lawful to promote a policy of designating council properties for sale in marginal wards for the purpose of securing an electoral advantage for the majority party at the forthcoming council elections. That question was put to Mr Sullivan and he answered it in the negative, as he was bound to do. The second, follow-up,

c question should have been whether, if that policy would be unlawful, the policy would become lawful if, with the same objective, and in order to conceal the targeting of sales in marginal wards, the designated sales policy were extended across the City of Westminster. That question was never put. No one, including Dame Shirley Porter and Mr Weeks, could have had any doubt at all what the

d answer would have been if it had. Mr Sullivan was never told of the course on which the council proposed to embark or had embarked. The second weakness is found in the history of pretence, obfuscation and prevarication which surrounded the policy from May 1987 onwards. If the policy was genuinely believed to be lawful, albeit controversial, there was no need for such intensive camouflage.

e [40] I can for my part see no reason to question the very clear findings made by the auditor and the Divisional Court on this question.

Inconsistency

f [41] The auditor's findings of wilful misconduct against Mr Hartley, Mr England and Mr Phillips were not upheld by the Divisional Court, and it is argued on behalf of Dame Shirley Porter and Mr Weeks that they cannot fairly or rationally be found liable if those others are to be exonerated. The inconsistency, as he saw it, of the Divisional Court findings was the main ground upon which Kennedy LJ allowed the appeal by Dame Shirley Porter and Mr Weeks.

g [42] In the case of Mr Hartley the Divisional Court found his conduct to be unlawful and so to amount to misconduct because of the improper motives of others of which he was aware. But the Divisional Court was prepared to accept that he did not appreciate the unlawfulness of his conduct and genuinely believed that his own overriding belief in wider home ownership rendered his conduct

h lawful (see (1997) 96 LGR 157 at 199). It accordingly found that his misconduct was not wilful.

[43] In the case of Mr England the Divisional Court found that he was not guilty of wilful misconduct down to 8 July 1987, whatever his doubts and equivocations, and although critical of his conduct thereafter the Divisional

j Court did not find him guilty of wilful misconduct (see (1997) 96 LGR 157 at 195).

[44] The Divisional Court found that Mr Phillips was guilty of misconduct. But it was not prepared to conclude that he must have known that what was proposed was unlawful as well as improper (see (1997) 96 LGR 157 at 202). The Divisional Court considered whether he was reckless. In the results it was not satisfied to the standard required that he had been reckless (see (1997) 96 LGR 157 at 203).

[45] Robert Walker LJ found this the most difficult aspect of the whole case *a* and it caused him some anxiety ([2000] 2 WLR 1420 at 1494) and unease (at 1496) and he thought there had perhaps been some element of mercy in the Divisional Court's conclusions (see [2000] 2 WLR 1420 at 1494, 1495). But he could not say they were not conclusions which were open to the Divisional Court ([2000] 2 WLR 1420 at 1496). I share Robert Walker LJ's anxiety and unease. It is understandable that the Divisional Court was reluctant to be excessively critical *b* of officers, who were subject to considerable pressure from elected members, as the Divisional Court pointed out (see (1997) 96 LGR 157 at 186). Mr Hartley's conduct does not earn that measure of indulgence. But the Divisional Court had the advantage of hearing these three witnesses. It was rightly alert to the high standard required before a finding of this gravity could be sustained. It may very well be that Messrs Hartley, England and Phillips were fortunate to be *c* exonerated, to the limited extent that they were exonerated. But the findings made against Dame Shirley Porter and Mr Weeks were, in truth, very strong. They were the leader and deputy leader of the council, and were respectively the prime architect and midwife of this policy. I am satisfied that no injustice is done to either of them by upholding the findings of the auditor and the Divisional *d* Court.

Causation

[46] At the forefront of their submissions on behalf of Dame Shirley Porter and Mr Weeks counsel advanced an argument to the effect that whatever the *e* impropriety or unlawfulness of their clients' purpose and motive this did not render the decision of the Housing Committee on 8 July 1987 unlawful. That was a decision lawfully made by the members of the committee (not including Dame Shirley Porter and Mr Weeks) for lawful housing reasons, untainted by the unlawful designated sales policy, and accordingly anything which happened thereafter was not attributable to any unlawful motivation on the part of Dame *f* Shirley Porter and Mr Weeks. As Schiemann LJ made plain in his judgment ([2000] 2 WLR 1420 at 1451–1453), this was an argument which particularly impressed him (although he made plain (at 1453) that he did not accept that Dame Shirley Porter had been either dishonest or improperly motivated). In my opinion this argument must be rejected. It is an agreed fact (recited in para [14] *g* above) that once the city-wide designated sales policy had been adopted by the majority party it was to all intents and purposes bound to be approved by the committee. The auditor concluded (p 325):

'885. In the event that taking into account party electoral advantage does *h* not invalidate a decision unless it becomes the dominant factor, I give my view as to whether party electoral advantage was such a dominant factor. I have concluded that the overwhelming inference to be drawn from the evidence is that party electoral advantage was the dominant consideration which influenced the Housing Committee in reaching a decision to adopt option 3 (increase designated sales by 500 per annum) and in selecting the *j* properties designated for sale. I find as a fact that the electoral advantage of the majority party was the driving force behind the policy of increased designated sales and that that consideration was the predominant consideration which influenced both the decision to adopt option 3 and the selection of the properties designated for sale.'

a   The conclusion of the Divisional Court on the committee's decision of 8 July 1987 is one that I would, for my part, accept:

'In our view this decision was substantially influenced by a wish to alter the composition of the electorate by increasing the Conservative vote in marginal wards by the sale of council properties, and was therefore unlawful. The
b   policy proposed at the meeting by [Mr Hartley] and adopted by the committee was one which gave effect to this purpose, whatever may have been the reasons for the votes of individual members. It is perfectly possible, in law and common sense, for a corrupt principal to cause a result through an innocent agent or (in the context discussed by Lord Nicholls of Birkenhead in *Royal Brunei Airlines Sdn Bhd v Tan* [[1995] 3 All ER 97 at 102,
c   [1995] 2 AC 378 at 385]) a dishonest third party to be liable for a breach of trust perpetrated by a trustee acting innocently. In the present case, whatever the reasons of individual members for voting as they did, the option for which they voted was placed before the committee, in part at least, in order to achieve the improper purpose to which we have referred.'
     (See (1997) 96 LGR 157 at 181.)
d

[47] If however it is appropriate to inquire into the motivation of the majority party members who voted for option 3 in the committee on 8 July 1987, the conclusion does not assist Dame Shirley Porter and Mr Weeks. Whatever his own reasons for supporting that option, Mr Hartley was very well aware of the purpose which underlay the policy. He was, as already noted, found guilty of
e   misconduct by the Divisional Court. In the auditor's decision he said that the late Dr Dutt, who was vice-chairman of the committee—

'was also aware of the objective to increase the majority party's voting strength in marginal wards by the adoption of an extended programme of designated sales in those wards. In my view, he took into account the
f   electoral advantage of the Conservative Party and sought to promote it in his voting and otherwise.'

(The auditor in his provisional findings expressed conclusions adverse to Dr Dutt, who disputed those findings and took his own life. The auditor, in his decision, made no finding of personal liability against Dr Dutt.) If those two tainted votes
g   are discounted, the majority party had no majority of votes on the committee. The auditor found that Cllr Warner tried to exercise an independent judgment but was influenced by the joint report laid before the committee (which contained no hint of the true purpose of the policy) and by the views of Mr Hartley (p 323 (para 879)). The same finding was made in relation to Cllrs Bianco and
h   Hooper, save that they were unable to and did not exercise any independent judgment in relation to adoption of the list of properties for designation circulated at the meeting, which had been devised by officers working with the chairman to achieve target numbers of sales in certain marginal wards in order to secure an electorate advantage for the majority party in those wards (pp 323–324
j   (para 880)). In the case of Cllrs Evans and Buxton the auditor found that they neither sought to exercise nor exercised any independent judgment in relation to voting for the adoption for option 3: they simply relied on the joint report and the views of Mr Hartley. The inescapable truth is that while the chairman and vice-chairman of the committee knew of the purpose which underlay option 3, the backbench members were in no position to exercise an informed independent judgment because they were never given a clear picture of why the policy had

been adopted and what it was intended to achieve. The committee was used by
the party leadership to secure approval of a policy of which the purpose was
never fully explained. In my opinion there was no informed exercise of
independent judgment by members of the committee such as could break the
chain of causation between the conduct of Dame Shirley Porter and Mr Weeks
and the consequences which followed.

The liability of Dame Shirley Porter and Mr Weeks

[48] The Divisional Court's findings adverse to Dame Shirley Porter and
Mr Weeks, reached on a mass of evidence, were fully justified, if not inevitable.
The Court of Appeal majority erred in departing from them. The passage of time
and the familiarity of the accusations made against Dame Shirley Porter and
Mr Weeks cannot and should not obscure the unpalatable truth that this was a
deliberate, blatant and dishonest misuse of public power. It was a misuse of
power by both of them not for the purpose of financial gain but for that of
electoral advantage. In that sense it was corrupt. The auditor may have been
strictly wrong to describe their conduct as gerrymandering, but it was certainly
unlawful and he was right to stigmatise it as disgraceful.

Preparation of papers

[49] The auditor held Dame Shirley Porter and Mr Weeks responsible for a
sum amounting (with interest) to £10,126 attributable to the cost of preparing
papers relating to the promotion of the electoral advantage of the majority party.
The basis of his finding was that this was an unlawful misuse of the time of
council officers. There is no dispute concerning the quantum of this sum. The
Court of Appeal held by a majority that since Dame Shirley Porter and Mr Weeks
did not transgress, the cost of preparing these papers could not be laid at their
door ([2000] 2 WLR 1420 at 1447). For reasons already given, I would hold that
they did transgress and would hold them liable to make good this sum.

Quantum

[50] The power of local authorities to dispose of land held by them under
s 32(1) of the Housing Act 1985 was subject to the consent of the Secretary of
State. By s 34(2) of that Act the Secretary of State's consent could be given
generally, and was so given by a ministerial letter issued in 1981 and continuing
to have effect under the 1985 Act by virtue of s 2(2) of the Housing (Consequential
Provisions) Act 1985. By para B(2) of this letter it was stated:

'A local authority may dispose of any house, if that house is vacant, to any
individual who intends to use it as his only or principal home, provided that
the disposal is effected for a price, consideration or rent which is equal to the
current market value of the house with vacant possession.'

It was also open to a local authority to dispose of properties at a discount of
between 30% and 70%, which is what the council in fact did.

[51] As explained by the Divisional Court in its judgment ((1997) 96 LGR 157
at 204), the auditor certified in accordance with s 20(1) of the 1982 Act that some
£31·67m was due jointly and severally from Dame Shirley Porter and Mr Weeks
(in addition, at that stage, to Mr Hartley, Mr England, Mr Phillips and another
officer). This was a net sum, arrived at by calculating the gross loss or deficiency
and then deducting from that figure the financial benefits enjoyed by the council
as a result of the sale of designated dwellings, such as the reduced cost of

a   management and maintenance of the council-owned housing stock. The net sum also allowed for interest on the net losses. Most of the items in the auditor's computation are not (subject to liability) in dispute. But there is one major issue: the treatment of the discounts allowed by the council on selling designated properties pursuant to what must, for present purposes, be treated as an unlawful policy. The auditor based his calculation on the open market value, with vacant *b*   possession, of the properties sold. He did not reduce his calculated figure of loss to reflect the discounted prices at which the council sold, and at which the council would have sold even if the policy had been a lawful one, if pursuant to a lawful policy the council would have sold at all. On this basis he reached a loss figure under this head of £15·476m.

    [52] Robert Walker LJ (with, as already noted, the assent of Kennedy LJ on
c   this point) took a different view. He said:

> 'In this case the relevant element of loss is the loss of part of the council's stock of social housing. It was not a loss in a commercial venture of selling dwellings with vacant possession. In my judgment the Divisional Court erred in its approach. It should have accepted the submission that there was
d   no loss if the discounted prices actually received by the council exceeded the value of the dwellings as tenanted social housing. There was ample evidence that the discounted prices did exceed that value, and it is not necessary to go into the subsidiary issue as to Ellis & Co.'s valuations. Any other approach would, it seems to me, be inconsistent with the auditor's separate investigation
e   and conclusion as to the additional costs of housing homeless persons which the council had to incur as a result of its own stock of social housing having been depleted by the designated sales policy.' (See [2000] 2 WLR 1420 at 1502.)

    On this basis he would have disallowed the full sum for which the auditor held Dame Shirley Porter and Mr Weeks liable under this head.

f   [53] Although the sum involved is very considerable, the point which divides the parties is (as it seems to me) a very narrow one. Should the prices at which the council actually sold be compared with the prices at which it would have sold if selling in lawful pursuance of its powers under s 32? If so, it has suffered no loss under this head. Or should the prices at which the council actually sold be compared with the open market value of the properties with vacant possession at
g   the time of sale? If so, it has suffered the loss certified by the auditor.

    [54] Section 20(1) of the 1982 Act provides for the certification by the auditor of the amount of a loss or deficiency incurred or caused by the wilful misconduct of any person. It is that amount which is due and recoverable for the benefit of the body which has suffered the loss or deficiency. The underlying principle is
h   one of compensation, to put the body which has suffered the loss or deficiency in the same position as it would have been in had the wilful misconduct which caused the loss or deficiency never occurred.

    [55] In this case the council was the freehold owner of a number of properties. The wilful misconduct of Dame Shirley Porter and Mr Weeks caused the sale of
j   some of those properties pursuant to an unlawful policy of designated sales. Thus the council parted with those properties. The council did not lose the full market value of the properties because it received discounted prices for them. But it lost the difference between the full market value of the properties and the discounted prices received. Had the council wished to replace the properties sold under the unlawful policy it would have had to pay the full market value of comparable properties. I do not think it is open to those responsible for an unlawful sales

policy to contend that if the properties had been sold under a lawful policy they
would have been sold at equally discounted prices since, if the policy of the   *a*
council had been lawful the council might never have sold the properties at all,
and it is in any event a matter for the owner of an asset to decide whether he will
exploit its value to the maximum extent or not. A wrongdoer is not entitled to
reap the benefit of a benign policy which might, but only might, have been
pursued by the owner had it not been unlawfully deprived of the asset.   *b*

[56] I do not for my part detect any element of double counting in the
auditor's calculation, which is in my opinion correct.

Impartiality, fairness and delay

[57] Before the Divisional Court and in the Court of Appeal, Dame Shirley
Porter and Mr Weeks challenged the impartiality of the auditor, the fairness of his   *c*
investigation and the time taken to carry out the audit. This challenge was very
fully considered by the Divisional Court, but failed both in that court and in the
Court of Appeal. The challenge has been further pursued before the House. It
must in my opinion be rejected for the detailed reasons given by my noble and
learned friend Lord Hope of Craighead.   *d*

[58] For all these reasons I would allow the auditor's appeal and restore his
certificate in the sum upheld by the Divisional Court. The parties (and Westminster
City Council, if so advised) are invited to make written submissions on costs.
I would in conclusion pay tribute to the clear and comprehensive judgment of the
Divisional Court.
e

LORD STEYN.

[59] My Lords, I am in complete agreement with the opinion of Lord Bingham
of Cornhill. I am also in complete agreement with the reasons given by my noble
and learned friend Lord Hope of Craighead in regard to the issues of impartiality,
fairness and delay. I would therefore also allow the auditor's appeal and restore   *f*
the certificate in the sum upheld by the Divisional Court.

LORD HOPE OF CRAIGHEAD.

[60] My Lords, I have had the advantage of reading in draft the speech of my
noble and learned friend Lord Bingham of Cornhill. I agree with all that he has
said on the issue of liability and, subject to some observations of my own, with   *g*
what he has said on the issue of quantum. I wish to concentrate in this speech
with the remaining issues in the case, which are those of impartiality, fairness and
delay.

Introduction   *h*

[61] In the Court of Appeal four matters were identified under the broad
heading of unfairness (see [2000] 2 WLR 1420 at 1453 per Schiemann LJ). These
were (a) apparent bias on the part of the auditor, (b) unreasonable delay on the
part both of the auditor and on the part of the Divisional Court in confirming the
decision by the auditor, (c) failure on the part of the Divisional Court to hold a   *j*
fair balance between the auditor and Dame Shirley Porter and (d) breach by the
Divisional Court of the presumption of innocence. The Court of Appeal was not
persuaded that there had been any unfairness which would justify allowing the
appeal.

[62] Before your Lordships the respondents have contended that the Court of
Appeal should have upheld their appeals on the ground that the proceedings were

a unfair, applying common law principles as understood before the coming into force of the relevant provisions of the Human Rights Act 1998. They also contend that the auditor violated their convention rights (European Convention for the Protection of Human Rights and Fundamental Freedoms 1950 (as set out in Sch 1 to the 1998 Act)) and that, as victims, they are entitled to rely directly on those rights under the 1998 Act. In addition they contend that the Divisional Court
b violated their convention rights, that these are legal proceedings brought by the auditor and they are entitled to rely on that violation in these proceedings under the Act. The main thrust of their contentions on the issue of unfairness was directed to their arguments that the auditor lacked the convention requirements of independence and impartiality, that he gave the appearance of bias contrary to the requirements of the common law and that there was unreasonable delay.

c [63] Before dealing with the substance of the points raised by these arguments I must first outline the statutory background and set out the facts. I shall then deal with a preliminary question which must be addressed. This is whether it is open to the respondents to rely directly on the provisions of the 1998 Act in this appeal. I shall explain why, notwithstanding the decision of this House in *R v*
d *Kansal (No 2)* [2001] UKHL 62, [2002] 1 All ER 257, [2001] 3 WLR 1562, I consider it appropriate to deal with the merits of the points which have been raised on the assumption that they can do so. As to the merits, I shall deal first with the questions relating to independence and impartiality and to the appearance of bias on the part of the auditor. I shall then deal with the issue of delay. Finally I shall deal with the points which have been raised about the conduct of the hearing by
e the Divisional Court.

The statutory background

[64] Provision has been made for many years in local government legislation to protect ratepayers against losses caused by unlawful expenditure or wilful
f misconduct on the part of members or senior officers of local authorities. Procedures were laid down for the audit of local authority accounts and, in the event of unlawful expenditure or wilful misconduct by of a member or senior officer, for the surcharge of that member or officer on a certificate given by the auditor. The provisions which were in force during the period to which this case relates were those in Pt III of the Local Government Finance Act 1982. These
g provisions were repealed by and re-enacted in the Audit Commission Act 1998, but I shall concentrate on those which are to be found in the 1982 Act.

[65] Prior to the coming into force of the 1982 Act local authorities and other bodies subject to audit were able to choose whether their accounts should be audited by a district auditor appointed by the Secretary of State or by a private
h auditor. The Layfield Committee of Inquiry into Local Government Finance considered that it was wrong in principle that any public body should be able to choose its own auditor. It recommended that the audit service should be made completely independent of both central government and local authorities, with a head of local audit reporting to a specially constituted higher institution ((Cmnd
j 6453), Ch 6, paras 18, 30–31). Section 11 of the 1982 Act provided for the establishment of a body to be known as the Audit Commission for Local Authorities in England and Wales. Section 12 provided that local authority accounts were in future to be subject to audit by an auditor or auditors appointed by the Commission. Section 13 provided that an auditor appointed by the Commission to audit the accounts might be an officer of the Commission, an individual with prescribed qualifications who was not such an officer or a firm of

such individuals. Section 14 provided that the Commission was to prepare and
keep under review a code of audit practice prescribing the way in which auditors *a*
were to carry out their functions under the Act. It was to be laid before Parliament
and approved by a resolution of each House. Section 15 sets out the general
duties of auditors when auditing accounts in accordance with Pt III of the Act.
Among these, in terms of sub-s (3), is the auditor's duty to consider whether in
the public interest he should make a report on any matter coming to his notice in *b*
the course of the audit.

[66] That, in brief, was the system under which Mr John Magill was appointed
by the Commission under ss 12 and 13 of the 1982 Act. His task was to audit the
council's accounts for the years 1987–1988 to 1994–1995. The Code of Audit
Practice for Local Authorities and the National Health Service in England and
Wales 1990 stated in para 10 that, in order that his opinions, conclusions, *c*
judgments and recommendations would be and would be seen to be impartial,
he was to maintain an independent and objective attitude of mind and ensure that
his independence was not impaired in any way. Paragraph 15 of the Code stated
that the audit was to be carried out in a professional and timely fashion. His
duties and powers in respect of hearing objections by local government electors *d*
and in regard to loss due to wilful misconduct were those set out in ss 17, 19 and
20 of the Act.

[67] Section 17(1) of the 1982 Act deals with the right of members of the public
to inspect the accounts to be audited and all books and other documents relating
to them, and sub-s (2) of the section provides that at the request of any local
government elector the auditor shall give the elector, or any representative of his, *e*
an opportunity to question him about the accounts. Section 17(3) and (4) provide:

> '(3) Subject to subsection (4) below, any local government elector ... or
> any representative of his, may attend before the auditor and make
> objections—(a) as to any matter in respect of which the auditor could take
> action under section 19 or 20 below; or (b) as to any other matter in respect *f*
> of which the auditor could make a report under section 15(3) above.
>
> (4) No objection may be made under subsection (3) above by or on behalf
> of a local government elector unless the auditor has previously received
> written notice of the proposed objection and of the grounds on which it is to
> be made.' *g*

[68] Section 19(1) of the Act provides that, where it appears to the auditor that
any item of account is contrary to law, he may apply to the court for a declaration
that the item of account was unlawful except where it is sanctioned by the
Secretary of State. Where the court is persuaded that it should make the declaration, *h*
it has power under s 19(2) to order any person responsible for incurring or
authorising the unlawful expenditure to repay it in whole or in part to the body
in question, if the expenditure exceeded £2,000 to order the person responsible
who was a member of a local authority to be disqualified from being a member
of a local authority and to order rectification of the accounts.

[69] Section 20(1) of the 1982 Act provides: *j*

> 'Where it appears to the auditor carrying out the audit of any accounts
> under this Part of this Act—(a) that any person has failed to bring into
> account any sum which should have been so included and that the failure has
> not been sanctioned by the Secretary of State; or (b) that a loss has been
> incurred or deficiency caused by the wilful misconduct of any person, he

a
shall certify that the sum or, as the case may be, the amount of the loss or the deficiency is due from that person and, subject to subsections (3) and (5) below, both he and the body in question (or, in the case of a parish meeting, the chairman of the meeting) may recover that sum or amount for the benefit of that body; and if the auditor certifies under this section that any sum or amount is due from two or more persons, they shall be jointly and
b
severally liable for that sum or amount.'

[70] Section 20(2)(b) of the 1982 Act provides that a person who is aggrieved by a decision of an auditor to certify under that section that a sum or amount is due from him may require the auditor to state in writing the reasons for his decision. Section 20(3) provides:

c
'Any such person who is aggrieved by such a decision may appeal against the decision to the court and—(a) in the case of a decision to certify that any sum or amount is due from any person, the court may confirm, vary or quash the decision and give any certificate which the auditor could have given; (b) in the case of a decision not to certify that any sum or amount is
d
due from any person, the court may confirm the decision or quash it and give any certificate which the auditor could have given; and any certificate given under this subsection shall be treated for the purposes of subsection (1) above and the following provisions of this section as if it had been given by the auditor under subsection (1) above.'

e
Section 20(4) provides for the disqualification of a member of a local authority if a certificate relates to a loss or deficiency caused by his wilful misconduct and the amount due from him exceeds £2,000.

The facts in outline

f
[71] This narrative begins where that set out in paras [4]–[18] of Lord Bingham's speech breaks off. Like him, I have taken much of it from the agreed statement of facts.

[72] By letters dated 18 and 20 July 1989 Cllr Neale Coleman, an opposition member of the Housing Committee, and a number of other local government electors made objections to the auditor under s 17(3) of the 1982 Act and invited
g
him to take action under ss 19 and 20 of the Act and to make a report in the public interest under s 15(3). Twenty-eight individuals were named or referred to in the objections as persons against whom the objectors invited the auditor to take action. They included the respondents Dame Shirley Porter and Mr Weeks. By letter dated 8 November 1989 Cllr Coleman made further submissions in support
h
of the original objection and added a further objection. Following receipt of the objections the auditor embarked on an investigation, the main stages of which were as follows.

[73] In October 1989 the auditor requested a formal response from the council to the initial objections. The council provided its formal response on
j
27 November 1989. On 5 December 1989 he asked the council if it wished to supplement that formal response to deal with the matters raised in the letter of 8 November. On 1 May 1990 the council provided its supplementary response to the auditor. During the period from June to December 1990 he carried out a review of the documentation at City Hall and obtained preliminary legal advice on matters arising from the objection. The documentation was extensive but it was incomplete, and he asked the council to provide further documents. In

December 1990 he commenced his programme of interviews. From January to
April 1991 he visited council offices to inspect further documents made available   *a*
by the council, requested further documents and continued his programme of
interviews. He completed his initial round of interviews in November 1992. He
reviewed the evidence which he had received by that date, obtained further legal
advice and in January 1993 began a second round of interviews which lasted from
January to July 1993. He found it necessary to conduct further interviews in   *b*
September and October 1993.

[74] On 29 September 1993, at the request of counsel and solicitors acting for
Dame Shirley Porter the auditor issued a preliminary provisional indication of net
expenditure and loss. He invited representations by 15 October 1993. Written
submissions on this preliminary indication were made on 15 October 1993 on
behalf of Dame Shirley Porter and on 27 October 1993 by Mr Weeks. On 13 January   *c*
1994 the auditor gave notice of his provisional findings to ten individuals and
provided copies of them to the objectors and to the council. He invited those
concerned to indicate whether they wished him to hold an oral hearing. He made
a public statement on the same date which representatives of the media were
invited to attend. This statement attracted widespread publicity. Recordings of   *d*
the auditor reading parts of the statement appeared on television news, and the
statement was referred to and discussed in Parliament and the media. Three
parties and the council, but not Dame Shirley Porter or Mr Weeks, then requested
the auditor to hold an oral hearing and the auditor agreed to do so. All parties
were informed on 25 March 1994 that there would be an oral hearing starting on
17 October 1994.   *e*

[75] The public statement by the auditor raised questions about his impartiality.
Solicitors for Mr Phillips and Dame Shirley Porter applied to the Audit Commission
on 29 March and 19 April 1994 to replace Mr Magill with a new auditor. The
Audit Commission refused to do so. At a preliminary meeting on June 1994
applications were made on behalf of Dame Shirley Porter and Mr Phillips that the   *f*
auditor should disqualify himself from further consideration of the objections.
On 7 October 1994 the auditor held a meeting to consider oral submissions on
this matter. Written representations in support of the application were made on
behalf of, among others, Mr Weeks. Further oral submissions were made on
behalf of Dame Shirley Porter on 17 October 1994. The auditor decided that he
should not disqualify himself. He gave his reasons in writing on 18 October 1994.   *g*

[76] The auditor held an audit hearing which sat for a total of 32 days between
19 October 1994 and 7 February 1995. He received further representations and
evidence after the hearing. On 17 August 1995 he circulated a revised provisional
calculation of net expenditure and loss. He invited representations on this
calculation by 5 October 1995. He received representations on it from the   *h*
objectors. The parties were informed by him that notification of the arrangements
for the issuing of his decision would be given on 21 March 1996. On 19 March
1996 the solicitors for Dame Shirley Porter wrote to the Audit Commission to
request an investigation into the auditor's conduct. On 16 April 1996 the Audit
Commission rejected her complaint. On 9 May 1996 the auditor issued his   *j*
decision on the objections, in which he issued certificates in the sum of £31·677m
against Dame Shirley Porter and Mr Weeks and four others. They appealed to
the Divisional Court. The appeal by one of the other four was stayed on the
ground of ill health. The appeals by Dame Shirley Porter and Mr Weeks and the
other three were heard between 1 October and 4 November 1997. On 19 December
1997 the Divisional Court dismissed their appeals but allowed the appeals by the

a three others. Their appeals to the Court of Appeal were heard between 22 and 26 March 1999. On 30 April 1999 the Court of Appeal allowed the appeals by Dame Shirley Porter and Mr Weeks.

[77] There are two key points in this history in regard to the respondent's argument about the fairness of the conduct of the proceedings by the auditor and the conduct of the Divisional Court when it dismissed their appeal. The first
b relates to the auditor's public statement on 13 January 1994. It is said that his conduct on this occasion gave rise to the appearance of bias on his part which could only be cured in the Divisional Court by quashing his certificate. The second relates to delay. The auditor issued his report and the certificate of surcharge on 9 May 1996. The respondents say that this was 15 months after the conclusion of the audit hearing on 7 February 1995, almost seven years after
c the objection was made on 18 July 1989, nearly nine years after the decision of the Housing Committee of 8 July 1987 against which the objection was taken and exactly ten years after start of the events following the local government elections on 8 May 1986. They contend that there had been such excessive delay that for the Divisional Court to quash the decision was the only appropriate remedy.

d
The 1998 Act

[78] The respondents' argument on unfairness was presented on the assumption that they were entitled under s 22(4) of the 1998 Act to rely in these proceedings on an alleged infringement of their convention rights by acts of the auditor and of the Divisional Court, all of which took place before the relevant sections of that
e Act were brought into force on 2 October 2000. It assumed that these are proceedings by or at the instance of Mr Magill as auditor, and that an auditor appointed by the Audit Commission under ss 12 and 13 of the 1982 Act was a public authority within the meaning of s 6(1) of the 1998 Act. It also assumed that s 22(4), which states that s 7(1)(b) applies to proceedings by or at the instigation of a public authority whenever the act in question took place, applies to an appeal
f in these proceedings.

[79] Mr Howell did not challenge the proposition, which I would accept, that an auditor appointed by the Audit Commission to audit the accounts of a local authority is a public authority. But he submitted that the proceedings which were conducted by the auditor and by the Divisional Court in the appeal to that
g court under s 20(3) of the 1982 Act were proceedings by or at the instigation of the objectors and not the auditor. He also submitted, following observations which I made in *R v Lambert* [2001] UKHL 37, [2001] 3 All ER 577, [2001] 3 WLR 206, that the acts of the Divisional Court which were complained of were outside the scope of s 7(1)(b) of the 1998 Act as they were acts of a court. I would reject
h both of these arguments.

[80] As to the first point, the function of the auditor under Pt III of the 1982 Act is to audit the accounts which require to be audited. It is his duty to satisfy himself by examination of the accounts and otherwise that the requirements of the statute have been complied with, that proper practices have been observed
j and proper arrangements have been made to obtain value for money in the use of resources (s 15(1)). He must also consider whether, in the public interest, he should make a report on any matter coming to his notice in the course of the audit in order that it may be considered by the body concerned or brought to the attention of the public (s 15(3)). He has power under ss 19 and 20 to declare an item of account unlawful and to recover a loss incurred or deficiency caused by wilful misconduct irrespective of whether there has been any objection to the

accounts. It is in that context that the right of any local government elector under
s 17(3) to attend before the auditor and make objections as to any matter in *a*
respect of which he could take action under ss 19 or 20, or as to any matter in respect
of which he could make a report under s 15(3), must be seen. The essence of
these proceedings, from start to finish, is that they are proceedings by the auditor.

[81] As to the second point, it has now been held in *R v Kansal (No 2)* [2002]
1 All ER 257, [2001] 3 WLR 1562 that s 7(1)(b) of the 1998 Act applies to acts of *b*
courts and tribunals in the same way as it applies to acts of other public
authorities. There has been no suggestion that the acts of the Divisional Court
which are complained of are acts to which s 6(2) of that Act applies. It has not
been argued that, as the result of primary legislation, the court could not have
acted differently or it was acting so as to give effect to primary legislation which
could not be read or given effect in a way which was compatible with the *c*
respondents' convention rights. It follows that the acts of the Divisional Court
which are under challenge are in the same position in this respect as the acts of
the auditor.

[82] There remains however the question whether the benefit of retrospectivity
under s 22(4) of the 1998 Act is available at the stage of an appeal. The hearing of *d*
this appeal took place before judgment was delivered in *R v Kansal (No 2)*. In that
case it was held that s 22(4) does not apply to an appeal against a conviction which
took place before 2 October 2000. One of the points which I made in my
dissenting judgment was that I did not see how it would be possible to confine
the decision in that case to criminal cases only (see [2002] 1 All ER 257 at [48]).
But this point has yet to be decided in a civil appeal, and it is perhaps still open to *e*
argument. As your Lordships did not hear any argument on it, I would prefer to
approach the respondents' submissions as to fairness on the assumption that they
are entitled to rely on their convention rights in this appeal irrespective of the fact
that all the acts in question took place before 2 October 2000.

f

Whether the proceedings are civil or criminal

[83] On the assumption that they were entitled in this appeal to rely on their
convention rights, the respondents submitted that in substance the proceedings
under s 20 of the 1982 Act were in the nature of a criminal charge. This argument
was considered and rejected by the auditor. It was also rejected by the Divisional
Court, which held that English law treats the matter as one of civil not criminal *g*
liability ((1997) 96 LGR 157 at 171). Schiemann LJ did not mention the question
of classification when he was dealing in the Court of Appeal with the issues of
fairness ([2000] 2 WLR 1420 at 1453–1463). But this question was addressed by
Mr McMullen in the course of his argument in this House, and it is the subject of
detailed submissions in his written case. The Strasbourg cases were reviewed by *h*
Lord Bingham of Cornhill in *McIntosh v Lord Advocate* [2001] UKPC D1 at
[16]–[28], [2001] 2 All ER 638 at [16]–[28], [2001] 3 WLR 107, where the issue was
whether a person against whom an application had been made for a confiscation
order was, by virtue of that application, charged with a criminal offence (see also
Phillips v UK (2001) 11 BHRC 280). *j*

[84] For the purposes of the convention the category into which the proceedings
are placed by domestic law, while relevant, is not the only consideration. The
court is required to look at the substance of the matter rather than its form, to
look behind the appearances and to investigate the realities of the procedure (see
Deweer v Belgium (1980) 2 EHRR 439 at 458 (para 44)). The nature of the offence
and the nature and degree of severity of the sanction must be taken into account

a also. As to the sanction, the question is whether, by reason of its nature and degree of severity, it amounts to a penalty in the sense of punishment (see *Engel v Netherlands* (1976) 1 EHRR 647 at 678–679 (paras 82, 83); *Lutz v Germany* (1987) 10 EHRR 182 at 197 (para 54); *Demicoli v Malta* (1991) 14 EHRR 47 at 62–63 (para 34)). For example, *Engel's* case concerned proceedings in a military court for disciplinary offences for which one of the sanctions liable to be imposed as b punishment was deprivation of liberty. In *Demicoli v Malta* (1991) 14 EHRR 47 too the applicant was at risk of imprisonment if the fine was not paid. In *AP, MP and TP v Switzerland* (1997) 26 EHRR 541 at 559 (para 42), the court said that it attached great weight to the domestic court's finding that the fine in question was penal in character and depended on the 'guilt' of the offending taxpayer. In *DC, HS and AD v UK* [2000] BCC 710 the European Court held that proceedings for the c disqualification of directors on the ground of unfitness under s 6 of the Company Directors Disqualification Act 1986 were inherently regulatory in character, and that for this reason they could not be said to involve the determination of a criminal charge within the meaning of art 6(1) of the convention.

[85] I consider that the nature of the proceedings under s 20 of the 1982 Act is d compensatory and regulatory, not punitive. Section 20(1) provides that the amount certifiable by the auditor, where it appears to him that a loss has been incurred or deficiency caused by wilful misconduct, is the amount of the loss or deficiency and that both he and the body in question may recover that amount for the benefit of that body. The object of the procedure is to compensate the body concerned, and the measure of the compensation is the amount of the loss e suffered. In the present case the amount certified was very large, but the nature of the proceedings does not alter depending on the amount certified. No fine is involved, nor does the section provide for a penalty by way of imprisonment. Section 20(4) provides for the respondents' disqualification from being members of a local authority. But this outcome is similar to that where a trustee is removed f after being found to have been in serious breach of trust, or a person is disqualified from acting as a director of a company. In my opinion measures of the kind provided for by s 20, which apply to persons having a special status or responsibility and are compensatory and regulatory rather than penal in character, lie outside the criminal sphere for the purposes of art 6 of the convention.

[86] For these reasons I would hold that s 20 of the 1982 Act does not involve g the making of a criminal charge within the meaning of art 6. But that does not mean that the respondents lack protection. They are entitled to all the protections afforded to them by art 6(1), the first sentence of which provides that in the determination of his civil rights and obligations everyone is entitled to a fair and public hearing within a reasonable time by an independent and impartial h tribunal established by law.

The independence and impartiality of the auditor
[87] The protections which art 6(1) lays down are that—

j 'In the determination of his civil rights and obligations ... everyone is entitled to a fair and public hearing within a reasonable time by an independent and impartial tribunal established by law.'

As I shall explain later when dealing with delay, I consider that this sentence creates a number of rights which, although closely related, can and should be considered separately. The rights to a fair hearing, to a public hearing and to a hearing within a reasonable time are separate and distinct rights from the right to a hearing before an independent and impartial tribunal established by law. This means that a complaint that one of these rights was breached cannot be answered by showing that the other rights were not breached. Although the overriding question is whether there was a fair trial, it is no answer to a complaint that the tribunal was not independent or was not impartial to show that it conducted a fair hearing within a reasonable time and that the hearing took place in public (see *Millar v Dickson* 2001 SLT 988 at 994 per Lord Bingham of Cornhill and my own observations (at 1003) in that case). Under this heading the question is whether the auditor lacked the independence and impartiality which is required by art 6(1).

[88] There is a close relationship between the concept of independence and that of impartiality. In *Findlay v UK* (1997) 24 EHRR 221 at 244–245 (para 73) the European Court said:

'The Court recalls that in order to establish whether a tribunal can be considered as "independent", regard must be had *inter alia* to the manner of appointment of its members and their term of office, the existence of guarantees against outside pressures and the question whether the body presents an appearance of independence. As to the question of "impartiality", there are two aspects to this requirement. First, the tribunal must be subjectively free from personal prejudice or bias. Secondly, it must also be impartial from an objective viewpoint, that is, it must offer sufficient guarantees to exclude any legitimate doubt in this respect. The concepts of independence and objective impartiality are closely linked ...'

In both cases the concept requires not only that the tribunal must be truly independent and free from actual bias, proof of which is likely to be very difficult, but also that it must not appear in the objective sense to lack these essential qualities.

[89] I shall leave over to the next heading the question whether the auditor's public statement on 13 January 1994 showed that he lacked the appearance of impartiality for the purposes of the art 6(1) convention right. At this stage the matter for consideration is the respondents' complaint that the circumstances and nature of his appointment and the investigation which he then conducted were such that the requirements of independence and impartiality in his case were not satisfied. At the heart of the argument is the multiplicity of roles which were being performed by the auditor. The respondents say that the procedure which he adopted on receipt of the objections violated their convention right because he acted as investigator, prosecutor and judge in the investigation which he carried out. He conducted the investigation, took the decision whether there was a case to answer, tried the case, assessed the loss and then appeared in the Divisional Court to defend his decision and his conduct.

[90] The Divisional Court said ((1997) 96 LGR 157 at 168) that the 1982 Act imposes on the auditor the roles of investigator, prosecutor and judge which might be thought an almost impossible burden, and it referred to the recommendation in para 223 of the *Third Report of the Nolan Committee on Standards in Public Life: Standards of Conduct in Local Government in England, Scotland and Wales* (1997) (Cm 3702-1), which has now been implemented for England and Wales by Pt III of the Local Government Act 2000, that surcharging by an auditor be abolished and replaced by other remedies. The court said (at 169), after reviewing his conduct of the hearing, that it was not persuaded that the auditor's final conclusions could be impeached on the grounds of unfairness. But

a (at 172), it said that it appeared to it that the roles which the auditor played would
   not meet the requirements of independence and apparent impartiality demanded
   by the convention.

   [91] In my opinion the conduct of the auditor requires to be looked at as a
   whole and in the context of the procedure which is laid down in the statute.
   Part III of the 1982 Act starts, as one would expect, by placing the responsibility
b for auditing the accounts on the auditor. It seeks to ensure his independence
   from the body whose accounts he is auditing by requiring in ss 12 and 13 that his
   appointment is to be by the Audit Commission and not by the body itself. His
   responsibilities include making reports under s 15 on any matter coming to his
   notice in the course of the audit and dealing with objections made by any local
   government elector under s 17. Where objections are made, it is his duty to
c consider under s 17(3) whether they relate to any matter in respect of which he
   could take action under s 19 (items contrary to law) or s 20 (wilful misconduct) or
   to any matter in respect of which he could make a report under s 15. The Act
   does not enable him to pass this responsibility to someone else. It is his duty, as
   the person in charge of the audit within the context of which the objections are
d made, to deal with them himself and, if they are well founded, to take such action
   as he is required to take on them by the statute. The auditing process, which is
   in his hands, is not complete until this has been done.

   [92] That being the structure of the procedure laid down by the statute, there is
   inevitably some force in the criticism that, where accusations of wilful misconduct
   are involved, the auditor is being required to act not only as an investigator but also
e as prosecutor and as judge. But this problem has been recognised and dealt with in
   s 20(3). It provides not only that any person aggrieved by his decision may appeal
   against the decision to the court but also that the court 'may confirm, vary or
   quash the decision and give any certificate which the auditor could have given'.
   The solution to the problem which s 20(3) provides is that of a complete
f rehearing by the Divisional Court. The court can exercise afresh all the powers
   of decision which were given to the auditor. In Lloyd v McMahon [1987] 1 All ER
   1118 at 1157, [1987] AC 625 at 697 Lord Keith of Kinkel said that, while there
   might be extreme cases where it would be appropriate to quash the auditor's
   decision, the court has a discretion, where it considers that justice can properly
   be done by its own investigation of the merits, to follow that course.

g [93] In Kingsley v UK (7 November 2000, unreported) the European Court said
   in para 51 that, even if an adjudicatory body determining disputes over 'civil
   rights and obligations' does not comply with art 6(1), there is no breach of the
   article if the proceedings before that body are subject to subsequent control by a
   judicial body that has full jurisdiction and does provide the guarantes of art 6(1);
h see also Bryan v UK (1995) 21 EHRR 342 at 360–361 (paras 44 and 46). The court
   went on to say this in Kingsley's case (para 58):

       'The court considers that it is generally inherent in the notion of judicial
       review that, if a ground of challenge is upheld, the reviewing court has
       power to quash the impugned decision, and that either the decision will be
j   taken by the review court, or the case will be remitted for a fresh decision by
       the same or a different body. Thus where, as here, complaint is made of a
       lack of impartiality on the part of the decision-making body, the concept of
       "full jurisdiction" involves that the reviewing court not only considers the
       complaint but has the ability to quash the impugned decision and to remit
       the case for a new decision by an impartial body.'

The powers which the Divisional Court has been given by s 20(3) fully satisfy
these requirements. Not only does it have power to quash the decision taken by   *a*
the auditor. It has power to rehear the case, and to take a fresh decision itself in
the exercise of the powers given to the auditor. In *R (on the application of Alconbury
Developments Ltd) v Secretary of State for the Environment, Transport and the Regions*
[2001] UKHL 23 at [52], [2001] 2 All ER 929 at [52], [2001] 2 WLR 1389 at [52] Lord
Slynn of Hadley observed that the principle of judicial control did not go so far as   *b*
to provide for a complete rehearing on the merits of the decision. In the case of
the procedure governed by s 20(3) however a rehearing on the merits can be
conducted, and that is what was done in this case.

[94] In these circumstances it is not necessary to examine the various grounds
on which the procedure adopted by the auditor was criticised. The issue at this
stage is whether the Divisional Court satisfied the requirements of art 6(1) in   *c*
regard to the scope of the jurisdiction which it was entitled to exercise. I would
answer this question in the affirmative. There has been no suggestion that the
proceedings in that court, which were conducted with conspicuous care and
attention to detail, lacked the appearance of independence and impartiality. In
my opinion those elements of the respondents' art 6(1) convention rights were   *d*
fully protected by the proceedings in the Divisional Court, having regard to the
powers which that court was entitled to exercise.

Apparent bias

[95] I turn now to the question whether the auditor's certificate should have
been quashed on the ground of apparent bias. The respondents submit that the   *e*
way in which the auditor conducted himself when he made his statement on
13 January 1994 indicated an appearance of bias on his part which affected all
stages of his investigation both before and after that date. Both the art 6(1)
convention right to an independent and impartial tribunal and the respondents'
rights to an unbiased judge at common law as it was understood before the   *f*
coming into effect of the relevant provisions of the Human Rights Act 1998 are
invoked under this heading.

[96] As I have said, the statement which the auditor made on 13 January 1994
received considerable publicity on television and in the newspapers. The
Divisional Court saw video recordings of the relevant item on the 1 pm and 9 pm
BBC TV news. The following description of the event is given in its judgment: *g*

'... a televised announcement was arranged at which the auditor himself
appeared and, although he said that his views were provisional, he expressed
them in florid language and supported them by reference to the thoroughness
of the investigation which he claimed to have carried out. There was a   *h*
further feature of the event which should have had no place in the middle of
a quasi-judicial inquiry. A stack of ring binders on the desk at which the
auditor sat bearing the name of his firm for the benefit of the cameras was,
ostensibly, under the protection of a security guard: unless it was being
implied that the persons under investigation might wish to steal the documents,
it is not clear what was the purpose of this posturing.' (See (1997) 96 LGR   *j*
157 at 173.)

[97] In the reasons which he gave on 18 October 1994 for deciding not to
disqualify himself the auditor said that he was mindful of the serious nature of the
allegations made against the respondents, that he had been careful to give them
a full opportunity to respond to these allegations and his provisional findings, that

a he retained an open mind and that he was not biased against any individual or the
council. He went on to say:

'114. I am not biased. I have acted fairly and will continue to do so. I will
exercise impartial, independent and objective judgment. I will reach a decision
on the evidence and submissions before me. I will not reach any decision adverse
to the council and/or to any respondent unless I am satisfied on the basis of
b the evidence that I am under a duty to do so. All parties will get a fair hearing
from me.

115. In my consideration of the disqualification application, I have sought
to apply the test formulated in *R v Gough* ([1993] 2 All ER 724, [1993] AC 646),
namely '*whether, in all the circumstances of the case, there appeared to be a real
danger of bias …*'. In my view, a person having ascertained the relevant
c circumstances would not consider that I will regard unfairly any person's
case with disfavour. It has been suggested that I will find it difficult to depart
from my provisional findings and views because of the publicity given to
these. I feel no such inhibition. Nor, in my view, is there any ground on
which I should reasonably be thought to be so inhibited. I have always made
d it plain that before reaching any conclusion I will consider any representations
made to me. In my view, that is a process which necessarily conveys to any
reasonable person the point that my conclusions may not coincide with my
provisional findings and views. My view is that no real danger of bias exists
and nor is there any other basis on which I should disqualify myself.'

e [98] The Divisional Court set out its conclusions on this issue in this way:

'In the light of the material before us, including, in particular, the auditor's
reasons for declining to recuse himself, we accept that, despite such inferences
to the contrary as might have been drawn from the press conference, the
auditor did have an open mind and was justified in continuing with the
f subsequent hearings. We note that he did not confirm his preliminary
findings in respect of those who gave evidence at those hearings. The error
of judgment which we find he made, in holding the press conference as he
did, did not, in our view, demonstrate bias on his part. He was at pains to
stress the provisional nature of his findings and it is pertinent that in his final
decision he made no finding of wilful misconduct against three people in
g relation to whom he had, provisionally, been minded so to find. In any
event, as with the investigation, any possible unfairness to the appellants has
been cured by the hearing before us.' (See (1997) 96 LGR 157 at 174.)

[99] The test for apparent bias which the auditor sought to apply to himself,
h and was applied in its turn by the Divisional Court, was that which was described
in *R v Gough* [1993] 2 All ER 724 at 737–738, [1993] AC 646 at 670 by Lord Goff of
Chieveley where he said:

'I think it unnecessary, in formulating the appropriate test, to require that
the court should look at the matter through the eyes of a reasonable man,
j because the court in cases such as these personifies the reasonable man; and
in any event the court has first to ascertain the relevant circumstances from
the available evidence, knowledge of which would not necessarily be
available to an observer in court at the relevant time. Finally, for the
avoidance of doubt, I prefer to state the test in terms of real danger rather
than real likelihood, to ensure that the court is thinking of possibility rather
than probability of bias. Accordingly, having ascertained the relevant

circumstances, the court should ask itself whether, having regard to those
circumstances, there was a real danger of bias on the part of the relevant
member of the tribunal in question, in the sense that he might unfairly
regard (or have unfairly regarded) with favour, or disfavour, the case of a
party to the issue under consideration by him ...'

[100] The 'reasonable likelihood' and 'real danger' tests which Lord Goff
described in *R v Gough* have been criticised by the High Court of Australia on the
ground that they tend to emphasise the court's view of the facts and to place
inadequate emphasis on the public perception of the irregular incident (see *Webb v R*
(1994) 181 CLR 41 at 50 per Mason CJ and McHugh J). There is an uneasy tension
between these tests and that which was adopted in Scotland by the High Court
of Justiciary in *Bradford v McLeod* 1986 SLT 244. Following Eve J's reference in
Law v Chartered Institute of Patent Agents [1919] 2 Ch 276, [1918–19] All ER Rep Ext
1237 (which was not referred to in *R v Gough*), the High Court of Justiciary
adopted a test which looked at the question whether there was suspicion of bias
through the eyes of the reasonable man who was aware of the circumstances (see
also *Millar v Dickson* 2001 SLT 988 at 1002–1003). This approach, which has been
described as 'the reasonable apprehension of bias' test, is in line with that adopted
in most common law jurisdictions. It is also in line with that which the
Strasbourg court has adopted, which looks at the question whether there was a
risk of bias objectively in the light of the circumstances which the court has
identified: *Piersack v Belgium* (1982) 5 EHRR 169 at 179–180 (paras 30–31); *De Cubber v
Belgium* (1984) 7 EHRR 236 at 246 (para 30); *Pullar v UK* (1996) 22 EHRR 391
at 402–403 (para 30). In *Hauschildt v Denmark* (1989) 12 EHRR 266 at 279 (para 48)
the court also observed that, in considering whether there was a legitimate
reason to fear that a judge lacks impartiality, the standpoint of the accused is
important but not decisive: 'What is decisive is whether this fear can be held
objectively justified.'

[101] The English courts have been reluctant, for obvious reasons, to depart
from the test which Lord Goff so carefully formulated in *R v Gough*. In *R v Bow
Street Metropolitan Stipendiary Magistrate, ex p Pinochet Ugarte (No 2)* [1999] 1 All ER
577 at 589, [2000] 1 AC 119 at 136 Lord Browne-Wilkinson said that it was
unnecessary in that case to determine whether it needed to be reviewed in the
light of subsequent decisions in Canada, New Zealand and Australia. I said that,
although the tests in Scotland and England were described differently, their
application was likely in practice to lead to results that were so similar as to be
indistinguishable (see [1999] 1 All ER 577 at 595, [2000] 1 AC 119 at 142). The
Court of Appeal, having examined the question whether the 'real danger' test
might lead to a different result from that which the informed observer would
reach on the same facts, concluded in *Locabail (UK) Ltd v Bayfield Properties Ltd,
Locabail (UK) Ltd v Waldorf Investment Corp, Timmins v Gormley, Williams v HM
Inspector of Taxes, R v Bristol Betting and Gaming Licensing Committee, ex p O'Callaghan*
[2000] 1 All ER 65 at 74, [2000] QB 451 at 477 (para 17) that in the overwhelming
majority of cases the application of the two tests would lead to the same outcome.

[102] In my opinion however it is now possible to set this debate to rest. The
Court of Appeal took the opportunity in *In re Medicaments and Related Classes of
Goods (No 2)* [2001] 1 WLR 700 to reconsider the whole question. Lord Phillips of
Worth Matravers MR, giving the judgment of the court, observed (at 711
(para 35)), that the precise test to be applied when determining whether a
decision should be set aside on account of bias had given rise to difficulty,

a reflected in judicial decisions that had appeared in conflict, and that the attempt to resolve that conflict in *R v Gough* [1993] 2 All ER 724, [1993] AC 646 had not commanded universal approval. He said (at 711 (para 35) that, as the alternative test had been thought to be more closely in line with Strasbourg jurisprudence which since 2 October 2000 the English courts were required to take into account, the occasion should now be taken to review *R v Gough* to see whether

b the test it lays down is, indeed, in conflict with Strasbourg jurisprudence. Having conducted that review he summarised the court's conclusions (at 726–727 (para 85)):

> 'When the Strasbourg jurisprudence is taken into account, we believe that a modest adjustment of the test in *R v Gough* is called for, which makes it
c > plain that it is, in effect, no different from the test applied in most of the Commonwealth and in Scotland. The court must first ascertain all the circumstances which have a bearing on the suggestion that the judge was biased. It must then ask whether those circumstances would lead a fair-minded and informed observer to conclude that there was a real possibility,
d > or a real danger, the two being the same, that the tribunal was biased.'

[103] I respectfully suggest that your Lordships should now approve the modest adjustment of the test in *R v Gough* set out in that paragraph. It expresses in clear and simple language a test which is in harmony with the objective test which the Strasbourg court applies when it is considering whether the circumstances

e give rise to a reasonable apprehension of bias. It removes any possible conflict with the test which is now applied in most Commonwealth countries and in Scotland. I would however delete from it the reference to 'a real danger'. Those words no longer serve a useful purpose here, and they are not used in the jurisprudence of the Strasbourg court. The question is whether the fair-minded

f and informed observer, having considered the facts, would conclude that there was a real possibility that the tribunal was biased.

[104] Turning to the facts, there are two points that need to be made at the outset. The first relates to the auditor's own assertion that he was not biased. The Divisional Court said ((1997) 96 LGR 157 at 174) that it had had particular regard to his reasons for declining to recuse himself in reaching its conclusion that

g he had an open mind and was justified in continuing with the subsequent hearings. I would agree that the reasons that he gave were relevant, but an examination of them shows that they consisted largely of assertions that he was unbiased. Looking at the matter from the standpoint of the fair-minded and informed observer, protestations of that kind are unlikely to be helpful. I think

h that Schiemann LJ adopted the right approach in the Court of Appeal when he said that he would give no weight to the auditor's reasons (see [2000] 2 WLR 1420 at 1457). The second point relates to the emphasis which the respondents place on how the auditor's conduct appeared from the standpoint of the complainer. There is, as I have said, some support in the jurisprudence of the Strasbourg court

j for the proposition that the standpoint of the complainer is important. But in *Hauschildt v Denmark* (1989) 12 EHRR 266 at 279 (para 48) the court emphasised that what is decisive is whether any fears expressed by the complainer are objectively justified. The complainer's fears are clearly relevant at the initial stage when the court has to decide whether the complaint is one that should be investigated. But they lose their importance once the stage is reached of looking at the matter objectively.

[105] I think that it is plain, as the Divisional Court observed (at 174), that the auditor made an error of judgment when he decided to make his statement in public at a press conference. The main impression which this would have conveyed to the fair-minded observer was that the purpose of this exercise was to attract publicity to himself, and perhaps also to his firm. It was an exercise in self-promotion in which he should not have indulged. But it is quite another matter to conclude from this that there was a real possibility that he was biased. Schiemann LJ said (at 1457) that there was room for a casual observer to form the view after the press conference that the auditor might be biased. Nevertheless he concluded (at 1457), having examined the facts more closely, that there was no real danger that this was so. I would take the same view. The question is what the fair-minded and informed observer would have thought, and whether his conclusion would have been that there was real possibility of bias. The auditor's conduct must be seen in the context of the investigation which he was carrying out, which had generated a great deal of public interest. A statement as to his progress would not have been inappropriate. His error was to make it at a press conference. This created the risk of unfair reporting, but there was nothing in the words he used to indicate that there was a real possibility that he was biased. He was at pains to point out to the press that his findings were provisional. There is no reason to doubt his word on this point, as his subsequent conduct demonstrates. I would hold, looking at the matter objectively, that a real possibility that he was biased has not been demonstrated.

Unreasonable delay

[106] The respondents' argument under this heading is directed to their art 6(1) convention right to the determination of their civil rights and obligations within a reasonable time. They contend that the auditor was guilty of inordinate delay in breach of the art 6(1) requirement and that they were at an unfair disadvantage due to delay when they were giving evidence before the Divisional Court. They also submit, under reference to constitutional provisions considered by the Privy Council, that they had a right to a determination within a reasonable time at common law which did not require them to demonstrate actual prejudice (see *Bell v DPP of Jamaica* [1985] 2 All ER 585, [1985] AC 937; *DPP v Tokai* [1996] AC 856, [1996] 3 WLR 149). The Divisional Court held ((1997) 96 LGR 157 at 169) that the test at common law was whether delay had given rise to such prejudice that no fair trial could be held (see *Tan v Cameron* [1993] 2 All ER 493, [1992] 2 AC 205 at 222–224, per Lord Mustill). In its judgment no such prejudice was shown, and in the Court of Appeal Schiemann LJ was of the same opinion (see [2000] 2 WLR 1420 at 1459). The respondents say that the approach taken by these courts was wrong in law, as there was no requirement to show actual prejudice. The nature of the common law right which they asserted in your Lordships' House appeared to me to be virtually indistinguishable in this respect from the right under art 6(1), so I do not need to dwell on this part of their argument. I shall deal with the issue of delay on the assumption that the test which they must satisfy is that which requires to be satisfied to demonstrate that there was a breach of the convention right and that prejudice, while relevant if it exists, does not require to be demonstrated.

[107] In their overall complaint about delay they have included the time which elapsed from the local government elections on 8 May 1986 and the decision of the Housing Committee on 8 July 1987. The period that has elapsed since the event in question may be a relevant factor when considering the

a question whether the delay was unreasonable. But they accept that the obligation under the convention relates only to the conduct of the proceedings. Time usually begins to run in civil cases for the purposes of art 6(1) from the date when the proceedings in question are initiated (see *Ausiello v Italy* (1996) 24 EHRR 568 at 571 (para 18)). I would hold that time began to run in this case from the date when the objections which gave rise to the investigation were received by the
b auditor, and that it includes the stage of the appeal to the Divisional Court. The period under review can therefore be divided into four distinct periods: (a) that from the receipt of the original objection on 18 July 1989 to the issuing by the auditor of his provisional views on 13 January 1994; (b) that from 13 January 1994 to the end of the audit hearing on 7 February 1995; (c) that from 7 February 1995 to the issuing by the auditor of his decision and the certificates of surcharge on
c 9 May 1996; and (d) that from 9 May 1996 to the decision of the Divisional Court, which was given on 19 December 1997. No complaint is made about any delay after that date.

[108] I would also hold that the right in art 6(1) to a determination within a reasonable time is an independent right, and that it is to be distinguished from the
d art 6(1) right to a fair trial. As I have already indicated, that seems to me to follow from the wording of the first sentence of the article which creates a number of rights which, although closely related, can and should be considered separately. This means that it is no answer to a complaint that one of these rights was breached that the other rights were not. To take a simple example, the fact that the hearing took place in public does not deprive the applicant of his right to a
e hearing before an independent and impartial tribunal established by law.

[109] I would respectfully follow Lord Steyn's observation in *Darmalingum v State* [2001] 1 WLR 2303 about the effect of s 10(1) of the Constitution of Mauritius when he said that the reasonable time requirement is a separate guarantee. It is not to be seen simply as part of the overriding right to a fair trial, nor does it
f require the person concerned to show that he has been prejudiced by the delay. In *Flowers v R* [2000] 1 WLR 2396 a differently constituted Board, following *Bell v DPP of Jamaica* [1985] 2 All ER 585, [1985] AC 937, held that prejudice was one of four factors to be taken into account in considering the right to a fair hearing within a reasonable time in s 20(1) of the Constitution of Jamaica. In the context
g of art 6(1) of the convention, however, the way this right was construed in *Darmalingum's* case seems to me to be preferable. In *Crummock (Scotland) Ltd v HM Advocate* 2000 SLT 677 at 679, Lord Weir, delivering the opinion of the High Court of Justiciary, said that under art 6(1) it was not necessary for an accused to show that prejudice has been, or is likely to be, caused, as a result of delay. The art 6(1) guarantee of a hearing within a reasonable time is not subject to any
h words of limitation, nor is this a case where other rights than those expressly stated are being read into the article as implied rights which are capable of modification on grounds of proportionality (see *Brown v Stott (Procurator Fiscal, Dunfermline)* [2001] 2 All ER 97 at 131, [2001] 2 WLR 817 at 851; *R (on the application of Pretty) v DPP* [2001] UKHL 61 at [90], [2002] 1 All ER 1 at [90], [2001]
j 3 WLR 1598). The only question is whether, having regard to all the circumstances of the case, the time taken to determine the person's rights and obligations was unreasonable.

[110] In *König v Federal Republic of Germany* (1978) 2 EHHR 170 at 197 (para 99) the European Court gave the following guidance as to the test to be applied in civil proceedings on the question of delay:

'The reasonableness of the duration of proceedings covered by Article 6(1) of the Convention must be assessed in each case according to its circumstances. When enquiring into the reasonableness of the duration of criminal proceedings, the Court has had regard, *inter alia*, to the complexity of the case, to the applicant's conduct and to the manner in which the matter was dealt with by the administrative and judicial authorities. The Court, like those appearing before it, considers that the same criteria must serve in the present case as the basis for its examination of the question whether the duration of the proceedings before the administrative courts exceeded the reasonable time stipulated by Article 6(1).'

[111] Applying this test to the facts, it will be convenient to examine separately the conduct of the auditor and that of the Divisional Court. I start with *c* the Divisional Court. It seems to me that there is no basis whatever for the suggestion that there was an unreasonable delay at this stage. The auditor issued his certificate in May 1996. It was not until December 1996 that the respondents filed their evidence on the main issues. The accounting evidence was not filed until April 1997. A procedural hearing was heard shortly afterwards in May 1997. *d* The case proceeded to a hearing in the Divisional Court in October 1997, which lasted for 23 days. Judgment was given on 19 December 1997. I would conclude without any difficulty, having regard to the complexity of the issues and the volume of evidence that had to be prepared and presented, that the proceedings in that court were concluded within a reasonable time.

[112] As for the conduct of the investigation by the auditor, there is a much *e* more extended timetable. A period of about three-and-a-half years elapsed between the receipt of the first objection in July 1989 and the issuing of the provisional findings in January 1994. A further period of about two years and five months then elapsed before he issued his decision and the certificates of surcharge. But this brief narrative has to be seen in the light of the nature of the *f* exercise on which he was engaged. The Divisional Court described his investigation as vast (see (1997) 96 LGR 157 at 161). It referred (at 169) to its mammoth nature, bearing in mind that the objections related to 28 individuals. I do not need to go over the details which are set out in the agreed statement of facts. I have already provided my own summary in an earlier part of this judgment, and some further details are given by the Divisional Court (see (1997) *g* 96 LGR 157 at 161–162, 168).

[113] In my opinion the most striking feature which emerges from all the facts relating to the conduct of the investigation by the auditor is that, far from causing delay by inaction, he was constantly in action. He was seeking out information wherever it could be found, often with considerable difficulty. He was interviewing *h* and re-interviewing many witnesses, recovering and perusing thousands of documents, calculating amounts of loss and expenditure and then gathering all this information together into a decision which eventually extended to almost 2,000 pages including the appendices. It has been suggested that his investigation was over-elaborate. There are comments to that effect in the Divisional Court's *j* judgment (see (1997) 96 LGR 157 at 161). But the auditor had to form his own judgment on this matter. He had to take account of the importance of the exercise to all parties, including those who were at risk of being surcharged, and he was entitled to have regard to its obvious political sensitivity. I would attach particular significance to these factors and to the fact that it has not been suggested that the auditor caused delay at any stage by inactivity.

a [114] Applying the test described in *König's* case (1978) 2 EHRR 170 at 197 (para 99) which directs attention to the complexity of the case, the applicant's conduct and the manner in which the matter was dealt with by the authorities, and leaving aside the question whether the respondents have shown that they were prejudiced, I would hold that the proceedings did not exceed the reasonable time requirement which art 6(1) lays down.

b [115] In view of the conclusion which I have reached I do not need to deal with the respondents' submissions about the remedy to which they were entitled if there had been undue delay. Schiemann LJ said that it would not have been appropriate in that event to quash the auditor's certificate (see [2000] 2 WLR 1420 at 1460). He had in mind the remedy which was available in the Divisional Court c to ensure that, despite the delay, there was a fair trial and the possibility instead of a remedy in damages. The appellant supported this approach. But these are difficult issues, and I would prefer to reserve my opinion on them.

The Divisional Court

d [116] The respondents submit that the Divisional Court made errors of law by applying the wrong tests to their arguments on apparent bias and delay. Their argument is that it dealt with the case as if their complaint was one of actual bias and with their complaint of delay on the basis that it was necessary to establish prejudice. It is true that the Divisional Court took particular account of the auditor's assertions that he was not biased and that, basing itself on the common e law authorities, it had regard to the question whether the delay resulted in prejudice. But I do not think that, read as a whole, the judgment is vulnerable to such serious criticism that their decision to uphold the certificates against Dame Shirley Porter and Mr Weeks should, as the respondents assert, have been set aside by the Court of Appeal on that ground alone. Mistakes of law of this kind, f if they are made, do not in themselves amount to breaches of the art 6 convention rights of the kind which must inevitably attract that remedy. They can be corrected on appeal. I have taken full account of the respondents' arguments in my review of their case on unfairness and of their criticisms of this part of the Divisional Court's reasoning.

g [117] They also submit that the Divisional Court ought to have quashed the certificates on the ground that the injury done to her public reputation by reason of the auditor's conduct in making his statement at a press conference was so severe that to quash the certificate was the only possible remedy. I would reject this argument also. The question which the Divisional Court had to address was whether the defects in the investigation conducted by the auditor were so h prejudicial to the respondents that it should in its discretion quash the certificates or whether it should proceed to a re-hearing on the merits and decide the issue on the evidence presented to the court (see *Lloyd v McMahon* [1987] 1 All ER 1118 at 1172, [1987] AC 625 at 716 per Lord Templeman). Various factors had to be taken into account in this case, including the inevitable consequence of the j passage of time on the recollection of witnesses to which the Divisional Court refers ((1997) 96 LGR 157 at 162). But the fact that the press conference gave rise to adverse publicity, albeit that this was severe, would not of itself have justified quashing the certificates. There were other interests to be taken into account, namely those of the objectors and of the council and its electors. The respondents were given the opportunity, to which they were entitled, to raise the issue in the context of their arguments on unfairness. In my opinion their rights were

sufficiently protected by the way in which this issue was examined in that court
and by the remedies that were available to them by way of appeal.   *a*

Conclusion on unfairness

[118] For these reasons I would hold that the proceedings as a whole did not
infringe the respondents' convention rights and that there was no unfairness at
common law on the ground either of apparent bias or of delay.   *b*

Quantum

[119] The auditor included in the amount which he certified under s 20(1)(b)
of the Local Government Finance Act 1982 as one of the items of loss in
consequence of the respondents' wilful misconduct a sum amounting to £15·476m
for discounts on the sale of dwellings sold at a discount. He took as the measure   *c*
of this loss the difference between the open market value of the dwellings with
vacant possession, as estimated at the time of the sales by the council's valuers
Ellis & Co for the purpose of arriving at a discounted price, and the discounted
prices at which they were actually disposed of. Most of the dwellings included in
this item were not sold outright but were let on long leases granted in   *d*
consideration of substantial premiums. For convenience however all the
transactions were referred to as sales. The discount was 30% to purchasers who
were not already tenants of the council. For existing tenants with the right to buy
it was a variable amount, but it was always more than 30%.

[120] As the Divisional Court said ((1997) 96 LGR 157 at 205), the question   *e*
whether this amount was properly certified was by far the most significant issue
in terms of quantum. Two main challenges to the auditor's approach to it were
advanced in that court. The first, which raised an issue of principle, was whether
the auditor was right to use the open market value of the unoccupied dwellings
as his starting point. The second was directed to the figures which he used for
assessing their market value which, it was said, were unreliable. The Divisional   *f*
Court upheld the auditor's approach on both points. It concluded (at 207) that
the loss arising from the sales at a discount was correctly calculated at £15·476m.

[121] The issue whether this amount was correctly calculated was raised again
in the Court of Appeal. Robert Walker LJ said that in his judgment the Divisional
Court erred in its approach, as it should have accepted the submission that there
was no loss if the discounted prices actually received by the council exceeded the   *g*
value of the dwellings as tenanted social housing (see [2000] 2 WLR 1420 at 1502).
His conclusion on this issue was rendered academic by the decision of the
majority to allow the appeals and discharge the certificates. Kennedy LJ said (at
1429) that he agreed with that part of the judgment of Robert Walker LJ which
dealt with quantum, but Schiemann LJ said (at 1447) that he preferred to express   *h*
no opinion on the point. As your Lordships have decided to allow the appeal, the
issue as to quantum is once again a live issue. The auditor submits that the
amount which was found to have been correctly calculated by the Divisional
Court should be included in the certificates.

[122] It may be convenient for me to set out again the provisions of s 20(1) of   *j*
the 1982 Act:

'Where it appears to the auditor carrying out the audit of any accounts
under this Part of this Act—(a) that any person has failed to bring into
account any sum which should have been so included and that the failure has
not been sanctioned by the Secretary of State; or (b) that a loss has been

a incurred or deficiency caused by the wilful misconduct of any person, he shall certify that the sum or, as the case may be, the amount of the loss or the deficiency is due from that person and, subject to subsections (3) and (5) below, both he and the body in question (or, in the case of a parish meeting, the chairman of that meeting) may recover that sum or amount for the benefit of that body ...'

b
[123] The task of the auditor in this case was to certify the amount of the loss or deficiency caused by the wilful misconduct. The loss or deficiency which he identified as due to wilful misconduct fell into two distinct parts. The first part consisted of expenditure incurred in the preparation of papers for the purpose of discussing the promotion of the electoral advantage of the majority party. This *c* part raised no issue of principle. It was simply a matter of arriving at an appropriate figure to restore to the council's account the amount of the expenditure. The auditor made a broad estimate under this heading of £5,000 which, when interest was added, amounted to £10,126. No appeal was taken against the calculation of this amount. By far the greater part of the loss which he identified fell into the *d* second part. This was the result of the resolution of the Housing Committee on 8 July 1987 to extend the programme of designated sales of dwellings from the council's social housing stock. After agreed corrections in the Divisional Court, the total amount of this loss was £26·462m. The figure of £15·476m for losses resulting from sales of dwellings at a discount is included in this figure.

[124] The auditor's approach, as explained by him in para 43 of his report, was *e* a simple one. He said that the sale of property such as housing accommodation at less than its market value involves a loss or deficiency to the authority which is equal to the difference between the market value of the asset and the proceeds of sale. In his view, the amount of this difference was the amount that should be certified as due from any person by whose wilful misconduct that loss or *f* deficiency has been incurred. It is this approach that the respondents have challenged as being wrong in principle.

[125] I agree that the sale of a dwelling which is unoccupied at less than its open market value with vacant possession can be regarded as producing a loss or deficiency for the purposes of s 20(1)(b) of the 1982 Act. This assumes that those who were responsible for the sale were under a duty to obtain a full price for it, *g* measured by its value with vacant possession in the open market. But I do not think that this can be regarded as a universal rule. The proper starting point is to identify the act of wilful misconduct. The next step is to determine what items of loss, if any, were caused by it. In the case of the designated dwellings, the act of wilful misconduct for which the respondents must be held accountable was the *h* promotion of the policy which the Housing Committee adopted on 8 July 1987. The effect of its resolution was to remove the designated dwellings from the council's social housing stock as they became vacant. What the council lost as a result of the adoption of the policy were 618 dwellings from its social housing stock. Its capacity to perform its obligation to house the homeless under Pt III of *j* the Housing Act 1985 was correspondingly reduced.

[126] Nevertheless, when these dwellings became vacant they could have been sold with vacant possession on the open market. Robert Walker LJ said that there was no loss to the council so long as the discounted prices actually received by it exceeded the value of the dwellings as tenanted social housing (see [2000] 2 WLR 1420 at 1502). They exceeded this value in all cases, so he was of the view that the auditor ought to have found that their sale did not result in any loss or

deficiency. But I agree with Lord Bingham that the principle which underlies the
statutory procedure is one of compensation. What the auditor is directed by
s 20(1) to certify is the amount of the loss or deficiency, and it is for the benefit of
the body that the amount certified is recoverable. The aim of the procedure is to
put the body in the same position that it would have been in but for the wilful
misconduct. Applying this approach, the loss to the council due to the sales for
which it ought to be compensated was the difference between the full market
price of the dwellings and the discounted prices which were received for them.

[127] That however does not conclude the argument. This is because the auditor
included in his calculation of this amount a sum amounting to £4·237m for extra
homelessness costs. These costs were directly attributable to the removal of the
designated dwellings from the social housing stock. Robert Walker LJ said (at
1502) that to include this figure in the amount of the loss or deficiency as well as
a figure for loss on the sale of the dwellings at a discount would result in double
counting. In his view it would be inconsistent with the auditor's decision to
include an amount for homelessness costs due to the depletion of the council's
social housing stock to assume that those dwellings would have been sold with
vacant possession at their full value on the open market.

[128] I think that there is considerable force in the point which Robert Walker LJ
made on this issue in his careful judgment. It seems to me that these two items
were arrived at by the auditor on two different and arguably inconsistent
assumptions. On the one hand the figure of £15·476m representing the loss
arising from sales at a discount assumes that the council would, but for the
unlawful policy, have obtained full value for dwellings as they no longer required
to be treated as part of the social housing stock when they were sold. On the
other hand the figure of £4·237m for extra homelessness costs is based upon costs
for which it is assumed the council should be compensated on the ground that the
dwellings ought to have been retained for social housing purposes. The principle
of compensation requires that the council should be fully compensated, but it
does not permit the council to be overcompensated. An auditor who seeks to
apply this principle must guard against the risk of double counting. The effect of
doing so would be to penalise the person from whom the amount was due, which
is not the object of the procedure. It would also enable the body to recover more
than was needed to make good the loss or deficiency.

[129] In my opinion however the point about double counting is not free from
difficulty. The principles are clear enough, but they depend for their application
on the facts. It seems to me that the point ought to have been raised when the
facts about the extra costs of homelessness were being inquired into by the
auditor or by the Divisional Court. That was not done, with the result that your
Lordships do not have the findings of fact which would be needed to disturb the
calculations made by the auditor on this issue. With some hesitation therefore I
have come to the conclusion, in agreement with your Lordships, that it would
not be right to hold that the auditor fell into the obvious trap of double counting
and that the sum upheld by the Divisional Court should not be departed from.

Conclusion

[130] I too would allow the auditor's appeal and restore his certificate in the
sum upheld by the Divisional Court.

LORD HOBHOUSE OF WOODBOROUGH.

a   [131] My Lords, I agree that the appeal should be allowed and the judgment of the Divisional Court ((1997) 96 LGR 157) restored as proposed by my noble and learned friends Lord Bingham of Cornhill and Lord Hope of Craighead and for the reasons which they have given. The question of quantum referred to in the penultimate section of Lord Bingham's speech gave me some anxiety but was effectively concluded by the limited way in which the arguments of the

b respondents were put. The respondents (no doubt for some good reason) did not deploy or support by evidence the arguments which might have displaced the valid primary measure of the council's capital account loss. I agree that what Robert Walker LJ said in his judgment ([2000] 2 WLR 1420 at 1502 (Court of Appeal)) did not, on examination, suffice to displace the primary measure nor did it show that there had been any double counting.

c

LORD SCOTT OF FOSCOTE.

[132] My Lords, this is a case about political corruption. The corruption was not money corruption. No one took a bribe. No one sought or received money for political favours. But there are other forms of corruption, often less easily

d detectable and therefore more insidious. Gerrymandering, the manipulation of constituency boundaries for party political advantage, is a clear form of political corruption. So, too, would be any misuse of municipal powers, intended for use in the general public interest but used instead for party political advantage. Who can doubt that the selective use of municipal powers in order to obtain party political advantage represents political corruption? Political corruption, if unchecked,

e engenders cynicism about elections, about politicians and their motives and damages the reputation of democratic government. Like Viola's 'worm i' the bud' it feeds upon democratic institutions from within (*Twelfth Night*).

[133] When detected and exposed it must be expected, or at least it must be hoped, that political corruption will receive its just deserts at the polls. Detection

f and exposure is, however, often difficult and, where it happens, is usually attributable to determined efforts by political opponents or by investigative journalists or by both in tandem. But, where local government is concerned, there is an additional very important bulwark guarding against misconduct. The Local Government Finance Act 1982 (now repealed but in force until 11 September 1998) required the annual accounts of a local authority to be audited by an

g independent auditor appointed by the Audit Commission (ss 12 and 13). The auditor had to satisfy himself that the local authority's accounts were in order (s 15(1) and (2)) and, also, had to—

> 'consider whether, in the public interest, he should make a report on any
> matter coming to his notice in the course of the audit in order that it may be
> *h*   considered by the [local authority] concerned or brought to the attention of
> the public ...' (Section 15(3).)

[134] If, in the course of the audit, it came to the attention of the auditor that municipal powers had been used not in the general public interest but, selectively, for party political advantage, it was plainly right that the political

j corruption in question should be exposed in a report under s 15(3).

[135] Section 16 of the Act gave the auditor extensive powers to obtain documents and information for the purposes of the statutory functions. These included the power to require any officer or member of the local authority 'to give him such information or explanation as he thinks necessary' (s 16(2)). Any report made by the auditor under s 15(3) became a public document open to inspection by any member of the public (s 18(5)(a)).

[**136**] The statutory provisions to which I have referred provided an *a* institutional means whereby political corruption consisting of the use of municipal powers for party political advantage might be detected and cauterised by public exposure. These provisions were repealed by the Audit Commission Act 1998 but replaced by provisions in Pt II of that Act which are to much the same effect (see, in particular, s 8 of the 1998 Act).

[**137**] In addition, however, where the misconduct in question had caused loss *b* to the local authority, s 20 of the 1982 Act enabled the auditor to require those responsible to make good the loss. Section 20(1) provided:

'Where it appears to the auditor carrying out the audit of any accounts under this Part of this Act … (a) … or (b) that a loss has been incurred or deficiency caused by the wilful misconduct of any person, he shall certify that *c* … the amount of the loss or the deficiency is due from that person and, subject to subsections (3) and (5) below, both he and the [local authority] in question … may recover that … amount for the benefit of that [local authority] …'

[**138**] Subsection (3) permitted an appeal against the auditor's certificate to be *d* made to the court. Subsection (4) applied where a certificate requiring payment of more than £2,000 had been made, or upheld, and disqualified the individual concerned from being a member of any local authority for a period of five years. And sub-s (5) required payment of the certified sum to be made within 14 days of the certificate becoming final. *e*

[**139**] The purpose of a s 20 certificate was compensatory, not penal. Its purpose was not to punish the wrongdoer but to require the quantified loss caused to the local authority by the 'wilful misconduct' to be made good. There was no element of discretion. If the officer or member had been guilty of 'wilful misconduct' as a result of which loss had been incurred it was the duty of the *f* auditor to issue a s 20 certificate specifying the amount of the loss. Of course, it will not be every case of political corruption, or other misconduct, in local government that will lead to financial loss to the local authority concerned. But many will do so and, in those cases, the powers and duties of auditors under s 20 of the 1982 Act (and under s 19 as well, although nothing turns on that section in *g* this case) constituted, in my opinion, powerful and valuable protection to the public.

[**140**] Section 20 of the 1982 Act was replaced by s 18 of the 1998 Act which was to the same effect. But s 18 of the 1998 Act has been repealed by the Local Government Act 2000 and not replaced. The 2000 Act also substantially re-cast *h* the investigation and report provisions that had been contained first in the 1982 Act and then in the 1998 Act. The institutional protection provided by statute against political corruption and other misconduct by members of local authorities is now confined to the investigation, report and publicity for which the 2000 Act and an amended version of s 17 of the 1998 Act (formerly s 19 of the 1982 Act) make provision. There is now no statutory provision directed to restitution *j* or compensation for loss caused by any wrongdoing that the investigation and report may have exposed. Certificates such as those issued against and challenged by Dame Shirley Porter and Mr David Weeks in the present case cannot now be issued. Local authorities that want to recover from delinquent councillors the loss caused by the delinquency must now do so by means of legal remedies available under the general law. However, s 20 of the 1982 Act was in force at the

a time the events material to this case took place and the propriety of the auditor's certificates against Dame Shirley and Mr Weeks must be tested on that footing.

[141] My Lords, I have had the advantage of reading in draft the opinion on this appeal of my noble and learned friend, Lord Bingham of Cornhill. As Lord Bingham has observed, the facts that have given rise to the appeal are set out at some length in the judgments of the Divisional Court ((1997) 96 LGR 157) and

b the Court of Appeal ([2000] 2 WLR 1420). Lord Bingham has highlighted some of the key events. I gratefully adopt and need not repeat those highlights.

[142] The factual findings made by the auditor, Mr John Magill, and by the Divisional Court against Dame Shirley Porter and Mr David Weeks were findings that justify being described as findings of political corruption. Dame Shirley and

c Mr Weeks, having appealed unsuccessfully to the Divisional Court, appealed successfully to the Court of Appeal. Mr Magill has appealed to this House. For the purposes of this appeal the parties have prepared a statement of agreed facts and issues. The contents of the statement were agreed by Mr Howell QC on behalf of Mr Magill, by Mr McMullen QC on behalf of Dame Shirley and by Mr Cakebread of counsel on behalf of Mr Weeks. The contents of the statement,

d in my opinion, endorse the essential findings of the auditor and of the Divisional Court regarding the conduct of Dame Shirley and Mr Weeks and justify the description of that conduct as political corruption. Thus: (1) As a consequence of local government elections in May 1986 reducing the Conservative majority from 26 to 4, Dame Shirley, the leader of the Conservatives on the Westminster Council, was determined that a greater majority should be achieved at the 1990

e elections. (2) Eight marginal wards, the 'key wards', were identified. The intention of Dame Shirley and Mr Weeks was to reduce the number of Labour voters and increase the number of Conservative voters in these key wards. The target was an overall increase of 2,200 Conservative supporters in these wards. (3) This increase was to be brought about by selling council-owned residential properties

f in the eight key wards when they became vacant. It was believed that owner-occupiers were more likely to vote Conservative than were council tenants. (4) The Director of Housing advised in May 1986 and again in March 1987 that if all council properties in the eight key wards were designated for selling, the council would not be able to meet its statutory housing obligations. (5) None the less, at a meeting on 24 March 1987, attended by Dame Shirley and Mr Weeks, it

g was decided to sell annually 250 properties in the eight key wards. (6) On 5 May 1987 Mr Sullivan QC met council officials in consultation. He was informed that the majority (Conservative) group wished to target sales in marginal wards for electoral advantage. He advised that this would not be lawful, that the designation of properties for sale had to be done for proper reasons and that, in

h identifying the properties to be sold, the same criteria had to be applied across the whole city. (7) The critical paragraph in the agreed statement of facts is para 42. It reads:

> *j* 'On the evening of 5 May 1987, the chairmen's group agreed to target designated sales city-wide in order to produce the agreed number of designated sales in marginal wards. The group decided to adopt the course ... of increasing the number of designated sales so as to be able to achieve the policy objective of 250 sales per annum in the marginal wards.'

[143] That was the policy eventually carried into effect via the Housing Committee decision on 8 July 1987. It led to the sale of 618 council properties (some were let on long leases for substantial premiums). It is clear that the policy

was adopted by the chairmen's group, led by Dame Shirley and Mr Weeks, and
was thereafter promoted by Dame Shirley and Mr Weeks, as well as by others,
not in order to achieve sales city-wide but in order to achieve 250 sales per annum
in the eight key wards. And those sales were for the purpose of replacing
probable Labour voters by probable Conservative voters. The city-wide policy
was no more than a cloak to give apparent legality to the sales in the eight key
wards which leading counsel had rightly warned would be unlawful unless part
of a city-wide policy adopted for a proper reason. The sales of the 618 properties
involved the exercise of local government powers to sell council properties (see
s 32 of the Housing Act 1985) not for the purpose for which those powers were
granted but in order to increase the number of Conservative voters in marginal
wards. It has not been in dispute before your Lordships that this purpose for
selling is an unlawful purpose.

[144] In the Court of Appeal Kennedy LJ commented on the political reality
that many government decisions, whether at local government level or in central
government, are taken with an eye to the electoral effect they may have. He said:

'Some of the submissions advanced on behalf of the auditor have been
framed in such a way as to suggest that any councillor who allows the
possibility of electoral advantage even to cross his mind before he decides
upon a course of action is guilty of misconduct ... In local, as in national,
politics many if not most decisions carry an electoral tag, and all politicians
are aware of it.' (See [2000] 2 WLR 1420 at 1444.)

The Lord Justice was, of course, correct. But there is all the difference in the
world between a policy adopted for naked political advantage but spuriously
justified by reference to a purpose which, had it been the true purpose, would
have been legitimate, and a policy adopted for a legitimate purpose and seen to
carry with it significant political advantage. The agreed statement of facts places
the policy adopted by the chairmen's group on 5 May 1987 fairly and squarely in
the former category.

[145] My Lords, there are three issues which arise on this appeal on which
I wish to comment. The first is whether Dame Shirley and Mr Weeks were, for
s 20 purposes, guilty of wilful misconduct. The second is whether, if they were,
that misconduct was causative of loss to the council. The third is how such loss
should be quantified. But, my Lords, the backcloth to each of these issues is that
Dame Shirley and Mr Weeks stand convicted of political corruption. They stand
so convicted on the basis of facts which are not now in dispute.

Wilful misconduct

[146] It has been submitted on behalf of Dame Shirley and Mr Weeks that
whether or not their conduct in promoting the policy of designated sales in the
eight key wards was misconduct, it lacked the quality of being 'wilful'. This, it is
said, is because, relying on advice which they believed had been given by
Mr Sullivan, they did not realise that the policy was unlawful. In *Lloyd v McMahon*
[1987] 1 All ER 1118 at 1151, [1987] AC 625 at 674 Woolf LJ said that misconduct—

'would only be wilful if the [councillors] were doing something which they
knew to be wrong or about which they were recklessly indifferent whether
it was wrong or not ...'

It has been common ground before your Lordships that this is the correct test.

[147] It is said that, in reliance on Mr England's note of what Mr Sullivan had
said in consultation on 5 May 1987, Dame Shirley and Mr Weeks thought that it

a would be lawful for them to achieve their purpose of designating properties for sale in the eight key wards in order to achieve annual sales of 250 properties in those wards provided that there were similar designations of properties for sale city-wide. Mr England's note reads, so far as material, as follows:

b 'Counsel advises that designated estates should be identified in marginal and non-marginal wards in order to protect the council. The group will, therefore, need to decide whether the 250 target applies across the city or whether in fact 250 sales in marginal wards are required in which case following counsel's advice, somewhere in the region of 300-350 properties will need to be sold across the city.'

c [148] But Dame Shirley and Mr Weeks knew that a policy adopted for the purpose of electoral advantage in the key wards would be unlawful. And nothing in Mr England's note of what Mr Sullivan had said, or indeed in what Mr Sullivan had actually said, indicated that the adoption of the city-wide policy in order to achieve the unlawful electoral purpose in the eight key wards would be any less unlawful than the adoption for that purpose of a policy in respect of the eight key *d* wards alone. As Lord Bingham has noted in para [39] of his opinion, Mr Sullivan was never asked the critical question, namely, whether the designated sales policy would become lawful if, with the same objective, the designated sales policy were extended city-wide. I agree with Lord Bingham that no reason for doubting the clear findings, adverse to Dame Shirley and Mr Weeks, of the *e* auditor and the Divisional Court has been shown.

Causation

[149] Dame Shirley and Mr Weeks rely on the Housing Committee's decision of 8 July 1987 as breaking the chain of causation. The designated sales policy was *f* implemented because the Housing Committee had resolved to adopt it. If the Housing Committee had not so resolved, the policy would not have been implemented. Neither Dame Shirley nor Mr Weeks was a member of the Housing Committee. Neither of them was present at the 8 July meeting. Mr McMullen submitted that a city-wide designated sales policy was a policy capable of being a lawful one. So it was. He submitted that the Housing Committee resolution that *g* adopted the policy was capable of being a lawful resolution. I agree. He submitted that if a majority of members of the committee voted in favour of the resolution for reasons that were lawful, then the resolution would have been lawful, notwithstanding that misconduct on the part of the leader of the council and her deputy had attended the formulation and promotion of the policy adopted by the *h* resolution. Again, I agree.

[150] It was argued on behalf of Mr Magill that even if the resolution were a lawful one, none the less the misconduct of Dame Shirley and Mr Weeks was not spent and could still be regarded, for s 20 purposes, as having 'caused the loss'. But for their misconduct, the designated sales policy would not have been *j* formulated and placed before the Housing Committee for approval. I agree that, applying a 'but for' test, it could be said that their misconduct had caused the loss. But I do not think that that is enough. If the Housing Committee resolution was a lawful one, then it was lawful for it to be implemented by the council. Its implementation was within the statutory powers of the council. This is not a case in which the council lacked power to carry out the property sales contemplated by the policy.

[151] So, if the improper electoral advantage in the eight key wards, the
purpose of the designated sales policy, had been made plain at the Housing   *a*
Committee meeting and had been repudiated by a majority of those present who
had then voted in favour of the policy for unimpeachable reasons, it would have
been plain that the misconduct had become spent even if, without the
misconduct, the policy would never have found its way to the committee. I find
it difficult to follow why the case would be different if, without an explicit   *b*
disclosure and repudiation of the policy, a lawful resolution adopting the policy
were passed. I accept that a corrupt principal can attain his unlawful object via
the medium of an innocent agent (see *Royal Brunei Airlines Sdn Bhd v Tan* [1995]
3 All ER 97 at 102, [1995] 2 AC 378 at 385), but I do not think a local authority
committee can be treated as merely an agent for the leader of the council, no
matter how influential he or she may be. I am, therefore, disposed to agree with   *c*
Mr McMullen, and to disagree with the Divisional Court (see (1997) 96 LGR 157
at 181), that if the Housing Committee resolution could be shown to have been
a lawful resolution, the causative effect of Dame Shirley's and Mr Weeks'
misconduct would, for s 20 purposes, be spent.

[152] There were 12 members of the Housing Committee. Seven of them   *d*
voted in favour of the designated sales policy. Five voted against. Of the seven,
two of them, Mr Hartley and Dr Dutt, were found guilty of misconduct by the
auditor. Each, in the auditor's opinion, 'took into account the electoral advantage
of the Conservative party and sought to promote it in his voting'. The auditor
issued a s 20 certificate against Mr Hartley but Mr Hartley succeeded on appeal
to the Divisional Court. In the view of the Divisional Court he was guilty of   *e*
misconduct but not of wilful misconduct (see (1997) 96 LGR 157 at 199). It
follows, however, from the finding of misconduct that Mr Hartley's vote at the
Housing Committee meeting was invalid.

[153] As to Dr Dutt, he took his own life before the auditor made his final
findings. The auditor, in his report, said (p 686):   *f*

> '1903. My provisional findings and views were adverse to Dr Dutt ... In
> letters to me, Dr Dutt disputed my provisional findings and views. Shortly
> thereafter, he took his own life. I make no findings ... of personal liability of
> Dr Dutt.'

[154] Mr McMullen has submitted that Dr Dutt must be treated as exonerated   *g*
from misconduct. I do not agree. Dr Dutt was exonerated from wilful misconduct,
but the provisional findings of misconduct were unchanged. In my opinion
Dr Dutt's vote falls into the same state as that of Mr Hartley. It was invalid. As
for the other five members of the committee who voted in favour of the
resolution, they so voted because the resolution was Conservative Party policy.   *h*
They did not know that the purpose of the resolution was to obtain electoral
advantage in the eight key wards. They did not know that that was the reason
why the policy had been adopted. They may very well have supposed that the
resolution reflected their party's general dislike of social housing and bias in
favour of owner occupation. I do not think, in these circumstances, that their   *j*
votes can be disregarded on the ground that they were invalid. But their votes
were insufficient in number to carry the resolution. Five valid votes in favour of
the resolution and five against would have produced a tie which, in theory, could
have been resolved by the chairman's casting vote. But the chairman was
Mr Hartley and any casting vote of his would, for the reasons already discussed,
have been an invalid vote.

a
[155] In my opinion, therefore, the resolution purportedly passed at the Housing Committee meeting was not a valid resolution, the wilful misconduct of Dame Shirley and Mr Weeks in promoting the policy purportedly adopted by the resolution was not spent and the chain of causation was not broken. In my opinion, their misconduct caused, for s 20 purposes, the 618 sales by the council that produced the loss.

b
Quantification of the loss

[156] The issue is whether Walker LJ's disagreement with the basis on which the Divisional Court had quantified the loss was correct.

[157] The 618 designated properties were sold with vacant possession. They
c were sold by the council at a discount against their vacant possession market value. The council had power to sell at a discount. If the sales had been lawful, no complaint about the discount could have been made. The question is whether, the sales being unlawful, the amount of the discount represents an item of loss caused by the wilful misconduct. The rival arguments, as I understand them, are these: (1) The properties were, before being designated for sale and becoming
d vacant, occupied by council tenants. Their value so tenanted was a good deal less than their value with vacant possession. If, on becoming vacant, they had been re-let to those on the council's waiting list for social housing, their value so re-let would, similarly, have been a good deal less than their value with vacant possession. The amount of the discount at which the properties were sold may
e be taken, on a rough and ready footing, as representing the difference in value between the properties let as social housing and the properties with vacant possession. So, if the council recover the amount of the discount the council will be in a better financial position than it would have been if the unlawful designated sales policy had never been adopted. This argument, expressed by Robert Walker LJ more lucidly than I have done, was concurred in by Kennedy LJ. It has been
f espoused by Mr McMullen and Mr Cakebread. (2) The alternative argument proceeds like this. The council has a statutory housing obligation and a long list of people who need to be housed. The unlawful sales reduced the council's stock of social housing. In order to replenish its stock and restore the position to what it was before the sales took place, the council would have to purchase properties in the open market. It would have to pay vacant possession prices. Accordingly,
g the loss it suffered by reason of the misconduct included the discounts at which the properties were sold. This was the approach of the Divisional Count. It was supported by Mr Howell.

[158] The answer to the question as to which approach is the right one does
h not, in my opinion, depend at all upon the manner in which the properties appeared in the council's accounts. The quantification of loss for s 20 purposes should, in my view, apply the same principles as are applicable to quantification of damages in tort. As a result of the wrongful acts of Dame Shirley and Mr Weeks the council suffered loss. What was that loss? It lost the properties that were sold, but it received the purchase price that was paid for them.
j Immediately before sale, the properties were vacant. They were sold with vacant possession but the council did not receive a vacant possession price. In my opinion, the discount represented a true loss suffered by the council. Interest on the discounted purchase price since its receipt and interest on the amount of the discount from the date of the sale ought, on the assumption that interest rates more or less reflect rates of inflation in property values, to enable the council to

replace the sold housing stock. Thus, to treat the discounts as items of loss seems to me to produce a just result, in line with the intentions underlying s 20.

[159] The problem, as it seems to me, with Robert Walker LJ's approach, is that it attributes no value to the benefit to the council of owning properties which are available to be used for social housing. The sale of the properties deprived the council of that benefit. The council can restore that benefit only by purchasing similar properties in the open market. The value of that benefit can be taken, again on a rough and ready basis, as being equivalent to the discounts.

[160] To allow the council to recover the discounts as items of loss does not, in my opinion, involve any element of double counting. A separate item of loss allowed by the Divisional Court was £4·237m, representing extra costs of housing homeless people which the council had to incur as a result of its own stock of social housing having been depleted by the sales of the 618 properties. Robert Walker LJ thought that to allow the discounts to be recovered as well as the £4·237m would be inconsistent and involve double counting. I do not think so. The £4·237m covered the extra costs of homelessness over the period starting from the date on which the properties, on becoming vacant, were available for re-letting and ending on the date of the auditor's certificate. Thereafter the loss of the 618 properties from the housing stock is covered by the capital sum received (or receivable) by the council (ie the discounted proceeds of sale plus the amount of the discounts) that enables it to replace the sold properties. There is no double counting.

Bias and unfairness

[161] There was a fourth issue raised by Dame Shirley and Mr Weeks. They submitted that the manner in which the auditor had gone about his task of fact finding was attended by at least the appearance of bias against them and that that feature of the case, coupled with the time it has taken for the case to come to finality, represented such a degree of unfairness as to infringe their right to a fair trial (see art 6 of the European Convention for the Protection of Human Rights and Fundamental Freedoms 1950 (as set out in Sch 1 to the Human Rights Act 1998)). These submissions fail, in my opinion, for the reasons given by my noble and learned friend Lord Hope of Craighead. I want to add just one comment on the issue of unfairness

[162] One of the most striking features of the case is the enormous amount that under the auditor's certificates Dame Shirley and Mr Weeks were adjudged liable to pay. The amount, £31m odd, seems enormous not because it does not accurately reflect the loss caused to the council by Dame Shirley's and Mr Weeks' misconduct but because it is so out of line with what most people would regard as a proportionate punishment for their misconduct. There is, I think, an almost instinctive feeling that the requirement that they pay the certified amount is unfair.

[163] This instinctive feeling, however, overlooks the very important fact that the purpose of a s 20 certificate is to compensate the local authority for loss. The purpose is not one of punishment. Nor does the amount to be certified lie in the discretion of the certifying auditor. If wilful misconduct has been proved it is his duty to certify the full amount of the loss thereby caused. The size of the amount so certified can no more represent an art 6 unfairness than can the size of an award of damages for tort or breach of contract. Since, for the reasons given by Lord Hope, there was no procedural unfairness in the proceedings which have

a culminated in the appeal to this House, there is no further convention point that can be taken.

Conclusion

[164] For the reasons given in this opinion in addition to those given by Lord Bingham, with which I am in full agreement, I would allow the appeal and restore the order of the Divisional Court.

Appeal allowed.

Dilys Tausz   Barrister.

R v Pendleton

[2001] UKHL 66

HOUSE OF LORDS

LORD BINGHAM OF CORNHILL, LORD MACKAY OF CLASHFERN, LORD STEYN, LORD HOPE
OF CRAIGHEAD AND LORD HOBHOUSE OF WOODBOROUGH

24, 25 OCTOBER, 13 DECEMBER 2001

Criminal law – Appeal – Fresh evidence – Test to be applied in deciding whether to allow appeal against conviction where fresh evidence received on appeal – Criminal Appeal Act 1968, s 2(1).

In 1985 the defendant, P, was charged with a murder committed in 1971. During a police interview, he admitted having been in the vicinity of the crime at the time of the murder, but denied having inflicted any violence on the victim. Although P subsequently instructed his lawyers that the admission had been false, they took the view that the jury would be unlikely to believe him if he gave evidence to that effect, and accordingly they put his case at trial on the basis that the statements made in interview were true. P was convicted, and in 1987 his renewed application for leave to appeal against conviction was refused. In 1999 the Criminal Cases Review Commission referred P's conviction to the Court of Appeal. P then applied to the Court of Appeal to receive evidence which had not been adduced at the trial. The reception of that evidence, which questioned the reliability of P's admission that he had been present at the scene of the crime, was not opposed. Having considered the new evidence, the court stated that it had no doubt about the reliability of P's admission and the safety of his conviction. On P's appeal to the House of Lords, the issue arose as to the correct test to be applied in deciding whether or not to allow an appeal against conviction where fresh evidence had been received on the appeal. P contended that where the Court of Appeal received fresh evidence it had to assess the quality of the evidence and allow the appeal if it judged that that evidence, combined with the original evidence, might have caused the jury, or a reasonable jury properly directed, to acquit. The test was therefore what impact the evidence, if called at trial, might have had on the jury, and accordingly it was not permissible for appellate judges, who had not heard any of the rest of the evidence, to make their own decision on the significance or credibility of the fresh evidence. The Crown contended that s 2(1)[a] of the Criminal Appeal Act 1968, which required the Court of Appeal to allow an appeal against conviction if 'they think' that the conviction was unsafe but to dismiss it in any other case, imposed on the court a duty of judgment in cases which involved fresh evidence as well as in other cases. It was therefore the court's judgment which mattered, and while the court might find it useful when forming that judgment to consider what impact the evidence, if called before the jury, might have had, that was not a necessary step, nor was it the only or final question the court had to ask.

Held – Where fresh evidence had been received on an appeal against conviction, the correct test to be applied by the Court of Appeal in determining whether to

---

a   Section 2 is set out at [8], below

a allow the appeal was the effect of the fresh evidence on the minds of the members of the court, not the effect that it would have had on the minds of the jury, so long as the court bore very clearly in mind that the question for its consideration was whether the conviction was safe and not whether the accused was guilty. It was undesirable that the exercise of the important judgment entrusted to the Court of Appeal by s 2(1) of the 1968 Act should be constrained by words not to be

b found in the statute and that adherence to a particular thought process should be required by judicial decision. Nevertheless, the jury-impact test did have a virtue in reminding the Court of Appeal that it was not and should never become the primary decision-maker, and that it had an imperfect and incomplete understanding of the full processes which had led the jury to convict. The court could make its assessment of the fresh evidence it had heard but, save in a clear case, it was at a

c disadvantage in seeking to relate that evidence to the rest of the evidence which the jury had heard. For those reasons it would usually be wise for the Court of Appeal, in a case of any difficulty, to test its own provisional view by asking whether the evidence, if given at the trial, might reasonably have affected the decision of the jury to convict. If it might, the conviction had to be thought to be unsafe. In the instant case, the Court of Appeal had directed itself in accordance

d with the correct test, but had strayed beyond its true function of review and had made findings which were not open to it in all the circumstances. Indeed, it had come perilously close to considering whether P was, in its judgment, guilty. Accordingly, the appeal would be allowed, and P's conviction quashed (see [19], [21], [28], [30]–[35], [38], [40], [47], below).

e *Stafford v DPP, Luvaglio v DPP* [1973] 3 All ER 762 followed.

Notes
For evidence on appeal, see 11(2) *Halsbury's Laws* (4th edn reissue) para 1380.

For the Criminal Appeal Act 1968, s 2, see 12 *Halsbury's Statutes* (4th edn) (1997
f reissue) 375.

Cases referred to in opinions
Franco v The Queen [2001] UKPC 38.
R v Barker (12 January 1971, unreported), CA.
g *R v Bowler* (24 July 1997, unreported), CA.
R v Callaghan (1989) 88 Cr App R 40, CA.
R v Clegg [1998] NIJB 68, NI CA.
R v D, R v J [1996] 1 All ER 881, [1996] QB 283, [1996] 2 WLR 1, CA.
R v Dwyer (16 November 1970, unreported), CA.
h *R v Evans* (3 December 1997, unreported), CA.
R v Flower (Richard), R v Siggins, R v Flower (Eric) [1965] 3 All ER 669, [1966] 1 QB 146, [1965] 3 WLR 1202, CCA.
R v Isaac [1964] Crim LR 721, CA.
R v Jones (1996) 33 BMLR 80, CA.
j *R v McIlkenny* [1992] 2 All ER 417, CA.
R v McNamee (17 December 1998, unreported), CA.
R v Parks [1961] 3 All ER 633, [1961] 1 WLR 1484, CCA.
R v Trevor [1998] Crim LR 652, CA.
Stafford v DPP, Luvaglio v DPP [1973] 3 All ER 762, [1974] AC 878, [1973] 3 WLR 719, HL.
Stirland v DPP [1944] 2 All ER 13, [1944] AC 315, HL.

Appeal

Donald Pendleton appealed with leave of the Appeal Committee of the House of *a*
Lords given on 12 February 2001 from the order of the Court of Appeal (Pill LJ,
Sachs and Steel JJ) on 22 June 2000 dismissing, on a reference by the Criminal
Cases Review Commission, his appeal against his conviction for murder in the
Crown Court at Leeds on 3 July 1986 after a trial before French J and a jury. The
Court of Appeal certified that a point of law of general public importance, set out *b*
at [5], below, was involved in its decision. The facts are set out in the opinion of
Lord Bingham of Cornhill.

Michael Mansfield QC and *Henry Blaxland* (instructed by *Taylor Nichol*) for the
appellant.
David Waters QC, Jeremy Benson QC and *David Perry* (instructed by the *Crown* *c*
Prosecution Service) for the Crown.

Their Lordships took time for consideration.

13 December 2001. The following opinions were delivered.   *d*

LORD BINGHAM OF CORNHILL.
[1] My Lords, this appeal concerns the role of the Court of Appeal (Criminal
Division) when fresh evidence is received on an appeal against conviction. The
legal question raised (although not the legal question certified) is whether in *e*
Stafford v DPP, Luvaglio v DPP [1973] 3 All ER 762, [1974] AC 878 this House
correctly defined the test to be applied in deciding whether or not to allow an
appeal in such a case.

The outline facts
[2] On the night of 2–3 June 1971 Mr Bernard Clark, a middle-aged newspaper *f*
seller, was murdered in Bradford. The appellant was interviewed by the police
during the inquiry which immediately followed the murder, and made a statement
dated 19 June 1971, but was eliminated as a suspect. Nearly 14 years later, as a
result of information given to the police by Gordon Sharpe, the appellant was
arrested on 23 March 1985. He was interviewed over a number of hours, in the *g*
absence of a solicitor, on that and the two ensuing days. After initial denials and
assertions of inability to remember what had happened on the night in question,
the appellant admitted being in the company of John Thorpe and in the vicinity
of the crime when the deceased had been murdered, although he adamantly
denied that he had himself inflicted any violence on the deceased. That violence
had been inflicted by Thorpe. The appellant and Thorpe were jointly charged with *h*
murder of the deceased and were tried at Leeds Crown Court before French J and
a jury.
[3] At trial the appellant was represented by solicitors and two counsel. His
instructions consistently were that he had not been in the vicinity at the time of
the murder. When arrested he had been so upset and distressed that he could not *j*
stop shaking. He had been put under pressure and had been prepared to say
anything to 'get the police off my back'. When he had come to make a statement
he had tried to recite what the police had said, although it was a complete pack
of lies. He had come to regret making the statement because it was so inaccurate.
The appellant was unable to call evidence (other than his own) to substantiate his
assertion that he had not been present at the time when the murder was

a committed, and that assertion was directly contradicted by the admissions he had repeatedly made in interview. The view was taken that, if he were to give evidence that his admissions of presence at the scene had been false, the jury would be unlikely to believe him. So (with, as the House understands, his consent) he was not called to give evidence and it was hoped that the jury would accept the truth of what he had said to the police in interview: that he had been present when
b the crime had been committed but had not himself been party to any violence. There was some evidence indirectly supporting this case. But the appellant's co-defendant Thorpe did give evidence, to the effect that it had been the appellant and not he who had murdered the deceased. The trial judge directed the jury that Thorpe's oral evidence was not evidence against the appellant, but on 3 July 1986 the jury convicted both defendants of murder. On 8 June 1987 the appellant's
c renewed application for leave to appeal was refused by the full Court of Appeal.

[4] On 4 February 1999 the Criminal Cases Review Commission referred the appellant's conviction to the Court of Appeal in exercise of its powers under s 9(1)(a) of the Criminal Appeal Act 1995. By s 9(2) the reference was to be treated for all purposes as an appeal against his conviction by the appellant under s 1 of the
d Criminal Appeal Act 1968. The appellant then made application to the Court of Appeal to receive evidence not adduced at the trial. This evidence consisted, first, of reports by Professor Gudjonsson and Dr Badcock and related to the reliability of the admissions made to the police by the appellant in interview. It consisted, secondly, of documents dating back to 1971, in particular the appellant's statement of 19 June 1971, bearing on his movements on the evening of 2–3 June, but not
e available at the time of the trial. The reception of this evidence was not opposed. Professor Gudjonsson and Dr Badcock both gave evidence before the court and were examined and cross-examined. The court read and considered the appellant's statement of 19 June 1971. But having considered this evidence the court had no doubt but that the appellant's conviction was safe and so dismissed his appeal.
f The House is now asked to decide whether the Court of Appeal formulated the right test and, if it did, whether the court erred in applying it.

[5] The certified question, not very pertinently expressed, is in these terms:

'Where, on an appeal against conviction, the Court of Appeal receives fresh evidence under s 23 of the Criminal Appeal Act 1968, in determining
g the safety of the conviction, is the court confined to answering the question, might a reasonable jury have acquitted the appellant had they heard the fresh evidence?'

The history and legislative background
h [6] Before 1907 issues of law arising in criminal trials could be resolved by writ of error and the reservation of legal questions under the Crown Cases Act 1848 and s 47 of the Supreme Court of Judicature Act 1873, but there was no readily available means of challenging a criminal conviction otherwise than on purely legal grounds. For very many years there was public pressure to establish a court
j of appeal with more general jurisdiction in criminal cases. Among other grounds for opposing such a court it was argued that to allow an appeal against conviction would undermine the role of the jury (see Radzinowicz and Hood *A History of English Criminal Law and its Administration from 1750* (1986) vol 5, p 765). This argument recognised what was, and remains, a central feature of trial on indictment in England and Wales, the extraordinary role of the trial jury. To it are entrusted, following a judicial direction on the law, the decision of the

all-important issues of fact and the determination whether or not the defendant
is proved to be guilty of the crime charged or some lesser alternative crime. In a a
civil trial by judge alone the judge will hear the evidence, consider the law and
deliver a reasoned judgment summarising the legal principles governing the case
and the facts to which they must be applied, and giving his decision. If the
decision is challenged, an appellate court may ordinarily review both the legal
ruling and the factual findings and the application of one to the other. But a b
criminal jury gives no reasons. Its answer is guilty or not guilty. While it is usually
safe to assume, in the absence of very good reason for holding otherwise, that the
jury will have heeded the judge's direction on the law, the process of reasoning
by which its decision is reached is never disclosed and can only be a matter of
inference. The role of an appellate court reviewing a conviction by a jury can
never be the same as that of a court reviewing the reasoned decision of a judge. c

[7] The Criminal Appeal Act 1907 did not intend to undermine the traditional
role of the trial jury but did intend to arm the new Court of Criminal Appeal with
powers sufficient to rectify miscarriages of justice, of which there had been
notorious recent examples. Section 1(7) of the Act provided that the court—

> 'shall, for the purposes of and subject to the provisions of this Act, have full d
> power to determine, in accordance with this Act, any questions necessary to
> be determined for the purpose of doing justice in the case before the court.'

A right of appeal was granted, with leave or with the certificate of the trial judge,
on any ground of fact or mixed fact and law (s 3(b)). The core provision of the Act e
was expressed in s 4(1):

> 'The Court of Criminal Appeal on any such appeal against conviction shall
> allow the appeal if they think that the verdict of the jury should be set aside
> on the ground that it is unreasonable or cannot be supported having regard
> to the evidence, or that the judgment of the court before whom the appellant f
> was convicted should be set aside on the ground of a wrong decision of any
> question of law or that on any ground there was a miscarriage of justice, and
> in any other case shall dismiss the appeal: Provided that the court may,
> notwithstanding that they are of opinion that the point raised in the appeal
> might be decided in favour of the appellant, dismiss the appeal if they
> consider that no substantial miscarriage of justice has actually occurred.' g

The subsection plainly called for an exercise of judgment by the court: 'if they
think', 'they are of opinion'. This core provision was buttressed by a range of
other powers, again calling for the court to exercise its judgment: power to affirm
or substitute a sentence 'If it appears' (s 5(1)); power to substitute conviction of a h
lesser offence if 'it appears' (s 5(2)); power to substitute such conclusion on the
effect of a special verdict 'as appears' (s 5(3)); power to quash the sentence passed
on a defendant if 'it appears' that he was insane when the act was done (s 5(4)).
A further and important range of powers was conferred on the court by s 9:

> 'For the purposes of this Act, the Court of Criminal Appeal may, if they j
> think it necessary or expedient in the interest of justice,—(a) order the
> production of any document, exhibit, or other thing connected with the
> proceedings, the production of which appears to them necessary for the
> determination of the case; and (b) if they think fit order any witnesses who
> would have been compellable witnesses at the trial to attend and be
> examined before the court, whether they were or were not called at the trial,

a   or order the examination of any such witnesses to be conducted in manner provided by rules of court before any judge of the court or before any officer of the court or justice of the peace or other person appointed by the court for the purpose, and allow the admission of any depositions so taken as evidence before the court; and (c) if they think fit receive the evidence, if tendered, of any witness (including the appellant) who is a competent but not compellable

b   witness, and, if the appellant makes an application for the purpose, of the husband or wife of the appellant, in cases where the evidence of the husband or wife could not have been given at the trial except on such application; and (d) where any question arising on the appeal involves prolonged examination of documents or accounts, or any scientific or local investigation, which cannot in the opinion of the court conveniently be conducted before the

c   court, order the reference of the question in manner provided by rules of court for inquiry and report to a special commissioner appointed by the court, and act upon the report of any such commissioner so far as they think fit to adopt it; and (e) appoint any person with special expert knowledge to act as assessor to the court in any case where it appears to the court that such

d   special knowledge is required for the proper determination of the case; and exercise in relation to the proceedings of the court any other powers which may for the time being be exercised by the court of appeal on appeals in civil matters, and issue any warrants necessary for enforcing the orders or sentences of the court: Provided that in no case shall any sentence be increased by reason of or in consideration of any evidence that was not given

e   at the trial.'

This section clearly expresses Parliament's overriding intention that the interests of justice should be served and also its expectation that the court would have to grapple with potentially difficult factual issues; the appointment of assessors would be inexplicable if the court were not itself to appraise the effect of evidence

f   which had been or was to be given.

[8] Although the 1907 Act has been repeatedly amended, the scheme of the Act has not been fundamentally altered. The most notable change has been the granting by the Criminal Appeal Act 1964 and the extension by the Criminal Justice Act 1988 of a power, on the allowing of an appeal against conviction, to

g   order a retrial. The core provision contained in s 4 of the 1907 Act is now expressed more shortly and simply in s 2 of the 1968 Act as amended: '(1) Subject to the provisions of this Act, the Court of Appeal—(a) shall allow an appeal against conviction if they think that the conviction is unsafe; and (b) shall dismiss such an appeal in any other case.' The powers contained in s 5 of the 1907 Act

h   have been re-enacted with some change of language but little, in principle, of effect. In s 23 of the 1968 Act, as amended, s 9 of the 1907 Act has been both simplified and elaborated:

'(1) For the purposes of an appeal under this Part of this Act the Court of Appeal may, if they think it necessary or expedient in the interests of

j   justice—(a) order the production of any document, exhibit or other thing connected with the proceedings, the production of which appears to them necessary for the determination of the case; (b) order any witness who would have been a compellable witness in the proceedings from which the appeal lies to attend for examination and be examined before the Court, whether or not he was called in those proceedings; and (c) receive any evidence which was not adduced in the proceedings from which the appeal lies.

(2) The Court of Appeal shall, in considering whether to receive any evidence, have regard in particular to—(a) whether the evidence appears to the Court to be capable of belief; (b) whether it appears to the Court that the evidence may afford any ground for allowing the appeal; (c) whether the evidence would have been admissible in the proceedings from which the appeal lies on an issue which is the subject of the appeal; and (d) whether there is a reasonable explanation for the failure to adduce the evidence in those proceedings.

(3) Subsection (1)(c) above applies to any evidence of a witness (including the appellant) who is competent but not compellable.

(4) For the purposes of an appeal under this Part of this Act, the Court of Appeal may, if they think it necessary or expedient in the interests of justice, order the examination of any witness whose attendance might be required under subsection (1)(b) above to be conducted, in manner provided by rules of court, before any judge or officer of the Court or other person appointed by the Court for the purpose, and allow the admission of any depositions so taken as evidence before the Court.'

[9] Under s 23, as under s 9 of the 1907 Act, the court's discretion to exercise the powers there conferred is governed by its judgment of what is necessary or expedient in the interests of justice. Section 23(1) is directed to the bringing of evidence, whether real, documentary or oral, before the court. To that end it may order the production of a document or other object or the attendance or examination of a witness, whether on request or of its own motion, and may receive evidence not adduced at the trial.

[10] There was no real issue between the parties to this appeal concerning the construction of s 23(1) and (2). The term 'receive' is used to describe the formal act of admitting the evidence referred to before the Court of Appeal. Deciding whether or not to receive the evidence is the first task the court must usually undertake when application is made that it should do so under s 23(1)(c). In considering whether or not it should receive such evidence, usually called 'fresh evidence', the court must have regard in particular to the matters listed in sub-s (2)(a) to (d). These are matters to which, as practice had developed over the years, the courts had come to pay attention (see *R v Parks* [1961] 3 All ER 633 at 634, [1961] 1 WLR 1484 at 1486–1487). They are matters of obvious significance. When considering an application to receive the fresh evidence of a witness, the court will have before it a written statement of the evidence which the witness will give: see form 6, prescribed by r 3 of the Criminal Appeal Rules 1968, SI 1968/1262. If the statement does not appear to the court on reading it to be even capable of belief, there will be little purpose in proceeding further. The statement may be obvious nonsense. Similarly, if it does not appear to the court when it reads the statement that it might, even if fully accepted, afford any ground for allowing the appeal (that is, for thinking that the conviction may be unsafe) there will again be little point in proceeding further. It is obviously relevant to consider whether the fresh evidence would be admissible at the trial, although the Court of Appeal has held that s 23(1)(a) of the 1968 Act is not limited to admissible evidence (see *R v D, R v J* [1996] 1 All ER 881, [1996] QB 283). The Court of Appeal will always pay close attention to the explanation advanced for failing to adduce the evidence at the trial, since it is the clear duty of a criminal defendant to advance any defence and call any evidence on which he wishes to rely at the trial. It is not permissible to keep any available defence or any available

a evidence in reserve for deployment in the Court of Appeal. Thus the practice of
the court is to require a full explanation of the reasons for not adducing the
evidence at the trial (see *R v Trevor* [1998] Crim LR 652). It is however clear that
while the court must, when considering whether to receive fresh evidence, have
regard in particular to the matters listed in s 23(2)(a) to (d), and while in practice
it is most unlikely to receive the evidence if the requirements of sub-paras (a), (b)
b and (c) are not met, the court has an overriding discretion to receive fresh
evidence if it thinks it necessary or expedient in the interests of justice to do so.

[11] I have described the decision whether or not to receive fresh evidence as
the court's first task when application is made under s 23(1)(c). But in practice,
and often with the consent of the Crown, the court will hear de bene esse the
evidence of the witness whose evidence it is sought to adduce, without
c preliminary argument whether the requirements of s 23(1) and (2) have been met
or not, as was done (for example) in *R v Parks*: see [1961] 3 All ER 633 at 635, [1961]
1 WLR 1484 at 1488. There is no objection to this practice. But if the court
receives the evidence, or hears it de bene esse, it must then undertake its second
task, of deciding whether or not to allow the appeal. What is the legal principle
d which should govern the court's approach to this task? That is the narrow but
important issue which divides the parties to this appeal.

The parties' submissions
[12] Mr Mansfield QC, for the appellant, took for his starting point that
recognised by the Privy Council in *Franco v The Queen* [2001] UKPC 38 at [18] of
e its advice:

'The starting point must always be that in a trial on indictment the jury is
the body to which the all-important decisions on the guilt of the accused
are entrusted. This does not mean that every deviation from procedural
regularity and legal correctness vitiates a jury's verdict of guilty. That would
f impose an unattainable standard of perfection and frustrate to an unacceptable
extent the effective administration of criminal justice. But it does mean that
an appellate court, which is not the trial tribunal, should be very cautious in
drawing inferences or making findings about how the jury would have
resolved issues which, for whatever reason, were never before it.'

g The Court of Appeal is a court of review, not a court of trial. It may not usurp
the role of the jury as the body charged by law to resolve issues of fact and
determine guilt. Where the Court of Appeal receives fresh evidence under s 23
of the 1968 Act it must assess the quality of the evidence and allow the appeal if
it judges that the fresh evidence combined with the original evidence might have
h caused the jury, or a reasonable jury properly directed, to acquit. The test is what
impact the evidence, if called at the trial, might have had on the jury. It is not
permissible for appellate judges, who have not heard any of the rest of
the evidence, to make their own decision on the significance or credibility of the
fresh evidence. Reliance was placed on Lord Devlin's famous address 'Sapping
j and Undermining' (1979) *The Judge* pp 148–176.

[13] The correct approach, Mr Mansfield submitted, was that indicated by Lord
Parker CJ in *R v Parks* [1961] 3 All ER 633 at 635, [1961] 1 WLR 1484 at 1488 when,
the court having received fresh evidence, he said: '... if the evidence to which I have
referred had been given at the trial, it is impossible to say that the jury might not
have had a reasonable doubt in the matter.' A similar test was applied in, for

example, *R v Isaac* [1964] Crim LR 721, *R v Flower (Richard)*, *R v Siggins*, *R v Flower (Eric)*
[1965] 3 All ER 669 at 671, [1966] 1 QB 146 at 150, *R v Dwyer* (16 November 1970, *a*
unreported), *R v Barker* (12 January 1971, unreported). Mr Mansfield submitted
that in rejecting Lord Parker CJ's jury-impact test as the necessary and appropriate
test, the House in *Stafford v DPP, Luvaglio v DPP* [1973] 3 All ER 762, [1974] AC 878
had erred in principle. That decision had been applied in a number of cases,
notably *R v Callaghan* (1989) 88 Cr App R 40 at 46–47. But in a number of cases in *b*
which appeals have been allowed, it was said, the older approach had been
followed. In *R v McIlkenny* [1992] 2 All ER 417 at 425 the limitations of the role of
the Court of Appeal were explicitly recognised. Mr Mansfield relied in particular
on the test formulated in *R v McNamee* (17 December 1998, unreported):

> 'The court's task in this appeal is to resolve the question as to whether the *c*
> conviction of this appellant is safe in the light of the fresh evidence. We test
> that question by asking whether the jury, if they had knowledge of the fresh
> evidence, would necessarily have come to the conclusion that they did. For
> reasons which we will set out we have concluded that it is not possible for us
> to say that the jury would necessarily have arrived at the same conclusion if
> they had knowledge of the fresh evidence ... We have, none the less, *d*
> concluded that the conviction is unsafe because we cannot be sure that the
> jury would have reached the conclusion that they were sure of guilt if they
> had the fresh evidence which we have heard. Furthermore the case as
> presented to us by both sides is very different to that presented at trial.'

In reliance on *Stirland v DPP* [1944] 2 All ER 13 at 15, [1944] AC 315 at 321, *e*
Mr Mansfield contended that the Court of Appeal should allow an appeal unless
it was inevitable that the jury would have convicted even if the fresh evidence had
been adduced at trial.

[14] Mr Waters QC, for the Crown, based his response on *Stafford v DPP*, a
modern and unanimous decision of the House which he submitted was correct *f*
in principle. Section 2 of the 1968 Act imposes on the Court of Appeal, in cases
which involve fresh evidence as in cases which do not, a duty of judgment. If the
court think the conviction is unsafe they must allow, otherwise they must
dismiss, the appeal. It is their judgment which matters: 'if they think ...' They
may find it useful when forming that judgment to consider what impact the *g*
evidence, if called before the jury, might have had, but that is not a necessary step
nor is it the only or final question the court must ask. *R v Clegg* [1998] NIJB 68 did
not, as contended in the Court of Appeal, impose a different test.

[15] The House was reminded of important passages in the speeches delivered
in *Stafford v DPP*. In the course of his leading speech Viscount Dilhorne said: *h*

> 'I do not suggest that in determining whether a verdict is unsafe or
> unsatisfactory, it is a wrong approach for the court to pose the question:
> "Might this new evidence have led to the jury returning a verdict of not
> guilty?" If the court thinks that it would or might, the court will no doubt
> conclude that the verdict was unsafe or unsatisfactory. Counsel for the appellant *j*
> Stafford in the course of his argument drew attention to the many cases in
> which, since 1908, and since the amendment made in 1966, the court has
> quashed a conviction saying that in the light of the fresh evidence the jury
> might have come to a different conclusion, but I do not think that it is
> established as a rule of law that, in every fresh evidence case, the court must
> decide what they think the jury might or would have done if they had heard

a   that evidence. That it is a convenient approach and a reasonable one to
    make, I do not deny. When a court has said that, it means and can only mean
    that they think that the fresh evidence might have led to a different result to
    the case, and that in consequence the verdict was unsafe or unsatisfactory.
    Counsel strongly urged that the court should recognise that reasonable men
    can come to different conclusions on contested issues of fact and that,
b   although the court came to the conclusion that the fresh evidence raised no
    reasonable doubt as to the guilt of the accused, they should nonetheless
    quash the conviction if they thought that a jury might reasonably take a
    different view. I do not agree. It would, in my opinion, be wrong for the
    court to say "in our view this evidence does not give rise to any reasonable
    doubt about the guilt of the accused. We do not ourselves consider that an
c   unsafe or unsatisfactory verdict was returned but as the jury who heard the
    case might conceivably have taken a different view from ours, we quash the
    conviction" for Parliament has, in terms, said that the court should only
    quash a conviction if, there being no error of law or material irregularity at
    the trial, "they think" the verdict was unsafe or unsatisfactory. They have to
d   decide and Parliament has not required them or given them power to quash
    a verdict if they think that a jury might conceivably reach a different
    conclusion from that to which they have come. If the court has no
    reasonable doubt about the verdict, it follows that the court does not think
    that the jury could have one; and, conversely, if the court says that a jury
    might in the light of the new evidence have a reasonable doubt, that means
e   that the court has a reasonable doubt. It is well settled that the Court of
    Appeal should only apply the proviso to s 2(1) if it is of the opinion that, if the
    jury had been properly directed, it would inevitably have come to the same
    conclusion. While, of course, the proviso cannot be applied where the court
    thinks the verdict unsafe or unsatisfactory, counsel for the appellant Stafford
f   argued that in a "fresh evidence" case the court should follow the same
    principle as that applicable to the proviso and only hold that a conviction was
    safe and satisfactory if they thought that a jury which heard the fresh
    evidence would inevitably have come to the conclusion that the accused was
    guilty. I cannot accept this argument. When the application of the proviso
    is under consideration, something has gone wrong in the conduct of the trial.
g   In a "fresh evidence" case nothing has gone wrong in the conduct of the trial
    and I see no warrant for importing the principles applicable to the proviso
    into the determination of whether a verdict is or is not safe and satisfactory.
    The words of s 2(1)(a) are clear and unambiguous and they are the words
    which have to be applied.' (See [1973] 3 All ER 762 at 765–766, [1974] AC 878
h   at 893–894.)

    After considering the fresh evidence in that case at length he observed:

        'While, as I have said the Court of Appeal and this House may find it a
        convenient approach to consider what a jury might have done if they had
j   heard the fresh evidence, the ultimate responsibility rests with them and
        them alone for deciding the question.' (See [1973] 3 All ER 762 at 766–767,
        [1974] AC 878 at 906.)

    Lord Pearson ([1973] 3 All ER 762 at 763, [1974] AC 878 at 890) agreed with
    Viscount Dilhorne. Lord Diplock agreed with Viscount Dilhorne and also
    with Lord Cross of Chelsea and Lord Kilbrandon, each of whom delivered

substantial speeches agreeing with Viscount Dilhorne's conclusion and with his essential reasoning (see [1973] 3 All ER 762 at 767–768, 768–770, [1974] AC 878 at 906–911, 911–914).

[16] In hearing any appeal against conviction the Court of Appeal will ordinarily have a considerable body of material before it: grounds of appeal; transcripts of the judge's summing up to the jury and any relevant passages in the evidence and of any material rulings given before or in the course of the trial; plans, photographs and so on. And although the court does not have the jury's reasons, it does have the jury's verdict. From this, some inferences may always be drawn. If the issue is consent, the jury must, to convict, have been sure that the victim did not consent. If the issue is pure identification, the jury must, to convict, have been sure that the evidence identifying the defendant was accurate and reliable. If a proper judicial direction has been given, it will ordinarily be safe for the Court of Appeal to infer that the factual ingredients essential to prove guilt have been established against the defendant to the satisfaction of the jury. But the Court of Appeal can rarely know, save perhaps from questions asked by the jury after retirement, at what points the jury have felt difficulty. The jury's process of reasoning will not be revealed and, if a number of witnesses give evidence bearing on a single question, the Court of Appeal will never know which of those witnesses the jury accepted and which, if any, they doubted or rejected.

[17] My Lords, Mr Mansfield is right to emphasise the central role of the jury in a trial on indictment. This is an important and greatly-prized feature of our constitution. Trial by jury does not mean trial by jury in the first instance and trial by judges of the Court of Appeal in the second. The Court of Appeal is entrusted with a power of review to guard against the possibility of injustice but it is a power to be exercised with caution, mindful that the Court of Appeal is not privy to the jury's deliberations and must not intrude into territory which properly belongs to the jury.

[18] Where the Court of Appeal has heard oral evidence under s 23(1)(c) of the 1968 Act (whether pursuant to its own decision, or by agreement, or de bene esse), the evidence will almost always have appeared, on paper, to be capable of belief and to afford a possible ground for allowing the appeal. By the time the court comes to decide whether the appeal should be allowed or dismissed, it will have heard the evidence, including cross-examination, and any submissions made on its effect. It may then conclude, without doubt, that the evidence cannot be accepted or cannot afford a ground for allowing the appeal. Such was the case, for example, in R v Jones (1996) 33 BMLR 80 at 88, where the court, having decided to receive and having heard opinion evidence from an expert, found conclusive objections to the acceptability of that opinion. The court may, on the other hand, judge the fresh evidence to be clearly conclusive in favour of allowing the appeal. Such might be the case, for example, if a witness who could not be in any way impeached testified, on oath and after all appropriate warnings, that he alone had committed the crime for which the appellant had been convicted. The more difficult cases are of course those which fall between these extreme ends of the spectrum.

[19] It is undesirable that exercise of the important judgment entrusted to the Court of Appeal by s 2(1) of the 1968 Act should be constrained by words not to be found in the statute and that adherence to a particular thought process should be required by judicial decision. Thus the House in Stafford v DPP were right to reject the submission of counsel that the Court of Appeal had asked the wrong question by taking as the test the effect of the fresh evidence on their minds and

a   not the effect that that evidence would have had on the mind of the jury (see [1974] AC 878 at 880). It would, as the House pointed out, be anomalous for the court to say that the evidence raised no doubt whatever in their minds but might have raised a reasonable doubt in the minds of the jury. I am not persuaded that the House laid down any incorrect principle in *Stafford v DPP*, so long as the Court of Appeal bears very clearly in mind that the question for its consideration is

b   whether the conviction is safe and not whether the accused is guilty. But the test advocated by counsel in *Stafford v DPP* and by Mr Mansfield in this appeal does have a dual virtue to which the speeches I have quoted perhaps gave somewhat inadequate recognition. First, it reminds the Court of Appeal that it is not and should never become the primary decision-maker. Secondly, it reminds the Court

c   of Appeal that it has an imperfect and incomplete understanding of the full processes which led the jury to convict. The Court of Appeal can make its assessment of the fresh evidence it has heard, but save in a clear case it is at a disadvantage in seeking to relate that evidence to the rest of the evidence which the jury heard. For these reasons it will usually be wise for the Court of Appeal, in a case of any difficulty, to test their own provisional view by asking whether the evidence, if

d   given at the trial, might reasonably have affected the decision of the trial jury to convict. If it might, the conviction must be thought to be unsafe.

[20] In some of the authorities, the decision to allow an appeal is closely associated with the decision to order a retrial. This is understandable but wrong. If the court thinks a conviction unsafe, its clear statutory duty is to allow the

e   appeal, whether or not there can be a retrial. A conviction cannot be thought unsafe if a retrial can be ordered but safe if it cannot. It is only when an appeal has been or is to be allowed because a conviction is thought to be unsafe that any question of a retrial can properly arise.

[21] In the present case, as adherence to precedent required, the Court of Appeal

f   formulated a test based on *Stafford v DPP* and other cases in which *Stafford v DPP* had been cited and applied. No criticism of its formulation is made if *Stafford v DPP* itself was correct. Since the principle laid down in *Stafford v DPP* was, in the opinion of the House, correct, the attack made on the Court of Appeal's self-direction in the present case must fail. The foregoing paragraphs, it is hoped,

g   make clear the approach which the Court of Appeal should follow. It would not be helpful to attempt to answer the certified question.

The appellant's conviction

[22] Professor Gudjonsson, a distinguished forensic psychologist, examined the

h   appellant in prison in October 1998 and studied a large quantity of documentation supplied by the Criminal Cases Review Commission. He wrote a report dated 18 January 1999. For purposes of this report he conducted tests to establish the appellant's intelligence, suggestibility, acquiescence, compliance, personality and socialisation. The appellant's intelligence was found to be at the upper end of the

j   low average range. He was found to be highly susceptible to giving in to leading questions and interrogative pressure. He had a very marked tendency to answer questions in the affirmative irrespective of the content of the question and to contradict himself. His profile was that of an unstable, neurotic extrovert. His personality was similar to that of persons found to be 'personality-disordered'. Professor Gudjonsson reviewed in detail the answers given by the appellant in interview. His conclusion was expressed in these terms:

'As far as the police interviews and Mr. Pendleton's self-incriminating *a* admission are concerned, I am of the view that in 1985 he was a psychologically vulnerable individual. He was an extremely anxious individual who was finding it difficult to cope with life (his medical records confirm this). The record of the police interviews gives an indication of his immense distress and agitation concerning his arrest and questioning, which appear to have been accompanied by a lack of concern or thought about the consequences *b* of his admissions. His anxiety proneness seems less pronounced now than it was in 1985, but in spite of this he proved to be abnormally suggestible, compliant and acquiescent. These vulnerabilities are likely to have been present, and possibly more marked, in 1985. Finally, it is evident from the transcripts of the police interviews that Mr. Pendleton was subjected to considerable pressure to confess, pressure he was clearly having difficulties *c* coping with ... Having considered this case carefully I have serious reservations about the reliability of the self-incriminating admissions Mr. Pendleton made to the police in 1985.'

When called to give oral evidence, the professor adhered to his opinion. He did *d* not assert that the appellant's admissions to the police had been false, acknowledging that he could not know whether they were false or not. But he considered that the circumstances of the questioning, for a man having the psychological character of the appellant, threw doubt on the reliability of what he had admitted.

[23] Dr Badcock, a consultant forensic psychiatrist, had previously examined *e* the appellant in April 1986 and reviewed his findings in the light of Professor Gudjonsson's report. His conclusion was expressed in these terms:

'I agree with Dr Gudjonsson that Mr Pendleton presented as a psychologically vulnerable individual during the period of the police interviews. I also agree that in some aspects of the interviews he appears to have been suggestible. *f* I am perhaps less confident than Dr Gudjonsson that all self incriminating admissions were obtained as a result of pressure to confess and, in the real life situation, he seems to have steadfastly maintained his belief that he was not directly involved in the death of Mr Clark.'

In his oral evidence he also adhered to the views he had expressed in his report. *g*

[24] The Court of Appeal in its judgment summarised all this evidence very fairly and fully. It also reviewed at some length the contemporaneously recorded, but not tape-recorded, summaries of the appellant's interviews with the police. It did not accept that the appellant had been put under unfair pressure and observed: *h*

'Given the contents of the appellant's statements to the police, and the manner in which they were elicited, we have no doubt as to the reliability of the admissions made by the appellant as to his presence at the scene of the murder. None of the vulnerabilities described by Professor Gudjonsson can, *j* upon a consideration of the interviews as a whole, put a flavour of falsity upon the admissions made. We find it inconceivable that his accounts were imagined or invented. Unless there is material, extraneous to the interviews and the issues surrounding them, which otherwise casts doubt upon the admissions, they provide a sound and sufficient basis for the safety of the conviction. Moreover upon being satisfied as to the appellant's presence, the

a   jury were entitled to convict him and it was not and could not reasonably be
     argued otherwise either in 1985 or now.'

     The Court of Appeal then considered the evidence of two witnesses, Sharpe and
     Gallimore. The first implicated the appellant indirectly in the commission of the
     crime, the second implicated him as being present but not as the author of the
b   violence. Having considered the fresh evidence to support an alibi the Court of
     Appeal expressed its final conclusion as follows:

         'A feature of the present appeal is the fact that the appellant wants the
         strength of the case against him assessed on the basis of the defence which he
         did not, but could have, put forward at the trial. Since his account that he
c   was not present at the scene of the murder has been consistent, albeit not put
         forward at the trial, he is entitled to do that. The court must assess the
         evidence at the trial and the further material which has since become
         available, on the basis of his case that not only did the appellant not
         participate in the attack on Clark but that he was not present at the scene.
d   We bear in mind the lapse of time between the murder and the trial. In our
         judgment there is no basis upon which an abuse of process submission could
         have succeeded at the trial, either on the law as it was in 1985 or as it is now,
         and making full allowance for subsequent events.
         We assess the reliability of the admissions made in interview on their own
         merits and also having regard to the additional material. If, notwithstanding
e   a provisional view as to their reliability, there was additional extraneous
         material which casts doubt on their reliability, that could affect the safety of
         the verdict. Nothing in the additional material, in our judgment, casts doubt
         upon the admissions made. Moreover, while the interviews of Thorpe are
         not evidence against the appellant, and the judge directed the jury that his
         oral evidence was not evidence against him either, we would accept that
f   there could be material emanating from him which, while not evidence
         against the appellant, could be used in his favour to cast doubt upon the
         reliability of his admissions. There is some doubt as to the circumstances in
         which the appellant and Thorpe met on 2 June 1971. That is not surprising
         and does not create a doubt about the reliability of admissions or as to what
g   occurred when they had met. There is nothing in the material emanating
         from Thorpe which supports a submission that the appellant's admissions
         were unreliable.
         The reliability of the appellant's admissions in interview are, in the present
         context, sufficient to ensure the safety of the verdict against him. Not only
h   does the material canvassed at the trial and the additional material canvassed
         upon the hearing of this appeal fail to cast doubt upon the reliability of the
         admissions, it provides other substantial evidence of the guilt of the appellant.
         Notwithstanding thorough investigation on behalf of the appellant, there is
         in our judgment substantial additional evidence of his guilt in the evidence
j   of Sharpe and Gallimore. We approached the case upon the basis of the law
         laid down in *Stafford v DPP, Luvaglio v DPP* [1973] 3 All ER 762, [1974] AC 878,
         R v Callaghan (1989) 88 Cr App R 40 and *R v Jones* (1996) 33 BMLR 80. We
         have no doubt that the conviction was safe. We add that if Carswell LCJ, in
         R v Clegg [1998] NIJB 68, had in mind a different test, which we doubt, we do
         not consider that a reasonable tribunal of fact might in the present case
         properly be left with a reasonable doubt about the safety of the conviction.'

Mr Mansfield criticised the quoted passages of the Court of Appeal judgment as
showing that the court was doing just what it should not have done, taking upon
itself the task of assessing the fresh psychological evidence and so trespassing
on the exclusive domain of the jury. The Court of Appeal was in effect undertaking
the retrial of a case which had never been before the jury. Mr Waters countered
that the Court of Appeal had undertaken the task which the statute imposes upon
it, had done so clearly and conscientiously, and had reached a conclusion which
should not be disturbed.

[25] In reviewing this case the House is at once confronted by the problem
that the appellant's true defence—that he had not been present when the crime
was committed and had lied to the police when telling them that he had
been—was never put to the jury at all. Mr Mansfield has at no stage made any
criticism of trial counsel in this regard, and the Court of Appeal considered that
no criticism could sensibly be made. It would not be right for the House on a
necessarily incomplete knowledge of the facts and without reference to trial
counsel to cast any aspersion on the handling of the defence. We do not doubt
that the appellant's advisors were seeking to achieve the best possible outcome
for him, although it should be clearly understood that counsel's duty is to give
effect to his instructions and not to present an affirmative case inconsistent with
them. But the inescapable fact is that the trial jury never had the opportunity to
consider an issue very close to the heart of the case: were the appellant's
admissions reliable and true? The jury were invited to acquit on the basis that the
appellant, in admitting presence and denying participation in the violence, had
spoken the truth. His instructions were that he had lied, since he had not been
present at all.

[26] This is not a unique situation. It occurred in *R v Evans* (3 December 1997,
unreported), when a trial had been conducted on the basis that the appellant had
either witnessed a murder or committed it and later evidence (also throwing
doubt on the reliability of his confessions) raised a doubt whether he had been
present at all, a question never investigated at the trial. It also arose in *R v Bowler*
(24 July 1997, unreported), when fresh evidence after the trial raised a possible
hypothesis that a death had been the result of accident, a hypothesis never raised
or investigated at the trial. In allowing the appeal in that case the court said:

> 'We are conscious that we have heard only a small part of the evidence in
> this case. We are also conscious that the witnesses at trial were not asked all
> the questions which they would have been asked had the accident hypothesis
> been before the jury. Our system provides for trial by jury, and a jury has not
> been asked to consider whether, in the light of all the evidence in the case,
> including the evidence for and against the accident hypothesis, it is sure of
> the appellant's guilt. In those circumstances we conclude that the appellant's
> conviction is unsafe.'

Given the primacy of the jury, it must always be a ground for concern if the jury
have never considered a potentially important aspect of the case.

[27] No one can now be sure what would have happened had the evidence of
Professor Gudjonsson been available at the time of the trial. But the defence
might in at least three respects have been conducted differently. First, the appellant
might have been called to give evidence on his own behalf. The prospect of the
jury believing that the appellant's disavowal of his admissions might be true
would plainly have been enhanced had he been able to rely, although necessarily
to a limited extent, on the evidence of a leading professional expert in this field.

a Giving evidence on his own behalf might of course have proved, in trial counsel's words, 'the certain road to disaster'. But the appellant would at least have had the satisfaction of giving his own account and his true case would have been before the jury. The outcome must be a matter of speculation. Secondly, there would have been much more searching investigation of the appellant's mental state during the interviews, which can only have been marginally relevant so long

b as the appellant's admissions were being accepted as true. This was not a case of oppression or abusive conduct by the police. But the appellant's behaviour was, it might be thought, somewhat extreme, even in a predicament which would upset the most phlegmatic. About halfway through the interview process, after the appellant had said 'Charge me, charge me, I did it, I don't care, you don't believe me', the police recorded:

c

'He then gripped his head in his hands and began moaning and wailing. He pulled his feet up onto the bench he was sitting on, and huddled into a ball in the corner of the interview room. He tugged at his hair and continued in this posture for two or three minutes before falling quiet and remaining

d curled up in the corner of the room.'

Thirdly, it seems likely that there would have been much more detailed inquiry into what passed between the police and the appellant which was not recorded. If it were shown that the appellant volunteered information which was true and which he could not have known had he not been present, this would plainly have

e given strong support to the Crown case. If, on the other hand, as he claimed, the appellant was merely repeating much that the police had told him, that would have been consistent with his disavowal. It would, for example, have been very relevant to explore what passed between the police and the appellant when he was taken to view the scene of the murder at 1400 hrs on 24 March 1985, following

f the episode recorded above. As it was, this aspect cannot have called for rigorous investigation.

[**28**] In the light of these uncertainties and this fresh psychological evidence it is impossible to be sure that this conviction is safe, and that is so whether the members of the House ask whether they themselves have reason to doubt the safety of the conviction or whether they ask whether the jury might have reached a

g different conclusion. The case against the appellant was not a strong one. Save in emotional outbursts which were rightly discounted, the appellant never admitted committing any violence. The jury were instructed not to rely on the oral evidence of Thorpe against him. Sharpe and Gallimore were criminals about whose evidence the jury could well have had reservations. And the jury never had the

h opportunity to consider what, on the appellant's instructions, had actually happened. Had the jury been trying a different case on substantially different evidence the outcome must be in doubt. In holding otherwise the Court of Appeal strayed beyond its true function of review and made findings which were not open to it in all the circumstances. Indeed, it came perilously close to

j considering whether the appellant, in its judgment, was guilty.

[**29**] It is unnecessary to consider the appellant's missing statement of 19 June 1971 in any detail. It reads as the somewhat artless statement of a disorganised and shiftless 25-year-old. It is consistent with his instructions that he had not been present when the crime was committed. But even if available to counsel at the trial it could scarcely have supported a convincing alibi. It is in itself of negligible significance.

[30] For reasons already given the appellant's appeal should be allowed and his conviction quashed.

LORD MACKAY OF CLASHFERN.

[31] My Lords, I am in agreement with the opinion of Lord Bingham of Cornhill. For the reasons he has given I would also allow the appeal.

LORD STEYN.

[32] My Lords, I am in agreement with the opinion of Lord Bingham of Cornhill. For the reasons he has given I would also allow the appeal.

LORD HOPE OF CRAIGHEAD.

[33] My Lords, I have had the advantage of reading in draft the speech of my noble and learned friend, Lord Bingham of Cornhill. I agree entirely with his analysis of the legislative background to this case and with his description of the approach which the Court of Appeal should follow where, in an appeal against conviction, it receives fresh evidence. I also agree with him, for the reasons which he has given, that it is impossible to be sure that this conviction is safe. I would allow the appeal and quash the conviction.

LORD HOBHOUSE OF WOODBOROUGH.

[34] My Lords, this appeal has been certified as raising a point of general public importance because the appellant has wished to argue that what your Lordships' House said in *Stafford v DPP, Luvaglio v DPP* [1973] 3 All ER 762, [1974] AC 878 should no longer be regarded as the law. I agree with your Lordships that this argument should be rejected. This means that the terms in which the Court of Appeal directed themselves in law were correct. However a further point has then arisen whether your Lordships agree with the assessment which the Court of Appeal made of the peculiar facts of this case and which led them to dismiss the appellant's appeal. I venture to doubt whether it was right for your Lordships to enter into that territory when all that is being suggested is that a different assessment to that made by the Court of Appeal is to be preferred. The structure of our criminal justice appellate system is that the assessment of the safety of the conviction, as opposed to the principles to be applied in doing so, is a matter for the Court of Appeal Criminal Division, a court specially constituted to carry out that task.

The point of principle

[35] On this aspect I wholly agree with what has been said by my noble and learned friend Lord Bingham of Cornhill. The criminal jurisdiction of the Court of Appeal is statutory, that is to say that its jurisdiction derives exclusively from statute and is defined by statute. Two fundamental considerations of policy underlie this: that no one should be convicted of an indictable crime save on his own plea or on the verdict of a jury; that the verdict of the jury should be final. This latter principle, originally absolute, was qualified by the creation of the Court of Criminal Appeal (and by its immediate predecessor) but from the outset the jurisdiction of the Court of Criminal Appeal was strictly limited. The Criminal Appeal Act 1968, the Act in force when *Stafford v DPP* was decided, still defined the jurisdiction in relatively elaborate terms. The amendment of that Act by the Criminal Appeal Act 1995 has simplified the definition and focussed it on a single criterion. Section 2(1) now reads: 'Subject to the provisions of this Act,

a the Court of Appeal—(a) shall allow an appeal against conviction if they think that the conviction is unsafe; and (b) shall dismiss such an appeal in any other case.' Therefore the sole criterion which the Court of Appeal is entitled to apply is that of what it thinks is the safety of the conviction. It has to make the assessment. That is made clear by the use of the words 'if they think'. The change in the language of the statute has reinforced the reasoning in *Stafford v DPP* and

b shows that appeals are not to be allowed unless the Court of Appeal has itself made the requisite assessment and has itself concluded that the conviction is unsafe. Lord Bingham of Cornhill CJ put the point clearly in *R v Jones* (1996) 33 BMLR 80 at 88 (cited also in the judgment of the Court of Appeal in the present case): 'It seems plain on the language of the statute and on authority that the court is obliged to exercise its own judgment in deciding whether, in the light of

c the new evidence, the conviction is unsafe.'

[36] The argument of the appellant was that this infringed the principle that a defendant should only be convicted on the verdict of the jury and any assessment by the Court of Appeal, after some possibility of a different verdict or some risk of unsafety had been shown, was contrary to this principle. Leaving on one side

d that this argument seeks to contradict the statute, the argument is radically unsound. The defendant has been convicted by a jury; no infringement of principle is involved. Indeed, it can be commented that it is the appellant's argument which is unprincipled since it is he who is seeking to escape from the verdict of a jury merely upon the possibility (which will exist in almost every case) that the jury might

e have returned a different verdict. Unless and until the Court of Appeal has been persuaded that the verdict of the jury is unsafe, the verdict must stand. Nothing less will suffice to displace it. A mere risk that it is unsafe does not suffice: the appellant has to discharge a burden of persuasion and persuade the Court of Appeal that the conviction *is* unsafe. It is ironic that the appellant has, under the banner 'the supremacy of the jury', sought to undermine that supremacy and the finality

f of the jury's verdict.

[37] A further point arises from the appellant's argument. In a 'fresh evidence' case, there has been no irregularity or error of law at the criminal trial. The verdict of guilty has been returned by a properly directed jury after a properly conducted and fair trial. The mere production on a later appeal of additional evidence which

g would have been admitted at the trial had it then been adduced demonstrates no unsafety of the verdict. It merely raises for the consideration of the Court of Appeal the question whether the Court of Appeal thinks that, taking into account the new evidence, the verdict has become unsafe. Whether or not to admit in the Court of Appeal new evidence not adduced at the trial has throughout been

h the subject of separate provision in the statutes, now the amended and simplified s 23 of the 1968 Act. Additional policy considerations of not destroying the ordinary finality and integrity of the criminal trial apply. These have been commented upon by the Court of Appeal on many occasions and call for no further repetition by me in this speech. But subject to those considerations, the Court of Appeal

j will have to look at the new evidence tendered and, if it thinks fit, listen to the witnesses giving it orally and being cross-examined, as happened in the Court of Appeal in the present case, in order to decide whether or not it thinks that the conviction is unsafe. The admission of the evidence in the Court of Appeal in no way prejudges or forecloses this question: s 23(2) refers to evidence which appears to the court to be '*capable*' of belief and which '*may*' afford a ground for allowing an appeal.

[38] It does not help and is in principle wrong to seek to explain or put a gloss on the words of s 2 of the 1968 Act. 'Unsafe' is an ordinary word of the English language. It connotes a risk of error or mistake or irregularity which exceeds a certain margin so as to justify the description 'unsafe'. It involves a risk assessment. Where the conviction results from a plea of guilty entered by the defendant, the circumstances in which the plea was entered are relevant. Where the conviction is after a trial, it is the trial and the verdict which are relevant. But, in my judgment it is not right to attempt to look into the minds of the members of the jury. Their deliberations are secret and their precise and detailed reasoning is not known. For an appellate court to speculate, whether hypothetically or actually, is not appropriate. It is for the Court of Appeal to answer the direct and simply stated question: do we think that the conviction was unsafe?

[39] I must also, again in agreement with my noble and learned friend Lord Bingham, emphasise a further point. No question of ordering a re-trial under s 7 of the 1968 Act arises unless the Court of Appeal has allowed the appeal and quashed the conviction appealed against as unsafe. There is no discretionary power to order retrials when the conviction has not already been held to be unsafe. It is not permissible to reason that it would be sensible to have a retrial therefore we will allow the appeal. The two questions must be kept distinct.

The conviction in the present case

[40] I will take this aspect as shortly as possible. Your Lordships are of the opinion that this conviction is unsafe. I agree. My difficulty is that I consider that it was unsafe in any event because the verdict was inconsistent with the directions of the trial judge as to how they should approach the evidence adduced at the trial. I remain unpersuaded that the new evidence now relied upon by the appellant would itself have disclosed any unsafety of the conviction. I consider that on that question the reasoning of the Court of Appeal was sound, that their assessment was painstaking and realistic and that it would not be proper to interfere with their conclusion on that point.

[41] This was an unusual case. There was a long interval of time between the time of the alleged offence and the time the appellant was arrested, interviewed, charged and brought to trial. The appellant was tried on an indictment which charged both him and one Thorpe with the murder of Bernard Clark. In the proof of evidence which was taken by his solicitors, the appellant did not complain about the conduct of the police and did not dispute their evidence as to what he had said to them in interview and elsewhere, but did state that he had not been at the scene of the crime and that what he had said in interview about having been there was made up and untrue. There was a witness (Gallimore) whose evidence was expected to have the effect of putting him at the scene but exonerating him of any actual involvement. Another witness (Sharpe) was expected to say that the appellant was both present and involved. Thorpe was to be expected to run the defence that the murderer was the appellant (just as the appellant had said in interview that the murderer was Thorpe). This presented the defence counsel with a problem of what advice to give the appellant. The upshot was that he was advised to put the prosecution to proof of their case against him. He would not go into the witness box. He would not raise an issue as to the credibility of what he had said in interview but rather build upon it to persuade the jury that the prosecution evidence did not prove that he was a party to the murder. Both Sharpe and Thorpe were witnesses who could be convincingly discredited. The

a   appellant's leading trial counsel has stated that the appellant accepted the advice
and counsel was sure that he understood it.

[42] No criticism has been made of counsel's advice either in the Court of
Appeal or in your Lordships' House. In my view this was clearly right. To advise
the appellant to go into the witness box and deny the truth of what he had said in
interview would probably have been disastrous. He was obviously an emotional
b   and immature person of very limited intelligence, as the record of the interviews
amply demonstrated, but he would have been a very vulnerable witness indeed
who could have been effectively cross-examined by both his co-defendant and the
Crown and it would inevitably have been put to him forcibly that he was a
murderer.

c   [43] Counsels' conduct of the trial on behalf of the appellant was remarkably
successful. When the judge summed up to the jury he told them, according to the
solicitor's note of the summing up, not to use the evidence of either Sharpe or
Thorpe against him. The result was that, whilst there was uncontradicted evidence
that the appellant was present, there was no evidence upon which the judge
considered that the jury should rely that he had joined in the attack on the victim
d   or had been a party to the murder. The jury nevertheless returned verdicts of
guilty against both defendants. Taking the summing up and the verdicts together,
I consider that the conviction of the appellant was unsafe and should be quashed.

[44] The thrust of the argument advanced before your Lordships on behalf of
the appellant was that if the defence at the trial had had the evidence of Professor
e   Gudjonsson and Dr Badcock, the defence would have been differently conducted,
the defence would have made a positive case that the appellant was not present
and the appellant would have gone into the witness box to say so and submit
himself to cross-examination. The psychologists would have gone into the witness
box to explain the susceptibility of a weak-minded man to suggestion and express
f   the view that this was what they believe had occurred. Like the Court of Appeal
whose judgment I would be happy to adopt on this aspect, I consider that this
course would have been no less disastrous than that already advised against. The
weak-mindedness of the appellant was already apparent from the interview
records as was the extreme care which the police took not to do anything which
could be criticised as oppressing the appellant or putting words into his mouth.
g   A highly debatable issue would have been opened up which would have done all
the damage which counsel were successfully avoiding by avoiding a positive
defence and putting the Crown to the proof of their case. In brief the introduction
of a psychological issue would have weakened the appellant's case not strengthened
it; it would have increased the risk of conviction not reduced it. Its absence does
h   not support a conclusion that the conviction was unsafe.

[45] Finally, I would sound two notes of warning. The first is that the courts
should be cautious about admitting evidence from psychologists, however eminent,
as to the credibility of witnesses. The assessment of the truth of verbal evidence
is save in a very small number of exceptional circumstances a matter for the jury.
j   The suggestibility of some persons is well within the experience of the ordinary
members of juries. To admit evidence from psychologists on such questions is
not only contrary to the established rules of evidence, but is also contrary to the
principle of trial by jury and risks substituting trial by expert. The present case
illustrates this danger with expert witnesses of unimpeachable reputation and
probity being led into expressing their own belief as to whether they would rely
on certain evidence, they having formed and taken into account disputable views

about other purely factual aspects of the case as well—e g, the way in which the interviews were conducted.

[46] The second note of warning concerns the use of subsequent psychological investigations of a defendant to attack his conviction. Sometimes this may be justified but it is always a risky exercise. Firstly, there may be a lapse of time and change of circumstance not only since the conviction but, more relevantly, since the commission of the relevant crime, which call into question the value of the later psychological investigation. Secondly, the psychologist has to rely to a significant extent upon his examination of the relevant person and his assessment of what that person tells him. What the psychologist is told is liable to be self-serving. It cannot be treated as reliable in so far as it consists of unproved contentious facts. An exculpatory account requires proof not merely transmission through the report of a psychologist. Of its nature, psychological evidence is liable to come into a different category to other types of expert evidence, such as DNA analysis, and to require a more critical approach to its use as new evidence for establishing the unsafety of an otherwise safe conviction.

[47] This said I agree to the response to the certified question and that the appeal should be allowed for the reasons which I have given.

Appeal allowed.

Kate O'Hanlon　Barrister.

a

Re Al-Fawwaz
Re Eiderous and another
[2001] UKHL 69

b HOUSE OF LORDS

LORD SLYNN OF HADLEY, LORD HUTTON, LORD MILLETT, LORD SCOTT OF FOSCOTE
AND LORD RODGER OF EARLSFERRY

22–24 OCTOBER, 17 DECEMBER 2001

c *Extradition – Fugitive offender – Relevant offence – Extra-territorial offence – United
States government seeking extradition of appellants in connection with conspiracy to
murder United States citizens abroad – Whether alleged offence having to be committed
within territory of United States – Extradition Act 1989, Sch 1, para 20 – United States
of America (Extradition) Order 1976, Sch 1, art I.*

d In the first of two conjoined appeals, the appellant, F, had been accused in a
United States district court of being party to a terrorist conspiracy, hatched
outside the United States, to murder citizens of that country in other parts of the
world. The alleged offence fell within the extra-territorial jurisdictions of both the
United States and England. After F was arrested in England, the United States
e government made a request for his extradition pursuant to the Extradition Treaty
between the Government of the United Kingdom and the Government of the
United States 1972 (as set out in Sch 1 to the United States of America (Extradition)
Order 1976). Under art I[a] of the treaty, each contracting party undertook to
extradite to the other any person found in 'its territory' who had been accused of
certain specified offences committed 'within the jurisdiction' of the other party.
f Extraditions to the United States were subject to Sch 1 of the Extradition Act
1989. Under para 20[b] of Sch 1, 'fugitive criminal' was defined as any person
accused or convicted of an 'extradition crime' committed 'within the jurisdiction'
of any foreign state who was in or suspected of being in some part of Her Majesty's
dominions. Paragraph 20 defined 'extradition crime' by reference to s 26[c] of the
g Extradition Act 1870. Section 26 provided that that term meant a crime which, if
'committed in England or within English jurisdiction', would have been one of
the crimes listed in one of the Schedules to that Act. The listed offences included
piracy by law of nations. In F's case, the stipendiary magistrate concluded that
there was a prima facie case and committed him to await the decision of the
h Secretary of State. On a subsequent application by F for habeas corpus, the
Divisional Court accepted his contention that, in cases governed by Sch 1 to
the 1989 Act, the extradition crime had to be committed within the territory of
the requesting state so that it would, as transposed, have been committed within
the territory of England and Wales. The court nevertheless dismissed F's
application, concluding that some of the alleged acts could be relied on to ground
j territorial jurisdiction in the United States. Subsequently, a differently-constituted
Divisional Court dismissed, for similar reasons, applications for habeas corpus by
the two appellants in the second case, whose extradition had been sought by the

---

a   Article I is set out at [16], below
b   Paragraph 20, so far as material, is set out at [12], below
c   Section 26, so far as material, is set out at [55], below

United States government in connection with the same conspiracy as had been
alleged against F. They appealed to the House of Lords, as did F. On the appeals, *a*
the United States government challenged the view of the Divisional Court in F's
case that jurisdiction had to be territorial in cases governed by Sch 1 of the 1989 Act.

Held – On its true construction, para 20 of Sch 1 to the 1989 Act did not require
the fugitive criminal to have committed the crime in respect of which extradition *b*
was sought within the territory of the requesting state. Rather, it was sufficient
that the crime was subject to the extra-territorial jurisdiction of the requesting
state and would, as transposed, be triable in England. Such a conclusion was
consistent with an ordinary meaning of the term 'the jurisdiction' of the state,
namely the power of that state to try an offence, which included extra-territorial
jurisdiction. It was also supported by the implied distinction in art 1 of the treaty *c*
between the 'territory' of the requested state and the 'jurisdiction' of the
requesting state, a distinction which suggested that the concept of jurisdiction
was wider than territory. Similarly, the words 'within English jurisdiction' in s 26
of the 1870 Act had to have been intended to add something to 'committed in
England'. Further, since the offence of piracy by law of nations could not be *d*
committed in the territory of a state, its inclusion in the 1870 Act showed that the
term 'jurisdiction' in that Act was not restricted to territorial jurisdiction. It
followed that the term 'within the jurisdiction' in para 20 of Sch 1 to the 1989 Act
included but was wider than 'in the territory' of the requesting state. A conclusion
to the contrary would make it impossible to extradite for some of the most
serious crimes now committed globally or across frontiers. Thus in the instant *e*
cases it was not necessary to show that the acts relied on for the conspiracy were
all done in the United States or that enough of them were done in that country to
ground jurisdiction. There was a prima facie case against all the appellants, and
accordingly the appeals would be dismissed (see [27], [30]–[32], [37], [38],
[42]–[46], [57], [64]–[66], [75], [77]–[79], [85], [89], [92], [93], [101], [102], [105], *f*
[106], [113]–[115], [117], [122], [140], [142]–[144], [146], [151], [164], [167], [170],
[172], below.)
      Government of Belgium v Postlethwaite [1987] 2 All ER 985 and *Liangsiriprasert v
United States Government* [1990] 2 All ER 866 considered.
      Decision of the Divisional Court [2001] 4 All ER 149 affirmed on different grounds. *g*

Notes
For jurisdiction in extradition proceedings, see 17(2) *Halsbury's Laws* (4th edn
reissue) para 1198.
      For the Extradition Act 1989, Sch 1, para 20, see 17 *Halsbury's Statutes* (4th edn) *h*
(1999 reissue) 745.

Cases referred to in opinions
Arton, Re (No 2) [1896] 1 QB 509, DC.
Brown v Stott (Procurator Fiscal, Dunfermline) [2001] 2 All ER 97, [2001] 2 WLR 817, PC. *j*
Doorson v Netherlands (1996) 22 EHRR 330, [1996] ECHR 20524/92, ECt HR.
Fitt v UK (2000) 30 EHRR 480, [2000] ECHR 29777/96, ECt HR.
Government of Belgium v Postlethwaite [1987] 2 All ER 985, sub nom *R v Governor of
      Ashford Remand Centre, ex p Postlethwaite* [1988] AC 924, [1987] 3 WLR 365, HL.
Government of Denmark v Nielsen [1984] 2 All ER 81, [1984] AC 606, [1984] 2 WLR
      737, HL.

a *Government of the Federal Republic of Germany v Sotiriadis* [1974] 1 All ER 692,
   sub nom *R v Governor of Pentonville Prison, ex p Sotiriadis* [1975] AC 1, [1974]
   2 WLR 253, HL.
   Kirkwood v UK (1984) 37 DR 158, E Com HR.
   Kossekechatkov v A-G for Trinidad [1932] AC 78, PC.
   Liangsiriprasert v United States Government [1990] 2 All ER 866, [1991] 1 AC 225,
b [1990] 3 WLR 606, PC.
   MacLeod v A-G for New South Wales [1891] AC 455, PC.
   Piracy Jure Gentium, Re [1934] AC 586, [1934] All ER Rep 506, PC.
   R v Bow Street Metropolitan Stipendiary Magistrate, ex p Pinochet Ugarte (No 3) [1999]
   2 All ER 97, [2000] 1 AC 147, [1999] 2 WLR 827, HL.
   R v Governor of Ashford Remand Centre, ex p Beese [1973] 3 All ER 250, [1973] 1 WLR
c 969, DC; *affd* sub nom *Beese v Governor of Ashford Remand Centre* [1973] 3 All ER
   689, [1973] 1 WLR 1426, HL.
   R v Governor of HM Prison Brixton, ex p Minervini [1958] 3 All ER 318, [1959] 1 QB
   155, [1958] 3 WLR 559, DC.
   R v Governor of Pentonville Prison, ex p Naghdi [1990] 1 All ER 257, [1990] 1 WLR
d 317, DC.
   R v Governor of Pentonville Prison, ex p Osman [1989] 3 All ER 701, [1990] 1 WLR 277,
   DC.
   R v Lavaudier (1881) 15 Cox CC 329, DC.
   R v Page [1953] 2 All ER 1355, [1954] 1 QB 170, [1953] 3 WLR 895, C-MAC.
   R v Taylor (Gary) (1994) TLR 484, CA.
e *R v United States Government, ex p Blair* (1985) Times, 21 June, DC.
   R v Watford Magistrates' Court, ex p Lenman [1993] Crim LR 388, DC.
   R v X, R v Y, R v Z (1989) 91 Cr App R 36, CA.
   Rees v Secretary of State for the Home Dept [1986] 2 All ER 321, [1986] AC 937, [1986]
   2 WLR 1024, HL.
f *Rey v Government of Switzerland* [1999] AC 54, [1998] 3 WLR 1, PC.
   Schtraks v Government of Israel [1962] 3 All ER 529, [1964] AC 556, [1962] 3 WLR
   1013, HL; *affg* [1962] 2 All ER 176, sub nom *R v Governor of Brixton Prison, ex p
   Schtraks* [1963] 1 QB 55, [1962] 2 WLR 976, DC.
   Sinclair v DPP [1991] 2 All ER 366, sub nom *R v Governor of Pentonville Prison, ex p
   Sinclair* [1991] 2 AC 64, [1991] 2 WLR 1028, HL.
g *Soering v UK* (1989) 11 EHRR 439, [1989] ECHR 14038/88, ECt HR.
   Tarling (No 1) v Government of the Republic of Singapore (1978) 70 Cr App R 77, DC
   and HL.
   Tivnan, Re (1864) 5 B & S 645, 122 ER 971.
   Tomlins' application, Re [1995] COD 192, DC.
h
   Appeals

   Re Al-Fawwaz
   Khalid Al-Fawwaz appealed with permission of the Appeal Committee of the
j House of Lords given on 11 June 2001 from the decision of the Divisional Court
   (Buxton LJ and Elias J) on 30 November 2000 ([2001] 4 All ER 149, [2001] 1 WLR
   1234) dismissing his application for a writ of habeas corpus ad subjiciendum
   directed to the governor of HM Prison, Brixton, where he had been detained
   following his committal on 8 September 1999 by the Bow Street Metropolitan
   Stipendiary Magistrate (Nicholas Evans) pending the decision of the Secretary of
   State for the Home Department on the request of the respondent, the government

of the United States of America, for his extradition on a charge of conspiracy to murder. The facts are set out in the opinion of Lord Slynn of Hadley.

Re Eiderous and anor

Ibrahim Eiderous and Adel Abdul Bary appealed from the decision of the Divisional Court (Kennedy LJ and Garland J) on 2 May 2001 ([2001] EWHC Admin 298, [2001] All ER (D) 24 (May)) dismissing their applications for writs of habeas corpus ad subjiciendum directed to the governor of HM Prison, Brixton, where they had been detained following their committal on 25 April 2000 by the Bow Street Metropolitan Stipendiary Magistrate (Nicholas Evans) pending the decisions of the Secretary of State for the Home Department on the requests of the respondent, the government of the United States of America, for their extradition on charges of conspiracy to murder. The facts are set out in the opinion of Lord Slynn of Hadley.

Edward Fitzgerald QC and *Keir Starmer* (instructed by *Raja & Partners*) for Al-Fawwaz. *Michael Mansfield QC* and *Tim Moloney* (instructed by *Birnberg Peirce*) for Eiderous. *Ben Emmerson QC* and *Julian Knowles* (instructed by *Ahmed & Co*) for Abdul Bary. *James Lewis* and *John Hardy* (instructed by the *Crown Prosecution Service*) for the United States government.

Their Lordships took time for consideration.

17 December 2001. The following opinions were delivered.

LORD SLYNN OF HADLEY.

[1] My Lords, your Lordships have heard three appeals together.

[2] In the first the appellant Al-Fawwaz is accused in the United States District Court for the Southern District of New York of conspiring with Osama bin Laden and others between 1 January 1993 and 27 September 1998. It is alleged that they agreed that United States citizens would be murdered in the United States and elsewhere and that American officials in the Middle East and Africa and soldiers deployed in the United Nations Peacekeeping Forces, American diplomats and other internationally protected persons would be killed and bombs planted at United States embassies and other American installations. It is alleged that in furtherance of the alleged conspiracy members of a terrorist group, Al-Qaeda which was founded and led by Osama bin Laden and was committed to violent opposition to the United States of America, bombed the United States embassies in Nairobi, Kenya and in Dar es Salaam, Tanzania. A large number of people were killed.

[3] The appellant was arrested in the United Kingdom on 27 September 1998 and a request made by the United States government for his extradition. On 9 December 1998 an order to proceed with the extradition was made by the Secretary of State on the basis that the appellant 'is accused of offences which, had they occurred in the United Kingdom, would have constituted the offence of conspiracy to murder, within the jurisdiction of the United States of America.' After a hearing the metropolitan stipendiary magistrate ruled that it was not necessary to allege that the offence had been committed in the territory of the United States of America. He found that there was a prima facie case against the appellant and committed him to await the decision of the Secretary of State. The appellant applied for habeas corpus but the application was dismissed by the

a Divisional Court on 30 November 2000 ([2001] 4 All ER 149, [2001] 1 WLR 1234) and it is from that order that the appellant comes before your Lordships.

[4] The Divisional Court held that it was necessary to show that the crime, in respect of which extradition was sought, was alleged to be committed within the actual territory of the United States and that it was not sufficient to allege that a crime was committed within the jurisdiction extra-territorially of the United
b States which would in similar circumstances be governed by the extra-territorial jurisdiction of the United Kingdom. The Divisional Court was, however, satisfied that three overt acts alleged by the United States of America could be relied on to found territorial jurisdiction in the United States, namely (a) the setting up and operating of a secure telephone line in the United States by the appellant through
c an organisation called MCI, (b) the purchase by the appellant of a satellite phone system in the United States, and (c) the issuing in pursuance of the conspiracy, of fatwahs and jihads, allegedly prepared with the concurrence of the appellant in the United States and elsewhere.

[5] The second appellant, Ibrahim Eiderous, and the third appellant, Abdul Bary, Egyptian nationals who were granted asylum in the United Kingdom, are
d likewise charged before the United States District Court for the Southern District of New York with what in the United Kingdom would have been a conspiracy to murder. On an application for extradition the same charge of conspiracy to murder, bomb and kill and the same bombing of two embassies relied on was alleged as that against Al-Fawwaz. Provisional warrants for arrest were executed in July 1999
e and the order to proceed with the examination was issued by the Secretary of State on 21 September 1999. On 25 April 2000 the appellants were committed to await the Secretary of State's decision on the basis that it was not necessary to allege that the acts were committed within the territory of the United States. As in Al-Fawwaz's case, the Divisional Court held ([2001] EWHC Admin 298, [2001]
f All ER (D) 24 (May)) on 2 May 2001, that there were in any event, overt acts within the territorial jurisdiction of the United States and on 2 May 2001 the Divisional Court dismissed the appeal. The overt acts alleged in the United States were challenged by the second and third appellants. There was no evidence to justify a finding that the satellite phone had been used to plan the explosions and that what happened was consistent with these two men being part of a dissident
g group who had been persecuted in their own country.

[6] There were thus some issues common to the appeals, others where the principle is the same but the factual material differs.

[7] It is convenient to consider first the question of principle and whether the extradition crime ruled on must be alleged to have been committed in the United
h States or whether it is sufficient that it is within the United States' jurisdiction in the sense that it is triable in the United States.

[8] The statutory provisions are not entirely simple and it is useful to set them out as far as relevant.

[9] Section 1 of the Extradition Act 1989 (which consolidated with amendments,
j provisions relating to extradition in the Criminal Justice Act 1988, the Fugitive Offenders Act 1967 and the Extradition Acts 1870 to 1935) provides that where an extradition procedure under Pt III of the 1989 Act is available as between the United Kingdom and a foreign state, a person in the United Kingdom who—

'(a) is accused in that state of the commission of an extradition crime; or
(b) is alleged to be unlawfully at large after conviction of an extradition crime

by a court in that state may be arrested and returned to that state in accordance with those procedures.'

[10] 'Extradition crime' except in Sch 1 is defined in s 2(1) as meaning:

'... (a) conduct in the territory of a foreign state ... which, if it occurred in the United Kingdom, would constitute an offence punishable with imprisonment for a term of 12 months ... and which, however described in the law of the foreign state ... is so punishable under that law; (b) an extra-territorial offence against the law of a foreign state ...'

so punishable which satisfies the conditions in sub-ss (2) and (3) of s 2.

[11] However s 1(3) provides that:

'Where an Order in Council under section 2 of the Extradition Act 1870 is in force in relation to a foreign state, Schedule 1 to this Act (the provisions of which derive from that Act and certain associated enactments) shall have effect in relation to that state, but subject to the limitations, restrictions, conditions, exceptions and qualifications, if any, contained in the Order.'

[12] Schedule 1, para 20 provides two important definitions:

'... "extradition crime", in relation to any foreign state, is to be construed by reference to the Order in Council under section 2 of the Extradition Act 1870 applying to that state as it had effect immediately before the coming into force of this Act and to any amendments thereafter made to that Order; "fugitive criminal" means any person accused or convicted of an extradition crime committed within the jurisdiction of any foreign state who is in or is suspected of being in some part of Her Majesty's dominions ...'

[13] The United States of America (Extradition) Order 1976, SI 1976/2144, as amended by the United States of America (Extradition) (Amendment) Order 1986, SI 1986/2020, was in force at all material times so that Sch 1 to the 1989 Act applied and the definitions there are to be followed.

[14] If a requisition is duly made for the surrender of a fugitive criminal of any foreign state under para 4(1) of the Schedule, the Secretary of State may require a metropolitan magistrate to issue a warrant for the arrest of the fugitive criminal. By para 6, as amended by s 158 of the Criminal Justice and Public Order Act 1994:

'(1) When a fugitive criminal is brought before the metropolitan magistrate, the metropolitan magistrate shall have the same powers, as near as may be, including power to adjourn the case and meanwhile to remand the prisoner either in custody or on bail, as if the proceedings were the summary trial of an information against him for an offence committed in England or Wales ...

(2) The metropolitan magistrate shall receive any evidence which may be tendered to show that the crime of which the prisoner is accused or alleged to have been convicted is an offence of a political character or is not an extradition crime.'

By para 7 of the Schedule as amended by s 158 of the 1994 Act:

'(1) In the case of a fugitive criminal accused of an extradition crime, if the foreign warrant authorising the arrest of such criminal is duly authenticated, and such evidence is produced as (subject to the provisions of this Schedule) would, according to the law of England and Wales, make a case requiring an

a   answer by the prisoner if the proceedings were for the trial in England and
Wales of an information for the crime, the metropolitan magistrate shall
commit him to prison, but otherwise shall order him to be discharged.'

By para 15 of the Schedule under the heading 'Deemed extension of jurisdiction
of foreign states':

b   'For the purposes of this Schedule any act, wherever committed, which is
any of the following offences—(a) an offence mentioned in paragraph (a) of
subsection (1) of section 1 of the Internationally Protected Persons Act 1978
which is committed against a protected person within the meaning of that
section ... (d) an offence under section 1(3) of the Internationally Protected
c   Persons Act 1978; [together with certain offences under the Taking of
Hostages Act 1982 and the Nuclear Material (Offences) Act 1983] ... and an
offence against the law of any state in relation to which this Schedule has
effect shall be deemed to be an offence committed within the jurisdiction of
that state.'

d   [15] The 1976 order cites the treaty between the government of the United
Kingdom and the government of the United States of America 'for the reciprocal
extradition of offenders' (Extradition Treaty between the Government of the
United Kingdom of Great Britain and Northern Ireland and the Government of
the United States of America 1972 (as set out in Sch 1 to that order) (the 1972
treaty). It provides in art III that: 'The Extradition Acts 1870 to 1935, as amended
e   or extended by any subsequent enactment, shall apply in the case of the United
States of America in accordance with the said treaty of the 8 June 1972.'

[16] The Schedule which sets out the treaty provides as follows:

ARTICLE I

f   Each Contracting Party undertakes to extradite to the other, in the
circumstances and subject to the conditions specified in this Treaty, any person
found in its territory who has been accused or convicted of any offence within
Article III, committed within the jurisdiction of the other Party ...

ARTICLE III

g   (1) Extradition shall be granted for an act or omission the facts of which
disclose an offence within any of the descriptions listed in the Schedule
annexed to this Treaty, which is an integral part of the Treaty, or any other
offence, if: (a) the offence is punishable under the laws of both Parties by
imprisonment or other form of detention for more than one year or by the
death penalty; (b) the offence is extraditable under the relevant law, being
h   the law of the United Kingdom or other territory to which this Treaty applies
by virtue of sub-paragraph 1(a) of Article II; and (c) the offence constitutes a
felony under the law of the United States of America.

(2) Extradition shall also be granted for any attempt or conspiracy to
commit an offence within paragraph (1) of this Article if such attempt or
j   conspiracy is one for which extradition may be granted under the laws of
both Parties ...'

By art IX:

'(1) Extradition shall be granted only if the evidence be found sufficient
according to the law of the requested Party either to justify the committal for
trial of the person sought if the offence of which he is accused has been

committed in the territory of the requested Party or to prove that he is the
identical person convicted by the courts of the requesting Party.'

[17] The Schedule to the 1976 order lists the offences referred to in art III of
the order. Those offences include 'murder' and 'attempt to murder'. By virtue
of art III(2) conspiracy to commit such an offence is also a crime for which
extradition can be granted as it was under the First Schedule to the 1870 Act.

[18] The Divisional Court in *Al-Fawwaz's* case concluded that the extradition
proceedings covered only crimes committed in the territory of the United States.
The acts done were transposed to the United Kingdom for the purpose of
deciding whether under s 26 of the 1870 Act the crimes committed in the United
States of America 'if committed in England or within English jurisdiction, would
be one of the crimes described in the first schedule to this Act'. Those crimes
include 'Murder, and attempt and conspiracy to murder'. The Divisional Court
considered that there were a number of pointers that jurisdiction in the 1870 Act
was limited to territorial jurisdiction. They relied in particular on (a) the speech
of Lord Mackay of Clashfern in *Rees v Secretary of State for the Home Dept* [1986] 2 All
ER 321, [1986] AC 937 and the speech of Lord Reid in *Schtraks v Government of
Israel* [1962] 3 All ER 529, [1964] AC 556; (b) the fact that the provision in s 25 of
the 1870 Act that 'every vessel of that state, shall ... be deemed to be within the
jurisdiction of and to be part of such foreign state'; (c) para 15 of Sch 1 to the 1989
Act which provided that certain offences of an international character (and in
particular the Internationally Protected Persons Act 1978) 'shall be deemed to be
an offence committed within the jurisdiction of that state'; (d) the fact that the
provisions of s 2 of the 1989 Act which included reference to extra-territorial
offences was specifically excluded from Sch 1 offences by s 2(1) of the 1989 Act.
They concluded that:

'... in cases governed by Sch 1 to the 1989 Act the extradition crime has to
be committed within the territory of the requesting state so that it would, as
transposed, be committed within the territory of England and Wales. It is
not enough that the latter crime would, as in Pt III cases as recognised in *Ex p
Pinochet (No 3) (R v Bow Street Metropolitan Stipendiary Magistrate, ex p Pinochet
Ugarte (No 3)* [1999] 2 All ER 97, [2000] 1 AC 147), be indictable under the
extra-territorial jurisdiction of the United Kingdom. We also think that the
concept of jurisdiction in art I of the treaty annexed to the 1976 Order is
subject to the same limitation. Whether this is a sensible rule in a world of
major international crime and of the regular passage of persons involved in
such crime between different jurisdictions is no doubt not for us to say.' (See
[2001] 4 All ER 149 at 158–159, [2001] 1 WLR 1234 at 1243 (para 32).)

[19] In the case of Mr Eiderous and Mr Abdul Bary the Divisional Court
(Kennedy LJ and Garland J) declined to reconsider the opinion of Buxton LJ and
Elias J in *Al-Fawwaz's* case on this issue since they were satisfied that there were
sufficient overt acts to confer jurisdiction.

[20] The matter is however one which your Lordships should now consider.

[21] Mr Fitzgerald QC, with whom Mr Emmerson QC and Mr Moloney
largely agreed, submits that Buxton LJ and Elias LJ were right to conclude that
jurisdiction has to be territorial. They accept that conspiracy to murder is a crime
within the First Schedule to the 1870 Act and in the 1976 order but they say that
the concept of jurisdiction in s 26 of the 1870 Act was limited to territorial
jurisdiction; this is in keeping with the historical notion of jurisdiction as being

a limited to crimes committed within the requesting state's territory. This they say is underlined by the fact that (a) in s 25 of the 1870 Act, it was necessary to provide for crimes committed on vessels and in colonies; (b) in the 1989 Act it was necessary to provide for extra-territorial crimes both in s 2 which lays down the definition of extradition crimes (but that is not applicable to Sch 1) and in s 22 dealing with crimes, the subject matter of international conventions. Moreover

b para 15 of Sch 1 to the 1989 Act would not be necessary if extra-territorial crimes were already covered. Reliance is placed on the cases referred to by the Divisional Court. Particular emphasis is placed on the fact that art I of the 1972 treaty is dealing with offences 'committed within the jurisdiction of the other party' which is different from susceptible to the jurisdiction of the requesting party and must be construed as meaning in the territory of the party. It is also said that

c art IX(1) of the treaty which requires evidence to justify 'the committal for trial of the person sought if the offence of which he is accused had been committed *in the territory* of the requested Party' supports their case (my emphasis).

[22] There is no doubt that the appellants can point to a number of cases where it has been said or assumed that the question at issue, depended on the act

d having been done in the territory of the state. See e g *R v Governor of Pentonville Prison, ex p Naghdi* [1990] 1 All ER 257, [1990] 1 WLR 317, *Kossekechatkov v A-G for Trinidad* [1932] AC 78, *R v Governor of HM Prison Brixton, ex p Minervini* [1958] 3 All ER 318, [1959] 1 QB 155. Detailed reference has been made to *Schtraks v Government of Israel* [1962] 3 All ER 529, [1964] AC 556. In that case however the question was whether the offence was committed within the territory rather than within the

e jurisdiction of one party to the treaty and in particular whether it was enough that there was de facto occupation and control by Israel rather than sovereignty over the territory. I do not find this directly in point. Closer is the statement in *Rees v Secretary of State for the Home Dept* [1986] 2 All ER 321 at 327, [1986] AC 937 at 955 where Lord Mackay of Clashfern said: 'When the 1870 Act was passed it dealt only with crimes committed within the territorial jurisdiction of a state with

f whom an extradition arrangement had been made ...'

[23] But the present question (territorial v extra-territorial) was not raised as an issue nor was it necessary to decide it and that question was not fully argued.

[24] At the same time if Lord Mackay's statement is to be read as referring to what the Act dealt with in fact at the time, and perhaps what it was thought at the

g time that it was directed to, it seems both to be correct and to be supported by views expressed after the date of the Act. See *Clarke on Extradition* (4th edn, 1903), though the case relied on, *R v Lavaudier* (1881) 15 Cox CC 329, does not seem to require as a matter of statutory interpretation that jurisdiction equals territory. See also *Oppenheim's International Law* (1st edn, 1905) vol 1, pp 196–197 and the

h argument of counsel for the government in *Re Tivnan* (1864) 5 B & S 645 at 672, 122 ER 971 at 981 that in extradition treaties of 1842 and 1843 'jurisdiction' was used in the sense of the territorial limit within which 'the right to deal with particular things or persons' is exercised.

[25] It does not seem to me, however, that any of these previous decisions or

j writings should be taken as concluding the matter conclusively today. The question, it seems for the first time, has to be decided directly; ie whether the 1972 treaty permits or requires extradition only in respect of crimes committed and acts done exclusively in the territory of the requesting state, and whether it is only acts done in that state which are transposed to the United Kingdom in order to decide whether the facts would constitute a crime triable in the United Kingdom.

[26] The respondents submit that the first chronological, and perhaps crucial, stage is to ask whether the person is a 'fugitive criminal' within the meaning of *a* para 20 of Sch 1 to the 1989 Act (which is the same as the definition in s 26 of the 1870 Act). This provision requires that the person shall be accused or have been convicted of an extradition crime committed within the jurisdiction of a foreign state. There is no reference to 'territory' although jurisdiction could be interpreted as meaning territory in the sense that the act done or the crime committed must *b* be done 'in' the state. Moreover conversely to take the view that jurisdiction does not mean only territory seems to require that the phrase 'crime committed within the jurisdiction' of any foreign state must be read as meaning 'a crime committed which is within the jurisdiction' of that state.

[27] It seems to me that the respondents' reading of the definition of 'fugitive criminal' as being one who has committed a crime within the jurisdiction of *c* rather than in the requested state, is consistent with art I of the 1972 treaty which requires the extradition of a person in the requested state of any person convicted of an offence specified in art III which is 'committed within the jurisdiction of the other Party'.

[28] 'Extradition crime' for the purposes of Sch 1 to the 1989 Act is to be *d* construed by reference to the Order in Council under s 2 of the 1870 Act. By para 3 of the 1976 order the Extradition Acts 1870 to 1935 are to apply in the case of the United States in accordance with the treaty. In the 1870 Act extradition crime means 'a crime which, if *committed in England or within English jurisdiction*, would be one of the crimes described in the first schedule' to the Act (my emphasis).

[29] This is different from the definition of fugitive criminal which refers only *e* to a crime committed within the jurisdiction of the foreign state and does not refer to the territory of the foreign state. It is thus looking at jurisdiction rather then territory.

[30] It seems to me that the words in the 1870 Act 'within English jurisdiction' must have been intended to add something to 'committed in England'. There is *f* nothing to indicate that those words are limited to specific statutory provisions deeming or declaring the offence to have been committed in England for the purposes of extradition.

[31] Accordingly unless there are other compelling reasons I would interpret 'within jurisdiction' as including but being wider than 'in the territory' of the foreign state. The question is thus whether the conduct complained of will be *g* triable in the United States and if that conduct were transposed to England, would be triable in England. The question is not whether the acts done in the United States (if any) regardless of other acts necessary to found jurisdiction committed elsewhere, would if transposed to England be triable in England. It is still necessary to decide whether all acts relied on or only those acts done in the *h* United States are transposed to England.

[32] In most cases, which approach is adopted may not matter. If only the events occurring in the United States are transferred to England and the other events occurring outside the United States of America are regarded as still occurring outside England, in asking whether the crime would be triable in England, it *j* seems likely that the English courts would have extra-territorial jurisdiction. I tend to the view that this is the right approach but I recognise the force of the argument that all events are transposed to England.

[33] The view that jurisdiction is wider than territorial jurisdiction is not in any way inconsistent with other provisions of the Schedule. Thus in para 4(2) of Sch 1 to the 1989 Act the Secretary of State can only order the issue of a warrant

a for arrest if the person is accused of an extradition crime committed within the jurisdiction of a foreign state and that person is already suspected of being in Her Majesty's dominions, i e present in the territory. If it had been intended only to cover acts done in the territory of a foreign state the territorial link would have been stated in both parts of the definition. The same approach is followed through in relation to the magistrate's power to order arrest, to bring the person

b before the magistrate (para 5) and to commit the person (paras 7 and 8). Each time the question is expressed as to whether the crime is alleged to have been committed in 'the jurisdiction' and not in the territory.

[34] It is to be noted that in art I of the 1972 treaty the obligation is to extradite a person found in the territory of the requested state who has been accused of an offence within art III 'committed within the jurisdiction of the other party'. The

c same applies to the power in para 4(2) of Sch 1 to the 1989 Act.

[35] I accept that where a person is authorised in para 8(3) of the Schedule not only to receive and hold in custody but also to 'convey within the jurisdiction of such foreign state' the criminal, that will normally mean taking the person to the territory of the foreign state. I would reserve the question as to whether it means

d only that but even if it does it seems to me to be a special provision which does not govern the meaning of the other parts of the Schedule and in particular para 20.

[36] It is to be noted also in the 1972 treaty that the request must be accompanied by a statement of the facts of the offence and of the law defining the offence and where the request is made to the United Kingdom a statement that

e the offence constitutes a felony 'under the law of the United States of America' (art VII). There must also be a warrant of arrest duly authenticated. There is no express requirement that any of these documents should state, let alone establish, that the offence alleged was committed in the territory of the United States. Nor is it to be implied that the procedure requires the magistrate, when the matter

f comes before him, to have evidence to show that the crime was committed in the territory of the United States.

[37] When the 1870 Act was passed crimes were no doubt largely committed in the territory of the state trying the alleged criminal but that fact does not, and should not, mean that the reference to the jurisdiction is to be so limited. It does not as a matter of the ordinary meaning of the words used. It should not because

g in present conditions it would make it impossible to extradite for some of the most serious crimes now committed globally or at any rate across frontiers. Drug smuggling, money laundering, the abduction of children, acts of terrorism, would to a considerable extent be excluded from the extradition process. It is essential that that process should be available to them. To ignore modern

h methods of communication and travel as aids to criminal activities is unreal. It is no less unreal to ignore the fact that there are now many crimes where states assert extra-territorial jurisdiction, often as a result of international conventions. Buxton LJ recognised the difficulties of the approach he felt bound to adopt when he commented: '[w]hether this is a sensible rule in a world of major international

j crime and of the regular passage of persons involved in such crime between different jurisdictions is no doubt not for us to say.' (See [2001] 4 All ER 149 at 159, [2001] 1 WLR 1234 at 1243 (para 32).)

[38] There is, moreover, one express provision of the 1870 Act which, as was emphasised during the argument, indicates that the jurisdiction of the requesting state is not limited to territorial jurisdiction. Even though most of the crimes listed in the First Schedule can be committed in England or on English vessels

which are to be treated as English territory it is clear that 'piracy by law of nations' not only may but has to be committed on the high seas, ie although within the jurisdiction it is not committed in the territory of the state. a

[39] Mr Fitzgerald stressed that if the test is one of jurisdiction unqualified by territoriality people may be extradited under what the United Kingdom would regard as an exorbitant jurisdiction. That, however, is in my view taken care of, even if the treaty is in general terms not excluding such exorbitant jurisdiction, by b the discretion of the Secretary of State either in not requiring the magistrate to arrest the person concerned or by refusing to extradite him at the end of the process. I find helpful two passages from previous speeches in your Lordships' House. The first is that of Lord Bridge of Harwich in *Government of Belgium v Postlethwaite* [1987] 2 All ER 985 at 991–992, sub nom *R v Governor of Ashford Remand Centre, ex p Postlethwaite* [1988] AC 924 at 947: c

> 'I also take the judgment in that case (*Re Arton (No 2)* [1896] 1 QB 509 at 517) as good authority for the proposition that in the application of the principle the court should not, unless constrained by the language used, interpret any extradition treaty in a way which would "hinder the working and narrow the operation of most salutary international arrangements" ... The second d principle is that an extradition treaty is "a contract between two sovereign states and has to be construed as such a contract. It would be a mistake to think that it had to be construed as though it were a domestic statute": *R v Governor of Ashford Remand Centre, ex p Beese* [1973] 3 All ER 250 at 254, [1973] 1 WLR 969 at 973 per Lord Widgery CJ. In applying this second principle, e closely related as it is to the first, it must be remembered that the reciprocal rights and obligations which the high contracting parties confer and accept are intended to serve the purpose of bringing to justice those who are guilty of grave crimes committed in either of the contracting states. To apply to extradition treaties the strict canons appropriate to the construction of domestic legislation would often tend to defeat rather than to serve this purpose.' f

[40] The second is that of Lord Griffiths in *Liangsiriprasert v United States Government* [1990] 2 All ER 866 at 878, [1991] 1 AC 225 at 251:

> 'Unfortunately in this century crime has ceased to be largely local in origin and effect. Crime is now established on an international scale and the g common law must face this new reality. Their Lordships can find nothing in precedent, comity or good sense that should inhibit the common law from regarding as justiciable in England inchoate crimes committed abroad which are intended to result in the commission of criminal offences in England. Accordingly, a conspiracy entered into in Thailand with the intention of h committing the criminal offence of trafficking in drugs in Hong Kong is justiciable in Hong Kong even if no overt act pursuant to the conspiracy has yet occurred in Hong Kong. This then is a sufficient reason to justify the magistrate's order ...'

[41] Finally I agree with what is said in *Jones on Extradition* (1995) p 88 j (para 3-023):

> 'Although the point was not argued, *Liangsiriprasert* is to be taken as clear authority for the proposition that the word "jurisdiction" in the definition of the words "extradition crime" in section 26 of the 1870 Act and paragraph 20 of Schedule 1 to the 1989 Act is not limited to "territory". Neither the

a   Secretary of State in issuing his order to proceed, nor the magistrate exercising his duties under section 10 (paragraph 7(1)), is required to consider whether there is evidence of criminal conduct committed within the territory of the requesting state. It is sufficient if, were the crime charged in England, he would be entitled to commit.'

b   [42] There is no doubt that conspiracy to murder is a crime within the jurisdiction of the United States and that if the acts were done here it would constitute the crime of conspiracy to murder under English law. In my opinion it was not necessary to show that the acts relied on for the conspiracy were all done in the United States of America, or that enough of them were done to ground jurisdiction.

c   [43] In these circumstances it is not necessary to prove overt acts in the territory of the United States. It is, however, still necessary to consider whether such evidence was produced as 'would according to the law of England and Wales, make a case requiring an answer by the prisoner if the proceedings were for the trial in England'.

d   [44] The first criticism made here of the magistrate's decision on the evidence was that he should not have taken account of the affidavit of an anonymous witness CS/1. It is obvious that at trial and also on an inquiry like the present the court should be cautious about admitting anonymous statements or affidavits. But that there is jurisdiction to admit them is clear. On the basis of what was said in *R v Taylor (Gary)* (1994) TLR 484, and by the European Court of Human Rights
e   in *Doorson v Netherlands* (1996) 22 EHRR 330, both for the purposes of the European Convention for the Protection of Human Rights and Fundamental Freedoms 1950 (as set out in Sch 1 to the Human Rights Act 1998) and the purposes of considering whether the legal proceedings have been fairly conducted at common law, there may have to be a balance of the interests of the defence and
f   of the protection of witnesses. It seems to me that the magistrate and the Divisional Court considered this matter carefully and were satisfied that the protection of the witness CS/1 made it necessary in all the circumstances to preserve his anonymity and that the interests of society in prosecuting required that the evidence be taken into account on the application for extradition. It would be a matter for the trial judge as to whether the statement should be
g   admitted. The parties in Al-Fawwaz agree that if the evidence of CS/1 is admitted there is sufficient to satisfy the requirement of para 7 of Sch 1 to the 1989 Act. That seems to me to be right. I consider that the decision of the Divisional Court in this case, that the magistrate's admission of the evidence, even if anonymous, was fully justified in all the circumstances to which the Divisional Court refer,
h   was correct.

[45] A more detailed argument was made in the cases of Eiderous and Abdul Bary to the effect that the matters relied on were insufficient for the purposes of para 7 of Sch 1. The Divisional Court on a detailed consideration rejected the submission that the purchase of the satellite telephone and the fact that the text
j   of the fatwahs were found in their possession were capable of an explanation which had nothing to do with the alleged conspiracy. I refer to, without repeating, their reasons but it is quite plain that the Divisional Court thought that the magistrate had, after consideration of all the material, taken the view that there was sufficient to justify a committal. I agree with that conclusion. I also agree with the Divisional Court's view that even if the reasons given by the magistrate were not detailed they were sufficient to indicate to both the

appellants and the court the basis of his decision so as to enable it to be challenged and reviewed on judicial review or appeal.   *a*

[46] In my opinion these three appeals should be dismissed.

LORD HUTTON.

[47] My Lords, the three appellants are accused in proceedings before the United States District Court for the Southern District of New York of conspiring *b* with Osama bin Laden and others between 1 January 1993 and 27 September 1998 by agreeing:

'(a) that citizens of the United States of America would be murdered in the United States of America and elsewhere; (b) that bombs would be planted and exploded at American embassies and other American installations; *c* (c) that American officials would be killed in the Middle East and Africa; (d) that American diplomats and other internationally protected persons would be murdered; which course of conduct would necessarily involve the commission of the offence of murder.'

The three appellants were arrested in London and the United States of America *d* seeks their extradition. An order to proceed with the extradition of Mr Al-Fawwaz was issued on 9 December 1998 in terms that he 'is accused of offences which, had they occurred in the United Kingdom, would have constituted the offence of conspiracy to murder, within the jurisdiction of the United States of America'.

[48] At a hearing on 8 September 1999, Mr Evans, a metropolitan stipendiary *e* magistrate, held that there was a prima facie case against Mr Al-Fawwaz and committed him to await the decision of the Secretary of State. Mr Al-Fawwaz moved an application of habeas corpus before the Administrative Court of the Queen's Bench Division, which was dismissed on 30 November 2000 (see [2001] 4 All ER 149, [2001] 1 WLR 1234).

[49] An order to proceed with the extradition of Mr Eiderous and Mr Abdul *f* Bary was issued in similar terms on 21 September 1999. On 25 April 2000 Mr Evans found that there was a prima facie case against both Mr Eiderous and Mr Abdul Bary and committed them to await the decision of the Secretary of State. The two appellants moved an application of habeas corpus before the Administrative Court of the Queen's Bench Division which was dismissed on 2 May 2001 (see [2001] EWHC Admin 298, [2001] All ER (D) 24 (May)).   *g*

[50] The principal question which arises on these three appeals is whether the extradition arrangements between the United States of America and the United Kingdom set out in the relevant legislation require the extradition crime to be committed within the territory of the United States of America, or whether it is sufficient that the offence for which extradition is sought is triable in the United *h* States of America and would be triable in England if the accused had been charged there.

[51] The magistrate ruled that it is sufficient that the alleged crime is triable in the United States of America. The Administrative Court in the case of Mr Al-Fawwaz ruled to the contrary and held, accepting the appellant's submission, that where *j* extradition is sought by the United States of America from England there is only jurisdiction to extradite where the crime had been committed within the territory of the United States of America so that it would, as transposed, be committed in England. In making its ruling the court observed that it was not for it to say whether this was a sensible rule in a world of major international crime and of the regular passage of persons involved in such crime between jurisdictions.

a   However the court also held that there was jurisdiction to extradite because there was prima facie evidence that overt acts in furtherance of the conspiracy had taken place within the territory of the United States of America. On the applications for habeas corpus by Mr Eiderous and Mr Abdul Bary a differently-constituted Administrative Court followed the ruling of the earlier Administrative Court on the issue whether territorial jurisdiction was required but, as in the case of

b   Mr Al-Fawwaz, ruled that there was jurisdiction because of the evidence of overt acts in furtherance of the conspiracy having taken place in the United States of America.

[52] My Lords, in considering the question whether on an application for extradition to the United States of America the alleged crime must have been committed within the territory of that state and before turning to consider the

c   statutory provisions it is relevant to observe that the general rule is that the courts of a state do not exercise criminal jurisdiction over offences committed outside the territory of that state. In *MacLeod v A-G for New South Wales* [1891] AC 455 at 458 Lord Halsbury LC stated: 'All crime is local. The jurisdiction over the crime belongs to the country where the crime is committed ...' Therefore, in practice,

d   most extradition requests relate to offences committed within the territory of the requesting state. But, increasingly, in modern times in order to combat international crime and terrorism, it has been recognised by democratic states that extra-territorial jurisdiction should be taken by individual states over certain crimes. Thus in 1982 in pursuance of an international convention the United Kingdom took extra-territorial jurisdiction over the offence of taking a hostage (see s 1 of

e   the Taking of Hostages Act 1982) and in 1988 in pursuance of an international convention extra-territorial jurisdiction was taken over the offence of torture by a public official or a person acting in an official capacity (see s 134 of the Criminal Justice Act 1988).

[53] In 1973 the United Nations General Assembly adopted the Convention

f   on the Prevention and Punishment of Crimes against Internationally Protected Persons, including Diplomatic Agents (New York, 14 December 1973; TS 3 (1980); Cmnd 7765). Under the Internationally Protected Persons Act 1978 'a protected person' includes a person who is a representative or an official of a state or an official or agent of an international organisation of an inter-governmental

g   character and who is entitled under international law to special protection from attack on his person (s 1(5)). Section 1(1) of the 1978 Act provides:

'If a person, whether a citizen of the United Kingdom and Colonies or not, does outside the United Kingdom—(a) any act to or in relation to a protected person which, if he had done it in any part of the United Kingdom, would

h   have made him guilty of the offence of murder [and other offences against the person] ... he shall in any part of the United Kingdom be guilty of the offences aforesaid of which the act would have made him guilty if he had done it there.'

j   It is common ground that internationally protected persons were to be the victims of the conspiracy of which the appellants are accused.

[54] Section 1(3) of the Extradition Act 1989 provides:

'Where an Order in Council under section 2 of the Extradition Act 1870 is in force in relation to a foreign state, Schedule 1 to this Act (the provisions of which derive from that Act and certain associated enactments) shall have effect in relation to that state, but subject to the limitations, restrictions, conditions, exceptions and qualifications, if any, contained in the Order.'   *a*

On the date on which the 1989 Act came into force an Order in Council (United States of America (Extradition) Order 1976, SI 1976/2144), setting out in a schedule the Extradition Treaty between the Government of the United Kingdom of Great Britain and Northern Ireland and the Government of the United States of America 1972 (the 1972 treaty), was in force. Therefore the extradition of an   *b*
offender to the United States of America is governed by Sch 1 to the 1989 Act.

[55] Paragraph 20 of Sch 1 defines an 'extradition crime' as follows:

'... "extradition crime", in relation to any foreign state, is to be construed by reference to the Order in Council under section 2 of the Extradition Act 1870 applying to that state as it had effect immediately before the coming into   *c*
force of this Act and to any amendments thereafter made to that Order ...'

The Order in Council (the 1976 order) provides in para 3: 'The Extradition Acts 1870 to 1935, as amended or extended by any subsequent enactment, shall apply in the case of the United States of America in accordance with the said Treaty of   *d*
the June 8, 1972.' Article III of the 1972 treaty provides:

'(1) Extradition shall be granted for an act or omission the facts of which disclose an offence within any of the descriptions listed in the Schedule annexed to this Treaty, which is an integral part of the Treaty, or any other offence, if ... (b) the offence is extraditable under the relevant law, being the   *e*
law of the United Kingdom of other territory to which this Treaty applies by virtue of sub-paragraph (1)(a) of Article II ...'

Therefore to determine the meaning of the term an 'extradition crime' at the present time when a request for extradition is made by the United States of America it is necessary to read s 26 of the Extradition Act 1870 which provides: *f*
'The term "extradition crime" means a crime which, if committed in England or within English jurisdiction, would be one of the crimes described in the first schedule to this Act ...'

[56] Paragraph 20 of Sch 1 to the 1989 Act defines a 'fugitive criminal' as follows:
    g
'... "fugitive criminal" means any person accused or convicted of an extradition crime committed within the jurisdiction of any foreign state who is in or is suspected of being in some part of Her Majesty's dominions ...'

Therefore two questions arise: (i) were the appellants 'fugitive criminals' as defined in para 20 of Sch 1 to the 1989 Act? and (ii) was the crime alleged against the   *h*
appellants an 'extradition crime' as defined by s 26 of the 1870 Act?

Were the appellants 'fugitive criminals'?

[57] The answer depends on whether the crime alleged was 'committed within the jurisdiction of [the] foreign state'—in this case the United States of   *j*
America. An ordinary meaning of the term 'the jurisdiction of the state', is the power of that state to try an offence and includes extra-territorial jurisdiction. Thus it is clear that under the 1978 Act a United Kingdom court has jurisdiction to try a charge of murder of a protected person when the murder is committed outside the United Kingdom. It is not in dispute that the court in the United States of America has extra-territorial jurisdiction under United States law to try

a the charge of conspiracy against the appellants notwithstanding that the conspiracy to murder was entered into outside the United States of America and that no overt acts by the appellants in pursuance of conspiracy may have been committed within the territory of the United States of America. Accordingly it would appear prima facie that the alleged conspiracy was committed 'within the jurisdiction' of the United States.

b [58] However, Mr Fitzgerald QC for Mr Al-Fawwaz submitted, and his submission was adopted by counsel for the other two appellants, that in the 1870 Act and the 1972 treaty with the United States of America the term 'jurisdiction' must be confined to 'territorial jurisdiction', though including vessels at sea and colonies, and must be so confined today because the 1989 Act provides in respect of extradition requested by the United States of America that, in effect,
c extradition under Sch 1 to that Act is to be governed by the provisions of the 1870 Act and the Order in Council made under it.

[59] Counsel submitted that in 1870 the common understanding of jurisdiction in relation to extradition was that it meant the territorial jurisdiction of the state and that an extradition crime was a crime committed within the territory of the
d requesting state. He relied on the judgments of the majority of the Divisional Court in Re Tivnan (1864) 5 B & S 645, 122 ER 971 where an act of piracy was committed on an American ship. The United States of America sought the extradition of persons charged with piracy from England and the terms of the 1842 treaty and the Extradition Act 1843 provided for the delivery of any person charged with certain crimes, among them piracy, committed 'within the jurisdiction'
e of the United States of America. The majority accepted the argument on behalf of the prisoners that 'jurisdiction' in the Act and the treaty meant the exclusive and peculiar jurisdiction of the United States of America and that as piracy jure gentium was triable by all states, the charge against the prisoners was not within the exclusive jurisdiction of the United States of America and therefore the
f prisoner should be discharged.

[60] Counsel cited Clarke on Extradition (4th edn, 1903) p 235 which stated in respect of the provisions of the 1870 Act: 'To justify a magistrate in committing there must be some evidence that the accused committed the crime within the jurisdiction, i.e., the territory of the country seeking his extradition ...' Counsel also pointed to s 25 of the 1870 Act which provided:
g
'For the purposes of this Act, every colony, dependency, and constituent part of a foreign state, and every vessel of that state, shall (except where expressly mentioned as distinct in this Act) be deemed to be within the jurisdiction of and to be part of such foreign state.'

h He submitted that the Act would not have deemed the jurisdiction of a state to extend to a vessel unless otherwise the term 'jurisdiction' was intended to apply only to the territory of the state.

[61] Section 2(1) of the 1989 Act expressly provides that, except in Sch 1 to that Act, 'extradition crime' includes an extra-territorial offence against the law of a
j foreign state provided that equivalent conduct would constitute an offence against the law of the United Kingdom. Counsel submitted that this provision in respect of extra-territorial crime, which expressly did not apply to Sch 1, supported his argument that proceedings under the 1870 Act and Sch 1 were confined to crimes committed within the territory of the requesting state.

[62] He made a similar point in respect of para 15 of Sch 1 to the 1989 Act which provides:

'For the purposes of this Schedule any act, wherever committed, which is
any of the following offences—(a) an offence mentioned in paragraph (a) of
subsection (1) of section 1 of the Internationally Protected Persons Act 1978
which is committed against a protected person within the meaning of that
section; (b) an offence mentioned in paragraph (b) of that subsection which
is committed in connection with such an attack as is so mentioned; (c) an
attempt to commit an offence mentioned in the preceding paragraphs; (d) an
offence under section 1(3) of the Internationally Protected Persons Act 1978;
(e) an offence under the Taking of Hostages Act 1982 or an attempt to
commit such an offence; (f) an offence mentioned in paragraphs (a) to (d) of
subsection (1) of section 1 of the Nuclear Material (Offences) Act 1983 which
is committed by doing an act in relation to or by means of nuclear material,
as defined in that Act; (g) an offence under section 2 of that Act; (h) an
attempt to commit an offence mentioned in paragraph (f) or (g) above; or
(i) torture, and an offence against the law of any state in relation to which this
Schedule has effect shall be deemed to be an offence committed within the
jurisdiction of that state.'

Counsel submitted that if the words 'within the jurisdiction of any foreign state'
in the definition of 'fugitive criminal' in para 20 of Sch 1 (derived from s 26 of the
1870 Act) included extra-territorial jurisdiction, there was no need for the deeming
provision of para 15.

[63] Counsel advanced an additional argument on the issue of jurisdiction
based on art IX of the 1972 treaty with the United States of America. Article IX(1)
provides:

'Extradition shall be granted only if the evidence be found sufficient
according to the law of the requested Party either to justify the committal for
trial of the person sought if the offence of which he is accused had been
committed in the territory of the requested Party or to prove that he is the
identical person convicted by the courts of the requesting Party.'

Counsel submitted that art IX required that before there can be extradition there
must be an offence committed within the territory of the requesting state which
is the counterpart of the hypothetical offence described in art IX as 'committed in
the territory of the requested party'. He submitted that there was no point in
making the hypothesis that the offence is committed within the territory of
the requested state if the offence had not been committed within the territory of the
requesting state.

[64] My Lords, I consider that the submissions advanced on behalf of the
appellants should not be accepted. My principal reason for forming this opinion
is that in the modern world of international terrorism and crime proper effect
would not be given to the extradition procedures agreed upon between states if
a person accused in a requesting state of an offence over which that state had extra-
territorial jurisdiction (it also being an offence over which the requested state
would have extra-territorial jurisdiction) could avoid extradition on the ground
that the offence was not committed within the territory of the requesting state.
In my opinion a court should not construe a statute or a treaty to have such an
effect unless the wording compels it to do so. I consider that the argument
advanced on behalf of the appellants that 'jurisdiction' means territorial jurisdiction
was powerfully answered by Cockburn CJ in his judgment in *Re Tivnan* (1864)
5 B & S 645 at 678, 122 ER 971 at 983, and although his judgment was a dissenting

a one the view which he expressed was a prescient one foreshadowing statements made in this House in more recent times by Lord Bridge of Harwich in *Government of Belgium v Postlethwaite* [1987] 2 All ER 985 at 991–992, sub nom *R v Governor of Ashford Remand Centre, ex p Postlethwaite* [1988] AC 924 at 947, and by Lord Griffiths in *Liangsiriprasert v United States Government* [1990] 2 All ER 866 at 878, [1991] 1 AC 225 at 251. Cockburn CJ stated:

b

> 'It is said, and with truth, that the primary and original mischief, which the statutes of extradition meant to prevent, was that of persons committing crimes in one state, and escaping beyond the reach of the law of that state, and so enjoying impunity; and it is also contended that for that purpose alone were those statutes passed. That that was their primary and principal object
> c I entertain no doubt, but that that was the *only* one I entertain great doubt; for it is impossible not to see that the mischief which it is the object of all civilized states to prevent is not limited to such cases.'

In *Government of Belgium v Postlethwaite* referring to the judgment of Lord Russell
d of Killowen CJ in *Re Arton (No 2)* [1896] 1 QB 509, Lord Bridge stated:

> 'I also take the judgment in that case as good authority for the proposition that in the application of the principle the court should not, unless constrained by the language used, interpret any extradition treaty in a way which would "hinder the working and narrow the operation of most salutary
> e international arrangements" ... The second principle is that an extradition treaty is 'a contract between two sovereign states and has to be construed as such a contract. It would be a mistake to think that it had to be construed as though it were a domestic statute': *R v Governor of Ashford Remand Centre, ex p Beese* [1973] 3 All ER 250 at 254, [1973] 1 WLR 969 at 973 per Lord Widgery CJ.
> f In applying this second principle, closely related as it is to the first, it must be remembered that the reciprocal rights and obligations which the high contracting parties confer and accept are intended to serve the purpose of bringing to justice those who are guilty of grave crimes committed in either of the contracting states. To apply to extradition treaties the strict canons appropriate to the construction of domestic legislation would often tend to
> g defeat rather than to serve this purpose.' (See [1987] 2 All ER 985 at 991–992, [1988] AC 924 at 947.)

I have no doubt that at the end of the penultimate sentence of that passage Lord Bridge would have added 'or within the extra-territorial jurisdiction of either of
h the contracting states' if the House had been considering an extra-territorial crime in that case.

[65] I further consider that there are provisions in the 1870 Act which support the argument advanced on behalf of the government of the United States by Mr Lewis. First, s 26 of the 1870 Act defines an 'extradition crime' as a crime
j which 'if committed in England or within English jurisdiction' would be one of the crimes described in the First Schedule to the Act. The implicit distinction between a crime committed in England and a crime committed within English jurisdiction points to the Act having an extra-territorial effect. Secondly, piracy by law of nations is one of the extradition crimes described in the First Schedule to the Act and shows that the term 'jurisdiction' in the Act is not restricted to territorial jurisdiction. Thirdly, s 6 of the 1870 Act provides:

'Where this Act applies in the case of any foreign state, every fugitive
criminal of that state who is in or suspected of being in any part of Her   a
Majesty's dominions, or that part which is specified in the order applying this
Act (as the case may be), shall be liable to be apprehended and surrendered
in manner provided by this Act, whether the crime in respect of which the
surrender is sought was committed before or after the date of the order, and
whether there is or is not any concurrent jurisdiction in any court of Her   b
Majesty's dominions over that crime.'

The recognition that a number of courts in Her Majesty's dominions may have
jurisdiction over the same crime suggests an extra-territorial jurisdiction in one of
those courts.

[66] Moreover art I of the 1972 treaty between the United Kingdom and the   c
United States of America provides:

'Each Contracting Party undertakes to extradite to the other, in the
circumstances and subject to the conditions specified in this Treaty, any person
found in its territory who has been accused or convicted of any offence
within Article III, committed within the jurisdiction of the other Party.'   d

Again the implied distinction between the 'territory' of the requested state and
the jurisdiction of the requesting state suggests that the concept of 'jurisdiction'
is wider than territory.

[67] I consider that the fact that s 2 of the 1989 Act includes certain   e
extra-territorial offences in the definition of 'extradition crime', but that s 2 does
not extend to Sch 1, does not advance the appellants' case, as in my opinion
Parliament recognised that the extradition crimes referred to in Sch 1 (the
provisions of which derive from the 1870 Act) already included extra-territorial
offences by virtue of the provisions of the 1870 Act.

[68] Article IX of the 1972 treaty is concerned with the sufficiency of the   f
evidence before the magistrate of the requested state to permit him to make an
order leading to the extradition of the accused person. In my opinion the
reference in art IX to 'if the offence of which he is accused had been committed
in the territory of the requested Party' relates only to the sufficiency of the
evidence and is not intended to restrict the jurisdiction of the magistrate to a   g
hypothetical crime committed in the territory of England and Wales.

[69] Nor do I think that the provision in para 15 of Sch 1 to the 1989 Act that
certain extra-territorial crimes be deemed to be committed within the jurisdiction
of certain states points to the conclusion that without that provision extra-
territorial crimes would not be within the scope of the extradition procedures to   h
which Sch 1 applies. I consider that para 15 is intended to simplify the task of the
magistrate and to obviate the need for him to decide the issue whether, when a
person is accused of an offence outside the territory of the requesting state, that
state has extra-territorial jurisdiction over that offence. As Lord Ackner stated in
Sinclair v DPP [1991] 2 All ER 366 at 386, sub nom *R v Governor of Pentonville Prison,
ex p Sinclair* [1991] 2 AC 64 at 91:   j

'I cannot accept that the legislature intended that it was to be part of the
function of the police magistrate to preside over lengthy proceedings
occupying weeks, and on occasions months, of his time hearing heavily
contested evidence of foreign law directed to whether there had been due
compliance with the many and varied obligations of the relevant treaty.'

a [70] Whilst there is no case which is decisive on the issue now before your Lordships, I think that the authorities give more support to the submissions of the government of the United States of America than to the submissions of the appellants. The appellants relied upon passages in the judgments in *Schtraks v Government of Israel* [1962] 3 All ER 529, [1964] AC 556 and *Rees v Secretary of State for the Home Dept* [1986] 2 All ER 321, [1986] AC 937. They relied on the statement
b by Lord Reid in *Schtraks'* case:

> 'In my judgment neither the Extradition Act, 1870, nor the order to which I have referred, is concerned with sovereignty; they are concerned with territory in which territorial jurisdiction is exercised.' (See [1962] 3 All ER 529 at 532, [1964] AC 556 at 579.)

c However the issue before the House in that case related to the wording of art I of the extradition treaty between the United Kingdom and Israel (Agreement of 4 April 1960 between the Government of the United Kingdom of Great Britain and Northern Ireland and the Government of the State of Israel on Extradition (as set out in the First Schedule to the Israel (Extradition) Order 1960, SI 1960/1660))
d and the relevant article did not contain the word 'jurisdiction' but rather the word 'territory'. Article 1 provided:

> 'The Contracting Parties agree to extradite to each other, in the circumstances stated in the present Agreement, those persons who, being accused or convicted of any of the offences enumerated in Article 3 and committed
e within the territory of the one Party, or on the high seas on board a vessel registered in the territory of that Party, shall be found within the territory of the other Party.'

One of the offences of which the prisoner was accused was alleged to have been committed in Jerusalem. The United Kingdom did not recognise the Israel
f government as having de jure sovereignty in Jerusalem but only de facto authority. Therefore the question before the House was whether Jerusalem was within the 'territory' of Israel. I consider that Lord Reid's observation must be read in that context and was not intended as a definitive statement that the 1870 Act could not apply to extra-territorial crimes.

g [71] In *Rees'* case the requesting state was the Federal Republic of Germany and the crime of which the prisoner was accused was the detention of a hostage (a West German national) in Bolivia. Lord Mackay of Clashfern stated:

> 'When the 1870 Act was passed it dealt only with crimes committed within the territorial jurisdiction of a state with whom an extradition arrangement
h had been made: see, for example, *Schtraks v Government of Israel* [1962] 3 All ER 529 at 532, [1964] AC 556 at 579 per Lord Reid.' (See [1986] 2 All ER 321 at 327, [1986] AC 937 at 955.)

However it is apparent that Lord Mackay's statement was based upon Lord Reid's observation and, with respect, is difficult to reconcile with the fact that piracy by the
j law of nations was an extradition crime within the ambit of the 1870 Act.

[72] I consider that the judgment of the Privy Council delivered by Lord Griffiths in *Liangsiriprasert v United States Government* [1990] 2 All ER 866, [1991] 1 AC 225 does give considerable support to the submissions of the government of the United States of America. In that case the accused conspired in Thailand to import heroin into the United States. He then went to Hong Kong and the United States of America requested his extradition from there. The extradition

procedures in Hong Kong were governed by the terms of the Extradition Acts
1870 to 1935 (see [1990] 2 All ER 866 at 870, [1991] 1 AC 225 at 241). The law of *a*
conspiracy in Hong Kong was the same as the common law of conspiracy in
England, and the accused argued that a conspiracy entered into abroad is not a
common law crime unless either some overt act pursuant to the conspiracy takes
place in England, or alternatively at least the impact of the conspiracy is felt in
England. This argument was rejected by the Privy Council. Lord Griffiths stated *b*
([1990] 2 All ER 866 at 871, [1991] 1 AC 225 at 241) that the task of the magistrate
was to apply Hong Kong law and to consider whether the evidence disclosed a
prima facie case against the accused upon the assumption that the drugs were to
be imported into Hong Kong rather than into the United States, and he stated:

> 'Unfortunately in this century crime has ceased to be largely local in origin *c*
> and effect. Crime is now established on an international scale and the common
> law must face this new reality. Their Lordships can find nothing in precedent,
> comity or good sense that should inhibit the common law from regarding as
> justiciable in England inchoate crimes committed abroad which are intended
> to result in the commission of criminal offences in England. Accordingly, a
> conspiracy entered into in Thailand with the intention of committing the *d*
> criminal offence of trafficking in drugs in Hong Kong is justiciable in Hong
> Kong even if no overt act pursuant to the conspiracy has yet occurred in
> Hong Kong.' (See [1990] 2 All ER 866 at 878, [1991] 1 AC 225 at 251.)

[73] Therefore it is clear that the Privy Council proceeded on the basis that
'jurisdiction' in the 1870 Act was not confined to the territory of the requesting *e*
state and to the territory of the requested state. But it is not entirely clear whether
this point was raised for decision by the Board because Mr Martin Thomas QC,
counsel for the accused, stated ([1991] 1 AC 225 at 229) that the principles related
to extradition were not in dispute and Mr Alun Jones QC, for the requesting
government, also stated (at 231) that there was no issue between the appellant *f*
and the respondents about the extradition aspects of the case and Lord Griffiths
stated ([1990] 2 All ER 866 at 871, [1991] 1 AC 225 at 241) that it was common
ground that the crimes were all extradition crimes.

[74] However, even if, as the Administrative Court stated in its judgment, the
Privy Council assumed, rather than decided, the point, it is clear that the Privy
Council was content to accept that 'jurisdiction' in the 1870 Act was not confined *g*
to territory, and I consider that the judgment does provide strong support for the
argument advanced by the respondent and that the effect of the decision was
correctly stated by *Jones on Extradition* (1995) p 88 (para 3-023):

> 'Although the point was not argued, *Liangsiriprasert* is to be taken as clear *h*
> authority for the proposition that the word "jurisdiction" in the definition of
> the words "extradition crime" in section 26 of the 1870 Act and paragraph 20
> of Schedule 1 to the 1989 Act is not limited to "territory".'

[75] Therefore for the reasons which I have stated I would reject the argument
on behalf of the appellants that in the 1870 Act, the Order in Council and Sch 1 to *j*
the 1989 Act 'jurisdiction' is limited to the territory of the state, and in my opinion
the Administrative Courts were in error in so holding.

[76] In *R v Governor of Pentonville Prison, ex p Osman* [1989] 3 All ER 701, [1990]
1 WLR 277 the Divisional Court gave consideration to s 7(5) of the Fugitive
Offenders Act 1967 (a provision similar to art IX of the 1972 treaty with the
United States of America) under which the magistrate must consider whether

a   there is sufficient evidence against the accused person to warrant his trial if the offence had been committed 'within the jurisdiction' of the magistrate. Lloyd LJ referred to the difficulty in relation to transposition which he described as follows:

> 'However, a difficulty arises when the act or omissions constituting the offence take place in two or more countries. Does one assume that all the acts or omissions constituting the offence took place within the United Kingdom?
b > Or only those which in fact took place within the territorial limits of the requesting country?' (See [1989] 3 All ER 701 at 713, [1990] 1 WLR 277 at 290.)

He then stated that in the light of the authorities only the acts or omissions which took place in the requesting state are to be treated as having taken place in England.
c   All else remains as it in fact happened. But I think it is important to note that Lloyd LJ was considering the issue of transposition on the basis that the English magistrate was considering a case where the offence alleged was not an extra-territorial offence and where the English magistrate would only have jurisdiction over the offence if it had been committed within his territorial jurisdiction. Thus in commencing his consideration of the subject Lloyd LJ stated: 'But if the defendant is alleged to have
d   committed an offence outside the territorial jurisdiction of the court, then unless the offence is an extra-territorial one, he has committed no offence against English law.' (See [1989] 3 All ER 701 at 712, [1990] 1 WLR 277 at 289.)

[77] In the present case it is common ground that the United States of America has extra-territorial jurisdiction over the alleged offence and that the United
e   Kingdom also has extra-territorial jurisdiction over the alleged offence. Therefore, in my opinion, no difficulty arises in respect of transposition. The offence is triable within the jurisdiction of the United States of America and, as transposed, is triable, as s 26 of the 1870 Act requires, 'within English jurisdiction'.

[78] Mr Fitzgerald submitted that the magistrate had to be satisfied that the
f   United States of America had jurisdiction to try the alleged offence and that there was also jurisdiction in England to try the alleged offence. In this case where both the United States of America and the United Kingdom have extra-territorial jurisdiction over the alleged offence that requirement is clearly satisfied. And, as I have already stated, I consider that the purpose of para 15 of Sch 1 to the 1989 Act is to ensure that in respect of the offences specified in it the magistrate will
g   not have to embark on a lengthy hearing to determine whether under the law of the requesting state it had extra-territorial jurisdiction over the alleged offence.

[79] Accordingly for the reasons which I have stated I consider that as both the United States of America and the United Kingdom have extra-territorial jurisdiction to try the alleged conspiracy there was jurisdiction for the magistrate to commit
h   the appellants to prison to await the warrants of the Secretary of State for their surrender to the United States of America. Therefore it is unnecessary to consider the ground on which the Administrative Courts held that the magistrate had jurisdiction, namely that overt action pursuant to the conspiracy had been carried out in the United States of America.

j   [80] The appellants raised other issues before the two Administrative Courts which were also raised before this House.

The admissibility of the evidence of the anonymous witness CS/1

[81] The evidence of CS/1 was described as follows by Buxton LJ in the judgment of the Administrative Court in *Al-Fawwaz*'s case ([2001] 4 All ER 149 at 161–162, [2001] 1 WLR 1234 at 1246–1247 (para 47)):

'CS/1 claims to have been directly involved in the conspiracy and to be in mortal fear by reason of his co-operation with the authorities. He needs anonymity at this stage to protect himself, though it is envisaged that he will give evidence revealing his identity at the trial in the United States. His evidence is of the first importance, because it directly involves Mr Al-Fawwaz in the conspiracy. Mr Fitzgerald was careful not to concede that CS/1's evidence, if admitted, concluded the issue of whether there was a prima facie case, since he said that the evidence was open to criticism on grounds of imprecision. In reality, however, it is impossible to conclude that a magistrate who acted on the evidence of CS/1 to commit Mr Al-Fawwaz, as the magistrate acted in this case, would be acting irrationally in *Ex p Osman* terms (*R v Governor of Pentonville Prison, ex p Osman* [1989] 3 All ER 701, [1990] 1 WLR 277).'

[82] The three appellants submitted that the magistrate was wrong in law and/or acted irrationally in admitting the evidence of CS/1. They relied on the judgment of the Court of Appeal in *R v Taylor (Gary)* (1994) TLR 484 where at the trial of the appellant, who had been convicted of perverting the course of justice by being involved in the disposal of the body of a murder victim, the judge permitted a witness to give corroborative evidence behind the screen without revealing her name and address. The defendant appealed on the ground that he had a fundamental right to see and hear the identity of the witness called against him save in rare or exceptional circumstances. The Court of Appeal dismissed the appeal. In delivering the judgment of the court Evans LJ stated:

'In so far as counsel for the appellant submitted that it was a fundamental right of a defendant to see and know the identity of his accusers, including witnesses for the Crown, which should only be denied in rare and exceptional circumstances, their Lordships agreed with him. The matter was pre-eminently one for the exercise of the judge's discretion, and the following factors were relevant to the exercise of that discretion. 1. There must be real grounds for fear of the consequences if the evidence were given and the identity of the witness revealed. In practical terms it might well be sufficient to draw a parallel with s 23(3)(b) of the Criminal Justice Act 1988, which concerned the admissibility of statements where the witness did not wish to give oral evidence through fear, but in principle it might not be necessary for the witness himself to be fearful or to be fearful for himself alone. There could be cases where concern was expressed by other persons, or where the witness was concerned for his family rather than for himself. 2. The evidence must be sufficiently relevant and important to make it unfair to make the Crown proceed without it. A distinction could be drawn between cases where the creditworthiness of the witness was in question rather than his accuracy. 3. The Crown must satisfy the court that the creditworthiness of the witness had been fully investigated and disclosed. 4. The court must be satisfied that there would be no undue prejudice to the accused, although some prejudice was inevitable, even if it was only the qualification placed on the right to confront a witness as accuser. There might also be factors pointing the other way, for example as in the present case where the defendants could see the witness on a video screen. 5. The court could balance the need for protection of the witness, including the extent of that protection, against unfairness or the appearance of unfairness. It seemed to their Lordships that there was no reason in principle why the same considerations should not *a*   apply to a witness for the defence. The judge's ruling in the present case was detailed and referred to the factors listed above. The law gave the trial judge the power to make an order that a witness remain anonymous in the exercise of his discretion, and the present case was not one where there were any grounds for supposing that the witness was not impartial or had an axe to grind. In their Lordships' view the judge was entitled to conclude that the

b   witness be allowed to give her evidence anonymously.'

[83] In the course of giving his decision in the case of Mr Al-Fawwaz the magistrate considered the judgment in *R v Taylor* and said:

c   'I am satisfied that there are real grounds for fear of the consequences if the identity of the witnesses were revealed. The evidence, particularly that of CS/1, is sufficiently important to make it unfair to make the government proceed without it ... the government seeks to satisfy this court that the creditworthiness of CS/1 has been fully investigated and disclosed. I am not so satisfied. Perhaps that is because no attempt was made in the preparation

d   of this extradition request to focus on that one issue. The time when it is most important that the court is so satisfied on these issues is at the effective trial. No doubt more information will be put before the trial judge in the event of extradition taking place. I know nothing to the detriment of CS/1's creditworthiness. What I do know is that the cumulative effect of all the circumstantial evidence is such that CS/1's evidence can not be described as

e   so inherently incredible that no jury properly directed could convict on it. The remaining evidence is exactly what one would expect to find if all that CS/1 says is true. The facts in (*Re Tomlins' application* [1995] COD 192) are unusual. It is rare for a defendant to be in a position where he is able to discredit a prosecution witness to the extent that a committal court will conclude that a

f   witness's evidence is worthless. The fact that one of the "principles" (*R v Taylor (Gary)* (1994) TLR 484) to be followed in this situation may not be satisfactorily met does not mean that this court, exercising its functions in extradition proceedings, is automatically bound to rule the evidence inadmissible. These are rare and exceptional circumstances in existence in this case. In all the circumstances, I am satisfied that there would be no undue

g   prejudice to Mr Al-Fawwaz by my admitting the evidence of CS/1 and CS/2. Accordingly I rule that evidence admissible in these committal proceedings.'

It is relevant to note that the United States government has now decided and confirmed that the identity of CS/1 would be disclosed in America.

h   [84] Further guidance as to the approach to be taken by a court hearing a challenge by an accused to the decision of a magistrate or judge to admit the evidence of an anonymous witness is given in the judgments delivered in *R v X, R v Y, R v Z* (1989) 91 Cr App R 36 and *R v Watford Magistrates' Court, ex p Lenman* [1993] Crim LR 388. In the former case Lord Lane CJ stated (at 40):

j   'The learned judge has the duty on this and on all other occasions of endeavouring to see that justice is done. Those are high sounding words. What it really means is, he has got to see that the system operates fairly: fairly not only to the defendants but also to the prosecution and also to the witnesses. Sometimes he has to make decisions as to where the balance of fairness lies. He came to the conclusion that in these circumstances the necessity of trying to ensure that these children would be able to give evidence outweighed any possible prejudice to the defendants by the erection of the screen.'

Although the judgment related to the anonymity of child witnesses the statement is of general application. In the latter case the court constituted by Beldam LJ and Laws J held:

'If a magistrate was satisfied that there was a real risk to the administration of justice, because a witness on reasonable grounds feared for his safety if his identity were disclosed, it was entirely within the powers of the magistrate to take reasonable steps to protect and reassure the witness so that the witness was not deterred from coming forward to give evidence. If, however, the rights of an accused, particularly his ability to prepare and conduct his defence were thereby prejudiced, justice required the court to balance the prejudice to him and the interests of justice. It might well be that on substantial grounds being shown justice would require the witness's identity to be disclosed. It was difficult to think of a decision more dependent on the exercise of discretion than the magistrate's decision in this case. The court would not interfere with such a decision unless it was shown that it was so unreasonable that no magistrate properly considering it and properly directing himself, could have reached that conclusion.'

[85] Therefore the authorities emphasise that the decision whether to admit evidence from an anonymous witness is a matter of deciding where the balance of fairness lies between the prosecution and the accused and that it is pre-eminently a matter for the discretion of the magistrate or judge conducting the hearing. I would reject the submission that the magistrate erred in law or acted irrationally in admitting the evidence of CS/1 where he was not satisfied that the United States government had fully investigated and disclosed the creditworthiness of the witness. This was one of the factors to be put into the balance when the magistrate was deciding how he would exercise his discretion and it is clear that he did take account of this factor. I consider that it cannot be said that his decision was so unreasonable that no magistrate properly considering the matter and properly directing himself could have reached the conclusion that he did. The magistrate was making a decision as to where the balance of fairness lay and he was entitled to find as he did.

[86] I would add that there is a degree of inconsistency between the statement of the Court of Appeal in *R v Taylor* that the accused has a fundamental right to see and know the identity of his accusers save in rare and exceptional circumstances and its statement of the factors which the judge should balance in the exercise of his discretion, some of which point to the preservation of the anonymity of a witness. The later judgments in *R v X* and *Ex p Lenman* lay emphasis on the magistrate or judge having to strike a balance of fairness between the prosecution and the accused, in which process the importance of the accused knowing the identity of his accuser is a factor of great weight, but I think that in some cases the balance of fairness may come down in favour of the prosecution notwithstanding that the circumstances could not be described as rare and exceptional. However in the case of a trial, as opposed to committal proceedings, account must now be taken of the Strasbourg jurisprudence relating to art 6 of the European Convention for the Protection of Human Rights and Fundamental Freedoms 1950 (as set out in Sch 1 to the Human Rights Act 1998).

a   [87] The appellants also submitted that the admission of the evidence of the anonymous witness CS/1 was in breach of art 6(3)(d) of the Human Rights Convention which provides that anyone charged with a criminal offence has the right to examine or have examined witnesses against him. The appellants recognised that they faced the difficulty that there is no provision for cross-examination in committal proceedings on an application for extradition, but they

b   submitted that their inability to cross-examine made it important that the defence should not be deprived of information as to the identity of a witness when knowledge of his identity might enable them to demonstrate that his evidence was unreliable because he was actuated by malice or hostility. In my opinion the two Administrative Courts were right to reject this argument as it is clear from the decision of the European Commission of Human Rights in *Kirkwood v UK*

c   (1984) 37 DR 158 that the provisions of art 6 do not apply to a committal hearing on an application for extradition, the Commission stating (at 191 (para 9)):

d   'Nevertheless, the Commission concludes that these proceedings did not in themselves form part of the determination of the applicant's guilt or innocence, which will be the subject of separate proceedings in the United States which may be expected to conform to standards of fairness equivalent to the requirements of Article 6, including the presumption of innocence, notwithstanding the committal proceedings. In these circumstances the Commission concludes that the committal proceedings did not form part of or constitute the determination of a criminal charge within the meaning of

e   Article 6 of the Convention.'

[88] The appellants further submitted that even if they could not rely on art 6, they were entitled to claim that the admission of the evidence of witness CS/1 was in breach of their right under art 5(4) of the convention to take proceedings for a speedy decision of the lawfulness of their detention. In my opinion the

f   Administrative Courts were also right to reject this submission. I consider that at the committal proceedings the appellants were able to challenge the lawfulness of their detention, and as they cannot rely on art 6 in respect of that hearing they cannot claim the rights given by art 6 by relying on art 5(4).

g

The sufficiency of the evidence

[89] The test for the magistrate to apply to the sufficiency of the evidence before him is that set out in para 7(1) of Sch 1 to the 1989 Act—whether the evidence produced would make a case requiring an answer by the prisoner at a trial. Counsel for Mr Al-Fawwaz accepted that if it was proper for the magistrate to admit the evidence of CS/1 this test was satisfied in his case. However in his

h   evidence CS/1 did not refer to either Mr Abdul Bary or Mr Eiderous by name and counsel for these two appellants submitted that the evidence against them was insufficient for the magistrate to commit. This submission was considered in the judgment of the Administrative Court delivered by Kennedy LJ ([2001] EWHC Admin 298, [2001] All ER (D) 24 (May)). As he observed, citing the judgment of

j   Lloyd LJ in *R v United States Government, ex p Blair* (1985) Times, 21 June, the question for the High Court to decide is not whether the evidence constitutes a case to answer but whether a reasonable magistrate, directing himself properly and in accordance with the law, could take that view. This question was carefully considered by Kennedy LJ who outlined in his judgment (at [17]–[30]), the various strands of evidence and concluded that the facts as a whole were capable of enabling a court to come to the conclusion that each defendant was guilty of the proposed charge. In my opinion the Administrative Court was fully entitled to come to this decision. *a*

[90] The two appellants further submitted that the decision of the magistrate to commit was flawed because he failed to give reasons for his decision and this submission was rejected by the Administrative Court. In *Rey v Government of Switzerland* [1999] AC 54 at 66–67, [1998] 3 WLR 1 at 10 Lord Steyn, in delivering the judgment of the Privy Council, said: *b*

'Despite a growing practice in England of stipendiary magistrates to give reasons in extradition proceedings it has not been held that magistrates are under a legal duty to do so. And the legal position in England is perhaps justified by the right of the fugitive to apply for habeas corpus to the Divisional Court if the decision of the stipendiary magistrate goes against *c* him: see section 11 of the Extradition Act 1989 ... In these circumstances their Lordships are not prepared to hold that there is a general implied duty upon magistrates to give reasons in respect of all disputed issues of fact and law in extradition proceedings. But their Lordships must enter a cautionary note: it is unnecessary in the present case to consider whether in the great diversity of cases which come before magistrates in extradition proceedings *d* the principle of fairness may in particular circumstances require a magistrate to give reasons.'

[91] Counsel for the appellant submitted that in the particular circumstance of this case fairness required the magistrate to give reasons. In fact the magistrate did give some reasons. He said in the course of delivering his decision and *e* referring to two faxes claiming responsibility for the Nairobi bombing and the Tanzania bombing:

'Nevertheless, I am satisfied that a jury, properly directed, *could* conclude, on the totality of the evidence that the claims were sent before the bombings. Similarly a jury *could* conclude, regardless of whether they conclude the *f* claims were sent before or after the bombings, that they were genuine. Similarly a jury *could* conclude that both defendants played a part in the dissemination of the claims to the international media. Further, a jury *could* conclude that Osama bin Laden was the moving force behind the bombings and played a central part in the conspiracy to cause the explosions. I have *g* carefully reread all the defence written submissions and my notes and considered those matters afresh. It does not seem to me to be either sensible or desirable that I should deal with each point in turn. Any review of my decision would necessitate those conducting the review to come to their own conclusion on whether there is a case to answer, rather than deciding *h* whether or not there are flaws in my approach or reasoning. I am satisfied that the facts taken as a whole are *capable* of enabling this court (or a jury properly directed) to come to the conclusion that the only reasonable inference to be drawn from them is that each defendant is guilty of the proposed charge. Thus each has a case to answer.'

j

However counsel submitted that these reasons were inadequate.

[92] In a case where there was such a mass of material and where the issue was whether a reasonable jury could draw the inference from that material that the prisoners were parties to the conspiracy alleged, striking a balance between stating his reasons briefly and over elaboration presented the magistrate with a task of some difficulty. Kennedy LJ said (at [40]) that he would have found it

a helpful if the magistrate had given more detailed reasons, but he rejected the
submission that his reasons were inadequate and he stated (at [41]):

'The magistrate did explain his approach, and it can be said that he was
being realistic. Even if he had attempted to explain in more detail the case
which he decided required an answer it is overwhelmingly likely that we
b would have still been required to carry out the exercise performed in this
court. Accordingly I do not accept that in law his reasons were inadequate,
and even if I were able to accept that submission I cannot see that it would
afford any basis for relief given that, in reality, in my judgment there were
good reasons for the magistrate deciding as he did.'

c I consider that Kennedy LJ was right so to hold.
[93] Accordingly for the reasons which I have given I would dismiss the three
appeals. I would add that the matters referred to by my noble and learned friend
Lord Scott of Foscote in para [121] of his speech were not referred to in argument
before the House and I express no opinion in relation to them.

d LORD MILLETT.
[94] My Lords, the double criminality rule lies at the heart of our law of
extradition. It is a precondition of extradition that the offence for which extradition
may be ordered should be within the criminal jurisdiction of both the requesting
and the requested state. The question for decision in the present case is whether
e this means the territorial jurisdiction of the states concerned or embraces their
extra-territorial jurisdiction also.
[95] In considering this question it is important to bear the objects of the
double criminality rule in mind, for its two requirements serve different purposes.
The first requirement, that the offence for which extradition is ordered should be
within the jurisdiction of the requesting state, serves a purely practical purpose.
f There is no point in extraditing a person for an offence for which the requesting
state cannot try him. The second requirement, that the offence should also be
within our own criminal jurisdiction, serves to protect the accused from the
exercise of an exorbitant foreign jurisdiction. Views as to what constitutes an
exorbitant jurisdiction naturally differ; the test adopted by our own law has been
g to accord to other countries the jurisdiction which we claim ourselves but no
more. As my noble and learned friend Lord Rodger of Earlsferry has observed,
this is not the only means of protection given by our system of extradition, for the
exercise of an exorbitant foreign jurisdiction may be forestalled by executive
action. But it is the only measure of judicial control which the law provides for
h this purpose.
[96] The first requirement is given effect by the definition of 'fugitive criminal'
in para 20 of Sch 1 to the Extradition Act 1989; the second by the definition of
'extradition crime' (where as in the present case the relevant Order in Council
was made before the coming into force of the 1989 Act) in s 26 of the Extradition
Act 1870.
j [97] The magistrate's power to commit a person to prison to await extradition
is contained in para 7 of Sch 1 to the 1989 Act as amended. This provides:

'(1) In the case of a fugitive criminal accused of an extradition crime, if the
foreign warrant authorising the arrest of such criminal is duly authenticated,
and such evidence is produced as (subject to the provisions of this Schedule)
would, according to the law of England and Wales, make a case requiring an

answer by the prisoner if the proceedings were for the trial in England and
Wales of an information for the crime, the metropolitan magistrate shall *a*
commit him to prison, but otherwise shall order him to be discharged.

(2) In the case of a fugitive criminal alleged to have been convicted of an
extradition crime, if such evidence is produced as (subject to the provisions
of this Schedule) would, according to the law of England and Wales, prove
that the prisoner was convicted of such crime, the metropolitan magistrate *b*
shall commit him to prison, but otherwise shall order him to be discharged.'

[98] Thus the magistrate must satisfy himself not only that the foreign warrant
is duly authenticated but also (1) that the accused is 'a fugitive criminal' (2) who
is accused or has been convicted of 'an extradition crime' and (3) that the
evidence would according to our own law make a case requiring an answer if the *c*
proceedings were for trial here.

Fugitive criminal

[99] 'Fugitive criminal' is defined as follows: '... "fugitive criminal" means any
person accused or convicted of an extradition crime committed within the *d*
jurisdiction of any foreign state who is in or is suspected of being in some part of
Her Majesty's dominions ...'

[100] Two points deserve particular attention. First, in order to found his
jurisdiction in an accusation case the magistrate must satisfy himself only that the
person brought before him is *accused* of an extradition crime committed within
the jurisdiction of the requesting state; for this limited purpose he is not required *e*
to satisfy himself that the accusation is well founded. Accordingly he will
ordinarily need to look no further than the allegations in the indictment and the
supporting documentation. Secondly, the requirement that the offence in question
should constitute an extradition crime committed within the jurisdiction of the
requesting state applies equally to both accusation and conviction cases. *f*
Accordingly the expression 'the jurisdiction of' the requesting state must bear a
meaning which is capable of accommodating both kinds of case.

[101] The question for decision is whether these words refer to the territorial
jurisdiction of the requesting state over crimes committed within its own territory
(expansively defined to include for example its ships or colonies) or whether they
also embrace its extra-territorial jurisdiction, however wide this may be. *g*

[102] I have no doubt that the latter interpretation is correct. My reasons are
as follows. (1) As I have already explained, it is not the function of this branch of
the double criminality rule to protect the accused from the exercise of an
exorbitant foreign jurisdiction. That is adequately catered for by the other branch
of the rule and by other means. (2) As a matter of ordinary language, the *h*
'jurisdiction of a state' in the criminal context simply means its power to try an
offender for an alleged offence, and includes both its territorial and extra-
territorial jurisdiction. The meaning of the expression may, of course, be controlled
by its context, as when we speak of 'leaving the jurisdiction'; but there is no
controlling context here. (3) Although the general rule is that '[t]he jurisdiction *j*
over the crime belongs to the country where the crime is committed' (see
MacLeod v A-G for New South Wales [1891] AC 455 at 458 per Lord Halsbury LC)
most countries exercise some degree of extra-territorial jurisdiction and were
doing so well before 1870. The English courts have for centuries claimed jurisdiction
to try British subjects for murder committed abroad; most civil law countries
exercise a similar jurisdiction based on the nationality of the victim rather than

a that of the accused. (4) There is high authority for and sound sense in the proposition that extradition treaties should not be construed in a way which would 'hinder the working and narrow the operation of most salutary international arrangements' (see *Government of Belgium v Postlethwaite* [1987] 2 All ER 985 at 991, sub nom *R v Governor of Ashford Remand Centre, ex p Postlethwaite* [1988] AC 924 at 947 per Lord Bridge of Harwich). This is even more the case in today's global

b village where national borders are no impediment to international terrorists and other criminals. (5) The 1989 Act is an enabling Act. It applies not only to existing treaties but also to future treaties yet to be entered into. These may, of course, place further restrictions on the powers of the English courts to order extradition but they may not extend them beyond those conferred by the Act. Such an Act should be given a wide construction in order not to fetter the power

c of the executive to enter into future treaties in future in whatever terms may be considered appropriate. (6) The Act would be unworkable in some conviction cases if the magistrate had to be satisfied that the crime been committed within the territorial jurisdiction of the requesting state. For this purpose, he should look no further than the conviction itself, yet this may not provide an answer.

d [103] While the other reasons are sufficient in themselves to indicate the correct interpretation of the word 'jurisdiction', I regard this last as conclusive. Take this very case, where the appellants are accused of conspiring to murder American citizens in the United States and abroad. The conspiracy is alleged to have been entered into and all the victims to have been murdered outside the United States. Very few overt acts are alleged to have taken place within the United

e States, and they may not be proved. The United States does not claim extra-territorial jurisdiction to try cases of murder on the basis of the nationality of the victims, yet it is conceded that the offences of which the appellants are accused are within its extra-territorial jurisdiction. Suppose the appellants had been convicted of the charges by a United States court and had escaped to the United Kingdom,

f so that it was a conviction and not an accusation case. The magistrate would look at the certificate of conviction in order to decide whether the offences of which they had been convicted were 'committed within the jurisdiction of the United States'. He would observe that the appellants had been found guilty of the offence of conspiracy and that it was alleged that some of the overt acts had taken place in the United States. But he would also observe from the summing up that the

g judge had instructed the jury that the offence was one over which the United States had extra-territorial jurisdiction and did not depend on the commission of any overt acts within its territory; so that they could convict even if they were not satisfied that any such acts had in fact taken place. In such a case it would be impossible to discover from the verdict or otherwise whether the jury had or had

h not been satisfied that overt acts had been committed in the United States as alleged. In these circumstances the magistrate would have no way of telling whether the accused had been convicted of an offence within the territorial jurisdiction of the United States or not.

Extradition crime
j
[104] 'Extradition crime' is defined as follows: 'The term "extradition crime" means a crime which, if committed in England or within English jurisdiction, would be one of the crimes described in the first schedule to this Act.' (See s 26 of the 1870 Act.)

[105] The same question arises here: whether the words 'within English jurisdiction' mean within our territorial jurisdiction or whether they extend to

our extra-territorial jurisdiction. I have no doubt that the latter interpretation is *a* correct. My reasons are as follows. (1) The contradistinction between 'in England' and 'within English jurisdiction' points strongly in favour of the wider interpretation. It is not in itself conclusive, since the latter expression could be intended merely to bring in British ships and colonies. But why stop there, when the English criminal jurisdiction has always been wider than this? (2) The only reason for distinguishing between one kind of jurisdiction and another is the need *b* to protect the accused from the exercise of an exorbitant foreign jurisdiction. But there is no justification for classifying as exorbitant a jurisdiction which, mutatis mutandis, we claim ourselves. The thinking behind this part of the definition is that we should not extradite for an offence which, in the corresponding circumstances, we could not try ourselves. (3) The policy which underlies the law of extradition is that a criminal should not escape trial and punishment by *c* leaving one country and going to another. If the offence with which he is charged or of which he has been convicted is also an offence triable in the country to which he has fled, he should be returned for trial or punishment to the country from which he came. (4) In *Liangsiriprasert v United States Government* [1990] 2 All ER 866, [1991] 1 AC 225 the Privy Council rejected a submission that a *d* conspiracy entered into abroad is not a crime at common law unless some overt act takes place in the territory of the forum, in that case Hong Kong. It was sufficient that the conspiracy was aimed at Hong Kong. Although the point was not argued by counsel, who agreed that the principles of extradition were not in dispute and that the offences in question were extradition crimes, it was clearly assumed that the words 'or within English jurisdiction' are not limited to English *e* territorial jurisdiction. The case has, in my view rightly, been taken as clear authority for that proposition in the leading textbook on the subject (see *Jones on Extradition* (1995) p 88 (para 3-023)). (5) The list of extradition crimes contained in the First Schedule includes piracy jure gentium. This is an offence which can only be committed on the high seas and (unlike municipal piracy) on a foreign *f* ship. Accordingly it *cannot* be committed in England or within the territorial jurisdiction of the English courts.

[106] I regard this last point as conclusive.

[107] Crimes which are the natural subject of extradition proceedings are almost invariably committed abroad and as such are usually outside the jurisdiction of the English courts, however widely that expression may be construed. So the *g* conduct which constitutes an extradition crime does not consist of acts which actually were committed in England or within English jurisdiction, but rather conduct which would constitute a crime under English law if the acts in question were so committed. The test, therefore, is a hypothetical one, which calls for some degree of transposition. *h*

[108] In *Tarling (No 1) v Government of the Republic of Singapore* (1978) 70 Cr App R 77 at 136 Lord Keith of Kinkel stated:

'In considering the jurisdiction aspect it is necessary to suppose that England is substituted for Singapore as regards all the circumstances of the case connected with the latter country, and to examine the question whether *j* upon that hypothesis and upon the evidence adduced the English courts would have jurisdiction to try the offences charged.'

This guidance was followed by the Divisional Court in *R v Governor of Pentonville Prison, ex p Osman* [1989] 3 All ER 701, [1990] 1 WLR 277. Lloyd LJ explained that only the acts which took place in the requesting state (Hong Kong) were to be *a*   treated as having taken place in England. All else remained as it in fact happened.

[**109**] For my own part, and subject to one point which I will mention in a moment, I think that this is the correct way to effect the transposition. The principle at work is mutatis mutandis. Given that the court is concerned with an extradition case, the crime will not have been committed in England but (normally) in the requesting state. So the test is applied by substituting England *b*   for the requesting state wherever the name of the requesting state appears in the indictment. But no more should be changed than is necessary to give effect to the fact that the court is dealing with an extradition case and not a domestic one. The word mutandis is an essential element in the concept; the court should not hypothesise more than necessary.

c   [**110**] The one point to which I would draw attention is that it is not sufficient to substitute England for the territory of the requesting state wherever that is mentioned in the indictment. It is necessary to effect an appropriate substitution for every circumstance connected with the requesting state on which the jurisdiction is founded. In the present case the appellants are accused, not merely of conspiring to murder persons abroad (who happened to be Americans), but of *d*   conspiring to murder persons unknown because they were Americans. In political terms, what is alleged is a conspiracy entered into abroad to wage war on the United States by killing its citizens, including its diplomats and other internationally protected persons, at home and abroad. Translating this into legal terms and transposing it for the purpose of seeing whether such conduct would constitute a crime 'in England or within English jurisdiction', the charges must be considered *e*   as if they alleged a conspiracy entered into abroad to kill British subjects, including internationally protected persons, at home or abroad. Such a conspiracy would constitute a criminal offence within the extra-territorial jurisdiction of our courts.

[**111**] I should not, however, wish it to be thought that the inclusion of internationally protected persons among the potential victims is necessary to *f*   found the jurisdiction. A conspiracy formed outside the jurisdiction to commit a crime in England is triable in England even though no overt act in furtherance of the conspiracy is committed in England: see *Liangsiriprasert*'s case [1990] 2 All ER 866 at 877, [1991] 1 AC 225 at 250 where Lord Griffiths pointed out that the inchoate crimes of conspiracy, attempt and incitement developed with the principal object of frustrating the commission of a contemplated crime by arresting and punishing *g*   the offenders before they committed the crime, and asked:

> 'If the inchoate crime is aimed at England with the consequent injury to English society, why should the English courts not accept jurisdiction to try it if the authorities can lay hands on the offenders, either because they come *h*   within the jurisdiction or through extradition procedures? If evidence is obtained that a terrorist cell operating abroad is planning a bombing campaign in London what sense can there be in the authorities holding their hand and not acting until the cell comes to England to plant the bombs, with the risk that the terrorists may slip through the net? Extradition should be sought before they have a chance to put their plan into action and they *j*   should be tried for conspiracy or the attempt as the case may be. Furthermore, if one of the conspirators should come to England, for whatever purpose, he should be liable to arrest and trial for the criminal agreement he has entered into.' (See [1990] 2 All ER 866 at 877–878, [1991] 1 AC 225 at 250.)

[**112**] When Lord Griffiths referred to a conspiracy 'aimed at England' he was clearly thinking of a conspiracy to commit a crime in England. If a conspiracy to

plant bombs in England would be triable in England even though it was entirely *a* inchoate and no bombs had yet been planted anywhere, a conspiracy to plant bombs in England and abroad where some bombs had already been planted abroad would be a fortiori. This is sufficient to uphold the jurisdiction in the present case, since a conspiracy to murder British subjects because they were British and for no other reason must be a conspiracy to murder them wherever they might be found, whether in England or elsewhere; and such a conspiracy is *b* (inter alia) a conspiracy to commit a crime in England. Moreover, while the point does not strictly arise for decision in the present case, I do not think that a definition of the offence which requires the prosecution to prove an intent to murder British subjects in England as opposed to elsewhere is either sensible or likely to prove to be stable. In my opinion, a conspiracy to plant bombs in British owned properties abroad and kill British subjects wherever they may be ought *c* not to be the less triable in England because the conspirators do not plan to carry out their murderous campaign in England itself.

Sufficiency of the evidence

[113] The final matter which the magistrate is required to consider is whether *d* the evidence is sufficient to make a case requiring an answer if the proceedings were for trial in England or Wales. This involves another hypothesis, but solely for the purpose of testing the sufficiency of the prosecution evidence. The magistrate is to consider this as if the proceedings were a purely domestic case. No transposition of facts and no feats of imagination are called for. *e*

Conclusion

[114] Subject to the foregoing and in all other respects I am in full agreement with the speeches of my noble and learned friends Lord Hutton and Lord Rodger. Like them, I would dismiss all three appeals. *f*

LORD SCOTT OF FOSCOTE.

[115] My Lords, I have had the advantage of reading in advance the opinions on these appeals given by my noble and learned friends Lord Slynn of Hadley, Lord Hutton, Lord Millett and Lord Rodger of Earlsferry. I am in agreement with them and propose simply to add a few comments of my own. *g*

[116] The purpose of extradition arrangements made between this country and other states is, in my view, twofold. First there is the desire that malefactors should not be able to escape the criminal justice consequences of their misdeeds by sheltering in a country other than that against whose laws they have offended. The comments of Cockburn CJ in *Re Tivnan* (1864) 5 B & S 645 at 678, 122 ER 971 *h* at 983 and of Lord Bridge of Harwich in *Government of Belgium v Postlethwaite* [1987] 2 All ER 985 at 991–992, sub nom *R v Governor of Ashford Remand Centre, ex p Postlethwaite* [1988] AC 924 at 947, cited by Lord Hutton in his opinion, are very much in point. But alleged malefactors who are present in this country, whether as permanent residents, as refugees or asylum seekers, or as visitors, are *j* entitled, while they are here, to the protection of our laws and our standards of criminal justice. They should not be exported abroad to face trial under a foreign criminal justice system unless, by our standards, there is a case against them that is fit for trial, and unless, by our standards, they will receive a fair trial in accordance with the requirements of art 6 of the European Convention for the Protection of Human Rights and Fundamental Freedoms 1950 (as set out in Sch 1

a to the Human Rights Act 1998). The second purpose of extradition arrangements is, or should be, to provide the requisite safeguards.

[117] In para [55] of his opinion, Lord Hutton has posed two questions. First, are the appellants 'fugitive criminals' and, second, is the crime alleged against them an 'extradition crime'? The answer to the questions depends upon the scope to be given to the references to 'jurisdiction' in the statutory definitions and other provisions which bear upon the meaning of these expressions. I am in complete

b agreement with the answers and the reasons for the answers given by my noble and learned friends. If a narrow meaning had to be attributed to 'jurisdiction', the extradition arrangements between this country and the United States, and indeed all extradition arrangements to which Sch 1 to the Extradition Act 1989 applied, would fall short of properly achieving the first of the two purposes to which

c I have referred.

[118] There are several aspects of the extradition arrangements applicable under Sch 1 to the 1989 Act that are relevant to the second purpose.

[119] There is the double criminality rule. No one is to be extradited unless the offence he is alleged to have committed would, if it had been committed in

d England 'or within English jurisdiction', have been an offence for which he could be tried under English law. It has been accepted in the argument before the House that if 'jurisdiction' is given the wide meaning for which the respondents contend and that your Lordships have accepted, there would have been extra-territorial jurisdiction under English law over the alleged offence.

e [120] A further safeguard for the fugitive criminal against whom extradition is sought is that the evidence relied on in support of the extradition request must be sufficient by the standards of English law to justify his committal for trial or to produce a case to answer (para 7(1) of Sch 1 to the 1989 Act) (art IX of the Extradition Treaty between the Government of the United Kingdom of Great Britain and Northern Ireland and the Government of the United States of

f America 1972 (as set out in Sch 1 to the United States of America (Extradition) Order 1976, SI 1976/2144)). As to this, I agree with my noble and learned friends that in relation to each of the appellants the test is satisfied.

[121] Paragraph 8 of Sch 1 contains the final safeguard for the fugitive criminal whose extradition is being sought. He will not be extradited unless the Secretary of State decides, as a matter of discretion, to order that the extradition may

g proceed. It has become the settled practice, as I understand it, for the Secretary of State, in a case where the law of the extraditing state might subject the extradited prisoner on conviction to the death penalty, to require a guarantee that a death sentence will not be imposed (see Soering v UK (1989) 11 EHRR 439). But there is, in the circumstances of the present cases, a further matter of concern.

h The media have, over the past few weeks, carried reports of the intention of the President of the United States, acting under emergency executive powers, to establish military tribunals to try non-United States citizens who are accused of terrorist offences. The offences with which these appellants are charged might well fall within the category of offences proposed to be dealt with by military

j tribunals. It is reported that the proposed military tribunals will be presided over by military personnel, not judges, will be able to admit evidence that would not ordinarily be admissible before a criminal court of law and will be able to conduct the trial behind closed doors. The charges against the appellants that have led to the extradition requests were laid before the United States District Court for the Southern District of New York. If the appellants are to be extradited I imagine that they will be tried before that court or some other Federal Court and not before a military tribunal that will not need to sit in public and that need not *a* observe the rules of evidence.

[122] I agree that these appeals should be dismissed.

LORD RODGER OF EARLSFERRY.

[123] My Lords, I gratefully adopt the summary of the facts and issues given in the speech of my noble and learned friend Lord Slynn of Hadley. *b*

[124] The appeals arise out of applications for habeas corpus in relation to requisitions by the United States for the extradition of the appellants. Extradition between the United Kingdom and the United States is regulated by a treaty signed between the two countries in 1972 and given effect in our law by the United States of America (Extradition) Order 1976, SI 1976/2144, an Order in Council *c* made by Her Majesty under s 2 of the Extradition Act 1870. Paragraph 3 of the 1976 order provides that the Extradition Acts 1870 to 1935, as amended or extended by any subsequent enactment, are to apply in the case of the United States in accordance with the Extradition Treaty between the Government of the United Kingdom of Great Britain and Northern Ireland and the Government of *d* the United States of America 1972 (as set out in Sch 1 to that order) (the 1972 treaty). This means that our domestic legislation regulating extradition has effect in relation to the United States, but 'subject to the limitations, restrictions, conditions, exceptions, and qualifications, if any, contained in the order' (s 5 of the 1870 Act). In other words the order may limit but cannot extend the scope of the extradition legislation. When the order was made, the relevant domestic *e* legislation comprised the Extradition Acts 1870 to 1935, but by virtue of s 1(3) of the Extradition Act 1989 it is now contained in Sch 1 to that Act. So in the absence of any relevant qualification in the treaty—and none was suggested in argument—the law governing the extradition of the appellants is to be found in Sch 1 to the 1989 Act. *f*

[125] The entire scheme of Sch 1 is built around the concept of the 'fugitive criminal'. He is the key figure. So, for instance, under para 3 every 'fugitive criminal' of a relevant state—but no one else—is liable to be apprehended and surrendered. Similarly, under para 4(1) the foreign state presents a requisition for the surrender of a 'fugitive criminal' and under para 4(2) the Secretary of State may require the metropolitan magistrate to issue his warrant for the apprehension of the 'fugitive *g* criminal'. If, eventually, the process ends in the magistrate making an order for his committal, under para 8(2) the Secretary of State orders the 'fugitive criminal' to be surrendered and he is handed over to the representative of the requesting state.

[126] Paragraph 20 shows who is to be regarded as a 'fugitive criminal' for *h* these purposes:

'... "fugitive criminal" means any person accused or convicted of an extradition crime committed within the jurisdiction of any foreign state who is in or is suspected of being in some part of Her Majesty's dominions; "fugitive *j* criminal of a foreign state" means a fugitive criminal accused or convicted of an extradition crime committed within the jurisdiction of that state ...'

These definitions are not free-standing: they cannot be understood unless one first knows what constitutes an 'extradition crime'. To discover that, one has to look at another definition in para 20:

a   '... "extradition crime", in relation to any foreign state, is to be construed by reference to the Order in Council under section 2 of the Extradition Act 1870 applying to that state as it had effect immediately before the coming into force of this Act and to any amendments thereafter made to that Order ...'

b   This in turn sends the reader back to the Order in Council as it had effect immediately before the 1989 Act came into force on 27 September 1989. For present purposes the relevant Order in Council gives effect to the 1972 treaty between the United Kingdom and the United States, art III(1)(b) of which provides:

c   '(1) Extradition shall be granted for an act or omission the facts of which disclose an offence within any of the descriptions listed in the Schedule annexed to this Treaty, which is an integral part of the Treaty, or any other offence, if ... (b) the offence is extraditable under the relevant law, being the law of the United Kingdom or other territory to which this Treaty applies by virtue of sub-paragraph (1)(a) of Article II ...'

d   In the case of proceedings such as these, involving the United States, the question whether a crime is an extradition crime must therefore be decided by considering whether it would have been an extradition crime under the 1870 Act and under the 1972 treaty, as they stood immediately before the 1989 Act came into force. In other words, it depends on whether the crime was an 'extradition crime' in

e   terms of s 26 of the 1870 Act. That section provided: '... The term "extradition crime" means a crime which, if committed in England or within English jurisdiction, would be one of the crimes described in the first schedule to this Act ...'

[127] At the end of the legislative paper-chase the position is this. The extradition process under Sch 1 to the 1989 Act applies only to fugitive criminals as defined

f   in para 20 of that Schedule. So defined, they are people who have been accused or convicted (a) of committing an extradition crime, as defined in s 26 of the 1870 Act, and (b) of committing that crime 'within the jurisdiction' of the requesting state. Since these appeals concern persons accused rather than convicted of crime, for ease of exposition I shall simply consider the legislation as it applies in such cases. In turning to look at the course of events in extradition proceedings, I do

g   so against the background of the classic account by Lord Diplock in his speeches in *Government of the Federal Republic of Germany v Sotiriadis* [1974] 1 All ER 692, sub nom *R v Governor of Pentonville Prison, ex p Sotiriadis* [1975] AC 1 and *Government of Denmark v Nielsen* [1984] 2 All ER 81, [1984] AC 606.

[128] Schedule 1 to the 1989 Act is the source of the Secretary of State's

h   powers to deal with a requisition for the surrender of an individual. Under para 4(2) he can issue an order for the arrest of the person concerned only if he is satisfied both that the person is accused of an extradition crime and that the crime is alleged to have been committed within the jurisdiction of the requesting state. If the Secretary of State is not so satisfied, then the process can go no further

j   unless and until he is provided with additional information which does satisfy him on these points. If, on the other hand, the Secretary of State is so satisfied, he may issue an order for the apprehension of the fugitive criminal. On receipt of the order to proceed the magistrate must issue an arrest warrant if he is presented with such evidence as would, in his opinion, justify the issue of such a warrant if the crime specified in the order had been committed in England or Wales.

[129] When the arrest warrant is executed and the individual is brought before
the magistrate, the magistrate may commit him to prison or order his discharge.
Paragraph 7(1) tells the magistrate what he is to do:

'In the case of a fugitive criminal accused of an extradition crime, if the
foreign warrant authorising the arrest of such criminal is duly authenticated,
and such evidence is produced as (subject to the provisions of this Schedule)
would, according to the law of England and Wales, make a case requiring an
answer by the prisoner if the proceedings were for the trial in England and
Wales of an information for the crime ...'

The functions of the magistrate are simply those set out in para 7(1), except that
the magistrate is also to receive any evidence tendered to show that the alleged
crime is of a political character (para 6(2)). The magistrate must look to see if the
foreign warrant is duly authenticated. In the case of an American extradition, the
authentication formalities are to be found in art VII(5) of the 1972 treaty. If the
magistrate is satisfied on that point, the other matter which he has to consider
under para 7(1) is whether such evidence of the extradition crime has been
produced as would make a case requiring an answer if the proceedings were for
trial in England and Wales of an information for the crime specified in the order
to proceed. If he is satisfied on this point, the magistrate commits the fugitive
criminal to prison; otherwise, he orders his discharge.

[130] Given the scheme of the legislation, it is helpful to keep distinct the
issues which the Secretary of State must consider and the issues which are for the
magistrate. Their roles are different. If need be, however, the proceedings may
be reviewed by the Administrative Court in the application for habeas corpus
which is specifically envisaged in para 8(1) of the Schedule.

[131] Counsel for the appellants argued that the magistrate has to consider
whether the individual is 'a fugitive criminal accused of an extradition crime'
since his jurisdiction under para 7(1) depends on that being the position. The
suggestion was that, in a case like the present, this would involve the magistrate
in hearing evidence and, on that basis, deciding where the crime had been
committed so that he could determine whether it had been committed within the
(territorial) jurisdiction of the requesting state. In reality this submission was tied
to the appellants' principal submission that the only relevant jurisdiction of a
requesting state is its territorial jurisdiction. At this stage I simply observe that
I am satisfied that Parliament did not envisage that the magistrate would need to
hear evidence in regard to his jurisdiction. A dispute as to whether the crime
specified in the order to proceed is an extradition crime will generally be legal
rather than factual. The nature of the jurisdiction upon which the requesting state
founds will appear, if not from the arrest warrant issued by the authorities in the
requesting state, at least from the supporting affidavits and other documents. On
neither issue is the magistrate likely to need to look beyond these documents.

[132] In the present proceedings the contention for the appellants is that the
conspiracy alleged against them was not committed 'within the jurisdiction' of
the United States. In other words, their contention is that they are not 'fugitive
criminals' in terms of para 20 of Sch 1 to the 1989 Act. If they are correct in that
contention, then none of the provisions in Sch 1 applies to them and the magistrate's
warrants for their committal will have to be quashed.

[133] The appellants' contention depends in the first place on the construction
of the phrase 'within the jurisdiction' in the definition of 'fugitive criminal' in
para 20. Most routine extradition cases will involve offences committed in the

a   territory of the requesting state. In such cases the jurisdiction element in the
    definition of a fugitive criminal will be uncontentious. Of course, as the appellants
    accept, in many states, especially nowadays, criminal jurisdiction is not limited to
    crimes committed within the territory of the state. They contend, however, that
    those accused of committing crimes outside the territory of the requesting state
    are not 'fugitive criminals' because the crime was not committed 'within the
b   (territorial) jurisdiction' of the requesting state. Those accused of such crimes are
    therefore immune to extradition.
        [134] On that approach the appellants in these cases who, it appears, have
    never set foot in the United States, would not count as 'fugitive criminals' and so
    would fall outside the entire extradition scheme in Sch 1 to the 1989 Act, unless
    something had been done in pursuit of the conspiracy within the United States.
c   Only in that way would their alleged crime of conspiracy to murder have been
    committed within the United States and so only in that way would the appellants
    fall within Sch 1 as 'fugitive criminals'.
        [135] The contention for the appellants was accepted by the Administrative
    Court in the case involving Al-Fawwaz ([2001] 4 All ER 149, [2001] 1 WLR 1234).
d   In the words of Buxton LJ to constitute an extradition crime, the offence—

        'has to be committed within the territory of the requesting state so that it
        would, as transposed, be committed within the territory of England and
        Wales. It is not enough that the latter crime would, as in Pt III cases as
        recognised in Ex p Pinochet (No 3) (R v Bow Street Metropolitan Stipendiary
e   Magistrate, ex p Pinochet Ugarte (No 3) [1999] 2 All ER 97, [2000] 1 AC 147), be
        indictable under the extra-territorial jurisdiction of the United Kingdom. We
        also think that the concept of jurisdiction in art 1 of the treaty annexed to the
        1976 Order is subject to the same limitation. Whether this is a sensible rule
        in a world of major international crime and of the regular passage of persons
        involved in such crime between different jurisdictions is no doubt not for us
f   to say.' (See [2001] 4 All ER 149 at 158–159, [2001] 1 WLR 1234 at 1243
        (para 32).)

    In the proceedings against Eiderous and Abdul Bary the Administrative Court
    found it unnecessary to reconsider the point (see [2001] EWHC Admin 298, [2001]
    All ER (D) 24 (May)). The United States government have taken the opportunity of
g   these appeals to challenge the decision of the Administrative Court on this point.
        [136] Plainly, Buxton LJ did not regard the rule which he stated as being sensible
    in today's world where easy communications mean that schemes may readily be
    laid and plots hatched in one country with the aim of committing major crime in
    another country. Drug trafficking is only the most obvious example. Counsel for
h   the appellants specifically acknowledged that modern circumstances might demand
    a different system which permitted extradition for crimes committed outside the
    territorial jurisdiction of the requesting state. The only trouble is, he said, that the
    system which we have in Sch 1 to the 1989 Act is an old model, dating back to
    1870, and it is not designed to operate in that way.
j   [137] 'Jurisdiction' is a word with a history in English stretching back some
    eight centuries. It can be used in a variety of contexts—not all of them legal—and
    with different shades of meaning. In this case we are concerned with 'jurisdiction'
    in the definition of 'fugitive criminal' in para 20 of Sch 1 to the 1989 Act where it
    refers to the jurisdiction of the requesting state, under its internal law, to regulate
    and punish conduct. Most of the conduct which states choose to regulate and
    punish is conduct occurring within their territory, including their ships and

aircraft. But states may also choose to regulate and punish certain conduct which
takes place outside their territory. For instance, the courts of England have for
centuries had jurisdiction to try cases of murder allegedly committed by English
and, later, British subjects anywhere in the world (*R v Page* [1953] 2 All ER 1355,
[1954] 1 QB 170). More generally, civil law countries have traditionally exercised
a wide jurisdiction to regulate and to punish within their own territory the
conduct of their citizens while they are living or travelling abroad. In the past, at
least, this extensive jurisdiction meant that such states were often reluctant to
extradite their own nationals. During the course of the last century, as a result of
various conventions, there was a great increase in the range of offences for which
international law specifically permits, or even obliges, states to assert extra-
territorial jurisdiction. The present case concerns an alleged conspiracy entered
into abroad to murder American citizens in the United States and elsewhere.
The appellants accept that, as a matter of the internal law of the United States, the
American courts have jurisdiction to try that charge. Moreover, while the exact
extent of the right of a state under international law to exercise jurisdiction over
the acts of aliens committed abroad may be a matter for debate (*Oppenheim's
International Law* (9th edn, 1992) vol 1, pp 466–467 (para 139) (ed Jennings and
Watts)), no issue of that kind arises in these proceedings. The appellants' contention
is simply that 'jurisdiction' in the relevant definition in para 20 is to be interpreted
as referring only to the requesting state's territorial jurisdiction, with the result
that our system of extradition applies only to criminals who have offended within
the territorial, as opposed to any wider, jurisdiction of the requesting state.

[138] Of course, even if 'jurisdiction' in para 20 includes all kinds of criminal
jurisdiction, in practice most extradition requests will concern crimes committed
within the territory of the requesting state and so falling within its territorial
jurisdiction. Not surprisingly, therefore, in some extradition treaties the states
agreed to surrender people accused of crimes committed within the 'territory' of
the requesting state. That was the language used, for example, in the first article
of the extradition treaty with France of 14 August 1876, given effect by an Order
in Council of 16 May 1878 under s 2 of the 1870 Act. The same applied in the case
of the treaty with Norway which was given effect by a similar Order in Council
of 30 September 1873. In each case, however, the treaty went on to provide for
the surrender of those accused of various crimes committed on the high seas.
The scope of the term 'territory' in the Norwegian treaty came before the
Divisional Court for decision in *R v Governor of HM Prison Brixton, ex p Minervini*
[1958] 3 All ER 318, [1959] 1 QB 155. Because the treaty covered the crimes on
the high seas, Lord Parker CJ held ([1958] 3 All ER 318 at 320, [1959] 1 QB 155 at
162) that 'territory' in the first article was not being used in its strict sense but as
an equivalent to 'jurisdiction'. Similarly, when considering the term 'jurisdiction'
in the definition of 'fugitive criminal' in para 20, the courts must interpret it in
such a way that it is apt to cover all the types of crime for which Parliament
intended that a fugitive criminal could be extradited under Sch 1 to the 1989 Act.

[139] Embedded within the definition of 'fugitive criminal' in para 20 is another
concept, 'extradition crime', which is defined in the same paragraph. The first
distinctive characteristic of a 'fugitive criminal' is indeed that he is alleged to have
committed an extradition crime. So the term 'jurisdiction' must be sufficiently
broad to cover all the kinds of jurisdiction which would be necessary to allow the
criminal to be prosecuted by the requesting state for any of the crimes included
in the term 'extradition crime'.

a [140] According to the definition in s 26 of the 1870 Act, an extradition crime is one which, 'if committed in England *or within English jurisdiction*', would constitute one of the crimes listed in the First Schedule to the 1870 Act (my emphasis). Here again we encounter the term 'jurisdiction'. And here again the context provides the guide to the proper interpretation. It shows clearly that the word is not being used to refer to the territorial jurisdiction of the English courts. If given that

b narrow interpretation, the words 'within English jurisdiction' would add nothing to the immediately preceding words 'in England'. It is not difficult, however, to see that they were inserted for a sound practical reason. They were intended to bring within the scope of 'extradition crime' conduct which, though it could not be committed in England, could none the less be committed within the jurisdiction of the English courts and would then amount to one of the crimes in

c the First Schedule to the 1870 Act. As originally enacted, the Schedule contained 19 items. The crimes in the first 15 items relate to conduct which could be committed in England. The last four items, by contrast, concern conduct which, by its very nature, could not be committed in England—piracy by the law of nations, sinking or destroying a vessel at sea, assaults on board a ship on the high

d seas and revolt or conspiracy to revolt by two or more persons on board a ship on the high seas. The extended definition in s 26 was obviously designed to ensure that the term 'extradition crime' would include conduct of this kind which would constitute an offence triable by the English courts and so would be within English jurisdiction, but which would be committed outside England. There would, of course, have been no point in including such crimes within the definition of

e 'extradition crimes' if, for some other reason, a criminal who committed them could never be a 'fugitive criminal' for purposes of extradition under the Act. The definition of 'fugitive criminal' in para 20 of Sch 1 to the 1989 Act must therefore be wide enough to cover those who commit any of these four crimes on the high seas.

f [141] The term 'jurisdiction' in the definition of a 'fugitive criminal' has to be read as including the vessels of the requesting state (para 19 of Sch 1). So, in the case of three of the four crimes committed on the high seas, it may be argued that the requesting state's jurisdiction would be founded on the fact that the crime was committed on, or in respect of, one of its vessels. On that basis the crime would be committed 'within the jurisdiction' of the requesting state.

g [142] It is unnecessary to decide whether that is the proper approach to these items. What matters for present purposes is that the first of this group of extradition crimes is 'piracy by law of nations'. The nature of the jurisdiction in such cases was described by Viscount Sankey LC when giving the advice of the Privy Council on a special reference in *Re Piracy Jure Gentium* [1934] AC 586 at 589,

h [1934] All ER Rep 506 at 507:

  'With regard to crimes as defined by international law, that law has no means of trying or punishing them. The recognition of them as constituting crimes, and the trial and punishment of the criminals, are left to the

j municipal law of each country. But whereas according to international law the criminal jurisdiction of municipal law is ordinarily restricted to crimes committed on its terra firma or territorial waters or its own ships, and to crimes by its own nationals wherever committed, it is also recognized as extending to piracy committed on the high seas by any national on any ship, because a person guilty of such piracy has placed himself beyond the protection of any State. He is no longer a national, but "hostis humani

generis" and as such he is justiciable by any State anywhere: Grotius
(1583–1645) "De Jure Belli ac Pacis," vol. 2, cap. 20, § 40.'   *a*

Since the jurisdiction over piracy by the law of nations is of this extensive nature,
it follows that the term 'jurisdiction' in the definition of 'fugitive criminal' is not
synonymous with 'territorial jurisdiction'. On the contrary, it must be wide enough
to cover even the extreme form of extra-territorial jurisdiction which is applied   *b*
to this kind of piracy. In other words even piracy committed on the high seas
must be a crime 'committed within the jurisdiction' of the requesting state in
terms of para 20 of Sch 1 to the 1989 Act. The same must have applied to the
equivalent provision in the 1870 Act.

[143] For this reason, I am respectfully unable to agree with the obiter
observation of Lord Mackay of Clashfern in *Rees v Secretary of State for the Home*   *c*
Dept [1986] 2 All ER 321 at 327, [1986] AC 937 at 955, to the effect that, when
passed, the 1870 Act dealt only with crimes committed within the territorial
jurisdiction of the requesting state. Lord Mackay cites some words of Lord Reid
in *Schtraks v Government of Israel* [1962] 3 All ER 529 at 532, [1964] AC 556 at 579.
That case concerned a request for the extradition of a man who was accused of   *d*
various offences committed in a part of Jerusalem over which Israel asserted a
sovereignty that the United Kingdom did not recognise. One relatively minor
question in the appeal was whether in these circumstances the offences had been
committed 'within the territory' of Israel, as required by the terms of the
extradition treaty between the United Kingdom and Israel. Lord Reid dealt with
the issue shortly and, in the course of doing so, he observed that neither the 1870   *e*
Act nor the Order in Council embodying the extradition treaty with Israel was
concerned with sovereignty: '... they are concerned with territory in which
territorial jurisdiction is exercised ...' Lord Reid's comment should be read in the
context of the issue that he was deciding. He was rejecting the argument that the
treaty would apply only where the requesting state exercised sovereignty over   *f*
the place where the offence had been committed. In his view it was sufficient that
the place was one over which the requesting state in fact exercised territorial
jurisdiction. It would be wrong to transform this very particular comment into a
general statement about the nature of jurisdiction under the 1870 Act. In any
event, the observation was obiter, since the decision of the House was based
essentially on their Lordships' acceptance of the reasoning of Lord Parker CJ as   *g*
to the interpretation of the term 'territory' in the treaty when the case was before
the Divisional Court ([1962] 2 All ER 176 at 181, sub nom *R v Governor of Brixton*
Prison, ex p Schtraks [1963] 1 QB 55 at 74–75). In these circumstances I find
nothing in *Rees'* or *Schtraks'* cases to displace the clear implication, as to
jurisdiction, of the inclusion of piracy by the law of nations among the crimes for   *h*
which criminals could be surrendered under the 1870 Act.

[144] In the course of his submissions Mr Fitzgerald pointed to other paragraphs
in Sch 1 to the 1989 Act in which, he said, the phrase 'within the jurisdiction'
refers to the territorial, rather than to any wider, jurisdiction of the requesting
state. For the sake of the argument I am prepared to assume that in some of the   *j*
provisions this is a proper inference to draw from the context. But, precisely
because the interpretation of a flexible term such as 'jurisdiction' depends on the
particular context in which it is used, other provisions cannot provide a reliable
guide to its interpretation in the context of para 20. That is particularly so where
the context is utterly different—for example, the delivery of the fugitive criminal
to the requesting state in para 8 and the flight of an aircraft in para 14. By contrast,

a   in para 20, for the reasons I have given, the context shows that 'jurisdiction' must be given a wide rather than a narrow interpretation.

[145] Mr Fitzgerald put particular emphasis on para 15. He argued that any conduct which was made an offence against the criminal law of a state was ipso facto 'within the jurisdiction' of that state, in the wider sense of that term. So, he said, the fact that Parliament had seen fit to deem the crimes in this paragraph to

b   have been committed within the requesting state's jurisdiction showed that 'jurisdiction' means 'territorial jurisdiction'. A glance at the international conventions lying behind what is now para 15 is sufficient, however, to show that, in this context, making conduct an offence is different from creating jurisdiction over that offence. See, for instance, arts 2 and 3 of the Convention on the Prevention and Punishment of Crimes against Internationally Protected Persons, including

c   Diplomatic Agents (New York, 14 December 1973; TS 3 (1980); Cmnd 7765). More particularly, since the term 'jurisdiction' in its wider sense includes territorial jurisdiction, in para 15 the United Kingdom could conveniently carry out its obligation under art 8(4) of the convention—to treat a crime as if it had been committed within a state's territory—by deeming that it had been 'committed

d   within the jurisdiction of that state'. The use of the term 'jurisdiction' for that purpose is therefore no indication that the same term means only 'territorial jurisdiction' in para 20.

[146] The terms of an extradition treaty cannot be used to construe the Act of Parliament under which the treaty is given effect in our domestic law. It is nevertheless worth noting that the language of art I of the 1972 treaty with the

e   United States does not suggest that the parties were treating 'territory' and 'jurisdiction' as synonymous. The contracting parties undertake to extradite any person found in their 'territory' who has been accused or convicted of any offence within art III of the treaty, 'committed within the jurisdiction of the other Party'. If the parties had thought that the only offences for which extradition could be

f   sought were those committed within the requesting state's territorial jurisdiction, a reference to 'territory' or 'territorial jurisdiction' would have been more consistent with the reference to the requested state's 'territory'. On the other hand, the very fact that the crimes for which extradition can be requested in terms of art III and the Schedule include 'piracy, involving ships or aircraft, according to international law' suggests that in art I the use of the term 'jurisdiction' was deliberate—to

g   ensure that all the relevant crimes were covered and to avoid the kind of argument that had caused difficulty in the Norwegian case. Indeed, since the treaty is framed in this way, only the assumption that the term was used in the wide sense in the 1870 Act too justifies what is in effect a conclusive presumption that the arrangement in the treaty complies with Sch 1 to the 1989 Act (see para 2).

h   These factors have to be kept in mind when, at this late date, your Lordships' House is asked to put a narrow interpretation on the term 'jurisdiction' in para 20 of Sch 1 to the 1989 Act.

[147] At first sight it might seem that, if 'jurisdiction' were given this wide interpretation, extradition could occur even if the requesting state founded its

j   request on an exorbitant assertion of jurisdiction. Mr Fitzgerald argued that, by using the term 'jurisdiction' as an equivalent to 'territorial jurisdiction' in para 20, Parliament had intended to guard against this eventuality. I consider that this argument ignores both the realities of the system of extradition and the protection afforded by the committal proceedings.

[148] In the first place it overlooks the fact that neither the 1870 Act, in its day, nor Sch 1 to the 1989 Act today has ever of itself provided for extradition between

the United Kingdom and any foreign state. Extradition arrangements are made
by treaty between Her Majesty, as the executive of the United Kingdom, and the
sovereign of the foreign state. What the 1870 and 1989 Acts do is to give the
framework within which the extradition arrangements made by the treaties are
given effect under our domestic law. The fact that extradition arrangements
are based on treaties provides the first line of defence against the abuse which
Mr Fitzgerald envisaged. In principle, the United Kingdom will have such treaty
arrangements only with states adopting what it regards as a proper approach to
the prosecution and trial of offenders. Among the relevant factors to be taken
into account in negotiating such treaties will, therefore, be the nature of the
jurisdiction exercised by the other state. If the jurisdiction is exorbitant, then
either the United Kingdom will simply not enter into a treaty with the state
concerned or else it will ensure that the provisions of the treaty are so drafted as
to provide for extradition only in cases where the state exercises an acceptable
jurisdiction. So, in any given case, it is to be assumed that the British government
of the day considered that the matter of the other state's jurisdiction had been
settled acceptably at the time when the treaty was concluded. If, later, the foreign
state begins to assert an exorbitant jurisdiction not excluded by the terms of the
treaty, then in the last resort the United Kingdom can give notice terminating
the treaty. The fact that it has not done so should, again in principle, indicate that
the government does not regard the state in question as exercising an exorbitant
jurisdiction.

[149] The exorbitant, or otherwise unacceptable, nature of a foreign state's
jurisdiction is therefore a matter for the executive to ponder when considering
whether to conclude an extradition treaty and whether to remain bound by it.
Similarly, when dealing with any particular requisition the Secretary of State can
take account of the exorbitant nature of the jurisdiction underlying the request.
Whatever the obligations of the United Kingdom under the relevant treaty may
be in international law, under para 4(2) of Sch 1 to the 1989 Act, the Secretary of
State has a discretion to issue or to decline to issue an order to proceed. Similarly,
under para 8(2) he has a discretion to issue or not to issue a warrant for the
surrender of the fugitive criminal. The Secretary of State could therefore decline
to take either of those steps if it appeared to him that the jurisdiction claimed by
the requesting state was exorbitant. This provides a further safeguard. Yet another
safeguard is to be found in the committal proceedings discussed below.

[150] Ultimately, issues as to the propriety of the jurisdiction claimed by a foreign
state depend on judgments as to comity among states in international law. By
their nature such judgments involve factors which must primarily be for the
consideration of the executive who have responsibility for our relations with foreign
states. Provided that the executive exercise their various powers appropriately,
I see no reason to fear that persons will in fact be surrendered to states asserting
an exorbitant jurisdiction, if the term 'jurisdiction' in para 20 has to be interpreted
broadly. It bears repeating that the appellants do not suggest that the jurisdiction
which the United States claims in their case is exorbitant. I deal with the judicial
safeguards below.

[151] I am accordingly satisfied that the term 'jurisdiction' in the definition of
'fugitive criminal' is broad enough to include the jurisdiction which the United
States asserts over a conspiracy formed abroad to murder United States citizens
within the United States and elsewhere.

[152] For practical reasons, in the hearing before this House the cross-appeal
relating to jurisdiction was heard first. I have also begun with the meaning of

a 'jurisdiction' in the definition of a 'fugitive criminal' in para 20. But, as I have already explained, this is only one of two important elements in that definition. The other is that the individual must be accused of an 'extradition crime'. It appears to me that this point would, more naturally, come first. In other words, when considering a requisition, the Secretary of State would, usually at least, first decide whether the crime in the requisition was an extradition crime and, only if b he was satisfied that it was, would he go on to consider whether it had been committed within the jurisdiction of the requesting state. Such an approach presupposes, however, that it is possible to determine whether a crime is an extradition crime without first considering the form of jurisdiction on which the requesting state founds. The contention for the appellants proceeds on a different basis. They say that the extra-territorial nature of the jurisdiction claimed by the c requesting state has a bearing on whether the crime is to be regarded as an extradition crime. In particular, they argue that, in making the transposition required by the definition in s 26 of the 1870 Act, it is necessary to transpose into England those actings that are alleged to have taken place in the requesting state but not those actings that are alleged to have taken place outside the territory of d the requesting state. The question then is whether, that qualified transposition having been made, the crime is an extradition crime under s 26. In this case, for instance, the appellants argue that only the overt acts alleged to have taken place in the United States should be supposed to have taken place in England, while all the other alleged actings of the appellants and their fellow conspirators must be supposed to have taken place abroad.

e [153] The Administrative Court in effect adopted that approach. They held that, in deciding whether an offence constituted an extradition crime under s 26:

'The law of England is applied on the hypothesised basis that the acts that took place in the requesting state, but no other acts, took place in England (see R v Governor of Pentonville Prison, ex p Osman [1989] 3 All ER 701 at 713, f [1990] 1 WLR 277 at 290). Mr Lewis, counsel for the government of the United States, accepted for present purposes that that decision bound us; though he wished to reserve for another day the possibility that what is transposed to England is not merely the acts done in the requesting state, but all the acts wherever done that constituted the offence charged.' (See [2001] g 4 All ER 149 at 154, [2001] 1 WLR 1234 at 1238 (para 11).)

[154] I would reject that approach. In doing so, I note that Ex p Osman [1989] 3 All ER 701 at 713, [1990] 1 WLR 277 at 290 and the authorities which Lloyd LJ cites all concern the Fugitive Offenders Act 1967, which differs in certain respects from the Extradition Acts. None the less, I consider that, when properly understood, h these authorities and, in particular, the passage from the speech of Lord Keith of Kinkel in Tarling (No 1) v Government of the Republic of Singapore (1978) 70 Cr App R 77 at 136 are consistent with the approach to transposition in the definition of 'extradition crime' which I prefer. They really deal with the separate matter of the test to be applied by the magistrate in considering the evidence at the committal j hearing.

[155] As I explained at [140] above, the phrase 'in England or within English jurisdiction' in the definition of 'extradition crime' in s 26 of the 1870 Act must have been framed so as to cover actings which could be supposed to have taken place in England and actings which, by their very nature, could not be supposed to have taken place in England because they occurred on the high seas. On that basis, all the alleged actings in the present case can be supposed, for the purposes

of s 26, to have taken place in England. The simple question then is whether, if they had taken place in England, those actings would have constituted the crime of conspiracy to murder in English law. For my part, I see no need for any more complex analysis at this stage since the test which I have outlined is sufficient to ensure that extradition is confined to allegations of crimes according to the law of the requesting state which would also be crimes according to English law and in respect of which Parliament has given the Secretary of State power to surrender accused persons.

[156] This interpretation of the relevant provisions is straightforward and the provisions when so interpreted are easy to apply. By contrast the approach advocated by the appellants and adopted by the Administrative Court leads inevitably to a blurring of two questions. The first is whether the individual concerned is a criminal accused of an 'extradition crime'. The second question is whether, even supposing that he is, there is evidence to justify ordering his committal to prison on that charge.

[157] When the magistrate is dealing with this second question, he may indeed require to take into account the extra-territorial nature of some of the alleged actings. As the Administrative Court noted in *Al-Fawwaz*'s case ([2001] 4 All ER 149 at 158, [2001] 1 WLR 1234 at 1243 (paras 30, 31)), this was the context in which the Privy Council approached the issues relating to the jurisdiction of the courts of the requested state in *Liangsiriprasert v United States Government* [1990] 2 All ER 866, [1991] 1 AC 225. The case concerned a conspiracy in Thailand to supply heroin for importation into the United States. The appellant went to Hong Kong to collect payment and was arrested. The United States requested his extradition. The parties were agreed that a conspiracy of this kind was an 'extradition crime' in terms of s 26 of the 1870 Act and the issue for the Board was whether the evidence disclosed a prima facie case against the appellant, upon the assumption that the drugs were to be imported into Hong Kong rather than into the United States ([1990] 2 All ER 866 at 871, [1991] 1 AC 225 at 241). It was within this context that the Board went on to decide that:

'... a conspiracy entered into in Thailand with the intention of committing the criminal offence of trafficking in drugs in Hong Kong is justiciable in Hong Kong even if no overt act pursuant to the conspiracy has yet occurred in Hong Kong.' (See [1990] 2 All ER 866 at 878, [1991] 1 AC 225 at 251.)

On that basis the Board upheld the magistrate's decision to commit the appellant on the first charge, a charge of conspiring to traffic in dangerous drugs. In my respectful opinion, although the point was not argued in *Liangsiriprasert*'s case, the approach which Lord Griffiths adopted was correct. I note in passing that counsel for the appellants conceded that, if their contention as to the interpretation of 'jurisdiction' in para 20 of Sch 1 to the 1989 Act was correct, the decision of the Privy Council upholding the committal of the appellant in *Liangsiriprasert*'s case must have been in substance wrong.

[158] The approach of the Privy Council was consistent with that of this House, some years earlier, in *Tarling*'s case, where the issues arose out of the evidence led before the magistrate in committal proceedings under the 1967 Act. The government of Singapore sought Mr Tarling's extradition, inter alia, on two charges of conspiring in Hong Kong to steal shares in a Hong Kong company, the property of a Singapore company. On the law as it stood then, Lord Wilberforce held that a conspiracy in Hong Kong to steal shares in a Hong Kong company, the

a   property of a English company, would not be triable in England. He therefore held that the charges were not supported (see (1978) 70 Cr App R 77 at 110–111).

[159] During the hearing before the House in the present case it was suggested that deciding the 'extradition crime' issue under s 26 of the 1870 Act by supposing that the whole conduct had taken place in England would weaken the safeguards for accused persons. I reject that criticism, precisely because the fact that some

b   of the alleged conduct took place abroad will be taken into account by the magistrate when deciding whether to commit the person concerned. The point is amply illustrated not only by *Tarling's* case but by the decision in *Liangsiriprasert's* case.

[160] The Privy Council first considered whether the evidence justified the appellant's committal on charge 1. On that matter, they held that a conspiracy to

c   commit a crime in Hong Kong was justiciable in Hong Kong even though there was no evidence of any overt act having been committed there. The magistrate had accordingly been entitled to order that the appellant should be committed on the first charge. Had they decided the issue of principle in favour of the appellant, however, the Board would, of course, have allowed his appeal against his

d   committal on that charge. So the whole issue of the jurisdiction of the court of the requested state could be, and was, duly considered in this context. The Board then went on to examine charges 2 and 4 which were charges of trafficking, and of doing acts preparatory to trafficking, in dangerous drugs contrary to s 4 of the Dangerous Drugs Ordinance (Laws of Hong Kong, 1988 rev, c 34). The evidence on these charges showed that the alleged activities had all taken place in Thailand.

e   The Board allowed the appellant's appeal against his committal on these charges on the view that s 4 did not have extra-territorial effect. This decision gave the appellant all the protection that he could ever have hoped to derive from the fact that the allegations related to extra-territorial conduct. The Board's prior assumption that the crimes were 'extradition crimes' did not impair that protection. Nor

f   would a prior judicial decision to the same effect impair it. The committal proceedings and any habeas corpus application therefore provide a full judicial safeguard against extradition based on a wider jurisdiction than is recognised under English law.

[161] For these reasons I would respectfully hold that the decision of the Administrative Court was wrong on this point.

g   [162] The appellants accept that, if the test for an extradition crime is applied as I would apply it—or indeed on the basis of a qualified transposition—the allegations against them in the present cases would amount to allegations of conspiracy to murder in English Law. That being so, they are persons accused of an extradition crime. Moreover, they are alleged to have committed the crime

h   within the jurisdiction of the United States. They are, therefore, fugitive criminals in terms of para 20 of Sch 1 to the 1989 Act.

[163] The principal remaining question is whether, applying the test in para 7(1), the magistrate was entitled to find that there was such evidence of conspiracy to murder as would have made a case requiring an answer if the

j   proceedings against the appellants had been for trial in England and Wales of an information for conspiracy to murder.

[164] In the case of Al-Fawwaz his counsel accepted that there was indeed sufficient evidence to justify his committal if the metropolitan magistrate had been correct to admit the affidavit of the anonymous witness referred to as 'CS/1'. So far as that matter is concerned, I am satisfied that, for the reasons given in the opinion of Buxton LJ, the decision of the Administrative Court on this

matter was correct. In particular I agree that, however detailed might be the list
of factors to be considered according to *R v Taylor (Gary)* (1994) TLR 484, the   *a*
decision as to admitting the evidence of an anonymous witness depends on
weighing a range of factors and is therefore one for the discretion of the trial judge
in all the circumstances. That was indeed the starting point of the discussion of
Evans LJ in *R v Taylor*. The same must apply to the magistrate in the committal
proceedings in these cases.   *b*

[165] Counsel for the appellants submitted that the approach adopted by the
Divisional Court had contravened their rights under art 5(4) of the European
Convention for the Protection of Human Rights and Fundamental Freedoms
1950 (as set out in Sch 1 to the Human Rights Act 1998) (the Human Rights
Convention) which required that basic principles of fairness should be applied to
extradition proceedings. These basic principles would reinforce the common law.   *c*
Even assuming that art 5 introduces some new element, it could not be suggested
that the requirements of fairness in respect of proceedings for detention for
extradition purposes could be higher than those enjoyed by a defendant at his trial
under art 6. In this connection it is useful to recall the observations of the
European Court of Human Rights in *Doorson v Netherlands* (1996) 22 EHRR 330   *d*
where the investigating judge had heard two anonymous witnesses in the
absence of the applicant's counsel during the preliminary investigation. The
court held that no issue under the Human Rights Convention arose in that
respect but that the subsequent use of their statements by the trial court to found
a conviction was capable of raising an issue under the convention. The court
observed (at 358, (para 69)) that the use of such statements was not under all   *e*
circumstances incompatible with the convention and continued (at 358
(para 70)):

> 'It is true that Article 6 does not explicitly require the interests of witnesses
> in general, and those of victims called upon to testify in particular, to be
> taken into consideration. However, their life, liberty or security of person   *f*
> may be at stake, as may interests coming generally within the ambit of
> Article 8 of the Convention. Such interests of witnesses and victims are in
> principle protected by other, substantive provisions of the Convention,
> which imply that Contracting States should organise their criminal
> proceedings in such a way that those interests are not unjustifiably   *g*
> imperilled. Against this background, principles of fair trial also require that
> in appropriate cases the interests of the defence are balanced against those of
> witnesses or victims called upon to testify.'

The court went on to consider the reason why the witnesses' anonymity had
been preserved and concluded that the reason was sufficient (at 358–359   *h*
(para 71)). As Lord Bingham of Cornhill pointed out in *Brown v Stott (Procurator
Fiscal, Dunfermline)* [2001] 2 All ER 97 at 106–107, [2001] 2 WLR 817 at 827 the
European Court have identified their decision in *Doorson v Netherlands* as a
particular example of a situation where there are competing interests which have
to be weighed when considering what constitutes a fair trial in criminal   *j*
proceedings (*Fitt v UK* (2000) 30 EHRR 480 at 510–511 (paras 44–45)).

[166] In my view, therefore, even taking account of the appellants' rights
under art 5(4), the Administrative Court were entitled to hold that, since the
magistrate accepted that there were real grounds to fear for the safety of CS/1 if
his identity were revealed, he had been justified in maintaining the anonymity of
CS/1 but nevertheless admitting his evidence in the committal proceedings. On

a the available information the fear for CS/1's safety was a sufficient reason for adopting that course at this stage. In reaching that decision the magistrate was entitled to have regard not simply to the interests of the appellants but to the interests of CS/1. Nor can it be said that in all the circumstances, including the other available evidence, it was irrational for the magistrate to take the evidence of CS/1 into account. On the contrary it was appropriate for the magistrate to do

b so in the circumstances, even though he was not satisfied that the creditworthiness of CS/1 had been fully investigated. Mr Fitzgerald accepts that, when that evidence is taken into account, there was sufficient evidence to justify the committal of Al-Fawwaz. No point is taken about the adequacy of the reasons given by the magistrate in his case. It follows that his appeal must be dismissed.

[167] In the case of Eiderous and Abdul Bary, so far as CS/1 is concerned, the
c Administrative Court adopted the approach of the court in the case of Al-Fawwaz and considered the circumstances in the light of that approach. On that basis the court came to the conclusion that the magistrate had been fully entitled to take the view that the statement of CS/1 had not been shown to be worthless and to hold it to be admissible. Again I am satisfied that the Administrative Court

d reached the correct conclusion on this matter. It follows that it was open to the magistrate to consider the issue of the sufficiency of the evidence against these appellants for the purpose of committal on the basis that it included the evidence of CS/1.

[168] Counsel for Eiderous and Abdul Bary sought to persuade us, however, that in their case, even taking the evidence of CS/1 into account, there was not a
e case to answer in terms of para 7(1) of Sch 1 to the 1989 Act. The evidence was of acts abroad and acts in pursuit of the conspiracy in the United States. They pointed out that certain of the items in the prosecution evidence were susceptible of an entirely innocent explanation. So, for instance, the purchase of the satellite telephone was said to be consistent with the appellants and the others concerned

f being involved in opposition to the government of Saudi Arabia. The possession of the faxed texts of the fatwahs was similarly said to be insufficient to point to involvement in a conspiracy to murder, not least because those fatwahs had been published. The explosions in Nairobi occurred at about 7.30 am GMT and the two faxes claiming responsibility, which were recovered from 1A Beethoven Street were timed at 4.45 am. It was argued that the time marked on the faxes

g would not show that they had been sent before the attack if that time was not GMT. So no sinister inference could be drawn from the apparent time when the appellants had received the faxes.

[169] Those submissions make the obvious point that, looked at in isolation, these various circumstances could be regarded as neutral. That is by no means an
h unusual feature of a circumstantial case such as the present. The Crown can only rarely lead direct evidence of the formation of a conspiracy, which by its very nature is likely to take place in secret. The prosecution case will tend to depend on evidence of various circumstances which, viewed severally and in isolation, could well be capable of an innocent explanation but which, taken together, the

j prosecution contend, point to a conspiracy. At trial the defence will seek to put forward an innocent explanation for these circumstances, whether in cross-examination or by leading evidence or in argument before the jury. The proper test of such a prosecution case at committal is not, however, to look at the various items of evidence separately but, as the jury would ultimately be asked to look at them, in relation to one another. Could the evidence as a whole justify a conviction? The question for the magistrate in this case was therefore whether, so regarded, the evidence of the circumstances on which the United States government rely was 'capable' of making a case which would require an answer in a trial of an information for conspiracy to murder.

[170] In his judgment Kennedy LJ rehearsed in considerable detail the relevant items of evidence and the criticisms made of them (see [2001] EWHC Admin 298, [2001] All ER (D) 24 (May)). Having done so, his conclusion was that the magistrate, who had looked at the evidence as a whole, had clearly been entitled to decide to order that the appellants be committed to prison. I respectfully agree with both his reasoning and his conclusion.

[171] The final point advanced before the House was that in the case of Eiderous and Abdul Bary the magistrate, when giving his decision to commit the appellants, had failed to give adequate reasons. Indeed, at times during his submissions, Mr Emmerson QC seemed to be contending that the magistrate had not given any reasons at all and so had been in breach of a duty to give reasons. Reference was made to the opinion of Lord Steyn giving the advice of the Privy Council in *Rey v Government of Switzerland* [1999] AC 54 at 66–67, [1998] 3 WLR 1 at 10 where he indicated that in extradition proceedings the principle of fairness may in particular circumstances require a magistrate to give reasons for committal. It is unnecessary, however, to enter into that issue in this case for the simple reason that the magistrate did in fact give reasons for his decision. The only possible criticism, therefore, was that those reasons had not been adequate. It may well be, as Kennedy LJ observed, that the magistrate could profitably have given more detail, but the issue is whether the reasons were adequate. Having considered what the magistrate said, I am left with no real doubt as to the import of his thinking in deciding as he did, even though he does not, of course, deal with all the points made in argument before him. In these circumstances I am satisfied that the reasons given by the magistrate were adequate. Certainly, the nature of his account of his reasons did nothing whatever to affect the appellants' ability to argue—as they did—that, on the evidence as a whole, no reasonable magistrate could have ordered that they should be committed to prison. In the event that argument has been rejected.

[172] I would accordingly dismiss the appeals of Eiderous and Abdul Bary.

[173] I should add one further remark. The entire argument in both appeals was conducted on the basis that the requisitions related to proceedings before the United States District Court for the Southern District of New York. There was no suggestion that the appellants would be tried before any other court of tribunal. In particular, no argument was advanced as to the matter mentioned at the end of the speech of my noble and learned friend Lord Scott of Foscote. I accordingly express no view on it.

Appeals dismissed.

Dilys Tausz   Barrister.

a

Cantabrica Coach Holdings Ltd v Vehicle Inspectorate

[2001] UKHL 60

b HOUSE OF LORDS

LORD SLYNN OF HADLEY, LORD STEYN, LORD HOPE OF CRAIGHEAD, LORD HUTTON AND
LORD SCOTT OF FOSCOTE

18, 19 JULY, 22 NOVEMBER 2001

c *Road traffic – Carriage of goods and passengers – Tachograph charts – Whether authorised officer empowered to require removal of tachograph charts from licensed transport operator's premises without prior written notice – Transport Act 1968, s 99(1) – Council Regulation (EEC) 3821/85, art 14(2).*

d The appellant company was a licensed coach operator and was therefore obliged to comply with Pt VI of the Transport Act 1968 (as amended). The Act provided that Part VI, which included s 99ᵃ, was to have effect with a view to securing the observance of proper hours or periods of work by persons engaged in the carriage of passengers or goods by road and thereby protecting the public against the risks which arose in cases where the drivers of motor vehicles were suffering from fatigue. In October 1998 a senior traffic examiner of the Vehicle Inspectorate
e visited the company's operating centre. The examiner, who was an authorised officer for the purposes of the 1968 Act, requested permission to remove the company's tachograph charts covering August 1998. The company was required to keep such charts by art 14(2)ᵇ of Council Regulation (EEC) 3821/85 (the regulation), a measure that was intended, in the interests of road safety, to
f provide for effective checking of records of drivers' hours. The company was prepared to allow the examiner to inspect the tachograph charts at its offices, but refused permission for removal on that and a subsequent occasion. The company was charged with failing to hand over tachograph charts required to be kept by art 14(2) of the regulation, contrary to s 99(1)(bb) and (4)(a) of the 1968 Act.
g Section 99(1) empowered an officer, on production if so required of his authority, to require any person 'to produce, and permit him to inspect and copy ... (bb) any record sheet' which that person was required to retain by art 14(2) of the regulation. In its concluding part, s 99(1) provided that the record sheet 'shall, if the officer so requires by notice in writing served on that person, be produced at the office of the traffic commissioner specified in the notice within such time
h (not being less than ten days) from the service of the notice as may be so specified'. If an officer had reason to believe that an offence had been committed under s 99(5) (making false entries) in respect of any record or document inspected by him under s 99, he was empowered, by s 99(6), to seize that record or document. Section 99(10) provided that references in s 99 to the inspection
j and copying of any record produced by means of equipment installed for specified purposes in a vehicle included references to the application to the record of any process for eliciting the information recorded thereby and to taking down the information elicited from it. The justices convicted the company, and the

---

a   Section 99, so far as material, is set out at [4], [6], below
b   Article 14(2) is set out at [2], below

Divisional Court dismissed its subsequent appeal by way of case stated. On
appeal to the House of Lords, the company submitted that s 99(1)(bb) empowered
the examiner to inspect and copy the tachograph records at its premises, but did
not give him power to require the records to be handed over. The company
relied, in particular, on the concluding part of s 99(1) and the power of seizure in
s 99(6), contending that they were inconsistent with the existence of a separate
power under s 99(1)(bb) to require that records be handed over.

Held – On its true construction, s 99(1) of the 1968 Act authorised an officer to
require the handing over, without prior notice, of record sheets required to be
kept under art 14(2) of the regulation, so that they could be examined and
analysed at the premises of the Inspectorate. The requirement in the first part of
s 99(1) 'to produce' records and to permit them to be inspected included by
necessary implication the handing over and retention for inspection of those
records. Moreover, the taking away of the records for effective and thorough
examination in the office of the Inspectorate was within the ambit of the power
of inspection given by the subsection. The powers contained in the first and
concluding parts of s 99(1) were not intended to be graduated steps so that
records could only be inspected at the office of the Inspectorate if ten days' notice
had been given. Rather, the powers were concurrent and it was a matter for the
discretion of the authorised officer, depending on the circumstances, to decide
whether to go to the office of the transport operator to require production of the
records which he might then take away for detailed inspection or to give ten days'
notice requiring the records to be produced at the office of the traffic commissioner.
Further, the power to seize records under s 99(6) related to a different procedure
in different circumstances than the procedure of inspection provided for in the
first part of s 99(1) and did not have the effect, as a matter of construction, that
the power to inspect was to be read as confined to inspection in the office of the
transport operator. The correct construction was also consistent with the purpose
of art 14(2) and s 99, namely to protect road users against the risk of accidents
arising from tiredness and lack of concentration by drivers of goods and
passenger vehicles who drove for excessive periods. A necessary part of the
procedure to give that protection was the careful checking and examination of
tachograph records and it was apparent that such checking and examination
would require on occasions that tachograph records were taken to an office of the
Inspectorate where the necessary specialised equipment and requisite number of
staff would be available. That conclusion was strongly supported by s 99(10)
which clearly envisaged that inspection and copying would require the application
to the records of processes for eliciting the information recorded in them. Those
processes would include the use of computers and other equipment which would
only be available for use in the offices of the Inspectorate. That was a compelling
reason to hold that the power to inspect given by s 99(1) included the power to
take away for the purpose of inspection. Accordingly, the appeal would be
dismissed (see [23], [30]–[32], [34]–[38], [54]–[56], [58], [102], below).

Notes

For inspection of records and documents, see 40(2) *Halsbury's Laws* (4th edn
reissue) para 1049.

For the Transport Act 1968, s 99, see 38 *Halsbury's Statutes* (4th edn) (2001
reissue) 199.

Appeal

a The defendant, Cantabrica Coach Holdings Ltd, appealed with leave of the Appeal Committee of the House of Lords given on 11 December 2000 from the order of the Divisional Court (Kennedy LJ and Butterfield J) on 31 March 2000 ([2000] RTR 286) dismissing its appeal by way of case stated against its conviction of an offence contrary to s 99(4) of the Transport Act 1968 by justices sitting at

b Dacorum Magistrates' Court on 10 May 1999, on an information preferred by the respondent, the Vehicle Inspectorate. The Divisional Court certified that a point of law of general public importance, set out at [10], below, was involved in its decision. The facts are set out in the opinion of Lord Slynn of Hadley.

David Phillips QC and *Richard Serlin* (instructed by *Wedlake Saint*, St Albans) for the
c defendant.
Richard Plender QC (instructed by *Foinette Quinn*, Milton Keynes) and *Christopher Hallsworth* of that firm for the Vehicle Inspectorate.

Their Lordships took time for consideration.
d
22 November 2001. The following opinions were delivered.

LORD SLYNN OF HADLEY.
[1] My Lords, on 10 May 1999 the appellant defendant was convicted of failing to comply with a requirement under s 99(1) of the Transport Act 1968 in that '[it]
e failed to produce a record sheet which [it was] required by art 14(2) of the Community Recording Equipment Regulation [Council Regulation (EEC) 3821/85] to retain contrary to s 99(4) of the Transport Act 1968 as amended'.
[2] The 1968 Act which originally provided a domestic regulatory code dealing with hours of driving of those engaged in the carriage of passengers and
f goods by road was amended to take account of Community regulations and in particular of the provisions of Council Regulations (EEC) 3820/85 and 3821/85 as amended. Council Regulation (EEC) 3820/85 was directed to harmonising conditions of competition between methods of inland transport, 'especially with regard to the road sector and the improvement of working conditions and road safety'. It laid down, inter alia, driving and rest periods for drivers. Council
g Regulation (EEC) 3821/85 provides for recording equipment to be installed and used in vehicles registered in a member state which are used for the carriage of passengers and goods and for monitoring compliance with the regulations. Article 14(1) of that regulation requires the employer to give to drivers a sufficient number of record sheets of an approved model. By art 14(2):
h
> 'The undertaking shall keep the record sheets in good order for at least a year after their use and shall give copies to the drivers concerned who request them. The sheets shall be produced or handed over at the request of any authorised inspecting officer.'

j [3] It is to be noted that by art 15(7), whenever a request is made by an authorised inspecting officer to do so, the driver must be able to produce the record sheets for the current week, and in any case for the last day of the previous week on which he drove. There the obligation is limited to producing.
[4] Part VI of the 1968 Act as amended provides for 'Drivers' Hours'. That part by s 95(1) 'shall have effect with a view to securing the observance of proper hours or periods of work' by the drivers covered by the legislation 'and thereby

protecting the public against the risks which arise in cases where the drivers of
motor vehicles are suffering from fatigue'. Subsequent sections of the 1968 Act
provide the detail of permitted hours and for the installation and use of recording
equipment and empower the Secretary of State by s 98 to make regulations to
achieve the objectives of the legislation. By s 99(1)(bb), with which this appeal is
concerned:

'(1) An officer may, on production if so required of his authority, require
any person to produce, and permit him to inspect and copy ... (bb) any
record sheet which that person is required by Article 14(2) of the Community
Recording Equipment Regulation to retain or by Article 15(7) of that
Regulation to be able to produce ... and that record sheet, book, register or
document shall, if the officer so requires by notice in writing served on that
person, be produced at the office of the traffic commissioner specified in the
notice within such time (not being less than ten days) from the service of the
notice as may be so specified.
(2) An officer may, on production if so required of his authority—(a) at
any time, enter any vehicle to which this Part of this Act applies and inspect
that vehicle and any recording equipment installed in it and inspect and copy
any record sheet on the vehicle on which a record has been produced by
means of the equipment or an entry has been made; (b) at any time which is
reasonable having regard to the circumstances of the case, enter any
premises on which he has reason to believe that such a vehicle is kept or that
any such record sheets, books, registers or other documents as are
mentioned in subsection (1) of this section are to be found, and inspect any
such vehicle, and inspect and copy any such record sheet, book, register or
document, which he finds there.'

[5] In sub-s (3) the officer is given power to detain the vehicle during such time
as is required for the exercise of his power under sub-s (2)(a).
[6] Subsection (5) creates offences of making false entries and by sub-s (6):

'If an officer has reason to believe that an offence under subsection (5) of
this section has been committed in respect of any record or document inspected
by him under this section, he may seize that record or document; and where
a record or document is seized as aforesaid and within six months of the date
on which it was seized no person has been charged since that date with an
offence in relation to that record or document under that subsection and the
record or document has not been returned to the person from whom it was
taken, a magistrates' court shall, on an application made for the purpose by
that person or by an officer, make such order respecting the disposal of the
record or document and award such costs as the justice of the case may
require ...
(10) In this section references to the inspection and copying of any record
produced by means of equipment installed for the purposes of section 97 of
this Act in a vehicle include references to the application to the record of any
process for eliciting the information recorded thereby and to taking down
the information elicited from it.'

[7] It is plain that for these provisions to be effective, adequate monitoring of
records of hours worked is essential for the protection both of the public and of
the drivers. Slackness and dishonest records could defeat the purpose of the
legislation. It is no less evident that drivers and employers are entitled to say that

a   the activities of enforcing officers must fall squarely within the powers conferred
on them. It is not to be assumed that there is a licence for unlimited intervention.
It is the balance between these two factors which has led to the present appeal.

[8]   The justices, when asked to state a case for the opinion of the High Court,
found the following facts.

b   'The appellant company was a coach operator and the holder of a public
services vehicle operator's licence, and as a result was obliged to comply
with Pt VI of the 1968 Act. Mr Harrison, a senior traffic examiner of the
Vehicle Inspectorate, an authorised officer for the purposes of the 1968 Act,
attended the appellant's company office on Thursday, 1 October 1998 and
met with the fleet manager, Mr Evans, and the general manager, Mr Collins,
c   and requested permission to remove the tachograph charts in respect of
August 1998, having previously made an appointment for the meeting.
Permission for removal was refused by the fleet manager, Mr Evans. The
appellant company was prepared to allow the officer to inspect the
tachograph charts at their offices. The tachograph charts for August 1998
were never produced for inspection or handed over to the Inspectorate.'

d
[9]   Having found the case proved the justices fined the defendant £400 and
ordered costs to be paid by it in the sum of £3,955·87. They put the following
question for the opinion of the High Court:

e   '1. Whether an offence under s 99(1)(bb) and 99(4)(a) of the Transport Act
1968 is committed by a refusal on the defendant's part to hand over
tachograph records to an authorised officer of the Vehicle Inspectorate upon
request in circumstances where: (i) the records are ready and available for
production to the officer; (ii) the officer refuses to accept production (and
inspection) at the defendant's premises of the records but requires them to
f   be handed over there and then for the officer to take away; (iii) the officer has
no reason to believe an offence under s 99(5) of the 1968 Act has been
committed in respect of any record or document inspected by him. Whether
the justices were right to conclude on the evidence before them that an
offence was committed under s 99(1)(bb) and 99(4)(a) of the 1968 Act of
failing to hand over tachograph records to be kept by art 14(2) of Council
g   Regulation (EEC) 3821/85.'

[10]   The Divisional Court answered each question in the affirmative. They
certified as a point of law of general importance involved in the decision:

'Whether it was right to construe the requirement imposed on an operator
h   under s 99(1) of the Transport Act 1968 to produce a record sheet required
to be kept under art 14(2) of Council Regulation 3821/85 as conferring a
power on the authorised officer to require the handing over of the record
sheet on demand without prior notice and without having reason to believe
that an offence has been committed contrary to s 99(5) of the 1968 Act.'

j   [11]   Both sides attach importance to the answer to this question in what is
being treated as a test case. Although the case only involves in effect tachograph
records it is to be borne in mind that the right to require the production and the
duty to permit the officer to inspect and copy apply not only to tachographs
under s 99(1)(bb) but also to other documents. Thus the power and the obligation
apply also to (a) any book or register which that person is required by regulation
to carry or have in his possession, or which is required to be 'carried on any

vehicle of which that person is the driver'; (b) any book or register which that
person is required to preserve; (c) if that person is the owner any other document a
which the officer may 'reasonably require to inspect' for the purposes of
ascertaining whether the 1968 Act and regulations made under it have been
complied with and (d) any book, register or document required by Community
rules which the officer may 'reasonably require to inspect' to ensure that
Community rules have been complied with. The scope of the power and duty b
provided for in s 99(1) must be referable to these too.

[12] The charge was of failing to 'hand over' the charts contrary to s 99(1)(bb)
and (4)(a) of the 1968 Act. As appears from the findings of fact the real problem
here was that whereas the company was willing to let the officer inspect the
charts at their office, they were not willing to let him take them away; he was
only satisfied by being given permission to take them away, presumably to c
inspect and perhaps to copy them at his office. It seems to me that the
requirement to 'produce' involves no more than providing them for the officer
to see. If the officer on notice, or in circumstances where they are readily
available and when they can be shown very quickly, requires production at the
company's premises a refusal to provide them for him to see would be an offence. d
Even though they were not in fact so provided or produced in this case that was
only because the officer was not interested in having them at the premises and
the company would not let him take them away. There was not in any sense a
refusal to 'produce' them to the officer at the company premises.

[13] If that had been all there would have been, it seems to me, no offence
under the section. The real question is whether the company had failed to 'permit e
him to inspect and copy' which seems to be what was intended by the allegation
that the company had failed 'to hand over' the charts, a phrase taken from
art 14(2) of Council Regulation (EEC) 3821/85 which requires that they shall be
'produced or handed over'.

[14] The defendant says that as a matter of language 'permit to inspect and f
copy' does not include taking away to inspect and copy. If production is satisfied
by providing the documents at the premises the company is only required to
permit inspection and copying at those premises. The defendant also says that
this is a deliberate part of the statutory scheme. Section 99(1)(bb) is concerned
with routine inspection. If more is required then the power in the concluding
words of s 99(1) must be used as it would be if the officer knew that by reason of g
the quantity of the records it would be necessary or more convenient to have
them at his office. A further stage is provided for in the power of seizure under
s 99(6) of the 1968 Act where it is suspected that the documents have been
falsified.

[15] I do not consider that the power to require documents to be taken to the h
office of the traffic commissioner in the final words of s 99(1) in itself necessarily
leads to the conclusion that documents can only be taken away by an officer if he
gives ten days' notice under that final provision. The question remains whether
the power to require the person to permit the officer to inspect and copy the
record sheets includes the power to take them away for that purpose.

[16] I accept the defendant's argument that, even acknowledging the importance j
of this monitoring process in the interests of road safety, it is necessary to be
satisfied that Parliament intended the opening words to confer a power to take
possession of business documents and to remove them from the company's
premises even if temporarily and for the specified purpose. It is perhaps easier to
accept that this was intended in respect of records which the 1968 Act or
regulations made by the Community or by the Secretary of State require to be

a kept in order to achieve the objectives of the legislation than in respect of 'any other document[s]' referred to in s 99(1)(c). The position however of all these documents has to be considered.

[17] I do not consider that any assistance is to be obtained on the question in this case from the provisions of s 99(2).

[18] It is essential to bear in mind that the power is given so that the officer can
b 'inspect and copy'. If the documents are few and copying facilities are available at the company's premises so that it is not reasonably necessary to take them away, production to the officer for inspection and copying there is in my opinion a compliance with the section. If on the other hand the documents are many or such that a proper inspection and copying is only possible with other equipment which is not immediately available then to enable the officer to inspect and copy
c he must be able to take them away but only for such period as is reasonably required for their inspection and copying.

[19] It is to be noted that the power to require documents in paras (c) and (d) of s 99(1) can only be exercised 'reasonably' and whether it is reasonably necessary to take documents away in order to inspect and copy is no more difficult to
d answer in my view than it is to answer the question whether under paras (c) and (d) the requirement is reasonable. It seems to me that this approach should not unusually cause any difficulties though I realise that there may be grey areas where the officer and the company may not agree as to what is reasonable. If, however, the officer reasonably requires to take the documents away and the company refuses it will of course risk prosecution. If the company's refusal is
e based on the claim that it is not reasonably necessary to take the documents away for inspection and copying and that defence is raised before the magistrates, then it seems to me at present (though the matter did not arise here and was not argued on this basis) that the prosecution must satisfy the magistrates that it was reasonable to take the documents away. The magistrates will of course have
f regard to the purpose and importance of the officer's inspection.

[20] I regard this conclusion as clearly compatible with the requirements of art 14(2) of Council Regulation (EEC) 3821/85 and do not find it necessary to refer a question to the Court of Justice of the European Communities as to the meaning of that article.

[21] It seems to me accordingly that where no notice has been served under
g the concluding words of s 99(1) and there is no reason to believe that an offence has been committed under s 99(5) of the 1968 Act an offence will be committed if the transport operator refuses to permit a vehicle inspector to take documents that it is reasonably necessary for him to take in order to inspect and copy them.

[22] I do not consider that such a conclusion can possibly be a violation of art 8
h of the convention rights set out in Sch 1 to the Human Rights Act 1998. As the Divisional Court held the provision is 'in accordance with the law' and 'necessary in a democratic society in the interests of … public safety'.

[23] As to the facts of the present case it seems to me that, it not having been contended that the officer's request to take away the documents in order to inspect and copy them was unreasonable and that that in itself was a defence, the
j justices were entitled to find the offence proved. I would accordingly dismiss the appeal.

LORD STEYN.

[24] My Lords, road safety is a high imperative. What can reasonably and sensibly be done to promote it, must be done. Driver fatigue is apparently a significant factor in road accidents in the United Kingdom. The risk affects both

drivers of heavy goods vehicles and ordinary car drivers. Added to this, however, it is a notorious fact that drivers of heavy vehicles are sometimes under commercial pressures, or feel under commercial pressure, to drive inordinately long hours. In order to reduce the risk of accidents resulting from fatigued drivers it is necessary to control the number of hours they drive per day. The tachograph has to-date been a prime tool in establishing and operating the regulatory system. A tachograph records the measurements of a tachometer: it notes the speed and times at which the vehicle was driven. An indispensable part of the regulatory system has been the regular and effective inspection and examination by the Vehicle Inspectorate of the relevant record sheets.

[25] Article 14(2) of Council Regulation (EEC) 3821/85 imposes on a transport operator obligations relating to the retention, production and handing over of tachograph records. It provides:

'The undertaking shall keep the record sheets in good order for a least a year after their use and shall give copies to the drivers concerned who request them. The sheets shall be produced or handed over at the request of any authorised inspecting officer.'

Article 15(7) of the regulation imposes on the driver of a vehicle fitted with a tachograph an obligation to produce certain record sheets to an inspecting officer. The regulation has direct effect. It is the backcloth to the corresponding provisions in our domestic legislation.

[26] The obligation under the law of England and Wales to produce records to an inspecting officer is contained in s 99(1)(bb) of the Transport Act 1968, which was added as part of the amendments made to Pt VI of the 1968 Act in order to give effect to the European code. The relevant part of s 99(1) reads:

'An officer may, on production if so required of his authority, require any person to produce, and permit him to inspect and copy ... (bb) any record sheet which that person is required by Article 14(2) of the Community Recording Equipment Regulation to retain or by Article 15(7) of that Regulation to be able to produce ... and that record sheet, book, register or document shall, if the officer so requires by notice in writing served on that person, be produced at the office of the traffic commissioner specified in the notice within such time (not being less than ten days) from the service of the notice as may be so specified.'

The words after para (bb) I will call the coda. Subsection (4)(a) of s 99 makes it an offence to fail to comply with a requirement under s 99(1).

[27] The appellant defendant, a coach operator, was prosecuted for an offence contrary to s 99(1)(bb) and s 99(4) of the 1968 Act in that 'on ... 15 September 1998 ... when asked by an authorised officer to hand over tachograph charts required to be kept by art 14(2) of Council Regulation (EEC) 3821/85 [it] failed to do so contrary to s 99(1)(bb) and (4)(a) of the Transport Act 1968'. It was common ground that on 15 September 1998 an authorised officer required the defendant to hand over the relevant records for August 1998. Through a senior employee the defendant agreed to allow the authorised officer to inspect the records but refused to allow the officer to remove the records from the defendant's premises. When the requirement was renewed on 1 October 1998 the defendant adopted the same position. A prosecution was launched. The information came before justices for hearing. The defendant contended that he was not legally obliged to hand over the records. On 10 May 1999 Hertfordshire

a justices convicted the defendant. The defendant was fined £400 and ordered to pay costs of £3,955·87. At the request of the defendant the justices stated a case for the Divisional Court of the Queen's Bench Division. The case stated in effect raised the question of law whether the authorised officer was entitled to require the records to be handed over to enable them to be examined and analysed at the premises of the Vehicle Inspectorate.

b [28] The Divisional Court (Kennedy LJ and Butterfield J) ([2000] RTR 286) answered the question in the affirmative and dismissed the appeal. The conclusion of the Divisional Court is contained in the following passage in the judgment of Butterfield J (at 304):

c '... it is within the discretion of the authorised officer whether he chooses to inspect the tachograph sheets at the operator's premises (which he might be content to do if the volume of documentation was small and if he had no real concern about it) or take the sheets away for more thorough and detailed analysis (which he might wish to do if, for example, he had concerns about the documentation or if his preliminary inspection suggested to him *d* that all was not as it should be or if the volume of it was such that it was difficult or impossible effectively to inspect at the premises).'

The Divisional Court refused leave to appeal but certified the following question:

e 'Whether it was right to construe the requirement imposed on an operator under s 99(1) of the Transport Act 1968 to produce a record sheet required to be kept under art 14(2) of Council Regulation 3821/85 as conferring a power on the authorised officer to require the handing over of the record sheet on demand without prior notice and without having reason to believe that an offence has been committed contrary to s 99(5) of the 1968 Act.'

f The rival contentions are as follows. The Vehicle Inspectorate contend that properly construed s 99(1) authorises a requirement that the relevant records be handed over so that they can be examined and analysed at premises of the Vehicle Inspectorate. The defendant argues that s 99(1) does not authorise a requirement that the records be handed over: it only authorises a requirement that the records be produced for inspection and copying on the defendant's premises. This is a *g* narrow point of statutory construction. It is the only issue before the House. In particular there is no issue as to whether the exercise of the power under s 99(1), whatever the precise scope of the power, was reviewable on public law grounds.

[29] It is of paramount importance to keep in mind the objective of the statutory power under s 99(1). The purpose is spelt out in s 95(1). It provides that *h* Pt VI of the 1968 Act, of which s 99(1) forms a part, shall have effect—

'with a view to securing the observance of proper hours [or periods] of work by persons engaged in the carriage of passengers or goods by road and thereby protecting the public against the risks which arise in cases where the drivers of motor vehicles are suffering from fatigue ...'
j

The preambles of Council Regulation (EEC) 3821/85 make clear that this 'social legislation' is intended 'in the interests of road safety' to provide for 'effective checking of records' of drivers' hours. The system is intended to 'minimise any possibility of fraudulent use'. This overriding objective of the European code is spelt out at length in Council Directive (EEC) 88/599 (OJ 1988 L325 p 55) of 23 November 1988. Significantly it provides in art 4(3):

'... checks carried out at the premises of the competent authorities, on the basis of relevant documents handed over by undertakings at the request of *a* the said authorities, shall have the same status as checks carried out at the premises of undertakings.'

The context, European and domestic, shows that a regulatory system of routine checks of records, which is effective to secure the objective, was contemplated by *b* the 1968 Act as amended.

[30] Counsel for the defendant contrasted the provisions of s 99(1) with the provisions of s 99(6) which authorises seizure of records when an officer has reason to believe that an offence of tampering with records under s 99(5) has been committed. He argued that s 99(6) shows that 'produce' in the opening words of s 99(1) does not authorise a requirement to hand over records. This argument *c* equates a handing over of records for examination and analysis with a seizure of records. That is not a legitimate position. The remedy of seizure under s 99(6) is a more draconian remedy than handing over records (if that is authorised by s 99(1)) for the limited purpose of examination and copying at the Vehicle Inspectorate's premises. The point does not assist the defendant.   *d*

[31] Similarly, I must reject the argument on behalf of the defendant based on the power contained in the coda of s 99(1) to require 'production' of records at the office of the traffic commissioner upon no less than ten days' notice. This is a different power: it involves not an obligation to produce or hand over but an obligation to deliver records at the office of a different agency, viz the traffic *e* commissioner. The subsection therefore provides for two distinct powers: the power under the opening words of s 99(1) requires no specified period of notice as a condition precedent to its exercise; and the power under the coda of s 99(1) requires ten days' notice to be given. The existence of two such separate powers are in no way inconsistent: the existence of separate powers is part of a coherent and rational statutory scheme. The two powers must not be confused or *f* conflated. It is impossible to read into the opening words the implication that ten days' notice must be given before that power is exercised.

[32] It will be observed that 'produce' under the coda unquestionably contemplates handing over of records. The result is therefore that on the defendant's interpretation the word 'produce' is used in different senses in the *g* opening words and in the coda of the subsection. While this is by no means a decisive argument, it is a pointer against the submission of the defendant.

[33] Another contextual indication against the narrow interpretation of the defendant is that under sub-s (2)(a) of s 99 an authorised officer is given power to enter certain vehicles 'at any time' and under sub-s 2(b) to enter any premises 'at *h* any time which is reasonable'. The defendant's restrictive interpretation of s 99(1) appears to be in disharmony with the admittedly strong powers of the Vehicle Inspectorate under s 99(2).

[34] Concentrating still on the statutory language, there is an even stronger indication in s 99(10) against the defendant's interpretation. It reads: *j*

'In this section references to the inspection and copying of any record produced by means of equipment installed for the purposes of section 97 of this Act in a vehicle include references to the application to the record of any process for eliciting the information recorded thereby and to taking down the information elicited from it.'

a Subsection (10) refers back to the words 'require any person to produce, and permit him to inspect and copy' in sub-s (1) when it provides for 'the application to the record of any process'. Plainly, sub-s (10) is wide enough to cover examination and analysis using a computer at the premises of the Vehicle Inspectorate. The fact that, due perhaps to an oversight, there has been no commencement order made in respect of s 99(10) is no answer. Subsection (10)
b is a sure guide to the best interpretation of the opening words of s 99(1).

[35] Finally, if the interpretation of the defendant is adopted the effectiveness of a regulatory system will be affected. Sometimes an examination and analysis of records at the premises of the Vehicle Inspectorate will be essential. It is true that on the defendant's interpretation the power in the coda exercisable on ten days' notice will still be available. But, if this was the only available power
c authorising handing over and removal of the records for examination at the Vehicle Inspectorate's premises, there will be a chance for unscrupulous operators to 'lose' the records at their premises or in the post. There may also be scope for tampering with the records. The interpretation of the Vehicle Inspectorate significantly reduces such risks. It therefore best promotes the objective of the
d statute, viz an effective checking system.

[36] The balance of arguments demonstrate convincingly that under s 99(1) an authorised officer may require the handing over of records. I would therefore endorse the interpretation of the Divisional Court. This conclusion is based on the interpretation of our domestic legislation but it is right to add that my reading of it is consistent with the United Kingdom's obligations under art 14(2) of
e reg 3821/85.

[37] For these reasons as well as the reasons given by my noble and learned friend Lord Hutton, I would therefore dismiss the appeal.

LORD HOPE OF CRAIGHEAD.

f [38] My Lords, I have had the advantage of reading in draft the speeches which have been prepared by my noble and learned friends Lord Steyn and Lord Hutton. I agree with them. For the reasons which they have given I too would dismiss the appeal.

[39] There is a division of opinion among us as to whether, in order to establish that an offence under s 99(1)(bb) of the Transport Act 1968 was
g committed in a case where the officer wishes to take the documents away for inspection and copying, the prosecution must satisfy the magistrate that it was reasonable for the officer to take the documents away. I note that counsel did not address their arguments to this point. But in any event I respectfully agree with Lord Steyn and Lord Hutton that the statute lays down no such requirement.

h [40] Section 99(1) confers power on the officer to do things. First, he may, on production if so required of his authority, require any person to produce any of the items listed in that subsection and permit him to inspect and copy them. Second, he may by notice in writing require that person to produce any of those items at the office of the traffic commissioner within such time of the notice as
j may be specified. Section 99(8), as amended by s 48 and Sch 4, para 2 of the Road Traffic Act 1991, provides that in that section 'officer' means an examiner appointed under s 66A of the Road Traffic Act 1988 and any person authorised for the purposes of that section by the traffic commissioner for any area. In neither case does the subsection provide that the requirement which the officer has made must be shown to have been reasonable. All that the prosecutor needs to show is that the officer made the requirement in the manner which the subsection lays

down and that the item which was not produced was one in respect of which he *a* was entitled to make the requirement.

[41] The various items in respect of which an officer is entitled to make the requirement fall into two categories. On the one hand there those which a person is required by regulations to carry or have in his possession, to preserve, to retain or to be able to produce: see s 99(1)(a), (b) and (bb). In their case all that needs to be shown is that the item was of the description laid down by the relevant *b* paragraph. On the other hand there are those which the officer reasonably requires to inspect for the purpose of ascertaining whether the provisions of regulations have been complied with: see s 99(1)(c) and (d). In their case it must be shown that it was reasonable for the officer to require to inspect the item for the purpose laid down in the paragraph.

[42] The question whether it was reasonable, or reasonably necessary, for the *c* officer to take any of these items away for the purpose of inspecting and copying them—which is the point at issue in this case—is a different question, which the subsection does not address. To say that this is a further condition that must be satisfied by the prosecutor would in effect be to insert into the subsection something which is not there. I prefer to base my decision on a construction of *d* the words used by the statute. That is not to say that a requirement made under s 99(1) may not be open to challenge on public law grounds. But that is not the issue in this case.

LORD HUTTON.

[43] My Lords, Pt VI of the Transport Act 1968 contains sections which were *e* enacted for the purpose of securing the observance of proper hours or periods of work by drivers of passenger or goods vehicles in order to protect the public against the risks which arise on the roads when those drivers are suffering from fatigue. Section 99 in Pt VI relates to the inspection of records and other documents by authorised officers in order to ensure that the permitted driving *f* times have not been exceeded. In 1986 sub-s (1) of s 99 was amended by the addition of para (bb) to give effect to Council Regulation (EEC) 3821/85 of 20 December 1985 on recording equipment in road transport.

[44] Article 14(2) of Council Regulation (EEC) 3821/85 provides:

'The undertaking shall keep the record sheets in good order for at least a *g* year after their use and shall give copies to the drivers concerned who request them. The sheets shall be produced or handed over at the request of any authorised inspecting officer.'

Article 19(1) provides:

h

'Member States shall, in good time and after consulting the Commission, adopt such laws, regulations or administrative provisions as may be necessary for the implementation of this Regulation. Such measures shall cover, inter alia, the re-organisation of, procedure for, and means of carrying out, checks on compliance and the penalties to be imposed in case of breach.' *j*

[45] The relevant parts of s 99 of the 1968 Act now read:

'(1) An officer may, on production if so required of his authority, require any person to produce, and permit him to inspect and copy ... (bb) any record sheet which that person is required by Article 14(2) of the Community Recording Equipment Regulation [(EEC) 3821/85] to retain or by Article a 15(7) of that Regulation to be able to produce; … and that record sheet, book, register or document shall, if the officer so requires by notice in writing served on that person, be produced at the office of the traffic commissioner specified in the notice within such time (not being less than ten days) from the service of the notice as may be so specified.

b (2) An officer may, on production if so required of his authority—(a) at any time, enter any vehicle to which this Part of this Act applies and inspect that vehicle and any recording equipment installed in it and inspect and copy any record sheet on the vehicle on which a record has been produced by means of the equipment or an entry has been made; (b) at any time which is reasonable having regard to the circumstances of the case, enter any premises on which he has reason to believe that such a vehicle is kept or that

c any such record sheets, books, registers or other documents as are mentioned in subsection (1) of this section are to be found, and inspect any such vehicle, and inspect and copy any such record sheet, book, register or document, which he finds there …

d (4) Any person who—(a) fails to comply with any requirement under subsection (1) of this section; or (b) obstructs an officer in the exercise of his powers under subsection (2) or (3) of this section, shall be liable on summary conviction to a fine not exceeding level 3 on the standard scale …

(5) Any person who makes, or causes to be made, any record or entry on a record sheet kept or carried for the purposes of the Community Recording

e Equipment Regulation or section 97 of this Act or any entry in a book, register or document kept or carried for the purposes of regulations under section 98 thereof or the applicable Community rules which he knows to be false or, with intent to deceive, alters or causes to be altered any such record or entry shall be liable—(a) on summary conviction, to a fine not exceeding the prescribed sum; (b) on conviction on indictment, to imprisonment for a

f term not exceeding two years.

(6) If an officer has reason to believe that an offence under subsection (5) of this section has been committed in respect of any record or document inspected by him under this section, he may seize that record or document; and where a record or document is seized as aforesaid and within six months of the date

g on which it was seized no person has been charged since that date with an offence in relation to that record or document under that subsection and the record or document has not been returned to the person from whom it was taken, a magistrates' court shall, on an application made for the purpose by that person or by an officer, make such order respecting the disposal of the

h record or document and award such costs as the justice of the case may require …

(10) In this section references to the inspection and copying of any record produced by means of equipment installed for the purposes of section 97 of this Act in a vehicle include references to the application to the record of any

j process for eliciting the information recorded thereby and to taking down the information elicited from it.'

A commencement order (Transport Act 1968 (Commencement No 6) Order 1970, SI 1970/259) made under s 166(2) and (3) of the 1968 Act brought sub-ss (1) to (9) of s 99 into force on 1 March 1970 but, perhaps due to an oversight, no commencement order has been made bringing sub-s (10) into force.

[46] The Hertfordshire justices convicted the defendant, a coach operator, of an offence under s 99(1)(bb) and (4)(a) and, rejecting its argument, held that an authorised officer was entitled to require it to hand over at its office tachograph records so that he could take them to be examined and analysed at the office of the Vehicle Inspectorate. The offence was charged in the summons as follows:

'Cantabrica Coach Holdings Ltd ... on Tuesday 15 September 1998 at Elton Way, Watford in the county of Hertfordshire, or elsewhere, when asked by an authorised officer to hand over tachograph charts required to be kept by art 14(2) of Council Regulation (EEC) 3821/85 failed to do so contrary to s 99(1)(bb) and (4)(a) of the Transport Act 1968.'

The certificate of conviction was worded:

'On 15 September 1998 at Elton Way, Watford [you] did fail to comply with a requirement made by an officer under s 99(1) of the Transport Act 1968 in that you failed to produce a record sheet which you were required by art 14(2) of the Community Recording Equipment Regulation [3821/85] to retain. Contrary to s 99(4) of the Transport Act as amended.'

[47] The defendant appealed by case stated to the Divisional Court which dismissed the appeal. The conclusion of the Divisional Court (Kennedy LJ and Butterfield J) was stated as follows in the judgment of Butterfield J ([2000] RTR 286 at 304):

'In my judgment the construction placed on section 99(1) of the Act of 1968 by the defendant is flawed. I conclude that the operator is required to produce and hand over tachograph record sheets on demand at the operator's premises if such a request is made of him. It is clear that in requiring the production of the document or the handing over of the records the Community legislature took account of the need to ensure effective checking. On the interpretation of section 99 of the Act of 1968 as I would hold, it is within the discretion of the authorised officer whether he chooses to inspect the tachograph sheets at the operator's premises (which he might be content to do if the volume of documentation was small and if he had no real concern about it) or take the sheets away for more thorough and detailed analysis (which he might wish to do if, for example, he had concerns about the documentation or if his preliminary inspection suggested to him that all was not as it should be or if the volume of it was such that it was difficult or impossible effectively to inspect at the premises). Alternatively he might require production and handing over of the records at the office of the traffic commissioner.'

[48] The Divisional Court refused leave to appeal but certified the following point of law of general public importance:

'Whether it was right to construe the requirement imposed on an operator under s 99(1) of the Transport Act 1968 to produce a record sheet required to be kept under art 14(2) of Council Regulation 3821/85 as conferring a power on the authorised officer to require the handing over of the record sheet on demand without prior notice and without having reason to believe that an offence has been committed contrary to s 99(5) of the 1968 Act.'

[49] My Lords, the point argued before the House by Mr Phillips QC for the defendant and Mr Plender QC for the respondent was a narrow one. It was

a whether s 99(1) empowered an authorised officer, who had not given at least ten days' notice as referred to in the concluding part of s 99(1), to go to the office of the coach operator and require it to hand over to him the tachograph records so that he could remove them for examination at the office of the Vehicle Inspectorate. This was the question set out in the point of law certified by the Divisional Court and it was the question to which the submissions of counsel

b were directed. It appears that the issue of the reasonableness of the request made by the authorised officer was not raised before the justices or the Divisional Court and counsel did not address the issue of reasonableness as a substantive point in their submissions to the House. Mr Phillips submitted that in the absence of at least ten days' notice the authorised officer had no power to take away the tachograph records whereas Mr Plender submitted that the first part of s 99(1)

c gave him that power and that the refusal to permit him to do so constituted an offence under s 99(1)(bb) and (4).

[50] My noble and learned friend Lord Scott of Foscote has considered the issue of reasonableness in his opinion, but having regard to the terms in which the Divisional Court formulated the certified question and to the way in which

d counsel have advanced their arguments, I confine my opinion to the issue of construction.

[51] I summarise Mr Phillips' submissions as follows. Pursuant to art 19(1) of Council Regulation (EEC) 3821/1985, s 99, as amended, implemented art 14(2) in graduated stages. The first stage was that an authorised officer was given power

e to require the production of the tachograph records at the transport operator's office and to inspect and copy those records in that office, but he was not given power to take them away for examination at the office of the traffic commissioner. The second stage was that if the Vehicle Inspectorate wished to inspect the tachograph records at the office of the traffic commissioner, then in pursuance of

f the concluding part of s 99(1) an officer must give at least ten days' notice in writing requiring production of the records at the office specified in the notice. In addition, if an officer had reason to believe that the offence of the falsification of a record had been committed contrary to s 99(5) he had power to seize the record under s 99(6).

[52] Mr Phillips placed reliance on the point that art 14(2) provided that the

g records shall be 'produced or handed over' at the request of any authorised officer whereas the first part of s 99(1) contained only the word 'produced' and not the words 'handed over'. Mr Phillips accepted that when records were produced at the office of the traffic commissioner pursuant to a notice under the concluding part of s 99(1) the Vehicle Inspectorate could retain the records for examination

h in that office, but he submitted that the separate power to require production at the traffic commissioner's office and the separate power to seize if there was reason to believe falsification pointed to the conclusion that there was no power under the first part of s 99(1) to take away the records from the office of the transport operator.

j [53] Mr Phillips also sought to derive support for the construction for which he contended from art 8 of the European Convention for the Protection of Human Rights and Fundamental Freedoms 1950 (as set out in Sch 1 to the Human Rights Act 1998) and submitted that when falsification is not suspected a power for the authorised officer to remove a transport operator's records from its office without notice is an interference with the operator's right of privacy which is excessive and is not proportionate to the legitimate aim of the legislation.

[54] In summary Mr Plender submitted that the requirement in the first part *a* of s 99(1) 'to produce' records and to permit them to be inspected includes by necessary implication the handing over and retention for inspection of those records, and that the taking away of the records for effective and thorough examination in the office of the Vehicle Inspectorate is within the ambit of the power of inspection given by the subsection. He submitted that on some occasions the volume of documentation to be inspected by an authorised officer *b* would be substantial and that a proper and effective inspection would not be possible unless the records could be taken away. A transport operator which produced documents in its office which could not be effectively inspected unless they could be taken away for examination by computer or other special equipment in an office of the Vehicle Inspectorate, could not be said to have produced those documents for inspection if it refused to let them be taken away, *c* having regard to the purpose for which art 14(1) of Council Regulation (EEC) 3821/1985 was adopted by the Council of the European Communities and the statutory purpose of s 99.

[55] I consider that the submissions on behalf of the Vehicle Inspectorate are correct. I do not think that the powers contained in the first and concluding parts *d* of s 99(1) were intended to be graduated steps so that the records could only be inspected in the office of the Vehicle Inspectorate if ten days' notice had been given. I agree with Butterfield J that the powers are concurrent and that it is a matter for the discretion of the authorised officer, depending on the circumstances, to decide whether to go to the office of the transport operator to require production of the records which he may then take away for detailed inspection *e* or to give ten days' notice requiring the records to be produced at the office of the traffic commissioner. I also consider that the power to seize records under s 99(6) where there is reason to believe falsification relates to a different procedure in different circumstances than the procedure of inspection provided for in the first part of s 99(1) and does not have the effect, as a matter of construction, that the *f* power to inspect is to be as read as confined to inspection in the office of the transport operator.

[56] The purpose of art 14(1) and of s 99 is to protect those who use the roads against the risk of accidents arising from tiredness and lack of concentration by drivers of goods and passenger vehicles who drive for excessive periods. A necessary part of the procedure to give this protection is the careful checking and *g* examination of tachograph records, and it is apparent that such checking and examination will require on occasions that the tachograph records be taken to an office of the Vehicle Inspectorate where the necessary specialised equipment and requisite number of staff will be available. In my opinion this conclusion is strongly supported by the terms of s 99(10) which can be taken into account on *h* the issue of construction notwithstanding that no commencement order has been made in respect of it. It relates to the inspection and copying of records as provided for by s 99(1) and clearly envisages that inspection and copying will require the application to the records of processes for eliciting the information recorded in them. These processes will include the use of computers and other *j* equipment which will only be available for use in the offices of the Vehicle Inspectorate. This is a compelling reason to hold that the power to inspect given by s 99(1) includes the power to take away for the purpose of inspection.

[57] I also consider that there is no substance in the defendant's reliance on art 8 of the convention. Even if art 8 can apply to the affairs of a limited liability company (a question on which I express no opinion) the power to take away

a   tachograph records for careful examination is 'in accordance with the law and is
necessary in a democratic society in the interests of ... public safety' (art 8(2)), and
in my opinion it is clear that the power to take away records for such examination
cannot be regarded as disproportionate to the legitimate aim of the legislation.

[58] Accordingly, I consider that the decision of the Divisional Court was
correct and I would dismiss this appeal.

b
LORD SCOTT OF FOSCOTE.

[59] My Lords, Tachographs must, subject to some exceptions, be fitted to all
commercial vehicles used for the carriage of goods or passengers. Their function
is to monitor the work performance of the driver, the speeds at which he is
c   driving, the hours he is at the wheel, the rest periods he takes and so on. The
purpose of this is two-fold, namely, first, the well-being of the driver, to try and
ensure that he is not being exploited by being required to be at the wheel for
longer hours than he should; and second, the safety of the public, who would be
at risk if drivers, through driving continuously for too many hours or taking
insufficient rest periods, became overtired while at the wheel. These are very
d   important purposes.

[60] The tachograph records must, in order to achieve these purposes, be
available for inspection by the authorities. In the United Kingdom, this is one of
the functions of the Vehicle Inspectorate. Their inspectors have statutory powers
to inspect and copy, and in certain circumstances to seize, tachograph records as
e   well as other records held by the vehicle owners or operators.

[61] The importance of the efficient functioning of the regulatory system to
which I have referred is not open to question. But there is another side to the coin
to which attention must also be paid. It is easy for officious officialdom to
become an offensive burden to the public whom the officials are supposed to
serve. It is important that the limits of the powers which allow officials to intrude
f   into the lives and affairs of citizens should be clearly defined and that the limits
should be observed. It is of course the function of the courts to support the
Vehicle Inspectorate's inspectors in operating the tachograph regulatory system
but it is also the function of the courts to guard against the assumption by the
inspectors of excessive powers not warranted by the terms of the statutory
g   system.

[62] It is the tension between these two imperatives that has led to the test
case that is now before your Lordships.

[63] The tachograph regulatory system consists in part of European legislation
and in part of domestic legislation. It is convenient to start with the former.

h   [64] The regulations currently in force are Council Regulation (EEC) 3820/85
and Council Regulation (EEC) 3821/85, both of 20 December 1985. Council
Regulation (EEC) 3820/85 sets out the rules relating to drivers and their work
that must be observed by the owners or operators of motor vehicles used for the
carriage of goods or passengers. Council Regulation (EEC) 3821/85 requires the
installation in these vehicles of recording equipment, ie tachographs, in order
j   that observance of the Council Regulation (EEC) 3820/85 rules may be monitored.

[65] Article 14(2) of Council Regulation (EEC) 3821/85 provides:

'The undertaking shall keep the [tachograph] record sheets in good order
for at least a year after their use and shall give copies to the drivers concerned
who request them. The sheets shall be produced or handed over at the
request of any authorised inspecting officer.'

The article does not say what the inspecting officer who has requested the
production or handing over of the sheets may then do with them. It is plain
enough, given the inspecting officer's monitoring function, that he may inspect
the sheets with a view to checking whether the Council Regulation (EEC)
3820/85 rules are being observed. But can he remove them for a more detailed
examination elsewhere? And, if so, how long can he retain them? The article is
silent. Can the inspecting officer take copies of the sheets? The article is silent.
Some form of statutory authority for the taking of copies would presumably be
necessary to avoid breach of copyright problems. If the inspecting officer is
entitled to remove the sheets from the premises of the operator, must any prior
notice be given before he does so? The removal of the sheets before the operator
has had a chance to take copies might disrupt the administration of the business.
On this, too, the article is silent. It seems to me that the cited sentence of art 14(2)
is of a skeletal character. Some detail, some flesh, seems to be needed for it to be
implemented.

[66] It is, therefore, not surprising to find that art 19(1) of Council Regulation
(EEC) 3821/85 provides:

'Member States shall, in good time and after consulting the Commission,
adopt such laws, regulations or administrative provisions as may be necessary
for the implementation of this Regulation. Such measures shall cover, inter
alia, the re-organisation of, procedure for, and means of carrying out, checks
on compliance and the penalties to be imposed in case of breach.'

[67] European Community regulations have, in general, a direct effect in
member states. But there is, in my opinion, no reason in principle why a
provision contained in a Regulation should not be so framed as to invite, or
require, individual member states to bring into effect domestic legislation to
implement the provision in question. Council Regulation (EEC) 3821/85 does
not contain provision for any criminal sanctions for breach of its provisions. It
has been common ground before your Lordships that provisions for offences and
penalties must be made by the domestic legislation contemplated by art 19(1).
The article expressly contemplates, also, domestic legislation relating to checks
on compliance.

[68] But the express references in art 19(1) to these matters are prefaced by the
words 'inter alia'. So it is quite clear that the scope of the domestic legislation
contemplated by the article is not limited to the matters expressly referred to. It
is a reasonable conclusion, therefore, that one of the things that art 19(1) left it
open to member states to provide by supplementary domestic legislation is the
detail that the second sentence of art 14(2) so notably omitted. In the framing of
any supplementary domestic legislation a margin of appreciation must be permitted
to each member state. Provided the domestic legislation establishes a regulatory
system consistent with the express provisions of Council Regulation (EEC)
3821/85 it is, in my opinion, franked by art 19(1).

[69] Part VI of the Transport Act 1968 established, among other things, a
United Kingdom regulatory system for passenger vehicles and goods vehicles
that predated by many years the tachograph requirements imposed by Council
Regulation (EEC) 3820/85. The domestic legislation contemplated by art 19(1)
of Council Regulation (EEC) 3821/85 took the form, so far as the United
Kingdom was concerned, of amendments to Pt VI of the 1968 Act. The amendments

a   were added by the Community Drivers' Hours and Recording Equipment
Regulations 1986, SI 1986/1457.

[**70**] Part VI of the 1968 Act, as amended, commences with a statement of the
purpose of the regulatory system:

b
'**95.**—(1) This Part of this Act shall have effect with a view to securing the
observance of proper hours or periods of work by persons engaged in the
carriage of passengers or goods by road and thereby protecting the public
against the risks which arise in cases where the drivers of motor vehicles are
suffering from fatigue …'

[**71**] The relevant operative provisions are to be found in s 99, headed
c   'Inspection of records and other documents'. Section 99, as amended, provides,
as far as relevant to tachograph records:

'(1) An officer may, on production if so required of his authority, require
any person to produce, and permit him to inspect and copy … (bb) any
record sheet which that person is required by Article 14(2) of the Community
d   Recording Equipment Regulation [(EEC) 3821/85] to retain or by Article
15(7) of that Regulation to be able to produce … and that record sheet …
shall, if the officer so requires by notice in writing served on that person, be
produced at the office of the traffic commissioner specified in the notice
within such time (not being less than ten days) from the service of the notice
as may be so specified.

e
(2) An officer may, on production if so required of his authority—(a) at
any time, enter any vehicle to which this Part of this Act applies and inspect
that vehicle and any recording equipment installed in it and inspect and copy
any record sheet on the vehicle on which a record has been produced by
means of the equipment or an entry has been made; (b) at any time which is
f   reasonable having regard to the circumstances of the case, enter any
premises on which he has reason to believe that such a vehicle is kept or that
any such record sheets … as are mentioned in subsection (1) of this section
are to be found, and inspect any such vehicle, and inspect and copy any such
record sheet … which he finds there …

(4) Any person who—(a) fails to comply with any requirement under
g   subsection (1) of this section; or (b) obstructs an officer in the exercise of his
powers under subsection (2) or (3) of this section, shall be liable on summary
conviction to a fine not exceeding level 3 on the standard scale …

(5) Any person who makes, or causes to be made, any record or entry on
a record sheet kept or carried for the purposes of the Community Recording
h   Equipment Regulation or section 97 of this Act or any entry in a book,
register or document kept or carried for the purposes of regulations under
section 98 thereof or the applicable Community rules which he knows to be
false or, with intent to deceive, alters or causes to be altered any such record
or entry shall be liable—(a) on summary conviction, to a fine not exceeding
j   the prescribed sum; (b) on conviction on indictment, to imprisonment for a
term not exceeding two years.

(6) If an officer has reason to believe that an offence under subsection (5) of
this section has been committed in respect of any record or document inspected
by him under this section, he may seize that record or document; and where a
record or document is seized as aforesaid and within six months of the date
on which it was seized no person has been charged since that date with an

offence in relation to that record or document under that subsection and the
record or document has not been returned to the person from whom it was *a*
taken, a magistrates' court shall, on an application made for the purpose by
that person or by an officer, make such order respecting the disposal of the
record or document and award such costs as the justice of the case may
require ...

(10) In this section references to the inspection and copying of any record *b*
produced by means of equipment installed for the purposes of section 97 of
this Act in a vehicle include references to the application to the record of any
process for eliciting the information recorded thereby and to taking down
the information elicited from it.'

[72] Subsections (1) to (9) of s 99 as originally enacted were brought into force *c*
on 1 March 1970: Transport Act 1968 (Commencement No 6) Order 1970,
SI 1970/259. Oddly, sub-s (10) has never been brought into force. This is, presumably,
an oversight. None the less the contents of sub-s (10) can properly be used as an
aid to construction of the other provisions of the section that refer to inspection
and copying. Parliament enacted the section as a whole, and it is as a whole that *d*
it should be read and construed.

[73] The issue before your Lordships arises out of a prosecution of the appellant
defendant, Cantabrica Coach Holdings Ltd, for an offence under s 99(4)(a). The
facts can be very shortly stated.

[74] The defendant is a licensed coach operator and, accordingly, under an *e*
obligation to comply with Pt VI of the 1968 Act. On 15 September and again on
1 October 1998 an official of the Vehicle Inspectorate attended the defendant's
office and requested permission to remove all the defendant's tachograph record
sheets in respect of August 1998. The defendant was willing to produce the sheets
and allow the officer to inspect them at the defendant's office. The defendant was
not willing to allow the officer to remove them from the office. Since, on each *f*
occasion, the officer's purpose in attending the defendant's office had been to take
away the record sheets, in view of the defendant's refusal to allow this the officer
withdrew, and the sheets were, in the event, not produced.

[75] On 29 January 1999 the defendant was charged in the Watford Magistrates'
Court with an offence under s 99(4)(a). The information said that the defendant *g*
'when asked by an authorised officer to hand over tachograph charts ... failed to
do so contrary to s 99(1)(bb) and 4(a) of the Transport Act 1968'.

[76] The information was not, in my opinion, strictly accurate. The defendant
had been agreeable to handing over the record sheets so as to enable them to be
inspected by the officer at the defendant's office, but had not been willing to hand *h*
them over so as to enable the officer to take them away.

[77] On 10 May 1999 the defendant was convicted by the magistrates. The
conviction was recorded as a conviction for having 'failed to produce a record
sheet which you were required by art 14(2) of the Community Recording
Equipment Regulation [(EEC) 3821/85] to retain. Contrary to s 99(4) of the Transport *j*
Act 1968 as amended'. This, too, was in my opinion inaccurate. The defendant's
failure was a failure to permit the officer to take the records away. It was not a
failure to produce them.

[78] The magistrates were requested by the defendant to state a case for the
Divisional Court. The case stated posed the following question for the opinion
of the High Court:

a   'Whether an offence under s 99(1)(bb) and s 99(4)(a) of the Transport Act
1968 is committed by a refusal on the defendant's part to hand over
tachograph records to an authorised officer of the Vehicle Inspectorate upon
request in circumstances where: (i) the records are ready and available for
production to the officer; (ii) the officer refuses to accept production (and
inspection) at the defendant's premises of the records but requires them to
b   be handed over there and then for the officer to take away; (iii) the officer has
no reason to believe an offence under s 99(5) of the 1968 Act has been
committed in respect of any record or document inspected by him?'

[79] The magistrates posed also the question whether they were right to
conclude on the evidence before them that the defendant had committed an
c   offence in failing to hand over the tachograph records.

[80] The reference in the second question to the evidence is important. The
facts found by the magistrates were set out in six short subparagraphs of para 2 of
the case stated. Subparagraphs (a) and (b) relate to the status of the official who
visited the defendant's premises and the status of the defendant. Nothing turns
d   on them. It is necessary, however, for me to set out the other four subparagraphs:

'(c) The senior traffic examiner attended the defendant's company office
on Thursday, 1 October 1998 and met with the fleet manager, Mr Evans, and
the general manager, Mr Collins, and requested permission to remove the
tachograph charts in respect of August 1998; having previously made an
e   appointment for the meeting.
(d) Permission for removal was refused by the fleet manager, Mr Evans.
(e) The defendant company was prepared to allow the officer to inspect
the tachograph charts at their offices.
(f) The tachograph charts for August 1998 were never produced for
inspection or handed over to the Inspectorate.'
f

[81] These four subparagraphs show, it is said, that an offence under
s 99(1)(bb) and (4)(a) of the 1968 Act had been committed. It is important to
notice, however, that there was no finding at all about copying; there was no
finding as to whether reasonable facilities for inspection of the records or for
copying the records existed at the defendant's offices; there was no finding as to
g   the purpose of the Inspectorate in wanting to remove the records. Your
Lordships were told by counsel for the Inspectorate, Mr Plender QC, that the
purpose was to subject the records to inspection by technologically advanced
equipment located at the Inspectorate's own offices. But the magistrates made
no finding about this. Your Lordships do not know, and there is nothing to
h   suggest that the magistrates knew, whether it would have been practicable for
the Inspectorate to have brought the equipment to the defendant's office and
operated it there. There is nothing to show that the defendant was told about the
reason why the Inspectorate deemed it necessary, or desirable, to remove the
records for inspection at their own office. There is nothing to indicate for how
j   long the Inspectorate might have needed to retain the records or that any
indication about the duration of the retention was given to the defendant.

[82] On the bare facts as found by the magistrates, the question posed for the
Divisional Court was a very stark one: is an offence committed simply by an
operator's refusal to permit an inspector to remove tachograph records and
without regard to whether the request was in the circumstances a reasonable
one?

[83] Mr Plender's response was that the law provides, by way of judicial review proceedings, a remedy for unreasonable behaviour by officials. I think that this response is correct. But its implications need to be followed through. A remedy in judicial review proceedings for an unreasonable request by an inspector for the removal of documents would have to be based on the premise that the request was in the circumstances an unlawful one in that it went beyond the power conferred by the statute. In that event the operator would have no obligation to comply with the request and an offence would not be committed by his refusal to comply with it. It must, therefore, in principle be open to an operator charged with failing to comply with a request made under s 99(1)(bb) to contend that the request was in all the circumstances an unreasonable one. It does not appear, however, that the defendant did so contend.

[84] The submissions made, both to your Lordships and in the Divisional Court, about the correct construction to be placed on s 99(1)(bb) of the 1968 Act did not mention at all the need that an inspector's request should not be one that in the circumstances was unreasonable. Mr Phillips QC, for the defendant, simply submitted that the vehicle operator did not have to comply with a request that the inspector be permitted to remove the records for inspection and copying elsewhere. If inspection at the Inspectorate's offices was desired, the inspector had to serve a notice of not less than ten days requiring the vehicle operator to produce the records at the office of the traffic commissioner. Otherwise, the only obligation placed on the operator was to permit inspection and copying at its own premises.

[85] Mr Plender, for the Inspectorate, submitted that s 99(1)(bb) obliged the operator to permit the inspector to remove the records for inspection and copying elsewhere whenever the inspector desired to do so.

[86] The Divisional Court ([2000] RTR 286) preferred the construction contended for by the Inspectorate, and concluded (at 304) that 'the operator is required to produce and hand over tachograph record sheets on demand at the operator's premises if such a request is made of him' and that 'it is within the discretion of the authorised officer whether he chooses to inspect the tachograph sheets at the operator's premises ... or take the sheets away for more thorough and detailed analysis' (para 36 of Butterfield J's judgment).

[87] While the basic approach to construction of Mr Plender is, in my opinion, to be preferred to that of Mr Phillips, Mr Plender's approach omits the limiting requirement that the inspector's request must not be an unreasonable one.

[88] Section 99(1) starts by saying that 'An officer may ... require any person to produce, and permit him to inspect and copy' the various documents specified. It is important to notice that this language does not give the officer any positive right other than to make a request. It places an obligation on the recipient of the request to comply with it. Failure to comply is an offence under sub-s (4)(a). The officer's request, and the operator's consequent obligation, has two elements to it. First, the request is for production of the documents. So the operator must produce them. Second, the request is for permission to inspect and copy the documents. So the operator must permit the officer to do so. As to production of the documents, the operator must be allowed a reasonable time for compliance. What constitutes a reasonable time will depend upon the content of the request. Many requests for production of documents could reasonably be expected to be complied with then and there. In respect of others, some time for compliance might be necessary. This was not a problem in the present case where the original request was made on 15 September 1998 and the repeat of the request

a took place on 1 October. The intervening period of two weeks was plainly ample for the August 1998 tachograph records to have been collected and produced.

[89] The request to be permitted to inspect and copy the records may present more difficulty. Both inspection and copying require facilities. The facilities may be available at the operator's premises or they may not. The equipment necessary for the inspection and copying, if not already available at the operator's premises,
b may or may not be able to be brought there. The statutory obligation on the operator to 'permit' the officer to inspect and copy must require the officer to be given a reasonable opportunity to inspect and copy. What constitutes a reasonable opportunity will depend on the circumstances of the case and the content of the particular request.

[90] The memorandum of conviction in the present case was drafted on the
c footing that a failure to permit records to be taken away constituted a failure 'to produce'. This, in my opinion, was an error. A failure to allow documents to be taken away for inspection and copying may constitute a failure to permit inspection and copying, but does not constitute a failure to produce, particularly where production for inspection on site is offered to the inspector but refused by
d him.

[91] Ordinarily, the obligation placed by s 99(1) on an operator 'to produce' the records is, in my opinion, discharged by their production at the operator's own premises. But the final four lines of s 99(1), referred to in argument as the 'coda', prescribes an alternative form of production if the requisite notice is given by the authorised officer.
e
[92] In the submissions to your Lordships both counsel tended to attribute to the word 'produced' in the coda a different meaning to that of the word 'produce' in the opening lines. In my opinion there is no difference in meaning. Both require the documents to be produced in the sense of being made physically available to the inspector. The only difference is as to the place where this is to happen. But, whether the production is at the operator's premises or at the traffic
f commissioner's office, the obligation on the operator to permit inspection and copying still applies. The coda prescribes a different place for the production but there apart the obligations placed on the person who is to produce the documents are the same. A reasonable opportunity for the inspector to inspect and copy must be afforded him.
g
[93] In summary, s 99(1) on its correct construction requires, in my opinion, that the vehicle operator provide the inspector with a reasonable opportunity to inspect and copy the tachograph records that under art 14(2) of Council Regulation (EEC) 3821/85 the operator is required to retain. A reasonable opportunity may require the inspector to be allowed to remove the records in order
h to subject them to examination by equipment located elsewhere. Subsection (10) makes clear that inspection need not be confined to visual inspection. But if the inspection and copying can be carried out at the operator's premises, if the removal of the records would have a disruptive effect on the operator's business, if the equipment in question can be taken to the operator's premises and operated
j there without too much difficulty, it may be that the request to be allowed to remove the records for inspection and copying will be an unreasonable one. If that is so, for those or any other reasons that may apply in a particular case, the operator will, in my opinion, have no obligation to comply with the unreasonable request for the removal of the records.

[94] This construction of s 99(1) seems to me consistent with the other subsections.

[95] Subsection (2) gives a positive right to an inspector (i) to enter a vehicle and (ii) to enter premises in order to inspect a vehicle and to inspect and copy any records which he finds in the vehicle or the premises. These rights of inspection and copying are independent of any permission granted by the operator and, in my opinion, would permit the officer to take away the records if it were reasonably necessary for him to do so for the purpose of inspection or copying.

[96] Subsection (6) confers on an inspector a positive right to seize records or other documents he has inspected under the section if he has reason to believe they have been falsified.

[97] The construction accords also with the second sentence of art 14(2). Article 14(2) requires the records to be 'produced or handed over'. One of the unsatisfactory features of the present case, to my mind, is that the verb 'hand over' has been given an extended meaning so as to cover the taking away of the documents and that the verb 'produce' has been given an extended meaning so as to cover the inspection of the documents. In my opinion these verbs should be confined to their ordinary meaning. A document is 'produced' to an inspector if it is physically presented to him. A document is 'handed over' to an inspector if it is placed for the time being in his possession. Section 99(1) provides expressly for the production of documents to an inspector and, unless the documents are handed over to the inspector, he cannot very well inspect or copy them. Neither art 14(2) nor s 99(1) provides any express right for an officer to take away elsewhere documents that have been handed to him for inspection and copying. But sub-s (1), in my opinion, requires the operator to permit him to do so, and sub-s (2) allows him to do so, unless the officer's decision to take them away is an unreasonable decision in all the circumstances.

[98] It appears that, at the trial before the magistrates, neither the appellant nor the Inspectorate directed itself to the reasonableness or otherwise of the inspector's request to be allowed to take the records away in order to subject them to examination at the Inspectorate's own offices. In my opinion, if an operator charged with an offence under ss 99(1)(bb) and 99(4)(a) wishes to contend that the officer's decision to take away the records for inspection and copying elsewhere was in all the circumstances an unreasonable one, it is for him to say so. And I think the officer must then be prepared to explain, why the removal of the documents was thought necessary. That explanation and its adequacy can then be tested.

[99] It has been made clear to your Lordships that this is a test case, brought to determine the extent of the obligations cast on vehicle operators by s 99(1)(bb) and of the corresponding legitimate expectations of the Inspectorate. In striking the balance between an effective regulatory system on the one hand and the interests of vehicle operators in being free of excessive intrusion by officials on the other, the key, in my opinion, is the reasonable requirements of the officials whose duty it is to monitor the regulatory system. Section 99 contemplates, in my view, that, in general, the inspection and copying should take place where the records are produced and handed over, ie at the operator's premises or, after the requisite notice, at the traffic commissioner's office. If, however, it is not reasonably practicable in the circumstances for the inspection and copying to take place at the operator's premises, the operator should, in my opinion, permit the records to be taken away for the purpose of inspection and copying elsewhere. On a prosecution under s 99(4)(a), or for that matter, s 99(4)(b), where the gravamen of the charge is that the operator has not permitted, or has hindered, the removal

a of the documents, the operator cannot, in my opinion, be convicted if the request to be permitted to remove them was so unreasonable as to be unlawful.

[**100**] It follows that I would deal with the first question posed in the case stated by answering that an offence would be committed in the postulated circumstances unless the request to be permitted to remove the records for inspection and copying to take place elsewhere than at the appellant's premises

b were unreasonable in all the circumstances. For the purposes of this answer, 'inspection' of a record includes 'the application to the record of any process for eliciting the information recorded thereby and … taking down the information elicited from it': see s 99(10).

[**101**] As to the second question, I would reply that, on the facts found as recorded in the case stated and in the absence of any contention that the officer's

c request to be allowed to remove the documents for inspection elsewhere was an unreasonable one, the justices were right to convict.

[**102**] I would, therefore, dismiss the appeal.

Appeal dismissed.

Dilys Tausz   Barrister.

Goode v Martin   *a*

[2001] EWCA Civ 1899

COURT OF APPEAL, CIVIL DIVISION

BROOKE, LATHAM AND KAY LJJ

22 NOVEMBER, 13 DECEMBER 2001   *b*

Pleading – Amendment – Permission to amend after expiry of limitation period – New claim – Claimant seeking permission for post-limitation amendment to statement of claim to add alternative claim based on facts put forward in the defence – Rule of procedure allowing post-limitation amendment to add new claim only if new claim *c* *arising out of same facts as a claim in respect of which claimant had already claimed a remedy – Whether possible to interpret rule in manner giving effect to claimant's right of access to court under human rights convention – Human Rights Act 1998, s 3(1), Sch 1, Pt I, art 6 – CPR 17.4(2).*

In August 1996 the claimant, a novice sailor, suffered serious head injuries in an *d* accident on board a racing yacht owned by the defendant, a very experienced sailor and yachtmaster. As a result of her injuries, the claimant suffered ten minutes pre-accident amnesia, and was therefore dependent on others to tell her what had happened. She commenced proceedings against the defendant in October 1997, the writ being endorsed with a statement of claim. The pleading *e* ascribed the accident to a 'car' having come free of the guide-rail in which it was designed to travel and having struck the claimant on the head. Seven different allegations of negligence were made, all concerned with different aspects of the defendant's failure to inspect the condition of the roller elements of the car. A curt defence was served in November 1997. In January 1998 the defendant's solicitors sent the claimant's solicitor a draft amended defence containing, for the *f* first time, the defendant's account of how the accident had happened. According to his version of events, the claimant had struck her head on the cockpit after being hit by the mainsheet. The defendant served an amended defence in February 1999, but a draft amended statement of claim, putting the claimant's case on an alternative basis to that already pleaded, was not served until April *g* 2000, some eight months after the expiry of the limitation period. The defendant opposed the claimant's application for permission to amend, even though the proposed amendment was founded on the version of the facts that he was setting out to prove at trial. He relied on CPR 17.4(2)[a] which permitted the court to allow a post-limitation amendment 'whose effect will be to add ... a new *h* claim, but only if the new claim arises out of the same facts or substantially the same facts as a claim in respect of which the party applying for permission has already claimed a remedy in the proceedings'. The master refused to allow the amendment, holding that the new claim did not arise out of the same facts as a claim in respect of which the claimant had already claimed a remedy within the meaning of r 17.4(2). His decision was affirmed on appeal by the judge, and the *j* claimant appealed to the Court of Appeal. On the appeal, the claimant contended that the proposed amendment was permissible if r 17.4(2) was interpreted as if it read: 'The court may allow an amendment whose effect will be to add ... a new claim, but only if the new claim arises out of the same facts or substantially the a same facts as *are already in issue on* a claim in respect of which the party applying for permission has already claimed a remedy in the proceedings.' The issues arose (i) whether r 17.4(2) could be so interpreted on normal principles of construction, and (ii) if not, whether it was possible under s 3(1)[b] of the Human Rights Act 1998 to read the italicised words into r 17.4(2) in order to give effect to the claimant's right of access to the court under art 6(1)[c] of the European

b Convention for the Protection of Human Rights and Fundamental Freedoms 1950 (as set out in Sch 1 to the 1998 Act).

Held – Although it would not have been possible, on conventional principles of construction, to interpret CPR 17.4(2) so as to produce a just result, the 1998 Act had altered the position. No sound policy reason could be detected why the

c claimant should not add to her claim the alternative plea which she proposed. No new facts were being introduced: she merely wished to say that if the defendant succeeded in establishing his version of the facts, she would still win because those facts, too, showed that he had been negligent and should pay her compensation. In those circumstances, to prevent her from putting that case

d before the court in the instant action would impose an impediment on her access to the court which would require justification. When applied to the facts of the instant case, r 17.4(2), as interpreted by the master and the judge, did not have any legitimate aim and, even if it did, the means used by the rule-maker would not be reasonably proportionate to that aim. Under s 3(1) of the 1998 Act, however, it was possible to interpret the rule in the manner suggested by the

e claimant. In that way there would be no violation of her rights under art 6 of the convention, and the court would be enabled to deal with the case justly, as it was adjured to do by the CPR. Accordingly, the appeal would be allowed (see [41]–[47], [49], [50], below).

Decision of Colman J [2001] 3 All ER 562 reversed.

f **Notes**

For the convention right of access to a court and for post-limitation amendments to statements of case, see respectively 8(2) *Halsbury's Laws* (4th edn reissue) para 141 and 37 *Halsbury's Laws* (4th edn reissue) para 677.

For the Human Rights Act 1998, s 3, Sch 1, Pt I, art 6, see 7 *Halsbury's Statutes*

g (4th edn) (1999 reissue) 502, 523.

Cases referred to in judgments

Ashingdane v UK (1985) 7 EHRR 528, ECt HR.

Cachia v Faluyi [2001] EWCA Civ 998, [2002] 1 All ER 192, [2001] 1 WLR 1966, CA.

Fannon v Backhouse [1987] CA Transcript 829, (1987) Times, 22 August.

h *Lloyds Bank plc v Rogers* [1996] CA Transcript 1904, [1997] TLR 154.

Mitchell v Harris Engineering Co Ltd [1967] 2 All ER 682, [1967] 2 QB 703, [1967] 3 WLR 447, CA.

R v A [2001] UKHL 25, [2001] 3 All ER 1, [2001] 2 WLR 1586.

Rodriguez v Parker [1966] 2 All ER 349, [1967] 1 QB 116, [1966] 3 WLR 546.

j *Weldon v Neal* (1887) 19 QBD 394, CA.

Welsh Development Agency v Redpath Dorman Long Ltd [1994] 4 All ER 10, [1994] 1 WLR 1409, CA.

b Section 3(1) provides: 'So far as it is possible to do so, primary legislation and subordinate legislation must be read and given effect in a way which is compatible with the Convention rights.'

c Article 6, so far as material, provides: '1. In the determination of his civil rights ... everyone is entitled to a fair ... hearing ... '

Appeal

The claimant, Virginia Goode, appealed from the decision of Colman J on
7 November 2000, for which reasons were given on 14 December 2000 ([2001]
3 All ER 562), dismissing her appeal from the order of the Admiralty Registrar
(Master Miller) on 16 June 2000 dismissing her application for permission to
amend her statement of claim in proceedings for negligence against the defendant,
Hugh Martin. The facts are set out in the judgment of Brooke LJ.

Peter Ralls QC and *Stuart Hornett* (instructed by *Barker Gillette*) for the claimant.
Jervis Kay QC and *John Russell* (instructed by *Lester Aldridge*, Bournemouth) for the
    defendant.

Cur adv vult

13 December 2001. The following judgments were delivered.

BROOKE LJ.

[1] This is an appeal by the claimant, Virginia Goode, against an order of
Colman J dated 7 November 2000 ([2001] 3 All ER 562), dismissing her appeal
against an order of the Admiralty Registrar, Master Miller, dated 16 June 2000,
refusing her permission to make certain amendments to her statement of claim.
In this respect the appeal to this court is a second appeal. The judge also dismissed
her application for permission to make these amendments on grounds not argued
before the master, namely that they did not raise claims or causes of action in
respect of which the relevant period of limitation had expired. She had contended
in this context that she did not acquire knowledge of relevant facts for the
purposes of ss 11 and 14 of the Limitation Act 1980 (the 1980 Act) until 23 January
1998, when the defendant's solicitor 'served' a draft amended defence. She also
appeals against that part of the judge's order. She does not appeal against his
refusal to exercise his discretion under s 33 of the 1980 Act to disapply the
provisions of that Act in her favour if all her other arguments failed, and I need
not say anything about that aspect of the case.

[2] The claimant is now 28. She obtained a law degree at London University
and completed the solicitors' legal practice course satisfactorily. She was due to
start a training contract with a well-known firm of London solicitors when
she suffered a catastrophic accident on the defendant's yacht on the Solent on
24 August 1996.

[3] The defendant, Hugh Martin, is a very experienced sailor and yachtsmaster.
Recently he was away from this country for about a year participating in the
Millennial Round the World yacht race. In 1996 he owned an Oyster SJ35 racing
yacht called the Ocean Cavalier. He invited a group of people to join him on the
yacht over the August bank holiday weekend. They included Mr Dominic
Nicholls and his wife Erica, and Erica Nicholls' brother Miles Holberry and his
wife Helen. Erica was also allowed to invite two friends, the claimant and a girl
called Sarah, to join the party of eight, which was completed by Ms Elspeth
Smedley.

[4] Dominic Nicholls had known the claimant's family for many years. His
wife Erica first met her in the summer of 1994, when they had worked together
for the same firm. They then became close friends. Mr Nicholls had served in the
army with the defendant, and he was a competent sailor himself. The defendant
had invited Mr and Mrs Nicholls to go sailing with him on a few previous

a occasions, so that Mrs Nicholls had a basic knowledge of how things operated on a yacht. The claimant, on the other hand, was a novice so far as sailing was concerned.

[5] It appears that the party sailed across to the Isle of Wight on the Friday evening and moored there. The following morning was sunny. They sailed on to Cowes, and had lunch on board. They were planning to stay overnight at
b Lymington or Yarmouth, but the weather deteriorated in the afternoon, and the defendant decided to alter course and sail up the Beaulieu river. It was while he was gybing that the accident happened.

[6] The claimant suffered a near fatal head injury. Soon after the accident happened, she was taken by a naval helicopter to a local naval hospital. Mr and
c Mrs Nicholls joined her there, and they accompanied her that night to a hospital at Southampton, not leaving until 4 or 5 am on the Sunday morning, by which time her parents had arrived. She was then in a coma for about four and a half days. She also suffered from ten minutes pre-accident amnesia. She has therefore always depended on others to tell her what happened. She was originally placed on a life-support machine; but she slowly recovered, and was discharged home
d from hospital on 9 September 1996. Her left frontal lobe, left cerebral hemisphere and left labyrinth were all damaged. There was no question of her being able to pursue her career as a solicitor for the time being. When she saw a consultant neurologist, Dr Savundra, a year later, her main concern was whether she would ever be able to return to her employment. She had problems with her concentration,
e she felt generally tired, and her physical and mental stamina were low. Dr Savundra believed that part of her symptoms were due to a failure to compensate for her peripheral vestibular lesion (which was susceptible to treatment), and part were due to her brain injuries for which no specific therapy was available.

f [7] During the first two years after the accident she was under the care of hospitals and clinics for much of the time. She then felt able to embark on her training contract, which she found extremely difficult. She was later to tell her solicitor that her life was entirely made up of working and sleeping. It was a daily struggle, and she never knew whether she would be able to work till the end of the week, or even for another day. On many occasions she had to be picked up
g from work because she was physically incapable of getting home by public transport. She focused on her work to the exclusion of everything else, because this was the only way she was able to carry on working. In July 2000 she told the court in a witness statement that it continued to be a great struggle for her to continue with her training contract. I mention these matters because it might
h otherwise have seemed strange that she did not pursue this litigation with the vigour that might have been expected of a trainee solicitor.

[8] I turn now to the history of this litigation. It appears that the claimant picked up some information about what happened from friends and family who visited her in hospital. In October 1996 she received letters from Mrs Nicholls and
j Ms Smedley. The former gave her contact addresses for everyone who was on the yacht at the time of the accident. She also told her that Sarah, Ms Smedley and the defendant had all written statements the day after the accident, which were being kept at the defendant's parents' home. She suggested that her lawyer should ask the defendant for them. Finally, she wished her good luck and encouraged her to get everything she was entitled to. In the other letter Ms Smedley explained that she had been at the bow, and did not actually see the incident. She

gave the claimant her telephone number in case she wanted to talk about the
boat.   *a*

[9] The claimant has engaged four firms of solicitors during the course of this litigation. She originally instructed a local firm of solicitors in Southgate, who wrote letters on her behalf to the defendant on 7 October and 8 November 1996. The defendant did not reply to either of them. The papers were then passed to a new firm, who wrote to him on 19 November. They urged him to furnish them   *b* immediately with the name, address and policy number of his insurers, and to confirm that he had notified them of their client's claim. They also required him to provide them with nine separate items of information or copy documents, and to undertake not to remove or interfere in any way with the boat, and in particular with the 'car' which they understood to be the cause of their client's injuries. They also told him they had applied for legal aid. Mr Martin maintained   *c* his policy of not replying.

[10] Nearly eleven months then elapsed before the writ was issued. It was endorsed with a statement of claim in which the accident was ascribed to the 'car' coming free of the guide-rail in which it was designed to travel and striking the claimant on the head. I will refer to the role of this 'car' in [16], below. Seven   *d* different allegations of negligence were made, all concerned with different aspects of the defendant's failure to inspect the condition of the roller elements of the car, all four of which were so worn as to require replacement.

[11] On 25 November Mr Martin finally broke his silence, although his defence was curt in the extreme. Paragraph 1 contained an admission that the claimant was on his yacht at his invitation on the day and in the place she had alleged. Paragraph 2   *e* contained general denials of negligence and causation. Paragraph 3 contained a non-admission of personal injuries, loss and damage. Paragraph 4 contained a positive averment that the accident was all her own fault, alternatively that she was guilty of contributory negligence. Paragraph 5 contained a general denial of the claim, and para 6 contained a general traverse. The only chink of light about   *f* Mr Martin's case was contained in the particulars of contributory negligence: (i) failing to heed the defendant's instructions to remain seated while the vessel was in the process of gybing towards the entrance to the Beaulieu river; (ii) failing to take any or any sufficient care for her own safety both generally and specifically whilst seated and in the vicinity of the mainsheet and traveller. On 26 November 1997 the claimant's solicitor served a notice to admit the fact that all four rollers   *g* of the car fractured just before the claimant suffered her injury. The defendant declined to admit anything.

[12] The claimant was still in a very shaky state of health, as Dr Savundra's September 1997 report shows. She encountered, however, an almost unbroken wall of silence when her solicitors wrote on her behalf in October 1997 to five of   *h* the people who had been in the boat when she had her accident. Mr and Mrs Holberry did not reply to their letter. Nor did Ms Smedley. Mrs Nicholls, however, did respond, and on 24 October 1997 the claimant's solicitor visited her at her home near Stockbridge to take a witness statement from her. He sent a draft for her approval to her four days later.   *j*

[13] In this draft statement Mrs Nicholls explained how the yachting party had been made up, and how Mr Martin had held a drill before they sailed, explaining how everything on the boat worked and how it was operated. She described the history of events until the weather deteriorated on the Saturday afternoon. She said that everyone became wet and miserable when it began to rain, and the wind got stronger. Mr Martin decided to head for Beaulieu, and he took over the helm

a   from the claimant, who came to sit with Mrs Nicholls in the cockpit, directly in front of him. She then described the gybe, and said that as they were performing it, the ropes suddenly went slack. She now believed that this was because the car had shattered. Although she did not actually see the shattered car strike the claimant, she saw her from the corner of her eye fall backwards very quickly. As she turned around she saw her hit her head on the cockpit floor. She had no

b   doubt in her mind that it was the car shattering that was the original cause of the accident.

[14] In his covering letter dated 28 October 1997 the claimant's solicitor invited her either to approve the draft statement or to make any changes to it she wished to make. He added that while he fully appreciated Mr Nicholls' position, he would like the opportunity of having a brief discussion with him, and he

c   invited her to ask him to telephone him at his own convenience. On 5 November 1997 Mrs Nicholls replied to the effect that she had decided to 'withdraw' her witness statement. Whilst she fully appreciated the claimant's unfortunate position, she was no longer willing to be a part of any proceedings that might have 'a negative effect' on Mr Martin. She added that her husband had also

d   chosen to take no part in any case against Mr Martin. The wall of silence was now complete.

[15] On 23 January 1998 the defendant's solicitors sent the claimant's solicitor a draft amended defence. This contained by amendment a limitation plea under s 185 and Pts I and II of Sch 7 of the Merchant Shipping Act 1995, on which nothing at present turns, except that this plea contained for the first time the

e   defendant's account of how the accident happened. It went along the following lines.

[16] The Ocean Cavalier was approaching the vicinity of the mouth of the Beaulieu River on a starboard gybe, with the boom out to port. The foresail was lowered. Mr Martin was on the helm. He warned the crew that he was going to

f   gybe and instructed them what to do during the gybe. He told them to be aware of the boom. The claimant was seated at the aft end of the cockpit to the starboard of the helmsman and aft of the mainsheet traveller track. This track ran athwart the vessel, and the mainsheet block and tackle was attached to it by a moving 'car'. Mr Martin told the claimant she was fine where she was.

g   [17] As the gybe commenced, Mrs Nicholls was situated in the cockpit, taking in the mainsheet in accordance with her instructions. The claimant then leaned over to help her, with the mass of her torso across the mainsheet track. Mr Martin shouted a warning to her, but the boom swung across at almost the same time, and the claimant was struck on her side by the mainsheet itself. She was knocked down as a result, and struck her head on the side of the cockpit.

h   [18] The defendant's solicitors did not obtain leave to amend their defence until 16 October 1998 when Moore-Bick J also gave the claimant leave to amend her statement of claim as to the matters contained in the amended defence within 21 days of the service of that pleading. He directed a trial as to liability and/or limitation of damage first. The defendant's solicitors then waited for a further

j   three-and-a-half months before serving the amended defence.

[19] A delay then occurred in the conduct of the proceedings between 2 February 1999, when the defendant's solicitors served their amended defence, and 10 March 2000 when the claimant's solicitors gave notice of intention to proceed. A third firm of solicitors came on the record on the claimant's behalf in February 1999, and that year appears to have been devoted to tidying up points of detail before the papers were submitted to counsel to consider amendments to

the statement of claim. In May 1999 the defendant's solicitors told them that the damaged car could not be found after the incident, despite extensive searches. A delay of seven months then occurred before effective arrangements were made for the claimant's expert to inspect the boat. In February 2000 the claimant changed her solicitors again. On 14 April 2000 the claimant's new solicitors served on the defendant's solicitors the draft amended statement of claim which they were now seeking leave to serve.

[20] The defendant's solicitors now contended that the claimant should not be allowed to make this amendment, notwithstanding that it was founded on the version of the facts which their own client was setting out to prove at the trial. They relied in this context on CPR 17.4(1) and (2) which provide, so far as is material:

'(1) This rule applies where—(a) a party applies to amend his statement of case in one of the ways mentioned in this rule; and (b) a period of limitation has expired under—(i) the Limitation Act 1980 ...

(2) The court may allow an amendment whose effect will be to add or substitute a new claim, but only if the new claim arises out of the same facts or substantially the same facts as a claim in respect of which the party applying for permission has already claimed a remedy in the proceedings.'

[21] On 16 June 2000 Master Miller refused to allow the amendment. He said that the defendant would suffer no prejudice from a factual point of view in dealing with the amendments, which flowed from what the defendant had said in his amended defence. He added that although there had been a remarkable delay in bringing the application, he would not have allowed this fact to tip the balance against the claimant so far as the exercise of his discretion was concerned. His difficulty, which he said he identified without any enthusiasm, was that the new claim did not arise out of the same facts as a claim in respect of which the claimant had already claimed a remedy. He said that he therefore had no jurisdiction to allow the amendment.

[22] When the claimant appealed to Colman J she added a new contention that the relevant limitation period had not in fact expired because she had not acquired knowledge of the relevant facts within the meaning of ss 11 and 14 of the 1980 Act until 23 January 1998 when the draft amended defence was served on her solicitors.

[23] Colman J upheld Master Miller's decision but shared his lack of enthusiasm for the result. In dismissing the appeal, he also considered and rejected a new argument founded on s 35 of the 1980 Act. He also rejected the new s 14 argument.

[24] In this context he applied a test set out in the decision of this court in *Welsh Development Agency v Redpath Dorman Long Ltd* [1994] 4 All ER 10 at 26, [1994] 1 WLR 1409 at 1425. He said that the claimant should only be given leave to amend if she could show that the defendant did not have a reasonably arguable case on limitation which would be prejudiced if he allowed the amendment. The defendant had argued that the only two matters of which the claimant did not have actual knowledge before November 1997 (three years before the hearing before Colman J) were the fact that she had been struck by the mainsheet and, less importantly, the fact that there was a wind speed of force seven from the west south west. Colman J held that it was arguable that if the solicitor then acting for the claimant had acted with reasonable diligence he would have been able to ascertain these two facts before that date. He was not willing to conclude that

a any earlier attempt that he had made to obtain additional evidence from those on board the yacht would necessarily have been futile.

[25] On this further appeal Mr Ralls QC, who appears for the claimant, has sought to bolster his primary case by the addition of a new argument based on art 6 of the European Convention for the Protection of Human Rights and Fundamental Freedoms 1950 (as set out in Sch 1 to the Human Rights Act 1998)

b which was not pursued before the judge. He says that if he fails in his contention that these amendments should be allowed on a conventional interpretation of CPR 17.4(2), then we ought to apply a more unconventional, yet possible, approach to interpretation. If we do not, the argument runs, his client's right of access to a court would be impaired by a restriction which impaired the essence of that right and did not have a legitimate aim. Even if a legitimate aim could be

c shown, the restriction employed means which were not reasonably proportionate to that aim (for these tests see *Ashingdane v UK* (1985) 7 EHRR 528 at 546–547 (para 57)). In order to consider the arguments on r 17.4(2) it is first necessary to say something about the legislative history.

[26] So far as primary legislation is concerned, it is necessary only to consider

d s 28 of the Limitation Act 1939 both in its original form and in its form as substituted by s 8 of the Limitation Amendment Act 1980. So far as the court is aware, there were no changes to s 28 in the intervening years. In its original form, the section provided:

e 'For the purposes of this Act, any claim by way of set-off or counterclaim shall be deemed to be a separate action and to have been commenced on the same date as the action in which the set-off or counterclaim is pleaded.'

[27] Between 1939 and 1980 no provision was made in primary legislation for the situation in which a party wished to add to its statement of claim a new cause

f of action founded on the same facts or substantially the same facts as had already been pleaded. Such provision was made for the first time in the greatly enlarged version of s 28 which was substituted in 1980, and consolidated in the same year as s 35 of the 1980 Act. The new s 35 (which is still in force) provides, so far as is material:

g '(1) For the purposes of this Act, any new claim made in the course of any action shall be deemed to be a separate action and to have been commenced— (a) in the case of a new claim made in or by way of third party proceedings, on the date on which those proceedings were commenced; and (b) in the case of any other new claim, on the same date as the original action.

h (2) In this section a new claim means any claim by way of set-off or counterclaim, and any claim involving either—(a) the addition or substitution of a new cause of action; or (b) the addition or substitution of a new party ...

(3) Except as provided by section 33 of this Act or by rules of court, neither the High Court nor any county court shall allow a new claim within

j subsection (1)(b) above ... to be made in the course of any action after the expiry of any time limit under this Act which would affect a new action to enforce that claim ...

(4) Rules of court may provide for allowing a new claim to which subsection (3) above applies to be made as there mentioned, but only if the conditions specified in subsection (5) below are satisfied, and subject to any further restrictions the rules may impose.

(5) The conditions referred to in subsection (4) above are the following— *a*
(a) in the case of a claim involving a new cause of action, if the new cause of
action arises out of the same facts or substantially the same facts as are
already in issue on any claim previously made in the original action ...'

[28] So much for primary legislation. So far as the practice of the High Court
was concerned, the rules governing amendments prior to the 1965 revision of the
Rules of the Supreme Court were set out in the judgment of this court in *Weldon v* *b*
Neal (1887) 19 QBD 394. In that case the court held that a plaintiff would not be
permitted to amend a statement of claim by setting up fresh claims in respect of
causes of action which had become statute-barred since the issue of the writ.
[29] In 1965 Ord 20, r 5 of the Rules of the Supreme Court 1965 was
introduced with the effect of changing this practice in certain ways. So far as is *c*
material, it provided:

'(2) Where an application to the Court for leave to make the amendment
mentioned in paragraph (3), (4) or (5) is made after any relevant period of
limitation current at the date of issue of the writ has expired, the Court may
nevertheless grant such leave in the circumstances mentioned in that *d*
paragraph if it thinks it just to do so ...
(5) An amendment may be allowed under paragraph (2) notwithstanding
that the effect of the amendment will be to add or substitute a new cause of
action if the new cause of action arises out of the same facts or substantially
the same facts as a cause of action in respect of which relief has already been
claimed in the action by the party applying for leave to make the amendment.' *e*

[30] The power of the Rules Committee to introduce these new rules without
the assistance of primary legislation soon came under fire, but it was upheld in
Rodriguez v Parker [1966] 2 All ER 349, [1967] 1 QB 116 and *Mitchell v Harris*
Engineering Co Ltd [1967] 2 All ER 682, [1967] 2 QB 703 for reasons which it is not *f*
now necessary to describe.
[31] The Law Reform Committee considered these rules in its *Twenty-First*
Report: Final Report on Limitation of Actions (Cmnd 6923), published in 1977. After
explaining the terms of RSC Ord 20, r 5 it said (at p 67 (para 5.12)):

'The Senior Master, who has suggested to us that the discretion of the *g*
court to allow an amendment of pleadings should be stated much more
widely than it now is, has helpfully drawn our attention to the terminology
used in Rule 15(c) of the American Federal Rules of Procedure, under which
a new cause of action may be added by amendment if "it arises out of the
conduct, transaction or occurrence of events set forth or attempted to be set
forth in the original proceedings". We have considered whether some such *h*
words as these might be preferable to those used in the existing R.S.C.; but
we doubt whether they add anything to the rule we have quoted above. The
object of any such rule must, as we see it, be twofold. First, it ought to
permit a plaintiff to amend his pleadings so as to make good the error of
failing to tell the complete legal story at the outset. Secondly, it ought to be *j*
drawn sufficiently narrowly so as to prevent the plaintiff from instituting,
under the guise of an amendment to an existing claim and after the limitation
period has run, proceedings which are wholly distinct from those covered by
the writ as originally framed. On the whole, we think that the existing rule
achieves this object and goes as far in giving the court a discretion as the
substantive law does, or should, permit. The American formula is probably

a consistent with our own substantive law, but we doubt whether its adoption would make any practical difference; nor do we think it is intrinsically superior to the existing words of the R.S.C.'

[32] It follows that the committee decided to make no change to the existing rules to cover a case like the present, where the claimant wishes to add a new *b* cause of action which arises out of the occurrence of events set forth in the proceedings as they stood before the proposed amendment. It does not appear to have considered the kind of situation with which we are at present concerned.

[33] The pre-consolidation Limitation Amendment Act 1980 was the vehicle by which many of the committee's recommendations were passed into law. I have already set out the new statutory scheme it introduced by way of *c* substitution of s 28 of the 1939 Act. Changes were subsequently made to the wording of RSC Ord 20, r 5(4), but r 5(5) remained unaltered. When the CPR were introduced in 1999, CPR 17.4(2) was in substantially the same terms as RSC Ord 20, r 5(5), with the substitution of the word 'claim' for the expression 'cause of action'.

d [34] I return now to s 35 of the 1980 Act (for its terms, see [27], above) in order to make two points. The first is that the language chosen by Parliament in s 35(5)(a) is apt to embrace the concept contained in r 15(c) of the American Federal Rules of Procedure and the situation that has arisen in the present case. The claimant's new cause of action does indeed arise out of the same facts as are already in issue on her claim. The second is that neither the former Rules *e* Committee nor the Civil Procedure Rules Committee have ever evinced any intention or desire to use their power under s 35(4) to add any additional restrictions to the rules permitting post-limitation amendments. So far as the first of these points is concerned, it has received judicial support from Hobhouse LJ, with whom Peter Gibson and Simon Brown LJJ both agreed, in *Lloyds Bank plc v* *f* *Rogers* [1996] CA Transcript 1904, [1997] TLR 154 when he said of s 35:

'The policy of the section was that, if factual issues were in any event going to be litigated between the parties, the parties should be able to rely upon any cause of action which substantially arises from those facts.'

g [35] We now possess more tools for enabling us to do justice than were available before April 1999. Since then, the CPR and the provisions of the 1998 Act have come into force. By the former we must seek to give effect to the overriding objective of dealing with cases justly when we interpret any rule (see CPR 1.2(b)). By the latter we must read and give effect to subordinate legislation, *h* so far as it is possible to do so, in a way which is compatible with the convention rights set out in Sch 1 to the Act (see s 3(1) of the 1998 Act).

[36] It is commonplace that the claimant must not be impeded in her right of access to a court for the determination of her civil rights unless any hindrance to such access can be justified in a way recognised by the relevant Strasbourg *j* jurisprudence (for the general principles, see *Cachia v Faluyi* [2001] EWCA Civ 998 at [17]–[20], [2002] 1 All ER 192 at [17]–[20], [2001] 1 WLR 1966). All she wants to do is to say that even if the accident happened in the way Mr Martin says it happened, he was nevertheless negligent for failing to take appropriate steps, as an experienced yachtsmaster, to protect her safety as a novice sailor. She does not want to rely on any facts which will not flow naturally from the way Mr Martin sets up the evidential basis of his defence at the trial.

[37] Mr Jervis Kay QC, who appeared for Mr Martin, encouraged us to adopt a narrow interpretation of both CPR 17.2 and s 35(5) of the 1980 Act. So far as the latter was concerned, he argued that the words 'the same facts as are already in issue on any claim' were not apt to embrace facts that were in issue on the defence to such a claim.

[38] He did not explain to us why, as a matter of policy, the meaning of the words should be restricted in this way. We suggested to him that it seemed to be unfair, if a defence was served at the end of, or just outside, the primary limitation period, a claimant could not riposte by saying: 'Well even if, which I dispute, the accident happened in that way, you were negligent because ...' His reply was that the claimant would have to issue a new claim, incorporating an appropriate plea under the 1980 Act, and consolidate that claim with her existing claim. It is hard to reconcile that expensive and cumbersome procedure with the philosophy of the overriding objective contained in the CPR.

[39] Mr Kay urged us to be cautious about relying on the dictum of Hobhouse LJ, because he was concerned with a quite different situation. He also took comfort from a dictum of Nourse LJ in *Fannon v Backhouse* [1987] CA Transcript 829, (1987) Times, 22 August when he said in a quite different factual context that he thought it clear that the words 'in issue on' meant 'material to' or the like. Again, Nourse LJ was not concerned with the situation which confronts us in the present case.

[40] As for the interpretation of CPR 17.4(2), Mr Kay encouraged us to adopt the narrow interpretation of the rule favoured by the judge and the master. The words 'out of the same facts or substantially the same facts as a claim' did not allow the court to consider facts which were put in issue by a defendant. This interpretation, he said, could work no injustice now that ss 11, 14 and 33 of the 1980 Act permitted the court to do justice in ways which were not possible before the amendments to the limitation legislation which came into effect from 1963 onwards. Even if the statute now allowed for a wider rule, we must interpret the rule as it stands, he said, and assume that the Rules Committee had deliberately decided to restrict its scope pursuant to its power under s 35(4).

[41] I have shown how there is no evidence that the committee ever did decide to introduce such a restriction. But for the introduction of the 1998 Act, however, an Act which was not in force when the master made his original ruling, I would have been of the view that Mr Kay's arguments on the construction of the rule (as opposed to the statute) were soundly based. Mr Ralls sought energetically to encourage us to read into the rule words which were not there. Without the encouragement of s 3(1) of the 1998 Act, I could see no way of interpreting the language of the rule so as to produce a just result.

[42] The 1998 Act, however, does in my judgment alter the position. I can detect no sound policy reason why the claimant should not add to her claim in the present action the alternative plea which she now proposes. No new facts are being introduced: she merely wants to say that if the defendant succeeds in establishing his version of the facts, she will still win because those facts, too, show that he was negligent and should pay her compensation.

[43] In these circumstances it seems to me that to prevent her from putting this case before the court in this action would impose an impediment on her access to the court which would require justification. If it cannot be justified, Mr Martin cannot then be heard to say that she could always bring another action. In such an action she would have to confront the argument that the six other people on the boat would probably have been willing to help her to

a understand what had happened if only her solicitor had approached them earlier, despite their later refusal to help her in any way. Why should she have to be troubled with this, one asks rhetorically, if there is no reasonable justification for the rule Mr Kay seeks to uphold.

[44] I do not consider that the rule, as interpreted by the master and the judge, has any legitimate aim when applied to the facts of the present case. Whether

b Mr Martin put forward his version of events (which the claimant now wishes to adopt) before or after the expiry of the primary limitation period ought to make no difference to her ability to adopt it as part of her case and say that if that was indeed what had happened, he had nevertheless been negligent. If she delayed unreasonably in putting forward her amended pleading, the master could have blocked it on those grounds, but he made it clear that he would not have

c exercised his discretion against her if the rule had permitted him to allow the amendment. Even if the rule had any legitimate aim in the circumstances of this case, the means used by the rule-maker (if we have to interpret the rule in the way favoured by the court below) would not be reasonably proportionate to that aim.

[45] The House of Lords has been showing us, most recently in *R v A* [2001]

d UKHL 25 at [44], [2001] 3 All ER 1 at [44], [2001] 2 WLR 1586, how we should approach the interpretative task imposed on us by s 3(1) of the 1998 Act. It is not necessary to read into this judgment the whole of the relevant passage in Lord Steyn's speech. It is sufficient only to quote two sentences:

e 'In accordance with the will of Parliament as reflected in s 3 it will sometimes be necessary to adopt an interpretation which linguistically may appear strained. The techniques to be used will not only involve the reading down of express language in a statute but also the implication of provisions.'

[46] Mr Ralls contended that we should interpret CPR 17.4(2) as if it contained the additional words 'are already in issue on'. It would therefore read, so far as is

f material:

'The court may allow an amendment whose effect will be to add ... a new claim, but only if the new claim arises out of the same facts or substantially the same facts as *are already in issue on* a claim in respect of which the party applying for permission has already claimed a remedy in the proceedings.'

g (Emphasis added.)

This would bring the sense of the rule in line with the language of the 1980 Act, which is the source of the authority to make the rules contained in CPR 17.4.

[47] In my judgment it is possible, using the techniques identified by Lord Steyn in *R v A*, to interpret the rule in the manner for which Mr Ralls contends.

h In this way there would be no question of a violation of the claimant's art 6(1) rights, and the court would be able to deal with the case justly, as we are adjured to do by the CPR. I would therefore permit the amendment and allow the appeal. A case management conference should be heard at an early date with a view to setting a timetable for an early trial after all the delays that have recently

j occurred.

[48] In these circumstances it is not necessary to consider Mr Ralls's alternative arguments in any detail. I can say quite briefly, however, that I consider that the judge was correct to reject the arguments which placed the claimant's date of knowledge unarguably at the time when her solicitors received the amended defence. Mr Martin was entitled as a matter of law, if he chose to descend to that level, to run the unattractive argument that his loyal trappist friends might have

been disposed, after all, to help the grievously injured claimant if only her
solicitor had approached them earlier. It would not have been right to shut out *a*
an argument along those lines, as would inevitably have been the case if
permission had been granted for the amendment on the basis of the claimant's
new s 14 argument which was not before the master.

LATHAM LJ.   *b*
   [49] I agree.

KAY LJ.
   [50] I also agree.

Appeal allowed. Permission to appeal refused.

Kate O'Hanlon   Barrister.

Practice Statement

a

QUEEN'S BENCH DIVISION (ADMINISTRATIVE COURT)
SCOTT BAKER J
1 FEBRUARY 2002

b

Practice – Administrative Court – Procedure for urgent applications – Listing policy.

SCOTT BAKER J (Lead Judge of the Administrative Court) gave the following annual statement of the Administrative Court at the sitting of the court.

c

(1) NOMINATED JUDGES

There are presently 25 judges nominated by the Lord Chief Justice to sit in the Administrative Court. They include two judges of the Chancery Division and two of the Family Division who act as additional judges of the Queen's Bench Division when dealing with Administrative Court cases. A list of those currently nominated is attached at annex A. The Administrative Court now has regular use of six courtrooms—courts 1, 2, 3, 10, 27 and 28. Routinely there are approximately eight judges allocated to single judge sittings and one or two Divisional Courts sit.

d

(2) MODERN JUDICIAL REVIEW

e

October 2000 saw the introduction of the Administrative Court and two fundamental changes to the work of the former Crown Office List—the introduction of CPR Pt 54 and the coming into force of the Human Rights Act 1998. There has now been time to assess the impact of those changes.

Part 54 followed the recommendations of the Bowman Review and has reformed the judicial review process. There are two particular areas of note. First, the requirement to serve the defendant and interested parties with the claim form and the ability of those parties to put summary grounds of defence before the court prior to the court considering whether permission should be granted to proceed. This change has enabled the court to dispose at the paper stage of many cases that are bound to fail. Secondly, the introduction of consideration of all applications for permission on paper in the first instance has meant a more structured allocation of cases to judges. Court time is now allocated for consideration of paper applications. The rate of renewal after refusal—an unknown factor in the Bowman recommendations—has stabilised at around 50%. Paper consideration has been a major contributor to the reductions in waiting times achieved over the past year. I shall return to the subject of waiting times.

f

g

h

Of the cases received from 2 October 2000 to 31 December 2001 some 19% were identified as raising Human Rights Act issues. The 1998 Act does not, however, appear to have generated a large increase in the receipts. Receipts for 2001 showed an overall increase of 11% on 2000. The increase was attributable to an increase in civil judicial review, in particular in asylum cases (2,159 compared to 1,876—an increase of 15%). There have been a number of high profile cases raising Human Rights Act issues such as *R (on the application of Alconbury Developments Ltd) v Secretary of State for the Environment, Transport and the Regions* [2001] UKHL 23, [2001] 2 All ER 929, [2001] 2 WLR 1389—the issue of the planning appeal system and *R v DPP, ex p Kebeline* [1999] 4 All ER 801, [2000] 2 AC 326—the issue of pre-Human Rights Act prosecutions.

j

(3) PERFORMANCE OF THE COURT IN 2001

During 2001 there were 274 Divisional Court sitting days, 1,447 single judge sitting days and 102 deputy High Court judge sitting days.

The statistics for 2001 show an increase in receipts but an improvement in waiting times.

Receipts: 5,298 (4,407 civil judicial review)

Disposals: 5,398 cases were determined in 2001

Adjourned generally	85
Determined by court	2,564
Discontinuance	372
No motion after grant of permission (pre-Bowman cases)	28
Not renewed	828
Withdrawn	1,521
Grand total	5,398

Waiting times during 2001:

The average waiting time for a decision on an application for *permission to apply for judicial review was eight weeks* (from lodging to decision).

The average waiting time for a *substantive determination (of all types of case) was 20 weeks* (from lodging to decision).

Expedited cases are being listed in a matter of weeks.

Legal representatives should bear these figures in mind when preparing cases.

In the light of the performance of the court a short warned list has been reintroduced to ensure the court is fully listed and time is not wasted when cases settle at the last minute. Parties in cases which are short warned will be notified that their case is likely to be listed from a specified date, and that they may be called into the list at less than a day's notice from that date. Approximately six cases are short warned for each week. If the case does not get on during that period, a date as soon as possible after that period will be fixed in consultation with the parties.

For the benefit of users the current listing policy of the Administrative Court is annexed to this statement (annex C).

(4) USERS GROUP

The Administrative Court Users Group provides a useful forum for discussion between the court users, the court staff and the nominated judges. Some of the forthcoming initiatives I am about to announce resulted from those discussions.

I intend for the group to continue to meet each term. I welcome suggestions for the agenda and the feedback which court users are uniquely placed to give.

(5) USE OF ALTERNATIVE MEANS OF RESOLUTION

a

I draw the attention of litigants and legal advisers to the decision of the Court of Appeal in R (*on the application of Cowl*) v *Plymouth City* [2001] EWCA Civ 1935, [2001] All ER (D) 206 (Dec). The nominated judges are fully committed to resolving disputes by alternative means where appropriate and are exploring ways of promoting this.

b

(6) FORTHCOMING INITIATIVES

Pre-action protocol for judicial review

The protocol was published in December 2001 and comes into force on 4 March 2002. Any claims for judicial review lodged on or after that date must *c* indicate that the protocol has been complied with. Reasons for non-compliance must be given in the claim form. The form is currently being reconsidered in the light of the experience of the past 16 months and the comments of users. The revised form will be available on the Court Service website shortly.

d *Urgent cases procedure*

CPR Pt 54 makes no express provision for urgent applications for permission to apply for judicial review to be made orally. As the result of users' concerns I now issue guidance on the procedure to be applied for urgent applications and for interim injunctions. Advocates must comply with this guidance; and where *e* a manifestly inappropriate application is made, consideration will be given to a wasted costs order. The full terms of the guidance and the form for use in this procedure are annexed to this statement (annex B).

1. The Administrative Court currently allocates paper applications for judicial review on a daily basis and one judge also act as the 'Urgent Judge'.

f 2. Where a claimant makes an application for the permission application to be heard as a matter of urgency and/or seeks an interim injunction, he must complete a prescribed form which states:
(a) the need for urgency;
(b) the timescale sought for the consideration of the permission application, e g within 72 hours or sooner if necessary (see para 6 below); and
g (c) the date by which the substantive hearing should take place.

3. Where an interim injunction is sought, a claimant must, in addition, provide:
(a) a draft order; and
(b) the grounds for the injunction.

h 4. The claimant must serve (by fax and post) the claim form and application for urgency on the defendant and interested parties, advising them of the application and that they may make representations.

5. Where an interim injunction is sought, the claimant must serve (by fax and post) the draft order and grounds for the application on the defendant and interested parties, advising them of the application and that they may make *j* representations.

6. A judge will consider the application within the time requested and may make such order as he considers appropriate.

7. If the judge directs that an oral hearing take place within a specified time the representatives of the parties and the Administrative Court will liaise to fix a permission hearing within the time period directed.

E-mail address for use for urgent post
    The Administrative Court Office now has e-mail addresses for *urgent post*.
The addresses are not available for formal filing of documents. When using these
addresses the office opening hours must be borne in mind and it cannot be assumed
that mail sent after 4.30 pm will be opened before 9 am on the following day.
    The e-mail addresses are:

For mail relating to paper applications—
Administrativecourtoffice.generaloffice@courtservice.gsi.gov.uk

For mail relating to listed cases—
Administrativecourtoffice.listoffice@courtservice.gsi.gov.uk

For mail relating to court orders—
Administrativecourtoffice.courtclerks@courtservice.gsi.gov.uk

Revised renewal form—judicial review
    With immediate effect, when completing the form used for renewing
applications for permission to apply for judicial review, claimants must set out
the grounds for renewal in the light of the reasons given by the single judge when
refusing permission on the papers. The revised form is annexed to this statement
(annex C).

ANNEX A

THE ADMINISTRATIVE COURT

The Hon Mr Justice Turner
The Hon Mr Justice Scott Baker
The Hon Mr Justice Hidden
The Hon Mr Justice Forbes
The Hon Mr Justice Mitchell
The Hon Mr Justice Evans-Lombe
The Hon Mr Justice Harrison
The Hon Mr Justice Lightman
The Hon Mr Justice Collins
The Hon Mr Justice Maurice Kay
The Hon Mr Justice Hooper
The Hon Mr Justice Newman
The Hon Mr Justice Moses
The Hon Mr Justice Sullivan
The Hon Mr Justice Richards
The Hon Mr Justice Burton
The Hon Mr Justice Jackson
The Hon Mr Justice Elias
The Hon Mr Justice Silber
The Hon Mr Justice Munby
The Hon Mr Justice Stanley Burnton
The Hon Mr Justice Ouseley
The Hon Mr Justice Wilson
The Hon Mr Justice Crane
The Hon Mr Justice Keith

a

ANNEX B

THE PROCEDURE FOR URGENT APPLICATIONS
TO THE ADMINISTRATIVE COURT

1. In October 2000 CPR Pt 54 was introduced which makes no express provision for urgent applications for permission to apply for judicial review to be made orally.

b   2. The Administrative Court is now issuing the following guidance on the procedure to be applied for urgent applications and for interim injunctions. It is the duty of the advocate to comply with this guidance; and where a manifestly inappropriate application is made, consideration will be given to a wasted costs order.

3. The Administrative Court currently allocates paper applications for judicial *c* review on a daily basis and one judge also acts as the 'Urgent Judge'.

4. Where a claimant makes an application for the permission application to be heard as a matter of urgency and/or seeks an interim injunction, he must complete a prescribed form which states:

• the need for urgency;

d • the timescale sought for the consideration of the permission application, e g within 72 hours or sooner if necessary (see para 8 below); and

• the date by which the substantive hearing should take place.

5. Where an interim injunction is sought, a claimant must, in addition, provide:

• a draft order; and

e • the grounds for the injunction.

6. The claimant must serve (by fax and post) the claim form and application for urgency on the defendant and interested parties, advising them of the application and that they may make representations.

7. Where an interim injunction is sought, the claimant must serve (by fax and *f* post) the draft order and grounds for the application on the defendant and interested parties, advising them of the application and that they may make representations.

8. A judge will consider the application within the time requested and may make such order as he considers appropriate.

g 9. If the judge directs that an oral hearing take place within a specified time the representatives of the parties and the Administrative Court will liaise to fix a permission hearing within the time period directed.

Judicial Review
Application for urgent consideration

This form (N463) must be completed by the claimant
or the claimant's advocate if exceptional urgency
is being claimed and the application needs to be
determined within a certain time scale.
The claimant, or the claimant's solicitors must serve
this form on the defendant(s) and any interested
parties with the N461 judicial review claim form.

To the defendant(s) and interested party(ies)
Representations as to the urgency of the claim
may be made by defendants or interested
parties to the Administrative Court Office by
fax—020 7947 6802

In the High Court of Justice Administrative Court	
Claim No	
Claimant(s)	
Defendant(s)	
Interested Parties	

SECTION 1 Reasons for urgency

SECTION 2 **Proposed timetable** (tick the boxes and complete the following statements that apply)

☐ (a) The N461 application for permission should be considered within ......
hours / days

☐ (b) Abridgement of time is sought for the lodging of acknowledgements
of service

☐ (c) If permission for judicial review is granted, a substantive hearing is
sought by ...... (date)

SECTION 3 **Interim relief** (state what interim relief is sought and why in the box below)
A draft order must be attached

SECTION 4 Service
A copy of this form of application was served on the defendant(s) and interested
parties as follows:

Defendant		**Interested party**	
by fax machine to	time sent	by fax machine to	time sent
Fax no.		Fax no.	
by handing it to or leaving it with		by handing it to or leaving it with	
Name		Name	
by e-mail to		by e-mail to	
e-mail address		e-mail address	
Date served		Date served	
Name of claimant's advocate		Claimant (claimant's advocate)	
Name		Signed	

a

ANNEX C
LISTING POLICY IN THE ADMINISTRATIVE COURT
February 2002

Fixing substantive hearings

b Where a case is ready to be heard substantively, it enters a warned list and all parties are informed of this by letter. Some cases require an early hearing date and take priority over other cases waiting to be fixed—these enter the expedited warned list.

Where counsel has been placed on the court record, their chambers are contacted by the Administrative Court list office in order to agree a convenient
c date for the hearing. Counsel's clerks are offered a range of dates and have 48 hours to take up one of the dates offered. If counsel's clerk fails to contact the list office within 48 hours, the list office will fix the hearing on one of the dates that was offered, without further notice and the parties will be notified of that fixture by letter. Where a hearing is listed in this way the hearing will only be
d vacated by the Administrative Court Office if both parties consent. Failing that, a formal application for adjournment must be made (on notice to all parties) to the court. The same procedure is followed where a claimant is in person.

Short warned list

Whilst the Administrative Court usually gives fixed dates for hearings, there is
e also a need to short warn a number of cases to cover the large number of settlements that occur in the list. Parties in cases that are selected to be short warned will be notified that their case is likely to be listed from a specified date, and that they may be called into the list at less than a day's notice from that date. Approximately six cases are short warned for any specified week. If the case does
f not get on during that period, a date as soon as possible after that period will be fixed in consultation with the parties.

Vacating fixtures

There are occasions when circumstances, outside the control of the List Office, may necessitate them having to vacate a hearing at very short notice. Sometimes
g this can be as late as 4.30 pm the day before the case is listed. This could be as a result of a case unexpectedly overrunning, a judge becoming unavailable, or other reasons. In deciding which hearing has to be vacated, the list office will assess the cases listed for the following day and take the following factors into consideration.
h • Which case(s), if removed, will cause the least disruption to the list (the aim is to adjourn as few cases as possible, ideally one).

• How many cases need to be adjourned given the reduced listing time available.

• Have any matters previously been adjourned by the court.
j • The urgency and age(s) of the matter(s) listed.

• Where the parties and/or their representatives are based (this is relevant as in some cases the parties travel to London the day before the hearing).

• Whether it is appropriate to 'float' the case in the event of another listed matter going short (cases will not be floated without the consent of the parties).

• The likelihood of a judge becoming available to hear a floated case.

After taking these factors into account, the List Office decide upon the case(s) which will have to be re-fixed and will inform the parties concerned that their hearing has been vacated. The case record will be noted that the matter is not to be adjourned by the court again. The court will also endeavour to re-fix the case on the next available date convenient to the parties.

a

---

b

Form 86B

In the High Court of Justice　　　　　　CO Ref no: CO/ ....
Queen's Bench Division
Administrative Court

c

In the matter of a claim for Judicial Review
The Queen on the application of

....

d

versus

....

Notice of RENEWAL of claim for permission to apply for Judicial Review (CPR 54.12)

e

1. *This notice must be lodged in the Administrative Court Office and served upon the defendant (and interested parties who were served with the claim form) within 7 days of the service on the claimant or his solicitor of the notice that the claim for permission has been refused.*

2. *If an extension of the time for lodging is required, please set out below the* **reasons for the delay:**

f

3. *Set out below the grounds for renewing the application:*

g

4. *Please supply*
    COUNSEL'S NAME:
    COUNSEL'S TELEPHONE NUMBER:

h

Signed　　　　　　　　　Dated

Claimant's Ref No.　　　　　Tel. No.　　　　　　Fax No.

To the Master of the Crown Office, Royal Courts of Justice, Strand, London, WC2A 2LL

Dilys Tausz　Barrister.

a   Re B (a child) (adoption by one natural parent)
[2001] UKHL 70

b   HOUSE OF LORDS

LORD NICHOLLS OF BIRKENHEAD, LORD MACKAY OF CLASHFERN, LORD HOFFMANN,
LORD MILLETT AND LORD RODGER OF EARLSFERRY

31 OCTOBER, 17 DECEMBER 2001

c   *Adoption – Application – Application for adoption by one natural parent –
Circumstances in which such an application could be granted – Adoption Act 1976,
s 15(3) – Human Rights Act 1998, Sch 1, Pt I, art 8.*

From August 1997 to April 1998 the appellant father, who was unmarried, had a
sexual relationship with an unmarried woman. She became pregnant early in
d   1998, and the child was born in October 1998. Without looking at the child, the
mother told hospital staff that she wished to have her adopted. The child was
placed with foster parents with a view to adoption, and since the birth the mother
had never met the child nor, save at a distance, seen her. The father was not
aware of the pregnancy or the birth until contacted by local social services. On
learning of the child's existence, he expressed a desire to look after her, and the
e   mother co-operated with him in making arrangements for her care. They entered
into a parental responsibility agreement, whereby the father was to have parental
responsibility as well as the mother. In December 1998 the child was placed with
her father, and he had looked after her ever since, having given up paid
employment in order to do so. He applied to adopt the child as sole parent,
f   primarily because he was anxious to secure the child's future in his sole care and
believed that he would feel more secure knowing that the mother's parental
responsibility had been removed. Although the mother consented to the making
of the adoption order, the Official Solicitor, acting as the child's guardian,
opposed the father's application, contending that an adoption order would not
promote the child's welfare and that there was no sufficient reason to justify
g   excluding the mother, as required by s 15(3)[a] of the Adoption Act 1976. Section 15(3)
provided that an adoption order was not to be made on the application of the
mother or father of the child alone unless the court was satisfied that '(a) the
other natural parent is dead or cannot be found or, by virtue of [anonymous
sperm donation], there is no other parent, or (b) there is some other reason
h   justifying the exclusion of the other natural parent'. The judge made the
adoption order, holding that the child's welfare demanded that there should be
such an order and that there were exceptional circumstances to justify the
mother's exclusion under s 15(3)(b), namely that she had rejected the child from
birth, had played no part in her upbringing, had consented to the adoption and
j   wished to play no part in the child's life other than to have indirect contact. On
the Official Solicitor's appeal, the Court of Appeal held that s 15(3)(b) was to be
interpreted restrictively, requiring a reason comparable to those set out in
s 15(3)(a) to justify the exclusion of the other natural parent. In reaching that
conclusion, the court held that such a construction was necessary in order to give

---

a   Section 15(3) is set out at [9], below

effect to s 15(3)(b) in a way that was compatible with the right to respect for the
child's family life under art 8[b] of the European Convention for the Protection of a
Human Rights and Fundamental Freedoms 1950 (as set out in Sch 1 to the Human
Rights Act 1998); that there was no pressing need to deprive the child of all legal
relationship with one half of her family of birth; and that it would be a
disproportionate response to her current needs to transform her from being the
child of two legal parents into the child of only one legal parent. The court therefore b
concluded that the judge had misdirected herself on the requirements of s 15(3)(b),
and allowed the appeal. The father appealed to the House of Lords.

Held – On its true construction, s 15(3)(b) of the 1976 Act did not require a reason c
comparable to those set out in s 15(3)(a) in order to justify the exclusion of the other
natural parent. The three exceptions listed in para (a) were instances where the
other natural parent could not have, or was unlikely to have, any further part in
the child's upbringing and life. Those three exceptions were not, however, an
exhaustive list of the circumstances in which a natural parent was unlikely in d
practice to have a further role in the child's life. There might be other situations,
such as abandonment, or persistent neglect or ill-treatment of the child, when the
welfare of the child justified the exclusion of a natural parent. It was not surprising,
therefore, that the exception stated in para (b) was altogether open-ended, and
there could be no ground for importing into it an unexpressed limitation whereby
'some other reason' had to be comparable with the death or disappearance of the e
other natural parent. What was required by para (b), and all that was required,
was that the reason, whatever it was, had to be sufficient to justify the exclusion
of the other parent. Whether any particular reason satisfied that test depended
on the circumstances, but the circumstances in which it would be in the best
interests of a child to make an adoption order in favour of one natural parent f
alone, thereby taking away one half of the child's legal family, were likely to be
exceptional. Moreover, s 15(3) had to be given effect in such a way as to avoid
the result that a court might make an adoption order excluding one natural parent
from the life of the child when that would represent an interference disproportionate
to the child's needs. There was, however, no discordance between the 1976 Act g
and art 8 of the convention on that point, and no need to 'read down' s 15(3)(b)
so as to avoid incompatibility which would otherwise exist. The balancing
exercise required by art 8 did not differ in substance from the like balancing
exercise undertaken by a court when deciding whether, in the conventional
phraseology of English law, adoption would be in the best interests of the child. h
Thus, unless the court misdirected itself in some material aspect when balancing
the competing factors, its conclusion that an adoption order was in the best
interests of a child identified the pressing social need for adoption and represented
the court's considered view on proportionality. In the instant case, the judge had
not misdirected herself and her decision was not plainly wrong. She had been j
entitled to conclude that the circumstances were exceptional, and that adoption
was in the child's best interests. Accordingly, the appeal would be allowed, and
the judge's order restored (see [22]–[24], [27], [28], [30]–[36], below).

---

b   Article 8 is set out at [10], below

Notes

a For adoption by one person and for the right to respect for family life, see respectively 5(3) *Halsbury's Laws* (4th edn reissue) para 558 and 8(2) *Halsbury's Laws* (4th edn reissue) paras 149, 151.

For the Adoption Act 1976, s 15, see 6 *Halsbury's Statutes* (4th edn) (1999 reissue) 224.

b For the Human Rights Act 1998, Sch 1, Pt I, art 8, see 7 *Halsbury's Statutes* (4th edn) (1999 reissue) 524.

Cases referred to in opinions

B v W (wardship: appeal) [1979] 3 All ER 83, [1979] 1 WLR 1041, HL.
G v G [1985] 2 All ER 225, [1985] 1 WLR 647, HL.
c *Grayan Building Services Ltd (in liquidation), Re* [1995] Ch 241, [1995] 3 WLR 1, CA.
Silver v UK (1983) 5 EHRR 347, [1983] ECHR 5947/72, ECt HR.

Appeal

The father of a child known as 'A' appealed with permission of the House of
d Lords given on 1 May 2001 from the decision of the Court of Appeal (Dame Elizabeth Butler-Sloss P, Potter and Hale LJJ) on 20 December 2000 ([2001] 1 FCR 600) allowing an appeal by the respondent, the Official Solicitor, acting as A's guardian, from the adoption order in respect of A made by Bracewell J on 29 June 2000 in favour of the father. The facts are set out in the opinion of Lord Nicholls
e of Birkenhead.

Andrew McFarlane QC and *David Hershman* (instructed by *Sharpe Pritchard*, agents
for *Brethertons*, Rugby) for the father.
Gordon Murdoch QC and *Michael Sternberg* for the Official Solicitor.

f Their Lordships took time for consideration.

17 December 2001. The following opinions were delivered.

LORD NICHOLLS OF BIRKENHEAD.

g [1] My Lords, this appeal concerns an adoption order, sought by one natural parent (the father) with the consent of the other (the mother). The child is a girl, now three years old. Bracewell J made the adoption order: see [2000] 2 FLR 717. The Court of Appeal, comprising Dame Elizabeth Butler-Sloss P, Potter and Hale LJJ, reversed her decision: see [2001] 1 FCR 600. The father has appealed to your Lordships' House. At no stage has the mother taken any part in the
h proceedings.

The story

[2] From August 1997 the mother and the father, neither of whom is married, had a sexual relationship. This ended in April 1998. Early in 1998 the mother
j became pregnant, although she did not realise this until some months later. The child (A) was born on 19 October 1998. The mother was then aged 28. Without looking at her baby the mother told the hospital staff that she wanted to have the child adopted. This was the mother's second child. Her first child, also a daughter, was born in 1993. On that occasion, and in accordance with the mother's wishes, the child had been adopted.

[3] So A, when four days old, was placed with foster parents with a view to adoption. Since the birth the mother has never met A nor, save at a distance, seen her. The father, then aged 25, was not aware of the mother's pregnancy or of A's birth. Purely by chance the local social services authority learned of the father's whereabouts. They contacted him, and he quickly expressed his desire to look after A. The mother then co-operated with the father in making arrangements for A's care. On 27 November 1998 they registered A's birth together, with the father's surname. On 7 December 1998 they entered into a parental responsibility agreement, whereby the father was to have parental responsibility as well as the mother. On 19 December 1998 A was placed with her father, and he has looked after her ever since. He gave up paid employment in order to do so. Child A is thriving. The issue in the case is not whether the father should continue to care for A as a single natural parent. That is not in doubt. The issue is whether he should become her sole adoptive parent.

The adoption proceedings

[4] The father made his adoption application to his local Family Proceedings Court on 26 April 1999. His understanding was that the mother was willing to agree. Subsequently her views wavered. The proceedings were transferred to the High Court because of their unusual nature.

[5] The father is seeking an adoption order primarily because he is anxious to secure A's future in his sole care. He feels insecure, and believes he will feel more secure knowing that the mother's parental responsibility for A has been removed. This can only be achieved by an adoption order. The mother has said repeatedly she does not wish to play any part in A's life. But the father is concerned that, without an adoption order, it will remain possible in future years for the mother to pose a threat to A's continued placement with him. He is concerned that the mother may marry and, with her new husband, ask to have A to live with her. The court might look favourably upon such an application. His vulnerability to an attempt by the mother to reclaim A is something which has caused him great anxiety. He is adamant in his wish for an adoption order, although whatever order is made will not affect the strength of his commitment to A. He does not, in principle, exclude the possibility of future contact by the mother with A, provided the placement with him is secure. He is willing to adhere to his arrangement with the mother to provide an annual progress report and photograph. The mother has a similar arrangement with the adoptive parents of her elder daughter.

[6] In his report to the court, the Official Solicitor, acting as A's guardian, opposed the application. The sole consequence of an adoption order would be to end the mother's relationship with A. This was not an order which could be said to safeguard and promote A's welfare. There was nothing in the history of the case to suggest that the mother would be likely to seek to disrupt the security of A's placement with her father. But any attempt by her to do so would not necessarily be to A's disadvantage. Further, the court has to be satisfied, before making an adoption order, that there is some reason justifying the exclusion of the mother, as required by s 15(3) of the Adoption Act 1976. There was no sufficient reason in this case. A's placement with her father should be secured by a residence order, suitable prohibited steps orders, and an order requiring the mother to obtain permission from the court before making any application for an order under s 8 of the Children Act 1989.

[7] After this report had been prepared the Official Solicitor was able to meet the mother. Her response to the Official Solicitor's report was that, although she

a considered the application was premature, she could understand the father's reasons and was not going to stand in his way. She made clear she would never seek to interfere with the lives of A and her father. She was not seeking direct contact with A. While she could not say this would always be her position, as a first step she would obtain legal advice. She would not simply turn up on the father's doorstep. She wished to maintain indirect contact with a yearly
b photograph and progress report. She then signed, in the presence of the Official Solicitor, the prescribed form of consent to the making of an adoption order. That was on 20 June 2000.

The decision of the judge

c [8] The application proceeded before Bracewell J on 29 June 2000 on the basis of affidavit evidence and reports. There was no oral evidence. The judge concluded that the welfare of A 'demands' there should be an adoption order 'in order to promote her welfare throughout her childhood'. To comply with the requirements of s 15(3) of the 1976 Act the circumstances must be exceptional. That was so here. The reasons for the exclusion of the mother were that she had
d rejected A from birth and played no part in her care or upbringing, and she had consented to the adoption and wished to play no part in A's life in the future, other than to have indirect contact. The judge said:

'This is not a case in which the mother has hesitated and weighed in the balance what she can provide for the child and what the father can provide.
e She has no interest in having any direct contact with A or participating in her upbringing. She is an intelligent, reflective woman, who has been able to consider the position and has reached a reasoned position of not wanting to play a part in A's life.'

f *The decision of the Court of Appeal*

[9] With the leave of the judge, the Official Solicitor appealed from her decision. Hale LJ gave the leading judgment in the Court of Appeal. She considered that Bracewell J had misdirected herself on the requirements of s 15(3)(b) of the 1976 Act. Section 15(3), as amended by the Human Fertilisation
g and Embryology Act 1990, s 49(5), Sch 4, para 4, provides:

'An adoption order shall not be made on the application of the mother or father of the child alone unless the court is satisfied that—(a) the other natural parent is dead or cannot be found or, by virtue of section 28 of the Human Fertilisation and Embryology Act 1990, there is no other parent, or
h (b) there is some other reason justifying the exclusion of the other natural parent, and where such an order is made the reason justifying the exclusion of the other natural parent shall be recorded by the court.'

Hale LJ noted that this provision is directed at sole adoption applications by
j natural parents. She continued ([2001] 1 FCR 600 at 610 (para 34)):

'It requires of this already very small and unusual group that there be some reason, comparable to the death, disappearance or anonymous sperm donation of the other natural parent, "justifying" his or her exclusion, not only from parental responsibility for but also from the whole life and lineage of the child.'

[10] Hale LJ found reinforcement for a restrictive interpretation of s 15(3)(b) ('some reason comparable to the death, disappearance or anonymous sperm donation of the other natural parent') in the need to read and give effect to this statutory provision, so far as possible, in a way which is compatible with the rights set out in art 8 of the European Convention for the Protection of Human Rights and Fundamental Freedoms 1950 (as set out in Sch 1 to the Human Rights Act 1998). Article 8 provides:

'1. Everyone has the right to respect for his private and family life, his home and his correspondence.
2. There shall be no interference by a public authority with the exercise of this right except such as is in accordance with the law and is necessary in a democratic society in the interests of national security, public safety or the economic well-being of the country, for the prevention of disorder or crime, for the protection of health or morals, or for the protection of the rights and freedoms of others.'

[11] Hale LJ noted that an adoption order is an interference by a public authority, in the shape of the court which makes it, with the exercise of the right to respect for family life. There are three components in the exceptions permitted under art 8(2): the intervention must be 'in accordance with the law', in pursuit of one of the legitimate aims defined in art 8(2), and 'necessary in a democratic society'. There is no difficulty with the first two components. The 1976 Act permits adoption in the circumstances of child A, but only if there is reason to exclude the mother. The intervention by the court is to protect the interests of the child. As to the third component, the interference must meet a pressing social need and be proportionate to that need. Hale LJ said (at 612 (para 40)):

'... it is difficult indeed to argue that there is a pressing social need to deprive A of all legal relationship with one half of her family of birth ... she already has a full and secure legal and factual relationship with her father. If there is any need to give her more, it can be provided for in a package of orders along the lines discussed. In my view, it would be a disproportionate response to her current needs to turn her from the child of two legal parents, with two legal families, into the child of only one parent, with only one legal family. Section 15(3) of the 1976 Act has to be given effect in such a way as to avoid that result.'

[12] Dame Elizabeth Butler-Sloss P and Potter LJ agreed. The Court of Appeal set aside the adoption order, and substituted a residence order in favour of the father and an order prohibiting the mother from making any application under the Children Act 1989 relating to A without the leave of a High Court judge, any application for such leave to be made on notice to the Official Solicitor but without notice to the father unless the court directs otherwise.

The grounds on which the Court of Appeal intervened
[13] The essence of the reasoning of Hale LJ in para 40 was that she formed a different view from the first instance judge on whether it was in the best interests of this little girl that the court should make an adoption order. Using the structure of art 8(2) of the convention as a framework, she expressed the view that adoption was not in A's best interests. Adoption by her father would be a 'disproportionate response' to her current needs.

a   [14] Unquestionably, on the facts in the present case this assessment of the
course which is in the best interests of A was a possible view. But before any
question can arise of the Court of Appeal making its own assessment of the
requirements of A's welfare and substituting this for the judge's assessment, it
must be shown that the judge erred in some relevant respect: by misdirecting
herself on the law or the evidence, or by being so plainly wrong that she must
b   have misdirected herself.

[15] This principle is so well established as scarcely to bear repetition: see, for
instance, the observations of Lord Scarman in B v W (wardship: appeal) [1979] 3 All
ER 83 at 96, [1979] 1 WLR 1041 at 1055, and Lord Fraser of Tullybelton in G v G
[1985] 2 All ER 225 at 227–230, [1985] 1 WLR 647 at 650–653. On the instant
appeals, leading counsel appearing for A's guardian submitted that, since this is
c   not a case in which oral evidence was heard, it was more readily open to the
Court of Appeal to substitute its view for that of the trial judge. He submitted
that in so far as the Court of Appeal differed from the judge's evaluation of the
inferences to be drawn from the primary facts, the Court of Appeal was in as good
a position as the judge and, therefore, it was entitled to form its own independent
d   opinion. In the light of this submission I must elaborate a little on this point.

[16] In cases such as the present the first instance judge decides which order,
if any, he considers is in the best interests of the child. When doing so the judge
is often said to be exercising his 'discretion'. In this context this expression is
descriptive of the judicial evaluation and balancing of a number of factors from
which an overall conclusion is reached on a concept whose application in any
e   given case is inherently imprecise. There is no objectively certain answer on
which of two or more possible courses is in the best interests of a child. In all save
the most straightforward cases, there are competing factors, some pointing one
way and some another. There is no means of demonstrating that one answer is
clearly right and another clearly wrong. There are too many uncertainties
f   involved in what, after all, is an attempt to peer into the future and assess the
advantages and disadvantages which this or that course will or may have for the
child.

[17] Hence the rationale underlying what I may call the principle in G v G.
Courts of appeal exist to remedy mistakes in the first instance process. The Court
of Appeal is not intended to be a forum in which unsuccessful litigants, where no
g   error occurred at first instance, may have a second trial of the same issue by
different judges under the guise of an appeal. The mere fact that appellate judges
might have reached a different conclusion had they been carrying out the
evaluation and balancing exercise does not mean that the first instance judge fell
into error. That fact does not, of itself, require or entitle the Court of Appeal to
h   intervene.

[18] Frequently a judge at first instance will exercise his discretion as described
above in proceedings where he will also have to evaluate witnesses and their oral
testimony. Depending on the circumstances, this feature may be an additional
reason why an appellate court should be slow to intervene. But the presence of
j   this additional feature is not an essential ingredient of the circumstances in which
the principle in G v G is applicable. The principle in G v G applies irrespective of
whether the evidence before the judge is oral or written, disputed or agreed. This
principle is applicable in the present case even though the evidence before
Bracewell J was wholly in written form.

[19] The matters discussed above are not peculiar to cases relating to children.
There are many types of case where the principle in G v G is applicable, with

greater or less force. In his valuable observations in *Re Grayan Building Services Ltd (in liq)* [1995] Ch 241 at 254–255, [1995] 3 WLR 1 at 12, my noble and learned friend Lord Hoffmann, then Hoffmann LJ, pointed out that the standards applied by the law in different contexts vary a great deal in precision 'generally speaking, the vaguer the standard and the greater the number of factors which the court has to weigh up in deciding whether or not the standards have been met, the more reluctant an appellate court will be to interfere with the trial judge's decision'. Cases relating to the welfare of children tend to be towards the edge of the spectrum where an appellate court is particularly reluctant to interfere with the judge's decision.

[20] It goes without saying that in the present case the highly-experienced members of the Court of Appeal had these principles in mind. Application of these principles is part of the staple diet of judges in that court. Two strands of criticism of the judge's judgment are discernible in the judgment of Hale LJ. The first, already mentioned, is that the judge materially misdirected herself on the proper interpretation and application of s 15(3) of the 1976 Act. If she did, the Court of Appeal was bound to carry out afresh the exercise of deciding whether, overall, it was in the best interests of A that an adoption order should be made in favour of her father. But if the judge did not err on this point, her decision must be allowed to stand unless, and this is the second criticism implicitly made by the Court of Appeal, her decision was plainly wrong.

Section 15(3): 'some other reason'

[21] The 1976 Act requires the court, when deciding whether to make an adoption order, to have regard to all the circumstances. First consideration is to be given to the need to safeguard and promote the welfare of the child throughout his childhood: s 6. An adoption order in favour of one natural parent alone will have the effect of excluding the other parent. In the present case an adoption order will mean that A is treated in law as if she were not the child of her mother: s 39(2).

[22] On its face this permanent exclusion of the child's mother from the life of the child is a drastic and detrimental consequence of adoption so far as the child is concerned. How serious this loss is likely to be depends on the circumstances of the case. In deciding whether to make an order having this consequence the court must always be satisfied that this course is in the best interests of the child. There must be some reason justifying the exclusion of the other natural parent. The reason must be sufficient to outweigh the adverse consequences such an order may have by reason of the exclusion of one parent from the child's life. Consent of the excluded parent is not of itself a sufficient reason, but it is a factor to be taken into account. Its weight will depend on the circumstances.

[23] In so far as the Court of Appeal construed s 15(3)(b) more restrictively than this, I am unable to agree. Section 15(3) imposes a prerequisite to the making of an adoption order on the application of the mother or father alone. One or other of the exceptions set out in paras (a) and (b) must be satisfied. The three exceptions listed in para (a) are instances where the other natural parent cannot have, or is unlikely to have, any further part in the child's upbringing and life. But these three exceptions are not an exhaustive list of the circumstances in which a natural parent is unlikely in practice to have a further role in a child's life. Further, there may be other situations when the welfare of the child justifies the exclusion of a natural parent. Abandonment, or persistent neglect or ill-treatment of the child, could be instances.

a [24] It is not surprising, therefore, that the exception stated in para (b) is altogether open-ended. No doubt this was a deliberate choice of language. I can see no ground for importing into this exception an unexpressed limitation whereby 'some other reason' must be comparable with the death or disappearance of the other natural parent. What is required by para (b), and all that is required, is that the reason, whatever it be, must be sufficient to justify the exclusion of the other *b* parent. Whether any particular reason satisfies this test depends on the circumstances. This is a matter left to the decision of the court. On this question of interpretation I respectfully consider the Court of Appeal was unduly restrictive in its approach.

[25] An adoption order in favour of a single natural parent alone will also have the effect of permanently extinguishing any parental responsibility of the other *c* natural parent: s 12(3)(a) of the 1976 Act. This will afford the adoptive parent a measure of additional security. But it is important here to keep in mind the wide range of powers the court now has under the Children Act 1989 to restrict the possibility of inappropriate intervention in the child's life by the other natural parent. Adoption is not intended to be used simply as the means by which to *d* protect the child's life with one natural parent against inappropriate intervention by the other natural parent.

[26] Another consequence adoption has in this type of case is that after adoption the child will be treated in law as if she had been born to her adoptive parent in wedlock: s 39(1)(b) of the 1976 Act. The significance of this benefit today should not be overstated. The social and legal status of children born outside *e* marriage has changed greatly in recent years. The social stigma and legal disabilities attendant upon 'illegitimacy' have now largely gone. Two children in every five born in this country are born outside marriage. Unless a contrary intention appears, statutes enacted after 1987 are to be interpreted without regard to whether a person's parents were married at any time. So also are wills and the *f* existing statutory provisions relating to intestacy: see ss 1, 18 and 19 of the Family Law Reform Act 1987.

[27] Having regard to all these matters, the circumstances in which it will be in the best interests of a child to make an adoption order in favour of one natural parent alone, thereby, in Hale LJ's words, taking away one half of the child's legal family, are likely to be exceptional. Bracewell J regarded the circumstances of the *g* present case as exceptional. She said so. The father's case was that the mother's continuing status as a parent with parental responsibility for A would perpetuate insecurity for him and that this would potentially affect A's stability. The judge accepted this. This is clear from the tenor of her extempore judgment, although she did not expressly so state. The chance circumstance which brought A's father *h* into A's life and upbringing was bound to add to his anxieties. Given the mother's attitude to A from the moment of A's birth, and her consent, adoption by the father was in A's best interests. Adoption was in A's best interests even though this would have the consequence of excluding the mother.

[28] In my view, on the evidence before her this conclusion was open to *j* Bracewell J. I can see no indication that she misdirected herself on the proper interpretation or application of s 15(3). Nor do I consider her decision can be said to be manifestly wrong. That an adoption order as sought by A's father will safeguard and promote A's welfare is a wholly tenable view. A residence order, together with an appropriate prohibited steps order, may not suffice to allay the father's genuine anxieties. In this type of case explicit analysis of the advantages and disadvantages of adoption must always be desirable. But I do not think the

absence of such an analysis from Bracewell J's judgment vitiates, or casts doubt, on her conclusion. The reasoning implicit in her judgment is sufficiently apparent.

Article 8: the right to respect for family life

[29] In reaching the contrary conclusion the Court of Appeal was influenced by its interpretation and application of art 8 of the convention. In considering this point it is important to keep in mind that in the present case the individual whose right has to be respected is the child. The mother has freely and unconditionally agreed to the making of an adoption order, with a full appreciation of the consequences. So there is no question of adoption being a violation of her rights under art 8.

[30] As to child A's rights, I agree with the Court of Appeal that the relationship of mother and child is of itself sufficient to establish 'family life'. I agree also that s 15(3) has to be given effect to in such a way as to avoid the result that a court might make an adoption order excluding one natural parent from the life of the child when this would represent an interference disproportionate to the child's needs. Where I part company with the Court of Appeal is that, unlike the Court of Appeal, I think this undesirable and unacceptable result is already precluded by the 1976 Act itself. There is no discordance between the statute and art 8 on this point. There is no need to 'read down' s 15(3)(b) so as to avoid incompatibility which otherwise would exist. There is no need to have recourse to s 3 of the Human Rights Act 1998.

[31] My reason for holding this view is as follows. Take a case, such as the instant case, where the natural father alone seeks an adoption order. The court hears evidence and representations from all concerned, including the child's guardian. The mother consents to the application. The court considers the advantages and disadvantages adoption would have for the child. The court decides that an adoption order is best for the child in all the circumstances. I do not see how an adoption order made in this way can infringe the child's rights under art 8. Under art 8 the adoption order must meet a pressing social need and be a proportionate response to that need: see, for example, *Silver v UK* (1983) 5 EHRR 347 at 376–377 (para 97(c)). Inherent in both these convention concepts is a balancing exercise, weighing the advantages and the disadvantages. But this balancing exercise, required by art 8, does not differ in substance from the like balancing exercise undertaken by a court when deciding whether, in the conventional phraseology of English law, adoption would be in the best interests of the child. The like considerations fall to be taken into account. Although the phraseology is different, the criteria to be applied in deciding whether an adoption order is justified under art 8(2) lead to the same result as the conventional tests applied by English law. Thus, unless the court misdirected itself in some material respect when balancing the competing factors, its conclusion that an adoption order is in the best interests of the child, even though this would exclude the mother from the child's life, identifies the pressing social need for adoption (the need to safeguard and promote the child's welfare) and represents the court's considered view on proportionality. That is the effect of the judge's decision in the present case. Article 8(2) does not call for more.

[32] I would allow this appeal and restore the order of Bracewell J.

LORD MACKAY OF CLASHFERN.

[33] My Lords, I have had the advantage of reading in draft the speech delivered by my noble and learned friend Lord Nicholls of Birkenhead. I agree

a with him that this appeal should be allowed and the order of Bracewell J restored for the reasons that he has given.

LORD HOFFMANN.

[34] My Lords, I have had the advantage of reading in draft the speech of my noble and learned friend, Lord Nicholls of Birkenhead. I agree with it, and for the *b* reasons he gives I too would allow the appeal and restore the order of Bracewell J.

LORD MILLETT.

[35] My Lords, I have had the advantage of reading in draft the speech of my noble and learned friend, Lord Nicholls of Birkenhead. I agree with it, and for the reasons he gives I too would allow the appeal and restore the order of Bracewell J.
c

LORD RODGER OF EARLSFERRY.

[36] My Lords, I have had the privilege of reading the speech of my noble and learned friend, Lord Nicholls of Birkenhead, in draft. For the reasons which he gives I too would allow the appeal and restore the order of Bracewell J.

Appeal allowed.

Kate O'Hanlon   Barrister.

Loutchansky v Times Newspapers Ltd and others (No 2)

[2001] EWCA Civ 1805

COURT OF APPEAL, CIVIL DIVISION

LORD PHILLIPS OF WORTH MATRAVERS MR, SIMON BROWN AND TUCKEY LJJ

12–15 NOVEMBER, 5 DECEMBER 2001

Libel and slander – Qualified privilege – Common law privilege – Duty to publish – Standard to be applied by court when considering whether newspaper had been under duty to publish defamatory words – Guidance.

Libel and slander – Limitation of action – Multiple publication rule – Whether multiple publication rule infringing right to freedom of expression by inhibiting maintenance of Internet archives of press reports – Limitation Act 1980, s 4A – Human Rights Act 1998, Sch 1, Pt I, art 10.

Libel and slander – Summary disposal of claim – Quantum – Whether procedure for summary disposal available in respect of quantum after separate trial on liability – Defamation Act 1996, s 8.

In September and October 1999 a newspaper published two articles alleging that the claimant, an international businessman, was the boss of a major Russian criminal organisation and was involved, inter alia, in money-laundering and the smuggling of nuclear weapons. Both articles were posted on the newspaper's website. In December 1999 the claimant commenced proceedings for libel against the newspaper's publishers, its editor and two of its journalists. In December 2000 the claimant brought a second action for libel against the defendants in respect of the continued Internet publication of the two articles, without qualification, on the newspaper's website after 21 February 2000, the date of the defence in the first action. The defendants did not plead justification in either action, but relied instead on the defence of qualified privilege. The two actions were eventually consolidated, and the judge ordered separate trials of liability and quantum. At the beginning of the trial of liability, the defendants sought to re-amend their defence in the second action in order to contend that the only actionable publication of a newspaper article on the Internet was that which occurred when the article was first posted on the Internet, that the second action had not therefore been brought within a year of the accrual of the cause of action and that accordingly it was time-barred under s 4A[a] of the Limitation Act 1980. The judge refused that application on the basis of the well-established principle that each individual publication of a libel gave rise to a separate cause of action with its own limitation period (the multiple publication rule). He also struck out the qualified privilege defence in the second action. After the jury had answered various questions of fact relating to the issue of qualified privilege in the first action, the judge ruled that the defendants had not been under a duty to publish the articles, and that accordingly the defence of qualified privilege was not available in respect of either article. In reaching that conclusion, the judge

a held that such a duty arose only if a failure to publish the information in question would leave the publisher open to legitimate criticism. At a subsequent hearing, the judge acceded to an application by the claimant for summary disposal of the issue of quantum under s 8[b] of the Defamation Act 1996, the provision dealing with the summary disposal of 'the plaintiff's claim'. On the defendants' appeals against those rulings, the Court of Appeal considered, inter alia, (i) the standard
b to be applied in determining whether there had been a duty to publish in cases involving publication to the whole world; (ii) whether, as the defendants contended, the multiple publication rule was in conflict with the right to freedom of expression in art 10[c] of the European Convention for the Protection of Human Rights and Fundamental Freedoms 1950 (as set out in Sch 1 to the Human Rights Act 1998) because, through inhibiting the willingness of the media to maintain
c web archives, it had a chilling effect upon that freedom that went beyond what was necessary and proportionate in a democratic society for the protection of the reputation of others; and (iii) whether, as the defendants also contended, s 8 of the 1996 Act applied only where the court was asked to make a determination before a trial on liability.

d
Held – (1) When the court was deciding whether there had been a duty to publish defamatory words to the world at large, the standard to be applied was that of responsible journalism, and in determining whether that standard had been satisfied the following considerations were likely to feature prominently in the court's thinking. First, a holding that a publication was privileged would, to
e all intents and purposes, provide the publishers with a complete defence since, in such a case, a finding of privilege would effectively pre-empt a finding of malice. Secondly, setting the standard of journalistic responsibility too low would inevitably encourage too great a readiness to publish defamatory matter. Journalists should be rigorous, not lax, in their approach. It was in the interest of the public, as well
f as the defamed individual, that, wherever possible, truths and not untruths should be told. That was also in the interests of the media. Once untruths could be published with impunity, the public would cease to believe any communication, true or false. Thirdly, however, setting the standard too high would be no less damaging to society because it would deter newspapers from discharging their proper function of keeping the public informed. When determining whether any
g given article should attract qualified privilege, the court had to bear in mind the likely impact of its ruling not only upon the case in hand but also upon the media's practices generally. Qualified privilege ordinarily fell to be judged as a preliminary issue before the truth or falsity of the communication was established. Accordingly, the question to be posed was not whether it was in the
h public interest to publish an untruth, but whether it was in the public interest to publish the article, true or false. Even when the untruth of the article was established, or where it was not formally disputed, it was important to remember that the defence of qualified privilege tolerated factual inaccuracy for two purposes, namely in order not to deter either the publication sued upon (which
j might have been true) or future publications of truthful information. In the

b   Section 8, so far as material, is set out at [90], below
c   Article 10, so far as material, provides: '1. Everyone has the right to freedom of expression. This right shall include freedom to ... impart information ... without interference by public authority ... 2. The exercise of these freedoms, since it carries with it duties and responsibilities, may be subject to such restrictions ... as are prescribed by law and are necessary in a democratic society ... for the protection of the reputation ... of others ... '

instant case, the judge had applied too stringent a test. Its application merely as
a 'cross-check' would be unexceptionable in a case where the test had been
satisfied: the publisher's claim to privilege would be indisputable if a failure to
publish would have laid him open to legitimate criticism. The converse, however,
was not true. Not all journalists could or should be expected to reach an identical
view in every case. Responsible journalism would in certain circumstances
permit equally of publication or of non-publication. Accordingly, the appeal on
the qualified privilege issue in the first action would be allowed to the extent of
remitting the case to the judge so that he could re-examine his findings of fact
with the correct standard in mind (see [41], [49], [50], [102], below); *Reynolds v
Times Newspapers Ltd* [1999] 4 All ER 609 considered.

(2) The multiple publication rule did not impose a restriction on the readiness
to maintain and provide access to archives that amounted to a disproportionate
restriction on freedom of expression, and thus did not conflict with art 10 of the
convention. Although the maintenance of archives, whether in hardcopy or on
the Internet, had a social utility, it was a comparatively insignificant aspect of
freedom of expression. Archive material was stale news and its publication could
not rank in importance with the dissemination of contemporary material. In any
event, the law of defamation did not have to inhibit the responsible maintenance
of archives. Where it was known that archive material was or might be defamatory,
the attachment of an appropriate notice warning against treating it as the truth
would normally remove any sting from the material. Moreover, whilst it was
true that to permit an action to be based on a fresh dissemination of an article
published long ago was at odds with some of the reasons for the introduction of
a one-year limitation period for defamation, the scale of such publication and any
resulting damage was likely to be modest compared with that of the original
publication. Accordingly, the appeal against the judge's refusal to allow the
amendment in the second action would be dismissed. Similarly, the appeal
against the striking out of the qualified privilege defence in that action would be
dismissed since the failure to attach any qualification to the articles published
over the period of a year on the newspaper's website could not possibly be
described as responsible journalism (see [74]–[76], [79], [102], below); *Duke of
Brunswick and Luneberg v Harmer* (1849) 14 QB 185 applied; *Berezovsky v Michaels,
Glouchkov v Michaels* [2000] 2 All ER 986 considered.

(3) The summary disposal procedure under s 8 of the 1996 Act was not
confined to cases in which the court was asked to make a determination before
there had been a trial on liability. The purpose of s 8 was to establish a procedure
for dealing with small claims in a time and cost-effective way. If it was appropriate
to have a summary procedure for disposing of issues of liability and quantum,
there was no reason why that procedure should not also be available in a suitable
case for disposing of quantum alone once liability had been determined or
admitted. The statute did not expressly limit the jurisdiction in that way and, on
a purposive construction, it was not intended to do so. A claim was not disposed
of by the court until both liability and quantum had been decided. Accordingly,
the appeal on the summary disposal point would also be dismissed (see [98], [99],
[101], [102], below).

Notes

For the right to freedom of expression, the defence of qualified privilege, the
limitation period and accrual of cause of action in defamation cases, and
summary disposal of defamation claims, see respectively 8(2) *Halsbury's Laws* (4th

a edn reissue) paras 158–159, 28 *Halsbury's Laws* (4th edn reissue) paras 109, 121, 123, 28 *Halsbury's Laws* (4th edn reissue) paras 902–903 and 28 *Halsbury's Laws* (4th edn reissue) paras 207–209.

For the Limitation Act 1980, s 4A, see 24 *Halsbury's Statutes* (4th edn) (1998 reissue) 703.

For the Defamation Act 1996, s 8, see 24 *Halsbury's Statutes* (4th edn) (1998
b reissue) 130.

For the Human Rights Act 1998, Sch 1, Pt I, art 10, see 7 *Halsbury's Statutes* (4th edn reissue) 524.

Cases referred to in judgment

Adam v Ward [1917] AC 309, [1916–17] All ER Rep 157, HL.
c *Al-Fagih v HH Saudi Research and Marketing (UK) Ltd* [2001] EWCA Civ 1634, [2001] All ER (D) 48 (Nov).
Baldwin v Rusbridger [2001] EMLR 1062.
Berezovsky v Michaels, Glouchkov v Michaels [2000] 2 All ER 986, [2000] 1 WLR 1004, HL; *affg* sub nom *Berezovsky v Forbes Inc, Glouchkov v Forbes Inc* [1999] EMLR
d 278, CA.
Blackshaw v Lord [1983] 2 All ER 311, [1984] QB 1, [1983] 3 WLR 283, CA.
Brunswick and Luneberg (Duke of) v Harmer (1849) 14 QB 185, 117 ER 75.
Burstein v Times Newspapers Ltd [2001] 1 WLR 579, CA.
Chase Securities Corp (t/a Amerex Holding Corp) v Donaldson (1945) 325 US 304, US SC.
GKR Karate (UK) Ltd v Yorkshire Post Newspapers Ltd [2000] 2 All ER 931, [2000] 1
e WLR 2571, CA.
Godfrey v Demon Internet Ltd [1999] 4 All ER 342, [2001] QB 201, [2000] 3 WLR 1020.
Gregoire v G P Putnam's Sons (1948) 81 NE (2d) 45, NY Ct of Apps.
Horrocks v Lowe [1974] 1 All ER 662, [1975] AC 135, [1974] 2 WLR 282, HL.
f *James v Baird* 1916 SC (HL) 158.
Lange v Atkinson (2000) 8 BHRC 500, NZ CA; *remitted from* [2000] 1 NZLR 257, PC.
Loutchansky v Times Newspapers Ltd [2001] EWCA Civ 536, [2001] 4 All ER 115, [2001] 3 WLR 404.
Lukowiak v Unidad Editoriale SA [2001] EMLR 1043.
g *McCartan Turkington Breen (a firm) v Times Newspapers Ltd* [2000] 4 All ER 913, [2001] 2 AC 277, [2000] 3 WLR 1670, HL.
Ogden v Association of the United States Army (a corporation) (1959) 177 F supp 498, US DC (District of Columbia).
Reynolds v Times Newspapers Ltd [1999] 4 All ER 609, [2001] 2 AC 127, [1999] 3 WLR 1010, HL.
h *Stuart v Bell* (1891) 2 QB 341, CA.
Toogood v Spyring (1834) 1 Cr M & R 181, [1824–34] All ER Rep 735, 149 ER 1044.
Whiteley v Adams (1863) 15 CB (NS) 392, 143 ER 838, CP.

Cases also cited or referred to in skeleton arguments

j *Abrams v United States* (1919) 250 US 616, US SC.
Age-Herald Publishing Co v Huddleston (1921) 207 Ala 40, Alabama SC.
Alexander v Arts Council of Wales [2001] EWCA Civ 514, [2001] 4 All ER 205, [2001] 1 WLR 1840.
Bata v Bata [1948] WN 366, CA.
Bergens Tidende v Norway (2001) 31 EHRR 430, [2000] ECHR 26132/95, ECt HR.
Beta Construction Ltd v Channel Four Ltd [1990] 1 WLR 1042, CA.

Bladet Tromsø v Norway (1999) 6 BHRC 599, ECt HR.
Bottomley v F W Woolworth & Co Ltd (1932) 48 TLR 521, CA.
Braddock v Bevins [1948] 1 All ER 450, [1948] 1 KB 580, CA.
Butler v Southam Inc (2000) 191 NSR (2d) 158, NS SC.
Castells v Spain (1992) 14 EHRR 445, [1992] ECHR 11798/85, ECt HR.
City of Chicago v Tribune Co (1923) 139 NE 86, Ill SC.
Cox v Feeny (1863) 4 F & F 13, 176 ER 445, NP.
De Freitas v Permanent Secretary of Ministry of Agriculture, Fisheries, Lands and Housing
    [1999] 1 AC 69, [1998] 3 WLR 675, PC.
De Haes v Belgium (1997) 25 EHRR 1, [1997] ECHR 19983/99, ECt HR.
Derbyshire CC v Times Newspapers Ltd [1993 1 All ER 1011, [1993] AC 534, HL.
Devlin v UK [2001] ECHR 29545/95, ECt HR.
Douglas v Hello! Ltd [2001] 2 All ER 289, [2001] 2 WLR 992, CA.
Fayed v UK (1994) 18 EHRR 393, [1994] ECHR 17101/90, ECt HR.
Firth v State of New York (2000) 706 NYS (2d) 835, NY Ct of Claims.
Goodwin v UK (1996) 1 BHRC 81, ECt HR.
Grobbelaar v News Group Newspapers Ltd [2001] EWCA Civ 33, [2001] 2 All ER 437.
Hartmann v Time (1947) 166 F (2d) 127, US Ct of Apps (3rd Cir).
Imutran Ltd v Uncaged Campaigns Ltd [2001] 2 All ER 385.
Jersild v Denmark (1994) 19 EHRR 1, [1994] ECHR 15890/89, ECt HR.
John v MGN Ltd [1996] 2 All ER 35, [1997] QB 586, CA.
Keeton v Hustler Magazine Inc (1984) 465 US 770, US SC.
Lange v Australian Broadcasting Corp [1997] 4 LRC 192, Aust HC.
Lee v Wilson & Mackinnon (1934) 51 CLR 276, Aust HC.
London Association for Protection of Trade v Greenlands Ltd [1916] 2 AC 15, [1916–17]
    All ER Rep 452, HL.
McDonald's Corp v Steel [1995] 3 All ER 615, CA.
McLean v David Syme & Co Ltd (1970) 92 WN (NSW) 611, NSW SC.
Means v MacFadden Publications Inc (1939) 25 F Supp 993, NY DC (SD).
Mohammed v The State [1999] 2 AC 111, [1999] 2 WLR 552, PC.
New York Times Co v Sullivan (1964) 376 US 254, US SC.
Nilsen v Norway (1999) 29 EHRR 125, [1999] ECHR 23118/93, ECt HR.
Oyston v Blaker [1996] 2 All ER 106, [1996] 1 WLR 1326, CA.
R v A [2001] UKHL 25, [2001] 3 All ER 1, [2001] 2 WLR 1546.
R v Lambert [2001] UKHL 37, [2001] 3 All ER 577, [2001] 3 WLR 206.
R v Secretary of State for the Home Dept, ex p Daly [2001] UKHL 26, [2001] 3 All ER
    433, [2001] 2 AC 532.
R v Secretary of State for the Home Dept, ex p Simms [1999] 3 All ER 400, [2000] 2 AC
    115, HL.
R v Wright (1799) 8 Term Rep 293, 101 ER 1396.
Rantzen v Mirror Group Newspapers (1986) *Ltd* [1993] 4 All ER 975, [1994] QB 670, CA.
Safeway Stores plc v Tate [2001] 4 All ER 193, [2001] QB 1120, CA.
Scott v Sampson (1882) 8 QBD 491, [1881–85] All ER Rep 628, DC.
Shah v Standard Chartered Bank [1998] 4 All ER 155, [1999] QB 241, CA.
Spring v Guardian Assurance plc [1994] 3 All ER 129, [1995] 2 AC 296, HL.
Stabilad Ltd v Stephen & Carter Ltd [1998] 4 All ER 129, [1999] 1 WLR 1201, CA.
Stern v Piper [1996] 3 All ER 385, [1997] QB 123, CA.
Stubbings v UK (1996) 23 EHRR 213, [1996] ECHR 22083/93, ECt HR.
Sun Life Assurance Co of Canada v W H Smith & Son Ltd (1933) 150 LT 211, [1933]
    All ER Rep 432, CA.
Sunday Times v UK (1979) 2 EHRR 245, [1979] ECHR 6538/74, ECt HR.

a *Sunday Times v UK (No 2)* (1991) 14 EHRR 229, ECt HR.
Sutcliffe v Pressdram Ltd [1990] 1 All ER 269, [1991] 1 QB 153, CA.
Templeton v Jones [1984] 1 NZLR 448, NZ CA.
Thorgeirson v Iceland (1992) 14 EHRR 843, ECt HR.
Venables v News Group Newspapers Ltd [2001] 1 All ER 908, [2001] Fam 430.
Vizetelly v Mudie's Select Library Ltd [1900] 2 QB 170, CA.
b *Wason v Walter* (1868) LR 4 QB 73, [1861–73] All ER Rep 105, DC.
Webb v Times Publishing Co Ltd [1960] 2 All ER 789, [1960] 2 QB 535.
Weldon v Times Book Co Ltd (1911) 28 TLR 143, CA.
Whitney v California (1927) 274 US 357, US SC.
Wolfson v Syracuse Newspapers Inc (1938) 254 App Div 211, NY SC.

c **Appeals**
Times Newspapers Ltd, Peter Stothard, David Lister and James Bone, the defendants to two actions for libel brought by the respondent claimant, Grigori Loutchansky, appealed (i) with permission of Latham LJ granted on 18 June 2001 from the orders of Gray J on 19 and 20 March 2001 ([2001] EMLR 876 and [2001]
d EMLR 885) dismissing the appellants' application for leave to re-amend their defence in the second action and striking out the defence of qualified privilege pleaded in that action; (ii) with permission of the Court of Appeal from the decision of Gray J on 22 March 2001 whereby he held that general damages in the first action were recoverable by the respondent in respect of the Russian publication of the alleged libels; (iii) with permission of Gray J from his decision
e on 27 April 2001 ([2001] EMLR 898) whereby he held that the defence of qualified privilege was not available to the appellants in the first action; and (iv) with permission of Gray J from his decision on 11 May 2001 ([2001] EMLR 933) acceding to the respondent's application for summary disposal of his claim for damages under s 8 of the Defamation Act 1996. The facts are set out in the
f judgment of the court.

Lord Lester of Herne Hill QC, Richard Spearman QC, Richard Parkes and Brian
    Kennelly (instructed by Reynolds Porter Chamberlain) for the appellants.
Desmond Browne QC and Hugh Tomlinson (instructed by Olswang) for the respondent.

g   *Cur adv vult*

5 December 2001. The following judgment of the court, to which all its members contributed, was delivered.

h **LORD PHILLIPS OF WORTH MATRAVERS MR.**
    [1] There are before us a number of interrelated appeals arising out of two consolidated libel actions brought by Dr Loutchansky (the respondent) against the publisher and editor of The Times and two of its journalists (the appellants). The first action was brought on 6 December 1999 in respect of two articles published in The Times respectively on 8 September 1999 (the first article) and 14 October 1999 (the
j second article); the second action was brought on 6 December 2000 in respect of the continued Internet publication of the same two articles on The Times website after 21 February 2000.
    [2] The appeals raise interesting and important questions variously as to the correct approach to qualified privilege following the House of Lords' decision in *Reynolds v Times Newspapers Ltd* [1999] 4 All ER 609, [2001] 2 AC 127, the proper construction of s 4A of the Limitation Act 1980 in the context of Internet

publication, the scope of general damages for defamation under Russian law, and
the availability of the summary disposal procedure under s 8 of the Defamation   *a*
Act 1996 once judgment has been entered, an issue of jurisdiction.

[3] Before attempting further to identify and address the particular points
arising, it is necessary to indicate something of the facts of the case although, for
reasons which will become clear, we can do so comparatively briefly; their fuller
exposition can be found in Gray J's judgment below ([2001] EMLR 898), and in   *b*
this court's judgment in *Loutchansky v Times Newspapers Ltd* [2001] EWCA Civ
536, [2001] 4 All ER 115, [2001] 3 WLR 404 (the appeal which decided, subject to
further appeal to the House of Lords, that a publisher claiming qualified privilege
cannot pray in aid facts unknown to him at the time of publication).

The facts   *c*
[4] The respondent is an international businessman of Russian and Israeli dual
nationality. He was born in Tashkent and subsequently based in Latvia. Prior to
December 1994 he was a regular visitor to England with numerous personal
business contacts here. In that month, however, the Home Secretary personally
directed his exclusion from the United Kingdom on the ground that his presence   *d*
here would not be conducive to the public good. That direction has been under
challenge ever since and an appeal is now pending before the Special Immigration
Appeals Commission.

[5] The first article was in these terms:

'SECOND RUSSIAN LINKED TO MONEY-LAUNDERING   *e*
   British and American investigators are examining the role of an alleged
second Russian mafia boss over possible involvement in money-laundering
through the Bank of New York. Investigators are understood to be looking
at links to Grigori Lutchansky [sic], whose company, Nordex, has been
described by the CIA as "an organisation associated with Russian criminal
activity". Mr Lutchansky's name surfaced in earlier money-laundering   *f*
investigations which may have links to the Bank of New York affair, in which
billions of dollars of Russian money are alleged to have been laundered. The
Russian-born businessman came to the attention of European and American
investigators in the early Nineties. They suspected Nordex of using its former
international base in Vienna as a front for a large-scale money-laundering   *g*
operation. His name also figured in a British police report in 1995, known as
Operation Ivan, which looked at the extent of the influence of the Russian
mob in London. Mr Lutchansky has repeatedly denied any wrong-doing or
links to criminal activity. Nordex, which has since moved out of Vienna, is
also alleged to have been involved in the smuggling of nuclear weapons and   *h*
by the mid-1990s reportedly controlled about 60 businesses in the former
Soviet Union and another 40 companies in the West. *The Times* has learnt
that these included between eight and ten offshore companies in British
jurisdictions, including the Channel Islands and the Isle of Man. They were
administered through a chartered accountant in central London whose
offices and homes were raided in 1996 by officers from the City of London   *j*
Police. The companies were suspected of being used to help launder money
from Russia, which was then channelled through European banks. No
charges were ever filed against the accountant. At about the same time, a
Yugoslav associate said to have been a front-man for Mr Lutchansky was
stopped and questioned after arriving at a London airport. No charges were
filed against him. The British investigation into Nordex is believed to have

a   failed because of the difficulty of establishing that the money funnelled
through offshore companies controlled by Nordex was linked to criminal
activities. Mr Lutchansky is alleged to be a former business associate of
Viktor Chernomyrdin, the former Russian Prime Minister, and in 1995 his
name hit the headlines after it emerged that he had been photographed with
President Clinton at a Democrat fund-raising event in 1993. He is also
b   alleged to have had business dealings with Semyon Mogilevich, the Hungarian-
based mafia figure at the centre of the Bank of New York investigation.'

[6] The words complained of in the second article read:

'TRADER LINKED TO MAFIA BOSS, WIFE CLAIMS
A Russian businessman under investigation by Swiss authorities pursuing
c   allegations of money-laundering was a friend of Grigori Lutchansky, a
suspected mafia boss, the businessman's wife claims ... If Mrs Chernoi's
allegation about a connection between her husband and Mr Lutchansky is
true, it will raise further questions about Mr Chernoi. In 1996 the CIA
described Nordex, a company operated by Mr Lutchansky and alleged to
d   have been used to launder money and smuggle nuclear weapons, as an
"organisation associated with Russian criminal activity".'

[7] The appellants never disputed that both articles were defamatory of the
respondent nor, indeed, was there any substantial dispute as to their meaning.
Both articles alleged that the respondent was the boss of a major Russian criminal
e   organisation and was involved in, amongst other things, money-laundering and
the smuggling of nuclear weapons either personally or through Nordex, a
company he owned and controlled. The first article stated more specifically that
either personally or by means of companies which he owned or controlled he was
involved in the criminal laundering of billions of dollars from Russia, alternatively,
by his conduct, had given reasonable cause to suspect him or his companies of
f   such involvement.

[8] Each article foreseeably prompted republication of the libellous matter by
the mass media in Russia in respect of which the respondent (in the first action)
also claimed damages.

[9] A further consequence of publication was that each article was posted on
g   The Times website where it has since remained accessible and, as ultimately
conceded, has from time to time been read. Despite the respondent's letter before
action on 17 November 1999 and subsequent complaints about the continuing
Internet publication of the articles, no qualification was added to the website until
23 December 2000 when the first article was prefaced by the words: 'This article
is subject to High Court libel litigation between Grigori Loutchansky and Times
h   Newspapers. It should not be reproduced or relied on without reference to
Times Newspapers Legal Department.'

[10] The sole defence pleaded to the first action was that of qualified privilege.
The appellants aver that it is the duty of a free press to communicate to the public
at large information regarding matters of public interest and that there is a
j   corresponding interest on the part of members of the public in receiving such
information. They contend that the subject matter of the articles complained of
was of the greatest general interest and importance to the public at large and to
the readers of The Times in particular, that is to say the corruption and
criminalisation of Russian society since the break up of the USSR, the involvement
of Russian organised criminal groups in money-laundering through western
banks, the smuggling of nuclear weapons and the activities of such groups,

including the acquisition of businesses in the West and in the United Kingdom in
particular. They rely upon various information which they say they were entitled a
to treat as reliable, responsible and authoritative. That comprised media reports
of the involvement of the Bank of New York in laundering the proceeds of
criminal activity in Russia; media reports of suspicions about and investigations
into serious crimes allegedly committed by the respondent, which have resulted
in his exclusion from various jurisdictions including the United Kingdom; a b
statement by the then director of the CIA about the respondent's company,
Nordex, being associated with Russian criminal activity; the respondent's
conviction by a Latvian court in 1983 of offences of dishonesty; and various
reports by intelligence services. In addition, the appellants rely on information
provided to Mr Lister, the author of both articles, by three unidentified sources
and a fourth source (eventually named as Jeffrey Robinson, the author of a book c
about organised crime) who asserted amongst other things that the respondent
either had been or was being investigated by various law enforcement agencies
in connection with money-laundering offences.

[11] The appellants have never sought to justify any aspect of these
defamatory publications: they recognise that they have been quite unable to d
obtain admissible evidence sufficient to plead and prove even the lesser form of
justification, reasonable grounds for suspicion. Rather their stance from first to
last has been that whilst it is no part of their case that the respondent is either
rightly or reasonably suspected of criminal activity, they for their part honestly
believe that he is. Certainly there has been no plea of malice in reply so that the
appellants' good faith is not in issue. e

[12] The second action was brought, as already noted, exactly a year after the
first. It related (so far as presently material) to the continuing Internet publication
of the articles and was prompted by the respondent's discovery that no
qualification whatever had been placed upon the appellants' website.

[13] The claim in the second action repeated the allegations that were made f
in the first. A claim for aggravated damages was added on grounds which
included:

'The defendant continued to publish the first and second libels on the
website despite the fact that they knew that they could not justify the g
allegations made and despite complaints by the claimant's solicitors in a
letter dated 25 October 2000.'

The defence adopted the plea of qualified privilege that had been pleaded in the
first action. Additional matters were relied upon in support of the plea of qualified
privilege. The first was that The Times maintained on its website a publicly h
available archive of past issues as a service to the public at large, both in this
country and abroad. In addition the appellants sought to rely upon various items
of information about the respondent or his companies that had come to their
attention between the date of the commencement of the first action and the date
of the commencement of the second action. j

[14] It is necessary next to indicate something of the course which these two
actions have taken, in particular to see just how the present series of appeals arise.

[15] Having ordered a split trial of the issues of liability and quantum, Gray J
began the liability trial of both actions on 19 March 2001 and on that day ([2001]
EMLR 876) made the first of the several orders now under appeal: an order
refusing the appellants leave to re-amend their defence in the second action—

a
'to contend that as a matter of law the only actionable publication of a newspaper article on the Internet is that which occurs when the article is first posted on the Internet. In consequence, the claimant's cause of action in respect of Internet publication of the articles of 8 September 1999 and 14 October 1999 did not accrue within one year before the commencement of the action and the defendant will rely on s 4A of the Limitation Act 1980.'

b
[16] In other words, the appellants were seeking to contend that a single publication rule should be applied when material which is initially published in hard copy is republished on the Internet. In rejecting that contention and holding that the single publication rule (prevalent in many states of the United States of America) is not applicable in this jurisdiction, the judge relied principally on two
c authorities, one old and one new: *Duke of Brunswick and Luneberg v Harmer* (1849) 14 QB 185, 117 ER 75 and *Berezovsky v Michaels, Glouchkov v Michaels* [2000] 2 All ER 986, [2000] 1 WLR 1004. The appellants submit that he was wrong to do so. This has been called the Internet single publication appeal.

[17] On the following day, 20 March 2001, the judge made the second of the orders now appealed, an order striking out the defence of qualified privilege in
d the second action on the basis that the appellants had no reasonable grounds to contend that after 21 February 2000 (the date of the appellants' defence in the first action) they remained under a duty to publish these articles over the Internet, nor could they sustain a separate argument for a special 'archive' privilege (see [2001] EMLR 885). The appellants' challenge to that order has been called the Internet
e qualified privilege appeal. These first two appeals (and a third appeal against the consequential order entering judgment for the respondent in the second action) are brought with the permission of Latham LJ.

[18] On 22 March 2001 the judge ruled that general damages in the first action are recoverable by the respondent in respect of the Russian publication of these libels since such damages would be recoverable under Russian law. We ourselves
f gave permission during the hearing for an appeal against this order and will call it the Russian publication appeal.

[19] The jury was finally empanelled on 26 March 2001 and the hearing then continued until 11 April when the jury gave their answers to 15 specific questions of primary fact which had been put to them as part of the process by which the
g judge had to decide whether the defence of qualified privilege was available to the appellants in the first action. In a very full and careful reserved judgment delivered on 27 April ([2001] EMLR 898), Gray J then ruled that the defence of qualified privilege was not available to the appellants in respect of either article so that in the first action too judgment was entered for the respondent for damages to be assessed. On this issue, however, the judge gave leave to appeal
h in the following terms:

'Success on the appeal may be problematic since the decision was ultimately one of fact. But I believe there is a compelling reason why the appeal should be heard, namely what standard the courts should apply when deciding
j whether there was a duty to publish defamatory words to the world at large.'

This has been called the first action liability appeal.

[20] Finally, on 11 May 2001, the judge acceded to the respondent's application 'that there be a summary disposal of the claimant's claim for damages under s 8 of the Defamation Act 1996' (see [2001] EMLR 933). This order, as stated, is challenged by the appellants on jurisdictional grounds. This has been called the summary disposal appeal.

[21] It is logical to consider first the first action liability appeal since its outcome must inevitably impact upon other appeals also, most obviously the Internet qualified privilege appeal.

The first action liability appeal

[22] This appeal must inevitably turn upon a proper understanding and application of the decision of the House of Lords in *Reynolds v Times Newspapers Ltd* [1999] 4 All ER 609, [2001] 2 AC 127. As to that let us begin by repeating para [26] of Simon Brown LJ's recent judgment in *Al-Fagih v HH Saudi Research and Marketing (UK) Ltd* [2001] EWCA Civ 1634, [2001] All ER (D) 48 (Nov):

> 'I must take as read the bulk of what was said in each of the five speeches in *Reynolds'* case. To cite even the most important passages would unduly lengthen this judgment. In essence the case held that the question whether a particular publication attracts qualified privilege at common law should be decided simply by asking whether in all the circumstances "the duty-interest test, or the right to know test" is satisfied (see [1999] 4 All ER 609 at 619, [2001] 2 AC 127 at 197 per Lord Nicholls of Birkenhead). Amongst the relevant circumstances are likely to be the ten specific factors identified by Lord Nicholls ([1999] 4 All ER 609 at 626, [2001] 2 AC 127 at 205). This approach reflects the European Court of Human Rights jurisprudence under art 10 of the European Convention of Human Rights and is designed to enable a proper balance to be struck between on the one hand the cardinal importance of freedom of expression by the media on all matters of public concern, and on the other the right of an individual to his good reputation. Neither right is absolute but the former, particularly in the field of political discussion, is of a higher order, a constitutional right of vital importance to the proper functioning of a democratic society. That is why "any curtailment of freedom of expression must be convincingly established by a compelling countervailing consideration, and the means employed must be proportionate to the end sought to be achieved" (see [1999] 4 All ER 609 at 622, [2001] 2 AC 127 at 200 per Lord Nicholls), and why "Any lingering doubts [as to how the balance should be struck] should be resolved in favour of publication" (see [1999] 4 All ER 609 at 626, [2001] 2 AC 127 at 205 per Lord Nicholls).'

[23] So far so good. At the end of the day the court has to ask itself the single question whether in all the circumstances the 'duty-interest test, or the right to know test' has been satisfied so that qualified privilege attaches. If, of course, it does, then, unless the claimant can prove malice, the defamatory publication is protected irrespective of whether it turns out to be true or false. So much at least of any analysis of *Reynolds'* case one might have thought to be uncontentious. There would then remain for determination the critical question as to what precisely these tests involve—or, as Gray J put it when granting permission to appeal, 'what standard the courts should apply when deciding whether there was a duty to publish defamatory words to the world at large'. Before reaching that question, however, it is necessary to deal first with a wider argument advanced by Lord Lester of Herne Hill QC for the appellants: the submission that this court should 'develop and clarify *Reynolds'* case' and—

> 'acknowledge that the traditional duty/interest test has been replaced by the following test: (1) whether, in all the circumstances other than the conduct of the newspaper, the subject matter of the communication is in the

a public interest ("the right to know"), giving rise to a prima facie occasion of qualified privilege; and (2) whether the newspaper failed to comply with the ethics of responsible journalism so as to abuse the occasion of privilege.'

[24] In support of this argument Lord Lester subjects *Reynolds'* case to a powerful and sustained critique, citing at length from the New Zealand Court of b Appeal's decision in *Lange v Atkinson* (2000) 8 BHRC 500 (the case having been remitted to that court by the Privy Council ([2000] 1 NZLR 257) specifically to allow for its reconsideration in the light of *Reynolds'* case). The New Zealand Court (at 510 (paras 24, 25)) declined to follow *Reynolds'* case, first because 'The blurring, perhaps even the removal, of the line between the occasion and its abuse in Lord Nicholls' non exhaustive list must add significantly to [the] c uncertainty [in both the principles of defamation law and their practical application]', and secondly, because 'it reduces the role of the jury in freedom of speech cases'. The essence of the decision is to be found in para 38 of the judgment (at 514):

d 'For reasons which can be briefly restated we would not strike the balance differently from the way it was struck in 1998. First, the *Reynolds* decision appears to alter the structure of the law of qualified privilege in a way which adds to the uncertainty and chilling effect almost inevitably present in this area of the law. We are not persuaded that in the New Zealand situation matters such as the steps taken to verify the information, the seeking of e comment from the person defamed, and the status or source of the information, should fall within the ambit of the inquiry into whether the occasion is privileged. Traditionally such matters are not of concern to that question in the kind of setting presently under discussion.'

[25] The New Zealand Court of Appeal then redefined (at 516 (para 44)) the f concept of actual malice to provide a stronger safeguard against abuse, stating:

'... while carelessness will not of itself be sufficient to negate the defence, its existence may well support an assertion by the plaintiff of a lack of belief or recklessness. In this way the concept of reasonable or responsible conduct on the part of a defendant in the particular circumstances becomes a legitimate g consideration.'

Malice, of course, here as in New Zealand, is an issue falling for determination by the jury.

[26] Powerful though this reasoning may appear, its effect can only be to accentuate the very different approaches which have been adopted in the two h jurisdictions. We, of course, are bound to follow that favoured by the House of Lords in *Reynolds'* case. Complain as he may that their approach conflates a two-part test and effectively pre-empts the jury's role in deciding malice, Lord Lester must recognise the constraints of binding authority. The most we can do is attempt to illuminate the single composite test which *Reynolds'* case undoubtedly j dictates and to identify certain of the crucial considerations likely to influence its application.

[27] Having now set out the parameters within which this court must operate, we think it helpful next to consider how the law of qualified privilege stood before the House of Lords in *Reynolds'* case came to determine how the defence should apply where matters of public interest and concern are published to the world at large.

[28] The origins of the common law defence of qualified privilege are to be found in *Toogood v Spyring* (1834) 1 Cr M & R 181 at 193, [1824–34] All ER Rep 735 *a* at 737–738, where Parke B said:

'In general, an action lies for the malicious publication of statements which are false in fact, and injurious to the character of another ... and the law considers such publication as malicious, unless it is fairly made by a person *b* in the discharge of some public or private duty, whether legal or moral, or in the conduct of his own affairs, in matters where his interest is concerned. In such cases, the occasion prevents the inference of malice, which the law draws from unauthorized communications, and affords a qualified defence depending upon the absence of actual malice. If *fairly* warranted by any reasonable occasion or exigency, and honestly made, such communications *c* are protected for the common convenience and welfare of society; and the law has not restricted the right to make them within any narrow limits.'

[29] Lindley LJ's judgment in *Stuart v Bell* (1891) 2 QB 341 at 350–351 illustrates the principle in operation:

d
'I take moral or social duty to mean a duty recognised by English people of ordinary intelligence and moral principle, but at the same time not a duty enforceable by legal proceedings, whether civil or criminal. My own conviction is that all or, at all events, the great mass of right-minded men in the position of the defendant would have considered it their duty, under the circumstances, to inform Stanley [the plaintiff's employer who in the light of *e* the communication dismissed him] of the suspicion which had fallen on the plaintiff. My own opinion is clear and strong that it was his moral or social, although not his legal, duty to do so; in other words, the occasion was privileged, and the judge should have directed the jury to this effect.'

[30] As Lord Nicholls observed, Lord Atkinson's dictum in *Adam v Ward* *f* [1917] AC 309 at 334, [1916–17] All ER Rep 157 at 170, is much quoted:

'... a privileged occasion is ... an occasion where the person who makes a communication has an interest or duty, legal, social, or moral, to make it to the person to whom it is made, and the person to whom it is so made has a corresponding interest or duty to receive it. This reciprocity is essential.' *g*

[31] Although, as Lord Nicholls explained in *Reynolds'* case [1999] 4 All ER 609 at 617–619, [2001] 2 AC 127 at 195–197, the common law has for many years recognised that on occasion the public interest may require that privilege be attached to publication even to the world at large, such instances are few and far *h* between. *Blackshaw v Lord* [1983] 2 All ER 311, [1984] QB 1, a decision of this court extensively cited and discussed by Brooke LJ in his helpful judgment in *Loutchansky v Times Newspapers Ltd* [2001] 4 All ER 115, [2001] 3 WLR 404, may have been, as Lord Cooke of Thorndon subsequently pointed out in *McCartan Turkington Breen (a firm) v Times Newspapers Ltd* [2000] 4 All ER 913 at 931, [2001] *j* 2 AC 277 at 301, 'somewhat discouraging' for newspapers contemplating this defence. In *Blackshaw v Lord* [1983] 2 All ER 311 at 327, [1984] QB 1 at 27, Stephenson LJ had put the possibility no higher than that—

'There may be extreme cases where the urgency of communicating a warning is so great, or the source of the information so reliable, that publication of suspicion or speculation is justified; for example, where there a is danger to the public from a suspected terrorist or the distribution of contaminated food or drugs ...'

[32] Although Lord Cooke in *Reynolds'* case spoke of the Court of Appeal in *Blackshaw v Lord* having 'adopted substantially the right approach', and said that 'In *Blackshaw v Lord* ... and now the present case, the law is being developed to meet the reasonable demands of freedom of speech in a modern democracy' (see
b [1999] 4 All ER 609 at 644, 645, [2001] 2 AC 127 at 224, 225), it is difficult to recognise in the approach to the defence conventionally adopted in the earlier jurisprudence the particular form of qualified privilege created by the House of Lords in *Reynolds'* case. Whatever else may be said about the decision of the New Zealand Court of Appeal in *Lange v Atkinson*, it was surely right to have
c recognised the striking departure which *Reynolds'* case made from the earlier approach. *Reynolds* privilege (as we shall call it), although built upon an orthodox foundation, is in reality sui generis.

[33] Whereas previously it could truly be said of qualified privilege that it attaches to the occasion of the publication rather than the publication, *Reynolds*
d privilege attaches, if at all, to the publication itself: it is impossible to conceive of circumstances in which the occasion of publication could be privileged but the article itself not so. Similarly, once *Reynolds* privilege attaches, little scope remains for any subsequent finding of malice. Actual malice in this context has traditionally been recognised to consist either of recklessness, ie not believing the statement to be true or being indifferent as to its truth, or of making it with the
e dominant motive of injuring the claimant. But the publisher's conduct in both regards must inevitably be explored when considering Lord Nicholls' ten factors, ie in deciding whether the publication is covered by qualified privilege in the first place. As May LJ observed in *GKR Karate (UK) Ltd v Yorkshire Post Newspapers Ltd* [2000] 2 All ER 931 at 940, [2000] 1 WLR 2571 at 2580:

f
'If the judge decides that the occasion was not privileged, the issue of malice does not arise. If the judge decides that the occasion was privileged, he must have decided that in all the circumstances at the time of the publication, including the extent of ... inquiries, the public was entitled to know the particular information available ... without [the journalist] making
g further inquiries. It is a little difficult to see how the same inquiries which objectively sustained the occasion as privileged would be capable of contributing to a conclusion that subjectively she was recklessly indifferent to the truth or falsity of her publication.'

[34] Similarly in *Al-Fagih's* case, when deciding that verification may well not
h be necessary or even appropriate in a case of neutral reportage, we concluded that the reckless form of malice could not run. Although that left outstanding the claimant's plea of malice on the basis that the publisher's dominant motive had been to injure him, it may be doubted whether in truth there remains room for such a principle in a case of *Reynolds* privilege. Once the publication of a particular
j article is held to be in the public interest on the basis of the public's right to know, can the privilege really be lost because the journalist (or editor?) had the dominant motive of injuring the claimant rather than fulfilling his journalistic duty? It is a surprising thought.

[35] The relevance of these observations to the present appeal is this. Once *Reynolds* privilege is recognised, as it should be, as a different jurisprudential creature from the traditional form of privilege from which it sprang, the

particular nature of the 'interest' and 'duty' which underlie it can more easily be understood.

[36] The interest is that of the public in a modern democracy in free expression and, more particularly, in the promotion of a free and vigorous press to keep the public informed. The vital importance of this interest has been identified and emphasised time and again in recent cases and needs no restatement here. The corresponding duty on the journalist (and equally his editor) is to play his proper role in discharging that function. His task is to behave as a responsible journalist. He can have no duty to publish unless he is acting responsibly any more than the public has an interest in reading whatever may be published irresponsibly. That is why in this class of case the question whether the publisher has behaved responsibly is necessarily and intimately bound up with the question whether the defence of qualified privilege arises. Unless the publisher is acting responsibly privilege cannot arise. That is not the case with regard to the more conventional situations in which qualified privilege arises. A person giving a reference or reporting a crime need not act responsibly: his communication will be privileged subject only to relevance and malice.

[37] Consider what Lord Diplock said in *Horrocks v Lowe* [1974] 1 All ER 662 at 669, [1975] AC 135 at 150:

> '... indifference to the truth of what he publishes is not to be equated with carelessness, impulsiveness or irrationality in arriving at a positive belief that it is true. The freedom of speech protected by the law of qualified privilege may be availed by all sorts and conditions of men. In affording to them immunity from suit if they have acted in good faith in compliance with a legal or moral duty or in protection of a legitimate interest the law must take them as it finds them. In ordinary life it is rare indeed for people to form their beliefs by a process of logical deduction from facts ascertained by a vigorous search for all available evidence and a judicious assessment of its probative value. In greater or in less degree according to their temperaments, their training, their intelligence, they are swayed by prejudice, rely on intuition instead of reasoning, leap to conclusions on inadequate evidence and fail to recognise the cogency of material which might cast doubt on the validity of the conclusions they reach. But despite the imperfection of the mental process by which the belief is arrived at it may still be "honest", ie a positive belief that the conclusions they have reached are true. The law demands no more.'

[38] *Reynolds* privilege could not arise in such circumstances: 'carelessness, impulsiveness or irrationality' would cost a journalist dear in the evaluation of his claim to privilege under several of the *Reynolds* factors, perhaps most notably factors 3, 4, 6, 7 and 8. As Lord Nicholls said:

> '[It] is for the court to have regard to all the circumstances when deciding whether the publication of particular material was privileged because of its value to the public. Its value to the public depends upon its quality as well as its subject matter. This solution has the merit of elasticity ... It can be applied appropriately to all information published by a newspaper, whatever its source or origin.' (See [1999] 4 All ER 609 at 623, [2001] 2 AC 127 at 202.)

[39] This court in *Al-Fagih's* case adopted the approach suggested by Lord Hobhouse of Woodborough in *Reynolds'* case, namely to ask: '... what it is in the public interest that the public should know and what the publisher could properly

a consider that he was under a public duty to tell the public' (see [1999] 4 All ER 609 at 658, [2001] 2 AC 127 at 239).

[40] Simon Brown LJ suggested that that approach seemed—

b

> 'properly to reflect on the one hand the importance of keeping the public informed and on the other the need for responsible journalism to guard against needless misinformation. A publisher could not "properly consider that he was under a public duty" to communicate the information to the public unless in deciding to do so he reasonably believed that he was acting responsibly.' (See *Al-Fagih*'s case [2001] All ER (D) 48 (Nov) at [46].)

c

It may be that the words 'reasonably believed that he' towards the end of that formulation are best omitted: they were intended, perhaps unnecessarily, to emphasise the objective nature of the test. In the final analysis it must be for the court, not the journalist, to decide whether he was acting responsibly. That appears clearly from several passages in *Reynolds'* case: in rejecting the newspaper's commended 'reliance upon the ethics of professional journalism', Lord Nicholls ([1999] 4 All ER 609 at 623, [2001] 2 AC 127 at 202) referred to 'the sad reality ...

d that the overall handling of these matters by the national press, with its own commercial interests to serve, does not always command general confidence'. Lord Cooke ([1999] 4 All ER 609 at 640, [2001] 2 AC 127 at 220) suggested that 'experience of libel litigation is apt to generate a suspicion that' the restriction of freedom of speech thought necessary to give reasonable protection to personal reputation tends rather to chill the publication of untruths than of material which

e may be true but cannot be proved to be true. Lord Hope of Craighead too spoke of situations in which the 'chilling' effect of the law 'is a necessary protection for the individual'. Perhaps one need look no further than Lord Nicholls' dictum in *Reynolds'* case:

f

> 'The common law does not seek to set a higher standard than that of responsible journalism, a standard the media themselves espouse. An incursion into press freedom which goes no further than this would not seem to be excessive or disproportionate.' (See [1999] 4 All ER 609 at 623, [2001] 2 AC 127 at 202.)

g [41] In deciding in any given case whether the standard of responsible journalism has been satisfied, the following considerations are likely to feature prominently in the court's thinking. (i) If the publication is held privileged, that, to all intents and purposes, will provide the publishers with a complete defence. In this class of case, as already observed, a finding of privilege will effectively pre-empt a finding of malice. Lord Nicholls described malice as 'notoriously

h difficult to prove', Lord Cooke as 'a dubious safeguard', and Lord Hope as 'very difficult, if not impossible, [to prove] if the sources of the information cannot be identified' (see [1999] 4 All ER 609 at 622, 640, 654, [2001] 2 AC 127 at 201, 219, 235 respectively). Accordingly, if the defence is established, that, as Gray J pointed out in his judgment below ([2001] EMLR 898 at 905 (para 16)), has 'the

j effect of denying any remedy, whether by way of compensation or other vindication, to a person who has been libelled'. The damaging consequences of that, not merely for the aggrieved individual but for society at large, are highlighted by Lord Nicholls in *Reynolds'* case:

> 'Reputation is an integral and important part of the dignity of the individual. It also forms the basis of many decisions in a democratic society which are fundamental to its well-being: whom to employ or work for,

whom to promote, whom to do business with or to vote for. Once besmirched
by an unfounded allegation in a national newspaper, a reputation can be
damaged for ever, especially if there is no opportunity to vindicate one's
reputation. When this happens, society as well as the individual is the loser.
For it should not be supposed that protection of reputation is a matter of
importance only to the affected individual and his family. Protection of
reputation is conducive to the public good. It is in the public interest that
the reputation of public figures should not be debased falsely.' (See [1999]
4 All ER 609 at 622, [2001] 2 AC 127 at 201.)

(ii) Setting the standard of journalistic responsibility too low would inevitably
encourage too great a readiness to publish defamatory matter. Journalists should
be rigorous, not lax, in their approach. It is in the interests of the public as well
as the defamed individual that, wherever possible, truths and not untruths should
be told. This is in the interests of the media too: once untruths can be published
with impunity, the public will cease to believe any communications, true or false.
(iii) Setting the standard too high, however, would be no less damaging to
society. This would deter newspapers from discharging their proper function of
keeping the public informed. When determining in respect of any given article
whether or not it should attract qualified privilege, the court must bear in mind
the likely impact of its ruling not only upon the case in hand but also upon the
media's practices generally. Qualified privilege ordinarily falls to be judged as a
preliminary issue and before, therefore, the truth or falsity of the communication
is established. The question to be posed is accordingly whether it was in the
public interest to publish the article, true or false, rather than whether it was in
the public interest to publish an untruth. Even, moreover, when the untruth of
the article *is* established (or when, as here, it is not formally disputed), it is
important to remember that the defence of qualified privilege tolerates factual
inaccuracy for two purposes: first so as not to deter the publication sued upon
(which might have been true); and secondly so as not to deter future publications
of truthful information.

[42] Such being, in our judgment, the correct approach to determining whether
Reynolds privilege attaches, it is time to consider how the matter was dealt with below.
In paras 15–34 of his judgment ([2001] EMLR 898 at 905–911), variously under the
headings 'The Law', 'Human Rights Jurisprudence', and 'The Considerations for
Determining Privilege', Gray J conducts what is for the greater part an admirably
clear and succinct survey of the development of the law to its present state. For
the moment we quote only paras 23 and 24 (at 907–908):

'23 Although *Reynolds* has rightly been perceived as enlarging the ambit of
qualified privilege, the conceptual foundation for the defence remains the
existence of a reciprocity of duty and interest on the part of the publisher and
the publishees respectively. This dual requirement was confirmed by all the
members of the House of Lords in *Reynolds* (see for example Lord Hobhouse
([1999] 4 All ER 609 at 659, [2001] 2 AC 127 at 240)). Brooke L.J. at paragraph 23
of his judgment on an interlocutory appeal in the present case reiterated the
existence of this dual requirement.

24 It follows that the mere existence of a legitimate interest on the part of
the readership of a newspaper to have the information imparted to them will
not of itself suffice to establish the privilege. It is possible to visualise cases
where it can be said that the readership has a legitimate interest in knowing

a   the information (perhaps because of the status or nature of the information in question) but where the claim to privilege will fail because the requisite duty to publish is not made out (perhaps because of the newspaper's failure to report the gist of the answers of Dr Loutchansky to the accusations against him).'

b   [43] Having then in para 35 (at 912–913) recorded the jury's answers to the 15 questions of primary fact put to them, the judge turned to consider with regard to each of the two articles in turn the application of the ten *Reynolds* factors. Unsurprisingly in the circumstances of the present case, the longest section of this part of the judgment (at 915–923 (paras 46–93)) concerns '3. The reliability and motivation of the sources of the information', and certain passages in it are *c*   for one reason or another critical of Mr Lister. So too are various views expressed by the judge with regard to '6. The urgency of the matter', '7. Whether comment was sought from the claimant', and '8. Whether the article contained the gist of the claimant's side of the story'. The judge then came to his conclusions and held in respect of each of the articles (respectively in paras 107 and 119 *d*   (at 930, 932)) that the appellants 'were not under a duty to publish the article' so that the defence of qualified privilege was not available to them.

[44] But for one particular paragraph in the earlier section headed 'The Law', we would not have felt able to disturb that conclusion. Argue about it as one might, and as, indeed, Mr Spearman QC sought to do, it followed upon a masterful analysis of a great deal of material (including evidence from Mr Lister *e*   over five days) and was in no way demonstrably wrong. Paragraph 18 of the judgment (at 906), however, appears to us to be critical and it needs to be set out in full:

'"Duty" in the sense in which that term is used in this context has been
f   judicially defined by Lindley L.J. in *Stuart v. Bell* [1891] 2 Q.B. 341 at 350 to mean:

a duty recognised by English people of ordinary intelligence and moral principle, whether civil or criminal. Would the great mass of right-minded men in the position of the defendant have considered it *g*   their duty under the circumstances to make the communications? In considering the question whether the occasion was an occasion of privilege, the court will regard the alleged libel and will examine by whom it was published, to whom it was published, when, why, and in what circumstances it was published, and will see whether these things establish a relation between the parties which gives rise to a social or *h*   moral right or duty, and the consideration of these things may involve the consideration of questions of public policy.

It is for the Judge to determine whether an occasion is privileged and therefore to decide whether the defendant was under a duty to make the communication. The judge will have no difficulty in determining *j*   whether there was a legal duty to make the communication, but there is no sure and unfailing criterion of what does or does not constitute a moral or social duty; as was pointed out by Erle C.J. in *Whiteley v. Adams* ((1863) 15 CB (NS) 392 at 418, 143 ER 838 at 848), 'Judges ... have all felt great difficulty in defining what kind of social or moral duty will afford a justification.'

I take that form of duty, albeit one not owed in law, to be a duty such that a
publisher would be open to legitimate criticism if he failed to publish the
information in question.'

[45] The first point to note about para 18 is that for whatever reason it
substantially misquotes Lindley LJ's judgment in *Stuart v Bell*. The first part of the
'quotation' falls to be contrasted with the accurate citation in [29], above. So far
from 'duty' being 'judicially defined' in the formulation of the question: 'Would
the great mass of right-minded men in the position of the defendant have
considered it their duty under the circumstances to make the communications?',
one sees that Lindley LJ was merely emphasising his own clear view on the facts
of that particular case. The second part of the quotation is in fact not from *Stuart
v Bell* but from *James v Baird* 1916 SC (HL) 158 at 163–164, and the last part is from
Gatley on Libel and Slander (9th edn, 1998) p 331 (para 14.6).

[46] Secondly, however, and altogether more importantly, para 18 then sets
out Gray J's understanding of the test to be satisfied before the defence of
qualified privilege can be invoked: the duty owed is 'such that a publisher would
be open to legitimate criticism if he failed to publish the information in question'.

[47] True it is, as Mr Browne QC points out, that the judge never explicitly
comes back to this test in any subsequent part of his judgment: all he does is to
refer in para 24 (already quoted above) to 'the requisite duty to publish', and to
conclude in paras 107 and 119 that the appellants 'are not under a duty to publish'
either article. But can the criticism of para 18 therefore be discounted, as
Mr Browne suggests, merely as a 'linguistic quibble'? In our judgment not. The
fact is that already, in two subsequent cases, Eady J appears to have had no doubt
as to the test Gray J was applying. In *Lukowiak v Unidad Editoriale SA* [2001]
EMLR 1043 at 1060 (para 64) Eady J said:

'A cross-check that is sometimes useful to carry out in such cases, as
suggested by Gray J. in *Loutchansky* ... ([2001] EMLR 898), is to ask whether
the particular defendant could have been the subject of legitimate criticism
if the material had not been published.'

[48] Three days later, in *Baldwin v Rusbridger* [2001] EMLR 1062, Eady J again
applied the same test 'by way of additional check'.

[49] To apply the test merely as a 'cross-check' is unexceptionable where the
test is satisfied. If, indeed, the publisher would have been open to legitimate
criticism had he not published, his claim to privilege will be indisputable. But the
converse is not true. That would be to impose too stringent a test. There will
undoubtedly be occasions when one newspaper would decide to publish and
quite properly so, yet a second newspaper, no less properly, would delay or
abstain from publication. Not all journalists can be or should be expected to reach
an identical view in every case. Responsible journalism will in certain circumstances
permit equally of publication or of non-publication.

[50] We therefore conclude that Gray J applied the wrong test to the question
whether there was a duty upon the appellants to publish these defamatory articles
to the world at large. He was right to grant permission to appeal to clarify the
standard. The standard required is that of responsible journalism in accordance
with the principles earlier explained. The judge's findings of fact will accordingly
need to be re-examined with this standard in mind. In our judgment there is no
good reason why this exercise should not be performed by the same judge and
every possible reason, in terms of expense and proportionality, why it should.
We shall so order.

The Internet single publication appeal

a [51] We have set out the facts giving rise to this appeal in the introduction to this judgment. It results from the judge's refusal to allow the appellants to re-amend their defence in the second action to rely on s 4A of the Limitation Act 1980 in respect of continuing publication of the offending articles on the Internet.

[52] Section 4A provides that no action for 'libel or slander ... slander of title,
b slander of goods or other malicious falsehood ... shall be brought after the expiration of one year from the date on which the cause of action accrued'.

[53] This section is subject to the provisions of s 32A of the same Act which provides:

c '(1) If it appears to the court that it would be equitable to allow an action to proceed having regard to the degree to which—(a) the operation of section 4A of this Act prejudices the plaintiff or any person whom he represents, and (b) any decision of the court under this subsection would prejudice the defendant or any person whom he represents, the court may direct that that section shall not apply to the action or shall not apply to any
d specified cause of action to which the action relates.

(2) In acting under this section the court shall have regard to all the circumstances of the case and in particular to—(a) the length of, and the reasons for, the delay on the part of the plaintiff; (b) where the reason or one of the reasons for the delay was that all or any of the facts relevant to the cause of action did not become known to the plaintiff until after the end of
e the period mentioned in section 4A—(i) the date on which any such facts did become known to him, and (ii) the extent to which he acted promptly and reasonably once he knew whether or not the facts in question might be capable of giving rise to an action; and (c) the extent to which, having regard to the delay, relevant evidence is likely—(i) to be unavailable, or (ii) to be less
f cogent than if the action had been brought within the period mentioned in section 4A.'

[54] The argument before the judge turned on how these provisions should be applied in the case of publication on the Internet. The amendment sought by the appellants was designed to enable them to advance the case that the
g limitation period would begin to run as soon as the allegedly defamatory article was first posted on the website and that subsequent occasions upon which the website was accessed did not give rise to separate causes of action, each with its individual limitation period. As stated, the judge refused leave to amend because he considered that this argument was unsustainable. Before us, counsel for the appellants have elaborated the submissions rejected by the judge.
h [55] Lord Lester opened this part of the appeal on behalf of the appellants, having provided the court in advance with lengthy written submissions. He accepted that the amendment that the appellants sought to plead would only succeed if the court were prepared to make new law. He submitted, however, that this area of the common law had developed to suit traditional hardcopy
j publication and was inimical to modern conditions. He urged that the law should develop to reflect those conditions and to accommodate the requirements of the Human Rights Act 1998 and the European Convention for the Protection of Human Rights and Fundamental Freedoms 1950 (as set out in Sch 1 to the 1998 Act).

[56] We propose first to consider the law as it now is, then the change that the appellants submit should be made to the law and finally whether the appellants have made out their case for effecting this change.

[57] It is a well-established principle of the English law of defamation that each
individual publication of a libel gives rise to a separate cause of action, subject to
its own limitation period. *Duke of Brunswick and Luneberg v Harmer* (1849) 14 QB
185, 117 ER 75 provides a striking illustration of this principle. On 19 September
1830 an article was published in the Weekly Dispatch. The limitation period for
libel was then six years. The article defamed the Duke of Brunswick. Seventeen
years after its publication an agent of the Duke purchased a back number
containing the article from the Weekly Dispatch's office. Another copy was
obtained from the British Museum. The Duke sued on those two publications.
The defendant contended that the cause of action was time barred, relying on the
original publication date. The Court of Queen's Bench held that the delivery of
a copy of the newspaper to the plaintiff's agent constituted a separate publication
in respect of which suit could be brought.

[58] In *Godfrey v Demon Internet Ltd* [1999] 4 All ER 342, [2001] QB 201 the
respondent brought an action in defamation against the appellants who were
Internet service providers. They had received and stored on their news server an
article, defamatory of the respondent, which had been posted by an unknown
person using another service provider. The issue was whether the appellants had
a defence under s 1(1) of the Defamation Act 1996. The judge held that they did
not. He observed:

> 'In my judgment the defendant, whenever it transmits and whenever there
> is transmitted from the storage of its news server a defamatory posting,
> publish that posting to any subscriber to its [Internet service provider] who
> accesses the newsgroup containing that posting. Thus every time one of the
> defendant's customers accesses "soc.culture.thai" and sees that posting
> defamatory of the plaintiff there is a publication to that customer.' (See
> [1999] 4 All ER 342 at 348, [2001] QB 201 at 208–209.)

[59] This decision was consistent with the *Duke of Brunswick*'s case and Lord
Lester did not suggest to the contrary.

[60] In *Berezovsky v Michaels, Glouchkov v Michaels* [2000] 2 All ER 986, [2000]
1 WLR 1004 the issue was whether England was the appropriate forum for
bringing an action in defamation for injury done to reputation in England as a
result of a defamatory article in an American business magazine. In the course of
his speech Lord Steyn ([2000] 2 All ER 986 at 993, [2000] 1 WLR 1004 at 1012)
observed that it was one of the distinctive features of English law that each
communication is a separate libel, citing the *Duke of Brunswick*'s case. Lord
Hoffmann also referred to that decision in the following passage:

> 'There was a good deal of interesting discussion at the Bar about whether an
> internationally disseminated libel constituted a number of separate torts in
> each country of publication or whether it should, at least for some purposes,
> be viewed as a "global tort". In this country the point is settled in the former
> sense by the decision in *Duke of Brunswick and Luneberg v Harmer* (1849) 14 QB
> 185, 117 ER 75. Dean Prosser has described the rule, which may lead to a
> multiplicity of suits, as possibly appropriate to "small communities and limited
> circulations" but "potentially disastrous today": "Interstate Publication"
> (1953) 51 Mich LR 959 at 961. In the context of the present case, this
> discussion is entirely academic. There is no question here of a multiplicity of
> suits. It is the plaintiffs who are for practical purposes treating the publication
> as a "global tort" by calling upon the English court and only the English court

a   to vindicate their reputations.' (See [2000] 2 All ER 986 at 1005, [2000] 1 WLR 1004 at 1024.)

[61] Lord Hope ([2000] 2 All ER 986 at 1007, [2000] 1 WLR 1004 at 1026) also observed that it was plain that separate causes of action arose in respect of each copy of the magazine, citing the *Duke of Brunswick*'s case. The law of Scotland was to the same effect.

b   [62] The outcome in *Berezovsky v Michaels* was not founded on these observations, indeed Lord Hoffmann and Lord Hope formed a dissenting minority. They underline, however, how firmly entrenched the principle in the *Duke of Brunswick*'s case is in our law. Why do the appellants suggest that that law should be changed? The answer appears from the following passage in their *c*   skeleton argument:

'The difficulties which [the multiple publication] rule poses for the new technology of the Internet, and in particular for website publication by newspapers of back numbers, are obvious. Above all, every day during which a back number remains on a website potentially gives rise to a new *d*   publication of that issue, and therefore a new cause of action, whether by actual accessing of a defamatory article by an Internet user, or (as the claimant argued was open to it) by reliance on an inference that someone must have accessed the article. The continuous and indefinite nature of that publication has the consequence that s 4A of the Limitation Act 1980 (which *e*   provides for a one-year limitation period in cases of libel and slander) is rendered nugatory, and that the maintainer of the website is liable to be indefinitely exposed to repeated claims in defamation. If it is accepted that there is a social utility in the technological advances which enable newspapers to provide an Internet archive of back numbers which the general public can access immediately and without difficulty or expense, instead of having to *f*   buy a back number (if available) or visit a library which maintains a collection of newspaper back numbers, then the law as it had developed to suit traditional hardcopy publication is now inimical to modern conditions, and (as has always been the strength of the common law) must evolve to reflect those conditions. As is developed below, it must evolve also to accommodate *g*   the requirements of the European Convention on Human Rights and of the Human Rights Act 1998.'

[63] How is it that the appellants suggest that the law should evolve? They focus on the provision of s 4A of the 1980 Act that no action shall be brought after the expiration of one year from the date on which *the cause of action accrued*. They *h*   contend that the words italicised should be interpreted to mean *the date of the initial publication*. The route by which they seek to achieve this is explained in the next paragraph of their skeleton argument as follows:

'The defendant seeks to adapt to an English context the rule known in the United States as the "single publication rule", whereby the distribution of a *j*   work involves only one publication, on the date of its first publication in a particular format. Hence, for example, the statute of limitations would start running on a libel in a book on the date of its first publication, even if it continued to be sold for months afterwards. Only one action for damages could be maintained, all damage suffered in all jurisdictions could be recovered in one action, and a judgment on the merits would bar any other actions for damages between the same parties in all jurisdictions. However,

if a new edition is published, or a softback edition, or even a reprinting, time   *a*
starts to run again.'

[64] Some time was taken during the appeal in exploring, with the help of
American authorities, the nature of the 'single publication rule' in the United
States. We take the following clear statement of that rule from the judgment of
District Judge Holtzoff sitting in the United States District Court for the District
of Columbia in *Ogden v Association of the United States Army (a corporation)* (1959)   *b*
177 F supp 498 at 502:

> 'From the foregoing discussion the conclusion is inescapable that the
> modern American law of libel has adopted the so-called "single publication"
> rule; and, therefore, this principle must be deemed a part of the common law
> of the District of Columbia. In other words, it is the prevailing American   *c*
> doctrine that the publication of a book, periodical or newspaper containing
> defamatory matter gives rise to but one cause of action for libel, which
> accrues at the time of the original publication, and that the statute of
> limitations runs from that date. It is no longer the law that every sale or
> delivery of a copy of the publication creates a new cause of action.'   *d*

[65] While the authorities suggest that the single publication rule was initially
introduced to combat the problem of a multiplicity of suits in different states
arising out of a single dissemination of a libel, the rule was also justified on the
basis that it gave effect to the purpose of limitation provisions as statutes of
repose designed 'to spare the courts from litigation of stale claims, and the citizen   *e*
from being put to his defense after memories have faded, witnesses have died or
disappeared, and evidence has been lost' (see *Chase Securities Corp (t/a Amerex
Holding Corp) v Donaldson* (1945) 325 US 304 at 314). It was for this reason that the
Court of Appeal of New York in *Gregoire v G P Putnam's Sons* (1948) 81 NE (2d) 45
at 48–49 held that the rule extended to the publication of a book:
                                                                                          f
> '... we conclude that the reasons mentioned above, which underlie the
> purpose of Statutes of Limitations, are as compelling when applied to cases
> involving the modern dissemination of printings or impressions of a book as
> when applied to cases involving the dissemination of issues of a newspaper
> or magazine. Otherwise, although a book containing libellous material may
> have been the product of but one edition or printing fifty years ago, if, by sale   *g*
> from stock or by display, a publisher continues to make unsold copies of the
> single publication available to the public today, such conduct would amount
> to a republication of any libel the book contains and thereby would become
> actionable. Under such a rule the Statute of Limitation would never expire
> so long as a copy of such book remained in stock and is made by the publisher   *h*
> the subject of a sale or inspection by the public. Such a rule would thwart
> the purpose of the Legislature...'

[66] In *Berezovsky's* case in the Court of Appeal ([1999] EMLR 278) the
appellants sought to persuade the court to approach the case as if it involved a
single global cause of action to be pursued in whatever jurisdiction was the most   *j*
appropriate. The single publication rule was invoked by way of analogy. This
argument was not advanced in the House of Lords and Lord Steyn observed that
it was 'contrary to the long-established principle of English libel law that each
publication is a separate tort' (see [2000] 2 All ER 986 at 993, [2000] 1 WLR 1004
at 1012). In the present case the appellants do not suggest that the English courts
should apply the single publication rule where a libel has been disseminated in

a more than one jurisdiction. They contend, however, that the rule should be applied when the issue is one of limitation in relation to an action commenced in this jurisdiction.

[67] The reasons advanced by the appellants for introducing this novel concept into our law are very similar to those adumbrated in the passage from *Gregoire*'s case which we have cited above. Section 4A of the 1980 Act imposes an
b unusually short limitation period in defamation cases. The object of this is to ensure that defamation claims are initiated promptly. If claims are brought within a year of the initial publication, the appellants will be able to marshal any available defence and data available. Lord Lester argued that these benefits will be defeated if, long after the initial publication, a respondent can base a claim on access by a single person to a copy of the publication in question.
c
[68] This was always true of documents in an archive or a library, as *Duke of Brunswick and Luneberg v Harmer* (1849) 14 QB 185, 117 ER 75 demonstrates. Lord Lester argued, however, that the position was much more acute where archives were provided on a website and thus very much more readily accessible.

d [69] Lord Lester accepted that situations could arise where application of the single publication rule in the context of limitation might give rise to injustice. An obvious example is the situation where a respondent does not become aware of the initial publication until over a year has elapsed. Lord Lester submitted, however, that as s 32A of the 1980 Act gives the court a discretion to allow an action to proceed out of time that removes any risk of injustice in such
e circumstances.

[70] Lord Lester buttressed these arguments by reference to the 1998 Act and the convention. He submitted that to permit defamation actions to be commenced more than a year after the initial publication was a restriction on the writer's freedom of expression enshrined in art 10 of the convention. Section 12 of the
f 1998 Act required the court to have particular regard to the importance of the convention right to freedom of expression. To be justified, any curtailment of freedom of expression has to be convincingly established by a compelling countervailing consideration, and the means employed had to be necessary and proportionate to the ends sought to be achieved.

g [71] Maintaining an archive of past press publications was a valuable public service. If a newspaper defendant which maintained a website of back numbers was to be indefinitely vulnerable to claims in defamation for years and even decades after the initial hardcopy and Internet publication, such a rule was bound to have an effect on the preparedness of the media to maintain such websites, and thus to limit freedom of expression.

h [72] In answer to these submissions Mr Browne started by emphasising that the principle in the *Duke of Brunswick*'s case that every publication of a libel gives rise to a separate cause of action is a well-established principle of English law that was recognised by the House of Lords in *Berezovsky v Michaels*. He submitted that this principle was not at odds with the convention. Article 10 recognised that the
j right of freedom of expression could properly be restricted 'for the protection of the reputation or rights of others'. The rule in the *Duke of Brunswick*'s case was part of the system of English law that balanced the right of freedom of expression against the entitlement to protection of one's reputation. If the appellants were exposed to liability in the second action they had only themselves to blame for persisting in retaining the offending articles on their website without qualifying these in any way.

Our conclusion

[73] Section 4A of the 1980 Act provides for a year within which to commence proceedings starting from the date on which the cause of action accrues. The appellants' submissions recognise that if they are to establish that the claims in the second action were time-barred they must, when applying s 4A, displace the rule in the *Duke of Brunswick's* case and replace it by the American single publication rule. They must also establish that under that rule, placing a publication on their website constitutes a single publication that occurs at the time it is placed on the website regardless of the period during which it remains there. The latter is by no means clear, but it is at least arguable. In our judgment the crucial question in relation to this part of the appeal is whether the appellants have made good their assertion that the rule in the *Duke of Brunswick's* case is in conflict with art 10 of the convention because it has a chilling effect upon the freedom of expression that goes beyond what is necessary and proportionate in a democratic society for the protection of the reputation of others.

[74] We do not accept that the rule in the *Duke of Brunswick's* case imposes a restriction on the readiness to maintain and provide access to archives that amounts to a disproportionate restriction on freedom of expression. We accept that the maintenance of archives, whether in hard copy or on the Internet, has a social utility, but consider that the maintenance of archives is a comparatively insignificant aspect of freedom of expression. Archive material is stale news and its publication cannot rank in importance with the dissemination of contemporary material. Nor do we believe that the law of defamation need inhibit the responsible maintenance of archives. Where it is known that archive material is or may be defamatory, the attachment of an appropriate notice warning against treating it as the truth will normally remove any sting from the material.

[75] Turning to the appellants' wider argument, it is true that to permit an action to be based on a fresh dissemination of an article published long ago is at odds with some of the reasons for the introduction of a 12-month limitation period for defamation. But the scale of such publication and any resulting damage is likely to be modest compared with that of the original publication. In the present case, as the judge observed, the action based on the Internet publication is subsidiary to the main action.

[76] The change in the law of defamation for which the appellants contend is a radical one. In our judgment they have failed to make out their case that such a change is required. The Internet single publication appeal is therefore dismissed.

The Internet qualified privilege appeal

[77] The judge struck out the defence of qualified privilege in the second action on the ground that he would be bound to hold that the privilege was not available. He gave six reasons for having reached this conclusion, which we shall summarise. (i) When the appellants published the articles on the Internet they knew that they were not in a position to justify them. (ii) They did not qualify the articles on the Internet by stating that they could not justify them or indicating that the respondent challenged them. (iii) The appellants had accepted that they had no basis for asserting that the respondent was even reasonably suspected of criminal activity and that they simply did not know if such suspicions were justified. (iv) The first article alleged that the respondent was, or was possibly, involved in the Bank of New York money-laundering scandal. This allegation was based on information from a single anonymous source that the respondent was being investigated on that account, not that he had been involved. (v) The

a second article was based on information supplied by Mrs Chernoi, but no reliance had been placed upon her in the pleaded claim of qualified privilege. (vi) Mr Alastair Brett, the appellants' in-house solicitor, had made a statement that could be taken to be definitive as to the appellants' state of mind. That statement contained no assertion on the part of the appellants of any honest belief in the truth of what was published about the respondent.

b [78] The reasoning of the judge, as explained in his short ex tempore judgment, was as follows:

c 'To succeed in a defence of qualified privilege the defendants had to show that they had been under a duty to publish the articles on the Internet. Only in exceptional circumstances can such a duty arise if the publisher has no honest belief in the truth of the matter published. No such special circumstances attended the publications on the Internet. Mr Brett had conceded that the defendants had no honest belief in the truth of what they had published. This was fatal to a defence of qualified privilege.'

d [79] We do not consider that a newspaper that is raising a defence of *Reynolds* qualified privilege has the onus of establishing an honest belief in the truth of the matter published. Nor do we consider that the judge was correct to deduce from the fact that Mr Brett made no positive assertion of honest belief that he lacked such belief. For these reasons we have concluded that the primary reason given by the judge for striking out the qualified privilege defence in the second action *e* was not well founded. It does not, however, follow that he was wrong to strike out the defence. A subsidiary reason given by the judge for striking out the defence was that the appellants had repeatedly republished on the Internet defamatory material that was the subject of a defamation action in which they were not seeking to justify the truth of the allegations without publishing any qualification to draw to the reader's attention the fact that the truth of the articles *f* was hotly contested. The judge considered that the republication of back numbers of The Times on the Internet was made in materially different circumstances from those obtaining at the time of the publication of the original hardcopy versions in September and October 1999. We agree. The failure to attach any qualifications to the articles published over the period of a year on The Times' *g* website could not possibly be described as responsible journalism. We do not believe that it can be convincingly argued that the appellants had a *Reynolds* duty to publish those articles in that way without qualification. It follows that we consider that the judge was right to strike out the qualified privilege defence in the second action although not for the primary reason that he gave for so doing. For these reasons the Internet single publication appeal is also dismissed.

h

The Russian publication appeal.

[80] This appeal is against the judge's ruling that damages for the Russian publication of the libels would be recoverable under Russian law. In other words the appellants say that the judge was wrong to rule that the respondent was able *j* to satisfy the double actionability test so that damages could be recovered for the Russian publication in the first action.

[81] Whether or not the judge was right depends upon a proper understanding of a joint experts' report from Russian lawyers who had been asked to provide the answers to a number of questions. These experts did not give oral evidence and in some respects their report is unclear and apparently contradictory. However, there is no doubt that libel is actionable under Russian civil law. The argument

is about remedy. The primary remedy is refutation (apology). But the claimant
has the additional right to claim compensation for financial losses and 'moral
damage' resulting from the publication. Article 151 of the civil code says:

> 'If an individual has sustained moral damage (physical or moral suffering)
> as the result of acts ... infringing upon other non-material benefits belonging
> to such individual ... the courts may order the defendant to pay monetary
> compensation for such damage.'

Non-material benefits include the dignity of the person, honour and good name.

[82] The appellants' argument is that moral damage has to be proved in much
the same way as English law requires proof of special damage to found an action
for slander. This, they say, is a matter of substantive Russian law and the
respondent has not pleaded or proved any such damage.

[83] The experts' report says that the claimant must prove his claim for moral
damage. However, in answer to the question 'Does a claimant have to prove
actual harm to his reputation and, if so, what loss or harm does he have to prove
(in this case the claimant claims to have suffered injury to his reputation and his
feelings)?' the experts said:

> 'As stated above the claimant does not have to prove actual harm to his
> reputation or good name, ie the claimant does not have to call any witnesses
> to testify that, in their eyes, the statement published has lowered the
> claimant's reputation. Russian courts are more actively involved in the
> proceedings than is the case in common law jurisdictions and more often
> than not they draw their own conclusions as to the damage inflicted on the
> claimant's reputation by the defamatory publication.'

[84] The judge relied on this last answer in the ruling which he made.
However, after referring to other passages in the experts' report he went on to
say:

> 'What the joint report appears to me to be saying is that damages can be
> recovered for moral harm consisting in injury to the honour, good name and
> dignity of the claimant. It appears to be agreed that there is no need for third
> party witnesses to be called to establish such damage. I accept that there may
> still be a measure of disagreement between the experts as to the manner in
> which such damage has to be proved, but I consider that [counsel for the
> respondent] is right when he says that that is a procedural rather than a
> substantive question and so falls for decision according to the lex fori, namely
> English law.'

[85] Mr Parkes who argued this appeal for the appellants, submits that the
judge failed to appreciate that, unlike English law, Russian law does not presume
injury to reputation and feelings as a result of the publication of a libel. We think
there is substance in this point. There is, it appears, no right to general damages
under Russian law for loss of reputation. If financial compensation is to be
awarded it must be for actual physical or financial loss which the claimant has
proved, or for moral damage. However, in the light of the experts' report, proof
of moral damage cannot be regarded as a matter of substantive law. There is
obviously some doubt as to what evidence is required, but, in an earlier report,
the appellants' expert said:

> 'The claimant must produce evidence as to the physical or moral suffering
> he endured. The evidentiary standard is far from clear however, and court

a   practice varies widely in this respect. Any damages awarded are intended
         solely to compensate the claimant for physical or moral suffering ...'

         [86] Therefore, it seems to us that as a matter of Russian law, this is a
         procedural rather than substantive question as the judge held. All matters of
         procedure are governed by the law of the lex fori, in this case, English law.
b   Furthermore, the respondent in his witness statement says in terms that
         publication of the two articles made him extremely upset. There is nothing in the
         experts' report to suggest that a claimant need provide any further proof in order
         to establish a claim for moral damage. In the course of argument Mr Browne QC
         agreed to limit the respondent's claim for damages in respect of the Russian
         publication to injury to feelings, so as to make it clear that the respondent was not
c   asking for general damages for injury to his reputation in Russia.
         [87] On this basis and for these reasons the Russian publication appeal is
         dismissed.

         The summary disposal appeal
d   [88] On 8 February 2001 Gray J dismissed an application by the respondent for
         trial by judge alone. However, as the trial date approached it became obvious
         that there would not be enough time to try liability and quantum in the time
         available before the end of the legal term at Easter. So, on 16 March 2001 the
         judge ordered a split trial. The trial on liability started three days later. The jury
         were empanelled on 26 March after a week of legal argument. It was common
e   ground that this jury could not be retained to deal with quantum if the need
         arose. The judge entered judgment for the respondent for damages to be assessed
         in the second action on 27 March and in the first action on 27 April. The
         respondent then applied for his claim for damages in each action to be summarily
         disposed of under s 8 of the Defamation Act 1996 and the judge made an order to
         this effect on 11 May.
f   [89] As well as arguing that he had no jurisdiction to make such an order, the
         appellants said that it would be wrong for the judge to proceed summarily in any
         event. They wanted the issue of damages to be tried by a jury on oral evidence
         which, together with legal argument, the judge thought would take at least five
         days and could probably not be heard until the end of the year. Summary
g   disposal could be done largely, if not exclusively, on paper and would probably
         last no more than a day or so. Of this state of affairs the judge said ([2001] EMLR
         933 at 936 (para 14)):

              'If ever there was an issue which calls for expeditious, proportionate and
              economic disposal, it is the issue of damages in this case. In case management
h   terms, the advantages of having damages summarily assessed are
              overwhelming.'

         This conclusion is not challenged on appeal. The issue is simply whether the
         judge had jurisdiction to make the order which he did on 11 May 2001. It turns
         entirely upon the proper construction of the statute.
j   [90] Section 8 of the 1996 Act says:

              '(1) In defamation proceedings the court may dispose summarily of the
              plaintiff's claim in accordance with the following provisions.
              (2) The court may dismiss the plaintiff's claim if it appears to the court that
              it has no realistic prospect of success and there is no reason why it should be
              tried.

(3) The court may give judgment for the plaintiff and grant him summary relief (see section 9) if it appears to the court that there is no defence to the claim which has a realistic prospect of success, and that there is no other reason why the claim should be tried. Unless the plaintiff asks for summary relief, the court shall not act under this subsection unless it is satisfied that summary relief will adequately compensate him for the wrong he has suffered.

(4) In considering whether a claim should be tried the court shall have regard to ... (c) the extent to which there is a conflict of evidence; (d) the seriousness of the alleged wrong (as regards the content of the statement and the extent of publication); and (e) whether it is justifiable in the circumstances to proceed to a full trial.

(5) Proceedings under this section shall be heard and determined without a jury.'

[91] Section 9 defines summary relief to mean 'as may be appropriate' a declaration of falsity, an order that the defendant publish an apology, damages not exceeding £10,000, or an injunction. For the purposes of summary disposal the respondent agreed to limit his damages in each action to £10,000. However, at the hearing before the judge on 11 May counsel made it clear that he would also be asking for an order that the appellants publish an apology.

[92] Section 10 enables rules of court to be made for summary disposal of defamation claims including provisions authorising a party to apply for summary disposal, the court to treat any application as an application for summary disposal or the court of its own notion to make an order for summary disposal 'at any stage of the proceedings'.

[93] In his judgment on this issue the judge accepted that the wording of s 8 reflected the fact that the summary disposal procedure was primarily designed for the early disposal of small claims at or shortly after their commencement. But he said that s 8 had to be read in conjunction with s 10 and its reference to 'at any stage of the proceedings'. He concluded (at 939):

'27 I accept that the word "claim" which is to be found in section 8(1) and elsewhere in the section will often be synonymous with "cause of action", ie that it will embrace both liability and damages. But it is, in my judgment, important not to lose sight of the fact that section 8 does not speak of the determination of a claim but, rather, of its "disposal". A claim is not disposed of by the court until both liability and quantum have been decided.

28 Bearing in mind the policy of the Act and the wording of section 10, it appears to me that the meaning to be ascribed to the term "claim" where it appears in section 8 is "so much of the plaintiff's claim as remains to be disposed of when the application under section 8 is made".'

[94] Mr Spearman starts by reminding us that any party to a libel action has a constitutional right to trial by jury subject to the limited exception provided by s 69(1) of the Supreme Court Act 1981. This right can, he says, only be restricted by clear statutory language. He submits that the summary disposal jurisdiction is to be found in s 8 and not s 10 of the 1996 Act and that s 8 is clearly concerned and concerned only with cases in which the court is asked to make a determination before there has been a trial on liability. The jurisdiction is to 'dispose of the plaintiff's claim in accordance with the following provisions'. Those provisions make it clear that the claim is not only the cause of action, but also one which is being considered prospectively by the court before a trial on

a liability has taken place. Thus, there can be no question of assessing the prospects
of success of a claim or deciding whether there is any reason for it to be tried after
there has been a trial on liability (sub-s (2) of s 8). Likewise, the court cannot give
a judgment or decide whether there is a defence to a claim which has a realistic
prospect of success or that there is some other reason why the claim should be
tried after liability has been decided (sub-s (3) of s 8). The judge's construction,
b Mr Spearman submits, would produce anomalous results. If a party was able to
ask for summary disposal after a trial on liability, he could obtain a declaration of
falsity or an apology under s 9 which he could not have got at trial.

[95] Mr Browne supports the judge's conclusions and relies, as did the judge,
on the decision of this court in *Burstein v Times Newspapers Ltd* [2001] 1 WLR 579.
There, the claimant complained of an article accusing him of organising bands of
c hecklers to wreck performances of modern atonal music. It was conceded that
the article was defamatory and at trial the judge struck out the defendant's only
defence of fair comment. This meant that the claimant had established liability.
The defendants then applied for summary disposal of his claim for damages. The
judge refused this application because he thought that £10,000 might not be
d adequate compensation. The defendants' appeal against this decision was
dismissed on the basis that it was within the judge's discretion, but the court
clearly proceeded on the basis that an order for summary disposal could have
been made after liability had been determined. However, as Mr Spearman says,
there was no argument about jurisdiction so this case is of little assistance.

e [96] Mr Spearman is obviously right that the court's jurisdiction to dispose of
claims summarily is only to be found in s 8. Section 10 is simply an enabling
provision. Subsections (2) and (3) of s 8 are, as the judge said, primarily directed
at the early disposal of small claims before any trial on liability has taken place.
But does this mean that the word 'claim' is used exclusively in this sense or does
it have a wider meaning so as to include so much of the plaintiff's claim as is still
f to be determined? Subsection (1) points to the following subsections to see what
the jurisdiction is so one must look at these provisions to see if the word 'claim'
can be given this wider meaning.

[97] As to sub-s (2) a court can obviously assess a claimant's prospects of
success after a trial on liability or rulings which effectively dispose of the defence,
g albeit the task is a simple one. Likewise the court can consider whether there is
any reason why a claim for damages should be tried (as opposed to summary
disposal) after liability has been determined. As to sub-s (3) on an application for
summary disposal of a quantum claim the court can give judgment on that claim
and grant summary relief. It might have to consider a causation or remoteness
defence. Obviously there is no difficulty in giving the wider meaning to 'claim'
h as it is used in sub-s (4). For these reasons we think that 'claim' in s 8 is capable
of bearing the wider meaning.

[98] The question then is: was it Parliament's intention that it should have this
wider meaning? We think it was. The section could obviously have been more
clearly drafted, but its purpose was to establish a procedure for dealing with small
j claims in a time and cost-effective way. We can see no reason in principle why
Parliament should have limited the jurisdiction in the way the appellants
contend. If it is appropriate to have a summary procedure for disposing of issues
of liability and quantum there is no reason why that procedure should not also be
available in a suitable case for disposing of quantum alone once liability has been
determined or admitted. The statute does not expressly limit the jurisdiction in
this way and giving its language a purposive construction we do not think it was

intended to do so. After all, as the judge said, a claim is not disposed of by the court until both liability and quantum have been decided.

[99] Summary disposal does of course give the claimant a right to ask for a declaration of falsity and an order that the defendant should publish an apology. Such remedies are not available ordinarily, so, in this case, the respondent would not be able to obtain an order for an apology if his claim for damages was not disposed of summarily. This is an anomaly but it is an anomaly which applies to any summary disposal at whatever stage this takes place. The defendant's position however will always be protected by the fact that the judge has a discretion as to whether to make such an order.

[100] In this case there must be a strong suspicion that one of the reasons the respondent applied for summary disposal was to enable him to ask the court to order the appellants to publish an apology. The judge does not refer to this in his judgment and nothing he said indicates that he would be prepared to make such an order. In these circumstances and while the appellants honestly maintain their belief in the truth of what they have published, we do not think there is any prospect of the judge ordering them to publish an apology if and when he summarily disposes of the respondent's claims.

[101] For these reasons we dismiss the summary disposal appeal.

Conclusion

[102] The first action liability appeal is allowed to the extent that the case will be remitted to Gray J to enable him to reconsider the appellants' claim to qualified privilege in the light of this judgment. All the other appeals are dismissed.

The first action liability appeal allowed to the extent specified. Other appeals dismissed. Permission to appeal refused.

Kate O'Hanlon   Barrister.

a

R v T
R v H
[2001] EWCA Crim 1877

b COURT OF APPEAL, CRIMINAL DIVISION
KEENE LJ, GARLAND AND BURTON JJ
26 JULY 2001

Criminal evidence – Sexual offence – Cross-examination of complainant about previous
c *sexual behaviour – Restrictions on evidence – Statutory provision restricting*
admissibility of evidence or questions about complainant's previous sexual behaviour –
Whether questions relating to complainant's failure on previous occasion to complain
about subject matter of charge when complaining of sexual abuse by others constituting
questions 'about' complainant's previous sexual behaviour – Whether questions
designed to establish that complainant had lied previously about sexual matters
d *constituting questions 'about' complainant's previous sexual behaviour – Youth Justice*
and Criminal Evidence Act 1999, s 41(1).

In the first of two appeals raising common issues, the defendant, T, was charged
with two counts of indecent assault and one of rape upon his niece. The alleged
offences were said to have taken place between 1987 and 1989, but the allegations
e against T were not made until 1999. The defence case was that none of the
alleged acts had taken place. At a preparatory hearing, the defence applied for
leave under s 41[a] of the Youth Justice and Criminal Evidence Act 1999, which
applied to the trial of a person charged with a sexual offence, to cross-examine the
complainant about two occasions, in 1987 and 1990, when she had made
f allegations of sexual abuse against other members of her family but not against T.
Under s 41(1) of the 1999 Act, the leave of the court was required before any
evidence could be adduced or any question asked in cross-examination, by or on
behalf of the accused, 'about any sexual behaviour' of the complainant. By virtue
of other provisions of s 41, such leave could not be granted if the questions would
be asked in order to impugn the complainant's credibility. The judge concluded
g that the questions were about the complainant's sexual behaviour, that they
would be asked in order to impugn her credibility and that accordingly it was not
open to him to grant leave. T appealed. In the second appeal, the defendant, H,
was charged with indecent assault on his stepdaughter. He denied that the
alleged act had taken place, and sought leave under s 41 to ask questions of the
h complainant in cross-examination in order to establish that she had made false
statements in the past about both sexual and non-sexual matters. The judge held
that the questions were rendered inadmissible for the same reasons as those given
by the judge in T's case. H appealed. On the appeals, the issue arose as to
whether the questions sought to be asked by the defendants were indeed 'about'
j any sexual behaviour of the complainants within the meaning of s 41.

Held – For the purposes of s 41 of the 1999 Act, questions or evidence about false
statements in the past by a complainant relating to sexual assaults, or about a
failure, while complaining of other sexual assaults, to complain of the alleged

---

a   Section 41, so far as material, is set out at [14], below

assault which formed the subject matter of the charge, were not normally
questions or evidence 'about' any sexual behaviour of the complainant. They
related not to her sexual behaviour but to her statements in the past or her failure
to complain. Such a construction was consistent with the purpose of s 41, which
had not been intended to exclude evidence or questions about previous false
complaints. It followed in the instant cases that the questions sought to be asked
were not automatically excluded by s 41, even if they were seen as going
principally to credibility. Accordingly, the appeals would be allowed (see [33],
[35], [36], [44], below); R v A [2001] 3 All ER 1 considered.

Per curiam. Where the defence wishes to put questions about alleged
previous false complaints, it will need to seek a ruling from the judge that they
are not excluded by s 41 of the 1999 Act. It will be professionally improper for
those representing the defendant to put such questions in order to elicit evidence
about the complainant's past sexual behaviour as such under the guise of
previous false complaints. In any event, the defence must have a proper
evidential basis for asserting that any such previous statement was (a) made and
(b) untrue. If those requirements are not met, then the questions will not be
about lies but about the sexual behaviour of the complainant within the meaning
of s 41(1). The judge is entitled to seek assurances from the defence that it has a
proper basis for asserting that the statement was made and was untrue (see [41],
below).

Notes
For the protection of complainants in proceedings for sexual offences, see Supp
to 11(1) Halsbury's Laws (4th edn reissue) para 518A.

For the Youth Justice and Criminal Evidence Act 1999, s 41, see 17 Halsbury's
Statutes (4th edn) (1999 reissue) 335.

Cases referred to in judgments
R v A [2001] UKHL 25, [2001] 3 All ER 1, [2001] 2 WLR 1546.
R v Cox (1986) 84 Cr App R 132, CA.
R v Funderburk [1990] 2 All ER 482, [1990] 1 WLR 587, CA.
R v Gibson [1993] Crim LR 453, CA.
R v Nagrecha (1997) 2 Cr App R 401, CA.
R v S [1992] Crim LR 307, CA.

Appeals

R v T
The defendant, RT, who was charged with two counts of indecent assault and
one of rape, appealed with leave of Judge Pollard from his decision, given at a
preparatory hearing in the Crown Court at Leicester on 3 April 2001, that certain
questions which the defence wished to put to the complainant were excluded by
s 41 of the Youth Justice and Criminal Evidence Act 1999. The facts are set out in
the judgment of the court.

R v H
The defendant, MH, who was charged with indecent assault, appealed with leave
of Judge Hammond from his decision, given at a preparatory hearing in the
Crown Court at Manchester on 2 April 2001, that certain questions which the
defence wished to put to the complainant were excluded by s 41 of the Youth

a Justice and Criminal Evidence Act 1999. The facts are set out in the judgment of the court.

Melbourne Inman QC and *Adrienne Lucking* (instructed by *Moss & Co*, Loughborough) for RT.

Frances Oldham QC and *Felicity Gerry* (instructed by the *Crown Prosecution Service*)
b for the Crown in RT's appeal.

Andrew Nuttall (instructed by *Draycott Browne*, Manchester) for MH.

Suzanne Goddard (instructed by the *Crown Prosecution Service*) for the Crown in MH's appeal.

KEENE LJ (delivering the judgment of the court).
c [1] These two appeals raise an important point as to the proper interpretation of s 41 of the Youth Justice and Criminal Evidence Act 1999, a section which imposes restrictions at trials for a sexual offence on producing evidence or asking questions about the complainant's sexual history.

[2] In both appeals rulings have been made in the context of a preparatory
d hearing that certain questions which the defence wish to put to the complainant were excluded by the provisions of s 41. In both cases leave to appeal to this court was granted by the crown court judge, it being very properly recognised that a novel point of law had arisen. The appeals are in consequence brought under 35(1) of the Criminal Procedure and Investigations Act 1996. With the consent of all parties, we give one combined judgment on both cases.
e [3] In the first appeal RT appeals against the ruling of Judge Pollard at the Crown Court at Leicester on 3 April 2001. The appellant is charged with two counts of indecent assault and one of rape, in all three cases the complainant being his niece. The alleged offences are said to have taken place between 1 November 1987 and 31 December 1989, when the complainant was aged
f between eight and eleven years old. At this time the complainant lived with her mother and three brothers. The defence case was that none of the alleged acts had taken place.

[4] It seems that the timing of the alleged incidents may be within a narrower compass than set out in the indictment, because they are alleged to have occurred while the appellant was temporarily living with the complainant's family, and
g there is some evidence that this was in the summer of 1987. The allegations by the complainant were not put forward until late 1999, and the defence seek to emphasise the various opportunities which she had had to put them forward on previous occasions. In particular, there were two occasions in late 1987 and in 1990 when she had been asked questions about sexual matters involving herself
h but did not raise the allegations about the appellant.

[5] The first of those two occasions was in November 1987, when the police were investigating allegations that one of her brothers had been sexually abused by another uncle. In the course of the investigations the complainant was asked whether 'anyone had ever touched her in a rude way'. She had replied 'Just
j granddad and M [one of her brothers] did once in Middlesbrough'.

[6] The second occasion was in 1990 when in the course of other investigations about sexual abuse of her she had made a statement alleging rape by one of her brothers. Once again there was no mention of anything done by the appellant.

[7] Leave was consequently sought on his behalf under s 41 to ask questions of the complainant about her failure to mention on those occasions in late 1987

and in 1990 the alleged incidents which form the basis of the current charges. The *a*
Crown Court judge summarised the questions which it was sought to put as
follows:

> 'Why did you not mention it when you were dealing with the police and
> social workers about sexual matters in late 1987 or in 1990? You did not
> mention it because it did not happen. Or, well, maybe things did happen to *b*
> you. Whatever happened to you, you have become confused about who did
> what to you, but in any event, your uncle never did anything to you.'

[8] There may also have been another opportunity for her to have mentioned
the alleged abuse in December 1988. If so, it comes into the same category as the
two occasions to which reference has already been made. *c*

[9] The judge took the view that it was not open to him to grant leave because
the questions were ones about sexual behaviour of the complainant, as defined
by s 42(1)(c), and did not relate to a relevant issue in the case because it was clear
that the questions would be asked in order to impugn the credibility of the
complainant (see s 41(4)).

[10] In the second appeal MH is charged with indecent assault of his *d*
stepdaughter in the summer of 2000 when she was aged 14. He denies that any
act took place. He appeals against the ruling of Judge Hammond at the Crown
Court at Manchester on 2 April 2001, whereby it was ruled that s 41 prevented
the defence from asking questions of the complainant to try to establish that she
had lied on a number of occasions in the past about sexual matters, as well as *e*
non-sexual matters. The questions proposed were as follows:

> '1. On a day prior to the events in this case, did you tell your brother, JH,
> that you had been raped?
> 2. Did you tell your friends that your brother had fought with the person
> that you said raped you? *f*
> 3. In late December 1997, did you tell GR that you had been raped by a
> boy called C, and did you whilst in her company and whilst walking to the
> Beech Public House on 28 December 1999 pretend to speak to C on your
> mobile phone?
> 4. Did you tell GR and your friend S (a prosecution witness) that you were
> pregnant and your mother had aborted it with a knitting needle? *g*
> 5. Did you tell AR that your mother treated you like a slave in the house?
> 6. Did you tell AR that you were involved in gangs?
> 7. Did you boast to your friends that you sold drugs and that your mother
> had condoned your use of?'
> *h*

[11] Some of those questions, of course, did not relate to sexual matters at all.

[12] In each case the defence proposes to contend that the statement alleged
to have been made by the complainant was untrue. It follows that, in so far as the
alleged statements by the complainant dealt with sexual matters, it was and is the
defence's position that those events never took place. *j*

[13] As in the first appeal, so here too the judge ruled that these were
questions about the complainant's sexual behaviour, given the definition in
s 42(1)(c), and that as the purpose in asking them would be to impugn her
credibility, they were rendered inadmissible because of s 41(4).

[14] In so far as it is relevant for present purposes, s 41 of the 1999 Act provides
as follows:

a
'(1) If at a trial a person is charged with a sexual offence, then, except with the leave of the court—(a) no evidence may be adduced, and (b) no question may be asked in cross-examination, by or on behalf of any accused at the trial, about any sexual behaviour of the complainant.

(2) The court may give leave in relation to any evidence or question only on an application made by or on behalf of an accused, and may not give such
b
leave unless it is satisfied—(a) that subsection (3) or (5) applies, and (b) that a refusal of leave might have the result of rendering unsafe a conclusion of the jury or (as the case may be) the court on any relevant issue in the case.

(3) This subsection applies if the evidence or question relates to a relevant issue in the case ...

(4) For the purposes of subsection (3) no evidence or question shall be
c
regarded as relating to a relevant issue in the case if it appears to the court to be reasonable to assume that the purpose (or main purpose) for which it would be adduced or asked is to establish or elicit material for impugning the credibility of the complainant as a witness.'

d 'Sexual behaviour' is defined by s 42(1)(c) as 'any sexual behaviour or other sexual experience, whether or not involving any accused or other person'.

[15] On behalf of the appellant in the first appeal, Mr Inman QC submits that the proposed questions are not ones 'about any sexual behaviour' of the complainant but about statements made by her in the past in response to certain questions. The cross-examination, it is said, relates only to her failure to make
e any reference to sexual abuse by the defendant at times when she was referring to such abuse by others. Indeed, on the November 1987 occasion it is argued that there was not merely a failure to comment about anything done by the appellant but an inconsistent statement—inconsistent, that is, with the present allegation— because of the reference to assault by 'just granddad and M'. Such cross-examination
f would not conflict with s 41, which was aimed at preventing questions of a complainant seeking to show that she, or for that matter he, was less worthy of belief because of previous sexual conduct. It is contended that the complainant need not be asked about any detail of the answers she had given on those previous occasions, save to show that she had been asked about sexual matters or had referred in her answers to sexual contact by someone other than a defendant.
g Mr Inman does not seek to run an allegation that the complainant had become confused because of past sexual experiences.

[16] Mr Inman also contends that if the provisions of s 41 were to be construed in such a way as to exclude questions of the kind described, then they would deprive the appellant of a fair trial, since the complainant's failure to raise these
h allegations at times when she was being asked about sexual abuse is clearly relevant to the issues in the case.

[17] Reliance is placed on s 3(1) of the Human Rights Act 1998:

'So far as it is possible to do so, primary legislation and subordinate legislation must be read and given effect in a way which is compatible with
j the Convention rights.'

[18] If the provisions of s 41 cannot be read in a way which is compatible with the appellant's right to a fair trial under art 6 of the European Convention for the Protection of Human Rights and Fundamental Freedoms 1950 (as set out in Sch 1 to the 1998 Act), then, argues Mr Inman, that section is incompatible with that convention right. However, his primary point on the 1998 Act is that the

provisions of s 41 can be read in a way which is compatible with his client's convention rights.

[19] Similar arguments are advanced on behalf of MH by Mr Nuttall in the second appeal. It is submitted that the questions which the defence seeks to ask are not ones about the complainant's sexual behaviour as defined in s 42(1)(c), but rather about her actions in telling lies, albeit some of those lies being about sexual matters. Mr Nuttall stresses that the Act is intended to relate to questions about sexual behaviour, not about fantasies or about fictional matters. The fact that, as the defence allege, the complainant tells lies is at the heart of the defence case and if such questions cannot be asked because of the terms of s 41 then that section is incompatible with the appellant's rights under art 6 of the convention.

[20] It is to be observed that, in the MH appeal, the Crown has changed its attitude towards this issue and adopts a neutral stance on the appeal. It now accepts, as Miss Goddard has told us, that s 41 can be read in a way which would allow the questions about previous lies about sexual assaults to be asked. This position is adopted because of the provisions of s 3 of the 1998 Act to which we have already referred. The Crown recognises that such questions are important and relevant when the jury comes to consider the complainant's credibility and that to exclude them might well breach the appellant's right to a fair trial.

[21] On the appeal by RT the Crown's position is somewhat different. Mrs Oldham QC submits that any question which involves the assertion of a previous sexual experience is a question 'about' that sexual experience. Questioning about previous inconsistent statements or previous opportunities to complain is prohibited by the 1999 Act unless it can be achieved without questions 'about any sexual behaviour'. This, it is said, does not deny the appellant a fair trial. A balance has to be struck between the rights of the accused and the rights of the complainant in such cases, and Parliament has decided where that balance should lie.

[22] The Crown's principal concern in RT is about the possible danger of questions along the lines summarised in the latter part of Judge Pollard's summary quoted earlier. Those dangers are ones which arise if questions are asked about the complainant being confused with her earlier sexual experiences so that in effect she is translating her recollection of sexual experiences with others and attributing them now to the appellant. However, Mrs Oldham concedes that if the questions go no further than Mr Inman has outlined—that is to say stressing her failure to refer to these allegations on occasions when she was making other sexual allegations or, indeed, to her making inconsistent statements in the past—then they are relevant questions and would not be 'about' sexual behaviour or experience.

[23] The interpretation of s 41 and its associated provisions is a matter which has been the subject of recent consideration by the House of Lords in R v A [2001] UKHL 25, [2001] 3 All ER 1, [2001] 2 WLR 1546. This is an authority to which reference has been made by all counsel who have addressed us.

[24] The issue with which this court is now faced did not fall for determination as such in that case, but the speeches in their Lordships' House do provide a valuable account of the background to, and the purposes of, these legislative provisions in the 1999 Act. Lord Steyn ([2001] 3 All ER 1 at [27]) noted that the purpose of s 41 was to prevent the defence advancing at trial what he described as 'the twin myths' that 'unchaste women were more likely to consent to intercourse and in any event, were less worthy of belief'. In the case of R v A, the requirements of s 3 of the 1998 Act and the importance of the right to a fair trial

a were emphasised by the House of Lords on the issue of interpreting s 41, Lord
Steyn stating (at [45]) that the language of the section had to be subordinated to
'broader considerations of relevance'.

[25] For our part we are quite satisfied that the questions sought to be put in
both cases under appeal are relevant in the normal, non-statutory sense of that
term.

b [26] In the RT appeal they go to the complainant's failure to mention the
alleged sexual assaults by the appellant on occasions when she was being asked
about such matters and was mentioning other sexual assaults. Such a failure, if it
could be established, would be likely to be highly material, though it would be
for the trial judge to decide whether the terms of s 41(2)(b), which deals with the
effect of a refusal of leave on the safety of the jury's conclusion, were met, assuming
c that the case fell within s 41 at all.

[27] In the case of MH, the fact that the complainant has fabricated in the past
allegations of sexual assault would again seem to this court to be clearly relevant,
if it can be established. That was so held in R v Nagrecha (1997) 2 Cr App R 401 by
this court in a case preceding the enactment of the 1999 Act. The reasoning in
d that case, relying on R v Gibson [1993] Crim LR 453, was that the evidence went
not merely to credit but to the crucial issue of whether there had been a sexual
assault at all. In R v Nagrecha, as in the well-known case of R v Funderburk [1990]
2 All ER 482 at 491, [1990] 1 WLR 587 at 597, emphasis was placed on the fact
that—

e   'where the disputed issue is a sexual one between two persons in private
the difference between questions going to credit and questions going to the
issue is reduced to vanishing point.'

[28] It seems to us that the line is a difficult one to draw, even though the
distinction was one which was often purportedly drawn under the previous
f legislation on this subject, s 2 of the Sexual Offences (Amendment) Act 1976,
when courts sought to spell out the principles which were applicable.

[29] Since the 1999 Act has come into force, in the case of R v A [2001] 3 All ER
1 at [79], Lord Hope of Craighead has indicated that questions about the sexual
behaviour of a complainant could be admissible if they went to show that the
complainant had a motive to fabricate the evidence, despite the ban in s 41(4) on
g questions as to credibility. That is a matter which needs to be borne in mind by
trial judges. If one finds on normal principles of interpretation that relevant and
significant evidence would be excluded by s 41, then it might be that a court
would need to go on to consider s 3 of the 1998 Act and to adopt the approach
suggested by Lord Hope in R v A (at [79]) and also by Lord Steyn (at [44], [45]). In
h appropriate cases, that could lead to a restrictive interpretation of s 41(4) because
of the provisions of s 3 of the 1998 Act and to a narrow definition as to credibility
as used in s 41(4).

[30] However, for the moment we proceed on the basis that the purpose or
the main purpose for which the questions would in both these appeals be asked
j would be 'to establish or elicit material for impugning the credibility of the
complainant as a witness'. If that is so, then those questions cannot be ones which
relate to a relevant issue in the case because s 41(4) expressly prevents them from
being so regarded.

[31] However, that is not the end of the matter. Section 41 only applies to
evidence or questions 'about any sexual behaviour of the complainant' (see
s 41(1)). That raises the issue of whether these proposed questions are, in either

case, ones 'about' her sexual behaviour. The previous legislation used the phrase
'about any sexual experience' (see s 2(1) of the 1976 Act). Although 'sexual
behaviour' is defined in the 1999 Act somewhat more broadly perhaps than just
'sexual experience', the concept of questions being 'about' such matters is
retained. It is, therefore, not without significance that in the case of R v Cox (1987)
84 Cr App R 132, dealing with the 1976 legislation, this court drew a distinction
between questions about the sexual behaviour itself and ones about statements
made about such behaviour by the complainant. Lord Lane CJ said (at 136):

> 'The result of that and the effect of the proposed questions and evidence is
> to indicate that it was not so much the sexual intercourse with Steven in the
> earlier event which was of importance, but what she said about it afterwards,
> and it was really that which was the subject of the application.'

[32] That distinction is one which has been drawn elsewhere. The courts in
the United States of America have held that evidence of prior false complaints is
not evidence of sexual conduct (see the article by H Galvin 'Shielding Rape
Victims in the State and Federal Courts' (1986) 70 Minn L Rev 763 at 859).

[33] It seems to this court that normally questions or evidence about false
statements in the past by a complainant about sexual assaults or such questions
or evidence about a failure to complain about the alleged assault which is the
subject matter of the charge, while complaining about other sexual assaults, are
not ones 'about' any sexual behaviour of the complainant. They relate not to her
sexual behaviour but to her statements in the past or to her failure to complain.

[34] In the event the Crown in RT does not contend that questions about
previous opportunities to complain involve the assertion of a previous sexual
experience on the part of the complainant. Certainly those questions which it is
sought to put in the RT case do not need to make such an assertion. They relate
essentially to statements in the past made by the complainant alleging sexual
experience but without needing to investigate whether those past statements by
the complainant were true or false. It is enough for the purposes of the defence
that she made such statements but said nothing about any sexual assault by the
present appellant.

[35] The interpretation which we have indicated of the wording of s 41(1)
would reflect the purpose of the 1999 Act, which was not to exclude such
evidence. At the report stage of the Bill, which became the 1999 Act, Lord
Williams of Mostyn, on behalf of the government, was clear that evidence about
previous false complaints was not to be excluded, saying of such evidence 'it is
about untruthful conduct on prior occasions. There is a very clear difference'
(598 HL Official Report (5th series) col 34 (8 March 1999)). Nothing in R v A
suggests that the purpose of s 41 was to exclude such evidence or questions.

[36] Consequently, a purposive approach to the interpretation of s 41, in
accordance with normal, pre-1998 Act principles of interpretation, leads this
court to conclude that the questions sought to be asked in both the present cases
were not automatically excluded by s 41, even if they are seen as going principally
to credibility.

[37] It is, therefore, unnecessary to invoke s 3 of the 1998 Act. However, had
we reached some different conclusion as a result of the traditional principles of
statutory interpretation, we should have found ourselves in these appeals obliged
to have adopted a narrow interpretation of s 41(1) because of the need to ensure
a fair trial.

a **[38]** In so saying we recognise that victims of crime have rights as well as defendants and that in cases of sexual offences the complainant has a right to a private life under art 8 of the convention which would include privacy in respect of her previous sexual conduct and experiences. A balancing exercise would be required. But in the present cases the balancing exercise must recognise the gravity of the charges faced by these two appellants and the serious consequences

b which they may face if convicted. We have no doubt that a fair trial in each case would require the interpretation of s 41(1) which has in the event been produced by more traditional methods. Section 41, therefore, is not to be seen as incompatible with a fair trial, given the approach which has been indicated.

[39] In arriving at that conclusion one is conscious of the potential dangers which Judge Hammond had in mind, so it seems, when he gave his ruling in the

c case of MH on whether questions about alleged false complaints could be asked. He said in that ruling at one point:

'... the answer to the question is unknown as to whether it took place or not [that is the sexual experience], and may very well elicit the issue that it

d did take place.'

[40] What seems to have concerned the judge is this. If a complainant is asked whether she had told a friend, X, on a previous occasion that she had been raped by Y (not the defendant) she may deny making the statement at all. However, she may admit making it, and, in accordance with the object which the defence

e has in mind, she would then normally be asked, 'That was not true, was it?' No problem arises if she agrees that it was a false statement. But she may answer that it was true. The defence will normally then be bound by that answer (see *R v S* [1992] Crim LR 307); but in some case its damage to the complainant's reputation may already be done. It is not difficult to postulate more damaging circumstances

f than in the example just given: if the complainant is alleged by the defence to have said to a friend in the recent past that she had just had intercourse with two complete strangers on leaving a disco, she admits making the statement to the friend and then goes on to deny that it was a lie, the very problem, or one of the problems which the 1999 Act was intended to guard against, could be created: her reputation in the eyes of the jury might well be severely injured and the deterrent

g effect on other potential complainants in sexual cases would continue to operate.

[41] As we say, this seems to have been the difficulty which Judge Hammond was troubled by and it is a matter for proper concern. However, it is open to a judge to guard against abuse of the system. The defence, wishing to put questions about alleged previous false complaints, will need to seek a ruling from the judge

h that s 41 does not exclude them. It would be professionally improper for those representing the defendant to put such questions in order to elicit evidence about the complainant's past sexual behaviour as such under the guise of previous false complaints. But in any case the defence must have a proper evidential basis for asserting that any such previous statement was (a) made and (b) untrue. If those

j requirements were not met, then the questions would not be about lies but would be 'about [the] sexual behaviour of the complainant' within the meaning of s 41(1). The judge is entitled to seek assurances from the defence that it has a proper basis for asserting that the statement was made and was untrue. That may not provide a watertight guarantee that in every single case evidence about the complainant's past sexual behaviour will be excluded, but it would normally prevent the sort of danger to which we have referred. We understand that in the present cases there is a proper evidential basis for the questions which the defence *a* seeks to put.

[42] In the case of RT, Mr Inman also seeks our guidance on one final matter where leave was not sought below. It concerns one of the complainant's brothers, who allegedly witnessed the rape incident but who made no mention of it when interviewed by the police in December 1990 but did refer to her grandfather 'interfering' with her. Guidance is sought as to whether questions *b* about her failure to mention the alleged rape are admissible under s 41, bearing in mind that the section applies to cross-examination generally, and not only to cross-examination of the complainant. Mr Inman submits that such questions would not be about the complainant's sexual behaviour but about her brother's veracity.

[43] We see the force of the point made. What is clear is that such questions do not go in any direct sense to the credibility of the complainant but rather to the issue of whether the rape happened. Such questions are not therefore excluded by s 41(4), which concerns only the credibility of the complainant. It is, however, it seems to us, a matter for the trial judge to determine, in the light of the way the arguments are put to him, the admissibility of such questions and this *d* court should not usurp his function. To do so would risk depriving one of the parties of its right of appeal to this court at some future date if he makes a ruling on that specific matter. The only guidance we can give is that which is set out earlier in this judgment, which we trust will be of some assistance.

[44] For the reasons given in this judgment, both these appeals are allowed.

Appeals allowed.

Kate O'Hanlon   Barrister.

a # Union Discount Co Ltd v Zoller and others (Union Cal Ltd, Pt 20 defendant)

[2001] EWCA Civ 1755

b COURT OF APPEAL, CIVIL DIVISION

LORD PHILLIPS OF WORTH MATRAVERS MR, SCHIEMANN AND MAY LJJ

24 OCTOBER, 21 NOVEMBER 2001

Damages – Costs – Recovery of legal costs as damages – Costs incurred in foreign
c *proceedings – Claimant bringing proceedings against defendant in England –*
Defendant bringing proceedings against claimant in New York contrary to exclusive
jurisdiction clause – New York court striking out defendant's proceedings – New York
law precluding claimant from recovering costs of strike out proceedings – Claimant
seeking to recover costs as damages in English proceedings – Whether costs incurred in
d *foreign proceedings capable of being recovered as damages in English action between*
same parties.

The appellant, UC, entered into contracts with the respondent, Z. Each contract
contained an exclusive jurisdiction clause nominating England. UC claimed that
money was owing under the contracts and sued Z in England. Z issued
e proceedings against UC in New York. On UC's application, the New York court
struck out Z's proceedings, holding that it had no jurisdiction by reason of the
exclusive jurisdiction clause. UC did not ask the New York court to award it costs
because under the law of New York costs would not have been awarded in such
circumstances. UC subsequently raised a new claim (the costs claim) in the
f English proceedings, seeking to recover the costs of the New York proceedings as
damages on the grounds that the exclusive jurisdiction clause was effective as a
contractual term; that breach of that term would sound in damages; and that Z
had breached it by issuing the New York proceedings. The costs claim was struck
out by the judge, who held that no proceedings could be brought before a civil
court in England to recover costs incurred by a party successfully prosecuting or
g defending an action in a foreign court. UC appealed.

Held – There was no rule that costs incurred in foreign proceedings could never
be recovered in an English action between the same parties. If there had been
such a rule, it could only have been justified by policy considerations. The public
h interest did not, however, require a claimant to be deprived of his reasonable
expenses of litigating in a foreign forum where (i) the costs which the claimant
sought to recover in the English proceedings had been incurred by him as a
defendant in foreign proceedings brought by the defendant in the English
proceedings; (ii) the claimant in the foreign proceedings had brought them in
j breach of an express term which had the effect of entitling the English claimant
to damages for breach; (iii) the rules of the foreign forum only permitted
recovery of costs in exceptional circumstances; and (iv) the foreign court had
made no adjudication as to costs. It followed in the instant case that, on the
assumption that the bringing of a suit in a foreign jurisdiction amounted to a
breach of contract, justice required that UC should receive the damages which it
had suffered by reason of the breach, namely the sum that it had reasonably

expended on the strike out proceedings in New York. Accordingly, the appeal would be allowed (see [8], [18], [34], [38], [39], below).

Berry v British Transport Commission [1961] 3 All ER 65 applied.

Jack L Israel Ltd v Ocean Dynamic Lines SA, The Ocean Dynamic [1982] 2 Lloyd's Rep 88 distinguished.

Notes

For the recovery as damages of costs incurred in previous proceedings between same parties, see 12(1) *Halsbury's Laws* (4th edn reissue) para 828.

Cases referred to in judgment

Agius v Great Western Colliery Co [1899] 1 QB 413, CA.
Berry v British Transport Commission [1961] 3 All ER 65, [1962] 1 QB 306, [1961] 3 WLR 450, CA.
Donohue v Armco Inc [2000] 1 All ER (Comm) 641, CA.
Hathaway v Barrow (1807) 1 Camp 151, 170 ER 909, NP.
Henderson v Henderson (1843) 3 Hare 100, [1843–1860] All ER Rep 378, 13 ER 301.
Jack L Israel Ltd v Ocean Dynamic Lines SA, The Ocean Dynamic [1982] 2 Lloyd's Rep 88.
Lonrho plc v Fayed (No 5) [1994] 1 All ER 188, [1993] 1 WLR 1489, CA.
Quartz Hill Consolidated Gold Mining Co v Eyre (1883) 11 QBD 674, CA.
Solway Prince, The (1914) 31 TLR 56.
Walshaw v Brighouse Corp [1899] 2 QB 286.

Cases also cited or referred to in skeleton arguments

Aggeliki Charis Cia Maritima SA v Pagnan SpA, The Angelic Grace [1995] 1 Lloyd's Rep 87, CA.
Cockburn v Edwards (1881) 18 Ch D 449, CA.
Continental Bank NA v Aeakos Compania Naviera SA [1994] 2 All ER 540, [1994] 1 WLR 588, CA.
Doleman & Sons v Ossett Corp [1912] 3 KB 257, CA.
Loton v Devereux (1832) 3 B & Ad 343, 110 ER 129, DC.
Schiffahrtsgesellschaft Detlev von Appen GmbH v Voest Alpine Intertrading GmbH [1997] 2 Lloyd's Rep 279, CA.
Seavision Investment SA v Norman Thomas Evennett, The Tiburon [1992] 2 Lloyd's Rep 26, CA.

Appeal

The Pt 20 defendant, Union Cal Ltd, appealed with permission of Judge Peter Heppel QC from his order of 11 April 2001, sitting as a judge of the High Court, granting an application by the defendants and Pt 20 claimants, Robert Zoller, Hans Maissen, Peter Atwood, Joseph Fleming, Frederick Lobatto, Jonathan Lobatto, Roderick Alasdair Steedman and Nancy Irene Steedman (Zoller), for summary judgment on Union Cal's counterclaim to recover as damages the costs of a successful application to the New York court to strike out proceedings brought against it by Zoller in New York. The claimant, Union Discount Co Ltd, took no part in the proceedings before Judge Heppel and the Court of Appeal. The facts are set out in the judgment of the court.

Guy Philipps (instructed by *Denton Wilde Sapte*) for Union Cal.
Mark Hubbard (instructed by *Harkavys*) for Zoller.

Cur adv vult

a 21 November 2001. The following judgment was delivered.

SCHIEMANN LJ.

[1] This is the judgment of the court. It concerns the correctness of the statement in 12(1) *Halsbury's Laws* (4th edn reissue) (damages) para 828 'Costs incurred in foreign proceedings cannot be recovered in an English action *b* between the same parties'. For this proposition the learned editors cite *Jack L Israel Ltd v Ocean Dynamic Lines SA, The Ocean Dynamic* [1982] 2 Lloyd's Rep 88, a decision of Robert Goff J.

[2] Union Cal Ltd (Union Cal) entered into contracts with Robert Zoller and others to whom we shall refer collectively as Zoller. Each contract contained an exclusive jurisdiction clause (EJC) nominating England.
c
[3] For present purposes the complicated procedural position can be summarised as follows. Union Cal claimed that money was owing under the contract and sued Zoller in England. Zoller issued proceedings against Union Cal in New York. Union Cal successfully applied in the New York court to strike out the New York proceedings against it on the ground that, by reason of the EJC, the *d* New York court had no jurisdiction. Thereafter Zoller served a defence and counterclaim in the English proceedings alleging misrepresentation by Union Cal. Union Cal raised a new claim (the costs claim) in the English proceedings against Zoller. This claim was struck out by Judge Peter Heppel QC sitting as a judge of the High Court. Union Cal, with the judge's permission, appeal the correctness of that striking out of the costs claim.
e
[4] The costs claim concerned Union Cal's costs incurred in the striking out proceedings in New York. In those proceedings Union Cal did not ask the New York court to award it costs because under the law of New York costs would not have been awarded in such circumstances. For the purposes of the proceedings before Judge Peter Heppel, Zoller conceded that there were real prospects of *f* Union Cal establishing at trial that; (1) the EJC was effective as a contractual term breach of which sounds in damages, and (2) by issuing the United States proceedings Zoller breached their contracts with Union Cal.

[5] Were this aspect of the case to proceed to trial the defendants would argue: (1) that the exclusive jurisdiction clause was not binding on them by reason of the provisions of the Unfair Terms in Consumer Contracts Regulations 1994, *g* SI 1994/3159, (2) that upon its true construction the clause did not prohibit the defendants from proceeding in the United States of America, (3) that Union Cal could have applied for and obtained an order for costs before the New York court, and (4) points regarding causation and mitigation of damage.

[6] The judge below, having considered *The Ocean Dynamic, Walshaw v* *h* *Brighouse Corp* [1899] 2 QB 286, *Berry v British Transport Commission* [1961] 3 All ER 65, [1962] 1 QB 306, *Lonrho plc v Fayed (No 5)* [1994] 1 All ER 188, [1993] 1 WLR 1489 and *Donohue v Armco Inc* [2000] 1 All ER (Comm) 641 held as follows: '... no proceedings may be brought before a civil court in England to recover costs incurred by a party successfully prosecuting or defending an action in the foreign *j* court.'

[7] The written submissions, outstandingly well formulated on behalf of the appellant by Guy Philipps, correctly identify the issue in the present appeal as follows:

'... whether the defendants are right to assert (in para 14 of the defence to counterclaim) that: "As a matter of law the costs of litigation can not be

recovered as damages for breach of contract by one party to the said
litigation against another" or whether the true principle of law is, as Union
Cal asserts (in para 12 of the amended reply to defence to counterclaim) that:
"The costs of prior proceedings between the same parties may be recovered
as damages for breach of contract if (as in the present case) the party seeking
to recover the costs of the prior proceedings as damages could not in the
circumstances of the prior proceedings have obtained an order for the
payment of those costs as costs."'

[8] The appellant submits and the respondents accept that if the rule is as
stated by the judge then this must be because of policy considerations. The judge
proceeded on this basis but failed to identify the policy considerations in play in
the present case apart from making reference to the cases to which we have
already referred. The appellant submits that those cases do not identify any
policy consideration which is applicable to the present case.

[9] The leading decision in this court is *Berry's* case. That had no foreign
element. It concerned the recoverability, in civil proceedings for malicious
prosecution, of costs incurred in criminal proceedings by the claimant who had
been unsuccessfully prosecuted but who had been awarded some of her costs but
who had not been awarded her remaining costs. This court held she could
recover the remaining costs as damages. Its approach was, first, to recognise that
in subsequent civil proceedings there are policy reasons which in some cases
inhibit recovery as damages of all the costs reasonably incurred in prior civil
proceedings, and, then, to hold that there was no policy reason in an action for
malicious prosecution for extending to costs in prior criminal proceedings the
rule which applied to prior civil proceedings. That is how it came about that
there was a lengthy and considered judgment by Devlin LJ (with whom Ormerod
and Danckwerts LJJ in their judgments agreed) about the reason for and nature
of the rule in relation to prior civil proceedings.

[10] The reasoning process of Devlin LJ appears from the following passages:

(i) '[*Quartz Hill Consolidated Gold Mining Co v Eyre* (1883) 11 QBD 674] was
a case in which the defendant presented a petition to wind-up the plaintiff
company. It was never served on the company and the defendant gave
notice that he was withdrawing it, but the company nevertheless appeared
to ask for its dismissal. It was dismissed by a vice-chancellor without costs
([1882] WN 27); I have no doubt that DANCKWERTS, L.J., was right when he
said in the course of the argument, after looking at the report of the case in
the Weekly Notes, that the reason why the plaintiff company was given no
costs was because their appearance was considered to be unnecessary. The
company brought an action for malicious prosecution and the damage they
alleged was the expenditure of costs incurred in opposing the petition which
they estimated at £30. The Court of Appeal held that the damage was not
recoverable. BRETT, M.R., said ((1883) 11 QBD 674 at 682): "The theory is
that the costs which the losing party is bound to pay, are all that were
necessarily incurred by the successful party in the litigation, and that it is
right to compel him to pay those costs because they have been caused by his
unjust litigation; but that those which are called 'extra costs', not being
necessarily incurred by the successful party in order to maintain his case, are
not incurred by reason of the unjust litigation." BOWEN, L.J., said (at 690):
"... the only costs which the law recognises, and for which it will compensate
him, are the costs properly incurred in the action itself ... If the judge refuses

a
to give him costs, it is because he does not deserve them: if he deserves them, he will get them in the ordinary action: if he does not deserve them, he ought not to get them in a subsequent action." ' (See [1961] 3 All ER 65 at 70, [1962] 1 QB 306 at 319–320.)

b
(ii) 'The rule is not easy to apply with justice because it embodies a presumption, which the law finds it convenient and maybe necessary to make; but which it has to, and does in other contexts, admit not to be in accordance with fact.' (See [1961] 3 All ER 65 at 70, [1962] 1 QB 306 at 320.)

c
(iii) 'The reason for the rule is not that the costs incurred in excess of the party and party allowance are deemed to be unreasonable; it is that what is presumed to be the same question cannot be gone into twice. The rule appears to have been first laid down by SIR JAMES MANSFIELD, C.J., in *Hathaway* v. *Barrow* ((1807) 1 Camp 151, 170 ER 909) where he put it on the ground that "… it would be incongruous to allow a person one sum as costs in one court, and a different sum for the same costs in another court." *If in*

d
the earlier case there has been no adjudication on costs (as distinct from an adjudication that there shall be no order as to costs), a party may recover all his costs assessed on the reasonable, and not on the necessary, basis. If a party has failed to apply for costs which he would have got if he had asked for them, a subsequent claim for damages may be defeated; but that would be because in such a case his loss would be held to be due to his own fault or omission. In any case in which the legal process does not permit an adjudication, the rule does not apply.' (See [1961] 3 All ER 65

e
at 71, [1962] 1 QB 306 at 320–321; our emphasis.)

(iv) '… if, as the result of a breach of contract (see *Agius* v. *Great Western Colliery Co* ([1899] 1 QB 413)) or a tort (see *The Solway Prince* ((1914) 31 TLR 56)), a person brings unsuccessfully an action against a third party or loses an

f
action brought by a third party, he may recover against the wrongdoer who has brought his contract or committed the tort the costs of the suit; and he will get all the costs which he has reasonably expended. The wrongdoer may not argue that the plaintiff is entitled only to party and party costs, notwithstanding that that is all he could or would have got from the third party if he had been successful. Thus the reason for the rule is that the law

g
cannot permit a double adjudication on the same point. It would be a rational rule and in accordance with the ordinary principle as to res judicata if in truth it were the same point. But it is not.' (See [1961] 3 All ER 65 at 71, [1962] 1 QB 306 at 321–322.)

h
(v) 'I find it difficult to see why the law should not now recognise one standard of costs as between litigants and another when those costs form a legitimate item of damage *in a separate cause of action flowing from a different and additional wrong* … The stringent standards that prevail in a taxation of party and party costs can be justified … It helps to keep down extravagance in litigation and that is a benefit to all those who have to resort to the law.

j
But the last person who ought to be able to share in that benefit is the man who ex hypothesi is abusing the legal process for his own malicious ends.' (See [1961] 3 All ER 65 at 72, [1962] 1 QB 306 at 322–323; our emphasis.)

(vi) 'If the matter were res integra, I should for myself prefer to see the abandonment of the fiction that taxed costs are the same as costs reasonably incurred and its replacement by a statement of principle that the law for reasons which it considers to be in the public interest requires a litigant to exercise a greater austerity than it exacts in the ordinary way, and which it will not relax *unless the litigant can show some additional ground for reimbursement over and above the bare fact that he has been successful.* Without a restatement of that sort, there is undoubtedly a practical need for the rule in civil cases. Otherwise, every successful plaintiff might bring a second action against the same defendant in order to recover from him as damages resulting from his original wrongdoing the costs that he had failed to obtain on taxation ... I have inquired into the reason for the rule, not because I think it open to us to reject it, but because we are asked to extend it. The question is whether it should be extended to costs in criminal cases as well as costs in civil cases.' (See [1961] 3 All ER 65 at 72–73, [1962] 1 QB 306 at 323; our emphasis.)

[11] From the passages which we have emphasised it is clear that Devlin LJ considered that, in a case such as the present where there was in the earlier action no prospect of obtaining costs although there had been no fault on behalf of the successful party, there was no policy inhibition on granting him the amount of those costs as damages in a later action if he had available to him an appropriate cause of action.

[12] Further, Devlin LJ was clearly unhappy with the reasoning which had led to the rule in English civil cases even where it did apply. In our judgment, just as a malicious prosecutor should not be able to rely for his own benefit on any policy consideration which is designed to keep down the cost of litigation, so a person who starts totally unnecessary proceedings in a foreign jurisdiction in breach of an EJC should not be able to rely on such policy considerations.

[13] There is nothing in *Berry's* case which supports the view that there are policy considerations which dictate that Union Cal should be kept out of its normal award of damages.

[14] The leading case at first instance upon which the judge below relied is a decision of Robert Goff J: *Jack L Israel Ltd v Ocean Dynamic Lines SA, The Ocean Dynamic* [1982] 2 Lloyd's Rep 88. In the judgment *Berry's* case is not referred to. *The Ocean Dynamic* is apparently the only reported case in which a litigant in United States proceedings has sought to recover its costs of those proceedings as damages in subsequent English proceedings. The facts of that case were very different from the facts here. The claimant commenced proceedings in England against the defendant, a United States company carrying on business in Wisconsin, alleging breach of a contract of carriage by sea. The defendant disputed the jurisdiction of the English court. The claimant therefore issued a protective writ in Wisconsin. The defendant's challenge to the jurisdiction of the English court was then dismissed. The claimant undertook to the English court to discontinue the United States proceedings, which it did. The claimant then sought in the English proceedings to recover as damages for breach of the contract of carriage its costs of the abortive United States proceedings in the sum of $US4,168·45.

[15] At the end of his unreserved judgment following the trial of the action, Robert Goff J (at 94) dismissed that minor head of claim in the following terms:

'[The United States] proceedings were between the parties to the present action in respect of the same claim. As such, the general principle is that they [sc the costs] cannot be recovered as damages, but can only be recovered if an order for costs was made by the appropriate Court. Indeed, there is no *a* evidence that if the United States action had been pursued to judgment, the relevant Court would have made any order for costs in favour of the plaintiffs recovering these particular costs, and bearing in mind the practice in the Courts of that country, I certainly cannot infer that this would have been done. The plaintiffs' submission involves therefore the bizarre consequence that, having discontinued the United States proceedings, they

b should now be able to recover as damages costs which they would not have been awarded in the United States action if they had won it. This plainly cannot be right. I therefore reject that head of damages.'

[16] Mr Philipps does not contend that the result reached by Robert Goff J is in any way to be criticised. He submits, and we accept, that the result was right

c because the costs sought to be recovered by the claimant were in no sense caused by the defendant's breach of the contract of carriage. Rather they flowed from the claimant's own decision to issue a protective writ in the United States of America.

[17] Mr Philipps submitted and we accept that Robert Goff J was not considering

d a case in which—as here—the plaintiffs had available to them a free-standing cause of action entitling them to seek to recover their costs as damages. His statement of the 'general principle' that 'costs cannot be recovered as damages' must be read in that light. Absent a separate cause of action, there is no doubt that costs, even if irrecoverable under the procedural rules of the foreign court, cannot be recovered as damages in separate proceedings in England. The

e claimant has suffered damnum sine injuria.

[18] It is important to emphasise that in the present case the following unusual features are all present. (i) The costs which the claimant seeks to recover in the English proceedings were incurred by him when he was a defendant in foreign proceedings brought by the defendant in the English proceedings. (ii) The

f claimant in the foreign proceedings brought those proceedings in breach of an express term, the EJC, which, it is assumed for present purposes, has the effect of entitling the English claimant to damages for its breach. (iii) The rules of the foreign forum only permitted recovery of costs in exceptional circumstances. (iv) The foreign court made no adjudication as to costs.

[19] It is common ground that there is no binding authority which inhibits us

g from granting Union Cal relief in damages in the present case. That relief is predicated on the assumption, not in issue before us, that the bringing of the New York proceedings itself constituted a breach of contract which has resulted in damages which are prima facie recoverable. Thus it is common ground that the action should not have been struck out unless there are policy reasons which

h prevent the recovery of these damages.

[20] Mark Hubbard, appearing for Zoller, put forward the following policy reasons which he submitted justified the conclusion of the judge.

The comity argument

j [21] He submitted that the rules of comity prevented the recovery of costs of civil proceedings in foreign jurisdictions as damages for breach of contract. The argument went as follows. Costs rules and practices in a state's jurisdiction are a matter for the state in question. One can advance policy arguments in favour of an approach, such as that which prevails in this country, that in general the successful party recovers his costs. Equally one can advance policy arguments in favour of an approach such as that which prevails in New York that in general each side pays its own costs. It would breach international comity if we sought *a* indirectly to apply our approach to litigation which had taken place in the foreign country.

[22] We accept that policy arguments can be made in favour of either approach but we reject the notion that by allowing a party in the position of Union Cal to recover these costs we would be breaching international comity. Comity is, as the editors of *Dicey and Morris on the Conflict of Laws* (13th edn, 2000) *b* point out in para 1-010 (pp 5–6), a term of very elastic content. Suppose the situation were reversed. A party from a jurisdiction which had an indemnity approach to costs more generous than our own is sued here in breach of an EJC. He persuades the English courts that we had no jurisdiction. He asks for costs but only recovers, let us say, a small amount of costs because our courts thought a larger amount was disproportionate to the amount at stake. He then sues for the *c* difference in the jurisdiction named in the EJC and recovers the difference. We can not think that such a happening would be the cause of the slightest concern to this country or its courts if indeed it ever came to their attention.

[23] There is in these cases no reason of comity why our courts should enforce a foreign jurisdiction's policy perception in preference to our own nor why they *d* should enforce ours in preference to theirs.

[24] If, as *Berry's* case demonstrates, an English civil court is prepared to give as damages in tort costs which have been refused by an English criminal court, we see no reason based on comity which would prevent an English civil court from giving as damages costs which a foreign court has not awarded. We would not expect to show a foreign court more comity than we show our own. *e*

The res judicata argument

[25] The courts manifestly should avoid two adjudications on the same point. That is common ground. However in cases such as the present where there is assumed to be an independent cause of action then, as Devlin LJ points out in the *f* fourth passage we cite at [10] from *Berry v British Transport Commission* [1961] 3 All ER 65, [1962] 1 QB 306 what is being adjudicated upon on the second occasion is not the same point.

[26] In the present case there is the additional point that in fact there was no adjudication upon costs in the New York court and so res judicata does not arise. *g*

The Henderson v Henderson point

[27] This founds on the well-known passage in *Henderson v Henderson* (1843) 3 Hare 100 at 115, [1843–1860] All ER Rep 378 at 381–382 in Wigram V-C's judgment in that case where he said:

h

'... where a given matter becomes the subject of litigation in, and of adjudication by, a court of competent jurisdiction, the Court requires the parties to that litigation to bring forward their whole case, and will not (except under special circumstances) permit the same parties to open the same subject of litigation in respect of matter which might have been brought forward as part of the subject in contest, but which was not brought *j* forward, only because they have ... omitted part of their case.'

[28] We accept of course that it is important that there should be an end to litigation but that principle has no sensible application to the present case. Since it was Union Cal's contention that the New York courts had no jurisdiction to consider breaches of the contract between Zoller and Union Cal, the latter could

a not in New York bring an action for damages caused to Union Cal by the bringing of the action in New York. If it wished to advance that contention it had to do so in England. The principle in *Henderson v Henderson* is manifestly inapplicable.

The unity of the law point

[29] Mr Hubbard submitted that since the English courts have for years *b* proceeded on the presumption referred to in the second of the quotations cited at [10] to the effect that the litigant who won the earlier proceedings will have got such costs as the law considers he deserves, the same presumption ought to apply whether those earlier proceedings were abroad or here. The law there referred to, it was implicit in his submissions, was the law of the courts in which the earlier proceedings were litigated. He submitted that either the general presumption *c* should be abandoned or it should be kept and universally applied.

[30] While in some ways an attractive proposition, it falls at first base because it was ruled in *Berry's* case by this court that it should not apply in malicious prosecution cases. Therefore the unity of the law after which he strives is not available—in any event in this court.

d [31] EJCs arise because the parties agree to litigate in one jurisdiction. It may be that one of the considerations which led to the adoption of the EJC in question was the costs regime in the nominated jurisdiction. We see no policy reason *connected with either party* for allowing one party to the contract to escape from liability for the damages which he has caused to the other by attempting to sue in a country where a different costs regime prevails.

e [32] There remains the question whether there is a policy reason *for the benefit of society at large* which argues in favour of applying the usual rule in cases where the costs sought to be recovered as damages represent the cost of litigation abroad in breach of an EJC. In the present case we can see none unless it be a desire to keep down litigation purely involving costs—often referred to as *f* parasitic litigation. A rationale behind the reluctance to facilitate parasitic litigation is that the state's legal resources should be devoted to central rather than parasitic questions. While this seems attractive, one must note that the amount of costs (or damages in the form of costs) at stake can be very much more than many a sum which otherwise is allowed to be recovered as damages.

g *The availability of an anti-suit injunction*

[33] Mr Hubbard submitted correctly that Union Cal had the option of obtaining an anti-suit injunction in England. The fact that they did not do this but instead chose to apply to strike out the New York proceedings was a tactical decision no doubt motivated, he submitted, by the desire not to expose *h* themselves to a costs order should they fail in the strike-out application. This in substance is an argument that Union Cal should have mitigated their damages by trying to obtain an anti-suit injunction. Even if this submission be correct, which we do not have to decide and do not decide, it goes to quantum not to the principle as to whether any damages are recoverable. We confess that it seems *j* to us unattractive for the New York claimant to submit that the English defendant should not have gone to New York to resist the proceedings which the New York claimant had, as a matter of choice, started there.

Conclusion

[34] In circumstances such as the present we do not consider that the public interest requires that the claimant should be deprived of its reasonable expenses

in litigating at the instance of the defendant in a jurisdiction which the defendant
chose in breach of an EJC. The proposition quoted at [1] of this judgment is too
widely stated.

[35] Treading cautiously in a field not much explored in recent litigation we
do not propose to go further. One can envisage more doubtful cases.

[36] Suppose, for instance, that the costs rules in Australia were broadly the
same as those which apply here. Suppose an attempt to litigate there in breach
of an EJC which nominated England. Assume successful proceedings there to
strike out the Australian litigation. Assume that costs are awarded to the
successful defendant but he only recovers two thirds of those costs although the
remainder was reasonably incurred. That defendant then sues here asking to be
awarded the remaining third as damages for breach of the EJC. Would our public
policy prevent him from recovering?

[37] Or suppose an arbitration clause which nominates arbitration in England.
One of the parties sues in the High Court. The other obtains a stay and a court
order for costs which does not fully recompense him for his costs reasonably
incurred.

[38] We prefer to leave such cases for the future. The present case concerns
someone who in breach of an EJC litigates in a jurisdiction which save exceptionally
does not award costs in strike out proceedings. Hence, no costs are asked for by
the party who successfully applied for the strike-out. It would have been
pointless to do so. In such a case, on the assumption that to bring suit in the
foreign jurisdiction amounts to a breach of contract, we consider that justice
requires that he should receive the damages which he has suffered by reason of
the breach. Those damages will be what he has reasonably expended on the
strike out proceedings. The situation appears to us to be akin to malicious
prosecution and the same rule as that established in *Berry*'s case should prevail.

[39] This appeal is allowed.

Appeal allowed. Permission to appeal refused.

Kate O'Hanlon   Barrister.

a

Veba Oil Supply & Trading Gmbh v Petrotrade Inc

[2001] EWCA Civ 1832

b COURT OF APPEAL, CIVIL DIVISION
SIMON BROWN, TUCKEY AND DYSON LJJ
22 NOVEMBER, 6 DECEMBER 2001

c

Contract – Condition – Breach – Effect – Contract for sale of gasoil – Contract providing for independent inspection – Contract stipulating method of inspection – Inspector employing different method – Whether inspector departing from instructions in material respect – Whether purchaser bound by inspector's decision.

By a contract made in August 1999, the defendant sellers sold 25,000 tons of gasoil to the claimant buyers. Clause 10 of the contract provided that the quantity and *d* quality of the cargo was 'to be determined by a mutually agreed independent inspector at the loading installation [Antwerp], in the manner customary at such installation. Such determination shall be final and binding for both parties save fraud or manifest error. Inspector to be appointed by seller ...' Clause 4 provided 'Gasoil meeting the following guaranteed specifications: Test: Density at 15 deg C; *e* Limit: +0·876 KG/L max; Method ASTM: D1298'. On 20 August 1999, some 34,000 tons of cargo were loaded on to a vessel and the mutually-agreed independent inspectors at Antwerp were instructed to carry out the determination under cl 10. The inspectors recorded that the cargo had been sampled and analysed and that its density at 15°C was 0·8750 kg/l (ie within the contractual specification) using the test method D4052 (rather than the specified method *f* D1298). The buyers brought an action claiming $US 250,000 from the sellers on the basis that they had on-sold the gasoil on similar quality terms, but that on arrival and testing the density of the oil was found to exceed the contractual maximum. The buyers disputed the inspectors' determination, submitting that it was not final and binding because the wrong testing method was used. The sellers applied for summary dismissal of the claim, contending that the inspectors' *g* determination was binding and conclusive and that the buyer's claim was accordingly bound to fail. The judge dismissed the application for summary judgment and the sellers appealed. On appeal, an issue arose as to what constituted a departure from instructions in a material respect.

h **Held** – A departure from instructions was material unless it could truly be characterised as trivial or de minimis in the sense of it being obvious that it could make no possible difference to either party. When parties entered into a contract on certain terms as to inspection it was important that the court should not lightly relieve one of them from being bound by those terms. Moreover, inspectors *j* should be astute to comply with their instructions and, if they departed from them, there should not then be much scope for dispute and litigation as to whether their determination was nevertheless binding. A departure from instructions was quite different from the situation where an expert had gone wrong in the course of carrying out his instructions, which required the court to consider whether that mistake had materially affected the ultimate result. Once a material departure from instructions was established, the court was not

concerned with its effect on the result. Such a determination was not binding on
the parties because if an expert departed from his instructions the parties would   *a*
not have agreed to be bound by his decision. In the instant case, as the inspectors
had not determined the quality of cargo using test method D1298, and as the
parties had not agreed to be bound by a determination as to quality by any other
method, the determination was not binding. Accordingly, the appeal would be
dismissed (see [15], [16], [26], [29], [39], [40], [49], below).   *b*

  Shell UK Ltd v Enterprise Oil plc [1999] 2 All ER (Comm) 87 and *Jones v Sherwood
Computer Services plc* [1992] 2 All ER 170 applied.

  Dean v Prince [1954] 1 All ER 749 and *Frank H Wright (Constructions) Ltd v Frodoor*
[1967] 1 All ER 433 distinguished.

  Decision of Morison J [2001] 1 All ER (Comm) 1051 affirmed.
                                                                                        c

Notes
For third party determinations, see 32 *Halsbury's Laws* (4th edn reissue) para 32.

Cases referred to in judgments
Arenson v Casson Beckman Rutley & Co [1975] 3 All ER 901, sub nom *Arenson v*   *d*
  Arenson [1977] AC 405, [1975] 3 WLR 815, HL.
Baber v Kenwood Manufacturing Co Ltd [1978] 1 Lloyd's Rep 175, CA.
British Shipbuilders v VSEL Consortium plc [1997] 1 Lloyd's Rep 106.
Campbell v Edwards [1976] 1 All ER 785, [1976] 1 WLR 403, CA.
Conoco (UK) Ltd v Phillips Petroleum Co (UK) Ltd (19 August 1996, unreported), DC. *e*
Dean v Prince [1954] 1 All ER 749, [1954] Ch 409, [1954] 2 WLR 538, CA.
Jones v Sherwood Computer Services plc [1992] 2 All ER 170, [1992] 1 WLR 277, CA.
Jones (M) v Jones (RR) [1971] 2 All ER 676, [1971] 1 WLR 840.
Nikko Hotels (UK) Ltd v MEPC plc [1991] 2 EGLR 103.
Shell UK Ltd v Enterprise Oil plc [1999] 2 All ER (Comm) 87.   *f*
Sutcliffe v Thackrah [1974] 1 All ER 859, [1974] AC 727, [1974] 2 WLR 295, HL.
Toepfer v Continental Grain Co Ltd [1974] 1 Lloyd's Rep 11.
Wright (Frank H) (Constructions) Ltd v Frodoor Ltd [1967] 1 All ER 433, [1967] 1
  WLR 506.

Cases cited or referred to in skeleton arguments   *g*
Bouygues (UK) Ltd v Dahl Jensen (UK) Ltd [2001] 1 All ER (Comm) 1041, CA.
Healds Foods Ltd v Hyde Dairies Ltd (1 December 1994, unreported), QBD; *affd*
  [1996] CA Transcript 1665.
Mercury Communications Ltd v Director General of Telecommunications [1996] 1 All
  ER 575, [1996] 1 WLR 48, HL.   *h*

Appeal
Petrotrade Inc (the sellers) appealed with permission of Waller LJ granted on
5 June 2001 from the decision of Morison J on 2 May 2001 ([2001] 1 All ER
(Comm) 1051) whereby he dismissed its application for summary dismissal of a *j*
claim for $US250,000 brought by the respondent, Veba Oil Supply & Trading
GmbH (the buyers), for damages arising from the alleged sale of 25,000 tons of
gasoil not of agreed density following an expert determination stipulated for by
the contract of, inter alia, density, which was not carried out according to the
method stipulated in the contract. The facts are set out in the judgment of
Simon Brown LJ.

a Michael Nolan (instructed by Davies Johnson & Co, Plymouth) for the sellers.
David Goldstone (instructed by Clifford Chance) for the buyers.

Cur adv vult

6 December 2001. The following judgments were delivered.

b **SIMON BROWN LJ.**

[1] If an independent expert departs from his instructions in a material respect his determination is not binding. What for these purposes is a material respect? That is the critical question before us. It arises on appeal from Morison J's order in the Commercial Court on 2 May 2001 ([2001] 1 All ER (Comm) 1051) dismissing *c* the appellants' application for summary judgment under CPR 24.2.

[2] The circumstances in which the point arises are not in dispute and can be briefly told. By a contract made in August 1999 the appellants (the sellers) sold a cargo of 25,000 plus metric tons of gasoil to the respondents (the buyers) FOB Antwerp.

d [3] The contract provided, amongst other things:

'4. PRODUCT/QUALITY   GASOIL MEETING THE FOLLOWING
GUARANTEED SPECIFICATIONS:

TEST	LIMIT	METHOD ASTM
DENSITY AT 15 DEG C	0.876 KG/L MAX	D1298 ...'

e That test was followed by 20 other specified tests.

'10. QUANTITY/QUALITY
Quantity and quality to be determined by a mutually agreed independent inspector at the loading installation, in the manner customary at such installation. Such determination shall be final and binding for both parties
f save fraud or manifest error. Inspector to be appointed by seller. Costs to be shared equally between buyer and seller.'

[4] On 20 August 1999 some 34,000 metric tons of cargo were loaded on board the vessel MT 'Robin' at the installation of the Belgian Refining Corp BV at Antwerp. Caleb Brett were the mutually agreed independent inspectors
g instructed to carry out the determination under cl 10. By their report dated 26 August 1999 they recorded that the cargo had been sampled and analysed and that its density at 15 °C was 0·8750 kg/l (ie within the contractual specification of 0·876), using test method D 4052 (rather than the specified method D 1298).

[5] In this action, brought on 17 August 2000, the buyers claim some
h $US250,000 from the sellers. They do so on the basis that they on-sold the cargo to the Lebanese Ministry of Oil on similar terms as to quality but that on arrival and testing the density of the oil was found to exceed the contractual maximum. They dispute the inspectors' determination. This, they say, is not final and binding because the wrong testing method was used.

j [6] The sellers contend that the inspectors' determination is binding and conclusive and that the buyers' claim is accordingly bound to fail. Hence their application for its summary dismissal and, following Morison J's rejection of their argument below, this appeal.

[7] Before coming to the arguments I should record certain further matters of agreement. First, that test method D 4052 is more modern and accurate than D 1298, having a margin of error of 0·0001% as opposed to 0·0007%. Second, that

had the inspectors used method D 1298, they would inevitably still have found
the density test satisfied in respect of the actual samples tested. Third, that
method D 4052 as opposed to D 1298 is that customarily used at Antwerp.

Was there a departure from instructions?

[8] Before turning to what I have already described as the critical issue, it is
necessary first to dispose of a preliminary argument: the sellers' contention that,
on the proper construction of the contract, the inspectors were not required to
use test method D 1298 and accordingly are not to be regarded as having
departed from their instructions, materially or otherwise.

[9] Mr Nolan's argument in this regard runs essentially as follows. Clause 4 is
a specification clause pure and simple requiring no more than that the cargo
should have a density up to the specified limit. Clearly one way of determining
as a matter of objective fact whether that specification was met was by using the
prescribed method. But it was not the only way. Another method could be used
if, as here, it would still be possible to demonstrate that the specification would
have been met even had the prescribed method been used. The only provision
in the contract expressly providing for how the independent inspector was to
determine the quality of the cargo was cl 10 which provided for this to be done
'in the manner customary at such installation'. The word 'manner' in that
context encompasses all aspects of the determination of cargo quality including
testing methods. Mr Nolan, indeed, went so far as to submit that the inspectors
were required to use customary method irrespective of whether it was better or
worse than the method prescribed by cl 4.

[10] For my part I would reject these arguments. Clause 4 does not require
that the cargo must be a cargo the specification of which is such that, if it were to
be tested by the specified method D 1298, it would meet the density specification
but that it need not be so tested. On the contrary, it provides that this test method
must be used. And, indeed, why else would the test method be specified? Why
should the parties care whether the cargo is theoretically capable of satisfying a
given test unless that particular test is to be used? Mr Nolan submits that test
D 1298 is specified merely as a standard or benchmark test and that any better test
would suffice. If his reasoning is sound, however, a *less* accurate test (provided
always it was 'customary' at the installation) would also suffice so long as it could
be shown that it would have produced the same result—as, indeed, it would have
done here (if one postulates the specification of test D 4052 and the use of
D 1298).

[11] There is this further objection to Mr Nolan's argument: in order to
determine whether the inspectors' determination is binding, the parties (or the
court) must go through the exercise of comparing the result of the actual test
used with the result of a hypothetical test using the specified method. True it is
that the parties here have sensibly agreed what the outcome of such an exercise
would be. That, however, will not always be so and often the exercise would be
problematic. It would certainly be uncommercial.

[12] In short, I share the view expressed by the judge below that cl 10 is not to
be read on its own. Clause 4 identifies both the standard and the method for
assessing whether the standard has been reached. What was required was a test
conducted by the stipulated method and none other. Clause 10 deals with the
'manner' of carrying out the required tests. This would, of course, include the
method where that was not otherwise specified (as was so in the case of some
tests under cl 4). But the 'manner' would include a host of other matters too, not

a least the sampling procedures to be followed. These are in fact what the buyers complain of and will seek to criticise if the inspectors' determination is set aside. The inspectors' evidence that the samples tested met the contractual specification will be well-nigh unassailable. Not so, however, the suitability or sufficiency of the samples taken.

b *Departure in a material respect*

[13] Having concluded that the inspectors departed from their instructions, I come then to the more difficult question of whether this departure was in a material respect. At an early stage of his submissions, and certainly in his written argument, Mr Nolan suggested that there is a distinction to be drawn between on the one hand a departure which is de minimis or trivial and on the other hand one

c which is immaterial. Ultimately, however, he came to accept that all these expressions are synonymous. The critical question is what in this context they entail. The sellers' argument in a nutshell is that a departure is not material unless it could have had an effect upon the ultimate result, ie could have affected the inspectors' determination that the cargo was of the specified quality, and here it

d is conceded it could not, and indeed did not.

[14] The buyers' contrary argument is that once, as here, a clear departure from instructions is established, the court should not be drawn into the exercise of determining what if any effect it might have had on the end result. Mr Goldstone submits that only the most trifling departure should properly be characterised as immaterial, where, for example, a valuer arrives late for an

e appointment. Failing that, Mr Goldstone submits that a departure should not be regarded as immaterial unless the court is satisfied that it could have made no conceivable difference not merely to the outcome of the determination itself but also in any other respect, as for example to a third party's readiness to accept, or pay against, the determination. There are many possible reasons, unconnected with the achievement of an accurate physical result, for choosing a particular test.

f It could have related to the on-sale contract. It could have related to a letter of credit. It could simply have been the test with which the buyers were most familiar and confident. It is not for the court to speculate. It is sufficient that the parties have agreed it.

[15] Before turning to the authorities most closely in point, it is convenient

g first to recognise two principles which inevitably touch on the issue. The first, and that on which understandably Mr Nolan places reliance, is to be found in Cairns LJ's judgment in *Toepfer v Continental Grain Co Ltd* [1974] 1 Lloyd's Rep 11 at 14:

h   'When parties enter into a contract on terms that the certificate of some independent person is to be binding as between them, it is important that the Court should not lightly relieve one of them from being bound by a certificate which was honestly obtained and not vitiated by fraud or fundamental mistake on the part of the certifier. When, for instance, as in this case, the certificate called for by the contract is one relating to the quality

j   of goods sold, the business purpose is to avoid disputes about quality, and that purpose is defeated unless it is made difficult for a party to go behind a valid certificate.'

[16] The second, clearly countervailing, principle is surely this: inspectors should be astute to comply with their instructions and, if they depart from them, there should not then be much scope for dispute and litigation as to whether their

determination is nevertheless binding. In short, the interests of finality cut both
ways although, of course, one bears in mind that if a determination is set aside the   *a*
underlying dispute is left unresolved.

[17] Coming then to the authorities I propose to take as my starting point the
first instance decision of *Jones (M) v Jones (RR)* [1971] 2 All ER 676, [1971] 1 WLR
840. The court there was concerned with a valuation produced by a valuer who
departed from his instructions in two respects: first he valued shares on a   *b*
break-up basis whereas he was instructed to use a going-concern basis; secondly
he valued certain machinery himself whereas his instructions required him to
have it valued by an expert valuer of his choice. Ungoed-Thomas J turned to
address—

> 'the defendant's contention that an error in principle does not vitiate a   *c*
> valuation unless it is shown by the person relying on it that it also results in
> a materially different valuation, both in the part of the valuation subject to
> error and in the overall valuation.' (See [1971] 2 All ER 676 at 681–682, [1971]
> 1 WLR 840 at 854.)

[18] The two cases with which he was principally concerned were *Dean v*   *d*
Prince [1954] 1 All ER 749, [1954] Ch 409 and *Frank H Wright (Constructions) Ltd v*
Frodoor Ltd [1967] 1 All ER 433, [1967] 1 WLR 506. The valuers in *Dean v Prince*,
as in *Jones v Jones* itself, had valued shares on a break-up rather than a
going-concern basis but, unlike in *Jones v Jones*, that had not been contrary to their
instructions; rather their instructions had simply been to determine a 'fair value'.   *e*
The Court of Appeal unanimously upheld the valuation although with some
reluctance. Sir Raymond Evershed MR said:

> '... I have felt compelled to the conclusion that though, as I think,
> Mr. Jenkinson [the valuer] erred in principle in treating himself as bound on
> accountancy principles to regard only the break-up value, Mrs. Dean has,   *f*
> nevertheless, failed sufficiently to establish that a consideration of the values
> of the plant "in situ" or otherwise would produce, in all the circumstances, a
> figure of value materially different from that at which Mr. Jenkinson
> arrived.' (See [1954] 1 All ER 749 at 758, [1954] Ch 409 at 426.)

Denning LJ stated the principle thus: '... if the courts are satisfied that the   *g*
valuation was made under a mistake, they will hold it not to be binding on the
parties.' (See [1954] 1 All ER 749 at 758, [1954] Ch 409 at 427.)

[19] The *Frank H Wright* case concerned an error on the face of the certificate
and decided that an immaterial error does not vitiate a valuation. But Roskill J
said: 'If this error had been material, it would have been enough to vitiate the   *h*
whole of the certificate, small as it might be and regrettable as the consequences
might be.' (See [1967] 1 All ER 433 at 457, [1967] 1 WLR 506 at 529.) He then
added with regard to the error in the case before him: '... this error is not material
because it does not affect the result ...'

[20] In *Jones v Jones*, Ungoed-Thomas J said of Roskill J's judgment: *j*

> 'He was not there dealing with any question of burden of proof; nor—what
> is crucial—was he, and nor indeed was Sir Raymond Evershed MR, dealing
> [in *Dean v Prince*] with a valuation made in a manner contrary to directions
> binding on the valuer as to the manner or method of valuation.' (See [1971]
> 2 All ER 676 at 682, [1971] 1 WLR 840 at 855.)

a

[21] A little later Ungoed-Thomas J continued:

'... I do not conclude that there is any requirement of general application that where a valuation is made on an erroneous principle, yet the valuation nevertheless stands unless it is also shown that a valuation on the right principle would produce a materially different figure from the figure of the valuation that he made. (This would incidentally place on the objector the

b

onus, not only of proving that the selected expert has acted on the wrong principle, but of incurring what might be the very heavy burden and expense of a completely new valuation, which itself might not be accepted as conclusive between the parties and merely leading to yet another valuation.) The authorities thus to my mind establish that if a valuation is erroneous in

c

principle, it is vitiated and cannot be relied on even though it is not established that the valuation figure is wrong.' (See [1971] 2 All ER 676 at 683, [1971] 1 WLR 840 at 856.)

I take 'erroneous in principle' in that final sentence to refer to a departure from instructions.

d

[22] I come next to this court's decision in *Jones v Sherwood Computer Services plc* [1992] 2 All ER 170, [1992] 1 WLR 277 upholding an expert's report on the basis that the experts had done precisely what they had been instructed to do. In the course of a judgment which considered a large number of authorities, Dillon LJ noted first, the development of the law in the mid-1970's establishing that an expert could be liable for damages if he had acted negligently in giving his

e

certificate (see the House of Lords' decisions in *Sutcliffe v Thackrah* [1974] 1 All ER 859, [1974] AC 727 and *Arenson v Casson Beckman Rutley & Co* [1975] 3 All ER 901, sub nom *Arenson v Arenson* [1977] AC 405); secondly, that this required reconsideration of the principle that a certificate could be vitiated for mistake (how could an expert be liable for a negligent mistake in giving a certificate if the

f

effect of that mistake was that the certificate was not binding on the parties?); and thirdly, that accordingly, in *Campbell v Edwards* [1976] 1 All ER 785, [1976] 1 WLR 403 and *Baber v Kenwood Manufacturing Co Ltd* [1978] 1 Lloyd's Rep 175, this court 'look[ed] at the question of setting aside certificates of experts on grounds of mistake afresh in the light of the principle that the expert or valuer can be sued for negligence' (see [1992] 2 All ER 170 at 179, [1992] 1 WLR 277 at 286). Lord

g

Denning MR had said in *Campbell v Edwards*:

'It is simply the law of contract. If two persons agree that the price of property should be fixed by a valuer on whom they agree, and he gives that valuation honestly and in good faith, they are bound by it. Even if he has

h

made a mistake they are still bound by it. The reason is because they have agreed to be bound by it.' (See [1976] 1 All ER 785 at 788, [1976] 1 WLR 403 at 407.)

[23] In *Jones v Sherwood Computer Services* Dillon LJ observed:

j

'Plainly Lord Denning MR came to change his views between 1954 [in *Dean v Prince* [1954] 1 All ER 749, [1954] Ch 409] and 1976 [in *Campbell v Edwards* [1976] 1 All ER 785, [1976] 1 WLR 403] ... We also therefore are free to look at the matter afresh on principle, and are not bound by the law as stated by common consensus in *Dean v Prince*. On principle, the first step must be to see what the parties have agreed to remit to the expert, this being, as Lord Denning MR said in *Campbell v Edwards*, a matter of contract. The

next step must be to see what the nature of the mistake was, if there is
evidence to show that. If the mistake made was that the expert departed a
from his instructions in a material respect, e g if he valued the wrong number
of shares, or valued shares in the wrong company, or if, as in *Jones (M) v Jones
(RR)* [1971] 2 All ER 676, [1971] 1 WLR 840 the expert had valued machinery
himself whereas his instructions were to employ an expert valuer of his
choice to do that, either party would be able to say that the certificate was b
not binding because the expert had not done what he was appointed to do ...
because Coopers [the valuers] did precisely what they were instructed to do,
the plaintiffs cannot challenge their determination of the amount of the sales.
There is another line of reasoning which points in the same direction, though
I do not found my judgment on it ... Therefore if there was any "mistake"
over the contracts subject to ratification it is a wholly immaterial mistake c
with no practical effect at all: see the judgment of Roskill J in *Frank H Wright
(Constructions) Ltd v Frodoor Ltd* ([1967] 1 All ER 433, [1967] 1 WLR 506) ...
where he refers to an error being "material" only if it materially affects the
ultimate result.' (See [1992] 2 All ER 170 at 178–179, 180, [1992] 1 WLR 277
at 286, 287, 288.) d

[24] The final authority to which I come on this part of the case is *Shell UK Ltd
v Enterprise Oil plc* [1999] 2 All ER (Comm) 87. Put shortly, the experts there, in
breach of contract, had used the wrong computer programme to map an oil field.
Lloyd J held in a reserved judgment following a six-day hearing that that
departure from the experts' instructions vitiated their final decision. In the e
section of the judgment headed 'The law as regards materiality of a breach',
Lloyd J discussed and quoted from, principally, the *Frank H Wright* case, *Jones v
Jones* and *Jones v Sherwood Computer Services*. The first two of those cases, he
noted, had not actually been cited to him although, of course, both were referred
to in *Jones v Sherwood Computer Services*. The relevant paragraphs in Lloyd J's
judgment are these (at 108–109): f

'97. Materiality must, of course, also be considered in the light of the
particular contract. In this case, the contract lays down the procedures for
submissions and documents passing between the parties and the expert
according to a carefully regulated procedure and timetable for what is likely
to be, at best, quite a lengthy process but one which is to be pursued at g
considerable speed. In that context, it seems to me that the test of materiality
has to be capable of being applied, at the latest, at the moment when the
error first comes to light, which is likely to be in the first formal document
produced by the expert after the error has occurred, or on a request for
clarification by one or another party soon thereafter. The ultimate effect of h
the error on the parties' position may not be known, or even capable of being
forecast with any accuracy, especially if it arises at an early stage. Both
parties agree that it cannot be necessary or possible to wait until the outcome
or effect of the error is known, which may be a long way down the line,
before being able to decide whether the error is sufficiently material to vitiate j
the expert's act. It is therefore a question of assessing materiality by reference
not to whether it actually affects the ultimate result, but according to its
potential effect on the result and, perhaps even more importantly, on the
process, including the ability of the parties to manage and deal with the
procedure in accordance with the contract. 98. I should also say that, if the
expert has committed a material breach of instructions, then as a matter of

a law the relevant act is not binding on any of the parties, leaving aside of course the effect of their subsequent acts. It is not a point on which the court has a discretion whether or not to allow the expert's act to stand. I do not consider that Lightman J intended to suggest that there was such a discretion when summarising the law in *British Shipbuilders v VSEL Consortium plc* [1997] 1 Lloyd's Rep 106 at 109, even though he said that the court "may" set the

b decision aside. That he did not mean to indicate that it was a discretionary issue appears in any event from the next following sentence. The relevant passage is: "(3) If the expert in … his determination fails to comply with any conditions which the agreement requires him to comply with in making his determination, the court may intervene and set his decision aside. Such a determination by the expert as a matter of construction of the agreement is

c not a determination which the parties agreed should affect the rights and duties of the parties, and the Court will say so."'

As Lloyd J had already noted, Lightman J in the *British Shipbuilders'* case was for this purpose drawing essentially upon *Jones v Sherwood Computer Services.*

d [25] Mr Nolan submits, as stated, that a departure is not material unless it affected, or at least could have affected, the outcome of the determination. In so submitting he relies upon a number of passages from the judgments I have discussed, most notably perhaps Sir Raymond Evershed MR's reference in *Dean v Prince* to 'a figure of value materially different from that at which [the valuer] arrived'; Roskill J's characterisation of the error in the *Frank H Wright* case as 'not

e material because it does not affect the result'; Dillon LJ's other 'line of reasoning' in *Jones v Sherwood* referring to 'a wholly immaterial mistake with no practical effect at all', with express reference back to Roskill J's judgment; and Lloyd J's reference in para 97 of his judgment in the *Shell UK* case ([1999] 2 All ER (Comm) 87 at 108) to not waiting to see 'whether the error is sufficiently material to vitiate

f the experts' act' so that materiality is to be assessed 'according to its potential rather than its actual effect upon the ultimate result'. All these passages, Mr Nolan argues, support the view that the essential touchstone of materiality is whether or not the departure might have affected the outcome of the determination. If demonstrably it could not have done so, or if, as here, that is conceded, the determination should stand.

g [26] Strongly and skilfully though the argument was advanced, for my part I cannot accept it. Rather I see the position as follows. (i) A mistake is one thing; a departure from instructions quite another. A mistake is made when an expert goes wrong in the course of carrying out his instructions. The difference between that and an expert not carrying out his instructions is obvious. (ii) Under the old

h law a mistake would vitiate the expert's determination if it could be shown that it affected the result. That was the concept of material mistake established in *Dean v Prince* and the *Frank H Wright* case. Not so, however, with regard to a departure from instructions—see Ungoed-Thomas J's judgment in *Jones v Jones* cited at [21] above. (iii) Under the modern law the position is the same as it was

j with regard to a departure from instructions, different with regard to mistakes. As Lord Denning MR explained in *Campbell v Edwards*, if an expert makes a mistake whilst carrying out his instructions, the parties are nevertheless bound by it for the very good reason that they have agreed to be bound by it. Where, however, the expert departs from his instructions, the position is very different: in those circumstances the parties have *not* agreed to be bound. (iv) The test of materiality devised for identifying vitiating mistakes does not carry across to the quite separate field of departures from instructions. This seems to me so both as a matter of principle and of authority. The position is as stated in *Jones v Jones* and in Dillon LJ's judgment in *Jones v Sherwood Computer Services* [1992] 2 All ER 170 at 179, [1992] 1 WLR 277 at 287 (quoted at [23] above) where he illustrates the principle by reference to *Jones v Jones*. (v) *Dean v Prince* and the *Frank H Wright* case—although on any view rightly decided—should no longer be regarded as authoritative with regard to experts' mistakes. That for the most part was made clear in *Jones v Sherwood Computer Services*. The contrary is not to be inferred from the dictum in Dillon LJ's judgment ([1992] 2 All ER 170 at 180, [1992] 1 WLR 277 at 288) (the other line of reasoning on which he did *not* found his judgment) referring back to the *Frank H Wright* case. It is time that *Dean v Prince* and the *Frank H Wright* case received their quietus. (vi) Once a material departure from instructions is established, the court is not concerned with its effect on the result. The position is accurately stated in para 98 of Lloyd J's judgment in the *Shell UK* case ([1999] 2 All ER (Comm) 87 at 108–109): the determination in those circumstances is simply not binding on the parties. Given that a material departure vitiates the determination whether or not it affects the result, it could hardly be the effect on the result which determines the materiality of the departure in the first place. Rather I would hold any departure to be material unless it can truly be characterised as trivial or de minimis in the sense of it being obvious that it could make no possible difference to either party.

[27] I should add that each side before us sought to draw some comfort from Lloyd J's judgment in the *Shell UK* case: Mr Nolan, as indicated, because of the references in para 97 (at 108) to the error (clearly there a departure from instructions) potentially if not actually affecting the ultimate result; Mr Goldstone because the judge's reference to the effect of the departure on the 'process' shows at least that he had broader considerations in mind than merely the result of the test itself. It is perhaps a pity that the *Frank H Wright* case and *Jones v Jones* were not explored in argument before the judge: the suspicion arises that he may not have appreciated that the former, as pointed out in the latter, was not concerned with a departure from instructions. This may explain what to my mind was Lloyd J's excessive concern with the effect of the expert's breach of instructions on the process if not the result.

[28] I therefore agree with what Morison J said in his judgment below ([2001] 1 All ER (Comm) 1051 at 1055 (para 15):

'The word "material" as used by Dillon LJ in *Jones v Sherwood Computer Services plc* [1992] 2 All ER 170 at 179, [1992] 1 WLR 277 at 287 ("If the mistake made was that the expert departed from his instructions in a material respect") is capable of meaning either that the mistake must be more than trivial or that the mistake must have made a material difference to the result. If it were the latter, then the protection afforded by a final certificate clause would become less effective since the court would have to try the facts to see if the error made a material difference. Since the whole purpose of the final determination provision is designed to avoid such a trial, I cannot think that the Court of Appeal meant more by the word "material" than "not de minimis." As Knox J pointed out in *Nikko Hotels (UK) Ltd v MEPC plc* [1991] 2 EGLR 103, it is not the business of the court to weigh the importance of a stipulation in a contract. If the requirement to use the method specified in cl 4 was contractual that is an end of the matter, whether or not the court thinks it was important or would have made a difference. The assumption *a* the court makes, on normal principles of construction, is that the parties have chosen to define their rights and obligations according to their own needs, whatever they may have been. In this case, with an on-sale, one can envisage the possibility that the buyers wanted the old-fashioned test for reasons connected with it. However, that is speculation. The position is, I think, that it is no business of the court to inquire why the buyers asked for

b this particular test. This is what was agreed ...'

[29] In short, the inspectors here were required to determine the quality of the cargo using test method D 1298. They did not do so and the parties had not agreed to be bound by a determination as to quality by any other method. The determination is accordingly not binding.

c

Manifest error

[30] Although that conclusion is sufficient to dispose of the appeal, I would touch briefly on the alternative basis for decision relied upon by the buyers, the reference in cl 10 to 'manifest error'. Morison J below went no further than to

d say that he was 'inclined to the view that there was a manifest error here, due to the wrong test being used'.

[31] Morison J had previously considered the meaning of 'manifest error' in *Conoco (UK) Ltd v Phillips Petroleum Co (UK) Ltd* (19 August 1996, unreported) where, following dicta in earlier cases, he held that manifest error referred to 'oversights and blunders so obvious as to admit of no difference of opinion'.

e

[32] The question then arising is whether it is relevant to consider whether the error is one that affected the result. Considering that question in the *Conoco (UK)* case, Morison J said:

'... it seems to me that there is no room for any debate as to whether the

f oversight or blunder would or would not have made any material difference to the result. If it could be shown that there was a manifest error then in my judgment that would be an end of the case. If fraud was shown, I cannot accept that it would be open to debate as to whether the fraud did or did not affect the result; so also would manifest error.'

g

[33] I confess to some difficulty with this approach. Fraud, of course, would vitiate the determination irrespective of whether it affected the result: 'Fraud or collusion unravels everything' (per Lord Denning MR in *Campbell v Edwards* [1976] 1 All ER 785, [1976] 1 WLR 403). The exception for 'manifest error', however, seems to me of a rather different character and to be designed

h essentially to fill the gap in the law created by the development to which I have already referred: the overthrow of the *Dean v Prince* principle of setting aside determinations for mistake. Nowadays, if parties wish to contract on the basis that they will not be held to mistakes made by the expert in the course of carrying out his instructions, they have no alternative but to include a term like this with

j regard to manifest error. But if they do, is it then really to be said that provided only the mistake is obvious, the determination will be avoided irrespective of whether it could affect the outcome? In this context I am inclined to think not. Take the very error committed in *Frank H Wright (Constructions) Ltd v Frodoor Ltd* [1967] 1 All ER 433, [1967] 1 WLR 506, the erroneous inclusion of a 'not' in the report. I do not think that that ought properly to be regarded as a 'manifest error'. Rather I would extend the 'definition' of manifest errors as follows:

'oversights and blunders so obvious *and obviously capable of affecting the determination* as to admit of no difference of opinion'. (My emphasis.)

[34] If, of course, the error consists of a departure from instructions, then, assuming I am right in my earlier conclusion, it will never be necessary to ask whether in addition that error amounts to a 'manifest error': it will vitiate the determination in any event. If, however, I am wrong in my earlier conclusion—if, in short, the inspectors' use of the wrong test method here ought properly to be regarded as an *immaterial* departure from their instructions—I would not conclude that it nevertheless constituted a manifest error such as to entitle the buyers to set aside the determination on that alternative basis.

[35] That, however, is by the way. For the reasons given earlier, I would hold the determination not to be binding because of the inspectors' material departure from their instructions, and accordingly dismiss this appeal.

TUCKEY LJ.

[36] Like Simon Brown and Dyson LJJ, I agree that this appeal should be dismissed. There is however, an apparent difference between them as to how to define a material departure from instructions about which I think I should express an opinion so that anyone looking for guidance from our judgment will know what the majority view about this is.

[37] My choice is between 'any departure is material unless it can truly be characterised as trivial or de minimis in the sense of it being obvious that it could make no possible difference to either party' (the first test—Simon Brown LJ at [26](vi)) or a departure which 'the parties would reasonably have regarded ... as sufficient to invalidate the determination' (the alternative test—Dyson LJ at [47]).

[38] I do not think the legal route which enables the test to be formulated matters although I prefer the implied term analysis. If, of course, there is an express term that is another matter, as Dyson LJ points out in para [44]. But the first test is just as capable of being an implied term as one which derives from the principle of de minimis non curat lex.

[39] I have to say I prefer the first test because I think it is more certain and direct. There may in fact be no difference between the two tests in practice, but an inquiry as to what the parties would reasonably have regarded as material appears at least to be less certain and direct than the inquiry required by the first test. Whichever test is applied the court would obviously need to consider the subject matter and express terms of the contract, the nature of the departure and any other relevant facts.

[40] I see no reason why application of the first test will only result in departures of form or procedure being excused. If, in the rare case postulated by Dyson LJ at [48], it is clear beyond argument that a departure of some other kind could not affect the result however the result is characterised, then it is obvious that it could make no possible difference to either party. If the passage from the judge's judgment referred to by Simon Brown LJ at [28] precludes this possibility, I agree with Dyson LJ's reservations about it, but I do not read it in this way. Rather I think it expounds the first test.

DYSON LJ.

[41] I agree with Simon Brown LJ that this appeal must be dismissed. I only wish to add a few observations on the 'departure in a material respect' point. The leading authority is *Jones v Sherwood Computer Services plc* [1992] 2 All ER 170,

a [1992] 1 WLR 277. Much of the debate in the present case has centred on the passage in the judgment of Dillon LJ:

'If the mistake made was that the expert departed from his instructions in a material respect, eg if he valued the wrong number of shares, or valued shares in the wrong company ... either party would be able to say that the certificate was not binding because the expert had not done what he was appointed to do.' (See [1992] 2 All ER 170 at 179, [1992] 1 WLR 277 at 287.)

b

The question is: what did he mean by 'in a material respect'?

[42] As he pointed out, the first step is to see what the parties have agreed to remit to the expert, this being a matter of contract. In the present case, as Simon Brown LJ has explained, the parties agreed to refer not merely the question of *c* whether the density of the oil was below 0·876kg/l at 15°C, but whether it was below that level when tested by ASTM method D 1298.

[43] In saying that the determination would not be binding if the expert departed from his instructions in a material respect, I believe that Dillon LJ was referring to what the parties must be taken to have agreed. Since they did not *d* agree this expressly, they could only have done so impliedly. In my view, a term should be implied in an expert determination clause such as cl 10 in the present case to the effect that the determination will not be binding if the expert departs from his instructions in a material respect. Such a term is reasonable and represents the obvious, but unexpressed, intention of the parties.

e [44] I prefer to analyse the problem in contractual terms than by reference to the general principle that the law does not concern itself with trifles: de minimis non curat lex. After all, it is possible, at least in theory, for the parties to a contract to specify the instructions to be followed by the expert in the utmost detail, and to stipulate expressly that any departure whatsoever, however trivial, is to be regarded as a material departure.

f [45] But where the parties have not defined what departures are to be regarded as material, the question remains: what is the yardstick by which materiality is to be judged? The judge contrasted a departure that was more than trivial or de minimis with one that must have made a material difference to the 'result'. He said that any departure would be material unless it was trivial. The fact that it made no difference to the result could not save the determination.

g [46] I have some misgivings about the suggested antithesis between on the one hand a departure that is de minimis and on the other hand a departure that must have affected the result. As I have already explained, the question is one of contract: what did the parties intend? It is not a question of the application of the general legal principle that de minimis non curat lex. Moreover, one has to be *h* careful to define what one means by the 'result' in this context. In the present case, if the result is that the sample, when tested, showed a density of less than 0·876kg/l at 15°C, then it is common ground that the departure did not affect the result. If, however, the result is that the sample, when tested *in accordance with D 1298*, showed a density of less than 0.876kg/l at 15°C, then the departure did *j* affect the result.

[47] So what is the test by which materiality is to be judged? Surely it is simply whether the parties would reasonably have regarded the departure as sufficient to invalidate the determination. At one end of the spectrum will be departures of form or procedure which could have no bearing on the substance of the determination. Unless the parties have so agreed expressly or by necessary implication, it will be a rare case in which a court would hold that they have

impliedly agreed that such a departure would invalidate a determination. At the
other extreme will be significant departures of substance. Dillon LJ gave two   *a*
good examples of these in the passage that I have quoted.

[48] In deciding what, the parties must be taken to have regarded as material,
the court will take into account the subject matter and express terms of the
contract and all the relevant circumstances. I would not rule out the possibility
that there may be cases in which a departure from instructions would reasonably   *b*
be regarded by the parties as immaterial because, although the expert's mistake
is not one of form or procedure, it is clear beyond argument that the departure
could not affect the result, however the result is characterised. Such a mistake is
immaterial because the parties could not reasonably consider it to be material.
But such cases are likely to be rare because it will not often be possible to say with
confidence that (a) the departure could not have affected the result, and (b) it was   *c*
unreasonable for a party to regard a departure that could not have affected the
result as material. Nevertheless, such cases may occur. It follows that I do not
entirely accept the analysis made by the judge in the passage that has been quoted
by Simon Brown LJ.

[49] Turning to the present case, I am in no doubt that the fact that the use of   *d*
the wrong method cannot have affected the 'result' does not save the
determination. As Mr Goldstone has pointed out, it cannot be assumed that the
choice of a particular method of testing is a consequence solely of the parties'
desire to achieve an accurate result. There may be different reasons which have
been dictated by the terms of other related contracts and/or letters of credit. The
possibility that there may be such other reasons is by no means far-fetched in the   *e*
context of a commercial contract which is likely to be one of a chain. These are
not matters about which the court can or should speculate. The starting point is
that if the parties have agreed that a determination using method A is to be
binding, then a determination using method B will not be binding because the
parties have not agreed that it will be. It follows that the determination is not
binding and the appeal must be dismissed.

Appeal dismissed.

Dilys Tausz   Barrister.

a   # Bank of China v NBM LLC and others
    ## [2001] EWCA 1933

COURT OF APPEAL, CIVIL DIVISION
PILL, TUCKEY AND JONATHAN PARKER LJJ
b   6, 18 DECEMBER 2001

Practice – Pre-trial or post-judgment relief – Freezing order – Worldwide freezing order
– Pre-trial order – Extra-territorial effect of order – Protection of third parties – Freezing
order in standard form – Proviso protecting third parties in respect of assets outside the
c   *jurisdiction – Appropriate terms.*

The claimant bank obtained a worldwide freezing order in aid of proceedings
brought in New York against companies and individuals associated with two
defendants to the action, C and L, who were alleged to have defrauded the bank
in the United States by various means. In evidence on the application for the
d   freezing order, the claimant stated that it believed that C and L had a historical
relationship with UBS, a third party bank. The freezing order was served on UBS,
which subsequently asked for the order to be varied to add, inter alia, that
nothing in the order should, in respect of assets outside England and Wales,
prevent UBS from complying with 'what it reasonably believes to be its
obligations, contractual or otherwise under the laws and obligations of the
e   country or state in which those assets are situated or under the proper law of any
bank account in question' (the *Baltic* proviso). The claimant was prepared to
agree to that proviso only in relation to UBS's obligations under criminal law,
whereas the proviso sought by UBS related to its civil obligations as well. The
judge held that as a matter of general principle it was important that a freezing
f   order should be clear and unequivocal so that both the parties to it and any third
parties knew exactly where they stood, in particular that banks which were
domiciled or otherwise present within the jurisdiction should not be required to
decide whether to act in conflict with the terms of the freezing order or in conflict
with their duties to customers under local law. The judge allowed the variation
of the wording to include the *Baltic* proviso and the claimant appealed against
g   that decision on the ground that there was no warrant for the inclusion of the
proviso in the present case or in the standard form of worldwide freezing order.
The claimant contended that the *Baltic* proviso gave too much protection to a
third party in the circumstances of the instant case because it enabled that third
party to decide for itself what its obligations were. The claimant instead argued
h   for a more exacting requirement that a third party should prevent breaches if it
were able to do so (the *Derby v Weldon* proviso).

Held – The limit of the court's territorial jurisdiction and the principle of comity
required that the effectiveness of freezing orders operating upon third parties
j   holding assets abroad should normally derive only from their recognition and
enforcement by the local courts. It was noteworthy that the English courts'
jurisdiction to grant freezing and disclosure orders was a good deal more
extensive than that of the courts in most other jurisdictions. Furthermore, third
parties amenable to the English jurisdiction should be given all reasonable
protection. It followed from those considerations that any order of the English
court which had the effect of requiring a third party to do or refrain from doing

something overseas would be exceptional. A third party should not be required
to breach its contractual obligations by virtue of the phrase 'able to prevent' in *a*
the *Derby v Weldon* proviso: contractual obligations could be enforced by order of
the local court which the third party would have to obey. There was no logical
justification for distinguishing between the third party's contractual and other
legal obligations under the local law and the onus should be on a claimant to
obtain relief from the local court rather than on the third party. The need to *b*
avoid unwarranted extra-territorial jurisdiction, the need to provide reasonable
protection for third parties affected by freezing orders, and the need to clarify the
Derby v Weldon proviso would usually entitle third parties to have the *Baltic*
proviso added to worldwide freezing orders unless the court considered on the
particular facts of the case that it was inappropriate. In the instant case, there was
no reason for not including the *Baltic* proviso as the case was an ordinary case of *c*
its kind, and accordingly the appeal would be dismissed (see [17]–[26], below).

Babanaft International Co SA v Bassatne [1989] 1 All ER 433, Derby & Co Ltd v
Weldon (No 2) [1989] 1 All ER 1002 and Baltic Shipping v Translink Shipping Ltd
[1995] 1 Lloyd's Rep 673 considered.

Decision of David Steel J [2001] 4 All ER 954 affirmed. *d*

Notes

For freezing orders (formerly called Mareva injunctions) over assets outside the
jurisdiction and the protection of third parties, see 3(1) *Halsbury's Laws* (4th edn
reissue) paras 331, 334. *e*

Cases referred to in judgments

Baltic Shipping v Translink Shipping Ltd [1995] 1 Lloyd's Rep 673.
Babanaft International Co SA v Bassatne [1989] 1 All ER 433, [1990] Ch 13, [1989] 2
    WLR 232, CA. *f*
Derby & Co Ltd v Weldon (No 2) [1989] 1 All ER 1002, [1990] Ch 65, [1989] 2 WLR
    412, CA.
MacKinnon v Donaldson Lufkin & Jenrette Securities Corp [1986] 1 All ER 653, [1986]
    Ch 482, [1986] 2 WLR 453.
Securities and Investments Board v Pantell SA [1989] 2 All ER 673, [1990] Ch 426, *g*
    [1989] 3 WLR 698.

Appeal

The claimant, the Bank of China, appealed from the decision of David Steel J on
5 July 2001 ([2001] 4 All ER 954) granting an application by Union Bank of *h*
Switzerland AG (UBS), a non-party, to vary a freezing order made by Tomlinson J
on 13 March 2001 in support of proceedings brought by the claimant in New York
against NBM LLC and 21 other defendants, including the fifteenth and sixteenth
defendants, John Chou and Sherry Liu. The facts are set out in the judgment of
Tuckey LJ. *j*

Susan Prevezer QC and *David Scorey* (instructed by *Coudert Brothers*) for the
    claimant.
Thomas Keith (instructed by *Simmons & Simmons*) for UBS.

Cur adv vult

a 18 December 2001. The following judgments were delivered.

TUCKEY LJ (giving the first judgment at the invitation of Pill LJ).

Introduction
[1] Paragraph F19.10 of the Commercial Court Guide says:

b
'As regards freezing injunctions in respect of assets outside the jurisdiction of the English Courts, the standard wording in relation to effects on third parties may in some cases appropriately incorporate wording to enable overseas branches of banks or similar institutions which have offices within the jurisdiction to comply with what they reasonably believe to be their
c   obligations under the laws of the country where the assets are located or under the proper law of the relevant banking or other contract relating to such assets.'

Such wording was incorporated into the worldwide freezing order in this case by David Steel J at the request of Union Bank of Switzerland AG (UBS), a Swiss bank
d with an English subsidiary and a branch in London. On this appeal Bank of China, the claimant, says that the judge should not have varied the order in this way.

The facts
e   [2] The claimant obtained the worldwide freezing order under the provisions of s 25 of the Civil Jurisdiction and Judgments Act 1982 in aid of proceedings in New York against companies and individuals associated with John Chou and his wife Sherry Liu (the fifteenth and sixteenth defendants) who are alleged to have defrauded the bank in the United States by various means. The claim is for $US34m plus interest, punitive damages and costs. None of the defendants are
f incorporated or resident in England and Wales and none of them has complied or is likely to comply with that part of the freezing order requiring them to disclose their assets.
[3] Although UBS are not defendants, in his evidence asking for the freezing order the deputy general manager of the claimant's New York branch said:

g
'I believe that defendants Chou and S Liu had an historical relationship with the Union Bank of Switzerland in Zurich Switzerland. The inquiry agents also reported that defendants Chou and S Liu had an historical relationship with the Union Bank of Switzerland in the Cayman Islands.'

h   [4] The freezing order made by Tomlinson J on 13 March 2001 was in the standard CPR/Commercial Court form (CPR PD 25 'Interim Injunctions'/app 5(2) to the Guide) which in the guidance notes under the heading 'Parties other than the Applicant and Respondent' says :

'(1) Effect of this Order:—It is a Contempt of Order for any person notified
j   of this Order knowingly to assist in or permit a breach of this Order. Any person doing do may be sent to prison, fined or have his assets seized.
(2) Effect of this Order outside England and Wales:—The terms of this order do not affect or concern anyone outside the jurisdiction of this Court until it is declared enforceable by or is enforced by a Court in the relevant country and then they are to affect him only to the extent that they have been declared enforceable or have been enforced UNLESS the person is: (i) a

person to whom this Order is addressed ... or (ii) a person who is subject to the jurisdiction of this Court and (a) has been given written notice of this Order at his residence or place of business within the jurisdiction of this Court and (b) is able to prevent acts or omissions outside the jurisdiction of this Court which constitute or assist in a breach of the terms of this Order.'

[5] When the order was served on UBS they asked for it to be varied to add after the words of the standard form which I have quoted:

'It is further ordered and directed that nothing in this order shall, in respect of assets located outside England and Wales, prevent UBS AG or its subsidiaries from complying with: (i) what it reasonably believes to be its obligations, contractual or otherwise under the laws and obligations of the country or state in which those assets are situated or under the proper law of any bank account in question; and (ii) any orders of the courts of that country or state provided reasonable notice of any application for such an order by UBS AG or any of its subsidiaries (to the extent such notice is permitted by the criminal law of such country or state) is given to the claimant's solicitors.'

[6] UBS's evidence suggests that they always ask for such a variation when they are served with a worldwide freezing order. The claimant was prepared to agree the second of the provisos and the first but only in relation to UBS's obligations under the criminal law of the country or state in which the assets were situated. The proviso sought by UBS related to its civil obligations as well. Thus, what is known as 'the *Baltic* proviso' refers to 'obligations contractual or otherwise'. So the judge had to decide whether the proviso in this form should be added to the order.

The judgment

[7] In deciding that it should the judge said:

'As a matter of general principle it is in my judgment important that the freezing order should be clear and unequivocal so that both the parties to it and any third party knows exactly where they stand. In particular banks which are domiciled or otherwise present within the jurisdiction should not be required to decide whether to act in conflict with the terms of the freezing order or in conflict with its duties to its customer under local law. Such an approach in my judgment is consistent with the interests of comity ...' (See [2001] 4 All ER 954 at [13].)

[8] After referring to the passage from the guide which I have quoted, the judge said (at [20]): 'As presently advised I would prefer the view that such a provision should be included unless inappropriate, rather than only included if appropriate.' He added that he thought the Rules Committee should consider whether the proviso should be included in the standard form.

The cases

[9] The standard form of freezing order has evolved since 1975. This court first had to consider a worldwide freezing order in *Babanaft International Co SA v Bassatne* [1989] 1 All ER 433, [1990] Ch 13, [1989] 2 WLR 232. The court recognised that third parties such as banks within the jurisdiction might be in contempt if

a their offices abroad permitted frozen overseas assets to be dealt with in breach of the terms of the order. So, Nicholls LJ said:

> 'It would be wrong for an English court by making an order in respect of overseas assets against a defendant amenable to its jurisdiction, to impose or attempt to impose obligations on persons not before the court in respect of acts to be done by them abroad regarding property outside the jurisdiction.
b That, self-evidently, would be for the English court to claim an altogether exorbitant, extra-territorial jurisdiction.' (See [1989] 1 All ER 433 at 453, [1990] Ch 13 at 44.)

The court therefore decided that a worldwide freezing order should only bind the defendants personally and would only be enforceable against third parties in *c* respect of assets outside the jurisdiction if it was declared enforceable in the country concerned (the *Babanaft* proviso). As has been pointed out the latter meant very little since enforceability against the third party would depend upon the order of the foreign court and not the English order.

[10] Shortly after the *Babanaft* case, *Derby & Co Ltd v Weldon (No 2)* [1989] 1 All ER *d* 1002, [1990] Ch 65 came before this court. The court again had to consider the effect of a worldwide freezing order on third parties such as banks. After referring to the problem and its solution by the court in the *Babanaft* case Lord Donaldson MR discussed a number of objections to the *Babanaft* proviso. Only the second is relevant to our case. He said:

e > 'The second objection is that it places an English corporate bank in a very difficult position. It may know of the injunction and may wish to support the court in its efforts to prevent the defendant from frustrating the due course of justice, but the proviso deprives it of the one justification which it would otherwise have for refusing to comply with his instructions.' (See [1989]
f 1 All ER 1002 at 1012, [1990] Ch 65 at 84.)

By this it appears he meant that the bank could not rely on the order of the English court because before it was effective an order of the foreign court had to be obtained. This led him to revise the *Babanaft* proviso by adding the requirement that persons who were subject to the jurisdiction of the English *g* court with notice of the order were required to prevent breaches of its terms if they were able to do so (the *Derby v Weldon* proviso).

[11] There the matter stood so far as the cases are concerned until the decision of Clarke J in *Baltic Shipping v Translink Shipping Ltd* [1995] 1 Lloyd's Rep 673 from which the *Baltic* proviso gets its name. But, on 30 July 1993 in his end of year *h* statement Saville J, the judge in charge of the Commercial Court, had said:

> 'A problem emerged earlier this year which was of great concern to those banks which are subject to the jurisdiction of both the English court and the courts of the country or countries where they may be holding assets of the defendant which are made the subject of a worldwide [freezing order].
j Certain countries may not recognise or give effect to ex parte orders made in this jurisdiction and indeed may make inconsistent orders. In such cases third party banks can be put in an impossible position, being required to do something by a court in this country and the opposite by a court abroad. The *Derby v Weldon* proviso does not seem to help as it does not apply to persons who are subject to the jurisdiction which of course is the case with most major banks. To solve this problem of double jeopardy we suggest in

appropriate cases that something along the lines of the following provision
be added to the order.'

He then set out the proviso in the terms which UBS sought in this case.

[12] In the *Baltic Shipping* case the claimant had obtained a post-judgment
freezing order in respect of a specific bank account in Noumea, New Caledonia.
The London branch of the French bank whose subsidiary held the account had
been served with the order and asked the court to include the proviso suggested
by Saville J. The claimant argued that this gave the bank too much protection
and that it would be sufficiently protected by the undertaking in damages. In
rejecting these submissions Clarke J said that there was no case in which this
particular point had been decided and accepted the submission that Lord
Donaldson MR in *Derby v Weldon* did not have in mind the position where the
English order constituted no justification as a matter of foreign law for refusing
to comply with the defendant's instruction. He said (at 678–679):

'The bank is not a party to these proceedings. It should be given all
reasonable protection. It is not in principle desirable for a bank to have to
rely upon the undertaking in damages ... I do not think that the bank should
have to run the risk that it would be in breach of its contract under the law
of Noumea for it to pay out pending an application by the plaintiff to the
local Court. That approach appears to me to be consistent with the general
approach of the Courts in the cases to which I have referred ...'

He added:

'So, it appears to me that in general and subject to the facts of the particular
case it would be desirable that a proviso along the lines of that proposed here
and along the lines of that proposed in Mr. Justice Saville's end of year
statement should be included in the standard [freezing order].'

[13] In his judgment in the *Baltic Shipping* case Clarke J referred to the decision
of Hoffman J in *MacKinnon v Donaldson Lufkin & Jenrette Securities Corp* [1986] 1 All
ER 653, [1986] Ch 482 which was not considered by the Court of Appeal in the
Babanaft case or *Derby v Weldon*. In that case the court had to consider whether
an order under the Bankers' Books Evidence Act 1879 should be made against an
American bank in respect of documents held at its head office in New York. In
deciding that no such order should be made, the judge said ([1986] 1 All ER 653
at 658, [1986] Ch 482 at 493): 'The principle is that a state should refrain from
demanding obedience to its sovereign authority by foreigners in respect of their
conduct outside the jurisdiction.' And:

'The nature of banking business is such that if an English court invokes
jurisdiction even over an English bank in respect of an account at a branch
abroad, there is a strong likelihood of conflict with the bank's duties to its
customer under the local law. It is therefore not surprising that any bank,
whether English or foreign, should as a general rule be entitled to the
protection of an order of a foreign court before it is required to disclose
documents kept at a branch or head office abroad.' (See [1986] 1 All ER 653
at 660, [1986] Ch 482 at 496.)

[14] Finally, we were referred to *Securities and Investments Board v Pantell SA*
[1989] 2 All ER 673 at 678, [1990] Ch 426 at 432–433 where Browne-Wilkinson V-C
said of the *Derby v Weldon* proviso:

a   'The result of that proviso in the present case is to ensure that my order has no operation within the Channel Islands and does not trespass on the jurisdiction of the Guernsey court. However, if the branch of Barclays Bank in Guernsey is holding moneys belonging to either of the defendants, the bank (being a bank locally resident in England) will, after service of the order, be required not to part with such moneys from the accounts held with the
b   bank with their Guernsey branch.'

It is not entirely clear from the report where the money to which the judge referred was, but, despite the eminence of its author, this statement was made on an ex parte application without any consideration of the point we have to decide and so I attach little weight to it.
c

Argument, discussion and conclusion
[15] Ms Prevezer QC, for the claimant, submits that there is no warrant for the inclusion of the *Baltic* proviso in this case or in the standard form of worldwide freezing order. She says this court struck the balance between
d   providing adequate protection for a claimant and avoiding double jeopardy for third parties such as banks in *Derby v Weldon*. There are no reported cases of third parties having had problems with the proviso and so we should leave well alone. The *Baltic Shipping* case was an exceptional case where the claimant knew that the money was in Noumea and yet failed to go to the local court to freeze it. In an ordinary case such as the present the *Baltic* proviso gives too much protection
e   because it enables a third party to decide itself what its obligations are. It effectively turns back the clock to the *Babanaft* case. A requirement that the third party should prevent breaches if it is able to do so is more exacting. She emphasises that an English court only has jurisdiction over the third party because it has chosen to do business here, so there is nothing exorbitant about the
f   *Derby v Weldon* proviso, particularly where the overseas assets in question are the frozen assets of, in this case, fraudsters. Here, it is conceded that the claimant has a strong case of fraud and that the worldwide freezing order was rightly made even though there were no assets or defendants within the jurisdiction so the court should do all it can to help.
[16] It does not seem to me that this court has ever properly considered the
g   point we have to decide. There is certainly no reference in any of the judgments to the difficulty which a third party might face under the law of the place where assets abroad are situated or the proper law of the contract under which they are held. Even if the point has been considered the cases show that this jurisdiction is an evolving one which means that we should not be inhibited by earlier
h   decisions on different facts.
[17] The cases to which I have referred do, I think, establish two general propositions. Firstly the limit of the courts' territorial jurisdiction and the principle of comity require that the effectiveness of freezing orders operating upon third parties holding assets abroad, should normally derive only from their
j   recognition and enforcement by the local courts. In this respect it is worth remembering that the English courts' jurisdiction to grant freezing and disclosure orders is a good deal more extensive than in most other jurisdictions, notably the United States. Secondly, third parties amenable to the English jurisdiction should be given all reasonable protection.
[18] It follows that any order of the English court which has the effect of requiring a third party to do or refrain from doing something abroad is exceptional.

With this in mind, what does 'able to prevent' in the *Derby v Weldon* proviso
mean? It was not spelt out in that case and Ms Prevezer accepts that it does not
require the third party to disobey the local criminal law or an order of the local
court. Her submission is, however, that it does require the third party to breach
its contractual obligations to its customer (its mandate) and that if it has to pay
damages as a result, it is adequately protected by the terms of the standard form
undertaking which the claimant gives which says:

'The applicant will pay the reasonable costs of anyone other than the
respondents which have been incurred as a result of this order ... and if the
court later finds that this order has caused such person loss and decides that
such person should be compensated for that loss, the applicant will comply
with any order the court may make.'

Ms Prevezer submits that if the bank was unwilling to breach its mandate it could
apply to the local court for relief so that anything it did or did not do would not
be in contempt of the English court.

[19] This analysis, if nothing else, shows that the *Derby v Weldon* proviso is
unclear. A third party would be 'able' to disobey the local criminal law or an
order of the local court, but it is rightly conceded that the proviso does not
require it to do this. Should it be required to breach its contractual obligations? I
do not think so. Those obligations could be enforced by order of the local court
which the third party would have to obey. I see no logical justification for
distinguishing between the third party's contractual and other legal obligations
under the local law. The onus should be upon the claimant to obtain relief from
the local court rather than upon the third party.

[20] Like Clarke J I do not think the undertaking in damages provides
sufficient protection for the claimant. Damage to reputation and regulatory
consequences abroad could not be adequately compensated. The bank might
also be forced into litigation abroad with a customer or a third party or be faced
with arguments here as to whether any particular loss fell within the terms of the
undertaking.

[21] Saville J's statement makes it clear that there have been problems with
the *Derby v Weldon* proviso and we were told by UBS that claimants usually agree
to the *Baltic* proviso being added to the standard form so I do not think it can be
assumed that the standard form has not given rise to problems in practice. The
Baltic proviso does of course only require the third party to have a reasonable
belief as to what its obligations are, but I think it is entitled to this degree of
protection. As Clarke J pointed out in the *Baltic Shipping* case if the court had to
decide whether the third party was able to prevent a breach of the order this
might involve a prolonged and contentious inquiry as to what the local law in fact
was.

[22] So, like the three experienced commercial judges who have previously
had to consider this point, I conclude that the need to avoid unwarranted
extra-territorial jurisdiction, the need to provide reasonable protection for third
parties affected by freezing orders and the need to clarify the *Derby v Weldon*
proviso will usually entitle third parties to have the *Baltic* proviso added to the
worldwide freezing order unless the court considers on the particular facts of the
case that this is inappropriate. As third parties are not represented when the order
is first made, I think the *Baltic* proviso should be included in the standard form.

[23] I see no reason for not including the *Baltic* proviso in this case. The
claimant deserves the best protection which this court can give, not least because

a it does not know where the defendants' assets, if any, are. On the other hand none of the defendants are domiciled or resident in this country and there is no evidence or suggestion that UBS have held any of their assets here. Ms Prevezer argued that this was an ordinary case of its kind and I agree.

[24] For these reasons I think this appeal should be dismissed and that the Rules Committee and the Commercial Court should consider the prescribed
b standard form in the light of this judgment.

JONATHAN PARKER LJ.
    [25] I agree.

PILL LJ.
c   [26] I also agree.

Appeal dismissed.

Melanie Martyn   Barrister.

Mousaka Inc v Golden Seagull Maritime Inc and another

a

QUEEN'S BENCH DIVISION (COMMERCIAL COURT)

DAVID STEEL J

b

20, 30 JULY 2001

Arbitration – Award – Leave to appeal against award – Judge refusing leave to appeal – Judge stating questions not of general public importance and that decisions of arbitrators not obviously wrong or open to serious doubt – Whether judge obliged to give *c* *full reasons for refusal of leave to appeal from arbitration award – Arbitration Act 1996, s 69 – Human Rights Act 1998, Sch 1, Pt I, art 6.*

The applicants were sellers and the respondents buyers of two product tankers. The respondents claimed damages for misrepresentation in relation to the *d* vessels' suitability for the carriage of certain cargoes and the dispute was referred to arbitration in accordance with the express terms of the relevant agreements. By a majority decision, the arbitrators held that the respondent buyers were entitled to damages. The applicants applied for permission to appeal under s 69[a] of the Arbitration Act 1996, contending that, reflecting the threshold requirements of s 69, the majority had been 'obviously wrong' in their conclusions on general *e* questions of law upon which leave to appeal was sought. In the alternative, they contended that the questions were of 'general public importance' and that the arbitrators' decision was open to 'serious doubt'. In accordance with s 69(5), the application was placed before the judge for consideration on paper. The judge held that 'If and to the extent that the questions posed by the Applicants are *f* questions of law (and in my judgment the second question is not): (1) the questions are not of general public importance ... (2) the decisions of the arbitrators are not obviously wrong (or even open to serious doubt)'. The applicants then applied for 'full reasons' for the judge's decision, contending that the judge was obliged to furnish such full reasons because of the right to a fair hearing provided by art 6[b] *g* of the European Convention for the Protection of Human Rights and Fundamental Freedoms 1950 (as set out in Sch 1 to the Human Rights Act 1998); the general duty on a court to give reasons for its decision; and principles of fairness and natural justice. The respondents submitted, inter alia, that the existing common law restrictions on providing reasons in applications under s 69 were still appropriate; *h* that the giving of detailed reasons would be worthless since there was no realistic prospect of further appeal; that the giving of further reasons would be subversive of the arbitral process; that the provisions of art 6 had been waived; and that the content of the decision satisfied the requirements of the convention.

j

___

a   Section 69, so far as material, provides: 'Leave to appeal shall be given only if the court is satisfied ... (c) that, on the basis of findings of fact in the award—(i) the decision of the tribunal on the question is obviously wrong, or (ii) the question is one of general public importance and the decision of the tribunal is at least open to serious doubt ...'

b   Article 6, so far as material, provides: '1. In the determination of his civil rights and obligations ... everyone is entitled to a fair and public hearing within a reasonable time by an independent and impartial tribunal established by law.'

a **Held** – The extent of the duty of courts to give reasons under art 6 varied according to the nature of the decision and the circumstances of the case. Full reasons ought to be given for a decision on the merits, although even then it was not necessary to provide a detailed answer to every argument. Although art 6 applied to the appeal process, it did not guarantee a right of appeal; none the less any limitation on the right of appeal had to be imposed pursuant to a legitimate

b aim, proportionately applied. If a right of appeal was rejected, the applicant had to be made aware of the grounds on which the decision was reached; in many cases that might take the form of an endorsement of the lower court's decision. Against that background, the continued implementation of the common law restraints on the provision of reasons for refusing leave to appeal against arbitral

c awards was fully compliant with the convention. In the instant case, the parties had agreed to arbitrate their dispute, and had thereby largely renounced the application of art 6. There had been a substantial hearing before the arbitrators, who had produced a detailed reasoned award on the merits. It was not suggested that the restrictions on the right of appeal were inconsistent with art 6, and it was

d further accepted that the limitations had a legitimate purpose and were not disproportionate to that purpose. An approach which went further than merely refusing leave, with or without express reference to the statutory criteria, and which gave some reasons why the arbitrators were correct on the merits, would be objectionable in principle. The giving of reasons which touched on the merits was at best pointless and at worst subversive: in practical terms the High Court

e was the court of last resort in arbitral proceedings and the provision of reasons touching on the merits might satisfy some degree of curiosity but would be completely worthless. Moreover, a response to such curiosity would import serious dangers, as although there might be cases in which the judge would be content to adopt the arbitrators' reasons, in the majority of cases the judge would

f be minded to express accord in different terms or with a different emphasis. Invidious comparisons might then be drawn by the parties, with the risk of applications being made under s 68 invoking some suggestion of irregularity. That problem was all the more acute in light of the absence of any right of appeal where the arbitrators were perceived as possibly, but not obviously, wrong.

g Accordingly, the scope and content of the judge's decision was not challengeable as being devoid of appropriate and relevant reasoning, and the application would therefore be dismissed (see [24]–[26], [30]–[33], [35], [36], [38], below).

Antaios Cia Naviera SA v Salen Rederierna AB, The Antaios [1984] 3 All ER 229 applied.

h *X v Germany* (1981) 25 DR 240, *Hadjianastassiou v Greece* (1992) 16 EHRR 219, *Tolstoy Miloslavsky v UK* (1995) 20 EHRR 442 and *Webb v UK* (1997) 24 EHRR CD 73 considered.

Notes

j For appeals on a point of law in arbitration proceedings, see Supp to 2 *Halsbury's Laws* (4th edn reissue) paras 690–713.

For the Arbitration Act 1996, s 69, see 2 *Halsbury's Statutes* (4th edn) (1999 reissue) 609.

For the Human Rights Act 1998, Sch 1, Pt I, art 6, see 7 *Halsbury's Statutes* (4th edn) (1999 reissue) 523.

Cases referred to in judgment

Aden Refinery Co Ltd v Ugland Management Co, The Ugland Obo One [1986] 3 All ER   *a*
737, [1987] QB 650, [1986] 3 WLR 949, CA.

Antaios Cia Naviera SA v Salen Rederierna AB, The Antaios [1984] 3 All ER 229, [1985]
AC 191, [1984] 3 WLR 592, HL.

Hadjianastassiou v Greece (1992) 16 EHRR 219, [1992] ECHR 12945/87, ECt HR.

Henry Boot Construction (UK) Ltd v Malmaison Hotel (Manchester) Ltd [2001] 1 All ER   *b*
257, [2001] QB 388, [2000] 3 WLR 1824, CA.

Pioneer Shipping Ltd v BTP Tioxide Ltd, The Nema [1981] 2 All ER 1030, [1982] AC 724,
[1981] 3 WLR 292, HL.

Tolstoy Miloslavsky v UK (1995) 20 EHRR 442, [1995] ECHR 18139/91, ECt HR.

Webb v UK (1997) 24 EHRR CD 73, E Com HR.   *c*

X v Germany (1981) 25 DR 240, E Com HR.

Application

By application dated 11 May 2001, Mousaka Inc applied to David Steel J to give
reasons for his decision on paper on 25 January 2001 dismissing its application for
permission to appeal from an award of arbitrators (Alexander Kazantzis, Robert   *d*
Gaisford and Michael Ferryman) on 30 October 2000 in arbitration proceedings
between it and the respondents, Golden Seagull Maritime Inc and Golden Seabird
Maritime Inc. The facts are set out in the judgment.

Michael Howard QC and *Simon Birt* (instructed by *Richards Butler*) for the applicant.   *e*
Peter Gross QC and *Sara Cockerill* (instructed by *Watson, Farley & Williams*, Piraeus)
for the respondents.

Cur adv vult

30 July 2001. The following judgment was delivered.   *f*

DAVID STEEL J.

Introduction

[1] The tentacles of the Human Rights Act 1998 reach into some unexpected
places. The Commercial Court, even when exercising its supervisory role as   *g*
regards arbitration, is not immune. A corporate body is a person with rights
protected by the 1998 Act and thus, for instance, can invoke art 6 of the European
Convention for the Protection of Human Rights and Fundamental Freedoms
1950 (as set out in Sch 1 to the 1998 Act) where it may be the victim of action
incompatible with its right to a fair trial. The particular issue that arises on the   *h*
present application is whether a judge, in refusing to give permission to appeal to
the High Court from an arbitration award, has a duty to state his reasons in full
for that refusal.

[2] The background can be stated briefly. The applicants were sellers and the
respondents were buyers of two product tankers pursuant to two MOAs   *j*
(memoranda of understanding) dated 28 August 1997. The respondents claimed
damages for misrepresentation in relation to the vessels' suitability for the
carriage of certain cargoes. The disputes was referred to arbitration in accordance
with the express terms of the MOAs.

[3] The arbitrators were well-known members of the London Maritime
Arbitrators Association, Mr Alexander Kazantzis, Mr Robert Gaisford and the late

a   Mr Michael Ferryman. There was an oral hearing between 8 and 26 May 2000. On
30 October, the arbitrators published an interim award. The reasons of the
majority (Mr Kazantzis and Mr Ferryman) were appended to the award and ran
to 64 pages. The majority held that the buyers were entitled to damages in an
amount to be assessed.

[4] By an arbitration application dated 24 November 2000, the applicants
b   sought permission to appeal under s 69 of the Arbitration Act 1996. The
questions of law on which leave to appeal were sought were: (i) In considering
multiple representations on the same subject matter which are made in a series
of documents prior to the conclusion of a contract, is the right approach to
consider the representations made together in their entirety so as to ascertain the
conjoint effect of what was being represented as at the date of contracting? (ii) Is
c   a party entitled to succeed in a claim for negligent misrepresentation even where
it is found as a fact: (a) that he had a reasonable opportunity to discover the
inaccuracy of the relevant misrepresentation; (b) that it was reasonable to expect
it to make use of that opportunity; and (c) that he acted carelessly in not making
use of that opportunity?

d   [5] It was the applicants' contention, reflecting the threshold requirements of
s 69, that the majority were 'obviously wrong' in their conclusions on these
questions of law. In the alternative, it was contended that the questions were of
'general public importance' and that their decision was open to 'serious doubt'.

[6] In accordance with the provisions of s 69(5) of the 1996 Act, the application,
together with witness statements filed by both sides containing detailed
e   arguments on the issues, was placed before me for consideration on paper. (I made
no order for an oral hearing nor was one requested.)

[7] My decision dated 25 January 2001 was as follows:

'If and to the extent that the questions posed by the applicants are
f   questions of law (and in my judgment the second question is not): (1) the
questions are not of general public importance; (2) the decisions of the
arbitrators are not obviously wrong (or even open to serious doubt).'

[8] On receipt of my decision, the applicants' solicitors wrote to me on
9 February 2001 as follows:

g   'We act for Mousaka Inc and have recently been passed your judgment on
your (sic) clients application for permission to appeal from the majority
Arbitrators award in this matter. For your ready reference we enclose a copy
of your decision.

Both we and our clients are puzzled that no reasons or explanations are
h   given for your decision particularly in view of the strong minority award of
Mr Gaisford. We would respectfully ask you to let us have your reasons so
we can pass them on to our clients.'

[9] I replied on 13 February 2001 as follows:

j   'Thank you for your letter dated the 9th February.
As you know, the approved practice under the Arbitration Act 1979 was
that prescribed by Lord Diplock in *The Antaios*, namely, in common with the
practice of the House of Lords on petitions for leave to appeal, not to give
reasons.
The Arbitration Act 1996 gave statutory force to the criteria for granting
leave, appear to make it appropriate as such to give reasons for the decision.

I recognise that it could be said that the right to a fair hearing under Article 6 of the Human Rights Act 1998 obliges the court to give reasons even upon such an application. But this raises a number of issues on which I would welcome argument.

Accordingly I am not prepared to respond to your written request for reasons. If your clients wish to pursue the matter, I will make arrangements for an oral hearing. In the event that the respondents do not oppose your application for the giving of reasons, it may be desirable for an amicus to be appointed.'

[10] My letter provoked the present application which was issued on 11 May whereby 'full reasons' are sought for my decision. According to the application notice, the obligation to do so arises from:

'1. The right to a fair hearing as provided by Article 6 of the European Convention on Human Rights ...
2. The general duty on a court to give reasons for its decision and
3. Principles of fairness and natural justice.'

Summary of the applicants' submissions

[11] In very summary form, the applicants submit: (i) the restrictions imposed by Lord Diplock in *Antaios Cia Naviera SA v Salen Rederierna AB, The Antaios* [1984] 3 All ER 229, [1985] AC 191 are not appropriate because the rationale for them is no longer relevant; (ii) the restrictions are in any event inconsistent with art 6 pursuant to which a court ought to give reasons for any decision; (iii) such an approach is in accord with the development of domestic law in this field; (iv) there has been no waiver in this respect; (v) the decisions of the Commission relating to the legitimacy of unreasoned decisions refusing leave to appeal are distinguishable.

Summary of the respondents' submissions

[12] Again in summary form, the respondents' submissions can be summarised as follows: (i) the restrictions imposed by Lord Diplock are still appropriate; (ii) the giving of detailed reasons would be worthless because there is no realistic prospect of further appeal; (iii) further or alternatively, the giving of detailed reasons would be subversive of the arbitral process; (iv) the provisions of art 6 have been waived; and (v) the content of my decision is a sufficient explanation of why leave has been refused and satisfies the requirements of Strasbourg jurisprudence.

The Antaios

[13] The starting point, as stated in my letter of 13 February, is the judgment of Lord Diplock in *The Antaios*. The House of Lords were concerned with the provisions of s 1 of the Arbitration Act 1979 (the predecessor of the 1996 Act) whereby, with the leave of the court, an appeal lay on an issue of law arising out of an arbitration award. The House reaffirmed its earlier decision in *Pioneer Shipping Ltd v BTP Tioxide Ltd, The Nema* [1981] 2 All ER 1030, [1982] AC 724 which had set out the criteria to be applied on the granting of leave.

[14] The House went on to consider two further matters: (i) whether in granting or refusing leave to appeal, the judge ought to give reasons; and (ii) whether, and in what circumstances, having granted or refused leave, the judge ought to give leave to appeal against his decision.

a   [15] On the latter point Lord Diplock said as follows:

'This brings me to "the s 1(6A) question" canvassed in Staughton J's second judgment of 19 November 1982: when should a judge give leave to appeal to the Court of Appeal from his own grant or refusal of leave to appeal to the High Court from an arbitral award? I agree with him that leave to appeal to the Court of Appeal should be granted by the judge under s 1(6A) only in
b   cases where a decision whether to grant or to refuse leave to appeal to the High Court under s 1(3)(b) in the particular case in his view called for some amplification, elucidation or adaptation to changing practices of existing guidelines laid down by appellate courts, and that leave to appeal under s 1(6A) should not be granted in any other type of case. Judges should have
c   the courage of their own convictions and decide for themselves whether, applying existing guidelines, leave to appeal to the High Court under s 1(3)(b) ought to be granted or not.' (See [1984] 3 All ER 229 at 236, [1985] AC 191 at 205.)

[16] On the first issue, the appellants' counsel Mr Gordon Pollock QC had
d   accepted that 'the only reason for giving judgment when the judge refuses leave to the High Court is to satisfy the curiosity of the disappointed party'. Counsel for the respondents Mr Mark Saville QC submitted 'strongly' that where the judge refused leave to appeal from the arbitration award, no reasons should be given.

e   [17] Lord Diplock's approach is set out as follows:

'However, save in the exceptional case in which he does give leave to appeal to the Court of Appeal under s 1(6A) because it falls within this limited category, a judge ought not normally to give reasons for a grant or refusal under s 1(3)(b) of leave to appeal to the High Court from an arbitral award. He should follow the practice that has been adopted in your Lordships'
f   House ever since a would-be appellant from a judgment of the Court of Appeal was required to petition this House for leave to appeal to it when leave to do so had not been granted by the Court of Appeal itself. It has been the practice of this House, at the close of the short oral argument on the petition, to say no more than that the petition is allowed or refused as the
g   case may be. Save in very exceptional circumstances, which I find myself unable at present to foresee, I can see no good reason why a commercial judge in disposing of an application under s 1(3)(b) should do more than that, and several good reasons why he should not. In the first place, he is not himself deciding at this stage the question of law arising out of the award which usually involves a question of construction of a commercial contract.
h   He is simply deciding whether the case is of a kind that is recognised, under the current guidelines laid down by appellate courts, as suitable to be admitted to appeal. In the second place, it adds to the already excessive volume of reported judicial semantic and syntactical analysis of particular words and phrases appearing in commercial contracts which judges are
j   inveigled to indulge in by the detailed oral arguments which it appears to be current practice to allow on applications ...' (See [1984] 3 All ER 229 at 237, [1985] AC 191 at 205–206.)

[18] Section 69 of the 1996 Act enacted in statutory form the very same limitations placed upon the right of appeal as provided for in *The Nema*: see para 286 of the Department Advisory Committee (DAC) Report (1996). In addition, it provided

that applications for leave to appeal should usually be dealt with without a
hearing. It follows, in my judgment, that, in the aftermath of the 1996 Act, there
are no good reasons to be elicited from the new Act itself that a different practice
should be adopted for the giving of reasons in the event of any refusal to grant
leave to appeal.

Human Rights Act 1998

[19] The principal thrust of the applicants' argument was that the giving 'of full
reasons' was now required by reason of Sch 1, Pt I, art 6 of the 1998 Act. It was not
suggested that the restrictions or limitations on the right of appeal were themselves
inconsistent with art 6. It was simply contended that the practice of not giving
reasons was no longer appropriate as not being consistent with art 6. In particular,
it was submitted, given that there was some potential for leave to appeal against
a refusal of leave to appeal (or in the alternative a remote possibility of a collateral
attack for impropriety in the approach to the application: see *Aden Refinery Co Ltd v
Ugland Management Co, The Ugland Obo One* [1986] 3 All ER 737, [1987] QB 650),
the requirements of due process, as developed in the Strasbourg jurisprudence,
necessitated the giving of at least some reasons since otherwise those rights of
appeal could not be effectively exercised.

[20] In this context the applicants made reference to *Hadjianastassiou v Greece*
(1992) 16 EHRR 219 at 237 in which the court said:

'32. The Court notes at the outset that although Article 93(3) of the Greek
Constitution requires all court judgments to be specifically and thoroughly
reasoned, under Article 96(5) the application of this requirement to the
military courts is subject to the adoption of a special law. Such a law has still
to be enacted. In the meantime the Court of Cassation can review the proper
application of the criminal law by those courts only through the questions
put by the Presidents and the replies given by their colleagues, from which
the reasoning is elicited.

33. The Contracting States enjoy a considerable freedom in the choice of
the appropriate means to ensure that their judicial systems comply with the
requirements of Article 6. The national courts must, however, indicate with
sufficient clarity the grounds on which they based their decision. It is this,
inter alia, which makes it possible for the accused to exercise usefully the
rights of appeal available to him. The Court's task is to consider whether the
method adopted in this respect has led in a given case to results which are
compatible with the Convention.'

[21] This approach, the applicants submitted, was further developed in *Tolstoy
Miloslavsky v UK* (1995) 20 EHRR 442 at 475 where the judgment of the court
contains the following passage:

'59. The Court reiterates that the right of access to the courts secured by
Article 6(1) may be subject to limitations in the form of regulation by the
State. In this respect the State enjoys a certain margin of appreciation.
However, the Court must be satisfied, firstly, that the limitations applied do
not restrict or reduce the access left to the individual in such a way or to such
an extent that the very essence of the right is impaired. Secondly a restriction
must pursue a legitimate aim and there must be a reasonable relationship of
proportionality between the means employed and the aim sought to be
achieved. It follows from established case law that Article 6(1) does not

a   guarantee a right of appeal. Nevertheless, a Contracting State which sets up
        an appeal system is required to ensure that persons within its jurisdiction
        enjoy before the appellate courts the fundamental guarantees in Article 6.
        However, the manner of application of Article 6 to the proceedings before
        such courts depends on the special features of the proceedings involved;
        account must be taken of the entirety of the proceedings in the domestic
b   legal order and of the role of the appellate court therein.'

        [22] But this emphasis on the crucial importance of the overall context in
        considering the extent of any obligation to provide reasons has led, in two decisions
        of the Commission in areas more closely analogous to the present case, to
        outcomes on which the respondents place considerable weight. In X v Germany
c   (1981) 25 DR 240, the applicant had accepted compensation under an urban
        reallocation scheme. He then sought damages for loss of rent. Having been
        successful at first instance, he lost on appeal. An attempt at a further appeal was
        rejected by the Federal Court without reasons. The Commission observed as
        follows (at 241):

d   'The Commission accepts that under specific circumstances the absence of
            reasons in a court decision might raise an issue as to the fairness of the
            procedure which is guaranteed by Article 6, paragraph 1 of the Convention.
            It recalls, however, its earlier jurisprudence according to which a right of
            appeal is not as such included among the rights and freedoms guaranteed by
e   the Convention. If the domestic law subjects the acceptance of the appeal to
            a decision by the competent court whether it considers the appeal raises a
            legal issue of fundamental importance and whether it has any chances of
            success, it may be sufficient for this court simply to refer to the provision
            authorising this procedure. This has been done in the present case and the
            applicant was thereby given to understand that the Federal Court of Justice
f   find no objection with the Hamm Court of Appeal second decision of ...
            March 1978. The Commission considers that in these circumstances there is
            no appearance that the proceedings have been unfair and contrary to the
            requirements of Article 6, paragraph 1 of the Convention and the applicant's
            complaint in this respect must be accordingly rejected as being manifestly
g   ill-founded within the meaning of Article 27, paragraph 2 of the Convention.'

        [23] Even closer to home is the decision in Webb v UK (1997) 24 EHRR CD 73
        in which the applicant complained that the Privy Council had failed to give
        reasons for refusing special leave to appeal. The Commission found as follows
        (at 74):
h

            'The Commission recalls that the manner in which Article 6(1) applies in
            relation to appeal proceedings depends on the special features of the
            proceedings involved. Account must be taken of the entirety of the proceedings
            in the domestic legal order and the role of the appeal court therein: in the case
j   of leave to appeal proceedings, the nature of those proceedings and their
            significance in the context of the proceedings as a whole must be considered,
            together with the powers of the appellate jurisdiction and the manner in which
            the proceedings are actually conducted ... Further, where a supreme court
            refuses to accept a case on the basis that legal grounds for such a case are not
            made out, very limited reasons may satisfy the requirements of Article 6 of the
            Convention ...

The Commission first notes that there was an oral hearing before the Privy Council in which Counsel for the applicant was heard. The Commission does not consider the facts disclosed any evidence of lack of equality of arms. The Commission further notes that special leave to appeal to the Privy Council will only be given where a case raises a "point of great and general importance" or in cases of "grave injustice". In the context of appeals to the Privy Council, where there has been a full appeal before the Court of Appeal, it must be apparent to litigants who have been refused leave that they have failed to satisfy the Privy Council that their case involved either a point of "great and general importance" or a "grave injustice". The factual position is therefore similar to the position before the Federal Constitutional Court in Germany, where no detailed reasons for rejection of a case are given.

The Commission, having considered the proceedings as a whole, considers there is no indication of unfairness in the present case such as would constitute a violation of Article 6(1).'

Conclusion on Strasbourg jurisprudence

[24] With this introduction, I seek to summarise the relevant Strasbourg jurisprudence. (1) Article 6 obliges courts to give reasons. The extent of this duty varies according to the nature of the decision and the circumstances of the case. (2) Full reasons should be given for a decision on the merits, although even then it is not necessary to provide a detailed answer to every argument. (3) Although art 6 applies to the appeal process, it does not guarantee a right of appeal: none the less any limitation on the right of appeal must be imposed pursuant to a legitimate aim, proportionately applied. (4) If a right of appeal is rejected, the applicant must be made aware of the grounds on which the decision was reached: in many cases this may take the form of an endorsement of the lower court's decision. (5) Where there are legitimate restraints on a right of appeal, such as the need for it to be a matter of general importance, it is sufficient for the court to refer to these limitations.

[25] Against that background, I regard the continued implementation of *The Antaios* restraints on the provision of reasons for refusing leave to appeal against arbitral awards (it being common ground that reasons for granting leave are not appropriate) as fully compliant with the Strasbourg jurisprudence.

(a) The parties have agreed to arbitrate their disputes. They have thereby largely renounced (in the interests of privacy and finality) the application of art 6 (albeit some incidents of this article are of course preserved by s 68 of the Act). (b) There has in fact been a substantial hearing before the arbitrators, who have produced a detailed reasoned award on the merits. (c) It is not suggested that the restrictions on the right of appeal are inconsistent with art 6. (Indeed the model law contemplates no right of appeal at all.) (d) It is further accepted that the limitations have a legitimate purpose and are not disproportionate to that purpose. (e) Those restrictions are clear and well known. In any event, they are referred to in my decision.

The domestic context

[26] The primary rationale for not giving reasons for refusing leave to appeal, as spelt out by Lord Diplock, is still valid. The nature of the exercise is to decide a threshold question whether the case is suitable for an appeal. Any detailed consideration of the issue of law would be misplaced. Whilst it is true (as already envisaged by Lord Diplock) that the hearing of applications in chambers (a fortiori

a on paper) put an end to the proliferation of reported judicial statements, the fact
remains that applications for leave attract even now protracted exchanges of
detailed written argument of the kind regarded by Lord Diplock as somewhat
unsatisfactory. Dealing with even the major arguments might often involve
lengthy reasons, with associated risks of delay.

[27] The applicants drew some comfort from a lecture by Bingham LJ (as he
b then was) in October 1987 in which he explained what he saw as the justification
for giving reasoned judgments. In the context of the proposition 'the parties are
entitled to be told why they have won or lost', he expressed a sense of
dissatisfaction arising from the practice of the rejection of petitions for leave to
appeal to the House of Lords being dismissed with no reasons. He added:

c   'I personally regret that commercial judges, when refusing applications for
          leave to appeal against arbitration awards, should have been enjoined against
          giving reasons, however briefly …'

[28] These concerns merit some reflection. But the fact remains that thereafter
the 1996 Act expressly adopted the approach to rights of appeal expressed in *The*
d *Nema*, with the added requirement that leave should only be furnished if it be just
and proper in all the circumstances for the court to determine the question of law.
So far as an application for leave is concerned, the 1996 Act further provided that
it should be usually determined without a hearing. As already observed, there is
no indication from the 1996 Act that it was appropriate to change the approach
e to such applications as spelt out in *The Antaios* so far as reasons were concerned.

[29] The direct analogy made by Lord Diplock was with applications to the
House of Lords for leave to appeal. Despite Bingham LJ's earlier reservations,
that procedure remains, I understand, unchanged.

f *Content of the decision*
[30] I confess that, until shortly before the decision in this case, it was my
personal practice to go further than merely refusing leave (with or without
express reference to the statutory criteria) and to give some reasons why I had
concluded that the arbitrators were correct (or at least not prima face wrong) on
the merits. When I became aware of the substantial variation in practice in this
g regard amongst the judges of the Commercial Court, I felt it appropriate to adopt
a common approach to the issue, giving rise to the form of decision in this very case.

[31] On further reflection I believe my former approach was, despite Lord
Bingham's concerns, objectionable in principle. I have not forgotten the need for
a party to know why he has won or lost. But given the terms of s 69 (and if
h necessary the terms of a decision in a form such as mine) the applicant can be in
no doubt why he has failed to obtain leave.

[32] Mr Peter Gross QC for the respondents went further and submitted that
the giving of reasons which touched on the merits was a practice at best pointless
and at worse subversive. In my judgment, he was correct so to submit.

j [33] In reality, the High Court is the court of last resort in arbitral proceedings.
Whilst there is a theoretical right of appeal, it is only to be exercised by the High
Court itself in quite exceptional circumstances. Lord Diplock contemplated that
leave should be confined to cases that called for a review of the guidelines. Since
those guidelines are now statutory and not laid down by the appellate courts, the
circumstances justifying leave, rather than reliance by the judge on his own
convictions, are not easy to foresee.

[34] Again, I accept the submission that intervention of the kind tentatively
envisaged in the *Aden Refinery* case is almost too remote a possibility to allow *a*
for—particularly as there is a right of challenge in respect of bias or other serious
irregularity under s 68.

[35] In practical terms the decision of the High Court is almost as immune to
challenge in this field as the House of Lords or the Privy Council in theirs (the decision
in the *Aden Refinery* case having been reaffirmed in *Henry Boot Construction (UK) Ltd v* *b*
Malmaison Hotel (Manchester) Ltd [2001] 1 All ER 257, [2001] QB 388). The provision
of reasons touching on the merits might satisfy some degree of curiosity but in
fact would be completely worthless.

[36] Furthermore, a response to this understandable curiosity imports with it,
in my judgment, serious dangers. Whilst there may be cases in which the judge
will be content to accept the arbitrators' reasons as his own, in the majority of *c*
cases he will be minded to express his accord in different terms or at least with a
different emphasis. Invidious comparisons would be drawn by the parties, with
the risk of applications under s 68 invoking some suggestion of irregularity. This
would all have the effect of undermining the arbitral process. The problem is all
the more acute bearing in mind the absence of any right of appeal where the *d*
arbitrators are perceived as possibly, but not obviously, wrong.

[37] The applicants were conscious of this risk and were at pains to say that the
scope and content of the reasons were within 'the discretion of the judge'. But in
the event I was never quite clear where the borderline was between a mere
declaration showing that the judge's mind had been applied to the relevant
threshold criteria on the one hand and the full reasons demonstrating the basis of *e*
concurrence (enthusiastic or otherwise) with the arbitrators' decision on the
other.

[38] In my judgment it is not appropriate to distinguish the present case from
the examples considered by the Commission cited above. The chosen tribunal
(in this case the arbitration panel) has adjudicated upon the dispute and provided *f*
a reasoned award. It was my view that the threshold requirements for granting
leave to appeal were not met. There is no effective right of appeal from that
conclusion. Accordingly, the scope and content of my decision dated 28 January
is not, in my judgment, challengeable as being devoid of appropriate and relevant
reasoning.

Application dismissed.

James Wilson   Barrister (NZ).

a # Moore's (Wallisdown) Ltd v Pensions Ombudsman

CHANCERY DIVISION

b FERRIS J

9, 10 OCTOBER, 21 DECEMBER 2001

Costs – Order for costs – Costs of appeal – Pensions Ombudsman – Liability of ombudsman for costs of successful appeal against his determination – Ombudsman appearing on appeal against his determination – Court allowing appeal – Appellants seeking order that ombudsman pay costs of appeal – Whether costs of successful appeal against Pensions Ombudsman's determination recoverable by appellant from Ombudsman when latter appearing on appeal.

c

G made a complaint to the Pensions Ombudsman concerning a pension scheme
d of which he was a member. In his determination, the Ombudsman upheld G's complaint and required M Ltd, which was the trustee and employer for the purposes of the scheme, to secure the provision of additional benefits for G. M Ltd appealed to the High Court, as did the scheme's insurer which feared that M Ltd might have a claim against it to recover the cost of complying with the decision and any further decision which might be made in favour of persons in
e similar positions to G. At the hearing of the appeals, M Ltd and the insurer were separately represented by solicitors and counsel. G took no part in the the appeals because of lack of means, but the Ombudsman appeared by solicitors and counsel, and sought to have his determination upheld. His appearance added at least a day to the length of the hearing. After the judge allowed the appeals,
f M Ltd and the insurer each sought an order for costs against the Ombudsman, but not against G. Accordingly, the judge was required to determine whether, and to what extent, such an order should be made against the Ombudsman when he had appeared on an appeal in an unsuccessful attempt to uphold his decision.

g **Held** – Where the Pensions Ombudsman made himself a party to the lis, he put himself at risk as to an order for costs, but whether such an order was actually made against him in a particular case was a matter on which the court would exercise its discretion in accordance with the principles set out in the CPR, including the general rule that the unsuccessful party would be ordered to pay the costs of the successful party. In the case of appeals from tribunals other than the
h Pensions Ombudsman, there was a settled practice that if the tribunal took no part in the appeal an order for costs would not be made against it, but if it did appear and made representations in support of its decision it made itself at least potentially liable for costs in the event that its decision was reversed. There was no reason to distinguish the position of the Pensions Ombudsman from that of
j other tribunals. Although, by appearing on an appeal, the Ombudsman might prevent the case of an aggrieved person of limited means from going unargued, that did not justify treating him differently from other tribunals. Furthermore, if the Ombudsman participated in an appeal and was successful in having his decision upheld, he was likely to be awarded his costs of the appeal against the unsuccessful appellant. It was difficult to see why there should be a lack of reciprocity in that respect. As to the exercise of discretion, there was nothing in

the instant case to cause the court to depart from the general rule that the *a*
unsuccessful party should be ordered to pay the costs of the successful party.
There was, however, no justification for ordering the Ombudsman to pay two
sets of costs. Accordingly, the court would only order him to pay M Ltd's costs
of the appeal (see [7], [25], [26], [29], [30], [32], [36], [45], [47], below).

Dictum of Chadwick J in *Providence Capitol Trustees v Ayres* [1996] 4 All ER 760
at 763–764 applied. *b*

Elliott v Pensions Ombudsman [1998] OPLR 21 and *University of Nottingham v Eyett*
(No 2) [1999] 2 All ER 445 not followed.

Notes

For the award of costs against the Pensions Ombudsman on an appeal from his *c*
determination, see 44(2) *Halsbury's Laws* (4th edn reissue) para 676.

Cases referred to in judgment

Bolton Metropolitan DC v Secretary of State for the Environment [1996] 1 All ER 184,
[1995] 1 WLR 1176, HL.
Dolphin Packaging Materials Ltd v Pensions Ombudsman [1995] OPLR 331. *d*
Edge v Pensions Ombudsman [1999] 4 All ER 546, [2000] Ch 602, [2000] 3 WLR 79,
CA; *affg* [1998] 2 All ER 547, [1998] Ch 512, [1998] 3 WLR 466.
Elliott v Pensions Ombudsman [1998] OPLR 21.
Law Debenture Trust Corp v Malley [1999] PLR 367.
Miller v Stapleton [1996] 2 All ER 449. *e*
Providence Capitol Trustees Ltd v Ayres [1996] 4 All ER 760.
R (on the application of Touche) v Inner London North Coroner [2001] EWCA Civ 383,
[2001] 2 All ER 752, [2001] 3 WLR 148.
R v Camborne Justices, ex p Pearce [1954] 2 All ER 850, [1955] 1 QB 41, [1954] 3 WLR
415, DC. *f*
R v Kingston-upon-Hull Rent Tribunal, ex p Black [1949] 1 All ER 260, DC.
R v Liverpool Justices, ex p Roberts [1960] 2 All ER 384, [1960] 1 WLR 585, DC.
R v Llanidloes Licensing Justices, ex p Davies [1957] 2 All ER 610, [1957] 1 WLR 809.
R v Newcastle-under-Lyme Justices, ex p Massey [1995] 1 All ER 120, [1994] 1 WLR
1684, DC. *g*
R v York City Justices, ex p Farmery (1988) 153 JP 257, DC.
Seifert v Pensions Ombudsman [1997] 1 All ER 214; *rvsd* [1997] 4 All ER 947, CA.
Steele Ford & Newton (a firm) v CPS [1993] 2 All ER 769, [1994] AC 22, [1993] 2 WLR
934, HL.
Sun Alliance and London Assurance Co Ltd v Pensions Ombudsman [2000] All ER (D) 1429. *h*
Thomas v Times Book Co Ltd [1966] 2 All ER 241, [1966] 1 WLR 911.
University of Nottingham v Eyett (No 2) [1999] 2 All ER 445, [1999] 1 WLR 594.

Applications

The appellant, Moore's (Wallisdown) Ltd (Moore's), and the third respondent, *j*
Royal and Sun Alliance Life and Pensions Ltd (R&SA) applied for orders requiring
the first respondent, the Pensions Ombudsman, to pay their costs of successful
appeals against his determination dated 4 April 2001 upholding a complaint by the
second respondent, Albert Edward Garwood. Mr Garwood took no part in the
appeal. The facts are set out in the judgment.

a *Peter Crampin QC* and *Piers Feltham* (instructed by *Frettens*, Christchurch) for Moore's.
Paul Newman (instructed by *CMS Cameron McKenna*) for R&SA.
Elisabeth Laing for the Pensions Ombudsman.

Cur adv vult

b 21 December 2001. The following judgment was delivered.

FERRIS J.

[1] On 21 November 2001 I handed down a judgment allowing two appeals from a determination of the Pensions Ombudsman dated 4 April 2001. I now have to decide certain questions relating to the costs of these appeals. As one of *c* these questions involves a point of principle I reserved my decision, which I now give.

[2] The Ombudsman's determination was made in respect of a complaint by Mr Garwood, who is a member of the pension scheme referred to in the determination as Moore's (Wallisdown) Ltd Co Retirement Account. The effect *d* of the determination was to uphold Mr Garwood's complaint and to require Moore's (Wallisdown) Ltd (Moore's), which is the trustee and employer for the purposes of the scheme, to secure the provision of additional benefits for Mr Garwood. The appeals on which I gave judgment were made by Moore's and the Royal & Sun Alliance Life and Pensions Ltd (R&SA) which is the insurer for the purposes of the scheme.

e [3] At the hearing of the appeals Moore's and R&SA were each separately represented by solicitors and counsel. Mr Garwood took no part in the appeals, although he had been duly served with the notices of appeal. The Ombudsman appeared by solicitors and counsel and argued in support of his determination.

[4] Neither of the successful appellants seeks any order for costs against *f* Mr Garwood, but both of them seek such an order against the Ombudsman. Their applications give rise to two questions. The first is whether and to what extent an order for costs should be made against the Ombudsman when he has appeared on an appeal and has unsuccessfully sought to uphold his decision. The second is whether any order for costs which is made against the Ombudsman should be in respect of the costs of both appellants or only one of them.

g
(A) *To what extent should an order for costs be made against the Ombudsman?*

[5] Appeals from a decision of the Pensions Ombudsman fall within a wider class of 'statutory appeals' to which CPR PD 52, para 17 applies. This class extends to all cases where—

h
'under any enactment an appeal (other than by way of case stated) lies to the court from a Minister of State, government department, tribunal or other person ...'

[6] It is a requirement of the practice direction that, in the case of every *j* statutory appeal, the notice of appeal must be served on the tribunal or other person from whose decision the appeal is brought (see CPR PD 52, para 17.5). A similar requirement was formerly imposed by RSC Ord 55, r 4. As I explained in my judgment on the substantive appeals, service of the notice of appeal on the Ombudsman does not automatically make him a respondent to the appeal, although the court hearing the appeal commonly permits him to be a party to the

appeal. The Ombudsman's participation in the appeal is frequently, indeed
usually, of considerable assistance to the court, particularly where, as in the
present case, the appeal is brought from a decision of the Ombudsman in favour
of a complainant who lacks the means to appear and seek to uphold that decision.

[7] In the case of appeals from tribunals other than the Pensions Ombudsman
there is a settled practice that if the tribunal takes no part in the appeal an order
for costs will not be made against it, but if it does appear and makes representations
in support of its decision it makes itself at least potentially liable for costs in the
event that its decision is reversed.

[8] In relation to appeals from magistrates the principles were recently stated
by Rose LJ giving the judgment of the Divisional Court in *R v Newcastle-under-
Lyme Justices, ex p Massey* [1995] 1 All ER 120, [1994] 1 WLR 1684. The third and
fourth of these principles are particularly relevant. So far as material they are as
follows:

'(iii) Justices who merely file affidavits and do not appear before the
Divisional Court or the High Court will not, without more, normally be
visited with a costs order (see s 2 of the [Review of Justices Decisions Act
1872, *R v Llanidloes Licensing Justices, ex p Davies* [1957] 2 All ER 610, [1957]
1 WLR 809] per Lord Goddard CJ and [*R v Liverpool Justices, ex p Roberts*
[1960] 2 All ER 384, [1960] 1 WLR 585] per Lord Parker CJ, recently
reasserted in [*R v York City Justices, ex p Farmery* (1988) 153 JP 257]). This is so
despite the fact that, in judicial review proceedings, justices are served with
notice of proceedings under Ord 53, r 5(3) and are therefore a party within
s 151(1) of the [Supreme Court Act 1981]. Albeit that they are a party, for
over a century it has not generally been the practice to award costs against
them in prerogative writ and judicial review proceedings and that practice,
reiterated by successive Lords Chief Justice, must have been known to
Parliament at the time of the 1977 and subsequent amendments to Ord 53
and of the enactment of ss 31 and 51 of the 1981 Act and of the [Statute Law
(Repeals) Act 1993]. (iv) Justices should not generally appear before the
Divisional Court or the High Court unless their bona fides are called into
question or there are other exceptional circumstances. If they do appear they
are unlikely to recover costs if successful (see [*R v Camborne Justices, ex p
Pearce* [1954] 2 All ER 850, [1955] 1 QB 41]) and they will be at risk as to costs
if they lose (see *Ex p Davies*).' (See [1995] 1 All ER 120 at 126–127, [1994]
1 WLR 1684 at 1692.)

[9] More recently still, the Court of Appeal has adopted a similar approach in
upholding an order for costs which had been made against a coroner who had
appeared and unsuccessfully resisted an appeal against his refusal to hold an
inquest (see *R (on the application of Touche) v Inner London North Coroner* [2001]
EWCA Civ 383, [2001] 2 All ER 752, [2001] 3 WLR 148).

[10] It appears that in the earlier years of the jurisdiction to hear appeals from
the Pensions Ombudsman a similar practice was applied. The matter was
considered by Chadwick J in *Providence Capitol Trustees Ltd v Ayres* [1996] 4 All ER
760. In that case a pensioneer trustee successfully appealed against a determination
of the Pensions Ombudsman in favour of a complainant. The Ombudsman took
no part in the appeal, but the pensioneer trustee sought an order that he should
nevertheless pay the costs of the appeal. This application was refused by
Chadwick J.

[11] In his judgment Chadwick J said (at 763):

a
'There is no inflexible rule that a successful litigant is entitled to expect to recover his costs from somebody (see the observations of Lord Bridge in *Steele Ford & Newton (a firm) v CPS* [1993] 2 All ER 769 at 779–780, [1994] 1 AC 22 at 39–40). Among the examples given by Lord Bridge is that of a party who has been the victim of a misjudgment by an inferior court or tribunal, and who obtains relief on an application for judicial review from the

b
Divisional Court in circumstances in which the court cannot hold either another party or the inferior tribunal itself liable in costs and there is no power to award costs from public funds. When the tribunal whose decision is overturned on appeal appears on the appeal and makes itself party to the lis, it puts itself at risk as to the costs of the appeal; and if the appeal against its decision is successful it may expect to pay the costs of the appeal: see the

c
observations of Lord Goddard CJ in *R v Kingston-upon-Hull Rent Tribunal, ex p Black* [1949] 1 All ER 260 and *R v Llanidloes Licensing Justices, ex p Davies* [1957] 2 All ER 610. But in circumstances where the tribunal does not appear and does not take part, it is only in exceptional cases that an order for costs will be made against it.'

d
He then quoted part of the extract from *Ex p Massey* [1995] 1 All ER 120, [1994] 1 WLR 1684 which I have set out above and continued (at 763–764):

'That that principle applies not only to justices but also to other tribunals appears from the decision of the Divisional Court in *R v Kingston-upon-Hull Rent Tribunal, ex p Black* [1949] 1 All ER 260; in particular in a trenchant

e
observation of Lord Goddard CJ, "If there had been no appearance by the Tribunal of course we should not have given costs in this case". In my view, those principles should guide me in the exercise of my discretion in the present case. It seems to me that it would be oppressive to make an order for costs against the Pensions Ombudsman in circumstances where his determination has been overturned on appeal but where he has not made

f
himself a party to the lis by appearing at the appeal or taking steps to defend his determination. It would be oppressive because the Ombudsman has no choice whether or not to be named as a respondent and no power, once named as a respondent, to set aside his own order so as to avoid the need for the appeal proceeding. He is necessarily a party and, whether or not on

g
further consideration he comes to the conclusion that his determination was wrong, there is nothing that he can do to prevent the appeal from proceeding. To visit a party with an order for costs in circumstances in which he is unable to take any steps to avoid the costs incurred on the appeal seems to me to be oppressive and unfair.'

h
[12] Later (at 765) Chadwick J referred to *Miller v Stapleton* [1996] 2 All ER 449, where Carnwath J had ordered the Ombudsman to pay the costs of an appeal against a determination made by him. He commented:

'That, as it seems to me, is an example of a case in which the Ombudsman,

j
for good and understandable reasons, had made himself a party to the lis; and so, in accordance with the principles to which I have referred, had put himself at risk as to an order for costs.'

[13] In concluding his judgment Chadwick J said (at 765):

'I do not intend to cast any doubt on the proposition that in suitable cases it may be appropriate for the Ombudsman to appear in order to argue

questions of law for the assistance of the court. But, if he does so on his own
initiative, he must risk the possibility that an order for costs will be made   *a*
against him if his arguments are unsuccessful.'

[14] It seems to me to be clear that in a case like the present, where the
Ombudsman has appeared and unsuccessfully sought to uphold his determination,
and the successful appellant reasonably decides not to seek an order for costs   *b*
against the complainant, Chadwick J would have thought it appropriate to make
an order that the Ombudsman is to pay the costs of the appeal.

[15] In *Seifert v Pensions Ombudsman* [1997] 1 All ER 214 the judge, on an
appeal, had set aside the entirety of the Ombudsman's determination and ordered
the Ombudsman to pay the costs of the appeal. On a further appeal to the Court
of Appeal ([1997] 4 All ER 947), on which the Ombudsman was represented by   *c*
solicitors and counsel and argued in support of his determination, that
determination was partially restored. Dealing with costs, Staughton LJ giving the
judgment of the court said (at 956):

'The two appeals from the ombudsman were necessary and achieved a
result, in that paras 37 and 38 of his determination were and remain set aside.   *d*
But that is not a sufficient ground to order him to pay the costs. The limited
circumstances in which an inferior tribunal, such as magistrates or an
arbitrator, should be ordered to pay the costs of an appeal from its decision
are well known. Now that this dispute, at first relatively simple but thereafter
to become complicated, has been fully argued before us, we do not consider   *e*
that it is a case for such an order. The judge's decision on that point is set
aside.'

[16] The list of authorities cited to the Court of Appeal includes *R v
Kingston-upon-Hull Rent Tribunal, ex p Black* [1949] 1 All ER 260; *R v Llanidloes
Licensing Justices, ex p Davies* [1957] 2 All ER 610, [1957] 1 WLR 809; *R v*   *f*
Newcastle-under-Lyme Justices, ex p Massey [1995] 1 All ER 120, [1994] 1 WLR 1684;
and *Providence Capitol Trustees Ltd v Ayres* [1996] 4 All ER 760. These must be the
authorities on which the Court of Appeal felt able to say that the limited
circumstances in which an inferior tribunal should be ordered to pay costs 'are
well known'. The Court of Appeal thus impliedly endorsed their applicability to
costs applications against the Pensions Ombudsman.   *g*

[17] Nevertheless in two other reported cases judges of the Chancery Division
have refused to make more than a limited order for costs against the Pensions
Ombudsman in cases where he has participated in the appeal and failed to uphold
his decision. In these cases the court ordered the Ombudsman to pay the costs of
the appeal only to the extent that they were increased by the Ombudsman's   *h*
participation.

[18] The first of these cases is *Elliott v Pensions Ombudsman* [1998] OPLR 21. In
that case Blackburne J set aside the Ombudsman's determination so far as it
affected the appellant. On the appellant's application that the Ombudsman should
pay his costs of the appeal, Blackburne J directed that the Ombudsman should pay   *j*
those costs only to the extent that they had been increased by the Ombudsman's
participation at the hearing of the appeal. The basis of this decision appears to be
as follows: (i) In his decision on the substantive appeal he had observed (at 24):

'In accordance with what has become the practice in these cases, at any
rate when the complainants are unrepresented, the Ombudsman appears
before me to assist the court and effectively to uphold his determination.'

a No doubt he was mindful, as the court always is, of the benefit of hearing adversarial argument. (ii) Referring to *Seifert*'s case [1997] 4 All ER 947, he said that it was clear that the fact that an appeal from the Ombudsman was necessary and that it was successful was not a sufficient ground for ordering the Ombudsman to pay the costs. (iii) He cited the passage from Chadwick J's judgment in the *Providence Capitol* case where he dealt with the position of a tribunal which b appears on the appeal and makes itself a party to the lis and, if the appeal is successful, must expect to pay the costs of the appeal. He said, however (at 37), that—

'it does not follow ... that, merely because the Ombudsman has taken part in the appeal, and that the appeal has been successful, he must bear *all* the c costs of the appeal.' (Blackburne J's emphasis.)

(iv) The reason which he gave for this is that the appellant, in order to escape the determination which is unfavourable to him, has no choice but to appeal and thus to incur some costs, whether the Ombudsman participates in the appeal or not. (v) He concluded (at 37):

d

'In these circumstances the guiding principle must, as it seems to me, be to assess the extent to which the appellant's costs have been increased as a result of the Ombudsman's participation in the appeal.'

[19] The second case is *University of Nottingham v Eyett (No 2)* [1999] 2 All ER e 445, [1999] 1 WLR 594, when the successful appellant argued before Hart J that *Elliott*'s case had been decided on a wrong principle and that a full order for costs should be made against the Ombudsman. The cases referred to in [16] above were cited to Hart J, although it seems that, with the exception of the *Providence Capitol* case [1996] 4 All ER 760, they had not been cited to Blackburne J. Hart J rejected the argument and followed *Elliott*'s case [1998] OPLR 21. He said that he f did so 'not merely from considerations of judicial comity but because it seems to me the preferable course to take' (see [1999] 2 All ER 445 at 447, [1999] 1 WLR 594 at 596).

[20] The reasons given by Hart J for taking this view can be summarised as follows: (i) 'Once it is accepted that the Ombudsman is not normally at risk as to g costs if he does not appear, there seems to be no good reason to discourage his appearance by making him potentially liable for the whole of the costs if he does' (see [1999] 2 All ER 445 at 447, [1999] 1 WLR 594 at 596). (ii) He emphasised the assistance which the court obtains from the participation of the Ombudsman in the appeal. (iii) He doubted the practicability of the suggestion, made by h Chadwick J in the *Providence Capitol* case, that the Ombudsman could protect himself from an order for costs by seeking the directions of the court as to his participation in the appeal. (iv) He said that to follow *Elliott*'s case in relation to the Ombudsman's liability for costs did not mean that a complainant who unsuccessfully participates in an appeal 'will be entitled to a similar indulgence from the court'. On the contrary he said that a complainant who seeks actively j to uphold the Ombudsman's determination on appeal is at risk as to costs in the normal way.

[21] In *Edge v Pensions Ombudsman* [1999] 4 All ER 546, [2000] Ch 602 the Ombudsman appealed unsuccessfully to the Court of Appeal from a decision of the High Court ([1998] 2 All ER 547, [1998] Ch 512) setting aside a determination made by him. One of the issues discussed by the Court of Appeal in its judgment (which was handed down by Chadwick LJ) was the standing of the Ombudsman

to appeal against a decision of the High Court setting aside his determination. This discussion includes the following passage:

> '... the High Court may take the view that it will be assisted by his submissions; and, if so, it will allow him to appeal (see *Dolphin Packaging Materials Ltd v Pensions Ombudsman* [1995] OPLR 331). If he does appear he risks the possibility that an order for costs may be made against him if his arguments are unsuccessful (see *University of Nottingham v Eyett (No 2)* [1999] 2 All ER 455, [1999] 1 WLR 594). An appeal from the High Court to this court requires permission. Where the ombudsman's arguments have been unsuccessful in the High Court and an order for costs has been made against him, it seems plain enough that he is entitled to apply for permission to appeal. But, now that the principles upon which an adverse order for costs will be made have become settled, it will be rare that the mere fact that there has been an order for costs against him in those circumstances will be sufficient to persuade this court that permission to appeal should be granted.'
> (See [1999] 4 All ER 546 at 581–582, [2000] Ch 602 at 642–643.)

[22] Before me it was submitted on behalf of the Ombudsman that the settled principles referred to by the Court of Appeal in this passage must be those applied in *Elliott's* and *Eyett's* cases, the latter of which was expressly mentioned in the passage. This is a matter to which I shall return.

[23] The decision of Sir Andrew Morritt V-C in *Sun Alliance and London Assurance Co Ltd v Pensions Ombudsman* [2000] All ER (D) 1429, must also be noted. Sir Andrew Morritt V-C allowed an appeal against a determination of the Ombudsman, the Ombudsman having participated in the appeal and argued unsuccessfully in support of his determination. The successful appellant sought an order for costs against the Ombudsman, limited in accordance with *Elliott's* and *Eyett's* cases, and this was not resisted by the Ombudsman. The transcript of the argument in respect of costs shows that Sir Andrew Morritt V-C was puzzled by the practice which was said to justify the order he was asked to make. He said:

> 'The order for costs sought by the successful party, the Sun Alliance, is in accordance with the decision of Hart J in *University of Nottingham v Eyett (No 2)* [1999] 2 All ER 445, [1999] 1 WLR 594—that is, where the Pensions Ombudsman fails to uphold his decision before this court on appeal, he is required to pay the appellant's costs to the extent to which they have been increased by the Ombudsman's appearance on the appeal. I am by no means happy with that practice, but that is the practice, and I am not invited to depart from it. I will accordingly make the order sought, but making it plain that the actual length of time taken by [counsel for the Ombudsman] is minimal compared to the costs of the proceedings as a whole.'

[24] It is convenient that I should say at once that, in the case before me, the time taken by the Ombudsman's participation was far from minimal. The hearing before me began at 10.30 am on 9 October 2001 and counsel for the two appellants had completed their submissions by 2.40 pm. If there had been no participation by the Ombudsman the hearing of the appeals would have been concluded soon afterwards, although I think I would still have wished to reserve my judgment. As it was, however, the argument was not concluded until about 3 pm on the next day, much of this time being taken up with the consideration of Miss Laing's argument concerning maladministration which I dealt with in paras [62]–[70] of my judgment on the substantive appeals. The participation of the

a Ombudsman thus added at least a day to the length of the hearing. (I say 'at least a day' because it seems likely that, in the absence of indications in Miss Laing's skeleton argument that she was seeking to support the decision as a finding of maladministration, the submissions of counsel for the appellants in support of the appeals would have been briefer.) I cannot assess the impact of the Ombudsman's participation on the costs of preparing the appeals, but it seems likely that the *b* appellants would recover a substantial amount in respect of costs even under an *Elliott* order.

[25] Turning to the issue of principle which I am asked to decide, I have to say that my own view is that the position was correctly stated by Chadwick J in *Providence Capitol Trustees Ltd v Ayres* [1996] 4 All ER 760 and that if the Ombudsman 'has made himself a party to the lis' he puts himself at risk as to an *c* order for costs. Whether an order is actually made against him in a particular case is a matter on which the court will exercise its discretion in accordance with the principles set out in CPR 44.3, including the general rule that the unsuccessful party will be ordered to pay the costs of the successful party.

[26] The main reason why I take this view is that I see no reason to distinguish *d* the position of the Pensions Ombudsman from that of the tribunals considered in the cases mentioned in [16] above. The effect of these cases was discussed by Chadwick J in the *Providence Capitol* case and what he said was in accordance with the principle which emerges from them. These cases were not, it seems, cited to Blackburne J in *Elliott's* case [1998] OPLR 21. They, or most of them, were cited to Hart J in *Eyett's* case and are mentioned by him in his summary of counsel's *e* arguments (see [1999] 2 All ER 445 at 446, [1999] 1 WLR 594 at 595). Hart J does not, however, explain why he thought they were not applicable to appeals from the Ombudsman, except to the extent that this is implicit in his primary reason for following *Elliott's* case, which was the desirability of the court being afforded the Ombudsman's assistance.

f [27] The assistance afforded to the court by the participation of the tribunal from whose decision an appeal is brought is not, however, peculiar to appeals from the Pensions Ombudsman. Its existence in the case of appeals from coroners was expressly mentioned in *R (on the application of Touche) v Inner London North Coroner* [2001] 2 All ER 752 at [54], where it was considered insufficient to justify a departure from the general principle. It manifestly exists in most, if not all, *g* other cases of statutory appeals.

[28] As was recognised in *Touche's* case [2001] 2 All ER 752 at [55], it would be a pity if the practice of making orders for costs against tribunals which seek unsuccessfully to uphold their own decisions were to make those tribunals reluctant to be represented at the hearing, but this too does not justify such a *h* departure, as the Court of Appeal held in *Touche's* case.

[29] There is one respect in which the position of the Pensions Ombudsman may be said to be different from that of other tribunals. The Pensions Ombudsman was established by Parliament as a means of affording informal and inexpensive justice to persons who perceive themselves to have suffered *j* prejudice in the administration of pension schemes. The court has recognised that, by appearing on an appeal, the Ombudsman may prevent the case of an aggrieved person of limited means from going unargued. But that does not appear to me to justify the treatment of the Ombudsman differently from other tribunals. The practice adopted in *Elliott's* and *Eyett's* cases means that the successful appellant is treated less favourably than he would be if the argument was presented by an amicus (cf *Touche's* case [2001] 2 All ER 752 at [55]).

[30] In addition to these considerations there is the fact that if the
Ombudsman participates in an appeal and is successful in upholding his decision
he is likely to be awarded his costs of the appeal against the unsuccessful
appellant. It is difficult to see why there should be a lack of reciprocity in this
respect.

[31] Am I, therefore at liberty to decline to follow *Elliott's* and *Eyett's* cases?
Although the point at issue concerns a question of discretion rather than a point
of law, I would naturally wish to follow recent decisions of other judges of this
division on a matter of this kind unless I were convinced that those decisions are
wrong and I am satisfied that in departing from them I am not going against any
ruling of a higher court.

[32] So far as my being convinced that the decisions are wrong, I have already
set out my position. I am encouraged by the fact that Chadwick J expressed a
view consistent with my own in the *Providence Capitol* case, even though this was,
I think, obiter. I am also encouraged by the view indicated by *Sun Alliance and
London Assurance Co Ltd v Pensions Ombudsman* [2000] All ER (D) 1429.

[33] As to a ruling of a higher court, the observations of the Court of Appeal
in *Edge v Pensions Ombudsman* [1999] 4 All ER 546, [2000] Ch 602 were relied upon
by the Ombudsman. But I do not read these observations as endorsing *Elliott's*
and *Eyett's* cases. While it is true that *Eyett's* case is expressly referred to, the
proposition in support of which it is cited is not that which underlies those parts
of the decision in *Elliott's* and *Eyett's* cases which are relied upon here. I do not
consider that the Court of Appeal was endorsing, as 'the principles upon which
an adverse order for costs will be made', anything beyond the proposition that, if
the Pensions Ombudsman does appear, he risks the possibility that an order for
costs may be made against him. Moreover this proposition is stated in *Edge's* case
[1999] 4 All ER 546 at 582, [2000] Ch 602 at 644 in terms which are substantially
the same as those used by Chadwick J in the *Providence Capitol* case [1996] 4 All ER
760 at 765. I cannot help thinking that if Chadwick LJ, in giving the decision of
the Court of Appeal in *Edge's* case, had thought that he was accepting a
qualification of what he himself had said in the *Providence Capitol* case, he would
have expressed himself differently and more fully on the point.

[34] I therefore conclude that what was said in *Edge's* case is more supportive
of the argument propounded on these appeals on behalf of the successful
appellants than those on behalf of the Ombudsman.

[35] Further it appears to me that the recent re-affirmation by the Court of
Appeal in *Touche's* case [2001] 2 All ER 752, [2001] 3 WLR 148 of the principles
applicable to orders for costs against other tribunals impliedly indicates that the
special treatment of the Pensions Ombudsman in *Elliott's* and *Eyett's* cases and the
unreported cases which have followed is an anomaly which ought not to be
continued.

[36] As to the exercise of discretion, it appears to me that there is nothing in
the case before me to cause a departure from the general rule that the
unsuccessful party should be ordered to pay the costs of the successful party.

(B) *Should the order for costs against the Ombudsman be in respect of the costs of
both appellants or only one of them?*

[37] The substantive decision of the Ombudsman was that Moore's were in
breach of a promise made to Mr Garwood which was binding on Moore's as a
trust obligation. He therefore gave directions requiring Moore's to pay the
contributions necessary to secure the fulfilment of that promise. He made no

a finding of any form of misconduct or maladministration against R&SA and gave no directions to R&SA.

[38] In the light of my judgment on the substantive appeals, Moore's was fully justified in appealing against this determination and, in accordance with what I have said previously in this judgment, I shall order the Ombudsman to pay Moore's costs of the appeal, not limited in accordance with the decisions in *b* *Elliott*'s and *Eyett*'s cases.

[39] R&SA is in a somewhat different position. It was not directly affected by the Ombudsman's decision. Its concern was that, if that decision stood, Moore's might have a claim against it to recover the cost of complying with the decision and with any further decision which might be made in favour of persons in a similar position to Mr Garwood. This was because R&SA had been Moore's *c* advisor in relation to the change from Moore's PLAS (Pension and Life Assurance Scheme) to the Plus Plan Scheme and later to the GPPP (Group Personal Pension Plan) and, as I understand it, was responsible for producing the documents which the Ombudsman regarded as giving rise to Moore's promise.

[40] In the skeleton argument on behalf of the Pensions Ombudsman, Miss Laing *d* submitted that R&SA had no standing to appeal against the Ombudsman's determination. I heard a certain amount of argument about this, both from her and from Mr Newman on behalf of R&SA. Reference was made to *Law Debenture Trust Corp v Malley* [1999] PLR 367 and *Bolton Metropolitan DC v Secretary of State for the Environment* [1996] 1 All ER 184, [1995] 1 WLR 1176. I prefer not to go into these issues and to assume, without deciding, that R&SA have the requisite *e* standing. The real question, as Miss Laing submitted, is whether in exercise of the court's discretion the Pensions Ombudsman should be ordered to pay two sets of costs.

[41] As to this, the court ordinarily sets its face against awarding separate sets of costs to two or more parties who appear in the same interest. This reluctance can *f* be displaced for good reason, but this calls for the separate representation of the parties to be properly justified.

[42] Mr Newman submitted that R&SA was not presenting the same case as Moore's, as could be seen from a comparison of their skeleton arguments. In my judgment this difference was more apparent than real. Both of them were seeking to attack the same decision on the ground that the material before the Ombudsman *g* did not justify his conclusion. The difference between the skeleton arguments was, it seems to me, merely a reflection of the views of two different counsel as to how to present in the most persuasive manner what was essentially the same case for each party.

[43] Mr Newman pointed out that R&SA had not taken up time by repeating *h* Mr Crampin QC's arguments on behalf of Moore's. Instead it had adopted these arguments. This is, of course, true. But it is not, to my mind, a justification for having separate representation.

[44] Mr Newman also submitted that the participation of R&SA in the appeal was rendered inevitable by the nature of the claimant's case, which had the *j* implications mentioned above in respect of R&SA. He suggested that the position was analogous to that in *Thomas v Times Book Co Ltd* [1966] 2 All ER 241, [1966] 1 WLR 911, where the plaintiff sued the defendant for conversion of the manuscript of a well-known play. The defendant joined as third party the person from whom it had obtained the manuscript, who in turn joined his supplier as fourth party. Plowman J, having found against the plaintiff, ruled that the plaintiff should pay the costs not only of the defendant but also of the third and

fourth parties. In my view the position in that case was quite different from the
position here. The claims against the defendant and the third and fourth parties
all depended on the same question of title. Had the plaintiff succeeded against
the defendant it is difficult to see what defence could have been raised in the third
and fourth party proceedings. In this case, however, the fear of R&SA that the
economic cost of complying with the Ombudsman's direction might be passed
on to it by Moore's was based upon wholly separate considerations, arising from
the relationship between R&SA and Moore's, which do not involve either the
Ombudsman or Mr Garwood. To put the matter in another way, the subsistence
of the Ombudsman's decision was only one ingredient of Moore's putative claim
against R&SA.

[45] In these circumstances I do not think it would be justified to order the
Ombudsman to pay two sets of costs.

[46] A possible order to make would be that Moore's and R&SA are to be paid
one set of costs between them, but this would involve difficult questions of
quantification. I did not understand any party to submit that it would be the right
order to make in the circumstances of this case.

(C) *Conclusion*

[47] My order will be that the Ombudsman is to pay Moore's costs of its
appeal, not limited as in *Elliott v Pensions Ombudsman* [1998] OPLR 21 and
University of Nottingham v Eyett (No 2) [1999] 2 All ER 445, [1999] 1 WLR 594, such
costs to be determined, in the absence of agreement, by detailed assessment.
I shall make no further order as to costs, thus leaving the Ombudsman and R&SA
to bear their own costs.

Order accordingly.

Celia Fox   Barrister.

a
Donohue v Armco Inc and others
[2001] UKHL 64

HOUSE OF LORDS

LORD BINGHAM OF CORNHILL, LORD MACKAY OF CLASHFERN, LORD NICHOLLS OF
b BIRKENHEAD, LORD HOBHOUSE OF WOODBOROUGH AND LORD SCOTT OF FOSCOTE

15–17 OCTOBER, 13 DECEMBER 2001

*Conflict of laws – Foreign proceedings – Restraint of foreign proceedings – Circumstances in
which court will restrain prosecution of foreign proceedings – Claimant seeking injunction
c from English court to restrain proceedings in New York arising out of alleged contractual
fraud – Defendants party to English jurisdiction clause – Alleged co-conspirators of
claimant defendants in New York proceedings – Whether English court should grant
anti-suit injunction in respect of New York proceedings – Supreme Court Act 1981,
s 37(1).*

d The A group of companies, the members of which were variously incorporated
in the United States and Singapore, alleged that it had been the victim of a scheme
of fraud devised in the United States by the claimant, D, and others, based on a
management buy-out of a UK-based insurance group. Three key contracts for the
sale of shares in the insurance group contained exclusive jurisdiction clauses
e providing that 'the parties hereby irrevocably submit themselves to the exclusive
jurisdiction of the English Courts to settle any dispute which may arise out of or
in connection with this Agreement'. The A group began proceedings in New
York against D and his alleged co-conspirators and D applied under s 37(1) of the
Supreme Court Act 1981 for an anti-suit injunction, which would have had the
effect of preventing the A group from bringing claims arising from the sale of
f the insurance group against D in any forum other than England. The judge at
first instance declined to grant the application, but his decision was reversed by
the Court of Appeal which exercised its discretion to grant the injunction sought.
D appealed to the House of Lords.

g **Held** – Where the parties had bound themselves by an exclusive jurisdiction
clause, effect should ordinarily be given to that obligation in the absence of strong
reasons for departing from it. Whether a party could show strong reasons
sufficient to displace the other party's prima facie entitlement to enforce the
contractual bargain would depend on all the facts and circumstances of the
particular case. Where the dispute was between two contracting parties, one of
h which sued the other in a non-contractual forum, and the claims fell within the
scope of the exclusive jurisdiction clause in their contract, and the interests of
other parties were not involved, effect would in all probability be given to the
clause. However, the court might well decline to grant an injunction or a stay
where the interests of parties other than parties bound by the exclusive jurisdiction
j clause were involved or grounds of claim not the subject of the clause were part
of the relevant dispute so that there was a risk of parallel proceedings and
inconsistent decisions. In the instant case, D's strong prima facie right to be sued
in England on claims made by the other parties to the exclusive jurisdiction clause
in so far as those claims fell within that clause was matched by the clear prima
facie right of the A group to pursue other claims in New York. The crucial
question was whether, on the facts, the A group could show strong reasons why

the court should displace D's prima facie entitlement. Moreover, if strong reasons were found, such reasons would have to lie in the prospect, if an injunction was granted, of litigation continuing partly in England and partly in New York, and that was a consideration to which great weight should be given. It would be necessary for any court determining the truth or falsity of the allegations against D and his alleged co-conspirators to form a judgment on their honesty and motives, and it was not conceivable, on the A group's case, that some of the four were guilty of the nefarious conduct alleged and the others not. It was therefore plain that the interests of justice would be best served by the submission of the whole dispute to a single tribunal which was best fitted to make a reliable and comprehensive judgment on all the matters in issue. The ends of justice would be served by a single composite trial in the only forum in which such a trial could be procured, namely New York, and accordingly there were strong reasons for not giving effect to the exclusive jurisdiction clause in favour of D. The Court of Appeal's exercise of its discretion to grant an injunction had been fundamentally vitiated by an incorrect view of the future shape of the litigation, as it had not been recognised that different conclusions might be reached in the case of certain of the alleged co-conspirators on the one hand and D on the other if parallel trials relating to the management buy-out took place in both England and New York. It followed that, subject to the A group undertaking not to enforce any multiple or punitive damages awarded in New York, D would be denied an anti-suit injunction. Accordingly, the appeal would be allowed (see [24], [25], [27], [33], [34]–[41], [49], [50], [71]–[76], below).

Citi-March Ltd v Neptune Orient Lines Ltd [1996] 2 All ER 545, *Bouygues Offshore SA v Caspian Shipping Co (Nos 1, 3, 4 and 5)* [1998] 2 Lloyd's Rep 461 and *Credit Suisse First Boston (Europe) v MLC (Bermuda) Ltd* [1999] 1 All ER (Comm) 237 considered.

Decision of the Court of Appeal [2000] 1 All ER (Comm) 641 reversed.

Notes

For injunctions to restrain foreign proceedings, see 8(1) *Halsbury's Laws* (4th edn reissue) para 1092.

For the Supreme Court Act 1981, s 37, see 11 *Halsbury's Statutes* (4th edn) (2000 reissue) 1076.

Cases referred to in opinions

Aggeliki Charis Cia Maritima SA v Pagnan SpA, The Angelic Grace [1995] 1 Lloyd's Rep 87, CA.

Airbus Industrie GIE v Patel [1998] 2 All ER 257, [1999] 1 AC 119, [1998] 1 WLR 686, HL.

Akai Pty Ltd v People's Insurance Co Ltd [1998] 1 Lloyd's Rep 90.

Aratra Potato Co Ltd v Egyptian Navigation Co, The El Amria [1981] 2 Lloyd's Rep 119, CA.

Beck v Value Capital Ltd (No 2) [1976] 2 All ER 102, [1976] 1 WLR 572, CA; *affg* [1974] 3 All ER 442, [1975] 1 WLR 6.

Bouygues Offshore SA v Caspian Shipping Co (Nos 1, 3, 4 and 5) [1998] 2 Lloyd's Rep 461, CA.

Bremen, The v Zapata Off-Shore Co (1972) 407 US 1, US SC.

British Aerospace plc v Dee Howard Co [1993] 1 Lloyd's Rep 368.

British Airways Board v Laker Airways Ltd [1984] 3 All ER 39, [1985] AC 58, [1984] 3 WLR 413, HL.

a   *Castanho v Brown & Root (UK) Ltd* [1981] 1 All ER 143, [1981] AC 557, [1980] 3 WLR
    991, HL.
    Channel Tunnel Group Ltd v Balfour Beatty Construction Ltd [1993] 1 All ER 664,
    [1993] AC 334, [1993] 2 WLR 262, HL.
    Citi-March Ltd v Neptune Orient Lines Ltd [1996] 2 All ER 545, [1996] 1 WLR 1367.
    Continental Bank NA v Aeokos Cia Naviera SA [1994] 2 All ER 540, [1994] 1 WLR 588,
b   CA.
    Credit Suisse First Boston (Europe) v MLC (Bermuda) Ltd [1999] 1 All ER (Comm) 237.
    DSV Silo-und Verwaltungsgesellschaft mbH v Sennar (owners), The Sennar (No 2)
    [1985] 2 All ER 104, [1985] 1 WLR 490, HL.
    Eleftheria, The [1969] 2 All ER 641, [1970] P 94, [1969] 2 WLR 1073.
c   *Evans Marshall & Co Ltd v Bertola SA* [1973] 1 All ER 992, [1973] 1 WLR 349, CA.
    *FAI General Insurance Co Ltd v Ocean Marine Mutual Protection and Indemnity
    Association* (1997) 41 NSWLR 559, NSW SC.
    Fehmarn, The [1958] 1 All ER 333, [1958] 1 WLR 159, CA.
    *Halifax Overseas Freighters v Rasno Export Technoprominport and Polskie Linie
d   Oceaniczne PPW, The Pine Hill* [1958] 2 Lloyd's Rep 146.
    Holland v Leslie [1894] 2 QB 450, CA.
    Johnson v Taylor Bros & Co Ltd [1920] AC 144, HL.
    Kidd v van Heeren [1998] 1 NZLR 324, NZ HC.
    Mackender v Feldia AG [1966] 3 All ER 847, [1967] 2 QB 590, [1967] 2 WLR 119, CA.
e   *Mahavir Minerals Ltd v Cho Yang Shipping Co Ltd, The MC Pearl* [1997] 1 Lloyd's Rep 566.
    Mercedes-Benz AG v Leiduck [1995] 3 All ER 929, [1996] AC 284, [1995] 3 WLR 718, PC.
    Siskina (cargo owners) v Distos Cia Naviera SA, The Siskina [1977] 3 All ER 803,
    [1979] AC 210, [1977] 3 WLR 818, HL.
    SNI Aérospatiale v Lee Kui Jak [1987] 3 All ER 510, [1987] AC 871, [1987] 3 WLR 59, PC.
f   *South Carolina Insurance Co v Assurantie Maatschappij 'de Zeven Provincien' NV; South
    Carolina Insurance Co v Al Ahlia Insurance Co* [1986] 3 All ER 487, [1987] AC 24,
    [1986] 3 WLR 398, HL.
    Spiliada Maritime Corp v Cansulex Ltd, The Spiliada [1986] 3 All ER 843, [1987] AC
    460, [1986] 3 WLR 972, HL.
    Taunton-Collins v Cromie [1964] 2 All ER 332, [1964] 1 WLR 633, CA.
g   *Unterweser Reederei GmbH v Zapata Off-Shore Co, The Chaparral* [1968] 2 Lloyd's Rep
    158, CA.
    Volkswagen Canada Inc v Auto Haus Frohlich Ltd [1986] 1 WWR 380, Alta CA.

    Appeal
h   Armco Inc, Armco Financial Services Corp, Armco Financial Services International
    Ltd, Armco Pacific Ltd and Northwestern National Insurance Co (the Armco
    group) appealed with permission of the Appeal Committee of the House of Lords
    given on 21 February 2001 from the order of the Court of Appeal (Stuart-Smith and
    Sedley LJJ, Brooke LJ dissenting) ([2000] 1 All ER (Comm) 641) on 29 March 2000
j   granting the respondent, Thomas Roger Donohue, an injunction restraining the
    Armco group from suing him in any forum other than England for claims said to
    arise out of the circumstances surrounding the collapse of an insurance business
    and a debt collection business, both based in England, and allowing his appeal
    from the order of Aikens J ([2000] 1 All ER (Comm) 425) on 15 July 1999 whereby
    he dismissed Mr Donohue's application for such an injunction. The facts are set
    out in the opinion of Lord Bingham of Cornhill.

Lord Grabiner QC and *Daniel Toledano* (instructed by *Freshfields*) for the Armco group.

Peter Leaver QC, Robert Howe and *Camilla Bingham* (instructed by *Simmons & Simmons*) for Mr Donohue.

Their Lordships took time for consideration.

13 December 2001. The following opinions were delivered.

LORD BINGHAM OF CORNHILL.

[1] My Lords, the issue in this appeal is whether an injunction should have been granted to restrain the prosecution of proceedings in New York and, if so, in whose favour it should have been granted.

[2] By a summons issued on 8 March 1999 Mr Donohue, the respondent to this appeal, sought such an injunction against the five companies, all of them in the Armco group, which are named as the appellants before the House. Aikens J at first instance declined to grant an injunction: [2000] 1 All ER (Comm) 425. His decision was reversed by a majority of the Court of Appeal (Stuart-Smith and Sedley LJJ, Brooke LJ dissenting) [2000] 1 All ER (Comm) 641, who granted an injunction. The facts giving rise to this appeal were helpfully summarised by the judge and Stuart-Smith LJ: see [2000] 1 All ER (Comm) 425 at 427–431 and [2000] 1 All ER (Comm) 641 at 644–648 of the respective judgments. Stuart-Smith LJ also appended to his judgment (at 672) an annex giving details of the companies and individuals involved in the proceedings and an explanation of the acronyms used in his judgment. Both the factual summary and the annex should be treated as incorporated in this opinion, which permits more economical reference to be made to the background history.

[3] The parties fall into two camps. One camp comprises Armco Inc, the parent company of the Armco group, a conglomerate based in the United States, and four other companies known by their initial letters (AFSC, AFSIL, APL and NNIC). These five companies are plaintiffs in the New York proceedings already mentioned and defendants (or potential defendants) in this English action and are named as appellants before the House. This camp also included Armco Financial Services Europe Ltd (AFSEL), a company which has now been dissolved.

[4] The second camp comprises, first of all, Mr Donohue, a defendant in the New York proceedings and the claimant here. It also comprises a number of potential co-claimants (PCCs), all of them defendants in the New York proceedings: Mr Rossi and his Ohio company known as ITRS; Mr Stinson and his Ohio company known as IROS; Wingfield Ltd, a Jersey company; and another Jersey company known as CISHL. Another defendant was sued in New York, Mr Atkins, but he settled the claim against him.

[5] The Armco group formerly included several insurance companies together known as the British National Insurance Group (BNIG). The BNIG ceased to write new business and entered run-off status in 1984. It thus represented a liability to Armco, since claims under existing policies had to be met, and negotiations for the sale of the business were set in train. On the Armco side, the negotiations were conducted by Messrs Rossi and Stinson, two senior and long-serving Armco executives, both of them United States citizens and residents. The prospective buyers were Mr Donohue and Mr Atkins, also senior and long-serving Armco executives, but United Kingdom citizens resident in Singapore and England respectively.

a
[6] The shares in the BNIG were owned by AFSIL and AFSEL. To effect the sale of the business Armco sold its shares in the BNIG. To this end it incorporated CISHL. AFSC injected $US 32·5m in cash and securities into CISHL. A further $US 10m was transferred from AFSEL to CISHL. On 3 September 1991 AFSIL and AFSEL each executed an agreement (referred to as 'the transfer agreements') transferring all their assets in the BNIG into CISHL. On the same day Wingfield
b
acquired all the shares in CISHL under a sale and purchase agreement bearing the same date under which Wingfield was named as the purchaser. After the sale the BNIG was renamed the North Atlantic Insurance Group (NAG), the leading company of which was called the North Atlantic Insurance Company Ltd (NAIC).

[7] Many of the facts surrounding these transactions are the subject of acute controversy between the parties. But two points central to this appeal are not in
c
doubt. First, the only parties to these three agreements were (on the Armco side) AFSIL, AFSEL and AFSC and (on what may be called the Donohue side) CISHL, Wingfield, Mr Donohue and Mr Atkins. It is now accepted that, on the dissolution of AFSEL, Armco Inc succeeded to the rights and obligations of that company, so it also is to be treated as a party to one of the transfer agreements and to the sale
d
and purchase agreement. But the other companies in the Armco group (APL and NNIC) and several of the PCCs (Messrs Rossi and Stinson and their respective companies ITRS and IROS) were not parties to any of the three agreements. Secondly, each of the three agreements contained an express stipulation that the contract was governed by English law, made provision for service on a nominated agent of the vendor's solicitors in England and, most importantly,
e
provided for the exclusive jurisdiction of the English court. In the sale and purchase agreement it was provided that 'the parties hereby irrevocably submit themselves to the exclusive jurisdiction of the English Courts to settle any dispute which may arise out of or in connection with this Agreement'. The exclusive jurisdiction clause in each of the transfer agreements was differently worded, but
f
no point has been taken on the difference of wording.

[8] Several years passed before, in early 1997, NAIC went into provisional liquidation with other group companies and a winding-up petition was presented to the High Court. From about this date, it appears that there were a series of discussions between a lawyer representing Armco and Mr Atkins, who had resigned from the NAG in 1995. Mr Atkins made a series of statements, the last
g
of them in evidence dated September 1998. On this statement Armco strongly rely in support of their case.

[9] On 5 August 1998 proceedings were issued by the five Armco appellants in New York against NAIC, Mr Donohue, Mr Atkins, all the six PCCs (Messrs Rossi and Stinson and their respective companies, Wingfield and CISHL), and NPV Ltd
h
(a Nevis company). The proceedings were based on what the amended complaint described as 'an international fraud of immense proportions'. The amended complaint is a substantial document, running to more than 70 pages and including 17 specific counts. It is not easily summarised, but the broad thrust of the Armco companies' case is clear enough. They contend that a secret agreement
j
(recorded in writing) was made between Messrs Donohue, Atkins, Rossi and Stinson in New York in April 1991. Pursuant to this agreement Armco would be fraudulently induced to inject an extra-large sum into the BNIG and the four would then buy the BNIG, thus enriched, through Wingfield, a Jersey company which they (or some of them) owned. Since Messrs Rossi and Stinson were Armco executives negotiating on behalf of their employer their conduct was a flagrant breach of the duty they owed to their employer. The plan was

implemented. Much of the money injected into the group has, it is alleged, been
siphoned off by the four for their own ends. But the alleged fraud did not end *a*
there. Armco also contend that, as part of the secret plan, the group of four
fraudulently induced Armco (by APL) to enter into debt collection contracts with
NPV, the Nevis company which they owned: these contracts are said to have
been unduly favourable to NPV and to have enabled the four to take exorbitant
fees for themselves. It is further alleged that the four fraudulently obtained *b*
money from two trust funds set up earlier to give financial protection to NNIC
against claims by policyholders of an insurer whose business NNIC had taken
over. In this way, it is said, the four fraudulently depleted the trust funds by some
$US 16m after the 3 September 1991 agreements. A further complaint is that,
between 1991 and 1997, the four diverted funds from the NAG to themselves by
means of various commission, consultancy and dividend payments. The New *c*
York proceedings also included claims under the Federal Racketeer Influenced
and Corrupt Organizations Act (18 USC § 1962(c)) (the RICO Act), which enables
a successful plaintiff to recover triple, punitive and exemplary damages.

[10] All the PCCs (Messrs Rossi and Stinson and their respective companies,
Wingfield and CISHL) moved to dismiss the New York proceedings against them *d*
on various grounds, a motion denied by Judge Schwartz sitting in the District
Court of the Southern District of New York on 30 September 1999. Mr Donohue
did not take part in that proceeding, but had instead issued the present summons
applying for an injunction on 8 March 1999. Application was also made in the
action to join the PCCs as claimants. APL and NNIC applied to set aside service
upon them.   *e*

[11] These three applications came before Aikens J who gave his reserved
judgment on 15 July 1999. On the third summons he ordered that service on APL
and NNIC be set aside ([2000] 1 All ER (Comm) 425 at 448 (para 68)). This
decision was upheld by the Court of Appeal ([2000] 1 All ER (Comm) 641 at 657
(para 46) and 667 (para 80)). It has not been challenged before the House.   *f*

[12] On the second summons, the judge decided that the PCCs should not be
joined as claimants in the English action ([2000] 1 All ER (Comm) 425 at 441
(para 50) and 447 (para 67)). The majority in the Court of Appeal took a different
view and held that they should be joined ([2000] 1 All ER (Comm) 641 at 660
(paras 52–53) and 671 (para 98)). Brooke LJ held that there were no grounds for
allowing any of the American PCCs (Messrs Rossi and Stinson and their *g*
respective companies) to be joined as claimants: [2000] 1 All ER (Comm) 641 at
669–670 (paras 89–92). The propriety of joining the PCCs as claimants in this
action is one of the major issues before the House.

[13] On the first summons, the judge held that an injunction restraining
proceedings in New York should not be granted to Mr Donohue. In reaching that *h*
conclusion he made two important findings. The first was expressed in paras 42
and 43 of his judgment ([2000] 1 All ER (Comm) 425 at 439):

'42. I have decided that the claims raised in the NY proceedings based on
a pre-existing conspiracy to defraud Armco are not claims that "arise out of" *j*
either the SPA [sale and purchase agreement] or the transfer agreements.
They "arise out of" the agreement to conspire against Armco to defraud it.
I have also concluded that the claims concerning the collection agreement
did not arise out of or in connection with the SPA or the transfer agreements.
I doubt the trust fund claims come within the EJCs [exclusive jurisdiction
clauses] too, but I was told that the trust fund claims may not be relevant

a
now that the NNIC/NAIC disputes have been settled subject to ratification by the Court. Thus at least the issues raised in counts 1 to 8 and 9 to 12 [of the amended complaint in the New York proceedings] are not within the EJCs.

    43. This means that much of the disputes raised in the NY proceedings are outside the scope of the EJCs.'

b
The second important finding was that Armco Inc had never succeeded to the rights and obligations of AFSEL under the transfer agreement and the sale and purchase agreement to which AFSEL had been party and so had never become bound by the exclusive jurisdiction clause in those agreements (at 435 (para 28)). The judge accordingly approached Mr Donohue's application by considering
c
whether the New York proceedings against him were vexatious and oppressive and concluded that they were not ([2000] 1 All ER (Comm) 425 at 445–457 (paras 65–66)). All three members of the Court of Appeal disagreed with these two findings, although with some qualifications by Brooke LJ concerning the first: [2000] 1 All ER (Comm) 641 at 652–653 (paras 30–31), 652 (para 27), 664
d
(para 67) and 671 (para 97). The Court of Appeal held that these errors vitiated the judge's exercise of discretion and so entitled the Court of Appeal to exercise its discretion afresh (at 653 (para 32) and 668–669 (para 87)).

    [14] The Court of Appeal's conclusions on these two points have not been in issue before the House. Armco Inc accepts that as the successor to AFSEL it is bound by the exclusive jurisdiction clauses in the transfer agreement to which
e
AFSEL was party and in the sale and purchase agreement to the extent that AFSEL would itself have been bound had it not been dissolved. Armco Inc also asserts that as the ultimate victim of the alleged conspiracy it has claims independent of those derived from AFSEL, an assertion challenged by Mr Donohue and the PCCs. On the scope of the clauses, the Armco companies accept that the clauses
f
cover claims based on the conspiracy which preceded the making of the agreements as well as the misrepresentations and concealment which procured them to be made. The scope of the clauses was not the subject of argument before the House and I do not think it appropriate to give detailed consideration to this aspect of the case. The exclusive jurisdiction clause in the sale and purchase agreement, quoted above, was in wide terms. The practice of the English courts
g
is to give such clauses, as between the parties to them, a generous interpretation.

    [15] The Court of Appeal granted an injunction against the first three Armco defendants (Armco Inc, AFSC and AFSIL) restraining them from commencing or continuing proceedings against any of the claimants (Messrs Donohue, Rossi and Stinson, IROS, ITRS, Wingfield and CISHL) in any court other than those of
h
England and Wales regarding any dispute arising out of the management buy-out, defined to mean the 1991 disposal of the BNIG. The injunction was expressed to apply in particular to the Armco companies' New York proceedings already referred to, and to the numbered counts which were held to cover the 1991 management buy-out. Thus the injunction did not apply to APL and NNIC,
j
the joinder of which companies had been disallowed, and was limited to the causes of action held to fall within the exclusive jurisdiction clauses. But the benefit of the exclusive jurisdiction clauses was extended to the four PCCs who were not party to them (Messrs Rossi and Stinson and their respective companies). The object of the injunction was plainly to give effect to the exclusive jurisdiction clauses and to ensure trial in England of the issues arising out of or connected with the management buy-out between all the parties involved.

[16] The grant of an anti-suit injunction, as of any other injunction, involves an exercise of discretion by the court. To exercise its discretion reliably and rationally, the court must have the fullest possible knowledge and understanding of all the circumstances relevant to the litigation and the parties to it. This is particularly true of an anti-suit injunction because, as explained below, the likely effect of an injunction on proceedings in the foreign and the domestic forum and on parties not bound by the injunction may be matters very material to the decision whether an injunction should be granted or not. Thus although the two main issues before the House cannot be regarded entirely independently of each other, it is preferable to consider the issue of joinder of the PCCs before considering the grant of an anti-suit injunction more generally.

Joinder of the PCCs

[17] CISHL was party to each of the transfer agreements. Wingfield was party to the sale and purchase agreement. All three agreements contained an English exclusive jurisdiction clause. Both companies have been sued by Armco in New York. Both have claims falling within RSC Ord 11, r 1(1)(d)(iii) and (iv) (now CPR 6.20(5)(c) and (d)) entitling them to seek leave to serve proceedings out of the jurisdiction. Under RSC Ord 15, r 6(2)(b)(ii) (now CPR 19.2(2)) the court has power to add these companies as claimants if it considers it desirable to do so. Thus if the court should consider it desirable to do so there is no jurisdictional objection to the grant of leave to add CISHL and Wingfield as claimants in Mr Donohue's action and to give leave (if it were needed) to CISHL and Wingfield to serve AFSIL and Armco Inc (as the successor to AFSEL) out of the jurisdiction. The basis of their claim is in principle the same as that of Mr Donohue, but since they seek to be added to existing proceedings they must persuade the court that it is desirable to add them. The decision whether it is desirable to add them will be heavily influenced by the decision whether to join the other PCCs and whether Mr Donohue upholds his claim to the grant of an anti-suit injunction.

[18] The other four PCCs (Messrs Rossi and Stinson and their respective companies) are in a different position. None was a party to either transfer agreement or to the sale and purchase agreement and so none has the benefit of the English exclusive jurisdiction clause. It is common ground that none has any cause of action which would entitle the court to give leave to serve proceedings out of the jurisdiction under RSC Ord 11, r 1 or CPR 6.20, and thus none could bring independent proceedings against any Armco company in England unless that company submitted to the jurisdiction. But these PCCs rely on the broad power of the court under RSC Ord 15, r 6 and CPR Pt 19, which is said to be unconstrained by the rules on service out of the jurisdiction, and it is said to be desirable to add them because they have a substantial cause of action entitling them to seek an anti-suit injunction. The Armco companies reply that a foreign party, even if already properly sued within the jurisdiction, may not be subjected to a claim for which leave to serve out could not be granted and further that, in the absence of any contractual right to rely on an exclusive jurisdiction clause, these PCCs have on the material before the House no cause of action entitling them to seek an anti-suit injunction. The first issue between the parties is whether these PCCs can show any cause of action which would entitle them to claim an injunction.

[19] The jurisdiction of the English court to grant injunctions, both generally and in relation to the conduct of foreign proceedings, has been the subject of

a consideration by the House of Lords and the Privy Council in a series of decisions in recent years which include *Siskina (cargo owners) v Distos Cia Naviera SA, The Siskina* [1977] 3 All ER 803, [1979] AC 210; *Castanho v Brown & Root (UK) Ltd* [1981] 1 All ER 143, [1981] AC 557; *British Airways Board v Laker Airways Ltd* [1984] 3 All ER 39, [1985] AC 58; *South Carolina Insurance Co v Assurantie Maatschappij 'de Zeven Provincien' NV; South Carolina Insurance Co v Al Ahlia Insurance Co* [1986] 3 All ER

b 487, [1987] AC 24; *SNI Aérospatiale v Lee Kui Jak* [1987] 3 All ER 510, [1987] AC 871; and *Airbus Industrie GIE v Patel* [1998] 2 All ER 257, [1999] 1 AC 119. Those decisions reveal some development of principle and there has in other decisions (for example, *Mercedes-Benz AG v Leiduck* [1995] 3 All ER 929, [1996] AC 284) been some divergence of opinion. But certain principles governing the grant of an injunction to restrain a party from commencing or pursuing legal proceedings in

c a foreign jurisdiction, in cases such as the present, as between the Armco companies and these PCCs, are now beyond dispute. They were identified by Lord Goff of Chieveley giving the opinion of the Judicial Committee of the Privy Council in the *SNI Aérospatiale* case [1987] 3 All ER 510 at 519, [1987] AC 871 at 892: (1) the jurisdiction is to be exercised when the ends of justice require it;

d (2) where the court decides to grant an injunction restraining proceedings in a foreign court, its order is directed not against the foreign court but against the parties so proceeding or threatening to proceed; (3) an injunction will only be issued restraining a party who is amenable to the jurisdiction of the court, against whom an injunction will be an effective remedy; and (4) since such an order indirectly affects the foreign court, the jurisdiction is one which must be exercised

e with caution.

In the *SNI Aérospatiale* case the issue was whether proceedings in Texas should be restrained in favour of Brunei, and Lord Goff summarised the guiding principles:

f   'In the opinion of their Lordships, in a case such as the present where a remedy for a particular wrong is available both in the English (or, as here, the Brunei) court and in a foreign court, the English (or Brunei) court will, generally speaking, only restrain the plaintiff from pursuing proceedings in the foreign court if such pursuit would be vexatious or oppressive. This presupposes that, as a general rule, the English or Brunei court must

g   conclude that it provides the natural forum for the trial of the action, and further, since the court is concerned with the ends of justice, that account must be taken not only of injustice to the defendant if the plaintiff is allowed to pursue the foreign proceedings, but also of injustice to the plaintiff is he is not allowed to do so. So, as a general rule, the court will not grant an injunction if, by doing so, it will deprive the plaintiff of advantages in the

h   foreign forum of which it would be unjust to deprive him. Fortunately, however, as the present case shows, that problem can often be overcome by appropriate undertakings given by the defendant, or by granting an injunction on appropriate terms, just as, in cases of stay of proceedings, the parallel problem of advantages to the plaintiff in the domestic forum which

j   is, prima facie, inappropriate can likewise often be solved by granting a stay on terms.' (See [1987] 3 All ER 510 at 522, [1987] AC 871 at 896.)

[20] If these principles are applied to the present case it is in my opinion plain that an anti-suit injunction could not properly be granted in favour of these PCCs. The judge (considering the position of Mr Donohue and all the PCCs) concluded that England was not the natural forum for these proceedings, that the connections

with England were slim and that the New York proceedings were not vexatious
and oppressive ([2000] 1 All ER (Comm) 425 at 445–447 (paras 65–66)).   *a*
Stuart-Smith LJ observed that if this were an alternative forum case he would not
necessarily disagree with the judge ([2000] 1 All ER (Comm) 641 at 655 (para 38)).
Brooke LJ considered that the convenient forum for the resolution of all disputes
between Messrs Rossi and Stinson and their former employers was clearly
situated on the other side of the Atlantic (at 669–670 (para 92)). Judge Schwartz   *b*
concluded that: 'Permitting this trial to proceed in New York would be neither
oppressive nor vexatious to defendants' and further said:

> 'This Court concludes that this action, involving US plaintiffs, mostly US
> or non-English defendants, and a fraudulent scheme that allegedly arose in
> New York, is far removed from the facts of those cases where courts granted   *c*
> the extraordinary remedy of forum non conveniens.'

The Armco companies are incorporated in Ohio, Delaware, Wisconsin and (in
the case of APL) Singapore. Messrs Rossi and Stinson and their companies have
no English links. The dispute between them and the Armco companies concerns
the alleged breach of the fiduciary duty they owed to their employers. It is plain   *d*
that England is not the natural forum for resolution of this dispute and that the
New York proceedings by the Armco companies against these PCCs are neither
vexatious nor oppressive.

[21] There is another more technical objection to the joinder of these PCCs.
In stating the third of his basic principles in the *SNI Aerospatiale* case, Lord Goff   *e*
made reference to 'a party who is amenable to the jurisdiction of the court'. This
echoed the language of Lord Diplock in his important statement of principle in
The Siskina [1977] 3 All ER 803 at 824, [1979] AC 210 at 256, which has been
understood to mean that the court may only grant an injunction where it has
personal jurisdiction over the defendant in the sense that he could be served
personally or under RSC Ord 11 (other than sub-r (i)): see *Channel Tunnel Group Ltd v*   *f*
Balfour Beatty Construction Ltd [1993] 1 All ER 664 at 668, [1993] AC 334 at 342 per
Lord Browne-Wilkinson. These PCCs could not, as already noted, have obtained
leave to serve out of the jurisdiction on any of the Armco companies in independent
proceedings. Service on APL and NNIC has been set aside. Does the amenability
of Armco Inc, AFSC and AFSIL to the jurisdiction of the English court by virtue   *g*
of their contractual relationship with Mr Donohue enable these PCCs to take
advantage of that relationship to effect service on the solicitors nominated by
those companies pursuant to the transfer and sale and purchase agreements, and
thus to prosecute a claim which could not otherwise have been prosecuted in this
forum? In my opinion it does not. Since *Holland v Leslie* [1894] 2 QB 450 the view
has prevailed that the court should refuse to allow an amendment of proceedings   *h*
which would introduce a new cause of action against a foreign defendant in
respect of which the court would have refused leave for service out of the
jurisdiction (see, for instance, *Beck v Value Capital Ltd (No 2)* [1974] 3 All ER 442,
[1975] 1 WLR 6, affirmed, although not on this point, [1976] 2 All ER 102, [1976]
1 WLR 572). This view seems to me to accord with principle. The jurisdiction   *j*
of the English court is territorial. A party resident abroad may be subjected to the
jurisdiction of the court to the extent (and only to the extent) that statute or rules
made under statute permit. It would emasculate that salutary rule if such a party,
properly served with notice of a claim falling within RSC Ord 11, r 1 or CPR 6.20,
were then to be exposed to claims falling outside the relevant rule. In exercising
its discretion to give leave to serve out of the jurisdiction the court will have

a regard to the substance of a claimant's complaint and not permit jurisdiction to be obtained by a mere device: *Johnson v Taylor Bros & Co Ltd* [1920] AC 144. It would be wrong in principle to allow these PCCs to use Mr Donohue's action as a Trojan horse in which to enter the proceedings when they could have shown no possible ground for doing so in their own right.

   [22] The majority of the Court of Appeal were in my opinion wrong to allow
b the joinder of these four PCCs, and I would accordingly set aside that order and refuse joinder.

The grant of an injunction to Mr Donohue

   [23] My Lords, I turn to the question whether an anti-suit injunction should be granted to Mr Donohue, recognising that as between him and the first three
c Armco appellants (Armco Inc, AFSC and AFSIL) there is a contractual obligation to submit any dispute which may arise out of or in connection with the sale and purchase agreement to the exclusive jurisdiction of the English court. It is plain that while some of the claims made by the Armco companies in the New York proceedings fall outside the scope of this clause, some claims central to the Armco
d companies' complaint fall within it. In this situation, exercise of the broad discretion conferred on the court by s 37 of the Supreme Court Act 1981 to grant an injunction in all cases in which it appears to the court to be just and convenient to do so is controlled by principles to be derived from a substantial line of authority here and abroad.

   [24] If contracting parties agree to give a particular court exclusive jurisdiction
e to rule on claims between those parties, and a claim falling within the scope of the agreement is made in proceedings in a forum other than that which the parties have agreed, the English court will ordinarily exercise its discretion (whether by granting a stay of proceedings in England, or by restraining the prosecution of proceedings in the non-contractual forum abroad, or by such other procedural
f order as is appropriate in the circumstances) to secure compliance with the contractual bargain, unless the party suing in the non-contractual forum (the burden being on him) can show strong reasons for suing in that forum. I use the word 'ordinarily' to recognise that where an exercise of discretion is called for there can be no absolute or inflexible rule governing that exercise, and also that a party may lose his claim to equitable relief by dilatoriness or other unconscionable
g conduct. But the general rule is clear: where parties have bound themselves by an exclusive jurisdiction clause effect should ordinarily be given to that obligation in the absence of strong reasons for departing from it. Whether a party can show strong reasons, sufficient to displace the other party's prima facie entitlement to enforce the contractual bargain, will depend on all the facts and circumstances of
h the particular case. In the course of his judgment in *The Eleftheria* [1969] 2 All ER 641 at 645–646, [1970] P 94 at 99–100, Brandon J helpfully listed some of the matters which might properly be regarded by the court when exercising its discretion, and his judgment has been repeatedly cited and applied. Brandon J did not intend his list to be comprehensive, but mentioned a number of matters,
j including the law governing the contract, which may in some cases be material. (I am mindful that the principles governing the grant of injunctions and stays are not the same: see the *SNI Aérospatiale* case [1987] 3 All ER 510 at 522, [1987] AC 871 at 896. Considerations of comity arise in the one case but not in the other. These differences need not, however, be explored in this case.)

   [25] Where the dispute is between two contracting parties, A and B, and A sues B in a non-contractual forum, and A's claims fall within the scope of the

exclusive jurisdiction clause in their contract, and the interests of other parties are not involved, effect will in all probability be given to the clause. That was the result in *Mackender v Feldia AG* [1966] 3 All ER 847, [1967] 2 QB 590; *Unterweser Reederei GmbH v Zapata Off-Shore Co, The Chaparral* [1968] 2 Lloyd's Rep 158; *The Eleftheria* [1969] 2 All ER 641, [1970] P 94; *DSV Silo-und Verwaltungsgesellschaft mbH v Sennar (owners), The Sennar (No 2)* [1985] 2 All ER 104, [1985] 1 WLR 490; *British Aerospace plc v Dee Howard Co* [1993] 1 Lloyd's Rep 368; *Continental Bank NA v Aeokos Cia Naviera SA* [1994] 2 All ER 540, [1994] 1 WLR 588; *Aggeliki Charis Compania Maritima SA v Pagnan SpA, The Angelic Grace* [1995] 1 Lloyd's Rep 87; and *Akai Pty Ltd v People's Insurance Co Ltd* [1998] 1 Lloyd's Rep 90. A similar approach has been followed by courts in the United States, Canada, Australia and New Zealand: see, for example, *The Bremen v Zapata Off-Shore Co* (1972) 407 US 1; *Volkswagen Canada Inc v Auto Haus Frohlich Ltd* [1986] 1 WWR 380; *FAI General Insurance Co Ltd v Ocean Marine Mutual Protection and Indemnity Association* (1997) 41 NSWLR 559; and *Kidd v van Heeren* [1998] 1 NZLR 324.

[26] *The Fehmarn* [1958] 1 All ER 333, [1958] 1 WLR 159 shows that this is not an invariable result. This was one of the earlier cases in the modern series. The Russian exclusive jurisdiction clause was a condition in a bill of lading, no doubt part of a standard form, and certainly not the subject of negotiation between the parties to the eventual dispute. That was between English owners of the bill and German owners of the vessel. The dispute was held to have a much closer connection with England than with Russia, and it was thought that the German owners did not object to the dispute being decided in England if they could avoid giving security. On those grounds, the judge having declined to stay the proceedings in England, the Court of Appeal upheld his decision.

[27] The authorities show that the English court may well decline to grant an injunction or a stay, as the case may be, where the interests of parties other than the parties bound by the exclusive jurisdiction clause are involved or grounds of claim not the subject of the clause are part of the relevant dispute so that there is a risk of parallel proceedings and inconsistent decisions. These decisions are instructive. In *Evans Marshall & Co Ltd v Bertola SA* [1973] 1 All ER 992, [1973] 1 WLR 349 there was a tripartite dispute but only two of the parties were bound by a clause conferring exclusive jurisdiction on the court in Barcelona. Kerr J at first instance was impressed by the undesirability of there being two actions, one in London and the other in Barcelona ([1973] 1 All ER 992 at 1001–1002, [1973] 1 WLR 349 at 363–364). The Court of Appeal took a similar view ([1973] 1 All ER 992 at 1002–1003, 1010, [1973] 1 WLR 349 at 377, 385). Sachs LJ thought separate trials particularly inappropriate where a conspiracy claim was in issue ([1973] 1 All ER 992 at 1002, [1973] 1 WLR 349 at 377). In *Aratra Potato Co Ltd v Egyptian Navigation Co, The El Amria* [1981] 2 Lloyd's Rep 119 the primary dispute was between cargo interests and the owner of the vessel, both parties being bound by a clause in the bill of lading conferring exclusive jurisdiction on the courts of Egypt. But the cargo interests had also issued proceedings against the Mersey Docks and Harbour Co, which was not bound by the clause. The Court of Appeal upheld the judge's decision refusing a stay. In the course of his leading judgment in the Court of Appeal Brandon LJ said (at 128):

'I agree entirely with the learned Judge's view on that matter, but would go rather further than he did in the passage from his judgment quoted above. By that I mean that I do not regard it merely as convenient that the two actions, in which many of the same issues fall to be determined, should be

a tried together; rather that I regard it as a potential disaster from a legal point
of view if they were not, because of the risk inherent in separate trials, one
in Egypt and the other in England, that the same issues might be determined
differently in the two countries. See as to this *Halifax Overseas Freighters Ltd. v.
Rasno Export Technoprominport and Polskie Linie Oceaniczne PPW, The Pine Hill*
([1958] 2 Lloyd's Rep 146) and *Taunton-Collins v. Cromie & Others* ([1964] 2 All ER
b 332, [1964] 1 WLR 633).'

Citi-March Ltd v Neptune Orient Lines Ltd [1996] 2 All ER 545, [1996] 1 WLR 1367
also involved third party interests and raised the possibility of inconsistent
decisions. Colman J regarded separate trials in England and Singapore as not only
inconvenient but also a potential source of injustice and made an order intended
c to achieve a composite trial in London despite a Singaporean exclusive jurisdiction
clause (see [1996] 2 All ER 545 at 553, [1996] 1 WLR 1367 at 1375–1376). *Mahavir
Minerals Ltd v Cho Yang Shipping Co Ltd, The MC Pearl* [1997] 1 Lloyd's Rep 566 again
involved third parties and raised the possibility of inconsistent findings. Despite
a clause conferring exclusive jurisdiction on the courts of Seoul, Rix J refused to
stay proceedings in England. He regarded the case as on all fours with the
d *Citi-March* case (at 575) and observed (at 569):

> 'It seems to me that so far the plaintiffs have shown strong cause why the
> jurisdiction clause should not be enforced. This is indeed a paradigm case for
> the concentration of all the relevant parties' disputes in a single jurisdiction.
> If in such a case a host of different jurisdiction clauses were to be observed,
e the casualty at the root of the action would become virtually untriable. The
> action would fragment and reduplicate, at vast cost.'

A similar approach is discernible in *Bouygues Offshore SA v Caspian Shipping Co
(Nos 1, 3, 4 and 5)* [1998] 2 Lloyd's Rep 461, in which the disputes involved four
f parties only two of whom were bound by an English exclusive jurisdiction clause.
Although the effect of the clause was described by Evans LJ as 'near-conclusive'
(at 467), an injunction to restrain proceedings in South Africa was refused. In
para 27 of his judgment (at 466) Evans LJ said:

> 'In my judgment, two questions arise, one a matter of principle. First,
g should the Court, when deciding whether or not to enforce the exclusive
> jurisdiction clause by means of an injunction which prevents Bouygues from
> continuing with its proceedings against Ultisol in South Africa, take into
> account the effects of such an injunction on persons who are not parties or
> entitled to enforce the contract containing the jurisdiction clause, Portnet
> and Caspian here, but who are both necessary and proper parties to the
h litigation wherever it is held? In my judgment, the clear answer to this
> question is "yes". Mr. Justice Clarke did so in his judgment and the contrary
> has not been argued before us. The relevance of the potential effects on third
> parties has been recognised in other authorities ...'

j Sir John Knox also held that proceedings should be allowed to continue in South
Africa because, among other reasons (at 470) 'this is the only way in which to
minimize, if not avoid altogether, the risk of inconsistent decisions in different
jurisdictions'.

[28] Not all cases can be so neatly categorised. In *Credit Suisse First Boston
(Europe) v MLC (Bermuda) Ltd* [1999] 1 All ER (Comm) 237 Rix J dealt with a case
in which there were four potential parties and three different agreements (or

classes of agreement) but only two of the parties were bound by an English a
exclusive jurisdiction clause under one of the agreements. There were
proceedings by C against A (the two parties to the clause) in England and
proceedings by A against C, B and D in New York alleging statutory breaches
relating to the agreement containing the clause and also under an agreement not
containing an exclusive jurisdiction clause, and including other claims such as a
claim for conversion. The judge gave leave, on their application, for B and D to b
be joined to C's action against A in England (at 248). A's application to stay the
proceedings by C in England was not pursued, but if it had been it would have
failed (at 257). On an application by C, B and D for an injunction to restrain A
suing them in New York, the judge granted an injunction but only to restrain the
prosecution of claims covered by the exclusive jurisdiction clause (at 259). The
judge was confronted in this case with a difficult procedural and jurisdictional c
tangle which permitted no wholly satisfactory solution. It was, however,
important to his decision that he did not judge it possible to make an order which
would ensure trial of all proceedings arising out of all the agreements in one
forum. He said (interpolating schematic references for the references he made to
named parties) (at 257): d

'(5) An important fact in this case, as it seems to me, is that, whether
I enforce [the exclusive jurisdiction clause] or not, I cannot ensure that all
litigation between [A] and [B, C and D] is carried forward in one jurisdiction
unless I would be prepared to extend my injunction to all the claims against
[B, C and D] in New York. That is because [the exclusive jurisdiction clause] e
does not bind [B and D]. That remains the case even if I assume that all the
claims against [C] come within [the exclusive jurisdiction clause], but I have
already stated that in my judgment that is not the case. It follows that unless
I am prepared not only to enforce [the exclusive jurisdiction clause] but also
to injunct [A's] claims against [B and D] and [A's] claims against [C] outside
[the exclusive jurisdiction clause], [A's] complaint in New York will continue f
in any event. On the other hand [counsel] has not pursued [A's] application
for a stay of [C's] action, but if he had, it would fail for the reasons for which
[counsel] cited *British Aerospace plc v Dee Howard Co* [1993] 1 Lloyd's Rep 368.
Thus the continuation of the proceedings in England is inevitable too.

(6) I would not, however, injunct the claims against [B and D] because, g
however undesirable it is in principle to have parallel litigation in two
jurisdictions, it seems to me the duplication of litigation does not in itself
make it in the interests of justice to injunct the New York proceedings in so
far as claims against [B] and [D] are concerned.'

[29] In seeking to apply this body of authority to the present case the first point h
to be made is that Mr Donohue has as against the first three Armco appellants a
strong prima facie right not to be the subject elsewhere than in England of claims
by those companies falling within the scope of the clause. Some of the claims
made against him by those companies in New York do fall within the clause. This
is an important and substantial, and not a formal or technical, right. At an earlier j
stage of this English litigation Armco sought to impeach the exclusive jurisdiction
clauses on the ground that they had been induced by the fraud of the four
conspirators. The judge not only rejected the contention that Armco executives
had been misled but also found that Armco's English and US lawyers had known
all about the clauses and their consequences and that Armco had had its own
good reasons for inserting English law and jurisdiction clauses in the contracts

a ([2000] 1 All ER (Comm) 425 at 437–439 (paras 35–40). There was no appeal against these conclusions. Thus Armco, having agreed to these clauses to serve their own ends, are now seeking to be released from their bargain. To permit them to do so exposes Mr Donohue to an obvious risk of injustice. This risk does not derive from the venue alone: Mr Donohue might, as a United Kingdom citizen, prefer to be sued in London rather than New York if he has to be sued
b anywhere, but to him, as a resident of Singapore, New York is not in itself an obviously more inconvenient forum than London. A more substantial objection may be founded on the perceived procedural disadvantages to him of being sued in New York: as the evidence suggests, the cost would be greater, trial would be by jury and costs would be very largely irrecoverable even if he were to succeed. But there are always points of this kind to be made when comparing one forum
c with another, and the standing, authority and expertise of the forum in which the New York proceedings are being pursued cannot be questioned. Much more significant, from Mr Donohue's viewpoint, are the RICO claims made against him. They could not be pursued against him in England. They could, if established in New York, lead to the award of swingeing damages against him.
d On agreement of the exclusive jurisdiction clause he could reasonably have felt confident that no RICO claim arising out of or in connection with the agreements could be pursued against him and it would represent an obvious injustice if he were now to be exposed to those claims.

[30] There is, as always, another side to the coin. All five Armco appellants have a clear prima facie right to pursue against Messrs Rossi, and Stinson and
e their respective companies any claim they choose in any convenient forum where they can found jurisdiction. They have successfully founded jurisdiction in New York. There is, as I have already concluded, no ground upon which this court could properly seek to restrain those proceedings. It would not be appropriate for the English courts to form any judgment, however tentative, on
f the merits of the Armco companies' claims, beyond noting that lack of merit was not one of the grounds on which the PCCs invited Judge Schwartz to dismiss the proceedings in New York. It must be assumed that the claims made by the Armco companies against their former employees Messrs Rossi and Stinson, including the RICO claims, are serious and substantial claims. There is nothing whatever to suggest that these claims will not proceed in New York whether or
g not an injunction is granted to Mr Donohue.

[31] It must further be noted that APL and NNIC have a clear prima facie right to pursue against Mr Donohue, Wingfield and CISHL also any claim they choose in any convenient forum where they can found jurisdiction. They have successfully founded jurisdiction in New York. I have already recorded that service of the
h English proceedings on APL and NNIC has been set aside. There is no ground upon which the English court could properly restrain their proceedings in New York. It appears, as Stuart-Smith LJ held ([2000] 1 All ER (Comm) 641 at 661 (para 54(3)), that the claims of APL and NNIC relate to the collection agreement and the trust fund withdrawals rather than the allegedly fraudulent management
j buy-out, but these claims also cannot be treated as lacking merit. They are proceeding in New York, and everything suggests that they will continue in New York whether or not the English court grants an injunction to Mr Donohue.

[32] Similarly, the first three Armco appellants have a clear prima facie right to pursue against Mr Donohue, Wingfield and CISHL any claim not covered by the exclusive jurisdiction clauses in any convenient forum where they can found jurisdiction. They have successfully founded jurisdiction in New York. To the

extent that the claims of these Armco companies do not arise out of or in
connection with the transfer agreements and the sale and purchase agreement,
they fall outside the exclusive jurisdiction clauses, and there is no ground upon
which the English court could properly restrain these proceedings. Everything
suggests that they will continue in New York whether or not the English court
grants an injunction to Mr Donohue.

[33] Thus Mr Donohue's strong prima facie right to be sued here on claims
made by the other parties to the exclusive jurisdiction clause so far as the
claims made fall within that clause is matched by the clear prima facie right of the
Armco companies to pursue in New York the claims mentioned in the last three
paragraphs. The crucial question is whether, on the fact of this case, the Armco
companies can show strong reasons why the court should displace Mr Donohue's
clear prima facie entitlement. If strong reasons are to be found (and the need for
strong reasons is underlined in this case by the potential injustice to Mr Donohue,
already noted, if effect is not given to the exclusive jurisdiction clauses) they must
lie in the prospect, if an injunction is granted, of litigation between the Armco
companies on one side and Mr Donohue and the PCCs on the other continuing
partly in England and partly in New York. What weight should be given to that
consideration in the circumstances of this case?

[34] I am driven to conclude that great weight should be given to it. The
Armco companies contend that they were the victims of a fraudulent conspiracy
perpetrated by Messrs Donohue, Atkins, Rossi and Stinson. Determination of the
truth or falsity of that allegation lies at the heart of the dispute concerning the
transfer agreements and the sale and purchase agreement. It will of course be
necessary for any court making that determination to consider any contemporary
documentation and any undisputed evidence of what was said, done or known.
But also, and crucially, it will be necessary for any such court to form a judgment
on the honesty and motives of the four alleged conspirators. It would not seem
conceivable, on the Armco case, that some of the four were guilty of the
nefarious conduct alleged against them and others not. It seems to me plain that
in a situation of this kind the interests of justice are best served by the submission
of the whole dispute to a single tribunal which is best fitted to make a reliable,
comprehensive judgment on all the matters in issue. A procedure which
permitted the possibility of different conclusions by different tribunals, perhaps
made on different evidence, would in my view run directly counter to the
interests of justice.

[35] Stuart-Smith LJ (at 656–657 (paras 42–44)) regarded the subject matter of
the collection agreement complaints as 'quite different' from that involving the
first three Armco appellants in relation to the transfer agreements and the sale
and purchase agreement. He discounted the significance of the trust fund
withdrawal claims on the ground that they had almost certainly been settled (at
657 (para 45)), although it is noteworthy that the settlement agreement made
with NAIC expressly preserved the right of NNIC to pursue claims against Messrs
Rossi, Stinson, Donohue and Atkins, ITRS, IROS, Wingfield, NPV and CISHL in
the New York proceedings. It is true that the collection agreement and the trust
fund withdrawals give rise to different grounds of claim. But the principal actors
are the same, and Armco contends, rightly or wrongly, that these were further
manifestations of the plot made by the four conspirators to enrich themselves at
the expense of Armco. I cannot for my part accept that the ends of justice would
be well served if Armco's allegations concerning the transfer and sale and
purchase agreements were determined in England and its allegations concerning

a the collection agreement and trust fund withdrawals were determined in separate proceedings in New York. The judgment made of the motives and honesty of the four alleged conspirators in the one context would plainly have an important bearing on the judgment made in the other.

[36] In my opinion, and subject to an important qualification, the ends of justice would be best served by a single composite trial in the only forum in which

b a single composite trial can be procured, which is New York, and accordingly I find strong reasons for not giving effect to the exclusive jurisdiction clause in favour of Mr Donohue. In New York proceedings Mr Donohue will be entitled to claim that the sale and purchase agreement is governed by English law. And Lord Grabiner, representing Armco, has accepted that Armco's breach of contract in suing elsewhere than in the contractual forum could found a claim by

c Mr Donohue for any damage he has suffered as a result. The qualification is that he should be protected against liability under the RICO claims made against him because of the obvious injustice to him which such liability would in the circumstances involve. But before considering whether such a protection can and should be afforded to Mr Donohue it is necessary to address an important

d preliminary question.

[37] The discretion whether or not to grant an injunction was in the first instance that of the judge. His exercise of discretion was entitled to be respected unless, on grounds of his error or misdirection, the Court of Appeal was entitled to exercise its discretion afresh. The Court of Appeal held, rightly, that such grounds existed, and did exercise its discretion afresh. But the exercise of

e discretion is not at large in this House: the Court of Appeal's exercise of discretion must in its turn be respected unless on grounds of error or misdirection the House is entitled to exercise its own discretion. Having regard to the long and closely-reasoned leading judgment of Stuart-Smith LJ, I would not lightly disregard the majority's conclusion.

f [38] I am, however, persuaded that the discretionary judgment made by the Court of Appeal is fundamentally vitiated by an incorrect view of the future shape of this litigation. In his judgment, Stuart-Smith LJ considered the grant of an injunction to Mr Donohue before considering whether Messrs Rossi and Stinson and their respective companies should be joined as claimants, and this enabled Mr Donohue to contend in argument that the Court of Appeal's decision on

g grant of an injunction should stand despite its conclusion, incorrect as I have held it to be, on joinder. But this reading of Stuart-Smith LJ's judgment cannot in my opinion be sustained. I think it is plain, in particular from para 42 of his judgment ([2000] 1 All ER (Comm) 641 at 656), that Stuart-Smith LJ contemplated that all disputes between the Armco companies and Messrs Donohue, Rossi and Stinson

h relating to the transfer and sale and purchase agreements would be resolved in the English forum. This enabled him to say:

> 'The issues in the claim of AFSC, AFSIL and the derivative claim of Armco Inc in relation to the MBO [management buy-out] are whether there was the secret agreement alleged, whether Mr Rossi and Mr Stinson were beneficially
>
> j interested in Wingfield at the time, whether $US 30m was an excessive sum and whether $US 10m worth of AFSEL's assets were secretly and fraudulently transferred. If these allegations are made out, Mr Donohue, Mr Rossi, Mr Stinson and Wingfield will be liable . . .'

He was not there recognising the possibility that different conclusions might be reached in the cases of Mr Rossi and Mr Stinson on the one hand and Mr Donohue and Wingfield on the other, a very unlikely event in the case of a single composite *a* trial but an entirely possible outcome if parallel trials relating to the management buy-out took place in both England and New York. This incorrect view was in my opinion compounded by his treatment of the collection and trust fund withdrawal claims as different and separate from the management buy-out claims. For reasons already given I cannot accept this view. Had Stuart-Smith LJ reached the view which I have reached on the joinder of Messrs Rossi and Stinson *b* and their companies, I feel sure that he would have been gravely concerned at the prospect of the same issue being determined in different tribunals, with the obvious and highly undesirable risk of inconsistent findings and decisions. For these reasons I am of the opinion that members of the House are entitled and bound to exercise their discretion afresh.

c

[39] The interests of justice are in my judgment best served if an anti-suit injunction is denied to Mr Donohue but an undertaking proffered on behalf of the Armco companies (defined to include the five Armco appellants) is accepted in the following terms:

'The Armco companies ... confirm that they undertake not to enforce *d* against Mr Donohue, Wingfield or CISHL any multiple or punitive damages awarded in the New York proceedings whether awarded pursuant to the RICO statute or common law.

For the avoidance of doubt, the above undertaking (i) shall not restrict the Armco companies from seeking to enforce any award made in the New York *e* proceedings for damages which are not multiple or punitive; (ii) shall relate only to enforcement; and (iii) as against any defendant in the New York proceedings other than Mr Donohue, Wingfield or CISHL, shall have no effect whatsoever in respect of the Armco companies pursuing or enforcing any claim or award in the New York proceedings whether for multiple or *f* punitive damages or otherwise.'

If there were any doubt about the efficacy of this proffered undertaking in relation not only to Mr Donohue but also Wingfield and CISHL, I would order the joinder of those companies. But I am satisfied that this is an unnecessary step which would serve no useful purpose. I would accordingly refuse the application *g* of these parties to be joined as claimants in the present action. In the result, I would allow the appeal, on the undertaking just recited, and set aside the orders of the Court of Appeal joining the PCCs as claimants and granting an injunction to Mr Donohue.

h

LORD MACKAY OF CLASHFERN.

[40] My Lords, I have had the advantage of reading in draft the speech delivered by my noble and learned friend Lord Bingham of Cornhill. For the reasons he gives with which I agree, I also would allow the appeal on the terms he has proposed. *j*

LORD NICHOLLS OF BIRKENHEAD.

[41] My Lords, I have had the advantage of reading in draft the speech of my noble and learned friend Lord Bingham of Cornhill. For the reasons he gives, and with which I agree, I too would allow this appeal.

LORD HOBHOUSE OF WOODBOROUGH.

a

[42] My Lords, I agree that the appeal should be allowed on the terms stated in the speech of my noble and learned friend Lord Bingham of Cornhill with which I agree. This appeal has not involved any disputed question of principle but has turned upon the application of established principles to the factual complexities of international multi-party disputes as exemplified by the facts of

b this particular case. It is because we are exceptionally differing from the Court of Appeal on a question of discretion that I will briefly add my own reasons for doing so.

[43] The case has two aspects. The primary aspect is whether Mr Donohue should be granted the 'anti-suit' injunction for which he has asked the court to restrain proceedings in New York or anywhere else other than in London. This ultimately turns upon the exercise of the court's discretion. The Court of Appeal

c were undoubtedly right to conclude ([2000] 1 All ER (Comm) 641 at 652–653) that, as the judge had made an error in holding that Armco Inc was not bound by the exclusive jurisdiction clause and had construed the clause as not having a wide enough scope to cover the disputes being raised in New York against Mr Donohue, this meant that his exercise of the discretion was wrongly based

d and the Court of Appeal were obliged to address the exercise of the discretion afresh. By a majority, the Court of Appeal decided to grant the injunction in a limited form, limited to the first three defendants and excluding claims in relation to the 'collection agreement' and the trust funds.

[44] The second aspect involves the subsidiary question whether Mr Rossi and Mr Stinson and their two companies, the four of the so-called 'PCCs' [potential

e co-claimants], should be joined as plaintiffs in Mr Donohue's English action and, if so, likewise granted an injunction. Formally, I agree that the question of joinder was dealt with by the majority of the Court of Appeal only after they had decided the primary question of whether Mr Donohue should be granted an injunction and that therefore it could be said, and the respondents so argued

f before this House, that the reversal of the Court of Appeal's decision on the second aspect would not invalidate their decision on the primary question. This, however, faces the respondents and the Court of Appeal with a dilemma. A central factor in the exercise of the discretion whether or not to grant any injunction was an assessment of what will be the position in New York and London if an injunction is granted. (If no injunction is granted the position is

g simple: the proceedings in New York will continue and there will be no proceedings, anyway at this stage, in London.) If the Court of Appeal have arrived at their decision of the primary question without fully carrying out that assessment they have been in error; they have left out of account a material factor. On the other hand, if they did carry out that assessment but made an error

h in doing so, proceeding on the basis that the four PCCs on would have to be sued in London and not in New York, their exercise of the discretion is likewise open to attack. I will therefore take the joinder issue first.

[45] The London action was an action brought by Mr Donohue. It was an action based upon the contractual right given by that clause to hold the other

j parties to that contract, and those claiming through them, to their promise only to sue Mr Donohue in England. Mr Donohue was entitled to sue and serve the first three defendants in accordance with that clause. Those defendants as they were bound to do acknowledged service and placed solicitors on the record to act on their behalf in the action. The four PCCs (and CISHL and Wingfield, who are not relevant for this purpose) then applied to be joined in the action. They simply relied upon the ground: 'The basis of the application is that England is the most appropriate forum for the resolution of the disputes between the applicants and the defendants.' Such an application is made by issuing and serving a summons or 'Application Notice' asking the court to order such joinder. The summons/notice had to be served on the existing parties by sending the summons to their solicitors on the record. No problem of service arises at that stage. But in order to obtain an order (save by the consent of all parties) for their joinder the applicants have to make out a case for their joinder. If they say, as did the four PCCs, that they should be joined because they too wish to claim 'anti-suit' injunctions against the existing defendants, they must be able to show that they could properly have brought proceedings against the defendants claiming that relief. It is at this stage that their application became unsustainable. The four PCCs had no procedural or contractual right to sue the defendants in the English jurisdiction; the English courts had no natural jurisdiction over the defendants. The applicants could not satisfy the tests laid down in *Spiliada Maritime Corp v Cansulex Ltd, The Spiliada* [1986] 3 All ER 843, [1987] AC 460. They could not show that London was clearly *the* appropriate forum (in contrast to New York) so as to justify them in commencing proceedings against the defendants in London ([1986] 3 All ER 843 at 858–859, [1987] AC 460 at 481). Further, by the same token, they could not show that they had any viable claim to an anti-suit injunction against the defendants based upon the contention that the defendants' chosen forum, New York, was a forum non conveniens to such a degree that it was vexatious for them to have sued the PCC parties there (*SNI Aérospatiale v Lee Kui Jak* [1987] 3 All ER 510, [1987] AC 871). New York was not an inappropriate forum (cf the *Spiliada* case [1986] 3 All ER 843 at 856, [1987] AC 460 at 477) nor could they show that they needed an injunction to protect proceedings in this country: *Airbus Industrie GIE v Patel* [1998] 2 All ER 257, [1999] 1 AC 119. The application by these parties to be joined in the action was misconceived and should have been refused. The majority of the Court of Appeal seem to have considered that the joinder and the grant of an anti-suit injunction to them followed from their decision to grant Mr Donohue an injunction. This was not correct. The position of a party who has an exclusive English jurisdiction clause is very different from one who does not. The former has a contractual right to have the contract enforced. The latter has no such right. The former's right specifically to enforce his contract can only be displaced by strong reasons being shown by the opposite party why an injunction should *not* be granted. The latter has to show that justice requires that he should be granted an injunction. The Court of Appeal should have refused the application of the four PCCs to be joined and should likewise have refused their application for an injunction.

[46] The Court of Appeal clearly had in mind that some proceedings would continue in New York, including some involving Mr Donohue himself. The limitations which they included in the injunction both as regards parties and as regards subject matter demonstrate this. The correct decision on the application of the four PCCs—that it should be dismissed—would have added to this prospect. The true balance between New York and London, therefore, was not that which must have been visualised by the majority of the Court of Appeal. The arguments in favour of refusing Mr Donohue the injunction for which he was applying would have been very materially strengthened.

[47] The Court of Appeal rightly attached importance to the fact that in New York Mr Donohue would be subject to 'RICO' claims and a liability in triple damages. To be protected against such a possibility was a legitimate concern of Mr Donohue to which a court should give weight in considering how to exercise

a its discretion. Lord Grabiner QC for the defendants recognised this and met it by offering the undertaking to which my noble and learned friend Lord Bingham has already referred. The offer of this undertaking does alter the position and indeed a court could have met the point by imposing equivalent terms upon the defendants as a condition of refusing to grant Mr Donohue an unqualified injunction. This too has changed the balance between the two jurisdictions and b should be taken into account.

[48] Lord Grabiner took his argument one step further. He acknowledged that some breaches of the exclusive jurisdiction clause have taken place and will continue, if the appeal is allowed and the injunction refused, and he likewise recognised that, if this leads to Mr Donohue incurring a greater liability or being put to a greater expense (eg, for unrecovered costs) in New York than would c have been the case in London, Mr Donohue may have a claim in damages against the defendants for breach of contract—breach of the exclusive jurisdiction clause. This does not appear to have been a point put to the Court of Appeal and it was only raised by Lord Grabiner in this House during his reply, no doubt as a result of his further consideration of the RICO point. I am prepared to accept this d submission and proceed on the basis that, if Mr Donohue can hereafter show that he has suffered loss as a result of the breach of the clause, the ordinary remedy in damages for breach of contract would be open to him. I say no more than this since the position is complex. The litigation in New York includes parties who are not parties to the jurisdiction agreement and against whom, and in relation to whom, Mr Donohue is not entitled to rely upon the clause. Further, when the e issues of fact have been fully tried in New York, a situation may be established whereby Mr Donohue's right to rely upon the contract as against the defendants may be affected or situations of circuity of action may arise. That is not presently the position but Lord Grabiner's point has merit and relevance in this exceptional and finely-balanced case.

f [49] The basis on which the exercise of the discretion has to be exercised is different from that before the Court of Appeal. In part this is because of a wrong decision on the joinder question and in part because of further arguments advanced by the defendants before this House. In my judgment in this case they exceptionally suffice to justify the House in deciding that the discretion should be exercised afresh by your Lordships and against the grant of the injunction.

g [50] I therefore agree that the appeal should be allowed on the terms proposed.

LORD SCOTT OF FOSCOTE.

[51] My Lords, I have had the advantage of reading in draft the opinion of my noble and learned friend, Lord Bingham of Cornhill, and gratefully adopt his h recital of the relevant facts.

[52] There seem to me to be two main issues that must be decided in the present case. They to some extent overlap one another. They are (i) whether the contractual exclusive jurisdiction clauses, contained in the transfer agreements dated 3 September 1991 under which AFSIL and AFSEL transferred their j respective shares in the BNIG to CISHL and in the sale and purchase agreement of the same date under which AFSIL and AFSEL transferred their shares in CISHL to Wingfield, should be enforced by injunction so as to bar proceedings in New York that fall within the scope of those clauses, properly construed; and (ii) if the answer to issue (i) is Yes, whether an injunction should be granted in order to bar also the prosecution in New York of proceedings that are not themselves caught by the exclusive jurisdiction clauses but are closely associated with those that are.

[53] The principles to be applied in order to decide on the one hand whether an exclusive jurisdiction clause should be enforced by an injunction and on the other hand whether the commencement or continuation of foreign proceedings which are not caught by an exclusive jurisdiction clause should be barred by an injunction seem now well settled and have not been the subject of any real disagreement before your Lordships. It is accepted that a contractual exclusive jurisdiction clause ought to be enforced as between the parties to the contract unless there are strong reasons not to do so. Prima facie parties should be held to their contractual bargain: see *The Fehmarn* [1958] 1 All ER 333, [1958] 1 WLR 159; *Unterweser Reederei GmbH v Zapata Off-Shore Co, The Chaparral* [1968] 2 Lloyd's Rep 158; *Aratra Potato Co Ltd v Egyptian Navigation Co, The El Amria* [1981] 2 Lloyd's Rep 119; *DSV Silo-und Verwaltungsgesellschaft mbH v Sennar (owners), The Sennar (No 2)* [1985] 2 All ER 104, [1985] 1 WLR 490; *Aggeliki Charis Cia Maritima SA v Pagnan SpA, The Angelic Grace* [1995] 1 Lloyd's Rep 87. If, on the other hand, there is no contractual bargain standing in the way of the foreign proceedings, 'the … court will, generally speaking, only restrain the plaintiff from pursuing proceedings in the foreign court if such pursuit would be vexatious or oppressive' (see *SNI Aérospatiale v Lee Kui Jak* [1987] 3 All ER 510 at 522, [1987] AC 871 at 896 per Lord Goff of Chieveley).

[54] There has been some debate before your Lordships as to the order in which the two issues referred to above should be considered but it seems to me convenient to start with the exclusive jurisdiction clauses and to try and decide what part, if any, of the New York proceedings the clauses cover, who is and who is not entitled to their benefit and who is and who is not bound by them.

The exclusive jurisdiction clauses

[55] In the transfer agreements, the parties to which were AFSIL and AFSEL, as transferors, and CISHL, as transferee, the exclusive jurisdiction clause said, simply, that 'each party submits to the exclusive jurisdiction of the Supreme Court of Judicature of England' (para 15.2).

[56] In the sale and purchase agreement the exclusive jurisdiction clause said that—

> 'the parties hereby irrevocably submit themselves to the exclusive jurisdiction of the English courts to settle any dispute which may arise out of or in connection with this agreement.'

[57] The parties to the sale and purchase agreement, in addition to AFSIL, AFSEL and Wingfield, included AFSC, Mr Atkins and Mr Donohue.

[58] The terms of the sale and purchase agreement clause are very wide, 'any dispute which may arise out of or in connection with this agreement', but it has not been suggested that the terms of the clauses in the transfer agreements should be given any lesser scope. So I propose to concentrate on the sale and purchase agreement clause and treat it as applicable also to any dispute arising out of or in connection with the transfer agreements.

[59] Armco Inc was not a party to any of these agreements but, on the dissolution of AFSEL, the assets of AFSEL, including its assignable choses in action, became vested, as I understand it, in Armco. It is accepted, rightly in my opinion, that, in respect of any causes of action vested in Armco as successor of AFSEL, Armco is subject to the same contractual inhibitions under the exclusive jurisdiction clause as AFSEL was subject to. But in respect of causes of action to which Armco is entitled in its own right, i e otherwise than as successor to AFSEL,

a   Armco is not bound by the exclusive jurisdiction clause, whether or not the causes of action relate to a dispute arising out of or in connection with one or other of the agreements.

[60] There is a point of construction of the exclusive jurisdiction clause that it is convenient to deal with at this point. It is accepted that the clause is not restricted to contractual claims. A claim for damages for, for example, fraudulent

b   misrepresentation inducing an agreement containing an exclusive jurisdiction clause in the same form as that with which this case is concerned would, as a matter of ordinary language, be a claim in tort that arose 'out of or in connection with' the agreement. If the alleged fraudulent misrepresentation had been made by two individuals jointly, of whom one was and the other was not a party to the agreement, the claim would still be of the same character, although only the

c   party to the agreement would be entitled to the benefit of the exclusive jurisdiction clause. The commencement of the claim against the two alleged tortfeasors elsewhere than in England would represent a breach of the clause. The defendant tortfeasor who was a party to the agreement would, absent strong reasons to the contrary, be entitled to an injunction restraining the continuance

d   of the foreign proceedings. He would be entitled to an injunction restraining the continuance of the proceedings not only against himself but also against his co-defendant. The exclusive jurisdiction clause is expressed to cover 'any dispute which may arise out of or in connection with' the agreement. It is not limited to 'any claim against' the party to the agreement. To give the clause that limited construction would very substantially reduce the protection afforded by the

e   clause to the party to the agreement. The non-party, if he remained alone as a defendant in the foreign proceedings, would be entitled to claim from his co-tortfeasor a contribution to any damages awarded. He could join the co-tortfeasor, the party entitled to the protection of the exclusive jurisdiction clause, in third party proceedings for that purpose. The position would be no different

f   if the claim were to be commenced in the foreign court with only the tortfeasor who was not a party to the exclusive jurisdiction clause as a defendant. He would be able, and well advised, to commence third party proceedings against his co-tortfeasor, the party to the exclusive jurisdiction clause.

[61] In my opinion, an exclusive jurisdiction clause in the wide terms of that with which this case is concerned is broken if any proceedings within the scope

g   of the clause are commenced in a foreign jurisdiction, whether or not the person entitled to the protection of the clause is joined as defendant to the proceedings. An injunction restraining the continuance of the proceedings would not, of course, be granted unless the party seeking the injunction, being someone entitled to the benefit of the clause, had a sufficient interest in obtaining the

h   injunction. It would, I think, be necessary for him to show that the claim being prosecuted in the foreign jurisdiction was one which, if it succeeded, would involve him in some consequential liability. It would certainly, in my opinion, suffice to show that if the claim succeeded he would incur a liability as a joint tortfeasor to contribute to the damages awarded by the foreign court.

j   [62] This point is of direct relevance in the present case. In the New York proceedings, which I must analyse more fully in a moment, several claims are made but most of them are based upon the allegation that Mr Donohue, Mr Atkins, Mr Rossi and Mr Stinson conspired together fraudulently to extract in various ways substantial sums of money from the Armco group of companies. If the allegations can be made good, the liability of the conspirators would be a joint and several liability. There are substantial issues as to which of the claims fall

within the language of the exclusive jurisdiction clause but I think it is clear that
some of them do. Of the four alleged conspirators only Mr Donohue and   *a*
Mr Atkins are contractually entitled to the benefit of the exclusive jurisdiction
clause. Mr Atkins has settled with Armco, so it was Mr Donohue alone who
commenced an action in this country for an injunction enforcing the clause. If
Mr Donohue is entitled to an injunction enforcing the clause he is entitled, in my
opinion, to an injunction that bars the continuance of the claims in question not   *b*
only against himself but also against Mr Rossi and Mr Stinson with whom he is
jointly and severally liable. If claims against Mr Donohue are within the clause,
then so too are the corresponding claims against Mr Rossi and Mr Stinson.
Mr Rossi and Mr Stinson are not contractually entitled to enforce the clause, but
Mr Donohue is, in my opinion, entitled to ask the court to enforce it by
restraining the prosecution in New York of all claims within its scope in respect   *c*
of which Mr Donohue would be jointly and severally liable.

The New York proceedings
   [63] It is necessary to analyse with some care the nature of the claims made in
the New York proceedings in order to decide which of them are caught by the   *d*
exclusive jurisdiction clause and which are not.
   [64] The amended complaint filed in New York describes the parties and then,
in paras 25 to 63, sets out the 'Facts'. Under the subheading 'The Secret Agreement'
it is alleged that the four individual defendants entered into a secret agreement
under which Mr Rossi and Mr Stinson, who owed Armco fiduciary duties as
directors and were responsible on behalf of Armco for negotiating with   *e*
Mr Donohue and Mr Atkins the terms under which the latter would purchase
from Armco the BNIG, became secret partners with them in that purchase. It is
alleged that pursuant to the secret agreement Mr Rossi and Mr Stinson agreed on
behalf of Armco to excessive sums being injected into CISHL before its shares
were sold to Wingfield. Recovery of the sums is sought. This claim seems to me   *f*
a fairly clear example of a 'dispute arising out of or in connection with' the sale
and purchase agreement.
   [65] The amended complaint goes on to allege that 'other aspects of the sale
were similarly tainted by the fraud' (para 41). Reference is made, as an example,
to the extraction of sums of money from two trust funds that had been
established in the United States to support insurance liabilities of NAIC. I find it   *g*
difficult to follow how this dispute could be brought within the exclusive
jurisdiction clause. The only 'connection' seems to me to be that if the BNIG had
not been purchased the scheme for milking the trust funds would not have been
implemented. It is a causa sine qua non, a 'but for', connection and I doubt
whether that is enough.   *h*
   [66] The amended complaint alleges, also, that 'as part of their secret
agreement' the four conspirators extracted funds from APL via a debt collection
agreement between APL, acting by Mr Rossi, and NPV, acting by Mr Donohue
and Mr Stinson, under which NPV obtained unjustifiably inflated rates of
commission. I cannot see any basis on which the claims based on this debt   *j*
collection agreement can be regarded as falling within the exclusive jurisdiction
clause.
   [67] In respect of each of the claims to which I have referred the plaintiffs in
the New York proceedings claim punitive as well as compensatory damages.
   [68] In addition it is alleged that the defendants' conduct constituted racketeering,
wire fraud and mail fraud for the purpose of the Federal Racketeer Influenced and

a Corrupt Organizations Act (18 USC § 1962(c)) (the RICO Act). Under the RICO Act claims triple damages are sought. In so far as the RICO Act claims are based on conduct in connection with the transfer agreements or the sale and purchase agreement, it might seem that they, too, fall within the language of the exclusive jurisdiction clause. But it is common ground that a RICO Act claim could not be brought in an English court. It cannot, in my opinion, be supposed that in *b* submitting to the exclusive jurisdiction of the English courts the parties had in mind claims which an English court would have no jurisdiction to entertain. The contractually expressed purpose of the submission to the English courts was 'to settle any dispute which may arise', etc. How can this language be sensibly thought apt to cover a dispute that the English courts would be jurisdictionally unable to settle? The choice of law provision that, in the sale and purchase *c* agreement, immediately preceded the exclusive jurisdiction clause, in my opinion, underlines the point 'this agreement shall be governed by and construed in accordance with' English law. The parties could not have intended that RICO Act claims would be governed by English law. English law does not recognise such claims. Nor can it be supposed that the parties, by the use of a fairly *d* commonplace choice of law provision and exclusive jurisdiction clause, were intending to contract out of any RICO Act liability that might be connected with the agreement. In my opinion, any such contractual intention would need to be clearly expressed. Accordingly, in my opinion, as a matter of construction of the exclusive jurisdiction clause, the RICO Act claims are not caught.

[69] The amended complaint included also breach of fiduciary duty claims *e* against Mr Rossi and Mr Stinson. These claims arise in part out of conduct of Mr Rossi and Mr Stinson in negotiating the terms of the sale by Armco of its BNIG. But I do not think a claim by Armco against its own officers for breach of fiduciary duty represents a 'dispute' caught by the exclusive jurisdiction clause. 'Dispute' in the clause means, in my opinion, a dispute in respect of which there *f* is, on each side, a party, or a person claiming through a party, to the agreement. A claim by Armco for breach of fiduciary duty by its directors is, in my opinion, no more caught than would be a claim by Armco for negligence by its lawyers whether or not the conduct complained of related to the transfer agreements or the sale and purchase agreement.

[70] There are, in addition, other claims made in the New York proceedings *g* but most of them are different formulations of the claims to which I have already referred. I think I have mentioned all those that bear upon the issues that arise on this appeal.

Should injunctions be granted?

h [71] Virtually all the claims in the New York proceedings are based upon the alleged secret agreement between the four individual defendants. Some of the claims, those made against Mr Donohue and those relating to the allegedly excessive funds injected into CISHL, are within the scope of the exclusive jurisdiction clause. Others seem to me to be plainly outside the scope of the *j* clause.

[72] The Court of Appeal granted injunctions restraining the continuance of claims 'to the extent that the claims arise out of or are connected with the management buy-out'. The injuncted claims included the RICO Act claims in so far as so arising or so connected. They included the breach of fiduciary duty claims against Mr Rossi and Mr Stinson in so far as so arising or so connected. For the reasons I have given I do not think that any of these claims were within the

scope of the exclusive jurisdiction clause on its true construction. But the
injuncted claims did not include the claims relating to the alleged milking of the *a*
trust funds nor those relating to the APL/NPV debt collection agreement. The
Court of Appeal's refusal to extend the injunction so as to bar these claims is not
the subject of any cross-appeal and it is accepted by Mr Donohue that the
prosecution in New York of these claims against him and the other defendants
will continue.   *b*

[73] So the injunction as granted by the Court of Appeal has left the alleged
secret agreement to be litigated both in the New York courts and in England. The
possibility of inconsistent conclusions on the facts is plain. The injunction has
barred the prosecution in New York of a part of the RICO Act claim. The claim
cannot be litigated in England and it follows that the part of the RICO Act claim *c*
that arises out of or in connection with the 'management buy-out' cannot be
litigated anywhere. The injunction has required Armco, an American company,
to prosecute in England a claim against its officers, Mr Rossi and Mr Stinson, for
breach of the fiduciary duty that they owe under Armco's domestic law.

[74] Many of the claims made in the New York proceedings, including the
RICO Act claims and the breach of fiduciary claims in so far as they do not arise *d*
out of or in connection with the management buy-out as well as all the trust fund
claims and the debt collection agreement claims, will be proceedings in New
York in any event. The common sense in all the claims based on the alleged
secret agreement being dealt with in the same court and at the same time seems
to me overwhelming. There are undoubted disadvantages to Mr Donohue in *e*
being sued in New York instead of in England. These have been referred to by
Lord Bingham. And the prosecution in New York of the claims, not only against
Mr Donohue but against Mr Rossi and Mr Stinson as well, that fall within the
exclusive jurisdiction clause constitutes a breach of a contractual term that
Mr Donohue is prima facie entitled to require to be observed. It is relevant to *f*
take into account, however, that the New York claims that do fall within the
exclusive jurisdiction clause on its true construction are somewhat peripheral, if
measured against the sort of contractual and tortious claims that the parties
might reasonably be supposed to have had in mind when agreeing to that clause.
The conspiracy constituted by the alleged secret agreement was aimed at
extracting money from the Armco group by using, or misusing, the authority of *g*
two of Armco's own officers who had become co-conspirators. It is one thing to
conclude that those claims based upon the conspiracy that arise out of or in
connection with the management buy-out are caught by the exclusive
jurisdiction clause properly construed; it is quite another to suppose that the
parties would have had claims of that sort in mind when agreeing to the clause. *h*

[75] In my opinion, however, it is the evident absurdity of requiring some
claims resulting from the alleged secret agreement to be litigated in England
notwithstanding that the rest will be litigated in New York that is the overriding
factor. There are, in my estimation, very strong reasons indeed for the normal
injunctive protection that the exclusive jurisdiction clause would warrant to be *j*
withheld in this case. I would have come to this conclusion in any event but the
undertaking offered by Armco to which Lord Bingham has referred confirms it.
If it should transpire that Mr Donohue is successful in the New York proceedings
but is unable to recover his costs, being costs that he would have expected to have
been awarded if he had successfully defended in England, I can see no reason in
principle why he should not recover, as damages for breach of the exclusive

a jurisdiction clause, such part of those costs as he incurred in his successful defence of the claims that fall within that clause.

[76] For these reasons I would allow the appeal and make the orders that Lord Bingham has suggested. As I have endeavoured to explain, I regard the exclusive jurisdiction clause, correctly construed, to the benefit of which Mr Donohue is but Mr Rossi and Mr Stinson are not contractually entitled, as covering some of
b the claims made against Mr Rossi and Mr Stinson whether or not Mr Donohue is a co-defendant and as not covering any of the RICO Act claims. Subject to that, I am in respectful and complete agreement with the reasons given by Lord Bingham for allowing the appeal.

Appeal allowed.

Celia Fox   Barrister.

R (on the application of Morgan Grenfell & Co Ltd) v Special Commissioner

a

[2001] EWCA Civ 329

COURT OF APPEAL, CIVIL DIVISION

b

SCHIEMANN, SEDLEY LJJ AND BLACKBURNE J

12, 13 FEBRUARY, 2 MARCH 2001

Privilege – Legal professional privilege – Solicitor and client – Communications between legal advisor and client – Inspector of taxes exercising statutory investigatory power to investigate tax-related scheme – Whether provision authorising inspector to require disclosure of material subject to legal professional privilege – Taxes Management Act 1970, s 20(1), (7).

c

MG, a merchant bank, devised a tax-related scheme under which it entered into certain property transactions with clients. Although MG had been open about the *d* scheme with the inspector of taxes and there was no question of tax evasion, the inspector decided to investigate the nature of the transactions, making use of the powers conferred on him by the Taxes Management Act 1970. Under s 20(1)[a] of that Act, an inspector could by notice in writing require a person to deliver to him such documents as were in the person's possession or power and as (in the inspector's reasonable opinion) contained, or might contain, information relevant to any tax *e* liability to which the person was or might be subject, or the amount of such liability. In contrast to various other investigatory provisions under the 1970 Act, s 20(1) did not expressly protect from disclosure material subject to legal professional privilege. By virtue of s 20(7), a notice under s 20(1) could only be given with the consent of a General or Special Commissioner. On an ex parte application by the *f* inspector and after receiving written submissions from MG, a Special Commissioner gave his consent to the issue of a s 20(1) notice against MG in respect of various documents, including material which the latter contended was protected from disclosure by legal professional privilege. MG applied for judicial review, contending that s 20(1) did not authorise the inspector to require disclosure of material subject to legal professional privilege. MG also challenged an earlier decision by *g* the commissioner that he had no jurisdiction or discretion to allow it to participate in an inter partes hearing of the application for consent to the s 20(1) notice. The Divisional Court rejected the challenges to both decisions and accordingly dismissed the application. MG appealed.

h

Held – (1) On its true construction, s 20(1) of the 1970 Act authorised an inspector of taxes to issue a notice requiring a taxpayer to disclose material subject to legal professional privilege. The provisions of the Act, taken as a whole, carried the inescapable implication that the rule of legal professional privilege was excluded except where it was expressly preserved, and the limit of available exceptions was *j* marked by the provisions in the Act which made express provision for documents which did not need to be produced. The code contained in the Act embodied an investigatory power of broad ambit to counter abuses of the tax system. It could not therefore be assumed that there was only one fundamental right at stake,

---

a   Section 20, so far as material, is set out at [11], below

a namely a person's right to keep from disclosure documents which were subject to legal professional privilege. The public interest in the prompt, fair and complete collection of the public revenue, as laid down by Parliament, was also in play (see [17], [18], below); *R v IRC, ex p Taylor (No 2)* [1990] 2 All ER 409 considered.

(2) A Special Commissioner had no power to allow a taxpayer to make oral representations against the issue of a notice under s 20(1). The possibility of an b oral hearing was excluded by the nature of the process in question. A right to be heard was axiomatically worth little without knowledge of the case which had to be met. Either, therefore, the inspector's hand had in some measure to be shown, or the taxpayer had to be content to make submissions in the dark. The former was plainly destructive of the whole purpose of the procedure: the latter would create a sustained pressure for disclosure. There were only two logical outcomes c if those two imperatives clashed in a face-to-face hearing. Either the taxpayer would learn nothing, in which case it was not easy to see what would have been achieved on his behalf that could not have been achieved in writing, or the Special Commissioner's opportunity to enjoy the benefit of advocacy would lead to accidental disclosure by him or (more probably) the inspector of material to d which the taxpayer was not entitled, disclosure of which at that stage would run counter to Parliament's purpose. Accordingly, the appeal would be dismissed (see [50], [51], below).

Decision of the Divisional Court [2001] 1 All ER 535 affirmed.

Notes
e For communications subject to legal professional privilege, see 3(1) *Halsbury's Laws* (4th edn reissue) para 526 and 44(1) *Halsbury's Laws* (4th edn reissue) para 90, and for an inspector's power to require a taxpayer to produce documents in respect of his own liability, see 23 *Halsbury's Laws* (4th edn reissue) para 1626.

For the Taxes Management Act 1970, s 20, see 42 *Halsbury's Statutes* (4th edn) f (1996 reissue) 178.

Cases referred to in judgment
B (a minor) v DPP [2000] 1 All ER 833, [2000] 2 AC 428, [2000] 2 WLR 452, HL.
Board of Education v Rice [1911] AC 179, [1911–13] All ER Rep 36, HL.
Coombs (T C) & Co (a firm) v IRC [1991] 3 All ER 623, sub nom *R v IRC, ex p T C* g *Coombs & Co* [1991] 2 AC 283, [1991] 2 WLR 682, HL.
Fetherstonaugh v IRC [1984] STC 261; sub nom *Finch v IRC* [1985] Ch 1, [1984] 3 WLR 212, CA.
Foxley v UK (2001) 8 BHRC 571, ECt HR.
Georgiou (t/a Marios Chippery) v UK [2001] STC 80, ECt HR.
h *Leech v Parkhurst Prison Deputy Governor* [1988] 1 All ER 485, [1988] AC 533, [1988] 2 WLR 290, HL.
Padfield v Minister of Agriculture, Fisheries and Food [1968] 1 All ER 694, [1968] AC 997, [1968] 2 WLR 924, HL.
Parry Jones v Law Society [1968] 1 All ER 177, [1969] 1 Ch 1, [1968] 2 WLR 397, CA.
j *R v Derby Magistrates' Court, ex p B* [1995] 4 All ER 526, [1996] AC 487, [1995] 3 WLR 681, HL.
R v IRC, ex p Taylor (No 2) [1990] 2 All ER 409, CA.
R v Secretary of State for the Home Dept, ex p Simms [1999] 3 All ER 400, [2000] 2 AC 115, [1999] 3 WLR 328, HL.
Walker (Inspector of Taxes) v Centaur Clothes Group Ltd [2000] 2 All ER 589, [2000] 1 WLR 799, HL.

Cases referred to in skeleton arguments

Baker v Campbell (1983) 153 CLR 52, Aust HC.   a

Campbell v UK (1983) 7 EHRR 165, [1983] ECHR 75511/76, ECt HR.

Campbell v UK (1992) 15 EHRR 137, ECt HR.

Crowley v Murphy (1981) 34 ALR 496, Aust Fed Ct.

General Mediterranean Holdings SA v Patel [1999] 3 All ER 673, [2000] 1 WLR 272.

Grazebrook (M & W) Ltd v Wallens [1973] 2 All ER 868, NIRC.   b

Invercargill City Council v Hamlin [1996] 1 All ER 756, [1996] AC 624, PC.

IR Comr v West-Walker [1954] NZLR 191, NZ CA.

Kirkness (Inspector of Taxes) v John Hudson & Co Ltd [1955] 2 All ER 345, [1955] AC
696, HL.

L (a minor) (police investigation: privilege), Re [1996] 2 All ER 78, [1997] AC 16, HL.   c

Lonrho plc v Secretary of State for Trade and Industry [1989] 2 All ER 609, [1989]
1 WLR 525, HL.

Marleasing SA v La Commercial Internacional de Alimentación SA Case C-106/89
[1990] ECR 4135.

Melluish (Inspector of Taxes) v BMI (No 3) Ltd [1995] 4 All ER 453, [1996] AC 454,
HL.   d

NAP Holdings UK Ltd v Whittles (Inspector of Taxes) [1994] STC 979, HL.

Niemietz v Germany (1992) 16 EHRR 97, [1992] ECHR 13710/88, ECt HR.

O'Reilly v Comr of State Bank of Victoria (1983) 153 CLR 1, Aust HC.

Ormond Investment Co Ltd v Betts (Inspector of Taxes) [1928] AC 143, [1928] All ER
Rep 709, HL.   e

Pepper (Inspector of Taxes) v Hart [1993] 1 All ER 42, [1993] AC 593, HL.

Price Waterhouse (a firm) v BCCI Holdings (Luxembourg) SA [1992] BCLC 583.

R v Doubtfire [2001] 2 Cr App R 209, CA.

R v DPP, ex p Kebeline [1999] 4 All ER 801, [2000] 2 AC 326, HL.

R v Gaming Board for GB, ex p Benaim [1970] 2 All ER 528, [1970] 2 QB 417, CA.   f

R v IRC, ex p Banque Internationale a Luxembourg SA [2000] STC 708.

R v IRC, ex p Lorimer [2000] STC 751.

R v Khan [1996] 3 All ER 289, [1997] AC 558, HL.

R v O'Kane, ex p Northern Bank Ltd [1996] STC 1249.

R v Special Comr of Income Tax, ex p IRC, R v IRC, ex p Ulster Bank Ltd [2000] STC 537.

Silver v UK (1983) 5 EHRR 347, [1983] ECHR 5947/72, ECt HR.   g

Sweet v Parsley [1969] 1 All ER 347, [1970] AC 132, HL.

Westcott (Inspector of Taxes) v Woolcombers Ltd [1986] STC 182; affd [1987] STC 600, CA.

Appeal

By notice dated 23 November 2000, Morgan Grenfell & Co Ltd (MG) appealed   h
with permission from the decision of the Divisional Court (Buxton LJ and
Penry-Davey J) on 8 November 2000, ([2001] 1 All ER 535) dismissing its
application for judicial review of (i) the decision of a Special Commissioner
(Stephen Oliver QC) on 28 September 1999 giving consent to the issue by an
inspector of taxes of a notice to MG under s 20(1) of the Taxes Management Act   j
1970; (ii) the notice itself, by which MG was required to deliver documents and
notes of meetings with advisors relating to a property transaction between it and
one of its clients; and (iii) a written decision of the commissioner dated 16 April
1999 ruling (a) that he had no jurisdiction or discretion to allow MG to participate
in an inter partes hearing of the application for consent to the issue of the s 20(1)
notice, and (b) that the provisions of s 20 of the 1970 Act overrode the taxpayer's

a ordinary right to legal professional privilege. The facts are set out in the judgment of the court.

Michael Beloff QC, Giles Goodfellow and *Sarah Dunn* (instructed by *Slaughter & May*) for MG.
Timothy Brennan and *Ingrid Simler* (instructed by the *Solicitor of Inland Revenue*) for

b the Crown.

Cur adv vult

2 March 2001. The following judgment of the court was delivered.

c **BLACKBURNE J.**

Introduction
   [1] This is an appeal against the dismissal by the Divisional Court (Buxton LJ and Penry-Davey J) ([2001] 1 All ER 535) of an application by Morgan Grenfell &

d Co Ltd (MG), the well-known merchant bank, for judicial review of: (1) a Special Commissioner's decision to give consent under s 20(7) of the Taxes Management Act 1970 (the 1970 Act) to the giving of a notice to MG under s 20(1) of that Act; (2) the notice itself, which is dated 28 September 1999, requiring MG to deliver documents and notes of meetings with advisors relating to a property transaction between MG and the Tesco Group entered into in February 1995; and (3) a

e written decision of the Special Commissioner dated 16 April 1999 (the preliminary decision) ruling (a) that he had no jurisdiction or discretion to allow MG to participate in an inter partes hearing of an application for consent to the issue of the s 20(1) notice and (b) that, as a matter of necessary inference, the provisions of s 20 of the 1970 Act override the taxpayer's ordinary right to legal

f professional privilege.
   [2] In issue before the Divisional Court were four questions which the court formulated in the following terms ([2001] 1 All ER 535 at 539 (para 8)):

   'I. Does s 20(1) of the 1970 Act authorise an inspector to issue a notice requiring disclosure by a taxpayer of LPP (legal professional privilege)

g material? II. Does a commissioner hearing an application by an inspector under s 20(7) of the 1970 Act have jurisdiction to permit the intended recipient of the inspector's notice to attend the hearing and make representations? III. In the present case, could the inspector have held the reasonable opinion that the LPP material contained or might contain information relevant to MG's tax liability, as s 20(1) of the 1970 Act requires?

h IV. To the extent that it is a separate issue from III, did the commissioner err in law in consenting to the issue of the notice in relation to the LPP material?'

   [3] The court concluded: (1) that s 20(1) of the 1970 Act authorised an inspector to issue a notice requiring disclosure by a taxpayer of material subject to legal

j professional privilege; (2) that MG had no right to require an oral hearing and, more generally, that the Special Commissioner had no jurisdiction to afford the intended recipient of the notice an inter partes hearing in respect of an application for consent under s 20(7); (3) that, on the basis of the disclosed information, the Special Commissioner could have held the reasonable opinion that the material subject to legal professional privilege contained or might contain information relevant to MG's tax liability; and (4) that, to the extent that it was a separate issue, the Special Commissioner had not erred in law in consenting to the issue of the notice. The application was therefore dismissed.

[4] MG's appeal, which is brought with the Divisional Court's permission, raises the following issues: (1) does s 20(1) of the 1970 Act authorise an inspector to issue a notice requiring disclosure by a taxpayer of material subject to legal professional privilege (the substantive issue); and (2) does the commissioner have a discretion to allow the taxpayer to make oral representations to him, inter partes, as to why consent should not be given to the giving of a notice under s 20(1) of that Act (the procedural issue)?

[5] The background to the proceedings, so far as it is necessary to set it out, is a tax-related scheme whereby, in essence, MG's client (in these proceedings it is a member of the Tesco Group), grants a long leasehold interest in property which it already owns to MG in return for a lump sum. MG then subleases the property back to the client in return for a periodic rent. The lump sum payment made by MG is claimed by it to qualify for tax relief against its trading income while the capital receipt by the client (in this case Tesco) will not be taxed as giving rise to any capital gain because of the availability of some form of relief such as a capital loss. The scheme is advertised by MG as enabling participants 'to secure extremely low cost funding through a tax arbitrage based on property' and is marketed as STELA (an acronym for Sale with Tax Enhanced Leasing Arbitrage).

[6] As the Divisional Court pointed out (at 538 (para 4)) MG have emphasised that they have throughout been open with the inspector of taxes: there is no suggestion here of tax evasion and, as MG contended, no question of tax avoidance either. Nevertheless, the inspector suspected (as he continues to do) that, on a true understanding of the matter, it might well emerge that the transactions, involving (as here) the purchase of supermarkets, are not trading transactions, but capital transactions, and should be treated as such for tax purposes. We were told by Mr Brennan, for the Crown, that the Revenue is aware of 16 such schemes involving payments made of £259m with tax at stake of £77m. It was with a view to investigating these matters further that—in regard to the particular transaction undertaken with Tesco in February 1995—the Revenue had recourse to its statutory powers of investigation under the 1970 Act.

[7] To this end, in November 1998, the inspector served on MG a so-called 'precursor notice' under s 20B(1) of the 1970 Act that, if the documents specified on an attached schedule were not produced within a stated period, he would consider applying to a Special Commissioner for permission to issue a s 20(1) notice. Among the items specified on the schedule were documents which MG contends are protected from disclosure by legal professional privilege.

[8] MG responded by requesting of the presiding Special Commissioner that they be granted the benefit of an inter partes hearing if and when the Revenue should apply for consent under s 20(7) to the issue of a s 20(1) notice. The letter requesting such a hearing also set out a summary of their reasons why consent should not be given among which was that, as the documents qualified for legal professional privilege, a s 20(1) notice could not require their disclosure.

[9] In the preliminary decision, given on 16 April 1999, the Special Commissioner, Stephen Oliver QC, concluded (so far as material); (1) that MG, as the intended recipient of an intended s 20(1) notice, had no right to attend the meeting at which the inspector seeks the commissioner's consent under s 20(7) and he had no discretion to admit them, (2) that arguments based on the European Convention for the Protection of Human Rights and Fundamental Freedoms (Rome, 4 November 1950; TS 71 (1953); Cmd 8969) (the Human Rights Act 1998

a not then being in force) did not alter this conclusion, and (3) that a taxpayer's ordinary right of legal professional privilege does not entitle him to refuse to comply with a s 20(1) notice.

[10] At an ex parte hearing on 28 September 1999 and notwithstanding further written representations by MG's legal advisors, the Special Commissioner gave his consent to the issue of a s 20(1) notice. On the same day the notice was issued

b to MG. These proceedings followed shortly thereafter.

The Taxes Management Act 1970

[11] Before coming to the two issues which arise on this appeal, it is necessary to set out the material provisions of the 1970 Act. We do so in their form as they existed in 1999. They were subsequently amended by the Finance Act 2000,

c effective from 28 July 2000, but in respects which do not affect the outcome of this appeal:

'**20.** *Power to call for documents of taxpayer and others.*—(1) Subject to this section, an inspector may by notice in writing require a person—(a) to deliver

d to him such documents as are in the person's possession or power and as (in the inspector's reasonable opinion) contain, or may contain, information relevant to—(i) any tax liability to which the person is or may be subject, or (ii) the amount of any such liability, or (b) to furnish to him such particulars as the inspector may reasonably require as being relevant to, or to the amount of, any such liability.

e (2) Subject to this section, the Board may by notice in writing require a person—(a) to deliver to a named officer of the Board such documents as are in the person's possession or power and as (in the Board's reasonable opinion) contain, or may contain, information relevant to—(i) any tax liability to which the person is or may be subject, or (ii) the amount of any such liability,

f or (b) to furnish to a named officer of the Board such particulars as the Board may reasonably require as being relevant to, or to the amount of, any such liability.

(3) Subject to this section, an inspector may, for the purpose of enquiring into the tax liability of any person ("the taxpayer"), by notice in writing require any other person to deliver to the inspector or, if the person to whom

g the notice is given so elects, to make available for inspection by a named officer of the Board, such documents as are in his possession or power and as (in the inspector's reasonable opinion) contain, or may contain, information relevant to any tax liability to which the taxpayer is or may be, or may have been, subject, or to the amount of any such liability; and the persons who

h may be required to deliver or make available a document under this subsection include the Director of Savings ...

(7) Notices under subsection (1) or (3) above are not to be given by an inspector unless he is authorised by the Board for its purposes; and—(a) a notice is not to be given by him except with the consent of a General or

j Special Commissioner; and (b) the Commissioner is to give his consent only on being satisfied that in all the circumstances the inspector is justified in proceeding under this section ...

(8A) If, on an application made by an inspector and authorised by order of the Board, a Special Commissioner gives his consent, the inspector may give such a notice as is mentioned in subsection (3) above but without naming the taxpayer to whom the notice relates; but such a consent shall not

be given unless the Special Commissioner is satisfied—(a) that the notice
relates to a taxpayer whose identity is not known to the inspector or to a class *a*
of taxpayers whose individual identities are not so known; (b) that there are
reasonable grounds for believing that the taxpayer or any of the class of
taxpayers to whom the notice relates may have failed or may fail to comply
with any provision of the Taxes Acts; (c) that any such failure is likely to have
led or to lead to serious prejudice to the proper assessment or collection of *b*
tax; and (d) that the information which is likely to be contained in the
documents to which the notice relates is not readily available from another
source ...

    20A. *Power to call for papers of tax accountant.*—(1) Where after the passing
of the Finance Act 1976 a person—(a) is convicted of an offence in relation to
tax (whenever committed) by or before any court in the United Kingdom; or *c*
(b) has a penalty imposed on him (whether before or after the passing of that
Act) under section 99 of this Act, and he has stood in relation to others as tax
accountant, an inspector authorised by the Board for the purpose of this
section may by notice in writing require the person to deliver to him such
documents as are in his possession or power and as (in the inspector's *d*
reasonable opinion) contain information relevant to any tax liability to
which any client of his is or has been, or may be or have been, subject, or to
the amount of any such liability ...

    20B. *Restrictions on powers under ss. 20 and 20A* ...

    (3) An inspector cannot under section 20(1) or (3), or under section 20A(1),
give notice to a barrister, advocate or solicitor, but the notice must in any such *e*
case be given (if at all) by the Board; and accordingly in relation to a barrister,
advocate or solicitor for references in section 20(3) and (4) and section 20A to
the inspector there are substituted references to the Board ...

    (8) A notice under section 20(3) or (8A) or section 20A(1) does not oblige a
barrister, advocate or a solicitor to deliver or make available, without his client's *f*
consent, any document with respect to which a claim to professional privilege
could be maintained.'

    [12] Section 20, under which the notice given to MG was issued, is part of an
elaborate series of provisions to be found in ss 20 to 20D of the 1970 Act dealing with
the production by taxpayers and others of such documents as, in the reasonable *g*
opinion of the inspector or, in some cases, the Commissioners of Inland Revenue,
contain information relevant either to any tax liability to which a person may be
subject or to the amount of any such liability. The provisions, which have been
amended and added to from time to time (s 20 itself being a wholesale replacement
by the Finance Act 1976 of the provisions originally contained in the 1970 Act), *h*
constitute a detailed code regulating to whom, by whom and subject to what
threshold requirements, both procedural and substantive, such notices can be given.
With the assistance of a most helpful schedule to his skeleton argument, Mr Brennan
reviewed the scope of these provisions, ranging from what he described as the
Revenue's most intrusive power, contained in s 20C, to enter and search specified
premises, if necessary by force, where there is a reasonable ground to suspect serious *j*
fraud and that evidence of it is likely to be found at the premises, to the relatively less
intrusive power, under s 20(1), to call on a taxpayer to deliver documents.

The substantive issue

    [13] After reviewing various provisions of the code, the Divisional Court (at 544
(para 27)) felt 'driven to conclude that the provisions of the 1970 Act taken as a

a whole do demonstrate a premise that the rule of LPP is excluded from them save where it is expressly incorporated'. It therefore concluded that, although s 20(1) was silent on the matter, it was a necessary implication from that premise that arguments based on legal professional privilege could not be used to resist an application for disclosure under s 20(1).

[14] Mr Beloff QC, for MG, attacked that conclusion on two bases: (1) the *b* Divisional Court's approach to statutory construction which, in certain respects he submitted, was inappropriate; and (2) its analysis of the 1970 Act which, he submitted, was flawed.

[15] With the exception of two particular matters, to which we come later, the general approach to the question of construction (as distinct from the application *c* of that approach to the 1970 Act) advanced before the Divisional Court and again before us was not a matter of controversy. It involved the following elements: (1) legal professional privilege, including legal advice privilege, is a fundamental right; (2) because of the principle of legality, legal professional privilege cannot be overridden by general or ambiguous words but only by express language or necessary implication; (3) because no language in the 1970 Act expressly overrides *d* legal professional privilege, to succeed, the Revenue must establish that, by necessary implication, legal professional privilege was excluded from s 20 (including s 20(1)) except where expressly preserved; and (4) the concept of necessary implication connotes an implication which is compellingly clear.

[16] Relevant to (1)—the fundamental nature of the rule of legal professional *e* privilege—is the statement of Lord Taylor of Gosforth CJ in *R v Derby Magistrates' Court, ex p B* [1995] 4 All ER 526 at 540–541, [1996] AC 487 at 507 that: 'Legal professional privilege is … much more than an ordinary rule of evidence, limited in its application to the facts of a particular case. It is a fundamental condition on which the administration of justice as a whole rests.' Relevant to (2)—the *f* significance of the principle of legality—is Lord Hoffmann's statement in *R v Secretary of State for the Home Dept, ex p Simms* [1999] 3 All ER 400 at 412, [2000] 2 AC 115 at 131 that:

> '… the principle of legality means that Parliament must squarely confront what it is doing and accept the political cost. Fundamental rights cannot be
g > overridden by general or ambiguous words. This is because there is too great a risk that the full implications of their unqualified meaning may have passed unnoticed in the democratic process. In the absence of express language or necessary implication to the contrary, the courts therefore presume that even the most general words were intended to be subject to the basic rights
h > of the individual.'

Relevant to (4)—what must be shown to give rise to a necessary implication that a fundamental right such as legal professional privilege is intended to be overridden—is the observation of Lord Nicholls of Birkenhead in *B (a minor) v DPP* [2000] 1 All ER 833 at 839, [2000] 2 AC 428 at 464 (a case concerned with whether *j* there was a need for a mental element in a particular sexual offence) that:

> '"Necessary implication" connotes an implication which is compellingly clear. Such an implication may be found in the language used, the nature of the offence, the mischief sought to be prevented and any other circumstances which may assist in determining what intention is properly to be attributed to Parliament when creating the offence.'

Also relevant was Lord Steyn's search for what he described ([2000] 1 All ER 833 at 847, [2000] 2 AC 428 at 473) as a 'consistency of theme' in the statutory provisions there under examination such as to justify overriding the presumption that general words in a statute are not intended to abrogate fundamental rights.

[17] We consider, in agreement with the Divisional Court, that, taken as a whole, the provisions of the code do carry the inescapable implication that the rule of legal professional privilege is excluded except where it is expressly preserved and that the provisions in the code which make express provision for documents which need not be produced mark the limits of the available exceptions. We reach that conclusion for the following reasons.

[18] The code embodies an investigatory power, of broad ambit, conferred by Parliament to counter abuses of the tax system as part of the core function of the Commissioners of Inland Revenue (under s 13(1) of the Inland Revenue Regulation Act 1890) 'to collect and cause to be collected every part of inland revenue'. It cannot therefore be assumed that there is only one fundamental right at stake, namely a person's right to keep from disclosure documents which are subject to legal professional privilege. The public interest in the prompt, fair and complete collection of the public revenue, as laid down by Parliament, is also in play. It lies within recognition by art 8(2) of the convention of the economic well-being of the country as a ground on which the right to respect for private life and correspondence may in a proper case be abrogated.

[19] The code is detailed in its provisions. The operation of s 20(1) well illustrates the point. The notice is to be given by an inspector of taxes, but only if he is authorised by the Board (ie the Commissioners of Inland Revenue) for its purposes (see s 20(7)). Even then, the inspector has no authority to give notice under s 20(1) to a barrister, solicitor or advocate. Only the Board can do this (see s 20B(3)). Before service of a s 20(1) notice, the taxpayer to be served must first be given a precursor notice under s 20B(1), ie he must first have been given a reasonable opportunity to deliver the documents in question. The inspector must hold the reasonable opinion that the documents he requires contain or may contain information relevant to the recipient's liability or the amount of that liability (see s 20(1)). Under s 20(7)(a) the notice is not to be given except with the consent of a General or Special Commissioner. The commissioner has been described as 'the monitor of the decision' of the inspector to serve the notice (see Lord Lowry in *T C Coombs & Co (a firm) v IRC* [1991] 3 All ER 623 at 637–638, sub nom *R v IRC, ex p T C Coombs & Co* [1991] 2 AC 283 at 302). Under s 20(7)(b) the commissioner must be satisfied that, in all the circumstances, the inspector is justified in proceeding. In addition to the service of the s 20(1) notice, s 20(8E) requires the inspector to give the recipient a written summary of his reasons for applying for consent by the commissioner to the giving of the notice.

[20] Against that background it is, to say the least, surprising that, if Parliament had intended that the inspector should have no power to require the delivery of documents covered by legal professional privilege, it has failed to spell this out. Can the same be said (as Mr Beloff says it) of the converse?

[21] Lawyers, ie barristers, advocates and solicitors, are dealt with separately by the code. A notice under s 20(1) or under s 20(3) (which relates to notices given to third persons, other than the taxpayer in question) or under s 20A(1) (which provides for the service of a notice on a person who has acted for others as a tax accountant and who has been convicted of a tax offence or has had a penalty imposed on him under s 99 of the 1970 Act) cannot be given to a lawyer except by the Board. The separate treatment of lawyers applies as much where it is their own

a tax liability that is involved (as would be the case where the notice is given under
s 20(1)) as where the tax liability of clients is at stake (as will be the case where the
notice is given under s 20(3)).

[22] With lawyers identified as a separate class of recipient of notices, s 20B(8)
provides that:

b   'A notice under section 20(3) or (8A) or section 20A(1) does not oblige a
barrister, advocate or a solicitor to deliver or make available, without his
client's consent, any document with respect to which a claim to professional
privilege could be maintained.'

This provision, it is to be noted, applies only where the lawyer, served with a
notice, is acting for a client. It does not apply to a lawyer served as a taxpayer.
c This is so even if the documents which the lawyer is required to deliver include
documents relating to advice given to a client with respect to which a claim to
legal professional privilege by the client could be maintained. What can be the
purpose of highlighting the preservation of legal professional privilege when
notices are served under those sections but not, as in the example just mentioned,
d where the lawyer is served as the taxpayer if there is an underlying assumption
that documents covered by legal professional privilege are in any event protected
from disclosure?

[23] Mr Beloff's suggested answer to this was to refer to the uncertain scope
in English law of the protection given to legal professional privilege in respect of
material held by solicitors outside judicial or quasi-judicial proceedings at the
e time the code, in its substituted form, was introduced into the 1970 Act in 1976.
In *Parry Jones v Law Society* [1968] 1 All ER 177, [1969] 1 Ch 1, the Court of Appeal
held that the Law Society was entitled under s 29 of the Solicitors Act 1957 to
make rules enabling it to inspect a solicitor's books and supporting documents in
order to see that the Solicitors' Accounts Rules and Solicitors' Trust Accounts
f Rules were being complied with, even if it meant disclosing the client's affairs,
thereby overriding any privilege or confidence which might otherwise subsist
between solicitor and client. Lord Denning MR ([1968] 1 All ER 177 at 178, [1969]
1 Ch 1 at 7) made reference, as a category separate from the privilege relating to
legal proceedings, to the privilege which 'arises out of the confidence subsisting
between solicitor and client similar to the confidence which applies between
g doctor and patient, banker and customer, accountant and client, and the like'. He
said that 'The law implies a term into the contract whereby a professional man is
to keep his client's affairs secret and not to disclose them to anyone without just
cause'. In the same case Diplock LJ said that:

h   '... privilege is irrelevant when one is not concerned with judicial or
quasi-judicial proceedings because, strictly speaking, privilege refers to a
right to withhold from a court, or a tribunal exercising judicial functions,
material which would otherwise be admissible in evidence. What we are
concerned with here is the contractual duty of confidence, generally implied
though sometimes expressed, between a solicitor and client.' (See [1968]
j   1 All ER 177 at 180, [1969] 1 Ch 1 at 9.)

The court held that, in the circumstances of that case, the contractual duty of
confidence was overridden.

[24] It was only later, said Mr Beloff, that this further category of protection,
now commonly referred to as legal advice privilege, was recognised to be as
much a part of legal professional privilege as was so-called litigation privilege. He

suggested that it was because, in 1976, it might well have been perceived that there
was a risk that the lawyer's duty of confidence would yield to the general words of   *a*
s 20(3), that s 20B(8) was inserted. Its function, he submitted, may therefore be seen
as making clear that legal professional privilege was not limited to quasi-judicial
proceedings, that the decision to disclose privileged material held by the solicitor
was the client's decision and not the solicitor's and that, accordingly, the solicitor
had to observe his duty of confidence.   *b*

[25] The difficulty about this submission is that, if Parliament's purpose was
to avoid any risk that the duty of confidence would yield to the general words of
s 20(3) (or the other provisions mentioned in s 20B(8)), it did so in a singularly
inappropriate way. Rather than state that the duty to disclose does not extend to
communications between a professional legal advisor and his client (or any   *c*
person representing his client) made in connection with the giving of legal advice
to the client, it limits it to notices under s 20(3) (or under the s 20(8A) and
s 20A(1)) and then only when served on the taxpayer's professional legal advisor.

[26] The Divisional Court ([2001] 1 All ER 535 at 542 (para 21)) was of the
opinion that the repetition in s 20B(8) of the rule as to legal advice privilege was
otiose unless the scheme of the 1970 Act was to exclude the legal professional   *d*
privilege rule unless expressly otherwise stated. We agree.

[27] The Divisional Court referred also to s 20C(4) of the 1970 Act. That provision
has since been amended by the Finance Act 2000 so that, since 28 July 2000, it
provides simply that 'Nothing in subsection (3) above authorises the seizure and
removal of items subject to legal privilege'. After drawing attention to the provision   *e*
as it existed and as amended by the 2000 Act, the Divisional Court said (at 542
(para 24)):

> '... it is very difficult to rationalise the successive versions of s 20C(4) ... if,
> as MG contended, references in the code to LPP are merely confirmatory of   *f*
> a general rule to which the code is necessarily subject. It is a necessary
> element in that argument that the exclusion of LPP material in the hands of
> legal advisers was merely a specifically stated instance of a general, though
> unexpressed, protection of LPP. But, if that were so, and the terms of the
> statute were originally thought sufficient to address every incidence of LPP,
> why was it changed to make specific reference to LPP as a whole?'   *g*

[28] Mr Beloff submitted that s 20C(4) was not redundant and that its purpose
was to clarify that a warrant under s 20C cannot authorise the seizure of material
covered by legal professional privilege in the hands of a lawyer and that,
accordingly, the lawyer's duty of confidentiality remains absolute. He also pointed *h*
out that, as the section is a power to seize (and not require disclosure of) documents
covered by the warrant so that the consent of the holder of the documents or of any
other person is irrelevant, the legislation distinguishes between s 20B(8) and
s 20C(4). That may be so but what the argument fails to address is why Parliament
has chosen to highlight this particular aspect of legal professional privilege. As the *j*
Divisional Court aptly observed (at 542 (para 25)):

> 'If it were thought necessary to give a special reminder of the importance
> of LPP in some particular case or cases, that might be thought more
> appropriate in a case such as the present, arising under s 20(1) of the 1970 Act,
> where no fraud is alleged or suspected.'

a   [29] Over and above the express preservation of legal professional privilege in
ss 20B(8) and 20C(4) there was a further provision to which we were referred. By
s 20B(2):

> 'A notice under section 20(1) does not oblige a person to deliver documents
> or furnish particulars relating to the conduct of any pending appeal by him;
b > a notice under section 20(3) or (8A) does not oblige a person to deliver or
> make available documents relating to the conduct of a pending appeal by the
> taxpayer; and a notice under section 20A does not oblige a person to deliver
> documents relating to the conduct of a pending appeal by the client.
> "Appeal" means appeal relating to tax.'

c   [30] The Divisional Court considered (at 542 (para 18)) that this provision did
not carry the matter further since appeals might be conducted by persons other
than lawyers, and the documents in question might therefore go beyond those
subject to legal professional privilege. It was suggested that the section was
introduced in view of the uncertain position—as regards matters of privilege—
where a taxpayer conducts his appeal in person or acts with the assistance of a
d person other than a qualified lawyer. Be that as it may, it is to be noted that the
privilege identified by s 20B(2) is confined to 'pending' appeals. MG's approach
to the code assumes, however, that the privilege continues indefinitely. (In *R v
Derby Magistrates' Court, ex p B* [1995] 4 All ER 526 at 540, [1996] AC 487 at 507
Lord Taylor CJ emphasised that 'The client must be sure that what he tells his
e lawyer in confidence will *never* be revealed without his consent' (emphasis
added).) Why then should Parliament express privilege in this provision in terms
merely of pending appeals if, in truth, the privilege is to continue after the appeal
has been disposed of? The documents to which the privilege attaches could well
be material notwithstanding disposal of the particular appeal.

f   [31] Thus far, we have considered the code without regard to decided
authority. In *R v IRC, ex p Taylor (No 2)* [1990] 2 All ER 409, a notice under s 20(2)
of the 1970 Act had been served on a solicitor as taxpayer. Among other
challenges advanced by him to the notice, the solicitor objected that some of the
documents covered by the notice might contain information protected by his
clients' legal professional privilege. In the course of his judgment dismissing the
g solicitor's appeal on this and other points, Bingham LJ (with whom Lord
Donaldson MR and Nourse LJ agreed) said (at 413–414):

> 'Counsel for the applicant … drew attention to the language of s 20B(2)
> and, in particular, the words "conduct of a pending appeal" and referred to
> the preservation of legal professional privilege which is made in s 20B(8). He
h > argued that Parliament could not have intended to override the client's
> ordinary right to legal professional privilege in respect of documents in the
> hands of a legal advisor. I am, for my part, and with all respect to that
> argument, unpersuaded by it. It is quite plain that Parliament had the
> position of professional legal advisors very much in mind. So much is plain
j > from s 20B(3) and (8). Parliament has expressly preserved the client's legal
> professional privilege where disclosure is sought from a lawyer or tax
> accountant in his capacity as professional advisor and not taxpayer. That is
> the position covered by s 20B(8). Parliament has, moreover, provided a measure
> of protection where the notice is given under s 20(1) or (3) concerning
> documents relating to the conduct of a pending appeal by the client. But
> there is no preservation of legal professional privilege and no limited

protection where the notice relates to a lawyer in his capacity as a taxpayer
who is served with a notice under s 20(2). The clear inference is, in my
judgment, that a client's ordinary right to legal professional privilege, binding
in the ordinary way on a legal advisor, does not entitle such legal advisor as
a taxpayer to refuse disclosure. That is not, to my mind, a surprising
intention to attribute to Parliament. In different circumstances the Court of
Appeal has held that the Law Society is entitled to override a client's right to
legal professional privilege when investigating a solicitor's accounts: see
Parry Jones v Law Society [1968] 1 All ER 177, [1969] 1 Ch 1. It is, as I think,
altogether appropriate that the Revenue, being charged with the duty of
collecting the public revenue, should enjoy a similar power.'

[32] Mr Beloff submitted to us, as he had to the Divisional Court, that that
decision was not binding on us as it concerned a notice under s 20(2) served on a
solicitor as a taxpayer who was concerned to urge his clients' legal professional
privilege as a reason for not disclosing various documents. He also submitted
that, in any event, Bingham LJ did not approach the issue of construction from
the premise of the principle of legality.

[33] The Divisional Court accepted Mr Beloff's first point and, although
seeing force in the second, considered that the Court of Appeal could not have
been ignorant of the significance of legal professional privilege, in its full sense,
which by 1989 (when *Ex p Taylor* was decided) was already well-established. The
court went on to say, first, that, although *Ex p B* was decided some years after, in
its statement of the importance of the principle of legal professional privilege, the
House of Lords made, and purported to make, no new law and, second, that it
was not possible to reconcile the outcome of *Ex p Taylor* with the position contended
for by MG in the present case.

[34] Mr Brennan submitted that the Court of Appeal in *Ex p Taylor* decided the
legal professional privilege point in favour of the Revenue and, that, since the
relevant provision in that case, s 20(2) is not, for this purpose, relevantly different
from s 20(1), the ratio in that case is decisive of the issue in the present case and
binding on this court. Alternatively, he submitted, the Divisional Court was
correct to hold that it is impossible to reconcile the outcome of *Ex p Taylor* with
Mr Beloff's submissions in the present case.

[35] We consider, like the Divisional Court, that the Court of Appeal in
Ex p Taylor could not have been unaware of the fundamental importance of legal
professional privilege. The fact that it may not have approached the issue of
construction in the full light of the principle of legality as it has now come to be
formulated does not, in our view, detract from this fact. We also agree with the
Divisional Court that it is impossible to reconcile the outcome of *Ex p Taylor* with
the submissions of MG in the present case. Since we have reached the same view
on the issue of legal professional privilege as the Court of Appeal did in
Ex p Taylor, it is idle to consider whether, in any event, we are bound by the ratio
in that case.

[36] We come now to Mr Beloff's particular criticisms of the Divisional Court's
approach to statutory construction. The first concerns the use of subsequent
legislation to construe an earlier provision. He submitted that, in construing the
ambit of s 20(1), it was not open to the Divisional Court to have regard to
amendments to the code introduced subsequent to 1976 when s 20(1) was first
enacted in what for all practical purposes is its current form. Subsequent
legislation, he submitted, can only be referred to if the original is ambiguous, i e if

a there are two or more equally tenable constructions and no other indications in the 1970 Act in question favouring one construction rather than the other or others (see *Fetherstonaugh v IRC* [1984] STC 261 at 272; sub nom *Finch v IRC* [1985] Ch 1 at 15). All the more was it not open to the Divisional Court to have regard to subsequent legislation, he submitted, where, as here, the court was considering whether there was a necessary implication that Parliament intended by s 20(1) to b override a fundamental right. The justification for holding that a fundamental right has been overridden is that Parliament, by passing the relevant provision, must have squarely faced up to the consequences of what it was doing and faced the political consequences. See the passage from Lord Hoffmann's speech in *R v Secretary of State for the Home Dept, ex p Simms* [1999] 3 All ER 400 at 412, [2000] 2 AC 115 at 131 set out at [16] above. The focus, he submitted, must therefore be c on the material before Parliament at the time it enacted the particular provision (here s 20(1)). This necessarily could not include subsequent amendments or new provisions.

[37] The short answer to this submission is that the conclusion on the question of construction is unaffected by any legislation passed subsequent to d 1976. The amendment to s 20C(4) of the 1970 Act introduced initially by the Finance Act 1989 and later replaced by the provision set out at [27] above was itself almost word for word the same as the corresponding provision to be found in a proviso to s 20C(3) as it was enacted in 1976. That proviso stated:

'But this [ie the seizure and removal of items in execution of a warrant] e does not authorise the seizure and removal of documents in the possession of a barrister, advocate or solicitor with respect to which a claim to professional privilege could be maintained.'

[38] It is true that, in its decision, the Divisional Court ([2001] 1 All ER 535 at 543 (para 23)) referred to s 20BA and para 5 of Sch 1AA to the 1970 Act which f were introduced by the 2000 Act. Section 20BA enables orders to be made by 'the appropriate judicial authority' for the delivery of documents in cases where there is reasonable ground for suspecting that an offence involving serious tax fraud has been or is about to be committed and that documents which may be required as evidence for the purpose of proceedings in respect of the offence are or may be in the possession any person. Paragraph 5 of Sch 1AA provides that the section g does not apply 'to items subject to legal privilege'. The reference to those provisions was not critical to the Divisional Court's decision but, even if it was, reference to them is not necessary to the conclusion which the Divisional Court reached and with which we agree that, except where otherwise expressly preserved, the rule of legal professional privilege cannot be maintained.

h [39] But, in any event, we question why, in a code such as this which Parliament has from time to time amended, it should be impermissible when determining what, at the date that the s 20(1) notice was issued, the true scope was of that provision, to consider what Parliament's intention was by reference to other provisions of the code. We see no reason why, in a case such as this, the j court's gaze must be confined to legislation as it existed at some much earlier date. Each amendment accrues to a text conveying an evolving but at each stage ascertainable intent.

[40] Mr Beloff's other criticism of the Divisional Court's approach to statutory construction concerned its failure, as he submitted, to pay proper regard to the view expressed by Lord Hoffmann in *Walker (Inspector of Taxes) v Centaur Clothes Group Ltd* [2000] 2 All ER 589 at 595, [2000] 1 WLR 799 at 805 that 'an argument

from redundancy [seldom] carries great weight, even in a Finance Act. It is not
unusual for Parliament to say expressly what the courts would have inferred *a*
anyway'. The importance of that approach, Mr Beloff submitted, is all the more
to be respected where, as here, what is in issue is the overriding of a fundamental
right. That is especially so, he said, given that there are no provisions of the 1970
Act which could not operate consistently with the general survival of legal
professional privilege.   *b*

[41] We consider that Mr Beloff has placed heavier reliance on Lord Hoffmann's
dictum than it was designed to bear. The strength or weakness of an argument
from redundancy must depend on the particular text. The question here is
whether Parliament's explicit protection of certain classes of privileged documents
would be redundant if its intention were that all such documents should be
protected. In other words, as the Divisional Court observed (at 543 (para 26)), the *c*
inquiry is into whether there can fairly be deduced from the terms of the code
taken as a whole a consistency of theme that requires, within that code, specific
provision to be made for the recognition of legal professional privilege. The
absence of any good reason why, in a detailed code of closely-related provisions,
Parliament has chosen to mention particular cases where legal professional *d*
privilege is to be preserved, confirms our view that they are intended to be
exceptions to an underlying rule that legal professional privilege is not to entitle
a person served with a notice to refuse disclosure. The inspector's argument from
redundancy is therefore one which, in the circumstances of this case, has some
force.

[42] There is, however, another argument from redundancy. We have mentioned *e*
it at the end of para [20] above; but consistency has, we suspect, caused Mr Beloff
to spell it out as a rhetorical question rather than in terms which, when they are
used by the Revenue, he attacks. It can nevertheless legitimately be asked, as a
riposte to the previous paragraph of this judgment, whether Parliament's explicit
exposure to production of certain classes of otherwise privileged document *f*
would be redundant if its intention were that all such documents should be
exigible by the Revenue. The answer, in our view, lies in what follows.

The principle of legality and the Human Rights Act 1998

[43] Mr Beloff made the powerful submission that a general abrogation of
legal professional privilege, save where otherwise specified, in the face of the *g*
Revenue's powers of search and seizure is not only as difficult to imply as it would
have been easy to express: it is all but blocked in the 1970 Act by the constitutional
principle that unequivocal legislative provision is necessary in order to override
fundamental rights. Here, he argues, the fundamentality of legal professional
privilege as a domestic legal right of the individual has now been reinforced by *h*
the constraints placed by art 8 of the convention on the construction of legislation
and on the acts of public authorities by ss 3 and 6 of the Human Rights Act 1998.
The decision of the European Court of Human Rights in *Foxley v UK* (2001) 8 BHRC
571 confirms that legal professional privilege is protected by art 8. Mr Beloff submits,
and we accept, that the 1998 Act requires us to revisit the reasoning in *R v IRC, ex p* *j*
Taylor (No 2) [1990] 2 All ER 409 in the light of the convention and its jurisprudence.

[44] Mr Beloff's initial recourse, however, is to the *Ex p B* decision and to the
protection afforded to it by s 11 of the 1998 Act: 'A person's reliance on a
Convention right does not restrict—(a) any other right or freedom conferred on
him by or under any law having effect in any part of the United Kingdom ...' This
is because art 8 affords a right to respect for private life and correspondence

a which can be qualified in a proper case, as we have said, by the interests of the economic well-being of the country. But legal professional privilege, as described in *R v Derby Magistrates' Court, ex p B* [1995] 4 All ER 526, [1996] AC 487, is unqualified by any considerations of public or private welfare. We accept this as the starting point for considering the meaning of the 1970 Act.

[45] Of Mr Beloff's argument that nothing would have been easier than to say
b in black and white what Mr Brennan has sought to spell out of the legislation, it would be unjustifiably cynical to say that it represents the triumph of hope over experience. What can more cogently be said is that not all legislators are ready to meet the 'political cost' which, as Lord Hoffmann said in *Ex p Simms* (at [16], above), might have to be paid for legislation that invades fundamental rights. One reason why there are many examples of statutory provisions which emerge
c only by implication is that some statutes are cast in broad and unspecific language: the 1998 Act is a good example, but ever since the Code Napoléon (and arguably for much longer) the advantages of legislating in brief and broad terms and leaving it to the courts to fill in the detail have been recognised. A related reason, however, and one which can make for complexity rather than simplicity,
d is that hinted at both by Lord Hoffmann and some years earlier by Lord Upjohn when in *Padfield v Minister of Agriculture, Fisheries and Food* [1968] 1 All ER 694 at 719, [1968] AC 997 at 1061, he spoke of the 'fear of parliamentary trouble' and the need for ministers on occasion 'to face the music in Parliament': it is sometimes simpler or safer to let the court as the interpreter of legislation, rather than ministers as its advocates, spell out its implications. There is nothing novel or
e necessarily sinister in this. Disraeli when moving the second Reform Bill of 1867, pressed as to whether women were meant to be included in the 'persons' who were being enfranchised, replied that this would be 'a matter for the gentlemen of the long robe'—as indeed it turned out to be; and as recently as 1997–1998, the Lord Chancellor and other ministers in moving the Human Rights Bill more than
f once made it clear that judicial exploration and development of simple and broad provisions was the way Parliament was being invited to go.

[46] The choice is, no doubt, a choice of risks; but if it is made in favour of exegesis by the court, the court must do its best to make a coherent whole of what has been enacted. Mr Beloff correctly submits that in doing this the court is not neutral. It starts from the principle of legality, which in this case means the
g upholding, unless Parliament has clearly said otherwise, of legal professional privilege. But the proviso brings us back to what, for reasons we have given, we consider to be the compellingly clear implication of the structure and wording of the segment of the Act which we have been examining. If, as we hold, it is Parliament's manifest intent that legal privilege should in general yield to the
h statutory disclosure regime, the principle of legality requires us to give effect to it.

A right to be heard?

[47] The submission that a taxpayer or advisor at risk of compulsory disclosure of confidential documents ought to have an opportunity of deflecting the
j application is at first sight attractive. To see why, one need go no further than Lord Loreburn LC's celebrated remark in *Board of Education v Rice* [1911] AC 179 at 182, [1911–13] All ER Rep 36 at 38 that acting in good faith and listening fairly to both sides 'is a duty lying upon every one who decides anything'. But in the same passage Lord Loreburn LC made clear, as other judges of high authority have done many times since, that how this is done is in principle a matter for each decision-maker: natural justice does not generally demand orality. And there is a

further, small, group of cases, of which Mr Brennan submits this is one, in which
the exigencies of the legislative scheme make an inter partes procedure impossible.

[48] What is said here by Mr Beloff is that although the disclosure procedure
is in one sense a first step which in itself determines nobody's rights or liabilities,
in another and more important sense it is conclusive of the Revenue's right to
invade somebody's privacy and (given our conclusions so far) to disrupt a
relationship of professional confidentiality. His position, he contends, is if anything
stronger than that of the applicant in *Georgiou (t/a Marios Chippery) v UK* [2001]
STC 80, in whose favour the European Court accepted that fine lines should not
be drawn, for art 6 of the convention purposes, between the civil and criminal
aspects of an assessment to a tax penalty. Here, where it is respect for private life
and correspondence under art 8 which in issue, the impugned decision constitutes
a completed invasion of the convention right. If the court is to sanction it, as we
have done, then Mr Beloff contends that it should only be by including at least a
power (he no longer says a duty) in the Special Commissioner to hear oral
submissions if he thinks they may help him to reach a sound conclusion. In this
way the common law will be doing what it can and should to prevent procedural
unfairness from being heaped on substantive injustice.

[49] It will be recalled that in the present case the Special Commissioner
accepted written submissions from the applicants without demur. But he held
that he had no power whatever to entertain oral submissions. Mr Brennan has
tenaciously, and in our ultimate view successfully, defended this entrenched and
in many ways unpromising position against Mr Beloff's assault. His argument is
that, both on principle and on authority, the self-evident risk of compromising
the investigation shuts out any possibility of an oral procedure.

[50] It has to be remembered that a right to be heard is axiomatically worth
little without knowledge of the case that has to be met. Either, therefore, the
inspector's hand has in some measure to be shown, or the taxpayer must be
content to make submissions in the dark. The former, it is plain, is destructive of
the whole purpose of the procedure; the latter, while some taxpayers may
consider it better than nothing, will create a sustained pressure for disclosure.
There are only two logical outcomes if these two imperatives clash in a face-to-
face hearing: one is that the taxpayer will duly learn nothing, in which case it is
not easy to see what will have been achieved on his behalf that could not have
been achieved in writing; the other is that the Special Commissioner's opportunity
(in Mr Beloff's happy phrase) to 'enjoy the benefit of advocacy' will lead to
accidental disclosure by him or (more probably) the inspector of material to
which Mr Beloff does not contend that the taxpayer is entitled and the disclosure
of which at this stage will run counter to Parliament's purpose. That purpose, we
apprehend, is in lieu of any inter partes procedure to install the General or Special
Commissioner as monitor of the exercise of the Inland Revenue's intrusive
powers and to require an inspector to put everything known to him, favourable
and unfavourable, before the commissioner when seeking his consent (*T C Coombs
& Co (a firm) v IRC* [1991] 3 All ER 623, sub nom *R v IRC, ex p T C Coombs & Co*
[1991] 2 AC 283). We accept Mr Brennan's contention, therefore, that the
possibility of an oral hearing is excluded by the nature of the process in question.
We do not accept his further ground that to establish a discretion to hold a
hearing is to invite judicial review of every decision not to do so and of every
failure to extract information from the inspector or to obtain reasons from the
commissioner. It is not legitimate, as Lord Bridge of Harwich said in *Leech v*

a *Parkhurst Prison Deputy Governor* [1988] 1 All ER 485 at 499, [1988] AC 533 at 566, to draw jurisdictional lines on a purely defensive basis. If the power exists, the possibility of judicial review comes with it. But, for the reasons we have given, we are satisfied that the Special Commissioner was right to conclude that he possessed no such power.

[51] The appeal will therefore be dismissed.

Appeal dismissed. Permission to appeal refused.

Kate O'Hanlon   Barrister.

Practice Direction

FAMILY DIVISION

Practice – Family Division – Incapacitated adults – Declaratory proceedings – Commencement and determination.

1. Proceedings which invoke the jurisdiction of the High Court to grant declarations as to the best interests of incapacitated adults are civil proceedings to which the Civil Procedure Rules 1998 apply. Although not assigned to any Division, having regard to their nature and the issues raised within them, such proceedings are more suitable for hearing in the Family Division.

2. Accordingly, these proceedings should be commenced, and will be determined, as follows. (a) Permanent vegetative state cases should be issued in the Principal Registry of the Family Division and will be determined by the President of the Family Division or by a judge nominated by her. Interlocutory applications will be heard by the President or by the nominated judge. (b) Other proceedings may be commenced in any registry but must be determined by a Judge of the Division. Interlocutory applications are to be heard by a judge of the Division.

3. The *Practice Note (Official Solicitor: declaratory proceedings: medical and welfare decisions for adults who lack capacity)* [2001] 2 FCR 569, dated 1 May 2001 and issued by the Official Solicitor [see annex below], provides valuable guidance in relation to these proceedings and should be followed.

4. Issued with the approval of the Lord Chief Justice and the Lord Chancellor.

14 December 2001   DAME ELIZABETH BUTLER-SLOSS P.

Annex[a]

Practice Note (Official Solicitor: declaratory proceedings: medical and welfare decisions for adults who lack capacity)

1. This practice note supersedes *Practice Note (Official solicitor: sterilization)* [1996] 3 FCR 95 and *Practice Note (Official Solicitor: vegetative state)* [1996] 3 FCR 606. It combines the guidance given in those earlier practice notes, and extends it to a wider range of medical and welfare disputes leading to litigation. This practice note deals only with adults who lack capacity. Medical treatment or welfare disputes about children will be dealt with under the Children Act 1989 or the inherent jurisdiction in relation to children (see *Practice Note (Official Solicitor: appointment in family proceedings)* [2001] 2 FCR 566 and *CAFCASS Practice Note (Officers of CAFCASS Legal Services and special casework: appointment in family proceedings)* [2001] 2 FCR 562).

JURISDICTION

2. The High Court has jurisdiction to make declarations as to the best interests of an adult who lacks decision-making capacity. The jurisdiction will be exercised when there is a serious justiciable issue requiring a decision by the court. It has been exercised in relation to a range of medical treatment issues, in particular

---

a   Editor's note: the annex does not form part of Dame Elizabeth Butler-Sloss P's Practice Direction, but has been set out for ease of reference.

a sterilisation operations and the continuance of artificial nutrition and hydration. It has also been exercised in relation to residence and contact issues. The jurisdiction is comprehensively reviewed and analysed in *Re F (adult: court's jurisdiction)* [2000] 3 FCR 30, [2001] Fam 38.

THE NEED FOR COURT INVOLVEMENT

b 3. Case law has established two categories of case that will in virtually all cases require the prior sanction of a High Court judge. The first is sterilisation of a person (whether a child or an adult) who cannot consent to the operation: *Re B (a minor) (wardship: sterilisation)* [1987] 2 All ER 206, [1988] AC 199 and *Re F (mental patient: sterilisation)* [1989] 2 All ER 545, [1990] 2 AC 1. The second is the discontinuance of artificial nutrition and hydration for a patient in a vegetative state: *Airedale NHS*
c *Trust v Bland* [1993] 1 All ER 821 at 833, [1993] AC 789 at 805. Further guidance about sterilisation and vegetative state cases is given below. In all other cases, doctors and carers should seek advice from their own lawyers about the need to apply to the court. In the Official Solicitor's view, applications should be made where there are disputes or difficulties as to either the patient's capacity or the
d patient's best interests. Guidelines were handed down by the Court of Appeal in *St George's Healthcare NHS Trust v S, R v Collins, ex p S* [1998] 3 All ER 673 at 702–704, [1999] Fam 26 at 62–65. It was stressed in that case that a declaration made without notice would be ineffective and ought not to be made.

THE APPLICATION

e 4. Applications should be made to the Family Division of the High Court (principal or district registry). The proceedings are not, however, 'family proceedings' for the puposes of CPR 2.1(2). The CPR will therefore apply.

THE CLAIM

f 5. In the Official Solicitor's view, the CPR Pt 8 alternative procedure is the more appropriate and a Pt 8 claim form should be used. The claimant should file all evidence with the claim form. The Official Solicitor is unlikely to be in a position to file all his evidence with his acknowledgment of service. A directions hearing should therefore be fixed when the claim form is issued.

6. The relief sought should be declarations that:

g '(1) [The patient] lacks capacity to make a decision about ... [specify treatment or welfare decision at issue, e g having a kidney transplant *or* where to live]. (2) It is [*or* is not] in the existing circumstances in the best interests of [the patient] for ... [specify treatment or other issue, e g him to undergo below-knee amputation of his left leg *or* her to have contact with the claimant for at
h least two hours each week].'

(See appendices below for suggested wording in sterilisation and permanent vegetative state (PVS) cases.)

THE EVIDENCE

j 7. The claimant must adduce evidence going to both capacity and best interests.

(1) *Capacity*

The court has no jurisdiction unless it is established that the patient is incapable of making a decision about the matter in issue. The test of capacity to consent to or refuse treatment is set out in *Re MB (an adult: medical treatment)* [1997] 2 FCR 541 at 553–554. In the Official Solicitor's view, this test can be used for a wide range of decisions. Evidence from a psychiatrist or psychologist who has assessed the patient applying the *Re MB* test to the particular decision in question is generally required. It follows from the terms of the *Re MB* test that global psychometric test results are unlikely to be relevant. The Official Solicitor's experience is that references to the outdated and discredited concept of 'mental age' are of no assistance at all. It is important for the expert assessing capacity to advise whether the patient is likely to develop capacity to make personal decisions about the matter in issue in the future.

(2) *Best interests*

In any medical case, the claimant must adduce evidence from a responsible medical practitioner not only (1) that performing the particular operation would not be negligent but also (2) that it is necessary in the best interests of the patient: *Re A (medical treatment: male sterilisation)* [2000] 1 FCR 193 at 200. The court's jurisdiction is to declare the best interests of the patient on the application of a welfare test analogous to that applied in wardship: *Re SL (adult patient) (medical treatment)* [2000] 2 FCR 452 at 467, [2001] Fam 15 at 30–31. The judicial decision will incorporate broader ethical, social, moral and welfare considerations (see [2000] 2 FCR 452 at 465, [2001] Fam 15 at 28). Emotional, psychological and social benefit to the patient will be considered: *Re Y (Mental incapacity: bone marrow transplant)* [1997] 2 FCR 172, [1997] Fam 110. The court will wish to prepare a balance sheet listing the advantages and disadvantages of the procedure for the patient. If potential advantages and disadvantages are to be relied on then the court will wish to assess in percentage terms the likelihood of them in fact occurring: *Re A* [2000] 1 FCR 193 at 206.

THE PARTIES

8. The claimant should be the NHS Trust or other body responsible for the patient's care, although a claim may also be brought by a family member or other individual closely connected with the patient. The body with clinical or caring responsibility should in any event be made a party: *Re S (hospital patient: court's jurisdiction)* [1995] 3 FCR 496, [1996] Fam 1.

9. The person concerned must always be a party and should normally be a defendant, with the Official Solicitor acting as litigation friend. The Official Solicitor has a standard form of medical certificate if there is any question about whether the person concerned is a 'patient' within the meaning of CPR r 21.1(2)(b). If the Official Solicitor does not act as litigation friend, the court will wish to consider whether he should be joined as an ex officio defendant or invited to act as a friend of the court. The Official Solicitor is invariably asked to be involved in sterilisation and vegetative state cases.

THE DIRECTIONS HEARING

10. Unless the matter is urgent, the claimant should fix a directions hearing for no less than eight weeks after the date of issue, to allow the Official Solicitor to make initial inquiries. The court should, if appropriate, be asked to hold the directions hearing in private to protect the interests of the patient: CPR 39.2(3)(d). The court will use the directions hearing to: (1) make orders where necessary to preserve the anonymity of the patient, family and other parties; (2) set a timetable for the Official Solicitor to conduct inquiries, obtain expert evidence and file his statement or report; (3) fix a further hearing, to serve either as a final hearing if the matter is unopposed or as a final directions hearing to fix a contested hearing.

a   11. The Official Solicitor's representative will always see the patient, review relevant medical/social work records and interview carers, family members and others close to the patient as appropriate.

12. The Official Solicitor will consider the patient's wishes and feelings, and will inquire as to any earlier views the patient may have expressed, either in writing or
b otherwise. The High Court may determine the effect of a purported advance statement as to future medical treatment: *Re T (adult: refusal of medical treatment)* [1992] 4 All ER 649, [1993] Fam 95 and *Re C (adult: refusal of medical treatment)* [1994] 1 All ER 819, [1994] 1 WLR 290. A valid and applicable advance refusal of treatment may be determinative. Previously expressed wishes and feelings which do not amount to an effective advance decision will still be an important component in the
c best interests decision.

THE FINAL HEARING
13. Any substantive hearing should be before a High Court judge of the Family Division. Cases proceeding unopposed may be disposed of without oral
d evidence. The final hearing may be in private if necessary to protect the interests of the patient: r 39.2(3)(d). If the hearing is in public, there may be orders that the identities of parties and witnesses (other than expert witnesses) should not be disclosed: r 39.2(4). An order restricting publicity will continue to have effect notwithstanding the death of the patient, unless and until an application is made to discharge it: *Re C (adult patient: restriction of publicity after death)* [1996] 1 FCR 60.
e The Official Solicitor will invite the court to make an appropriate order in relation to his costs.

CONSULTATION WITH THE OFFICIAL SOLICITOR
14. Members of the Official Solicitor's legal staff are prepared to discuss adult
f medical and welfare cases before proceedings are issued. Inquiries should be addressed to a family litigation lawyer at:

The Official Solicitor
81 Chancery Lane
London WC2A 1DD
g Telephone: 020 7911 7127
Fax: 020 7911 7105
e-mail: enquiries@offsol.gsi.gov.uk

Inquiries about *children* medical and welfare cases should be directed to:

CAFCASS Legal Services and Special Casework
h Newspaper House
8–16 Great New Street
London EC4A 3BN
Telephone: 020 7904 0867
Fax: 020 7904 0868/9
j e-mail: legal@cafcass.gsi.gov.uk

Staff of CAFCASS Legal will liaise with the Official Solicitor where it is unclear which office can best represent a child.

LAURENCE OATES

1 May 2001   Official Solicitor

Appendix 1: Sterilisation cases

a

1. If a sterilisation procedure is necessary for therapeutic as opposed to contraceptive purposes then there may be no need for an application to court: *Re GF (a patient)* [1991] FCR 786. If, however, any case lies anywhere near the boundary line it should be referred to the court: *Re SL (adult patient) (medical treatment)* [2000] 2 FCR 452 at 469, sub nom *Re S (adult patient: sterilisation)* [2001] Fam 15 at 32.

b

THE CLAIM
2. The relief sought in relation to an adult should be declarations that:

'(1) [The patient] lacks capacity to consent to an operation of ... [specify procedure proposed, e g tubal occlusion by Filshie clips *or* laparoscopic sub-total   c
hysterectomy *or* vasectomy]. (2) It is in the existing circumstances in the best interests of [the patient] for her/him to undergo an operation of ... [specify procedure as above].'

THE EVIDENCE   d
3. The court must be satisfied that the patient lacks capacity and that the operation will promote the best interests of the patient, rather than the interests or convenience of the claimant, carers or public. In sterilisation cases, the best interests test has at least three particular components.

(1) Likelihood of pregnancy   e
An operation must address a current real need. It must be shown that the patient is capable of conception and is having or is likely to have full sexual intercourse. In relation to a young woman who has no interest in human relationships with any sexual ingredient a high level of supervision is an appropriate protection: *Re LC (medical treatment: sterilisation)* [1997] 2 FLR 258.   f
Any risk of pregnancy should be identifiable rather than speculative: *Re S (adult: sterilisation)* [1999] 1 FCR 277.

(2) Damage deriving from conception and/or menstruation
The physical and psychological consequences of pregnancy and childbirth for the patient should be analysed by obstetric and psychiatric experts. In the case of   g
a male, these considerations will be different: *Re A (medical treatment: male sterilisation)* [2000] 1 FCR 193 at 202–203. Psychiatric evidence as to the patient's likely ability to care for and/or have a fulfilling relationship with a child should be adduced. Evidence as to any child having a disability is likely to be irrelevant: *Re X (adult patient: sterilisation)* [1999] 3 FCR 426 at 431. If the proposed procedure is intended   h
to affect the patient's menstruation, then evidence about any detriment caused by her current menstrual cycle must also be adduced.

(3) Medical and surgical techniques
The court will require a detailed analysis of all available and relevant methods of addressing any problems found to be substantiated under (1) and (2) above.   j
This analysis should be performed by a doctor or doctors with expertise in the full range of available methods. The expert should explain the nature of each relevant method and then list its advantages and disadvantages (in particular, morbidity rates, mortality rates and failure rates) for the individual patient, taking into account any relevant aspects of her physical and psychological health. The Royal College of Obstetrics and Gynaecology has published relevant evidence-based

a clinical guidelines (No 4: *Male and Female Sterilisation*, April 1999 and No 5: *The Management of Menorrhagia in Secondary Care*, July 1999).

Appendix 2: Permanent vegetative state cases

1. It is futile to provide medical treatment, including artificial nutrition and hydration, to a patient with no awareness of self or environment and no prospect
b of recovery: *Airedale NHS Trust v Bland* [1993] 1 All ER 821 at 870, [1993] AC 789 at 869. The purpose of the proceedings is to establish whether the patient is in this condition. It is not appropriate to apply to court to discontinue artificial feeding and hydration until the condition is judged to be permanent. Diagnostic guidelines are not statutory provisions and a precise label may not be of importance. The court's
c concern is whether there is any awareness whatsoever or any possibility of change: *Re D (adult: medical treatment)* [1998] 1 FCR 498 at 508 and *Re H (adult: medical treatment)* [1998] 3 FCR 174. The approach of the court has been reviewed in the light of the Human Rights Act 1998 and held to be compatible with convention rights: *NHS Trust A v M, NHS Trust B v H* [2001] 1 All ER 801, [2001] Fam 348 (see also European Convention on Human Rights and Fundamental Freedoms 1950
d (as set out in Sch 1 of the 1998 Act)). There has as yet been no decided case dealing with the discontinuance of artificial feeding and hydration for an adult patient with any (however minimal) awareness of self or environment.

The claim

e 2. All claims in these cases should be issued in the Principal Registry and will normally be heard by the President of the Family Division unless she releases the case to another Family Division judge. The relief sought should be declarations that:

f '(1) [The patient] lacks capacity to consent to continued life-sustaining treatment measures and is in the permanent vegetative state. (2) It is not in the existing circumstances in the best interests of [the patient] to be given life-sustaining medical treatment measures (including ventilation, nutrition and hydration by artificial means) and such measures may lawfully be discontinued. (3) It is in [the patient's] best interests to be given such treatment and nursing care whether at hospital or elsewhere under medical supervision as may be
g appropriate to ensure he/she retains the greatest dignity until such time as his/her life comes to an end.'

The medical evidence

h 3. The diagnosis should be made in accordance with the most up-to-date generally accepted guidelines for the medical profession. A review by a working group of the Royal College of Physicians has been endorsed by the Conference of Medical Royal Colleges (*The Permanent Vegetative State*, Royal College of Physicians Publication Unit (1996); with addendum published in (1997) 31 JR Coll Physns 260). The review concludes that the diagnosis of permanent vegetative state should
j not be made until the patient has been in a continuing vegetative state following head injury for 12 months or following other causes of brain damage for six months. The addendum to the review emphasises that there is no urgency in making the diagnosis and the assessors should take into account descriptions given by relatives, carers and nursing staff who spend most time with the patient. *The International Working Party Report on the Vegetative State* (1996), produced by the Royal Hospital for Neuro-disability, sets out in an appendix a range of vegetative presentations.

4. The claimant should, as a minimum, adduce evidence from (1) the treating
physician and (2) a neurologist or other expert experienced in assessing disturbances *a*
of consciousness. Both should deal with the diagnosis and their professional
judgment of whether continued treatment would be in the patient's best interests.
The duties of doctors making the diagnosis are described in the Royal College of
Physicians review.

5. The court will generally wish to see at least two reports from experts, one of *b*
whom must be independent of the treating clinical team and claimant. The Official
Solicitor will usually commission the second expert report.

Other evidence

6. The claimant should also adduce evidence about the views of family members.
The views of family members or others close to the patient cannot act as a veto *c*
to an application but they must be taken fully into account by the court: *Re G
(persistent vegetative state)* [1995] 2 FCR 46 at 51.

The final hearing

7. It is usual for the final hearing to be in public, with protection for the identities
of parties and witnesses. Even if the matter is unopposed, it may be appropriate *d*
for at least one expert to attend to give oral evidence. Family members need not
attend if this would cause distress.

a

R v Rezvi
[2002] UKHL 1

HOUSE OF LORDS

b LORD SLYNN OF HADLEY, LORD BROWNE-WILKINSON, LORD STEYN, LORD HOPE OF CRAIGHEAD AND LORD HUTTON

29–31 OCTOBER 2001, 24 JANUARY 2002

Sentencing – Confiscation order – Proceeds of crime – Whether statutory provisions governing confiscation orders compatible with human rights – Criminal Justice Act
c *1988, s 72AA – Human Rights Act 1998, Sch 1, Pt I, art 6, Pt II, art 1.*

The defendant pleaded guilty to two counts of theft and was subsequently given a custodial sentence. On the day of sentencing, which took place before the implementation of the Human Rights Act 1998, a confiscation order was made
d against the defendant pursuant to Pt VI of the Criminal Justice Act 1988. One of the provisions of that Part, s 72AA[a], provided for the making of certain statutory assumptions. On the defendant's appeal against the confiscation order, which was heard after the implementation of the 1998 Act, the principle issue was whether those assumptions were compatible with art 6(2)[b] of the European Convention for the Protection of Human Rights and Fundamental Freedoms 1950
e (as set out in Sch 1 to the 1998 Act), which provided that everyone charged with a criminal offence was presumed innocent until proved guilty. On the basis, as then understood, of the retrospective effect of the 1998 Act, the Court of Appeal considered the position as if that Act was directly applicable. It nevertheless held that the 1988 Act was compatible with the convention, and dismissed the appeal.
f The defendant appealed to the House of Lords.

Held – The 1998 Act did not apply to the outcome of criminal trials which were concluded before the implementation of that Act even if an appeal was heard after its implementation. It followed in the instant case that the defendant's convention rights were not engaged. The confiscation order had been properly
g made, and accordingly the appeal would be dismissed (see [1], [2], [5], [21]–[23], [26], [38], below); *R v Kansal (No 2)* [2002] 1 All ER 257 applied.

Per curiam. Article 6(2) of the convention does not apply to confiscation proceedings under the 1988 Act. Such proceedings are part of the sentencing process following a conviction, and do not, therefore, involve a fresh criminal
h charge within the meaning of art 6(2). That conclusion does not leave unprotected a person who is subject to confiscation proceedings under the 1988 Act. Such a person is protected, inter alia, by the general right to a fair hearing under art 6(1) of the convention. However, Pt VI of the 1988 Act is a proportionate response to the problem which it addresses, namely the fact that professional and habitual criminals frequently take steps to conceal their profits from crime. Article 1[c] of
j the First Protocol to the convention, which provides that no one shall be deprived of his possessions except in the public interest and subject to conditions provided by law, does not require a different conclusion on proportionality.

---

a   Section 72AA, so far as material, is set out at [8], below
b   Article 6, so far as material, is set out at [8], below
c   Article 1 is set out at [17], below

Accordingly, there is no incompatibility when the provisions of the 1988 Act are measured against the rights under the convention and the First Protocol (see [1], [2], [10], [11], [13], [14], [16]–[18], [23], [30], [32], [38], below); *McIntosh v Lord Advocate* [2001] 2 All ER 638 and *Phillips v UK* (2001) 11 BHRC 280 followed.

Decision of the Court of Appeal [2001] 2 All ER 609 affirmed on different grounds.

Notes

For the presumption of innocence and the right to property, see 8(2) *Halsbury's Laws* (4th edn reissue) paras 142, 165, and for confiscation orders in respect of the proceeds of an offence, see 11(2) *Halsbury's Laws* (4th edn reissue) para 1284.

For the Criminal Justice Act 1988, s 72AA, see 12 *Halsbury's Statutes* (4th edn) (1997 reissue) 1028.

For the Human Rights Act 1998, Sch 1, Pt I, art 6, Pt II, art 1, see 7 *Halsbury's Statutes* (4th edn) (1999 reissue) 523, 525.

Cases referred to in opinions

Allenet de Ribemont v France (1995) 20 EHRR 557, ECt HR.
de Freitas v Permanent Secretary of Ministry of Agriculture, Fisheries, Lands and Housing [1999] 1 AC 69, [1998] 3 WLR 675, PC.
Engel v Netherlands (No 1) (1976) 1 EHRR 647, ECt HR.
McIntosh v Lord Advocate [2001] UKPC D1, [2001] 2 All ER 638, [2001] 3 WLR 107.
Minelli v Switzerland (1983) 5 EHRR 554, ECt HR.
Phillips v UK (2001) 11 BHRC 280, ECt HR.
Pierson v Secretary of State for the Home Dept [1997] 3 All ER 577, [1998] AC 539, [1997] 3 WLR 492, HL.
R v Benjafield, R v Leal, R v Rezvi, R v Milford [2001] 2 All ER 609, [2001] 3 WLR 75, CA.
R v DPP, ex p Kebeline, R v DPP, ex p Rechachi [1999] 4 All ER 801, [2000] AC 326, [1999] 3 WLR 972, HL.
R v Kansal (No 2) [2001] UKHL 62, [2002] 1 All ER 257, [2001] 3 WLR 1562.
R v Lambert [2002] UKHL 37, [2001] 3 All ER 577, [2001] 3 WLR 206.
R v Secretary of State for the Home Dept, ex p Simms [1999] 3 All ER 400, [2000] 2 AC 115, [1999] 3 WLR 328, HL.
Salabiaku v France (1988) 13 EHRR 379, ECt HR.
Saunders v UK (1996) BHRC 358, ECt HR.
Sekanina v Austria (1993) 17 EHRR 221, ECt HR.

Appeal

The appellant, Syed Zargham Rezvi, appealed with leave of the Appeal Committee of the House of Lords given on 14 February 2001 from the decision of the Court of Appeal (Lord Woolf CJ, Judge LJ and Collins J) on 21 December 2000 ([2001] 2 All ER 609, [2001] 3 WLR 75) dismissing his appeal against a confiscation order in the sum of £214,839 imposed on him by Judge Ader in the Crown Court at Snaresbrook on 10 April 2000 under Pt VI of the Criminal Justice Act 1988. The Court of Appeal certified that a point of law of general public importance, set out at [4], below, was involved in its decision. The facts are set out in the opinion of Lord Steyn.

Tim Owen QC and *Danny Friedman* (instructed by *Magrath & Co*) for the appellant.
David Perry, Kennedy Talbot and *Duncan Atkinson* (instructed by the *Crown Prosecution Service*) for the Crown.

a Their Lordships took time for consideration.

24 January 2002. The following opinions were delivered.

LORD SLYNN OF HADLEY.

b [1] My Lords, I have had the advantage of reading in draft the speech of my noble and learned friend Lord Steyn. I agree with him that this appeal should be dismissed on the basis of the decision of your Lordships' House in *R v Kansal (No 2)* [2001] UKHL 62, [2002] 1 All ER 257, [2001] 3 WLR 1562. I also agree with the views he expresses as to the relationship between rights under the European Convention for the Protection of Human Rights and Fundamental Freedoms 1950 (as set out in Sch 1 to the Human Rights Act 1998) and the provisions of the *c* Criminal Justice Act 1988.

LORD BROWNE-WILKINSON.

[2] My Lords, I have had the advantage of reading in draft the speech of my *d* noble and learned friend Lord Steyn. I agree with it and, for the reasons he has given, I too would dismiss this appeal.

LORD STEYN.

[3] My Lords, at present the powers of the court to order the confiscation of *e* the proceeds of crime are contained in three statutes, viz Pt VI of the Criminal Justice Act 1988, the Drug Trafficking Act 1994 and Pt III of the Terrorism Act 2000. If the Proceeds of Crime Bill (Bill 31 of 2001), which is presently before Parliament, is enacted it will create a uniform and more comprehensive system for confiscation orders in relation to persons who benefit from criminal conduct.

f [4] In outline the circumstances of the appeal before the House are as follows. On 11 October 1999 in the Crown Court at Snaresbrook the appellant pleaded guilty to two counts of theft on an indictment containing 14 counts of theft. On 10 April 2000 he was sentenced to 15 months' imprisonment on each count. On the same day after a hearing under the 1988 Act a judge made a confiscation order against the appellant in the sum of £214,839. He appealed to the Court of *g* Appeal against the confiscation order (see [2001] 2 All ER 609, [2001] 3 WLR 75). His appeal was heard together with other appeals including the appeal *R v Benjafield*, that case being concerned with a confiscation order under the 1994 Act. The principal point in both cases before the Court of Appeal was whether the making of confiscation orders under the 1988 Act and under the 1994 Act was *h* compatible with the Human Rights Act 1998 which incorporated the European Convention for the Protection of Human Rights and Fundamental Freedoms 1950 (as set out in Sch 1 to the 1998 Act) into our law. On the basis of the position as to retrospectivity as then understood, the Court of Appeal considered the position as if the 1998 Act was directly applicable to the two appeals. The Court *j* of Appeal held that both the 1988 Act and the 1994 Act were compatible with the convention. The Court of Appeal dismissed the appeal of the appellant (Rezvi) and adjourned the appeal of Benjafield for further argument. The Court of Appeal certified that a point of law of general public importance is involved, viz:

'Are the provisions of s 72AA of the Criminal Justice Act 1988, as amended, and s 4 of the Drug Trafficking Act 1994 incompatible with art 6 of the convention and/or art 1 of the First Protocol?'

With the leave of the House both Rezvi and Benjafield appealed to the House. The appeals raise in some respects similar questions but are otherwise *a* unconnected. This opinion is only concerned with the appeal of Rezvi (and the 1988 Act). I will consider the appeal of Benjafield (and the 1994 Act) in a separate opinion (see [2002] UKHL 2, [2002] 1 All ER 815). However, some reference to the 1994 Act will be necessary.

[5] It is now necessary to return to the assumption that the 1998 Act is *b* applicable to the present appeal. The appellant's plea of guilty, the sentence of the court, and the making of the confiscation order preceded the coming into operation of the 1998 Act on 2 October 2000. After the hearing of the appeals of Rezvi and Benjafield in the House of Lords, the decision of the House in *R v Kansal (No 2)* [2001] UKHL 62, [2002] 1 All ER 257, [2001] 3 WLR 1562, settled the issue of retrospectivity of the 1998 Act in respect of the outcome of criminal trials *c* which were concluded before 2 October 2001: the 1998 Act is not applicable to such cases even if an appeal is heard after the relevant date. It follows that the appellant's convention rights are not engaged. Nevertheless, given the fact that the Court of Appeal dealt with the convention issues and bearing in mind the importance of the points, it would be sensible to give consideration to the *d* potential impact of the convention on the 1988 Act.

[6] Before I turn to the principal issues it is necessary to explain the circumstance of the case in some more detail. On 24 February 1999 the police arrested the appellant on suspicion of theft from his employer. He had held the position of assistant financial controller at the St Giles Hotel, Bedford Avenue, London WC1 for more than three years and had worked at the hotel for *e* approximately nine years. His salary was £23,000 p a. The appellant admitted two counts of theft of £5,000 on 2 and 14 February 1999. The hotel asked security consultants to investigate the possibility of other thefts. They discovered that between April 1997 and February 1999, the hotel suffered losses totalling approximately £283,000. On 19 May 1999 the police interviewed the appellant in *f* relation to these other losses. He denied that he was involved. He said others had been responsible for other thefts. He was charged with 14 specimen counts of theft and deception covering a period from April 1997 to February 1999. On 11 October 1999, in accordance with the admissions he made in interview, the appellant pleaded guilty to counts 13 and 14 which covered a period of ten days only. Counsel for the Crown indicated that the pleas were not acceptable and *g* that a trial was necessary. Witnesses from Malaysia were required and so the court ordered a delayed fixture. On 21 January 2000, the Crown served a prosecutor's statement in accordance with s 71(1)(a) of the 1988 Act. The statement stated that it was appropriate to proceed with confiscation proceedings under s 72AA. The prosecutor's statement explained that though he was entitled under the 1988 Act *h* to examine the appellant's assets for a six-year period, he had chosen the period January 1997 to the commencement of proceedings (May 1999) as this is the period during which the appellant's financial lifestyle appears to change significantly. He had made large and regular deposits of cash into the various accounts which he controlled. And during a period when he was in receipt of a moderate income he had expended large amounts of cash. Applying the statutory *j* assumptions, the prosecutor assessed the appellant's total benefit from his criminal activities at £622,375·64 and his realisable assets as £353,742·17. On 24 January 2000 counsel for the Crown told the judge that the appellant's plea brought him within s 72AA of the 1988 Act, that the relevant notices had been served, and that the Crown had decided not to proceed on the main counts on this indictment. He mentioned questions of expense as being one of the factors

a the Crown had taken into account. He applied for counts 1 to 12 to lie on the file and for sentence (including issues of confiscation) to be adjourned until April. Counsel for the appellant did not oppose the application. He said it was to his client's advantage that the prosecution were not proceeding on counts 1 to 12. Although the Crown offered to explain why it had chosen not to proceed with all counts in the indictment, the court did not require an explanation. The judge

b acceded to the Crown's application and counts 1 to 12 were ordered to lie on the file on the usual terms. On 28 March 2000 the appellant served a defence statement under s 73(2) of the 1988 Act in response to the prosecutor's statement. He relied on the fact that on 24 January the Crown had elected not to proceed on counts 1 to 12 of the indictment and asserted that there was no evidence to substantiate the Crown's claim as to wider losses. Counsel submitted that the

c court should not exercise its discretion under s 72AA(3) of the 1988 Act, and should not make the assumptions specified in s 72AA(4). The Crown responded to the defence statement on 4 April 2000 and rejected the argument that the court should not exercise its discretion to proceed under the assumptions provisions because counts 1 to 12 had not been proceeded with. On 10 April 2000, the judge

d heard evidence from the prosecution and defence as well as argument. He made a confiscation order. After considering the appellant's explanations for his ownership of various assets and moneys over the relevant period the judge concluded that he was unable to accept the appellant's version where it was unsupported. He said that the appellant's evidence was noteworthy for the lack of support where it could have easily been forthcoming. Applying the assumptions

e he concluded that the total benefit should be fixed at £539,734·60 and the realisable assets should be fixed at £214,839. He made a confiscation order in that sum.

[7] The principal issues to which I will now turn are: (i) Whether a person against whom a confiscation order is sought under s 71 of the 1988 Act is charged

f with a criminal offence within the meaning of art 6(2) of the convention. (ii) If such a person is charged with a criminal offence, whether the assumptions in s 72AA of the 1988 Act are compatible with the defendant's convention rights. (iii) Whether it is an abuse of the process of the court for the Crown, in exercise of its discretion under ss 71(1)(a) and 72AA(1)(b) of the 1988 Act, to ask the court to make a confiscation order in respect of conduct which overlaps with criminal

g charges to which the defendant has pleaded not guilty and which remain undetermined. There are also additional points which I will briefly mention.

[8] The confiscation provisions contained in Pt VI of the 1988 Act enable the Crown Court or a magistrates' court to confiscate the proceeds of crime following conviction of offences to which the Act applies. It is unnecessary to set out the

h legislation in extenso. Subject to complying with the qualifying conditions and safeguards of the regime it empowers a judge to proceed to make a confiscation order. Section 71 spells out steps in the confiscation regime. And s 71(7A) provides that the standard of proof required to determine any question arising under Pt VI as to whether a person has benefited from an offence, and the amount to be recovered, is the balance of probabilities. Section 72AA deals with

j confiscation relating to a course of criminal conduct. At the heart of the matter are the statutory assumptions in aid of the making of a confiscation order which are to be found in s 72AA of the 1988 Act. Section 72AA(3) provides for the making of assumptions. So far as material the section then provides:

'(4) Those assumptions are—(a) that any property appearing to the court—(i) to be held by the defendant at the date of conviction or at any time in the period between that date and the determination in question, or (ii) to have been transferred to him at any time since the beginning of the relevant period, was received by him, at the earliest time when he appears to the court to have held it, as a result of or in connection with the commission of offences to which this Part of this Act applies; (b) that any expenditure of his since the beginning of the relevant period was met out of payments received by him as a result of or in connection with the commission of offences to which this Part of this Act applies; and (c) that, for the purposes of valuing any benefit which he had or which he is assumed to have had at any time, he received the benefit free of any other interests in it.

(5) Where the court has determined that the assumptions specified in subsection (4) above are to be made in any case it shall not in that case make any such assumption in relation to any particular property or expenditure if—(a) that assumption, so far as it relates to that property or expenditure, is shown to be incorrect in the defendant's case; (b) that assumption, so far as it so relates, is shown to be correct in relation to an offence the defendant's benefit from which has been the subject of a previous confiscation order; or (c) *the court is satisfied that there would (for any other reason) be a serious risk of injustice in the defendant's case if the assumption were to be made in relation to that property or expenditure.*' (My emphasis.)

These provisions must now be examined in the light of the 1998 Act and the convention. The 1998 Act provides:

'**3.**—(1) So far as it is possible to do so, primary legislation and subordinate legislation must be read and given effect in a way which is compatible with the Convention rights ...

4.—(1) Subsection (2) applies in any proceedings in which a court determines whether a provision of primary legislation is compatible with a Convention right.

(2) If the court is satisfied that the provision is incompatible with a Convention right, it may make a declaration of that incompatibility.'

Article 6 of the convention provides:

'1. In the determination of ... any criminal charge against him, everyone is entitled to a fair and public hearing within a reasonable time by an independent and impartial tribunal established by law. Judgment shall be pronounced publicly ...

2. Everyone charged with a criminal offence shall be presumed innocent until proved guilty according to law.

3. Everyone charged with a criminal offence has the following minimum rights: (a) to be informed promptly, in a language which he understands and in detail, of the nature and cause of the accusation against him ...'

The criminal charge issue

[9] Counsel for the appellant submitted that the 'assumptions' amount in effect to a clear breach of the guarantee under art 6(2) that everyone 'charged with a criminal offence' shall be presumed innocent until proved guilty according to law and that accordingly the relevant provisions of the 1988 Act are incompatible with the 1998 Act. Article 6(2) is triggered whenever a person is 'charged with a criminal offence'. The issue is whether confiscation proceedings are a discrete process which involved the appellant being 'charged with a criminal offence'.

a   **[10]** This point was recently considered by the Privy Council in relation to
confiscation proceedings in drugs legislation in Scotland (see *McIntosh v Lord
Advocate* [2001] UKPC D1, [2001] 2 All ER 638, [2001] 3 WLR 107). The Privy
Council unanimously held that an application for a confiscation order under the
Proceeds of Crime (Scotland) Act 1995 is not a charge under domestic Scottish
law or within the meaning of art 6(2): see in particular the judgments of Lord
b   Bingham of Cornhill (at [13]–[28]), and Lord Hope of Craighead (at [41]–[43]).
The issue was considered in depth in the context of the law of Scotland and
European jurisprudence. In these circumstances it is unnecessary to cover all the
same ground again. The Privy Council categorised (at [25]) the confiscation
order as 'a financial penalty (with a custodial penalty in default of payment) but
it is a penalty imposed for the offence of which he has been convicted and
c   involves no accusation of any other offence'. This is an accurate description of
the confiscation procedure under the 1988 Act. Lord Bingham observed (at [28])
in conclusion on this aspect:

'In concluding, as I do, that art 6(2) has no application to the prosecutor's
application for a confiscation order, I would stress that the result is not to
d   leave the respondent unprotected. He is entitled to all the protection
afforded to him by art 6(1), which applies at all stages, the common law of
Scotland and the language of the statute. If the court accedes to the
application of a prosecutor under s 1(1) of the 1995 Act, it will order an
accused to pay "such sum as the court thinks fit". In making a confiscation
e   order the court must act with scrupulous fairness in making its assessment to
ensure that neither the accused nor any third person suffers any injustice.'

These observations apply mutatis mutandis to confiscation under the 1988 Act.
      [11] Since *McIntosh's* case was decided a chamber of the European Court of
Human Rights (Section IV) has dealt with a similar point in relation to confiscation
f   proceedings under the 1994 Act (see *Phillips v UK* (2001) 11 BHRC 280). By a
majority the court came to the following conclusion (at 290–291 (paras 35–36)):

'35 ... whilst it is clear that art 6(2) governs criminal proceedings in their
entirety, and not solely the examination of the merits of the charge (see, for
example, [*Minelli v Switzerland* (1983) 5 EHRR 554 at 565 (para 30), *Sekanina
g   v Austria* (1993) 17 EHRR 221 and *Allenet de Ribemont v France* (1995) 20 EHRR
557]), the right to be presumed innocent under art 6(2) arises only in
connection with the particular offence "charged". Once an accused has
properly been proved guilty of that offence, art 6(2) can have no application
in relation to allegations made about the accused's character and conduct as
h   part of the sentencing process, unless such accusations are of such a nature
and degree as to amount to the bringing of a new "charge" within the
autonomous convention meaning referred to in para 28, above (see [*Engel v
Netherlands (No 1)* (1976) 1 EHRR 647 at 681 (para 90)]).
      36. In conclusion, therefore, the court holds that art 6(2) was not
applicable to the confiscation proceedings brought against the applicant.'
j
The majority added (at 291 (para 40)):

'The court considers that, in addition to being specifically mentioned in
art 6(2), a person's right in a criminal case to be presumed innocent and to
require the prosecution to bear the onus of proving the allegations against
him or her forms part of the general notion of a fair hearing under art 6(1)
(see, mutatis mutandis, *Saunders v UK* (1996) BHRC 358 at para 68). This

right is not, however, absolute, since presumptions of fact or of law operate in every criminal law system and are not prohibited in principle by the convention, as long as states remain within certain limits, taking into account the importance of what is at stake and maintaining the rights of the defence (see *Salabiaku v France* [(1988) 13 EHRR 379 at 400 (para 28)])'.

Overall, the majority held, the application to the applicant of the relevant provisions of the 1994 Act 'was confined within reasonable limits given the importance of what was at stake and that the rights of the defence were fully respected' (see (2001) 11 BHRC 280 at 293 (para 47)).

[12] There is a powerful partly dissenting opinion of Judge Bratza joined by Judge Vajic to the effect that the majority took too narrow a view of art 6(2). If this view had prevailed it would in my respectful view have caused difficulties in English law and in other national legal systems. After all, a 'criminal charge' gives rise to a 'minimum right' under art 6(3)(a) 'to be informed promptly ... of the nature and cause of the accusation against him'. This provision fits in uneasily with confiscation proceedings with its elaborate step-by-step machinery designed to obtain information to enable the court eventually to decide whether a confiscation order should be made and, if so, in what sum. At the very least, if art 6(2) is held to be directly applicable, it will tend to undermine the effectiveness of confiscation procedures generally. Finally, it is to be noted that on the issue of proportionality the minority share the views of the majority.

[13] It follows that in my view confiscation proceedings are part of the sentencing process following a conviction and do not involve a fresh criminal charge.

The proportionality issue

[14] It is a notorious fact that professional and habitual criminals frequently take steps to conceal their profits from crime. Effective but fair powers of confiscating the proceeds of crime are therefore essential. The provisions of the 1988 Act are aimed at depriving such offenders of the proceeds of their criminal conduct. Its purposes are to punish convicted offenders, to deter the commission of further offences and to reduce the profits available to fund further criminal enterprises. These objectives reflect not only national but also international policy. The United Kingdom has undertaken, by signing and ratifying treaties agreed under the auspices of the United Nations and the Council of Europe, to take measures necessary to ensure that the profits of those engaged in drug trafficking or other crimes are confiscated (see United Nations Convention against Illicit Traffic in Narcotic Drugs and Psychotropic Substances (Vienna, 20 December 1988; TS 26 (1992) Cm 1927); Council of Europe Convention on Laundering, Search, Seizure and Confiscation of the Proceeds from Crime (Strasbourg, 8 November 1990 (Cm 1561)). These conventions are in operation and have been ratified by the United Kingdom.

[15] It is clear that the Criminal Justice Act 1988 was passed in furtherance of a legitimate aim and that the measures are rationally connected with that aim (see *de Freitas v Permanent Secretary of Ministry of Agriculture, Fisheries, Lands and Housing* [1999] 1 AC 69 at 80, [1998] 3 WLR 675 at 684 for the three-stage test). The only question is whether the statutory means adopted are wider than is necessary to accomplish the objective. Counsel for the appellant submitted that the means adopted are disproportionate to the objective in as much as a persuasive burden is placed on the defendant. The Court of Appeal ([2001] 2 All ER 609 at 634–635, [2001] 3 WLR 75 at 103) carefully considered this argument and ruled:

a '87. The onus which is placed upon the defendant is not an evidential one but a persuasive one, so that the defendant will be required to discharge the burden of proof (see Lord Hope's third category of provisions in [R v DPP, ex p Kebeline, R v DPP, ex p Rechachi [1999] 4 All ER 801 at 843, [2000] AC 326 at 379]). This is therefore a situation where it is necessary to carefully consider whether the public interest in being able to confiscate the ill-gotten

b gains of criminals justifies the interference with the normal presumption of innocence. While the extent of the interference is substantial, Parliament has clearly made efforts to balance the interest of the defendant against that of the public in the following respects. (a) It is only after the necessary convictions that any question of confiscation arises. This is of significance, because the trial which results in the conviction or convictions will be one

c where the usual burden and standard of proof rests upon the prosecution. In addition, a defendant who is convicted of the necessary offence or offences can be taken to be aware that if he committed the offences of which he has been convicted, he would not only be liable to imprisonment or another sentence, but he would also be liable to confiscation proceedings. (b) The

d prosecution has the responsibility for initiating the confiscation proceedings unless the court regards them as inappropriate ... (c) There is also the responsibility placed upon the court not to make a confiscation order when there is a serious risk of injustice. As already indicated, *this will involve the court, before it makes a confiscation order, standing back and deciding whether there is a risk of injustice.* If the court decides there is, then the confiscation order

e will not be made. (d) There is the role of this court on appeal to ensure there is no unfairness.

88. It is very much a matter of personal judgment as to whether a proper balance has been struck between the conflicting interests. Into the balance there must be placed the interests of the defendant as against the interests of

f the public, that those who have offended should not profit from their offending and should not use their criminal conduct to fund further offending. However, in our judgment, if the discretions which are given to the prosecution and the court are properly exercised, the solution which Parliament has adopted is a reasonable and proportionate response to a substantial public interest, and therefore justifiable.' (My emphasis.)

g For my part I think that this reasoning is correct, notably in explaining the role of the court in standing back and deciding whether there is or might be a risk of serious or real injustice and, if there is, or might be, in emphasising that a confiscation order ought not be made. The Crown accepted that this is how the

h court, seized with a question of confiscation, should approach its task. In my view this concession was rightly made.

[16] In agreement with the unanimous views of the Court of Human Rights in *Phillips v UK* (2001) 11 BHRC 280 I would hold that Pt VI of the 1988 Act is a proportionate response to the problem which it addresses.

j *Issue on art 1 of the First Protocol*

[17] Article 1 of the First Protocol to the convention provides:

'Every natural or legal person is entitled to the peaceful enjoyment of his possessions. No one shall be deprived of his possessions except in the public interest and subject to the conditions provided for by law and by the general principles of international law.

The preceding provisions shall not, however, in any way impair the right *a* of a State to enforce such laws as it deems necessary to control the use of property in accordance with the general interest or to secure the payment of taxes or other contributions or penalties.'

Counsel argued that art 1 of the First Protocol requires a different conclusion on proportionality. That cannot be right. The legislation is a precise, fair and *b* proportionate response to the important need to protect the public. In agreement with the European Court of Human Rights in *Phillips'* case I would hold that the interference with art 1 of the First Protocol is justified.

Conclusion on compatibility *c*

[18] Even if convention rights were directly engaged I would hold that there is no incompatibility when the provisions of the 1988 Act are measured against the rights under the convention and the First Protocol.

The principle of legality *d*

[19] Counsel for the appellant also sought to rely on the domestic principle of legality. The principle is that ambiguous or general words in a statute cannot override fundamental rights. Many illustrations of the application of this principle are to be found in the speech of Lord Browne-Wilkinson, and in my speech, in *Pierson v Secretary of State for the Home Dept* [1997] 3 All ER 577, [1998] AC 539. It *e* was endorsed by the House in *R v Secretary of State for the Home Dept, ex p Simms* [1999] 3 All ER 400, [2000] 2 AC 115. Lord Hoffmann explained the rationale of the principle (see [1999] 3 All ER 400 at 412, [2000] 2 AC 115 at 131). There is, however, no scope for the application of this principle in the present case. The legislation is explicit in its terms and represents a fair balance between the interests of the individual and those of the community. *f*

Abuse of process

[20] The thrust of the final argument of counsel for the appellant was that in making the confiscation order the court took into account counts which were undetermined. The premise of this argument is wrong: the judge rightly relied *g* on the evidence before him in relation to confiscation and not on any undetermined counts. The confiscation regime is a fair procedure which takes account of the offender's rights as well as the public interest. In *McIntosh v Lord Advocate* [2001] 2 All ER 638 at [35], Lord Bingham observed:
h

'It is only if a significant discrepancy is shown between the property and expenditure of the accused on the one hand and his known sources of income on the other that the court will think it right to make the s 3(2) assumptions, and unless the accounting details reveal such a discrepancy the prosecutor will not in practice apply for an order. It would be an obviously *j* futile exercise to seek an order where the assets and expenditure of the accused are fully explained by his known sources of legitimate income. If a significant discrepancy is shown, and in the first instance it is for the prosecutor to show it, I do not for my part think it unreasonable or oppressive to call on the accused to proffer an explanation. He must know the source of his assets and what he has been living on.'

a   The same reasoning applies in the present case. The application by the Crown to apply primary legislation (subject to control by the court and subject to a full right of appeal on the part of a convicted defendant) could not amount to an abuse of the process of the court. The procedure is fair in as much as the sentencing court is duty bound not to make the assumptions if it might be unfair to do so. There was therefore no abuse of the process of the court.

b
Conclusion

[21] The judge had to determine disputed issues of fact. The appellant and his wife testified. He rejected their evidence. That was a decision open to him on the evidence. On the evidence before the judge the order of confiscation was properly made.

c

Disposal

[22] For these reasons as well as the reasons given by Lord Hope of Craighead I would dismiss the appeal.

d   **LORD HOPE OF CRAIGHEAD.**

[23] My Lords, I have had the advantage of reading in draft the speech of my noble and learned friend Lord Steyn. I agree with it, and for reasons which he has given I too would dismiss this appeal. I should like however to add these observations.

e   [24] The confiscation order to which the appellant was made subject was made before s 7(1)(b) of the Human Rights Act 1998 came into force. Nevertheless he seeks to rely on s 22(4) of that Act, which provides that s 7(1)(b) applies to proceedings brought by or at the instigation of a public authority whenever the act in question took place. His appeal is based in part on the proposition that the legislation under which the order was made is incompatible with his rights under

f   art 6 of the European Convention for the Protection of Human Rights and Fundamental Freedoms 1950 (as set out in Sch 1 to the 1998 Act) and that, for this reason, the prosecutor's act in applying for the making of the order was unlawful within the meaning of s 6(1) of that Act.

[25] The Court of Appeal ([2001] 2 All ER 609 at 625, [2001] 3 WLR 75 at 93

g   (para 51)) held that, as his appeal was part of the proceedings to which s 7(1)(b) of the 1998 Act applied, the appellant was entitled to rely in this appeal on his convention rights. It also held ([2001] 2 All ER 609 at 625, [2001] 3 WLR 75 at 94 (para 53)) that s 3(1) of the 1998 Act had to be given retrospective effect if s 7(1)(b) was to be applied retrospectively, with the result that for the purposes of this

h   appeal that the Criminal Justice 1988 Act had to be read and given effect in a way which was compatible with his convention rights.

[26] Since the date of that decision your Lordships have delivered judgments on the issue of retrospectivity which has had the effect of overruling the decision reached on it by the Court of Appeal. In *R v Kansal (No 2)* [2001] UKHL 62, [2002]

j   1 All ER 257, [2001] 3 WLR 1562 your Lordships decided not to depart from the reasoning of the majority in *R v Lambert* [2002] UKHL 37, [2001] 3 All ER 577, [2001] 3 WLR 206. Those were cases where the defendant was appealing against his conviction. In this case your Lordships are concerned not with an appeal against conviction but with an appeal which is to be treated as an appeal against sentence. But the reasoning of the majority in *R v Lambert* applies to all appeals whatever their subject matter. In this situation I agree that it must be applied in this case also. I would hold that it is not open to the appellant in this appeal to

rely on s 7(1)(b) of the 1998 Act in regard to the pre-commencement act of the
prosecutor in asking the court to make the confiscation order.

[27] As Lord Woolf CJ observed, however, the ability of the court to give
guidance in future cases is an important consideration (see [2001] 2 All ER 609 at
625, [2001] 3 WLR 75 at 93–94 (para 53)). I agree with Lord Steyn that it would
be sensible for your Lordships to take the opportunity of considering the
potential impact of the convention on confiscation proceedings under Pt VI of
the 1988 Act as amended. With that in mind, I add these comments on art 6 of
the convention in the light of the decision of the European Court of Human
Rights in *Phillips v UK* (2001) 11 BHRC 280. I should also like to add a few words
on the issue of abuse of process.

Article 6 of the convention
[28] The decision of the Judicial Committee of the Privy Council in *McIntosh v
Lord Advocate* [2001] UKPC D1, [2001] 2 All ER 638, [2001] 3 WLR 107 was, as
Lord Steyn has observed, concerned with confiscation proceedings under the
Proceeds of Crime (Scotland) Act 1995 following a conviction for a drug-trafficking
offence. There is a close similarity between the provisions with which that case
was concerned and those in the present case, and I agree that much of the
reasoning in that case can be applied here too. There are however two points
about it that are worth mentioning in view of the comments on that decision by
the European Court in *Phillips'* case.

[29] The first point is that the Scottish legislation, as applied to cases where
there is a conviction for drug trafficking, does not require the assessment of the
value of the accused's proceeds from drug trafficking to be based on assumptions
that he has been engaged on other conduct which would be treated as criminal.
As Lord Bingham of Cornhill said in *McIntosh's* case [2001] 2 All ER 638 at [6] (7),
the expression 'drug trafficking' in the 1995 Act has a meaning distinct from and
wider than that of the expression 'drug trafficking offence'. It includes conduct
which would, but also conduct which would not, give rise to criminal offences
under Scots law. This made it a little easier in that case to hold that art 6(2) of the
convention was not engaged than it perhaps would have been in this case.

[30] But the activity of drug trafficking is in general an essentially criminal
activity, and it seems likely that the purpose of the definition was to enable
conduct falling within that description to be brought into account even if it could
not have been prosecuted in a criminal court in Scotland. So I do not think that
this difference between the two legislative regimes provides a reason for not
applying the decision in *McIntosh's* case to this case. The important point is that
the procedure which s 72AA of the 1988 Act lays down does not involve the
bringing of a fresh charge or charges against the defendant. The process cannot
begin until he has been convicted of the qualifying offences, and it is only those
offences that may be taken into account in determining his sentence. The process
which then follows is based upon the assumption that the criminal charges
against the defendant in the indictment have been proved. I continue to think
that art 6(2) is not directly engaged in these circumstances.

[31] The second point is that counsel for the respondent in *McIntosh's* case
made it clear at the outset of his argument that he was not seeking to rely to any
extent on art 6(1). He relied exclusively on art 6(2) and did not attempt to argue
that there was any breach of art 6(1). Nevertheless the Board did not overlook
art 6(1), as Lord Bingham made clear (see [2001] 2 All ER 638 at [28]). As he said,
the conclusion that art 6(2) did not apply did not leave the accused unprotected,
as he was entitled to all the protection afforded to him by art 6(1). In my opinion

that observation applies with equal force where a confiscation order is sought
under Pt VI of the 1988 Act. This means that the defendant is entitled to the
benefit of all the general requirements of art 6 to which Judge Bratza and Judge
Vajic referred in their partly dissenting opinion in *Phillips v UK* (2001) 11 BHRC
280 at 295–296.

[32] The critical question in the present case therefore is that on which the
European Court in *Phillips'* case were unanimous. That is the question whether,
as applied to the appellant in this case, the provisions of s 72AA exceeded the
reasonable limits within which they are required to be confined by art 6(1) as
regards the general implied right under that article in a criminal case to be
presumed innocent: see para 40 of the judgment in that case. On that issue,
I would apply the test indicated in para 47 of that judgment. The question is
whether the application of the procedure to the appellant was confined within
reasonable limits given the importance of what was at stake, and whether his
rights were fully respected. No criticism has been made in this case of the
approach which the judge took to the facts when he was calculating the amount
of the confiscation order. Having regard to that fact, to what was said in
paras 40–43 of the judgment in *Phillips'* case and to the whole structure of the
procedure which the section lays down including the discretion which is given to
the court and the duty which is placed on it to avoid a serious risk of injustice, I
would hold that this test is satisfied.

Abuse of process

[33] Thus argument is not affected by the decision in *R v Kansal (No 2)* [2002]
1 All ER 257, as it depends upon common law principles and is not founded on an
alleged breach of any convention right. The essence of the appellant's point is
that the s 72AA confiscation procedure was intended to be used against lifestyle
criminals. It was appropriate for use in cases where the Crown had established a
course of criminal conduct, as the sidenote to s 72AA indicates. In this case the
appellant had been charged with 14 counts spanning a 22-month period from
April 1997 to February 1999. It was accepted that if convictions had been obtained
on all 14 counts, that would have been sufficient to make it appropriate to resort
to s 72AA. But it was submitted that, by accepting the appellant's pleas of guilty
to two offences only relating to a ten-day period in February 1999, the Crown
came nowhere near establishing a course of criminal conduct.

[34] There is no doubt that the initial requirements for the making of a
confiscation order under s 72AA were satisfied. Section 72AA(1)(a) provides that
that section applies in case where an offender is convicted of a qualifying offence
which is an offence of a relevant description if the prosecutor gives written notice
to the court that he considers that the case is one in which it is appropriate for the
provisions of that section to be applied and the offender is convicted in those
proceedings of at least two qualifying offences. The definition of 'qualifying
offence' in s 72AA(2) provides, among other things, that the court must be
satisfied that it is an offence from which the defendant has benefited. In this case
the requisite notice was given and the appellant pled guilty in the same
proceedings to two offences which were offences from which he had benefited.
They were offences of theft contrary to s 1(1) of the Theft Act 1968 in which the
sum involved was said in each case to be £5,000.

[35] The alleged abuse is directed to the fact that the 12 other offences in the
indictment, which comprised nine offences of theft contrary to s 1(1) of the 1968
Act and three offences of obtaining money transfers by deception contrary to
s 15A of that Act, had not been proceeded with. The prosecutor's notice was

given after the appellant had pled guilty to the last two counts of theft but not guilty to the other 12, which pleas had not been acceptable to the prosecutor. This statement referred to the fact that the appellant was due to appear at the Crown Court in respect of eleven charges of theft and three charges of deception totalling £35,105. It also stated that an examination of the accounts of the hotel where the appellant had been employed as assistant financial controller had identified £283,000 of losses since April 1997 attributable to transactions conducted by him and that the 14 charges were specimen counts of theft and deception. It would clearly have been unfair for the prosecutor to rely on everything that was said in that statement once he had decided, as he did when the case came up for trial, to accept pleas of guilty to the last two charges only and not to proceed with the other 12.

[36] In the event the prosecutor did not do this. He produced a further statement in which he referred in terms to the fact that counts 1 to 12 were not proceeded with. Under reference to the provisions of the statute he then explained the approach which he invited the court to take, based on the fact that the appellant had been convicted only of two qualifying offences and on the assumptions which the court was entitled to make under s 72AA(4). It has not been suggested that anything that he said in this later statement was misleading or inaccurate. In these circumstances I consider that he dealt correctly with the situation which arose when the case came up for trial. I do not think that his act in asking the court to make the assumptions which it was entitled to make in the event of the appellant's conviction of two qualifying offences only can be described as an abuse of the process.

[37] Furthermore, as the prosecutor correctly said in his second notice, s 72AA does not require the prosecutor to specify any offences other than the qualifying offences. The matter proceeds from then on upon assumptions which the court makes if it thinks fit. It is the offences from which in accordance with those assumptions the defendant is assumed to have benefited that are treated under s 72AA(6) as relevant criminal conduct. But the whole exercise is subject to the provision in s 72AA(5)(c) that the court shall not make an assumption if it is satisfied that there would be serious risk of injustice in the defendant's case. In the whole context I do not think that the prosecutor can be said to have acted unfairly in this case.

LORD HUTTON.

[38] My Lords, I have had the advantage of reading in draft the speech of my noble and learned friend Lord Steyn. I agree with it, and for the reasons which he has given I too would dismiss this appeal.

Appeal dismissed.

Kate O'Hanlon　Barrister.

a

R v Benjafield
[2002] UKHL 2

HOUSE OF LORDS
LORD SLYNN OF HADLEY, LORD BROWNE-WILKINSON, LORD STEYN, LORD HOPE OF
b CRAIGHEAD AND LORD HUTTON
29, 30, 31 OCTOBER 2001, 24 JANUARY 2002

Sentencing – Confiscation order – Drug trafficking – Whether statutory provisions governing confiscation orders compatible with human rights – Drug Trafficking Act
c 1994, s 4(3) – Human Rights Act 1998, Sch 1, Pt I, art 6, Pt II, art 1.

The defendant pleaded guilty to two counts of conspiracy to supply drugs, and was sentenced to a total of 14 years' imprisonment. Subsequently, the court made a confiscation order against him pursuant to the provisions of the Drug
d Trafficking Act 1994. That order was imposed before the implementation of the Human Rights Act 1998. On the defendant's appeal against the confiscation order, which was heard after the implementation of the 1998 Act, the Court of Appeal considered whether the reverse burden assumptions in s 4(3)[a] of the 1994 Act were compatible with certain provisions of the European Convention for the Protection of Human Rights and Fundamental Freedoms 1950 (as set out in Sch 1
e to the 1998 Act), namely art 6(1)[b] (the general right to a fair hearing) and art 6(2) (the presumption of innocence in respect of those charged with a criminal offence). After giving judgment on that issue, the court adjourned consideration of the merits of the defendant's appeal. The appeal was eventually dismissed, and the defendant appealed to the House of Lords.

f
Held – A defendant who was the subject of criminal proceedings before the implementation of the 1998 Act was not entitled to rely on convention rights in an appeal after the implementation of that Act. It followed in the instant case that the defendant's convention rights were not engaged, and his appeal would be dismissed (see [1], [2], [6], [14]–[16], below); *R v Kansal (No 2)* [2002] 1 All ER 257
g applied.

Per curiam. Article 6(2) of the convention does not apply to confiscation proceedings under the 1994 Act. Such proceedings are part of the sentencing process following a conviction, and are not a criminal charge within the meaning of art 6(2). Although a person who is subject to confiscation proceedings has the
h full protection of art 6(1), the reverse burden provisions in s 4(3) of the 1994 Act are compatible with art 6(1). The 1994 Act pursues an important objective in the public interest and the legislative measures are rationally connected with the furtherance of that objective. The procedure devised by Parliament is a fair and proportionate response to the need to protect the public interest. The critical point is that under the 1994 Act, as under the Criminal Justice Act 1988, the judge
j must be astute to avoid injustice. If there is a serious or real risk of injustice, he

---

a   Section 4 is set out at [8], below
b   Article 6, so far as material, provides: '1. In the determination of ... any criminal charge against him, everyone is entitled to a fair ... hearing ...
2. Everyone charged with a criminal offence shall be presumed innocent until proved guilty according to law ...'

must not make a confiscation order. Furthermore, any interference with the
right to peaceful enjoyment of possessions under art 1 of the First Protocol of the   *a*
convention is also justified (see [1], [2], [7]–[9], [15], [16], below); *McIntosh v Lord
Advocate* [2001] 2 All ER 638 and *Phillips v UK* (2001) 11 BHRC 280 followed.

    Decision of the Court of Appeal [2001] 2 All ER 609 affirmed on different
grounds.

                                                 b

Notes

For the presumption of innocence and the right to property, see 8(2) *Halsbury's
Laws* (4th edn reissue) paras 142, 165, and for confiscation orders in respect of
drug trafficking, see 11(2) *Halsbury's Laws* (4th edn reissue) para 1305.

    For the Criminal Justice Act 1994, s 4, see 12 *Halsbury's Statutes* (4th edn) (1997
reissue) 1500.   *c*

    For the Human Rights Act 1998, Sch 1, Pt I, art 6, Pt II, art 1, see 7 *Halsbury's
Statutes* (4th edn) (1999 reissue) 523, 525.

Cases referred to in opinions

McIntosh v Lord Advocate [2001] UKPC D1, [2001] 2 All ER 638, [2001] 3 WLR 107.   *d*
Phillips v UK (2001) 11 BHRC 280, ECt HR.
R v Kansal (No 2) [2001] UKHL 62, [2002] 1 All ER 257, [2001] 3 WLR 1562.
R v Rezvi [2002] UKHL 1, [2002] 1 All ER 801, [2002] 2 WLR 235.

Appeal

Karl Robert Benjafield appealed with leave of the Appeal Committee of the   *e*
House of Lords given on 4 April 2001 from (i) the decision of the Court of Appeal
(Lord Woolf CJ, Judge LJ and Collins J) on 21 December 2000 ([2001] 2 All ER
609, [2001] 3 WLR 75) whereby it held that s 4 of the Drug Trafficking Act 1994
was compatible with the European Convention for the Protection of Human
Rights and Fundamental Freedoms 1950 (as set out in Sch 1 to the Human Rights   *f*
Act 1998), and (ii) the order of the Court of Appeal (Judge LJ and Collins J) on
8 March 2001 dismissing the appellant's appeal against the confiscation order in
the sum of £327,971 imposed on him by Judge Downes in the Crown Court at
Norwich on 1 July 1999 under the 1994 Act. Consideration of the appeal on the
merits had been adjourned by the Court of Appeal in its earlier decision. The
Court of Appeal certified that a point of law of general public importance was   *g*
involved in that decision, namely whether s 4 of the 1994 Act was incompatible
with art 6 of the convention and art 1 of the First Protocol of the convention. The
facts are set out in the opinion of Lord Steyn.

Charles Miskin QC and *Danny Friedman* (instructed by *Stewarts*, Stowmarket) for   *h*
    the appellant.
David Perry, Kennedy Talbot and *Duncan Atkinson* (instructed by the *Crown
    Prosecution Service*) for the Crown.

Their Lordships took time for consideration.   *j*

24 January 2002. The following opinions were delivered.

LORD SLYNN OF HADLEY.

    [1] My Lords, for the reasons to be given by my noble and learned friend Lord
Steyn I too would dismiss this appeal.

LORD BROWNE-WILKINSON.

a   [2] My Lords, I have had the advantage of reading in draft the speech of my noble and learned friend Lord Steyn. I agree with it and, for the reasons he has given, I too would dismiss this appeal.

LORD STEYN.

b   [3] My Lords, this appeal was heard at the same time as the appeal in *R v Rezvi* [2002] UKHL 1, [2002] 1 All ER 801, [2002] 2 WLR 235 in which the House deliver speeches today. In many respects the two appeals involve substantially similar questions. Having regard to the conclusions and reasons in *R v Rezvi* it will be possible to deal with this appeal quite briefly.

c   [4] In outline the circumstances of the appeal are as follows. On 8 September 1998 the appellant pleaded guilty to two counts of an indictment, thereby admitting that he had conspired with others to supply class A and B drugs between 6 May and 24 July 1997. On 19 October 1998 a Crown Court judge sentenced him to 14 years and 5 years respectively, the terms to run concurrently. A preliminary hearing to determine the extent to which the appellant benefited *d* from drug trafficking took place between 29 and 31 March 1999. On 1 July 1999 the court made a confiscation order in the sum of £327,971. In default of payment of the said sum, a term of three years' imprisonment was imposed. On 5 October 1999 a High Court judge gave the appellant leave to appeal against the confiscation order. On 6 December 2000 the appeal came before Lord Woolf CJ, Judge LJ and Collins J ([2001] All ER 609, [2001] 3 WLR 75). The Court of Appeal *e* considered the compatibility of s 4(3) of the Drug Trafficking Act 1994 with the Human Rights Act 1998 which incorporated the European Convention for the Protection of Human Rights and Fundamental Freedoms 1950 (as set out in Sch 1 to the 1998 Act) into our law. On 20 December 2000 the Court of Appeal gave judgment on the application of art 6(1) and (2) to confiscation proceedings. The *f* Court of Appeal adjourned consideration of the merits of the appellant's appeal to a later date. On Thursday 8 March 2001 the adjourned hearing took place. In a judgment which is unreported the Court of Appeal (Judge LJ and Collins J) dismissed the appeal.

  [5] On this appeal the following issues arise for determination: (i) Whether a defendant who was the subject of criminal proceedings before the coming into *g* force of ss 6 and 7(1)(b) of the 1998 Act is entitled, after they come into force, to rely, in the course of appellate proceedings, on an alleged breach of his convention rights by the trial court or prosecuting authority. (ii) Whether a person against whom a confiscation order is sought under s 4 of the 1994 Act is 'charged' with a criminal offence within the meaning of art 6(1) of the convention. (iii) If such a *h* person is charged with a criminal offence, whether the reverse burden assumptions in s 4 of the 1994 Act are compatible with art 6(2) of the convention and/or art 1 of the First Protocol. (iv) Whether it was appropriate and just to make the confiscation order in the circumstances of this case.

j *The retrospectivity issue*

  [6] The answer to issue (i) is No. The appellant pleaded guilty and was sentenced and a confiscation order was imposed on him before the 1998 Act came into force. Following the decision of the House in *R v Kansal (No 2)* [2001] UKHL 62, [2002] 1 All ER 257, [2001] 3 WLR 1562, it is now clear that the appellant's convention rights are not engaged. Nevertheless, I will briefly summarise the position on the assumption that the convention is applicable.

The criminal charge issue

[7] The answer to issue (ii) is No. Relying on the decision of the Privy Council *a* in *McIntosh v Lord Advocate* [2001] UKPC D1, [2001] 2 All ER 638, [2001] 3 WLR 107 and the decision of a chamber of the European Court of Human Rights in *Phillips v UK* (2001) 11 BHRC 280, as well as on the relation between art 6(2) and (3)(a), I explained in *R v Rezvi* why the bringing of confiscation proceedings is not a criminal charge under art 6(2) of the convention. There are material differences *b* between the confiscation regimes under the Criminal Justice Act 1988 (applicable in *R v Rezvi*) and the 1994 Act (applicable in the present case). But in regard to the applicability of art 6(2) the position is the same. Article 6(2) does not apply to confiscation proceedings. But the appellant has the full protection of art 6(1).

Compatibility of reverse burden provisions with art 6(1) *c*

[8] It is unnecessary to set out the legislation. Counsel for the appellant concentrated on the following provisions of the 1994 Act:

'4.—(1) For the purposes of this Act—(a) any payments or other rewards received by a person at any time (whether before or after the commencement of this Act) in connection with drug trafficking carried on by him or another *d* person are his proceeds of drug trafficking; and (b) the value of his proceeds of drug trafficking is the aggregate of the values of the payments or other rewards.

(2) Subject to subsections (4) and (5) below, the Crown Court shall, for the purpose—(a) of determining whether the defendant has benefited from *e* drug trafficking; and (b) if he has, of assessing the value of his proceeds of drug trafficking, make the required assumptions.

(3) The required assumptions are—(a) that any property appearing to the court—(i) to have been held by the defendant at any time since his conviction, or (ii) to have been transferred to him at any time since the beginning of the period of six years ending when the proceedings were *f* instituted against him, was received by him, at the earliest time at which he appears to the court to have held it, as a payment or reward in connection with drug trafficking carried on by him; (b) that any expenditure of his since the beginning of that period was met out of payments received by him in connection with drug trafficking carried on by him; and (c) that, for the *g* purpose of valuing any property received or assumed to have been received by him at any time as such a reward, he received the property free of any other interests in it.

(4) The court shall not make any required assumption in relation to any particular property or expenditure if—(a) that assumption is shown to be *h* incorrect in the defendant's case; or (b) *the court is satisfied that there would be a serious risk of injustice in the defendant's case if the assumption were to be made*; and where, by virtue of this subsection, the court does not make one or more of the required assumptions, it shall state its reasons.' (My emphasis.)

Making due allowance for the differences between the confiscation procedures *j* under the 1988 Act and under the 1994 Act, the reasoning in *R v Rezvi* [2002] 1 All ER 801 applies with equal force in this case. The 1994 Act pursues an important objective in the public interest and the legislative measures are rationally connected with the furtherance of this objective. The procedure devised by Parliament is a fair and proportionate response to the need to protect the public interest. The critical point is that under the 1994 Act, as under the 1988 Act, the a   judge must be astute to avoid injustice. If there is or might be a serious or real risk of injustice, he must not make a confiscation order. In these circumstances a challenge to the compatibility of the legislation must fail.

Article 1 of the First Protocol
b   [9] For the reasons given in *R v Rezvi* I would hold that any interference with art 1 of the First Protocol is justified.

The merits
[10] The main issue in the confiscation proceedings concerned two properties known as 'The Bentleys' (which was in the appellant's sole name) and 'La Siesta' (which was in the joint names of the appellant and his mother). The question was
c   whether the appellant's father had provided the money for the purchase of the properties or whether the money was the appellant's own income derived from drug trafficking. The appellant's case was that his father completed a number of property sales between June and November 1986. The total realised moneys were in the region of £92,000. The appellant contended that this figure would
d   have constituted a sufficient pool for the purchase of the properties. Summaries of the conveyancing files were provided to the Court of Appeal. The appellant submitted that these files suggested that his father had had sufficient funds. The property was acquired when the appellant was 24 years old, several years before there was any direct evidence that he was involved in drug trafficking. Mr Heywood, the vendor of one of the properties, gave evidence that he thought the appellant
e   was 'skint'.
[11] On the other hand, the trial judge found that he was satisfied that Benjafield was at the head of a very considerable organisation dealing in large quantities of class A and class B drugs. He was not an addict and was motivated purely through profit. The appellant did not give evidence and so the judge was
f   deprived of any explanation by him. The appellant's father was called to give evidence but the judge rejected his evidence. The Crown's case was that there was no evidence of the source of the funds for the appellant to buy the properties.
[12] Counsel for the appellant argued that on the evidence the making of a confiscation order was inappropriate. He said that it was probable that the appellant's father paid for the properties. The fact that the appellant did not
g   testify is, however, a powerful point against him. Collins J (with whom Judge LJ agreed) further observed (para 19):

h   'The indictment covered the dates March to July 1997, but it was clear from the conversations that were overheard that this appellant must have been involved in drug trafficking to a major extent for a period before that. He was, as the judge found, the prime mover, indeed the leader, of the enterprise. As a matter of common sense it can be said that one does not get to that pinnacle in drug trafficking immediately, so it was clear that it would have been a perfectly proper inference to draw that this appellant had been engaged in drug trafficking for some time before May 1997.'

j   And later Collins J added (para 46):

'... where the drug trafficking was at such a high level it is perfectly proper to conclude that it must have been going on for a considerable time before the appellant built himself up to reach the position that on the evidence he clearly did reach.'

For my part I see no reason to disagree with the reasoning of the Court of Appeal.

[13] A less than satisfactory aspect of the case is, however, that the judge had *a* misdescribed his function by saying 'it has not been shown on the balance of probabilities that there was any risk of injustice'. As is apparent from the judgments in *R v Rezvi* [2002] 1 All ER 801, [2002] 2 WLR 235 and on this appeal that is putting it too high. The judge must avoid any real risk of injustice. But I am satisfied that no injustice or prejudice resulted from this misdirection as is *b* convincingly shown by the careful review of the case by the Court of Appeal.

Disposal
[14] I would dismiss the appeal.

LORD HOPE OF CRAIGHEAD.   *c*
[15] My Lords, I have had the advantage of reading in draft the speech of my noble and learned friend Lord Steyn. I agree with it, and for the reasons which he has given I too would dismiss the appeal.

LORD HUTTON.   *d*
[16] My Lords, I have had the advantage of reading in draft the speech of my noble and learned friend Lord Steyn. I agree with it, and for the reasons which he has given I too would dismiss this appeal.

Appeal dismissed.

Kate O'Hanlon   Barrister.

a
BHP Great Britain Petroleum Ltd v Chesterfield Properties Ltd
[2001] EWCA Civ 1797

b COURT OF APPEAL, CIVIL DIVISION
JUDGE, JONATHAN PARKER LJJ AND BODEY J
23, 24 OCTOBER, 30 NOVEMBER 2001

Landlord and tenant – Covenant – Release – Assignment of lease – Statutory provisions
c *providing mechanism for release of 'landlord covenants' on assignment – Whether*
personal covenants capable of being released under statutory provisions – Landlord and
Tenant (Covenants) Act 1995, ss 3(6), 8, 28(1).

By an agreement made in April 1997, CP Ltd agreed to grant a lease over part of
a building to the claimant tenant following the completion of works of
d refurbishment. That agreement constituted a collateral agreement as defined in
s 28(1)[a] of the Landlord and Tenant (Covenants) Act 1995, and covenants
contained in such an agreement fell within the definition of 'covenant' contained
in that provision. Section 28(1) further provided that 'landlord covenant' meant
a covenant falling to be complied with by the landlord of the premises demised
by the tenancy, while 'landlord' was defined as the person 'for the time being'
e entitled to the reversion expectant on the term of the tenancy. Section 3(6)(a)[b]
provided that nothing in s 3, which dealt with the transmission of the benefit and
burden of covenants, operated in the case of a covenant which was expressed to
be personal to any person, to make the covenant enforceable by or against any
other person. In cl 12.2 of the agreement, CP Ltd covenanted to remedy or
f procure the remedy of any 'Building Works Defect' of which it had been notified
by the tenant. That obligation was expressly stated to be personal to CP Ltd.
'Building Works Defect' was defined in cl 1.1.8 as any physical damage to the
demised premises manifesting itself during a period of six years commencing on
the completion of the lease (the first limb of the definition) or any defect in the
premises which 'will' result in such damage 'manifesting itself' during that period
g (the second limb of the definition). In July 1997 CP Ltd granted the lease to the
tenant in accordance with the terms of the agreement. In July 1999 CP Ltd
transferred its interest in the property, subject to the lease, to another company.
Later that month, CP Ltd served a notice on the tenant under s 8[c] of the 1995 Act,
seeking its release from the landlord's obligations under the tenancy. By virtue
h of s 8, a release of the landlord covenants took effect if the tenant did not serve a
notice objecting to the release within a specified period. The tenant served no
such counternotice. In September 1999 and April 2000 certain toughened glass
units in which the building was clad fractured, and one of them (a non-vertical
unit) fell to the ground. In subsequent proceedings, the tenant claimed that
j CP Ltd was liable to replace not only the units that had fractured but also all the
other non-vertical units, on the footing that the use of the toughened glass in a
non-vertical plane constituted a defect in the property which CP Ltd was liable to

a   Section 28, so far as material, is set out at [32], below
b   Section 3, so far as material, is set out at [34], below
c   Section 8, so far as material, is set out at [40], below

make good under cl 12.2. CP Ltd contended that its liability was limited to
replacing the units that had actually fractured, but submitted that, in any event, *a*
it had been released from liability by the operation of the s 8 notice. On
applications by both parties for summary judgment, the judge found for CP Ltd
on the extent of its liability on the ground that the tenant could not say that any
further physical damage would definitely result from the defect. He further held,
however, that a personal covenant could not constitute a landlord covenant as *b*
defined in s 28(1), and that accordingly the operation of the s 8 notice had not
discharged CP Ltd's liability in respect of the fractured windows. CP Ltd
appealed against that part of the judge's decision, contending that it had the effect
of reinstating the distinction between covenants which 'touch and concern' the
land on the one hand, and personal covenants on the other—a distinction that
Parliament had set out to abolish when it had passed the 1995 Act. The tenant *c*
cross-appealed against the judge's decision on the extent of CP Ltd's liability. On
the cross-appeal, CP Ltd contended that the tenant could rely on the second limb
of the definition in cl 1.1.8 only if it could establish as a matter of certainty that
further physical damage would occur before the end of the six-year period.

d

Held – (1) A covenant personal to the original landlord could not be a 'landlord
covenant' within the definition in s 28(1) of the 1995 Act, and accordingly it could
not be released by the operation of a notice served under s 8 of the Act. The crux
was the definition of 'landlord' as the person 'for the time being' entitled to the
reversion expectant on the term of the tenancy. Those words clearly connoted
the person who might from time to time be entitled to the reversion. Transposing *e*
that definition into the definition of the expression 'landlord covenant', it
followed that that was an obligation falling to be complied with by the person
who might from time to time be entitled to the reversion. An obligation that was
personal to the original landlord was, by definition, not such an obligation since
it did not fall to be performed by the person who might from time to time be *f*
entitled to the reversion of the tenancy. Moreover, there was no direct antithesis
between a personal covenant on the one hand and a covenant which 'touches and
concerns', or related to, the land on the other. A covenant which related to the
land might nevertheless be expressed to be personal to one or other or both of the
parties to it. That was a matter for the contracting parties. Furthermore, there
was nothing in the 1995 Act to fetter the freedom of contracting parties to place *g*
a contractual limit on the transmissibility of the benefit or burden of obligations
under a tenancy. On the contrary, s 3(6)(a) clearly demonstrated that no such
fetter had been intended by Parliament. It followed that CP Ltd's obligations in
cl 12 of the agreement were not landlord covenants within the meaning of the
1995 Act, and that the s 8 notice was ineffective to release CP Ltd from such *h*
obligations. Accordingly, the latter's appeal would be dismissed (see [58]–[64],
below).

(2) On the true construction of cl 1.1.8 of the agreement, CP Ltd's liability
under the second limb of the definition extended to remedying the underlying
defect not merely by repairing any damage that had already occurred but also by *j*
ensuring that the defect was remedied, so that it would not result in physical
damage (or, as the case might be, further physical damage) occurring in the
future. The words 'manifesting itself [during the six-year period]' in the second
limb of the definition of 'Building Works Defect' applied not to the physical
damage but to the defect. Thus, in order to bring the second limb of the definition
into play, the tenant had to be able, prior to the cut-off date, to point to a defect

a in the property which 'will' result in physical damage to the property at some time in the future, not necessarily prior to the cut-off date. That requirement was met by establishing, with the benefit of hindsight, that the defect had in fact resulted in physical damage. Otherwise, the tenant would be in a worse position if physical damage had in fact occurred than if it had not, in that the existence of actual physical damage would preclude it from requiring the remedying of the

b underlying defect unless it could prove that further physical damage would result from the defect. It followed that while the first limb of the definition was directed at physical damage which had actually occurred, the second limb was directed at the existence of an underlying defect which either had caused or would cause physical damage. Accordingly, the tenant's cross-appeal would be allowed (see [59]–[62], [64], [75]–[79], [81], [82], below).

c   Decision of Lightman J [2001] 2 All ER 914 reversed in part.

Notes
For the release of landlord and tenant from covenants on the assignment of interest, see Supp to 27(1) *Halsbury's Laws* (4th edn reissue) para 466B.

d   For the Landlord and Tenant (Covenants) Act 1995, ss 3, 8, 28, see 23 *Halsbury's Statutes* (4th edn) (1997 reissue) 717, 725, 750.

Cases referred to in judgment
Spencer's Case (1583) 5 Co Rep 16a, [1558–1774] All ER Rep 68, 77 ER 72.
Swift (P & A) Investments (a firm) v Combined English Stores Group plc [1988] 2 All ER

e   885, [1989] AC 632, [1988] 3 WLR 313, HL.
System Floors Ltd v Ruralpride Ltd [1995] 1 EGLR 48, CA.

Appeal and cross-appeal
The first defendant, Chesterfield Properties Ltd (Chesterfield), appealed with

f permission of Lightman J granted on 7 March 2001 from that part of his decision on 27 February 2001 ([2001] 2 All ER 914, [2001] 3 WLR 277) whereby he held, on applications for summary judgment, that a notice served by Chesterfield on the claimant, BHP Petroleum Great Britain Ltd (BHP), on 30 July 1999 under s 8 of the Landlord and Tenant (Covenants) Act 1995 had not discharged Chesterfield from its liability to BHP under cl 12.2.1 of an agreement for a lease made between

g the parties on 30 April 1997. BHP cross-appealed with permission of Chadwick LJ granted on 29 March 2001 from that part of Lightman J's decision dealing with the extent of Chesterfield's liability. The second defendant, Chesterfield (Neathouse) Ltd, was not a party to the proceedings in the Court of Appeal. The facts are set out in the judgment of the court.

h
Kim Lewison QC and *Andrew PD Walker* (instructed by *Dechert*) for Chesterfield.
Michael Barnes QC (instructed by *Herbert Smith*) for BHP.

Cur adv vult

j 30 November 2001. The following judgment of the court was delivered.

JONATHAN PARKER LJ.

INTRODUCTION
    [1] Before the court are an appeal and a cross-appeal against an order made by Lightman J dated 27 February 2001. The appellant (the first defendant in the

action) is Chesterfield Properties Ltd (Chesterfield). The respondent and
cross-appellant (the claimant in the action) is BHP Petroleum Great Britain Ltd   *a*
(BHP).

[2] The second defendant in the action, Chesterfield (Neathouse) Ltd, is not a
party to the appeal or the cross-appeal.

[3] By its particulars of claim, BHP seeks relief against Chesterfield in respect
of alleged breaches by Chesterfield of its obligations under an agreement for lease   *b*
made between them dated 30 April 1997 (the Agreement). By its defence
Chesterfield denies liability, contending (among other things) (a) that under the
terms of the Agreement, on their true construction, its liability for the alleged
breaches (which are denied) is materially less than that contended for by BHP,
and (b) that it has in any event been released from such liability by the operation   *c*
of a notice dated 30 July 1999 which it served on BHP under s 8 of the Landlord
and Tenant (Covenants) Act 1995. By its reply, BHP joins issue on both those
contentions.

[4] Both BHP and Chesterfield applied for summary judgment under CPR Pt 24.
The applications were heard by Lightman J and led to the order part of which is
the subject of the appeal and cross-appeal. In his judgment, which is reported at   *d*
[2001] 2 All ER 914, [2001] 3 WLR 277, the judge determined the issue as to the
construction of the Agreement in favour of Chesterfield and the issue as to
the effect of the notice in favour of BHP: that is to say, he concluded that the
extent of Chesterfield's liability under the Agreement was as contended for by
Chesterfield, and that Chesterfield was not released from that liability by the   *e*
operation of the notice. BHP now appeals against the judge's conclusion as to the
true construction of the Agreement; Chesterfield appeals against the judge's
conclusion as to the effect of the notice. In procedural terms, as already
mentioned, the appellant is Chesterfield and the cross-appellant is BHP.

[5] Chesterfield appears by Mr Kim Lewison QC and Mr Andrew PD Walker
of counsel; BHP appears by Mr Michael Barnes QC.   *f*

THE FACTUAL BACKGROUND

[6] By the Agreement, Chesterfield agreed with BHP to undertake certain
specified works to a substantial office building at One Neathouse Place, London
SW1 and to grant a 20-year lease of the greater part of the building to BHP. Since   *g*
it is unnecessary for present purposes to differentiate between the building as a
whole and the part of it which was to be leased (and which in the event was
leased) to BHP, we will refer to the latter as 'the property'. The Agreement
contains obligations on the part of Chesterfield (to the terms of which we shall
have to return) relating to the making good of defects in the property and to the   *h*
repair of physical damage to the property.

[7] On 1 July 1997, Chesterfield granted a lease of the property to BHP in
accordance with the terms of the Agreement. On 9 July 1999 Chesterfield transferred
its interest in the property, subject to the lease, to Chesterfield (Neathouse) Ltd.

[8] On 30 July 1999 Chesterfield served the notice on BHP. By the notice,   *j*
Chesterfield applied to be released from 'the landlord's obligations under the
tenancy' with effect from the date of the transfer of its reversionary interest
(9 July 1999), pursuant to s 8 of the 1995 Act.

[9] Section 8 of the 1995 Act (to the detailed terms of which we turn below)
entitles a tenant on whom a notice has been served by his landlord under the
section to serve a counter-notice on the landlord objecting to the release of the

a   obligations referred to in the landlord's notice. In the event, however, no counter-notice was served by BHP.

[10] The exterior of the property is clad largely in units of toughened glass, some of which are fixed in a non-vertical plane. In September 1999 two of the vertical units fractured. In April 2000 two further units fractured, one of which (a non-vertical unit) fell to the ground and injured a passer-by. This led to the
b   service of a dangerous structure notice on 5 May 2000. Since then, two further units have fractured. Neither of these fell to the ground.

[11] In the action, which was commenced on 10 October 2000, BHP claims that under the terms of the Agreement and in the events which have happened Chesterfield is liable not merely to replace the units which have fractured (that is to say, to repair the physical damage which has occurred) but also to replace all
c   the other non-vertical units in the property, on the footing that the use of the toughened glass in a non-vertical plane constitutes a defect in the property which Chesterfield is liable to make good. Chesterfield, on the other hand, contends that on the true construction of the Agreement its liability is limited to replacing the units which have actually fractured, with the further proviso that in the case
d   of each such unit the cost of replacement must exceed £50,000 (excluding VAT). Chesterfield did not contend before the judge that its liability is further limited by the proviso as to cost of replacement (although the point is missed in its application notice), but no objection is taken by BHP to this contention being raised on BHP's cross-appeal. In the alternative, as noted earlier, Chesterfield contends that it has in any event been released from liability by the operation of
e   the notice. We refer hereafter to the issues as to the true construction of the Agreement as 'the Agreement issue', and to the issue as to the effect of the notice as 'the 1995 Act issue'.

THE AGREEMENT

f   [12] As already noted, the Agreement provided that following completion of works of refurbishment to be carried out by Chesterfield, Chesterfield would grant BHP a 20-year lease of the property.

[13] Clause 1.1 of the Agreement contains a number of definitions, of which only the following are material for present purposes:

g   '1.1.8 "**Building Works Defect**" any physical damage to the Demised Premises manifesting itself during the Defects Period or any defect in the Demised Premises which will result in physical damage to the Demised Premises manifesting itself during the Defects Period and in either case:—

1.1.8.1. which is caused by defective design materials or workmanship in the construction of the Building Works and
h   1.1.8.2. which one or more of the Warrantors is responsible to the Landlord to remedy pursuant to the provisions contained in any contract appointment or warranty between the Landlord and the Warrantors and

1.1.8.3. the cost of remedying which will in each such case exceed £50,000 (excluding VAT);
j   but excluding:—

1.1.8.4. any such damage which occurs or arises directly or indirectly as a result of any works undertaken by or on behalf of the Tenant to the Demised Premises or the Tenants use of the Demised Premises otherwise than in accordance with the provisions of the Lease and

1.1.8.5. (subject and without prejudice to the provisions of clause 12.2.7) any such damage to the extent that the cost of remedying such damage

would result in the Landlord incurring costs and expenses pursuant to clause
12.2 of this agreement in excess of the Maximum Aggregate Sum ...   *a*

1.1.15 "**the Defects Period**" the period of six years commencing on and
including the date of the actual completion of the Lease or if completion of
the Lease is delayed otherwise than by reason of the default of the Landlord
the period commencing on and including the date upon which the Lease
should have been completed pursuant to the provisions of this agreement.'   *b*

[14] Clause 1.2 is headed 'Interpretation'. Clause 1.2.5, under that heading,
reads as follows (so far as material):

'References in this agreement to the Landlord are references to
Chesterfield Properties PLC and shall not include the Landlord's successors
in title. All obligations on the part of the Landlord in this agreement ... are   *c*
personal obligations of the Landlord.'

[15] Clause 12 of the Agreement is headed 'Concrete Frame Defects and
Building Works Defects'. Clause 12.2 deals with 'Building Works Defects'. Its
opening words are: 'If on one or more occasions during the Defects Period a
Building Works Defect manifests itself the following provisions shall apply ...'   *d*

[16] Clause 12.2.1 provides that BHP shall notify Chesterfield in writing of a
'Building Works Defect' as soon as reasonably practicable. Clause 12.2.3.2 is in
the following terms:

'... the Landlord shall with the minimum practical inconvenience to the
Tenant and as economically as reasonably practicable remedy or procure the   *e*
remedying of each Building Works Defect as quickly as reasonably practicable
after obtaining the necessary building consents and after (if reasonably
required by the Landlord) the Tenant and all other occupiers shall have
vacated the Demised Premises or the part or parts of the Demised Premises
affected by such Building Works Defects.'   *f*

[17] Clause 12.5 of the Agreement is headed 'General Provisions'. Clause
12.5.1 provides as follows:

'12.5.1. For the avoidance of doubt:—
12.5.1.1. the Tenant acknowledges that the obligations on the part of the
Landlord contained in this clause 12 are personal obligations of Chesterfield   *g*
Properties Plc and the Tenant acknowledges and confirms that the Tenant
shall have no claim of any nature whatsoever against the Landlords
successors in title to the Demised Premises arising out of or otherwise in
connection with the obligations on the part of the Landlord contained in this
clause 12;   *h*
12.5.1.2. the benefit of the provisions contained in this clause 12 shall
enure for the Tenants successors in title and the Tenant and the Tenants
successors in title shall be entitled to assign the benefit of the provisions
contained in this clause 12 to each subsequent assignee of the Lease but not
otherwise.'   *j*

THE 1995 ACT
The previous law
[18] Prior to the sixteenth century a lease of land was regarded in law as no
more than a personal contract, giving rise to no proprietary rights or obligations.
In the sixteenth century, however, it was established that on the transfer of the

a reversion or of the leasehold interest the benefit and the burden of those covenants in the lease which 'touched and concerned' the land demised by the lease passed to, and were enforceable by and against, successors in title of the original parties. In the Conveyancing Act 1881 and the Law of Property Act 1925 the equivalent expression to 'touch and concern' is 'has reference to the subject-matter of the lease'.

b [19] So far as transfers of the reversion were concerned, this change in the law was effected by the Grantees of Reversions Act 1540. The law as so enacted was re-enacted in the 1881 Act and in ss 141 and 142 of the 1925 Act.

[20] So far as transfers of the leasehold interest were concerned, the change in the law was effected at common law, by *Spencer's Case* (1583) 5 Co Rep 16a, [1558–1774] All ER Rep 68. The principle established by *Spencer's Case* remained

c as a common law principle up to the passing of the 1995 Act.

[21] However, the development of the law as to the transmissibility of the benefit and burden of covenants in a lease did not impinge upon the contractual liability of the original parties to the lease. They remained contractually liable throughout the term of the lease, despite transfers of the reversion and/or of the

d leasehold interest.

[22] Hence the law as to the enforceability of covenants in a lease prior to the passing of the 1995 Act depended upon, and was regulated by, the application of the twin concepts of privity of contract and privity of estate. As it was put by the Law Commission in the opening paragraph of its report on *Landlord and Tenant Law, Privity of Contract and Estate* (Law Com no 174), published in 1988 (the 1988

e report):

'In the law of landlord and tenant privity of contract means that the original landlord and the original tenant normally remain liable to perform their respective obligations for the whole of the period for which the lease was granted, even if they have parted with all interest in the property.

f Privity of estate means that the landlord and the tenant for the time being automatically assume responsibility for the lease obligations which relate directly to the property for the period during which they own an interest in it, but they are not necessarily bound to comply with all the terms of the lease.'

g
[23] In Pt II of the 1988 report, under the heading 'The Present Law', the Law Commission summarised the law in relation to the enforceability of covenants in a lease (as it then stood) as follows:

'2.1 A lease creates a new legal estate, vesting the property in the tenant

h for a defined period; it also constitutes a contract between the original parties, who normally undertake liabilities under the covenants for the whole term created by the lease. The direct contractual relationship— privity of contract—between the original landlord and the original tenant means that they remain liable to perform their respective covenants for the

j whole period of the lease, notwithstanding that they have parted with all interest in the property. Thus, e.g., the original tenant remains liable to pay rent if the person to whom he has assigned the term defaults; "of course the expectation, commercially speaking, is that the assignee will pay, but the assignor does not by assignment get rid of one jot or tittle of his original liability". Although the privity of contract principle applies equally to landlords and tenants, examples of tenants being made liable are more

common. The main reason for this is probably that in the majority of leases
the tenant undertakes many more obligations than does the landlord.   *a*

2.2 Privity of estate means that the parties stand for the time being in the
relationship of landlord and tenant, which of itself involves certain
enforceable obligations. As between the original parties to a lease, there is at
first privity both of contract and of estate. However, if either the original
landlord or the original tenant parts with his interest in the property, the   *b*
privity of estate between them comes to an end. There is then privity of
estate between the person who is landlord for the time being and the person
who is tenant for the time being. The parties currently in the position of
landlord and tenant become bound by, and can enforce, certain types of
covenant in a lease. The covenants so enforceable are, in general, those
which have a direct bearing on their relationship as landlord and tenant—   *c*
said technically to be, covenants which "touch and concern" the land or have
"reference to the subject-matter of the lease", terms which are treated as
synonymous. In practice, almost all the most important covenants in a lease
fall within this category. Those covenants which impose merely personal
obligations bind only the original parties, and not their successors.   *d*

2.3 Once the lease is assigned, there will be privity of estate between the
landlord and the assignee. When a lease requires the landlord's consent to
an assignment by the tenant, it is not uncommon for the landlord to require
the proposed assignee to covenant directly with him to observe and perform
the tenant's covenants in the lease. In that case, as soon as the assignee
covenants directly with the landlord, there will additionally be privity of   *e*
contract between them. As a result, the new tenant's liability will go beyond
the normal privity of estate liability of an assignee in two respects. First, his
liability will extend to all the tenant's covenants in the lease and not merely
those which touch and concern the land. Secondly, if his covenant is
expressed to bind him for the remainder of the lease, he remains liable even   *f*
if he subsequently assigns his interest.'

[24] Later in the 1988 report, the Law Commission considered the concept of
privity of estate in greater detail, noting that covenants in a lease could be divided
into two groups: those which 'touched and concerned' the land, and those which
did not. It described the latter category as covenants which 'impose personal or   *g*
collateral obligations' (see ibid para 2.20). The Law Commission went on to refer
to the lack of any guiding principle for deciding into which of the two categories
a particular covenant fell. In paras 2.21–2.23 it said:

'2.21 Thus, when the original tenant assigns his lease, the assignee (and
any subsequent assignee) automatically becomes directly liable to the   *h*
landlord, with whom he has privity of estate, in respect of those covenants
which "touch and concern" the land. Examples of such covenants are
covenants to pay the rent; to repair buildings; to insure them against fire; to
use the property for domestic purposes only; and a covenant not to assign
the lease without the landlord's consent. Similarly, when the original   *j*
landlord parts with the reversion, his successor becomes responsible for
complying with those obligations which have "reference to the subject
matter of the lease". Examples of such obligations undertaken by the
landlord are covenants to repair or insure the premises, to supply water to
the property, and to give the tenant quiet possession of the premises.
Personal covenants bind only the original parties, and not their successors.

a
Examples of such covenants are a landlord's covenant not to compete with the tenant's business; a covenant requiring payment of an annual sum to a third party; and one promising to pay the tenant a sum of money at the end of the lease or until a new lease is granted.

2.22 The test for distinguishing between those covenants which touch and concern the land and those which are merely personal has been
b
variously formulated in the decided cases over the years. The covenant will touch and concern the land if it *per se* affects the nature, quality or value of the land; if it affects the landlord in his normal capacity as landlord or the tenant in his normal capacity as tenant; if the covenant is beneficial to the owner for the time being of the covenantee's land and to no one else.

2.23 The rules concerning covenants which run with the land were
c
criticised some fifty years ago as "purely arbitrary, and the distinctions, for the most part, quite illogical". As we indicated in the Working Paper, there are a number of difficult borderline cases from which it is hard to discern a clear guiding principle. To take a few examples. A landlord's covenant to renew a lease runs with the land, but a covenant that a landlord will make a
d
payment to the tenant at the end of the lease, or in default will grant a new lease does not. A covenant not to employ a named person on business premises binds the tenant's successors; a covenant not to employ a particular class of people on the property does not.'

e
The Law Commission's proposals for reform
[25] In Pt IV of the 1988 report, under the heading 'Reform Proposals', the Law Commission said:

'*Basis*
4.1 Our proposals for reform recognise the importance of two principles:
f
First, a landlord or a tenant of property should not continue to enjoy rights nor be under any obligation arising from a lease once he has parted with all interest in the property.

Secondly, all the terms of the lease should be regarded as a single bargain for letting the property. When the interest of one of the parties changes hands the successor should fully take his predecessor's place as landlord or
g
tenant, without distinguishing between different categories of covenant.

4.2 The majority of those who responded to the Working Paper believed that the effect of transferring property which has been leased should be the "clean break" which results from applying the two principles. Nevertheless, the consultation convinced us that there are cases in which, for good reason,
h
landlords can only agree to a proposed assignment if they are assured that their existing tenant will continue to be responsible for complying with the lease terms. We are therefore proposing a scheme based on the general abrogation of the privity of contract principle, but which stops short of abolishing it in all cases.

j
Outline
4.3 We propose a general rule that the liability of the original tenant, and his entitlement to benefits under the lease, should not survive an assignment of the lease. For this purpose, we propose that all the covenants in a lease should be treated in the same way, whether or not at present they touch and concern the land. Nevertheless, it would be possible for the landlord, when granting consent to the assignment, to impose a condition that the tenant

will be liable to guarantee the performance of some or all of the lease *a*
covenants by his immediate successor.

4.4 The Landlord and Tenant Act 1988 implements our recommendations
generally to impose a duty on landlords not unreasonably to withhold
consent. The effect would be that in cases where the landlord is not entitled
to withhold his consent to assign, he would only be able to impose a
condition that the tenant have continuing liability where it was reasonable *b*
to do so.

4.5 For landlords, we propose a rule that when they part with their
interest in the property let by a lease they will escape further responsibility
for the lease obligations if, but only if, they comply with the prescribed
conditions. These will involve their giving notice to the tenant and his being *c*
able to withhold consent if it is reasonable for him to do so. Again, the
benefits of being landlord, so far as they can enure to an owner who has
parted with the property, would only continue for a former landlord who
had continuing liability.

4.6 Landlords and tenants will generally have different forms of continuing *d*
liability, where they have any at all. Former landlords will be jointly and
severally liable with the current landlord, and any other former landlord
who is still liable. A former tenant, on the other hand, will normally be
guarantor of the current tenant; the only exceptional case is where a tenant
only assigns part of the property and remains jointly and severally liable with *e*
the assignee for some covenants which affect the whole property. Making
former tenants liable as guarantors avoids the major injustice to tenants
which can arise where the terms of the lease are, in effect, later varied to
increase the tenant's liability. That will now release the tenant, except where
the court varies an unsatisfactory lease of a flat.'
f

[26] Later in the 1988 report, under the heading 'Assignment of whole
property by landlords', the Law Commission said:

'4.16 In relation to the liability of landlords, we should have preferred our
proposals to have mirrored precisely our recommendations for tenants' *g*
covenants. However, that is not possible because tenants rarely, if ever, have
a right to give or withhold consent to dispositions by their landlord. They
would therefore not be in a position to require continuing liability after an
assignment of the reversion and to block an assignment if the condition is not
agreed. Moreover, there is less need here for radical change. In most leases, *h*
the landlord undertakes far fewer obligations that the tenant and landlords
may not be troubled by the prospect of continuing responsibility.

'4.17 For these reasons, we do not propose that an assignment of the
landlord's reversionary interest should automatically affect his continuing
liability. Rather, we recommend that an assigning landlord should have an *j*
option to operate a procedure which could end his liability, and his entitlement
to benefits, under the lease. A landlord who wished to escape further
responsibility would have to give the tenant notice of his proposal to assign.
In the notice the landlord would propose that after the assignment he should
no longer have any liability under the lease. It would give the tenant four
weeks in which to reply.'

a [27] In para 5.1, in Pt V of the 1988 report, the Law Commission summarised its recommendations. The following recommendations are material for present purposes:

   '(1) A tenant who assigns all the property let by a lease should generally cease to be liable to comply with the lease covenants, and similarly should cease to have the benefit of the lease. The assignee should become liable to
b perform the covenants and should have the benefit.

   (2) A landlord consenting to an assignment should be able to impose a condition that the tenant guarantees the performance of the lease covenants by his successor, but only until the following assignment.

   (3) A landlord who assigns the whole of his reversion should have the
c option to escape further liability, and to forego benefits, under the lease by serving a prescribed notice on the tenant.

   (4) The incoming landlord should be liable to perform all the lease covenants, and be entitled to the benefits of the lease. Any previous landlord remaining bound by the covenants should be jointly and severally liable with the new landlord.
d
   (5) On a later assignment of the reversion, a previous landlord should be able to serve notice to escape further liability, but should have no statutory right to be notified in advance of a proposed assignment ...

   (10) The distinction between lease covenants which touch and concern the land and those which do not should be abolished.'
e

The 1995 Act itself

   [28] It is common ground that the 1995 Act was intended to implement the proposals made by the Law Commission in the 1988 report. Its preamble proclaims it to be (among other things): 'An Act to make provisions for persons
f bound by covenants of a tenancy to be released from such covenants on the assignment of the tenancy ...'

   [29] The judge said ([2001] 2 All ER 914 at [14]):

   'There were significant intermediate stages between the [1988] report and the enactment of the 1995 Act which are conveniently referred to in *Megarry*
g *& Wade: The Law of Real Property* (6th edn, 2000) p 975, para 15-064. It is accordingly not possible to assume that the 1995 Act gave unqualified effect to the recommendations in the [1998] report. There were modifications and additions. But I can find no indication in *Hansard* or elsewhere of any intention to qualify the adoption of the principle that the release of a landlord
h or tenant from a covenant was intended to be sequential upon, and only sequential upon, a parting by the landlord or tenant with his interest in the property let and the successor taking his predecessor's place as the party responsible for complying with that covenant.'

j [30] No suggestion to the contrary has been made in this court: indeed both sides rely on the 1988 report as setting the context in which the true meaning and effect of the 1995 Act falls to be considered.

   [31] Section 1(1) of the 1995 Act provides that the provisions relating to the transmission of covenants and to the release of covenants on assignment contained in ss 3 to 8 inclusive apply only to tenancies coming into existence on or after 1 January 1996.

[32] Before turning to the particular sections which are relevant for present
purposes it is convenient to turn first to the definitions in s 28(1). The material
definitions are these:

'... "collateral agreement", in relation to a tenancy, means any agreement
collateral to the tenancy, whether made before or after its creation ...
"covenant" includes term, condition and obligation, and references to a
covenant ... of a tenancy include a covenant ... contained in a collateral
agreement ...
"landlord" and "tenant", in relation to a tenancy, mean the person for the
time being entitled to the reversion expectant on the term of the tenancy and
the person so entitled to that term respectively;
"landlord covenant", in relation to a tenancy, means a covenant falling to
be complied with by the landlord of premises demised by the tenancy ...
"tenant covenant", in relation to a tenancy, means a covenant falling to be
complied with by the tenant of premises demised by the tenancy.'

[33] Section 2(1)(a) implements recommendation (10) in para 5.1 of the 1988
report that the distinction between those lease covenants which touch and
concern the land and those which do not should be abolished. It is in the
following terms:

'(1) This Act applies to a landlord covenant or a tenant covenant of a
tenancy—(a) whether or not the covenant has reference to the subject
matter of the tenancy ...'

[34] Section 3 is entitled 'Transmission of benefit and burden of covenants'. It
provides as follows (so far as material):

'(1) The benefit and burden of all landlord and tenant covenants of a
tenancy—(a) shall be annexed and incident to the whole, and to each and
every part, of the premises demised by the tenancy and of the reversion in
them, and (b) shall in accordance with this section pass on an assignment of
the whole or any part of those premises or of the reversion in them.
(2) Where the assignment is by the tenant under the tenancy, then as
from the assignment the assignee—(a) becomes bound by the tenant
covenants of the tenancy except to the extent that—(i) immediately before
the assignment they did not bind the assignor, or (ii) they fall to be complied
with in relation to any demised premises not comprised in the assignment;
and (b) becomes entitled to the benefit of the landlord covenants of the
tenancy except to the extent that they fall to be complied with in relation to
any such premises.
(3) Where the assignment is by the landlord under the tenancy, then as
from the assignment the assignee—(a) becomes bound by the landlord
covenants of the tenancy except to the extent that—(i) immediately before
the assignment they did not bind the assignor, or (ii) they fall to be complied
with in relation to any demised premises not comprised in the assignment;
and (b) becomes entitled to the benefit of the tenant covenants of the
tenancy except to the extent that they fall to be complied with in relation to
any such premises.
(4) In determining for the purposes of subsection (2) or (3) whether any
covenant bound the assignor immediately before the assignment, any

a

waiver or release of the covenant which (in whatever terms) is expressed to be personal to the assignor shall be disregarded.

(5) Any landlord or tenant covenant of a tenancy which is restrictive of the user of land shall, as well as being capable of enforcement against an assignee, be capable of being enforced against any other person who is the owner or occupier of any demised premises to which the covenant relates,

b

even though there is no express provision in the tenancy to that effect.

(6) Nothing in this section shall operate—(a) in the case of a covenant which (in whatever terms) is expressed to be personal to any person, to make the covenant enforceable by or (as the case may be) against any other person; or (b) …'

c

[35] Subsections (2) and (3) of s 3 implement, in part, the recommendations in the 1988 Report (see above). Subsection (6)(a) is material in the instant case, given that the Agreement provides in terms that the obligations of Chesterfield under the Agreement are personal to Chesterfield (see cll 1.2.5 and 12.5.1.1. quoted above).

d

[36] Section 4 deals with rights of re-entry, and is not material for present purposes.

[37] Sections 5 to 8 inclusive are headed 'Release of Covenants on Assignment'. Section 5 applies where a tenant assigns premises demised to him under a tenancy. Section 5(2) provides as follows (so far as material):

e

'If the tenant assigns the whole of the premises demised to him, he— (a) is released from the tenant covenants of the tenancy, and (b) ceases to be entitled to the benefit of the landlord covenants of the tenancy, as from the assignment.'

[38] Section 6 applies where a landlord assigns the reversion in the premises subject to the tenancy. Section 6(2) provides as follows:

f

'If the landlord assigns the reversion in the whole of the premises of which he is the landlord—(a) he may apply to be released from the landlord covenants of the tenancy in accordance with section 8; and (b) if he is so released from all of those covenants, he ceases to be entitled to the benefit of the tenant covenants of the tenancy as from the assignment.'

g

[39] Section 7 deals with the position of a former landlord, and is not material for present purposes.

[40] Section 8 lays down the procedure for seeking release from a covenant under s 6. It provides as follows:

h

'(1) For the purposes of section 6 or 7 an application for the release of a covenant to any extent is made by serving on the tenant, either before or within the period of four weeks beginning with the date of the assignment in question, a notice informing him of—(a) the proposed assignment or (as the case may be) the fact that the assignment has taken place, and (b) the request

j

for the covenant to be released to that extent.

(2) Where an application for the release of a covenant is made in accordance with subsection (1), the covenant is released to the extent mentioned in the notice if—(a) the tenant does not, within the period of four weeks beginning with the day on which the notice is served, serve on the landlord or former landlord a notice in writing objecting to the release, or (b) the tenant does so serve such a notice but the court, on the application of

the landlord or former landlord, makes a declaration that it is reasonable for
the covenant to be so released, or (c) the tenant serves on the landlord or
former landlord a notice in writing consenting to the release and, if he has
previously served a notice objecting to it, stating that that notice is
withdrawn.

(3) Any release from a covenant in accordance with this section shall be
regarded as occurring at the time when the assignment in question takes
place.

(4) In this section—(a) "the tenant" means the tenant of the premises
comprised in the assignment in question (or, if different part of those
premises are held under the tenancy by different tenants, each of those
tenants); (b) any reference to the landlord or former landlord is a reference to
the landlord referred to in section 6 or the former landlord referred to
in section 7, as the case may be; and (c) "the court" means a county court.'

[41] Finally, s 27(1) provides that the form of notice under s 8 shall be
prescribed by regulations made by statutory instrument. It is common ground
that the notice was in the prescribed form.

THE JUDGMENT OF LIGHTMAN J

[42] Addressing the 1995 Act issue, the judge ([2001] 2 All ER 914, [2001] 3
WLR 277) said this:

'[22] I turn to the first question. The rival contentions by the parties put
the issue into perspective. Mr Berry for [Chesterfield] submits any form of
obligation on the part of a landlord in a tenancy or collateral agreement,
whatever its character or topic, constitutes a landlord covenant and likewise
any form of obligation on the part of a tenant constitutes a tenant covenant.
On the other hand Mr Barnes QC for [BHP] submits that the obligation in
either case must be capable of being annexed to the premises demised by the
tenancy and the reversion and accordingly transmissible under s 3 of the Act,
and that this excludes personal covenants. It is common ground that the
Agreement is a "collateral agreement" in relation to the Lease. It is sufficient
to say the Agreement is an agreement "running side by side" and "parallel to"
the Lease (see the definition of "collateral" in The Oxford English Dictionary
(2nd edn)). (It is unnecessary for this purpose, though it may be sufficient,
that the Agreement constitutes the species of contract known as a collateral
contract.) It is clear that the personal covenant, since it is "a covenant in a
collateral agreement", is for the purposes of the 1995 Act (in accordance with
the definition of the term "covenant") a covenant of the Lease. The critical
question is whether that covenant falls within the definition in s 28 of a
landlord covenant. For this purpose it must be a covenant "falling to be
complied with by the landlord of premises demised by the tenancy", and the
landlord for this purpose means "the person for the time being entitled to the
reversion expectant on the term of the tenancy". Focus, as it seems to me,
must be placed on the words "for the time being". These words to my mind
connote, not merely that the covenant falls to be complied with by the
landlord at any particular point in time (as submitted by Mr Berry for
[Chesterfield]), but that it falls to be complied with by the person who may
from time to time be entitled to the reversion. It may be noted that a tenant
covenant is likewise defined as a covenant falling to be complied with by the
person "so" (ie like the landlord in the case of the landlord covenant) for the

a   time being entitled to the tenancy. In short the only covenant that can constitute a landlord or tenant covenant is a covenant which is capable of subsisting (in the language of s 3 of the Act) as a transmissible covenant and accordingly a personal covenant cannot qualify.

[23] Mr Berry submitted that this construction could not stand with the two specific references in the 1995 Act to personal covenants. Section 3(6)

b   provides that nothing in s 3 (which is concerned with the transmission of the benefit and burden of covenants) shall operate to make a covenant expressed to be personal to any person enforceable by or (as the case may be) against any other person; and s 15(5) again provides that nothing in that section (which is concerned with enforcement of covenants) shall operate to make a covenant expressed to be personal to any person enforceable by or (as the

c   case may be) against any other person. I do not find any contra-indication to the construction which I have adopted in either of those provisions. They are cautionary provisions designed to prevent any question arising whether the sections might have the unexpected and unintended result there referred to. They do not elevate, or reflect any intention to elevate, personal into

d   landlord or tenant covenants.'

[43] The judge went on to observe that he was relieved to reach the conclusion he had, for a number of reasons. In the first place, his conclusion accorded with the recommendations in the 1988 report. Secondly, the judge pointed out that one of the consequences of a contrary conclusion would be that

e   a tenant (who is automatically released from 'tenant covenants' on an assignment: see s 5(2)) would thereby be automatically released from any obligation owed to his landlord under an agreement collateral to the tenancy, notwithstanding that such obligation might be wholly unconnected with the tenancy.

[44] The judge accordingly held that the personal obligations of Chesterfield under the Agreement survived, and were unaffected by, the service of the notice.

f   [45] Addressing the Agreement issue, the judge said this:

'[28] The Tenant maintains that under cl 12.2.3.2 of the Agreement he is entitled to require [Chesterfield] to remedy, not merely the physical damage that has occurred by reason of the building work defect (ie replace the windows if the total cost exceeds £50,000) but also the underlying defect,

g   namely the use of the wrong and untested glass. This claim turns on the definition of Building Work Defect in cl 1.1.8, namely—"any physical damage to the Demised Premises manifesting itself during the Defects Period or any defect in the Demised Premises which will result in physical damage to the Demised Premises manifesting itself during the Defects

h   Period." [BHP] cannot say that further physical damage will result from this defect, nor could he say that further physical damage would result when [BHP] gave notice of the defect between the date of the resultant damage to the second and third window. All he can say now is, and all he could say then was, that the defect gives rise now and gave rise then to a significant risk of

j   further damage. But Mr Barnes for [BHP] submits that the issue whether there is a defect which will cause damage (and accordingly requires remedying) must be looked at as at the date of the Agreement: looked at from that viewpoint it can now be seen and said that the defect would result in physical damage. It is, however, clear (most particularly from cl 12.2 of the Agreement) that the situation must be looked at as at the date of [BHP's] notification of the defect. Accordingly [BHP] cannot require [Chesterfield]

to remedy the alleged defect: he can only require remedy of the accrued
physical damage and then only if the cost of the remedy exceeds £50,000.
Any complaint about this on the part of [BHP] must be in respect of the
negotiation or drafting of this term of the Agreement.'

THE 1995 ACT ISSUE

The arguments

[46] Mr Lewison QC, for Chesterfield, submits that the Agreement is a
'collateral agreement', and that the obligations in question constitute a 'landlord
covenant', within the definitions of those expressions in s 28(1) of the 1995 Act.
Accordingly, he submits, by virtue of s 3(1) of the 1995 Act the burden of those
obligations passed to Chesterfield (Neathouse) Ltd on the transfer of the
reversion, notwithstanding that the obligations are expressed to be personal to
Chesterfield (see cll 1.2.5 and 12.5.1.1 of the Agreement, quoted earlier).
Similarly, he submits, it was open to Chesterfield to serve a notice under s 8
seeking to be released from its obligations under the Agreement. It follows, he
submits, that since no counter-notice was served Chesterfield was released from
those obligations with effect from the date of the transfer of the reversion.

[47] Mr Lewison submits that the effect of the judge's decision is to reinstate
the distinction between covenants which 'touch and concern' the land demised
on the one hand, and personal covenants on the other: a distinction which
Parliament, on the recommendation of the Law Commission, set out to abolish
when it passed the 1995 Act.

[48] He also relies on the fact that the benefit of the obligations in question
was intended to pass to assignees of the lease (see cl 12.5.1.2. of the Agreement,
quoted earlier).

[49] As an illustration of the way in which the 1995 Act operates, Mr Lewison
takes the example of obligations entered into by a management company. He
submits that in virtually all cases where a lease imposes obligations on a
management company such obligations will be personal to the management
company, but by virtue of the 1995 Act the benefit and the burden of such
obligations will nevertheless be transmissible. By contrast, he submits, if the
judge is right neither the benefit nor the burden of those obligations will be
transmissible.

[50] Mr Lewison cites the decision of the Court of Appeal in *System Floors Ltd v
Ruralpride Ltd* [1995] 1 EGLR 48 (decided before the coming into force of the 1995
Act) as an example of a case in which the burden of a personal covenant has been
held to be transmissible, notwithstanding that the benefit of it was not. In that
case the landlord agreed, by a side-letter which was expressed to be personal to
the tenant, to accept a surrender of the lease on certain terms. The landlord
subsequently transferred the reversion to a third party who took without notice
of the side-letter. The court at first instance held that the terms of the side-letter
were not binding on the new landlord. On appeal by the tenant, the Court of
Appeal (Leggatt, Millett and Morritt LJJ) held that the side-letter was drafted in
terms which indicated that it was intended to be binding on those entitled to the
reversion for the time being and was accordingly enforceable against a successor
in title to the reversion pursuant to s 142 of the Law of Property Act 1925,
notwithstanding that the benefit would not pass to any subsequent tenant. In the
course of his judgment, Morritt LJ said (at 50):

a   'I do not see why the transmission of the burden should depend on transmissibility of the benefit if all the other conditions are satisfied when, as the decision in *P&A Swift Investments* v *Combined English Stores Group plc* ([1988] 2 All ER 885, [1989] AC 632) shows, the transmission of the benefit does not depend on the transmissibility of the burden.'

b   [51] Mr Lewison submits that, by analogy with the *P & A Swift Investments* case, under the old law the obligations of Chesterfield under cl 12.2 of the Agreement would have been regarded as touching and concerning the property, since the benefit of the obligations was transmissible notwithstanding that the burden of the obligations was not.

[52] Mr Lewison stresses the width of the definitions in s 28(1) of the 1995 Act. c   He submits that, in passing the 1995 Act, Parliament cannot have intended to exclude obligations such as those contained in cl 12.2 of the Agreement from the rules applicable to 'landlord covenants', and that to exclude such obligations from the definition of 'landlord covenants' would be contrary to the whole scheme of the 1995 Act.

d   [53] Mr Barnes QC, for BHP, submits that the requirement under the old law that, in order to be transmissible, the benefit and burden of covenants in a lease should 'touch and concern' the land did not affect the freedom of the original contracting parties to agree that the benefit or the burden of an obligation should be personal to one or other or both of them.

[54] Mr Barnes submits that the effect of the 1995 Act is essentially twofold. In e   the first place, it abolishes the former rule that an original tenant remains liable on the covenants of his tenancy notwithstanding an assignment of the tenancy. In the second place it deals with the unsatisfactory former rule that, in order to be transmissible, a covenant had to 'touch and concern' the land. Nothing in the 1995 Act, he submits, fetters the freedom of the original landlord and the original f   tenant, as the contracting parties, to provide that the benefit and/or the burden of a covenant shall be personal and not capable of transmission on a disposition of the relevant interest.

[55] Mr Barnes denies that the exclusion from the definition of a 'landlord covenant' of a covenant the burden of which is expressed to be personal to the landlord involves reinstating the former distinction between covenants which g   'touch and concern' the land and those which do not. He points out that there is no necessary contra-distinction between covenants which 'touch and concern' the land on the one hand and personal covenants on the other. He gives as an example a covenant by a tenant to carry out improvements to the land. Such a covenant plainly 'touches and concerns' the land, notwithstanding that it may be h   expressed to be personal to the tenant.

[56] Turning to the definition of 'landlord covenant' in s 28(1) of the 1995 Act, Mr Barnes submits that it is clear from the definition of 'landlord' as 'the person for the time being entitled to the reversion expectant on the term of the tenancy' that a 'landlord covenant' does not include a covenant the burden of which is j   personal to the original grantor of the tenancy.

[57] He tests this submission by considering the situation where a tenant has assumed a personal obligation to the landlord. If Chesterfield's interpretation of the 1995 Act is correct, the tenant will be automatically released from that obligation on an assignment of the tenancy (see s 5(2)), and the assignee of the tenancy will not become liable to perform it because s 3(6)(a) will apply. So, on that basis, the obligation will terminate on the first assignment of the tenancy.

Conclusions

[58] In resolving the 1995 Act issue, we do not find it necessary to have recourse to the recommendations of the Law Commission in the 1988 report. In our judgment the 1995 Act issue can readily be resolved by reference to the provisions of the 1995 Act itself.

[59] The crux, as we see it, is the definition of 'landlord' in s 28(1) as meaning 'the person *for the time being* entitled to the reversion expectant on the term of the tenancy' (my emphasis). We find it impossible to read that definition as meaning only the original landlord. In agreement with the judge ([2001] 2 All ER 914 at [22]) we consider that those words clearly connote the person who may *from time to time* be entitled to the reversion on the tenancy. It follows that, transposing that definition into the definition of the expression 'landlord covenant', what one has is an obligation 'falling to be complied with by [the person who may from time to time be entitled to the reversion on the tenancy]'. An obligation which (that is to say, the burden of which) is personal to the original landlord is, by definition, not such an obligation, since it does not fall to be performed by the person who may from time to time be entitled to the reversion on the tenancy.

[60] It follows that in our judgment Chesterfield's obligations in cl 12 of the Agreement, being expressed to be personal to Chesterfield, are not 'landlord covenants' within the meaning of the 1995 Act, and that the notice was accordingly ineffective to release Chesterfield from such obligations.

[61] With respect to Mr Lewison, Chesterfield's argument on the 1995 Act issue seems to us to be based on the fallacy that there is a direct antithesis between a personal covenant (that is to say a covenant which is personal in the sense that the burden of it is expressed to be personal to the covenantor) on the one hand and a covenant which 'touches and concerns', or which relates to, the land on the other. As Mr Barnes correctly submits, there is no such direct antithesis. A covenant which relates to the land may nevertheless be expressed to be personal to one or other or both of the parties to it. That is a matter for the contracting parties.

[62] Nor can we see anything in the 1995 Act to fetter the freedom of contracting parties to place a contractual limit on the transmissibility of the benefit or burden of obligations under a tenancy. On the contrary, that no such fetter was intended by Parliament is clearly demonstrated, in our judgment, by s 3(6)(a) (quoted earlier).

[63] Nor do we find the two authorities on which Mr Lewison relies (the *System Floors* and *P & A Swift Investments* cases) to be of any assistance in the instant case. The fact that the transmissibility of the burden of a covenant does not depend on the transmissibility of the benefit of it does not seem to us to throw any light on the meaning and effect of the 1995 Act.

[64] Accordingly, we conclude that the judge was right to resolve the 1995 Act issue in favour of BHP.

THE AGREEMENT ISSUE

The arguments

[65] Mr Barnes repeats the submission which he made to the judge, to the effect that the fact (which is to be assumed for present purposes) that physical damage to the property has resulted from the use of defective materials means that the conditions for the application of the second limb of the definition of 'Building Works Defect' in cl 1.1.8 of the Agreement have been fulfilled. He

a submits that, at whatever point in time one is required to consider whether physical damage 'will result' from such a defect—whether the appropriate point in time be the date of the Agreement or the date when notice is given under cl 12.2.1 of the Agreement or some other point in time—the (assumed) fact that physical damage *has resulted* from the use of defective materials proves that, viewed as at the appropriate point in time, physical damage *would*, as a matter of certainty, result therefrom. Accordingly, he submits, Chesterfield is obliged to

b remedy the defect by replacing all non-vertical units of toughened glass.

[66] As an alternative submission, prompted by the court in the course of argument and adopted by Mr Barnes (albeit with, perhaps, less than complete enthusiasm) Mr Barnes submits that under the second limb of the definition of 'Building Works Defect' it is the defect which has to manifest itself within the

c six-year period, not the physical damage: in other words, that for the purposes of cl 12.2 of the Agreement it is enough if BHP can point, within the six-year period, to a defect which 'will' at some time in the future (not necessarily within the six-year period) result in physical damage.

d [67] If, however, the court were to hold that the physical damage which has occurred falls within the first, but not the second, limb of the definition of 'Building Works Defect', with the consequence that Chesterfield's obligation is limited to replacing the four units which have fractured, then Mr Barnes submits that the proviso in cl 1.1.8.3 of the Agreement that the cost of so doing will 'in each such case' exceed £50,000 (excluding VAT) refers not to separate items of

e damage but to damage resulting from separate causes. Hence, he submits, the fact that the cost of replacing a single fractured unit may not exceed the specified figure will not avail Chesterfield if the total cost of replacing all four fractured units exceeds that figure.

[68] Mr Lewison submits that in construing the definition of 'Building Works

f Defect' in cl 1.1.8 of the Agreement it is relevant to bear in mind, as part of the commercial context in which the Agreement was concluded, that in assuming the obligations in question Chesterfield was in effect providing BHP with protection against the insolvency of the professional team which was contracted to carry out the works of refurbishment. Reading the definition in that context, it is clear (he

g submits) that for the purposes of the second limb of the definition it is the physical damage, not the defect, which has to manifest itself within the six-year period.

[69] In support of this submission, Mr Lewison relies on the definition of the expression 'Concrete Frame Defect' in cl 1.1.12 of the Agreement, which refers expressly to 'any defect in the concrete frame which will result in physical

h damage to the Concrete Frame manifesting itself during the contractual term of the Lease'. Mr Lewison submits that there is no commercial reason why Chesterfield should undertake to make good a 'Concrete Frame Defect' which has not given rise to any physical damage prior to the expiry of the lease.

[70] Mr Lewison submits, therefore, that in order to bring the second limb of

j the definition into play BHP cannot rely on physical damage which has already occurred: rather, it has to establish that physical damage (that is to say, in a case where some physical damage has already occurred, *further* physical damage) *will* as a matter of certainty occur before the expiry of the six-year period.

[71] As to cl 1.1.8.3, Mr Lewison submits that the clause means what it says, and that in the instant case the words 'in each case' refer to the replacement of each fractured unit.

Conclusions

[72] For convenience, we will begin by setting out once again the material part of the definition of the expression 'Building Works Defect' in cl 1.1.8 of the Agreement. The material part of the definition reads as follows:

'... any physical damage to the Demised Premises manifesting itself during the Defects Period or any defect in the Demised Premises which will result in physical damage to the Demised Premises manifesting itself during the Defects Period ...'

[73] Given that it is extremely difficult, if not impossible, to prove as a matter of absolute certainty that, for example, the use of defective materials 'will' result in physical damage occurring—let alone within a specified period of time— Mr Lewison's interpretation of the definition of 'Building Works Defect' seems to us to place the tenant in something of a straitjacket. If the tenant considers that there is a defect in the demised premises as a result of, for example, the use of defective materials, it is faced with a choice. If it gives notice of the alleged defect *before* any physical damage has occurred, it will (on Mr Lewison's interpretation) be faced with the well-nigh impossible task of establishing that the defect *will* cause physical damage to manifest itself prior to 30 June 2003 (the end of the six-year period). If, on the other hand, it waits until some physical damage *has* occurred before it serves a notice, it will (on Mr Lewison's interpretation) be met with the response that under the first limb of the definition the landlord is only obliged to repair the physical damage which has actually occurred (subject always to the proviso as to cost), and that so far as the risk of any further damage is concerned, the tenant must establish that further damage *will* occur prior to 30 June 2003.

[74] We cannot believe that the parties to the Agreement could have intended such an unworkable, unfair, and indeed irrational, result. Accordingly we look to see whether there is some legitimate way of construing the definition in a more sensible and workable way.

[75] In our judgment there is. Despite Mr Barnes' lack of enthusiasm for the point, it seems to us that the words 'manifesting itself during the Defects Period' in the second limb of the definition of 'Building Works Defect' apply not to the physical damage but to the defect. In our judgment, in order to bring the second limb of the definition into play BHP has to be able, prior to 30 June 2003, to point to a defect in the property (e g the use of defective materials) which 'will' result in physical damage to the property at some time in the future—not necessarily prior to 30 June 2003.

[76] We do not find a comparison with the terms of the definition of 'Concrete Frame Defect' to be of assistance on this point, given that Chesterfield's liability in respect of such a defect is not limited to the six-year defects period. The existence of the cut-off date of 30 June 2003 seems to us to be of crucial importance in considering the extent of Chesterfield's liability for building works defects. In the context of that cut-off date it seems to us to make complete commercial sense that Chesterfield's liability in respect of such defects should not be limited to making good physical damage which has occurred prior to that date but should also include making good defects the existence of which has come to light prior to that date, provided that the tenant can establish that such defects will result in physical damage occurring, whether before or after the cut-off date.

[77] Further, where the defect relied on has in fact resulted in physical damage, it seems to us to fly in the face of common sense to construe the word

a 'will' as requiring BHP to establish that further damage will occur in the future. We accept Mr Barnes' submission that, as a matter of construction of the second limb of the definition, the requirement of establishing that an alleged defect 'will' result in physical damage is met by establishing, with the benefit of hindsight, that it has *in fact* resulted in physical damage. Otherwise, the tenant will be in a worse position if physical damage has in fact occurred than if it has not, in that the *b* existence of actual physical damage will preclude it from requiring the remedying of the underlying defect unless it can prove that *further* physical damage *will* result from the defect.

[78] In our judgment, therefore, the first limb of the definition is directed at physical damage which has actually occurred, whereas the second limb is directed at the existence of an underlying defect which either has caused or will *c* cause physical damage. Under the first limb, Chesterfield's liability is limited to repairing the damage which has actually occurred (subject to the proviso as to cost): under the second limb, its liability extends to remedying the underlying defect by not merely repairing any damage which has already occurred but also ensuring that the defect is remedied, so that it will not result in physical damage *d* (or, as the case may be, further physical damage) occurring in the future.

[79] Accordingly, in disagreement with the judge, we would resolve the Agreement issue in favour of BHP.

[80] In the light of our conclusions, it is unnecessary to address the arguments as to the true construction of the proviso as to cost contained in cl 1.1.8.3 of the Agreement.

e

RESULT

[81] In the result, therefore, we conclude that Chesterfield's liability under cl 12.2 of the Agreement is as contended for by BHP, and that Chesterfield was not released from such liability by the operation of the notice.

f [82] We would accordingly dismiss Chesterfield's appeal and allow BHP's cross-appeal.

Appeal dismissed. Cross-appeal allowed.

Kate O'Hanlon   Barrister.

Lilly Icos Ltd v Pfizer Ltd   *a*
[2002] EWCA Civ 02

COURT OF APPEAL, CIVIL DIVISION
ALDOUS, BUXTON AND LONGMORE LJJ
17 DECEMBER 2001, 23 JANUARY 2002   *b*

Discovery – Collateral use of information obtained – Undertaking not to use disclosed
documents for collateral or ulterior purpose – Application to maintain after trial
confidentiality in respect of document referred to in open court – Approach to be adopted
on such an application – CPR 31.22(1)(a), (2).
                                                                   c

During the course of proceedings for the revocation of a pharmaceutical patent
on the ground of obviousness, the patentee disclosed to the opponent various
material designated as confidential. The confidentiality of that material during
the proceedings was subject to an agreement between the parties, permitting the
material to be seen only by a strictly limited number of people on either side (the *d*
confidentiality club) who were bound by undertakings of confidence. The
agreement adopted conditions laid down by CPR 31.22(1)(a)[a] and (2). Under
r 31.22(1), a party to whom a document had been disclosed could use it only for
the purpose of the proceedings in which it had been disclosed, except, inter alia,
where the document had been read to or by the court, or had been referred to, at
a hearing which had been held in public (para (1)(a)). Paragraph (2) provided that *e*
the court could make an order restricting or prohibiting the use of a disclosed
document even where it fell within the para (1)(a) exception. The agreement
between the parties was reinforced by a consent order, effectively made under
r 31.22(2), retaining confidentiality for the documents in the confidentiality club
until the end of the trial. The disclosed material included a two-page schedule *f*
showing, on the first page, the sales figures for the patentee's product and, on the
second page, the patentee's advertising expenditure since the product's launch.
The provision of such a schedule was common practice in revocation
proceedings since patentees frequently contended that the commercial success of
the patented product was one indication that the invention was not obvious,
while opponents often argued that the commercial success of the patentee's *g*
product was attributable not to its unique merits but to the patentee's
promotional efforts. In the event, the opponent did not pursue such an
argument, either in the pleadings or at trial. However, the commercial success
of the product remained central to the patentee's case, and the schedule was
referred to in passing by one of its scientists in a witness statement which also *h*
disclosed further important commercial information. After the end of the trial,
all of which was held in public, the patentee made an unopposed application
for an order under r 31.22(2), maintaining confidentiality in respect, inter alia, of
the second page of the schedule, ie the figures for advertising and promotion.
Such figures were generally regarded in the pharmaceutical industry as highly *j*
commercially sensitive. In considering the application, the judge invoked the test
of necessity which justified the exclusion of the public from the hearing of cases
involving secret processes, where publicity would destroy the subject-matter of
the proceedings (the necessity test). He concluded that, since patent claims were

---

a   Rule 31.22 is set out at [3], below

a   of general public importance, the party seeking to withhold material from
    disclosure had to make out particularly clearly that there was a necessity for such
    an order and that, as other important commercial information had been disclosed
    by the patentee, there were great difficulties in its making out a case of necessity
    in respect of the advertising and promotional figures. On that basis, he refused to
    make an order maintaining confidentiality in relation to those figures. On the
b   patentee's appeal, the Court of Appeal considered the approach to be adopted on
    an application under r 31.22(2) and whether the test applied by the judge was
    appropriate.

    Held – (1) The necessity test, which involved necessity in the context of enabling
    the action to be heard at all, was not a test that directly addressed the issue of
c   limited confidentiality within an action, and could not be directly transposed
    from one case to the other. A test of necessity, generally stated, only went a
    limited way towards illuminating the court's task in a case involving confidential
    information which would be damaged by publicity. The court had to approach
    the issue more broadly, starting from the principle that very good reasons were
d   required for departing from the normal rule of publicity. That was the normal
    rule because publicity was the very soul of justice and the surest of all guards
    against improbity, keeping the judge himself under trial. When considering an
    application in respect of a particular document, the court should take into
    account the role that it had played or would play in the trial, and thus its relevance
    to that process of scrutiny (the scrutiny considerations). It should start from the
e   assumption that all documents in the case were necessary and relevant for that
    purpose, and the court should not accede to general arguments that it would be
    possible, or substantially possible, to understand the trial and judge the judge
    without access to a particular document. However, in particular cases the
    centrality of the document to the trial was a factor to be placed in the balance. In
f   dealing with issues of confidentiality between the parties, the court had to have
    in mind the 'chilling' effect of an order upon the interests of third parties.
    Moreover, simple assertions of confidentiality and of the damage that would be
    done by publication, even if supported by both parties, should not prevail. The
    court would require specific reasons why a party would be damaged by the
    publication of a document, and those reasons would, in appropriate cases, be
g   weighed in the light of the scrutiny considerations. The court should bear in
    mind that if too demanding a standard were imposed under CPR 31.22(2) in
    respect of documents that had been referred to inferentially or in short at the trial,
    it might be necessary, in order to protect genuine interests of the parties, for more
    trials or parts of trials to be held in private, or for parts of witness statements or
h   skeletons to be in closed form. As for patent cases, they were subject to the same
    general rules as any other cases, but they presented some particular problems.
    Patent litigation was of peculiar public importance, and that meant that the
    public had to be properly informed. At the same time, it also meant that the
    issues had to be properly explored in the sense that parties should not feel
j   constrained to hold back from relevant or potentially relevant issues because of
    legitimate fears of the effect of publicity (see [23]–[25], below); *Scott v Scott*
    [1911–13] All ER Rep 1 and *Smithkline Beecham Biologics SA v Connaught
    Laboratories Inc* [1999] 4 All ER 498 considered.

    (2) In the instant case, the most important feature was the very limited role
    that the second page of the schedule had played in the trial. In order to keep the
    trial judge, or the Court of Appeal, under trial, it was not necessary, and indeed

was not relevant, for the interested spectator to have access to the second page of the schedule, however much it might fall under CPR 31.22(1)(a). That consideration enabled the court to take a somewhat less demanding approach to the claim for confidentiality than would otherwise be appropriate, and to act upon the fears of everyone in the pharmaceutical industry about the disclosure of advertising figures. Accordingly, the appeal would be allowed to the extent of making an order under r 31.22(2) in respect of the second page of the schedule (see [26]–[28], below).

Notes

For subsequent use of disclosed documents, see 37 *Halsbury's Laws* (4th edn reissue) para 565.

Cases referred to in judgments

A-G v Times Newspapers Ltd [1991] 2 All ER 398, [1992] 1 AC 191, [1991] 2 WLR 994, HL.

App No 9480/82 v UK (1985) 7 EHRR 146, E Com HR.

Barings plc (in liq) v Coopers & Lybrand [2000] 3 All ER 910, [2000] 1 WLR 2353, CA.

Bonzel v Intervention Ltd (No 2) [1991] RPC 231.

GIO Personal Investment Services Ltd v Liverpool and London Steamship Protection and Indemnity Association Ltd (FAI General Insurance Co Ltd intervening) [1999] 1 WLR 984, CA.

Home Office v Harman [1982] 1 All ER 532, [1983] 1 AC 280, [1982] 2 WLR 338, HL.

R (on the application of Pelling) v Bow County Court [2001] UKHRR 165, DC.

Scott v Scott [1913] AC 417, [1911–13] All ER Rep 1, HL.

Smithkline Beecham Biologics SA v Connaught Laboratories Inc [1999] 4 All ER 498, CA.

Appeal

The patentee, Pfizer Ltd, appealed with permission of Laddie J from his refusal of its application for an order under CPR 31.22(2) maintaining after trial confidentiality in respect of the second page of a schedule referred to in open court in the trial of an action brought against the patentee by the opponent, Lilly Icos Ltd, for revocation of European Patent No 0702555. The facts are set out in the judgment of the court.

Richard Meade (instructed by *Bird & Bird*) for the patentee.
Colin Birss (instructed by *Taylor Joynson Garrett*) for the opponent.

23 January 2002. The following judgment of the court was delivered.

BUXTON LJ.

Introduction

[1] The background to this appeal, and the issues in the substantive dispute out of which it arises, are fully set out in appeal A3/2000/3811[b], and need not be repeated here.

---

b Editor's note: this was an appeal from Laddie J's decision on 10 November 2000 ([2001] IP & T 190) to revoke the patent on grounds of obviousness. The Court of Appeal dismissed that appeal in judgments ([2002] EWCA Civ 01, [2002] All ER (D) 172 (Jan)) handed down immediately before the delivery of the judgment in the instant appeal.

a [2] The present dispute concerns various material disclosed by the patentee during the revocation proceedings, which was treated as confidential in the hands of the opponent during those proceedings, and which the patentee wishes to remain confidential even after those proceedings have terminated. Originally there was a significant amount of material in respect of which the judge had declined to make such an order and in respect of which the patentee wished to

b seek the view of this court; and further material in respect of which such an order had been made, some part of which the opponent wished to challenge. However, after discussions between the parties the opponent has abandoned its cross-appeal, and the patentee wishes to maintain its appeal in respect of only one document. Before the judge the opponent had not sought the release of the then existing confidentiality order in respect of that document, but the judge himself,

c of his own motion, refused to make an order maintaining confidentiality. Understandably, therefore, the opponent indicated that it would not oppose the patentee's appeal. We however considered that issues of some general importance might be involved in the appeal, and we indicated that we would appreciate assistance from both parties. The opponent was thereupon good

d enough to instruct Mr Birss to assist us, and he afforded us considerable help, as did Mr Meade on behalf of the patentee.

Legal framework
[3] The issue arises under CPR 31.22, which reads:

e   '(1) A party to whom a document has been disclosed may use the document only for the purpose of the proceedings in which it is disclosed, except where—(a) the document has been read to or by the court, or referred to, at a hearing which has been held in public; (b) the court gives permission; or (c) the party who disclosed the document and the person to whom the document belongs agree.

f   (2) The court may make an order restricting or prohibiting the use of a document which has been disclosed, even where the document has been read to or by the court, or referred to, at a hearing which has been held in public.'

g As is well known, provisions to this broad effect, though formulated in slightly different terms, were introduced into RSC Ord 24, r 14A as a result of the decision of the government of the United Kingdom not to contest the complaint declared admissible by the European Commission on Human Rights, *App No 9480/82 v UK* (1985) 7 EHRR 146, in relation to the law declared by the House of Lords in *Home Office v Harman* [1982] 1 All ER 532, [1983] 1 AC 280.

h [4] It may be mentioned that we have described the issue as one of confidentiality, and we will for convenience continue to describe it as such. However, it will be seen from CPR 31.22 that the basic prohibition in relation to disclosed documents is in terms of their *use*. A breach of that prohibition, such as in a patent case the use by the opponent of processes disclosed by the patentee,

j might not involve anything that would usually be characterised as a breach of *confidence*.

[5] The provisions of CPR 31.22 relate only to, and in this appeal we are directly concerned only with, documents produced to the other side on disclosure, and the subsequent obligations of the other side in relation to those documents. We are not directly concerned with issues of access to court documents on the part of non-parties, such as have recently been considered by this court in

GIO Personal Investment Services Ltd v Liverpool and London Steamship Protection and Indemnity Association Ltd (FAI General Insurance Co Ltd intervening) [1999] 1 WLR 984 and *Barings plc (in liq) v Coopers & Lybrand* [2000] 3 All ER 910, [2000] 1 WLR 2353. The issue before us does however appear to impact indirectly upon the position of non-parties in two ways, which it will be necessary to have in mind. First, if a party is at liberty to 'use' a disclosed document, he may no doubt make it available to a non-party, in the absence of a special order preventing that. Second, if the court does make an order under CPR 31.22(2), but the document in question comes into the possession of a third party, for instance by accident or theft, then any use by the third party of the document with knowledge of the court's order will arguably be a contempt. We heard no sustained argument on that point, but as at present advised the conclusion just stated would appear to follow by analogy with the view taken by the House of Lords in *A-G v Times Newspapers Ltd* [1991] 2 All ER 398, [1992] 1 AC 191.

[6] The special condition releasing the normal rule of confidentiality arises when a document 'has been read to or by the court, or referred to, at a hearing which has been held in public'. It was conceded that that condition was fulfilled in respect of the document in issue before us. However, since the width of this provision may affect the proper approach to cases arising under it, we should say a little more about it.

[7] Although the principle of the orality of the English trial remains untouched, practice has moved greatly in the direction of the presentation of evidence and arguments in writing; the use of documents by reference to them in those writings rather than by their being read out in open court; and the consideration by the judge of a large part of that material before the trial opens, so that it is not necessary to make specific reference to it during the trial itself. In *Smithkline Beecham Biologics SA v Connaught Laboratories Inc* [1999] 4 All ER 498 this court pointed out that the intent of (as it was then) RSC Ord 24, r 14A would be substantially frustrated if the rule were literally restricted to what had physically happened in open court. The rule was passed in the interests of the publicity properly attaching to the administration of justice, and of the interests of the recipient of the document under art 10 of the European Convention for the Protection of Human Rights and Fundamental Freedoms 1950 (see [1999] 4 All ER 498 at 510). To achieve those ends under modern practice it was necessary to take as falling under CPR 31.22(1)(a) any document pre-read by the judge, or referred to in for instance witness statements taken to stand as evidence, even if the document or the witness statement was not actually read out in court. Some further details of that regime may be mentioned, and then some comments offered.

[8] First, there are taken to fall under the rule certain categories of document, in particular those coming within the pre-reading of the judge. It does not have to be established that the judge has actually read the documents: once the category is established, it is for a party alleging that they have not in fact been read to establish that fact, something that has to be achieved without inquiry of the judge (see *Barings plc (in liq) v Coopers & Lybrand* [2000] 3 All ER 910 at 922, [2000] 1 WLR 2353 at 2367). Second, it therefore follows that not everything that is disclosed or copied in court bundles falls under this rule: the *Connaught* approach is restricted to documents to which the judge has been specifically alerted, whether by reference in a skeleton argument or by mention in the 'reading guide' with which judges are now provided at least in patent cases. Third, since the *Connaught* approach is based upon the assumed orality of a trial, documents,

a however much pre-read by the judge, remain confidential if no trial takes place, but the application is, for instance, dismissed by consent, albeit by a decision announced in open court (see the *Connaught* case [1999] 4 All ER 498 at 509).

[9] The central theme of these rules is the importance of the principle that justice is to be done in public, and within that principle the importance of those attending a public court understanding the case. They cannot do that if the *b* contents of documents used in that process are concealed from them: hence the release of confidence once the document has been read or used in court. As this court recognised in the *Connaught* case, there may be some artificiality about that approach. That is because full access to documents deemed to have been read or used in court may give third parties at least the possibility of much more fully studying and understanding the case and the issues in it than if they merely heard *c* the documents read aloud. Nevertheless, that paradox helps to underline this court's concern that economical means of using and referring to the documents, understood amongst the lawyers, should not exclude the spectators from comprehension of the case.

[10] One further preliminary issue needs to be mentioned. At the start of *d* these proceedings the parties followed the normal practice in patent actions of entering into what is called, perhaps slightly unfortunately, a 'confidentiality club'. That is an agreement that during the proceedings documents designated as confidential shall be seen only by a strictly limited number of people on each side, almost entirely professional advisors, who are bound by undertakings of confidence in relation to them. The agreement in the present case however *e* further provides, we were told in accordance with normal practice, that the undertakings cease to apply in respect of any document that has been read to the court or referred to at a hearing in public, unless the court orders otherwise: that is, the parties adopted the condition laid down by CPR 31.22(1)(a) and (2).

[11] This agreement was reinforced by an order made by consent, again we *f* were told in accordance with normal practice, retaining confidentiality for the documents in the confidentiality club, effectively under CPR 31.22(2), until the end of the trial. That enables reference to be made to documents falling under the *Connaught* rubric without at that stage surrendering confidentiality, an arrangement that is seen as facilitating the smooth running of the trial. We shall have to revert to that aspect of the arrangements at a later stage. Such an order *g* however only applies to the trial. Once the trial is completed the order, and the agreement, expire: hence the need for specific application in relation to documents that are still sought to be maintained as confidential, such as the application made in this case to Laddie J.

[12] When making its decision under CPR 31.22(2) at the end of the *h* proceedings the court will note, but will not be constrained by, any such confidentiality agreement (see the *Connaught* case [1999] 4 All ER 498 at 511). There are two reasons for that approach. First, as this court pointed out in the *Connaught* case, patent litigation is of considerable public importance, involving as it does potential restrictions on competition in respect of goods of great public *j* benefit. It should so far as possible take place in public, whatever the contrary wishes of the parties. Second, as pointed out in [5], above, a confidentiality obligation, whether undertaken by agreement or imposed by order, incidentally affects the access to information, and thus freedom of expression, of third parties. For the court to sanction such agreements in circumstances other than those of real need would therefore give rise to serious questions under art 10 of the convention.

The document and its history

[13] With that regrettably long introduction we come at last to the document in issue in this case.

[14] As is frequently the case in proceedings for revocation on grounds of obviousness, the patentee argued that one indication that the invention was not obvious was the striking commercial success of the product when eventually marketed. If it was obvious that such rewards were available, why had no one else got there first? A counter to that argument often advanced by opponents is that the commercial success was explicable not by the unique merits of the product but by the promotional efforts of the large organisation that had marketed it. Each of these claims potentially requires substantial and inconvenient disclosure. It has therefore become the practice, in order to save the expense of disclosing thousands of documents, for the patentee to be ordered, by consent, to produce a schedule showing (p 1) sales figures in value terms; and (p 2) advertising expenditure on a month-by-month basis since the launch of the product. Such an order was made, and such a schedule produced by the patentee, in this case.

[15] The patentee persisted to trial in its argument in relation to commercial success. However, the opponent did not in the event seek to argue, either in its pleadings or at trial, that that success had been attributable to promotional efforts. The patentee, in support of the claim to commercial success, adduced evidence from one of its senior scientists, who set out examples of the interest expressed in the product by the press, and gave details of amounts prescribed, numbers of patients treated, and estimated market share. These details went beyond, and gave more disclosure than, the information on p 1 of the schedule. The only reference to advertising and promotion was in the last sentence of this section of the witness statement, which said:

'I understand that details of sales of sildenafil cirate, broken down into the USA and the rest of the world, together with advertising and promotional expenses, on a month by month basis to August 1999 have been provided to the Claimant's solicitors in confidence.'

[16] The patentee does not seek to retain confidentiality for p 1 of the schedule, inter alia because the information that it contains, or something approaching it, can be reconstructed from various publicly available sources. The patentee does, however, seek to retain confidentiality for p 2 of the schedule, contending that figures for advertising and promotion are not publicly available, and are regarded generally in the pharmaceuticals industry as highly commercially sensitive. It will be recalled that the opponent did not oppose a confidentiality order in respect of p 2 of the schedule, but the judge of his own motion declined to make the order.

The judge's ruling

[17] It should first be said that the matter of orders under CPR 31.22(2) came before the judge in a somewhat unsatisfactory manner. There was more than one hearing, and the judge does not seem to have been given any detailed exposition of why, as in the case of p 2, certain orders were not opposed. In view of the observations of this court in the *Connaught* case, referred to in [12] above, it should be clearly understood that the court will require to be persuaded, and will require detailed submissions as to why it should be persuaded, that the confidentiality agreement should subsist in respect of any particular documents.

a   [18] The judge at the start of his judgment referred to *Scott v Scott* [1913] AC
417, [1911–13] All ER Rep 1, concerning the central principle that trials must be
held in public, and then cited some well-known words of Lord Haldane:

> 'While the broad principle is that the Courts of this country must, as
> between parties, administer justice in public, this principle is subject to
> apparent exceptions ... But the exceptions are themselves the outcome of a
b   > yet more fundamental principle that the chief object of Courts of justice
> must be to secure that justice is done. In the two cases of wards of Court and
> of lunatics the Court is really sitting primarily to guard the interests of the
> ward or the lunatic ... It may often be necessary, in order to attain its primary
> object, that the Court should exclude the public ... The other case referred
c   > to, that of litigation as to a secret process, where the effect of publicity would
> be to destroy the subject-matter, illustrates a class which stands on a different
> footing. There it may well be that justice could not be done at all if it had to
> be done in public. As the paramount object must always be to do justice, the
> general rule as to publicity, after all only the means to an end, must
> accordingly yield. But the burden lies on those seeking to displace its
d   > application in the particular case to make out that the ordinary rule must as
> of necessity be superseded by this paramount consideration. The question is
> by no means one which, consistently with the spirit of our jurisprudence, can
> be dealt with by the judge as resting in his mere discretion as to what is
> expedient. The latter must treat it as one of principle, and as turning, not on
> convenience, but on necessity.' (See [1913] AC 417 at 437–438, [1911–13]
e   > All ER Rep 1 at 9.)

Basing himself upon this classic statement, the judge held in his judgment:

> 'Where the court is dealing with a matter of general public concern, then
> the party seeking to withhold material from disclosure has to make out
f   > particularly clearly that there is a necessity for the order he seeks.'

[19] In respect of the schedule, the judge pointed out that commercial success
had not been a side issue, but crucial to the patentee's case. He then said:

> 'I can see very great difficulties in [the patentee's] way in making out a case
g   > of necessity for secrecy in respect of the figures relating to advertising and
> promotional expenses in view of the central nature of this issue to the task
> facing the court in considering the validity of this patent and in view of the
> extensive disclosure in [the patentee's witness's] statement which seems to
> me to disclose the most important commercial information, that is to say,
h   > sale, numbers of customers, and so on.'

However, the patentee having indicated that it would wish to appeal any order
adverse to it in relation to p 2 of the schedule, the judge agreed to maintain the
confidentiality order that otherwise he would have made until this court could
consider the matter, with the benefit of such evidence as the patentee saw fit to
j   put before us.

[20] The evidence now to hand really does no more than reiterate the belief
held by the patentee and others in the industry that information of the order to
be found on p 2 is highly commercially sensitive, and to state that it cannot be
gleaned from anywhere other than the manufacturer's confidential records. We
have no doubt that if that evidence had been before the judge it would not have
altered the view that he was minded to take. We are therefore effectively in the

position of hearing an appeal from a refusal by the judge to make an order under
CPR 31.22(2) in respect of p 2 of the schedule.

Criticisms of the judge's analysis

[21] Two matters may be mentioned. The first, to which we will have to
return, concerns the judge's analysis of the nature of the substantive case. While
it is quite true that commercial success was an important issue, as we have seen
there was not, in the event, introduced into the case any actual consideration of
the effect of advertising. Page 2 had been drawn up, by order of the court, but as
a matter of convenience, against the possibility of such an argument being raised.
Therefore, although p 2 was indeed referred to at a public hearing, by reason of
its having been mentioned in the witness statement referred to in [15], above, that
reference was only as a matter of record or in passing, and not as part of any
argumentative submissions. Anyone sitting in court and trying to understand the
issues in the case and why it was decided as it was would not have needed, indeed
would not have been helped by, access to p 2.

[22] Further, we think that it goes too far, as at one stage was tentatively
suggested by Mr Birss, to argue that the p 2 figures were important to the case
because they may have persuaded the opponent that the 'promotion' argument
was unsustainable, and therefore explained to a spectator why a common
argument had not been advanced on this occasion. The material might well be
of interest for that purpose, but that in itself plainly does not bring the material
within the ambit of CPR 31.22(1)(a).

[23] The second point is of more general importance. The judge imposed a
test of 'necessity', drawing that from *Scott v Scott*. The general emphasis in *Scott v
Scott* on public hearings is all-pervasive, and of central importance. However, as
the passage cited in [18], above, demonstrates, the 'necessity' there discussed is
necessity in the context of enabling the action to be heard at all. It is not,
therefore, a test that directly addresses the issue of limited confidentiality within
an action, and cannot be directly transposed from the one case to the other.

[24] We are fortified in our belief that these two problems, although
stemming from a common principle, are different in their implications by the
form of CPR 39.2, relating to the holding of hearings in private. That provides:

'(1) The general rule is that a hearing is to be in public ...

(3) A hearing, or any part of it, may be in private if—(a) publicity would
defeat the object of the hearing ... (c) it involves confidential information
(including information relating to personal financial matters) and publicity
would damage that confidentiality; (d) a private hearing is necessary to
protect the interests of any child or patient ...'

It may be noted in passing that the validity of CPR 39.2 and its conformity to
arts 6 and 10 of the convention was upheld by the Divisional Court in *R (on the
application of Pelling) v Bow County Court* [2001] UKHRR 165, a decision in respect
of which permission to appeal was refused by this court. The rule makes a clear
distinction between the types of case addressed in *Scott v Scott*, which are dealt
with in sub-rr (a) and (d) above, and problems such as that in our case, which is
addressed in sub-r (c). A test of 'necessity', generally stated, only goes a limited
way towards illuminating the court's task in the latter case, which has to be
approached more broadly: whether the question is whether to hold the hearing
in private, or whether to make or refuse an order under CPR 31.22(2).

The court's approach

a
[25] It may be convenient to set out a number of considerations that have guided us. (i) The court should start from the principle that very good reasons are required for departing from the normal rule of publicity. That is the normal rule because, as Lord Diplock put it in *Home Office v Harman* [1982] 1 All ER 532 at 537, [1983] 1 AC 280 at 303, citing both Jeremy Bentham and Lord Shaw of
b Dunfermline in *Scott v Scott*:

> ' "Publicity is the very soul of justice. It is the keenest spur to exertion and the surest of all guards against improbity. It keeps the judge himself while trying under trial." '

c The already very strong English jurisprudence to this effect has only been reinforced by the addition to it of this country's obligations under arts 6 and 10 of the convention. (ii) When considering an application in respect of a particular document, the court should take into account the role that the document has played or will play in the trial, and thus its relevance to the process of scrutiny referred to by Lord Diplock. The court should start from the assumption that all
d documents in the case are necessary and relevant for that purpose, and should not accede to general arguments that it would be possible, or substantially possible, to understand the trial and judge the judge without access to a particular document. However, in particular cases the centrality of the document to the trial is a factor to be placed in the balance. (iii) In dealing with issues of
e confidentiality between the parties, the court must have in mind any 'chilling' effect of an order upon the interests of third parties (see [5] above). (iv) Simple assertions of confidentiality and of the damage that will be done by publication, even if supported by both parties, should not prevail. The court will require specific reasons why a party would be damaged by the publication of a document.
f Those reasons will in appropriate cases be weighed in the light of the considerations referred to in sub-para (ii) above. (v) It is highly desirable, both in the general public interest and for simple convenience, to avoid the holding of trials in private, or partially in private. In the present case, the manner in which the documents were handled, together with the confidentiality agreement during trial, enabled the whole of the trial to be held in public, even though the judge
g regarded it as justified to retain confidentiality in respect of a significant number of those documents after the trial was over. The court should bear in mind that if too demanding a standard is imposed under CPR 31.22(2) in respect of documents that have been referred to inferentially or in short at the trial, it may be necessary, in order to protect genuine interests of the parties, for more trials
h or parts of trials to be held in private, or for instance for parts of witness statements or skeletons to be in closed form. (vi) Patent cases are subject to the same general rules as any other cases, but they do present some particular problems and are subject to some particular considerations. As this court pointed out in *Smithkline Beecham Biologics SA v Connaught Laboratories Inc* [1999] 4 All ER 498, patent litigation is of peculiar public importance, as the present case itself
j shows. That means that the public must be properly informed; but it means at the same time that the issues must be properly explored, in the sense that parties should not feel constrained to hold back from relevant or potentially relevant issues because of (legitimate) fears of the effect of publicity. We venture in that connection to repeat some words of one of our number in *Bonzel v Intervention Ltd (No 2)* [1991] RPC 231 at 234:

'... the duty placed upon the patentee to make full disclosure of all relevant documents (which is required in amendment proceedings) is one which *a* should not be fettered by any action of the courts. Reluctance of this court to go into camera to hear evidence in relation to documents which are privileged which could be used in other jurisdictions, would tend to make patentees reluctant to disclose the full position. That of course would not be in the interest of the public.' *b*

In our view, the same considerations can legitimately be in the court's mind when deciding whether to withdraw confidentiality from documents that are regarded by a party as damaging to his interests if used outside the confines of the litigation in which they were disclosed.

c

The principles applied to this case

[**26**] In our view, the most important feature of this case, and one that we think with respect was not sufficiently addressed by the judge (see [21] above), is the very limited role that p 2 played in the trial. If it had been placed in a physically separate document from p 1 of the schedule, and had not been, unnecessarily, referred to in passing by the patentee's deponent, it would not *d* have fallen under the terms of CPR 31.22(1)(a) at all. To keep the trial judge, or ourselves in hearing the appeal, under trial, in the terms referred to in [25](ii) above, it is not necessary, and indeed it is not relevant, for the interested spectator to have access to p 2, however much it may fall under CPR 31.22(1)(a). That consideration enables the court to take a somewhat less demanding approach to *e* the claim for confidentiality than would otherwise be appropriate.

[**27**] We are of course familiar from our general experience with the very great reluctance of businessmen to disclose advertising figures, though we would not claim to understand the full reasons for that reluctance, and the evidence in this case does not enlighten us. None the less, we are told, in strong terms, that information of the order contained in p 2 is regarded as axiomatically confidential, *f* not only by the patentee, but also by everyone else engaged in this industry. Despite the warning that we gave in [25](iv) above, and maintain here, we consider that that is a fear that we can, in an appropriate case, legitimately act upon. This is in our view a legitimate such case for the reasons given in [26], above. We should not by any means be taken as thereby deciding that figures for *g* advertising expenditure can be kept confidential in every case, without further reason.

[**28**] We therefore allow the appeal to the extent of making an order under CPR 31.22(2) in respect of p 2, only, of the patentee's confidential schedule of commercial success.

Appeal allowed as specified.

Kate O'Hanlon   Barrister.

Director General of Fair Trading v Proprietary Association of Great Britain and another

[2001] EWCA Civ 1217

COURT OF APPEAL, CIVIL DIVISION

LORD PHILLIPS OF WORTH MATRAVERS MR, BROOKE AND ROBERT WALKER LJJ

11 JUNE, 26 JULY 2001

Costs – Wasted costs – Restrictive trade practices – Associations resisting application for discharge of exemption order – Rule of procedure providing for appointment of representative respondent but no such order made – Court rejecting application that it should recuse itself on grounds of apparent bias – Court of Appeal reversing that decision – Associations seeking order requiring Lord Chancellor to pay wasted costs caused by infringement of right to fair trial by independent and impartial tribunal – Whether trade association 'victim' of unlawful act in absence of representation order – Whether cure of defect by Court of Appeal precluding award of wasted costs – Human Rights Act 1998, s 7, Sch 1, Pt I, art 6(1) – Restrictive Practices Court (Resale Prices) Rules 1976, r 9(b).

The Director General of Fair Trading applied to the Restrictive Practices Court for the discharge of an exemption order made in respect of medicines sold over the counter. The application was opposed by two associations, PATA and PAGB. The latter was an association of manufacturers, importers and suppliers of medicines sold over the counter. Under r 9(b)[a] of the Restrictive Practices Court (Resale Prices) Rules 1976, the court could order some or all of the suppliers, retailers or trade associations who were before it to be represented by a representative respondent. No such order was made in the instant case. The associations sought an order vacating the trial on the grounds that one of the members of the court had disclosed apparent bias, and that the whole of the court should recuse itself since the other members were infected by her apparent bias. The court rejected that application, but the associations appealed successfully to the Court of Appeal. As a result, the proceedings began again before a reconstituted court. That hearing came to a premature end when the associations withdrew their opposition following an indication by the court that it was unsympathetic to the points they were making. The associations estimated that they had wasted costs of about £1m because the proceedings had had to begin again. They sought the recovery of those costs from the Lord Chancellor, contending that there had been an infringement of their right to a trial by an impartial tribunal under art 6(1)[b] of the European Convention for the Protection of Human Rights and Fundamental Freedoms 1950 (as set out in Sch 1 to the Human Rights Act 1998) and that they were entitled to be compensated for the costs wasted as a result of that infringement by the Lord Chancellor, the emanation of the state responsible for providing impartial tribunals to conduct trials of civil litigation. Article 6(1) provided that everyone had the right to a fair hearing by an impartial tribunal in the determination of 'his civil rights and

---

a   Rule 9(b) is set out at [12], below
b   Article 6, so far as material, is set out at [6], below

obligations'. The Lord Chancellor contended that the court had no jurisdiction to grant PAGB any relief since it was not a 'victim' of an unlawful act within the *a* meaning of s 7(1)^c of the 1998 Act. Section 7(7) provided that a person was the victim of an unlawful act only if he would be a victim for the purposes of art 34 of the convention if proceedings had been brought in respect of that act in the European Court of Human Rights. The Lord Chancellor further contended that, in any event, the associations could not claim that their rights under art 6(1) had *b* been infringed since the Court of Appeal had corrected the situation that had arisen at first instance.

Held – A complainant who claimed a breach of art 6(1) of the convention was required to show that his own civil rights and obligations had been directly affected *c* by the proceedings and were the subject matter of the dispute. It was on that basis that the European Commission of Human Rights had declared inadmissible applications made by trade unions or other representative bodies which had an interest on behalf of their members in general or were otherwise interested in the point at issue in the case, but were not themselves directly affected. That was *d* because the applicants themselves did not qualify as 'victims' for the purposes of art 34 of the convention. In the instant case, r 9(b) of the 1976 rules provided a route by which the individual parties could have been formally represented by PAGB, but they had chosen not to follow that route. In those circumstances PAGB could not properly be regarded as a victim for the purposes of making a claim under s 7(1) of the 1998 Act, and could not, therefore, claim that its rights under art 6(1) had been *e* violated, because the proceedings in the Restrictive Practices Court were not determinative of its civil rights and obligations within the meaning of art 6(1). In any event, it was trite convention law that an appeal court could remedy defects in first instance decisions where the appeal was in the nature of a rehearing or otherwise involved a careful review of the merits. The Court of Appeal had *f* remedied such a defect in the instant case, so that there had been no violation of art 6(1). No authority had been shown to the court to justify the contention that, notwithstanding that fact, the associations were nevertheless entitled to recover wasted legal costs as compensation for an art 6(1) breach. Accordingly, the associations' application for costs against the Lord Chancellor would be refused (see *g* [6], [7], [19], [21], [23], [34], [35], below).

Ahmed v UK (1995) 20 EHRR CD 72 applied.

Notes

For the right to a fair trial by an independent and impartial tribunal, see 8(1) *h* *Halsbury's Laws* (4th edn reissue) paras 134, 140.

For the Human Rights Act 1998, s 7, Sch 1, Pt 1, art 6, see 7 *Halsbury's Statutes* (4th edn) (1999 reissue) 505, 523.

---

c   Section 7, so far as material, provides: '(1) A person who claims that a public authority has acted ... *j*
    in a way which is made unlawful by section 6(1) [acting in a way which is incompatible with a
    convention right] may—(a) bring proceedings against the authority under this Act in the
    appropriate court or tribunal, or (b) rely on the Convention right or rights concerned in any legal
    proceedings, but only if he is (or would be) a victim of the unlawful act ...
    (7) For the purposes of this section, a person is a victim of an unlawful act only if he would be a
    victim for the purposes of Article 34 of the Convention if proceedings were brought in the
    European Court of Human Rights in respect of that act ...'

Cases referred to in judgment

a   *Ahmed v UK* (1995) 20 EHRR CD 72, E Com HR.

Barberà v Spain [1994] ECHR 10588/83, ECt HR.

Bowman v UK (1996) 21 EHRR CD 79, E Com HR.

De Cubber v Belgium (1984) 7 EHRR 236, [1984] ECHR 9186/80, ECt HR.

De Haes v Belgium (1997) 25 EHRR 1, [1997] ECHR 19983/92, ECt HR.

b   *Edwards v UK* (1992) 15 EHRR 417, ECt HR.

Findlay v UK (1997) 24 EHRR 221, [1997] ECHR 9186/80, ECt HR.

Hodgson v UK (1987) 10 EHRR 503, [1987] ECHR 9580/81, ECt HR.

Kingsley v UK (2001) 33 EHRR 288, [2000] ECHR 35605/97, ECt HR.

Medicaments and Related Classes of Goods (No 2), Re [2001] 1 WLR 700, CA.

c   *Oberschlick v Austria (No 2)* (1997) 25 EHRR 357, [1997] ECHR 20834/92, ECt HR.

R (on the application of Shields) v Crown Court at Liverpool [2001] EWHC Admin 90, [2001] UKHRR 610, DC.

Riepan v Austria [2000] ECHR 35115/97, ECt HR.

Steele Ford & Newton (a firm) v CPS [1993] 2 All ER 769, sub nom *Holden & Co v CPS (No 2)* [1994] 1 AC 22, [1993] 2 WLR 934, HL.

d   *TP v UK* [2001] 2 FCR 289, ECt HR.

Twalib v Greece (2001) 33 EHRR 584, [1998] ECHR 24294/94, ECt HR.

Cases also cited or referred to in skeleton arguments

Agrotexim v Greece (1996) 21 EHRR 250, [1995] ECHR 14807/89, ECt HR.

e   *Aiden Shipping Co Ltd v Interbulk Ltd* [1986] 2 All ER 409, [1986] AC 965, HL.

Airey v Ireland (1979) 2 EHRR 305, [1979] ECHR 6289/73, ECt HR.

Ait-Mohoub v France (2000) 30 EHRR 382, [1998] ECHR 22924/93, ECt HR.

Albert v Belgium (1983) 5 EHRR 533, [1983] ECHR 7299/75, ECt HR.

Ashingdane v UK (1985) 7 EHRR 528, [1985] ECHR 19175/91, ECt HR.

f   *Bryan v UK* (1996) 21 EHRR 342, [1995] ECHR 19178/91, ECt HR.

Christians against Racism and Fascism v UK (1980) 21 DR 138, E Com HR.

Cutter v Eagle Star Insurance Co Ltd, Clarke v Kato [1998] 4 All ER 417, [1998] 1 WLR 1647, HL.

Condron v UK (2000) 8 BHRC 290, ECt HR.

Fahy's Will Trusts, Re [1962] 1 All ER 73, [1962] 1 WLR 17.

g   *Gibson's Settlement Trusts, Re* [1981] 1 All ER 233, [1981] Ch 179.

Golder v UK (1979) 1 EHRR 524, [1975] ECHR 4451/70, ECt HR.

Goose v Wilson Sandford & Co [1998] TLR 85, CA.

Le Compte v Belgium (1982) 4 EHRR 1, [1982] ECHR 6878/75, ECt HR.

Lustig-Prean v UK (2001) 31 EHRR 601, [2000] ECHR 31417/96, ECt HR.

h   *Maharaj v A-G of Trinidad and Tobago (No 2)* [1978] 2 All ER 670, [1979] AC 385, PC.

Osman v UK (1998) 5 BHRC 293, ECt HR.

Papamichalopoulos v Greece (1996) 21 EHRR 439, [1995] ECHR 14556/89, ECt HR.

Poplar Housing and Regeneration Community Association Ltd v Donoghue [2001] EWCA Civ 595, [2001] 4 All ER 604, [2001] 3 WLR 183.

j   *R v A* [2001] UKHL 25, [2001] 3 All ER 1, [2002] 1 AC 45.

R v Canterbury Crown Court, ex p Regentford Ltd [2001] HRLR 362, DC.

R v Hendon Rural DC, ex p Chorley [1933] 2 KB 696, [1933] All ER Rep 20, DC.

R v Lord Chancellor, ex p Lightfoot [1999] All ER 583, [2000] QB 597, CA.

R v Lord Chancellor, ex p Witham [1997] 2 All ER 779, [1998] QB 575, DC.

R v Secretary of State for the Home Dept, ex p Anderson [1984] 1 All ER 920, [1984] QB 778, DC.

R v Secretary of State for the Home Dept, ex p Leech [1993] 4 All ER 539, [1994] QB
198, CA.

*R (on the application of Alconbury Developments Ltd) v Secretary of State for the
Environment, Transport and the Regions* [2001] UKHL 23, [2001] 2 All ER 929,
[2001] 2 WLR 1389.

R v Secretary of State for the Home Dept, ex p Daly [2001] UKHL 26, [2001] 3 All ER
433, [2001] 2 AC 532.

Raymond v Honey [1981] 2 All ER 1084, [1981] QB 874, DC; *affd* [1982] 1 All ER 756,
[1983] 1 AC 1, HL.

Rentall Ltd v D S Willcock Ltd (30 July 1997, unreported), QBD.

Ross v Bowbelle (owners) [1997] 1 WLR 1159, CA.

Schuler-Zgraggen v Switzerland (1996) 21 EHRR 404, [1995] ECHR 14518/89, ECt HR.

Smith v UK (2001) 31 EHRR 620, [2000] ECHR 33985/96, ECt HR.

Stanford v UK [1994] TLR 130, ECt HR.

Stran Greek Refineries v Greece (1995) 19 EHRR 293, [1994] ECHR 13427/87, ECt HR.

Tolstoy Miloslavsky v UK (1995) 20 EHRR 442, [1995] ECHR 18139/91, ECt HR.

W (children) (care plan), Re, Re W (children) (care plan) [2001] EWCA Civ 757, [2001]
2 FCR 450.

Wright v Bennett [1948] 1 All ER 410, [1948] 1 KB 601, CA.

X v Netherlands (1975) 1 DR 66, E Com HR.

Z v UK (2001) 34 EHRR 97, [2001] 2 FCR 246, ECt HR.

Application

On 21 December 2000 the Court of Appeal handed down a judgment ([2001] 1 WLR
700) giving its reasons for its decision on 21 November 2000 to allow an appeal by
the applicant associations, the Proprietary Association of Great Britain and the
Proprietary Articles Trade Association, against the refusal of the Restrictive
Trade Practices Court on 17 November 2000 to recuse itself on the grounds of
apparent bias in proceedings in which the associations were opposing an
application by the Director General of Fair Trading for the discharge of an
exemption order made in 1970. The Court of Appeal adjourned the issue of costs.
On the adjourned hearing, the associations, relying on art 6(1) of the European
Convention for the Protection of Human Rights and Fundamental Freedoms
1950 (as set out in Sch 1 to the Human Rights Act 1998), sought an order
requiring the Lord Chancellor to pay their wasted costs. The Director General
took no part in the application. The facts are set out in the judgment of the court.

Catharine Otton-Goulder QC, Margaret Gray and *Andrew Henshaw* (instructed by
CMS Cameron McKenna) for the associations.

Philip Sales and *Jason Coppel* (instructed by the *Treasury Solicitor*) for the Lord
Chancellor.

Cur adv vult

26 July 2001. The following judgment of the court, prepared by Brooke LJ, was
delivered.

BROOKE LJ.

[1] On 21 December 2000 we allowed an appeal by the Proprietary Association
of Great Britain (PAGB) and the Proprietary Articles Trade Association (PATA)
against an order of the Restrictive Practices Court on 17 November 2000 whereby

a   it had declined to vacate a trial of a contested application which was then proceeding before it (see *Re Medicaments and Related Classes of Goods* [2001] 1 WLR 700). The grounds of the application to vacate the trial were that one member of the court had disclosed apparent bias, and that the whole of the court should recuse itself on the grounds that the other members were infected by her apparent bias.

b   [2] The consequence of our direction was that the proceedings had to begin again before a reconstituted court. The new hearing started before a panel of the court presided over by Buckley J, but it came to a premature end without the need for a judgment of the court when PAGB and PATA withdrew their opposition to the relief being sought by the Director General of Fair Trading following an indication by the court that it was unsympathetic to the points they were making.

c   [3] Although substantial costs savings were achieved in the way the parties presented the case to the second panel, PAGB and PATA estimate that they wasted costs of about £1m because the proceedings had to begin again.

d   [4] Before the enactment of the Human Rights Act 1998 the Lord Chancellor on occasion made ex gratia payments out of the funds allocated to his department by Parliament when litigants complained that they had been put to unnecessary expense by reason of some form of maladministration in the operation of the courts. In those days the House of Lords had made it clear in *Steele Ford & Newton (a firm) v CPS* [1993] 2 All ER 769, sub nom *Holden & Co v CPS (No 2)* [1994] 1 AC 22 that s 51 of the Supreme Court Act 1981 gave a court no implied power to

e   make an order out of central funds in civil litigation to compensate a litigant for wasted costs. The appellants maintain, however, that the position has been altered since the 1998 Act came into force on 2 October 2000. They say that their art 6(1) right to a trial by an impartial tribunal has been infringed, and that they are entitled to be compensated for the costs they have wasted as a result of the

f   infringement of that right by the Lord Chancellor, being the emanation of the state responsible for providing impartial tribunals to conduct trials of civil litigation.

[5] Mr Philip Sales has appeared for the Lord Chancellor to resist this claim. He takes two preliminary points. If they are good points, there will be no need for us to consider any of the other matters that were debated before us. His first

g   point is that PAGB is not a victim within the meaning of s 7(1) of the 1998 Act (see also s 7(7)) so that the court has no jurisdiction to grant them any relief under the Act. This in itself would not be sufficient to bar PATA's claim under that section. Mr Sales' second point is that these proceedings are completely misconceived. This court has corrected the situation that arose at first instance, so that an

h   impartial tribunal was made available for the determination of the civil rights in issue. The appellants are therefore quite unable to claim that any art 6 rights have been infringed.

[6] Mr Sales' first point was developed along the following lines. Article 6(1) of the European Convention for the Protection of Human Rights and Fundamental

j   Freedoms 1950 (as set out in Sch 1 to the 1998 Act) provides, so far as is material, that:

'In the determination of his civil rights and obligations or of any criminal charge against him, everyone is entitled to a fair and public hearing within a reasonable time by an independent and impartial tribunal established by law.'

This language has been held to mean that a complainant must be able to show
that his own civil rights and obligations have been directly affected by the
proceedings and be the subject matter of the dispute.

[7] In this context Mr Sales showed us a number of Strasbourg decisions which
declared inadmissible applications made by trade unions or other representative
bodies which had an interest on behalf of their members in general or were
otherwise interested in the point in issue in the case, but were not themselves
directly affected. The reason why they were declared inadmissible was because
these applicants did not qualify as 'victims' for the purposes of art 34 of the
convention, which is given effect under our domestic law by s 7(7) of the 1998
Act. The cases themselves were primarily concerned with alleged breaches of
arts 10 and 11 of the convention, but their effect is equally applicable to the status
of a complainant under art 6.

[8] The decisions in *Hodgson v UK* (1987) 10 EHRR 503 at 506, *Ahmed v UK*
(1995) 20 EHRR CD 72 at 77–78, and *Bowman v UK* (1996) 21 EHRR CD 79 are
examples of this approach to the interpretation of art 34. It is sufficient for present
purposes to refer only to *Ahmed v UK*, in which four local government officers and
their trade union (UNISON) complained about the effect of statutory regulations
which restricted the political activities of the four individual applicants. In
declaring the application admissible in relation to the four individuals, but
inadmissible in relation to UNISON, the European Commission of Human
Rights said ((1995) 20 EHRR CD 72 at 78):

> 'The Regulations at issue in the present case do not affect any rights which
> UNISON may have under Article 11 of the Convention, and UNISON's
> freedom of expression is not limited in any way by the Regulations.
> Moreover, the Regulations were not addressed to trade unions but to local
> authority employees, and they do not refer to limitations on individuals'
> union activity. To the extent that an individual may be affected by the
> Regulations in the exercise of the Convention rights, for example in his
> freedom of expression by speaking in public in a union context, he is the
> person affected and not the union. Accordingly the Commission finds that
> UNISON is not directly affected by the provisions of the Regulations within
> the meaning of the Convention organs. It may not therefore claim to be a
> victim of a violation of the Convention within the meaning of the Article 25.'

[9] After this point was first raised in relation to both appellants, PATA
adduced evidence which showed that the proceedings in the Restrictive Practices
Court were indeed determinative of PATA's own civil rights and obligations
because the outcome sought by the Director General rendered illegal an activity
which constituted one of PATA's constitutional objects and its primary practical
objective. It is not necessary to say any more about this, because Mr Sales
accepted that this evidence rebutted his challenge to that association's standing.
He stood his ground, however, in relation to PAGB. It is therefore necessary to
consider its position in rather more detail. We gave all parties the opportunity
to provide us with further evidence and/or submissions on the point. As a result
the position, though not agreed, is now a good deal clearer than it was at the time
of the hearing.

[10] The material application to the Restrictive Practices Court was made by
the Director General pursuant to s 17 of the Resale Prices Act 1976. This Act,
among other things, consolidated with other related enactments those provisions
of the Resale Prices Act 1964 which still had effect, and s 17 created a power in the

a   court to discharge any direction it had previously made to the effect that goods of any class should be exempted goods for the purposes of this legislation. In our judgment dated 21 December 2000, which is now reported under the title *Re Medicaments and Related Classes of Goods (No 2)* [2001] 1 WLR 700, we set out in paras 8–10 (at 704) the history leading up to the application made by the Director General to discharge the earlier exemption order made in respect of 'OTCs' *b*   (medicines etc sold over the counter) in 1970. For present purposes it is sufficient to quote only part of para 8:

> 'PAGB is an association of manufacturers, importers and suppliers of branded "pharmacy only" and "general sales list" medicines, vitamins and mineral supplements sold over the counter (without the need for a *c*   prescription) in the United Kingdom. The majority of PAGB members have established and maintain a system of resale price maintenance in relation to the sale of such branded goods in the United Kingdom.'

[11] The parties who represented the various industry interests in the 1970 application were PAGB, PATA and an association called ABPI. ABPI were *d*   concerned only with prescription medicines, in respect of which resale price maintenance had withered away before 1998. Boots Pure Drugs Co Ltd formally entered an appearance in the 1970 proceedings, but was not represented at the final hearing. Apart from that company, no individual undertaking was at any time a party to those proceedings, and the judgment in 1970 identified only the three industry bodies we have mentioned above and the Registrar of Restrictive *e*   Practices (now the Director General) as parties to the proceedings. No formal order was made to the effect that those bodies should represent their members.

[12] Rules 19 to 21 of the Restrictive Practices Court (Resale Prices) Rules 1976, SI 1976/1899, prescribe the procedure to be followed in relation to an application under s 17 of the 1976 Act to discharge an order previously made by the court. In *f*   particular, r 20(2) provides in effect that a copy of the notice of application for leave to apply for such an order must generally be served on every party who appeared on the hearing of the previous proceedings, and r 21 provides for the directions which may be made if leave is granted. For this purpose the provisions of the rules relating to an application under s 16 of the Act apply with any *g*   necessary modifications. These include r 9(b), which provides that on the hearing of the preliminary application for directions the court may order that 'some or all of the suppliers, retailers or trade associations who are before the Court be represented by such representative respondent as the Court may direct'.

[13] The Director General's application for leave was opposed by PATA and PAGB, and when leave was granted by the court in March 1999 he undertook to *h*   the court that he would advertise the existence of the proceedings, so that other interested parties would have an opportunity to take part, if so advised. In the event, only two persons responded to the advertisement, and both ultimately decided not to become parties.

[14] The court at no time made any representative order pursuant to r 9(b). *j*   The two associations' solicitors always accepted that in a formal sense they acted only for those two clients, for whom they were the solicitors on the record. When the Treasury Solicitor invited them in September 1999 to confirm that this was the case, the solicitors replied:

> 'In a formal sense and for the purposes of the record given the nature of the proceedings, we act for the respondent association as parties in this litigation.

Whilst clearly we could not and cannot take our instructions from each of
the members of the association individually, the associations are the sum of
their membership from time to time and we do consider the members as our
clients in this sense.'

[15] Two days later, at an interlocutory hearing before Lightman J, the fact
that the individual manufacturers were not formally parties to the proceedings
surfaced again in the following dialogue between Mr Turner (who appeared for
the Director General) and the judge:

> '*The Judge*: I understand Mr Cran accepts that all the members of the
> Association are his clients and effectively parties to the proceedings.
> *Mr Turner*: My Lord, for the record the Director General's understanding
> is that they are not parties to the proceedings. There is a procedure by which
> they may be made parties to the proceedings, which has not been engaged
> in. They are simply member companies of the trade association which is the
> respondent in this ...
> *The Judge*: This again is a far reaching question which if it is going to be live
> I will deal with at an appropriate stage with skeleton arguments.'

[16] That was how the matter was left. Rule 15(1) of the 1976 rules makes
special provision for orders for disclosure of documents against individual
suppliers or retailers who are members of a trade association which is a party to
proceedings, and this rule enabled the Director General to make applications for
such orders even though no representative order had been made under r 9(b).
We have been told by the Director General that a different procedure was adopted
in proceedings affecting the Premier League, because in those proceedings the
league was formally made a representative respondent for all the football clubs
which had been members of it at one time or another since its inception. In those
circumstances disclosure from the members was given as a matter of course, as if
they were individually parties to the proceedings, without the need to have
recourse to r 15(1).

[17] We have been told that counsel for the associations remembers a
conversation with her opposite number in which both sides agreed that they did
not want the manufacturers to appear individually, because of the huge additional
administrative burden and additional cost which would be entailed. However
that may be, the Director General seems to have been content with a situation in
which the rules enabled him to obtain the disclosure he sought from individual
members of PAGB. Rule 15(1), in conjunction with r 29 of the Restrictive Practices
Court Rules 1976, SI 1976/1897, also enabled a joint accountants' investigation to
be ordered. For their part, the associations seem to have been content to spare
their members the expense and nuisance of individual representation. In those
days when the 1998 Act was on the statute-book but had not yet come into force,
nobody seems to have turned their attention to the question whether the absence
of a representative order would disentitle both PAGB and, of necessity, its
non-party members, from making any complaint about a breach of their art 6(1)
rights during the course of the proceedings.

[18] Miss Otton-Goulder QC made brief submissions to the effect that the
cases of *Ahmed, Hodgson* and *Bowman*, on which Mr Sales relied, produced results
which were not at all surprising on the facts, but that the present situation was
different. She referred us to the views expressed by John Wadham and Helen
Mountfield in a passage in their book *Blackstone's Guide to the Human Rights Act
1998* (1999) pp 39–41 in which they discuss problems of standing in judicial review

a   proceedings. In that context they differentiated between public interest groups which are really an association of interested individuals who may be regarded as a group of persons each of whom may be regarded as a victim, and representative groups such as Amnesty or the Joint Council for the Welfare of Immigrants who may have special expertise but who cannot be classified in the first category.

b   [19] On this occasion we do not have to go into those deep waters. Each case has to be decided in its own context, and in the present context the rules provided a route by which the individual parties could have been formally represented by PAGB, but they chose not to follow that route. In those circumstances PAGB cannot be properly regarded as a victim for the purposes of making a claim under s 7(1) of the 1998 Act.

c   [20] Anticipating that the court might reach this conclusion, the appellants in the alternative sought an order pursuant to CPR Pt 19 whereby PATA and PAGB might be made representatives of all persons who had the same right (in other words, all those who contributed to the costs and whose rights were affected by the main proceedings). Alternatively they invited us to adjourn so as to permit the joinder of all the affected parties. In our judgment it is far too late to grant

d   them relief in either form, so as to enable the manufacturers retrospectively to become victims of the alleged breach of the convention.

[21] For these reasons, in our judgment, PAGB cannot be heard to say that the proceedings in the Restrictive Practices Court violated any of its convention rights, because they were not determinative of PAGB's civil rights and obligations within the meaning of art 6(1).

e   [22] Mr Sales' second preliminary point was that in the events that had occurred there had been no violation of anyone's art 6 rights. He said that this point could be put in a number of ways. It might be said that this court did not find a breach of art 6: it merely averted a breach which might have occurred in the future. Alternatively, he said that there was no breach of art 6, since the

f   appellants did obtain a fair hearing before the reconstituted first instance court which represented an independent and impartial tribunal. His third way of putting the matter was that any breach of art 6 was remedied by this court and/or by the retrial before the Restrictive Practices Court.

[23] It is trite convention law that an appeal court can remedy defects in first

g   instance decisions where the appeal is in the nature of a full rehearing or otherwise involves a careful review of the merits (see, for example *Edwards v UK* (1992) 15 EHRR 417 and *Twalib v Greece* (2001) 33 EHRR 584). In giving the judgment of the Divisional Court in *R (on the application of Shields) v Crown Court at Liverpool* [2001] EWHC Admin 90 at [34], [2001] UKHRR 610 at [34]) Brooke LJ

h   said of two cases (*De Cubber v Belgium* (1984) 7 EHRR 236 at 248–249 (paras 32–33) and *Findlay v UK* (1997) 24 EHRR 221) which had been cited to contrary effect:

> 'These cases do not establish that an appeal court cannot remedy defects in first instance decisions by holding those decisions to be invalid. Indeed, that is one way in which an effective remedy for breaches of Convention rights
j   > can be secured, as required by Art 13 of the Convention. In such cases the appeal court is not saving the decision, notwithstanding the blemishes at first instance, rather it is invalidating the decision because of the blemishes at first instance. The court is then ruling in a criminal case that the original verdict cannot be allowed to stand and that if there is to be a conviction, it can only be after a fresh trial in which the Convention rights are respected. It is simply upholding Convention rights.'

If that court had had the benefit of Mr Sales' argument in the present case, the second sentence of this passage might well have been phrased in a different way.   a

[24] The case of *Kingsley v UK* (2001) 33 EHRR 288 provides a good illustration of the point Mr Sales was making to us. The European Court of Human Rights held (at 302 (para 50)) that a panel of the Gaming Board had not presented the necessary appearance of impartiality to constitute a tribunal which complied with art 6(1). It went on to say, however, in para 51:   b

'However, even where an adjudicatory body determining disputes over "civil rights and obligations" does not comply with Article 6(1), there is no breach of the Article if the proceedings before that body are "subject to subsequent control by a judicial body that has full jurisdiction and does provide the guarantees of Article 6(1)". The issue in the present case is   c
whether the High Court and the Court of Appeal satisfied the requirements of Article 6(1) as far as the scope of jurisdiction of those courts was concerned.'

[25] The unusual feature of that case was that the courts on judicial review had no power to remit the case to any tribunal other than the one whose impartiality had   d
been successfully impugned. This was the reason why the applicant was successful on the facts of that case (see at 304 (para 59)). More importantly, however, in the present context, the European Court made it quite clear (at 303–304 (para 58)) that if the reviewing court had had the power to quash the impugned decision and either to make the relevant decision afresh or to remit the case for a new decision by an impartial body, then there would have been no breach of art 6(1).   e

[26] Despite this powerful recent authority to contrary effect, Miss Otton-Goulder maintained that the hearing before the reconstituted Restrictive Practices Court was not in itself sufficient to give effect to the requirements of art 6, and that her clients must have compensation for their wasted costs as well. Unless they were granted this relief, she argued that there would be no restitutio in   f
integrum and the breach of art 6 would remain uncured.

[27] In this context she referred us to the decision of European Court in *Barberà v Spain* [1994] ECHR 10588/83. In that case, she said, the European Court had awarded the applicants compensation in respect of a period of time they spent in prison, holding that their subsequent release and acquittal could not in themselves afford complete reparation for the damage derived from their   g
detention (see para 16). What she overlooked was that in that case the European Court in December 1988 had found that there had been a violation of art 6(1). It was only in the course of the events which followed that judgment that the applicants were released and acquitted. They recovered compensation for the damage they suffered as a direct consequence of the trial found by the court to be   h
in violation of the convention, at a time when there had been no question of any appellate proceedings nullifying the breach.

[28] Miss Otton-Goulder also relied on Strasbourg cases in which, she said, the court awarded wasted legal costs as part of the applicants' compensation where the violation of their legal rights related to the conduct of legal proceedings. In   j
this context she cited the awards in *De Haes v Belgium* (1997) 25 EHRR 1 at 59 (paras 67–69) and *Oberschlick v Austria (No 2)* (1997) 25 EHRR 357 at 369 (paras 40–42).

[29] In each of these cases the European Court had held that the applicants' convention rights had been violated in the national courts, and awarded them their legal expenses and costs in those courts as part of the just satisfaction to which they were entitled under art 50 of the convention. If, however, there has

a been no breach of art 6(1) at national level, these decisions do not take the matter any further.

[30] Miss Otton-Goulder argued that the decision of the European Court in *Riepan v Austria* [2000] ECHR 35115/97 also advanced her cause. In that case the court held that the criminal trial of a prisoner in a small room in the closed area of a prison did not comply with the requirement of publicity laid down in art 6(1)

b of the convention. The question therefore arose whether the absence of publicity at the trial court could be remedied by anything other than a complete rehearing before the appeal court, and the European Court held, on the facts, that the public hearing before the Linz Court of Appeal did not remedy the matter (see para 41). Apart from questioning the applicant, the appellate court did not take any evidence and in particular did not rehear the witnesses. This is, therefore, merely

c an example of the application of the principles set out in *Kingsley v UK* (see para [24], above). It is clear that the European Court considered that the matter could have been effectively remedied if the Court of Appeal had heard all the relevant evidence itself in public.

[31] Miss Otton-Goulder conceded, on the authority of *De Cubber v Belgium*

d (1984) 7 EHRR 236 at 249 (para 33), that a higher court might in some circumstances make reparation for an initial violation of one of the convention's provisions, but she said that while certain of the consequences of the violation comprised by the lack of impartiality at first instance remained unremedied, it could not be said that full reparation had been made, still less that the violation had ceased to exist.

e [32] She relied in this context on the very recent European Court decision in *TP v UK* [2001] 2 FCR 289. In that case a child aged four years and nine months was interviewed on video, and a place of safety order was made the same day in the belief that the child was saying her mother's boyfriend had sexually abused her (see at 251–252 (paras 13–17)). A transcript of the video interview was not

f disclosed to the mother or her solicitors for nearly 12 months, and they then pointed out that the girl had shaken her head when asked whether the abuser was living at home, and that she had identified her abuser as having been thrown out of the house by her mother. The muddle had occurred because her mother's boyfriend and the abuser shared the same first name. The child was reunited with her mother very soon after the muddle had been rectified (see at 253–254

g (paras 27–29)). The European Court held (at 267 (para 83)) that the question whether to disclose the video of the interview and its transcript should have been determined promptly to allow the mother an effective opportunity to deal with the allegations that her daughter could not be returned safely to her care, and that there had therefore been a breach of art 8 of the convention.

h [33] It is hardly surprising in those circumstances that the court ordered compensation to reflect the damage caused by the removal of this girl from her mother for a year (see at 320–321 (paras 112–113, 116)). This was not an art 6 case, and mother and child were entitled to restitutio in integrum in relation to the violation of their art 8 rights. The mere fact that they were reunited after a

j year pursuant to a consent order made by a High Court judge was insufficient to remedy the wrong they had been done.

[34] Miss Otton-Goulder was unable to show us any authority which justified her contention that notwithstanding the fact that this court remedied the situation so that no violation of art 6(1) occurred, her clients were nevertheless entitled to recover wasted legal costs as compensation for an art 6(1) breach. Indeed, Strasbourg authority is to contrary effect. In *Kingsley v UK* (2001) 33 EHRR 288 where the

European Court did hold that there had been an art 6(1) breach, it nevertheless
did not allow Mr Kingsley his costs incurred in the domestic proceedings as costs
(still less as pecuniary damages). It appeared to accede to the submission made
on behalf of the United Kingdom government (at 305 (para 65)) to the effect that the
court's normal practice was to disallow costs incurred in the domestic proceedings.

[35] For these reasons we are satisfied that Mr Sales' second preliminary objection
is also well-founded. In these circumstances it is unnecessary to consider any of
the other issues raised on this application.

[36] All that remains, therefore, is the question whether the appellants can
recover from the Director General any of the costs of the issue on which they
succeeded in this court. Since the hearing we have received written submissions
from the Director General on this question, but we do not know whether this is
a course which the appellants still seek to pursue. If they do, a further hearing
would have to be arranged for this purpose unless the parties are willing to permit
the court to determine that issue on the basis of written submissions.

Application dismissed. Permission to appeal refused.

Kate O'Hanlon   Barrister.

Clibbery v Allan
[2002] EWCA Civ 45

a

COURT OF APPEAL, CIVIL DIVISION
DAME ELIZABETH BUTLER-SLOSS P, THORPE AND KEENE LJJ
b   6–8 NOVEMBER 2001, 30 JANUARY 2002

Family proceedings – Chambers hearings – Confidentiality of proceedings – Whether family proceedings could only be held in private in children cases – Whether all family proceedings heard in private confidential – Administration of Justice Act 1960, s 12 –
c   *Contempt of Court Act 1981, s 11 – Family Law Act 1996, Pt IV – Family Proceedings Rules 1991.*

For several years, C had a sexual relationship with a prominent businessman, A. After the breakdown of their relationship, C commenced proceedings under Pt IV of the Family Law Act 1996, seeking, inter alia, an occupation order in
d   respect of a flat owned by a company of which A was the beneficial owner. In accordance with the Family Proceedings Rules 1991 (made under the Matrimonial and Family Proceedings Act 1984), the case was heard, and judgment given, in chambers, but no special direction was given as to the confidentiality of the proceedings. The judge dismissed the application on the grounds of lack of
e   jurisdiction. C then took her story to a national newspaper, giving a journalist direct extracts from an affidavit sworn by A. The story was published several times in that newspaper and others. A sought a written undertaking from C not to repeat the publication or disclose confidential information. After C refused to give such an undertaking, A successfully applied without notice for injunctions restraining her from disclosing, save to her legal advisors, any affidavit, statement,
f   other document, oral evidence or the judgment in the proceedings. On A's subsequent application to continue the injunctions, the judge held that there was in principle no difference between the procedures to be adopted in the Family Division and those in the other two Divisions of the High Court; that the guiding principle, which applied across the board, was that of open justice; that the
g   practice of hearing cases in chambers was largely for administrative convenience and did not denote privacy or confidentiality of the proceedings or of the documents used in the proceedings; that the only derogations from that position were to be found in (a) the common law principles setting out the circumstances (including wardship cases) in which proceedings were confidential and (b) the statutory restrictions on the publication of information relating to proceedings,
h   contained, inter alia, in s 12[a] of the Administration of Justice Act 1960 (which included issues concerning children) and s 11[b] of the Contempt of Court Act 1981 (exemption from disclosure in court); that accordingly no confidentiality attached to proceedings in the Family Division, or to information conveyed in the course of such proceedings, merely because those proceedings took place in
j   chambers; and that none of the exceptions to the general principle applied in the instant case. The judge therefore dismissed the application. On A's appeal, the Court of Appeal considered (i) whether, as the judge had stated, family proceedings could be held in private only in children cases; and (ii) the

---

a   Section 12 is set out at [52], [53], below.
b   Section 11 is set out at [78], below.

circumstances in which family proceedings, held in private, should be treated as
secret or confidential with the effect that there could be no subsequent publication
of the documents, the oral evidence, the submissions, the judgment or any of
them.

Held – (1) Family proceedings could be heard in private even when they were
not children cases. Parliament had provided for rules to be made to regulate the
statutory framework of the family justice system. The 1991 rules, which were
properly based upon the 1984 Act, gave the court power to exclude the public in
family proceedings. There could be no problem in the application of that
procedure under the 1991 rules, designed as it was to provide a measure of
privacy, not necessarily confidentiality, to family proceedings. The CPR gave a
similar degree of privacy to groups of civil cases, and there remained a power to
allow the public in if the judge directed. Thus the 1991 rules were not ultra vires,
and there was no objection to family courts hearing cases in private and excluding
the public where those rules permitted them to do so (see [42], [50], [86],
[122]–[124], below); *Scott v Scott* [1913] AC 417, *Forbes v Smith* [1998] 1 All ER 973
and *Hodgson v Imperial Tobacco Ltd* [1998] 2 All ER 673 considered.

(2) Save in children cases, cases involving issues of ancillary relief or other
situations which could be shown manifestly to require permanent confidentiality,
family proceedings were not, and should not be seen to be, in a separate category
from other civil proceedings as regards the confidentiality of the proceedings and
of information relating to them. Information about children cases was
indubitably covered by privacy and secrecy, and no information could be
disclosed after the end of the case without the leave of the court. Similarly, all
cases involving ancillary relief were protected from publication by anyone
without leave of the court. Information disclosed under the compulsion of
ancillary relief proceedings was protected before, during and after the proceedings
by the implied undertaking that such information would be used only for the
purpose of the proceedings. That undertaking extended to voluntary disclosure
in ancillary relief proceedings, to the information contained in the documents and
to affidavits, statements of truth and witness statements. The obligation to
respect the implied undertaking would also be imposed by the court in cases
analogous to ancillary relief and found in Pt III of the 1991 rules, e g applications
in cases of failure to provide reasonable maintenance or applications to alter
maintenance agreements. There were, however, other family proceedings, of
which the instant case was an example, which were not automatically covered by
secrecy, although they could be heard in private. Whether they were so
protected would depend upon the type of proceedings, and whether they came
within, or part of the information came within, the ambit of s 12 of the 1960 Act
or whether the administration of justice would otherwise be impeded or
prejudiced by publication. Applications under Pt IV of the 1996 Act did not
necessarily come within s 12, nor was the element of compulsion, triggering an
implied undertaking, always present. Although there might be cases in which it
was appropriate for the court hearing the case in private to decide whether, under
s 11 of the 1981 Act, any or even all of the information should not be disclosed, it
could not properly be a blanket protection of non-publication in all cases heard in
private in chambers under the 1991 rules. However, in applications for
occupation orders where children were involved, the welfare of those children
was likely to be the major issue, and consequently the exemption in s 12 of the
1960 Act would probably apply. If the financial affairs of any of the parties had to

a be investigated, that information would probably be protected, and the general principles of discovery would apply. The parties and the court would, however, have to consider in each case whether the proper working of the administration of justice required there to be continuing confidentiality after the end of the proceedings. In the instant case, there was no basis for prohibiting publication of the proceedings. Accordingly, the appeal would be dismissed (see [72], [73], [75],

b [77], [79], [83], [85], [86], [122], [125], below).

Notes

For the general requirement of openness of judicial proceedings, see 1(1) *Halsbury's Laws* (4th edn) (2001 reissue) para 109.

For the Administration of Justice Act 1960, s 12, see 11 *Halsbury's Statutes*
c (4th edn) (2000 reissue) 185.

For the Contempt of Court Act 1981, s 11, see 11 *Halsbury's Statutes* (4th edn) (2000 reissue) 201.

For the Family Law Act 1996, Pt IV, see 27 *Halsbury's Statutes* (4th edn) (2000 reissue) 752.

d For the Family Proceedings Rules 1991, see 12 *Halsbury's Statutory Instruments* (2000 Issue) 82.

Cases referred to in judgments

A v A, B v B [2000] 1 FCR 577.

A-G v Leveller Magazine Ltd [1979] 1 All ER 745, [1979] AC 440, [1979] 2 WLR 247,
e HL.

B v UK [2001] 2 FCR 221, ECt HR.

Bourns Inc v Raychem Corp [1999] 3 All ER 154, CA.

Crest Homes plc v Marks [1987] 2 All ER 1074, [1987] AC 829, [1987] 3 WLR 293, HL.

Derby & Co Ltd v Weldon (1988) Times, 20 October.

f *Forbes v Smith* [1998] 1 All ER 973.

GIO Personal Investment Services Ltd v Liverpool and London Steamship Protection and Indemnity Association Ltd (FAI General Insurance Co Ltd intervening) [1999] 1 WLR 984, CA.

Hodgson v Imperial Tobacco Ltd [1998] 2 All ER 673, [1998] 1 WLR 1056, CA.

Home Office v Harman [1982] 1 All ER 532, sub nom *Harman v Secretary of State for*
g *the Home Dept* [1983] 1 AC 280, [1982] 2 WLR 338, HL.

Jenkins v Livesey (formerly Jenkins) [1985] 1 All ER 106, [1985] 1 AC 424, [1985] 2 WLR 47, HL.

J-PC v J-AF [1955] P 215, PD and CA.

Kelley v Corston [1997] 4 All ER 466, [1998] QB 686, [1998] 3 WLR 246, CA.

h *Kelly v BBC* [2001] 1 All ER 323, [2001] Fam 59, [2001] 2 WLR 253.

Medway v Doublelock Ltd [1978] 1 All ER 1261, [1978] 1 WLR 710.

Morris (Jenny), In the matter of [1902] P 104.

P-B (a minor) (child cases: hearing in open court), Re [1997] 1 All ER 58, CA.

Prudential Assurance Co Ltd v Fountain Page Ltd [1991] 3 All ER 878, [1991] 1 WLR 756.

j *R (on the application of Pelling) v Bow County Court* [2001] UKHRR 165, DC.

R v R (disclosure to Revenue) [1998] 1 FCR 597.

Riddick v Thames Board Mills Ltd [1977] 3 All ER 677, [1977] QB 881, [1977] 3 WLR 63, CA.

S v S (disclosure to Revenue) [1997] 1 WLR 1621.

Scott v Scott [1913] AC 417, [1911–13] All ER Rep 1, HL.

SmithKline Beecham Biologicals SA v Connaught Laboratories Inc [1999] 4 All ER 498, CA.

Taylor v Director of Serious Fraud Office [1998] 4 All ER 801, [1999] 2 AC 177, [1998]   a
3 WLR 1040, HL.

Cases also cited or referred to in skeleton arguments
Ali Shipping Corpn v Shipyard Trogir [1998] 2 All ER 136, [1999] 1 WLR 136, CA.
Axen v Germany (1984) 6 EHRR 195, [1983] ECHR 8273/78, ECt HR.
B v UK [2001] 2 FCR 221, ECt HR.   b
Dar v Taylor (17 May 2001, unreported), QBD.
F (a minor) (publication of information), Re [1977] 1 All ER 114, [1977] Fam 58, CA.
G (minors) (celebrities: publicity), Re [1999] 3 FCR 181, CA.
Hildebrand v Hildebrand [1992] 1 FLR 244.
Naylor v Preston Area Health Authority [1987] 2 All ER 353, [1987] 1 WLR 958, CA.
R v Bow County Court, ex p Pelling [1999] 4 All ER 751, [1999] 1 WLR 1807, CA.   c
Stephens v Avery [1988] 2 All ER 477, [1988] Ch 449.
Trustor AB v Smallbone [2000] 1 All ER 811.
X v UK (7 March 1977, unreported), E Com HR.
Z v Finland (1997) 25 EHRR 371, [1997] ECHR 22009/93, ECt HR.
                                                                                                               d

Appeal
The appellant, Ivan William Allan, appealed with permission of Thorpe LJ granted
on 12 July 2001 from the order of Munby J on 14 June 2001 ([2001] 2 FCR 577)
dismissing his application to continue injunctions, granted on his without notice
application by Connell J on 3 May 2001, restraining the respondent, Glory Anne   e
Clibbery, from in any way disclosing to any person save her legal advisors in the
proceedings (i) the text or a summary of the whole or any part of any affidavit,
statement or other document filed in the proceedings, (ii) the text or a summary of
the whole or any part of any oral evidence given by the parties or by any other
witness in the proceedings, and (iii) the text or a summary of the whole or any part
of the judgment delivered by Judge Krikler on 12 April 2001. The facts are set out   f
in the judgment of Dame Elizabeth Butler-Sloss P.

Andrew Moylan QC and *Christopher Pocock* (instructed by *Kinglsey Napley*) for the
appellant.
James Price QC and *Andrew Monson* (instructed by *Reynolds Porter Chamberlain*) for   g
the respondent.

Cur adv vult

30 January 2002. The following judgments were delivered.
                                                                                                               h

DAME ELIZABETH BUTLER-SLOSS P.
[1] This is an appeal by Ivan Allan (the appellant), from the refusal of Munby J
on 14 June 2001 to continue injunctions granted ex parte by Connell J on 3 May
restraining Glory Anne Clibbery (the respondent), from disclosing information
about the appellant. The appeal raises fundamental issues over the procedures   j
for hearing family cases in the High Court and in county courts round the
country. The specific question raised on this appeal is whether the practice of
hearing the majority of family cases in chambers has the consequence that
information about those proceedings may not be reported.
[2] The background to this appeal is an application by the respondent in the
Royal Courts of Justice under Pt IV of the Family Law Act 1996 seeking a

a non-molestation order against the appellant and an occupation order in respect of a flat in Piccadilly owned by a company of which the appellant was the beneficial owner. The application was heard by Judge Krikler on 9 April 2001. The respondent abandoned her application for a non-molestation order. The issues before Judge Krikler were whether the court had jurisdiction to make an occupation order, and if there was jurisdiction whether, in the exercise of his

b discretion, he should make such an order. The respondent accepted that she had no beneficial interest in the flat and that she and the appellant did not marry nor agree to do so. Judge Krikler found for the appellant and held that the respondent and appellant had never lived together as husband and wife and that the flat had never been their home. Under the provisions of the 1996 Act, s 36(1), he had no jurisdiction to make an occupation order. He also decided that, if he had

c had jurisdiction, he would not have made an order. He dismissed the application and ordered the respondent to pay the appellant's costs. The respondent then vacated the flat in which she had been living.

[3] The case before Judge Krikler appears to have generated a considerable volume of paper, numerous affidavits and documents disclosed on discovery.

d The trial bundle was contained in six lever arch files. None of the documents filed, nor the evidence given to the circuit judge, nor the orders made, nor his judgment was shown either to Munby J or to us. The case was heard in accordance with r 3.9 of the Family Proceedings Rules 1991, SI 1999/1247, in chambers and judgment was given in chambers. Munby J, in his judgment, described the next step as the reaction 'of the woman scorned'.

e
[4] The respondent took her story to the Daily Mail. She appears to have been particularly upset and angry by an affidavit sworn by the appellant and, it would seem, she gave direct extracts from it to the Daily Mail journalist. She set out her side of the story in emotive language. The appellant is a prominent businessman, living mainly in Hong Kong, who had a sexual relationship with her over a

f number of years, and the story has been published several times in the Daily Mail and more recently in other newspapers.

[5] On 30 April 2001, the appellant's solicitor wrote to her solicitor seeking a written undertaking from her not to repeat the publication nor to disclose confidential information. On her behalf, her solicitor refused to do so and said

g that his client wished to alert members of the general public to the lack of a concept of 'common law marriage' and that women should be aware of how little rights they have on the breakdown of such a relationship. Her solicitor asserted her right to publish the information. The appellant then learned that she had been in touch with a journalist in the Far East and that she had suggested that she might sell a number of ideas for articles about the appellant. Malice or bad faith

h on the part of the respondent has not however been argued as part of this appeal.

[6] On 3 May the appellant issued an application in the High Court Family Division for injunctions to restrain the respondent from—

j   'in any way disclosing to any person save her legal advisers in these proceedings: (a) the text or a summary of the whole or any part of any affidavit, statement (whether or not sworn) or other document filed or disclosed in any proceedings; (b) the text or a summary of the whole or any part of any oral evidence given by the parties or by any other witness in the … proceedings; (c) the text or a summary of the whole or any part of the judgment delivered by His Honour Judge Krikler on 12 April 2001.'

[7] On a without notice application made on 3 May Connell J granted the *a*
injunctions as requested and the respondent was served the same day. On 10 May
the appellant issued an application to commit the respondent for contempt of
court in respect of the disclosure of information to the Daily Mail and to the
journalist in the Far East. Those proceedings were adjourned pending the hearing
before Munby J and on appeal. After the oral submissions were completed, we
were informed that the contempt proceedings have been withdrawn.   *b*

[8] The judgment of Munby J has been reported ([2001] 2 FCR 577). He set
out the facts (at [3]–[16]) and said (at [6]):

> 'As required by r 3.9(1) of the Family Proceedings Rules 1991 ... the
> proceedings before Judge Krikler were conducted and judgment was given
> in chambers. It is common ground that no application was made for the *c*
> proceedings or any part of them to be heard otherwise than in chambers.
> Equally, it is common ground that at no time was Judge Krikler asked to
> make any special direction as to the confidentiality of the proceedings before
> him, nor did he do so. In short, the proceedings were conducted in precisely
> the same way, and no doubt on the same assumptions by those involved as
> to the implications of the fact that they had been heard in chambers, as *d*
> hundreds of similar cases are heard up and down the land every day, whether
> in the Family Division of the High Court or in county courts exercising
> family jurisdiction.'

[9] He set out the issues (at [18]) as follows:
                                                                          e
> 'Put very shortly—and expressed in somewhat general terms—the question
> which I have to consider can be summarised as follows: when proceedings in
> relation to money or property (as opposed to children) are heard in the
> Family Division in chambers, as they almost invariably are, is it, as the
> respondent would have it, unlawful and a contempt of court for one of the
> parties to make public disclosure of what has gone on in chambers? Or, as *f*
> the applicant would have it, is such disclosure permissible in the absence of
> any lawfully imposed direction of the trial judge to the contrary?'

[10] He said (at [21]):

> 'Anyone with any experience of practice in this Division probably *g*
> approaches the solution to the present problem with a number of more or
> less firmly rooted preconceptions and beliefs. However, and as I recently
> had occasion to point out in a not wholly dissimilar context, such
> assumptions, however inveterate and however distinguished those who
> hold them, can be a less than accurate guide to the true legal position (see *h*
> *Kelly v BBC* [2001] 1 All ER 323 at 337–338, [2001] Fam 59 at 71). Accordingly
> it is best to go back to basics.'

[11] He then, in the remainder of his long and careful judgment, demolished
those preconceptions and held that there was in principle no difference in the
procedures to be adopted in the Family Division of the High Court from the *j*
other two Divisions. The guiding principle was open justice and this applied
across the board. The practice of hearing cases in chambers was largely for
administrative convenience and did not denote privacy or confidentiality of the
proceedings or the documents used in the proceedings. The only derogation
from that position was to be found in the express exceptions set out by the House
of Lords in *Scott v Scott* [1913] AC 417, [1911–13] All ER Rep 1, in the statutory

a exceptions in the Judicial Proceedings (Regulation of Reports) Act 1926 (as amended), the Administration of Justice Act 1960, s 12 and the Contempt of Court Act 1981, s 11.

[12] His conclusion is found at [2001] 2 FCR 577 at [117]–[118]:

b '[117] In my judgment Mr Monson is correct in his submission that no confidentiality attaches to proceedings, or to information conveyed in the course of proceedings, in the Family Division merely because those proceedings take place in chambers. He is correct in his submission that rr 3.9(1), 10.20 and 10.15 do not, either individually or together, create any general obligation of confidence in relation to proceedings in the Family Division heard in chambers. More specifically, having regard to the
c complaint made in the present case, he is correct in his submission that information which is not already inherently confidential does not become confidential merely because it is packaged in an affidavit sworn and filed in the Family Division.

[118] Putting the matter the other way round, in the Family Division, as in the other divisions of the High Court, the starting point has to be the
d principles to be found in *Scott v Scott, Forbes v Smith* ([1998] 1 All ER 973) and *Hodgson's* case (*Hodgson v Imperial Tobacco Ltd* [1998] 2 All ER 673, [1998] 1 WLR 1056). Restrictions on the use that can be made of information deployed in proceedings in the Family Division, and analogous obligations of confidentiality, are to be found, for example, in relation to
e children in s 12(1)(a) of the 1960 Act, in relation to matrimonial and certain other classes of proceedings in s 1(1)(b) of the 1926 Act and generally in relation to material obtained under compulsion in the operation of the implied undertaking. This list is not intended to be exhaustive. But none of these restrictions apply in the present case. Nor does any other restriction to which Mr Moylan has directed my attention.'

f
[13] Munby J then considered further arguments based on the European Convention for the Protection of Human Rights and Fundamental Freedoms 1950 (as set out in Sch 1 to the Human Rights Act 1998) and found the balance of the rights of the parties to be in favour of publication. He accordingly dismissed the application for an injunction and discharged the injunction granted by
g Connell J. The injunction has however been continued pending the outcome of this appeal.

[14] On appeal to this court, in the most interesting and helpful submissions of Mr Moylan QC for the appellant and Mr Price QC for the respondent, three main issues have emerged.

h (A) Are proceedings held in chambers private in the sense that the public can properly be excluded?

(B) The issue on the appeal: in what circumstances are proceedings which are held in private, to be treated as in secret or confidential with the effect that there can be no subsequent publication of the documents, the oral evidence, the
j submissions, the judgment or any of them?

(C) If these proceedings can properly be treated as secret or confidential, and injunctions could therefore be granted, should they be granted in the present appeal to prohibit further publication?

[15] It is necessary, in my judgment, to look at the first issue, (A), since Munby J expressed his conclusions on this issue also, and it is also important to look at it separately from the question of publication since the one may not and,

in certain cases, clearly does not cover the other. The first issue also raises the question whether the 1991 rules may be ultra vires in providing for private hearings, which exclude the public, in non-children cases.

Public or private hearing

[16] The starting point must be the importance of the principle of open justice. This has been a thread to be discerned throughout the common law systems:

> 'Publicity is the very soul of justice. It is the keenest spur to exertion and the surest of all guards against improbity. It keeps the judge himself while trying under trial.' (Bentham)

Consequently, and I respectfully agree with the approach of Munby J, the exclusion of the public from proceedings has objectively to be justified. It is not good enough for it to be said that we have always done it this way so it has to be right. That principle of open justice applies to all courts and in principle the family courts are not excluded from it, although for good reasons which I shall set out later, many family cases, as Mr Price accepted, require confidentiality.

[17] Proceedings in the courts are either held in open court, where the public is entitled to enter and listen or in circumstances in which the public is largely excluded either by rule of court or by practice. This exclusion does not, of itself, have the consequence of a ban on later publication. There was some confusion in argument in this court, as there has been in the past, as to the meaning given to the words 'chambers', 'private', or 'in camera'. I start with the meaning of the word 'chambers'. It is not defined in s 67 of the Supreme Court Act 1981 which states:

> 'Business in the High Court shall be heard and disposed of in court except in so far as it may, under this or any other Act, under rules of court or in accordance with the practice of the court, be dealt with in chambers.'

[18] In the 1997 edition of the *Supreme Court Practice* vol 2, Pt 17, para 5276, 'chambers' was contrasted with 'in court' to mean 'in private, secret, secluded behind closed doors'. That definition was not considered an accurate description by Lord Woolf MR in *Hodgson v Imperial Tobacco Ltd* [1998] 2 All ER 673, [1998] 1 WLR 1056. Jacob J, in *Forbes v Smith* [1998] 1 All ER 973 in the passage I cite below, treated 'in chambers' as the same as 'in private', as I did in *Re P-B (a minor) (child cases: hearing in open court)* [1997] 1 All ER 58 at 61. Jacob J's definition was approved by Lord Woolf MR in *Hodgson's* case and now adopted in CPR 39.2 (see below).

[19] The other phrase in use, in particular, in the Chancery Division, was 'in camera'. This phrase sometimes denoted proceedings which were confidential or secret with the effect that the public were excluded and in respect of which there could be no subsequent publication of information. That situation was recognised by Lord Woolf MR in *Hodgson's* case. The phrase sometimes meant the same as 'in chambers'. The exclusion of the public from the hearing, as such, did not necessarily have the effect of prohibiting later publication of the proceedings. In s 12(3) of the 1960 Act, hearings 'in chambers' and 'in camera' were treated equally: '... references to a court sitting in private include references to a court sitting in camera or in chambers'. That would appear also to be the case in adoption. In s 64 of the Adoption Act 1976 proceedings are held in private: '... proceedings under this Act—(a) in the High Court, may be disposed of in

a chambers; (b) in a county court, shall be heard and determined in camera'. I am driven to recall Humpty Dumpty: 'When *I* use a word—it means just what I choose it to mean—neither more nor less.'

[20] I would therefore suggest that there are three categories of case, those heard in open court, those heard in private and those heard in secret where the information disclosed to the court and the proceedings remain confidential.

b
Civil proceedings held in private

[21] I start with the civil courts, whose procedures in many ways differ from family proceedings, but not entirely. The majority of cases in civil proceedings, whether at High Court or county court level, have been heard in public, whereas interlocutory proceedings have been heard in private, formerly in chambers. The *c* practice of hearing cases in chambers has varied over the years and Munby J set out in his judgment ([2001] 2 FCR 577 at [24]–[25]) a detailed analysis of the procedure in the Queen's Bench and Chancery Divisions. It suffices to quote from the judgment of Jacob J in *Forbes v Smith* [1998] 1 All ER 973 at 974:

d
> 'A chambers hearing is in private, in the sense that members of the public are not given admission as of right to the courtroom. Courts sit in chambers or in open court generally merely as a matter of administrative convenience. For example, in the Chancery Division the normal practice for urgent interlocutory cases is for the matters to be heard in open court, the application being made by way of motion. Corresponding applications in *e* the Queen's Bench Division are normally made in chambers. There is no logic or reason as to why exactly the same sort of case in one Division should be in open court and, in another Division, in chambers. Furthermore, until about ten years ago, appeals in the Chancery Division ... were normally taken in open court. Now they are taken in chambers. The change was the result of an administrative decision, not a change in the law.'

f
While respectfully agreeing with Jacob J with respect to the administrative convenience of hearing civil matters in chambers, in my view the allocation of work to chambers in the family courts has a somewhat different basis.

[22] In *Hodgson's* case Lord Woolf MR set out the then existing procedure in the civil courts and a foretaste of his civil procedure reforms encapsulated in the *g* Civil Procedure Act 1997 and the CPR. He endorsed the passage from the judgment of Jacob J which I set out above. He said ([1998] 2 All ER 673 at 685–686, [1998] 1 WLR 1056 at 1070):

> 'A distinction has to be clearly drawn between the normal situation where a court sits in chambers and when a court sits in camera in the exceptional *h* situations recognised in *Scott v Scott* [1913] AC 417, [1911–13] All ER Rep 1 or the court sits in chambers and the case falls in the categories specified in s 12(1) of the 1960 Act (which include issues involving children, national security, secret processes and the like). Section 12(1) also refers to the court having prohibited publication. Such proceedings are appropriately described *j* as *secret*; proceedings in chambers otherwise are not appropriately so described.'

[23] Lord Woolf MR then described the advantages of hearing cases in chambers and pointed out the surprising absence of authority for what could be repeated in public in respect of what went on in chambers. He continued ([1998] 2 All ER 673 at 686–687, [1998] 1 WLR 1056 at 1071–1072):

'However, it remains a principle of the greatest importance that, unless
there are compelling reasons for doing otherwise, which will not exist in the *a*
generality of cases, there should be public access to hearings in chambers and
information available as to what occurred at such hearings ... In relation to
hearings in chambers the position may be summarised as follows. (1) The
public has no right to attend hearings in chambers because of the nature of
the work transacted in chambers and because of the physical restrictions on *b*
the room available, but if requested, permission should be granted to attend
when and to the extent that this is practical. (2) What happens during the
proceedings in chambers is not confidential or secret and information
about what occurs in chambers and the judgment or order pronounced can,
and in the case of any judgment or order should, be made available to the
public when requested. (3) If members of the public who seek to attend *c*
cannot be accommodated, the judge should consider adjourning the
proceedings in whole or in part into open court to the extent that this is
practical or allowing one or more representatives of the press to attend the
hearing in chambers. (4) To disclose what occurs in chambers does not
constitute a breach of confidence or amount to contempt as long as any *d*
comment which is made does not substantially prejudice the administration
of justice. (5) The position summarised above does not apply to the
exceptional situations identified in s 12(1) of the 1960 Act or where the court,
with the power to do so, orders otherwise.'

[24] The procedure in all civil courts is now regulated by the Civil Procedure *e*
Act 1997, which, by s 2 gave authority to the Civil Procedure Rules Committee,
presided over by the Master of the Rolls, to make rules to be approved by the
Lord Chancellor. The current rules are the CPR. The general rule for hearings
in court is set out in CPR 39.2:

'(1) The general rule is that a hearing is to be in public. *f*

(2) ...

(3) A hearing, or any part of it, may be in private if—(a) publicity would
defeat the object of the hearing; (b) it involves matters relating to national
security; (c) it involves confidential information (including information
relating to personal financial matters) and publicity would damage that *g*
confidentiality; (d) a private hearing is necessary to protect the interests of
any child or patient; (e) it is a hearing of an application made without notice
and it would be unjust to any respondent for there to be a public hearing;
(f) it involves uncontentious matters arising in the administration of trusts or
in the administration of a deceased person's estate; or (g) the court considers *h*
this to be necessary, in the interests of justice.

(4) The court may order that the identity of any party or witness must not
be disclosed if it considers non-disclosure necessary in order to protect the
interests of that party or witness.'

[25] CPR PD 39A states: *j*

'1.3 Rule 39.2(3) sets out the type of proceedings which may be dealt with
in private.

1.4 The decision as to whether to hold a hearing in public or in private
must be made by the judge conducting the hearing having regard to any
representations which may have been made to him.

a   1.4A The judge should also have regard to Article 6 (1) of the European
Convention on Human Rights.
1.5 The hearings set out below shall in the first instance be listed by the
court as hearings in private under rule 39.2(3), namely ...'

[26] The Practice Direction then lists 11 types of hearings which are to be
b heard in private. They include claims for possession, suspending a warrant of
execution or possession, variation of a judgment debt, charging, garnishee,
attachment of earnings, or similar applications, oral examination, application in
relation to an LSC funded client, security for costs in an application under s 726(1)
of the Companies Act 1985, applications by trustees and under the Inheritance
(Provision for Family and Dependants) Act 1975 or the Protection from
c Harassment Act 1997.
[27] Paragraph 1.6 deals with hearings relating to a child or a patient. Paragrah
1.8 states:

'Nothing in this practice direction prevents a judge ordering that a hearing
taking place in public shall continue in private, or vice-versa ...
d   1.9 If the court or judge's room in which the proceedings are taking place
has a sign on the door indicating that the proceedings are private, members
of the public who are not parties to the proceedings will not be admitted
unless the court permits.'

[28] In the civil courts governed by the 1997 Act and the CPR, cases within the
e group set out in CPR 39.2, can be, but do not have to be heard in private, and the
judge or district judge has the power to exclude the public. CPR 39.2 and the
Practice Direction were challenged as ultra vires by way of judicial review in the
Divisional Court in R (on the application of Pelling) v Bow County Court [2001]
UKHRR 165. In his judgment Buxton LJ held that the CPR were intra vires and
f that r 39.2 was facultative. A hearing in private in civil proceedings may mean
more than just administrative convenience and may include a confidential
hearing. The implementation of the CPR has simplified life for all judges and
practitioners in civil proceedings. The same cannot be said of the family
procedures.

g *Scott v Scott*
[29] It is a major plank of the submission advanced by Mr Price on behalf of
the respondent that to hold the present proceedings in private is contrary to the
principles laid down in *Scott v Scott* [1913] AC 417, [1911–13] All ER Rep 1. It is
therefore necessary to look with some care at the background to the facts of that
h case and the approach of the House of Lords. Parliament, by enacting the
Matrimonial Causes Act 1857, terminated the ecclesiastical jurisdiction to deal
with petitions for divorce a mensa et thoro and nullity and the ancillary orders
which would have to be made following such decisions. Judicial separation was
substituted for divorce a mensa et thoro and a new jurisdiction was given to allow
petitions for dissolution of marriage. Ever since 1857 the jurisdiction to deal with
j matrimonial breakdown and its consequences has been regulated by statute and
not by the common law. A major exception to the statutory framework was the
parens patriae jurisdiction in wardship. References to children in the speeches
were to wardship and not to statutory provisions relating to children. At the time
of *Scott v Scott* the relevant legislation was the Matrimonial Causes Acts 1857 to
1907, and the Divorce Rules made thereunder (the relevant Divorce Rules were
those enacted on 26 December 1865, as subsequently added to/amended).

Section 22 of the 1857 Act provided that, in cases other than those involving the
dissolution of marriage, the principles and procedure of the Divorce Court were *a*
to follow so far as possible those which had been followed in the Ecclesiastical
Courts, subject to the provisions of the 1857 Act. Section 46 stated:

> 'Subject to such rules and regulations as may be established as herein
> provided, the witnesses in all proceedings before the court where their *b*
> attendance can be had shall be sworn and examined orally in open Court;
> Provided that parties, except as hereinafter provided, shall be at liberty to
> verify their respective cases in whole or in part by affidavit, but so that the
> deponent in every such affidavit shall, on the application of the opposite
> party or by direction of the Court, be subject to be cross-examined by or on
> behalf of the opposite party orally in open Court, and after such *c*
> cross-examination may be re-examined orally in open Court as aforesaid by
> or on behalf of the party by whom such affidavit was filed.'

[30] The Divorce Rules did little to restrict this general principle of openness.
Some of them provided for the hearing in chambers of specific applications, such *d*
as r 124, which concerned a deserted wife's applications for a protection order
over her post-desertion earnings and property—see *In the matter of Jenny Morris*
[1902] P 104. Others provided for certain hearings to take place by way of
summons (which were heard in the judge's private room—see r 162), such as
applications to stay proceedings for restitution of conjugal rights (r 176)
and applications to vary or rescind a Registrar's order on alimony (r 192). *e*
Rules 40 and 205 dealt explicitly with the mode of trial or hearing in matrimonial
causes, but neither in any way qualified or restricted the general principle set
down by s 46 of the 1857 Act. Therefore, although some of the Divorce Rules
made express provision for the private hearing of certain specified applications,
the majority of matrimonial hearings (including nullity suits) were left to be *f*
governed by the provisions of s 46.

[31] In *Scott v Scott* the petitioner wife sought a declaration of nullity on the
ground of non-consummation of the marriage, due to the impotency of the
respondent husband. Among the directions for the hearing of the petition was
that the cause be heard in camera. The case proceeded undefended and was
heard in private. The President of the Probate, Divorce and Admiralty Division *g*
pronounced a decree nisi. The petitioner obtained an official transcript of
the proceedings and sent copies to members of her husband's family. He
instituted proceedings to commit her, her solicitor and others for contempt of
court for disclosing information about the nullity hearing and sought injunctions
to restrain them from making similar or other communications about the nullity *h*
proceedings. The trial judge found the petitioner and her solicitor to be in
contempt. The Court of Appeal dismissed the appeal as incompetent. It would
appear that there had grown up a practice in the Division of hearing nullity suits
in camera and with this petition the High Court followed the same practice.

[32] The House of Lords had two issues to consider, the propriety of the *j*
hearing of the nullity petition in camera and the power to prohibit subsequent
publication of those proceedings. The House of Lords in their speeches made it
clear that the 1857 Act and the rules made under it, and not the practices of the
Ecclesiastical Courts as they had been believed subsequently to be (see [1913] AC
417 at 470–473, [1911–13] All ER Rep 1 at 27–28 per Lord Shaw of Dunfermline),

a were to be followed in the Probate, Divorce and Admiralty Division. Viscount
Haldane LC said ([1913] AC 417 at 434, [1911–13] All ER Rep 1 at 8):

b 'I think that the effect of s. 46 of the Divorce Act was substantially to put
an end to the old procedure, and to enact that the new Court was to conduct
its business on the general principles as regards publicity which regulated the
other Courts of justice in this country. These general principles are of much
public importance, and I think that the power to make rules, conferred by
ss. 46 and 53, must be treated as given subject to their observance. They lay
down that the administration of justice must so far as the trial of the case is
concerned, with certain narrowly defined exceptions to which I will refer
later on, be conducted in open Court. I think that s. 46 lays down this principle

c generally, and that s. 22 is, so far as publicity of hearing is concerned, to be read
as making no exception in any class of suit or proceeding save in so far as
ordinary Courts of justice might have power to make it.'

[33] He said ([1913] AC 417 at 435–436, [1911–13] All ER Rep 1 at 8–9):

d 'Whatever may have been the power of the Ecclesiastical Courts, the
power of an ordinary Court of justice to hear in private cannot rest merely
on the discretion of the judge or on his individual view that it is desirable for
the sake of public decency or morality that the hearing should take place in
private. If there is to be any exception to the broad principle which requires
the administration of justice to take place in open Court, that exception must

e be based on the application of some other and overriding principle which
defines the field of exception and does not leave its limits to the individual
discretion of the judge ... In proceedings, however, which, like those in the
Matrimonial Court, affect status, the public has a general interest which the
parties cannot exclude ...'

f [34] He set out as exceptions, the cases of wards and lunatics in which the
court exercised it paternal jurisdiction. He said ([1913] AC 417 at 437, [1911–13]
All ER Rep 1 at 9):

'While the broad principle is that the Courts of this country must, as
between parties, administer justice in public, this principle is subject to

g apparent exceptions, such as those to which I have referred. But the
exceptions are themselves the outcome of a yet more fundamental principle
that the chief object of Courts of justice must be to secure that justice is done
... It may often be necessary, in order to attain its primary object, that the
Court should exclude the public. The broad principle which ordinarily
governs it therefore yields to the paramount duty, which is the care of the

h ward or the lunatic.'

[35] He referred to the other case, of litigation as to a secret process—

'where the effect of publicity would be to destroy the subject-matter,
[which] illustrates a class which stands on a different footing. There it may

j well be that justice could not be done at all if it had to be done in public. As
the paramount object must always be to do justice, the general rule as to
publicity, after all only the means to an end, must accordingly yield.' (See
[1913] AC 417 at 437–438, [1911–13] All ER Rep 1 at 9.)

[36] He said ([1913] AC 417 at 439, [1911–13] All ER Rep 1 at 10):

'A mere desire to consider feelings of delicacy or to exclude from publicity details which it would be desirable not to publish is not, I repeat, enough as the law now stands. I think that to justify an order for hearing in camera it must be shewn that the paramount object of securing that justice is done would really be rendered doubtful of attainment if the order were not made. Whether this state of the law is satisfactory is a question not for a Court of justice but for the Legislature.'

[37] In due course Parliament passed the Judicial Proceedings (Regulation of Reports) Act 1926, later amended by the Domestic and Appellate Proceedings (Restriction of Publicity) Act 1968 which prohibited reporting by the press, inter alia, of the evidence in cases of divorce, nullity, judicial separation and restitution of conjugal rights, although the hearings remained in open court.

[38] The other members of the court gave similar judgments underlining the clear principles of open justice. Earl Loreburn said ([1913] AC 417 at 445, [1911–13] All ER Rep 1 at 13):

'The inveterate rule is that justice shall be administered in open Court. I do not speak of the parental jurisdiction regarding lunatics or wards of Court, or of what may be done in chambers, which is a distinct and by no means short subject, or of special statutory restrictions. I speak of the trial of actions including petitions for divorce or nullity in the High Court.'

[39] He set out the same exceptions as Viscount Haldane LC but included circumstances in which the court might be cleared or closed if such a precaution was necessary for the administration of justice. He said ([1913] AC 417 at 446, [1911–13] All ER Rep 1 at 14):

'It would be impossible to enumerate or anticipate all possible contingencies, but in all cases where the public has been excluded with admitted propriety the underlying principle, as it seems to me, is that the administration of justice would be rendered impracticable by their presence, whether because the case could not be effectively tried, or the parties entitled to justice would be reasonably deterred from seeking it at the hands of the Court.'

[40] He recognised that rules might be framed to regulate hearings otherwise than in court which would be valid if they did not go beyond the limitations he indicated. He pointed out that no such rules had been made.

[41] Lord Shaw of Dunfermline was of the opinion that the order to hear the nullity suit in camera and to suppress thereafter all reports of what happened at the trial was beyond the power of the judge to pronounce. He said ([1913] AC 417 at 476, [1911–13] All ER Rep 1 at 29–30):

'... they appear to me to constitute a violation of that publicity in the administration of justice which is one of the surest guarantees of our liberties, and an attack upon the very foundations of public and private security.'

[42] This clear reminder of the requirement for open justice in the hearing of actions not only set out the common law principles underlying the procedures in court but also reflected the statutory requirements in s 46. It is clear that judges cannot decide arbitrarily whether a case should be heard in public or in private or that the entire proceedings should or should not remain secret. The general

a principles stated in *Scott v Scott* cannot, however, be treated as a fetter upon the power of Parliament to change the law as it did in the 1926 Act (see above) and, indeed, as it did in the Matrimonial Causes Act 1950, s 32(4) which required evidence of sexual capacity in the course of nullity proceedings to be heard in camera (subject to the judge's discretion to hear it in open court where the interests of justice so required). Nor can the decision in *Scott v Scott* be taken in
b any way to prevent or restrict the enactment of rules for regulating the trial of family cases.

Current procedures in family proceedings

[43] I turn now to the current procedures in family cases. With the exception of wardship and certain declarations in medical cases heard in the High Court, the
c jurisdiction of the High Court Family Division and of the county courts with family jurisdiction, whether public or private, remains based on statute and regulated by the statutory framework. The hearing of cases is divided into those which are heard in open court and those heard in chambers. The way in which those cases are heard is regulated by rules and not by custom. In all cases, except
d adoption which has its separate Adoption Rules 1984, SI 1984/265, the Family Proceedings Rules 1991, SI 1991/1247, direct the court and the parties to the procedure to be adopted and the way in which each case is to be heard. The 1991 rules, as subordinate legislation, depend for their legitimacy upon the Matrimonial and Family Proceedings Act 1984. Section 40 of the 1984 Act provides that the
e power to make rules of court for the purposes of family proceedings shall be exercisable by the Lord Chancellor, together with four or more of a group of people including the President of the Family Division. Section 40(3A) was inserted by, and s 40(4) was amended by, the Civil Procedure Act 1997. Subsection (3A) states:

f   'Rules made under this section may make different provision for different cases or different areas, including different provision—(a) for a specific court; or (b) for specific proceedings, or a specific jurisdiction, specified in the rules.'

Subsection (4): 'Rules made under this section may ... (a) modify or exclude the application of any provision of the County Court Act 1984; and (b) ...'
g [44] The 1991 rules have been amended from time to time, most recently in 1999. Where the 1991 rules provide for the procedure to be adopted in the High Court or in the relevant county court, they are to be followed. The 1991 rules have not yet been revised to take account of the CPR introduced in 1999. Where the 1991 rules do not cover the situation before the court, recourse still has to be
h had to the relevant Rules of the Supreme Court, (otherwise superseded by the CPR). The statutory basis of the jurisdiction in family cases is of great importance in the light of the submissions made to Munby J and to this court.

[45] The arrangement of the 1991 rules is in ten Parts. Part II covers matrimonial proceedings which subdivide into the petition, the pleadings, preparation for trial
j etc and ancillary relief. Under Pt II, the directions and interlocutory proceedings and ancillary relief applications are heard in chambers but the substantive hearing of the petition, including a nullity petition, is in open court (see r 2.32). As in 1857 and in 1913, oral evidence in divorce, nullity and judicial petitions is heard in open court and cannot be heard in secret (save that nowadays, evidence of sexual capacity in nullity proceedings is normally heard in camera—see s 48(2) of the Matrimonial Causes Act 1973). One has to remember, however, that in

uncontested divorce petitions, the major part of the procedure is dealt with on paper by the district judge, but the decree nisi is pronounced in public.

[46] The procedure for hearing ancillary relief applications, during the continuance of the main proceedings and after the grant of a decree nisi or absolute, is regulated by r 2.66(2) which provides: 'The hearing or consideration shall, unless the court otherwise directs, take place in chambers.' Applications for ancillary relief are almost invariably heard in chambers.

[47] Part IV of the 1991 rules deals with children applications under the Children Act 1989. There is no disagreement that children applications fall to be determined in private. Confidentiality in wardship cases was specifically recognised in *Scott v Scott,* and s 12(1)(a) of the Administration of Justice Act 1960 treated children cases as an exception to the general rule of publication of court proceedings; see below. The procedure in children cases is set out in careful detail in the 1991 rules and the confidentiality of all aspects of the proceedings, the evidence of the parties, the reports filed, and the documents disclosed is specifically provided for in r 4.23, headed 'Confidentiality of documents'. Rule 4.16 deals with the hearing: '(7) Unless the court otherwise directs, a hearing of, or directions appointment in, proceedings to which this Part applies shall be in chambers.'

[48] The public is almost always excluded from children proceedings which almost invariably remain confidential, subject to judgments, made suitably anonymous in cases of wider interest, being given in public or made available for publication.

[49] Part IV of the Family Law Act 1996, with which we are concerned in this appeal, is to be found among non-matrimonial proceedings under Pt III. This Part of the 1991 rules includes a variety of other applications, including maintenance agreements and other financial relief applications, the Married Women's Property Act 1882, s 17, declarations of legitimacy or as to marital status, or consents to marriage of a minor. Some of those applications are heard in open court. Others, for instance, those that are analogous to ancillary relief applications, are heard in chambers, see for instance an application in case of failure to provide reasonable maintenance, r 3.1(10). By r 3.9(1):

'An application for an occupation order or a non-molestation order under Part IV of the Family Law Act 1996 shall be dealt with in chambers unless the court otherwise directs.'

This subrule is similar in its terms to the other proceedings heard in chambers under the 1991 rules.

Conclusion on family proceedings heard in private

[50] Parliament has provided for rules to be made to regulate the statutory framework of the family justice system. The 1991 rules are properly based upon the 1984 Act. In those rules the court has the power to exclude the public in family proceedings. For my part, I can see no problem in the application of this procedure under the 1991 rules, designed as it is to provide a measure of privacy, not necessarily confidentiality, to family proceedings. The CPR give a similar degree of privacy to groups of civil cases. There remains also the power to allow the public in if the judge or district judge directs. This discretion is similar to that set out by Buxton LJ in *R (on the application of Pelling) v Bow County Court,* see above. In the 1984 Act the authority to make the 1991 rules was provided by s 40. There is no statutory prohibition against providing for hearings in chambers in

a the family cases; on the contrary, there is a statutory basis for the rules. Section 12 of the 1960 Act (see below) does not concern itself with the legitimacy of hearings in private but with the publication of information from those proceedings. In my judgment, Munby J's judgment was expressed in too broad terms in stating that family proceedings could not, with the exception of children cases, be heard in private. The 1991 rules are not ultra vires any Act of Parliament
b and there is no objection to family courts hearing cases in private and excluding the public where the 1991 rules permit them to do so.

ISSUE (B)

Publication of information relating to proceedings

c   [51] As I have already said above, the hearing of a case in private does not, of itself, prohibit the publication of information about the proceedings or given in the proceedings. The general rule is that it is not a contempt of court to report what has happened at a hearing in chambers; see *Scott v Scott* [1913] AC 417 at 444, 484, [1911–13] All ER Rep 1 at 13, 34 per Earl Loreburn and Lord Shaw respectively.
d The principle of open justice is to be derogated from only to the extent that it is strictly necessary to do so and applies equally to publication of information. In *A-G v Leveller Magazine Ltd* [1979] AC 440 at 465, [1979] 1 All ER 745 at 761, Lord Edmund-Davies said:

e   'And what appears certain is that at common law the fact that a court sat wholly or partly in camera (and even where in such circumstances the court gave a direction prohibiting publication of information relating to what had been said or done behind closed doors) did not of itself and in every case necessarily mean that publication thereafter constituted contempt of court. For that to arise something more than disobedience of the court's direction needs to be established. That something more is that the publication must
f   be of such a nature as to threaten the administration of justice either in the particular case in relation to which the prohibition was pronounced or in relation to cases which may be brought in the future.'

      [52], [53] Section 12 of the 1960 Act sets out the circumstances in which it shall
g be a contempt of court to publish information given in private proceedings. Section 12 states:

        '(1) The publication of information relating to proceedings before any court sitting in private shall not of itself be a contempt of court except in the following cases, that is to say—(a) where the proceedings—(i) relate to the
h   exercise of the inherent jurisdiction of the High Court with respect to minors; (ii) are brought under the Children Act 1989; or (iii) otherwise relate wholly or mainly to the maintenance or upbringing of a minor; (b) where the proceedings are brought under Part VIII of the Mental Health Act 1959, or under any provision of that Act authorising an application or reference to be
j   made to a Mental Health Review Tribunal or to a county court; (c) where the court sits in private for reasons of national security during that part of the proceedings about which the information in question is published; (d) where the information relates to a secret process, discovery or invention which is in issue in the proceedings; (e) where the court (having power to do so) expressly prohibits the publication of all information relating to the proceedings or of information of the description which is published.

(2) Without prejudice to the foregoing subsection, the publication of the
text or a summary of the whole or part of an order made by a court sitting in   *a*
private shall not of itself be contempt of court except where the court
(having the power to do so) expressly prohibits the publication.

(3) In this section references to a court include references to a judge and
to a tribunal and to any person exercising the functions of a court, a judge or
tribunal; and references to a court sitting in private include references to a   *b*
court sitting in camera or in chambers.

(4) Nothing in this section shall be construed as implying that any
publication is punishable as contempt of court which would not be so
punishable apart from this section.'

[54] The exceptions set out in s 12 are not however exhaustive. Lord Woolf MR   *c*
recognised in *Hodgson v Imperial Tobacco Ltd* [1998] 2 All ER 673 at 687, [1998] 1
WLR 1056 at 1072 that—

'To disclose what occurs in chambers does not constitute a breach of
confidence or amount to contempt as long as any comment which is made
does not substantially prejudice the administration of justice.'   *d*

There are situations outside the exceptions in s 12 which have been long
recognised as requiring confidentiality. They are based upon the potential
prejudice to the proper administration of justice. The best-known example is the
implied undertaking in the compulsory disclosure of documents in proceedings.
The importance of the implied undertaking has been accepted in decisions of the   *e*
House of Lords and Court of Appeal.

[55] In *Riddick v Thames Board Mills Ltd* [1977] 3 All ER 677, [1977] QB 881 this
court held that a party who disclosed a document on discovery was entitled to the
protection of the court against any use of it otherwise than in the action in which
it was disclosed. In that case the proceedings by a dismissed employee had been   *f*
settled. A memorandum setting out the facts of the dismissal was disclosed in
those proceedings. The employee subsequently brought an action in defamation
based upon the memorandum. Lord Denning MR said ([1977] 3 All ER 677 at
687–688, [1977] QB 881 at 896):

'The memorandum was obtained by compulsion. Compulsion is an   *g*
invasion of a private right to keep one's documents to oneself. The public
interest in privacy and confidence demands that this compulsion should not
be pressed further than the course of justice requires ... In order to
encourage openness and fairness, the public interest requires that documents
disclosed on discovery are not to be made use of except for the purposes of   *h*
the action in which they are disclosed. They are not to be made a ground for
comments in the newspapers, nor for bringing a libel action, or for any other
alien purpose.'

He then referred to Bray *The Principles and Practice of Discovery* (1885) and
continued: *j*

'Since that time such an undertaking has always been implied ... A party
who seeks discovery of documents gets it on condition that he will make use
of them only for the purposes of that action, and no other purpose.'

[56] Stephenson LJ said ([1977] 3 All ER 677 at 694–695, [1977] QB 881 at 902):

a   '... in my judgment the court has and should generally use the power to protect parties who make full and frank disclosure of documents, and the public interest in such disclosure, by discouraging the use by a plaintiff in a later action of a document obtained on discovery in an earlier action. If the court can require an undertaking from a plaintiff not to misuse a document before it is produced to him, it should have the power to restrain him from
b   misusing it after it has been produced.'

[57] In *Home Office v Harman* [1982] 1 All ER 532, [1983] 1 AC 280 the House of Lords, by a majority, held that a solicitor who had obtained copies of documents disclosed on discovery by the other party to the litigation, gave an implied undertaking to the court not to use the copies, nor allow them to be used for any
c   purpose other than the proper conduct of the action on behalf of his client; that the fact that they had been read out in open court at the hearing of the action, whether admitted in evidence or not, did not bring that implied undertaking to an end and that breach of the undertaking was a civil contempt.

[58] Lord Keith of Kinkel said ([1982] 1 All ER 532 at 540–541, [1983] 1 AC 280
d   at 308):

'Discovery constitutes a very serious invasion of the privacy and confidentiality of a litigant's affairs. It forms part of English legal procedure because the public interest in securing that justice is done between parties is considered to outweigh the private and public interest in the maintenance of
e   confidentiality. But the process should not be allowed to place upon the litigant any harsher or more oppressive burden than is strictly required for the purpose of securing that justice is done ... The implied obligation not to make improper use of discovered documents is, however, independent of any obligation under the general law relating to confidentiality. It affords a particular protection accorded in the interests of the proper administration
f   of justice. It is owed not to the owner of the documents but to the court, and the function of the court in seeing that the obligation is observed is directed to the maintenance of those interests, and not to the enforcement of the law relating to confidentiality.'

[59] In *Crest Homes plc v Marks* [1987] 2 All ER 1074, [1987] AC 829 the House
g   of Lords again considered the issue of use of material disclosed on discovery, this time by way of an Anton Piller order. Lord Oliver of Aylmerton said ([1987] 2 All ER 1074 at 1078, [1987] AC 829 at 854):

'... the implied undertaking applies not merely to the documents discovered themselves but also to information derived from those
h   documents whether it be embodied in a copy or stored in the mind.'

[60] In *Taylor v Director of Serious Fraud Office* [1998] 4 All ER 801, [1999] 2 AC 177 the House of Lords held that, in order to ensure that the privacy and confidentiality of those who made, and those who were mentioned in, statements contained in unused material which had come into existence as a result of
j   criminal investigation were not invaded more than was absolutely necessary for the purposes of justice, compliance by the prosecution with its obligation to disclose all such material to the defence generated an implied undertaking not to use the material for any purpose other than the conduct of the defence. Consequently the plaintiff was not able to use that material in his action for defamation. Lord Hoffmann ([1998] 4 All ER 801 at 808, [1999] 2 AC 177 at 208)

repeated the requirement of public policy in securing the proper administration of justice. He said:

> 'In the case of information which has not been made public ... the fact that publication may have been foreseeable as a possibility at the time when the documents were written does not mean that privacy and confidentiality should not be preserved so far as it is possible to do so. It is equally foreseeable that documents disclosed in civil discovery will be published in open court but that does not mean that there is no point in the court retaining control over the use of documents which have not been published or even, for some purposes, over those which have.' (See [1998] 4 All ER 801 at 810, [1999] 2 AC 177 at 210.)

[61] In *Bourns Inc v Raychem Corp* [1999] 3 All ER 154 an attempt was made to use documents disclosed for the purposes of taxation of costs for a collateral purpose. An implied undertaking was held to arise to use those documents only for the purposes of those proceedings. In that case there was no order for discovery but the court held that, if the documents had not been provided by voluntary disclosure, an order for production would have been necessary. Aldous LJ said (at 162): 'It is also necessary for the proper administration of justice that parties should co-operate, in so far as they can, thereby avoiding repeated applications to the court.'

[62] Although that case depended to a large extent upon the special requirements in connection with taxation of costs, the co-operation referred to by Aldous LJ is of general application.

[63] There are, of course, limits to the ambit of the protection of confidentiality of documents disclosed in litigation. Browne-Wilkinson V-C in *Derby & Co Ltd v Weldon* (1988) Times, 20 October rejected the submission that there was a general implied obligation not to disclose documents prior to use in court. His judgment was analysed in detail by Hobhouse J in *Prudential Assurance Co Ltd v Fountain Page Ltd* [1991] 3 All ER 878, [1991] 1 WLR 756. Hobhouse J said:

> '... it is clear that there is no blanket restriction on the use of documents and information acquired in the course of litigation. Prima facie there is no restriction. The *compulsion* exception is confined to documents and information which a party is compelled, without any choice, to disclose. Where a party has a right to choose the extent to which he will adduce evidence or deploy other material, then there is no compulsion even though a consequence of such choice is that he will have to disclose material to other parties.' (See [1991] 3 All ER 878 at 891, [1991] 1 WLR 756 at 769.)

[64] In *GIO Personal Investment Services Ltd v Liverpool and London Steamship Protection and Indemnity Association Ltd (FAI General Insurance Co Ltd intervening)* [1999] 1 WLR 984 there was an application to allow a non-party to inspect written submissions and documents required for parallel litigation. Potter LJ referred (at 990–991) to RSC Ord 38, r 2A and said:

> 'Thus, on the one hand, service of a witness statements under the rule does not operate to waive the confidentiality of the statement or documents to which it refers until the statement has been put in evidence at the trial. On the other hand, once it is put in evidence, the confidentiality is lost and, in principle, the witness statement is available to the public for inspection and copying, subject only to the procedures ...'

a [65] In *SmithKline Beecham Biologicals SA v Connaught Laboratories Inc* [1999] 4 All ER 498 the Court of Appeal applied with approval the decision in the *Prudential Assurance* case. This was a patent action in which the court had to consider the changing forensic practice whereby counsel no longer read out all the relevant documents and much of the argument was provided in written skeleton arguments read by the judge prior to the hearing of the case. This court *b* held that the documents in dispute had been read by the judge and referred to in open court and therefore came within the provisions of RSC Ord 24, r 14A. It is to be observed that in the above cases, each of them was heard or to be heard in open court where oral evidence was likely to be given and/or the documents and skeleton arguments referred to.

[66] Both in civil and in family proceedings the court controls the use of *c* documents during the proceedings and in certain instances after the end of the proceedings. So, for example, by virtue of CPR 5.4(2)(c) the court must give permission for a non-party to search for, inspect and take a copy of any court document other than a claim form which has been served or a judgment or order given or made in public (similar, though not identical, provisions are contained *d* in the 1991 rules, r 10.20(3)). Similarly, CPR 31.22(2) empowers the court to restrict or prohibit the use of documents disclosed in proceedings, even if they have been read to or by the court, or referred to, at a public hearing. It would appear, although we have not heard argument on the point, that r 39.2 is wider than s 12 and that the exceptions set out in r 39.2(3) may be treated as heard in secret and the information about them may not be made public without the *e* permission of the court. I do not however consider that is necessarily the position with regard to cases heard in private in chambers under the 1991 rules.

Confidentiality of documents in the Family Division

[67] The approach of the courts to applications in family proceedings is to *f* some extent inquisitorial, even in non-children cases. The court is enjoined to have regard to all the circumstances in ancillary relief applications and in applications under s 36 of the 1996 Act; see below. In ancillary relief cases, the requirement of full and frank disclosure and that the parties to a claim for adjustment of their financial positions after divorce are obliged to provide information, places a considerable degree of compulsion upon both parties; see *g* *Jenkins v Livesey (formerly Jenkins)* [1985] 1 All ER 106, [1985] 1 AC 424, the 1991 rules, r 2.61B; Form E.

[68] In several first instance judgments the issue has arisen in attempts to use for collateral purposes documents disclosed in family financial proceedings. In *Medway v Doublelock Ltd* [1978] 1 All ER 1261, [1978] 1 WLR 710 the plaintiff had *h* sworn affidavits in ancillary relief proceedings in the Family Division pursuant to a court order. In Ord 14 proceedings in the Chancery Division, the defendant company sought to make use of the affidavits in an application for security for costs. The defendant company argued that the implied undertaking applicable to discovery of documents did not apply to disclosures made by the plaintiff in his *j* affidavits of means. Goulding J said that the principle of the implied undertaking—

'rests on a wider ground, namely that public interest requires that a party, compelled by process of law to make what may be damaging disclosures for the purpose of a particular suit, should not thereby be at risk of their use for other purposes. It is a strong thing, though necessary for matrimonial litigation, to make a man disclose all the details of his means.' (See [1978] 1 All ER 1261 at 1264, [1978] 1 WLR 710 at 713.)

[69] He referred to the practice of the Family Division in hearing ancillary relief applications in chambers and the effect of r 130 of the Matrimonial Causes Rules 1977, SI 1977/344 (now the 1991 rules, r 10.20) that documents filed with the court were not open for inspection without leave nor could a copy be taken without leave. Affidavit evidence was treated to a considerable extent as confidential. He then considered the balance of public interest and said:

'... in the present case it is necessary to weigh against one another not two competing interests, public or private, but two applications of the same public interest in different sets of proceedings.' (See [1978] 1 All ER 1261 at 1265, [1978] 1 WLR 710 at 714.)

He decided that the confidentiality afforded to disclosure of means made by a party under compulsion in matrimonial proceedings was a matter of great public importance which weighed more heavily than the giving of security for costs and refused the application.

[70] In *S v S (disclosure to Revenue)* [1997] 1 WLR 1621 Wilson J gave a written judgment in chambers in an application for ancillary relief. The wife's brother sent an official transcript of the judgment to the Inland Revenue, who sought leave from the judge, under r 10.15(6) of the 1991 rules, to keep the transcript and obtain a transcript of the oral evidence, and, under r 10.20(3) to inspect the documents in order to investigate the husband's tax position. Wilson J weighed the public interest of due payment of tax and punishment of tax evaders against the public interest in parties in ancillary relief applications making full and frank disclosure of their resources. He refused the application. In 1998 Wilson J heard a similar application where the Inland Revenue had received a copy of the transcript of a judgment delivered by him in chambers in ancillary relief proceedings, in *R v R (disclosure to Revenue)* [1998] 1 FCR 597. In that case upon receipt of the judgment the Inland Revenue made assessments based upon the husband's undisclosed income. The judge held that the disclosure of the judgment given in chambers without leave of the court was irregular. He applied the same principles as set out in *S v S* above but on the facts in *R v R* gave leave to the Inland Revenue to retain the transcript of his judgment.

[71] Charles J in *A v A, B v B* [2000] 1 FCR 577 heard together the ancillary relief applications by two wives whose husbands were in business together. Consent orders were made after it became clear that both husbands admitted attempting to hide the true extent of their assets. Charles J indicated his intention of disclosing the papers to the Inland Revenue and to the DPP and others. He gave a judgment setting out the appropriate response by the court to revelations of tax evasion or other tax impropriety. He referred to the duty on the parties to provide full and frank disclosure and cited *Jenkins v Livesey* and pointed out that parties do not have a choice as to what information they provide relating to their means and other relevant information. He said that such information, whether provided by affidavit, or in answer to questions (before or after orders of the court), was provided under compulsion for the purposes of the application.

[72] In each of the above cases, the obligation on the parties to make full and frank disclosure in their financial disputes was of such importance that it was in the public interest to preserve confidentiality of that information by means of the implied undertaking. In order to achieve compliance with disclosure by the party under the obligation to do so, the party seeking the disclosure is required by the court only to use that information for the purposes of the proceedings. It is the protection provided by the court in cases of compulsion. Ancillary relief

applications are appropriately heard in private in accordance with the 1991 rules, see above. The public may not, without leave of the court, hear the evidence given in these applications. It would make a nonsense of the use of an implied undertaking if information about the means of a party, in some cases sensitive information, could be made public as soon as the substantive hearing commenced. Information disclosed under the compulsion of ancillary relief proceedings is, in my judgment, protected by the implied undertaking, before, during and after the proceedings are completed. Munby J, in his judgment, did not suggest to the contrary. He also pointed out that the 1926 Act (as amended in 1968) protects ancillary relief proceedings from press publication. This may be the case but we heard no argument on it.

[73] The implied undertaking extends, as the cases to which I have referred above show, to voluntary disclosure in ancillary relief proceedings, to the information contained in the documents and to affidavits and statements of truth and witness statements. All such information is required for the full and frank exchange of financial information and all the relevant circumstances which may be necessary to enable the court to know, in order to come to a fair conclusion in accordance with the exercise of its statutory jurisdiction. In my judgment, the obligation to respect the implied undertaking will also be imposed by the court in cases analogous to ancillary relief and found in Pt III of the 1991 rules (see for instance applications in cases of failure to provide reasonable maintenance or application to alter maintenance agreements, rr 3.1, 3.5).

[74] Protection is given by the 1991 rules to information filed during the proceedings and the requirement for permission for such information or for the judgment to be provided to third parties; see, for instance, rr 10.15, 10.20. Confidentiality with regard to documents in children proceedings is in wider terms in r 4.23 than r 10.20(3). None of these rules, is, however in my view, relevant to whether or not confidentiality continues between the parties after the case heard in private is over.

Cases under Pt IV of the 1996 Act

[75] In the types of proceedings covered by the 1991 rules, information about children cases is indisputably covered by privacy and secrecy and no information can be disclosed after the end of the case without the leave of the court. For the reasons set out above, I am satisfied that all cases involving issues of ancillary relief are also protected from publication by anyone without the leave of the court. There are however other family proceedings, of which the present appeal is an example, which are not, in my judgment, automatically covered by secrecy, although they can be heard in private. Whether they are so protected, will depend upon the type of proceedings and whether they come within, or part of the information comes within, the ambit of s 12 or whether the administration of justice will otherwise be impeded or prejudiced by publication.

[76] Section 36 of the 1996 Act provides a mechanism for a non-married partner to claim against the other partner for an order entitling him/her to the occupation of a dwelling-house in certain circumstances. It is analogous to applications between spouses also found in Pt IV. Section 36(6) sets out the checklist to be applied by the court:

'(6) In deciding whether to make an order under this section containing provision of the kind mentioned in subsection (3) or (4) and (if so) in what manner, the court shall have regard to all the circumstances including—(a) the housing needs and housing resources of each of the parties and of any relevant child; (b) the financial resources of each of the parties; (c) the likely effect of any order, or of any decision by the court not to exercise its powers under subsection (3) or (4), on the health, safety or well-being of the parties and of any relevant child; (d) the conduct of the parties in relation to each other and otherwise; (e) the nature of the parties' relationship; (f) the length of time during which they have lived together as husband and wife; (g) whether there are or have been any children who are children of both parties or for whom both parties have or have had parental responsibility; (h) the length of time that has elapsed since the parties ceased to live together; and (i) the existence of any pending proceedings between the parties (i) for an order under paragraph 1(2)(d) or (e) of Schedule 1 to the Children Act 1989 (orders for financial relief against parents); or (ii) relating to the legal or beneficial ownership of the dwelling-house.'

Further relevant considerations are to be found in s 36(7) and (8).

[77] Mr Moylan submitted that the requirement for the court in s 36(6) to have regard to all the circumstances had the effect of extending the concept of confidentiality imposed by the court on all documents and information provided in applications under Pt IV of the 1996 Act. I agree with Munby J that that submission goes too far. It does not, in my view, follow that a hearing of a s 36 application which is in private, even one which is to some extent inquisitorial with the requirement that 'the court shall have regard to all the circumstances', is to remain for ever entirely confidential. Part IV applications do not necessarily come within s 12 nor is the element of compulsion, thereby triggering an implied undertaking, always present. In my judgment the court must look at the application before it and come to a conclusion whether that application falls within the ambit of s 12 or within the recognised categories of cases, those of children and ancillary relief issues, or whether there are other factors as a result of which, if the proceedings are not treated as secret, there will be prejudice to the administration of justice. Family proceedings are not and should not be seen to be in a separate category from other civil proceedings, other than in recognised classes of cases or in other situations which can be shown manifestly to require permanent confidentiality.

[78] Parliament in the Contempt of Court Act 1981 has provided by s 11 exemption from disclosure in court:

'In any case where a court (having power to do so) allows a name or other matter to be withheld from the public in proceedings before the court, the court may give such directions prohibiting the publication of that name or matter in connection with the proceedings as appear to the court to be necessary for the purpose for which it was so withheld.'

[79] This section gives statutory protection for non-disclosure of information which should remain secret, where, and only where, a court has the power to do so. This requirement takes the court back to the general principles and the recognised exceptions to them. It has not been the practice of the family courts in the past to apply this section, but there may be cases, as possibly the present appeal might have been, for the court hearing the case in private to decide whether any or even all the information should not be disclosed. It cannot properly be a blanket protection of non-publication in all cases heard in private in chambers under the 1991 rules. It can however apply not only to the actual case before the court but also to groups of cases arising out of the same type of

a circumstances; see Lord Edmund-Davies in *A-G v Leveller Magazine Ltd* [1979] 1 All ER 745, [1979] AC 440. Rule 3.9 of the 1991 rules has no requirement to file evidence, unless the court requires it and makes an order. I would suggest, however, that in applications for occupation orders where there are children, the welfare of those children is likely to be a major issue or often the major issue. Consequently the s 12 exemption would be likely to apply. If the financial affairs b of any of the parties have to be investigated, and bearing in mind the requirement that the court shall have regard to all the circumstances, that information, if required or likely to be required by the court, would probably be protected. The general principles of discovery would apply. It will however require the parties and the court to consider in each case whether the proper working of the administration of justice requires there to be continuing confidentiality after the c end of the proceedings. That is, in my view, no bad thing.

[80] Before the speeches in *Scott v Scott* set out in ringing tones the crucial importance of open justice it had already been a corner stone of the common law. The statutory framework, providing the procedures in civil and family cases, recognises the necessity to hold some proceedings in private and that there d should be protection against publication of some of those proceedings. Such protection must be proportionate to the requirements of the administration of justice. It might be thought to be inconvenient and time-consuming to have to look at this problem in individual cases heard in private. There are groups of cases in which the answer is obvious and, in my view, there will only be a small number of cases, in particular under Pt IV, where the advocates and the court e may have to consider the point.

The European Convention for Human Rights

[81] In my judgment there is nothing in art 6 of the convention which requires all cases, willy nilly, to be heard in open court. To hear them in private and to f debar publication of the proceedings heard in private must be necessary in a democratic society and proportionate to that necessity. The European Court recognised in *B v UK* [2001] 2 FCR 221 that the art 6 requirement to hold a public hearing was subject to exceptions. The court said (at 233 (para 37)):

g '... the requirement to hold a public hearing is subject to exceptions. This is apparent from the text of art 6(1) itself, which contains the proviso that: "the press and public may be excluded from all or part of the trial ... where the interests of juveniles or the private life of the parties so require, or to the extent strictly necessary in the opinion of the court in special circumstances where publicity would prejudice the interests of justice." Moreover, it is established in the Court's case-law that, even in a criminal law context where h there is a high expectation of publicity, it may on occasion be necessary under art 6 to limit the open and public nature of proceedings in order, for example, to protect the safety or privacy of witnesses or to promote the free exchange of information and opinion in the pursuit of justice ...'

j The Human Rights Act 1998 and the European jurisprudence underline our own long-established principles of open justice which are entirely in conformity with the convention and which our exceptions do not, in my judgment, breach.

[82] The other argument raised both on appeal and below is the balancing exercise between the right to respect for family life and privacy in art 8 and the right to freedom of expression in art 10. It is widely recognised in European jurisprudence that the balance in children cases is in favour of confidentiality; see *B v UK*. The principles underlying the recognition of implied undertakings do not

appear to me to breach the requirements of art 10. I agree however with the
analysis by Munby J ([2001] 2 FCR 577 at [151]–[153]). Both in our domestic law *a*
and in compliance with the convention, there cannot be a blanket approach. The
balance between art 8 and art 10 was, in my judgment, correctly struck by
Munby J.

[83] In the present appeal, the court has no information at all about the
evidence which was adduced at the hearing in the county court, other than that *b*
reported in the newspapers. There is a blanket objection by the appellant to
publication, based on the general premise that the case was heard in chambers
and consequently must remain secret. On the information available to this court
and to Munby J it was an issue of jurisdiction. How that issue could require six
lever arch files of evidence is baffling, but it is not my business to speculate. This
appeal has to be decided on what the court knows. Applying the principles which *c*
I have set out above, I can see no ground upon which, on the present facts, there
cannot be publication of the proceedings. Although I consider, for the reasons set
out above that he has expressed his general propositions too widely, I agree with
the conclusions of Munby J on the facts of the appeal.

d

ISSUE (C)

Relief

[84] I also agree with Munby J that, if I had found that the court had jurisdiction
to grant relief to the appellant, this was, on the information available to us, not a
case to grant an injunction against the respondent. *e*

[85] I would therefore dismiss the appeal and discharge the existing injunction.

THORPE LJ.

[86] I have had the advantage of reading in draft the judgment of Dame
Elizabeth Butler-Sloss P. I am in complete agreement with the first 51 paragraphs *f*
of the judgment in which she sets the scene and decides the first issue, issue A. I
can add nothing in that regard. I also agree that this appeal should be dismissed.
However, in view of the importance of the second issue on the appeal, issue B,
I should like to add some views of my own.

The historical background *g*

[87] Following the enactment of s 46 of the Matrimonial Causes Act 1857 the
tension between the principle of open justice and the consequent revulsion of
respectable opinion at the salacious details of trials in the divorce court appearing
in the popular press surfaced almost immediately. Prior thereto evidence in the
ecclesiastical courts had been taken in private and private Acts of Parliament for *h*
divorce were rare. So it is evident that the application of the open justice principle
to the new statutory remedy for divorce created an enduring problem. Legislative
attempts to suppress the publication of evidence in divorce cases in the nineteenth
century proved unsuccessful.

[88] The judgment of the House of Lords in *Scott v Scott* [1913] AC 417, *j*
[1911–13] All ER Rep 1 was decided against the background of the 1912 Royal
Commission on Divorce and Matrimonial Causes which had concluded that,
although proceedings for divorce should continue to be heard in open court,
some restrictions on publication should be introduced, if necessary by statute,
enabling judges both to close the court and to prohibit reporting in the exercise
of their discretion. That recommendation lay fallow for a decade. However the

a press coverage of the Russell case in 1922 and the Dennistoun case in 1925 propelled the passage of the Judicial Proceedings (Regulation of Reports) Act 1926. No doubt the aim of the statute was to strike a balance between the principle of open justice and the need to kerb reports from the divorce court for the protection of public morality.

[89] For this brief review I have drawn exclusively on ch 4 of Cretney *Law,*
b *Law Reform, and The Family* (1998) where the whole saga is traced with a judicious balance of scholarship and wit.

[90] The objectives of the statute were partially achieved. Over the next almost 50 years the principal business of the specialist judges and practitioners in the Probate Divorce and Admiralty Division was the dissolution of marriage, all petitions being heard and determined in public, whether defended or undefended.
c Of course there were ancillary issues dealt with in chambers to settle disputes as to maintenance or as to children. These ancillary proceedings were always held in private and it was never doubted that publication of such private proceedings was prohibited. Of course where the chambers proceedings related to children, their exceptional character was never in doubt. It had been expressly recognised
d by the House of Lords in *Scott v Scott* (for instance see the speech of Lord Shaw of Dunfermline [1913] AC 417 at 482, [1911–13] All ER Rep 1 at 33). As for maintenance hearings, they were, of course, ancillary to 'judicial proceedings for dissolution of marriage, for nullity of marriage, or for judicial separation' and therefore at least arguably caught by s 1(1)(b) of the 1926 Act.

[91] However, in and after 1970 law and practice changed almost out of
e recognition. Uncontested divorces are dealt with without any hearing at all, other than the formal pronouncement of decrees nisi en bloc. Contested divorces in open court are almost unknown. Specialist professional efforts are now largely devoted to proceedings under the Children Act 1989 or to ancillary relief proceedings. Of course there are many other lesser fields of litigation including
f enforcement and variation, wardship, adoption, injunctive relief, child abduction, declaratory relief and Inheritance Act claims. But it is self-evident that the 1926 Act no longer bites on the business of the courts in our modern family justice system.

[92] Statutory enactments to reflect this almost total transformation are hard to find. Section 39(1) of the Children and Young Persons Act 1933 empowered
g any court in any proceedings to prohibit the publication of details relating to any child or young person concerned in the proceedings. The Administration of Justice Act 1960 introduced the restraints in s 12(1)(a) and (e) relevant to family proceedings. The Domestic and Appellate Proceedings (Restriction of Publicity) Act 1968 empowered the Court of Appeal to sit in private and, by s 2, extended
h s 1(1)(b) of the 1926 Act to proceedings under s 27 of the Matrimonial Causes Act 1973 and proceedings under Pt III and under s 56(1) of the Family Law Act 1986. (I have not understood, but have not had time to research, what motivated the extension of the 1926 Act to cover these three relatively esoteric areas of the court's statutory jurisdiction.) The 1973 Act by s 48(2) re-enacted an earlier
j provision that evidence on the question of sexual capacity in nullity proceedings should ordinarily be heard 'in camera'. Equally the Adoption Act 1976 made similar provision for proceedings under that Act.

[93] It therefore seems to me that parliament has been sparse in its contribution to unravelling the question of what, if anything, may be extracted from family proceedings in private for subsequent publication. That may be because there seemed to be little need for parliament to legislate. In the family

justice system the designation 'in chambers' has always been accepted to mean
strictly private. Judges, practitioners and court staff are vigilant to ensure that no
one crosses the threshold of the court who has not got a direct involvement in the
business of the day. One of the parties may have formed a new relationship. But
if the new partner has not party status in the litigation application must be made
to the judge despite the obvious and direct involvement in the life of the family.
This strict boundary has always been scrupulously observed by the press. Of
course the judge always retains a residual discretion and, accordingly, a hearing
in chambers may culminate in a judgment in open court. Alternatively the judge
may make an abbreviated statement in order that the public interest in the
proceedings may be at least partially satisfied.

[94] This practice may have been supported by shifts in public opinion. In
1974 para 4.408 the *Report of the Committee on One Parent Families* (Cmnd 5629) (the
Fines Committee) recommended that the practice of hearing proceedings in
private in the High Court should be extended to all hearings which the public
interest did not decisively demand should be conducted in open court. In 1985 the
Booth Committee considered that there was a powerful argument for private
hearings of divorce suits.

[95] However by the 1990s the pendulum was perhaps swinging in the other
direction. The Cleveland Report (1988) urged a rationalisation of restrictions on
reporting by the media and in 1990 the Calcutt Committee drew attention to the
variety of different provisions in existence and recommended review. Accordingly
in 1993, 'as part of the Lord Chancellor's rolling programme of reform of family
law and business' his department issued a consultation paper entitled 'Review of
Access to and Reporting of Family Proceedings'. The consultation paper was the
work of a group from the Lord Chancellor's Department, the Home Office, the
Department of Health and the Law Commission. The result was an extremely
thorough and scholarly paper. After a brief introduction Pt II endeavoured to
summarise the current law over the course of 50 pages. Part III set out the rival
arguments for open justice and privacy and Pt IV set out the options for change.
The final section headed 'Summary and Consultation Points' contained the
group's proposals. At para 5.9 there is this:

> 'We believe there is a need for rationalisation of the law and practice
> relating to access to and reporting of family proceedings to remove unnecessary
> complexity and inconsistency and to establish provisions which are as clear
> and simple as possible while retaining flexibility where necessary. However
> the current balance between openness and privacy seems to be generally
> accepted, and therefore we do not consider there is a need for change for its
> own sake.'

[96] More specifically under the subheading 'Reporting' the group stated at
para 5.13:

> 'The position as regards reporting of family proceedings is, if anything, yet
> more complex than that relating to access. Again, there are different
> statutory provisions according to the type of case and level of court. There
> is widespread inconsistency, not only as to what details may be reported and
> those who are bound by the restrictions, but also as to the consequences
> when the restrictions are not observed. As with access, we believe there is a
> powerful case for rationalisation of reporting restrictions.'

a [97] No doubt another impetus to publication of the consultation paper was the increasing influence of the European Convention for the Protection of Human Rights and Fundamental Freedoms 1950 on our domestic law and practice. I believe that there were widespread responses to the consultation paper. Certainly the Family Division bench, of which I was then a member, submitted a paper supported by a substantial majority of the judges of the Family

b Division and the district judges of the Principal Registry. It is to my mind a matter of regret that the government did not carry this initiative forward. However, just as at the beginning of the decade family justice reforms made major demands, so in the second half of the decade were even greater demands made by the reform of the civil justice system. In recent years the family justice system has seemed something of a Cinderella. In reality the reforms as to access and reporting

c introduced in the wake of civil justice reforms have not been replicated in the family justice system. Certainly the judgment of Munby J in the present case has re-emphasised the uncertainties and inconsistencies in our law as to access to and reporting of family proceedings. Those difficulties and inconsistencies could, in my opinion, be resolved by government, particularly since much of the

d groundwork has already been done. The description of the law in relation to the reporting of family proceedings as being uncertain is made good by a study of p 118 of the consultation paper which seeks to reveal in tabular form the position as to the reporting of the individual types of family proceedings.

[98] The horizontal divisions of the table into categories large, medium and small refer to volume of business as established by judicial statistics. The table

e comes with a health warning that its statements 'have, out of necessity, been simplified, and should not be relied upon as a wholly accurate picture of the law'. Until such time as the law can be clarified and rationalised to reflect current public policy issues, I would favour the minimum departure from the present well-established and well-tried practice. Of course the extent to which the

f present line can be held depends upon a review of the current law.

The present law

[99] From all that I have written above it is obvious that I do not consider the present practice as to the reporting of family proceedings can be justified in every respect by reference to statute. However extensively the 1926 Act, as amended,

g and the 1960 Act are construed they cannot be held to cover all family proceedings, as the present appeal illustrates. Accordingly I advance a series of propositions.

[100], [101] The first is that family proceedings are easily distinguishable from civil proceedings in the other Divisions of the High Court. Speaking of ancillary relief proceedings in the case of *Kelley v Corston* [1997] 4 All ER 466 at 494, [1998]

h QB 686 at 715, Butler-Sloss LJ referred to 'the more inquisitorial atmosphere of family proceedings'. I believe that this means that in family proceedings the relationship between the court and the litigants is clearly distinguishable from the relationship between the litigants and the court in civil proceedings. In the latter the parties bring into the arena such material as they choose to bring

j together with such material as they may be ordered to bring during the development of the case. At the completion of that process the judge determines the outcome applying the law to such facts as have been admitted or have been found proved. The determination of an ancillary relief application proceeds on a very different basis. First it is to be noted that litigants may not bring into the proceedings such material as they think fit. All parties are under a duty of full and frank disclosure, clearly recognised well before the advent of the statutory

powers for equitable redistribution of assets on divorce. The duty was succinctly
stated by Sachs J at first instance in the case of *J-PC v J-AF* [1955] P 215 at 228–229
when he said:

> 'For a husband in maintenance proceedings simply to wait and hope that
> certain questions may not be asked in cross-examination is wholly wrong. In
> the light of this apparent misapprehension it is as well to state expressly
> something which underlies the procedure by which husbands are required in
> such proceedings to disclose their means to the court. Whether that
> disclosure is by affidavit of facts, by affidavit of documents or by evidence on
> oath (not least when that evidence is led by those representing the husband)
> the obligation of the husband is to be full, frank and clear in that disclosure.'

[102] Next it is important to draw attention to the words of s 25 of the 1973
Act. Subsection (1) reads:

> 'It shall be the duty of the court in deciding whether to exercise its powers
> under any of sections 22A to 24BB above and, if so, in what manner, to have
> regard to all the circumstances of the case ...'

[103] Section 25A, introduced by amendment, states:

> 'If the court decides to exercise any of its powers under any of sections 22A
> to 24BB above in favour of a party to a marriage ... it shall be the duty of the
> court to consider whether it would be appropriate so to exercise those
> powers that the financial obligations of each party towards the other will be
> terminated as soon ... as the court considers just and reasonable.'

[104] Thus the duty that parliament has cast upon the court must be matched
by a duty on the parties to supply the court with the fullest relevant information.
Once the statutory duty is engaged by the issue of an application for relief under
ss 22A to 24BB then both parties are under the duty of full, frank and clear
disclosure. A breach of that duty forces the court to draw inferences, inferences
which will inevitably be adverse to the party in breach of the duty. There is the
clearest authority for the above propositions in the speech of Lord Brandon of
Oakbrook in the case of *Jenkins v Livesey (formerly Jenkins)* [1985] 1 All ER 106 at
113, [1985] 1 AC 424 at 436 when he said:

> 'My Lords, the terms of s 25(1) of the 1973 Act which I have set out above
> are, in my opinion, of crucial importance in relation to the questions raised
> by this appeal. The scheme which the legislature enacted by ss 23, 24 and 25
> of the 1973 Act was a scheme under which the court would be bound, before
> deciding whether to exercise its powers under ss 23 and 24, and, if so, in what
> manner, to have regard to all the circumstances of the case, including, inter
> alia, the particular matters specified in paras (a) and (b) of s 25(1). It follows
> that, in proceedings in which parties invoke the exercise of the court's
> powers under ss 23 and 24, they must provide the court with information
> about all the circumstances of the case, including, inter alia, the particular
> matters so specified. Unless they do so, directly or indirectly, and ensure that
> the information provided is correct, complete and up to date, the court is not
> equipped to exercise, and cannot therefore lawfully and properly exercise, its
> discretion in the manner ordained by s 25(1).'

[105] In civil proceedings restrictions on dissemination of litigation material
for ulterior purposes are usually put on the basis of an implied undertaking not to

a do so. However it is plain that the concept of the implied undertaking is founded on the duty to the court. In *Prudential Assurance Co Ltd v Fountain Page Ltd* [1991] 3 All ER 878 at 895, [1991] 1 WLR 756 at 774 Hobhouse J said:

> 'It may be thought desirable to express the duty as an implied undertaking to the court. But, whether it is so expressed or not, it is in my judgment a duty that is owed to the court and which can be enforced by the court …
b > Breach of the duty amounts to a contempt of court, which may be trivial or serious depending upon the circumstances. The court has the power wholly or partially to release the recipient from the duty, or undertaking, and to permit use to be made of the documents nevertheless.'

c [106] Accordingly I have no difficulty in concluding that in the important area of ancillary relief, where the table confirms that the volume of business is large, all the evidence (whether written, oral or disclosed documents) and all the pronouncements of the court are prohibited from reporting and from ulterior use unless derived from any part of the proceedings conducted in open court or otherwise released by the judge.

d [107] The authors of the review expressed the proposition that ancillary relief proceedings could be taken to be covered by the provisions of s 1(1)(b) of the 1926 Act namely 'in relation to any judicial proceedings for dissolution of marriage, for nullity of marriage, or for judicial separation, or for restitution of conjugal rights'.

[108] The proposition seems to me to be inherently unsound. As I have indicated the primary business of the Probate, Divorce and Admiralty Division in *e* 1925 was the trial of divorce and nullity suits. Ancillary relief as we now know it was unknown. The exceptions provided in the subsection are expressed in language that is only comprehensible by reference to the trial of divorce and nullity suits. The exceptions are incapable of application by adoption to a contested ancillary relief application held by a district judge sitting in his room at *f* a family hearing centre anywhere in England and Wales. However the view expressed in the review was adopted by Munby J ([2001] 2 FCR 577 at [68]).

[109] Before us neither counsel referred to the review and Mr Moylan did not address the status of ancillary relief proceedings by reliance on that paragraph of the judgment below. Accordingly my opinion as to whether or not s 1(1)(b) of the 1926 Act applies to ancillary relief proceedings must remain provisional. But *g* even if the subsection does apply to ancillary relief it will not prohibit either party from selling or otherwise releasing the judgment in reliance on the exception provided by s 1(1)(b)(iv). I therefore prefer to rest the regulation of the parties to ancillary relief proceedings on their duty to the court as I have explained above.

[110] Of course Mr Price QC in his submissions made much of the decision in *h* this court in *Hodgson v Imperial Tobacco Ltd* [1998] 2 All ER 673, [1998] 1 WLR 1056. In his judgment Lord Woolf MR nowhere refers to the 1991 rules or the practice in family proceedings or to any of the relevant authorities in the Family Division. Lord Woolf MR, in delivering an important judgment, clearly presaged one aspect of the wholesale reform of procedure in civil justice on which he was *j* then engaged. He was well aware that at that time sweeping reforms of the practice in ancillary relief proceedings were well advanced. There is in my mind the clearest inference that the application of the judgment of this court was limited to civil proceedings.

[111] Mr Moylan mounts an attractive argument that the language of parliament in Pt IV of the Family Law Act 1996 is parallel to the parliamentary language in s 25 of the 1973 Act. He stresses the fact that s 36(6) of the 1996 Act replicates the

obligations contained in s 25(1) and (2) to have regard to all the circumstances of
the case and in particular to have regard to the matters in a statutory checklist.   *a*
Certainly sub-s (6) states: 'In deciding whether to make an order under this
section ... and (if so) in what manner, the court shall have regard to all the
circumstances including ...'

[112]–[115] Within the statutory checklist there then follows a number of
specifics including: *b*

> '... (b) the financial resources of each of the parties ... (d) the conduct of
> the parties in relation to each other and otherwise; (e) the nature of the
> parties' relationship; (f) the length of time during which they have lived
> together as husband and wife ...'

[116] In my opinion it is strongly arguable that that language thrusts upon the   *c*
court an obligation amounting to a duty to bring into account an extensive range
of factors, many of them highly personal to the parties. The court's ability to
perform that duty must equally rest upon an obligation on the parties to make
full, frank and clear disclosure of evidence on each of the subheadings of s 36(6)
as are relevant to the particular case. The court's duty is equally engaged by the *d*
issue of the application. The respondent has a choice either to participate fully,
discharging his consequential duty, or to risk the outcome of unopposed
proceedings. For myself I would accept that submission were it raised by the
present appeal. However, s 36(6) is only engaged if the applicant satisfies the
conditions set out in sub-s (1). It is my understanding of the issue decided by
Judge Krikler that the appellant resisted the application on the grounds that the   *e*
respondent could not satisfy sub-s (1) since the dwelling house in respect of which
the order was sought was not 'The home in which they lived together as husband
and wife or a home in which they at any time so lived together or intended so to
live together.'

[117] Since the respondent to this appeal failed to prove that requirement *f*
contained in s 36(1)(c) the court never arrived at its obligation under s 36(6). In
effect the appellant challenged the jurisdiction of the court successfully. That
being the narrow issue I find it difficult to discern a sufficiently clear duty in the
court to give rise to a corresponding duty on the parties to refrain from ulterior
use of the litigation material.

[118] I agree with Dame Elizabeth Butler-Sloss P that cases such as the present *g*
are likely to form relatively rare exceptions to the general rule. This case has
attracted a great deal of interest and comment amongst the specialist
practitioners. In so far as they look to our judgments for clear signposts as to the
way ahead, the best generalisation that I can offer for cases not involving children
is that, wherever the nature of the proceedings is at least quasi-inquisitorial, the *h*
duty to the court will probably be discernible.

[119] As Dame Elizabeth Butler-Sloss P has pointed out, the effect of CPR 39.2
and the Practice Direction may be to put the restraints in civil proceedings on a
higher plain than in family proceedings. The only class of proceedings that are
truly cross boundary are claims under the Inheritance (Provision for Family and *j*
Dependants) Act 1975. For they may be issued either in the Chancery Division or
in the Family Division. They specifically fall within the protection of CPR 39.2. It
would be anomalous were the protection less in family proceedings. Therefore I
have not found the conclusion in this appeal either easy or satisfactory. That state
of affairs only heightens the case for the resumption of the rolling programme for
the reform of family law and practice.

a   **[120]** I would not wish it to be inferred that I am opposed to change or an advocate for the present practice. There are strong arguments for the introduction of greater openness in family proceedings. There is strong evidence that a substantial section of public opinion would favour such a change. However the arguments for and against are complex and finely balanced, as the government's consultation paper demonstrated. The resolution of those conflicting considerations must, in my opinion, be for government on an inter-departmental

b   review.

[121] The outcome of these proceedings seems to me far from satisfactory. A system that rigorously excludes the press from access to litigation material but permits the parties to disseminate it elsewhere may in some cases put a considerable monetary value on the litigation material. We have no knowledge

c   of the respondent's motives, but it would not be unreasonable to infer that amongst her motivation for her disclosure to the Daily Mail and her approach to the Hong Kong press was a desire for revenge or a desire to recoup the costs order before Judge Krikler. The appellant no doubt participated in the proceedings before Judge Krikler on the advice, or perhaps only on the assumption,

d   that the proceedings were private and secure against wider dissemination. In that he has been disappointed.

KEENE LJ.

[122] I also agree that this appeal should be dismissed for the reasons given by Dame Elizabeth Butler-Sloss P and wish only to add a few limited comments on

e   the issues in this case.

[123] On the topic of hearings taking place in public or private, I would endorse the need to scrutinise more closely than has happened in practice in the past whether a hearing in private can be justified. Of course, in many cases in the Family Division, especially those involving children, there can be no doubt that

f   the hearing should take place in private, and this situation is reflected in the Family Proceedings Rules 1991, SI 1991/1247.

[124] I agree that those rules are not ultra vires. Apart from any other consideration, the rules do repeatedly allow the court a discretion as to whether it sits in public or in private. But in some cases, such as in some instances of applications for occupation orders, there may be little justification for the

g   proceedings to be heard in private, and as and when a court comes to exercise its discretion on this matter it will, as a result of s 6 of the Human Rights Act 1998, have to take into account art 6(1) of the European Convention for the Protection of Human Rights and Fundamental Freedoms 1950 (as set out in Sch 1 to the 1998 Act). It will not be possible in all cases to show that an application for an

h   occupation order falls within one of the exceptions to art 6(1) where the press and public may be excluded. That burden is likely to be particularly difficult to discharge where children are not involved.

[125] So far as publication is concerned, I find myself in agreement with the description given by Dame Elizabeth Butler-Sloss P of the law applicable in

j   litigation generally, including the legal principles governing the occasions when the implied undertaking arises. Applying those principles to proceedings in the Family Division, I accept that in ancillary relief proceedings such an undertaking would normally operate because of the duty on the parties to make full disclosure: *Jenkins v Livesey (formerly Jenkins)* [1985] 1 All ER 106, [1985] 1 AC 424. But the requisite element of compulsion to disclose will not exist in all family proceedings. I share the view of Dame Elizabeth Butler-Sloss P, as expressed in

[77] hereof, that such an element will not necessarily exist in cases arising under
s 36 of the Family Law Act 1996, merely because of the provisions of sub-s (6) of *a*
that section. I doubt whether the duty of the *court* under that subsection to have
regard to all the circumstances, including certain specified matters, creates in all
circumstances a sufficient obligation and degree of compulsion on the *parties* to
disclose information so as to give rise to the implied undertaking.

Appeal dismissed.

Kate O'Hanlon   Barrister.

a   # R (on the application of McLellan) v Bracknell Forest Borough Council
      # Reigate and Banstead Borough Council v Benfield and another
b   ## [2001] EWCA Civ 1510

COURT OF APPEAL, CIVIL DIVISION

WALLER, LATHAM AND KAY LJJ

c   10, 11, 13 JULY, 16 OCTOBER 2001

Housing – Local authority houses – Possession – Introductory tenancy – Whether mechanism for recovering possession of property let under introductory tenancy compatible with human rights – Housing Act 1980, s 89 – Housing Act 1996, s 127 –
d   *Human Rights Act 1998, Sch 1, Pt I, arts 6, 8 – Introductory Tenants (Review) Regulations 1997.*

In two conjoined appeals by local authority introductory tenants who were facing eviction, the Court of Appeal considered the impact of the European Convention for the Protection of Human Rights and Fundamental Freedoms
e   1950 (as set out in Sch 1 to the Human Rights Act 1998) on the introductory tenants' scheme introduced by Pt V of the Housing Act 1996. Section 124(1) of the 1996 Act gave local authorities a discretion whether or not to elect to operate such a scheme in respect of new lettings. The purpose of the power to adopt such a regime was to enable authorities to deal more effectively with any tendency on the part of new tenants to engage in anti-social behaviour which emerged during
f   the first 12 months of the tenancy, and with tenants who, during the same period, fell into arrears of rent and appeared to the authority to be bad payers. Provided the authority had followed the correct procedures as laid down in the 1996 Act for terminating an introductory tenancy, the county court was obliged under s 127(2)[a] to make a possession order. Section 128[b] required the authority first to
g   serve a notice on the tenant saying that it would be asking the court to make an order for possession, and setting out its reasons for doing so. Section 129(2)[c] gave the tenant the right to a review of the decision by the authority. The procedures to be followed by an authority when conducting such a review were laid down in the Introductory Tenants (Review) Regulations 1997. They required, in particular,
h   that the review should be carried out by a person who was not involved in the decision to apply for an order for possession and who was more senior than the original decision-maker; that the tenant could request an oral hearing; that he should be given not less than five days' notice of any oral hearing; and that a tenant who had requested an oral hearing had the right to be accompanied and/or represented, to call persons to give evidence, to question any witness and
j   to make representations in writing. If, on review, the original decision was upheld, the authority could then commence proceedings for possession in the

_____

a   Section 127 is set out at [20], below
b   Section 128 is set out at [21], below
c   Section 129, so far as material, provides: ' ... (2) On a request duly made to it, the landlord shall review his decision ...'

county court. Although the county court had no power to entertain a defence
based on a denial of the allegations of the breaches of the tenancy agreement
provided for in the s 128 notice, a pre-1998 Act Court of Appeal decision had
established that the judge had power to adjourn the possession proceedings,
pending determination of High Court judicial review proceedings, if he thought
that there was a real chance of permission to apply being granted. On making a
possession order, the county court also had power under s 89(1)^d of the Housing
Act 1980 to postpone the giving up of possession for a period of no more than six
weeks. On the appeals in the instant cases, the Court of Appeal considered
whether the termination of an introductory tenancy engaged the right to respect
for private life, family life and home under art 8(1)^e of the convention; if so,
whether a tenant was entitled to argue that his particular eviction had to be
justified as falling within the grounds for interfering with that right permitted in
art 8(2), namely that it was in accordance with the law and was necessary in a
democratic society for the protection of the rights and freedoms of others; and if
he was so entitled, whether the existing procedures enabled the tenant to
establish that there was no such justification for interference with his art 8(1)
rights. The court further considered whether the decision of the review panel
engaged art 6(1) of the convention which provided that, in the determination of his
civil rights, everyone was entitled to a fair hearing by an independent and
impartial tribunal. If it did, the question further arose as to whether the procedure
was compatible with art 6(1).

Held – (1) Although the eviction of a tenant under the introductory tenants'
scheme would engage art 8(1) of the convention and such a tenant was entitled
to raise the question whether, in his particular case, art 8(2) justified the eviction,
the review procedure, taken together with judicial review, provided adequate
protection for a possible breach of art 8. The overall scheme had been put in
place by Parliament which had decided that it was necessary in the interests of
tenants generally and local authorities to have a scheme whereby, during the first
12 months, tenants were on probation and could be evicted without long battles
in the county court. There was in place a review procedure and that procedure
was quasi-judicial in the sense that it was required to be fair. It contained a
number of important safeguards. If, following the review, the local authority
decided to continue with the possession proceedings, it had to give its reasons. If
there were challenges to those reasons and/or the tenant asserted that the
exceptions in art 8(2) did not apply in the particular case, the judge would, if he
thought it arguable, adjourn to allow an application to be made for judicial
review. Should the decision of the review panel be found to have been reached
without a proper evidential basis or upon a view of the facts that could not
reasonably be entertained or on the basis of a material error of fact, that would
be a ground for review in the High Court. In addition, if the judge thought that
the pace of the eviction was out of proportion and an infringement of the tenant's
human rights, he could use s 89 of the 1980 Act to grant an extension of time,
albeit for a limited period. If the tenant had not sought to review the decision to
seek possession, that would be relevant, but it would not deprive the county
court of the power to consider whether the particular decision might arguably be
in breach of the convention. In relation to arguability, the county court would

---

d   Section 89, so far as material, is set out at [22], below
e   Article 8 is set out at [28], below

a bear in mind that the scope of judicial review was not set in stone. It followed that the introductory tenancy scheme was not incompatible with art 8, and there was no reason to think that individuals' rights would be infringed without remedy from the courts (see [42], [43], [58]–[67], [107], [108], below); *Manchester City Council v Cochrane* [1999] 1 WLR 809 and *Poplar Housing and Regeneration Community Association Ltd v Donoghue* [2001] 4 All ER 604 considered.

b   (2) Although the decision of the review panel involved a determination of the tenant's civil rights, and thus engaged art 6 of the convention, there was no infringement of that provision. The review panel in itself could not have the degree of independence necessary to comply with art 6, but the decision-making procedure had to be considered as a whole. There was no reason why the procedure could not be operated fairly, and no reason why the remedy of judicial
c review would not provide an adequate safeguard to tenants, enabling them to challenge any unfairness and/or infringement of their convention rights, particularly under art 8. Accordingly, neither s 127 of the 1996 Act nor the scheme was incompatible with art 6. The appeals themselves would be dismissed (see [83], [101], [102], [105]–[108], below); *R (on the application of Alconbury*
d *Developments Ltd) v Secretary of State for the Environment, Transport and the Regions* [2001] 2 All ER 929 considered.

     Per curiam. Where a review has taken place, it should be the norm for the local authority, in a case in which it is seeking to take possession, to spell out in affidavits before the county court judge the manner in which the review procedure was operated in the individual case, dealing with the degree of independence of the
e tribunal from persons who took the original decision, the way the hearing was conducted and the reason for taking the decision to continue with the proceedings. In that way, the judge will have the information on which he can take an informed view as to whether the matter should be adjourned to allow for an application to be made for judicial review (see [103], [107], [108], below).

f
Notes

For the right to a fair hearing and the right to respect for private life, family life and home, see 8(2) *Halsbury's Laws* (4th edn reissue) paras 134–140, 149–152, and for introductory tenancies, see 22 *Halsbury's Laws* (4th edn reissue) paras 227–233.

     For the Housing Act 1980, s 89, see 23 *Halsbury's Statutes* (4th edn) (1997
g reissue) 336.

     For the Housing Act 1996, ss 127, 128, 129, see 21 *Halsbury's Statutes* (4th edn) (1997 reissue) 858, 859.

     For the Human Rights Act 1998, Sch 1, Pt I, arts 6, 8, see 7 *Halsbury's Statutes* (4th edn) (1999 reissue) 523, 524.

h   For the Introductory Tenants (Review) Regulations 1997, see 10 *Halsbury's Statutory Instruments* (2001 Issue) 206.

Cases referred to in judgments

Albert v Belgium (1983) 5 EHRR 533, ECt HR.
j *Associated Provincial Picture Houses Ltd v Wednesbury Corp* [1947] 2 All ER 680, [1948] 1 KB 223, CA.
Avon CC v Buscott [1988] 1 All ER 841, [1988] QB 656, [1988] 2 WLR 788, CA.
Bryan v UK (1995) 21 EHRR 342, E Com HR and ECt HR.
Buckley v UK (1997) 23 EHRR 101, ECt HR.
Edwards (Inspector of Taxes) v Bairstow [1955] 3 All ER 48, [1956] AC 14, [1955] 3 WLR 410, HL.

Handyside v UK (1976) 1 EHRR 737, ECt HR.

Kaplan v UK (1980) 4 EHRR 64, E Com HR.

Kingsley v UK (7 November 2000, unreported), ECt HR.

König v Germany (1978) 2 EHRR 170, ECt HR.

Manchester City Council v Cochrane [1999] 1 WLR 809, CA.

Mayor and Burgesses of the London Borough of Lambeth v Howard [2001] EWCA Civ 468, (2001) 33 HLR 58.

Mellacher v Austria [1989] 12 EHRR 391, ECt HR.

P v UK (12 December 1990, unreported), E Com HR.

Poplar Housing and Regeneration Community Association Ltd v Donoghue [2001] EWCA Civ 595, [2001] 4 All ER 604, [2001] 3 WLR 183.

R (on the application of Alconbury Developments Ltd) v Secretary of State for the Environment, Transport and the Regions [2001] UKHL 23, [2001] 2 All ER 929, [2001] 2 WLR 1389, HL.

R (on the application of Bewry) v Norwich City Council [2001] EWHC Admin 657, [2001] All ER (D) 461 (Jul).

R (on the application of Mahmood) v Secretary of State for the Home Dept [2001] 1 WLR 840, CA.

R v Criminal Injuries Compensation Board, ex p A [1999] 2 AC 330, [1999] 2 WLR 974, HL.

R v DPP ex p Kebeline, R v DPP, ex p Rechachi [1999] 4 All ER 801, [2000] 2 AC 326, [1999] 3 WLR 972, HL.

R v Secretary of State for the Home Dept, ex p Simms [1999] 3 All ER 400, [2000] 2 AC 115, [1999] 3 WLR 328, HL.

R v Secretary of State for the Home Dept, ex p Turgut [2001] 1 All ER 719, CA.

Ringeisen v Austria (No 1) (1971) 1 EHRR 455, ECt HR.

S v UK (1986) 47 DR 274, E Com HR.

Secretary of State for Education and Science v Tameside Metropolitan BC [1976] 3 All ER 665, [1977] 1 AC 1014, [1976] 3 WLR 641, HL.

Trustees of Dennis Rye Pension Fund v Sheffield City Council [1997] 4 All ER 747, [1998] 1 WLR 840, CA.

W v UK [1988] 10 EHRR 29, ECt HR.

Wiggins v UK (1978) 13 DR 40, E Com HR.

Zumtobel v Austria (1993) 17 EHRR 116, ECt HR.

Appeals

R (on the application of McLellan) v Bracknell Forest BC

The claimant, Nina McLellan, appealed with permission of Keene LJ from the decision of Longmore J on 21 December 2000 whereby, in dismissing her proceedings for judicial review against the defendant, Bracknell Forest BC, he held that the provisions of the Housing Act 1996 in relation to introductory tenancies were not incompatible with arts 6, 8 and 14 of the European Convention for the Protection of Human Rights and Fundamental Freedoms 1950 (as set out in Sch 1 to the Human Rights Act 1998). The Secretary of State for Transport, Local Government and the Regions participated in the proceedings as an interested party. The facts are set out in the judgment of Waller LJ.

Reigate and Banstead BC v Benfield and anor

The second defendant, Penelope Forrest, appealed from the order of Judge Cook at Epsom County Court on 11 January 2001 granting the claimant, Reigate and *a* Banstead BC, possession of premises occupied by her. The first defendant, Rebecca Benfield, took no part in the appeal. The Secretary of State for Transport, Local Government and the Regions participated in the proceedings as an interested party. The facts are set out in the judgment of Waller LJ.

Nigel Pleming QC and *Robert Latham* (instructed by *Dexter Montague & Partners,*
b Berkshire) for McLellan.
Timothy Straker QC and *Sarah Jane Davies* (instructed by *Alex Jack*) for Bracknell Forest.
David Watkinson and *Beatrice Prevatt* (instructed by *John Gallagher, Shelter*) for Forrest.
Andrew Arden QC and *Christopher Baker* (instructed by *Alice Maddison*) for Reigate
c and Banstead.
Philip Sales and *Daniel Stilitz* (instructed by the *Treasury Solicitor*) for the Secretary of State.

Cur adv vult

d 16 October 2001. The following judgments were delivered.

WALLER LJ.

INTRODUCTION
e [1] These two appeals raise important questions relating to the impact of the European Convention for the Protection of Human Rights and Fundamental Freedoms 1950 (as set out in Sch 1 to the Human Rights Act 1998) on the provisions of the Housing Act 1996 in relation to introductory tenancies for council tenants.
[2] The first appeal, *R (on the application of Johns and McLellan) v Bracknell Forest BC*
f (*McLellan*) comes from a decision of Longmore J dated 21 December 2000. Before him it was argued that the introductory tenants' scheme under the 1996 Act was incompatible with arts 6, 8 and 14 of the convention. Longmore J ruled that the provisions of the 1996 Act were not incompatible with the convention on any of the grounds argued. Leave to appeal that decision was given by Keene LJ but
g only in so far as the decision turned on art 6.
[3] The second appeal, *Reigate and Banstead BC v Benfield and Forrest (Forrest)*, is an appeal from a decision of Judge Cook sitting in the Epsom County Court dated 11 January 2001. He granted the respondent in that case possession of the premises occupied by Forrest ruling that there was no reasonable prospect of a finding that the mandatory provisions of the 1996 Act were affected by the
h convention and the 1998 Act. The appeal against his decision was transferred to the Court of Appeal pursuant to s 57 of the Access to Justice Act 1999. The issues on this appeal relate not only to art 6, but arts 8 and 14 of the convention. The notice of appeal has been amended, with leave, seeking various declarations of incompatibility by reference to arts 8 and 14. Those amendments also contain a
j declaration of incompatibility of s 89 of the Housing Act 1980, the relevance of which will become clear.

INTRODUCTORY TENANCIES
[4] It is convenient to trace the history of introductory tenancies and to consider the proper construction of the 1996 Act which introduced them, without regard at first to the provisions of the convention and the 1998 Act.

[5] The background I can take very largely from the submissions of the
Secretary of State prepared by Mr Sales and Mr Stilitz.   *a*

[6] Under the Housing Act 1985, all tenancies of dwelling houses granted by
local authorities (with certain exceptions listed in Sch 1 to the Act) are secure
tenancies. The local authority can only terminate secure tenancies by obtaining
a county court order. The grounds for terminating such tenancies are set out in
Sch 2 to the 1985 Act. However, under the scheme of the 1985 Act, even where   *b*
an authority has satisfied the court that a ground for possession exists, the court
has a discretion whether or not to order possession.

[7] In April 1995 the Department of the Environment produced a consultation
paper entitled 'A consultation paper on probationary tenancies'. That paper is
exhibited to the witness statement of Michael Barclay Gahagan. Certain findings
are recorded in that consultation paper including the following: *c*

'Anti-social behaviour by a small minority of tenants and others is a
growing problem on council estates ... the misery caused to tenants when
the enjoyment of their home is spoilt by the activities of their neighbours or
others can destroy their whole quality of life. Whole estates can be
stigmatised by the anti-social behaviour of a few. Such behaviour manifests   *d*
itself in many different ways, including vandalism, noise, verbal and physical
abuse, threats of violence, racial harassment, damage to property, trespass,
nuisance from dogs, car repairs on the street, joyriding, domestic violence,
drugs and other criminal activities, such as burglary. Tackling the causes and
consequences of such behaviour represents a major drain on the resources   *e*
and time of housing managers. Research has shown that up to 20% of
housing managers' time is spent in dealing with questions of neighbour
nuisance, and that between 2 and 10% of tenants of any given estate have
been the subject of complaint.'

[8] Mr Straker QC on behalf of the council (Bracknell) in McLellan's appeal   *f*
also sought to emphasise that tenants who failed to pay their rents imposed a
serious burden on other tenants. If a tenant simply will not pay the rent then the
position is that that shortfall has to be shared as a burden to other tenants and that
is a serious matter so far as the council and other tenants are concerned.

[9] In the context of the above issues the above consultation paper also made
the following finding: *g*

'... the way in which the courts work results in difficulties in following
through possession cases quickly because of delays in getting the cases before
the court; inconsistency over what is regarded as acceptable evidence,
witness intimidation exacerbated by delays in court hearings, and what   *h*
authorities see as their difficulty in convincing the courts of the serious
nature of the nuisance caused by the tenant.'

[10] To the above Mr Straker would add also the serious nature of the burden
that is imposed on other tenants when there are arrears of rent.

[11] Part V of the 1996 Act therefore introduced the concept of introductory   *j*
tenancies into new lettings made by local authorities. The local authorities had a
discretion whether or not to elect to operate an introductory tenancy regime.
The purpose of the power to opt to establish such a regime was to enable
authorities to deal more effectively with any tendency on the part of new tenants
to engage in anti-social behaviour which emerged during the first 12 months of
the tenancy. Again Mr Straker would add and stress that the option also enabled

a authorities to deal more effectively with tenants who got into arrears with the rent and appeared to the authority to be bad payers during that first 12 months of the tenancy.

[12] Where a local authority has opted for introductory tenancies in relation to their tenants, the nub of the scheme is that (provided the authority followed the correct procedures as laid down in the 1996 Act for terminating an b introductory tenancy), under s 127(2) of the 1996 Act, the county court is obliged to make a possession order.

THE REGIME OF INTRODUCTORY TENANCIES

[13] The regime of introductory tenancies works as follows: s 124(1) of the 1996 Act gives local authorities a discretionary power to establish introductory c tenancies (although they are obliged by s 105 of the 1985 Act to consult with existing tenants on any such proposal). If an election to establish a scheme is made, then all new tenancies granted by an authority which would otherwise have been secure tenancies will be introductory tenancies.

[14] Section 125 of the 1996 Act provides that, so long as possession proceedings d have not been commenced, the introductory tenancy will automatically become a secure tenancy on the expiry of the one-year trial period.

[15] During the period of the introductory tenancy the tenant has some but not all the safeguards of a secure tenant. In particular, like a secure tenant, the introductory tenant has: (i) the right to succession of spouse or family member, (ii) the right to repair, (iii) the right to be consulted on housing management e issues, (iv) the right to assign, (v) the right to be consulted on decisions to delegate housing management and (vi) the right to participate in housing management contract monitoring. But, unlike the secure tenant, the introductory tenant does not have (i) the right to buy, (ii) the right to take in lodgers, (iii) the right to sub-let, (iv) the right to improve, (v) the right to exchange or (vi) the right to vote f prior to a transfer to a new landlord.

[16] Section 136 obliges authorities to publish and supply tenants with information that explains, amongst other things, the express terms of their introductory tenancies and the relevant provisions of the 1996 Act concerning introductory tenancies.

[17] Guidance was issued under circular 2/97 exhibited again to Mr Gahagan's g statement. That provided, amongst other things, that an introductory tenancy will usually be brought to an end because the tenant has breached the terms of the tenancy agreement, and stated that it was therefore important that the introductory tenancy agreements clearly set out the responsibilities of both the tenant and the landlord (see para 18).

h [18] To end an introductory tenancy, the authority must first serve a notice on the tenant saying that the authority will be asking the court to make an order for possession (s 128(1) of the 1996 Act). Section 128(3) of the 1996 Act states that the notice must set out the authority's reasons. The tenant has the right to a review of that decision by the authority: ie the tenant can require the authority to think j again (s 129(2) of the 1996 Act).

[19] The Introductory Tenants (Review) Regulations 1997, SI 1997/72 lay down the procedures that an authority must follow when conducting a review. In particular: (i) the review must be carried out by a person who was not involved in the decision to apply for an order for possession and by a person who is more senior than the original decision-maker; (ii) the tenant can request an oral hearing; (iii) the tenant must be given not less than five days' notice of any oral hearing; (iv) a

tenant who has requested an oral hearing has the right to be accompanied and/or represented, to call persons to give evidence, to question any witness and to make representations in writing.

[20] If on review the original decision is upheld, the authority may then commence proceedings for possession in the county court. By s 127(2) of the 1996 Act, the court must make an order for possession unless the authority has failed to comply with the requirements of s 128 of the 1996 Act. Section 127 provides:

'(1) The landlord may only bring an introductory tenancy to an end by obtaining an order of the court for the possession of the dwelling-house.

(2) The court shall make such an order unless the provisions of section 128 apply.'

[21] Section 128 provides:

'(1) The court shall not entertain proceedings for the possession of a dwelling-house let under an introductory tenancy unless the landlord has served on the tenant a notice of proceedings complying with this section.

(2) The notice shall state that the court will be asked to make an order for the possession of the dwelling-house.

(3) The notice shall set out the reasons for the landlord's decision to apply for such an order.

(4) The notice shall specify a date after which proceedings for the possession of the dwelling-house may be begun. The date so specified must not be earlier than the date on which the tenancy could, apart from this Chapter, be brought to an end by notice to quit given by the landlord on the same date as the notice of proceedings.

(5) The court shall not entertain any proceedings for possession of the dwelling-house unless they are begun after the date specified in the notice of proceedings.

(6) The notice shall inform the tenant of his right to request a review of the landlord's decision to seek an order for possession and of the time within which such a request must be made.

(7) The notice shall also inform the tenant that if he needs help or advice about the notice, and what to do about it, he should take it immediately to a Citizens' Advice Bureau, a housing aid centre, a law centre or a solicitor.'

[22] Finally, s 89(1) of the 1980 Act provides that, subject to a number of exceptions, a court making a possession order, including a possession order pursuant to s 127(2) of the 1996 Act, may in its discretion postpone the giving up of possession for a limited period. It provides so far as material:

'Where a court makes an order for the possession of any land ... the giving up of possession shall not be postponed ... to a date later than fourteen days after the making of the order, unless it appears to the court that exceptional hardship would be caused by requiring possession to be given up by that date; and shall not in any event be postponed to a date later than six weeks after the making of the order.'

MANCHESTER CITY COUNCIL V COCHRANE [1999] 1 WLR 809

[23] Prior to the coming into force of the 1998 Act, the Court of Appeal considered the nature of the above provisions of the 1996 Act and in particular the role of the county court when it came to consider whether to make a possession

a order under s 127(2). The Court of Appeal ruled that the private law right of a tenant under the introductory tenancy was no more than a right to possession until an order for possession in favour of the council was made by the court. In particular the court had no discretion not to make such an order once the requirements of s 128 regarding notice of proceedings had been complied with. It would be a clear contravention of the mandatory terms of s 127(2) for the county court to entertain a defence based on a denial of allegations of breaches of
b the tenancy agreement provided for in the notice under s 128. The Court of Appeal further held that by s 38(3) of the County Courts Act 1984 a county court was prohibited from reviewing the exercise or failure to exercise a public duty in the absence of Parliamentary authority to do so, and, since Pt V of the of the 1996 Act conferred no such authority, the county court's powers were limited to
c granting an adjournment of possession proceedings pending determination of judicial review proceedings in the High Court, if the county court formed the view there was a real chance of leave to apply for judicial review being granted. Sir John Knox who gave the judgment of the court, put the matter this way (at 819):

d 'If one were to treat the provisions of section 128 as a form of Scylla and those of section 127(2) as Charybdis, the channel in between available for navigation is remarkably narrow but I see no escape from that analysis even though it does reduce the functions of the court to that of ascertaining that it does have jurisdiction to entertain the proceedings at all. Once it has done so it is required to make a possession order and that, in my view, necessarily
e involves that it has no discretion in the matter at all.'

[24] In relation to the power to adjourn for the purpose of enabling judicial review to take place, Sir John Knox said (at 819):

f 'It is common ground that the council's duty to comply with section 129(2) is subject to judicial review. Equally it is clear that this duty is a public law duty and the correlative right in the tenants to have it lawfully performed must be a public law right. The county court must in my view have at least jurisdiction to grant an adjournment if satisfied that there is a real chance of leave to apply for judicial review being granted.'

g [25] Thus, prior to the coming into force of the 1998 Act, it is clear that the county court had no power other than to consider whether it had jurisdiction. In particular it had no power to consider whether the tenant might or might not have been in breach of the introductory tenancy agreement. Only if the county court considered that there was a real chance of leave to apply for judicial
h review being granted, could the court in those circumstances adjourn the matter in order to enable that challenge to take place.

The relevant provisions of the 1998 Act
[26] These are as follows:

j '**3.** *Interpretation of legislation.*—(1) So far as it is possible to do so, primary legislation and subordinate legislation must be read and given effect in a way which is compatible with the Convention rights.

(2) This section—(a) applies to primary legislation and subordinate legislation whenever enacted; (b) does not affect the validity, continuing operation or enforcement of any incompatible primary legislation …

4. *Declaration of incompatibility.*—(1) Subsection 2 applies in any proceedings in which a court determines whether a provision of primary legislation is compatible with a Convention right.

(2) If the court is satisfied that the provision is incompatible with a Convention right, it may make a declaration of that incompatibility.

(3) Subsection (4) applies in any proceedings in which a court determines whether a provision of subordinate legislation, made in the exercise of a power conferred by primary legislation, is compatible with a Convention right.

(4) If the court is satisfied—(a) that the provision is incompatible with a Convention right, and (b) that (disregarding any possibility of revocation) the primary legislation concerned prevents removal of the incompatibility, it may make a declaration of that incompatibility.

(5) In this section "court" means ... (e) in England and Wales ... the High Court or the Court of Appeal.

(6) A declaration under this section ("a declaration of incompatibility")— (a) does not affect the validity, continuing operation or enforcement of the provision in respect of which it is given; and (b) is not binding on the parties to the proceedings in which it is made ...

6. *Acts of public authorities.*—(1) It is unlawful for a public authority to act in a way which is incompatible with a Convention right.

(2) Subsection (1) does not apply to an act if—(a) as the result of one or more provisions of primary legislation, the authority could not have acted differently; or (b) in the case of one or more provisions of, or made under, primary legislation which cannot be read or given effect in a way which is compatible with the Convention rights, the authority was acting so as to give effect to or enforce those provisions.

(3) In this section "public authority" includes—(a) a court or tribunal, and ...

7. *Proceedings.*—(1) person who claims that a public authority has acted (or proposes to act) in a way which is made unlawful by section 6(1) may—(a) bring proceedings against the authority under this Act in the appropriate court or tribunal, or (b) rely on the Convention right or rights concerned in any legal proceedings, but only if he is (or would be) a victim of the unlawful act.

(2) In subsection (1)(a) "appropriate court or tribunal" means such court or tribunal as may be determined in accordance with rules; and proceedings against an authority include a counterclaim or similar proceeding.

(3) If the proceedings are brought on an application for judicial review, the applicant is to be taken to have a sufficient interest in relation to the unlawful act only if he is, or would be, a victim of that act ...

8. *Judicial remedies.*—(1) In relation to any act (or proposed act) of a public authority which the court finds is (or would be) unlawful, it may grant such relief or remedy, or make such order, within its powers as it considers just and appropriate.'

[27] Relevant provisions of the convention:

'*Article 6*

Right to a fair trial

1. In the determination of his civil rights and obligations or of any criminal charge against him, everyone is entitled to a fair and public hearing within a reasonable time by an independent and impartial tribunal established by law.

a

Judgment shall be pronounced publicly but the press and public may be excluded from all or part of the trial in the interests of morals, public order or national security in a democratic society, where the interests of juveniles or the protection of the private life of the parties so require, or to the extent strictly necessary in the opinion of the court in special circumstances where publicity would prejudice the interests of justice ...

b

Article 8

Right to respect for private and family life

1. Everyone has the right to respect for his private and family life, his home and his correspondence.

c

2. There shall be no interference by a public authority with the exercise of this right except such as is in accordance with the law and is necessary in a democratic society in the interests of national security, public safety or the economic well-being of the country, for the prevention of disorder or crime, for the protection of health or morals, or for the protection of the rights and freedoms of others ...

d

Article 14

Prohibition of discrimination

The enjoyment of the rights and freedoms set forth in this Convention shall be secured without discrimination on any ground such as sex, race, colour, language, religion, political or other opinion, national or social origin, association with a national minority, property, birth or other status.'

e

THE FACTS RELATING TO THE APPEALS

f

McLellan

[**28**] On 1 June 2000 McLellan was granted an introductory tenancy by Bracknell of premises known as 1 Enid Wood House, Bracknell, Berkshire. The tenancy commenced on 5 June 2000 and the weekly rent was £62·45. McLellan was aged 19 years and occupied the building with her partner Nicholas Martin, aged 17 years.

g

[**29**] On 21 July 2000 Bracknell served a notice of proceedings for possession notifying McLellan that proceedings for possession might be commenced after 21 August 2000. The stated reason was 'arrears of rent in the sum of £374·70 remained outstanding at the close of account on 14 July 2000'. McLellan requested a review which, on 18 August 2000, upheld the decision to serve the notice of proceedings for possession. The reviewing officer did however agree to postpone court proceedings provided that McLellan's housing benefit was (when obtained) backdated and that McLellan pay £10 per week to clear the arrears. McLellan issued a draft claim form for judicial review and served it on Bracknell whereupon Bracknell agreed to withdraw the notice of possession. Matters were effectively resolved prior to the hearing before Longmore J, however, all parties desired Longmore J to deal with the impact of the 1998 Act and the convention and he was in the circumstances prepared so to do.

h

j

[**30**] Since the hearing before Longmore J we are told that there had been further developments. On 18 May 2001 Bracknell issued a summons claiming possession of the premises. It seems the reasons for so doing were allegations of nuisance. McLellan accepts that there have been occasions when noise has

emanated from her flat, but disputes it should justify eviction. The county court
was to hear the summons on 18 June 2001 but the hearing was adjourned pending
this appeal.

Johns

[31] No appeal arises in relation to Johns but the facts in her case exemplify
matters that can occur under the introductory tenancy scheme. Johns was a
young single woman and was granted an introductory tenancy on 29 November
1999. On 26 May 2000 the council sent a notice of proceedings for possession
giving the reason that Johns was causing a nuisance to other residents. Johns
sought a review of that decision by the council. On 14 June 2000 a review panel
was constituted, and on 16 June 2000 the panel decided that Johns allowed her
visitors to cause a nuisance to other residents. The panel therefore upheld the
original decision to seek possession. On 18 September 2000 Johns issued an
application for judicial review of the decision of the council to proceed with their
notice of proceedings for possession. Turner J granted permission on 6 October
2000 whereupon the council withdrew their notice. However, on 20 October
2000 the council issued a second notice, with the result that on 15 November
there was a second review hearing. This second hearing decided that there was
no case for Johns to answer on the allegations of nuisance committed by her or
her visitors. The council decided not to seek an order for possession and on the
anniversary of the grant of the tenancy, 29 November 2000, Johns became a
secure tenant who could not be evicted without a court order. As a secure tenant
the court order could only be granted if the judge was satisfied that there was a
ground for obtaining possession and that it was reasonable for the council to be
granted possession.

Benfield and Forrest

[32] Benfield and Forrest were mother and daughter who were granted an
introductory tenancy by Reigate and Banstead Borough Council (Reigate) on 27
December 1999. They fell into rent arrears and on 28 April 2000 Reigate served
a notice of possession proceedings. Benfield and Forrest did not request a review
of that decision as (so they alleged but which is disputed) they had been informed
(or understood) that unless the arrears were cleared before the review, the matter
would proceed to court. On 9 August 2000 Reigate issued possession proceedings.
Benfield and Forrest paid £2,000 towards the rent arrears on 29 September 2000,
reducing the arrears to £576. Benfield and Forrest paid a further £200 in late
December 2000. On 3 October 2000 Reigate decided that the claim for
possession would proceed. Benfield and Forrest maintain that they have an
outstanding claim for housing benefit and should be able to clear the arrears with
the assistance of her mother who is selling her house (as to which she had so
informed the housing officer on 14 July 2000).

BAD PAYERS

[33] In support of Mr Straker's submission in relation to bad payers, it is right
to record the evidence of Robert Cripps given in his second statement of
28 November 2000. There he says (para 5):

'The Claimant has adopted a regime of Introductory Tenancies, the
purpose of this regime being to try to gauge whether persons will be good,
reliable tenants, fulfilling their financial responsibilities regarding payment of
rent and their social responsibilities, such persons being suitable to become

a   secure tenants. Introductory tenancies have been introduced by the council
    to ensure that problems with the non-payment of rent and neighbour
    nuisance are minimised. The regime encourages persons to regularly pay
    their rent, and generally only those persons who demonstrate that they will
    reliably pay their rent, become secure tenants. Local Authorities, such as the
    Claimant, are under a statutory duty to avoid a deficit on the Housing
b   Revenue Account and non-payment of rent causes the Claimant a serious
    problem in terms of honouring avoidance of the Housing Revenue Account
    deficit and may have the consequence of passing financial burdens on to
    those who are already tenants of the Claimant. There is a pressing social
    need to encourage financial accountability among tenants. That is, if some
    tenants do not pay rent and run up arrears, other tenants are liable to make
c   up the budgetary shortfall, in the long term, by shouldering rent increases.'

    IMPACT OF THE CONVENTION

    Article 8
d   [34] The provisions of this article of relevance are in sub-para (1) that
    '[e]veryone has the right to *respect* for his private and family life, his home ...' (my
    emphasis); and in sub-para (2):

        '... there shall be no interference by a public authority with the exercise of
        this right except such as is in accordance with the law *and* is necessary in a
e   democratic society ... for the protection of the rights and freedoms of
        others.' (My emphasis.)

    [35] Mr Andrew Arden QC for Reigate in the second appeal submitted that
    art 8(1) is not engaged, and thus that art 8 has no application because there is no
    interference with the right to 'respect' for the home through the mere exercise of
f   a power of termination within the terms pursuant to which the home has been
    made available. This, it should be said, was an argument which Mr Straker QC
    for Bracknell pursued before Longmore J in *McLellan*'s case. Longmore J rejected
    it but also held that the interference was necessary in a democratic society for the
    protection of the rights and freedoms of others. Keene LJ refused leave to appeal
    on the art 8 aspect in that appeal, and this aspect of the art 8 point was accordingly
g   not argued on that appeal.
    [36] Mr Sales, for the Secretary of State, whilst standing shoulder to shoulder
    with many aspects of the councils' arguments on other points, on this point
    positively asserted that art 8 was engaged. It was part of his defence to the art 6
    attack, that eviction of a tenant fell within art 8(1), and that judicial review would
h   provide a remedy where there was a failure to justify the eviction under art 8(2).
    As Mr Arden conceded, part of the reason why the council were keen to succeed
    on this point, as opposed to being content with arguing that they could justify
    under art 8(2), was that the council wished if it could to limit judicial review of its
    decisions as far as it could, otherwise some of the benefit of the procedure of
j   introductory tenancies would be lost.
    [37] Mr Arden's argument in short was this. He suggested that since a tenant
    would know the basis on which he or she had become a tenant, ie on the basis
    that the statutory provisions and procedures of the introductory tenancy scheme
    applied to it, the rights of the tenant to occupy the premises were simply in
    accordance with that scheme. Thus if the council complied with the provisions
    of the introductory tenancy scheme in order to bring the tenancy to an end, that

involved no want of respect for the tenant's home. So, it is argued, the question *a* whether the scheme had been complied with would be the first question which, if answered in favour of the council, would lead to the conclusion that art 8(1) was not engaged. It would then follow that the question whether the eviction could be justified under art 8(2) would not arise.

[38] Mr Arden suggested that he obtained support for this approach from the following authorities: *Wiggins v UK* (1978) 13 DR 40; *S v UK* (1986) 47 DR 274 and *b* *P v UK* (12 December 1990, unreported).

[39] In *Wiggins'* case the Commission acknowledged that Guernsey's resident laws meant that lawful occupation of the home was conditional upon the applicant either living with his wife or obtaining a permit. On the particular facts the Commission held that the applicant could not have expected to foresee the circumstances in which the condition would cease to be available to him and thus *c* found that art 8(1) was engaged. In *S v UK* the Commission concluded that the same sex partner of a deceased secure tenant could not use art 8 to complain about her eviction by the local authority landlord on the basis that the landlord's entitlement to possession under the general law meant that the house could no longer be considered to be 'home'. In *P v UK* the Commission found it unnecessary *d* to decide whether the termination of a tenancy of a caravan pitch could be considered to be an interference under art 8(1) but questioned whether it was.

[40] In my view the above are scant support for the approach advocated by Mr Arden, and there are more compelling authorities against it. In *Mayor and Burgesses of the London Borough of Lambeth v Howard* [2001] EWCA Civ 468, (2001) 33 HLR 58 Sedley LJ assumed that any eviction of a tenant fell within art 8(1). He *e* said (at [30]):

'Respect for a person's home is neither an absolute concept, nor, given Article 8(2), an unqualified right. I do find myself puzzled by the learned judge's remark that Article 8 "at first sight ... has no application in the present circumstances". It seems to me that any attempt to evict a person, whether *f* directly or by process of law, from his or her home would on the face of it be a derogation from the respect, that is the integrity, to which the home is prima facie entitled.'

Sedley LJ said (at [32]):
g
'A legal threat to a secure home will, in the ordinary way, engage Article 8(1). In situations where the law affords an unqualified right to possession on proof of entitlement, it may be that Article 8(2) is met, but that is not the present class of case and nothing in this judgment should be taken as impinging on it.'
h
[41] In *Poplar Housing and Regeneration Community Association Ltd v Donoghue* [2001] EWCA Civ 595 at [67], [2001] 4 All ER 604 at [67], [2001] 3 WLR 183 Lord Woolf CJ delivering the judgment of the court said:

'To evict the defendant from her home would impact on her family life. The effect of art 8(2) ... is therefore critical. The starting point is the fact that *j* after the order for possession was obtained, Tower Hamlets continued to owe a limited duty ...'

[42] In my view the terms of art 8(2) demonstrate that Mr Arden's approach is not a proper approach to art 8. It is not a preliminary question whether the tenancy has been properly terminated in accordance with its terms. It is under

a art 8(2) that the question to be considered is whether an eviction was in accordance with the law, and whether it was necessary for the protection of the rights and freedoms of others. In the *Poplar* case the Court of Appeal decided that Poplar was a public authority and thus that art 8(2) was directly applicable, but it seems to me that even if it had been a private landlord seeking to evict a tenant under an assured shorthold tenancy, the court as a public authority would have
b had to approach s 21(4) (the section under consideration in that case) in much the same way. It would have concluded that s 21(4) did not infringe any art 8 right but not because art 8 did not apply at all, but because the eviction was in accordance with the law and because it was not disproportionate to allow the tenancy to be brought to an end in accordance with the rights of the landlord. The wording of art 8(2) is apposite to allow consideration not only of the tenants'
c rights, and not only the rights of persons other than the landlord and the tenant ie other tenants for example, but the rights of the landlord as well. In *S v UK* [1986] 47 DR 274 at 278 the Commission put their conclusion in these terms:

> *d* 'Further, even if the applicant's right to respect for her home, as guaranteed by Article 8, could be regarded as having been interfered with by order of the County Court for possession against her, the Commission considers that such interference was clearly in accordance with the law and was also necessary for the protection of the contractual rights of the landlord to have the property back at the end of the tenancy.'

e [43] I would accordingly reject Mr Arden's argument that art 8 has no application.

Impact of art 8

[44] The issues which need to be considered are at what Mr Sales called the
f macro level as well as at the micro level. At the macro level the question is whether s 127 is incompatible with the convention in that it allows a tenant to be evicted from the home without scrutiny by the court making the order. The argument is that there is no justification under art 8(2) for having such a draconian provision. At the micro level the question is whether the decision to use s 127 in relation to the particular tenant; (a) has to be justified in every case
g by reference to art 8(2); (b) if so, whether the tenant is deprived by s 127 and the decision in *Manchester City Council v Cochrane* [1999] 1 WLR 809 of the ability to contest that justification; and (c) in Forrest's appeal whether at the micro level the tenant has an arguable case that her art 8 rights are being infringed. The argument in the proceedings before Longmore J provides a good example of the two levels
h of the argument. The proceedings originally asserted both arguments at the micro level, and also at the macro level. Because Miss McLellan and Miss Johns no longer needed relief in relation to their personal position by the time of the hearing before Longmore J, the argument only proceeded at the macro level and it was only at the macro level that the judge addressed the matter. So far as
j Forrest's appeal is concerned, argument has certainly concentrated at the macro level, but the micro level must not be overlooked.

[45] Serious questions are in my view raised despite the conclusion of Keene LJ not to grant permission to appeal in *McLellan*'s case, but that flows from consideration of what I am terming the micro level. As I have indicated Longmore J considered the position at the macro level, ie by reference to whether the introductory tenancy scheme could be justified by reference to the factors under

art 8(2). He considered the evidence relating to the reasons why the scheme was adopted, and said as follows:

'There can be no doubt that the scheme of introductory tenancies does interfere with the exercise of this right (art 8(1)), but it is of course in accordance with the law as laid down in the Housing Act 1996. The question, therefore, is whether the interference is necessary in a democratic society for the protection of the rights and freedoms of others. Necessary in a democratic society does not mean indispensable; nor does it mean desirable. Convention jurisprudence has decided that it means: (a) that the reasons given to justify the interference must be relevant and sufficient; (b) that the interference must correspond to a pressing social need; and (c) that the interference must be proportionate to the aim pursued (see *Handyside v UK* (1976) 1 EHRR 737) ...'

[46] This formulation was expressly approved by the Court of Appeal in *Howard*'s case (2001) 33 HLR 58 (see the judgment of Sedley LJ at [34]). Longmore J having examined the matter then finally concluded in this way:

'It does not seem to me that it is in any way inevitable that the legislation will act disproportionately and for all these reasons there is, in my judgment, no incompatibility with art 8. Nor, if relevant, do I consider there to be any compatibility with art I of Protocol I for all the same reasons. The infringement of that article was not argued as a separate point.'

[47] The force of the reasoning of Longmore J is clear and if the only question was whether the scheme could be justified I would accept his conclusion. It has furthermore the support of Keene LJ who refused leave to appeal on this aspect. The point in essence is that it is very much for Parliament to make the relevant judgments in this area. Furthermore, since the decision of Longmore J, it seems to me that *Poplar Housing and Regeneration Community Association Ltd v Donoghue* [2001] 4 All ER 604, [2001] 3 WLR 183 has provided further support for the view that he formed.

[48] The *Poplar* case indeed provides a good starting point for further consideration of this issue. The issue in that case was whether the fact that a court was bound by s 22(4) to make an order for eviction to terminate a shorthold tenancy involved a breach of the tenant's convention rights under arts 8 and 6. The court held that there was no breach of art 6 because if the court held that the section was not within the exception identified in art 8(2), and if the court had held that the county court could consider whether in the particular circumstances of the tenant in that case, the action of the landlord could be justified under art 8(2), there would have to be a remission to the county court for the purpose of trying that issue.

[49] What however the court held was that the section imposed on the court a duty to make the order for possession without considering the particular circumstances of the individual tenant, and that the section was compatible with the convention, saying (at [72]):

'We are satisfied, that notwithstanding its mandatory terms, s 21(4) of the [Housing Act 1988] does not conflict with the defendant's right to family life. Section 21(4) is certainly necessary in a democratic society in so far as there must be a procedure for recovering possession of property at the end of a tenancy. The question is whether the restrictive power of the court is a legitimate and proportionate. This is the area of policy where the court should defer to the decision of Parliament. We have come to the conclusion that there was no contravention of art 8 or of art 6.'

[50] The distinction between the *Poplar* case and the cases under the introductory tenancy scheme which create the difficulty seems to me to be the fact that the
b circumstances of the particular tenant are brought directly into focus under the introductory tenancy scheme by virtue of the requirement under s 128(3) to provide reasons for seeking possession, and the machinery for the reviewing of those reasons.

[51] In other words so far as individual tenants are concerned their positions have to be considered at the micro level, and the decision of a council to use s 127
c may itself have to be tested. Do those reasons have to be tested by reference to art 8(2), ie do the reasons on their face have to demonstrate that if they are right, it is necessary for the protection of the rights and freedom of others for the procedure under s 127 to be used? If so, is there machinery which allows the tenant to establish that the exceptions in art 8(2) do not apply?

d [52] The decision to take possession proceedings may be taken without the tenant opting to have a review (as in Forrest's appeal) or it may be taken after a review, the review forming part of the process leading to termination. The following questions seem to me to arise. Does the mere existence of the scheme mean that a local authority will not be, or cannot be, guilty of a breach of art 8 by reference to the individual rights of the particular tenant or will art 8(1) require
e the local authority to justify the particular decision by reference to the criteria in art 8(2)? Will it be sufficient justification to assert that the local authority has complied with the provisions of the scheme (ie acted in accordance with the law), and that Parliament has provided the remedy? Should the tenant be entitled to say in his or her particular case however justified the scheme may be generally, it
f is unnecessary for the local authority either (a) to enforce the scheme against him or her in order to protect the rights of other tenants or the rights of the local authority; or (b) opt for the scheme at all in the particular area because the conditions do not exist in that area as contemplated by those introducing the legislation?

[53] In the *Poplar* case there was no question of the situation of the particular
g tenant and the reasonableness or otherwise of the decision being in issue. Thus there was no discussion as to whether judicial review would provide a remedy which was art 6 compliant. But if the answer to the above questions is that the tenant should be entitled to raise matters, the question will arise as to whether the contemplation in *Cochrane's* case [1999] 1 WLR 809 that judicial review may
h be available is sufficient, or whether some modification to *Cochrane's* case is required and if so whether that modification can be achieved on the wording of the present legislation. This may be akin to the question that will arise when art 6 comes to be considered, but it needs consideration at this stage in relation to art 8.

[54] Mr Sales positively asserted that a tenant does have the right to raise
j points by reference to his or her own particular situation, but he also asserted that it does not follow that there needs to be any departure from *Cochrane's* case. His submission was that the tenant has the opportunity to raise points on the review; the tenant then before the county court judge has an opportunity to raise the question whether there is an arguable case for judicial review, and that the procedure in *Cochrane's* case allowing the judge to consider whether there was an arguable case for judicial review provided the tenant with protection against any

breach of art 8. Mr Sales would further suggest that the scope of judicial review
will be wider than the traditional approach, and could be wider still if necessary.

[55] Mr Watkinson also asserted in his appeal that the tenant should have the
right to raise points by reference to the facts of the particular case, but he asserted
that the alternatives were as follows:

'The judge could have (i) adjourned the claim for possession to enable the
appellants to discharge the rent arrears; (ii) suspended the possession order
for up to six weeks (section 89 HA 1980) which might have enabled arrears
to have been discharged; (iii) adjourned the possession proceedings to allow
application for judicial review to be made of the decision to institute or
pursue possession proceedings (see [Cochrane's case] [1999] 1 WLR 809 at
819); (iv) adjourned the possession proceedings to enable an application to
the High Court for a declaration of incompatibility; or (v) transferred the
case to the Administrative Court list for hearing as a judicial review which
could lead to a quashing of the decision as incompatible with a Convention
right with consequent invalidity of the possession proceedings (see Trustees
of Dennis Rye Pension Fund v Sheffield City Council [1997] 4 All ER 747 at 755,
[1998] 1 WLR 840 at 849 and Avon CC v Buscott [1988] 1 All ER 841, [1988] QB
656).'

[56] Mr Arden submitted that the review allowed the tenant if he or she opted
for it to raise particular facts, and that s 127 was clear in its terms and did not allow
for the tenant to raise points before the county court. He accepted that if he was
wrong on his first argument then judicial review would be available although he
would argue for a limited scope to that review.

[57] As to Mr Watkinson's suggestions the position seems to me to be as
follows. The wording of s 127 is clear, and indeed it is not suggested by him, or
indeed by any counsel, that by virtue of s 3 of the 1998 Act, words could be read
into that section so as to reverse their effect, and reverse Cochrane's case. He
submitted that if there has been an infringement of a convention right, the tenant
must be entitled to raise it in the possession proceedings (see s 7(1)(a) of the 1998
Act), and that it follows the judge must be bound to consider it. If the judge finds
the breach established he must be bound to give effect to that decision, the court
itself being a public authority, and that the court should in those circumstances
adjourn the possession proceedings generally so that the tenant's rights are not
infringed. His alternatives are fall-back positions one of which allows for
suspending possession under s 89 for a limited period of time, leading
Mr Watkinson into the argument that that section is also incompatible because it
imposes the time limits. His final two fall-backs, adjourning for judicial review or
a transfer to the Administrative Court, seem to adopt Cochrane's case.

[58] It seems to me that a tenant under an introductory tenancy must have the
right to raise the question whether it is reasonable in his or her particular case to
insist on eviction ie the question whether art 8(2) justifies the eviction. That
much has in reality to be conceded because under the relevant section reasons
must be given and there is then an entitlement to review ie an opportunity to
argue, that it is not reasonable in the particular case.

[59] The tenant must then have the right to rely on his or her convention
rights in any proceedings (see s 7(1)(b) of 1998 Act). That does not mean any
more than it says and because the point can be raised, it does not follow that the
court is bound to do any more than Cochrane's case envisaged ie consider the
arguability of the point, and then adjourn to allow the point to be properly

a considered if the point is arguable. The court is making the order it considers appropriate (see s 8(1)). Section 127 does not prevent the tenant relying on a convention right if the procedure in *Cochrane*'s case is followed.

[60] In this area, as with the arguments that will arise under art 6, what at root has to be considered is whether the review procedure taken together with judicial review provides adequate protection for a possible breach of art 8, and thus b whether the procedure advocated by *Cochrane*'s case where the county court judge considers whether there is a case for judicial review, and then adjourns it if there is, conforms with s 7 of the 1998 Act.

[61] In my view it does for the following reasons. Although as indicated the circumstances of particular tenants must be looked at, the overall scheme was one put in place by Parliament and that is an important point as it was in the c *Poplar* case [2001] 4 All ER 604, [2001] 3 WLR 183 as appears from the paragraph already quoted. The same point appears from *Buckley v UK* (1997) 23 EHRR 101 at 129 (para 74) where it is stated:

d 'As is well established in the Court's case law, it is for the national authorities to make the initial assessment of the "necessity" for an interference, as regards both the legislative framework and the particular measure of implementation. Although a margin of appreciation is thereby left to the national authorities, their decision remains subject to review by the Court for conformity with the requirements of the Convention. The scope of this margin of appreciation is not identical in each case but will vary e according to the context. Relevant factors include the nature of the Convention right in issue, its importance for the individual and the nature of the activities concerned.'

[62] Furthermore, in the context of art I Protocol I, the court has stated in *Mellacher v Austria* (1989) 12 EHRR 391 at 408–409 (para 45):

f '[Laws to control the use of property in accordance with the general interest] are especially called for and usual in the field of housing, which in our modern societies is a central concern of social and economic policies. In order to implement such policies, the legislature must have a wide margin of appreciation both with regard to the existence of a problem of public g concern warranting measures of control and as to the choice of the detailed rules for the implementation of such measures. The Court will respect the legislature's judgment as to what is in the general interest unless that judgment be manifestly without reasonable foundation.'

[63] Thus in the context of the introductory tenancy scheme Parliament h decided that it was necessary in the interest of tenants generally and the local authorities to have a scheme whereby during the first 12 months tenants were on probation and could be evicted without long battles in the county court. The scheme does not require the local authorities to be satisfied that breaches of the tenancy agreements have taken place, although alleged behaviour that would j constitute a breach will be relevant. There is in place a review procedure and that procedure is quasi-judicial in the sense that it is required to be fair. It contains a number of important safeguards. First, the local authority has a statutory obligation to set out a full statement of reasons for terminating the introductory tenancy in the notice for possession. Second, an attempt is made to remove any bias that there may be by requiring the review to be conducted by an officer senior to the officer who took the decision to issue the notice for possession, and

someone who was not involved in that previous decision. Third, the tenant has
an opportunity to make representation at an oral hearing or to make written *a*
representations (see paras 2, 4, and 5 of the 1997 regulations). Fourth, the tenant
has the right to representation including legal representation (see para 5(2)(a) of
the 1997 regulations). Fifth, the tenant has the right to call witnesses to give
evidence (see para 5(2)(b) of the 1997 regulations). Sixth, the tenant has the right
to put questions to any person who gives evidence at the hearing (see para 5(2)(c) *b*
of the 1997 regulations).

[64] If following the review the council decide to continue with the
possession proceedings, they again must give their reasons. The application
for possession then comes before the county court. If there is a challenge to the
reasons given and/or if the tenant asserts that the exceptions in art 8(2) do not *c*
apply in the particular case, and the judge thinks that arguable, the judge will
adjourn to allow an application to be made for judicial review. Should the
decision of the review panel be found to have been reached without proper
evidential basis or upon a view of the facts which could not reasonably be
entertained or on the basis of a material error of fact, then that would be a ground
for a review in the High Court (see *Secretary of State for Education and Science v* *d*
Tameside Metropolitan BC [1976] 3 All ER 665, [1977] 1 AC 1014 and *R v Criminal
Injuries Compensation Board, ex p A* [1999] 2 AC 330 at 344–345, [1999] 2 WLR 974
at 982). In addition, if the judge thought that although the decision to evict was
not in breach of art 8 the pace of the eviction which was taking place was out of
proportion and an infringement of the tenant's human rights, he could use s 89 *e*
and grant an extension of time, albeit for a limited period.

[65] What then if the tenant has not sought to review the decision to seek
possession under the section as in Forrest's appeal? This will be relevant but it
would not deprive the county court of the power to consider whether the
particular decision might arguably be a breach of the convention. If the judge
concludes that the point is arguable then he can adjourn to allow an application *f*
to be made for judicial review.

[66] In relation to arguability the county court will in any event bear in mind
that the scope of judicial review is not necessarily set in stone (see further below).

[67] In my view therefore the introductory tenancy scheme is not as such
incompatible with art 8, and there is no reason to think that individuals' rights *g*
will be infringed without remedy from the courts.

Section 89 compatibility

[68] It would not be right to consider the effect of this section outside the
ambit of the introductory tenancy scheme. I say that because in the light of the *h*
Poplar case [2001] 4 All ER 604, [2001] 3 WLR 183 it certainly cannot be said that
any limit placed on a county court's powers in relation to making an order for
possession must be incompatible with art 8. The *Poplar* case clearly demonstrates
that simply is not right. In the context of introductory tenancies and in the light
of my reasoning based on *Cochrane's* case [1999] 1 WLR 809 it seems to me there *j*
is no tenable argument that s 89 will provide a basis for saying that a tenant's art 8
rights are being infringed. The court has the power to adjourn if it is arguable that
a tenant's right is being infringed. If it does that, s 89 is simply not in play.
Section 89 only comes into play if either the court thinks its use with its
limitations will prevent an infringement of human rights, or if there is no
arguable infringement of those rights.

Article 6

a
[69] Is art 6 engaged? Article 6 is concerned with the 'determination of civil rights' ie with the resolution of a dispute between persons as to their civil rights. The initial decision by the council's housing section to serve notice of proceedings is said not to be such a determination. If that decision were simply characterised as a decision by one party to seek termination of a contract or tenancy that might

b no doubt be right. That was how it was characterised before Longmore J and on that basis it was so accepted by Longmore J (see paras 18 and 19 of his judgment). Indeed it is right to emphasise by way of introduction to the first point argued by Mr Sales on art 6 that no decision by one party to terminate a contract will be a determination within the meaning of that term in art 6.

[70] But it also is right to emphasise that art 6 may be engaged where the

c decision is of an administrative nature which affects the civil rights of individuals. Lord Clyde in R *(on the application of Alconbury Developments Ltd) v Secretary of State for the Environment, Transport and the Regions* [2001] UKHL 23 at [150], [2001] 2 All ER 929 at [150], [2001] 2 WLR 1389 said this:

d
'It is thus clear that art 6(1) is engaged where the decision which is to be given is of an administrative character, that is to say one given in an exercise of a discretionary power, as well as a dispute in a court of law regarding the private rights of the citizen, provided that it directly affects civil rights and obligations and is of a genuine and serious nature.'

e
[71] The decision of the council to terminate an introductory tenancy involves not only consideration of whether the introductory tenant has acted in certain ways which may be a breach of the tenancy agreement but it involves a balancing exercise so far as the position of other tenants or other would be tenants are concerned. Linda Wells on behalf of Bracknell, said in her witness statement:

f
'33. As Social Housing Professionals in a Joint Social Services and Housing Department, our role is to encourage and enable tenants to maintain successful tenancies. Eviction is very much a last resort, and is very often considered to be a failure. We regularly engage with other support agencies to prevent tenants losing their homes, and that remains so under the Introductory Tenancy Scheme.

g
34. However, as indicated above, the Scheme is a vital tool in the Council's fulfilment of its housing functions and its duties and responsibilities towards all its tenants and forms key part of the Council's strategy for dealing with anti-social behaviour.

35. Introductory Tenancies help to impress on new tenants the

h significance of their responsibilities under the Tenancy Agreement, and the fact that such an agreement should not be entered into lightly. They also provide a more expedient and certain route to possession in the small proportion of cases in which tenants persistently fail to pay rent or engage in behaviour that seriously affects other residents' peaceful enjoyment of their home and neighbourhood. In these ways they have proved to be a crucial

j Housing Management tool, both as a deterrent to anti-social behaviour and in minimising rent arrears.'

[72] Those paragraphs, and those already quoted from the second statement of Mr Cripps, have not been suggested to be in any way inaccurate as reflecting the attitude of a council. They demonstrate that decisions involve weighing up competing interests of tenants as a whole. It is the nature of the introductory

tenancy scheme giving the council powers to terminate a tenancy in the way
provided for which brings into play public law remedies and not private law
remedies as *Cochrane's* case recognised.

[73] However, the decisions do affect the property rights of the particular
tenant and in relation thereto the decision is of a 'genuine and serious nature'.
I stress that aspect because as it seems to me even if there was not an express
procedure laid down for some form of review and hearing, a decision of this
nature to terminate this type of tenancy might well bring into play an obligation
to provide an opportunity to be heard, and indeed under European jurisprudence,
art 6 might well in any event be engaged in relation to that decision in the way
hereafter explained.

[74] Before turning to art 6 and the cases relevant thereto, it is worth
examining what the attitude of the English courts would have been prior to the
coming into force of the 1998 Act. As already indicated in relation to a decision
of the council which complied with the review procedure, the introductory
tenant would not have had a private law remedy. The remedy would have been
by judicial review. What challenge could have been made? Could there have
been a challenge to the fairness of the procedure if the regulations had been
followed? It seems to me that the court would have accepted that there was
imposed on the council a duty to act fairly. The precise content of that duty
would have depended on the circumstances. In each case it would have been
recognised that a tenant would be at risk of losing the right to a secure tenancy,
and thus that the consequences for the tenant were great. But in relation to the
assertion that an obligation to act fairly would not normally allow someone to act
as judge in their own cause, the response would have been (a) that Parliament
had authorised that the review should be carried out as per the regulations and
(b) that in any event the procedural safeguards of having persons not involved in
the first decision reviewing the decision was fair. It has never been suggested in
these appeals that at common law an introductory tenant would succeed either
in challenging the regulations or in challenging any decision of a review panel
under the regulations, on the basis that no decision of a review panel could be
valid since the body was bound to be disqualified as a judge in its own cause.

[75] In *R (on the application of Bewry) v Norwich City Council* [2001] EWHC
Admin 657, [2001] All ER (D) 461 (Jul) (to which we have been referred after
completion of the arguments in this case), Moses J seems to have held that a
decision of the Review Board under the Housing Benefit (General) Regulations
1987, SI 1987/1971 was invalid at common law on the basis that only primary
legislation could authorise a body to be judge in its own cause. I am not sure that
that is right. The matter has not been fully argued out before us. But the relevant
principle seems to me to be the principle of legality as described by Lord
Hoffmann in *R v Secretary of State for the Home Dept, ex p Simms* [1999] 3 All ER 400
at 412, [2000] 2 AC 115 at 131:

'Parliamentary sovereignty means Parliament can, it if chooses, legislate
contrary to fundamental principles of human rights. The Human Rights Act
1998 will not detract from this power. The constraints upon its exercise by
Parliament are ultimately political, not legal. But the principle of legality
means that Parliament must squarely confront what it is doing and accept
the political cost. Fundamental rights cannot be overridden by general or
ambiguous words. This is because there is too great a risk that the full
implications of their unqualified meaning may have passed unnoticed in the

a   democratic process. In the absence of express language or necessary implication to the contrary, the courts therefore presume that even the most general words were intended to be subject to the basic rights of the individual. In this way the courts of the United Kingdom, though acknowledging the sovereignty of Parliament, apply principles of constitutionality little different from those which exist in countries where the power of the

b   legislature is expressly limited by a constitutional document.'

[76] After 2 October 2000 the principle was subsumed by s 3 of the 1998 Act, but before that date the principle was a rule of construction of some importance. First, it recognised the need for primary legislation to take away a fundamental right. Second, general words in primary legislation would not be

c   enough.

[77] Before the coming into force of the 1998 Act it would accordingly have been open to persons in the position of the appellants on these appeals, to argue that it needed primary legislation to take away fundamental rights, and to seek to argue that the regulations fell foul of that principle. The attack, so far as I know,

d   was never made, and I would suggest that it would have failed. It would have failed because a fundamental right is not to a tribunal which may not be perceived as judge in its own cause; the right is to access to the courts for the determination of civil rights as described in art 6 of the convention. The question at common law would accordingly have been whether the primary legislation empowered

e   regulations setting up the review panel, bearing in mind an introductory tenant's right to seek judicial review. I suggest that there would be no question that it did. On judicial review I suggest that if an attack on the decision of the review body were to be successful, it would have been necessary to establish some factor beyond the mere constitution of the review body in accordance with the regulations. It would not have been enough to argue that, albeit constituted

f   strictly in accordance with the regulations, the review body would be perceived as a judge in its own cause making all decisions void.

[78] As I say the matter has not been argued out but one can say at least this. Before the 1998 Act came into force it has not been suggested that the review body set up under these regulations simply cannot reach a fair decision; nor has

g   it been suggested that the decision reached by the review body cannot be properly reviewed by judicial review.

[79] How then does art 6 impinge on the above? The argument of Mr Pleming QC, putting it at its simplest, is that the sections of the 1996 Act recognise that the local authority must have reasons for terminating an

h   introductory tenancy (see s 128(3)); if the tenant takes issue with the validity of those reasons and seeks a review, the validity is determined by the review panel whose fact-finding is then implemented by the county court making an order. He thus submits there is a determination of a civil right and art 6 applies to the decision-making process. Since the county court takes no part in the decision relating to the facts and since the review panel is not an independent tribunal

j   taking decisions in public, art 6 is prima facie infringed. Furthermore, by the information provided to tenants who enter into introductory tenancies, introductory tenants will be led to believe that only if they are in breach of the terms of the introductory tenancy agreement will the local authority consider that there are reasons for taking proceedings for possession; thus the issue determined by the review panel will more often than not be whether the tenant

is in breach of the introductory tenancy agreement. Again he submits a civil right
is determined, art 6 is thus engaged and art 6 is prima facie infringed.

[80] Mr Sales' argument in reliance on *Kaplan v UK* (1980) 4 EHRR 64 is that
on a proper analysis there is no determination of civil rights by the review panel.
He submitted that under the introductory scheme the local authority is free to
determine a tenancy without reliance on any breach and without any
determination of any issue between the parties. The fact that one party to the
tenancy allows another party to come and seek to explain why the tenancy
should not be terminated, does not mean that a rejection of the explanation
amounts to a determination of any civil right. In one sense the very fact that the
review panel is part of the local authority demonstrates that the body is not
determining issues; it is deciding for itself whether to exercise the right of
obtaining possession having given the other party a fair opportunity to explain
why it should not. Not every administrative decision which affects private rights
brings into play art 6. Mr Sales would not go so far as to say that the local
authority need have no reason for termination, because he would accept that the
decision of the local authority can be made the subject of judicial review where
for example it could be shown to be an unreasonable decision, or, he would add,
where it can be shown that the taking of the decision in the particular
circumstances infringes the art 8 rights of the tenant.

[81] Mr Sales relied particularly on the following citations from *Kaplan's* case
(at 87–88, 90):

'151. As the Court has held in [*Ringeisen v Austria (No 1)* (1971) 1 EHRR 455
and *König v Germany* (1978) 2 EHRR 170] Article 6(1) may be applicable in
cases concerning the exercise of such public powers. Nevertheless, Article 6
does not, in the Commission's opinion, prohibit the conferment on public
authorities of powers to take action affecting the private rights of citizens. It
does not go so far as to provide that all acts, decisions or measures which
affect private rights must themselves be taken by a tribunal. Such a
conclusion, apart from being in conflict with the common position in the
contracting States both today and when the Convention was drafted, would
also not be warranted, in the Commission's opinion, by a proper
interpretation of Article 6(1).

152. It is plain from the text of Article 6(1) that it does not directly protect
the individual's "civil rights" as such against acts or decisions which modify,
annul or otherwise interfere with them. In many circumstances the private
rights of an individual are liable to be affected not only by the lawful acts of
public authorities but also by those of other individuals or entities exercising
countervailing private rights of their own, and indeed by circumstances of a
purely factual nature such as the effluxion of time. The mere fact that an
individual's private rights are adversely affected by the acts of another party,
whether a public authority or not, does not therefore involve a violation of
Article 6(1) ...

154. In the Commission's view the essential role of Article 6(1) in this
sphere is to lay down guarantees concerning the mode in which claims or
disputes concerning legal rights and obligations (of a "civil" character) are to
be resolved. A distinction must be drawn between the acts of a body which
is engaged in the resolution of such a claim or dispute and the acts of an
administrative or other body purporting merely to exercise or apply a legal
power vested in it and not to resolve a legal claim or dispute. Article 6(1)

a would not, in the Commission's opinion, apply to the acts of the latter even if they do affect "civil rights". It could not be considered as being engaged in a process of "determination" of civil rights and obligations. Its function would not be to decide (*"decidera"*) on a claim, dispute or *"contestation"*. Its acts may, on the other hand, give rise to a claim, dispute or *"contestation"* and Article 6 may come into play in that way …

b 161. An interpretation of Article 6(1) under which it was held to provide a right to a full appeal on the merits of every administrative decision affecting private rights would therefore lead to a result which was inconsistent with the existing, and long-standing, legal position in most of the Contracting States.'

c [82] Mr Sales' argument is similar to that put forward on behalf of the Lord Advocate in R (*on the application of Alconbury Developments Ltd*) v *Secretary of State for the Environment, Transport and the Regions* [2001] 2 All ER 929, [2001] 2 WLR 1389 and dealt with by Lord Hoffmann from [131]–[135]. Lord Hoffmann indeed quotes para 154 of *Kaplan*'s case and then says:

d '[134] My Lords, this reasoning is in accordance with the way in which, at the outset of this speech, I suggested to your Lordships that, apart from European authority, the case ought to be decided. But it provides a short answer only if it is assumed that art 6 requires no more than that judicial review proceedings be decided by an independent and impartial tribunal. If,

e however, art 6 is construed as going further and mandating some minimum content to the judicial review jurisdiction, then it is necessary to ask, as I have done at some length, whether the extent of the judicial review jurisdiction available in England and Scotland is sufficient to satisfy the requirements of the European Court jurisprudence. As appears from my analysis of that

f jurisprudence, there is no doubt that the European Court of Human Rights has construed art 6 as requiring certain minimum standards of judicial review. This appears most clearly from the Swedish cases to which I have referred.

[135] Once one accepts this construction, it makes little difference whether one says, as in *Kaplan*'s case, that the administrative act does not fall

g within art 6 at all and the question is concerned only with the adequacy and impartiality of the judicial review, or whether one says, as the European Court of Human Rights and Commission have done in other cases, that the administrative act does in theory come within art 6 but the administrator's lack of impartiality can be cured by an adequate and impartial judicial

h review. The former seems to me a more elegant analysis, but the latter may be necessary in order to explain, in the context of civilian concepts, why the administrative process can be treated as involving at any stage a determination of civil rights and obligations. So, tempting as it is, I am unable to accept [counsel for the Lord Advocate's] short cut.'

j [83] It seems to me that Mr Sales is suggesting that in this case we should take the short cut. In my view we are not free to do so. Thus I reject Mr Sales' first point. The decision of the review panel is certainly involved in the determination of an introductory tenant's civil rights and I accept that the real issue to be addressed at this stage is whether the combination of the review panel plus judicial review is enough to meet the requirements of art 6 to which I now turn.

Is combination of review panel plus judicial review enough to meet the requirements of art 6?

[84] It is accepted that the review panel itself could not have the degree of independence to comply with art 6. But it is also accepted that it is necessary to consider the decision making process as a whole in determining whether the requirements of art 6 are met. *Albert v Belgium* (1983) 5 EHRR 533 at 542 (para 29) puts it this way:

'... the Convention calls for at least one of the two following systems: either the jurisdictional organs themselves comply with the requirements of Article 6(1), or they do not so comply but are subject to subsequent control by a judicial body that has full jurisdiction and does provide the guarantees of Article 6(1).'

[85] There are further aspects of the speech of Lord Hoffmann in the *Alconbury* case to which I would draw attention. First he points out (at [73]) how judicial review gives effect to the rule of law ensuring that 'administrative decisions will be taken rationally, in accordance with a fair procedure and within the powers conferred by Parliament'. Second he points out (at [74]) that decisions on policy are not a '"determination" of civil rights' although they may 'affect civil rights' although some decisions may in fact 'determine civil rights' and should thus be made by independent and impartial tribunals. Third he traces how the European jurisprudence arrived at the view that art 6(1) could have an application to administrative decisions concluding (at [79]) that the court has accepted that 'civil rights' means only rights in private law and has applied art 6(1) to administrative decisions on the ground that they can determine or affect rights in private law. He then cites the above passage from *Albert's* case which refers to control by a judicial body with 'full jurisdiction', and continues:

'[79] These views of the meaning of "civil rights and obligations" are only of historical interest, because, as we shall see, the European Court of Human Rights has not restricted art 6(1) to the determination of rights in private law. The probable original meaning, which Judge Wiarda said in [*König v Germany* (1978) 2 EHRR 170 at 205], was the "classical meaning" of the term "civil rights" in a civilian system of law, is nevertheless important. It explains the process of reasoning, unfamiliar to an English lawyer, by which the Strasbourg court has arrived at the conclusion that art 6(1) can have application to administrative decisions. The court has not simply said, as I have suggested one might say in English law, that one can have "civil right" to a lawful decision by an administrator. Instead, the court has accepted that "civil rights" means only rights in private law and has applied art 6(1) to administrative decisions on the ground that they can determine or affect rights in private law ...

[86] In the later case of *Albert* (1983) 5 EHRR 533 at 542 (para 29), in which a similar situation arose, the court said, that although disciplinary jurisdiction could be conferred upon professional bodies which did not meet the requirements of art 6(1) (e g because they were not "established by law" or did not sit in public)—"Nonetheless, in such circumstances the Convention calls at least for one of the two following systems: either the jurisdictional organs themselves comply with the requirements of Article 6(1), or they do not so comply but are subject to subsequent control by a judicial body that has full jurisdiction and does provide the guarantees of Article 6(1)."

a
[87] The reference to "full jurisdiction" has been frequently cited in subsequent cases and sometimes relied upon in argument as if it were authority for saying that a policy decision affecting civil rights by an administrator who does not comply with art 6(1) has to be reviewable on its merits by an independent and impartial tribunal. It was certainly so relied upon by counsel for the respondents in these appeals. But subsequent
b
European authority shows that "full jurisdiction" does not mean full decision-making power. It means full jurisdiction to deal with the case as the nature of the decision requires.

[88] This emerges most clearly from the decisions on the English planning cases, which I shall analyse later in some detail. But the leading European authority for the proposition that it is not necessary to have a
c
review of the merits of a policy decision is *Zumtobel v Austria* (1993) 17 EHRR 116. The Zumtobel partnership objected to the compulsory purchase of their farming land to build the L52 by-pass road in the Austrian Vorarlberg. The appropriate government committee heard their objections but confirmed the order. They appealed to an administrative court which said
d
that the government had taken proper matters into account and that it was not entitled to substitute its decision for that of the administrative authority. They complained to the commission and the European Court of Human Rights that, as the administrative court could not "independently assess the merits and the facts of the case", it did not have "full jurisdiction" within the meaning of the *Albert* formula. The European Court of Human Rights said
e
(at 133 (para 32)) that its jurisdiction was sufficient in the circumstances of the case, '[r]egard being had to the respect which must be accorded to decisions taken by the administrative authorities on grounds of expediency and to the nature of the complaints made by the Zumtobel partnership".'

f
[86] What however about the review of factual decisions? On this Lord Hoffmann cites with approval a passage from the opinion of Mr Nicolas Bratza (as he then was) when concurring with the majority of the Commission on the admissibility of Mr Bryan's complaint in *Bryan v UK* (1995) 21 EHRR 342. Mr Bratza said (at 354):

g
'It appears to me that the requirement that a court or tribunal should have "full jurisdiction" cannot be mechanically applied with the result that, in all circumstances and whatever the subject matter of the dispute, the court or tribunal must have full power to substitute its own findings of fact, and its own inferences from those facts, for that of the administrative authority concerned. Whether the power of judicial review is sufficiently wide to
h
satisfy the requirements of Article 6 must in my view depend on a number of considerations, including the subject matter of the dispute, the nature of the decision of the administrative authorities which is in question, the procedure, if any, which exists for review of the decision by a person or body acting independently of the authority concerned and the scope of that power
j
of review.'

[87] Lord Hoffmann then said:

'[110] Mr Bratza's particular insight, if I may respectfully say so, was to see that a tribunal may be more or less independent, depending upon the question it is being called upon to decide. On matters of policy, the inspector was no more independent than the Secretary of State himself. But this was a matter on which independence was unnecessary—indeed, on democratic *a* principles, undesirable—and in which the power of judicial review, paying full respect to the views of the inspector or Secretary of State on questions of policy or expediency, was sufficient to satisfy art 6(1). On the other hand, in deciding the questions of primary fact or fact and degree which arose in enforcement notice appeals, the inspector was no mere bureaucrat. He was an expert tribunal acting in a quasi-judicial manner and therefore sufficiently *b* independent to make it unnecessary that the High Court should have a broad jurisdiction to review his decisions on questions of fact.'

[**88**] Lord Hoffmann pointed out that the European Court adopted Mr Bratza's approach in its judgment saying:

'[114] On ground (b) [(issues of fact)], the European Court of Human *c* Rights noted (at 360–361 (para 46)) what it described as: "... the uncontested safeguards attending the procedure before the inspector: the quasi-judicial character of the decision-making process; the duty incumbent on each inspector to exercise independent judgment; the requirement that inspectors must not be subject to any improper influence; the stated mission of the *d* Inspectorate to uphold the principles of openness, fairness and impartiality.

[115] It went on to say (at 361 (para 47)) that if Mr Bryan had pursued his appeal on ground (b), the High Court, while not being able to substitute its own findings of fact, "had the power to satisfy itself that the inspector's findings of fact or the inferences based on them were neither perverse nor irrational". This was enough to satisfy art 6: "Such an approach by an appeal *e* tribunal on questions of fact can reasonably be expected in specialised areas of the law such as the one at issue, particularly where the facts have already been established in the course of a quasi-judicial procedure governed by many of the safeguards required by Article 6(1). It is also frequently a feature in the systems of judicial control of administrative decisions found throughout *f* the Council of Europe Member States.'

[**89**] What those passages support are the following propositions in considering whether judicial review, plus the procedures, are art 6 compliant: (1) it is relevant whether findings of fact are material to the decision; (2) if findings of fact are material to the decision, that will not finally determine whether judicial *g* review provides a remedy in compliance with art 6; (3) if the facts have themselves been found by 'an expert tribunal' sufficiently independent to make it unnecessary for the court to have a broad jurisdiction to review those decisions of fact that is likely to lead to the conclusion that judicial review is sufficient.

[**90**] The above propositions are made in the context of the traditional ambit *h* of judicial review. If that was the correct ambit to contemplate then clearly, if the facts are material, it might be said that the less expert the fact-finder and the less independent the fact-finder then the less likely it would be that judicial review would be sufficient. Perhaps the first question is whether it is right to contemplate only the traditional form of judicial review. In *W v UK* [1988] 10 EHRR 29 the decision referred to by Keene LJ in giving leave in *McLellan*'s case, *j* the court took a limited view of the scope of judicial review as appears from para 82 (at 58):

'An application for judicial review or the institution of wardship proceedings does enable the English courts to examine a local authority's *a*   decision in the matter of access by a parent to his child who is in public care. These two remedies provide valuable safeguards against exercise by the authority of its discretion in an improper manner. Nevertheless, on an application for judicial review, the courts will not review the merits of the decision but will confine themselves to ensuring, in brief, that the authority did not act illegally, unreasonably or unfairly. Where a care order or a

b   parental rights resolution is in force, the scope of the review effected in the context of wardship proceedings will normally be similarly confined.'

[91] One question is whether it is right to contemplate that judicial review would be as limited as there suggested.

c   [92] In *R (on the application of Alconbury Developments Ltd) v Secretary of State for the Environment, Transport and the Regions* [2001] 2 All ER 929, [2001] 2 WLR 1389 Lord Hoffmann was not contemplating, or perhaps not needing to contemplate, any extension in relation to judicial review (see his speech at [73]). Lord Nolan said (at [62]):

d   'The reversal of a finding of fact in the field of planning would no doubt be highly unusual. I mention *Edwards (Inspector of Taxes) v Bairstow* [1955] 3 All ER 48, [1956] AC 14 simply to illustrate the generosity with which the courts, including your Lordships' House, have interpreted their powers to review questions of law. A similarly broad and generous approach has been adopted in the development of judicial review extending as it does not only to points

e   of law in the strict and narrow sense but to such matters as the rationality of the decision and the fairness of the decision-making process. One possibility canvassed in argument was that the powers of review as at present exercised by the courts might be enlarged in order to accommodate the requirements of the 1998 Act. For my part, at least in the context of the present case, I see

f   no need for that.'

[93] Lord Clyde said:

         '*The scope of judicial review*

g   [169] The suggestion was advanced that if the respondents were correct in their contention that the present proceedings are in breach of art 6(1), the scope of judicial review might somehow be enlarged so as to provide a complete remedy. The point in the event does not arise, but I consider that it might well be difficult to achieve a sufficient enlargement to meet the stated purpose without jeopardising the constitutional balance between the

h   role of the courts and the role of the executive. The supervisory jurisdiction of the court as it has now developed seems to me adequate to deal with a wide range of complaints which can properly be seen as directed to the legality of a decision. It is sufficient to note the recognition of the idea of proportionality, or perhaps more accurately, disproportionality, and the

j   extent to which the factual areas of a decision may be penetrated by a review of the account taken by a decision-maker of facts which are irrelevant or even mistaken (*R v Criminal Injuries Compensation Board, ex p A* [1999] 2 AC 330 at 344–345, [1999] 2 WLR 974 at 982). But consideration of the precise scope of the administrative remedies is not necessary for the purposes of the present appeals.'

[94] Lord Slynn said:

a

'[51] The Court of Justice does of course apply the principle of proportionality when examining such acts and national judges must apply the same principle when dealing with Community law issues. There is a difference between that principle and the approach of the English courts in *Associated Provincial Picture Houses Ltd v Wednesbury Corp* [1947] 2 All ER 680, [1948] 1 KB 223. But the difference in practice is not as great as is sometimes supposed. The cautious approach of the Court of Justice in applying the principle is shown inter alia by the margin of appreciation it accords to the institutions of the community in making economic assessments. I consider that even without reference to the 1998 Act the time has come to recognise that this principle is part of English administrative law, not only when judges are dealing with community acts but also when they are dealing with acts subject to domestic law. Trying to keep the *Wednesbury* principle and proportionality in separate compartments seems to me to be unnecessary and confusing. Reference to the 1998 Act however makes it necessary that the court should ask whether what is done is compatible with convention rights. That will often require that the question should be asked whether the principle of proportionality has been satisfied: see *R v Secretary of State for the Home Department, ex p Turgut* [2001] 1 All ER 719; *R (Mahmood) v Secretary of State for the Home Dept* [2000] 1 WLR 840.

b

c

d

[52] This principle does not go as far as to provide for a complete rehearing on the merits of the decision. Judicial control does not need to go so far. It should not do so unless Parliament specifically authorises it in particular areas.'

e

[95] Judicial control over the legality of a decision does not require a complete rehearing of the merits. But it seems to me that in considering whether a section of a statute is compatible or not, this court should be inclined to assume that the administrative court will at least be likely to ensure that its procedures will enable it to test the legality of a decision, and in particular whether that decision infringes the human rights of a tenant such as the tenants in the appeals before us. Support for this view appears from 1(1) *Halsbury's Laws* (4th edn) (2001 reissue) para 89, where it says:

f

g

'Where the exercise of a discretionary power is liable to interfere with fundamental human rights, the courts will examine the decision maker's actions more rigorously than where such interests are not directly affected by the action taken ...'

—citing Lord Hope of Craighead in *R v DPP ex p Kebeline, R v DPP, ex p Rechachi* [1999] 4 All ER 801 at 843–844, [2000] 2 AC 326 at 380.

h

[96] With the above in mind I return to the relevant considerations. Are material facts likely to be an issue? That seems to me to depend on the circumstances of individual cases. In relation to rent arrears, for example, the facts can be established with certainty, and the question in issue as between the council and an individual tenant is likely to be whether in the circumstances it was reasonable for the council to proceed with terminating the introductory tenancy. That question, if it is to be reviewed by a court, seems to me to be clearly suitable for judicial review even of the traditional variety.

j

[97] There may however be circumstances of a more difficult nature. If the council in providing reasons alleges acts constituting nuisance, and if the

a allegations themselves are disputed that at first sight seems to raise issues of fact. But under the introductory tenancy scheme it is not a requirement that the council should be satisfied that breaches of the tenancy agreement have in fact taken place. The right question under the scheme will be whether in the context of allegation and counter-allegation it was reasonable for the council to take a decision to proceed with termination of the introductory tenancy. That is again

b a matter which can be dealt with under judicial review either of the traditional kind or if it is necessary so to do intensified so as to ensure that the tenant's rights are protected.

[98] What about the quality of the tribunal carrying out the review and what about the important point taken by Mr Pleming that if the administrative court formed the view that the decision of a review panel ought to be quashed then its

c only power would be to remit the matter to the landlord? This was a point of significance in *Kingsley v UK* (7 November 2000, unreported), see in particular paras 58 and 59.

[99] It is in my view legitimate to take into account in this context that the review panel is a body chosen by Parliament. If, of course, it was simply

d impossible for such a tribunal to reach a fair decision, that would lead inevitably to the conclusion that the scheme could not work without infringement of art 6. Would it be impossible for there to be a fair decision from any person who would be appointed to review matters under the introductory tenancy scheme? Would a court inevitably come to the conclusion that any officer, however senior, could

e not constitute a fair tribunal for hearing the matter? Is the position such that judicial review could not provide the check as to whether a decision had been reached fairly and lawfully?

[100] One has to remember that the council are in reality making decisions which are not simply decisions as to whether it has a right to terminate. The council is not anxious to terminate unless other considerations prevail. The council

f is having to have regard to competing interests of other tenants and the competing interest of others who need the housing that they can supply. In my view there is no reason to think that such a decision cannot be taken fairly at a senior level of the council reviewing the decisions already reached by less senior people. Furthermore it seems to me that judicial review will be able to check the

g fairness and legality of decisions taken.

[101] Thus, it is my view (i) that there is no reason to hold that the review procedure cannot be operated fairly, and (ii) that there is no reason to hold that the remedy of judicial review will not provide an adequate safeguard to tenants enabling them to challenge any unfairness and/or any infringement of their

h convention rights particularly under art 8.

[102] Thus, as it seems to me, it cannot be said that s 127 or the scheme at the macro level is incompatible with art 6.

[103] What I would stress is that where a review has taken place, in a case in which the council is seeking to take possession, it should be the norm for the

j council to spell out in affidavits before the county court judge, how the procedure was operated in the individual case dealing with the degree of independence of the tribunal from persons who took the original decision, the way the hearing was conducted and the reason for taking the decision to continue with the proceedings. In that way the judge will have the information on which he can take an informed view as to whether the matter should be adjourned to allow for an application to be made for judicial review. In this way also s 7 of the 1998 Act

can be complied with so that the question whether it is arguable that any breach
of human rights occurred can be considered at the county court stage.

Article 14

[**104**] Having regard to the views expressed on arts 6 and 8 no point arises in
relation to art 14, art 14 only having any operation within the ambit of another
convention right. I should however just say that in my view the argument that
the introduction of an introductory tenancy scheme is in some way discriminatory,
seems to me misplaced. Once introduced the scheme applies to all would-be
tenants, and there is no question of persons in factually similar circumstances
being treated differently.

CONCLUSION

[**105**] In relation to McLellan's appeal the appeal must be dismissed.

[**106**] In relation to Forrest's appeal the position is as follows. Forrest did not
seek a review by the council of its decision. There is an issue as to how that came
about. However, no request was made to the county court judge to adjourn the
case so that an application for judicial review could be made, and the argument
proceeded on what I have called the macro level. It seems to me that it is too late
now to apply for permission to move for judicial review. I should add that on the
facts as presented to us, I have no reason for thinking that permission to move for
judicial review would ever have been granted. In the circumstances this appeal
must be dismissed also.

LATHAM LJ.

[**107**] I agree.

KAY LJ.

[**108**] I also agree.

Appeals dismissed. Permission to appeal refused.

Kate O'Hanlon   Barrister.

a Adan v Newham London Borough Council and another

[2001] EWCA Civ 1916

b COURT OF APPEAL, CIVIL DIVISION
BROOKE, HALE LJJ AND DAVID STEEL J
23, 24 OCTOBER, 14 DECEMBER 2001

Housing – Homeless person – Duty of housing authority to provide accommodation – Appeals procedure – Local authority reviewing officer not an independent and impartial
c *tribunal – Applicant having right of appeal on point of law to county court from reviewing officer's decision – Whether appeals procedure as a whole complying with right to fair hearing – Housing Act 1996, ss 202, 204 – Human Rights Act 1998, Sch 1, Pt I, art 6(1) – Local Authorities (Contracting Out of Allocation of Housing and Homelessness Functions) Order 1996, art 3.*

d
The respondent, A, applied to the appellant local housing authority for assistance under Pt VII of the Housing Act 1996. Her application was rejected by one of the authority's housing officers, and that decision was affirmed by its appeal officer on a review under s 202[a] of the 1996 Act. A then exercised her right of appeal to the county court under s 204(1)[b] of the Act which gave a dissatisfied applicant a
e right of appeal 'on any point of law' arising from the review decision or the original decision. The judge allowed the appeal and quashed the decision. However, he expressed concern about the compatibility of the normal review procedure with art 6(1)[c] of the European Convention for the Protection of Human Rights and Fundamental Freedoms 1950 (as set out in Sch 1 to the
f Human Rights Act 1998) which provided that everyone was entitled, in the determination of his civil rights and obligations, to a fair hearing by an independent and impartial tribunal. The judge therefore directed that the further review should be conducted by a different reviewing officer who possessed the appropriate impartiality and independence required by art 6(1) of the convention (the further direction). On appeal to the Court of Appeal, the authority did not
g challenge the judge's decision to allow A's appeal, but did challenge his power to make the further direction.

Held – The judge had no power to make the further direction. Section 204 of the 1996 Act specified the powers given to the county court on such an appeal, and
h since the matter was a public law matter, the authority was obliged to review the matter again as soon as the original determination was quashed. As a public authority, the authority would know that it would be unlawful for it to act in a way that was incompatible with a convention right, and the County Courts Act 1984 expressly provided that the county court had no power to order mandamus.
j The judge was doing just that when he ordered the authority to carry out a public

---

a   Section 202, so far as material, provides: '(1) An applicant has the right to request a review of—(a) any decision of a local housing authority as to his eligibility for assistance …
(4) On a request being duly made to them, the authority or authorities concerned shall review their decision.'
b   Section 204, so far as material, is set out at [69], below
c   Article 6 is set out at [54], below

duty in a particular way. Accordingly, the appeal would be allowed (see [7], [51], [84], below). *a*

Per curiam. Although a local housing authority appeal officer, employed by the authority to review its decisions on applications for assistance by homeless persons under Pt VII of the 1996 Act, is not an independent and impartial tribunal for the purposes of art 6(1) of the convention, the powers of the county court on an appeal against his decision on a point of law under s 204 of the 1996 Act, which *b* are akin to those of judicial review exercisable in the High Court, are sufficient to ensure that the procedure as a whole is compliant with art 6(1), provided that there is no material dispute as to the primary facts. If there is no such dispute, the county court will have power to correct any errors of law which may have arisen in the way in which those facts were considered for the purpose of the ultimate *c* decision. Where, however, there is such a dispute, the irregularity in the procedure cannot be cured by an appeal under s 204. It is not possible to interpret the words 'appeal ... on any point of law' in s 204(1) as if they included an appeal on a point of fact. Similarly (per Brooke LJ and David Steel J, contra Hale LJ), it it not possible to interpret them in such a way as to confer on a county court jurisdiction to decide whether the decision-making process as a whole complies *d* with art 6(1) in the particular circumstances of the case, and to decide disputed questions of fact itself if it concludes that that is the only way to achieve compliance with art 6(1). It follows that if, on a s 202 review, there is a dispute about primary facts which has to be resolved because it is material to the decision-making process, the danger will arise that the proceedings, taken as a *e* whole, will not be convention-compliant. It is, nevertheless, open to an authority to contract out its reviewing function pursuant to the powers conferred on it by art 3^dof the Local Authorities (Contracting Out of Allocation of Housing and Homelessness Functions) Order 1996 in such a way that an independent and impartial tribunal might be appointed to conduct the review in those cases where *f* a material dispute as to the facts has to be resolved (see [9], [17], [20], [26], [42]–[44], [48]–[50], [67], [70], [76], [87], [94], below); *R (on the application of Alconbury Developments Ltd) v Secretary of State of the Environment, Transport and the Regions* [2001] 2 All ER 929, *R v A* [2001] 3 All ER 1 and *R (on the application of McLellan) v Bracknell Forest BC, Reigate and Banstead BC v Benfield* [2002] 1 All ER 899 considered. *g*

Notes

For the right to a fair hearing before an independent and impartial tribunal, see 8(2) *Halsbury's Laws* (4th edn reissue) paras 134, 140, and for appeals to the county *h* court on a point of law from a reviewing officer's decision, see 22 *Halsbury's Laws* (4th edn reissue) para 264.

For the Housing Act 1996, ss 202, 204, see 21 *Halsbury's Statutes* (4th edn) (1997 reissue) 910, 911.

For the Human Rights Act 1998, Sch 1, Pt 1, art 6, see 7 *Halsbury's Statutes* (4th edn) (1999 reissue) 523. *j*

For the Local Authorities (Contracting Out of Allocation of Housing and Homelessness Functions) Order 1996, see 10 *Halsbury's Statutory Instruments* (2001 issue) 205.

d   Article 3, so far as material, is set out at [9], below

Cases referred to in judgments

a *Albert v Belgium* (1983) 5 EHRR 533, [1983] ECHR 7299/75, ECt HR.
Associated Provincial Picture Houses Ltd v Wednesbury Corp [1947] 2 All ER 680, [1948] 1 KB 223, CA.
Begum v Tower Hamlets London BC [2000] 1 WLR 306, CA.
Benmax v Austin Motor Co Ltd [1955] 1 All ER 326, [1955] AC 370, [1955] 2 WLR
b   418, HL.
Brutus v Cozens [1972] 2 All ER 1297, [1973] AC 854, [1972] 3 WLR 521, HL.
Bryan v UK (1996) 21 EHRR 342, [1995] ECHR 19178/91, E Com HR and ECt HR.
C v S (minor: abduction: illegitimate child) [1990] 2 All ER 961, sub nom *Re J (a minor) (abduction: custody rights)* [1990] 2 AC 562, [1990] 3 WLR 492, HL.
Daganayasi v Minister of Immigration [1980] 2 NZLR 130, NZ CA.
c *Deumeland v Germany* (1986) 8 EHRR 448, [1986] ECHR 9384/81, ECt HR.
Director General of Fair Trading v Proprietary Association of Great Britain [2001] EWCA Civ 1217, [2002] 1 All ER 853, sub nom *Re Medicaments and Related Classes of Goods (No 4)* [2002] 1 WLR 269.
Edwards v UK (1992) 15 EHRR 417, ECt HR.
d *Edwards (Inspector of Taxes) v Bairstow* [1955] 3 All ER 48, [1956] AC 14, [1955] 3 WLR 410, HL.
Feldbrugge v Netherlands (1986) 8 EHRR 425, [1986] ECHR 8562/79, ECt HR.
Ghosh v General Medical Council [2001] UKPC 29, [2001] 1 WLR 1915.
ISKCON v UK (1994) 76A DR 90, E Com HR.
Khawaja v Secretary of State for the Home Dept [1983] 1 All ER 765, [1984] AC 74,
e   [1983] 2 WLR 321, HL.
Minister for Aboriginal Affairs v Peko-Wallsend Ltd (1985–86) 162 CLR 24, Aust HC.
Nessa v Chief Adjudication Officer [1999] 4 All ER 677, [1999] 1 WLR 1937, HL.
New Zealand Fishing Industry Association Inc v Minister of Agriculture and Fisheries [1988] 1 NZLR 544, NZ CA.
f *Poplar Housing and Regeneration Community Association Ltd v Donoghue* [2001] EWCA Civ 595, [2001] 4 All ER 604, [2002] QB 48, [2001] 3 WLR 183.
Priess v General Dental Council [2001] UKPC 36, [2001] 1 WLR 1926.
Puhlhofer v Hillingdon London BC [1986] 1 All ER 467, [1986] AC 484, [1986] 2 WLR
     259, HL.
R v A [2001] UKHL 25, [2001] 3 All ER 1, [2002] 1 AC 45, [2001] 2 WLR 1546; *affg*
g   [2001] ECWA Crim 4, sub nom *R v Y* [2001] All ER (D) 66 (Jan).
R v Criminal Injuries Compensation Board, ex p A [1999] 2 AC 330, [1999] 2 WLR 974, HL.
R v London Residuary Body, ex p Inner London Education Authority (1987) [1998] JR
     238, DC.
h *R v P* [1991] 3 All ER 337, sub nom *DPP v P* [1991] 2 AC 447, [1991] 3 WLR 161, HL.
R (on the application of Alconbury Developments Ltd) v Secretary of State of the Environment, Transport and the Regions [2001] UKHL 23, [2001] 2 All ER 929, [2001] 2 WLR 1389.
R (on the application of Bewry) v Norwich City Council [2001] EWHC Admin 657,
j   [2001] All ER (D) 461 (Jul).
R (on the application of Husain) v Asylum Support Adjudicator [2001] EWHC Admin 852, [2001] All ER (D) 107 (Oct).
R (on the application of Kathro) v Rhondda Cynon Taff County BC [2001] EWHC Admin 527, [2001] All ER (D) 130 (Jul).
R (on the application of McLellan) v Bracknell Forest BC, Reigate and Banstead BC v Benfield [2001] EWCA Civ 1510, [2002] 1 All ER 899.

R (on the application of Wilkinson) v Responsible Medical Officer Broadmoor Hospital
  [2001] EWCA Civ 1545, [2001] All ER (D) 294 (Oct).   *a*
Schuler-Zgraggen v Switzerland (1993) 16 EHRR 405, [1993] ECHR 14518/89 ECt
  HR.
Secretary of State for Education and Science v Metropolitan Borough of Tameside [1976]
  3 All ER 665, [1977] AC 1014, [1976] 2 WLR 641, HL.
Secretary of State for Employment v Associated Society of Locomotive Engineers and   *b*
  Firemen (No 2) [1972] 2 All ER 949, [1972] 2 QB 455, [1972] 2 WLR 1370, CA.
Shah v Barnet London BC [1983] 1 All ER 226, [1983] 2 AC 309, [1983] 2 WLR 16,
  HL.
Simplex GE (Holdings) Ltd v Secretary of State for the Environment [1988] 3 PLR 25,
  CA.
Stefan v UK (1998) 25 EHRR CD 130, E Com HR.   *c*
Twalib v Greece (2001) 33 EHRR 584, [1998] ECHR 24294/94, ECt HR.
Zumtobel v Austria (1993) 17 EHRR 116, [1993] ECHR 12235/86, ECt HR.

Cases also cited or referred to in skeleton arguments

Azimi v Newham London BC (2001) 33 HLR 569, CA.   *d*
Bugdaycay v Secretary of State for the Home Dept [1987] 1 All ER 940, [1987] AC 514,
  HL.
Campbell v UK (1985) 7 EHRR 165, [1984] ECHR 7819/77, ECt HR.
Chapman v UK (2001) 10 BHRC 48, ECt HR.
Dombo Beheer BV v Netherlands (1994) 18 EHRR 213, ECt HR.
Håkansson v Sweden (1990) 13 EHRR 1, [1990] ECHR 11855/95, ECt HR.   *e*
Kemper Reinsurance Co v Minister of Finance [2000] 1 AC 1, [1998] 3 WLR 630, PC.
König v Germany (1979) 2 EHRR 170, [1978] ECHR 6232/73, ECt HR.
Langborger v Sweden (1990) 12 EHRR 416, [1989] ECHR 11179/84, ECt HR.
Lombardo v Italy (1996) 21 EHRR 188, [1992] ECHR 11519/85, ECt HR.
Marckx v Belgium (1979) 2 EHRR 330, [1979] ECHR 6833/74, ECt HR.   *f*
Pudas v Sweden (1988) 10 EHRR 380, [1987] ECHR 10426/83, ECt HR.
R v Brent London BC, ex p Bariise (1999) 31 HLR 50, CA.
R v Croydon London BC, ex p Graham (1994) 26 HLR 286, CA.
R v Islington London BC, ex p Hinds (1996) 28 HLR 302, CA.
R v Lambert [2001] UKHL 37, [2001] 3 All ER 577, [2001] 3 WLR 206.
R v Newham London BC, ex p Bibi (28 July 2000, unreported), QBD.   *g*
R v Newham London BC, ex p Begum [2000] 2 All ER 72.
R v Secretary of State for the Home Dept, ex p Salem [1999] 2 All ER 42, [1999] AC 450,
  HL.
R v Tower Hamlets London BC, ex p Rouf (1989) 21 HLR 294.
R v Wyre BC, ex p Joyce (1984) 11 HLR 73, DC.   *h*
Racal Communications Ltd, Re [1980] 2 All ER 634, [1981] AC 374, HL.
Reid v Secretary of State for Scotland [1999] 1 All ER 481, [1999] 2 AC 512, HL.
Ringeisen v Austria (No 1) (1971) 1 EHRR 455, [1971] ECHR 2614/65, ECt HR.
Ruiz-Mateos v Spain (1993) 16 EHRR 505, [1993] ECHR 12952/87, ECt HR.
Salesi v Italy (1998) 26 EHRR 187, [1993] ECHR 13023/87, ECt HR.   *j*
Scanfuture UK Ltd v Secretary of State for Trade and Industry [2001] IRLR 416, EAT.
Soering v UK (1989) 11 EHRR 439, [1989] ECHR 14038/88, EC HR.
Surdonja v Ealing London BC, Mohamed v Hammersmith and Fulham London BC [2000]
  2 All ER 597, [2001] QB 97, CA.
Tickner v Mole Valley DC (2 April 1980, unreported), CA.
Varey v UK [2001] TLR 72, [2001] ECHR 26662/95, ECt HR.

a *Vilvarajah v UK* (1992) 14 EHRR 248, [1991] ECHR 13163/87, ECt HR.
W v UK (1987) 10 EHRR 29, [1987] ECHR 9749/82, ECt HR.

Appeal

Newham London Borough Council appealed with permission of Robert Walker LJ granted on 19 March 2001 from that part of the order of Judge Laurie,
b made at Bow County Court on 6 October 2000, whereby, after quashing a decision by Newham's appeal officer on 23 June 2000 affirming on review Newham's decision to reject an application by the respondent, Fardous Adan, for assistance under Pt VII of the Housing Act 1996, he directed that the matter be remitted for a further review decision within 28 days, to be conducted by a different reviewing officer who, in respect of independence and impartiality,
c complied with art 6(1) of the European Convention for the Protection of Human Rights and Fundamental Freedoms 1950 (as set out in Sch 1 to the Human Rights Act 1998). The Secretary of State for Transport, Local Government and the Regions participated in the appeal as an interested party. The facts are set out in the judgment of Brooke LJ.

d

Cherie Booth QC and *Kerry Bretherton* (instructed by *Mark Bowing*) for Newham.
Nigel Pleming QC and *Kate Markus* (instructed by *Eve Wee Solicitors*) for Mrs Adan.
Mark Hoskins and *Martin Chamberlain* (instructed by the *Treasury Solicitor*) for the
    Secretary of State.

e
                                                                    Cur adv vult

14 December 2001. The following judgments were delivered.

BROOKE LJ.

f   [1] This is an appeal by the London Borough of Newham (Newham) against an order made by Judge Laurie in the Bow County Court on 6 October 2000 (and later amended under the slip rule on 9 October 2001) whereby after quashing a decision made on a review of a homelessness application under Pt VII of the Housing Act 1996 he directed that the matter be remitted for a further review decision within 28 days, to be conducted by a different reviewing officer (being
g an officer who in respect of independence and impartiality complies with art 6 of the European Convention for the Protection of Human Rights and Fundamental Freedoms 1950 (as set out in Sch 1 to the Human Rights Act 1998)). The judge made his direction only four days after that Act came into force, but the difficulty (and importance) of the issue he faced was recognised by all three of the
h experienced members of the Bar who appeared on the hearing of this appeal more than a year later.

[2] The facts of the case are relatively straightforward. Mrs Adan is a Dutch citizen of Somali origin. Her three children, now aged ten, seven and five, are also Dutch citizens. Her husband was murdered outside the family home in the
j Netherlands in March 1996. A murder investigation conducted by the Dutch police was inconclusive. In January 2000 she decided to bring her family to England. She had found it increasingly difficult to live in the Netherlands on her own, and her children wanted to move because they were frightened that their father's murderer would return and kill them. In particular her oldest child, a girl, was suffering from behavioural problems which were affecting her educational development. She had frequent nightmares, and her younger brothers shared her

fears. When the family came to England, Mrs Adan terminated her tenancy and brought all the family's possessions with her. They lived at first with her sister-in-law and her six children in a three-bedroomed property in Stratford. Her sister-in-law then required them to leave, because her home was so crowded, and Mrs Adan turned to Newham to seek housing assistance.

[3] Section 185(1) of the 1996 Act provides that a person is not eligible for assistance under Pt VII of the Act if he is a person from abroad who is ineligible for housing assistance. The effect of reg 4(a) of the Homelessness Regulations 1996, SI 1996/2754, is that Mrs Adan had to show that she was habitually resident in this country (or the Republic of Ireland) in order to be eligible. Her application was initially rejected by a Newham housing officer in March 2000 on these grounds. She was told that she was not habitually resident in this country because she had made no arrangements for accommodation or work here and she was in receipt of social security payments from the Netherlands. Officers had looked at the circumstances of her case, and had decided that she did not have a settled and viable pattern of living here as a resident.

[4] She exercised her right to a review of this decision pursuant to s 202 of the 1996 Act, and the review was conducted by Mr Paul Clark, who is Newham's appeal officer. On 23 June 2000 he gave his reasons for declining to alter the original decision. After setting out the facts (which he took from her history of events) at some length and summarising the effect of the submissions he had received from her solicitors, he told her that although she had had difficulties in the Netherlands, there was no evidence that she planned to settle in this country. She did not make any inquiries about accommodation in this country, she did not learn English and she remained financially dependant on the Dutch authorities (who were paying her a widow's pension). He had therefore decided that she was not habitually resident in this country.

[5] Mrs Adan then exercised her right of appeal to the county court pursuant to s 204(1) of the 1996 Act which gives a dissatisfied applicant a right to appeal 'on any point of law arising from the decision or, as the case may be, the original decision'. She did not suggest in her grounds of appeal that Mr Clark had got any of the underlying facts wrong. Her complaint was that he had taken into account irrelevant factors and failed to take into account relevant factors; that he had not properly applied the correct legal test or conducted a proper balancing exercise of the relevant factors; and that his decision, in all the circumstances, was irrational. Her appeal was supported by a short witness statement and by a skeleton argument which deployed all the relevant evidence and concluded that in all the circumstances it was irrational for Mr Clark to say that there was no evidence that she had planned to settle in the United Kingdom.

[6] This argument was sufficient to persuade Judge Laurie to allow the appeal. He said 'It is a statement of fact that there is no evidence, but there is tons of evidence that she planned to do just that' (viz settle in the United Kingdom). Newham does not now challenge his decision to allow the appeal and quash Mr Clark's determination on those grounds. What is in issue on this appeal is his direction that Newham's further review should be conducted by a different reviewing officer who possessed the appropriate impartiality and independence required by art 6 of the convention. The judge had expressed concern about the compatibility of the normal review procedure with that article of the convention, and decided that he needed to spell out in his order what the convention required.

[7] I am satisfied that he did not have power to make this further direction.
Section 204 of the 1996 Act specifies the powers given to the county court on
these appeals, and because this is a public law matter, as soon as the original
determination was quashed Newham was obliged to review the matter again. By
now the 1998 Act was in force. As a public authority Newham would know that
it would be unlawful for it to act in a way which was incompatible with a
convention right, and s 38(3)(a) of the County Courts Act 1984 expressly
prescribes that the county court shall not have the power to order mandamus,
which is what the judge was doing when he ordered Newham to carry out a
public duty in a particular way.

[8] In the ordinary course of things this judgment could end at this point,
particularly since things have changed with the passage of time. When it was
decided that Mrs Adan is habitually resident in this country for social security
purposes, she made a fresh application to Newham under Pt VII of the 1996 Act.
This application has recently been determined against her on the ground that she
made herself intentionally homeless by relinquishing her tenancy in the
Netherlands. We have been told that a review of that decision is now pending.
Notwithstanding the existence of this new application, the parties were very
anxious that this court should express its opinion on the remaining, much more
important, issues that have been argued, and we have been told that a number of
other cases have been held up pending our judgment in this case. Because
Mrs Adan served a respondent's notice seeking a declaration that the relevant
statutory provisions were incompatible with the requirements on art 6(1) of the
convention in the event that her other arguments failed, Mr Hoskins appeared for
the Secretary of State as a party to the proceedings pursuant to CPR 19.4A(2).

[9] The issues can be stated quite briefly. Mr Hoskins and Mr Pleming QC
accepted that the procedure under Pt VII of the 1996 Act involved the
determination of Mrs Adan's civil rights within the meaning of art 6(1) of the
convention. Ms Booth QC accepted this proposition in this court, but reserved
her position in the event that the case went further. It was common ground
that a Newham employee, like Mr Clark, could not constitute an independent
and impartial tribunal for art 6(1) purposes, and it is unnecessary in these
circumstances to consider any of the other complaints Mr Pleming made about
the review procedure. The central questions were whether the county court had
'full jurisdiction' on an appeal pursuant to s 204 of the 1996 Act, so that there
would be no art 6 irregularity in the procedure taken as a whole, alternatively
whether if Newham contracted out its reviewing function pursuant to powers
conferred on it by art 3 of the Local Authorities (Contracting Out of Allocation of
Housing and Homelessness Functions) Order 1996, SI 1996/3205, this exercise
would cure the position. Article 3 of this order provides, so far as is material, that:

> 'Any function of an authority which is conferred by or under Part VII of the
> [Housing Act 1996] (homelessness) … may be exercised by, or by employees
> of, such person (if any) as may be authorised in that behalf by the authority
> whose function it is.'

[10] Ms Booth told us that Newham found the prospect of having to use these
contracting out powers a singularly unattractive one. She said that in practice a
local appeals officer like Mr Clark is able to deal with a number of these vulnerable
applicants' problems in an attractively informal way. Newham receives 3,000
Pt VII applications each year, of which half are allowed. Five hundred go on for
a review, at which one in three are then allowed. There are then 30 to 40 appeals

each year to the county court. Her clients did not wish to see a more formal
procedure put in place. She said that for the most part disputes arose over the
inferences to be drawn from the facts furnished by the applicants, and disputes on
issues of primary fact were comparatively uncommon. Homeless women suffering
violence from their partners were particularly attracted to the informality of
Newham's procedures.

[11] The scope for argument in this case was considerably reduced by the recent
decision of another division of this court in *R (on the application of McLellan) v
Bracknell Forest BC, Reigate and Banstead BC v Benfield* [2001] EWCA Civ 1510,
[2002] 1 All ER 899. That appeal was concerned with a similar art 6(1) challenge
to the procedures for terminating an introductory tenancy created under Pt V of
the 1996 Act. To put the matter briefly, such a tenant has some but not all of the
safeguards of a secure tenancy for the first one-year trial period of his/her
tenancy. If the local authority landlord wishes to terminate the tenancy before
the year is up (usually because the tenant has breached the terms of the tenancy
agreement) it has power to decide that it will seek an order for possession. Once
it has done this, it must serve a notice on the tenant giving notice of its intention,
and setting out its reasons, and the tenant then has the right to require a review
of that decision, and also a right to request an oral hearing. If the local authority
remains unmoved, the tenant's only remedy is by way of judicial review: the
county court is bound to grant the order sought. For the details of this procedure,
see [2002] 1 All ER 899 at [13]–[22].

[12] The reason why this court considered that that procedure was compatible
with the convention was that it was satisfied that the Administrative Court on
judicial review had full jurisdiction to cure any defect in the legality of the local
authority's decision in the circumstances of that type of case. It was particularly
concerned to ascertain whether material facts were likely to be in issue.
Waller LJ, with whom Latham and Kay LJJ agreed, concluded ([2002] 1 All ER 899
at [96]–[97]) that if the local authority's reasons for seeking possession related to
rent arrears, the facts could be established with certainty, and that if its reasons
related to a complaint that the tenant was being a nuisance—

> 'under the introductory tenancy scheme it is not a requirement that the
> council should be satisfied that breaches of the tenancy agreement have in
> fact taken place. The right question under the scheme will be whether in the
> context of allegation and counter-allegation it was reasonable for the council
> to take a decision to proceed with termination of the introductory tenancy.'

[13] Waller LJ concluded (at [97]) that as with a rent arrears complaint (where
the issue was also likely to be whether in the circumstances the council's decision
was reasonable), this was a matter which could be dealt with under judicial
review either of the traditional kind or (if it was necessary to do so) intensified so
as to ensure that the tenant's rights were protected.

[14] Mr Pleming, who appeared for one of the appellants in that case, accepted
that at this level *McLellan*'s case was binding on us as to the approach a court
should adopt towards a complaint of this kind. He argued, however, that there
were different considerations to be applied on the case of an application under
Pt VII of the 1996 Act. Although it might be that in many cases the local authority
might accept the version of the facts presented by the applicant, there were many
other cases which bristled with disputes over primary facts (for example, as to the
reasons why the applicant had left his/her last home). In those cases a court to
which appeals lay only on a point of law did not have the full jurisdiction required

a by art 6(1) jurisprudence. It was common ground that the county court's powers on an appeal under s 204 of the 1996 Act are akin to those of judicial review exercisable in the High Court (see *Begum v Tower Hamlets London BC* [2000] 1 WLR 306 at 312–314, 327).

[15] The circumstances in which the power of the Administrative Court in judicial review proceedings to review the legality of administrative decisions
b might be sufficient to ensure compatibility with art 6(1) of the convention were so comprehensively discussed by the House of Lords in *R (on the application of Alconbury Developments Ltd) v Secretary of State of the Environment, Transport and the Regions* [2001] UKHL 23, [2001] 2 All ER 929, [2001] 2 WLR 1389 that it is unnecessary to cover that ground again, except so far as is necessary for the purpose of resolving the issues in the present case.

c [16] Ms Booth told us that in practice the grounds for dissatisfaction with a reviewing officer's decision usually amount to a question of law within the ambit of the county court's jurisdiction, and that issues of disputed primary fact are comparatively rare. She instanced as grounds of legitimate challenge a failure to make adequate inquiries; a failure to put relevant matters to the applicant; a
d failure to allow the applicant to comment on matters which the authority was minded to weigh against the applicant; a failure to take into account relevant matters and the consideration of irrelevant matters; making a perverse decision; reaching a decision which no local authority properly directing itself could properly reach; a failure to follow procedures, including those provided by the Code of Guidance; and a failure to give adequate reasons for the decision.

e [17] This list is not an exhaustive list, and it is reasonably clear from what she told us on behalf of a local authority which has vast experience in these matters that the appellate jurisdiction of the county court on points of law will usually be sufficient to ensure that the proceedings, taken as a whole, are art 6 compliant. If there is a dispute of fact, but the local authority does not find it necessary to
f resolve the dispute in order to adjudicate fairly on the application, then the situation will be on all fours with that considered by this court in *McLellan*'s case. It is only where housing officers have to resolve a dispute of fact which is material to the decision, and the appeal against their finding cannot properly be categorised as an appeal on a point of law, however elastic that expression may be taken to be, that difficulties are likely to arise over convention compliance.

g [18] Ms Booth went on to suggest that s 204 of the 1996 Act, read in conjunction with CPR Pt 52, has the potential to provide the solution to any residual problems over convention compliance. Section 204(3) gives the county court power to 'make such order confirming, quashing or varying the decision as it thinks fit'. Although Pt 52 is 'subject to any ... enactment ... which sets out
h special provisions with regard to any particular category of appeal' (r 52.1(4)), she submitted that there was nothing in the 1996 Act to prevent the county court (which is an 'appeal court' for this purpose—see r 52.1(3)(b)) from receiving oral evidence (r 52.11(2)). She also relied on other powers given to an appeal court by r 52.11, including the power to draw any inference of fact which it considered
j justified on the evidence. She argued that in these circumstances the county court had ample power to correct any decision by a review officer even if the complaint relates to the way in which a factual dispute was resolved.

[19] The trouble about this argument is that statute has limited the powers of this particular appeal court to appeals on points of law. It follows that both r 52.10 (to which we were also referred) and r 52.11 must be read subject to the proviso that rules which confer powers wider than the powers conferred by

Parliament on the county courts in this particular statutory scheme are expressly
excluded from the county court's range of powers by r 52.1(4). When Parliament
has expressly narrowed an appeal court's powers so as to leave intact the
jurisdiction of an administrative body as the fact-finding tribunal, the rule-makers
have no authority to widen them. I do not consider that the court's power to
'vary the decision', which enables it to correct the wording of a decision without
having to quash it completely, are apt to turn an appeal on a point of law into an
appeal on a point of fact.

[20] I have little doubt, on the basis of what Ms Booth told us, that in very
many Pt VII cases no art 6(1) difficulty will arise. To take a case like the present,
where there is no dispute about the underlying facts but a dispute whether, given
those facts, the applicant was habitually resident in this country, it is not
necessary to go further than two decisions of the House of Lords to see that the
central dispute raises a question of law over which the county court will have
jurisdiction.

[21] In *Edwards (Inspector of Taxes) v Bairstow* [1955] 3 All ER 48, [1956] AC 14
Mr Bairstow and Mr Harrison contended that they were engaged in an adventure
in the nature of trade within the meaning of Case I of Sch D to the Income Tax
Act 1918. Mr Edwards, the Inspector of Taxes, disagreed. With no previous
experience in buying and selling machinery the two men had bought a complete
spinning plant for the purpose of making a quick resale. In the event they took
longer than expected to find a purchaser, and incurred a number of expenses in
connection with the sale, insurance, renovation, necessary office work, travelling
and entertaining, and rent for the housing of the plant. In due course they made
a significant profit on the resale.

[22] Mr Edwards' rejection of their contention was upheld by the General
Commissioners, and the High Court and the Court of Appeal both decided that
they had no power to interfere with a finding of fact. The House of Lords adopted
a different approach. Viscount Simonds said:

> 'The primary facts as they are sometimes called do not, in my opinion,
> justify the inference or conclusion which the commissioners have drawn; not
> only do they not justify it but they lead irresistibly to the opposite inference
> or conclusion. It is, therefore, a case in which, whether it be said of the
> commissioners that their finding is perverse or that they have misdirected
> themselves in law by a misunderstanding of the statutory language or
> otherwise, their determination cannot stand.' (See [1955] 3 All ER 48 at 53,
> [1956] AC 14 at 29.)

See also Lord Radcliffe [1955] 3 All ER 48 at 56–57, [1956] AC 14 at 33–35.

[23] In *Shah v Barnet London BC* [1983] 1 All ER 226, [1983] 2 AC 309, five
overseas students had been pursuing courses of study in this country for three
years or more when they applied to their local education authorities for an award
in respect of their studies for a first degree, or comparable, course of further
education. Their applications were refused on the statutory ground that they had
not been ordinarily resident in this country for three years, the view being taken
that they had been granted limited leave to enter for the purposes of their initial
studies and that leave had now expired.

[24] After observing ([1983] 1 All ER 226 at 233, [1983] 2 AC 309 at 340) that
the relevant statutory provisions were to be construed by giving to the words
'ordinarily resident in the United Kingdom' their natural and ordinary meaning,
Lord Scarman said:

'Though the meaning of ordinary words is, as Lord Reid observed in *Brutus v Cozens* [1972] 2 All ER 1297 at 1299, [1973] AC 854 at 861, a question of fact, the meaning to be attributed to enacted words is a question of law, being a matter of statutory interpretation. So in this case a question of law arises as to the meaning of "ordinarily resident in the United Kingdom", even though it arises only at a preliminary stage in the process of determining a question of fact, namely whether the "propositus" (in these appeals, the student applicant) has established the fact of ordinary residence for the prescribed period (ie three years immediately preceding the course in respect of which he seeks an award). It is with this preliminary stage that the courts are concerned. If a local education authority gets the law right, or, as lawyers would put it, directs itself correctly in law, the question of fact ie has the student established the prescribed residence? is for the authority, not the court, to decide. The merits of the application are for the local education authority, subject only to judicial review to ensure that the authority has proceeded according to the law.' (See [1983] 1 All ER 226 at 233, [1983] 2 AC 309 at 341.)

[25] When Lord Brandon of Oakbrook said in *C v S (minor: abduction: illegitimate child)* [1990] 2 All ER 961 at 965, sub nom *Re J (a minor) (abduction: custody rights)* [1990] 2 AC 562 at 578 that the question whether a person is or is not habitually resident in a specified country is a question of fact to be decided by reference to all the circumstances of any particular case, there is no indication that he intended to depart from Lord Scarman's proposition that there is a preliminary question of law to be determined before the facts can be decided. See, too, for a similar discussion about the meaning of the words 'habitually resident' in the Income Support (General) Regulations 1987, SI 1987/1967, *Nessa v Chief Adjudication Officer* [1999] 4 All ER 677 at 680–683, [1999] 1 WLR 1937 at 1940–1943.

[26] In these circumstances I am satisfied that in the context of the 'habitual residence' type of issue on which Mrs Adan's application originally foundered it is likely that there would be no difficulty about convention compliance. If there is no dispute about the primary facts, the county court will have power to correct any errors of law which may have arisen in the way in which those facts were considered for the purpose of the ultimate decision.

[27] As to the residue of cases which call for decisions on disputed facts, Mr Hoskins boldly submitted that even though the county court has only been given jurisdiction to entertain appeals on a point of law, it was possible for us to interpret s 204(1) of the 1996 Act as if it gave the county court power to resolve disputed issues of fact if this was necessary to ensure that the procedure was art 6 compliant.

[28] He accepted that this was not a case in which a court with supervisory powers was obliged to resolve an issue of precedent fact in order to determine whether a public authority had power to take the decision complained of (see *Khawaja v Secretary of State for the Home Dept* [1983] 1 All ER 765 at 722, [1984] AC 74 at 97). He relied, however, on a recent line of authority, buttressed by academic writing, in support of his contention that a court of supervisory jurisdiction has power to consider whether a public authority has reached a mistaken conclusion of fact, not on traditional *Wednesbury* or even super-*Wednesbury* grounds (see *Associated Provincial Picture Houses Ltd v Wednesbury Corp* [1947] 2 All ER 680, [1948] 1 KB 223), but because it has believed other witnesses when it ought to have believed the applicant.

[29] His starting point was a dictum of Lord Slynn of Hadley in *R v Criminal Injuries Compensation Board, ex p A* [1999] 2 AC 330 at 344–345, [1999] 2 WLR 974 at 981–982. The board had rejected the applicant's claim for compensation after being misled by a police witness as to the effect of a report by a police doctor which was not before it. The House of Lords quashed the board's decision on procedural grounds. In his speech, however, Lord Slynn alluded to arguments to the effect that jurisdiction existed to quash the board's decision on the grounds of a material error of fact. He said that he would accept that there was jurisdiction to quash the board's decision on that ground, but he preferred to decide the matter on the alternative procedural basis. Lord Hobhouse of Woodborough ([1999] 2 AC 330 at 348, [1999] 2 WLR 974 at 985), agreeing as to the result, said that he expressed no opinion about the problems to which the acceptance of 'error of fact' as a ground for judicial review would give rise, nor would he discuss the soundness of the views expressed in the two textbook passages to which Lord Slynn referred: Wade and Forsyth, *Administrative Law* (7th edn, 1994) pp 316–318 (see now eighth edition (2000) pp 282–284), and De Smith, Woolf and Jowell, *Judicial Review of Administrative Action* (5th edn, 1995) p 288.

[30] Lord Slynn returned to this topic in *R (on the application of Alconbury Developments Ltd) v Secretary of State of the Environment, Transport and the Regions* [2001] UKHL 23 at [53]–[54], [2001] 2 All ER 929 at [53]–[54], [2001] 2 WLR 1389, when he said that the potential ability of a supervisory court to review material errors of fact made the argument that the scope of judicial review was sufficient to comply with convention standards in the case before the House even stronger. The only other member of the House to consider this topic was Lord Clyde, who approached it very cautiously ([2001] 2 All ER 929 at [169]):

'The suggestion was advanced that, if the respondents were correct in their contention that the present proceedings are in breach of art 6(1), the scope of judicial review might somehow be enlarged so as to provide a complete remedy. The point in the event does not arise, but I consider that it might well be difficult to achieve a sufficient enlargement to meet the stated purpose without jeopardising the constitutional balance between the role of the courts and the role of the executive. The supervisory jurisdiction of the court as it has now developed seems to me adequate to deal with a wide range of complaints which can properly be seen as directed to the legality of a decision. It is sufficient to note the recognition of the idea of proportionality, or perhaps more accurately, disproportionality, and the extent to which the factual areas of a decision may be penetrated by a review of the account taken by a decision-maker of facts which are irrelevant or even mistaken (*R v Criminal Injuries Compensation Board, ex p A* [1999] 2 AC 330 at 344–345, [1999] 2 WLR 974 at 982). But consideration of the precise scope of the administrative remedies is not necessary for the purposes of the present appeals.'

[31] In *R (on the application of McLellan) v Bracknell Forest BC, Reigate and Banstead BC v Benfield* [2002] 1 All ER 899 at [64] Waller LJ said that if the decision of a review panel considering a tenant's objections to his/her introductory tenancy being terminated was found to have been reached on the basis of a material error of fact, then that would be a ground for review in the High Court. He supported this proposition by reference to Lord Slynn's dictum in *Ex p A* and by the following passage in the speech of Lord Wilberforce in *Secretary of State for*

a *Education and Science v Metropolitan Borough of Tameside* [1976] 3 All ER 665 at 681–682, [1977] AC 1014 at 1047:

b
> 'If a judgment requires, before it can be made, the existence of some facts, then, although the evaluation of those facts is for the Secretary of State alone, the court must enquire whether those facts exist, and have been taken into account, whether the judgment has been made on a proper self direction as to those facts, whether the judgment has not been made on other facts which ought not to have been taken into account. If these requirements are not met, then the exercise of judgment, however bona fide it may be, becomes capable of challenge …'

c   [32] Finally, Mr Hoskins relied on the even more recent decision of this court in *R (on the application of Wilkinson) v Responsible Medical Officer Broadmoor Hospital* [2001] EWCA Civ 1545, [2001] All ER (D) 294 (Oct) as suggesting that a supervisory court could turn itself into an ordinary appellate court in the changed climate created by the Human Rights Act 1998.

d   [33] In that case a patient detained at Broadmoor Hospital challenged the lawfulness of a decision to administer injections to him without his consent. The responsible medical officer (RMO) had no power to administer any treatment to him in those circumstances unless it constituted treatment for his mental disorder, and there were disputes of fact, which this court held could only be resolved by cross-examination, as to the nature of that disorder, whether the

e patient was (as the RMO believed) incapacitated, whether the proposed treatment would benefit his condition and be justified even with his consent, and whether such treatment was justified if it had to be given under constraint. It was a feature of the case that subject to an unresolved question as to whether leave was required under s 139 of the Mental Health Act 1983, there was nothing to stop the patient from bringing a private law action in these circumstances, where

f cross-examination would certainly be permitted.

[34] I consider that one would have to delve much deeper than this line of authority to find support for the proposition that where Parliament has decided that a particular body should decide questions of fact, a court of supervisory jurisdiction should be able to look at the factual evidence before that body and

g decide that it had made a mistake of fact susceptible of review when it preferred to believe one witness rather than another.

[35] In *Wade and Forsyth* (8th edn, 2000) p 286 the authors suggest that a supervisory court now has jurisdiction to quash a decision if an erroneous and decisive fact was: (a) jurisdictional; (b) found on the basis of no evidence; or

h (c) wrong, misunderstood or ignored. Except for the concept that an erroneous and decisive fact was wrong, these grounds are all familiar grounds for judicial review. The concept of 'wrongness' is a more elusive one. On one side of the line are the simple examples discussed in the text at pp 282–283, some of which were deployed by the appellants in argument in *Ex p A* [1999] 2 AC 330 at 333–334. On the other are the cases in which complaint is made that an administrative

j decision-maker got the facts wrong by preferring one version of the facts to another when it could reasonably have accepted either version.

[36] There are very powerful judicial statements throughout the common law world which suggest that in this second type of case a court of supervisory jurisdiction has no power to interfere. It is necessary only to quote a few of them.

[37] In *Secretary of State for Employment v Associated Society of Locomotive Engineers and Firemen (No 2)* [1972] 2 All ER 949 at 967–968, [1972] 2 QB 455 at 493

Lord Denning MR, who in general preferred an expansionist view of the court's
supervisory powers which has not won universal acceptance, said: a

'... if he plainly misdirects himself in fact or in law, it may well be that a
court would interfere; but when he honestly takes a view of the facts or the
law which could reasonably be entertained, then his decision is not to be set
aside simply because thereafter someone thinks that his view was wrong.'
                                                                          b
[38] In *Puhlhofer v Hillingdon London BC* [1986] 1 All ER 467 at 474, [1986] AC
484 at 518 Lord Brightman said:

'Parliament intended the local authority to be the judge of fact ... Where
the existence or non-existence of a fact is left to the judgment and discretion
of a public body ... it is the duty of the court to leave the decision of that fact c
to the public body to whom Parliament has entrusted the decision-making
power save in a case where it is obvious that the public body, consciously or
unconsciously, are acting perversely.'

[39] In Australia, Mason J said in *Minister for Aboriginal Affairs v Peko-Wallsend Ltd*
(1985–86) 162 CLR 24 at 40–41:   d

'The limited role of a court reviewing the exercise of an administrative
discretion must constantly be borne in mind. It is not the function of the
court to substitute its own decision for that of the administrator by exercising
a discretion which the legislature has vested in the administrator. Its role is
to set limits on the exercise of that discretion, and a decision within those e
boundaries cannot be impugned: *Wednesbury Corporation (Associated Provincial
Picture Houses Ltd v Wednesbury Corp* [1947] 2 All ER 680, [1948] 1 KB 223).'

[40] In New Zealand, Cooke P, who had been unable to carry his two
colleagues in the Court of Appeal with him in relation to the more expansionist
views he had expressed in *Daganayasi v Minister of Immigration* [1980] 2 NZLR 130 f
at 149, said in *New Zealand Fishing Industry Association Inc v Minister of Agriculture
and Fisheries* [1988] 1 NZLR 544 at 552:

'... to jeopardise validity on the ground of mistake of fact the fact must be
an established one or an established and recognised opinion; and that it
cannot be said to be a mistake to adopt one of two differing points of view of g
the facts, each of which may be reasonably held.'

This formulation contains an echo of the opinion expressed by Scarman LJ in
Secretary of State for Education and Science v Metropolitan Borough of Tameside [1976]
3 All ER 665 at 675, [1977] AC 1014 at 1030 when he said that 'misunderstanding h
or ignorance of an established and relevant fact' fell within the scope of judicial
review.

[41] This is not the occasion—because we do not have to decide the point—to
take further the discussion initiated by Lord Slynn in *Ex p A* and the *Alconbury
Developments* case. In very many cases, although it could be said that an
administrative body has made a material mistake of fact the decision is vulnerable j
on other more conventional grounds: for procedural impropriety (as in *Ex p A*),
or because a factor has been taken into account which should not have been
taken into account (as in *Simplex GE (Holdings) Ltd v Secretary of State for the
Environment* [1988] 3 PLR 25) or because there was no evidence on which the
decision could have been safely based (see *R v London Residuary Body, ex p Inner*

a *London Education Authority* (1987) [1998] JR 238 at 240: '... a mistake as to fact can vitiate a decision as where ... the fact was the only evidential basis for [the] decision'). What is quite clear is that a court of supervisory jurisdiction does not, without more, have the power to substitute its own view of the primary facts for the view reasonably adopted by the body to whom the fact-finding power has been entrusted.

b [42] In my judgment, if we were to be beguiled by the arguments of Mr Hoskins into holding that we should interpret the words 'may appeal to the county court on any point of law arising from the decision' in s 204(1) of the 1996 Act as meaning 'any point of law, or if it is necessary to do so in order to ensure that an appellant's convention rights are not violated, any point of fact', we

c would be doing exactly what Lord Woolf CJ adjured courts not to do in *Poplar Housing and Regeneration Community Association Ltd v Donoghue* [2001] EWCA Civ 595, [2001] 4 All ER 604, [2002] QB 48 when he distinguished between interpretation, which is a matter for the courts, and legislation, which is a matter for Parliament. The danger of blurring of the distinction between the judicial role and the legislative role was no doubt what Lord Clyde had in mind when he spoke in the

d *Alconbury Developments* case [2001] 2 All ER 929 at [169] of 'jeopardising the constitutional balance' (see [30], above). I can see nothing in the speeches in the House of Lords in *R v A* [2001] UKHL 25, [2001] 3 All ER 1, [2002] 1 AC 45 which would enable us in any circumstances to interpret the words 'appeal on any point of law' as meaning, or including, 'appeal on any point of fact'.

e [43] It follows that if a case arises on a s 202 review where there is a dispute about the primary facts of a kind which has to be resolved because it is material to the decision-making process, then the danger will arise that the proceedings, taken as a whole, will not be convention compliant. The reviewing officer will lack the independent status of the planning inspector in the *Alconbury Developments*

f case and the county court does not have full jurisdiction to decide questions of disputed fact (except in a *Wednesbury*, or super-*Wednesbury*, sense). If such a case arises before the law is changed in order to correct the deficiencies identified in this judgment, then it appears to me that the local authority will have to exercise its contracting-out powers so as to ensure that any such dispute is determined by a tribunal with the appropriate attributes of independence and impartiality.

g [44] It was suggested in argument that this escape route would not be open because s 202(4) of the 1996 Act prescribes that on a review 'the authority or authorities concerned shall review their decision', so that the review power would still be being exercised, even if it was contracted out, by an authority which lacked independence and impartiality. I do not consider that this argument

h is soundly based. Article 3 of the Local Authorities (Contracting Out of Allocation of Housing and Homelessness Functions) Order 1996, SI 1996/3205, (for whose terms see [9], above) makes it clear that the performance of the authority's function (in this case the function of reviewing the earlier decision) is transferred to the third party to whom the function has been contracted out. It would be

j inappropriate in this judgment to discuss on a hypothetical basis any of the practical difficulties that may arise when trying to ensure that the third party has the requisite independence.

[45] For the sake of completeness, I would add that there is nothing in the Allocation of Housing and Homelessness (Review Procedures) Regulations 1999, SI 1999/71, or para 17.8 of the Code of Guidance which prevents this function

from being contracted out to someone who is not an officer of the relevant local authority.

[46] We were shown during the course of argument some recent decisions in disciplinary cases in the medical field. The Privy Council decisions in *Ghosh v General Medical Council* [2001] UKPC 29, [2001] 1 WLR 1915 and *Priess v General Dental Council* [2001] UKPC 36, [2001] 1 WLR 1926 show that no convention difficulties will usually arise where an appeal court's jurisdiction is truly appellate and not merely supervisory, although in *Priess'* case Lord Cooke of Thorndon observed ([2001] 1 WLR 1926 at [10]) that there may be some risk of unpredictable circumstances where even a full Privy Council hearing is not enough. I do not consider that the decision of the European Commission of Human Rights in *Stefan v UK* (1998) 25 EHRR CD 130, where a Strasbourg challenge to the Privy Council's dismissal of an appeal against a decision of a General Medical Council Health Committee on the medical question of the applicant's mental fitness to practise was declared inadmissible, assists very much outside the specialist context of that particular jurisdiction.

[47] Finally, we were shown three recent judgments in the Administrative Court in which conclusions were reached which are similar to that to which I have found myself driven in the present case. I refer to the judgments of Richards J in *R (on the application of Kathro) v Rhondda Cynon Taff County BC* [2001] EWHC Admin 527 at [28]–[29], [2001] All ER (D) 130 (Jul) at [28]–[29], Moses J in *R (on the application of Bewry) v Norwich City Council* [2001] EWHC Admin 657 at [58]–[62], [2001] All ER (D) 461 (Jul) at [58]–[62], and Stanley Burnton J in *R (on the application of Husain) v Asylum Support Adjudicator* [2001] EWHC Admin 852 at [78]–[79], [2001] All ER (D) 107 (Oct) at [78]–[79]. It is sufficient for present purposes to recite a passage in the last of these judgments. In *Husain's* case Stanley Burnton J said:

'[78] ... where the decisions of a tribunal are likely to depend to a substantial extent on disputed questions of primary fact, and the tribunal is clearly not independent, judicial review should not suffice to produce compliance with art 6. The scope for review of findings of primary facts is too narrow to be considered a "full jurisdiction" in such a context. Fact-dependent decisions must be made by fully independent tribunals: the scope for judicial review of primary findings of fact, and particularly of findings as to the credibility of witnesses, is generally too narrow to cure a want of independence at the lower level.

[79] I think that the courts should lean against accepting judicial review as a substitute for the independence of tribunals. If the availability of judicial review is too easily regarded as curing a want of independence on the part of administrative tribunals, the incentive for the executive and the legislature to ensure the independence of tribunals is considerably weakened.'

I agree.

[48] I would add that I have had the opportunity of reading in draft the judgment of Hale LJ. I admire the ingenious way in which she seeks to interpret the words 'point of law arising from the decision' so as to include the question whether the decision-making process as a whole complies with art 6 of the convention in the particular circumstances of the case. This, she asserts, is plainly a point of law (see [75], below).

[49] Much as I would like to follow her along that path, I do not consider it is constitutionally open to us to do so. It would involve using judicial sleight of

a hand to enlarge the jurisdiction of the county court beyond that given to it by Parliament. Parliament has decided that the local authority should be the final arbiter on the facts, not the courts, and the courts do not, in my judgment, have the power to put these arrangements into reverse.

[50] It is trite convention law, as I said in *Director General of Fair Trading v Proprietary Association of Great Britain* [2001] EWCA Civ 1217 at [23], [2002] 1 All ER
b 853 at [23], [2002] 1 WLR 269, that an appeal court can remedy defects in first instance decisions where the appeal is in the nature of a full rehearing or otherwise involves a careful review of the merits (see, for example, *Edwards v UK* (1992) 15 EHRR 417 and *Twalib v Greece* (2001) 33 EHRR 584). In such cases it invalidates the first decision because of the blemishes in procedural fairness which it contains, so that the proceedings, viewed as a whole, do not violate art 6.
c But it is a giant leap from there to hold that an appeal court has power to arrogate itself a jurisdiction which Parliament clearly did not give it, in order to ensure that the proceedings, taken as a whole, are art 6 compliant. The issue identified by Hale LJ does indeed raise a point of law on a second appeal, which is the reason why this court has been considering it. It is not possible, in my judgment, to
d interpret s 204 of the 1996 Act as if it raised a point of law for the county court itself. We must be very careful not to substitute decision-making by the judges for decision-making by the executive when we try to make the law convention compliant. I agree with what David Steel J says about this issue in his judgment, which I have also read in draft.

[51] For these reasons, I would allow the appeal and direct that the judge's
e order should be altered with the deletion of the direction I have recited in para [6] of this judgment.

HALE LJ.

[52] I agree that the judge did not have power to make the direction he did.
f He did have power to quash the decision, thus requiring that the local authority take it again. Hence the simple answer is to allow this appeal, but only to the extent of deleting the judge's direction that the matter be 'remitted for further review decision within 28 days to be conducted by a different Reviewing Officer (being an Officer who in respect of independence and impartiality complies with art 6 of Sch 1 of the Human Rights Act 1998)'. It is also the sensible answer, as
g matters have now moved on and there would be little point in sending the case back to the circuit judge. However, in my view, that would otherwise have been the right solution.

[53] Although it is not necessary for the disposal of the appeal, all parties have asked us to consider two issues: (1) whether the regime for deciding homelessness
h cases, as presently operated and understood, always complies with art 6(1) of the European Convention for the Protection of Human Rights and Fundamental Freedoms 1950 (as set out in Sch 1 to the Human Rights Act 1998); and (2) if it does not, can it be changed and if so how?

[54] Article 6(1) reads as follows:

j   'In the determination of his civil rights and obligations ... everyone is entitled to a fair and public hearing within a reasonable time by an independent and impartial tribunal established by law. Judgment shall be pronounced publicly ...'

Ms Booth QC has accepted for the purpose of this hearing that the determination of an application for accommodation, or for assistance in obtaining accommodation,

under Pt VII of the Housing Act 1996 is 'the determination of his civil rights and
obligations'. The European Court of Human Rights has held that 'the general   *a*
rule is that Article 6(1) does apply in the field of social insurance, including even
welfare assistance' (see *Schuler-Zgraggen v Switzerland* (1993) 16 EHRR 405 at 430
(para 46), also *Feldbrugge v Netherlands* (1986) 8 EHRR 425, *Deumeland v Germany*
(1986) 8 EHRR 448). Those cases concerned what we would call social security
benefits, but the court pointed out that—   *b*

> '... despite the public law features pointed out by the Government, the
> applicant was not only affected in her relations with the administrative
> authorities as such but also suffered an interference with her means of
> subsistence; she was claiming an individual economic right flowing from
> specific rules laid down in a federal statute.' (See (1993) 16 EHRR 405 at 431   *c*
> (para 46).)

[55] A claim for accommodation under Pt VII of the 1996 Act is also, it is
accepted for present purposes, such a right. Once the local authority are satisfied
that the statutory criteria for providing accommodation exist, they have no
discretion. They have to provide it, irrespective of local conditions of demand   *d*
and supply. Hence this is more akin to a claim for social security benefits than it
is to a claim for social or other services, where the authorities have a greater
degree of discretion and resource considerations may also be relevant.

[56] Nevertheless, as Ms Booth points out, the nature of the decision-making
process required by art 6(1) differs according to the nature of the right being
claimed. The European Court in *Albert v Belgium* (1983) 5 EHRR 533, adopted the *e*
concept of 'full jurisdiction'. But as Lord Hoffmann explained, in *R (on the
application of Alconbury Developments Ltd) v Secretary of State of the Environment,
Transport and the Regions* [2001] UKHL 23 at [87], [2001] 2 All ER 929 at [87], [2001]
2 WLR 1389, 'subsequent European authority shows that "full jurisdiction" does
not mean full decision-making power. It means full jurisdiction to deal with the *f*
case as the nature of the decision requires'.

[57] In assessing the sufficiency of the decision-making process under Pt VII of
the 1996 Act, it must be relevant that local authorities, with all the internal and
external controls to which they are subject, are involved. On the other hand,
decisions to house the homeless are quite different from the Secretary of State's
decisions in planning and compulsory purchase, with which the House of Lords   *g*
was concerned in the *Alconbury Developments* case. In that case, Lord Hoffmann
([2001] 2 All ER 929 at [74]) drew a distinction between policy decisions 'as to
what the public interest requires', which one would expect to see taken by
democratically accountable bodies, and the determination of rights. He applied
it (at [90]):   *h*

> 'In applying the distinction between policy decisions and the determination
> of rights, one would expect that, while the question of whether planning
> permission should be granted was a matter of policy, the questions of
> whether a breach of planning control had taken place would involve a
> determination of right.'   *j*

Decisions under Pt VII of the 1996 Act are not in any sense 'policy' decisions as to
what the public interest requires (as Lord Hoffmann put it) or 'questions of
expediency' (as the European Commission put it in *ISKCON v UK* (1994) 76A DR
90, echoing the court in *Zumtobel v Austria* (1993) 17 EHRR 116). The policy
decisions were taken by Parliament when it enacted the 1996 Act. Individual

a eligibility decisions are taken in the first instance by local housing authorities but policy questions of the availability of resources or equity between the homeless and those on the waiting list for social housing are irrelevant to individual eligibility.

[58] Even then, however, art 6 does not necessarily require that the decision be made by a body which possesses all the court-type characteristics which a *b* literal reading of the article would suggest. It may be enough if it possesses some of those characteristics and those which it does not possess are safeguarded by access to the courts. One might have thought, as Lord Hoffmann went on to observe in the *Alconbury Developments* case [2001] 2 All ER 929 at [90], that decisions as to whether or not there has been a breach of planning control 'fall within the category in which one was entitled to the judgment of an independent *c* and impartial tribunal'. However, the European Court held otherwise in *Bryan v UK* (1996) 21 EHRR 342. The planning inspector did not possess all those characteristics, because he was 'still the creature of the Secretary of State'. But there were important safeguards attending the procedure before him: the quasi-judicial character of the process, the inspector's duty to exercise independent *d* judgment, the requirement that inspectors should not be subject to any improper influence, and the inspectorate's mission to uphold the principles of openness fairness and impartiality. These, coupled with the court's power to intervene if his findings of fact were perverse or irrational, were sufficient.

[59] Hence, in *R (on the application of McLellan) v Bracknell Forest BC, Reigate and Banstead BC v Benfield* [2001] EWCA Civ 1510 at [89], [2002] 1 All ER 899 at [89], *e* Waller LJ concluded that the relevant passages from Lord Hoffmann's speech in the *Alconbury Developments* case—

> '[supported] the following propositions in considering whether judicial review, plus the procedures, are art 6 compliant: (1) it is relevant whether findings of fact are material to the decision; (2) if findings of fact are material *f* to the decision, that will not finally determine whether judicial review provides a remedy in compliance with art 6; (3) if the facts have themselves been found by an "expert tribunal" sufficiently independent to make it unnecessary for the court to have a broad jurisdiction to review those decisions of fact that is likely to lead to the conclusion that judicial review is *g* sufficient.'

Richards J drew a similar conclusion in *R (on the application of Kathro) v Rhondda Cynon Taff County BC* [2001] EWHC Admin 527 at [28], [2001] All ER (D) 130 (Jul) at [28]:

h > 'Looking at the overall tenor of the speeches in the *Alconbury Developments* case and at the underlying decisions of the Strasbourg court ... I accept that the finding that the Secretary of State's decision-making process was compatible in principle with art 6 was based to a significant extent on the fact-finding role of the inspector and its attendant procedural safeguards ...'

j [60] In this case, however, the internal decision-making process does not share the essential features of the planning inspectorate. Both the initial decision-maker and the reviewing officer are officers of the local authority concerned. They have no independence from that authority, no matter how conscientiously they fulfil their obligations. Those obligations do not require anything in the nature of a quasi-judicial hearing. That is not a criticism: many applicants will no doubt welcome the speed, privacy, and informality of the process, as well as the knowledge of the local community which the reviewing officer will often bring to it. But these are the features of a good initial decision-making process: they are not the features of an art 6 determination.

[61] An appeal which is limited to points of law as that has traditionally been understood cannot fill all the gaps. Until this case, the understanding was that the county court acted on the same principles as the High Court had previously acted when judicial review was the only remedy in homelessness cases (see *Begum v Tower Hamlets London BC* [2000] 1 WLR 306). This means that it has a jurisdiction over errors both in procedure and in law which is, as Sedley LJ observed (at 327), 'at least as wide as that of a court of judicial review'. Its powers are in some respects wider, as s 204(3) permits it to 'make such order confirming, quashing or varying the decision as it thinks fit'.

[62] There are three broad types of judgment which may need to be made in any determination of rights and liabilities. (i) What are the primary facts? Who did what and when and with what intention? (ii) What are the inferences to be drawn from those facts? (iii) What are the legal rules applicable to those findings?

[63] As to (i) we are told that the local authority in this case took Mrs Adan's account of the primary facts from her. They did not conduct any independent inquiries of their own. They did not challenge anything she told them. No doubt this will often be the case. But there will be cases where the local authority are sceptical about what they have been told or at least wish to find out what others involved, for example previous landlords, have to say. Their determination of these primary facts will not be attended by any of the safeguards expected of a judicial or quasi-judicial determination. As currently understood, the county court could not resolve any such dispute as to the primary facts.

[64] As to (ii), there is more than one kind of inference to be drawn from primary facts. For example, s 177(1) of the 1996 Act provides that 'It is not reasonable for a person to continue to occupy accommodation if it is probable that this will lead to domestic violence against him'. The primary facts will be those relied on by the applicant, such as previous violence, threats of violence, stalking, or the like. The inference to be drawn is whether this means that domestic violence is probable in the future. That is an inference of fact.

[65] In this case, the question of whether an applicant is 'ineligible for housing assistance' within the meaning of s 185(1) of the 1996 Act, depends upon whether the applicant is 'not habitually resident in the Common Travel Area' for the purpose of reg 4 of the Homelessness Regulations 1996, SI 1996/2754. Once the correct legal test has been identified, habitual residence has commonly been described as a question of fact. As Lord Scarman put it in *Shah v Barnet London BC* [1983] 1 All ER 226 at 233, [1983] 2 AC 309 at 341:

> 'Though the meaning of ordinary words is, as Lord Reid observed in *Brutus v Cozens* [1972] 2 All ER 1297 at 1299, [1973] AC 854 at 861, a question of fact, the meaning to be attributed to enacted words is a question of law, being a matter of statutory interpretation. So in this case a question of law arises as to the meaning of "ordinarily resident in the United Kingdom," even though it arises only at a preliminary stage in the process of determining a question of fact, namely whether the "propositus" ... has established the fact of ordinary residence for the prescribed period ... It is with this preliminary stage that the courts are concerned. *If a local education authority gets the law right, or, as lawyers would put it, directs itself correctly in law, the question of fact*

a   *ie has the student established the prescribed residence? is for the authority, not the court, to decide.'* (My emphasis.)

This approach does not differ significantly from that of the House of Lords in *Edwards (Inspector of Taxes) v Bairstow* [1955] 3 All ER 48, [1956] AC 14, where the question was whether a particular transaction was 'an adventure in the nature of *b*   trade'. Viscount Simonds said:

     '... in my opinion, whatever test is adopted, that is whether the finding that the transaction was not an adventure in the nature of trade is to be regarded as a pure finding of fact, or as the determination of a question of law, or of mixed law and fact, the same result is reached in this case ... For it is *c*   universally conceded that, though it is a pure finding of fact, it may be set aside on grounds which have been stated in various ways but are, I think, fairly summarised by saying that the court should take that course *if it appears that the commissioners have acted without any evidence, or on a view of the facts which cannot reasonably be entertained* ... The primary facts as they are *d*   sometimes called do not, in my opinion, justify the inference or conclusion which the commissioners have drawn; not only do they not justify it but they lead irresistibly to the opposite inference or conclusion.' (See [1955] 3 All ER 48 at 53, [1956] AC 14 at 29; my emphasis.)

Lord Radcliffe said:

e
     'I do not think that inferences drawn from other facts are incapable of being themselves findings of fact, although there is value in the distinction between primary facts and inferences drawn from them. When the Case comes before the court, it is its duty to examine the determination having regard to its knowledge of the relevant law. If the Case contains anything ex *f*   facie which is bad law and which bears on the determination, it is, obviously, erroneous in point of law. But without any such misconception appearing ex facie, *it may be that the facts found are such that no person acting judicially and properly instructed as to the relevant law could have come to the determination under appeal* ... I do not think that it much matters whether this state of affairs is *g*   described as *one in which there is no evidence to support the determination, or as one in which the evidence is inconsistent with, and contradictory of, the determination, or as one in which the true and only reasonable conclusion contradicts the determination.'* (See [1955] 3 All ER 48 at 57, [1956] AC 14 at 36; my emphasis.)

   [66] I have quoted these well-known passages at length to demonstrate that *h*   the circumstances in which an inference drawn from primary facts can be treated as a question of law are not unlimited. They are different from the circumstances in which such inferences can be drawn in an appeal on fact and law (cf *Benmax v Austin Motor Co Ltd* [1955] 1 All ER 326, [1955] AC 370). The cases do not support the proposition that *any* conclusion that a legal or statutory concept applies to a *j*   particular set of facts is a question of law, although in practice they permit considerable elasticity in their application. In any particular case, it may not be easy for the county court judge to know on which side of the line the particular inference is to fall: if it had been easy, Judge Laurie would have gone on in this case to decide whether, on the agreed primary facts, Mrs Adan was habitually resident here. Even if a case does fall on the error of law side of the boundary, it may not be easy to know whether it is a case in which there is only one possible

answer, so that the judge can vary the decision accordingly, or whether it should
be quashed so that the authority can make it again.

[67] Hence it is not surprising that Mr Pleming QC, on behalf of Mrs Adan,
argues that homelessness decisions are rich in factual questions over which the
court may have limited or no control. These are in no sense 'specialist issues'
which might properly be referred to an expert tribunal: they are bread and butter
questions of the kind which county courts encounter regularly in the course of
their work. I have no doubt that, although the present decision-making process
will comply with art 6 of the convention in some cases, there are many others in
which it will not do so. The only question, therefore, is what can be done to put
it right. The question of a declaration of incompatibility does not strictly arise
here, given that all this discussion is obiter dicta, but it is not difficult to imagine
a case in which such a question would arise. All parties here would prefer us to
find an alternative solution.

[68] We were presented with two possibilities, which in my view are
cumulative rather than alternative: (1) interpreting the court's jurisdiction and
powers under s 204 of the 1996 Act to enable it to cure those cases in which the
procedure as a whole would not otherwise comply with art 6; and (2) contracting
out the local authority's reviewing function under s 202 of the 1996 Act to a body
which meets the art 6 criteria, both in terms of its independence and impartiality
and in terms of the procedures adopted.

[69] Mr Hoskins for the Secretary of State argued eloquently that we could
take a bold approach to the interpretation of s 204(1) so as to enable the system
to be operated compatibly in all cases. Section 204(1), it will be recalled, provides
that:

'If an applicant who has requested a review under section 202—(a) is
dissatisfied with the decision on the review, or (b) is not notified of the
decision on the review within the time prescribed under section 203, he may
appeal to the county court on any point of law arising from the decision or,
as the case may be, the original decision.'

[70] Mr Hoskins' first approach was to invite us to take a more than generous
view of the concept of a 'point of law'. This involved the widest possible view of
the inferences permitted by *Edwards v Bairstow*. It also involved an extension of
the concept of a 'material mistake of fact', in *R v Criminal Injuries Compensation
Board, ex p A* [1999] 2 AC 330, [1999] 2 WLR 974, to encompass the power to retake
the actual decision as to what the facts were. These bold propositions would, as I
understood him, apply generally to appeals on a point of law, irrespective of
whether compliance with the convention rights was involved. I would find
that difficult to accept, not only because I do not think that either concept can be
taken so far, but also because of the effect it would have on the many other
situations in which appeals are limited to points of law. In many of these, the first
instance tribunal already complies with art 6, or will do so if it is combined either
with judicial review or an appeal on a point of law, or it is not required to comply
with art 6 because compliance has been waived (as will normally be the case with
arbitration). It is neither necessary nor appropriate to stretch the concept of an
appeal on a point of law for all purposes simply to enable Pt VII of the 1996 Act
to become convention compatible in all cases.

[71] Mr Hoskins' second approach was to suggest that we could interpret *this
particular provision* so as to secure compatibility in all cases. This is much more

a attractive. We would be solving the problems posed by homelessness cases without affecting any other area of the law. Section 3(1) of the Human Rights Act 1998 requires that: 'So far as it is possible to do so, primary legislation ... must be read and given effect in a way which is compatible with the Convention rights.' Lord Steyn has given us guidance in *R v A* [2001] UKHL 25 at [44], [2001] 3 All ER 1 at [44], [2002] 1 AC 45:

b 'On the other hand, the interpretative obligation under s 3 of the 1998 Act is a strong one. It applies even if there is no ambiguity in the language in the sense of the language being capable of two different meanings. It is an emphatic adjuration by the legislature ... Section 3 of the 1998 Act places a duty on the court to strive to find a possible interpretation compatible with

c convention rights. Under ordinary methods of interpretation a court may depart from the language of a statute to avoid absurd consequences: s 3 goes much further. Undoubtedly, a court must always look for a contextual and purposive interpretation: s 3 is more radical in its effect. It is a general principle of the interpretation of legal instruments that the text is the primary source of interpretation ... Section 3 of the 1998 Act qualifies this general

d principle because it requires a court to find an interpretation compatible with convention rights if it is possible to do so ... In accordance with the will of Parliament as reflected in s 3 it will sometimes be necessary to adopt an interpretation which linguistically may appear strained. *The techniques to be used will not only involve the reading down of express language in a statute but also*

e *the implication of provisions.* A declaration of incompatibility is a measure of last resort. It much be avoided unless it is plainly impossible to do so.' (My emphasis.)

[72] The statutory provision in question, s 41 of the Youth Justice and Criminal Evidence Act 1999, permitted the court to give leave to adduce evidence

f or ask questions in cross-examination about the sexual behaviour of the complainant in sexual offence prosecutions only in certain defined circumstances. These included, in s 41(3)(c), cases where—

'it is an issue of consent and the sexual behaviour of the complainant to which the evidence or question relates is alleged to have been, in any respect, so similar—(i) to any sexual behaviour of the complainant which (according

g to the evidence adduced or to be adduced by or on behalf of the accused) *took place as part of the event which is the subject matter of the charge against the accused* ... that the similarity cannot reasonably be explained as a coincidence.' (My emphasis.)

h Lord Steyn ([2001] 3 All ER 1 at [46]) construed this to mean that—

'due regard always being paid to the importance of seeking to protect the complainant from indignity and from humiliating questions, the test of admissibility is whether the evidence (and questioning in relation to it) is nevertheless so relevant to the issue of consent that to exclude it would

j endanger the fairness of the trial under art 6 of the convention. If this test is satisfied the evidence should not be excluded.'

[73] Lord Slynn of Hadley, Lord Clyde and Lord Hutton all agreed with this interpretation and must therefore have agreed that s 3(1) of the 1998 Act permitted them to do so. Lord Hope of Craighead disagreed ([2001] 3 All ER 1 at [108]):

'... s 3 of the 1998 Act does not entitle the court to legislate; its task is still
one of interpretation. The compatibility is to be achieved only so far as this
is possible. Plainly this will not be possible if the legislation contains
provisions which expressly contradict the meaning which the enactment
would have to be given to make it compatible. It seems to me that the same
result must follow if they do so by necessary implication ...'

He thought that the entire structure of the provision in question contradicted the
idea that it was possible to give the court a wider power to allow cross-
examination in rape cases.

[74] Those who took the view that they could interpret the section in such a
way may have done so because they thought that it was not contradicted either
expressly or by necessary implication. Alternatively, they may have agreed with
Lord Steyn's approach to s 3(1) of the 1998 Act. The case does, however, indicate
how far the House has been prepared to go in striving for compatibility.

[75] That case concerned a statute passed after the 1998 Act upon which the
government took a contrary view. This case concerns a relatively recent statute
but one passed well before the 1998 Act. That case involved interpreting the
words 'took place as part of the event which is the subject matter of the charge'
to include any similar sexual behaviour which the court thinks so relevant to the
issue of consent that it would endanger the fairness of the trial to exclude it. This
case would involve interpreting the words 'point of law arising from the decision
or, as the case may be, the original decision' to include the question whether the
decision-making process as a whole complies with art 6 of the convention in the
particular circumstances of the case. This seems to me to be plainly a point of
law. If the court reaches the conclusion that the process will only comply with
art 6 if the court reaches its own conclusion on disputed questions of fact, then it
can, indeed must, 'give effect to' its disposal powers under s 204(3) of the 1996 Act
and its procedural powers under CPR Pt 52 so as to make good the deficiency.
Given that the court has power under s 204(3) to vary the local authority's
decision as it thinks fit, this does less violence to the statutory language than
implying a power to send the case back to the local authority with a direction to
comply with art 6.

[76] An alternative is to read the Local Authorities (Contracting Out of
Allocation of Housing and Homelessness Functions) Order 1996, SI 1996/3205,
made under s 70(2) of the Deregulation and Contracting Out Act 1994, so as to
require the local authority to contract out their reviewing function under s 202 of
the 1996 Act in any case in which they fear that the overall decision-making
process will not comply with art 6. The local authority may always do this if they
wish. They might contract it out to a body which resembled the planning
inspectorate or a social security appeal tribunal. They might require that body to
adopt procedures which were sufficient to comply with art 6: in particular in
offering an oral hearing in more circumstances than is at present required by the
Allocation of Housing and Homelessness (Review Procedures) Regulations 1999,
SI 1999/71. If so, the county court would no doubt reach the conclusion that the
procedures as a whole were sufficient to comply with art 6 and confine its own
role to correcting errors of law in the more traditional sense.

[77] But some local authorities may be reluctant to do this. It would change
the character of reviews in at least as fundamental a fashion as would the
proposed interpretation of the court's jurisdiction. The reviewing function is part
of a good internal decision-making process. It enables the authority to stand back

a a little from the pressures affecting the original decision-maker and look at that decision again. It is, we are told, welcomed by many applicants. A goodly proportion of them benefit from it. Parliament intended them to have that benefit. They would be deprived of it if it were turned into something rather different by contracting it out to a more formal process conducted by someone else.

b [78] More importantly, however, it will not always be clear to the local authority before the review takes place whether this is a case in which an independent fact-finding body is required: the issues may only become clear to the local authority from the representations made by or on behalf of the applicant during the review. The only safe solution would be for them to contract out reviews in every case. But that would be to require them to take a step in all cases c to meet a need for compliance which is only present in some. Furthermore, it is to place upon the local authority the whole burden of compliance, when the jurisprudence both here and in the European Court of Human Rights makes it clear that it is the decision-making process as a whole which must comply. The court is part of that process and the court is much better placed than the local d authority to decide whether, in the particular case in question, the process as a whole complies with art 6. The court comes at the end of the process and by then it is known, or ought to be known, what the case is about.

[79] Hence, if the local authority for whatever reason do not provide a reviewing system which is adequate to comply with art 6 in the particular case, the county court would have to say so. As we are agreed that the court cannot e send the case back with a direction to comply, the court is required to fill the gap itself. This is no more radical an interpretation of s 204 of the 1996 Act as a whole than is the suggestion that the local authority be required as a matter of law to adopt a different decision-making process. Of course, if they were so required, but did not do so, this would clearly be a question of law for the court to resolve.

f [80] I therefore see the two possibilities as cumulative rather than alternative. I am prepared to accept that the local authority may choose to contract out some or all of its reviews to a body whose constitution and procedures enable the decision to comply with art 6 (even though this would change the character of reviews and deprive applicants of much that is valuable in them). But if they do g not do so, and the particular issues in the case require an independent decision, then the court should fill the gap.

[81] I do not see this approach as jeopardising the constitutional balance: the issue before the court is properly characterised as one of law and Parliament and the CPR have given the court appropriate powers to resolve the problem. I am h to some extent fortified in that view by the fact that all three parties in this case regard it as a possible approach to construction of the 1996 Act. Mr Hoskins initially appeared to go further, inviting us to read the words 'fact or' into s 204(1). That would have opened up the possibility of a complete rehearing in almost every case; but it became clear that the proposed implication was only in those cases where it was necessary to make the process art 6 compliant. Ms Booth was j clear that Newham London BC does not want to have to set up a new contracted-out reviewing system for the large numbers of cases they have: she too argued for a wide view of the court's powers if it turns out that art 6 will not be complied with in a particular case. Mr Pleming is concerned that there should be a process which overall has full jurisdiction to consider any questions or inferences of fact which may be involved in his client's renewed application. Of

course the arguments of counsel cannot prevail over the limits of the possible in
the interpretation of statutory language. But for the reasons already explained, *a*
this interpretation is indeed possible.

[82] If Mr Hoskins and Ms Booth are right, this approach will not open the
floodgates to retrying all the issues in every homelessness case. But if they are
wrong, the obvious solution for the Secretary of State would be to set up a
specialist tribunal system to fill the gap. Such tribunals already exist for social *b*
security benefits and have recently been extended to housing and council tax
benefit: see the Housing Benefit and Council Tax Benefit (Decisions and Appeals)
Regulations 2001, SI 2001/1002. There are even examples in the provision of
services, such as the special educational needs tribunal. For the reasons given
earlier, claims under Pt VII of the 1996 Act are not discretionary and have much
in common with claims for social security and other financial benefits. In *c*
principle, therefore, there is nothing at all radical in subjecting individual claims
to independent scrutiny on questions of fact as well as law. The Pt VII procedure
is the exception rather than the rule.

[83] For these reasons, therefore, I would have sent this case back to the
county court, with a direction to consider whether the requirements of art 6 were *d*
complied with in this case, and to decide the case itself in accordance with those
requirements if they were not.

DAVID STEEL J.

[84] I also agree with the order proposed by Brooke LJ.   *e*

[85] I propose to dwell solely on the hypothetical issue on which Brooke and
Hale LJJ are divided, namely whether it is legitimate, in order to ensure that
review proceedings are convention compliant (European Convention for the
Protection of Human Rights and Fundamental Freedoms 1950 (as set out in Sch 1
to the Human Rights Act 1998)), to interpret s 204(1) of the Housing Act 1996 in *f*
such a way as to allow the county court, where it concludes that the review
process will only comply with art 6 if it reaches its own conclusion on disputed
questions of fact, to allocate to itself jurisdiction to entertain an appeal on those
issues of fact.

[86] On this issue I am in agreement with Brooke LJ that any temptation to
confer such an enlargement of the jurisdiction of the county court must be *g*
resisted, both as a matter of authority and of constitutional propriety.

[87] I start with authority and the decision of the House of Lords in *R v A*
[2001] UKHL 25, [2001] 3 All ER 1, [2002] 1 AC 45. Ironically, just as in the present
case, the decision had an entirely hypothetical base, namely an appeal by the
Crown against an obiter dictum, but not the decision, of the Court of Appeal *h*
([2001] EWCA Crim 4, sub nom *R v Y* [2001] All ER (D) 66 (Jan)). The detailed
views of their Lordships on the proper approach to interpretation of the relevant
section of the Youth Justice and Criminal Evidence Act 1999 in the face of s 3 of
the 1998 Act varied.

[88] Some passages from Lord Steyn's speech have already been cited *j*
including his summary of the effect of the decision in para [46]. I draw attention
to the following additional passages:

'[43] … In my view ordinary methods of purposive construction of
s 41(3)(c) (of the 1999 Act) cannot cure the problem of the excessive breadth
of s 41, read as a whole, so far as it relates to previous sexual experience

a
between a complainant and the accused. Whilst the statute pursued desirable goals, the methods adopted amounted to legislative overkill ...

[45] In my view s 3 of the 1998 Act requires the court to subordinate the niceties of the language of s 41(3)(c) of the 1999 Act, and in particular the touchstone of coincidence, to broader considerations of relevance judged by logical and commonsense criteria of time and circumstances. *After all, it is*

b
realistic to proceed on the basis that the legislature would not, if alerted to the problem, have wished to deny the right to an accused to put forward a full and compete defence by advancing truly probative material. It is therefore possible under s 3 of the 1998 Act to read s 41 of the 1999 Act, and in particular s 41(3)(c), as subject to the implied provision that evidence or questioning which is required to ensure a fair trial under art 6 of the convention should

c
not be treated as inadmissible.' (My emphasis.)

[89] In a short judgment, Lord Slynn of Hadley expressed agreement with Lord Steyn's statement as to the effect of the decision. But his reasoning put emphasis on the imprecision of the relevant part of the subsection:

d
'[13] Section 41(3)(c) of the 1999 Act raises a different issue. Although if read literally or even perhaps purposively this provision is very restrictive, I think disproportionately restrictive, it is less precise than s 41(3)(b). The section must be read and given effect in a way "which is compatible with the Convention rights" in so far as it is possible to do so. It seems to me that your

e
Lordships cannot say that it is not possible to read s 41(3)(c) together with art 6 of the convention rights in a way which will result in a fair hearing. In my view s 41(3)(c) is to be read as permitting the admission of evidence or questioning which relates to a relevant issue in the case and which the trial judge considers it necessary to make the trial a fair one.'

f
[90] Lord Hope of Craighead also agreed that the appeal should be dismissed, but was not minded to accept that s 41 as such had made excessive inroads into convention rights. The matter, in his judgment, could only be determined at the trial by construing the words of the section applying the test adumbrated by Lord Steyn *'so far as it is possible to do so'*:

g
'[109] In the present case it seems to me that the entire structure of s 41 of the 1999 Act contradicts the idea that it is possible to read into it a new provision which would entitle the court to give leave whenever it was of the opinion that this was required to ensure a fair trial ...

[110] I would not have the same difficulty with a solution which read down the provisions of sub-ss (3) or (5) of s 41, as the case may be, in order

h
to render them compatible with the convention right. But if that were to be done it would be necessary to identify precisely (a) the words used by the legislature which would otherwise be incompatible with the convention right, and (b) how these words were to be construed, according to the rule which s 3 of the 1998 Act lays down, to make them compatible. That, it

j
seems to me, is what the rule of construction requires. The court's task is to read and give effect to the legislation which it is asked to construe ... I would leave that exercise to be undertaken by the trial judge in the light of such further information about the nature and circumstances of his relationship with the complainant that the respondent can make available if and when he renews his application. If he finds it necessary to apply the interpretative

obligation under s 3 of the 1998 Act to the words used in s 41(3)(c) of the 1999
Act, he should do so by construing those words, so far as it is possible to do
so, by applying the test indicated at [46] of the speech of my noble and
learned friend Lord Steyn.'

[91] Lord Clyde agreed with Lord Steyn's summary of the outcome. His
approach was by way of the need to strain the language:

'[136] ... If a case occurred where the evidence of the complainant's sexual
behaviour was relevant and important for the defence to make good a case
of consent, then it seems to me that the language would have to be strained
in order to avoid the injustice to the accused of excluding from a full and
proper presentation of his defence ...'

[92] Lord Hutton also agreed that the appeal should be dismissed but his
approach was altogether different. He concluded that, on the facts, there was
sufficient similarity to the behaviour alleged to satisfy s 41(3)(1):

'[163] I have observed (at [159]) that on ordinary principles of construction
and having regard to the change in emphasis in *R v P* [1991] 3 All ER 337,
sub nom *DPP v P* [1991] 2 AC 447 away from "striking similarity" to
"probative force" there is a possible argument that relevant evidence of a
previous close and affectionate relationship in which sexual intercourse took
place is admissible under s 41(3) of the 1999 Act. Therefore pursuant to the
obligation imposed by s 3(1) of the 1998 Act that s 41 must be read and given
effect in a way which is compatible with art 6 of the convention, I consider
that s 41(3)(c) should be read as including evidence of such previous
behaviour by the complainant because the defendant claims that her sexual
behaviour on previous occasions was similar, and the similarity was not a
coincidence because there was a causal connection which was her affection
for, and feelings of attraction towards, the defendant. It follows that I am in
full agreement with the test of admissibility stated by my noble and learned
friend Lord Steyn at [46] of his speech.'

[93] Making full allowance for the peculiar difficulties created by s 3 of the
1998 Act in the criminal law context, perhaps I should not disguise my attraction
to Lord Hope's approach. In any event, straining the language is one thing:
implying words to ensure that the statutory provision does not infringe the
convention is perhaps another.

[94] Whatever may be the true analysis of the decision, I still agree with the
conclusion of Brooke LJ that it does not permit an interpretation, so as to allow
the county court to fill any 'gap', that renders the words 'appeal on a point of law'
as including 'appeal on a point of fact'. Straining the language cannot achieve that
end. Nor is a dispute of fact rendered a dispute of law by reason of what would
otherwise be a shortfall in convention compliance as regards the provision for
resolution of that dispute. Nor, in the further alternative, is there any need to
imply words to that effect. The court is simply not boxed into a corner where the
only option is the implication of the words 'fact or' or a declaration of
incompatibility. The local authority simply has to contract out the review process,
either generally or in appropriate cases.

[95] There is no need to cite further authority for the proposition that legislation
is a matter for Parliament. Importantly, I am unable to proceed on the basis that
'if alerted' to the problem, Parliament would have adopted the course suggested

a by Hale LJ. The consequential need for caution is spelt out in the conclusion of Lord Hoffmann's Combar Lecture 2001 on the 'Separation of Powers': 'However slow, obtuse and maddening the democratic process may be, there is a legitimacy about the decisions of elected institutions to which judges, however enlightened, can never lay claim.'

Appeal allowed.

Kate O'Hanlon   Barrister.

Note
Turner v Grovit and others
[2001] UKHL 65

a

HOUSE OF LORDS

LORD NICHOLLS OF BIRKENHEAD, LORD HOFFMANN, LORD HOBHOUSE OF
WOODBOROUGH, LORD MILLETT AND LORD SCOTT OF FOSCOTE
7 FEBRUARY, 13 DECEMBER 2001

b

*Conflict of laws – Jurisdiction – Challenge to jurisdiction – Claimant working as
solicitor for group of companies but having employment contract with Irish member of* *c*
*group – Claimant relocating from London to Madrid – Claimant resigning and suing
for constructive dismissal in England – Spanish member of group suing claimant in
Spain for breach of contract – Whether inconsistent with Brussels Convention for
English court to grant on grounds of abuse of process anti-suit injunction in respect of
proceedings in another convention state – Civil Jurisdiction and Judgments Act 1982,* *d*
Sch 1, arts 5(1), 21, 22.

On the hearing of an appeal by the defendants, Felix Fareed Ismail Grovit,
Harada Ltd (trading as Chequepoint UK) and Changepoint SA, from the decision
of the Court of Appeal (Stuart-Smith and Laws LJJ, Jonathan Parker J) on 28 May
1999 ([1999] 3 All ER 616, [2000] QB 345) allowing an appeal by the claimant, *e*
Gregory Paul Turner, from the decision of David Donaldson QC, sitting as a
deputy judge of the Chancery Division, on 24 February 1999 ([1999] 1 All ER
(Comm) 445) refusing his application for restraining orders in respect of
proceedings brought against him in Spain, the House of Lords referred the
following question to the Court of Justice of the European Communities: *f*

> 'Is it inconsistent with the Convention on Jurisdiction and the Enforcement
> of Judgments in Civil and Commercial Matters 1968 (as set out in Sch 1 to the
> Civil Jurisdiction and Judgments Act 1982) for the courts of the United
> Kingdom to grant restraining orders against defendants who are threatening
> to commence or continue legal proceedings in another convention country
> when those defendants are acting in bad faith with the intent and purpose of *g*
> frustrating or obstructing proceedings properly before the English courts?'

Dilys Tausz   Barrister.

a
Roerig v Valiant Trawlers Ltd
[2002] EWCA Civ 21

COURT OF APPEAL, CIVIL DIVISION

b SIMON BROWN, WALLER AND SEDLEY LJJ

17 DECEMBER 2001, 28 JANUARY 2002

Conflict of Laws – Tort – Damages – Assessment – Dutch national employed by Dutch company and living in Holland killed in accident while working on English-registered
c *trawler – Deceased's partner bringing action in England on behalf of Dutch dependants for loss of dependency – Whether substantially more appropriate for damages to be assessed under Dutch law rather than English law – Fatal Accidents Act 1976, s 4 – Private International Law (Miscellaneous Provisions) Act 1995, s 12.*

The claimant was a Dutch woman whose partner, another Dutch national, had
d been killed in an accident on a trawler which was registered in England and owned by the defendant, an English-registered company. That company was the subsidiary of a Dutch company, and the deceased had been on board the trawler as an employee of another Dutch company in the same group. Since, however, the accident had occurred on an English-registered trawler, English law was the
e applicable law governing the tort under the general rule prescribed by s 11 of the Private International Law (Miscellaneous Provisions) Act 1995. Though living in Holland, the claimant brought an action in England against the defendant under the Fatal Accidents Act 1976, on behalf of herself and her children, for loss of dependency. Section 4[a] of the 1976 Act provided that, in assessing damages in respect of a person's death in an action 'under this Act', benefits which had accrued or would or might accrue to any person from his estate or otherwise as
f a result of his death were to be disregarded. The defendant nevertheless contended that the claimant would have to give credit for benefits arising from her partner's death since such benefits would be taken into account under Dutch law and it was that law which governed the assessment of damages in the case. The defendant relied on s 12(1)[b] of the 1995 Act which displaced the general rule
g under s 11 if it appeared, in all the circumstances, from a comparison of (a) the significance of the factors which connected a tort with the country whose law would be the applicable law under the general rule, and (b) the significance of any factors connecting the tort with another country, that it was 'substantially' more appropriate for the applicable law for determining the issues arising in the case, or any of those issues, to be the law of the other country. The defendant
h accordingly contended that when a comparison was made of the significant factors connecting the tort with England, and the significant factors connecting it with Holland, it was substantially more appropriate for the applicable law relating to the issue of damages to be the law of Holland. That contention was rejected
j by the judge on the determination of preliminary issues. The defendant appealed, relying on the fact that the deceased was Dutch, that he was employed by a Dutch company paying Dutch taxes and making contributions to obtain Dutch benefits, and that the dependants would suffer the loss of their dependency in Holland.

---

a   Section 4 is set out at [2], below
b   Section 12 is set out at [7], below

Held – Where the defendant was English and the tort had taken place in England, it could not be said that it was substantially more appropriate, within the meaning of s 12 of the 1995 Act, for damages to be assessed by the law of another country simply because the deceased had been a national of that country, and had been living and employed in that country. The key word was 'substantially', and the general rule was not to be dislodged easily. It followed in the instant case that the judge had been correct to conclude that the defendant had failed in its attempt to dislodge that rule. Accordingly, the appeal would be dismissed (see [12], [48], [49], below).

Per curiam. (1) The question whether deductions are to be made for benefits in assessing damages for loss of dependency is a matter of procedural rather than substantive law, and is therefore subject to the lex fori. In any event, once an action has been brought under the 1976 Act, s 4 must apply simply as a matter of construction since it refers to the assessment of damages in an action under 'this Act' (see [23], [25], [28]–[30], [48], [49], below); *Chaplin v Boys* [1969] 2 All ER 1085 considered.

(2) In determining whether a decision made at the conclusion of the hearing of a preliminary issue constitutes a 'final decision' for the purposes of para 2A.2 of CPR PD 52, which provides that an appeal from such a decision in a claim allocated to the multi-track lies to the Court of Appeal, the court should apply a broad commonsense test, asking whether (if not tried separately) the issue would have formed a substantive part of the final trial. The fact that an issue has sensibly been taken separately should not deprive a party of their right to go to the Court of Appeal. If it does, that will be an active discouragement to parties to support the trial of preliminary issues (see [45], [46], [48], [49], below).

Notes

For displacement of the general choice of law rule and for assessment of damages for loss of dependency, see respectively 8(1) *Halsbury's Laws* (4th edn reissue) para 899 and 12(1) *Halsbury's Laws* (4th edn reissue) para 935.

For the Fatal Accidents Act 1976, s 4, see 31 *Halsbury's Statutes* (4th edn) (2000 reissue) 485.

For the Private International Law (Miscellaneous Provisions) Act 1995, s 12, see 45 *Halsbury's Statutes* (4th edn) (1999 reissue) 1027.

Cases referred to in judgments

Breavington v Godleman (1988) 169 CLR 41, Aust HC.

Caltex Singapore Pte Ltd v BP Shipping Ltd [1996] 1 Lloyd's Rep 286.

Chaplin v Boys [1969] 2 All ER 1085, [1971] AC 356, [1969] 3 WLR 322, HL.

Coupland v Arabian Gulf Petroleum Co [1983] 2 All ER 434, [1983] 1 WLR 1136; *affd* [1983] 3 All ER 226, [1983] 1 WLR 1136, CA.

Edmunds v Simmonds [2001] 1 WLR 1003.

Esso Malaysia, The, Cox v Owners of the Esso Malaysia [1974] 2 All ER 705, [1975] QB 198, [1974] 3 WLR 341.

Holmes v Bangladesh Biman Corp [1988] 2 Lloyd's Rep 120, CA; *rvsd* [1989] 1 All ER 852, [1989] AC 1112, [1989] 2 WLR 481, HL.

McKain v R W Miller & Co (South Australia) Pty Ltd (1991) 174 CLR 1, Aust HC.

Parry v Cleaver [1969] 1 All ER 555, [1970] AC 1, [1969] 2 WLR 821, HL.

Perrett v Robinson (1988) 169 CLR 172, Aust HC.

Stevens v Head (1993) 176 CLR 433, Aust HC.

Tanfern Ltd v Cameron-MacDonald [2000] 2 All ER 801, [2000] 1 WLR 1311, CA.

White v Brunton [1984] 2 All ER 606, [1984] QB 570, [1984] 3 WLR 105, CA.

a
Appeal
The defendants, Valiant Trawlers Ltd, appealed with permission of May LJ granted on 24 August 2001 from the decision of Judge Reddihough at Grimsby County Court on 15 March 2001 whereby he determined in favour of the claimant, Alexandra Marie Roerig, certain preliminary issues relating to the assessment of damages in an action under the Fatal Accidents Act 1976 brought
b by her against the defendants on her own behalf and on behalf of her children for loss of dependency arising from the death of her partner. The facts are set out in the judgment of Waller LJ.

Robert Leonard (instructed by *Ince & Co*) for the defendants.
Robert Weir (instructed by *Bridge McFarland*, Grimsby) for the claimant.
c
Cur adv vult

28 January 2002. The following judgments were delivered.

d **WALLER LJ** (giving the first judgment at the invitation of Simon Brown LJ).

Introduction
[1] This is an appeal from the judgment of Judge Reddihough dated 15 March 2001. He decided certain preliminary issues in relation to the assessment of damages in favour of the claimant. Although the judge was asked to answer four
e issues summarised at para 5 of his judgment, the issues were drafted in order to enable the court to answer one question, namely in assessing damages for loss of dependency should benefits resulting from the loss be deducted from the damages?
[2] The claimant is a Dutch lady and brings the action as a dependant of a
f Dutchman. She does so on her own behalf and on behalf of their Dutch children in the English courts under the Fatal Accidents Act 1976, the Dutchman having been tragically killed on a trawler registered in England and owned by the defendants, an English-registered company. There is no dispute about liability or about the claimant's entitlement to bring the action under the above Act. It is furthermore not in issue that under s 4 of the 1976 Act it is provided that in
g relation to actions brought under that Act:

> 'Assessment of damages: disregard of benefits.—In assessing damages in respect of a person's death in an action under this Act, benefits which have accrued or will or may accrue to any person from his estate or otherwise as a result of his death shall be disregarded.'
h

[3] The defendants (appellants in this court) however contend, and for the present it must be assumed, accurately, that under Dutch law the position is different. In the witness statement of Mr Van der Zwan, para 23 which is the limit of the evidence that has been obtained on Dutch law, the position is put in
j this way:

> 'Compensation is also paid to accident victims and their dependants through civil court proceedings. However, under Dutch law the level of compensation is determined by the financial requirements of the claimant. All benefits received by the claimant—whether emanating from social security or from a collective labour agreement's provision—will be taken into account and deducted from compensation. The reasoning behind this

is that society provides for its victims and their dependants to an acceptable and reasonably high minimum, which is usually elevated by provisions arranged by the industry they are/were working in. In Ms Roerig's and her children's case this social security system works out as follows ...'

[4] There then follows a full explanation of the various benefits which have been paid, or will be payable to the claimant and her children following the death of Mr Van der Plas. From preceding paragraphs of Mr Van der Zwan's statement it seems that the benefits are accrued as a result of substantial contributions deducted from the deceased's earnings, as well as substantial contributions by the deceased's employers in Holland. The benefits include (i) a payment under Dutch labour law; (ii) a payment made without legal obligation covered by a personal accident insurance; (iii) a state surviving relatives' pension including amounts for the children; (iv) a widow and orphans' pension from the workers' pension fund for the Offshore Fishing Industry. It is further said that in relation to this last pension, the deceased's employers after his death negotiated with the relevant authorities to ensure the benefits were available to the claimant and her children despite the fact that she and the deceased were not married. The preliminary issues are thus designed to find the answer to the one question—does s 4 of the 1976 Act apply to the claimant's claim, or must she give credit for the benefits which she and her children would have to give if the damages were being assessed under Dutch law?

[5] To succeed on this issue in the Court of Appeal the defendants must establish that the judge was wrong in relation to all, or practically all, the issues he decided.

[6] The first issue he decided related to the proper law of the tort. Section 11 of the Private International Law (Miscellaneous Provisions) Act 1995 (the Private International Law Act) provides as follows:

'Choice of applicable law: the general rule.—(1) The general rule is that the applicable law is the law of the country in which the events constituting the tort or delict in question occur.

(2) Where elements of those events occur in different countries, the applicable law under the general rule is to be taken as being—(a) for a cause of action in respect of personal injury caused to an individual or death resulting from personal injury, the law of the country where the individual was when he sustained the injury; (b) for a cause of action in respect of damage to property, the law of the country where the property was when it was damaged; and (c) in any other case, the law of the country in which the most significant element or elements of those events occurred.

(3) In this section "personal injury" includes disease or any impairment of physical or mental condition.'

[7] It is not in dispute that under the general rule there laid down the applicable law is English law because the accident to the deceased occurred on an English-registered trawler, and thus that is the law 'in which the events constituting the tort or delict in question' occurred, or at the very least, the law of the country 'where the individual was when he sustained the injury'. But the defendants rely on s 12 of the same Act which provides as follows:

'Choice of applicable law: displacement of general rule.—(1) If it appears, in all the circumstances, from a comparison of—(a) the significance of the factors which connect a tort or delict with the country whose law would be the

a   applicable law under the general rule; and (b) the significance of any factors
     connecting the tort or delict with another country, that it is substantially
     more appropriate for the applicable law for determining the issues arising in
     the case, or any of those issues, to be the law of the other country, the general
     rule is displaced and the applicable law for determining those issues or that
     issue (as the case may be) is the law of that other country.

b   (2) The factors that may be taken into account as connecting a tort or
     delict with a country for the purposes of this section include, in particular,
     factors relating to the parties, to any of the events which constitute the tort
     or delict in question or to any of the circumstances or consequences of those
     events.'

c   [8] They contended accordingly that when a comparison is made of the
     significant factors connecting the tort with England, and the significant factors
     connecting the tort with Holland, it is substantially more appropriate for the
     applicable law relating to the issue of damages to be the law of Holland. The
     judge found against the defendants on that issue.

d   [9] As regards the second issue it seems that after liability was admitted, and
     one presumes in case the judge were to be against the claimant on the first issue,
     the claimant amended her claim to allege a claim in contract as between the deceased
     and the defendants. The claim as pleaded alleged a contract of employment. It
     also alleged that the proper law of the contract was English. There thus were two
     aspects of this issue. The contract relied on was a contract in writing which on its
e   face purported to be such. It was (indeed is) in English and purports to be made
     between the defendants and the deceased (see p 208A of the bundle). On the trial
     of the preliminary issue the judge found (contrary to the claimant's argument),
     that the deceased had a contract of employment with a Dutch company (Diepzee)
     not with the defendants, and that the arrangement was that Diepzee provided its
f   employees to the defendants. Those findings are not challenged. But the judge,
     by virtue of the document at p 208A, spelt out another form of contract, and he
     further found that that contract was governed by English law. He thus decided
     both aspects of this issue in favour of the claimant.

     [10] The final issue, which the judge resolved on the basis that he might be
     wrong about both the previous issues, was whether s 4 of the 1976 Act was
g   substantive or procedural. If it was procedural, then (as was common ground)
     even if the proper law of the tort was Dutch and/or even if the proper law of any
     relevant contract was Dutch, the English court would apply s 4. The judge found
     that s 4 was procedural, and thus ruled against the defendants on this aspect also.

     [11] We have been very much assisted by a full and comprehensive judgment,
h   and by full and comprehensive skeleton arguments, all of a high standard. At the
     oral hearing we heard full submissions from Mr Leonard for the defendants on all
     issues. At the invitation of the court Mr Weir concentrated his submissions
     entirely on issues 1 (proper law of the tort) and 3 (procedural or substantive),
     success on either of which would be enough for his client to succeed. The court
j   further suggested to Mr Weir that if he did not succeed on one or other of those
     issues he was in fact unlikely to be able to uphold the judge on issue 2 (the
     contract issue). It would not have been possible to complete the oral hearing on
     the day allotted for the appeal if issue 2 had been further developed. Mr Weir was
     offered the opportunity of considering whether he wanted to address further oral
     argument to the court on some other day on issue 2 with (as was made clear)
     possible costs consequences if that issue were to be determined against his client.

Since there also remained at the conclusion of the oral hearing a further point on
the procedure adopted by the defendants in seeking permission to appeal and the
costs consequences of adopting that procedure on which both sides were content
to put in written submissions, we invited Mr Weir to make clear by those written
submissions what his position was in relation to issue 2. In the result Mr Weir has
confirmed that his client does not seek to be allowed further oral argument on
issue 2 and relies simply on the full skeleton argument previously lodged. Mr Weir
has also put in written submissions on the appeal procedure point.

Issue 1—Proper law of the tort

[12] (i) At first sight s 12 of the Private International Law Act seems less than
clear when the question is whether some other law should be applied in relation
to an issue such as damages or a head of damage. It requires comparison of the
significance of the factors which connect a *tort* (not the issue) with the *country*
whose law would be the applicable law under the general rule, and the
significance of any factors connecting the *tort* (*not* the issue) with another *country*,
and from that comparison to decide in all the circumstances whether it is
substantially more appropriate for the law of that other country to be the law to
determine the *issue*. It may be that the words 'or any of those issues' were
inserted in the section as an amendment without further amendment of para (a)
or (b) of sub-s (1) (that seems possible since those words were apparently not in
the Bill originally put forward by the Law Commission and not in the Bill
originally placed before Parliament (see *Dicey and Morris on the Conflict of Laws*
(13th edn, 2000) vol 2, para 35-095)). It may also be that it was a deliberate
decision to draft the section in a way which forced concentration primarily on
factors which connected the tort generally to a particular country, even in
considering whether there should be an exception for a particular issue. For our
purposes it matters not how it happened, the section requires an approach by
reference to factors that connect the tort generally to a particular country, and an
assessment by reference to those factors as to whether it is substantially more
appropriate that an issue be tried by some law other than the law which governs
the tort generally.

(ii) The first exercise is to identify the issue in relation to which it might be
suggested that the general rule should not be applicable. It is not I think seriously
argued that in relation to issues giving rise to liability the general rule should not
have applied. The argument relates to the assessment of damages, and in
particular to the assessment of a particular head of damage accepted as
recoverable under both Dutch and English law, 'dependency', and ultimately to
the question whether benefits accruing from the death of the deceased should be
deducted when making that assessment. The characterisation for the purposes of
private international law of issues arising in a claim as issues relating to tort or
delict is a matter for the courts of the forum (see s 9(2) of the Private International
Law Act). This will be relevant again when considering issue 3 (procedural or
substantive). The question is whether the issue in the instant case should be
defined as damages generally, or that head of damage 'dependency' or even more
refined to the issue whether benefits should be deducted. In *Chaplin v Boys* [1969]
2 All ER 1085, [1971] AC 356 the House of Lords wrestled with the question
whether damages for pain and suffering which were irrecoverable under Maltese
law, Malta being the country where the motor accident took place, but
recoverable under English law, the law of the country of both parties, and of the
forum, should be decided under English law or Maltese law. That points the way

a as it seems to me to defining and refining the issue in this case at least to that relating to recoverability of damages for loss of dependency. I would however limit the refinement of the issue to 'loss of dependency' as opposed to further refining the issue as to whether 'benefits should be deducted in assessing loss of dependency'. This may not be so important when considering this issue, but it is at this stage that there seems to me to be an overlap between issue 3 and issue 1.

b The question whether a head of damage is recoverable is clearly a matter of substantive law which could be decided by reference to a law other than the law of the forum. An issue of what should be deducted in calculating the damages under a specific head should be for the law of the forum. For reasons which I shall develop when considering issue 3, the deduction of benefits seems to me a matter of calculation and thus for the forum. Under s 12 of the Private International Law

c Act the law of the forum is not an option unless that law is also a law of a country with which the tort has significant connecting factors. Thus an issue which is for the law of the forum cannot be a relevant issue under s 12. I accept that at this stage in the context of this case in any event that distinction may be unimportant.

(iii) The next task is to identify the factors that connect the tort with England

d and those that connect the tort with Holland. The factors that connect with England seem to me to be that the events occurred on a boat registered in England, and that the defendants are an English company. What then are the factors that connect with Holland? The deceased was a Dutchman, and his death would lead to damage being suffered by his dependants, who are Dutch, in Holland where they live. The incident occurred when the deceased was under

e the supervision of the Dutch fishing master albeit the skipper of the boat was English. In real terms the vessel was on a Dutch fishing expedition in that the boat set off from a Dutch port and would return with its catch to a Dutch port. The defendants were a subsidiary of a Dutch company, and the deceased was on board the trawler as an employee of a Dutch company also a member of the same

f group.

(iv) What then is the significance of the Dutch factors when compared to the significance of the English factors which might make it substantially more appropriate for Dutch law to determine the loss of dependency issue? Mr Leonard submits that it is the fact that the deceased was Dutch, employed by a Dutch company paying Dutch taxes and making contributions to obtain Dutch security

g benefits, and the fact that the dependants will suffer their loss of dependency in Holland as Dutch citizens, which are the most significant factors. That, he submits, makes it logical to assess this aspect of the damages by Dutch law. But it seems to me that the logic of that argument leads almost inevitably to the consequence that where a claimant, injured in England, is a foreigner living and

h employed in that foreign country, any head of damage should be assessed in accordance with the law of his or her country. Indeed in one sense I suppose it could be said to be 'appropriate' that that should be so since the injured party or the dependants thereof are likely to feel their loss only in that foreign country. But it seems to me that it was not intended that the general rule should be

j dislodged so easily. Where the defendant is English, and the tort took place in England, it cannot surely be said that it is *substantially* more appropriate for damages to be assessed by Dutch law simply because the claimant or the deceased is Dutch. One can entirely understand that if fortuitously two English persons are in a foreign country on holiday and one tortiously injures the other, the significant factors in favour of England being the place by reference to which the damages should be assessed may make it *substantially* more appropriate that

damages should be assessed by English law. But say the position were that an
English defendant under English principles relevant to assessment of damage
would have to pay aggravated damages to a claimant, and would thus have to pay
English plaintiffs such damages, why should a foreigner not be entitled to have
such damages awarded in his or her favour simply because by the law of where
they reside those damages would be unavailable?

(v) In my view the word 'substantially' is the key word. The general rule is
not to be dislodged easily. I thus think the judge was right in the view he formed
that the defendants had failed in their attempt to do so.

Issue 3—Substantive or procedural

[13] This issue only arises on the assumption that the above view on issue 1 is
wrong, ie on the basis that Dutch law must be taken to be the appropriate law by
reference to which the loss of dependency should be assessed. As already
indicated, if Dutch law were the appropriate law by which to decide the benefits
which will accrue to the claimant and her children in Holland as a result of the
deceased's death, then a deduction would have to be made in assessing the loss
of dependency. But the claimant argues that even if Dutch law was the
appropriate law for determining what heads of damage were recoverable
including loss of dependency, English law as the lex fori should still apply to the
issue whether benefits should be deducted. It is common ground that all matters
of procedure are governed by the law of the country to which the court wherein
any legal proceedings are taken belongs (see *Dicey and Morris*, vol 1, rule 17
(para 7R-001)). What is argued on behalf of the claimant is that although 'heads
of damage' are substantive (see *Dicey and Morris*, para 7-036), quantification and
assessment of damages are procedural and thus a matter for the lex fori, English
law. The question whether benefits should be deducted is argued to be a matter
of quantification or assessment and thus procedural.

[14] Mr Weir would further suggest that such authority as there is relating
expressly to the deduction of benefits is in his favour. In *Coupland v Arabian Gulf
Petroleum Co* [1983] 2 All ER 434 at 446, [1983] 1 WLR 1136 at 1149 in the
judgment of Hodgson J at first instance appears the following passage:

'It is clear that the ordinary rule in tort is that the law of the place where
the action is being brought (the lex fori) is the law to be applied. To find an
exception to that rule one has to find an issue, which is decided differently by
the two jurisprudences, which is capable of being segregated and which can
then be decided by an application of what, in effect by the back door, is the
proper law of that issue. But before one can do that one has to have some
substantial difference between the two systems of law. In this case (as I have
demonstrated) the only possible candidate for segregation would be the rule
in Libyan law that social security benefits are not deductible from an award
of general damages. But that contention is not advanced by counsel for the
plaintiff (and properly so, it seems to me), for that rule is, in my judgment, a
rule for the quantification of damage and not a rule dealing with a head of
damage. And, if it is a rule dealing with the quantification of damage, then it
is for the law of this country to prevail.'

[15] Further, more recently, Garland J in a dictum not necessary for his
decision in *Edmunds v Simmonds* [2001] 1 WLR 1003 at 1011 said:

a   'Even if I had not decided the section 12 point in the claimant's favour,
      I would, unless persuaded that Spanish law did not recognise any head of
      damage recoverable by the claimant, have decided that quantification was
      purely procedural and should be carried out according to English law in any
      event.'

b   [16] The above passage from Hodgson J's judgment in *Coupland*'s case is
      clearly the basis for the following passage in *Dicey and Morris* (vol 2, para 35-053):

      'It has also been said that whether social security benefits are deductible
      from an award of general damages is a rule for the quantification of damages
      and not a rule dealing with a head of damage. The question will, accordingly,
c   be referred to English law.'

      [17] Mr Leonard suggested that the language in the above quote from *Dicey
      and Morris* is not a strong endorsement of what was a concession in *Coupland*'s
      case. He further argued that to suggest in general terms that 'quantification' or
      'calculation' is for the lex fori is misleading. He quoted a further passage from
d   *Dicey and Morris* (para 35-055):

      'On the other hand, questions such as whether loss of earning capacity or
      pain and suffering or (in fatal accident claims) solatium or loss of society are
      admissible heads of damage, all questions of remoteness of damage, the
      existence and extent of the claimant's duty to mitigate damage, whether
e   exemplary damages are recoverable, the existence and extent of financial
      ceilings on recoverable damages, and whether recovery can be had for any
      head of damage unknown to English law are questions of substantive law.'

      [18] If mitigation is a matter of substantive law then he submitted that the
f   question whether a deduction should be made for benefits received as a result of
      death should also be substantive. Indeed he suggested that the common law rule
      that the claimant should give credit for benefits received, subject to the
      exceptions in personal injury cases—no credit for the proceeds of insurance
      policies and the like, and no credit for charitable donations (see *Parry v Cleaver*
      [1969] 1 All ER 555, [1970] AC 1), are matters of substantive law. Thus he
g   submitted that the Dutch rule relating to the deduction of benefits and s 4 of the
      1976 Act are also substantive. He suggested that he gains some support from
      passages in the speeches in *Chaplin v Boys* and from the way in which the court
      has treated financial limits (see *Caltex Singapore Pte Ltd v BP Shipping Ltd* [1996]
      1 Lloyd's Rep 286). Ultimately his submission was that the assessment of
h   damages should be regarded as an exercise in calculating and reconciling a
      balance sheet consisting of debit and credit entries. He submitted that the law
      governing what type of debit and what type of credit goes into the balance sheet
      is substantive, the calculation and quantification thereafter being procedural.

      [19] There is a marked absence of evidence as to the true nature of the law in
j   Holland. The view expressed in the statement of Mr Van der Zwan (see [3],
      above) provides very little clue as to whether the rule relating to deductions is a
      statutory provision equivalent to our 1976 Act or is simply an equivalent to our
      common law rule. The best the court can do is to presume that there is nothing
      in the nature of the rule as applied in Holland which indicates that any different
      approach should be taken to it as compared to the approach to be taken to the
      rule in England whether at common law or by statute.

[20] The claimant brings these proceedings under the 1976 Act. She does not
rely on any provision of Dutch law or on any appointment as administrator under
Dutch law nor could she do so. Procedurally an action on behalf of a person
killed in an accident is only available in the English courts by virtue of what is
now ss 1 and 2 of the 1976 Act. The defendants asserted by their defence that it
was more appropriate for the applicable law for determining the issues that arose
in the proceedings including at that stage liability to be determined by the law of
the Netherlands. But no application was made to stay the proceedings nor would
such an application have succeeded. Thus it must be accepted that the proceedings
were properly brought under the Act.

[21] It is perhaps also right to bear in mind that we do not know precisely how
the law in Holland in relation to deducting benefits has developed in personal
injury actions generally or how interconnected that development is with the way
in which damages for dependency generally are assessed in Holland. Nor do we
know whether in Holland, as in England, public policy considerations have come
into play. In relation to the question whether benefits should be deducted in
assessing damages for personal injury (not fatal accident cases) English common
law has developed not without difficulty to the stage where in principle credit
must be given for benefits received as a result of personal injuries, but there are
identified exceptions. The exceptions at common law are insurance proceeds and
the like and charitable gifts, which have been made exceptions on the grounds of
public policy. As Lord Reid said in *Parry v Cleaver* [1969] 1 All ER 555 at 557, [1970]
AC 1 at 13: 'The common law has treated this matter as one depending on justice,
reasonableness and public policy.' (See also Lord Reid's reliance on public policy
as reflected by what was then s 2(1) of the Fatal Accidents Act 1959 ([1969] 1 All
ER 555 at 563 [1970] AC 1 at 19–20).)

[22] Mr Leonard would suggest that s 4 of the 1976 Act simply provides
another example of an exception to the common law rule, and would seek to
argue that the common law rule and its exceptions are part of the substantive law,
and that the rule in Holland must thus be presumed to be substantive. If Dutch
law were the proper law to be applied in deciding the issue of loss of dependency
he concludes that deductions must be made as per the Dutch rule. I reject
Mr Leonard's submission in relation to the deduction of benefits at common law
and in relation to s 4 in particular.

[23] It seems to me that the question whether or not deductions should be
made for benefits in assessing damages for the loss of dependency should be a
matter for the lex fori. That seems to me so looking at the matter as if the
common law and s 4 had to be approached in the same way, which was how the
matter was argued before us and was how the matter was approached by the
judge. I accept that the courts have struggled to define the difference between
procedural and substantive. As Lord Pearson said in *Chaplin v Boys* [1969] 2 All ER
1085 at 1106, [1971] AC 356 at 395: 'I do not think there is any exact and
authoritative definition of the boundary between substantive and procedural (or
adjectival or non-substantive) law.' The Australian decision *Stevens v Head* (1993)
176 CLR 433, which by a majority of four to three decided that a New South
Wales statute was procedural and not substantive, bears testament to the
difficulties in this area. *Dicey and Morris* had this to say about that decision and
the decision of Clarke J in the *Caltex* case to which we were also referred:

'7-038 Statutory provisions limiting a defendant's liability are prima facie
substantive; but the true construction of the statute may negative this view.

a
The proper classification of rules which limit the amount of damages recoverable was considered by the High Court of Australia in *Stevens v. Head*, a case involving an action arising out of a road accident in New South Wales brought by the plaintiff in Queensland. One of the questions facing the court was whether or not a provision in the Motor Accidents Act 1988 of New South Wales which limited the amount of damages which could be

b
recovered in respect of non-economic loss was a substantive rule to be applied as part of the *lex causae*. Although a minority took the view that a rule which imposes a ceiling on damages is substantive—because it is not directed to governing or regulating the mode or conduct of court proceedings—the majority held that the statutory provision in question was procedural as it did not touch the heads of liability in respect of which

c
damages might be awarded, but simply related to the quantification of damages. In *Caltex Singapore Pte Ltd. v. BP Shipping Ltd.* ([1996] 1 Lloyd's Rep 286) Clarke J., while accepting that rules limiting liability are prima facie substantive, relied on *Stevens v. Head* and held that section 272 of the Singapore Merchant Shipping Act 1970 (and the equivalent English

d
provision), under which the defendant in a collision action has the right to limit liability, is not a substantive rule.

7-039 It may be questioned whether the approach adopted in these cases is either desirable in terms of policy or entirely consistent with the authorities. The primary purpose of classifying a rule as substantive or procedural is "to determine which rules will make the machinery of the

e
forum court run smoothly as distinguished from those determinative of the rights of [the] parties." From this perspective provisions or rules dealing with the measure of damages should not be seen as procedural in nature. Furthermore, a close reading of the leading authorities (in particular *Boys v. Chaplin* ([1969] 2 All ER 1085, [1971] AC 356)) suggests that the scope of the

f
choice of law rule that the quantification of damages is governed by the *lex fori* should be restricted to rules relating to the method whereby damages are assessed (e.g. the English rule that damages are assessed once and for all) and should not encompass rules which fix or limit the extent of the defendant's liability.'

g
[24] In my view however the judgment of the majority in *Stevens v Head* (1993) 176 CLR 433 is compelling. Furthermore the passages in *Chaplin v Boys* relied on by the majority lend full support for the view expressed. I will quote what seems to me to be the core passage (at 456–457) so far as principle is concerned:

h
'In determining whether, by the lex loci, the relevant facts give rise to a civil liability of the kind which the plaintiff seeks to enforce, the courts of the forum distinguish between substantive and procedural laws. Procedure is governed exclusively by the laws of the forum, but the substantive laws of the place of the tort determine whether, by those laws, there exists a civil liability of the kind which the plaintiff seeks to enforce. In [*McKain v R W

j
Miller & Co (South Australia) Pty Ltd* (1991) 174 CLR 1], it was held that a South Australian law which imposed a limitation on the time within which to bring an action in the courts of that State for damages for a tort committed within that State but which did not extinguish the cause of action was not a substantive law which precluded the bringing of an action in the courts of New South Wales for damages for a tort committed in South Australia. The majority followed a line of authority which distinguished between a statute

of limitation which does no more than cut off resort to the courts for the
enforcement of a claim and a statute which extinguishes civil liability and
destroys a cause of action. The former is classified as a procedural law, the
latter as substantive. A similar distinction has been drawn between a law
which denies a remedy in respect of a particular head of damage in
negligence (a substantive law) and a law which affects the quantification of
damages in respect of a particular head of damage (a procedural law). That
distinction was drawn by a majority in *Chaplin v. Boys* ([1969] 2 All ER 1085,
[1971] AC 356) and by Brennan J. and Dawson J. in *Breavington v. Godleman*
((1988) 169 CLR 41), followed in *Perrett v. Robinson* ((1988) 169 CLR 172). In
McKain, the Chief Justice accepted that "the question of what heads of
damage are recoverable is now treated as a substantive issue" and that a
matter concerning quantification of damage, "on traditional analysis, has
been treated as a procedural consideration." But his Honour's preferred
view was that the measure of damages for personal injury is a question of
substantive law, as he held in *Breavington v. Godleman*. We are respectfully
unable to accept that view.'

[25] The passages in the speeches of the majority in *Chaplin v Boys* relied on are
at [1969] 2 All ER 1085 at 1093, 1095, 1105, [1971] AC 356 at 378–379, 381–382, 393
per Lords Hodson, Guest and Wilberforce respectively (see (1993) 176 CLR 433
at 457, footnote 94). The passages referred to support the view that so far as
damages are concerned it is a question for the substantive law whether a head of
damage is recoverable, but quantification of the actual head is procedural. If one
poses the question whether the issue in this case is about the right to recover
certain benefits or whether it is about the quantification of the damages for loss
of dependency the answer seems to me to be that it is about the quantification of
the damages. The concern of the court in considering a tortious claim should be
as to liability including liability for particular heads of damage without the
existence of which liability might not be complete. The question whether
deductions should be made for benefits is not a question which goes to liability;
it is a question going to assessment.

[26] It also seems to me that there is good reason why once it is established
that a particular head of damage is recoverable by whatever is the appropriate
law, the assessment of the appropriate figure for that head of damage should be
for the forum, including in particular what deductions should be made according
to the public policy of the forum. As *Dicey and Morris* (vol 1, para 7-004) says: 'The
primary object of this Rule [ie that procedure should be governed by the lex fori]
is to obviate the inconvenience of conducting the trial of a case concerning
foreign elements in a manner with which the court is unfamiliar'. They add
(I accept) that 'If, therefore, it is possible to apply a foreign rule ... without causing
any such inconvenience, those rules should not necessarily ... be classified as
procedural'. In my view the question whether deductions of benefits should be
made is likely to be bound up both with policy considerations and with the way
in which damages under the particular head are to be assessed overall.

[27] In this case the judge records that although he had not heard an expert on
Dutch law—

'it appears that the dependants' claim for damages under Dutch law is
assessed on a similar basis to English law, save that the dependants would
have to give credit against such damages for various insurance, pension,

a   social security and inherited benefits accruing to them as a result of the
     deceased's death.'

I am unclear on what basis one can draw any inference that that would be so save
on a presumption that without evidence of Dutch law, it must be presumed to be
the same as English law. However to make that presumption in this case seems
to me to be rather unreal, because one knows that the approach of the Dutch
b   court, at least in one respect, is radically different. The truth seems to me to be
that we simply do not know on what basis a dependant can bring an action in
Holland, nor the basis on which damages are assessed, nor what precisely has led
the Dutch courts to apply the rule it does. What we do know is that under the
Fatal Accidents Acts dependants, even foreign dependants, can bring their
proceedings, and that as a matter of policy in the framework of the Act as a whole,
c   it has been provided by s 4 of the 1976 Act that no benefits of any kind shall be
deducted. We also know that in ordinary personal injury actions the courts in
England have developed rules and exceptions so far as the deduction of benefits
are concerned by reference to English public policy, and in the context of making
general assessments of loss. If s 4 was to be disapplied, or if the English common
d   law rules were to be disapplied, it would seem to me that it might be said with
some force that it was also necessary to investigate how damages for dependency
would be assessed in Holland generally, in order to make sure that by making the
relevant deduction the Dutch claimant was not being deprived in some way. To
make that assessment would involve the court examining how general damages
for loss of dependency were quantified in Holland, an exercise which should not
e   be undertaken by the English court and which in any event it would be very
inconvenient to undertake.

     [**28**] I now turn to a point which was not argued but which seems to me
possibly to provide a short answer to this particular case. As I have already said
we are concerned with an action which can only be brought in this country by
f   virtue of the 1976 Act. The Act is available for the benefit of foreigners (see *The
Esso Malaysia, Cox v Owners of the Esso Malaysia* [1974] 2 All ER 705, [1975] QB 198),
provided proceedings can be properly issued and served. Surely then, simply as
a matter of statutory construction, once an action is brought in reliance on the
provisions of that Act then the sections which refer to assessments 'under the Act'
or refer to assessment of damages 'in the action' (clearly referring to actions
g   brought 'under the Act') simply apply. Thus I would in fact suggest that if
damages for bereavement were a head of damage recoverable under Dutch law
with a limit in excess of that provided for by s 1A, s 1A would still apply so as to
impose a limit; I would suggest that if bereavement were not a head of damage
recoverable under Dutch law, then since by virtue of s 1A 'An action under this
h   Act may consist of or include a claim for damages for bereavement', damages for
bereavement would be recoverable in the sum provided for by s 1A. Furthermore
since s 3(1) of the 1976 Act provides that 'In the action' ie an action under the Act,
'such damages ... may be awarded as are proportioned' etc, and s 3(3) for
example provides for the prospect of remarriage not to be taken into account 'In
j   an action under this Act', clearly it is s 3 which provides the basis on which
damages are to be 'assessed' in relation to actions brought under the Act and not
some provision of Dutch law.

     [**29**] Section 4 is in the same vein—it provides that 'In assessing damages in
respect of a person's death in an action *under* this Act ... benefits ... shall be
disregarded'. Since the action is under 'this Act', it follows, I would suggest, that
simply as a matter of construction of the statute s 4 must apply. That seems to

me to make s 4 'procedural' or 'adjectival or non-substantive' in the sense that it is a part of the law which the English court must apply to actions brought under this particular statute. That would provide a short answer to this particular case concerned with the application of s 4 to a 1976 Act claim.

[30] Thus I would uphold the judge's decision on this issue both on the basis relied by him and on the narrower basis of statutory construction.

Issue 2—Contract

[31] As already indicated since in my view the claimant should succeed on issues 1 and 3, it is strictly unnecessary to consider either aspect of this issue in great detail. The contract point was only raised after admission of liability, and the claimant does not need to succeed on this point unless she fails on the other issues. When pleaded it should be said that what was alleged was that there was a contract of employment between the defendants and the deceased, and there was no suggestion of two contracts one with Diepzee and one with the defendants. I do not however understand Mr Leonard to take a pleading point other than forensically.

[32] The contract point, as it has become in this court, arises in the following way. The deceased was employed on any view by Diepzee and the arrangement between the defendants and Diepzee was that Diepzee provided the deceased to the defendants in return for payment. Diepzee paid all wages, and made all social security deductions etc. The documents support the above (see p 174 of the bundle for the contract of employment and p 110 for an example of an invoice from Diepzee to the defendants). As the judge put it 'there is overwhelming evidence that the deceased's contract of employment was with Diepzee', and there is no appeal from that finding.

[33] However when boarding the Atlantic Princess the deceased was asked to sign a further document headed 'List of crew and signatures of seamen who are parties to the crew agreement'. The relevant terms of that document provided for 'employment' by cl 1 'at the rate of wages expressed'; for the parts of the local port industrial agreement to be incorporated without so specifying, simply putting in the words 'shares'.

[34] When the deceased signed the same there appeared in the column next to his signature under the heading rate of wages 'as agreed'.

[35] It will be seen that the deceased was purporting to agree to be employed by the defendants even though he had a contract of employment with Diepzee. The clause relating to the applicable terms and conditions does not specify an appropriate local port industrial agreement, but refers to 'shares'. It would seem that it was the British crewmen and not the Dutch who were on a sharing arrangement, though even in the British crewmen's case the agreement does not accurately describe the arrangement (see para 4 of Mr Harper's statement (p 116)).

[36] The reason why the deceased was asked to sign this particular form is not in issue. By s 25 of the Merchant Shipping Act 1995 it is provided:

'*Crew agreements.*—(1) Except as provided under subsection (5) below, an agreement in writing shall be made between each person employed as a seaman in a United Kingdom ship and the persons employing him and shall be signed both by him and by or on behalf of them.

(2) The agreements made under this section with the several persons employed in a ship shall be contained in one document (in this Part referred to as a crew agreement) except that in such cases as the Secretary of State

a   may approve—(a) the agreements to be made under this section with the persons employed in a ship may be contained in more than one crew agreement; and (b) one crew agreement may relate to more than one ship.

(3) The provisions and form of a crew agreement must be of a kind approved by the Secretary of State; and different provisions and forms may be so approved for different circumstances.

b   (4) Subject to the following provisions of this section, a crew agreement shall be carried in the ship to which it relates whenever the ship goes to sea.

(5) The Secretary of State may make regulations providing for exemptions from the requirements of this section—(a) with respect to such descriptions of ship as may be specified in the regulations or with respect to voyages in such areas or such description of voyages as may be so specified; or (b) with *c*   respect to such descriptions of seamen as may be specified in the regulations; and the Secretary of State may grant other exemptions from those requirements (whether with respect to particular seamen or with respect to seamen employed by a specified person or in a specified ship or in the ships of a specified person) in cases where the Secretary of State is satisfied that the *d*   seamen to be employed otherwise than under a crew agreement will be adequately protected.

(6) Where, but for an exemption granted by the Secretary of State, a crew agreement would be required to be carried in a ship or a crew agreement carried in the ship would be required to contain an agreement with a person employed in a ship, the ship shall carry such document evidencing the *e*   exemption as the Secretary of State may direct.

(7) Regulations under this section may enable ships required under this section to carry a crew agreement to comply with the requirement by carrying a copy thereof, certified in such manner as may be provided by the regulations.

f   (8) If a ship goes to sea or attempts to go to sea in contravention of the requirements of this section the master or the person employing the crew shall be liable on summary conviction to a fine not exceeding level 4 on the standard scale and the ship, if in the United Kingdom, may be detained.'

g   [37] Furthermore, by regulations made from time to time, the requirement of what was to be contained in such an agreement was laid down, and certain standard forms of agreement were approved. This particular standard form was approved under Merchant Shipping Notice No M 1425 (see p 122), and it seems that it was out of date at the time when the voyage with which this action is concerned took place, since in July 1992 Merchant Shipping Notice No M 1498 *h*   superseded M 1425. So far as I can see nothing in the regulations or in the memorandum providing for standard forms would approve a crew agreement under which the ship pays a company for the supply of labour. Such an arrangement would seem to need to have specific approval.

[38] What then is the answer to the question whether the document signed by *j*   the deceased gave rise to a contract? One possible answer is that it should be rejected in toto as a document signed without any intention to create legal relations, that argument being founded on the inconsistency between its terms and the terms of the deceased's actual contract of employment plus the absence of any reference to appropriate terms, and the absence of any consideration at least in financial terms. An alternative is to construe it as a contract under which independently of the deceased's contract of employment with the defendants, the

defendants undertook contractual obligations vis-à-vis the deceased. In considering
those alternatives I would suggest that albeit we are not concerned with whether
there has been some breach of the regulations or a breach of the Merchant
Shipping Act, it is relevant that the purpose that lay behind s 25 was to protect
seamen employed on ships by providing that there should be a contract between
the ship and its crew in one document.

[39] I have not found the resolution of this question easy. Rejection of the
document as being inconsistent with the contract of employment already entered
into at first sight seems attractive. But although in most circumstances it would
be very surprising for someone to enter into two contracts overlapping so far as
his or her employment was concerned, unless one contract is inconsistent with
the other I cannot see any reason why two such contracts should not be signed.
Furthermore, there is no reason to think that both the defendants and the
deceased did not intend to enter into legal relations when they signed the
document. Why, it might be asked, if the defendant chooses to sign a document
of a contractual nature performing as it believes its statutory obligation to do so,
should there not be imposed on that defendant implied contractual duties in
addition to the duties in tort? The argument that no consideration would be
provided for such promises seems at first sight powerful but it is unattractive.
Furthermore the defendants were providing the vessel on which the deceased
was being asked to work and asked for the signature before the deceased was
allowed on board.

[40] On the second aspect of this issue, if what is under consideration is an
independent contract between the defendants (an English company) and the
deceased, under which the deceased was to be allowed on board an
English-registered vessel, the argument for that contract to be governed by
English law seems to me to be overwhelming. I would agree with the judge
(following the language of art 3(1) of the Rome Convention on the Law Applicable
to Contractual Obligations 1980, contained in Sch 1 of the Contracts (Applicable
Law) Act 1990), that the choice of law as English is demonstrated with reasonable
certainty by the terms of the contract and/or the circumstances of the case.

[41] It is unnecessary to come to a final conclusion on these points having
regard to the views expressed on the other issues, but my inclination is to feel that
the judge's decision on both points, and thus this issue, also ought to be upheld.

Appeal procedure point

[42] Since we will be dismissing the appeal, this point is probably of academic
interest so far as the parties are concerned, but it is important to clarify the
appropriate appeal route where preliminary points are tried. The submissions of
the parties are set out in Mr Leonard's original supplemental skeleton, in Mr Weir's
most recent written submissions, and Mr Leonard's written response thereto.

[43] There is no dispute about the applicable rules. The claimant's skeleton
on that aspect is thus not in issue:

'Appropriate Appeal Court
    The rules governing the appropriate appeal court are set out in the Access
to Justice Act 1999 (Destination of Appeals) Order 2000, SI 2000/1071. The
rules on appeal as set out at CPR PD 52, paras 2A.1–2A.4 (White Book,
Autumn 2001 edn, vol 1, pp 995–996) simply rehearse the rules set out in this
order. This claim has been allocated to the multi-track, (see order of
9 September 2000) accordingly art 4 of the order (PD 52, para 2A.2) applies.

a This provides that an appeal shall lie to the Court of Appeal where the decision to be appealed is a final decision. Article 1(2)(c) (PD 52, para 2A.3) provides that "final decision" means: a decision of a court that would finally determine (subject to any possible appeal or detailed assessment of costs) the entire proceedings whichever way the court decided the issues before it. In addition, by art 1(3) (PD 52, para 2A.4) a decision of a court shall be treated
b as a final decision where it: (a) is made at the conclusion of part of a hearing or trial which has been split into parts; and (b) would, if made at the conclusion of that hearing or trial, be a final decision under para 2(c).'

[44] The question is whether the judge's decision in this case must be treated as a 'final decision'. The defendants thought not and it was in those circumstances
c that they applied to Sullivan J in Leeds for permission to appeal. They still seek to defend that view. The claimant says that it was, and they rely on the wording of the rule, and they further rely on the dictum of Brooke LJ in *Tanfern Ltd v Cameron-MacDonald* [2000] 2 All ER 801 at 806, [2000] 1 WLR 1311 at 1315 (para 17) as follows:

d   'A final decision includes the assessment of damages or any other final decision where it is "made at the conclusion of part of a hearing or trial which has been split up into parts and would, if made at the conclusion of that hearing or trial, be a final decision" (the 2000 order, art 1(3)); it does not include a decision only on costs. This means that if a judge makes a final decision on any aspect of a claim, such as limitation, or on part of a claim
e   which has been directed to be heard separately, this is a final decision within the meaning of this provision.'

[45] Mr Leonard referred to the old rules, RSC Ord 59, r 1A(4) and the notes thereunder including the reference to *White v Brunton* [1984] 2 All ER 606, [1984]
f QB 570 and *Holmes v Bangladesh Biman Corp* [1988] 2 Lloyd's Rep 120 (see *Annual Practice 1999* pp 1011–1012), and sought to gain some assistance therefrom. In my view Mr Weir is right in saying strictly those authorities are of little assistance in construing the new rules. But, that said, it seems to me that what the present rules in fact reflect, in relation to treating a decision as final where it is made at the conclusion of the hearing of a preliminary issue, is the commonsense
g approach of Bingham LJ (as he then was) in his judgment in *Holmes'* case where he said (at 124):

'... a broad common-sense test should be applied, asking whether (if not tried separately) the issue would have formed a substantive part of the final trial. Judged by that test this judgment was plainly final, even though it did
h   not give the plaintiff a money judgment and would not, even if in the airline's favour, have ended the action.'

[46] If one poses the question—if no preliminary issue had been ordered would the decision as to the appropriate law have formed a substantive part of
j the final decision on damages?—the answer would undoubtedly be that it would, and that an appeal would have lain to the Court of Appeal against that final decision. The fact that the issue is sensibly taken separately should not deprive a party of their right to go to the Court of Appeal, and furthermore it would be an active discouragement to parties to support the trial of preliminary issues if the result was to so deprive them. That is the principle that the new rules in my view seek to uphold.

[47] In my view thus the decision on this preliminary issue was made at the conclusion of part of a hearing which the order ordering a preliminary issue had split into parts. The decision should have been treated as a final decision for appeal purposes. Thus the appropriate route for an appeal from the decision of the judge was to the Court of Appeal and that was the court from which permission to appeal should have been sought.

SEDLEY LJ.
[48] I agree.

SIMON BROWN LJ.
[49] I also agree.

Appeal dismissed.

James Wilson   Barrister (NZ).

a # Konamaneni and others v Rolls-Royce Industrial Power (India) Ltd and others

CHANCERY DIVISION

b LAWRENCE COLLINS J

21–23, 26–28 NOVEMBER, 20 DECEMBER 2001

Company – Minority shareholder – Representative action – Foreign company – Whether English court having jurisdiction to hear derivative claim in relation to foreign company – Whether appropriate forum for determining shareholders' entitlement to
c *bring derivative claim to be taken into account by English court when considering appropriate forum for trial of action – CPR 6.20(3), 19.9.*

The claimants were minority shareholders in SPGL, an Indian company. All the directors of SPGL were Indian citizens, and all but two of them lived in India.
d The shareholders brought a derivative claim in England against two English companies, seeking to enforce a claim by SPGL in respect of bribes allegedly paid by the English companies to SPGL's managing director, an Indian living in India, for the purpose of securing contracts for the construction and maintenance of a power station in India. A large number of actions or criminal complaints relating to the project were pending in India, some of which raised issues of wrongdoer
e control that also arose in the English action. In that action, the shareholders alleged that the general meeting of SPGL was indirectly under the control of the wrongdoers; that it was therefore plain that the general meeting would not pass a resolution authorising or approving the pursuit of proceedings against the English companies; that at least half of SPGL's board were closely associated with
f the managing director; that it was therefore unlikely that the board would pass any resolution that might facilitate a decision to pursue proceedings against the English companies; and that accordingly the shareholders were entitled to rely on the 'fraud on the minority' exception to the usual rule that a company was the proper claimant in an action to redress a harm done to it or to enforce a cause of action vested in it (the fraud exception). In accordance with CPR 19.9[a], the rule
g of procedure governing derivative claims brought on behalf of a 'company' by its members, the shareholders joined SPGL as defendant to the proceedings. They therefore sought the court's permission under CPR 6.20(3)[b] to serve the proceedings on SPGL out of the jurisdiction. Under r 6.20(3), the court could grant such permission if a claim was made against someone on whom the claim
h form had been or would be served, and (a) there was between the claimant and that person a 'real issue' which it was reasonable for the court to try, and (b) the claimant wished to serve the claim form on another person who was a necessary or proper party to the claim. The master granted permission, and the defendants subsequently applied, inter alia, for that order to be set aside. On the application,
j SPGL contended that in a derivative action there was no 'real issue', within the meaning of r 6.20(3), between the shareholder claimant and the substantive

---

a Rule 19.9, so far as material, provides: '(1) This rule applies where a company ... is alleged to be entitled to claim a remedy and a claim is being made by one or more members of the company ... for it to be given that remedy ...
   (2) The company ... for whose benefit a remedy is sought must be a defendant to the claim ...'
b Rule 6.20, so far as material, is set out at [42], below

defendant, that in any event 'company' in r 19.9 referred only to English companies and that accordingly the English court had no jurisdiction to hear a derivative claim in relation to a foreign company. Alternatively, the defendants contended that England was not the appropriate forum for the action. The issue arose whether the court was concerned purely with the identification of the appropriate forum for the trial of the bribery allegations or whether it was also concerned with the appropriate forum for determining the issue of the shareholders' entitlement to bring a derivative action.

Held – (1) The English court did have jurisdiction to hear a derivative claim in relation to a foreign company. There was no basis for restricting CPR 19.9 to English companies, and in any event to do so would not have the effect of depriving the court of jurisdiction to entertain a derivative claim. As for r 6.20(3), the requirement that there should be a real issue between the claimant and those served, or to be served, within the jurisdiction was intended to ensure that the claim was brought bona fide against the defendant in the jurisdiction, and not merely in order to bring in the foreign defendant as a necessary or proper party (see [44], below).

(2) In determining the appropriate forum for a derivative action in relation to a foreign company, the questions which arose in considering whether the fraud exception applied were a significant factor to be taken into account. Those questions were an integral part of the claim in a derivative action, and it would be wholly unjust and inappropriate to treat them as a purely procedural matter to be excluded from the equation. Moreover, if issues arose relating to the exercise of discretionary powers of management, considerable weight should be accorded to the potential role of the courts of the place of incorporation. It was doubtful whether they had exclusive jurisdiction to deal with such issues: it might, for example, be wholly unjust to require recourse to an offshore haven to pursue fraudulent directors in a case which had no connection with the jurisdiction other than that it was the place of incorporation. Nevertheless, the courts of the place of incorporation would almost invariably be the most appropriate forum for the resolution of the issues which related to the existence of the right of shareholders to sue on behalf of the company. In the instant case, the Indian connections were overwhelming, and the shareholders had fallen far short of satisfying the burden to show clearly that England was the appropriate forum for the derivative claim. Accordingly, the master's order would be set aside (see [65]–[67], [128], [188], below); *Pergamon Press Ltd v Maxwell* [1970] 2 All ER 809 considered.

Per curiam. The law of the place of the incorporation of a company governs the right of a shareholder to bring a derivative action in England since the basic rule is that shareholders have no direct rights. Although for purely English domestic purposes, the exceptions to that rule have been regarded as a purely procedural device, their real nature is not procedural in the international context. They confer a right on the shareholders to protect the value of their shares by giving them a right to sue and recover on behalf of the company. It would be very odd if that right could be conferred on the shareholders of a company incorporated in a jurisdiction which has no such rule, and under which they have acquired their shares (see [50], below).

Notes

For actions in respect of corporate wrongs and for service out of the jurisdiction with permission of the court, see respectively 7(2) *Halsbury's Laws* (4th edn reissue) para 1171 and 37 *Halsbury's Laws* (4th edn reissue) para 346.

Cases referred to in judgment

Amin Rasheed Shipping Corp v Kuwait Insurance Co, The Al Wahab [1983] 2 All ER 884, [1984] AC 50, [1983] 3 WLR 241, HL.

Arab Monetary Fund v Hashim [1993] 1 Lloyd's Rep 543; *affd* [1996] 1 Lloyd's Rep 589, CA.

Atlantic Star, The, Owners of the Atlantic Star v Owners of the Bona Spes [1973] 2 All ER 175, [1974] AC 436, [1973] 2 WLR 795, HL.

Bahrein Petroleum Co Ltd v P J Pappu AIR 1966 SC 634, India SC.

Barrett v Duckett [1995] 1 BCLC 243, CA.

Batchelder v Kawamoto (1998) 147 F (3d) 915, US Ct of Apps (9th Cir).

Bhamboo Mal v Ram Narain AIR 1928 Lahore 297, Lahore CA.

BP Exploration Co (Libya) Ltd v Hunt [1976] 3 All ER 879, [1976] 1 WLR 788.

Brink's-MAT Ltd v Elcombe [1988] 3 All ER 188, [1988] 1 WLR 1350, CA.

Burland v Earle [1902] AC 83, PC.

Connelly v RTZ Corp plc [1997] 4 All ER 335, [1998] AC 854, [1997] 3 WLR 373, HL.

CTS Corp v Dynamics Corp of America, Indiana v Dynamics Corp of America (1987) 481 US 69, US SC.

Edwards v Halliwell [1950] 2 All ER 1064, CA.

Electric Furnace Co v Selas Corp of America [1987] RPC 23, CA.

Far Eastern Steamship Co (Kakinada, petitioner) v Koika Trading Co Ltd AIR 1978 Andhra Pradesh 433, Andhra Pradesh HC.

Fargro Ltd v Godfroy [1986] 3 All ER 279, [1986] 1 WLR 1134.

Ferguson v Wallbridge [1935] 3 DLR 66, PC.

Foss v Harbottle (1843) 2 Hare 461, 67 ER 189.

Hagen, The [1908] P 189, [1908–10] All ER Rep 21, CA.

Hausman v Buckley (1962) 299 F (2d) 696, US Ct of Apps (2nd Cir).

Heyting v Dupont [1964] 2 All ER 273, [1964] 1 WLR 843, CA.

Hira Lal Patni v Kali Nath Co Ltd AIR 1962 SC 199, India SC.

Hovenden & Sons v Millhoff (1900) 83 LT 41, [1900–3] All ER Rep 848, CA

Industries and General Mortgage Co v Lewis [1949] 2 All ER 573.

Jalakrishna, The [1983] 2 Lloyd's Rep 628.

Kiran Singh v Chaman Paswan AIR 1954 SC 340, India SC.

Lubbe v Cape plc [2000] 4 All ER 268, [2000] 1 WLR 1545, HL.

Mahesan v Malaysia Government Officers' Co-operative Housing Society Ltd [1978] 2 All ER 405, [1979] AC 374, [1978] 2 WLR 444, PC.

McDermott Inc v Lewis (1987) 531 A (2d) 206, Delaware SC.

Nurcombe v Nurcombe [1985] 1 All ER 65, [1985] 1 WLR 370, CA.

Oppenheimer v Louis Rosenthal & Co AG [1937] 1 All ER 23, CA.

Pergamon Press Ltd v Maxwell [1970] 2 All ER 809, [1970] 1 WLR 1167.

Petrotrade Inc v Smith [2000] 1 Lloyd's Rep 486.

Prudential Assurance Co Ltd v Newman Industries Ltd (No 2) [1982] 1 All ER 354, [1982] Ch 204, [1982] 2 WLR 31, CA.

Radhakrishna Hospitality Service Private Ltd v EIH Ltd [1999] 2 Lloyd's Rep 249.

Raja Setrucharlu Ramabhadra Raju Bahadur v Maharaja of Jeypore AIR 1919 PC 150, PC.

Smith v Croft (No 2) [1987] 3 All ER 909, [1988] Ch 114, [1987] 3 WLR 405.

Spiliada Maritime Corp v Cansulex Ltd, The Spiliada [1986] 3 All ER 843, [1987]
AC 460, [1986] 3 WLR 972, HL.

a

Spokes v Grosvenor and West End Railway Terminus Hotel Co Ltd [1897] 2 QB 124, CA.
Vishva Ajay, The [1989] 2 Lloyd's Rep 558.

Applications

By application dated 10 May 2001 the first and second defendants, Rolls-Royce
Industrial Power (India) Ltd and Heaton Power Ltd (the Rolls-Royce defendants),
applied for a declaration that the court had no jurisdiction to hear a derivative
action brought against them by the claimants, Lakshmi Konamaneni, Santha
Reddy Pekety, Vansanth Rao Mitta and Spectrum Technologies USA Inc, as
members of the third defendant, Spectrum Power Generation Ltd (SPGL), an
Indian company. Alternatively, the Rolls-Royce defendants applied for a stay of
proceedings on the grounds of forum non conveniens or for an order setting aside
the order of Master Moncaster on 2 February 2001 granting the claimants
permission to serve proceedings on SPGL out of the jurisdiction. SPGL also
applied for an order setting aside the master's order. The facts are set out in the
judgment.

b

c

d

Robert Hildyard QC and *Robert Miles* (instructed by *Freshfields Bruckhaus Deringer*)
for the Rolls-Royce defendants.
David Mackie QC and *Sarah Garvey* of *Allen & Overy* for SPGL.
Leslie Kosmin QC and *Andrew Thompson* (instructed by *S J Berwin*) for the claimants.

e

Cur adv vult

20 December 2001. The following judgment was delivered.

LAWRENCE COLLINS J.

f

I. INTRODUCTION

[1] These proceedings involve a derivative claim by four claimants. Two of
the claimants are individuals resident in India, one is an individual resident in the
United States, and the fourth claimant is a company incorporated in Mauritius.
They sue as members of Spectrum Power Generation Ltd (SPGL), an Indian
company which is joined as a defendant. The claimants seek to enforce a claim
by the company against two English companies in the Rolls-Royce group which,
it is alleged, paid bribes, through a British Virgin Islands company, Towanda
Services Ltd, to the managing director of the company, an Indian resident in
India, to secure contracts for the construction and maintenance of a power
station in India. The 208MW power station has been fully operational since 1998
and was one of the first power plants in India to be operated in the private sector.
The plant was constructed by the Rolls-Royce defendants, and the Rolls-Royce
group remains involved in the maintenance of the plant.

g

h

[2] There are pending in India some 18 actions or criminal complaints relating
to the interests in, and conduct of, the project, in which the principal protagonists
are, on the one hand, the managing director of the company, Mr Kishan Rao, and,
on the other hand, Dr Mohan Rao, who is related to Kishan Rao by marriage, and
who was a principal promoter of the project. The information on which the
claimants base their action is derived from Mohan Rao, and he gives instructions
to their lawyers. The proceedings are funded by his business associate and
relative by marriage, Mr Ravi Reddy, who is also a relative by marriage of two of

j

a the individual claimants (the other claimant being the wife of a senior employee of one of his companies) and who owns, indirectly, shares in the fourth claimant and thereby in SPGL.

[3] The defendants challenge the existence and/or exercise of jurisdiction by the English court. When Master Moncaster was asked to give permission to serve the Indian company outside the jurisdiction he expressed concerns about whether
b the English court had jurisdiction to entertain a derivative action brought for the benefit of a foreign company, but those concerns were allayed by the claimants' advisors on the without notice application. This case raises, apparently for the first time in England, the question of the operation in the international context of derivative claims and the exceptions to the rule in *Foss v Harbottle* (1843) 2 Hare 461, 67 ER 189.

c

II. THE CLAIM AND THE PROTAGONISTS

[4] The claim was brought originally by the first three claimants. Between them they hold 9,000 shares in the third defendant, SPGL. The number of issued shares in SPGL is about 141m, and the claimants' shares amounted in aggregate
d to about 0·005% of the issued share capital, and are worth about the equivalent of £2,000 in aggregate. The fourth claimant, Spectrum Technologies USA Inc, a company incorporated in Mauritius (STUSA (Mauritius)), is a company which owns about 22% of the issued shares in SPGL. It is managed by Mohan Rao, who has an indirect interest in some of its shares. STUSA (Mauritius) was added as a
e claimant to allay the concern of Master Moncaster whether the court would allow a derivative action by shareholders who had no significant interest in the outcome of the proceedings and who were acting on the directions of Ravi Reddy.

Ravi Reddy

f [5] Mr Ravi Reddy is a successful businessman who has been resident in the United States since 1978, and who is a non-resident Indian (NRI). He is connected with each of the claimants in ways on which I shall elaborate in [8]–[10], below. He is an NRI, and is now a United States citizen. His business interests are primarily in the United States, and he says his net worth is more than $US 100m. He is related, through marriage, to Mohan Rao. Mr Reddy, who is indirectly a
g substantial shareholder in SPGL and in STUSA (Mauritius), is funding the claimants (including the provision of security for costs) and has agreed to indemnify SPGL in relation to its costs of the action if leave to continue is obtained by the claimants under CPR 19.9. He says he is funding the litigation because he feels morally bound to support the shareholders, and they do not
h necessarily have the sophistication or financial means to chase down fraud within the company.

[6] For reasons which will be mentioned below (at [100]) the Rolls-Royce group became substantial shareholders in SPGL, through Rolls-Royce Godavari Power Ltd. Ravi Reddy sought to purchase its interest in SPGL. That would have
j given him and Mohan Rao a controlling interest in SPGL. The negotiations for the purchase terminated in 1999. The Rolls-Royce evidence (from Mr Mead, who was a project development manager with Rolls-Royce, and who left earlier this year) is that Ravi Reddy said on various occasions that if the deal did not proceed he would seek other avenues to exert control over SPGL, and Mr Mead says he understood that to be a threat of further legal action against, amongst others, Rolls-Royce.

Dr Mohan Rao

[7] Dr Mohan Rao is a United States citizen of Indian origin. He has been involved all his working career in the power generation field. After taking a first degree in engineering in Hyderabad, he obtained a PhD in Mechanical and Electrical Engineering from an American university, and then worked for 18 years from 1972 with GE Power Systems, a leading manufacturer of power equipment, where he was a development engineer and subsequently a manager of mechanical systems. Since about 1990 he has been associated with the STUSA group of companies. He was said to be the source of much of the information relied upon by Mrs Konamaneni, the first claimant, and by Mr Mervis, the claimants' solicitor, in their witness statements in support of the application for permission to serve out of the jurisdiction. In his own witness statement he says that he is responsible for the day-to-day affairs of STUSA with regard to the litigation concerning the project.

The individual claimants

[8] The first claimant, Mrs Konamaneni, is resident in Hyderabad. She is a deputy manager with Vysya Bank in Hyderabad. She owns 3,600 shares of ten rupees nominal value each in SPGL out of a total issued share capital of 141m shares (ie about 0·0025% of the issued share capital). She is the wife of Mr K Satish, a senior employee of STUSA. She says that her husband told her that Mohan Rao had told him that Kishan Rao had taken bribes from Rolls-Royce. She was shocked and she jumped at the chance to take legal action when her husband told her that Ravi Reddy (who is a good friend of her husband) was prepared to bear the legal expenses.

[9] The second claimant, Mrs Pekety, who lives in the United States, owns 2,700 shares in SPGL (approximately 0·0019% of the issued share capital). Mrs Pekety is the mother-in-law of Ravi Reddy, and she is also the aunt of Mohan Rao's wife. She says she heard about the bribery allegation from Ravi Reddy in about 1999. She is a claimant in eight derivative actions on behalf of SPGL in Hyderabad in India against, inter alios, Rolls-Royce Industrial Power (India) Ltd and Heaton Power Ltd. She is also the complainant in three actions brought against SPGL and various directors of SPGL before the criminal courts in Hyderabad. I deal in sections IX and XII below with these proceedings.

[10] The third claimant, Mr Mitta, is resident in Hyderabad, and owns 2,700 shares in SPGL (approximately 0·0019% of the issued share capital). He is the first named claimant in the eight derivative actions in Hyderabad. Mr Mitta's brother is Mohan Rao's brother-in-law. He says that most of his information about the allegations comes from Ravi Reddy.

Kishan Rao and Jaya Food Industries

[11] Kishan Rao has, at all material times, been the managing director of SPGL. He is resident in India. He is Mohan Rao's relation by marriage, Kishan Rao's daughter-in-law being Mohan Rao's niece. Mohan Rao involved Kishan Rao and his company Jaya Food Industries Pvt Ltd (Jaya Food) in the project at its outset in 1992. Jaya Food was engaged in the production of dry foods, such as pasta and was Kishan Rao's principal business and his vehicle for his original investment in SPGL. It was incorporated in India, and is now called Bambino Agro Industries Pvt Ltd. His sons, M Raghuveer and M Subramanyam, are associated with him in business and are directors of SPGL.

SPGL

a
　　[12] SPGL was incorporated on 26 October 1992 under the Indian Companies Act 1956. The current shareholders are as follows: (a) Rolls-Royce Godavari Power Ltd (a Mauritius company) and part of the Rolls-Royce group (47·5%); (b) Kishan Rao and associates (about 26%); (c) Mohan Rao and associates (about 25%). The remaining shares are held by the general public.

b
　　[13] All the directors of SPGL are Indian citizens and, apart from Mohan Rao and his nominee director Mr Bharteey, are resident in India. Mohan Rao and Mr Bharteey have been directors since 1994. Rolls-Royce is not represented on the board.

　　[14] According to SPGL, the affiliations of the other directors are as follows:

c

Name	Affiliation
Mr Raghuveer	Kishan Rao's son
Mr Subramanyam	Kishan Rao's son
Mr Bhattacharyya	No affiliation, and formerly the deputy managing director of the State Bank of India
Mr Shukla	No affiliation, and a chartered accountant who also sits on the board of companies owned by Kishan Rao
Professor Narain	No affiliation, a leading Indian economist from Osmania University in Andhra Pradesh
Mr Krishnan	No affiliation, nominated by State Bank of India, of which he was former chief general manager
Mr Upasani	No affiliation, nominated by Industrial Development Bank of India a former chief secretary to the government of Maharashtra and a former chairman of the Indian Company Law Board
Mr Loonkar	No affiliation, nominated by the Industrial Finance Corp of India Ltd, of which he is the chief general manager, Hyderabad

d

e

f

g
　　[15] The present debt to equity ratio is about 8:1, and it is obvious that the board members nominated by the financial institutions are there to look after the interests of the lenders, and not simply to decorate the board. I should mention at this point that although SPGL says that Mr Bhattacharyya, Mr Shukla and Professor Narain have no affiliation with either of the Kishan Rao and Mohan Rao camps, the first claimant says that Mohan Rao has told her that they are all close

h
friends of Kishan Rao.

The STUSA group

　　[16] The relevant companies in the STUSA group are: (a) Spectrum Technologies USA Inc, a New York company (STUSA), which is owned by

j
Mohan Rao and Brij Bharteey, and holds about 2m shares in SPGL; (b) STUSA (Mauritius), which holds about 26m shares in SPGL, and which is 100% owned by Spectrum Infrastructure Ltd (SIL) (Mauritius); (c) SIL (Mauritius), which is owned by Spectrum Power Investors Group (SPIG), various individuals, and SIL (Jersey); (d) SIL (Jersey), which holds about 900,000 shares in SPGL, and is owned by Mohan Rao and Brij Bharteey; (e) SPIG, which is owned as to 50% by Ravi Reddy.

Rolls-Royce
a
[17] The defendants are two companies in the Rolls-Royce engineering group.
I shall refer to them together as the 'Rolls-Royce defendants'. The first defendant,
Rolls-Royce Industrial Power (India) Ltd (RRIP), and the second defendant,
Heaton Power Ltd (Heaton), contracted with SPGL in 1994 for the engineering,
procurement and construction (EPC) of the plant. RRIP contracted with SPGL
in 1995 for the operation and maintenance (O&M) of the plant. The Rolls-Royce   b
companies were associated with companies in the Westinghouse Electric Corp
group in these contracts, with Westinghouse as a co-contractor or principal
sub-contractor. Heaton will be referred to by its current name, although its name
was Parsons Turbine Generations Systems Ltd until 1997, following the sale in
1996 of most of its business to Siemens. RRIP and Heaton are wholly-owned
subsidiaries of Rolls-Royce Power Engineering plc, which itself is a subsidiary   c
of Rolls-Royce plc. As I have mentioned already, another company in the group,
Rolls-Royce Godavari Power Ltd (which is incorporated in Mauritius), put equity
into SPGL between 1995 and 1998 and holds about 47·5% of its issued shares, but
is not represented on its board.

[18] At all times material to this action, the only business of RRIP related to   d
power projects in India. RRIP has several offices in India, and conducts all of its
operations in India. It is registered in India as a foreign company, and has filed
the names of persons there to accept service on its behalf. Heaton's business was
principally concerned with power projects in India. It now has only two full-time
employees. According to their published accounts, RRIP and Heaton did not   e
trade on their own account but acted as agents for Rolls-Royce Power
Engineering plc until 1996, and thereafter as agents for Rolls-Royce plc.

The allegations
[19] After setting out some of the history of the project (with which I deal in   f
greater detail in section VI) the particulars of claim allege that on 1 November
1993 Heaton and RRIP entered into two agency agreements (the agency
agreements) with a British Virgin Islands company, Towanda Services Ltd
(Towanda), under which Towanda was to assist them in presenting bids for, and
promoting the securing of, the EPC and O&M contracts for the Rolls-Royce
defendants. If the contracts were secured, $US 19·3m was to be paid to Towanda   g
in respect of the EPC contract and £1·5m was to be paid in respect of the O&M
contract.

[20] It is alleged that the agency agreements were shams, that Towanda was a
creature of Kishan Rao which had no relevant expertise and was not intended to
perform any genuine services; and that the agency agreements were intended by   h
Kishan Rao and the parties to the agency agreements as a cloak for payments
to Kishan Rao in the nature of bribes, intended by RRIP and Heaton to induce
Kishan Rao as managing director of SPGL to procure or do his best to procure
that SPGL awarded the EPC contract and the O&M contract to companies in the
Rolls-Royce group; that the payments were made by the Rolls-Royce defendants   j
or other companies in the Rolls-Royce group to Towanda; that the Rolls-Royce
defendants knew that Towanda was beneficially owned and/or controlled by
Kishan Rao; that the bribes were not disclosed to shareholders of SPGL,
either in general meeting or otherwise; or disclosed to the board of SPGL; and
that Kishan Rao was influenced by the bribes to procure or use his best endeavours
to procure that SPGL granted the EPC contract and the O&M contract to

a companies in the Rolls-Royce group (or that is in any event to be irrebuttably presumed as a matter of law).

[21] The claim is for restitution of the amounts paid or for damages in the same amounts. The particulars of claim make it clear that this is a derivative claim by the claimants as members of SPGL to enforce causes of action vested in SPGL and to seek relief on its behalf. In order to bring the claim within one of

b the exceptions to the rule that a shareholder cannot normally sue for a wrong done to the company (the rule in *Foss v Harbottle,* with which I deal below in section III), the particulars allege that the general meeting of SPGL is controlled or is capable of being controlled by Rolls-Royce Godavari Power Ltd and Kishan Rao and his group of companies and thereby indirectly by Rolls-Royce plc and/or the Rolls-Royce group and Kishan Rao. Accordingly, it is said, it is plain

c that the general meeting of SPGL would not pass a resolution authorising or approving the pursuit of proceedings by SPGL against RRIP and Heaton; and that of the ten directors (including Kishan Rao) at least five are closely associated with him, and it is highly unlikely that the board would pass any resolution which might facilitate a decision that the company should pursue proceedings against

d the Rolls-Royce defendants and/or Kishan Rao seeking the relief sought in the claim.

Applications

[22] There are before the court: (a) the application of the Rolls-Royce defendants for a declaration that the court has no jurisdiction, or for a stay of the proceedings on grounds of forum non conveniens, or for an order to set aside the

e order of Master Moncaster of 2 February 2001 granting permission to serve SPGL out of the jurisdiction and service made thereunder; and (b) the application by SPGL to set aside the order of Master Moncaster.

[23] The applications raise, among others, the following issues: (a) whether the English court ever has jurisdiction to hear a derivative claim in relation to a

f foreign company; (b) whether the action falls within the provisions of CPR Pt 6, which allows service to be permitted on a person outside the jurisdiction who is 'a necessary or proper party' to a claim against someone who is served or is to be served within the jurisdiction, and whether there is between the claimant and the person within the jurisdiction 'a real issue which it is reasonable for the court to try' (r 6.20(3)); (c) whether England is the appropriate forum; and (d) whether

g there was any material non-disclosure on the without notice application to Master Moncaster and, if so, whether the order should be set aside as a result.

III. DERIVATIVE ACTIONS

[24] It is an elementary principle that 'A cannot, as a general rule, bring an

h action against B to recover damages or secure other relief on behalf of C for an injury done by B to C' (*Prudential Assurance Co Ltd v Newman Industries Ltd (No 2)* [1982] 1 All ER 354 at 357, [1982] Ch 204 at 210).

[25] The usual rule is that a company is the proper claimant in an action to redress a harm done to the company or enforce a cause of action vested in the

j company (the so-called 'rule in *Foss v Harbottle*'). There are, however, a number of exceptions to the rule. The exception relied upon in this case is an alleged 'fraud on the minority'. The remedy was 'introduced on the ground of necessity alone in order to prevent a wrong doing without redress' (see *Smith v Croft (No 2)* [1987] 3 All ER 909 at 957, [1988] Ch 114 at 185). Where what has been done amounted to a fraud and the wrongdoers are themselves in control of the company, the rule is relaxed in favour of the aggrieved minority who are allowed to bring a minority shareholders' action on behalf of themselves and all others. The reason for this is that if they were denied that right, their grievance would *a* never reach the court because the wrongdoers themselves, being in control, would not allow the company to sue (see *Edwards v Halliwell* [1950] 2 All ER 1064 at 1067, the *Prudential Assurance* case [1982] 1 All ER 354 at 358, [1982] Ch 204 at 211). As Browne-Wilkinson LJ said in *Nurcombe v Nurcombe* [1985] 1 All ER 65 at 71, [1985] 1 WLR 370 at 378:   *b*

> 'Since the wrong complained of is a wrong to the company, not to the shareholder, in the ordinary way the only competent plaintiff in an action to redress the wrong would be the company itself. But, where such a technicality would lead to manifest injustice, the courts of equity permitted a person interested to bring an action to enforce the company's claim.'   *c*

[26] A 'fraud on the minority' involves two elements. The first is a cause of action in the company that can be characterised as an equitable fraud. Fraud includes all cases where the wrongdoers are endeavouring, directly or indirectly to appropriate themselves money, property or advantages which belong to the company or in which the other shareholders are entitled to participate (see   *d* *Burland v Earle* [1902] AC 83 at 93). The second element is control of the company by the wrongdoers.

[27] Wrongdoer control may be established by proof that the wrongdoers own a majority of the shares carrying votes, but the essential question is whether the claimant (or perhaps, more accurately, the company) is being prevented from pursuing a claim which the company legitimately has: see *Smith v Croft (No 2)*   *e* [1987] 3 All ER 909 at 956–957, [1988] Ch 114 at 185 per Knox J, who said:

> 'Ultimately the question which has to be answered in order to determine whether the rule in *Foss v Harbottle* ((1843) 2 Hare 461, 67 ER 189) applies to prevent a minority shareholder seeking relief as plaintiff for the benefit of the company is: is the plaintiff being prevented improperly from bringing these   *f* proceedings on behalf of the company? If it is an expression of the corporate will of the company by an appropriate independent organ that is preventing the plaintiff from prosecuting the action he is not improperly but properly prevented and so the answer to the question is No. The appropriate independent organ will vary according to the constitution of the company   *g* concerned and the identity of the defendants, who will in most cases be disqualified from participating by voting in expressing the corporate will.'

[28] For present purposes, the following propositions may be derived from the modern cases: (1) Since the bringing of the derivative claim requires the exercise of the equitable jurisdiction of the court on the grounds that the interests   *h* of justice require it, the court will not allow such an action to be used in an inequitable manner so as to produce an injustice: *Nurcombe v Nurcombe* [1985] 1 All ER 65 at 71, [1985] 1 WLR 370 at 378 per Browne-Wilkinson LJ. (2) Accordingly, a claimant who has participated in the wrong of which complaint is made will be disqualified from bringing the action: Gower's *Principles of Modern Company Law*   *j* (6th edn, 1997) p 669, the then equivalent passage of which was approved in *Nurcombe v Nurcombe* [1985] 1 All ER 65 at 69, [1985] 1 WLR 370 at 376 per Lawton LJ. (3) The claimant must be acting bona fide for the benefit of the company (see *Nurcombe v Nurcombe* and *Barrett v Duckett* [1995] 1 BCLC 243 at 250).

[29] The defendants also rely on a further proposition, namely that there must be no other adequate remedy available, which is derived from *Barrett v Duckett*.

a That was a case in which the alternative remedy was a claim by the liquidator, since a petition had been presented to wind up the company. Both Peter Gibson and Beldam LJJ considered that the decision whether to pursue an action against directors alleged to have diverted the business of the company was best left to the judgment of an independent liquidator. Peter Gibson LJ relied on two other decisions: *Ferguson v Wallbridge* [1935] 3 DLR 66, *Fargro Ltd v Godfroy* [1986] 3 All ER

b 279, [1986] 1 WLR 1134, in which derivative actions failed because there was a liquidator who was in a position to take action. This is not the occasion to express a final view, but it seems to be that the notion that there must be no alternative remedy expressed in *Barrett v Duckett* is not an independent bar to a derivative action, but simply an example of a case where there will be no relevant wrongdoer control.

c

Procedural aspects

[30] A derivative action is brought in representative form, and the company is joined as a defendant in order for it to be bound by any judgment and to receive the fruits (if any) of the judgment, and because the action has not been authorised

d by its board or general meeting (see *Spokes v Grosvenor and West End Railway Terminus Hotel Co Ltd* [1897] 2 QB 124).

[31] In the *Prudential Assurance* case the Court of Appeal considered what course was to be taken by the court if, as happened in *Foss v Harbottle* and in the *Prudential Assurance* case itself, the court was confronted by a motion on the part of the delinquent or by the company, seeking to strike out the action. A dilemma

e would emerge if the claimant could require the court to assume, as a fact, every allegation made by the claimant, since this would absolve the claimant from the burden of bringing himself within the exception simply by alleging fraud and control. But if the claimant had to prove fraud and control before he could establish his title to prosecute the action, then the action may need to be brought

f to a conclusion before the court could decide whether or not the claimant should be permitted to prosecute it.

[32] Accordingly, the Court of Appeal held:

'... whatever may be the properly defined boundaries of the exception to the rule, the plaintiff ought at least to be required before proceeding with his

g action to establish a prima facie case (i) that the company is entitled to the relief claimed and (ii) that the action falls within the proper boundaries of the exception to the rule in *Foss v Harbottle* ((1843) 2 Hare 461, 67 ER 189). On the latter issue it may well be right for the judge trying the preliminary issue to grant a sufficient adjournment to enable a meeting of shareholders to be

h convened by the board, so that he can reach a conclusion in the light of the conduct of, and proceedings at, that meeting.' (See [1982] 1 All ER 354 at 366, [1982] Ch 204 at 221–222.)

[33] In *Smith v Croft* Knox J considered that the striking out procedure was appropriate for the determination of the right of the shareholders to sue, since

j questions of fact could be gone into on such applications and in exceptional cases cross-examination could be permitted on affidavits, although in that case there was no application for cross-examination. He said:

'My conclusion is that it is the question stated by the Court of Appeal that has to be decided as a preliminary matter, that it is a special form of procedure concerned with giving sensible operation to the rule in *Foss v Harbottle*, and which is concerned with avoiding the Scylla and Charybdis, on the one hand, of having a preliminary issue which effectively requires one to try the whole action where the rule serves no useful purpose and, on the other side of the strait, of assuming that everything that the plaintiffs allege is necessarily correct as a matter of fact, which is of course the technique the court adopts when it has what was called a strict demurrer. The Court of Appeal, it seems to me, has laid down a halfway house for this very special type of case, one in which the legal issues in this particular case are sufficiently well defined for the parties to be able to argue them. Further, I am satisfied that they will determine the result of the action completely if answered in one particular way (not if answered in the other way, but that is seldom obtainable).' (See [1987] 3 All ER 709 at 921, [1988] Ch 114 at 138–139.)

[34] Knox J said ([1987] 3 All ER 909 at 921, [1988] Ch 114 at 138) that the purpose of the adjournment referred to in the *Prudential Assurance* case to enable a meeting of shareholders to be convened was not to discern whether the defendants had control, but was to secure for the benefit of the judge, who was deciding whether to allow the minority shareholder's action on behalf of the company to go forward, the commercial assessment whether the prosecution of the action was likely to do more harm than good or, the phrase used in argument in the *Prudential Assurance* case, 'kill the company by kindness'. He said that the whole tenor of the Court of Appeal's judgment was directed at securing that a realistic assessment of the practical desirability of the action going forward should be made by the organ that has the power and ability to take decisions on behalf of the company.

[35] In 1994 RSC Ord 15, r 12A was added to introduce a filter, and its provisions are substantially reproduced in CPR 19.9, which applies to 'derivative claims', ie 'where a company, other incorporated body or trade union is alleged to be entitled to claim a remedy and a claim is made by one or more members ... for it to be given that remedy'. In such a case, after the claim has been issued the claimant must apply, with written evidence in support to the court for permission to continue the claim. There is no reported case on how the power under the rule is to be applied in order to deal with the concerns expressed in the *Prudential Assurance* case, although it has been suggested that the rule is not providing an effective filter (see Reed 'Derivative Claims: the application for permission to continue' (2000) 21 Company Lawyer 156).

IV. THE FOREIGN ELEMENT

[36] SPLG is an Indian company. Four shareholders pursue a derivative action on its behalf against two companies incorporated in England. Two of the individual claimants are resident in India, a third is resident in the United States and the corporate claimant is incorporated in Mauritius.

[37] Three questions arise: (a) does the English court have jurisdiction in a derivative claim on behalf of a foreign company? (b) if so, what law applies to determine whether a derivative claim can be brought? (c) if there is jurisdiction, and the applicable law permits a derivative claim, how do forum conveniens rules apply in the context of applications to stay proceedings or to set aside service outside the jurisdiction?

[38] The position of the claimants is that if the company has a cause of action against wrongdoers within the jurisdiction, then the court has jurisdiction in a shareholders' derivative action against the wrongdoers and the company can be joined as a necessary or proper party under r 6.20(3); that whether a derivative

a claim can be brought is a matter of procedure, and therefore governed by English law as the lex fori, and the necessary procedure is regulated by r 19.9. On the principles for staying of actions or setting aside service outside the jurisdiction, the claimants argue that the normal rules apply, and the court is primarily concerned with the appropriate forum for the underlying claim, and that the derivative nature of the claim is insignificant in the context of the question of the

b appropriate forum.

[39] The claimants say that it makes practical sense for there to be no blanket rule excluding jurisdiction in respect of all derivative claims made on behalf of foreign companies. Such a rule would make no practical sense at all. (1) There might be no other court which would be competent to hear the action (which, ex hypothesi, the English court does have jurisdiction to hear). (2) If there were

c another competent court, it might not be the appropriate court. (3) In particular, the courts of the place of incorporation of the company might well be either not competent or not appropriate. (4) Further, there is no reason why a derivative claim on behalf of a foreign company would necessarily be inconvenient to hear in England. For example, procedural issues arising from the derivative nature of

d the claim may be insignificant or even non-existent (as in this case).

[40] SPGL's position is that the court either does not have jurisdiction to determine a derivative claim because there is no applicable provision in CPR Pt 6 for service on the foreign company, or, if there is in theory a basis for the application of Pt 6, then the court will not exercise jurisdiction because (a) r 19.9 does not or may not apply to foreign companies or (b) there is a general rule that

e the court will not interfere in the management of a foreign company. Alternatively it is argued that if the court has jurisdiction under Pt 6, and if r 19.9 applies to foreign companies, then the jurisdiction should be exercised very rarely and not extraterritorially.

f *CPR Pt 6*

[41] The provisions for service out of the jurisdiction, replacing RSC Ord 11, are in Pt 6. The overriding principle is that the court will not give permission unless satisfied that England is the proper place in which to bring the claim: see r 6.21(2A).

[42] The effect of r 6.20(3) is that a claim form may be served out of the
g jurisdiction if—

> 'a claim is made against someone on whom the claim form has been or will be served and—(a) there is between the claimant and that person a real issue which it is reasonable for the court to try; and (b) the claimant wishes to serve the claim form on another person who is a necessary or proper party
h to that claim.'

By r 6.21(2) in such a case the written evidence must state the grounds on which it is said that there is between the claimant and the person on whom the claim form has been, or will be served, a real issue which it is reasonable for the court
j to try.

[43] SPGL argues that there are two reasons why the court has no jurisdiction in a derivative claim in relation to a foreign company. First, there is no real issue between the claimants and the Rolls-Royce defendants, because the underlying claim is by the company and not by the claimants, who are suing on behalf of the company. The second is that the reference in r 19.9 to companies and other incorporated bodies should be interpreted to mean only English companies.

[44] In my judgment, there is no basis for restricting r 19.9 to English companies, and in any event to do so would not have the effect of depriving the court of jurisdiction to entertain a derivative claim. There is more substance in the argument on r 6.20(3), but I do not consider that it is right. The requirement that there should be a real issue between the claimant and those served, or to be served, within the jurisdiction is intended to ensure that the claim was brought bona fide against the defendant in the jurisdiction, and not merely in order to bring in the foreign defendant as a necessary or proper party: see the cases cited in *Civil Procedure* (White Book, 2001) para 6.21.28. If that conclusion is right then there can be no doubt that, if it were an appropriate case for service outside the jurisdiction, SPGL would be a necessary party since it has long been the rule, confirmed by r 19.9(2), that the company for whose benefit a derivative claim is brought must be a defendant to the claim.

Governing law

[45] The arguments in this case canvassed the question of what law governs the right of a shareholder to bring a derivative action in England. The first main candidate is English law as the lex fori on the basis that the right of shareholders to sue is a matter of procedure, and the second is the law of incorporation as the law governing the relationship of the company and its shareholders. Master Moncaster, when considering the without notice application, canvassed the possibility that the English court might not allow a derivative action unless and until it had been authorised by the foreign court. There is little to be said for another possible candidate, the law of the underlying claim which it is sought to bring on behalf of the company.

[46] In favour of English law as the lex fori is that in English law, but not necessarily in cases with a foreign element, the exceptions to the rule that only the company which is injured may sue are regarded as remedial or procedural. It was probably in this sense that Browne-Wilkinson LJ spoke of the courts of equity permitting the action if a technicality led to manifest injustice (see *Nurcombe v Nurcombe* [1985] 1 All ER 65 at 71, [1985] 1 WLR 370 at 378). *Gower* (p 665) goes as far as to say that the basic rule in *Foss v Harbottle* is part of the law of civil procedure, although it is not easy to see how the basic rule stated in *Prudential Assurance Co Ltd v Newman Industries Ltd (No 2)* [1982] 1 All ER 354 at 357, [1982] Ch 204 at 210 that 'A cannot, as a general rule, bring an action against B to recover damages or secure other relief on behalf of C for an injury done by B to C' can be regarded as a merely procedural rule.

[47] The application of English law as the lex fori is supported by a decision of the Court of Appeal, albeit a decision in which the point does not appear to have been taken, still less arisen for decision. In *Heyting v Dupont* [1964] 2 All ER 273, [1964] 1 WLR 843 the plaintiff was a minority shareholder in a Jersey company which had been incorporated to exploit an invention of the defendant. The articles had deadlock provisions. The plaintiff contended that the defendant had by misfeasance damaged the company. In the Court of Appeal it was observed that it was 'essentially a dispute between two discordant partners' (see [1964] 2 All ER 273 at 275, [1964] 1 WLR 843 at 848). The plaintiff obtained leave to serve the company out of the jurisdiction (see [1964] 1 WLR 843 at 846). It was held that on the assumption that there was a general exception to the rule in *Foss v Harbottle* (1843) 2 Hare 461, 67 ER 189 where the interests of justice so require (an assumption no longer justified since the *Prudential Assurance* case), there was no

a basis for the application of that exception. Although no point on jurisdiction or choice of law appears to have been taken, Russell LJ said:

> 'I dare say that the rule in *Foss* v. *Harbottle* is a conception as unfamiliar in the Channel Islands as is the Clameur de Haro in the jurisdiction of England and Wales; but clearly this is a matter of procedure to be decided according
> *b* to the law of this forum.' (See [1964] 2 All ER 273 at 275, [1964] 1 WLR 843 at 848.)

[48] The second candidate for the law applicable to the question whether a shareholder has a right to claim in respect of wrongs to a company is the law of the place of incorporation. There is no authority in England which is directly on
c point, but the question has been considered in the United States, where derivative actions are frequently brought in one state in relation to the affairs of corporations which have been incorporated in another state. The approach in these cases is that the right of the shareholder to bring the derivative action is governed by the law of the state of incorporation, but that the wrongdoers may be sued in a state which has personal jurisdiction over them, but subject to the American principles
d of forum non conveniens. In the international context it has been held also that the right to bring a derivative action depends on the law of the place of incorporation.

[49] In *Batchelder v Kawamoto* (1998) 147 F (3d) 915, a holder of American Depository Receipts (ADRs) for shares of the Japanese corporation Honda Motor Co Ltd brought a derivative action for wrongs allegedly committed by
e directors and other officers and employees of Honda Japan and its American subsidiary. Under Japanese law only shareholders, and not holders of ADRs, had a right to bring a derivative action. The action in the Federal Court in California was dismissed. The principal ground was that Japanese law did not give the holder of ADRs a right to sue and that Japanese law applied because the plaintiff
f purchased his ADRs pursuant to a deposit agreement expressly providing for the law of Japan to govern shareholder rights. But it was held that even if there had not been the choice of law provision in the deposit agreement (at 920):

> '... ordinary conflicts-of-law principles would direct us to apply Japanese law to Batchelder's claim. Batchelder holds an interest in Honda Japan, not
> *g* American Honda. Under the "internal affairs" doctrine, the rights of shareholders in a foreign company, including the right to sue derivatively, are determined by the law of the place where the company is incorporated. See *Hausman v. Buckley* ((1962) 299 F (2d) 696); *McDermott Inc. v. Lewis* ((1987) 531 A (2d) 206 at 214–217); *cf. CTS Corp v Dynamics Corp of America, Indiana v*
> *h* *Dynamics Corp of America* (1987) 481 US 69 at 89 ("This beneficial free market system depends at its core upon the fact that a corporation—except in the rarest situations—is organized under, and governed by, the law of a single jurisdiction, traditionally the corporate law of the State of incorporation").'

[50] It is possible that this approach is influenced by the notion (mentioned by
j Browne-Wilkinson LJ in *Nurcombe v Nurcombe*) that in the United States the derivative action is really two actions, one of which is a claim by the minority shareholder against the company for failure to enforce the company's rights, and the other being the claim by the company against the wrongdoer. In the present case, the important question of choice of law does not arise for decision, because there is no material difference between English law and Indian law. It is clear

from the evidence, and the texts on Indian company law (Ramaiya *Guide to the Companies Act* (15th edn, 2001) pp 165 et seq) that the Indian courts follow English case law on the point and permit derivative actions based on the exceptions to the rule in *Foss v Harbottle*. If it had arisen for decision I would have held that the law of the place of incorporation governs. That is because the basic rule is that the shareholders have no direct rights, as the *Prudential Assurance* case makes clear. Although for purely English domestic purposes, the exceptions to the rule have been regarded as a procedural device, I do not consider that in the international context their real nature is procedural. They confer a right on shareholders to protect the value of their shares by giving them a right to sue and recover on behalf of the company. It would be very odd if that right could be conferred on the shareholders of a company incorporated in a jurisdiction which had no such rule, and under which they had acquired their shares.

Discretionary powers and jurisdiction

[51] The question of choice of the applicable law is therefore not decisive for present purposes. But in contending that the law of the place of incorporation governs, Mr David Mackie QC for SPGL has relied on material which I do consider is relevant to the issues. He relies on *Dicey and Morris on the Conflict of Laws* (13th edn, 2000) rule 154(2), p 1110: 'All matters concerning the constitution of a corporation are governed by the law of the place of incorporation'; and on the comment (p 1112):

'English courts are reluctant to intervene in domestic issues between members of a foreign corporation. In particular they will not seek to exercise powers which are given to officers of a foreign corporation by its constitution. The reluctance of the courts to intervene is perhaps responsible for the dearth of authority on the subject of Rule 154(2), but none the less it is submitted that the Rule is soundly based in that reference to any other legal system would be absurd.'

[52] The authority cited for the reluctance of the English court to intervene is *Pergamon Press Ltd v Maxwell* [1970] 2 All ER 809, [1970] 1 WLR 1167, a decision of Pennycuick J. The case arose out of the first main Maxwell cause celebre in the late 1960s. In 1969 an American company, Leasco, was proposing to make a bid for Pergamon Press Ltd (Limited), an English public company. Limited held 70% of the shares of a New York company, Pergamon Press Inc (Inc). The byelaws of Inc provided that special meetings of shareholders were to be called at any time at the request in writing of shareholders earning a majority of the shares. While the Leasco takeover of Limited was still in prospect, Robert Maxwell, who was then chairman and managing director of Limited, used the voting powers of Limited in Inc to procure the byelaws of Inc to be amended by removing the power of shareholders to call a meeting. The Leasco bid was withdrawn when accounting irregularities were discovered.

[53] Maxwell was ousted from the board of Limited, but he and his co-directors refused to give up control of Inc. The new board of Limited failed in proceedings in New York to obtain an order convening a meeting of shareholders to remove the directors of Inc. Limited then brought proceedings in England against Maxwell for an order that he should, under the byelaw which gave the president of Inc power to convene a meeting, forthwith convene a special meeting of Inc for the purpose of the shareholders removing him and his co-directors and of re-amending the byelaws so as to restore the pre-existing

a   rights. Limited contended that Maxwell had acted in breach of his fiduciary duty to Limited by casting its votes in favour of the resolution of Inc since he had thereby deprived Limited of the valuable right of insisting that a special meeting of Inc should be called.

[54] The argument of Limited was that Maxwell had been in breach of his fiduciary duty to Limited by procuring the alteration of the byelaws of Inc and
b   that he should be ordered to use his power as director of Inc to convene a meeting to restore the position. But it was held that, because his power under the byelaws of Inc to convene a special meeting was a fiduciary power of a discretionary nature invested in him as president of Inc, the only proper court in which to seek to control the exercise of that power was the New York court, and that an English court could not control the exercise of a fiduciary power arising in the internal
c   management of a foreign company. Pennycuick J said:

'... the power [to call a meeting of the New York subsidiary in his capacity as president] is a fiduciary power of a discretionary nature, vested in the defendant in the capacity of an officer of Incorporated. It follows that the defendant is bound to exercise that power in good faith in the interest of
d   Incorporated as a whole. There is no suggestion that the law of New York is different in this respect from that of England. That being the position, it seems to me, in the first place, that the court of New York is the only proper tribunal in which the members of Incorporated could seek to control the exercise of this discretionary power. It cannot be open to an English court
e   to control the exercise of a fiduciary power arising in the internal management of a foreign company.' (See [1970] 1 WLR 1167 at 1171–1172, [1970] 2 All ER 809 at 813–814.)

[55] Two points are being made by Pennycuick J. The first is that the extent of the duties of the director of a foreign company is governed by the law of that
f   company's place of incorporation. The second is that the courts of that place are 'the only proper tribunal' in which the members can seek to control the exercise of that power. The first point is unexceptional and indeed obvious, but it may be that the second proposition goes too far, in allocating exclusive responsibility to the courts of the place of incorporation for making orders controlling the exercise of discretionary powers. The decision predates the development of the modern
g   forum non conveniens principles from later in the 1970s (see *The Atlantic Star, Owners of the Atlantic Star v Owners of the Bona Spes* [1973] 2 All ER 175, [1974] AC 436), and was given at a time when the prevailing view was that if the English court had jurisdiction, there was not normally a discretion to refuse to exercise it. If a similar point were to arise for decision today, I consider that the correct
h   approach would be to say that the courts of the place of incorporation are very likely indeed to be the appropriate forum, but not so overwhelmingly that they will necessarily be the exclusive forum. So understood, the *Pergamon Press* case confirms that questions of internal management are governed by the law of the place of incorporation, and that the courts of that place are best suited to give
j   decisions on the control and extent of the powers of the management.

Forum and discretion

[56] The relevant forum conveniens principles on the application to set aside service out of the jurisdiction and the application for a stay of proceedings are set out authoritatively in *Spiliada Maritime Corp v Cansulex Ltd, The Spiliada* [1986] 3 All ER 843, [1987] AC 460. English defendants may take advantage of these

principles in stay applications, although there are very few cases in which English defendants have succeeded.

a

[57] There is an important difference between the principles applicable to the discretion to set aside service and the discretion to order a stay. In the case of service out of the jurisdiction the claimant has to show that England is 'the proper place in which to bring the claim' (see CPR 6.21(2A)). But also because the exercise of jurisdiction involves bringing foreign parties to England:

b

'The effect is, not merely that the burden of proof rests on the plaintiff to persuade the court that England is the appropriate forum for the trial of the action, but that he has to show that this is clearly so. In other words, the burden is, quite simply, the obverse of that applicable where a stay is sought of proceedings started in this country as of right.' (See [1986] 3 All ER 843 at 858, [1987] AC 460 at 481 per Lord Goff of Chieveley.)

c

[58] In order to obtain a stay of proceedings the basic principle is that a stay will only be granted on the ground of forum non conveniens where the court is satisfied that there is some other available forum, having competent jurisdiction, which is the appropriate form for the trial of the action, ie in which the case may be tried more suitably for the interests of all the parties and the ends of justice; the defendant must show not only that England is not the natural or appropriate forum for the trial but to establish that there is another available forum which is clearly or distinctly more appropriate than the English forum (see [1986] 3 All ER 843 at 855, [1987] AC 460 at 476–477).

d

[59] If the defendant does satisfy that test, then the proceedings will be stayed unless the claimant establishes that there are circumstances by reason of which justice requires that a stay should nevertheless not be granted (see [1986] 3 All ER 843 at 856, [1987] AC 460 at 478, *Connelly v RTZ Corp plc* [1987] 4 All ER 335 at 345, [1998] AC 854 at 872, *Lubbe v Cape plc* [2000] 4 All ER 268 at 275, [2000] 1 WLR 1545 at 1155). *Connelly's* case shows, by the citation of *Oppenheimer v Louis Rosenthal & Co AG* [1937] 1 All ER 23, that in some circumstances a similar policy may work in cases of service outside the jurisdiction. There are some circumstances where the claimant would not obtain a fair trial in the foreign court, or where the injustice which would be done by restricting the claimant to the foreign court would be so great that the foreign court would not be regarded as an available forum. In such circumstances, provided the case came within the provisions for service out of the jurisdiction, England would be regarded as the appropriate forum.

e

f

g

[60] In *Connelly's* case Lord Goff said, in relation to stay applications:

'[The] general principle ... is that, if a clearly more appropriate forum overseas has been identified, generally speaking the plaintiff will have to take that forum as he finds it, even if it is in certain respects less advantageous to him than the English forum. He may, for example, have to accept lower damages, or do without the more generous English system of discovery ... Only if the plaintiff can establish that substantial justice cannot be done in the appropriate forum, will the court refuse to grant a stay ...' (See [1997] 4 All ER 335 at 345, [1998] AC 854 at 872–873.)

h

j

[61] The relevant factors 'include not only factors affecting convenience or expense (such as availability of witnesses), but also other factors such as the law governing the relevant transaction ... and the places where the parties

a   respectively reside or carry on business' (see *The Spiliada* [1986] 3 All ER 843 at 856, [1987] AC 460 at 478). 'In considering this question the court must take into account the nature of the dispute, the legal and practical issues involved, such questions as local knowledge, availability of witnesses and their evidence and expense' (*Amin Rasheed Shipping Corp v Kuwait Insurance Co, The Al Wahab* [1983] 2 All ER 884 at 896, [1984] AC 50 at 72 per Lord Wilberforce).

b   [62] There are two points of principle which I should deal with at this stage. The first is whether this is a case for the application both of the principles relating to stay of proceedings and the principles with regard to service out of the jurisdiction. The second is whether I am concerned purely with the identification of the appropriate forum for trial of the bribery allegations or whether I am also concerned with the appropriate forum for determination of the question whether

c   this is a proper case for a derivative action.

[63] On the first question I am satisfied that I should approach the matter on the basis of the application of the principles relating to service out of the jurisdiction. SPGL are necessary parties to the action, and unless the claimants can show that England is clearly the appropriate forum, service will be set aside,

d   and the action cannot proceed in the absence of SPGL. Conversely, if the claimants can show that England is clearly the appropriate forum, then any application for a stay by the Rolls-Royce defendants would be doomed to failure.

[64] The Rolls-Royce defendants have joined SPGL in arguing the service out of the jurisdiction points, and have also applied to set aside the order of Master Moncaster permitting service on SPGL. The point taken by the claimants that

e   the Rolls-Royce defendants have no standing to apply to set aside an order which does not directly affect them is sterile, since they can only succeed if SPGL succeeds, and if SPGL succeeds then there will be no proceedings in England against the Rolls-Royce defendants by the claimants. Nor do I consider that SPGL can be criticised for making the application to set aside the order granting

f   permission. The claimants say that a company in relation to which a derivative action is brought should be essentially neutral. SPGL says that it is entirely neutral with regard to the underlying dispute, but that it is entitled to say that these matters should not be dealt with in England at great expense and inconvenience. I do not consider that this attitude is open to criticism.

g   [65] On the second question, I am satisfied that the questions which arise on whether the fraud exception to the rule in *Foss v Harbottle* applies are to be taken into account in determining the appropriate forum, and that they are a significant factor. This is so notwithstanding that the forum conveniens cases habitually speak of the appropriate forum for trial of the action, and that the peculiarly *Foss v Harbottle* issues may be determined at a preliminary stage without trial. But it is

h   clear that these issues are an integral part of the claim in a derivative action, and it would be wholly unjust and inappropriate to treat them as a purely procedural matter to be excluded from the equation.

[66] I also consider that the effect of the *Pergamon Press* case is, at the least, that if issues arise relating to the exercise of what Pennycuick J described as discretionary

j   powers of management, then I should accord considerable weight to the potential role of the courts of the place of incorporation. I doubt whether they have exclusive jurisdiction to deal with such issues. For example it may be wholly unjust to require recourse to an offshore haven to pursue fraudulent directors in a case which has no connection with the jurisdiction other than that it is the place of incorporation.

[67] I therefore proceed on the following basis. The court has power to permit service on SPGL in a derivative claim by shareholders against English defendants, but the order for service can stand only if the claimants can show that England is the clearly appropriate forum for determination of the questions whether they are entitled to bring a derivative action and whether the defendants are liable to SPGL for the alleged bribery.

V. THE AVAILABILITY OF THE INDIAN FORUM

[68] There were several rounds of written evidence on the Indian law relating to jurisdiction. The evidence for the claimants was that of former Chief Justice Ahmadi and Mr Raghunandan Rao, a practising lawyer; for the Rolls-Royce defendants, Ms Goswami, an advocate of the Supreme Court who acts for the Rolls-Royce group in India; and for SPGL, Mrs Shroff, a partner in a firm of advocates and solicitors acting for SPGL in India, and Mr Vaidyanathan, a senior advocate, practising chiefly before the Supreme Court.

[69] Most, but not all, of the rules relating to the jurisdiction of the Indian courts are statutory. For present purposes they derive from the Code of Civil Procedure of 1908, which appears to have been designed to deal primarily with territorial jurisdiction as between the different parts of India, but has been applied to international cases to determine the jurisdiction of Indian courts in relation to persons outside India; and from the Indian Companies Act 1956, which contains provisions in ss 591 to 597 equivalent to those in Pt XXIII of the Companies Act 1985 relating to registration of foreign companies with places of business within India and the filing of the name and address of one or more persons authorised to accept service of process.

[70] The potentially relevant provisions of the 1908 Code are ss 19 to 21. The broad effect of these provisions is as follows: (a) an action for damages may be brought within the jurisdiction where the wrong was done or in the place where the defendant resides, or carries on business, or personally works for gain: s 19; (b) an action may be brought in a jurisdiction in which the defendant (or, if more than one, each of them) actually and voluntarily resides, or carries on business, or personally works for gain: s 20(a); (c) an action may be brought against more than one defendant in the jurisdiction in which one of them actually and voluntarily resides, or carries on business, or personally works for gain, provided that in such a case either (i) the leave of the court is given or (ii) the defendants who do not reside etc in the jurisdiction acquiesce in the institution of the suit: s 20(b); (d) an action may be brought in the jurisdiction within which the cause of action, wholly or in part, arises: s 20(c); and (e) for the purposes of determining where a corporation carries on business, it is deemed to carry on business at its sole or principal office in India, or, in respect of any cause of action arising at any place where it has also a subordinate office, at such place: explanation to s 20.

[71] There are two relevant statutory provisions recognising the possibility of submission to the jurisdiction. The first is in s 20(b), referred to above, the effect of which is that if an action is properly brought against someone within the jurisdiction, another defendant may acquiesce in the institution of the proceedings. The second is in s 21(1), which deals only with the effect on appeal of a failure in the court below to object to jurisdiction, and provides: 'No objection as to the place of suing shall be allowed by any Appellate or Revisional Court unless such objection was taken in the Court of first instance at the earliest possible opportunity ...'

a   [72] In order to guard against the possibility that there would be some doubt as to whether they might otherwise be subject to the jurisdiction of the Indian courts, the Rolls-Royce defendants have agreed to submit. If that is effective under Indian law, then that would make India an available forum for the purposes with which I am concerned (see *Lubbe v Cape plc* [2000] 4 All ER 268 at 272–277, [2000] 1 WLR 1545 at 1552–1556).

b   [73] It is also clear that if the claimants were to sue Kishan Rao in India the Rolls-Royce defendants could be joined either if leave were given, or if they submit. This is conceded by the claimants, and is confirmed by the course of the litigation in sections VIII, IX and XI below, in which parties outside India have been joined in actions in which there are Indian defendants.

c   [74] On the other possible bases of jurisdiction, the defendants' evidence is to the effect that: (a) the Indian courts have jurisdiction to give leave to serve out of the jurisdiction, because the alleged wrong was done in India, or the cause of action arises wholly or partly in India, because SPGL is wholly in India and it suffered the damage there: ss 19 and 20(c); (b) RRIP has an office in India, and therefore falls within definition of carrying on business or personally working for gain in Indian jurisdiction. Heaton operates plant and so carries on business or

d   personally works for gain. Consequently there is jurisdiction under s 20(a) and (b); (c) RRIP has a liaison office in Delhi which is registered with the Registrar of Companies, and several project/site offices, and has filed under s 592 of the 1956 Act the name of a person authorised to accept service; (d) a foreign party could submit to the jurisdiction of an Indian court.

e   [75] The claimants' evidence, from former Chief Justice Ahmadi, is: (a) no part of the cause of action arose in India because no part of the wrong/fraud took place in India; (b) there is no jurisdiction over a foreign corporate defendant unless it has either (i) its principal office in India, or (ii) a subordinate office in India in circumstances where the cause of action also arose in India; and

f   accordingly since neither of the Rolls-Royce defendants has its principal office in India, the Indian court would not have jurisdiction; if a company has more than one place of business, then the cause of action must arise at the place where the action is brought; (c) parties cannot submit because parties cannot by consent confer jurisdiction where none otherwise exists under the 1908 Code, except where two courts potentially have jurisdiction.

g   [76] Following the conclusion of argument in these applications, I sent a note on 4 December 2001 to the parties to say that it seemed to me that the evidence did not sufficiently deal with the question whether a party could simply submit to the jurisdiction of the Indian court by appearing and not objecting to territorial jurisdiction; and that having looked at statements in Mulla on the *Code of Civil*

h   *Procedure* (16th edn, 2001) (the leading work in India on the subject), and two decisions of the Supreme Court of India, it seemed to me that a party could submit to the jurisdiction of a court with general competence and could waive any objection based on territorial jurisdiction. I asked leading counsel to take instructions from the experts. On 12 December all parties lodged further opinions

j   from their experts.

[77] The cases to which I referred the parties were *Hira Lal Patni v Kali Nath Co Ltd* AIR 1962 SC 199 and *Bahrein Petroleum Co Ltd v P J Pappu* AIR 1966 SC 634. In *Patni's* case the Supreme Court of India said (at 201):

'The objection to its territorial jurisdiction is one which does not go to the competence of the court and can, therefore, be waived … It is well settled that the objection as to local jurisdiction of a court does not stand on the same footing as an objection to the competence of a court to try a case. Competence of a court to try a case goes to the very root of the jurisdiction, and where it is lacking, it is a case of inherent lack of jurisdiction. On the other hand an objection as to the local jurisdiction of a court can be waived and this principle has been given a statutory recognition by enactments like S. 21 of the Code of Civil Procedure.'

[78] In the *Bahrein Petroleum* case the Supreme Court of India confirmed (at 636) that s 21 of the 1908 Code was a statutory recognition of the principle that the defect as to the place of suing under ss 15 to 20 may be waived. Mulla *Code of Civil Procedure* p 461, says precisely the same (but without any citation to the case).

[79] The experts for the defendants, Ms Goswami and Mr Vaidyanathan, both give clear evidence that the effect of the decisions of the Supreme Court of India, as confirmed by *Mulla* is that a party may submit to the jurisdiction of a court of general competence and may waive any objection based on territorial jurisdiction.

[80] Former Chief Justice Ahmadi gave an opinion that the parties to a legal dispute could not by agreement confer jurisdiction as to competence and territorial jurisdiction on an Indian court, although there was a form of statutory estoppel available in certain limited circumstances provided by s 21 of the 1908 Code which applied only at an appellate or revisional level. He relied on decisions of the Supreme Court and of the Privy Council, each relating to jurisdiction over land, and a decision in 1928 of the Lahore Court of Appeal. *Kiran Singh v Chaman Paswan* AIR 1954 SC 340 dealt with an action for recovery of possession of land, and in that case it was said (at 342):

'A defect of jurisdiction, whether it is pecuniary or territorial, or whether it is in respect of the subject-matter of the action, strikes at the very authority of the Court to pass any decree, and such a defect cannot be cured even by consent of parties.'

[81] In *Raja Setrucharlu Ramabhadra Raju Bahadur v Maharaja of Jeypore* AIR 1919 PC 150, the action at first instance in Vizagapatam was for the sale of land subject to a mortgage. Section 17 of the 1908 Code provided that a suit to obtain relief in respect of immovable property might be instituted in the court within the local limits of whose jurisdiction any portion of the property was situate. The land was outside the jurisdiction of the court, but no point was taken on jurisdiction at trial. It was held by the Privy Council that the point could be taken on appeal, notwithstanding s 21, which provides that no objection could be taken on appeal (in this case before the Madras court) 'as to the place of suing' unless the objection had been taken in the court below. The reason was (at 152): 'This is not an objection as to place of suing; it is an objection going to the nullity of the order on the ground of want of jurisdiction.'

[82] The decisions of the Supreme Court and of the Privy Council do not appear to me to be inconsistent with the later decisions of the Supreme Court in 1962 and 1966, each of which state that s 21 is declaratory of the principle that, at least in actions in personam, objections to territorial jurisdiction can be waived. All that *Singh*'s case appears to say is that a court has no authority to make a decree in relation to land outside its jurisdiction. So also *Raju Bahadur*'s case holds that the provision that objections as to 'place of suing' which cannot be raised on appeal if they have not been taken below does not apply to jurisdiction over land

a in the agency tracts which was excluded from the operation of the 1908 Code. If the former Chief Justice were right in saying that objections to territorial jurisdiction could not be waived under s 21, not only would it be contrary to the two decisions of the Supreme Court in 1962 and 1966, but it would deprive s 21 of all meaning.

[83] The decision of the Lahore Court of Appeal in *Bhamboo Mal v Ram Narain* b AIR 1928 Lahore 297 cited by former Chief Justice Ahmadi does say that s 21 has no application to foreigners not otherwise subject to the jurisdiction. But the opposite was decided in 1978 in Andhra Pradesh in *Far Eastern Steamship Co (Kakinada, petitioner) v Koika Trading Co Ltd* AIR 1978 Andhra Pradesh 433, and the decision in the *Bahrein Petroleum* case, where it was held there had been a submission to the Cochin court, was an international case and does not appear c (despite the references to Bahrein Petroleum having an agent in Bombay) to have depended on there being another court in India with jurisdiction.

[84] My conclusion is that India is an available forum for these reasons: (a) RRIP has a place of business in India and has registered an agent to accept service, and the claimants have not disputed this either as a matter of fact or law, d and Heaton could be joined with leave to an action against RRIP, or could acquiesce in such an action under s 20(b) of the 1908 Code; or (b) Kishan Rao is amenable to the jurisdiction of the Indian courts, and the Rolls-Royce defendants could be joined with leave, or could acquiesce under s 20(b): if the claimants are right in their allegations, Kishan Rao is liable, and any failure to sue him would be purely tactical; or (c) the strong weight of authority is that a submission to the e jurisdiction of the Indian court would be effective, and the Rolls-Royce defendants have offered to submit.

[85] The claimants purported to introduce new matters in the final opinion of former Chief Justice Ahmadi, for which they had neither sought nor been granted permission. The point on jurisdiction is that because the action would be a f derivative action, permission is required to commence it and the court might refuse permission if it appeared that the cause of action had not arisen within its jurisdiction or that the defendants did not reside or carry on business within the jurisdiction; and that third parties interested in the suit might join the proceedings and raise the issue of jurisdiction. The defendants have not had an opportunity to answer this evidence, which should not have been sought to be g introduced at this stage. But former Chief Justice Ahmadi does not appear to have been instructed on RRIP's registration under the 1956 Act as a foreign company and its having filed the name of a person authorised to accept service. In any event, the problem would not arise if Kishan Rao were a defendant, and has not arisen in the eight derivative actions in Hyderabad to which the Rolls-Royce h defendants (and other foreign companies) are parties. A point on limitation is taken, to the effect that if time had begun to run in India, it would not have been prevented from running by the institution of the English proceedings. If that is so, then the remedy for that has always been in the hands of the claimants. But I take no account of this point, raised as it is without permission after numerous j rounds of evidence.

VI. HISTORY OF THE PROJECT

[86] In this section I shall set out the history of the project. Not all of the facts are common ground, and in setting out the history, which is derived from the witness statements and exhibits, I am not intending to make any finding of disputed fact.

The project

[87] In the late 1980s National Thermal Power Corp (NTPC) was given a licence to set up a gas-based power project at Kakinada, Andhra Pradesh. NTPC is a state-owned power utility company, and the largest supplier of power in India. In the early 1990s the Andhra Pradesh State Electricity Board invited tenders for the construction and maintenance of the plant. With the encouragement of the then chief minister of Andhra Pradesh, Mohan Rao resigned from GE Power Systems, and established STUSA to make a bid for the project.

[88] In March 1992 the government of Andrah Pradesh issued a letter of intent to STUSA to give it the responsibility of setting up the project. Following meetings with NTPC and officials of the power ministry in India, it was decided that the project would be established and run by a joint venture company in which CMS (a major United States power generation company), STUSA and NTPC would participate. It was also decided that Kishan Rao's Jaya Food would be added as a promoter to and participant in the project due to the close family relationship between Mohan Rao and Kishan Rao, and his access to local capital.

[89] A joint venture company was formed using the STUSA name, ie Spectrum, and it was registered on 26 October 1992, as Spectrum Power Generation Ltd. Because STUSA and Mohan Rao could not purchase shares in the Indian company without first obtaining exchange control approvals, Kishan Rao and his sons were the notional promoters of the company. In January 1993 the Indian Ministry of Energy required NTPC's participation in the equity on a minority basis.

[90] Once the joint venture company had been formed, it became necessary to formalise the relationship between the three joint venture partners in a promoters' agreement. A promoters' agreement was executed on 20 June 1993 between STUSA, Jaya Food and NTPC, on which I elaborate below at [96] and [97]. In June 1994 the relationship between CMS and the other parties broke down, and CMS agreed to a lump sum payment for the expenses it had incurred was agreed. SPGL was unable to obtain exchange control clearance and as a result CMS instituted proceedings in a Michigan Federal Court for the money. The only relevance of this for the purposes of these proceedings is that the Rolls-Royce defendants rely on statements made by Mohan Rao in those proceedings.

Award of contracts

[91] SPGL sought tenders for the project from 1992. The main contracts were to be contracts for engineering, procurement and construction (EPC) and operation and maintenance (O&M). Tenders for the EPC contract were received from ABB, Siemens, a Rolls-Royce/Westinghouse consortium, Bharat Heavy Electricals of India, and General Electric. There was a separate tendering process for the O&M contract, in which the tenders were Rolls-Royce/Westinghouse, NTPC and three United States companies.

[92] Both sets of contracts were awarded to Rolls-Royce/Westinghouse. Following a series of letters of intent and the signature of an outline version, and after consideration of the tenders, the EPC contracts were entered into on 12 December 1994: between SPGL, RRIP, and Westinghouse International Service Co Ltd for the erection, supervision and commissioning of the plant; and between SPGL, Heaton and Westinghouse Electric Corp for the manufacture and supply of plant. Following board approval in March 1995, Mohan Rao and

a Kishan Rao were authorised to execute the O&M contract with RRIP. The contract was executed on 14 March 1995, with Westinghouse as principal sub-contractor.

Agency agreements

[93] On 1 November 1993 two agency agreements were entered into with Towanda, which had been incorporated in the British Virgin Islands on 5 October
b 1993. One was with Heaton for the purpose of securing an EPC contract with SPGL, and the other with RRIP to secure an O&M contract. The commission in the former was to be $US 19·3m (in instalments commencing on signature), and in the latter agreement the commission was to be $US 1·5m. The agreements were to be governed by English law.

c [94] There is a major conflict of evidence on the role of Mohan Rao in the inception and conclusion of these agreements. He says that he did not see them until 1997 and did not appreciate their significance until 1999, when, in proceedings against him by Kishan Rao in Hyderabad (to which I shall refer below in section XI) Kishan Rao alleged that Towanda was owned and controlled by him. The Rolls-Royce witnesses say that Mohan Rao was not only aware of the agency
d agreements, but that he pressed for them to be completed and participated in the negotiations for their conclusion.

[95] Rolls-Royce has produced a contemporary memorandum to the then head of Rolls-Royce Power Generation Systems Ltd in October 1993, attaching the 'Draft Agency Agreement for handing over during your discussions with
e Mohan Rao in Hyderabad next week'. It is accepted by some of the Rolls-Royce witnesses that the draft was probably not handed over, and I shall revert to the evidence on this below in section XV.

Promoters' agreement

f [96] On 29 June 1993 NTPC, Jaya Food and STUSA entered into a promoters' agreement to set out the terms on which the promoters would set up and run the power project. It included terms as to the division between equity and debt funding and the extent to which equity would be made available to the public. The promoters' agreement also provided that of the 90% to be allotted to Jaya Food and STUSA, 50% of such shares could be issued to an 'Affiliate' of those
g parties. According to Rolls-Royce, it was agreed that Kishan Rao would become managing director, and that representatives of Jaya Food, STUSA and NTPC would sit on the board.

[97] Ninety per cent of the initial issued and paid up equity capital was to be subscribed and held by Jaya Food, STUSA and its affiliates including CMS, and
h 10% by NTPC. Out of the 90% held by Jaya Food and STUSA they could offer up to 20% to the public for subscription at par.

[98] On 27 July 1995 STUSA and STUSA (Mauritius) entered into an agreement under which STUSA (Mauritius) as an affiliate of STUSA would invest $US 8,335,070 as equity.

j [99] According to the evidence of SPGL, no equity contributions were made by NTPC and no shares were issued to it. As a result of NTPC's failure to make its equity contribution the financial position of the project became difficult. In addition it is said that, in breach of the promoters' agreement, Mohan Rao failed to furnish guarantees on behalf of STUSA to financial institutions to secure SPGL's debt. As a result, Kishan Rao arranged for further funds to be contributed from his own resources and those of his companies. He also arranged a loan with

ANZ Grindlays of £50m in 1995 which was guaranteed by the State Bank of India.
He also guaranteed other loans, and arranged unsecured loans of £4m.   *a*

[100] As a result of the non-Indian debt the company was required to obtain
non-Indian equity, and the board therefore agreed on 24 February 1994 a different
shareholding structure: NRIs 4·5%; overseas corporate bodies 13·5%; foreign
companies/foreigners 42%; resident Indians 40%. To meet the foreign equity
requirement SPGL obtained in 1995 an equity contribution from a Mauritian   *b*
company in the Rolls-Royce group, Rolls-Royce Godavari Power Ltd, which
became, following further contributions in 1998, the largest shareholder with
47·53%. STUSA and its associates took up 24·76%.

[101] According to Rolls-Royce, it was asked to take up equity to demonstrate
its confidence in SPGL and to get the project kick-started. It thought that SPGL
would issue a substantial number of shares to other subscribers, but this was   *c*
prevented by the dispute between Kishan Rao and Mohan Rao, leaving
Rolls-Royce in the position which it had not anticipated of owning a substantial
long-term stake.

[102] Relations between the Mohan Rao camp and the Kishan Rao camp
broke down after about December 1995 when the board of SPGL rescinded its   *d*
adoption of the promoters' agreement. There ensued litigation in India concerning
the validity of the board decision to rescind the promoters' agreement, but the
dispute has significantly escalated since 1999 following a criminal complaint
made by Kishan Rao against Mohan Rao and his associate Mr Brij Bharteey in the
Court for the Special Judge for Economic Offences at Hyderabad. Kishan Rao
accused them of having defrauded NRI investors by persuading them to invest in   *e*
SPGL and then misappropriating the money by purchasing shares in the name of
STUSA (Mauritius).

[103] Shortly afterwards Mohan Rao wrote a long and angry letter to
Kishan Rao, in which he said:

> 'Maybe you forgot, but let me try to recollect for your sake that you were   *f*
> in the Chutta, Atta and Vermicelli business in a very small way and knew
> nothing of POWER or power generation, excepting that you were greedy
> for power, money and had a flair for show of power. Dear Mr. Kishan Rao,
> is it not out of trust and the faith I had in you that I associated you with this
> project right from the time after STUSA responded to the tender of the   *g*
> AP State Electricity Board. Did I not trust you and treated you as an elder,
> take you to all the meetings and discussions we had with the various
> departments of Government—both at State level and Central level? You had
> every knowledge of the entire project right from the beginning, as you were
> so close to all our functioning. Mr. Kishan Rao were you not aware of how   *h*
> we ie, for STUSA generated funds abroad and how we channelled them into
> the project after obtaining all the necessary approvals? Which aspect of our
> involvement is not known to you Mr. Kishan Rao? Being a relative of mine
> that too close relative, you knew each and every aspect of my life including
> my bankruptcy proceedings in USA of the year 1983. You had my every
> particular and detail with you, which would not have been available to you   *j*
> had we been mere business partners. Mr. Kishan Rao, I really am amazed at
> your memory and memory retrieval capacities. What you knew happened
> in 1983 you found it relevant to use against me now in the year 1999. And
> that too when we started working on the project from 1990. Mr. Kishan Rao
> your action in doing all these is very apparent. You are doing all these with

a   a deliberate scheming and purpose. Your aim is to harm my name and reputation and ruin me even as a person. This is nothing but sheer slander and criminal intimidation ... Dear Mr. Kishan Rao, as it is you started acting malafide and developed a greedy intent towards SPGL, and wanted to have a monopoly and total control over the project. You acted malafide and worked hard trying to throw out NTPC, which was there in this project right

b   since the inception of thought for this power project. You had no qualms in cruelly cutting it out from the project. You then targeted STUSA and started using all the tricks in your hat to throttle and suffocate us and make our existence in SPGL miserable ... Dear Mr. Kishan Rao, I know that you filed this criminal case against me in the Economic Offences Court without any

c   legal basis. I gave any amount of thought as to why you did this. Your letter to Ms Mangala J. Reddy and other NRI Investors gives out the answer and made your malintents clear and transparent. You both got the Court issue summons and address a letter to the US Embassy at Delhi. You obtain copies of the said letter and summons. You then bundle them up copy of the complaint, copy of the letter issued by Court to US Embassy and the

d   summons of Court, and send them to the NRI Investors in US ... If you fail to act on my letter and comply with calls made by me herein, I will be having no other option but to initiate necessary legal action against you to safeguard myself, my name and reputation, and seek legal remedies including Civil and Criminal against you in all available forums.'

e
VII. INDIAN LITIGATION: OVERVIEW

[104] The Indian litigation consists of 18 separate civil and criminal cases, with some considerable overlap in the allegations and the issues. In all but one of the cases (the NTPC action to invalidate the rescission of the promoters' agreement)

f   the principal protagonists are Kishan Rao and Jaya Food, and SPGL, on the one side and Mohan Rao and his companies or his nominees on the other.

[105] A broadly chronological account of the litigation will show how the dispute has escalated. The proceedings are as follows: (1) Delhi proceedings by STUSA in 1996 (followed by a similar case by NTPC in 1997) to set aside the board decision rescinding the promoters' agreement; (2) eight derivative actions

g   brought in Hyderabad in January 1999 on behalf of SPGL by nominees of Mohan Rao or Ravi Reddy (including the second and third claimants in this action) against Kishan Rao alleging that he had acquired shares in SPGL by fraudulently paying out its money on bogus construction contracts to entities controlled by him; (3) a 1999 criminal complaint in Hyderabad by Kishan Rao against Mohan

h   Rao alleging that he had defrauded NRIs by using their money to buy STUSA's interest in SPGL; (4) proceedings by Kishan Rao in Hyderabad in May 1999, alleging that he had advanced money through Towanda to Mohan Rao for the purchase of shares in SPGL, which had not been repaid; (5) three criminal complaints in Hyderabad in January 2000 brought by the second claimant in this

j   action, alleging fraud by Kishan Rao in siphoning off money from SPGL to the same bogus contractors alleged in the derivative actions; (6) proceedings in 2001 by STUSA to challenge the settlement of the NTPC proceedings in connection with the promoters' agreement; (7) three criminal complaints brought against Kishan Rao and his sons in July 2001 alleging forgery of revenue-stamped contracts.

[106] In the proceedings to challenge the rescission of the promoters' agreement there have been many interlocutory applications, involving applications relating to control over the issues of shares and the taking of management decisions. In 1998 the court in Delhi unsuccessfully endeavoured to procure a settlement by making an order under which the Industrial Development Bank of India convened a meeting of all parties to negotiate a settlement. In the course of those negotiations Mohan Rao sought to be made joint managing director with equal representation of STUSA and Jaya Food on the board.

VIII. ACTIONS IN DELHI BY STUSA IN 1996 AND BY NTPC IN 1997 TO CHALLENGE SPGL'S RESCISSION OF THE PROMOTERS' AGREEMENT

[107] The defendants are SPGL, Jaya Food, and NTPC. The proceedings alleged that SPGL and Jaya Food were seeking to avoid their obligations under the promoters' agreement; that the board minutes of 14 December 1995 to rescind the promoters' agreement had been falsified; that SPGL had failed to issue shares to STUSA and NTPC; that Jaya Food was attempting to grab control and management of SPGL by hijacking the project. The proceedings sought a declaration of invalidity of the board resolution and orders prohibiting any increase in SPGL's share capital and directing that no steps were taken in SPGL's management without its and NTPC's consent.

[108] NTPC's claim was similar, except that it joined as defendants many more parties, including the Rolls-Royce defendants. The action was settled in April 2001. But the Supreme Court of India said that this did not preclude STUSA from challenging the settlement agreement, and a derivative action was brought by STUSA on its own behalf and on behalf of other shareholders against Jaya Food, and Kishan Rao and his sons, to challenge the settlement agreement. In September 2001 Justice Kapok refused to grant an injunction to prevent implementation of the settlement agreement.

Interim applications and appeals

[109] There were numerous interim applications in these actions and on appeal, including applications to restrain management of SPGL without the consent of STUSA (and NTPC), for injunctions to restrain the issue of further shares, for orders that STUSA should jointly operate SPGL, and for the appointment of a receiver. All of these applications were unsuccessful at first instance and on appeal in the Delhi Civil Appellate Division. STUSA has applied for special leave to appeal from the Supreme Court of India, and in that application has asked for the appointment of a receiver. In the course of these appeals STUSA joined the defendants in the NTPC proceedings (including the Rolls-Royce defendants) as additional defendants to its proceedings.

[110] On 24 July 2000 the Supreme Court of India ordered that, pending the appeals, 'In the mean time the parties shall maintain status quo as on today and shall not take any major decision except the decisions to carry on day-to-day functions' (the status quo order). The evidence of SPGL is that the effect of the status quo order has been to make it difficult for it to raise additional capital without permission of the court. Mohan Rao has successfully challenged an order giving such permission, and made an offer (which was declined) to make capital contributions.

IX. HYDERABAD DERIVATIVE ACTIONS: JANUARY 1999

a   [111] The eight derivative actions in the Hyderabad City Civil Court were commenced in January 1999. The same six plaintiffs sue in each action, in each case as shareholders claiming to hold 2,700 shares in SPGL. The first plaintiff, Mr Mitta, is Mohan Rao's brother-in-law and is the third claimant in these proceedings, and the second plaintiff, who sues as Ms Santha Reddy, is Ravi

b Reddy's mother-in-law and is the second claimant in these proceedings. The other four plaintiffs are members of the Reddy family.

[112] The claim in each action is that shares in SPGL held by Kishan Rao's company, Bambino Finance Pvt Ltd, were paid for from money fraudulently diverted from SPGL through bogus contracts with fictitious entities or entities

c controlled by Kishan Rao and his sons. The entities concerned are Blue Star Constructions Co and Real Builders, which are said to be sham partnerships, and Kris Engineers, which is said to be owned by Kishan Rao's sons. Consequently it is alleged that the shares were issued for no consideration, and that the funds of SPGL were used for the purchase of its own shares. The actions seek an order

d that shares in SPGL held by Bambino be declared null and void, and that the register of SPGL be rectified by cancelling the shares. The Rolls-Royce companies (including Rolls-Royce Godavari Power Ltd) are parties (for the purpose of requiring them to furnish information) and jurisdiction to try the suit is said to arise from the fact that Bambino, the principal defendant, is within the territorial jurisdiction of the court.

e   [113] The derivative actions claim that (a) the persons in control of SPGL are close relatives of Kishan Rao; (b) no purpose would be served 'in moving the domestic forum'; (c) where the wrongdoers are in control, the shareholders can move the court for the necessary relief; (d) the issue of the shares was wrongful and ultra vires, and a fraud on the minority, and the majority directors would

f have no interest in protecting the interests of SPGL since they acquired their majority by fraudulent means; (e) there is no alternative remedy before the Indian Company Law Board.

[114] The significant features for present purposes are: (a) the plaintiffs are associated with Mohan Rao and Ravi Reddy; (b) the information for the action

g comes from STUSA; (c) the actions raise questions of wrongdoer control and the honesty of Kishan Rao.

X. HYDERABAD CRIMINAL PROCEEDING BY KISHAN RAO AGAINST MOHAN RAO AND BRIJ BHARATEEY: 1999

h   [115] The criminal complaint was made by Kishan Rao against Mohan Rao and Brij Bharateey in the Court of the Special Judge for Economic Offences in Hyderabad. The complaint alleges fraud under the Indian Companies Act 1956. The essence of the complaint is that the accused induced NRIs to invest in SPGL, and misappropriated the funds so as to buy shares in SPGL in the names of

j STUSA, Spectrum Infrastructure (Jersey) and STUSA (Mauritius).

[116] Mohan Rao claims that the purpose of these proceedings is to cause damage to the STUSA companies and to retain control of SPGL in order 'to further siphon off funds with the active connivance of the so-called independent professional directors': judgment of Judge Raghavaiah in the Hyderabad debt proceedings.

XI. HYDERABAD DEBT ACTION BY KISHAN RAO: MAY 1999

[117] In this action, commenced in May 1999, Kishan Rao sues Mohan Rao, STUSA, Spectrum Infrastructure Ltd (Jersey) and STUSA (Mauritius). Kishan Rao claims $US4·9m, which he says he lent to Mohan Rao in February 1995, because Mohan Rao could not afford to pay for his equity contribution in SPGL. Kishan Rao claims that it was agreed that Mohan Rao would repay the money once he had sufficient funds. There is said to be a document in Mohan Rao's handwriting giving the payment instructions. Kishan Rao claims that the money was paid to Mohan Rao's nominee's account in Panama, and Kishan Rao's sons were present in Lugano when Mohan Rao withdrew the money. Mohan Rao then used this money to pay for shares in SPGL that were allotted to the STUSA group of companies. It is also alleged (as in the criminal complaint) that Mohan Rao had collected $US9·3m from NRIs for investment in SPGL but had failed to use the money for that purpose. Kishan Rao claims that Mohan Rao concealed from him that he had been adjudged insolvent by a New York federal bankruptcy court in 1983.

[118] Kishan Rao says that he owns and controls Towanda and that its bank statements indicated that $US4·9m was remitted to Mohan Rao's nominee accounts in February 1995: $US4m to Darofe SA, Panama, account with Banco di Credito, Lugano and $US900,000 to Mount Stevens Investment Ltd, account with BNPI Mauritius. Mohan Rao denies the allegations and says he knows nothing of the companies alleged to be his nominees. Kishan Rao has replied that in an application made in an appeal against the dismissal of an interim application in the 1996 action, Mohan Rao claimed that Mount Stevens Investments Ltd was associated with him, and that his sons were present when Mohan Rao and Ravi Reddy received cash in Lugano. The defendants put Kishan Rao to proof of his assertion that Towanda was his company, and say that no material had been put forward to show that Towanda was owned by Kishan Rao. In the course of dismissing an application for attachment of the defendants' assets Judge Raghavaiah took the view that Kishan Rao had not placed satisfactory evidence on record to show that Towanda was owned by Kishan Rao, or that the payees were connected with Mohan Rao.

XII. CRIMINAL COMPLAINTS BY MRS SANTHA REDDY PEKETY: JANUARY 2000

[119] Mrs Pekety, the second claimant in these proceedings and the mother-in-law of Ravi Reddy, made three separate criminal complaints in the Court of the Special Judge for Economic Offences in Hyderabad. Each of the complaints was brought in January 2000. In each case Mrs Pekety, as the holder of 2,700 shares in SPGL, says that she 'met Dr A V Mohan Rao, one of the promoter directors of SPGL and inquired into the reasons for non-payment of dividends by SPGL in spite of making the investment in the shares way back in the year 1995'. In each case it is alleged that 'several crores [hundred of millions] of rupees were siphoned off by giving bogus contracts to family or friends of' Kishan Rao. It is alleged that contracts relating to site levelling and construction work were awarded to companies established by Kishan Rao as a device to transfer funds from SPGL; and that Kishan Rao and his sons, having been entrusted with control over the funds of SPGL, have committed criminal breaches of trust. The principal entities alleged to be involved are the same as in the eight Hyderabad derivative actions, Kris Engineers, Blue Star Constructions and Real Builders.

XIII. CRIMINAL COMPLAINTS BY STUSA: JULY 2001

a   **[120]** In July 2001 STUSA lodged three criminal complaints against Kishan Rao and his sons, alleging that the contracts with Kris Engineering, Real Builders, and Blue Star Constructions had been executed on revenue stamped paper which had been obtained fraudulently. STUSA has been seeking to have Kishan Rao arrested.

b   XIV. ALLEGATIONS OF FRAUD AND BRIBERY
[121] In the course of the applications and appeals at first instance and on appeal in the Delhi High Court Mohan Rao alleged that 'cost overruns ... resulted from the mismanagement and suspected siphoning of funds' by Kishan Rao (6 January 1998) and that rescission of the promoters' agreement was part of a *c*   strategy of concealing 'financial mismanagement and siphoning away of funds from SPGL' and 'several crores of rupees were siphoned off by giving bogus contracts to family of friend's owned companies' of Kishan Rao (18 November 1999).

[122] In the eight derivative actions and three criminal complaints in Hyderabad, the complainants allege that Kishan Rao defrauded SPGL by *d*   siphoning off money to pay for bogus construction work. In the three new criminal complaints by STUSA, Kishan Rao is accused of forgery in relation to the same contracts.

[123] In the application to the Supreme Court of India for the appointment of a receiver, Mohan Rao made an affidavit on 5 January 2001 that he had:

e   '... recently come to know that two agency agreements were executed for procuring the operation and maintenance contract (O&M) as well as engineering procurement and construction (EPC) contract. While one agreement was executed between Rolls Royce Industrial Power (India) Ltd and Towanda Services Ltd for procuring the O&M contract, the second *f*   agency agreement was executed between Parsons Turbine Generators Ltd and Towanda Services Pvt Ltd for procuring the EPC contract ... From the said agreement it transpires that a sum of £1·5m and $US19·3m was to be paid to Towanda Services Ltd by Rolls-Royce Group as agency fee/kick-back for obtaining/procuring O&M contract as well as EPC contract in respect of the power project at Kakinada ie SPGL. The fact that Towanda Services is *g*   owned and controlled by Mr. Kishan Rao is admitted fact in the suit being OS No 239 of 1999 filed in the Court of Chief Judge, City Civil Courts, Hyderabad by Mr. Kishan Rao as plaintiff ... From a collective reading of the above documents, it is apparent that not only bribes have been paid by Rolls-Royce to Mr. Kishan Rao for procuring the engineering procurement *h*   and construction (EPC) contract as well as operation and maintenance (O&M) contract but also a major amount of the alleged bribe has been re-circulated into the company as equity contribution of RRGP. In fact, as no real funds have actually been invested by RRGP, RRGP has never taken any stand in the matter in courts below.'

j   **[124]** On 6 November 2001 STUSA made an application to the Supreme Court of India for the following relief: (a) that the present management of SPGL, comprising Kishan Rao and his sons, and Mr Shukla and Mr Bhattacharyya be removed, (b) that the board of directors be reconstituted in accordance with the promoters' agreement, (c) that SPGL be operated, run and managed in accordance with the promoters' agreement and that a representative of STUSA should be appointed as managing director/CEO of the company with all executive powers, (d) that Kishan Rao and sons be ordered to repay all moneys siphoned from SPGL, totalling at least Rs58·21 crores.

[125] According to the application (which remains pending):

> 'From the limited inspection of SPGL records, it is apparent that the present management of SPGL comprising of Kishan Rao, his family members and friends have not only committed fraud but they have also siphoned off money from SPGL.'

[126] In the proceedings commenced earlier this year to set aside the NPTC settlement agreement, Mohan Rao on behalf of STUSA said:

> 'There is evidence of any amount of collusion between [Kishan Rao] and Rolls-Royce group of companies in the matter of management of SPGL. Rolls-Royce group of companies has assisted, colluded and actively aided siphoning out huge sums of money by bogus agency agreements ... (a) huge amounts have been siphoned of [sic] from SPGL by Kishan Rao, his family members and the corporates owned-controlled by them in the name of land and site development contracts and bogus book entries and was already included in the EPC contract with Rolls-Royce (b) the amount so siphoned off was brought in by them as alleged equity contribution in SPGL.'

XV. THE APPROPRIATE FORUM

General

[127] I have given reasons why India is an available forum for resolution of this claim. The thrust of the claimants' case on forum is that in determining the question of forum it is not sufficient for there to be Indian contacts with the case and that the essential question is with what country the issues are connected, and the relevant issues are primarily those relating to the allegations of bribery rather than the issues relative to the claimants' right to bring the action.

[128] It is clear that in the normal case the starting point must be the identification of the issues which are likely to arise. In section IV, I expressed the view that it was for the claimants to establish that England was clearly the more appropriate forum for the determination of the issues not only in relation to the bribery allegations but also in relation to the question of their standing to sue, even if that question is resolved without any form of trial or oral evidence. In my judgment the courts of the place of incorporation will almost invariably be the most appropriate forum for the resolution of the issues which relate to the existence of the right of shareholders to sue on behalf of the company.

[129] Apart from a reference in the latest opinion of former Chief Justice Ahmadi to permission being required to commence a representative action, there is no material in the evidence to indicate how Indian courts would deal with the problem (recognised in the Indian text on company law) which came to the fore in *Prudential Assurance Co Ltd v Newman Industries Ltd (No 2)* [1982] 1 All ER 354, [1982] Ch 204 and which is the subject of CPR 19.9. But whether the problem is dealt with by way of a preliminary issue or at trial, the issues will arise at some stage. In any event it is not easy to compartmentalise all of the issues. For example, the Rolls-Royce defendants say that Mohan Rao was well aware of the agency agreements, and benefited from the payments to Towanda. This may be relevant to several issues: whether the action is brought for ulterior purposes;

a whether Mohan Rao participated in the alleged wrongs; and whether the payments were legitimate.

Connections with England and India

[130] I accept that there is an important connection of the proceedings with England, and it is that the Rolls-Royce defendants are English companies. But
b they conduct no operations in England, and the operations they conduct in India are conducted as agents for other companies in the Rolls-Royce group. In any event Heaton now has a minimal staff. But it seems that most of the Rolls-Royce executives who dealt with the project can be made available in England without difficulty. Of the four individuals who have so far given evidence on their behalf, two live in England, one is in India and the fourth is in Norway.
c
[131] No doubt many of the relevant documents in the Rolls-Royce group will be in England (although the evidence is that the documents of RRIP are in India), but those which are in India could no doubt be made easily available in England. I do not regard as significant the claimants' suggestion that an Indian judgment would have to be enforced in England: there has been no suggestion that the
d Rolls-Royce defendants would not satisfy any judgment against them, and in any event Indian judgments are enforceable in England under the Foreign Judgments (Reciprocal Enforcement) Act 1933.

[132] The only other connections with England are, first, that the agency agreements were, it would seem, executed by a Rolls-Royce executive in
e England. Although the place where transactions take place is a relevant factor, the actual place of signature is often accidental, and there is no reason to believe that in this case it is a significant factor. So also the fact that the agency agreements are expressed to be governed by English law and subject to English jurisdiction is of no relevance. If they are shams and utterly bogus, then the choice of law and jurisdiction clauses are equally bogus. If they are genuine the
f choice is effective, but is irrelevant for the purposes of this case because this is not a claim under the agreements. It is alleged (and not yet contested) that the payments were made under the agency agreements from England. If so, this is not a matter which will require much investigation, and does not point to England as an appropriate forum.

g [133] On the other hand, there are very strong connections with India. The claim is a derivative claim by Indians and an NRI, and an NRI-controlled Mauritian company. The nominal claimants are linked with NRIs who have substantial investments in India. The claim is made on behalf of an Indian company complaining of a fraud consisting of bribes taken by the managing director in connection with construction and maintenance contracts executed in
h India for a power project in India. The board which is said to be controlled by the wrongdoers is entirely, apart from Mohan Rao and his colleague, in India. There are many civil and criminal actions pending in India which relate to the project, to the shareholding in the company, and to allegations of mismanagement by the company. As a result of the status quo order of the Supreme Court of India the
j operations of the company are subject to close scrutiny by the courts.

Other countries

[134] The fact that Mohan Rao and Ravi Reddy (and one of the individual claimants) are mainly resident in the United States does not detract from India being the country with the overwhelmingly strong connections with the case. It

is obvious that they have strong connections with India, and there is no evidence
that they have substantial connections with England. Their companies are
incorporated in New York, Mauritius and Jersey, but no doubt they are in practice
controlled from the United States. The fact that Towanda is a British Virgin
Islands company and is administered from Switzerland, and that the Towanda
payments by Rolls-Royce (and, allegedly, to Mohan Rao) were made to
Switzerland, have little or no bearing on the forum issues in this case. Nor is it
material that Rolls-Royce's partner in the project is a United States group,
Westinghouse.

The issues

[135] The principal issues which, on the proceedings so far, are likely to arise
are these: (a) is the derivative action brought bona fide for the benefit of the
company by shareholders, as the claimants contend, or is it, as the defendants
claim, a claim brought by nominees of Mohan Rao and Ravi Reddy as part of their
continuing struggle with Kishan Rao for control of SPGL and designed to involve
Rolls-Royce in a resolution of that struggle? (b) is SPGL being improperly
prevented from bringing or adopting the claim? (c) if the payments to Towanda
were illegitimate, did Mohan Rao know about them and/or knowingly benefit
from them so as to disqualify his nominees from bringing the action? (d) is there
any other remedy available? (e) were the payments under the agency agreements
legitimate, and if not, did the Rolls-Royce defendants know?

Ulterior motive

[136] The defendants' position is this: the current English action is part of the
wider factional battle between the two main camps of joint venturers in SPGL.
The action has been brought by the Mohan Rao/STUSA/Ravi Reddy camp to
seek to pressurise the Rolls-Royce defendants into becoming involved in settling
the overall disputes between the two camps. The English proceedings were first
threatened at about the time when STUSA's attempts to achieve results through
the Indian courts had been frustrated. The Rolls-Royce defendants say that in the
course of settlement negotiations which took place in January to March 2001, part
of the settlement proposed was the termination of the English proceedings. The
individual claimants say in their witness statements that they knew nothing about
that proposal, and the defendants say that this shows that the proceedings in the
various jurisdictions are being controlled and maintained by others, and that the
individual claimants have allowed their names to be put forward as participants
in the wider dispute.

[137] Ravi Reddy has tried and failed to purchase the Rolls-Royce interest in
SPGL, and the defendants say that he still has ambitions of acquiring it. They say
that the purpose of the proceedings is to seek to force the Rolls-Royce defendants
to involve themselves in breaking the impasse between the groups of promoters.
This amounts to an ulterior purpose, ie the furtherance of sectional or factional
interests rather than the interests of the company itself.

[138] The resolution of this question is, of course, for the court which decides
whether the derivative claim can be brought. The three original individual
claimants have no financial interest in the outcome. Even if the proceedings were
to succeed and SPGL were to be paid the full amounts claimed, the individual
claimants' proportionate interest would be about £5 each. It would be wholly
unrealistic on the material before me to suppose that this is not a claim in reality being

a pursued by Mohan Rao and Ravi Reddy for their own purposes. The claimants are being funded by Ravi Reddy and get their information from Mohan Rao.

[139] It must be they who took the decisions and gave the instructions even before STUSA (Mauritius) was joined as a party, for example not to make Kishan Rao a defendant to the English proceedings. I have no doubt that this was purely tactical, and designed to support the case for English jurisdiction, just like the recent

b application by Mohan Rao on behalf of STUSA in the Indian court to remove the Rolls-Royce defendants because of their claim in England that the proceedings should be stopped because of the Indian proceedings.

[140] It is a striking feature of the case that the claimants have chosen not to join Kishan Rao as a defendant. Their stated reasons are these: they need to

c recover only once; there would be difficulty of enforcement against Kishan Rao; joining him would increase the costs and complexity, and he would delay the proceedings, whereas Rolls-Royce would have to consider the merits (ie settle). But their case is that he has received many millions of dollars; and that the bribery case is a simple one.

d [141] Ravi Reddy says he feels 'morally bound to support the individual claimants' and that he is supporting them because (among other reasons) they do not have the 'financial means to chase down the fraud within the company'. But if their object is 'to chase down fraud within the company' proceedings in England are an absurd method of accomplishing that mission, when it is clear that the Indian authorities have wide powers of investigation under the Indian

e Companies Act 1956.

Role of Mohan Rao

[142] I have already said that the role of Mohan Rao is relevant to different aspects of this case. There can be no doubt that he and Ravi Reddy are behind

f the claimants, and that there is therefore a probability that any court seised with the derivative action issues would be prepared to treat him as a claimant for the purposes of those issues. There would then be a serious issue as to whether he had participated in the alleged wrongdoing.

[143] There is a clear conflict of evidence on the role played by Mohan Rao in the negotiations for the contracts in the period 1993 to 1995. According to

g Mohan Rao, he was in the negotiating team, but was only responsible for the technical side, and Kishan Rao dealt exclusively with the financial/commercial side.

[144] According to the Rolls-Royce evidence, there were intense and very difficult negotiations, principally with Mohan Rao, who led them. At the time of the negotiations Kishan Rao had inadequate command of English to undertake

h the negotiations without the presence of either of Mohan Rao or one of his own sons. Kishan Rao was a local Indian businessman with no previous experience in power projects but who could bring his governmental and other contacts to assist the development of the project. The Rolls-Royce defendants rely on board minutes in 1994 and 1995 as indicating that Mohan Rao played a very active role

j in evaluating the tenders and in awarding the contracts. He signed the EPC contract and witnessed the O&M contract. In October 1993 Mohan Rao signed an application on behalf of SPGL addressed to the Industrial Development Bank of India (IDBI) for financial assistance, and in August 1994 he signed the loan agreement between SPGL and IDBI, who are its main bankers, and have board representation in SPGL.

[145] This conflict is of course not to be resolved in these applications, but it is plain that the issues raised are relevant to the issues and are far from frivolous. Apart from the Rolls-Royce evidence to which I have referred there are statements made by Mohan Rao which belie his account of his role, and which suggest strongly that Mohan Rao has significantly downplayed his role in SPGL in these proceedings, and support the contention of the defendants that he was the driving force behind the project, and was involved in negotiating all aspects of SPGL's involvement in the project, including the funding and financial arrangements.

[146] When he verified the 1996 claim by STUSA in Delhi he stated that 'the entire project was thought of and conceived' by him and that 'he has been the life and soul of the entire project since 1990'. In the course of an appeal in interlocutory proceedings in the same litigation he said in January 1998:

'... [the] EPC contract and O&M contract have been completely initiated, discussed, negotiated and finalised by Dr Mohan Rao. His vital role has been acknowledged ... by the EPC contractors and [SPGL]. Both the EPC and O&M contracts have been signed by Dr Mohan Rao on behalf of [SPGL]. All this time, the managing director Mr Kishan Rao and his so-called experienced in-house technical team played a passive role and did not make any significant contributions to either the deliberations and it was the technical expertise and effort of [STUSA] and NTPC which are behind the success of the project.'

[147] In the proceedings in the Federal Court in Michigan by CMS for its unpaid expenses a brief on behalf of STUSA stated out that even before his appointment to the board in March 1994 Mohan Rao had held himself out, and acted, as a board member in dealings with potential project partners.

[148] There is also a major conflict of evidence on the role of Mohan Rao in the negotiation and conclusion of the agency agreements. The Rolls-Royce defendants say that he played a major role. His position is that he did not know of them until 1997, when he first saw them but did not appreciate their significance. He first became aware of their significance when Kishan Rao alleged in the Hyderabad debt action in 1999 that Towanda was owned and controlled by him. But in those proceedings he put Kishan Rao to proof that Towanda was owned by him, and Mohan Rao told the Supreme Court of India in January 2001 that he had 'recently come to know' of the execution of the agency agreements.

[149] The documents in this case indicate that a draft agency agreement for the EPC contract was drafted on behalf of RRIP (with a date in June 1993). On 27 October 1993 Mr Hynd, who was then the sales and marketing director of Heaton, wrote a memorandum to Dr Singleton, who was then the head of Rolls-Royce Power Generation Systems Ltd. The memorandum said: 'Attached is the draft agency agreement for handing over during your discussions with Mohan Rao in Hyderabad next week.'

[150] Dr Singleton's evidence in these proceedings was that he does not believe that he did in fact hand over the draft to Mohan Rao on that occasion. But he says that he is confident that Mohan Rao was, at that time, already well aware of what became known as the Towanda agreements and that he was involved in the negotiations of those agreements. Mr Hynd says that he does not recall what happened regarding the agency agreement after the date of his memorandum, but the fact that the draft was to be handed over to Mohan Rao is consistent, he

a says, with his understanding about the knowledge of and involvement in the negotiations on the terms of what became as the Towanda agreements. Mr Hynd says that given his knowledge of the role of Mohan Rao as the originator of the project and the extent of his involvement in all aspects, he does not accept the statement by Mohan Rao to the effect that he did not appreciate the true nature of the Towanda agreements.

b [151] Mr Lockton, who was then the managing director of Rolls-Royce (India) Ltd says that he believes that the draft agreement was handed over to both Kishan Rao and Mohan Rao, but his evidence is that it is inconceivable to him that Mohan Rao would not have received or at least been shown a copy of the draft by Kishan Rao, or at the very least have been told about the content. Mr Lockton says that he had several conversations with both Kishan Rao and *c* Mohan Rao in relation to those agreements during 1993, and in particular a meeting in Delhi in June 1993 with Kishan Rao and Mohan Rao at which they discussed, among other topics, a planned visit to the United Kingdom by both of them in July 1993 for discussions in relation to the agency agreements. He recalls a further meeting with Mohan Rao in Delhi towards the end of September 1993 *d* in which he pressed for the agency arrangements to be finalised. Mr Lockton says that Mohan Rao pressed him, as his main Rolls-Royce contact in the initial stages of the project, to exert his influence to have the necessary arrangements put in place.

[152] Kishan Rao has alleged in the Hyderabad debt proceedings that Mohan Rao received substantial payments from Towanda, which were used *e* by Mohan Rao to invest in shares in SPGL via STUSA. These allegations are denied by Mohan Rao, and in interlocutory proceedings the judge in Hyderabad ruled that Kishan Rao did not adduce sufficient evidence of his ownership of Towanda or that the payees were connected with Mohan Rao. But there are documents linking Mohan Rao with one of the payees, Mount Stevens Ltd. If the *f* allegations are ultimately made out, it will show that Mohan Rao and STUSA not merely knew of and participated in the production of the original agency agreements, but also benefited from payments made by Towanda.

Wrongdoer control

g [153] It is already apparent that this unusual case differs from the typical derivative action. One respect in which it differs is that in the normal case the principal defendants are the allegedly fraudulent directors who are said to control the board and the general meeting. In this case not only is the director not a party, but the company has a board which includes senior bankers who are there to look after the interests of lending institutions including the IDBI, the Industrial *h* Finance Corp of India, and the State Bank of India. The banks have contributed in loans some eight times the capital which has been introduced by Mohan Rao/ Ravi Reddy and their associates, Kishan Rao and his associates, and Rolls-Royce. The IDBI was entrusted by the Delhi court with the task of settling the shareholder disputes, but its efforts failed, apparently because of Mohan Rao's *j* demands.

[154] The board has independent members of considerable standing. The court seised with the dispute could stay the proceedings until the board has been given an opportunity to consider whether to commence or continue proceedings. The board would have to consider (inter alia) the broad commercial implications of suing SPGL's most important and vital trading partners and continuing

contractors, and whether by suing the Rolls-Royce defendants those defendants may resurrect and bring forward cross-claims against SPGL, the size and importance of the likely return in the context of the commercial project involving a total cost of $US250m. If the board decided that there should be proceedings then the action would continue in the name of the company. If it decided not do so, then issues of good faith might arise, and there might have to be evidence from the independent board members.

[155] If the true question is, as I think it is, whether the company is being wrongly prevented from seeking redress then India is plainly the appropriate forum for determining whether the relevant organ is the company in general meeting or the board, and if it is the board, whether there is an independent board which can properly consider whether the prosecution of the action is likely to do more harm than good (cf *Prudential Assurance Co Ltd v Newman Industries Ltd (No 2)* [1982] 1 All ER 354 at 365, [1982] Ch 204 at 221). The Indian courts, as the courts of the place of incorporation and business of SPGL, are far better placed as a practical matter to determine questions of wrongdoer control and whether the proceedings are being brought bona fide in the interests of SPGL.

Alternative remedy

[156] The court seised with the question of whether the derivative action is justified will also have to consider whether there is an alternative remedy as expressed by Peter Gibson LJ in *Barrett v Duckett* [1995] 1 BCLC 243 at 250, and what is meant by that expression. The defendants argue that the remedies available to the Company Law Board are alternative in a relevant sense. In view of what I have said above (at [29]), I need say no more than I am doubtful whether the remedy in the Company Law Board is the type of alternative remedy that the case envisages. But even if it did, I am satisfied that the remedies available in the Company Law Board would not be a substitute for this action if it is held to have the bona fide intention of recovery from the Rolls-Royce defendants. But the remedies under the 1956 Act are sufficient if the true purpose of the claimants is, as is said, to chase down the fraud and root out corruption. There are several various avenues under the 1956 Act whereby minority shareholders may apply for an investigation into the affairs of the company by the Company Law Board or inspectors appointed by the central government: see ss 235, 237 and 388B to 388E of the Indian Companies Act 1956.

Bribery issues

[157] In relation to the underlying allegations of bribery, the claimants say that the focus is simply on the conduct of the Rolls-Royce companies, rather than SPGL's internal affairs. A claimant may claim the sum paid by the briber from either the briber itself or the bribed fiduciary on a comparatively narrow basis, in restitution and/or in tort, with the benefit of certain irrebuttable presumptions in the claimants' favour. The claimants say that the Rolls-Royce defendants have consistently refused to answer the bribery allegations in correspondence, and that even now their case amounts to no more than a bare denial. The claimants say that since the Rolls-Royce defendants have really put forward no case which amounts to a defence of the bribery claim then there are no issues which will go to trial, and therefore England as the place where the defendants are is the appropriate forum for what would in substance be a claim for summary

a judgment. None of the usual forum factors, location of witnesses, location of documents, governing law etc would have any significant role to play.

[158] The argument is this. A bribe is a secret commission paid to an agent or other fiduciary by the payer, who knows that the payee is an agent or fiduciary and fails to disclose the payment to the principal or other person to whom the fiduciary duty is owed (see *Industries and General Mortgage Co v Lewis* [1949] 2 All ER

b 573 at 575, *Petrotrade Inc v Smith* [2000] 1 Lloyd's Rep 486 at 489–490). The motive of the briber when giving the bribe is not relevant and evidence as to such motive will not be allowed; there is an irrebuttable presumption in favour of the claimant that the fiduciary was influenced by the bribe; at least where the agent is 'a confidential buyer of goods for his principal from the briber', there is an

c irrebuttable presumption in favour of the claimant that the true price of the goods as between him and the purchaser company must be taken to have been less than the price paid by at least the amount or value of the bribe (see *Hovenden v Millhoff* (1900) 83 LT 41, [1900–3] All ER Rep 848, *Mahesan v Malaysia Government Officers' Co-operative Housing Society Ltd* [1978] 2 All ER 405, [1979] AC 374).

d [159] Accordingly the claimants contend: (1) Rolls-Royce has paid very substantial sums of money to Towanda; (2) Towanda was beneficially owned by Kishan Rao; (3) Rolls-Royce must have known that Towanda was beneficially owned by Kishan Rao; (4) unless the agency agreements were fully disclosed by either Kishan Rao or Rolls-Royce to SPGL's shareholders, and sanctioned by them in general meeting, those arrangements constituted bribery for civil

e purposes; (5) therefore, it is to be presumed irrebuttably that Rolls-Royce's motive was corrupt, that those arrangements did influence Kishan Rao, and that Rolls-Royce would have been prepared to enter into the EPC and O&M contracts at prices less than the actual prices by the amount of money it promised, or alternatively actually paid, to Towanda. SPGL is therefore entitled to recover

f those sums promised or actually paid to Towanda.

[160] The claimants argue that it is insufficient for present purposes for Rolls-Royce to do no more than simply assert in evidence that the agency agreements 'are purely commercial arrangements and do not constitute kick-backs for obtain/procuring [the] O&M contract as well as the EPC contract'

g (David Bale, Rolls-Royce plc's principal legal advisor, in the proceedings in the Supreme Court of India in answer to Mohan Rao's allegation of bribery). The claimants say that Rolls-Royce is in no position to deny that Towanda was owned by Kishan Rao. They also say that the evidence is that Rolls-Royce knew that Towanda was a Kishan Rao creature.

h [161] But the evidence on which the claimants rely is the evidence of the Rolls-Royce executives who dealt with Kishan Rao and Mohan Rao, and I have set it out fully in [149]–[151], above. The evidence does not indicate that Towanda was Kishan Rao's creature. But if, as the claimants say, it would have been plain to Roll-Royce that Towanda must have been Kishan Rao's creature

j then the same evidence would show that it was also Mohan Rao's creature and that he was deeply implicated, as a de facto director and agent of SPGL, in the bribery which they allege. The claimants' assertion that the evidence that Rolls-Royce knew that Towanda was a Kishan Rao creature is to be derived from their account of the 1993 meetings can only suggest that there is a real issue as to whether Mohan Rao was also to benefit from payments to Towanda.

Evidence and evaluation

[162] I am satisfied that prima facie the court of the place of incorporation is *a* best fitted to deal with the derivative action issues. But in my judgment on any view of the facts of this case the Indian court is clearly the appropriate forum to consider whether the action is brought for ulterior purposes; whether the appropriate organ for the purposes of wrongdoer control is the board or the general meeting; if it is the board, whether it is capable of taking independent *b* decisions, and, if so, how they should be taken; and how to deal with the allegation that Mohan Rao was deeply involved in the impugned transactions. I accept that there may be little need for cross-examination on all but the last issue, but that is a matter for whichever court decides (if it does) to deal with these questions as a preliminary matter.

[163] The negotiations and conclusion of the contracts for the commissioning *c* and maintenance of the project will be relevant even if the claimants are right in contending that they will have the benefit of some irrebuttable presumptions.

[164] It is plain that determination of these issues will involve the evidence of a number of participants in the transactions. The Rolls-Royce defendants say that they will wish to say that the agency agreements were known to all those then *d* concerned with SPGL, which was then to be identified with Mohan Rao and Kishan Rao; that Kishan Rao had no authority to commit SPGL to the EPC and O & M contracts, and therefore the presumption that the alleged bribe influenced the contract price does not operate. They wish to have the opportunity to adduce evidence of the surrounding circumstances, including the competitive tendering *e* process, the scrutiny given to the tenders by STUSA (ie by Mohan Rao), by foreign consultants employed by STUSA and by representatives of NTPC. They do not suggest that the existence of a tendering process is a conclusive answer in itself to the bribe allegations. On the other hand, they say that the existence of a competitive tendering process and the steps taken thereunder are clearly part of the surrounding circumstances which will bear on the court's determination of *f* the status of the agency agreements and their effect.

[165] Apart from three of the Rolls-Royce witnesses, most of the potential witnesses in both the derivative action issues (particularly on motive, wrongdoer control, and 'clean hands') and the bribery issues are in India or are closely connected with India as NRIs, and none are in England. They include (a) the *g* three individual claimants; (b) Kishan Rao; (c) the two sons of Kishan Rao; (d) representatives of NTPC; (e) Mohan Rao; (f) Ravi Reddy; and (g) the other directors of SPGL. The evidence of Westinghouse executives may also be relevant. They may be in the United States, but there is no reason to suppose that they are in England.

[166] This is already an odd case without Kishan Rao as a party. His *h* importance as a witness in these proceedings is obvious. On the claimants' case he is the principal wrongdoer. He was the managing director of SPGL at the time the allegedly corrupt transactions were entered into, and it is to SPGL that he owed fiduciary duties. He is the person alleged to have received bribes. The Indian courts would be able to compel his attendance as a witness (both to give *j* oral evidence and to provide documents). If the proceedings were to continue in England no such powers of compulsion would be available in relation to his evidence, and the parties would have to resort to letters rogatory, which would be of doubtful utility in a case of this kind. The same considerations apply to his two sons and his advisers, who were involved in the relevant transactions.

a   [167] The other main protagonist is Mohan Rao. His evidence will be central in relation to many of the issues. It will plainly be relevant to two central questions in the derivative action issues, namely that of ulterior motive and participation in the wrongdoing. Rolls-Royce will seek to show that he has been centrally involved in all the relevant transactions, from the inception of the project; that he was aware of and involved in the negotiation of the agency agreements and was *b* also the main contact as SPGL involved in negotiating the EPC and O&M contracts; that he was also centrally involved in the competitive tendering process and the decisions of the SPGL board to award the contracts to the Rolls-Royce defendants.

[168] Ravi Reddy is also likely to be able to give evidence in relation to many of the same issues. In particular, his evidence is likely to be relevant to the *c* question of the purposes for which this litigation has been commenced and, in particular, whether the proceedings can be properly regarded as having been brought in the best interests of SPGL.

[169] The documents of SPGL and NTPC are almost certainly located in India. Mohan Rao accepts his own documents are located in India. The documents *d* of STUSA are located in the United States. It is likely that the documents of Kishan Rao are in India. The documents of RRIP are in India, and those of Heaton are in England. There is no evidence about the location of documents of other Rolls-Royce companies, including those for which they were agents. Most of the relevant documents are likely to be located outside England, and if the *e* proceedings were in England it would be very difficult and cumbersome to use the Convention on the Taking of Evidence Abroad in Civil or Commercial Matters (The Hague, 18 March 1970, TS 20 (1977); Cmnd 6727) to reach Indian documents in the possession of non-parties.

f *Applicable law*

[170] This is not a factor of great significance in this case because there is no evidence of any difference between English law and Indian law on the relevant matters. But the case does involve some developing and controversial areas of law such as the scope of the right to bring derivative actions and the law of bribery. I have expressed the view that the question of the right to bring a *g* derivative action is governed by Indian law, and it is likely that the bribery issues are governed by Indian law (see *Arab Monetary Fund v Hashim* [1993] 1 Lloyd's Rep 543; affirmed on this aspect [1996] 1 Lloyd's Rep 589). To the extent that there are controversial issues it would be better for them to be decided by the court which can authoritatively rule on them, and whose judgments are subject to *h* appeal. But since there is no evidence of any differences, and since the application of foreign law is an everyday occurrence in English courts, this is not a significant pointer to India as the proper forum.

Indian litigation

j [171] I regard the Indian litigation as a significant factor in India being the forum conveniens. I do so not on the basis of the 'Cambridgeshire factor', identified in *Spiliada Maritime Corp v Cansulex Ltd, The Spiliada* [1986] 3 All ER 843, [1987] AC 460, ie the saving in convenience and costs which would be occasioned by the claim being dealt with by the Indian lawyers who have acquired knowledge and expertise through the Indian proceedings.

[172] This is not a case where there is strictly a lis alibi pendens. The bribery allegations in India are made only in the context of an interim application for a receiver, and will not arise as such at trial, and the Rolls-Royce defendants are only parties to some of the Indian proceedings for the purpose of obtaining discovery or as nominal defendants in their capacity as shareholders.

[173] But there are extensive allegations of mismanagement and fraud in the Indian proceedings against Kishan Rao, and the derivative actions in Hyderabad raise the same questions of wrongdoer control as would arise in these proceedings. There is therefore a risk of inconsistent findings in the broader sense. I have set out in section XIV some of the principal allegations and I will not repeat them. In addition, looked at broadly, the Indian proceedings are to a large extent about control of voting power and of management of SPGL, and support the conclusion that these proceedings are part of a power struggle for control of SPGL. The Indian courts are far better equipped to evaluate them.

Cross-claims

[174] I do not consider the fact that the Rolls-Royce defendants may assert cross-claims is of any significance to the forum issues. Earlier this year RRIP repeated to SPGL that it was still owed more than £3m under the EPC contract. There is also a claim in excess of £10m under the O&M contract. The contract contains a clause which provides that in the case of currency fluctuation the price may be adjusted following negotiation. If agreement is not reached the either party may terminate the agreement. Rolls-Royce says that the true effect is that a revised price may become due notwithstanding that the only express remedy is termination. The contract is subject to Indian law and arbitration in Switzerland. I heard argument on the merits of the cross-claim and whether it is capable of being a defence to the restitutionary claim made in these proceedings. Those questions do not arise for decision now, but I am satisfied that they are neutral on the issue of forum.

Delay

[175] In a case involving service out of the jurisdiction under CPR 6.20 the burden is on the claimants to show that England is clearly the more appropriate forum, and if they do not discharge that burden, that is the end of the matter and there is no room (as there is in the case of staying of actions) for the English court to retain jurisdiction if the claimant shows that it would be unjust for him to be deprived of a remedy on the ground that, in the words of Lord Goff in *Connelly v RTZ Corp plc* [1997] 4 All ER 335 at 345, [1998] AC 854 at 873, 'substantial justice cannot be done in the appropriate forum'.

[176] I have expressed the view (above, at [59]) that in the context of service out of the jurisdiction there is room only for such an argument if the injustice in what would otherwise be the appropriate forum is such that it cannot be regarded as an 'available forum'. In such a case it might be argued that England is clearly the more appropriate forum, because there is no effective alternative. The main objection to India advanced by the claimants is that there is likely to be greater delay there. Mr Raghunandan Rao says that it might take up to five years to get to trial in India, and the earliest disposal that could be expected would be about four years. Former Chief Justice Ahmadi says that it might be up to ten years.

[177] Delay has been a factor taken into account in cases involving applications to stay on the ground that India is the appropriate forum (see *The*

a *Jalakrishna* [1983] 2 Lloyd's Rep 628 and *The Vishva Ajay* [1989] 2 Lloyds Rep 558; but contrast *Radhakrishna Hospitality Service Private Ltd v EIH Ltd* [1999] 2 Lloyd's Rep 249). It is well known that in the past there were substantial delays in the Indian legal system, caused by the combination of an enormous population and an overworked and understaffed judiciary, but it is also well known that very great efforts have been made in recent years to reduce the backlog of cases. The

b evidence in this case goes nowhere near showing that it is so serious as to amount to a substantial injustice, and nowhere near showing that it is such as to deprive the claimants of any remedy at all. It is not seriously arguable that 'substantial justice cannot be done' in India in relation to claims by Indian residents and NRIs (and their companies) in relation to an Indian company and its affairs, and it would be a substantial breach of comity to stigmatise the Indian legal system in

c that way. This is typically the situation in which the claimant will have to 'take [the appropriate] forum as he finds it' (see *Connelly's* case [1997] 4 All ER 335 at 345, [1998] AC 854 at 872).

[178] In any event, these claimants and parties associated with them have brought a series of actions in the courts of India, and they have had ready access

d to the Indian court system at all levels up to the Supreme Court of India. They have not shown concern about delay. They took more than a year between writing their first letter before action (3 December 1999) and obtaining permission to serve out of the jurisdiction (2 February 2001).

e XVI. NON-DISCLOSURE

[179] In view of the conclusion which I have reached that the order for service should be set aside because the claimants have not clearly shown that England is the appropriate forum, I will deal shortly with the allegations of non-disclosure. About 50 pages of witness statements and more than 400 pages of documents were before Master Moncaster when he made his order in February 2001.

f [180] On an application without notice the duty of the applicant is to make a full and fair disclosure of all the material facts, i e those which it is material (in the objective sense) for the judge to know in dealing with the application as made: materiality is to be decided by the court and not by the assessment of the applicant or his legal advisors; the duty is a strict one and includes not merely material facts known to the applicant but also additional facts which he would

g have known if he had made proper inquiries (see *Brink's-MAT Ltd v Elcombe* [1988] 3 All ER 188 at 192–193, [1988] 1 WLR 1350 at 1356–1357). But an applicant does not have a duty to disclose points against him which have not been raised by the other side and in respect of which there is no reason to anticipate that the other

h side would raise such points if it were present.

[181] These principles have long been applied to applications for permission to serve out of the jurisdiction (see, e g *The Hagen* [1908] P 189 at 201, [1908–10] All ER Rep 21 at 26). In that context it has been held that it would not be reasonable to expect an applicant for permission to serve out to anticipate all the

j arguments or points which might be raised against his case (see *Electric Furnace Co v Selas Corp of America* [1987] RPC 23 at 29). A failure to refer to arguments on the merits which the defendant might raise at trial should not generally be characterised as a 'failure to make full and fair disclosure', unless they are of such weight that their omission may mislead the court in exercising its jurisdiction under the rule and its discretion whether or not to grant permission (see

BP Exploration Co (Libya) Ltd v Hunt [1976] 3 All ER 879 at 889, approved in the
Electric Furnace case [1987] RPC 23 at 29).

[182] In the *BP Exploration* case, Kerr J warned (at 894):

> '... the court should not consider the supporting affidavit as though it were
> marking an examination paper, deciding one way or the other merely on the
> basis of the extent to which the affidavit could have been improved. The
> primary question should be whether in all the circumstances the effect of the
> affidavit is such as to mislead the court in any material respect concerning its
> jurisdiction and the discretion under the rule.'

[183] I do not consider that, subject to one point, there is any case for setting
aside for non-disclosure. The witness statements may have been somewhat
partial and overzealous, but the criticism made by the defendants amounts to no
more than the evidence did not fully anticipate all the points on the exercise of
the discretion which they have now made.

[184] There was one material fact which was not disclosed before the master
made his order on 2 February 2001. Before that date he had been told that the
bribery allegations formed no part of the Indian proceedings. The first claimant's
witness statement denied that the issues were substantially the same as those in
the Indian proceedings, and stated: '... in fact they are completely different. In
particular, I am informed by Dr A V Mohan Rao, the issue of bribery by
Rolls-Royce is simply not raised in the Indian proceedings.'

[185] The claimants' solicitor, Mr Mervis, said: 'From my review of extracts of
the Delhi and Hyderabad proceedings, it would not appear that those
proceedings relate to the bribes to which the English proceedings relate. Dr Rao
has informed me that they do not in fact concern the bribes.'

[186] After reviewing the papers Master Moncaster wrote to the claimants'
solicitors to say that he was not minded to give permission, and raised a number
of concerns about the application, including the question whether there was an
overlap with the Indian proceedings. In response the claimants' solicitors put
before Master Moncaster in December 2000 a draft skeleton argument and a
further witness statement of Mr Mervis, each of which stated (in slightly
different terms) that there was no allegation of bribery in the Indian proceedings
and little or no overlap between the issues in these proceedings and the Indian
proceedings.

[187] But on 5 January 2001 Mohan Rao swore an affidavit in the proceedings
before the Supreme Court of India making those allegations in support of
STUSA's application for the appointment of a receiver. It is clear from the
witness statement of Mr Mervis to which I have referred that he was well aware
of the importance of the bribery allegations in relation to the English
proceedings. When the claimants' solicitors learned of this they informed the
master, who decided not to revoke his order (as he was entitled to do:
CPR 3.1(7)). The claimants accept that the fact that the bribery allegations were
referred to in that affidavit should have been disclosed. The non-disclosure was
serious, and culpable, but in the circumstances I see no basis for setting aside for
non-disclosure, since the non-disclosure cannot be said to have led to the
continuance of the order giving permission to serve out of the jurisdiction.

XVII. CONCLUSIONS

a   [188] The Indian connections of this case are overwhelming. Even though the first and second defendants are English companies, the joinder of SPGL is a necessary element in the claim, and the claimants have fallen far short of satisfying the burden to show clearly that England is the appropriate forum for the derivative claim. I will therefore set aside the order of Master Moncaster.

b   [189] I should add this: an order for service out of the jurisdiction can be set aside if the claimant fails to show that there is a serious issue to be tried. SPGL relied on the alternative remedy point in support of the proposition that there would have been no serious issue to be tried on the derivative aspects of the claim. I have already expressed the view that it would be unrealistic to view these proceedings as anything other than as being pursued by Mohan Rao and Ravi Reddy

c for their own purposes. If that view is right, then the claimants would not have succeeded at the stage of the application under CPR 19.9 in obtaining permission to continue with the claim, and therefore there would be no serious issue to be tried on the derivative claim. That, however, will now be a question for the judge in India.

Order accordingly.

Neneh Munu   Barrister.

Practice Direction

a

FAMILY DIVISION

Practice – Family Division – Video conferencing – Procedure – Facilities in Royal Courts of Justice.

b

1. Video conferencing facilities are available in the Royal Courts of Justice (RCJ) in Court 38. In proceedings pending in the Principal Registry of the Family Division which are to be heard in the RCJ or in First Avenue House and in which it is desired to use these facilities, the following procedure should be observed.

2(a). Directions for the video conferencing hearing should be given by an order made in the proceedings. The order may be made without attendance, provided all parties consent.

c

(b). The order should specify, in general terms, the purpose of the hearing and give the date, time, place and duration of the hearing and the place or country with which the link is to be effected.

d

(c). Availability of the facilities must be ascertained prior to the order being made fixing the appointment. This can be done by communicating with those responsible for managing the video conferencing facility in the RCJ ('the video managers'—Roger Little and Norman Muller, telephone 020 7947 6581; fax 020 7947 6613). If the order is made at a hearing, the court associate or clerk will be able to make the telephone call to ascertain an available date. For orders to be made without attendance, the parties must ascertain the availability of the facilities prior to submitting the application.

e

(d). In every case, the parties must communicate with the video managers as soon as possible after the order has been made to ensure that all the necessary arrangements for the telephone link to be established are settled well in advance of the appointed date.

f

3. Where in any case the main hearing may be delayed because video conferencing facilities at the RCJ are not conveniently available, consideration should be given to using video conferencing facilities at the Bar Council or the Law Society. If facilities away from the RCJ are to be used, it will be the responsibility of the party applying for the video conferencing hearing to make all the necessary arrangements with the video conferencing provider.

g

4. Issued with the approval of the President.

Gerald Angel
Senior District Judge

14 January 2002

End of Volume 1